Formation *and* Development *for* Catholic School Leaders

Volume I

The Principal as *Educational* Leader

Formation *and* Development *for* Catholic School Leaders

Expectations in the Areas of Leadership, Curriculum, and Instruction

Volume I
The Principal as *Educational* Leader

Maria J. Ciriello, OP, Ph.D., Author/Editor
Dean of the School of Education
University of Portland, Oregon

Department of Education
United States Catholic Conference
Washington, D.C.

2nd Edition

In its planning document, as approved by the general membership of the United States Catholic Conference in November 1992, the Department of Education was authorized to prepare materials for the preparation of educational leaders. This present revision of *The Principal as Educational Leader,* containing references to the *Catechsim of the Catholic Church*, is the first of a three-volume series, *Formation and Development for Catholic School Leaders.* It is a collaborative project with the National Catholic Educational Association in consultation with NCEA/CACE members from Catholic colleges and universities, approved by the Most Reverend Robert J. Banks, Chairman of the Committee on Education, and authorized for publication by the undersigned.

Monsignor Dennis M. Schnurr
General Secretary
NCCB/USCC

First Printing, September 1993
Revised Printing, April 1998

ISBN 1-57455-077-2

Acknowledgments

Academic Press, Inc.

Mann, V. 1991. Language problems: A key to early reading problems. In *Learning about learning disabilities*, edited by B. Y. L. Wong, 129–62. Copyright © 1991 by Academic Press, Inc. Reprinted by permission of the author.

Swanson, H. L, and J. B. Cooney. 1991. Learning disabilities and memory. In *Learning about learning disabilities*, edited by B. Y. L. Wong, 104–22. Copyright © 1991 by Academic Press, Inc. Reprinted by permission of the publisher.

Wong, B. Y. L. 1991. The relevance of metacognition to learning disabilities. In *Learning about learning disabilities*, edited by B. Y. L. Wong, 231–57. Copyright © 1991 by Academic Press, Inc. Reprinted by permission of the publisher.

Willows, D. M. 1991. Visual processes in learning disabilities. In *Learning about learning disabilities*, edited by B. Y. L. Wong, 163–93. Copyright © 1991 by Academic Press, Inc. Reprinted by permission of the publisher.

Allyn and Bacon

Bos, C., and S. Vaughn. *Strategies for teaching students with learning and behavior problems*, 24–57. Copyright © 1991. Reprinted by permission of Allyn and Bacon.

Glickman, C. D. *Supervision of instruction: A developmental approach*, 189–91. Copyright © 1990. Reprinted by permission of Allyn and Bacon.

Parke, B. *Gifted students in regular classrooms*, 3–16, 42–63, 127–42. Copyright © 1989. Reprinted by permission of Allyn and Bacon.

American Association of School Administrators

Savary, L. M. 1992. *Creating quality schools*, 27–32. Copyright © 1992. Reprinted by permission of the American Association of School Administrators, Arlington, Va.

Association for Supervision and Curriculum Development

Brophy, J. 1992. Probing the subtleties of subject-matter teaching. *Educational Leadership* 49(7):4–8. Reprinted with permission of the Association for Supervision and Curriculum Development. Copyright © 1992 by ASCD. All rights reserved.

Caine, R. N., and G. Caine. 1991. *Making connections: Teaching and the human brain*, 48–50, 59–61, 80–87, 102–05, 105–06, 112–13, 154–58. Copyright © 1991 by ASCD. Reprinted by permission of the author.

Dunn, R. 1990. Rita Dunn answers questions on learning styles. *Educational Leadership* 48(2):15–19. Copyright © 1990. Reprinted by permission of the author.

Glatthorn, A. A. 1987. *Curriculum renewal: A rationale for a consensus curriculum*, 20–27. Reprinted with permission of the Association for Supervision and Curriculum Development. Copyright © 1987 by ASCD. All rights reserved.

Marzano, R. J. 1992. *A different kind of classroom*, 25–27, 124–26, 135–39. Reprinted with permission of the Association for Supervision and Curriculum Development. Copyright © 1992 by ASCD. All rights reserved.

Nolan, J., and P. Francis. 1992. Changing perspectives in curriculum and supervision. In *Supervision in transition, 1992 yearbook*, 52–60. Reprinted with permission of the Association for Supervision and Curriculum Development. Copyright © 1992 by ASCD. All rights reserved.

Sheive, L. T., and M. B. Schoenheit. 1987. Vision and the work of educational leaders. In *Leadership: Examining the elusive*, 94, 96–98. Reprinted with permission of the Association for Supervision and Curriculum Development. Copyright © 1987 by ASCD. All rights reserved.

Corwin Press, Inc.

Blase, J., and P. C. Kirby. 1992. *Bringing out the best in teachers*, 10–21, 99–111. Copyright © 1992 by Corwin Press, Inc. Reprinted by permission of Corwin Press, Inc.

Maehr, M. L., C. Midgley, and T. Urdan. 1992. School leader as motivator. *Educational Administration Quarterly* 28(3):410–29. Copyright © 1992 by Corwin Press, Inc. Reprinted by permission of Corwin Press, Inc.

Delacorte Press

Clifton, D. O., and P. Nelson. 1992. *Soar with your strengths*, 111–22. Copyright ©1992 by Selection Research, Inc. and Paula Nelson. Reprinted by permission of Delacorte Press, a division of Bantam Doubleday Dell Publishing Group, Inc.

Contents

Foreword

A Brief History

For many years, the identification and preparation of talented and qualified leadership for Catholic schools had been primarily the responsibility and priority of religious congregations whose members together with some priests served as principals.

Since the Second Vatican Council, staffing patterns of Catholic schools have changed dramatically. Today the majority of both teachers and principals are lay women and men. The tasks of identifying and preparing Catholic school principals have developed largely through the efforts of the education leaders in Catholic colleges and universities.

In 1982, with a grant from the Knights of Columbus Michael J. McGivney Fund for New Initiatives in Catholic Education, the National Catholic Educational Association (NCEA) began a project to study new approaches, to recommend new directions, and to identify needs for training materials. In 1985, the results of this work were published by NCEA in *Those Who Would Be Catholic School Principals: Their Recruitment, Preparation, and Evaluation* (Manno 1985).

Recognizing that many potential Catholic school administrators are not able to participate in the on-site programs of Catholic colleges and universities, a joint committee from the United States Catholic Conference (USCC) Department of Education, the National Catholic Educational Association Department of Chief Administrators of Catholic Education (CACE), and the National Catholic Graduate Educational Leadership Programs (NCGELP) of Colleges and Universities met for several years to develop alternative means to prepare school leaders. In particular, the goal was to help dioceses prepare those who aspire to be Catholic school principals and who are without the means and/or resources to earn traditional degrees at Catholic colleges.

Out of the efforts of the joint committee a set of forty-five competencies for Catholic school principals was developed. The competencies address three roles: Spiritual leader, Educational leader, and Managerial leader. NCEA/CACE received a final report from the joint committee in October 1991 and endorsed the project.

At that point, Regina Haney, OSF, of NCEA assumed responsibility for developing an assessment process for future administrators. Lourdes Sheehan, RSM, of USCC agreed to coordinate the preparation of training modules based on the agreed-upon competencies.

Maria Ciriello, OP, Ph.D., then of the Department of Education at The Catholic University of America, was hired as the project-director in November 1991. Her first step was to form an advisory committee composed of persons with both practical and theoretical experience in Catholic school administration. The members of the committee who lent guidance to the project and who critiqued drafts of the writing are: Nancy Gilroy, assistant superintendent of the Catholic Schools Division of the Archdiocese of Baltimore; Joel Konzen, SM, principal of Saint Michael Academy in Austin, Texas; Dr. Elizabeth Meegan, OP, superintendent of schools in the Diocese of Pittsburgh; Dr. Jerome Porath, superintendent of schools in the Archdiocese of Los Angeles; Bernadine Robinson, OP, experienced principal from the Diocese of Cleveland; Dr. Mary Frances Taymens, SND, assistant superintendent of schools in the Archdiocese of Washington and the vice-president of the Executive Committee of the NCEA Department of Secondary Schools; Gary Wilmer, principal of Saint Charles Borromeo Elementary School in the Archdiocese of St. Paul and Minneapolis and north central states regional representative of the NCEA Department of Elementary Schools.

Because Sr. Maria and the Advisory Committee were concerned that the knowledge and experience of persons dedicated to and successful in Catholic school administration have input into the project, a two-step process was developed. First, the [arch]dioceses were surveyed to determine the present practice concerning the preparation of Catholic school administrators. Of the sixty dioceses replying, few had systematic programs in place. Virtually all respondents indicated a need for support in developing such programs. Second, over three hundred persons well versed in Catholic school administration were invited to submit proposals addressing competencies to prepare Catholic school administrators.

Obviously, as this brief history illustrates, this publication, *Formation and Development for Catholic School Principals: A Three-Volume Preparation Program for Future and Neophyte Principals*, owes its existence to the interest and the hard work of a great many people. Among all the persons already noted, Lourdes Sheehan, RSM, Secretary for Education, USCC, deserves special recognition for her support and facilitation at every stage of the work. Other people who provided invaluable support services were Patricia Bain, administrative assistant at the USCC and Phyllis Kokus, manager of publications/sales at the NCEA. In addition this project is indebted to Bernadette Sykes of the USCC who spent many hours organizing the copyrighted material and ensuring that it was properly managed.

Added Feature to this Second Edition

The original edition of this first volume, concerning educational leadership, was developed largely through the collaborative efforts of Rita O'Leary, IHM; Donna Innes, CSA; Bernadine Robinson, OP; and Maria Ciriello, OP, Ph.D. Jean Barton, Ph.D., and Claire Helm, Ph.D., contributed the concept papers.

The added feature in this edition is listing the sections of the *National Catechetical Directory* and the *Catechism of the Catholic Church* that relate to the specific competencies. I am indebted to Catherine Dooley, OP, who selected the appropriate sections from the *Directory* and the *Catechism* which are included.

Two additional volumes complete this program of study. The volume on spiritual leadership addresses competencies related to faith development, building Christian community, moral and ethical development, and history and philosophy in Catholic schools. The volume on managerial leadership includes competencies regarding personnel management, institutional management, and finance and development.

Supplementary Resources

Self-assessment Survey: This instrument is keyed to correspond to the nine areas of responsibility involved in Catholic school leadership addressed in this three-volume series. Designed to be self-administered and self-scored, this guide will assist individuals to estimate their current knowledge and skills, and guide subsequent study.

Handbook: A companion publication designed to be a compact reference for pastors and parish school committees to enhance their understanding of the responsibilities of the parish school principal is also available. Called *Expectations for the Catholic School Principal: A Handbook for Pastors and Parish School Committees*, it contains a brief description of the position of the principal. Major components include the concept papers reprinted from the three volumes and new, additional chapters addressing the relationship of the pastor and superintendent to the parish school. All chapters include reflection questions and bibliography.

Finally, this work is dedicated to the countless committed, successful Catholic school principals, past and present. This program hopes to extend your work by nurturing future principals of Catholic schools.

Thank you.

Maria J. Ciriello, OP, Ph.D
Dean of the School of Education
University of Portland, Oregon

Introduction

How does a diocese prepare those who aspire to be Catholic school principals? How does a religious community provide a guided internship experience for its future administrators? How does a person interested in administration in a Catholic school system prepare? How does a practicing Catholic school administrator "update," renew, improve, or gain other insights?

In an effort to address the task of developing Catholic school leaders, a committee was formed of persons associated with the USCC Department of Education, NCEA/CACE, and the National Catholic Graduate Educational Leadership Programs (NCGELP) of Catholic Colleges and Universities. The fruits of this committee were a set of competencies encompassing the basic knowledge and skills expected of well-prepared Catholic school administrators.

The content of the individual competencies is the focus of the learning experiences presented in *Formation and Development for Catholic School Leaders* in this and two other companion volumes. These three volumes in the series constitute a program of study which may be pursued either by an individual or by a group to prepare to become a Catholic school administrator.

Each volume addresses that portion of the competencies that applies most directly to one of the three Catholic school leadership roles: educational, spiritual, and managerial. Briefly, the contents of each publication are as follows:

Volume I—Educational leadership role, which includes two areas of responsibility: 1. promoting vision using principles of good leadership and 2. directing the curricular and instructional aspects of the school.

Volume II—Spiritual leadership role, which encompasses four areas of responsibility: 1. faith development, 2. Christian community building, 3. moral and ethical formation, and 4. familiarity with the history and philosophy of Catholic schools.

Volume III—Managerial leadership role, which comprises three areas of responsibility: 1. personnel, 2. the institution, and 3. finance and development skills.

The purpose of this preparation program of study is to provide the learner with some theoretical insight into the context of Catholic school administration and some practical direction toward gaining systematic experience which will prepare and enhance one's ability to be a competent Catholic school leader.

In this educational leadership volume, the theoretical perspective is developed in a chapter preceding each practical experience chapter. Dr. Claire Helm provides a context for a new model of Catholic school leadership using a review of the literature to explore the ways leadership has been studied in the past. Dr. Donna Innes, CSA, presents a model of curriculum for Catholic educators by proposing several components to be considered in a comprehensive Catholic school curriculum.

An Overview of Catholic School Leadership Expectations

The following outline is presented to help the reader understand the scope of the complete program of study envisioned for the preparation for the Catholic school principal. This overview contains the expectations of the Catholic school principal related to three roles: educational, spiritual, and managerial leadership. Each role has several areas of responsibility. Each area of responsibility is further delineated by specific competencies.

Expectations for the Catholic School Principal

ROLE: THE PRINCIPAL AS *EDUCATIONAL LEADER*

Area of responsibility: *Leadership*

L1. Demonstrates symbolic and cultural leadership skills in developing a school climate reflecting Catholic identity

L2. Applies a Catholic educational vision to the daily activities of the school

L3. Promotes healthy staff morale

L4. Recognizes and fosters leadership ability among staff

L5. Interprets and uses research to guide action plans

L6. Identifies and effects needed change

L7. Attends to personal growth and professional development

Area of responsibility: *Curriculum and Instruction*

C1. Demonstrates a knowledge of the content and the methods of religious education

C2. Knows of the developmental stages of children and youth

C3. Recognizes and provides for cultural and religious differences

C4. Provides leadership in curriculum development, especially for the integration of Christian values

C5. Demonstrates an understanding of a variety of educational and pedagogical skills

C6. Recognizes and accommodates the special learning needs of children within the inclusive classroom

C7. Supervises instruction effectively

C8. Demonstrates an understanding of effective procedures for evaluating the learning of students

C9. Demonstrates the ability to evaluate the general effectiveness of the learning program of the school

ROLE: THE PRINCIPAL AS *SPIRITUAL LEADER*

Area of responsibility: *Faith Development*

F1. Nurtures the faith development of faculty and staff through opportunities for spiritual growth

F2. Ensures quality Catholic religious instruction of students

F3. Provides opportunities for the school community to celebrate faith

F4. Supports and fosters consistent practices of Christian service

Area of responsibility: *Building Christian Community*

B1. Fosters collaboration between the parish(es) and the school

B2. Recognizes, respects, and facilitates the role of parents as primary educators

B3. Promotes Catholic community

Area of responsibility: *Moral and Ethical Development*

M1. Facilitates the moral development and maturity of children, youth, and adults

M2. Integrates gospel values and Christian ethics into the curriculum, policies, and life of the school

Area of responsibility: *History and Philosophy*

H1. Knows the history and purpose of Catholic schools in the United States

H2. Utilizes church documents and Catholic guidelines and directives

H3. Develops and implements statements of school philosophy and mission that reflect the unique Catholic character of the school

ROLE: PRINCIPAL AS *MANAGERIAL LEADER*

Area of responsibility: *Personnel Management*

P1. Recruits, interviews, selects, and provides an orientation for school staff

P2. Knows and applies principles of adult learning and motivation

P3. Knows and applies the skills of organizational management, delegation of responsibilities, and communication skills

P4. Uses group process skills effectively with various school committees

P5. Manages conflicts effectively

P6. Evaluates staff

Area of responsibility: *Institutional Management*

I1. Provides for an orderly school environment and promotes student self-discipline

I2. Understands Catholic school governance structures and works effectively with school boards

I3. Recognizes the importance of the relationship between the school and the diocesan office

I4. Recognizes the importance of the relationship between the school and religious congregation(s)

I5. Knows civil and canon law as it applies to Catholic schools

I6. Understands state requirements and government-funded programs

I7. Understands the usefulness of current technologies

Area of responsibility: *Finance and Development*

D1. Demonstrates skills in planning and managing the school's financial resources toward developing and monitoring an annual budget

D2. Understands the basic strategies of long-range planning and applies them in developing plans for the school

D3. Provides for development in the broadest sense, including effective public relations programs (parish[es], church, and broader community) and a school marketing program

D4. Seeks resources and support beyond the school (and parish[es])

Who Will Profit from These Experiences?

Anyone interested in pursuing a self-study program to gain current knowledge and professional insights into Catholic education administration will benefit from the series of readings and activities presented here. However, the impetus for this program of training and formation grew out of the recognition that most persons do not have the opportunity to attend a Catholic college or university which offers programs to prepare Catholic school leaders. Most current and aspiring Catholic school administrators have, by necessity, received their formal education in public or non-Catholic private institutions of higher learning. Yet the expectations and responsibilities of Catholic and public school administrators are radically different. Because, by nature, these degree and certification programs do not address the unique circumstances and integral mission orientation of Catholic schools, public school administration sequences (though often excellent in their own right) are simply not adequate for Catholic school administrators.

The following set of experiences is presented to address primarily the unique mission of the Catholic school and the special demands placed upon Catholic school administrators. These activities presume that the learner has or is obtaining a graduate degree in education administration.

The appropriate use of this material is to supplement the standard education degree. These training and formation activities are in no way intended to replace or supplant standard professional preparation in education administration.

Since the following set of experiences presumes that the participant will possess prior or concurrent experience studying education administration topics, it does not pretend to be comprehensive in its treatment of any particular area of responsibility or competency. Rather, these activities are intended to build on previous knowledge and to lend a specifically "Catholic" perspective to all aspects of administration.

How to Use These Experiences

In the pages that follow each area of responsibility that is part of the spiritual leadership role is treated as a separate, freestanding learning unit. The design of each unit/area of responsibility is the same:

1. An **overview** is presented that lists the competencies included.
2. A separate **rationale** is provided to clarify the importance of each specific competency for a Catholic school administrator.
3. **Learning activities**, including integral readings, and interactions with experienced professionals are prescribed.
4. **Outcome activities** are listed to provide the learner opportunities to demonstrate mastery of the specific competency.
5. A **bibliography** organized by competency and citing additional sources of information relevant to the particular area of responsibility is included to help the learner extend personal knowledge and insights.
6. **Reprints** of many of the selections listed in the integral readings sections are included. Special permission was obtained for these reprints which should be used solely by the learner. No permission is granted for duplication of these materials. Any attempt to do so is against the law.
7. Each volume concludes with a **general bibliography** of all the sources cited in the volume.

Because people's background, life experiences, and past professional opportunities will differ widely, it is assumed that the appropriate configuration of preparation experiences will be shaped to the particular needs of the individual. Since not every aspirant will need additional education in every competency/expectation in all three roles of leadership, the experiences are deliberately designed to contain some redundancy in presentation. Such overlap is intended to provide consistency and to present each competency as a discrete part of the larger area of responsibility. The intention of this format is to make it easier to "pick and choose" those competencies that are the "best fit" for an individual's needs, while maintaining the integrity of focus of each set of learning activities.

This study program is designed to encourage the development of an active *portfolio* record containing examples of learning and outcome activities indicating both the depth and breadth of preparation experience. Such a portfolio should be a valuable resource:

1. for the applicant seeking a specific position or to give evidence of updating, and
2. for the employing agency to evaluate the candidate's readiness to assume a position.

The learning activities and proof of mastery for each of the competencies also will depend upon the structure and circumstances of the study program. Accordingly, two models are suggested:

Model I—*The experiences are being completed under the direction of a diocese or a religious community.* The diocese or religious community may choose to provide a structured program with a person or persons appointed to direct and monitor the learning activities and to review and evaluate the outcome activities of those learners participating in the program. The learners, in turn, will be expected to participate in the activities assigned and to present evidence of mastery by completing the designated outcome activities.

Model II—*The learner is an individual pursuing this study program on his/her own.* In this case, the learner is urged to seek out individual(s) who have knowledge and experience with elementary and/or secondary Catholic school administration to act as mentor(s).

Regardless of the mode used to pursue this study program, the learner is encouraged to keep an ongoing *journal* of all reading and learning experiences. Such a record will serve as an invaluable resource when one assumes administrative responsibilities.

Integral to education administration is the protracted expectation for the leader to be constantly interacting with various constituencies. One of the best ways to prepare for this demand is in a social, rather than individual or isolated, context. For that reason, the learner is encouraged to seek out a *mentor*. The stimulation of working with one or more persons willing and able to share ideas and expertise while providing guidance and support will add immeasurably to the learner's confidence and experience.

Leadership

A Leadership Perspective for Catholic Schools

Claire M. Helm, Ph.D.

Where there is no vision, the people perish. (Prv 29:18)

If you can help them [faculty] meet needs, if you can inspire them to do it gladly, you are leading; if you are telling them, you're not leading! (Helm 1989, p. 148)

"When people ask me what I do all day, I say 'I walk around is what I do . . . and sometimes I think—at the end of the day—do I have anything to show for it?'" This admission by an experienced Catholic school principal (Helm 1989, p. 100) would not be surprising to most veteran administrators. What usually stuns new principals is, in fact, the sheer scope and complexity of the typical job description for the principal. After looking at a proposed checklist of the principal's responsibilities, one would-be administrator groaned and exclaimed, "I do wonder if the Lord himself could do this job!"

Thus the common question facing Catholic school administrators is "What should be the primary focus of the Catholic school principal?" or, put another way, "What do I need to do myself and what should I delegate?" The answer to this simple but critical question is rooted in a thorough understanding of leadership theory and a deep appreciation for the unique mission of the Catholic school.

In search of leaders

A trip through the dense forest of leadership literature to the present interest in cultural and symbolic leadership requires more than a compass. Few authors are able to agree even on a definition of leadership (Stogdill 1974). Yukl (1981) notes that "The most commonly used measure of leader effectiveness is the extent to which the leader's

group or organization performs its task successfully and attains its goals" (p. 5). Kellerman (1984) asserts that leadership is "getting people to follow" (p. ix).

Regardless of the definition favored, most agree that leadership is at the heart of the successful organization. So from Galton's (1870) "great man" theory to Roberts' (1985) light-hearted summary of the leadership secrets of Attila the Hun, scholars and researchers have searched for clues to identify effective leaders. Research on leadership in the formal sense, however, is less than a century old (Stogdill 1974). Yukl (1981) notes that most of the research on leadership can be classified according to one of the following approaches: 1) trait, 2) behavior, 3) situational/contingency, and 4) power/influence.

Trait studies

One of the earliest attempts to study leadership used the trait approach. Leaders were thought to possess certain traits not found in others. The focus of most preliminary studies was the comparison of leaders with nonleaders with respect to physical characteristics, personality, and ability. This initial research did not surface traits that appeared to correlate with leadership effectiveness. Yukl (1981) asserts that this line of research tended to treat the factors "in an atomistic fashion, suggesting that each trait acted singly to determine leadership effects" (Stogdill 1974, p. 82). Hollander (1985) pointed out that the relationship of the leader to the situation was neglected as a relevant factor in these studies.

Later research used more relevant traits and improved measures and focused on patterns rather than isolated traits and skills. This later approach suggests that certain general characteristics can differentiate leaders from followers (Yukl 1981). For example an important predictor of managerial success is the broad category of managerial motivation, in particular, the desire to exercise power, a drive to compete with peers, and a positive attitude toward authority figures (McClelland 1975, Miner 1978).

Stogdill (1974) summarized trait research by noting that the characteristics of effective leaders could be grouped into *task*-related traits, such as the need for achievement, enterprise, and initiative, and *social* traits, such as the ability to enlist support, cooperation, and nurturance. Along with studies highlighting the importance of the motivational patterns of leaders, Katz (1955) and Mann (1965) focused their attention on the three types of skills associated with all effective leaders:

- human relations skills (e.g., the ability to communicate clearly and effectively),
- technical skills (e.g., specialized knowledge of methods and procedures), and
- conceptual skills (e.g., problem-solving ability).

Behavior studies

Studies of leader behavior have been both popular and useful (Yukl 1981), but the lack of agreement across studies and "the absence of a widely accepted taxonomy" of leader behaviors are "disturbing" (p. 120). Some of the earliest studies of effective and ineffective leader behaviors were done through the Ohio State Leadership Studies organized in 1945. Items on the Leader Behavior Description Questionnaire (LBDQ) yielded two patterns of behavior of particular interest. *Consideration* behavior was helpfulness, friendliness, and availability to subordinates. *Initiating structure* behavior was getting subordinates to follow rules and maintaining performance standards.

Stogdill (1974) concluded that research on the relationship of these two factors (consideration and initiation) to group productivity, satisfaction, and cohesiveness has been positive. "The most effective leaders tend to be described as high on both scales" (Stogdill 1974, p. 394). However, Yukl (1981) points out, "[T]he more general a behavior category is, . . . the less useful it is for determining what makes a leader effective in a particular situation" (p. 120).

In addition to the use of questionnaires such as the LBDQ, leader behavior has been studied using observation, activity sampling, self-report diaries, interviews, and the use of the critical incident (Yukl 1981). Efforts to develop a useful taxonomy that reconciles the discrepancies of earlier studies continue even today. Yukl and Nemeroff's (1979) list of nineteen discriminating leader behaviors includes the following:

- emphasis on subordinate performance,
- consideration given to subordinates,
- inspiration provided by the leader,
- planning by the leader,
- the management of conflict,
- the training of subordinates, and
- the extent to which praise and recognition is offered.

Situational/contingency studies

Situational theories of leadership assume that different situations require different patterns of traits and behaviors for a leader to be effective. Situational theories underscored the need to identify the factors or "moderator variables" that enhanced or nullified the influence of a leader's traits, skills, or behavior (Yukl 1981). The variables to be considered are the task itself and the past history, culture, norms, and size of the group (Hollander 1985). Situational theories have been studied by several researchers including

- Fiedler's Contingency Model (1964),
- Hershey and Blanchard's Situational Theory (1977),
- House's Path Goal Theory (1971),
- Vroom and Yetton's Decision-Making Model (1973), and
- Yukl's Multiple Linkage Model of Leadership (1981).

These theories are similar in that each deals with the effects of leaders on the satisfaction, motivation, and performance of subordinates.

Hollander (1985) notes that Fiedler's Contingency Model of Leadership Effectiveness has helped "to bridge the trait and situational approaches and opened the way for other useful contingency concepts" (p. 499). Yukl (1981) summarized his analysis of situational theories of leadership by concluding that they are "complex, imprecisely formulated, and difficult to test" (p. 169).

Power/influence studies

The fourth major approach to the study of leadership, that of power/influence, attempts to explain leader effectiveness in terms of the source of power, whether position or personality, or amount of power available to leaders and the manner in which leaders exercise power or influence over followers. Power/ influence research has also attempted to identify the impact of subordinates on leaders.

One of the most prominent power/influence theories is the Social Exchange Theory which examined the reciprocal influence between leaders and subordinates. According to this theory a fundamental form of social interaction is an exchange of benefits or favors which over time contributes to expectations of rewards (Yukl 1981). Leaders and followers both achieve their separate purposes because each has something perceived to be valuable or needed by the other. This "valuable" is used as a "bargaining chip" to satisfy the other's need. This theory is usually called upon to explain one-to-one interactions.

How leaders use power in situations where there are several subordinates is another focus of research. French and Raven (1959) propose a particularly useful topology to explain the uses of power (Yukl 1981). This topology identifies five sources of power for a leader:

- reward power: the subordinate does something in order to be rewarded;
- coercive power: the subordinate does something to avoid punishment;
- legitimate power: the leader is acknowledged to have the right or authority;
- expert power: the leader is perceived to have special knowledge or skills; and
- referent power: the subordinate admires and tends to identify with the leader.

McClelland (1970) asserts that leaders can use any of these types of power in two ways: to dominate—keeping subordinates dependent—or to empower—building the skills and confidence of subordinates. Yukl (1981) observes that historically, charismatic leaders often employ a blend of uplifting and domineering power in their leadership. This has had both good (Gandhi) and disastrous (Hitler) effects. Since almost all leadership entails some

degree of charisma, the concept is worthy of our further study.

Charisma, according to Weber (1947) is applied "to a certain quality of an individual's personality by virtue of which he [*sic*] is set apart from ordinary men [*sic*] and treated as endowed with supernatural, superhuman, or at least specifically exceptional powers or qualities" (p. 358). House (1977) first summarized the effects of charismatic leadership on followers as

- causing followers to model their behavior, affect, and beliefs after their leaders;
- articulating a transcendent goal or mission for the followers;
- inspiring self-confidence in the followers; and
- bringing about some change in the status quo.

House (1977) hypothesized that charismatic leaders behave in ways that set them apart from other leaders. Such behaviors include

- role modeling of a specific value system for the follower;
- goal articulation, particularly of a futuristic or transcendent nature (e.g., Martin Luther King's "I Have a Dream" speech);
- demonstration of confidence and high expectations for others; and
- motive-arousal leader behavior which refers to the behaviors that arouse motives in followers related to the accomplishment of the goal or mission.

Although there are some serious methodological limitations in the power studies (Yukl 1981), there have also been some significant findings for leaders. Effective leaders tend to rely more on their personal power (e.g., helping behavior) rather than their position power (e.g., insistence on proper titles) even though both types are necessary (Whyte 1969).

Stogdill (1974) uses the word "bewildering" (p. vii) to summarize his assessment of the leadership research. Yukl (1981) notes that while the field is presently in a "state of ferment and confusion" (p. 268), progress has been made in the development of our understanding of leadership processes and in the identification of the determinants of leadership effectiveness. He highlights three approaches for the improvement of leadership:

- an emphasis on research-based selection processes,
- training for effectiveness, and
- situation engineering which involves changing the situation to be more compatible with the leader's strengths.

A new paradigm of leadership

As this brief summary of the literature concludes, the study of leadership is neither straightforward nor simple. A glance at recent titles related to leadership effectiveness makes it evident that the last word on leadership has yet to be written! Many of the recent paradigms of leadership study the dynamic involved in leader-follower interactions. Burns (1978) argued that it was time to bring the literature on leadership and the literature on followership together. He asserts that there are two kinds of leadership: one transactional and the other transformational in nature.

Transactional leadership occurs when one person makes contact with another for the purpose of exchanging something of value or to satisfy personal needs (Burns 1978). It recognizes what it is we want from our work and attempts to provide it based on the performance given (Bass 1985). Transactional leadership responds to the subordinate's immediate self-interests. It is thus a reciprocal relationship in which both the leader and the subordinate exert influence or power over one another. It has many overtones of exchange theory. Bass (1985) argued, however, that a purely transactional or exchange approach to leadership was not enough to explain all types of leadership. For instance it would not explain the leadership of a Winston Churchill or a Lee Iacocca.

Burns (1978) suggests that transformational leadership recognizes the immediate needs and demands of followers but also seeks to satisfy higher needs and engages the "full person of the follower" (p. 4). The result is a kind of moral leadership because it "elevates" both the follower and the leader through a "mutual stimulation" to a "new awareness about issues of consequence" (Bass 1985, p. 17). This type of leadership embodies many of the characteristics of charismatic leadership.

Burns (1978) pointed to the significance of transformational leadership when he said, "I define leadership as leaders inducing followers to act for certain goals that represent the values and motivations—the wants and needs, the aspirations and expectations—of both leader and followers" (p. 19). Transformational leadership in the words of Bass (1985) is "leadership that motivates followers to work for transcendental goals and for aroused higher-level needs for self-actualization rather than for immediate self-interest" (p. 11). Bass maintains that this form of leadership results in achievement of higher levels of performance among individuals than previously thought possible.

The Catholic school has a mission orientation that integrates religious and academic purposes. The leader in this context must possess a strong faith and firm allegiance to the goals of the Catholic Church which is combined with an unshakable conviction about the potency of an excellent education. It appears that the characteristics of a transformational leadership style are an appropriate "fit" for one charged with preserving the integrity of the Catholic school mission. The seminal work of such researchers and writers as House (1977), Burns (1978), Bennis (1984), Bass (1985), and Sergiovanni (1990, 1992) all speak to values and expectations held for Catholic school leadership. Transcendental goals, the emphasis on value-added leadership, moral leadership, and servant leadership (Sergiovanni 1992)—the language of transformational leaders—is all quite compatible with the traditions and desires of Catholic school leaders in this country.

School effectiveness and the culture of the school

Before turning our attention to the unique environment that is the Catholic school, the next stop on the journey to understanding the demands on leadership in Catholic schools is to examine the institution to be led. A brief review of the growing body of research now popularly termed "school effectiveness research" will give form to the responsibilities of the Catholic school principal.

Some troubling reports on U.S. public education (e.g., *A Nation at Risk: The Imperative for Educational Reform* [United States Department of Education 1983]), helped to spawn the search for effective school practices as well as the leadership that contributes to this success. The research indicates that, despite socioeconomic differences, effective schools share common characteristics:

- strong instructional leadership;
- high expectations for student achievement;
- well-defined goals, in particular, a strong academic program;
- local control over instruction and staff in-service programs;
- a safe, orderly environment;
- a cohesive approach to discipline;
- a system of monitoring student progress; and
- regular student attendance (Edmonds 1979, Purkey and Smith 1982).

Attempts to understand how the characteristics of effective schools influence student learning have provided current researchers with a fascinating agenda. Briefly, the findings note that a school, as an institution, possesses a climate which permeates all aspects of school life. Describing precisely the nature of climate is often challenging. An oft-used example of the presence of climate is that a visitor walking into a school will get a "feel" for the place. This intuitive reaction is noted more objectively by Tagiuri (1968), who described climate as the total environmental quality within the school. He proposed it had four dimensions: ecology, milieu, social systems, and culture. Ecology is manifested in the physical aspects of the school such as the amount and type of student work or religious symbolism evident in the school. The milieu or social dimension includes teacher morale. The social systems incorporate the teacher-principal relationships. Finally, the culture encompasses the school's belief systems, values, cognitive structures, and meanings.

Deal and Kennedy (1983) state that culture is "the way we do things around here" (p. 14). For example, school people, whether children or adults, often try to adjust to a situation by conforming or fitting in. They "learn the ropes" by observing how others successfully maneuver in a situation and frequently follow suit with similar behavior. Put more formally, Deal (1987) asserts that those in school acquire a learned pattern of unconscious or semiconscious thought which is reflected in beliefs and reinforced by behavior. Culture then becomes embedded in the history, values, legends, stories, and ceremonies of the school and shapes the experiences of those associated with it.

Deal and Kennedy (1983) state that strong school cultures go hand in hand with school improvement.

Strong cultures provide a bonding spirit that helps "teachers to teach; students to learn; and for parents, administrators, and others to contribute to the instructional process." Culture provides ways schools can communicate their identity to outside groups "through shared values, heroes and heroines, and rituals" (p. 15). To summarize: the school as an organization exudes a climate/culture that in turn affects student outcomes, behaviors, values, growth, and satisfaction (Anderson 1982).

Leadership and the Catholic school

Drawing on the work of Burns (1978) and the effective schools literature, leadership that attends to the unique culture and symbolism as part of a transformational style should ensure a school environment that embodies the characteristics of effective schools. In a Catholic school environment the administrator is challenged to develop a school climate that demonstrates the characteristics of effective schools but that is influenced and shaped by the values and beliefs of Catholicism. Thus Catholic school principals are challenged to be transformational leaders who are also cultural and symbolic.

A symbolic leader takes on the role of "chief." By emphasizing selective attention and modeling important goals through behaviors, the chief (leader) signals to others what is of importance and value (Sergiovanni 1984). "Purposing" is of major concern to the symbolic leader. Vaill (1984) defines purposing to be those "actions . . . which have the effect of inducing clarity, consensus, and commitment regarding the organization's basic purposes" (p. 91).

The cultural leader is portrayed as a "high priest" by Sergiovanni (1984). "Seeking to define, strengthen, and articulate those enduring values, beliefs, and cultural strands that give the school its unique identity" (p. 9) is the role of the high priest. The result of successful cultural leadership is the bonding together of students, teachers, and others as "believers in the work of the school" (p. 9).

Sergiovanni (1984) in his earlier writing specifies three functions necessary for the competent public school principal:

- the technical or sound management function,
- the human or interpersonal function, and
- the educational or instructional function.

More recently Sergiovanni (1992) has come to appreciate and emphasize a fourth dimension: fostering the cultural and symbolic aspects of the school. Attention to this latter dimension is essential in a complete Catholic education that encompasses both a religious and an academic purpose.

The specific mission of the Catholic school is "the critical, systematic transmission of culture in the light of faith and the bringing forth of the power of Christian virtue by the integration of culture with faith and of faith with living" (*The Catholic School* 1977, p. 119).

What might the Catholic school visitor experience that would distinguish this school and its "culture" from its public- or private-school neighbor? The authors of *The Religious Dimension of Education in a Catholic School* (Congregation for Catholic Education 1988, no. 25) express the hope that from "the first moment that a student sets foot into a Catholic school, he or she ought to have the impression of entering a new environment, one illumined by the light of faith, . . . having its own unique characteristics" and "permeated by the Gospel spirit of love and freedom."

Byrk, Holland, Lee, and Carriedo (1984) in their study of effective Catholic elementary schools made reference to the "distinctive character that transcends religious programs and personnel" (p. 15). This character was reflected in the perceptions of the school community about the religious purpose of the Catholic school, in the social interactions among faculty and students, and in the description by teachers of their role as ministers within the Church.

In *Evangelizing the Uncoverted*, O'Malley (1991) contends that at the secondary level the challenge facing the administrators and mostly lay faculties of today is to continue to find ways to "evangelize the baptized but unconverted," "to discomfit the comfy," and to challenge the assumption of many adolescents that because they are "nice" they are necessarily good Christians (p. 3). The counter-cultural message of the Gospel in other words means that Catholic schools must continue to find ways to communicate the difficult truths of Christianity: its insecurity, apostleship, service, and suffering as well as an understanding of the Church as the "living presence of Jesus Christ in the world" (Heft 1991, p. 21).

McDermott (1985) categorized the four roles of the Catholic school leader as manager, academic leader, creator of the school environment, and religious leader. As academic leaders Catholic school principals must first seek not only "co-workers in the apostolate of teaching" (p. 43) with the appropriate credentials but also those who are going to participate as role models in the building of a Christian community. As creators of the school's climate or environment, principals are in the best position to provide the leadership necessary to create the unique sense of purpose, mission, and identity Sergiovanni (1984) claims is the mark of the truly excellent school. As religious leaders, "activators of the school's apostolic mission," Catholic school principals ensure that "growth in faith is central to the program of the school" . . . (and they summon) "the school's community to worship—the highest form of human activity" (McDermott, p. 45).

Observations of four Catholic elementary school principals, identified as transformational using Bass's Multifactor Leadership Questionnaire (Helm 1989), revealed that these principals appeared to use every opportunity to focus attention on the primacy of the school's purpose. Some of the strategies employed to this end were

- their example of practicing (modeling) as well as "preaching" the values espoused by the school,
- careful selection of teachers who "fit in" with their vision of what the school should be,
- reiteration of high expectations of the teachers as role models, and
- the emphasis placed on the central place occupied by religion class and religious services.

High visibility by the principal, attention paid to religious symbolism, and the high priority placed on positive teacher-principal and parent-principal relationships were also characteristic of all four administrators despite differences in personality and leadership style. Efforts to involve teachers in decision making appeared to contribute significantly to the high morale and positive climate apparent in these schools. Frequent, positive feedback and regular communication with teachers and parents were reflected in the high degree of cohesiveness of values identified as central to each school's mission. "The bottom line," as one teacher explained, "is that Christian values, witness, and religion are central to everything" (Helm 1989, p. 203).

Catholic school leaders for the 21st century

The answer to what should be the primary focus of a Catholic school principal thus lies in a thorough understanding and appreciation of the unique role of the Catholic school administrator. It begins with an understanding of the specific mission which is at the heart of the Catholic school: the integration of religious truth and values with life. Nurturing the dual purpose of providing an effective religious education with a quality academic education is the particular responsibility and charge of the Catholic school leader. In responding to this challenge the principal is the champion and protector of the Catholic identity of the school.

Effective principals have a clear understanding of the impact of a school's culture. More importantly, they must possess an acute awareness that as trustees of the school's identity they are in the focal position to provide the leadership necessary to create the special sense of purpose, mission, and identity that Sergiovanni (1984) claimed is the mark of the truly excellent school. This leadership is best described as cultural and symbolic or transformational. Catholic school leaders must exercise an educational vision that flows from the Catholic identity of the school and is respectful of its dual purpose. By promoting healthy staff morale and developing the leadership potential of the faculty, the Catholic school principal sustains the vision and strengthens the culture of the school. Identifying areas of needed change and developing action plans that are consistent with research are ways the leader preserves the mission and refreshes the school's identity.

It is not unusual for new principals as well as the "veterans" to express anxiety at the apparently formidable agenda facing them, particularly with respect to their religious leadership role. The words and actions of Jesus offer their own challenge as well as model. Jesus called a little child to stand in the midst of the disciples and, putting his arms around the child, Jesus said to the disciples: "Whoever welcomes a child such as this for my sake, welcomes me. And whoever welcomes me, welcomes not me, but him who sent me" (Mk 9:37). And in another place, Jesus said: "Let the children come to me and do not hinder them. It is to just such as these that the kingdom of God belongs" (Mk 10:14). Principals also could recall that Jesus clearly said: "It was not you who chose me, it was I who chose you to go forth and bear fruit. Your fruit must endure so that all you ask the Father in my name he will give you. The command I give you is this, that you love one another" (Jn 15:16–17).

U.S. Catholic school leaders of the twenty-first century inherit the legacy of all those who have gone before them—a legacy and rich tradition embedded in the histories of our schools and in the biographies of the clergy and the religious men and women whose faith, courage, and vision nurtured and inspired us all. May their legacy live on in the next generation of leaders!

Reflection Questions

1. Some say "leaders are born not made." What conclusions do you draw after reviewing the leadership literature?

2. Are there any specific personal traits needed to function effectively in the particular context of Catholic education?

3. What, if any, particular behaviors are expected of Catholic school leaders by the parish? parents? civic community? public school counterparts?

4. Much of the literature specifies that the "situation" must be taken into account when examining the effectiveness of the leader. Catholic schools serve diverse communities nationwide that have widely divergent economic conditions, resources, and needs. How do the particular circumstances of a school community influence the leadership of the Catholic school principal?

5. Because most of the administration of the Catholic school is decided and managed at the local school level (in contrast to the more centralized public school system), the Catholic school principal has a broad scope of responsibilities. Emerging needs such as the necessity for systematic public relations, marketing, development programs, political action demands, and the family's expanding child care needs further tax the resources of the school and its personnel. In the face of these formidable obligations how ought the Catholic school principal proceed?

6. In the Catholic school context is it more appropriate for the principal to rely on "personal" or "position" power to effect change?

7. Practically speaking, in the overall leadership context of the Catholic school, are there any characteristics of a transactional style versus a transformational style that Catholic school leaders might emphasize in order to achieve the dual purpose of the Catholic school?

8. How would you apply the cultural and symbolic behavior of leaders theoretically presented in this chapter to a specific Catholic school familiar to you?

9. Keeping in mind the expectations of the Catholic school principal: What if any, aspects of leadership must ordinarily be reserved to the principal or head of the school? Which aspects are more appropriately shared?

Resources

Anderson, C. S. 1982. The search for school climate: A review of the research. *Review of Educational Research* 52(3):368–420.

Bass, B. M. 1985. Leadership and performance beyond expectations. New York: The Free Press.

Bennis, W. 1984. Transformation power and leadership. In *Leadership and organizational culture*, ed. T. J. Sergiovanni and J. E. Corbally, 64–71. Urbana-Champaign: University of Illinois Press.

Bryk, A. S., P. B. Holland, V. E. Lee, and R. A. Carriedo. 1984. *Effective Catholic schools: An exploration.* Washington, D.C.: National Catholic Educational Association.

Burns, J. M. 1978. *Leadership.* New York: Harper and Row.

Congregation for Catholic Education. 1977. *The Catholic school.* Washington, D.C.: United States Catholic Conference.

———. 1988. *The religious dimension of education in a Catholic school: Guidelines for reflection and renewal.* Washington, D.C.: United States Catholic Conference.

Deal, T. E. 1987. The culture of schools. In *Leadership: Examining the elusive, 1987 Yearbook*, 3–15. Alexandria, Va.: Association for Supervision and Curriculum Development.

Deal, T. E., and A. A. Kennedy. 1983. Culture and school performance. *Educational Leadership* 40(5):14–15.

Deal, T. E., and K. D. Peterson. 1990. *The principal's role in shaping school culture*. Washington, D.C.: United States Department of Education.

Drahmann, T., and A. Stenger. 1989. *The Catholic school principal: An outline for action*. Revised. Washington, D.C.: National Catholic Educational Association.

Edmonds, R. R. 1979. Effective schools for the urban poor. *Educational Leadership* 37(2):15–27.

Fiedler, F. E. 1964. A contingency model of leadership effectiveness. In *Advances in experimental social psychology*, ed. L. Berkowitz. New York: Academic Press.

French, J. R., and B. Raven. 1959. The bases of social power. In *Studies in social power*, ed. D. Cartwright. Ann Arbor, Mich.: Institute for Social Research.

Galton, F. 1870. *Hereditary genius*. New York: Appleton.

Heft, J. 1991. Catholic identity and the Church. In *What makes a school Catholic?*, ed. F. D. Kelly, 14–21. Washington, D.C.: National Catholic Educational Association.

Helm, C. M. 1989. Cultural and symbolic leadership in Catholic elementary schools: An ethnographic study. Ph.D. diss., The Catholic University of America, Washington, D.C.

Hersey, P., and K. H. Blanchard. 1977. *Management of organizational behavior*. 3d ed. Englewood Cliffs, N.J.: Prentice-Hall.

Hollander, E. P. 1985. Leadership and power. In *Handbook of social psychology*. Vol. II. *Special fields and applications*, ed. E. Aronson, 3d ed., 485–537. New York: Random House.

House, R. J. 1971. A path goal theory of leader effectiveness. *Administrative Science Quarterly* 16:321–39.

———. 1977. A 1976 theory of charismatic leadership. In *Leadership: The cutting edge*, ed. J. G. Hunt and L. L. Larson, 189–207. Carbondale: Southern Illinois University Press.

Katz, R. L. 1955. Skills of an effective administrator. *Harvard Business Review* January-February: 33–42.

Kellerman, B., ed. 1984. *Leadership: Multidisciplinary perspectives*. Englewood Cliffs, N.J.: Prentice-Hall.

Kelly, F. D., ed. 1991. *What makes a school Catholic?* Washington, D.C.: National Catholic Educational Association.

Larranaga, R. 1990. *Calling it a day: Daily meditations for workaholics*. San Francisco: Harper and Row.

Mann, F. C. 1965. Toward an understanding of the leadership role in formal organization. In *Leadership and productivity*, ed. R. Dubin, G. C. Homans, F. C. Mann, and D. C. Miller. San Francisco: Chandler.

McClelland, D. 1970. The two faces of power. *Journal of International Affairs* 24(1):29–47.

———. 1975. *Power: The inner experience*. New York: Irvington.

McDermott, E. 1985. Distinctive qualities of the Catholic school. In *NCEA Keynote Series No. 1*. Washington, D.C.: National Catholic Educational Association.

Miner, J. B. 1978. Twenty years of research on role motivation theory of managerial effectiveness. *Personnel Psychology* 31:739–60.

Nouwen, H. 1989. *In the name of Jesus: Reflections on Christian leadership*. New York: Crossroad Publishing Company.

O'Malley, W. J. 1991. Evangelizing the unconverted. In *What makes a school Catholic?*, ed. F. D. Kelly, 3–9. Washington, D.C.: National Catholic Educational Association.

Purkey, S., and M. S. Smith. 1982. Synthesis of research on effective schools. *Educational Leadership* 40(3):64–69.

Roberts, W. 1985. *Leadership secrets of Attila the Hun*. New York: Warner Books.

Sergiovanni, T. J. 1984. Leadership and excellence in schooling. *Educational Leadership* 41(5):4–13.

———. 1990. *Value-added leadership: How to get extraordinary performance in schools*. San Diego: Harcourt, Brace, Jovanovich Publishers.

———. 1992. *Moral leadership: Getting to the heart of school improvement*. San Francisco: Jossey-Bass Publishers.

Stogdill, R. M. 1974. *Handbook of leadership: A survey of theory and research*. New York: The Free Press.

Tagiuri, R. 1968. The concept of organizational climate. In *Organizational climate: Exploration of a concept*, ed. R. Tagiuri and G. H. Litwin. Boston: Harvard University, Division of Research, Graduate School of Business Administration.

United States Department of Education. 1983. *A nation at risk: The imperative for educational reform*. Washington, D.C.

Vaill, P. B. 1984. The purposing of high-performing systems. In *Leadership and organizational culture*, ed. T. J. Sergiovanni and J. E. Corbally, 85–104. Urbana-Champaign: University of Illinois Press.

Vroom, V. H., and P. W. Yetton. 1973. *Leadership and decision-making*. Pittsburgh: University of Pittsburgh Press.

Weber, M. 1947. *The theory of social and economic organization*. New York: Oxford University Press.

Whyte, W. F. 1969. *Organizational behavior: Theory and applications*. Homewood, Ill.: Irwin.

Yukl, G. A. 1981. *Leadership in organizations*. Englewood Cliffs, N.J.: Prentice-Hall, Inc.

Yukl, G. A., and W. Nemeroff. 1979. Identification and measurement of specific categories of leadership behavior: A progress report. In *Crosscurrents in leadership*, ed. J. G. Hunt and L. L. Larson. Cardondale: Southern Illinois University Press.

Area of Responsibility: Leadership

Bernadine Robinson, OP; Rita O'Leary, IHM; Maria Ciriello, OP, Ph.D.

Frequently one hears the phrase, "The leadership makes the difference." The role of leader in a Catholic school goes beyond the generic definition, "the position or office of a leader." According to Ristau (1991), leaders are those who hold a strong belief about what needs to be done and why it should happen; they see ways to get things accomplished. They are risk-takers with only a bit of sensible fear about the future. Fullan (1991) confirms this in a succinct manner by stating that leadership relates to mission, direction, and inspiration.

The principal as educational leader in a Catholic school is called to the following expectations:

L1. To demonstrate *symbolic and cultural leadership* skills in developing a school climate reflective of its Catholic identity

L2. To apply a *Catholic educational vision* to the daily activities of the school

L3. To promote healthy *staff morale*

L4. To recognize *leadership ability among staff* and to foster this ability

L5. To interpret and use *research to guide action plans*

L6. To identify and *effect* needed *change*

L7. To attend to *personal growth and* professional *development*

The following pages address each leadership expectation separately. In an introduction a rationale is presented to clarify the importance of the expectation as a basic competency for the Catholic school administrator. Learning activities including readings and interactions with experienced professionals are prescribed. To foster optimum growth and insight the learner is encouraged to seek a mentor and to make every effort to interact with personnel actively involved in the day-to-day functioning of Catholic educational institutions. A written record (journal) of all related readings and activities is integrated to enhance personal development and to provide a systematic chronicle of professional experiences. Finally, outcome activities are listed to provide the learner opportunities to demonstrate mastery of the specific competency.

Role: Principal as Educational Leader

Area: Leadership

Competency: L1
Symbolic and Cultural Leadership

The leadership function required of a Catholic school principal goes beyond sound management, educational knowledge, and interpersonal skills. The principal is called to symbolic and cultural leadership.

Sergiovanni (1990) describes the symbolic leader as one who assumes the role of *chief* and who, by emphasizing selective attention (the modeling of important goals and behaviors), signals to the others what is of importance and value.

Owens (1987) emphasizes that there is a precondition for symbolic leadership. Leaders must think clearly about what is of importance and value. They must develop a vision about a desired state of affairs that is clear to them—one they can articulate to others. He maintains, however, that *symbolic* leadership is insufficient to provide excellence in schooling. Each school has a particular *culture*—a uniqueness, a history, traditions, and customs that leaders must emphasize and make coherent.

Attention to building the skills of symbolic and cultural leadership can create a school climate of purpose that reflects a Catholic identity since the school has a religious and moral character as well as an academic focus.

To support and give evidence of professional growth in demonstrating a knowledge of symbolic and cultural leadership skills, the learner will engage in the listed activities under the direction of the diocese (Model I) or through a self-directed program and/or with the guidance of a mentor (Model II).

The primary means of keeping a consistent record of activities is to keep an ongoing JOURNAL which would contain:
1) a *Dated Log* section recording when activities were undertaken and completed,
2) a *Reading/Response* section in which notes from suggested readings and the response reactions are systematically organized, and

3) an *Experience(Activity)/Reflection* section in which one records ideas and insights gained through interacting with people or seeking out additional information in the course of completing the activities.

Learning Activities: L1
Symbolic and Cultural Leadership

1. Read the following and respond with reactions in a journal.* Ideally, you should discuss these readings and your reactions with a mentor. These integral readings are reprinted for your convenience on pages 30–46.

Congregation for Catholic Education. 1988. *The religious dimension of education in a Catholic school: Guidelines for reflection and renewal.* Washington, D.C.: United States Catholic Conference, nos. 24–46.

Deal, T. E., and K. D. Peterson. 1990. *The principal's role in shaping school culture.* Washington, D.C.: United States Department of Education, Office of Educational Research and Improvement, 16–33.

National Conference of Catholic Bishops. 1979. *Sharing the light of faith: National catechetical directory for Catholics of the United States.* Washington, D.C.: United States Catholic Conference, nos. 206–11, 215.

Reck, C. 1991. Catholic identity. In *The Catholic identity of Catholic schools*, eds. J. Heft and C. Reck, 26–27. Washington, D.C.: National Catholic Educational Association.

Sergiovanni, T. J. 1990. *Value-added leadership.* New York: Harcourt, Brace, Jovanovich, 82–90, 151–52.

Also, read the following sections from the *Catechism.*

Libreria Editrice Vaticana. 1994. *Catechism of the Catholic Church.* Washington, D.C.: United States Catholic Conference.

Nos. 1897–98: The role of authority is to ensure the common good.

Nos. 1902–03: The responsibility of authority is to be just and act as a moral force respecting the common good.

* In your journal, note insights you gleaned concerning ways of creating bonds and commitment to values within a school community,

---

making use of existing connections that already link families, school, and Church in the Catholic school. What further questions do you have? What ideas do you have for application in the future?

2. Visit two Catholic schools. Learn the history of each school. What symbols and slogans representing values do the schools utilize? What rituals and practices provide special occasions for celebrating and binding the school community to traditions and values? (If access to Catholic schools is not feasible, visit other schools, day care institutions, a college, or places where working with children occurs in a structured/educational setting. The purpose of this activity is to help you understand how culture is developed and sustained by educational institutions.) In any case, compare and contrast the many ways symbolic and cultural leadership is expressed.

3. Many Catholic schools have a video or printed matter which advertises the school's special qualities and values. Collect as many different examples as possible. How are the symbols, slogans, and ritual practices depicted? What impression of the institution do these artifacts convey to you? What messages do these materials convey? Begin developing a resource file by noting the ideas that appeal to you. (Again, if schools are not available for comparison, investigate nonprofit organizations that work with or for children or other social causes.)

4. If the diocese has a principals' handbook, look for the section that states the educational philosophy of the diocese. How does the philosophy address the religious and moral focus the Catholic school is to maintain? Do you think the perspective is complete? How is the philosophy implemented in the remaining sections of the handbook? If you had not read the philosophy, could you gain insights into the beliefs of the diocese from the other material presented? (If there is no handbook in the diocese or if you cannot obtain one, write a philosophy for the diocese that supports a religious and moral focus for Catholic schools.)

As a result of study, reflection, and interaction with knowledgeable individuals, the learner will be able to complete the following activities. The quality of response to these activities should give some indication of the level of expertise the learner is able to bring to the situation.

Outcome Activities: L1
Symbolic and Cultural Leadership

1. Make a list of the values you believe should be emphasized by the leader who is building a strong culture through symbolism. For each value list at least two things you would do to make these values real to the faculty, parents, and students.

2. Name at least three special occasions in a school year that would be cause for celebration. Develop a specific plan that could be used to provide opportunities for binding students, faculty, parents, and, if applicable, parishioners to traditions and values.

3. Using your educational experience as a student, teacher or administrator, think of a situation in the past that is an example of individuals either exhibiting or not exhibiting appropriate cultural and symbolic leadership. In light of what you have read and learned, describe and evaluate the experience. Tell what you would affirm and, perhaps, imitate or what you might change or improve. In general, what insights do you have for the situation using the "advantage of hindsight"?

4. Design a brochure which could be used to represent a Catholic school in which you have worked. What elements should be included to convey the speical qualities and values of the school?

Role: Principal as Educational Leader

Area: Leadership

Vision is an important dimension of leadership. Sheive (1987) observes that less effective principals have no vision, no blueprint for their schools. They spend time maintaining tranquility in the here and now. Leaders with vision focus on possibilities.

Perri (1989) maintains that the competent visionary leader is well-informed about cutting-edge developments in education, is well-grounded in tried and true practices of the profession, and is able to see where the school is to be in three to five years. The Catholic school educator seeks to actualize academic and organizational excellence, but also to communicate a world vision with a clear sense of Gospel values.

Peters (1985) suggests that a principal talk openly and frequently about what the school stands for and believes in, and where the school should be headed, allowing people to buy into and take part in shaping the way.

Attention given to applying a Catholic educational vision to the daily activities of the school through the vision of the leader and the covenant the group shares is key to a successful program and basic to the purpose of Catholic education.

To support and give evidence of professional growth in demonstrating a knowledge of the procedures for applying a Catholic educational vision to the daily activities of the school, the learner will engage in the listed activities under the direction of the diocese (Model I) or through a self-directed program and/or with the guidance of a mentor (Model II).

The primary means of keeping a consistent record of activities is to keep an ongoing JOURNAL which would contain:

1) a *Dated Log* section recording when activities were undertaken and completed,
2) a *Reading/Response* section in which notes from suggested readings and the response reactions are systematically organized, and
3) an *Experience(Activity)/Reflection* section in which

one records ideas and insights gained through interacting with people or seeking out additional information in the course of completing the activities.

Learning Activities: L2
Catholic Educational Vision

1. Read the following and respond with reactions in a journal.* Ideally, you should discuss these readings and your reactions with a mentor. These integral readings are reprinted for your convenience on pages 47–55.

National Conference of Catholic Bishops. 1973. *To teach as Jesus did: A pastoral message on Catholic education.* Washington, D.C.: United States Catholic Conference, no. 82.

———. 1979. *Sharing the light of faith: National catechetical directory for Catholics of the United States.* Washington, D.C.: United States Catholic Conference, nos. 30, 232.

———. 1990. *In support of Catholic elementary and secondary schools.* Washington, D.C.: United States Catholic Conference, 6.

Perri, S. 1989. The principal as teacher of teachers. In *Reflections on the role of the Catholic school principal,* ed. R. Kealey, 67–74. Washington, D.C.: National Catholic Educational Association.

Sergiovanni, T. J. 1990. *Value-added leadership.* New York: Harcourt, Brace, Jovanovich, 56–63.

Sheive, L. T., and M. B. Schoenheit. 1987. Vision and the work of educational leaders. In *Leadership: Examining the elusive, 1987 yearbook,* 94, 96–98. Alexandria, Va.: Association for Supervision and Curriculum Development.

Also, read the following sections from the *Catechism.*

Libreria Editrice Vaticana. 1994. *Catechism of the Catholic Church.* Washington, D.C.: United States Catholic Conference.

Nos. 737–38: The mission of the Church is the sign of the mission of Christ in the world . . . to announce, bear witness, make present, and spread the mystery of the Trinity.

* In your journal, note insights concerning ways in which a principal converts "vision" to "actuality." How does he or she make informed decisions? inspire? share decision-making?

---

2. In 1990, the bishops issued a statement of support of Catholic schools that referred to their 1973 statement, *To Teach as Jesus Did.* Compare the mission set for schools in the earlier document with the goals of the 1990 statement. Has the emphasis changed in the ensuing years? What is the continuity between the statements? What are the issues and challenges for persons leading the schools today?

3. Part of the Catholic educational mission and vision is to be open to the *Message*, to build upon it in *Community*, to witness it in *Worship,* and to live it through *Service.* Interview at least three people—principals and/or youth ministers and pastors concerning the ways they work with faculty, students, and parents to make them aware of areas of human need and provide opportunities for the practice of Christ-like service. How would you describe the "vision" of the personnel? Did you get the impression that the personnel have a systematic plan or program in place to raise awareness in these areas? Did the described activities take into consideration the developmental level and/or allow for individual differences or circumstances of the recipients? Was there an attempt to involve families and others in the implementation?

4. Discuss with a school principal the role of parents in the school in terms of complementing the "vision."
   a. What types of activities, involvement, and/or roles are parents encouraged to assume? What groups are established to support the school (e.g., a functioning school board, school finance committee, home-school association)? Are there training programs in place for school board members and volunteers? How does the principal assess the contribution of parents?
   b. If possible, talk with one or two parents who have children in the school. Are these particular parents active in the school? What reasons do they give for their level of involvement? Then, specifically seek out two "active" parents. How do they view the importance of their contributions to the school?

   c. In general, how would you assess the general level of parent involvement? What potential is or is not being tapped? If asked, what suggestions or comments would you make to the leadership of the school?

5. Research the resources and agencies within the civic and diocesan community that the school may call upon to help children and families who may have special needs. Seek out a school principal to learn if the school has in place any programs which specifically address families or children in crisis (e.g., alcohol, abuse, death, etc.) or for situations that are often dangerous (e.g., latchkey children) and/or overwhelming (e.g., loss of job, etc.). How will you use this information as you develop your own "vision" for fostering *Message, Community, Worship,* and *Service* in the Catholic school you may one day administer?

As a result of study, reflection, and interaction with knowledgeable individuals, the learner will be able to complete the following activities. The quality of response to these activities should give some indication of the level of expertise the learner is able to bring to the situation.

Outcome Activities: L2
Catholic Educational Vision

1. You have accepted a position as a principal at a parish school (grades K–6) where the neighborhood is unsafe, families are poor, and parental nurturing appears wanting. The school, at present, has no definite program to address these problems. Develop a section of a mission statement in which support for children and families is mentioned. Then, based on your research, outline a possible one-year and three-year plan that is consistent with that mission statement.

2. Choose one of the recent recommendations proposed by a national committee (e.g., National Teachers of Mathematics) to improve teaching/learning, communication, evaluation, or materials for teaching a particular subject. If you are convinced of its educational value, what

steps will you take to gain consensus and commitment and begin implementation? If you think the recommendation is unworthy, give the rationale for your opinion and suggest a course of action or recommendation to replace it. What steps would you take to move this idea to reality within the school and parish and in the larger community?

3. Describe the "ideal school" which uses every opportunity to work in partnership with parents/guardians in the religious/educational (academic) formation of their children. What would these opportunities include? Name all the factors that would be needed to allow for such a program. What means would need to be taken (by administration, teachers, parish, parents) to accomplish such a program?

Role: Principal as Educational Leader

Area: Leadership

Compentency: L3
Staff Morale

There are at least two reasons for an educational leader to promote healthy staff morale: (1) It leads to higher levels of commitment and performance and (2) it is right and good for teachers and others to find their work satisfying and meaningful (Sergiovanni 1992).

Many researchers have tried to determine what creates job satisfaction and commitment in an individual. Few dispute that the work itself can count as an important motivator. Personal satisfaction can be gained from achievement, recognition, and responsibility (Csikszentimihalyi 1990).

Blase (1992) conducted research to ask teachers to name the qualities and/or activities of principals that most affected them in a positive way. Teachers frequently mentioned that sincere positive reinforcement (praise) from the administrator left them feeling "encouraged, appreciated, recognized." Most admired qualities of administrators were honesty (a consistency between words and actions) and optimism (positive thinking).

Levine (1989) states that at times staff morale can drop because of "turning points" in adults' lives. Opportunities to learn of stage and phase theories of adult development can be helpful. With increased awareness, a staff can support each other through predictable cycles of personal development while working to meet professional responsibilities.

Administrators also need to be cognizant of the wealth of information concerning generally accepted principles of adult learning. Many attempts at in-service or staff development are met with resistance because adults want to be involved in the planning and design of their development (Ristau 1989).

Attention given by the Catholic school principal to promoting healthy staff morale is performing an essential and unique service not only for improving educational practices, but also for the betterment of the lives of the adults and children involved.

To support and give evidence of professional growth in demonstrating a knowledge of the procedures for promoting healthy staff morale, the learner will engage in the listed activities under the direction of the diocese (Model I) or through a self-directed program and/or with the guidance of a mentor (Model II).

The primary means of keeping a consistent record of activities is to keep an ongoing JOURNAL which would contain:

1) a *Dated Log* section recording when activities were undertaken and completed,

2) a *Reading/Response* section in which notes from suggested readings and the response reactions are systematically organized, and

3) an *Experience(Activity)/Reflection* section in which one records ideas and insights gained through interacting with people or seeking out additional information in the course of completing the activities.

Learning Activities: L3
Staff Morale

1. Read the following and respond with reactions in a journal.* Ideally, you should discuss these readings and your reactions with a mentor. These integral readings are reprinted for your convenience on pages 56–69.

Blase, J., and P. C. Kirby. 1992. *Bringing out the best in teachers.* Newbury Park, Calif.: Corwin Press, 10–21, 99–111.

Knipper, C., and D. Suddarth. 1991. Involving staff in the in-service process. In *Capital wisdom: Papers from the Principals Academy 1991,* 29–34. Washington, D.C.: National Catholic Educational Association.

Ristau, K. 1989. The role of the principal in the ongoing education of teachers. In *Reflections on the role of the Catholic school principal,* ed. R. Kealey, 60–62. Washington, D.C.: National Catholic Educational Association.

Sergiovanni, T. J. 1992. *Moral leadership: Getting to the heart of school improvement.* San Francisco: Jossey-Bass, 59–65.

Also, read the following sections from the *Catechism*.
Libreria Editrice Vaticana. 1994. *Catechism of the Catholic Church*. Washington, D.C.: United States Catholic Conference.

Nos. 1913–17: The concept of participation is explored along with its value to the common good.

No. 1917: Specifies the responsibilities of the leader to encourage participation.

* In your journal, note insights concerning ways one promotes healthy staff morale. How can a principal utilize knowledge of human growth and development and adult learning in staff relationships? What kind of support do teachers need from administrators?

2. Visit at least two schools. Talk with the principals and other personnel (e.g., secretary, teachers, housekeeping staff) if possible. What indicators, based on your readings, did you observe that indicated a healthy staff morale is promoted within the school? What might be areas of possible concern? If the school is associated with a parish, find out what activities are used to foster home, school, and parish unity. If possible, interview the pastor to learn his ideas about his responsibility and involvement with the school. What other nonverbal indications did you notice that contribute to staff morale? What were the similarities and differences between the schools? What lessons have you learned from this experience that you will want to apply in the future?

3. Interview at least three or four teachers (preferably from different schools). What personal traits do they admire most in the leaders with whom they have been associated? What behaviors on the part of the principal enable the teacher to do his or her best work? What motivates each of these teachers? Is it the same for everyone? How did the experiences of these persons affirm or differ from your own experiences of being enabled (or hampered) by a

principal when you were a teacher? What lessons have you learned about leaders and "followers"? What have you learned about yourself?

As a result of study, reflection, and interaction with knowledgeable individuals, the learner will be able to complete the following activities. The quality of response to these activities should give some indication of the level of expertise the learner is able to bring to the situation.

Outcome Activities: L3
Staff Morale

1. Name five specific ways a school principal helps to create a positive working/learning environment. Are there cautions one should keep in mind in planning motivational strategies to build healthy staff morale? If you were to implement these strategies, which would be easy or "natural" for you and which might you need to "work at"? What support or preparation would you need to implement these ideas?

2. Drawing on your past or present experience as a teacher, list ten factors or characteristics of the job of teaching that can be improved or enriched. Name at least two strategies to address the improvement or enrichment of each factor. How do you support your choice of strategies?

3. List the steps you would take to involve teachers in determining topics of interest and concern to begin to design an in-service plan for the year. Then give the details of the procedure you would use once possible topics have surfaced.

4. Develop a specific plan of daily, weekly, monthly, and yearly activities that will encourage healthy staff morale in your school. What assumptions have you made in developing this plan?

Role: Principal as Educational Leader

Area: Leadership

Compentency: L4
Leadership Ability Among Staff

Burns (1978) identifies two basic types of leadership: the transactional and the transforming. With a *transactional* style, the leader approaches followers with an eye to exchanging one thing for another (rewards for satisfactory work). *Transforming* leadership recognizes an existing need, looks for potential motives and higher needs in followers, and engages the full person of the follower. The result is a relationship of mutual stimulation and elevation that converts followers into leaders.

In schools of today, the numerous complex tasks are too much for one person (the principal) to deal with. There is also an increasing specialization of teachers and a desire on their part for a higher valuation of their capabilities. According to Barth (1991), these are promising issues for the improvement of schools from within. It is possible for a principal, adopting a transformational style of leadership, to enable staff members to discover and be eager to share their skills and talents. The school can become a community of leaders offering independence, interdependence, resourcefulness, and collegiality.

Ristau (1991) states that the idea of a great leader at the top who has all the answers and who can make anything happen is out of date and will not work today. The emerging model for the Catholic school principal is a circular one—"top down authoritarianism yielding to a networking style."

Attention given by the Catholic school principal to recognizing leadership ability among staff members and then fostering this ability through encouragement, modeling, and especially commitment will lead to full participation and professionalism that adequately responds to the challenges of a new age.

To support and give evidence of professional growth in demonstrating a knowledge of the procedures for recognizing and fostering leadership abilities among staff members, the learner will engage in the listed activities under the direction of the diocese (Model I) or through a self-directed program and/or with the guidance of a mentor (Model II).

The primary means of keeping a consistent record of activities is to keep an ongoing JOURNAL which would contain:

1) a *Dated Log* section recording when activities were undertaken and completed,

2) a *Reading/Response* section in which notes from suggested readings and the response reactions are systematically organized, and

3) an *Experience(Activity)/Reflection* section in which one records ideas and insights gained through interacting with people or seeking out additional information in the course of completing the activities.

Learning Activities: L4
Leadership Ability Among Staff

1. Read the following and respond with reactions in a journal.* Ideally, you should discuss these readings and your reactions with a mentor. These integral readings are reprinted for your convenience on pages 70–79.

   Barth, R. S. 1991. *Improving schools from within.* San Francisco: Jossey-Bass, 133–46.

   Ristau, K. 1991. The challenge: To provide leadership within Catholic schools. In *Leadership of and on behalf of Catholic schools*, 12–17. Washington, D.C.: National Catholic Educational Association.

   Sergiovanni, T. J. 1992. *Moral leadership: Getting to the heart of school improvement.* San Francisco: Jossey-Bass, 67–72.

   Also, read the following sections from the *Catechism*.
   Libreria Editrice Vaticana. 1994. *Catechism of the Catholic Church.* Washington, D.C.: United States Catholic Conference.

   Nos. 1878–80: Working together in love and friendship mirrors the love of the Trinity. Through society individuals receive gifts which enrich themselves as well as the group.

   Nos. 1882–85: The principal of subsidiarity allows for the individual gifts of the members to develop capacities for the good of the group. It aims at harmony and order.

No. 1889: Grace strengthens individuals and inspires a life of self-giving.

Nos. 1905–12: The concept of the "common good" along with its essential elements of respect for the person, social well-being and development, and peace is explored at length.

* In your journal, note insights concerning ways one identifies and fosters leadership ability. How does a principal give needed assistance? Should everyone on staff be offered opportunities for leadership? If so, how is this accomplished?

2. Interview a school principal about his or her views regarding the characteristics of the ideal teacher. Identify the philosophical perspectives that the principal seems to prefer in the ideal teacher. Was leadership ability mentioned? In what context?

3. If possible, observe a meeting of department heads, specialty groups in education, a parish council meeting, etc. (where everyone at the meeting has some expertise to offer). Take notes on how the meeting was organized and conducted. Who led or presided at the meeting? What roles did the individuals take in the course of the meeting? Where did the "real" leadership reside? Was it always with the same person? When is one style more effective than another style?

4. Interview five or six teachers. Ask: (1) If you were asked and given time, what assignment or responsibility in the school would you find exciting? (2) Other than teaching in the classroom, what responsibilities do you now have that are enriching to the school as well as to yourself? (3) How do you exhibit leadership in the school? What conclusions can you draw about the potential, expertise, and commitment each of these individuals could bring to a leadership situation?

As a result of study, reflection, and interaction with knowledgeable individuals, the learner will be able to complete the following activities. The quality of response to these activities should give some indication of the level of expertise the learner is able to bring to the situation.

Outcome Activities: L4
Leadership Ability Among Staff

1. Develop a ten-item attitude questionnaire which could be given to teachers to assess their feelings about staff involvement and empowerment. Give a rationale for your choice of items. How would you use such an instrument? What would you do with the results?

2. "Transformational leadership begins with followership based on compelling ideas" (Sergiovanni 1992). But most teachers (like most principals) need assistance in putting compelling ideas into successful actions. Based on your readings and experience, develop a plan which principals might use to help them bring compelling ideas to reality. How would you advise principals to work with the faculty and staff to promote fresh ideas and then bring them to fruition?

3. Oftentimes, teachers or staff complain that "going to meetings and working on plans is just a waste of time." Teachers complain that, in the past, they have worked hard to develop an idea and then, after spending much time and effort on the project, "nothing happens."
   a. When this situation describes actual experience: How does this affect the progress of the school? What is the apparent effect on teachers? How does this affect the role of the principal? What advice would you give a principal to address this situation?
   b. Based upon your research and experience, develop several guidelines a principal might use in identifying important responsibilities and deciding why, when, and to whom they shall be delegated. How shall accountability be built into the process for both the principal and the teachers/staff?

Role: Principal as Educational Leader

Area: Leadership

School improvement is a constant theme for effective principals. Even though the data from research studies on students from Catholic schools consistently indicate findings of high performance, Convey (1992) cautions against complacency, reminding educational leaders that the effectiveness of a particular school must be individually ascertained.

Glickman (1990) suggests that research, which once was the province of experts and consultants, now becomes part of the day-to-day operation in schools where principals and staff seek to promote continuous growth. This research becomes a basis for determining professional actions as to the what and how of improving learning for students.

To make intelligent, thoughtful responses, formulate action plans, and engage others in the resolution of problems, the educational leader must have a knowledge base that provides substance. In addition to the large body of scholarly research in the field of education, McCleary (1992) proposes drawing concepts from related and supporting fields—management, philosophy, and social sciences as well as communications and computer science.

Attention given by the Catholic school principal to interpreting and using research to guide action plans increases credibility and leads to the use of effective approaches in improving education.

To demonstrate increased knowledge of procedures for interpreting and using research to guide action plans, the learner will engage in the listed activities under the direction of the diocese (Model I) or through a self-directed program and/or with the guidance of a mentor (Model II).

The primary means of keeping a consistent record of activities is to keep an ongoing JOURNAL which would contain:

1) a *Dated Log* section recording when activities were undertaken and completed,
2) a *Reading/Response* section in which notes from suggested readings and the response reactions are systematically organized, and

3) an *Experience(Activity)/Reflection* section in which one records ideas and insights gained through interacting with people or seeking out additional information in the course of completing the activities.

Learning Activities: L5
Research to Guide Action Plans

1. Read the following and respond with reactions in a journal.* Ideally, you should discuss these readings and your reactions with a mentor. These integral readings are reprinted for your convenience on pages 80–112.

   Convey, J. J. 1992. *Catholic schools make a difference: Twenty-five years of research*. Washington, D.C.: National Catholic Educational Association, 6–8, 33–34, 59, 62.

   National Conference of Catholic Bishops. 1979. *Sharing the light of faith: National catechetical directory for Catholics of the United States*. Washington, D.C.: United States Catholic Conference, no. 223.

   United States Department of Education. 1986. *What works: Research about teaching and learning*. Washington, D.C.: Office of Educational Research and Improvement, 19, 21–23, 25, 27, 29, 31–39, 41–43, 45–47, 49–53, 55, 57, 59–62.

   Wang, M. C., G. D. Haertel, and H. J. Walberg. 1990. What influences learning? A content analysis of review literature. *Journal of Educational Research* 84(1):30–43.

   * In your journal, note insights you gained concerning the correct way to interpret and engage in educational research as well as some methods for formulating action plans based on credible research.

2. Using a copy of *What Works: Research about Teaching and Learning* (op. cit.), compare practices recommended in the publication with activities at your school. Which recommendations in *What Works* would you uphold? With which would you disagree? Why? (If you are not presently associated with a school, ask a principal to assess the advisability of the recommendations.)

3. Interview two or three principals. Depending on the circumstances (an elementary or secondary school), discuss some appropriate curriculum or policy issue (e.g., discipline, implementing technology, reading and writing across the curriculum). Regarding the issue: How was the decision made and implemented? Did any research projects, pilot programs, etc. influence or justify choices and decisions? If you were called upon as a consultant, what commendations and recommendations would you make about the program/policy? What research would you rely on to make your final report?

As a result of study, reflection, and interaction with knowledgeable individuals, the learner will be able to complete the following activities. The quality of response to these activities should give some indication of the level of expertise the learner is able to bring to the situation.

Outcome Activities: L5
Research to Guide Action Plans

1. Using a recent copy of *Journal of Educational Research*, study one of the accounts of research that interests you because of its possible implications for future use. Analyze and critique the procedure or method used. Summarize the results and/or implications. Finally, give a personal reaction to the research in terms of your possible future use of the information gained.

2. Select an innovation (team teaching, cooperative learning, computer-based instruction, year-round education, modular scheduling, etc.). Assess the possible implications of an adoption of the practice for (a) learners, (b) teachers, (c) principal, (d) parents, and (e) the larger community. Note at least one positive and one negative effect of the innovation for each of the four groups. Base your statements on a thorough understanding of the topic through research.

3. The public school in your area has no formal admission criteria for its kindergarten program except a birth deadline date. Parents think this is too arbitrary since children develop differently and some have greater formal prekindergarten experience than in the past. The pastor, eager to serve parents and concerned about the school finances, feels pressured to have you admit children into the parish kindergarten program who would be too young by the public school criteria. The pastor wants the school board included in whatever decision is made. You, as principal, have been asked to prepare a balanced case for the next school board meeting that speaks to this issue. How would you proceed? What resources and personnel might you consult and/or include in the presentation? What research would you call upon to support both sides of this issue?

Role: Principal as Educational Leader

Area: Leadership

Compentency: L6
Effect Change

Change is a necessary condition for improvement of organizations. Lipham (1981) states that, since principals are the key internal agents, no change of substantial importance can occur in any school without their understanding and support.

There are lessons to be learned from current knowledge of successful change. Fullan (1992) suggests some basic orientations for anyone initiating improvement efforts:

1. even well-developed innovations take time to assimilate;
2. ownership is stronger in the middle of a change process than at the beginning; and
3. problems should be treated as natural phenomena which, if accepted, can lead to creative solutions and deeper satisfaction.

Luby, Moser, and Posey (1991) state that challenges for change come from various agents in the form of concepts, people, and events. If the administrator chooses to respond, he or she will need to conduct preliminary research and also evaluate the suggested change in the light of the school mission statement and philosophy. If the change appears viable, and there is support, work on an action plan can begin. The action plan will include the why, what, who, when, and how. Finally, monitoring and evaluating the implementation of the change is essential.

Attention given by the Catholic school principal to identifying and affecting needed change will provide a necessary condition for improvement and enable the school to live its philosophy more fully and faithfully.

To support and give evidence of professional growth in demonstrating a knowledge of the procedures for identifying and affecting needed change, the learner will engage in the listed activities under the direction of the diocese (Model I) or through a self-directed program and/or with the guidance of a mentor (Model II).

The primary means of keeping a consistent record of activities is to keep an ongoing JOURNAL which would contain:

1) a *Dated Log* section recording when activities were undertaken and completed,
2) a *Reading/Response* section in which notes from suggested readings and the response reactions are systematically organized, and
3) an *Experience(Activity)/Reflection* section in which one records ideas and insights gained through interacting with people or seeking out additional information in the course of completing the activities.

Learning Activities: L6
Effect Change

1. Read the following and respond with reactions in a journal.* Ideally, you should discuss these readings and your reactions with a mentor. These integral readings are reprinted for your convenience on pages 113–25.

   Daresh, J. C. 1991. *Supervision as a proactive process.* Prospect Heights, Ill.: Waveland, 129–30, 137–40.

   Fullan, M. G., and M. B. Miles. 1992. Getting reform right: What works and what doesn't. *Phi Delta Kappan* 73(10):745–52.

   Luby, M. A., M. S. Moser, and L. Posey. 1991. Introducing change with success. In *Capital wisdom: Papers from the Principals Academy 1991,* 48–54. Washington, D.C.: National Catholic Educational Association.

   * In your journal, note insights you gained concerning ways to introduce change, as well as methods of assisting the staff in the implementation and evaluation of new programs. Who in leadership should be responsible for the various stages of change?

2. Discuss with a school principal his or her "agenda" for change or improvement in the school. What is the impetus for change? What factors facilitate and/or retard change? What role does the administrator play? What, if any, processes does the leader use? What needs are being addressed? How are decisions made and implemented?

3. Interview three or more teachers from separate schools who have been teaching ten or more years. Ask them to comment on innovations that have been proposed during the years they have been teaching. Which innovations did they find beneficial? Which ones did they find unsuccessful? What, in their opinions, contributed to the failure?

4. Begin a file of newspaper, magazine, and journal articles that detail ideas and efforts of people making changes in schools to improve the quality of instruction. Determine which of these ideas might have future usefulness for you. Would you adapt them in any way?

As a result of study, reflection, and interaction with knowledgeable individuals, the learner will be able to complete the following activities. The quality of response to these activities should give some indication of the level of expertise the learner is able to bring to the situation.

Outcome Activities: L6
Effect Change

1. Assume that you are a principal in a school where much attention and recognition is given to athletes. You and your staff are concerned that excellence in academics is not held in high esteem by the majority of the student body. The goal agreed upon for the upcoming school year is that of bringing about changes in the academic learning climate. Develop an outline of the procedures you will use to direct and guide the necessary changes.

2. As an educational leader, what specific steps would you take to improve receptivity to change on the part of teachers?

3. Name a current situation in the field of curriculum that you would like to see improved. (If at present you are not associated with a school, get this information from a principal.) As principal, describe the methods you would use to make the necessary changes toward improvement.

Role: Principal as Educational Leader

Area: Leadership

Compentency: L7
Personal Growth and Development

Principals need replenishment, invigoration, and an expanded repertoire of ideas and practices with which to respond to a demanding and complex job. Learning is replenishing and the best antidote to routinization. The importance of continuous professional education for principals is highlighted by research which shows the quality of the school and the "know-how" of the principal to be highly correlated. Many of the skills recognized as important for an effective principal are learned skills. The critical element in the principal's learning, as in all adult learning, is ownership. In well-designed programs, there are opportunities to share problems, be helpful to others, and get help in clarifying and becoming confident about goals, ideas, and practices (Barth 1991).

In the school leadership position, feelings of exhaustion and discouragement can occur. Rathus and Nevid (1986) encourage people dealing with stress to discover ways of controlling self-defeating thoughts and to learn to use relaxation techniques. Since time and energy are limited, time-management methods, such as those recommended by Smith and Andrews (1989), can also prove helpful.

McBrien (1987) emphasizes the importance of being more than a competent, efficient minister. The Catholic school principal must embody and live by spiritual values that he or she represents, proclaims, and tries to persuade others to embrace. Prayer, reflection, and discernment are vital.

Attention given by the Catholic school principal to personal growth and professional development influences the quality of life and the best interests of all involved with the school community.

To support and give evidence of a knowledge of the procedures for attending to personal growth and professional development, the learner will engage in the listed activities under the direction of the diocese (Model I) or through a self-directed program and/or with the guidance of a mentor (Model II).

The primary means of keeping a consistent record of activities is to keep an ongoing JOURNAL which would contain:

1) a *Dated Log* section recording when activities were undertaken and completed,
2) a *Reading/Response* section in which notes from suggested readings and the response reactions are systematically organized, and
3) an *Experience(Activity)/Reflection* section in which one records ideas and insights gained through interacting with people or seeking out additional information in the course of completing the activities.

Learning Activities: L7
Personal Growth and Development

1. Read the following and respond with reactions in a journal.* Ideally, you should discuss these readings and your reactions with a mentor. These integral readings are reprinted for your convenience on pages 126–37.

   Barth, R. S. 1991. *Improving schools from within.* San Francisco: Jossey-Bass, 68–78.
   Clifton, D. O., and P. Nelson. 1992. *Soar with your strengths.* New York: Delacorte Press, 111–22.
   McBrien, R. P. 1987. *Ministry: A theological, pastoral handbook.* New York: Harper Collins, 77–81.
   Rathus, S. A., and J. S. Nevid. 1986. *Adjustment and growth: The challenges of life.* New York: Holt, Rinehart, and Winston, 273–79.

   * In your journal, note ways one deals with the stresses of the principalship, maintains a balance in work and relaxation, and promotes one's personal, spiritual, and professional growth.

2. Investigate programs in your area that are designed to promote principals' learning. How are they designed? Is there opportunity at these gatherings for principals to share what they know and to use that knowledge to help others? If meetings are held on a diocesan level, what prayer or spiritual growth experiences are offered?

3. Talk with the pastor of your parish or with anyone in a retreat center who can tell you of

opportunities for spiritual enrichment. What programs are offered for reflection and prayer?

4. Interview a principal. How does he or she create a balance in life through time management? What other suggestions can that person offer to acheive balance in important matters?

5. If possible, visit a health center for the purpose of learning healthful ways of improving one's quality of life. What suggestions do they give for maintaining a healthy lifestyle? (If a visit to a health center is not possible, get reading material offered in hospital or doctors' waiting rooms or begin to watch for scheduled programs about health on public television stations.)

As a result of study, reflection, and interaction with knowledgeable individuals, the learner will be able to complete the following activities. The quality of response to these activities should give some indication of the level of expertise the learner is able to bring to the situation.

Outcome Activities: L7
Personal Growth and Development

1. Write an analysis of your own knowledge, skills, and personal traits as they bear on the role of Catholic school principal. Describe your strengths and indicate areas in which you feel you have room to grow. Give specific details of a personal development plan that describes how you will bring your strengths to excellence and manage the areas in your life that need improvement.

2. Design a weekly program that you, as a busy principal, could follow to keep your life in balance. Include specific times and days and make provision for spiritual growth, professional reading and enrichment, and periods of mental and physical relaxation.

3. Reflect on your life goals and hopes for your personal and professional life. In writing, specify what you hope to give and contribute to others or to the good of the Church and society through the ministry of serving as a Catholic school administrator. In detail, list the sacrifices of time, finances, etc. that might be involved for you and perhaps your family in making such a life decision. Include the rewards and compelling reasons why this life choice is "right" for you. After looking at both sides, reflect honestly whether (or not) you want to persist. Specify clearly the reasons for your decision.

Leadership Bibliography

Role: Principal as Educational Leader

Area of Responsibility Leadership

Introduction

Fullan, M. G. 1991. *The new meaning of educational change.* New York: Teachers College, 157–60.

Ristau, K. 1991. The challenge: To provide leadership within Catholic schools. In *Leadership of and on behalf of Catholic schools.* Washington, D.C.: National Catholic Educational Association, 12–17.

L1. To demonstrate symbolic and cultural leadership skills in developing a school climate reflective of its Catholic identity

Beaudoin, D. M. 1990. Diversity in spirituality in the Catholic elementary school. *Momentum* 21(2):34–36.

Congregation for Catholic Education. 1988. *The religious dimension of education in a Catholic school: Guidelines for reflection and renewal.* Washington, D.C.: United States Catholic Conference, nos. 24–46.

Convey, J. J. 1992. *Catholic schools make a difference: Twenty-five years of research.* Washington, D.C.: National Catholic Educational Association, 89–93.

Deal, T. E., and K. D. Peterson. 1990. *The principal's role in shaping school culture.* Washington, D.C.: United States Department of Education, Office of Educational Research and Improvement, 16–33.

Libreria Editrice Vaticana. 1994. *Catechism of the Catholic Church.* Washington, D.C.: United States Catholic Conference, nos. 1897–98, 1902–03.

National Conference of Catholic Bishops. 1979. *Sharing the light of faith: National catechetical directory for Catholics of the United States.* Washington, D.C.: United States Catholic Conference, nos. 206–11, 215.

Owens, R. G. 1987. The leadership of educational clans. In *Leadership: Examining the elusive, 1987 yearbook.* Alexandria, Va.: Association for Supervision and Curriculum Development, 23–26.

Reck, C. 1991. Catholic identity. In *The Catholic identity of Catholic schools,* eds. J. Heft and C. Reck, 26–27. Washington, D.C.: National Catholic Educational Association.

Sergiovanni, T. J. 1990. *Value-added leadership.* New York: Harcourt, Brace, Jovanovich, 82–90, 151–52.

L2. To apply a Catholic educational vision to the daily activities of the school

Libreria Editrice Vaticana. 1994. *Catechism of the Catholic Church.* Washington, D.C.: United States Catholic Conference, nos. 737–38.

National Conference of Catholic Bishops. 1973. *To teach as Jesus did: A pastoral message on Catholic education.* Washington, D.C.: United States Catholic Conference, no. 82.

———. 1979. *Sharing the light of faith: National catechetical directory for Catholics of the United States.* Washington, D.C.: United States Catholic Conference, nos. 30, 232.

———. 1990. *In support of Catholic elementary and secondary schools.* Washington, D.C.: United States Catholic Conference, 6.

Perri, S. 1989. The principal as teacher of teachers. In *Reflections on the role of the Catholic school principal,* ed. R. Kealey, 67–74. Washington, D.C.: National Catholic Educational Association.

Peters, T., and N. Austin. 1985. *A passion for excellence.* New York: Random House, 286.

Sergiovanni, T. J. 1990. *Value-added leadership.* New York: Harcourt, Brace, Jovanovich, 56–63.

Sheive, L. T., and M. B. Schoenheit. 1987. Vision and the work of educational leaders. In *Leadership: Examining the elusive, 1987 yearbook,* 94, 96–98. Alexandria, Va.: Association for Supervision and Curriculum Development.

L3. To promote staff morale

Blase, J., and P. C. Kirby. 1992. *Bringing out the best in teachers.* Newbury Park, Calif.: Corwin Press, 10–21, 99–111.

Csikszentmihalyi, M. 1990. *Flow: The psychology of optimal experience.* New York: Harper Collins, 74.

Knipper, C., and D. Suddarth. 1991. Involving staff in the in-service process. In *Capital wisdom: Papers from the Principals Academy 1991,* 29–34. Washington, D.C.: National Catholic Educational Association.

Levine, S. L. 1989. *Promoting adult growth in schools.* Boston: Allyn and Bacon, 209–17.

Libreria Editrice Vaticana. 1994. *Catechism of the Catholic Church.* Washington, D.C.: United States Catholic Conference, nos. 1913–17, 1917.

National Association of Secondary School Principals. 1990. Developing staff morale. *Practitioner* 16(4):1–8.

Ristau, K. 1989. The role of the principal in the ongoing education of teachers. In *Reflections on the role of the Catholic school principal*, ed. R. Kealey, 60–62. Washington, D.C.: National Catholic Educational Association.

Sergiovanni, T. J. 1992. *Moral leadership.* New York: Harcourt, Brace, Jovanovich, 59–65.

L4. To recognize leadership ability among staff members and to foster this ability

Barth, R. S. 1991. *Improving schools from within.* San Francisco: Jossey-Bass, 133–46.

Blase, J., and P. C. Kirby. 1992. *Bringing out the best in teachers.* Newbury, Calif.: Corwin Press, 55–75.

Burns, J. M. 1978. *Leadership.* New York: Harper and Row, 4.

Glickman, C. D. 1990. *Supervision of instruction.* Boston: Allyn and Bacon, 366–72.

Kealey, R., ed. 1989. *Reflections on the role of the Catholic school principal.* Washington, D.C.: National Catholic Educational Association, 7–9.

Libreria Editrice Vaticana. 1994. *Catechism of the Catholic Church.* Washington, D.C.: United States Catholic Conference, nos. 1878–80, 1882–85, 1889, 1905–12.

Ristau, K. 1991. The challenge: To provide leadership within Catholic schools. In *Leadership of and on behalf of Catholic schools*, eds. K. Ristau and J. Rogus, 12–17. Washington, D.C.: National Catholic Educational Association.

Sergiovanni, T. J. 1992. *Moral Leadership.* New York: Harcourt, Brace, Jovanovich, 67–72.

L5. To interpret and use research to guide action plans

Blase, J., and P. C. Kirby. 1992. *Bringing out the best in teachers.* Newbury, Calif.: Corwin Press, 82–86.

Convey, J. J. 1992. *Catholic schools make a difference: Twenty-five years of research.* Washington, D.C.: National Catholic Educational Association, 6–8, 33–34, 59, 62.

Glatthorn, A. A. 1987. *Curriculum renewal.* Alexandria, Va.: Association for Supervision and Curriculum Development, 99–104.

Glickman, C. D. 1990. *Supervision of instruction.* Boston: Allyn and Bacon, 253–54.

McCleary, L. E. 1992. The knowledge base for school leaders. In *School leadership: A blueprint for change*, ed. Thomson, 21–22. Newbury Park, Calif.: Corwin.

National Conference of Catholic Bishops. 1979. *Sharing the light of faith: National catechetical directory for Catholics of the United States.* Washington, D.C.: United States Catholic Conference, no. 223.

United States Department of Education. 1986. *What works: Research about teaching and learning.* Washington, D.C.: Office of Educational Research and Improvement, 19, 21–23, 25, 27, 29, 31–39, 41–43, 45–47, 49–53, 55, 57, 59–62.

Wang, M. C., G. D. Haertel, and H. J. Walberg. 1990. What influences learning? A content analysis of review literature. *Journal of Educational Research* 84(1):30–43.

L6. To identify and effect needed change

Blase, J., and P. C. Kirby. 1992. *Bringing out the best in teachers.* Newbury Park, Calif.: Corwin Press, 22–53, 77–81.

Daresh, J. C. 1991. *Supervision as a proactive process.* Prospect Heights, Ill.: Waveland Press, 129–30, 137–40.

Fullan, M. G. , and M. B. Miles. 1992. Getting reform right: What works and what doesn't. *Phi Delta Kappan* 73(9):745–52.

Lipham, J. M. 1981. *Effective principal, effective school.* Reston, Va.: National Association of Secondary School Principals, 15–17.

Luby, M. A., M. S. Moser, and L. Posey. 1991. Introducing change with success. In *Capital wisdom: Papers from the Principals Academy 1991*, 48–54. Washington, D.C.: National Catholic Educational Association.

Parks, D., and W. Warner. 1992. Four essentials of leadership. *Streamlined Seminar* 10(3):1–4.

L7. To attend to personal growth and professional development

Barth, R. S. 1991. *Improving schools from within.* San Francisco: Jossey-Bass, 68–78.

Clifton, D. O., and P. Nelson. 1992. *Soar with your strengths.* New York: Delacorte Press, 111–22.

McBrien, R. P. 1987. *Ministry: A theological, pastoral handbook.* New York: Harper Collins, 77–81.

Rathus, S. A., and J. S. Nevid. 1986. *Adjustment and growth: The challenges of life.* New York: Holt, Rinehart and Winston, 273–79.

Sergiovanni, T. J. 1992. *Moral leadership.* New York: Harcourt, Brace, Jovanovich, 52–56.

Smith, W. F., and R. L. Andrews. 1989. *Instructional leadership.* Alexandria, Va.: Association for Supervision and Curriculum Development, 135–56.

Integral Readings for Leadership

The Religious Dimension of Education in a Catholic School: Guidelines for Reflection and Renewal

Congregation for Catholic Education. 1988. Nos. 24–46.
Washington, D.C.: United States Catholic Conference.

1. What is a Christian school climate?

24. In pedagogical circles, today as in the past, great stress is put on the climate of a school: the sum total of the different components at work in the school which interact with one another in such a way as to create favorable conditions for a formation process. Education always takes place within certain specific conditions of space and time, through the activities of a group of individuals who are active and also interactive among themselves. They follow a program of studies which is logically ordered and freely accepted. Therefore, the elements to be considered in developing an organic vision of a school climate are: persons, space, time, relationships, teaching, study, and various other activities.

25. From the first moment that a student sets foot in a Catholic school, he or she ought to have the impression of entering a new environment, one illumined by the light of faith, and having its own unique characteristics. The Council summed this up by speaking of an environment permeated with the Gospel spirit of love and freedom.[15] In a Catholic school, everyone should be aware of the living presence of Jesus the "Master" who, today as always, is with us in our journey through life as the one genuine "Teacher," the perfect Man in whom all human values find their fullest perfection. The inspiration of Jesus must be translated from the ideal into the real. The Gospel spirit should be evident in a Christian way of thought and life which permeates all facets of the educational climate. Having crucifixes in the school will remind everyone, teachers and students alike, of this familiar and moving presence of Jesus, the "Master" who gave his most complete and sublime teaching from the cross.

26. Prime responsibility for creating this unique Christian school climate rests with the teachers, as individuals and as a community. The religious dimension of the school climate is expressed through the celebration of Christian values in Word and Sacrament, in individual behavior, in friendly and harmonious interpersonal relationships, and in a ready availability. Through this daily witness, the students will come to appreciate the uniqueness of the environment to which their youth has been entrusted. If it is not present, then there is little left which can make the school Catholic.

2. The physical environment of a Catholic school

27. Many of the students will attend a Catholic school—often the same school—from the time they are very young children until they are nearly adults. It is only natural that they should come to think of the school as an extension of their own homes, and therefore a "schoolhome" ought to have some of the amenities which can create a pleasant and happy family atmosphere. When this is missing from the home, the school can often do a great deal to make up for it.

28. The first thing that will help to create a pleasant environment is an adequate physical facility: one that includes sufficient space for classrooms, sports and recreation, and also such things as a staff room and rooms for parent-teacher meetings, group work, etc. The possibilities for this vary from place to place; we have to be honest enough to admit that some school buildings are unsuitable and unpleasant. But students can be made to feel "at home" even when the surroundings are modest, if the climate is humanly and spiritually rich.

29. A Catholic school should be an example of simplicity and evangelical poverty, but this is not inconsistent with having the materials needed to educate properly. Because of rapid technological progress, a school today must have access to equipment that, at times, is complex and expensive.

This is not a luxury; it is simply what a school needs to carry out its role as an educational institution. Catholic schools, therefore, have a right to expect the help from others that will make the purchase of modern educational materials possible.[16] Both individuals and public bodies have a duty to provide this support.

Students should feel a responsibility for their "school-home"; they should take care of it and help to keep it as clean and neat as possible. Concern for the environment is part of a formation in ecological awareness, the need for which is becoming increasingly apparent.

An awareness of Mary's presence can be a great help toward making the school into a "home." Mary, Mother and Teacher of the Church, accompanied her Son as he grew in wisdom and grace; from its earliest days, she has accompanied the Church in its mission of salvation.

30. The physical proximity of the school to a church can contribute a great deal toward achieving the educational aims. A church should not be seen as something extraneous, but as a familiar and intimate place where those young people who are believers can find the presence of the Lord: "Behold, I am with you all days."[17] Liturgy planning should be especially careful to bring the school community and the local Church together.

3. The ecclesial and educational climate of the school

31. The declaration *Gravissimum educationis*[18] notes an important advance in the way a Catholic school is thought of: the transition from the school as an institution to the school as a community. This community dimension is, perhaps, one result of the new awareness of the Church's nature as developed by the Council. In the Council texts, the community dimension is primarily a theological concept rather than a sociological category; this is the sense in which it is used in the second chapter of *Lumen gentium,* where the Church is described as the People of God.

As it reflects on the mission entrusted to it by the Lord, the Church gradually develops its pastoral instruments so that they may become ever more effective in proclaiming the Gospel and promoting total human formation. The Catholic school is one of these pastoral instruments; its specific pastoral service consists in mediating between faith and culture: being faithful to the newness of the Gospel while at the same time respecting the autonomy and the methods proper to human knowledge.

32. Everyone directly involved in the school is a part of the school community: teachers, directors, administrative and auxiliary staff. Parents are central figures, since they are the natural and irreplaceable agents in the education of their children. And the community also includes the students, since they must be active agents in their own education.[19]

33. At least since the time of the Council, therefore, the Catholic school has had a clear identity, not only as a presence of the Church in society, but also as a genuine and proper instrument of the Church. It is a place of evangelization, of authentic apostolate and of pastoral action—not through complementary or parallel or extracurricular activity, but of its very nature: its work of educating the Christian person. The words of the present Holy Father make this abundantly clear: "the Catholic school is not a marginal or secondary element in the pastoral mission of the bishop. Its function is not merely to be an instrument with which to combat the education given in a State school."[20]

34. The Catholic school finds its true justification in the mission of the Church; it is based on an educational philosophy in which faith, culture and life are brought into harmony. Through it, the local Church evangelizes, educates, and contributes to the formation of a healthy and morally sound life-style among its members. The Holy Father affirms that "the need for the Catholic school becomes evidently clear when we consider what it contributes to the development of the mission of the People of God, to the dialogue between Church and the human community, to the safeguarding of freedom of conscience . . ." . Above all, according to the Holy Father, the Catholic school helps in achieving a double objective: "of its nature it guides men and women to human and Christian perfection, and at the same time helps them to become mature in their faith. For those who believe in Christ, these are two facets of a single reality."[21]

35. Most Catholic schools are under the direction of Religious Congregations, whose consecrated members enrich the educational climate by bringing to it the values of their own Religious communities. These men and women have dedicated themselves to the service of the students without thought of personal gain, because they are convinced that it is really the Lord whom they are serving.[22] Through the prayer, work and love that make up their life in community, they express in a visible way the life of the Church. Each Congregation brings the richness of its own educational tradition to the school, found in its original charism; its members each bring the careful professional preparation that is required by the call to be an educator. The strength and gentleness of their total dedication to God enlightens their work, and students gradually come to appreciate the value of this witness. They come to love these educators who seem to have the gift of eternal spiritual youth, and it is an affection which endures long after students leave the school.

36. The Church offers encouragement to these men and women who have dedicated their lives to the fulfillment of an educational charism.[23] It urges those in education not to give up this work, even in situations where it involves suffering and persecution. In fact, the Church hopes that many others will be called to this special vocation. When afflicted by doubts and uncertainty, when difficulties are multiplied, these Religious men and women should recall the nature of their consecration, which is a type of holocaust[24]—a holocaust which is offered "in the perfection of

love, which is the scope of the consecrated life."[25] Their merit is the greater because their offering is made on behalf of young people, who are the hope of the Church.

37. At the side of the priests and Religious, lay teachers contribute their competence and their faith witness to the Catholic school. Ideally, this lay witness is a concrete example of the lay vocation that most of the students will be called to. The Congregation has devoted a specific document to lay teachers,[26] meant to remind lay people of their apostolic responsibility in the field of education and to summon them to participate in a common mission, whose point of convergence is found in the unity of the Church. For all are active members of one Church and cooperate in its one mission, even though the fields of labor and the states of life are different because of the personal call each one receives from God.

38. The Church, therefore, is willing to give lay people charge of the schools that it has established, and the laity themselves establish schools. The recognition of the school as a Catholic school is, however, always reserved to the competent ecclesiastical authority.[27] When lay people do establish schools, they should be especially concerned with the creation of a community climate permeated by the Gospel spirit of freedom and love, and they should witness to this in their own lives.

39. The more the members of the educational community develop a real willingness to collaborate among themselves, the more fruitful their work will be. Achieving the educational aims of the school should be an equal priority for teachers, students and families alike, each one according to his or her own role, always in the Gospel spirit of freedom and love. Therefore channels of communication should be open among all those concerned with the school. Frequent meetings will help to make this possible, and a willingness to discuss common problems candidly will enrich this communication.

The daily problems of school life are sometimes aggravated by misunderstandings and various tensions. A determination to collaborate in achieving common educational goals can help to overcome these difficulties and reconcile different points of view. A willingness to collaborate helps to facilitate decisions that need to be made about the ways to achieve these goals and, while presenting proper respect for school authorities, even makes it possible to conduct a critical evaluation of the school—a process in which teachers, students and families can all take part because of their common concern to work for the good of all.

40. Considering the special age group they are working with, primary schools should try to create a community school climate that reproduces, as far as possible, the warm and intimate atmosphere of family life. Those responsible for these schools will, therefore, do everything they can to promote a common spirit of trust and spontaneity. In addition, they will take great care to promote close and constant collaboration with the parents of these pupils. An integration of school and home is an essential condition for the birth and development of all of the potential which these children manifest in one or the other of these two situations—including their openness to religion with all that this implies.

41. The Congregation wishes to express its appreciation to all those dioceses which have worked to establish primary schools in their parishes; these deserve the strong support of all Catholics. It also wishes to thank the Religious Congregations helping to sustain these primary schools, often at great sacrifice. Moreover, the Congregation offers enthusiastic encouragement to those dioceses and Religious Congregations who wish to establish new schools. Such things as film clubs and sports groups are not enough; not even classes in catechism instruction are sufficient. What is needed is a school. This is a goal which, in some countries, was the starting point. There are countries in which the Church began with schools and only later was able to construct Churches and to establish a new Christian community.[28]

4. The Catholic school as an open community

42. Partnership between a Catholic school and the families of the students must continue and be strengthened: not simply to be able to deal with academic problems that may arise, but rather so that the educational goals of the school can be achieved. Close cooperation with the family is especially important when treating sensitive issues such as religious, moral, or sexual education, orientation toward a profession, or a choice of one's vocation in life. It is not a question of convenience, but a partnership based on faith. Catholic tradition teaches that God has bestowed on the family its own specific and unique educational mission.

43. The first and primary educators of children are their parents.[29] The school is aware of this fact but, unfortunately, the same is not always true of the families themselves; it is the school's responsibility to give them this awareness. Every school should initiate meetings and other programs which will make the parents more conscious of their role, and help to establish a partnership; it is impossible to do too much along these lines. It often happens that a meeting called to talk about the children becomes an opportunity to raise the consciousness of the parents. In addition, the school should try to involve the family as much as possible in the educational aims of the school—both in helping to plan these goals and in helping to achieve them. Experience shows that parents who were once totally unaware of their role can be transformed into excellent partners.

44. "The involvement of the Church in the field of education is demonstrated especially by the Catholic school."[30] This affirmation of the Council has both historical and

practical importance. Church schools first appeared centuries ago, growing up alongside monasteries, cathedrals and parish churches. The Church has always had a love for its schools, because this is where its children receive their formation. These schools have continued to flourish with the help of bishops, countless Religious Congregations, and laity; the Church has never ceased to support the schools in their difficulties and to defend them against governments seeking to close or confiscate them.

Just as the Church is present in the school, so the school is present in the Church; this is a logical consequence of their reciprocal commitment. The Church, through which the Redemption of Christ is revealed and made operative, is where the Catholic school receives its spirit. It recognizes the Holy Father as the center and the measure of unity in the entire Christian community. Love for and fidelity to the Church is the organizing principle and the source of strength of a Catholic school.

Teachers find the light and the courage for authentic Religious education in their unity among themselves and their generous and humble communion with the Holy Father. Concretely, the educational goals of the school include a concern for the life and the problems of the Church, both local and universal. These goals are attentive to the Magisterium and include cooperation with Church authorities. Catholic students are helped to become active members of the parish and diocesan communities. They have opportunities to join Church associations and Church youth groups, and they are taught to collaborate in local Church projects.

Mutual esteem and reciprocal collaboration will be established between the Catholic school and the bishop and other Church authorities through direct contacts. We are pleased to note that a concern for Catholic schools is becoming more of a priority of local Churches in many parts of the world.[31]

45. A Christian education must promote respect for the State and its representatives, the observance of just laws, and a search for the common good. Therefore, traditional civic values such as freedom, justice, the nobility of work and the need to pursue social progress are all included among the school goals, and the life of the school gives witness to them. The national anniversaries and other important civic events are commemorated and celebrated in appropriate ways in the schools of each country.

The school life should also reflect an awareness of international society. Christian education sees all of humanity as one large family, divided perhaps by historical and political events, but always one in God who is Father of all. Therefore a Catholic school should be sensitive to and help to promulgate Church appeals for peace, justice, freedom, progress for all peoples and assistance for countries in need. And it should not ignore similar appeals coming from recognized international organizations such as UNESCO and the United Nations.

46. That Catholic schools help to form good citizens is a fact apparent to everyone. Both government policy and public opinion should, therefore, recognize the work these schools do as a real service to society. It is unjust to accept the service and ignore or fight against its source. Fortunately, a good number of countries seem to have a growing understanding of and sympathy for the Catholic school.[32] A recent survey conducted by the Congregation demonstrates that a new age may be dawning.

Notes

15. Cf. *Gravissimum educationis*, 8. For the Gospel spirit of love and freedom, cf *Gaudium et spes*, 38: "[The Lord Jesus] reveals to us that God is love (1 Jn 4:8), and at the same time teaches us that the fundamental rule for human perfection, and therefore also for the transformation of the world, is the new commandment of love". See also *2 Cor* 3:17: "Where the Spirit of the Lord is present, there is freedom."

16. This question was treated in *The Catholic School*, 81–82.

17. *Mt* 28:20

18. 6.

19. Cf the address of John Paul II to the parents, teachers and students from the Catholic schools of the Italian Province of Lazio, March 9, 1985. *Insegnamenti*, VIII/1, p. 620.

20. Address of John Paul II to the bishops of Lombardy, Italy, on the occasion of their "Ad limina" visit, January 15, 1982, *Insegnamenti*, V/1, 1982, p. 105.

21. *Insegnamenti*, VIII/1, pp. 618 f.

22. *Mt* 25:40: "For indeed I tell you, as often as you have done these things to one of these least of my brothers, you have done it to me".

23. Cf *Perfectae caritatis*, 8: "There are in the Church a great number of institutes, clerical or lay, dedicated to various aspects of the apostolate, which have different gifts according to the grace that has been given to each: 'some exercise a ministry of service, some teach' (cf *Rom* 12:5-8)". Also see *Ad gentes divinitus*, 40.

24. *Summa Theol.* II-II, q. 186, a. 1: "By antonomasis those are called 'religious' who dedicate themselves to the service of God as if they were offering themselves as a holocaust to the Lord",

25. *Ibid*, a. 2.

26. *Lay Catholics in Schools: Witnesses to the Faith*.

27. The norms of the Church in this respect are to be found in canons 800–803 of the Code of Canon Law.

28. Cf the address of Pope Paul VI to the National Congress of Diocesan Directors of the Teachers' Organizations of Catholic Action, *Insegnamenti*, I, 1963, p. 594.

29. Cf *Gravissimum educationis*, 3.

30. *Gravissimum educationis*, 8.

31. A number of recent documents from national Episcopal Conferences and from individual local ordinaries have had the Catholic school as their theme. These documents should be known and put into practice.

32. See, for example, the Resolution of the European Parliament on freedom of education in the European Community, approved by a large majority on March 14, 1984.

The Principal's Role in Shaping School Culture

Deal, T. E., and K. D. Peterson. 1990. 16–33. Washington, D.C.: United States
Department of Education, Office of Educational Research and Improvement.

Sizing Up the Situation

Key Questions for Symbolic Leaders

A principal, consciously or unconsciously, is always alert to *read* the school culture, and to decide whether and how to try to *shape* it. Principals approaching a new school—or trying to understand their own—should ask themselves three basic questions:

◆ What is the culture of the school now—its history, values, traditions, assumptions, beliefs, and ways?

◆ Where it matches my conception of a "good" school, what can I do to strengthen existing patterns?

◆ Where I see a need for new direction, what can be done to change or reshape the culture?

Reading the Current School Culture

This section will present some practical steps many principals take to read and shape the cultures of their respective schools. In doing so we both borrow anthropological language of symbols, rituals, and ceremonies and coin our own metaphors for the principal's role as potter, poet, actor, and healer.

In each instance our purpose is to remind school leaders of the formidable nature of their unofficial power to reshape school culture toward an "ethos of excellence" and make quality an authentic part of the daily routine of school life.

A principal must understand his or her school—its patterns, the purposes they serve, and how they came to be. Changing something you do not understand is a surefire recipe for stress—and ultimate failure. A principal must inquire below the surface of what is happening to formulate a deeper explanation of what is really going on. To be effective, principals must *read* their school and community culture.

Reading culture takes several forms: watching, sensing, listening, interpreting, using all of one's senses, and even employing intuition when necessary. First, the leader must listen to the echoes of school history.

The process of constructing an "organizational genealogy" or family tree is one of the best strategies of coming to know the personality—or culture—of a school. A principal can reconstruct the history through listening, watching, interviewing, and examining artifacts and records.

A more active re-creation of a school's history through group storytelling is both instructive and helpful in connecting a school with its ancestral roots.

Example:
One school focused an in-service day on the history of the school. The faculty was assigned to two

groups on the basis of their tenure. Both old-timers and newcomers were assigned the task of remembering events and heroes and retelling memorable stories. As each group reported, the history of the school came to life. Emotionally powerful for all the participants, the event re-presented a mosaic of the school culture.

The Informal Network

A principal must also listen to the key voices of the present. These people may be thought of as cultural "players" in various dramas at the school. Experienced principals will recognize the cast of characters. They include:

◆ Priests and priestesses—long-time residents who "minister" to the needs of the school.[21] They take confession, preside over rituals and ceremonies, and link the school to the ways of the past;

◆ Storytellers—recreate the past and personify contemporary exploits through lore and informal history;

◆ Gossips—keep everyone current on contemporary matters of importance, as well as trivia of no special merit. They form the informal grapevine that carries information far ahead of formal channels of communication; and

◆ Spies, counterspies, and moles—carry on subterranean negotiations which keep informal checks and balances among various power centers in the school. Through such covert operations, much of the work of the school is transacted.

Each of these sources—and others—is an informant on the present as well as the past. Far below the level of rational discourse and public conversation, the informal network provides a regular update on the current culture of the school.

The Past as Key to the Future

Most important, the leader must listen for the deeper dreams and hopes the school community holds for the future. Every school is a repository of unconscious sentiments and expectations that carry the code of the collective dream—the high ground to which they aspire.

This represents emerging energy the principal can tap and a deep belief system to which he or she can appeal when articulating what the school might become.

A principal can get an initial reading of a school by asking these key questions about the founding, traditions, building, current realities, and future dreams of the school:

◆ How long has the school existed?

◆ Why was it built, and who were the first inhabitants?

◆ Who had a major influence on the school's direction?

◆ What critical incidents occurred in the past, and how were they resolved, if at all?

- What were the preceding principals, teachers, and students like?
- What does the school's architecture convey? How is space arranged and used?
- What subcultures exist inside and outside the school?
- Who are the recognized (and unrecognized) heroes and villains of the school?
- What do people say (and think) when asked what the school stands for? What would they miss if they left?
- What events are assigned special importance?
- How is conflict typically defined? How is it handled?
- What are the key ceremonies and stories of the school?
- What do people wish for? Are there patterns to their individual dreams?

Shaping a School Culture

When principals have reflected to the point they feel they understand a school's culture, they can evaluate the need to *shape* or reinforce it. Valuable aspects of the school's existing culture can be reinforced; problematic ones require revitalizing. Shaping the culture is not an exact science. Shaping a culture is indirect, intuitive, and largely unconscious.

This section is to help principals identify the cultural dimensions of their job and concrete things they can do, in concert with others, to shape school culture.

1. The principal as *symbol:* affirm values through dress, behavior, attention, routines.
2. The principal as *potter:* shape and be shaped by the school's heroes, rituals, ceremonies, symbols.
3. The principal as *poet:* use language to reinforce values and sustain the school's best image of itself.
4. The principal as *actor:* improvise in the school's inevitable dramas.
5. The principal as *healer:* oversee transitions and change in the life of the school.

The Principal as Symbol

Everyone watches a new principal. His or her selection is a symbolic event, indicating to the school community where the culture is and where it might be headed. Age, gender, philosophy, reputation, demeanor, and other characteristics are important signals that will be read by members of the culture in a variety of ways.

Who a principal is—what he or she does, attends to, or seems to appreciate—is constantly watched by students, teachers, parents, and members of the community.

How a principal listens to and reads the school's existing culture communicates an interest, concern, or disdain for existing traditions. All that the principal does, says, and reacts to signals the values he or she holds. Above all else, a principal is a teacher in the best sense of the word.

Like other managers, principals engage in an enormous number of very routine actions. Maintaining the school building, budget, staff, discipline, and schedule takes up time. But these seemingly routine actions can be transformed into more meaningful symbolic events that reinforce the basic values and purposes of the school.

We rarely "see" an action's symbolic value at the time it occurs. More often we realize it later, if at all. For example, the "building tour" that many principals take in the morning may be simply a walk through the building to investigate potential trouble spots or building maintenance problems. In some schools, the teachers and students see the same walk as a ritual demonstrating that the principal cares and is involved in the learning environment.

Routine tasks are most likely to take on symbolic meaning when the principal shows sincere personal concern for core values and purposes while performing them. A classroom visit, building tour, or staff meeting may be nothing more than the technical observation of a routine activity, or, it may be a symbolic expression of the deeper values the principal holds for the school.

Almost all actions of the principal can have symbolic content when a school community understands their connection to its shared values.

Seemingly innocuous actions send signals as to what the principal values. The community may see a signal in any of the following arrangements or behaviors of the principal:

The Office

Its location, accessibility, decoration, and arrangement reflect the principal's values. One principal works from her couch in an office in the school's entryway; another is hidden in a corner suite behind a watchful secretary. One principal decorates with students' work on the office walls; others with athletic trophies, public service awards, posters of favorite works of art, or photographs of the family. These social artifacts signal to others what is considered important.

Demeanor

What car the principal drives, his or her clothes, posture, gestures, facial expression, sense of humor, and personal idiosyncrasies send signals of formality or informality, approachability or distance, concern or unconcern. A wink following a reprimand can have as much effect on a child as the verbal reprimand itself. A frown, a smile, a grimace, or a blank stare each may have a potent effect.

Time

How principals spend their time and what they focus their attention on send strong signals about their values. The community quickly discerns discrepancies between espoused values and actual values indicated by what issues receive time and attention.[22] The appointment book and daily routines signal what a principal values.

Appreciation

Principals signal their appreciation formally through official evaluations and public recognition and rewards. Informally, their daily behavior and demeanor communicate their preference in quality teaching, admirable behavior, and desired cultural traditions. Teachers and students are particularly attentive to the values displayed and rewarded by the principal in moments of social or organizational crisis within the school.

Writing

The form, emphasis, and volume of memos and newsletters communicate as strong a signal from the principal as what he or she writes in them. Memos may be a source of inspiration, a celebration of success, or a collection of bureaucratic jargon, rules, and regulations. Even the appearance of written material will be noticed, from the informality of the blue smudge of the mimeograph to the care evidenced by the new typewriter ribbon. Pride, humor, affection, and fatigue displayed in writing send signals about what a principal values.

Taken together, all these aspects of the principal's behavior, conscious and unconscious, form a public persona which carries symbolic meaning. They come with the territory of being a principal and help to shape the culture of the school.

The Principal as Potter

A principal may try to shape the elements of school culture (its values, ceremonies, and symbols) the way a potter shapes clay—patiently and with much skill.[23]

In doing so, he or she articulates the shared values, celebrates school heroes or heroines, observes rituals and ceremonies, and nurtures important school symbols.

Articulating Shared Values

It often falls to the principal, formally and informally, to articulate the philosophy that embodies what the school stands for. A valuable service is rendered if the principal can express those values in a form that makes them memorable and easily grasped.

In one district, the values are crystallized in the simple, single phrase: "Every child a promise."[24] Another school district developed the motto: "A commitment to People. We care. A commitment to Excellence. We dare. A commitment to Partnership. We share."[25] Again, to ring "true," mottos must reflect the actual practices and beliefs of the school.

In other schools, symbols function like slogans. One middle school's values are embodied in the symbol of a frog. The frog reflects the school's commitment to caring and affection that makes all children "princes and princesses."[26]

Celebrating School Heroes and Heroines

There are important individuals in most schools, past and present, who exemplify the values of the school. Heroes and heroines, living and dead, personify values and serve as role models for others. Students, teachers, parents, and custodians may qualify for special status through words or deeds.

Like stories about Paul Bunyan or Charles Lindbergh, the stories of these local heroes motivate and teach the ways of the culture. When they exemplify qualities a principal wants to reinforce, he may recognize these individuals

publicly. Schools can commemorate teachers or administrators in pictures, plaques, or special ceremonies just as businesses, hospitals, or military units do.

Observing Rituals

The school principal can shape the culture by participating in and encouraging the rituals that celebrate important values. Everyday tasks take on added significance when they symbolize values. School activities may become "rituals" when they express shared values and bind people in a common experience. These rituals are stylized, repeated behavior that reinforces shared values and beliefs.

Example:
A new superintendent of schools opened his first district-wide convocation by lighting a small lamp, which he labeled the "lamp of learning." After the event, no one mentioned the lamp. The next year, prior to the convocation, several people inquired: "You are going to light the lamp of learning again, aren't you?" The lighting of the lamp had been accepted as a symbolically meaningful ritual.[27]

Rituals take various forms. Some rituals are social and others center around work. Americans shake hands, Italians hug, and French kiss both cheeks when greeting or parting. Surgical teams scrub for 7 minutes, although germs are destroyed by modern germicides in 30 seconds. Members of the British artillery, when firing a cannon, still feature an individual who holds his hand in a position that once kept the horse from bolting because "that's the way it has always been done."

Meetings, parties, informal lunches, and school openings or closings provide opportunity for rituals. Fraternities often close meetings with an open opportunity for anyone to share anything of importance. In this setting, issues can be aired, accomplishments recognized, disagreements expressed, or exploits retold. These rituals bind people to each other—and to the deeper values of the organization.

Observing Ceremonies

School ceremonies allow us to put cultural values on display, to retell important stories, and to recognize the exploits and accomplishments of important individuals. These special events tie past, present, and future together. They intensify the social commitment to the organization and revitalize individuals for challenges that lie ahead.

When a ceremony is held, a special place, a special touch, and a special rhythm and flow may build momentum and express sincere emotions. Planning and staging these events are often done with extreme care. Encouraging and orchestrating such special ceremonies provide another opportunity for principals to shape—and be shaped by—the culture of the school.

Example:
One group of parents—with input from the high school principal—planned a celebration for the

school's teachers. They decorated the cafeteria, using white tablecloths and silver candle holders. They went to the superintendent and asked permission to serve wine and cheese and arranged for a piano bar where teachers and parents could sing together. Each teacher was given a corsage or a ribbon. The supper was potluck, supplied by the parents. After dinner, the school choir sang. Several speakers called attention to the significance of the event. The finale came as the principal recognized the parents and asked everyone to join her in a standing ovation for the teachers. The event was moving for both the teachers and the parents, and has become a part of the school's tradition.[28]

The Principal as Poet

We should not forget the straightforward and subtle ways that principals communicate with language—from memos to mottos to sagas and stories and informal conversation.

The words and images and sincerity principals use to talk about the school or students convey sentiments as well as ideas. "The achievement scores of *my* school are above the norm" conveys a very different image from "*Our* school is a special place to be."

Acronyms can separate insiders from outsiders to the school community. PSAT, CTBS, or NAEP may carry different meaning to educators than to their publics. Idioms and slogans ("Every child a promise" or "We Care; We Dare; We Share") may condense shared understandings of a school's values. However, hypocrisy in such slogans can alienate those who hear it. Consider the principal in the satirical book *Up the Down Staircase* who would say, "Let it be a challenge to you" in the face of problems that were obviously impossible to solve.[29]

Metaphors may provide "picture words" that consolidate complex ideas into a single, understandable whole. Whether students and teachers think of a school as a factory or a family will have powerful implications for day-to-day behavior.

One of the highest forms of "principal talk" is the story. A well-chosen story provides a powerful image that addresses a question without compromising its complexity. Stories ground complicated ideas in concrete terms, personifying them in flesh and blood. Stories carry values and connect abstract ideas with sentiment, emotions, and events.

Stories told by or about leaders help followers know what is expected of them. They emphasize what is valued, watched, and rewarded for old-timers and greenhorns alike.

Example:
The parents of a third grade student informed the principal that they were planning to move into a new house at Christmas and would therefore be changing schools. He suggested they tell the teacher themselves, since she took a strong personal interest in each of her students. They returned later with the surprising announcement that they were postponing their move. The principal asked why. The mother replied, "When we told Mrs. Onfrey about our decision she told us we couldn't transfer our child from her class. She told us that she wasn't finished with him yet."[30]

By repeating such stories, principals reinforce values and beliefs and so shape the culture of the school. "Sagas," stories of unique accomplishment, rooted in history and held in sentiment by the whole school community, can define the core values of a school to its members. They can convey to the outside world an "intense sense of the unique" that captures imagination, engenders loyalty, and secures resources and support from outsiders.[31]

The Principal as Actor

Cultures are often characterized as theater, the stage on which important events are acted out. If "all the world's a stage," then aspects of the life of a school are fascinating soap operas. Technically they have been called "social dramas."[32]

Much of this drama occurs during routine activities of the school. Periodic ceremonies, staged and carefully orchestrated, provide intensified, yet predictable theater. The outcome is usually known in advance (of graduation or an assembly), but both the players and the spectators are caught up in the spirit of the play.

There are also moments of unpredictable drama in any organization. In crises, or critical incidents (like a student suicide or the explosion of the space shuttle Challenger) are moments of unforeseen school drama.

A critical incident like a school closing provides the principal a significant opportunity to act in a social drama that can reaffirm or redirect cultural values and beliefs.

Example:
A principal was concerned about the effect of a school merger on the students and the community. He convened a transition committee to plan, among other things, a ceremony for the last day of school. On that day, the closing school was wrapped in a large red ribbon and filmed by a helicopter. When wreckers had demolished the building, each student, teacher, parent, and observer was given one of the bricks tied with a red ribbon and an aerial photograph of the school tied with a red bow.[33]

Such drama provides a heightened opportunity to mark a historical transition and reaffirm cultural ties within the school community. Rather than inhibiting or stifling such dramas, the principal may seize them as an opportunity to resolve differences and redirect the school.

Social dramas can be improvisational theater with powerful possibilities to reaffirm or alter values. In a political sense, such events as faculty or student conflicts are arenas —with referees, rounds, rules, spectators, fighters, and seconds. In the arena, conflicts are surfaced and decided, rather than lingering and seething because they have been avoided or ignored.

Critical incidents, from this perspective, provide the principal a significant opportunity to participate in a social drama that can reaffirm or redirect the values and beliefs of the school.

The Principal as Healer

Most school cultures are stable, but not static, and changes do occur. The principal can play a key role in acknowledging these transitions, healing whatever stress they create, and helping the school adapt to change in terms of its traditions and culture.

Schools celebrate the natural transitions of the year. Every school year has a beginning and an end. Beginnings are marked by convocations to end the summer and outline the vision and hopes for the coming year. Endings are marked by graduations, which usually unite members in a common celebration of the school culture.

The observation of national and seasonal holidays, from Halloween to President's Day, may make the school an important cultural center for events in the local community and reaffirm the school's ties to the wider culture. One school convenes a schoolwide festival each fall, winter, and spring, at which they demonstrate the way the students' religions honor a particular holiday.[34] Because of the diversity among students, such festivals provide an opportunity for students to learn different customs and foods. Such observances create a schoolwide unity around differences that could otherwise become divisive.

The beginning and end of employment are episodic transitions that a principal may use to reaffirm the school's culture and its values. What newcomers must learn about the school is a good definition of what is important in its culture.

Retirement marks the end of a career and the loss of a member of the school community. A retirement ceremony reviews and commemorates the contributions of the individual and also the ongoing traditions of the school. Both the retiree and the school need to crystallize what the person meant and the legacy they leave behind.

Even transfers, reductions in force, terminations, and firings-for-cause are transitions that can be marked by cultural events. In one Massachusetts elementary school, primary students named hallways after teachers who had been let go in the wake of a taxpayer rebellion that required tremendous cost reductions in nearly every school in the State.[35]

Unpredictable, calamitous events in the life of the school, like a death or school closing, will be upsetting to all members of the school community. These transitions require recognition of pain, emotional comfort, and hope. Unless transitions are acknowledged in cultural events, loss and grief will accumulate.

Example:
At one school closing, all the students, teachers, alumni, and the principal joined the mayor and other dignitaries in a parade from the old schoolhouse to the new. The parade was launched ceremonially from the old school with speeches and stories. The parade was accompanied by firetrucks and marching bands. At the receiving school, the children were met by their new classmates and teachers. The principal of the old school passed his symbolic authority to the principal of the new school.[36]

The principal as healer recognizes the pain of transitions and arranges events that make the transition a collective experience. Drawing people together to mourn loss and to renew hope is a significant part of the principal's culture-shaping role.

School Subcultures and the Wider Community

Subcultures will always exist within the culture of the school. Student subcultures form around neighborhoods, interests, gender, class, and race. Among students, subcultural differences are often the basis for arguments and fights.

For teachers, subcultures form around grade levels, departments, length of tenure, race, and sex. Teachers may define themselves in terms of their profession, association, or union. There is always some tension between a teacher's loyalty to the profession and to the school.

There can be tension among the subcultures of the school. Tensions between the subcultures of teachers and administrators may be expressed as disputes about professional autonomy and systemwide coordination. Tensions between students and teachers may be more graphically expressed. "No more pencils, no more books, no more teachers' dirty looks" is a piece of year-end student lore that has survived through generations.

A successful principal recognizes these differences among the various subcultures of the school but can, at the same time, articulate the shared values that bind them. This in turn binds various subcultures to the school as a whole.

An ongoing dialogue with the local community and responsibility to the local superintendent has long been a vital part of the principal's role. Increasingly, however, the principal must also implement new State policy directives. These policies, in turn, may reflect national concerns about America's relative position in the world economy. Effective principals identify how these new policies can reinforce existing school values and take on meaning in terms of local hopes and dreams.

It is the principal who casts the expectations of the larger community in terms of the unique flavor and traditions of the school. The school culture and the principal's leadership either encourage the school-community dialogue—or dramatically cut the school off from its community roots. The principal's roles as listener, symbol, potter, poet, actor, and healer must also extend to the greater community.

Symbolic Leadership and School Context

Symbolic leadership is more an art form than an exact science. Actions that might otherwise be only individually, technically, or politically inspired can take on much greater meaning. At the core of symbolic leadership is the importance of understanding the culture of a particular school—where it has been, where it is, and where it wants to go.

Principals who are successful as symbolic leaders can infuse daily routines with symbolic value to the school community. Their office, demeanor, and behavior send signals about school values. The ceremonies and rituals they emphasize, and the language they use to discuss them can have an influence in shaping the culture of the school.

But much of what happens in a school is not directly within the principal's control. This requires the symbolic leader to join the troupe of the school community's improvisational actors and actresses.

Principals who enjoy the security of control will find discomfort in the ambiguity and unpredictability of improvisational theater. But a symbolic leader will, if necessary, learn the merits of improvising in a comfortable way.

Even further outside a principal's control are the powerful reform pressures for schools to change. Whether changes are inspired at the national, State, district, or school level, the principal must either assume the role of healer or encourage the healing process. Otherwise, efforts to improve schools may actually scar the cultural system that gives meaning to the enterprise.

School Culture and Symbolic Leadership

We believe that the more principals understand about school culture and their roles in shaping it, the better equipped they will be to avoid the common pitfalls of change and reform. Culture involves all dimensions of life in schools. It determines individual needs and outlooks, shapes formal structures, defines the distribution of power, and establishes the means by which conflicts are dealt with. Understanding the specific culture of a school helps principals make external reforms locally meaningful. As principals become more sensitive symbolic leaders, they must not ignore their other important leadership roles, those of

counselor (meeting needs and helping to build skills), administrator of a formal structure (adjusting goals and roles), and arbitrator (creating arenas in which to resolve the normal conflicts in a school). Symbolic leadership goes hand in hand with these other aspects of school leadership.

Notes

21. Deal, T. E. (1987). "The culture of schools." In L. T. Sheive and M. B. Schoenheit (Eds.), *Leadership: Examining the elusive.* (1987 Yearbook of the Association for Supervision and Curriculum Development.) Arlington, VA: Association for Supervision and Curriculum Development.

22. Argyris, C., & Schon, D. A. (1978). *Theory in practice.* San Francisco: Jossey-Bass.

23. Greenfield, W. (1987). "Moral imagination and interpersonal competence: Antecedents to instructional leadership." In W. Greenfield (Ed.), *Instructional leadership.* Boston: Allyn & Bacon.

24. This example was contributed by a district superintendent from Tennessee.

25. The motto is from the Edina (Minnesota) School District. It was developed through an extensive dialogue involving the entire school community. Ray Smith, Superintendent of Schools, initiated the process following the suicide of his predecessor, Dr. Roberta Block.

26. This example was shared by a middle school principal during a session at Harvard's Principals Institute.

27. Dr. Seldon Whitaker began this tradition in his first year as Superintendent of State College Area School District in State College, Pennsylvania.

28. This celebration was held at Concord High School in Concord, Massachusetts. One of the authors (Deal) attended this event.

29. Kaufman, B. (1966). *Up the down staircase.* New York: Avon.

30. This story was generated as groups of administrators in the Richmond (Virginia) School District reconstructed the system's history.

31. Clark, B. (1973). "The saga in higher education." In V. Baldridge and T. E. Deal, *Managing change in educational organizations.* Berkeley, CA: McCutchen.

32. Turner, V. (1975). *Dramas, fields and metaphors: Symbolic action in human society.* Ithaca, NY: Cornell University Press.

33. This example is from Fulton County, Georgia. It is one of a series in a school system that has been forced to close a large number of its schools.

34. This example is based on the authors' confidential case notes.

35. This example was shared by Dr. Tom Johnson, then Assistant Superintendent in Needham, Massachusetts.

36. This example is also taken from Fulton County, Georgia.

Sharing the Light of Faith:
National Catechetical Directory for Catholics of the United States

National Conference of Catholic Bishops. 1979. Nos. 206–11, 215.
Washington, D.C.: United States Catholic Conference.

Chapter IX.*
Catechetical Personnel

Part A: Ideal Qualities of Catechists

206. Response to a Call

As important as it is that a catechist have a clear understanding of the teaching of Christ and His Church, this is not enough. He or she must also receive and respond to a ministerial call, which comes from the Lord and is articulated in the local Church by the bishop. The response to this call includes willingness to give time and talent, not only to catechizing others, but to one's own continued growth in faith and understanding.

207. Witness to the gospel

For catechists to be effective, the catechist must be fully committed to Jesus Christ. Faith must be shared with conviction, joy, love, enthusiasm, and hope. "The summit and center of catechetical formation lies in an aptitude and ability to communicate the Gospel message."[1] This is possible only when the catechist believes in the gospel and its power to transform lives. To give witness to the gospel, the catechist must establish a living, ever-deepening relationship with the Lord. He or she must be a person of prayer, one who frequently reflects on the scriptures and whose Christlike living testifies to deep faith. Only men and women of faith can share faith with others, preparing the setting within which people can respond in faith to God's grace.

208. Commitment to the Church

One who exercises the ministry of the word represents the Church, to which the word has been entrusted. The catechist believes in the Church and is aware that, as a pilgrim people, it is in constant need of renewal. Committed to this visible community, the catechist strives to be an instrument of the Lord's power and a sign of the Spirit's presence.

The catechist realizes that it is Christ's message which he or she is called to proclaim. To insure fidelity to that message, catechists test and validate their understanding and insights in the light of the gospel message as presented by the teaching authority of the Church.

209. Sharer in community

The catechist is called to foster community as one who has "learned the meaning of community by experiencing it."[2] Community is formed in many ways. Beginning with acceptance of individual strengths and weaknesses, it progresses to relationships based on shared goals and values.

It grows through discussion, recreation, cooperation on projects, and the like.

Yet it does not always grow easily; patience and skill are frequently required. Even conflict, if creatively handled, can be growth-producing, and Christian reconciliation is an effective means of fostering community. Many people have had little experience of parish community and must be gradually prepared for it.

Christian community is fostered especially by the Eucharist, "which is at once sign of community and cause of its growth."[3] The catechist needs to experience this unity through frequent participation in the celebration of the Eucharist with other catechists and with those being catechized. Awareness of membership in a Christian community leads to awareness of the many other communities in the world which stand in need of service. The catechist seeks to cooperate with other parish leaders in making the parish a focal point of community in the Church.

210. Servant of the community

Authentic experience of Christian community leads one to the service of others. The catechist is committed to serving the Christian community, particularly in the parish, and the community-at-large. Such service means not only responding to needs when asked, but taking the initiative in seeking out the needs of individuals and communities, and encouraging students to do the same.

Sensitive to the community's efforts to find solutions to "a host of complex problems such as war, poverty, racism, and environmental pollution, which undermine community within and among nations,"[4] the catechist educates to peace and justice, and supports social action when appropriate. The Church often becomes involved in efforts to solve global problems through missionaries, who also carry out in a special way its mission of universal evangelization. The catechist should show how support for missionary endeavors is not only required by the Church's missionary nature but is an expression of solidarity within the human community.

211. Knowledge, skills, and abilities

Although even the best preparation for catechetical ministry will have little effect without the action of the Holy Spirit in the hearts of catechists and those being catechized, catechists should certainly seek to acquire the knowledge, skills, and abilities needed to communicate the gospel message effectively. They must have a solid grasp of Catholic doctrine and worship; familiarity with scripture; communication skills; the ability to use various methodologies; understanding of how people grow and mature and of how persons of different ages and circumstances learn.

---

* Editor's note: Chapter notation refers to this excerpt.

Part B: Catechetical Roles and Preparation

215. School principals

The Catholic school principal plays a critical role in realizing the goals of Catholic education. While specifics of this role vary according to circumstances, certain functions relating to catechesis are basic.

Recognizing that all faculty members share in catechetical ministry,[8] principals recruit teachers with appropriate qualifications in view of the Catholic school's apostolic goals and character. They provide opportunities for ongoing catechesis for faculty members by which they can deepen their faith and grow in the ability to integrate in their teaching the fourfold dimensions of Catholic education: message, community, worship, and service. In collaboration with the faculty, principals see to it that the curriculum reflects these dimensions.

Principals foster community among faculty and students. They understand the Catholic school as a part of larger communities, religious and secular. They collaborate with parish, area, or diocesan personnel in planning and implementing programs for a total, integrated approach to catechesis. They also establish norms and procedures of accountability and evaluation within the school, and in relation to the larger community.

Notes

1. *General Catechetical Directory*, 111.
2. *To Teach as Jesus Did*, 23.
3. *Ibid.*, 24.
4. *Ibid.*, 29.
8. *Teach Them*, A Statement of the Catholic Bishops. United States Catholic Conference, May 6, 1976. United States Catholic Conference, 1976, p. 7.

Catholic Identity

Reck, C. 1991. In *The Catholic identity of Catholic schools*, eds. J. Heft and C. Reck, 26–27.
Washington, D.C.: National Catholic Educational Association.

Climate—The Call

Elementary schools especially are called to create a school climate that reproduces, as far as possible, the warm atmosphere of family life (RD, no. 40). Vatican II documents describe the Catholic school climate like this: "From the first moment that a student sets foot in a Catholic school, he or she ought to have the impression of entering a new environment, one illumined by the light of faith, and having its own unique characteristics, an environment permeated with the Gospel spirit of love and freedom" (*Christian Education*, no. 8). In this setting, the pupils experience their dignity as persons before they know the meaning of the word dignity (*To Teach*, no. 155).

Education is one of the most important ways by which the church fulfills its commitment to the dignity of the person (*To Teach*, nos. 9, 13). Although collaboration is vital to meet this commitment, the prime responsibility for creating this unique Christian school climate rests with the teachers, as individuals and as a community (RD, no. 26).

Students, however, are not spectators as the school climate is developed; they help to determine the quality of this climate. The more that students can be helped to realize that a school, with all its activity, has only one purpose—to help them in their growth toward maturity—the more those students will be willing to become actively involved (RD, no. 106).

Climate—The Research

The strongest motivator attracting teachers to the Catholic school is the desire to teach in its educational environment. Second strongest is their view of teaching as ministry, and, third, their love of teaching (*CHS: Their Impact*, no. 194).

Teachers in Catholic schools—despite lower pay—have high morale, a factor in positive school climate. Even teachers in Catholic high schools, where many students' families are below the poverty level, claim high (85 percent) job satisfaction (*Heart of Matter*, no. 9).

Students, from their vantage point, report that teachers "overwhelmingly express respect and appreciation for their school colleagues" (*CHS: Their Impact*, no. 19).

Service—The Call

Values are essential, but "every true educator knows that a further step is necessary: values must lead to action; they are the motivation for action" (RD, no. 107). After studying a Christian social ethic, with its focus on the dignity of the human person, on justice, honesty, and freedom, students ought to be ready to reach out to those who are in need (RD, nos. 89–90).

Service—The Research

Research shows that Catholic high school students rate higher than their public school peers in community involvement, contributing money to the poor, and concern for others (*Heart of Matter*, 22). After graduation, Catholic school-educated parishioners are the people who "do more of the volunteer work" (McCready, 224). In fact, "more than 20 years of solid research has shown that the schools are an important source of adult Catholic resources in terms of contributions and volunteerism" (McCready, 230).

References

Benson, P. L., et. al. *Catholic High Schools: Their Impact on Low-Income Students*. Washington, D.C.: National Catholic Educational Association, 1986.

Congregation for Catholic Education. *The Religious Dimension of Education in a Catholic School: Guidelines for Reflection and Renewal*. Rome: Vatican Polyglot Press, 1988. [The most recent church document on the Catholic school.]

Guerra, M. J., Donahue, M. J., Benson, P. L. *The Heart of the Matter: Effects of Catholic High Schools on Student Values, Beliefs and*

Behaviors. Washington, D.C.: National Catholic Educational Association, 1990. [The most recent research on the Catholic high school with a summary of prior findings.]

McCready, W. C. "Catholic Schools and Catholic Identity: 'Stretching the Vital Connection'," pp. 217–31.

National Conference of Catholic Bishops. *To Teach as Jesus Did*. Washington, D.C.: United States Catholic Conference, 1972.

Vatican II. "Declaration on Christian Education." In Flannery, A. (ed.) *Vatican Council II: The Conciliar and Post-Conciliar Documents*. Volume 1, 1965, pp. 725–37.

Value-Added Leadership

Sergiovanni, T. J. 1990. 82–90. New York: Harcourt, Brace, Jovanovich.

Symbolic Leadership: Enhancing Meaning

"All of us hunger for that which is sacred."

Sam Bellows

If purposing is to have value, it must be lived in the everyday interactions and actions of everyone in the school. The challenge of leadership is to translate values and ideas into actions and programs. Symbolic leadership can provide the bridge between ideas developed and ideas in use, stated values and values embodied in school practice. John Meyer knows how to practice symbolic leadership.

In 1973 John Meyer became principal of the Garvin School in the Garrett School District near St. Louis, Missouri.[1] Garvin, built in 1950, had fallen on hard times. It had become known as a "combat zone," "the armpit of the district," and as the "dumping ground for teachers" not succeeding elsewhere. Teachers described teaching at Garvin as rough and a newly arrived sixth-grade teacher, assigned to replace another who was leaving because of a nervous breakdown, was greeted by students with "GO HOME" signs hung from his classroom windows. By 1984 the school had earned a reputation as one that not only worked but one that worked well. The 1983 achievement test scores at Garvin, for example, were received with disbelief by some central office administrators. One commented that "Something must be wrong with the tests if Garvin did that well."

Deciding that tackling all the problems at Garvin at the same time would be counterproductive, Meyer began on the road to school improvement by concentrating first on bringing about a level of competence in the areas of discipline, student achievement, and teacher performance. The result was a consistently applied discipline plan that, while demanding, had clear moral overtones. The plan was based on such basic principles as caring, praise, love, and concern coupled with high expectations and clearly defined personal accountability for one's behavior. An instructional management system was developed which involved close monitoring and coaching of teachers and teaching by Meyer. Comfortable with his knowledge of curriculum and teaching, Meyer did not hesitate to let teachers know when performance was not up to standard. He was quick to provide individual help when needed and emphasized teaching-oriented staff development programs for everyone. He refused to accept excuses from teachers when students were not learning. He helped one teacher who was having difficulty develop a plan for improvement and followed persistently to see that it was carried out, offering help as needed.

Though progress was slow and efforts time-consuming for Meyer, his pushing and persistence paid off. As one central office person put it, "John Meyer is stubborn. He will work with the teacher who has potential and won't give up. He has straightened out more staff and made good professional teachers of them. Some are on his staff now." Less promising teachers were let go or were encouraged to take early retirement.

Meyer was a superb manager with highly refined situational leadership skills. He developed, for example, a file folder system with folders numbered consecutively one to thirty-one for each day of the month. As issues, demands and other requirements crossed his desk he would decide whether to take immediate action or to mark "the item with ff23 indicating into which folder his secretary would place the task. Items are placed according to the time needed for completion." Each morning Meyer's secretary placed the day's file folder on his desk for his perusal. The contents then became the day's scheduled tasks.

Other situational leadership skills he practiced were "calculated neglect" and the use of nonverbal communications. In his words he was good at putting "things on hold, to wait and see later, to get more information. It may be defined by others as not doing the job, but eventually I get around to doing what's best. . . . Calculated neglect leaves it on your mind so you can think it through."

He was skilled at the subtle use of body language. When people visited the office he always gave enough time to thoroughly deal with the issues and concerns at hand but rarely gave any more. As researchers Stanfield and Walter report, "Meyer is able to get up from his chair, walk someone to the door, and end the conversation before the person realizes that the conversation is over."

Though initially many teachers were uncomfortable with Meyer's approach to leadership and the demands he was to make, the majority of staff came to respect and admire him. As time went on he delegated more of the burden of schooling to them and built a climate of caring and collegiality. Solid management and good interpersonal relationships—the raw materials of situational leadership —combined with an emphasis on coaching of teachers were the conditions that helped Meyer to secure a level of competence that would make Garvin work. He knew how to practice leadership by bartering and building.

Researchers Stanfield and Waller point out, however, that "It is obvious in this study of John Meyer and Garvin School that it required more than these (situational leadership, management and human relations) skills to cause Garvin School to be identified as a 'turnaround school' brought from the 'armpit of the district' to a school recognized for its exemplary programs and achievements." The *key* ingredient these researchers found was Meyer's ability to convincingly play the role of *principal teacher* on the one hand and to *bond* staff, students, and parents together around a common set of values and ideals on the other. This bonding would help them derive sense and meaning from their school lives and to make a commitment to excellence. Meyer was also a master at symbolic and cultural leadership, the value-added dimensions that can lead to extraordinary performance. Stanfield and Waller describe Meyer in action as follows:

> Meyer visits the classrooms, the cafeteria, the playground, and the teachers' lounge. He supports the building of traditions at Garvin and takes an active role in developing rituals that are performed daily, monthly, and yearly. He begins each day with announcements and the Pledge of Allegiance. . . . He involves the families in the enterprise of schooling when he calls the parents at home or at work to inform them that their child was the "good news" student that day. He supports the staff at Garvin with his Friday classroom visits to award pencils to the students who have completed all their work for the week. He is actively involved in the yearly reading program and involves parents in the program by requiring a signed contract agreeing that a special time will be set aside daily for reading. The annual visit of the headless horseman is another Garvin school tradition that is important to staff, students and community.

The horseman tradition was played out each year at Halloween when the headless horseman would ride across the schoolyard to the squeals and laughter of delighted children. As he galloped high on his black horse head in hand, he would lift his cape to reveal his identity to everyone's delight but to no one's surprise. On one occasion Meyer, wearing a "Miss Piggy" costume complete with wig, dress, and beads, rode into each classroom of the building on a motorcycle. The purpose was to motivate students to participate in the winter home reading program. (Miss Piggy was just one of a series of characters who have been employed through the years to kick off the annual program.) Stanfield and Waller note further:

> Meyer also carefully works to construct the reality that he sees as vital for the students at Garvin to succeed. He stresses to the students the importance of using their abilities, of doing their best in all endeavors and in realizing that one person can make a difference in their lives. They are told that they also have a responsibility to make a difference in someone else's life. He models his positive regard for the children when he stops in the hallway to hear a child's tale of weekend baseball accomplishments. He states his beliefs and models daily that the children at Garvin can learn and succeed. He is consistent in his expression of beliefs that the school can make a difference in the lives of children, and that what is best for the children should guide decision making.

Symbolic and cultural leadership can help communicate messages to parents, students, and staff that highlight the values, principles, and directions that are considered important to the leader and the school. When Bob Macklin, the principal of the Fox Lane High School in New Bedford, New York, moved his office from an interior location in the building to one that opened on a main thoroughfare of the school, he was extending an invitation to the students that his door was open.[2]

Steve Johnson, the principal of Mark Twain Middle School in San Antonio, frequently phones students who don't show up for his daily scheduled mentor group session. He phones in the evening, especially asking to talk to the missing student, not the parents. His message? "I was worried about you today—are you coming tomorrow?" Armonk, New York, Byram Hills High School principal Joseph Dipalermo tries to stand at the main entrance of the school each day to greet students and to say goodbye to them.[3] This is his way of taking to heart William Purkey's advice, "Show me your greetings and show me your leave takings and I will know your relationship." The relationship Dipalermo wants for all the students at Byram Hills is communicated loudly and clearly.

Pope Crook, the principal of Castle Hills Elementary School in San Antonio, gives coupons to students that they may then exchange for hugs from staff. The "good for one free hug" coupons communicate to students that the school cares about them and help them to feel good about themselves. The coupons also communicate to staff and parents the importance of building self-esteem in students. These principals are practicing symbolic leadership. Symbolic leadership provides an important link between the school's covenant and the meaning and significance that students and teachers enjoy as part of their daily school lives.

The Forces of Leadership

Successful leadership requires that one know how to make the right choices—choices that maintain a delicate balance among competing requirements. Think of leadership, for example, as a set of forces available to principals and other school leaders as they work in the school. Five forces comprise this set: technical, human, educational, symbolic, and cultural. All of the forces are important but they play different roles in achieving extraordinary performance.

Sound management techniques comprise the power of the technical force. Proper management is a basic requirement of all organizations if they expect to function properly day by day and to maintain support from external constituents. Furthermore, poorly managed enterprises can have negative effects on workers. The noted motivation psychologist Ray C. Hackman, for example, found that "poor organization of work" resulted in such negative feelings among workers as frustration and aggression, anxiety, personal inadequacy, and even social rejection.[4] Management provides the order and reliability that make the workplace secure and that free people to focus wholeheartedly on major purposes and central work activities.

The human force of leadership derives its power from harnessing the school's social and interpersonal potential, its human resources. Schools are human-intensive and the interpersonal needs of students and teachers are of sufficient importance that should they be neglected school problems are likely to follow.

Expert knowledge about matters of education and schooling is the power of the educational force. This force is concerned with the educational aspects of leadership. When principals rely on the educational force they assume the role of principal teacher.

The technical, human, and educational forces of leadership provide that critical mass needed for basic school competence. A shortage in any of the three forces upsets this critical mass and less effective schooling is likely to occur. In this sense they provide value; but the presence of the three forces does not guarantee excellence.

Symbolic leadership comprises the fourth force. When expressing this force, school leaders assume the role of "chief" emphasizing selective attention to or modeling of important goals and behaviors, and signaling to others what is important and valuable in the school. Touring the school; visiting classrooms; seeking out and visibly spending time with students; downplaying management concerns in favor of educational; presiding over ceremonies, rituals, and other important occasions; and providing a unified vision of the school through proper use of words and actions are examples of leadership behaviors associated with this force.

The power of the fifth force, cultural leadership, comes from defining, strengthening, and articulating enduring values, beliefs, and cultural strands that give the school its identity over time. This is the "high priest" function of being a leader. The behaviors associated with cultural leadership include articulating school purposes and mission; socializing new members to the school; telling stories and maintaining or reinforcing myths, traditions, and beliefs; explaining "the way things operate around here";

developing and displaying a system of symbols over time; and rewarding those who reflect the culture. The net effect of the cultural force of leadership is to bond together students, teachers, and others to the work of the school in a common cause.

Building a Culture of Excellence

One of the leading experts on the topic of school culture, Vanderbilt University professor Terrence E. Deal, believes that symbolic leadership is key to achieving extraordinary commitment and performance. His book *Corporate Cultures*, co-authored with McKinsey consultant Allan A. Kennedy, provides a template for understanding the culture of an enterprise and the leadership dimensions that help strengthen this culture.[5] Deal maintains that "the pathway" to educational excellence is inside each school. It exists in the traditions and symbols that make a school special to students, teachers, administrators, parents and the community.

Deal believes that a school's culture can be strengthened by first beginning to explore and document its history. Each school has its own story of origin, of the key people that were involved, and of the circumstances that launched it. "Throughout a school's history, a parade of students, teachers, principals, and parents cast sustaining memories. Great accomplishments meld with dramatic failures to form a potentially cherishable lore. This legacy needs to be codified and passed on."[6] Deal acknowledges the importance of developing a set of core values that comprise the shared covenant for students, teachers, administrators, parents, and others. He points out, however, that this set of shared values does not appear mystically but rather evolves from the school's experience and has historical analogues. He maintains that values detached from the school's history rarely have the kind of meaning that counts.

A second step on the road to strengthening the school's culture is to "anoint and celebrate heroes and heroines." These are the figures that Deal maintains provides tangible examples of shared values and provide necessary role models for others to emulate. These people should be identified and celebrated as heroes and heroines. Examples he provides are "a teacher who turned down a corporate offer to stay in the classroom close to students; a student who learned to read despite major learning handicaps; a custodian who knows each student by name; a principal who successfully fought the district superintendent and initiated a new program for parents; or a former student who once struggled with math and caused trouble and now is a well-recognized physicist."[7]

Strong cultures, Deal points out, build traditions and celebrate rituals that testify to the importance and significance of shared values. In good schools, for example, teaching is considered to be a sacred ritual. Principals go into classes not to monitor teachers or to check up on students but to celebrate the sacred ritual of teaching, thus enhancing the meaning and significance of teaching and learning in the minds and hearts of teachers and students. Deal believes that the use of ceremonies and dramatic events are important strategies for building a school culture. Pep rallies, assemblies, and graduation ceremonies are examples that quickly come to mind. Too often these standard ceremonies become routinized and their value is then diminished. The secret is to make the ceremony as sacred as possible. Sometimes new ceremonies have to be inaugurated and old ones revamped. Very few elementary, middle, or high schools, for example, have a matriculation ceremony. This is an ancient rite designed to enroll a person as a member of a body or enterprise. Its origins are in ancient colleges and universities but the idea is readily adaptable to the modern school.

Here's how such a ceremony might work in a high school or a junior high school. The ceremony would be held in the evening so that parents could come and witness the enrollment of their children as members of the unique student body that comprises the Evergreen School. They would, of course, be dressed in their best clothes. The new students, properly attired, would then be marched into the auditorium or gymnasium taking seats up front. The stage would be filled with flower arrangements and a candelabra or two burning brightly. At the signal, "Pomp and Circumstance" rings out over the loudspeakers and the faculty marches down the center aisle wearing their academic robes. They take positions on the stage facing the students. There would be a parade of short speeches by representatives of the local school board, the principal or principals of the sending schools, the principal of Evergreen, the president of Evergreen's PTA and so on. The superintendent in academic robes and other local dignitaries, formally attired, would be introduced and duly recognized. The students would then rise and take a matriculation oath promising to study hard and do their best to uphold the values and traditions of the school, promising not to let down their parents, promising to prepare to take their positions as those who will run the country someday. At the conclusion of the matriculation oath a well-rehearsed chorus would sing the first stanza of the Evergreen school song. The newly matriculated students would join them for the second stanza. Everyone present would sing the third stanza. Closing remarks would be made. A suitable exit song would be played as the faculty marches out, followed by the dignitaries, and then by the students. A reception would follow. The event would be covered fully by the media.

To some, a matriculation ceremony and similar events might be considered as clever tricks designed to deceive people. The noted organizational theorist James C. March would respond to such criticism as follows: "The stories, myths and rituals of management are not merely ways some people fool other people or a waste of time. They are fundamental to our lives. We embrace the mythologies and symbols of life and could not otherwise easily endure."[8] Deal believes that it is important for teachers and administrators who want to revitalize a school culture to tell good stories—vivid stories of memorable events and important accomplishments that embody the values of the school. Finally, Deal recommends that the cultural network of the school be strengthened and officially rewarded. He states, "People often wonder why the school secretary, custodian, or elderly teacher seem to have so much power. Their power usually derives from their unofficial role as priest, gossip, or storyteller. Schools need to identify these people, to integrate them into the mainstream of activity, and to reward them for the important positive contributions they make. A principal who fights the informal network usually loses; one who works with the cultural cast of characters can have a powerful effect on a school."[9]

Notes

1. The "Meyer story" is summarized from Pamela C. Stanfield and James E. Waller, "The Principal as White Knight." Paper presented to the American Educational Research Association (Washington, D.C., 1987). The researchers reached an agreement with the school district to maintain confidentiality. Thus the name, Meyer, is a pseudonym and the names Garvin School and Garrett School District are fictitious.
2. "How Do You Make Your School an Inviting Place?" *Principals Exchange.* vol. 3, no. 2, Westchester Principals' Center (1988), p. 6.
3. *Ibid.*
4. Ray C. Hackman, *The Motivated Working Adult* (New York: American Management Association, 1969), p. 158.
5. Terrence E. Deal and Allan A. Kennedy, *Corporate Cultures.* (Reading, Mass.: Addison-Wesley, 1982).
6. Terrence E. Deal, "The Symbolism of Effective Schools." *The Elementary School Journal.* vol. 85, no. 5 (1985), p. 615.
7. *Ibid.*, p. 616.
8. James G. March, "How We Talk and How We Act: Administrative Theory and Organizational Life" Thomas J. Sergiovanni and John E. Corbally, eds., *Leadership and Organizational Culture* (Urbana: University of Illinois Press, 1984), p. 31.
9. Deal, *op.cit.*, p. 616.

Value-Added Leadership

Sergiovanni, T. J. 1990. 151–52. New York: Harcourt, Brace, Jovanovich.

Avoiding the mantle of messiah is a worry for Ruby Cremaschi-Schwimmer, principal of the Lincoln High School in San Diego, California. Prior to her arrival, Lincoln was near the bottom of the heap among high schools in San Diego. The building was in disrepair and students scored low on district tests of reading, mathematics, and language. The school's dropout rates were among the highest. Today Lincoln is a school that works and works well. Much of the credit for its success goes to its principal, who saw her job as a "sacred mission." She was, in many respects, the "messiah" who transformed Lincoln. In her words, "My fears about this 'Guru' approach are that when everything rests on the personality of one individual there is the danger of things regressing when he or she must move on and that too much power residing in one individual leader may lead to the 'Jim Jones' syndrome of leadership with negative results." In her view, leadership must be driven by ideas and obligation—not personality. She is now at work trying to shift the emphasis from what "Principal Cremaschi-Schwimmer believes in and wants" to what Lincoln High School believes in, stands for, and can be. For Lincoln's success to become real, leadership-by-banking must become real.

In his book *Servant Leadership*, Robert K. Greenleaf tells the story of the 18th century American Quaker John Woolman, who almost singlehandedly convinced the society to renounce slavery. He didn't accomplish this by raising a big storm or by the force of charismatic personality. "His method was one of gentle but clear and persistent persuasion. . . . The burden of his approach was to raise questions: What does the owning of slaves do to you as a moral person? What kind of institution are you binding over to your children? Man by man, inch by inch, by persistently returning and revisiting and pressing his gentle arguments over a period of 30 years, the scourge of slavery was eliminated from this society, the first religious group in America formally to renounce and forbid slavery among its members."[13] The concept of servant leadership is popular among Catholic school educators. With Jesus cited as the authority: "You know that rulers of the Gentiles lord it over them and their great men exercise authority over them. It shall not be so among you, but whoever would be great among you must be your servant" (Matthew 20:25).

Servant leadership describes well what it means to be administrator. School administrators are responsible for "ministering" to the needs of the schools they serve. The needs are defined by the shared values and purposes that comprise school covenants. They administer by furnishing help and being of service to parents, teachers, and students. They minister by highlighting and protecting the values of the school. The school leader as minister is one who is devoted to a cause, mission, or set of ideas and accepts the duty and obligation to serve this cause.

Note

13. Robert K. Greenleaf, *Servant Leadership*. (New York: Paulist Press, 1977.) p. 29 as quoted in Arthur Blumberg, "Some Not Quite Random Thoughts About Leadership." *Wingspan*. Vol.4, No. 1, 1988, p. 5.

To Teach as Jesus Did:
A Pastoral Message on Catholic Education

National Conference of Catholic Bishops. 1973. No. 82. Washington, D.C.: United States Catholic Conference.

82. "The future of humanity lies in the hands of those who are strong enough to provide coming generations with reasons for living and hoping." (*The Church Today*, 31) Here as in other areas of educational ministry the threefold purpose of Christian education provides a guide for developing and evaluating programs. Educational programs for the young must strive to teach doctrine, to do so within the experience of Christian community, and to prepare individuals for effective Christian witness and service to others. In doing this they help foster the student's growth in personal holiness and his relationship with Christ.

Sharing the Light of Faith:
National Catechetical Directory for Catholics of the United States

National Conference of Catholic Bishops. 1979. Nos. 30, 232.
Washington, D.C.: United States Catholic Conference.

Chapter II.* The Catechetical Ministry of the Church

30. Mission of the Church

The Church continues the mission of Jesus, prophet, priest, and servant king. Its mission, like His, is essentially one—to bring about God's kingdom—but this one mission has three aspects: proclaiming and teaching God's word, celebrating the sacred mysteries, and serving the people of the world. Corresponding to the three aspects of the Church's mission and existing to serve it are three ministries: the ministry of the word, the ministry of worship, and the ministry of service. In saying this, however, it is important to bear in mind that the several elements of the Church's mission are inseparably linked in reality (each includes and implies the others), even though it is possible to study and discuss them separately.

Chapter X.* Organization for Catechesis

Part B: The Parish

232. Catholic schools

Catholic schools are unique expressions of the Church's effort to achieve the purposes of Catholic education among the young. They "are the most effective means available to the Church for the education of children and young people."[7]

Catholic schools may be part of the parish structure, interparochial or regional, diocesan or private. Growth in faith is central to their purpose.

As a community and an institution, the school necessarily has an independent life of its own. But a parochial school is also a community within the wider community, contributing to the parish upon which it depends and integrated into its life. Integration and interdependence are major matters of parish concern; each program in a total catechetical effort should complement the others.[8]

Similarly, regional, diocesan, and private schools should work in close collaboration with neighboring parishes. The experience of community in the schools can benefit and be benefited by the parishes.

Teachers in Catholic schools are expected to accept and live the Christian message and to strive to instill a Christian spirit in their students. As catechists, they will meet standards equivalent to those set for other disciplines and possess the qualities described in Chapter IX, Part A [nos. 205-11].

The school should have a set religion curriculum, with established goals and objectives, open to review and evaluation by parish boards and diocesan supervisory teams. It is recommended that an integrated curriculum provide options for catechists and students by offering electives along with the core curriculum.

It is desirable that Catholic high schools in a diocese work together to share resources, provide opportunities for teacher training and development, and cooperate in establishing program guidelines.

The school's principal and faculty are responsible for making clear the importance of religion. The quality of the catechetical experience in the school and the importance attached to religious instruction, including the amount of time spent on it, can influence students to perceive religion as either highly important or of little importance.

Its nature as a Christian educational community, the scope of its teaching, and the effort to integrate all learning

*   Editor's note: Chapter notations refer to this excerpt.

with faith distinguish the Catholic school from other forms of the Church's educational ministry to youth and give it special impact. In Catholic schools children and young people "can experience learning and living fully integrated in the light of faith,"[9] because such schools strive "to relate all human culture eventually to the news of salvation, so that the life of faith will illumine the knowledge which students gradually gain of the world, of life and of mankind."[10] Cooperative teaching which cuts across the lines of particular disciplines, interdisciplinary curricula, team teaching, and the like help to foster these goals of Catholic education.

"Building and living community must be prime, explicit goals of the contemporary Catholic school."[11] Principal and faculty members have a responsibility to help foster community among themselves and the students. Creative paraliturgies and sacramental celebrations for particular age groups can strengthen the faith community within the school.

Catholic school students should be introduced gradually to the idea and practice of Christian service. In early years, efforts to instill a sense of mission and concern for others help lay a foundation for later service projects, as does study of the lives of the saints and outstanding contemporaries.

Junior and senior high school programs should foster a social conscience sensitive to the needs of all. Familiarity with the Church's social encyclicals and its teaching on respect for human life will be part of this formation. (Cf.

Chapter VII) Opportunities for field and community experiences are high desirable. Teachers, administrators, parents, and students should be involved in planning service projects. One measure of a school's success is its ability to foster a sense of vocation, of eagerness to live out the basic baptismal commitment to service, whether this is done as a lay person, religious, deacon, or priest.

Catechesis speaks of the missionary nature of the Church. It points out that all Christians are responsible for missionary activity by reason of the love of God, which prompts in them a desire to share with everyone the spiritual goods of this life and the life to come. Catholic schools provide opportunities for participation in missionary projects through the Holy Childhood Association, the Society for the Propagation of the Faith, etc. They also provide students with opportunities to search for the gifts that the Holy Spirit offers them for this ministry.

Through a carefully planned process, the entire school community—parents, students, faculty, administrators, pastors, and others—needs to be involved in the development of its goals, philosophy, and programs.

Notes

7. *To Teach as Jesus Did*, 118; cf. also, *The Catholic School*, Sacred Congregation for Catholic Education. United States Catholic Conference, 1977.
8. Cf. *To Teach as Jesus Did*, 92.
9. *Ibid.*, 103.
10. Christian Education, 8.
11. *To Teach as Jesus Did*, 108.

In Support of Catholic Elementary and Secondary Schools

National Conference of Catholic Bishops. 1990. P. 6. Washington, D.C.: United States Catholic Conference.

Our Future
Goals for 1997

By the twenty-fifth anniversary of *To Teach As Jesus Did* in 1997, we commit ourselves unequivocally to the following goals:

1. That Catholic schools will continue to provide high quality education for all their students in a context infused with gospel values.

2. That serious efforts will be made to ensure that Catholic schools are available for Catholic parents who wish to send their children to them.

3. That new initiatives will be launched to secure sufficient financial assistance from both private and public sectors for Catholic parents to exercise this right.

4. That the salaries and benefits of Catholic school teachers and administrators will reflect our teaching as expressed in *Economic Justice for All*.

The Principal as Teacher of Teachers

Perri, Susanne, OP. 1989. In *Reflections on the role of the Catholic school principal*, ed. R. Kealey, 67–74. Washington, D.C.: National Catholic Educational Association.

The latest school research shows a close creative linkage between the principal as strong educational leader and an effective school.

This strong connection suggests that those professionals interested in good schools should study and reflect upon the qualities of the principal as an educational leader. It is to that end that this chapter is dedicated.

Educational Leaders Are Visionaries and Decision-Makers

Imagine the effective educational leader looking into a mirror. In the reflection the leader sees two characteristics that deserve careful study: that of a visionary and that of a key decision-maker.

Visionary. A visionary is well-informed about the cutting-edge developments in education while, at the same time, well-grounded in the tried and true practices of the profession: able to see where the school is to be in three to five years, and able to inspire the staff to internalize the vision and work to actualize it.

Even more so, the educational visionary has a world vision. For us in Catholic schools, this world vision embraces a clear sense of Gospel values, the teachings of the Catholic church, and, as the bishops' pastoral on campus ministry teaches, the ability to appropriate the faith in the light of the Gospel. Basic to the formulation of this vision is a clear sense of the world into which students of Catholic schools will enter. Such a person communicates the vision in a clear and caring manner to all parties involved: teachers, students, parents, pastoral-team members, school board members, and community.

A central tenet of our educational philosophy is that the school's primary business is the instruction of students. This philosophy, actualized through systematic, well-articulated goals established by the school staff under the leadership of the principal, empowers teachers to lead students to the desired vision of the future,

Decision-Maker. The educational decision-maker always has an eye on the future. But, at the same time, the principal is grounded in the realities of today. As a result this leader prods the teachers to do their professional best as they work to actualize the work of the school. Simultaneously, the principal holds them accountable for the quality of their performance. At all times, the principal holds high standards and expectations for staff performance. The educational leader also accepts the responsibility to help the teachers meet those standards as well as working hard personally to achieve them. The principal fosters effective teaching and learning through productive faculty meetings, insightful classroom observations, thoughtful curriculum renewal and other professional development opportunities.

A person cannot be an educational decision-maker unless committed to life-long learning and models being a student of the profession by constantly learning, integrating, and sharing what is learned. The principal expects the staff to do the same, and learns from them as they gain new information about education.

As noted earlier, we consider the leader to be someone who does the right thing, while the manager does things right. In business, these roles of leader and manager are often differentiated and assigned to different people. However, in the school business, the building-principal performs both tasks. As we continue our reflections on the principal as decision-maker, we should look a little more deeply into this duality of role expectations for the principal because both roles affect one's choices as the key leader for the school.

As leader, the principal chooses risk and innovation in order to do the right thing. At other times, this educator chooses the safe route to do things right. Educational leaders need the ability to use both analytical induction and intuitional deduction when making decisions.

At times, the principal divides a decision into its component parts, predicts the costs and benefits of each of the various options, and uses hard data to make a final decision. At other times, the educational leader acts instantaneously, trusting the inner voice or making decisions based on faith.

The school leader, having a clear vision of the school, knows when to involve and not to involve the staff in the decision-making process.

For a moment, let's look a little more closely at the principal's role as decision-maker. In analyzing the teaching act, I have often heard Madeline Hunter state in her presentations that the classroom teacher makes between 2,000 and 5,000 decisions in a single day. The educational leader is the same. Decisions are made about people, about processes, and about products. People-decisions include such things as communication, school-climate, self-esteem, conflict resolution, stress management, and staff wellness. Key process decisions about the school include models for instruction, mastery teaching, thinking skills, presenting skills, learning styles, leadership, supervision, and the change process. Product decisions include such items as curriculum and instructional materials.

One major area of decision-making is in the area of a comprehensive curriculum. The principal is the ultimate decision-maker in creating, adjusting, and annually evaluating the school's curriculum. The principal utilizes curriculum sources that support coordination and accountability among school personnel. In the world of rapid change, Catholic schools can no longer accept the limited approach of the textbook's content as the curriculum focus. It is the school's own curriculum which articulates, in practical form, the collective goals of an individual school.

Catholic school students are called upon to be competent and confident, responsible and happy, hope-filled and wholesome American adults of the 21st century. These are some of the focal points of the principal's decision making for curriculum design and implementation.

Educational Leaders Are Models and Coaches

Modeling. The principal models those specific behaviors which teachers are expected to practice in their classrooms. This modeling occurs particularly at staff meetings and in the classroom. The principal designs the staff meetings according to the principles of effective instruction. By the end of each staff meeting, the teachers have learned something, and have observed the principal as a model for their own teaching.

The principal periodically volunteers to teach classes in each teacher's room. These provide models of good teaching. The principal may videotape herself teaching the class and invite the teachers to critique the tape at a staff meeting. Such a procedure models effective teaching, the ability to accept evaluation, an appreciation for lifelong learning, and the willingness to take a risk in order to grow professionally.

Coaching. As "The Teacher of Teachers," the principal not only models, but also coaches. Coaching is a process by which principal and teacher first agree on a procedure for observing and recording the teaching act. The principal provides feedback by describing the teaching event. Finally, principal and teacher jointly interpret and assay the consequences of the lesson and plan a future course of action.

This helps the teacher refine teaching and other skills such as planning, human relations, classroom management, curriculum management, knowledge of content, use of materials, and classroom climate. Coaching is a process that increases teacher-principal dialogue, skill development, and formative evaluation.

As a coach, the principal knows, models, and practices the various elements of good teaching. This educator observes teachers also in order to reinforce and refine the use of these elements through effective systematic feedback.

This caring, sensitive, accurate feedback helps the teacher make major decisions related to the instructional skills required for success. In the process, the principal-coach emphasizes one or another of the major instructional decisions. These guidelines include the following:

1) Select an objective at the correct level of difficulty for the students. The coach helps the teacher assess the current abilities and previous experience of the students so that the lesson can be targeted to the outer edge of the students' potential. In other words, the coach helps the teacher match lesson to learner.

2) Teach to an objective. The principal helps the teacher make decisions about how to best deliver the content to the students. This involves decisions about what to include and how to include it as well as what not to include.

3) Monitor the learning and adjust the teaching. This category of decision-making includes the teacher's ability to elicit observable student behaviors which indicate whether or not the student has learned the content. The coach helps the teacher a) obtain the behavior from the student, b) analyze that behavior, and c) make appropriate adjustments, if needed.

4) Use the principles of learning. The coach helps the teacher take an intentional and active role in affecting the rate and degree of learning achieved by the students, retaining what is learned, and in increasing productive behavior, through the effective use of reinforcement theory. In so doing, the coach helps the teacher raise the probability of successful student learning.

Another integral component of coaching is motivation. Just as successful teachers challenge students to learn, the educational leader motivates teachers to increase their instructional competence and confidence in order that they may pass those skills and attitudes on to their students.

Three motivational factors that the principal must be able to inculcate in the teacher are 1) success, 2) knowledge of results, and 3) feeling tone.

Success is a strong tool for increasing motivation: "Nothing succeeds like success." The more success teachers experience, the more optimistic they will be about future performance. On the other hand, the more they fail, the less willing they will be to expose themselves to risk because their prediction is "I won't make it." The principal has the opportunity and obligation to help the teacher succeed and to celebrate that success through passing it on to the students.

Knowledge of results is another factor for increasing teacher motivation. The amount, the specificity, the immediacy, and the frequency of feedback which teachers receive about their performance affects how they improve professionally. Just doing something again, without knowing how well we did it, is, in the long run, neither satisfying nor stimulating. The result will be that we will not be motivated to continue or improve our performance.

When we find out what we are doing well, what needs to be improved, how to improve it, and, finally, feel that there is reasonable probability that we can improve it, we are motivated to try to achieve higher goals.

Feeling tone is the way particular teachers feel in particular situations. Feeling tone affects the amount of effort they are willing to put forth to increase their instructional skills. Teachers are most apt to work hard at their teaching if they find that the teaching environment is pleasant. The principal plays the key role in effecting a pleasant environment for the school.

We might sum up coaching by defining its purposes as follows: 1) to help the principal improve as a teacher, 2) to help the teacher improve instruction skills, 3) to correct problems which surface in the classroom observation, 4) to support the choice of an alternate teaching practice(s), 5) to support a uniform use of effective teaching practices by all teachers in the school, 6) to promote adoption of a shared-language for teaching theory, 7) to get new teachers off to a good start, 8) to help new teachers move to higher levels of teaching at a quicker pace, and 9) to achieve professional growth for all involved.

Conclusion

As an educational leader, the principal leads, manages, motivates, models, and coaches. That adds up to many expectations. In order to meet those expectations, the educational leader studies, learns, grows, and collaborates.

Sometimes, to achieve the above goals, a given principal will pair up with a companion principal from another school. As a pair, they might share readings, learning, problems, and experiences. They can also visit each other's schools and observe each other in staff meetings, teacher observations, evaluations, and share feedback with one another.

A Catholic school needs a principal who is intimately involved in the school's instructional program at all levels.

In the foregoing paragraphs I have used many words to describe this principal: leader, manager, visionary, communicator, life-long learner, decision-maker, curriculum developer, and instructor.

But above all else, the principal of tomorrow must be the teacher of teachers in the school and in that capacity serve as a model, and even more importantly as a coach. The attitude of the teacher-coach should be one of excitement and commitment to the importance of Catholic education in general and instructional enablement in particular.

Other kinds of coaches have a significant role to play in our society but their role is relatively insignificant when compared to the impact which a principal can have on society. The Catholic school principal chooses to become an instructional enabler whose all consuming purpose is to raise the probability that each and every teacher in the school is a successful and artistic instructor of the total person—spiritually, academically, socially, emotionally, and morally. This is carried out in a climate which manifests God's unconditional love.

About the Author

Sister Susanne Perri is a member of the Sisters of St. Dominic, Tacoma. Washington. She holds masters degrees in school administration and in religious education. Sister served as an elementary school teacher and principal and since 1969 has been the Director of Instructional Services for the Archdiocese of Seattle. She has taught graduate courses at Seattle Pacific University and at Seattle University and has conducted several sessions of the NCEA Leadership Training Program. She has served on the committees of the NCEA Department of Elementary Schools and the Supervision, Curriculum and Personnel section of CACE.

Value-Added Leadership

Sergiovanni, T. J. 1990. 56–63. New York: Harcourt, Brace, Jovanovich.

Purposing: The Building of a Covenant

Purposing involves both the vision of the leader and the covenant that the group shares. The notion of leader vision is widely accepted but the effect of purposing on school excellence falls short if this is where it ends. Covenants provide the value-added dimension needed for extraordinary performance.

Vision gets the most attention in the leadership literature. Leaders, according to the noted leadership theorist Warren Bennis, need to have "the capacity to create and communicate a compelling vision of a desired state of affairs, a vision . . . that clarifies the current situation and induces commitment to the future."[7] Vision is an important dimension of leadership and without it the very point of leadership can be missed. However, the vision of the school must also reflect the hopes and dreams, the needs and interests, the values and beliefs of everyone that has a stake in the school. Ultimately it is what the school stands for that counts.

In their book, *Passion for Excellence*, Tom Peters and Nancy Austin point out that vision should start with a single person and suggest that one should be wary of "committee visions."[8] This is good advice. Principals and superintendents have a responsibility, even obligation, to talk openly and frequently about their beliefs and commitments, their hopes and dreams, their values and ideals.

They are the ones who are responsible for starting the dialogue about what the school stands for, believes in, and about where the school or district should be headed.

The development of a vision, however, should not be construed as a strategic plan that functions as a "road map" charting the turns needed to reach a specific reality that the leader has in mind. It should instead, as Diamond Shamrock CEO William Bricker points out, be viewed more as a compass that points the direction to be taken, that inspires enthusiasm and that allows people to buy into and take part in the shaping of the way that will constitute the school's mission.[9] The fleshing out of this vision requires the building of a shared consensus. The building of a consensus about purposes and beliefs creates a powerful force that bonds people together around common themes, on the one hand, and that provides them with a sense of what is important and some signal of what is of value, on the other.

In successful schools consensus runs deep. It is not enough, for example, to have worked out what people stand for and what is to be accomplished. A binding and solemn agreement needs to emerge that represents a value system for living together and that provides the basis for decisions and actions. This binding and solemn agreement represents the school's covenant. When both the value of vision and the value-added dimension of covenant are present, teachers and students respond with increased motivation and commitment and their performance is well beyond the ordinary.

As the school covenant is built, the leader's behavioral style becomes less important than what the leader stands for and communicates to others. It is important for school leaders to do something. It is also important to be someone—to have ideas, values, and beliefs about what is right and good and what is worth accomplishing. The realm of purposing, vision, and covenants is that of the high ground that inspires and provides moral leadership. This realm should not be confused with the stating of technical objectives and the development of tactical plans for their implementation. The "technical" and "high ground" mix in purposing and planning are illustrated below.

Purposing is concerned with vision (leader's hopes and dreams), school covenant (shared values and expectations, and the *development* of the school's mission (shared purpose). By contrast, planning is concerned with *defining* the mission and developing goals (strategy) and objectives (tactics). Purposing is an expression of leadership, and planning a management function.

Leadership, according to General Motors training manager Ralph Frederick, "creates vision and energy" while management directs resources and channels energy created by leadership.[10] In this light, plans are important for they help guide the day-to-day activities of the school. Raising test scores in reading on the Iowa Test of Basic Skills, for example, is an important outcome of schooling but it hardly speaks to school purposes. Purposes are much more inspiring, urgent, and sacred. Planning represents the rungs on the ladder that must be climbed, but purposes speak to where the ladder leads.

Michigan State University professor Jay Featherstone made the point recently that if we want to highlight the importance of schooling it might be a good idea to mention to students and their parents, "Look, we are taking all this trouble with you (students) because you are going to run the country someday."[11] If the school's mission is indeed to get kids ready to run the country someday, then it would need to get them ready to:

Take charge of our cultural heritage and cherished ideas as embodied in the academic knowledge that comprises our history, literature, mathematics, the arts, and other disciplines.

Provide the capital needed to support our health, commerce, educational, cultural, military, and other critical institutions; thus ensuring that we will live with safety, in dignity, and with grace.

Break new frontiers in the sciences and the arts that will result in newer and better ways for us to live together and work together.

Make wise decisions as wards and stewards of our democratic society.

Find dignity, meaning, and happiness in their lives as they assume adult roles of parent, spouse, child, and friend.

And finally, to take responsibility for their own personal health and for the health of others.

In a sense these purposes of schooling comprise a litany of sacred responsibilities that students must be prepared to undertake *and a* set of sacred responsibilities for those in the schools who have to get them ready.

Marva Collins, the founder of Chicago's West Side Prep, had a vision that revolutionized the lives of her students. Her school was founded in a basement with a handful of disadvantaged children as students. A recent U.S. Department of Education publication spoke of Collins's vision as follows: "Her vision of what they could become transformed socially maladjusted children who could not read or write into winners of statewide educational awards, into 'citizens of the world,' who saw education as their way out of poverty. The 'school creed' that she wrote embodies the vision that made West Side Prep a success: 'My success and . . . education can be companions that no misfortune can depress, no crime can destroy, and no enemy can alienate. Without education, (one) is a slave. . . . Time and chance come to us all. I can be either hesitant or courageous. I can . . . stand up and shout: "This is my time and my place. I will accept the challenge." ' "[12]

Not only should statements of school purpose sound good, they should influence the direction that the school takes and the decisions that parents, teachers, students, and administrators make as they travel in the appropriate direction. Purposes with the following characteristics are most likely to have the greatest influence:

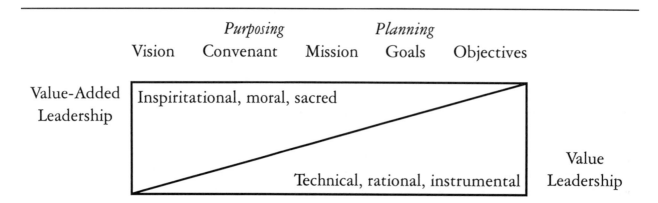

1. They are clear enough so that you know you are achieving them.
2. They are accessible enough so that they can be achieved with existing resources.
3. They are important enough to reflect the core values and beliefs that are shared by those with a stake in the school.
4. They are powerful enough that they can inspire and touch people in a world that is managerially loose and culturally tight.
5. They are focused enough and few in number so that it is clear as to what is important and what isn't.
6. They are characterized by consonance. Most of the purposes hang together as a group. Contradictory purposes can be managed.
7. They encourage cooperation within the school and not competition. Cooperative purposes encourage people to work together by allowing each member to share in what the group achieves or attains. Everyone benefits when anyone is successful. Competitive purposes, by contrast, pit one person against another. Each member receives rewards independent of the success of the group and contingent only upon his or her own performance regardless of how well the group does.
8. They are difficult enough to evoke challenge and cause people to "gambare," to persist.
9. They are resilient enough to stand the test of time and thus are not easily changed.

Some school covenants include an operational platform that provides the rules and standards for living and working together. This is the approach being considered by the Alliance for Better Schools. The Alliance is comprised of the Hawthorne Elementary School and the Mark Twain Middle School in the San Antonio Independent School District; the Jackson-Keller Elementary School and Lee High School from the North East Independent School District; and Trinity University and the Psychological Corporation. The Alliance schools are committed to guaranteeing academic excellence for all students and are trying to identify the conditions needed for excellence. They want their platform to serve as a basis for evaluating decisions that teachers, principals, and others make. Decisions would be okay providing that they are consistent with the conditions for excellence. No decision would be allowed that was not consistent with the conditions for excellence. The Alliance schools have the following platform under consideration:

The Alliance for Better Schools is committed to the principle that academic excellence applies to all students and everyone can achieve excellence if conditions are right. Conditions for excellence:

1. Form follows function.

Schools exist to promote and provide for teaching and learning. Thus decisions about organizing for schooling, scheduling, faculty assignments, curriculum, and teaching should reflect and facilitate this purpose. By contrast, decisions based on political expediency, bureaucratic convenience, or predetermined conceptions of management practice result in function following form and should be avoided.

2. Innovation and risk taking are encouraged and rewarded.

Academic excellence involves inventing new solutions to old problems, viewing old problems in different ways, and confronting new problems swiftly and effectively. It is better to try and fail than not to try at all. Mistakes are okay providing that we learn from them.

3. Reflective teaching is encouraged and nurtured.

Academic excellence requires that teachers develop teaching strategies and change teaching strategies in response to situations they face. Different students, different goals and objectives, different subject matter content, and different teaching contexts all require different strategies. Teaching is situationally specific. Excellence does not come in a can. No seven steps to heaven exist. No list of generic teaching behaviors can provide the magic answer. Instead teaching strategies are created in use as teachers teach and reflect and teach again. Models of teaching do not prescribe but help inform reflective teaching.

4. Teachers and administrators are motivated and committed.

Academic excellence requires that teachers and administrators work hard and give a good deal of themselves to teaching and learning. They regularly exceed giving "a fair day's work for a fair day's pay." Motivation and commitment are enhanced when professionals are in charge of their practice, have ownership in school affairs, and find teaching and schooling to be rewarding.

5. Collegiality is encouraged and enhanced.

Academic excellence requires that teachers work together and with administrators as colleagues. Colleagues are familiar with each other's work, talk clinically about teaching practice, share ideas, and help each other.

6. Rewards are shared.

Academic excellence requires that rewards for teachers be distributed cooperatively rather than individually. Reward systems need to bring professionals together, not divide them; encourage them to share ideas, help and support each other, not to compete with each other. Intercompetition for teachers (school to school) is okay but not intracompetition (teacher to teacher within the same school). "The success of one is the success of all and the failure of one is the failure of all," is our motto.

7. Accountability is genuine.

Academic excellence requires schools to be accountable. When teachers teach, students should be expected to learn. But accountability cannot be genuine unless it is accompanied by responsibility. Teachers and administrators, schools and school communities cannot be held accountable unless they are given the responsibility for making decisions about teaching and learning in the school.

8. Standards are high.

Academic excellence requires more than competence. Schools should be run in a competent manner. Teachers should teach competently and students should achieve a level of acceptable competence in learning. But excellence requires that schools make a commitment beyond competence. Good is not good enough: If we are to give more, we must expect more. If we expect more, students will achieve more.

9. Developmental needs of students are connected to academic achievement.

Academic excellence requires that we give attention to the heart and soul as well as the mind. When the three are brought together, each benefits. When it comes to learning we cannot choose between what is good for a student academically and what is good developmentally.

10. Open-mindedness and inquiry are encouraged.

Academic excellence requires that we be open to new ideas and search for new and better ways. Any idea should be considered if it can help us to teach better and students to learn better.

Notes

7. Warren Bennis, "Transformative Power and Leadership" Sergiovanni and Corbally, *op.cit.*, p. 66.
8. Tom Peters and Nancy Austin, *A Passion for Excellence* (New York: Random House, 1985), p. 286.
9. Robert H. Hayes, "Strategic Planning—Forward in Reverse?" *Harvard Business Review* (Nov.-Dec. 1985).
10. Doron Levin, "G.M. Bid to Rejuvenate Leadership." *New York Times* (Sept. 3, 1988).
11. Jay Featherstone, comments to the seminar "Tomorrow's Schools: Models of Learning, Models of Schooling." Michigan State University (July 16, 1988).
12. *Principal Selection Guide*. (Washington, D.C.: Department of Education, 1987), p. 5.

Vision and the Work of Educational Leaders

Sheive, L. T., and M. B. Schoenheit. 1987. In *Leadership: Examining the elusive, 1987 yearbook*, 94, 96–98. Alexandria, Va.: Association for Supervision and Curriculum Development.

The Nature of Vision

A vision is a blueprint of a desired state. It is an image of a preferred condition that we work to achieve in the future. In chapter 3, David C. Dwyer, Bruce Barnett, and Ginny Lee call vision "an overarching goal." Hickman and Silva (1984, 151) call it a "mental journey from the known to the unknown." Blumberg and Greenfield (1986, 228) relate vision to "moral imagination" that "gives that individual the ability to see that the world need not remain as it is—that it is possible for it to be otherwise—and to be better." Vision is what people work toward. One leader, a school superintendent, spoke about vision in personal terms:

I believe you need to carry around dreams. You begin to see scenarios in your head. We're going to combine our two high schools some day, and I can already see the first assembly when all the kids come together. I can already see the parade through town when we celebrate it. When you're in a place long enough, you actually attend one of those scenarios [that you dreamed]. That really is exciting.

Do all leaders have a vision? After our discussions with these 12 educators, we inferred that each has *a professional mission.*[3] When we asked for confirmation that they were describing a vision or a dream of theirs, each agreed. This group of educational leaders is not unique. Bennis and Nanus (1985), who interviewed 90, "trend-directing" leaders in the corporate and public sector, also report that all their subjects "had an agenda, an unparalleled concern with

---

Figure 7.2. Two Categories of Vision

	ORGANIZATIONAL	UNIVERSAL
Goal	Excellence in the organization	Equity for a target group
Orientation	One school or district	All schools or districts
Central concern	Creating the best	Righting a wrong

outcome." Their finding, which is similar to ours, suggests that a focus on the possibilities is central to the work of leaders recognized as change agents.

Effectiveness is a key notion. Rutherford (1985), reporting on a University of Texas at Austin study, notes that, when asked, effective principals can describe their visions. He also concludes that "the less effective principals had no vision for their schools; they've focused on maintaining tranquility in the here and now" (p. 32).

Although all our leaders have an image of a preferred future, a vision, none has the same vision in mind. Two categories of vision exist for our leaders: organizational and universal. Visions in the organizational category focus on the school or district where the leader works. Visions in the universal category are broader; they extend across several organizations. (See Fig. 7.2.)

Organizational Vision

The first category of vision relates to *organizational excellence*. Four principals talked at length about building superb schools. One stated, "I wanted to make the kids realize that they had the best high school in the North Country." Another said, "I want every teacher in the school to be glad they're here and every other teacher in town to wish they were here."

Two others with an organizational vision are superintendents. Like the principals, their purpose is to work toward excellence, although these district leaders focus on creating an outstanding school district. One said, "My goal is a very simple one. It's just to be sure that good teaching is going on in every classroom."

All the leaders with visions of organizational excellence seem to have a clear notion of where they are going. Somehow each, by a different path, has developed a sense of what the excellent, healthy organization is. They use this silhouette or template of the healthy school much as a physician uses an understanding of the healthy, well-functioning body. With the vision or silhouette of excellence in mind, the school leader assesses the organization and finds a discrepancy. On the basis of the diagnosis, the educator conceives a prescription to alleviate the situation.

Dwyer and the other authors of chapter 3 identify this vision as an "overarching goal." Manasse (1984) and Rutherford (1985) also describe principals with personal visions of effective, excellent schools. A recent ASCD publication by Patterson, Perkey, and Parker (1986) offers excellent suggestions about developing and actualizing an organizational vision.

Blumberg and Greenfield (1986) point out the moral component of how to apply competing standards of goodness that leaders need to address when discussing vision. They note that, "to lead a school well, one must have a vision of what is desirable and possible in that school's context" (p. 226). Reading the transcripts of the leaders with visions of excellence, we had the impression that these educators are driving or pushing their organizations toward the preferred future they have in mind.

Universal Visions

The second category of vision extends beyond the organization in which the leader works. The six whose vision fell in this category have a dual image of their preferred futures. They have the organizational excellence vision already described. They also exert considerable energy toward a second, more universal purpose which centers on an *issue of equity* that encompasses the entire educational scene. All the issue-related visions described to us concern righting a wrong.

Although the leaders with a universal vision have a passion for equity, their target groups differ. One's vision is that underprivileged children will achieve an equal education. Another's vision of equity focuses on racial integration. A third concerns an equal role for women administrators. The vision of a fourth relates to professional development. A fifth leader's vision of equity is of a community school where children and adults learn from each other. A sixth leader is deeply committed to effective-schools research.

But the same silhouette or notion of health that assists these leaders with their organizational visions does not guide their universal visions. They are dreamers as well as physicians. In several cases, their universal images of a preferred future have no template. These leaders are not following a pattern—they are making one.

The dreams of these visionaries do not impede their competence. They convinced us that they can balance their dreams and the reality of competing priorities in the schools. These leaders know how to get things done. They accomplish the many tasks that keep an organization out of trouble and on the road toward excellence. At the same time, their passion for equity spurs them to goals and actions that reach for the more perfect world they envision.

Although they are activists, the leaders with a universal vision of equity are not cultists. While each identified important significant others in their lives who also strive toward their image of a preferred future, none seems to have a group of "followers." These leaders described their relationships with like-minded individuals in collegial rather than cultish ways. But after reading their transcripts, we decided these leaders are far ahead of their subordinates and their colleagues in other schools or districts. We had the sense that these leaders are pulling all of us toward a future that we would all prefer.

Note

3. We tried not to bias the sample. When asking for nominations, we avoided the term *vision*. Instead, we asked for the names of educators who are committed to school and schooling; who are clear about what they are trying to achieve; and who bring diverse people together to accomplish a goal, that is, their preferred future. When interviewing subjects we also avoided the term *vision*. We began by asking about the leader's goals as an educator. Only after a subject described what we thought was a vision did we verify our perception by asking, "Is your vision, then, to _____?"

Bringing Out the Best in Teachers

Blase, J., and P.C. Kirby. 1992. 10–21, 99–111. Newbury Park, Calif.: Corwin Press.

Chapter 2.* The Power of Praise

When I am in [the principal's] office taking care of business and he sees me, or when I peek into his office to say hello, he takes time to give me some kind of feedback. Sometimes it is as casual as: "You look peppy today." Sometimes it is to comment on something I'm involved in: "The Drill Team sure was impressive last night. How cohesive, proud, and disciplined they looked!" He'll tell me about a student's comment that I have a lot of energy and organizational skills which makes my class fun.

The main thing, no matter what he says, is he is sincere. It's not B.S. and isn't dished out just for the sake of it. . . . Credibility is important. I'm not sure he does this consciously, . . . it's just the way he is. He has good interpersonal skills and that probably carries him a long way and is responsible for his effectiveness.

I feel good, inspired, motivated. It reminds me that it sure is easy to make someone's day and we need to take time to [do so] more often. Being motivated makes us do a better job. I'm sure it helps me remain positive and flexible.

—A high school teacher

Of all the strategies used to influence teachers' work, praise was the most frequently reported and was perceived as one of the most effective by teachers in our study. Interestingly, however, praise does not appear in lists of the characteristics of strong school leaders identified in the school effectiveness literature. As William Greenfield (1987) noted, the significance of interpersonal factors in influencing teachers "may *seem obvious,* [yet] it is an aspect of the principal's role that is largely unattended by those concerned with understanding the nature of leadership in schools" (p. 69, emphasis added).

Our teachers, however, clearly recognized the value of personal compliments and individual attention from their principals. Why then the discrepancy between what teachers perceive to be such a crucial role for principals and what school effectiveness researchers discuss as key correlates of leader effectiveness?

Perhaps, as Greenfield hinted, it may be *taken for granted* that principals do routinely praise teachers. After all, teacher performance assessment instruments invariably include indicators of how *teachers* reinforce *student* behavior; positive reinforcement is universally accepted as a correlate of effective teaching. Principals, as former teachers, may be expected automatically to translate this teaching behavior to the leadership domain. That some principals are effective in doing so is revealed in our data for effective and open principals. Nevertheless, praise remains conspicuously absent in the literature about effective instructional leadership. For this reason, it may be underutilized by school principals.

Perhaps principals are familiar with the power of praise, but in their haste to attend to the *research-recognized* components of instructional leadership, the importance of praising teachers may be displaced. Terrence Deal (1987) also recognized that the school effectiveness literature (with regard to the principal's role) ignores important aspects of schools. He argued that schools should be examined through multiple lenses. Principals must attend to other critical organizational dimensions in addition to instruction. They must be instructional leaders as well as counselors or parents, engineers or supervisors, contenders or referees, and heroes or poets. As counselors/parents, principals add to personal growth and development with praise, advice, and affection. This nurturing function, according to Deal, is one of the most time-consuming demands of the principalship. Unfortunately, principals who are eager to develop their "instructional leadership" skills may do so at the expense of advancing their interpersonal relations with teachers.

It may be possible that viewing principals as counselors or parents, as Deal suggests, would appear a bit paternalistic to many teachers, thereby reducing teachers' stature. Even if Deal's analogy is scorned, his counsel nonetheless may be valid. Again, we reiterate that in our data, praise was the most frequently mentioned influence strategy used by open and effective principals. Its role in leader effectiveness should not be ignored or taken for granted.

Why Praise?

Given that principals are expected to assume many roles in schools and that the role of instructional leader alone is a multifaceted one, why do effective principals devote so much time to praising teachers? Although one intent in conducting this study was to identify effective strategies used by principals to *influence teacher performance,* it may be true that praise also satisfies *personal needs* of the principals themselves. Arthur Blumberg and William Greenfield (1986) described the effective principals they

---

* Editor's note: Chapter notation refers to this excerpt.

studied as having high needs for both expressing and receiving warmth and affection. Principals who are effective may attend to the interpersonal needs of teachers because they themselves receive satisfaction from that role.

In addition to the *personal satisfaction* they may derive from praising teachers, according to our data, effective principals also use praise as a strategy for influencing teachers' attitudes and behavior. Teachers in our study linked the use of praise specifically to the principals' goals of *promoting and reinforcing classroom performance*. As an influence strategy, praise was used most often with individual teachers; open and effective principals commended teachers for their instructional and classroom management efforts. Recognition of individual teachers' strengths was viewed as a means of maintaining and developing teachers' skills while promoting teachers' confidence and satisfaction.

Whereas other influence strategies were intended to encourage teachers' involvement in aspects of schooling that transcended the classroom, goals associated with the use of praise were related primarily to enhancing instructional performance. Praise also was used (but less frequently) to build school climate, faculty cohesiveness, and support for school goals.

Teacher Reactions to the Use of Praise

We have all heard the occasional grumblings of administrators uncomfortable with overt displays of affection or encouragement; they claim not to be the "touchy-feely" type. Similarly, we have heard the teacher who disdains such expressions of approval, viewing them as condescending or patronizing. Is the use of praise *necessary* and *effective* for improving teaching performance? To answer this question, we again turn to the responses of our teachers.

The teachers in our study viewed praise as a positive and effective influence strategy. Praise from their principals helped boost their confidence and pride. Many reported that positive reinforcement left them feeling "encouraged," "appreciated," and "recognized":

> The principal often writes personal notes to individual faculty members, encouraging, complimenting, and just giving "strokes." These are found in our mailboxes at school or sometimes sent out to our homes. She also sends out notes to the entire faculty complimenting them for a job well done. She makes me feel that what I do is appreciated and these actions give me positive thoughts about the principal. . . . I know how busy her schedule is. When I feel that what I do is noticed and appreciated, I have a better feeling about my job and try to do a better job.
> —A middle school teacher

In addition to greater esteem and satisfaction, the use of praise increased teachers' sense of *belonging*. Because their principals took the time to recognize their contributions, teachers felt that they were "important members of the team." Others said they felt "loved" and "respected" by their principals.

As a strategy for influencing teacher behavior, the use of praise was particularly successful. Teachers reported that the positive feelings associated with praise led to increased *motivation*. They felt "inspired" and "enthusiastic." Their loyalty and dedication grew. Because of her principal's appreciation, one teacher declared, "I wouldn't think of *not* doing a good job. I would feel guilty." Another concurred: "I try to do my best to live up to his comments."

Praise affected teacher behavior along several dimensions. Generally, teachers attempted to comply with the expectations of principals that were implied in the use of praise. According to teachers, performance compliance concerned *instruction* and *use of time*:

◆ "I try harder to be creative in my teaching."
◆ "Indeed, more time is spent planning."
◆ "I work harder. This means I don't just put in eight hours a day. I work until I'm finished."

Recognizing how praise positively affected them, teachers often modeled the practice by using a more positive discipline approach, including frequent praise, with students. *Modeling* was used both in the classroom and throughout the school building:

◆ "I'm more positive . . . open and patient with students."
◆ "I look for something to praise the kids about."
◆ "I find myself trying to emulate [the principal's] positiveness not only with my students but with parents and other teachers."

Finally, teachers reported that praise affected their *support* for principals. Some teachers acknowledged *reciprocating*:

◆ "I praise him in return."
◆ "I'm quicker to support the principal."

Others volunteered their time and energy to help principals:

◆ "I'll do 'extras' for her."
◆ "I'm more apt to volunteer for projects she needs help on."

It appears then that praise is an effective strategy for improving school climate because it enhances teacher morale and teachers' attitudes toward students. It also enhances teachers' instructional practices and the amount of effort they put forth.

On Potency and Ubiquity

Our research has produced indisputable evidence of the power of praise as an influence strategy with teachers. We have suggested that some educators—teachers and principals—may feel uncomfortable with this strategy;

still, we cannot deny its potency. We have gathered substantial evidence of the positive effects of praise on both attitudes and behaviors of teachers. Two questions surface with regard to this finding. First, how do we account for the singular impact of a strategy that may be viewed as "obvious" or "common sense"? And if the potency of the strategy is "obvious," why is it not used by more school principals?

Educators invariably agree that their work is plagued by difficulties. Means and ends are only loosely connected; seldom are we certain that what we actually do in the classroom positively affects students' lives. In one of the most respected studies of the sociology of teaching, Dan Lortie (1975) observed that teaching is filled with "endemic uncertainties" related to difficulties of assessing individual student outcomes and the quality of teaching, as well as of multiple role expectations (pp. 134–161). Because the link between what teachers do and its impact on students is uncertain, teachers must rely on self-evaluations of performance. Yet most individuals have needs for recognition and approval that remain unfulfilled by self-evaluation alone.

Uncertainties and self-doubts could be mollified by approval from others. Unfortunately, formal performance evaluations, no matter how outstanding, offer teachers little consolation. A positive evaluation indicates minimal competence; seldom is it used for purposes of recognition or advancement. And, as Lortie (1975) noted, veteran teachers work day after day knowing that they can be replaced by novices!

Because teaching also is characterized by the isolation of the classroom, there are few opportunities for interaction with other adults. Teachers rarely observe or are observed by other teachers. They spend nearly every working minute communicating with children—often as many as 150 children per day. It is not surprising that they respond so appreciatively and enthusiastically to adult interaction and feedback. Unless cooperative experiences such as peer coaching become commonplace, administrators are the only external adult referents by which teachers judge their work.

Perhaps the most revealing observation from our study is that teachers only reported being influenced by praise when it was related to their *professional* performance. Although they may have been complimented for appearances (for example, a new suit or hairstyle) or praised for accomplishments outside the school, only work-related praise was reported as a source of *influence*. To be effective with teachers, it seems, praise must be connected to their professional accomplishments.

Earlier, we asked the question, "Why praise teachers?" The more obvious question now seems to be, "Why not?" Unfortunately, the same barriers that inhibit teacher interaction also limit teacher-administrator communication. With many teachers to observe, each in a different enclosed location, even informal assessments of teacher performance are time-consuming. But in order to reinforce positive teacher behaviors, observation is mandatory. (What would

we praise them for if we did not find out how well they were doing?) Thus even for principals who value informal classroom visits and are comfortable expressing compliments and gratitude, the demands on their time are exacerbated by the structural isolation of teaching. Nevertheless, despite the difficulties in observing and acknowledging classroom performance, we found that some principals are particularly adept at recognizing teacher contributions to school success.

Opportunities and Methods

How and when do effective and open principals praise teachers' professional performance? The answer, according to our teachers: Principals capitalize on every available opportunity to compliment teachers; their praise consists of brief but sincere remarks and gestures.

Although time and structure may limit the number of opportunities to praise individual teachers, open and effective principals take advantage of other situations. Many teachers reported that their principals regularly use *group praise*. Principals are able to reach many teachers at once by complimenting them at *faculty meetings* with smaller groups of teachers, or over the *intercom*. As evidenced by the remarks of several teachers, principals use such occasions to express praise without qualification:

◆ "He expresses a complete faith and belief in his faculty . . . says we are the chosen ones . . . the best faculty in the state."
◆ "He starts and ends every meeting by complimenting the faculty for their hard work."
◆ "Every Friday she tells us how hard we worked."

We learned from our study that praise can be an effective influence strategy even when it is not communicated directly to teachers. Teachers reported knowing how their principals felt about their work from comments the principals made to others. Although perhaps not *intended* as a means of influence, teachers did learn of these remarks to others and were impressed by them. As one teacher boasted, "He brags on us every chance he gets."

Group praise is not, we found, used by effective principals to compensate for a lack of individual praise. Quite the contrary, principals intersperse frequent and specific *individual praise* with group praise. They mention individuals by name at faculty meetings and in conversations with others. Informal verbal compliments are commonplace; one teacher called them "one-minute praises." Another noted the deliberate effort of his principal to praise teachers: "She catches me doing something right and says so." Although principals most often comment on some aspect of teacher performance that they have witnessed, compliments from students or parents also are related to teachers.

In addition to oral praise, the principals described in our study wrote brief notes to individual teachers. After observing classes, many principals left brief notes of praise on teachers' desks. Others placed complimentary notes in the mailboxes of individual teachers.

Finally, principals often express praise *nonverbally*. Especially effective during the classroom observation where the principal hopes to be unobtrusive, the nonverbal gesture communicates immediate approval. This technique takes several forms, all appreciated by our teachers:

◆ "She touches me on the shoulder to show her appreciation."
◆ "A few literal pats on the head are one of his strategies."
◆ "Simple smiles tell me a lot."

Thus effective principals rely on brief, usually informal, verbal and nonverbal praise to influence individual teachers and teacher groups. It should be noted that variety and frequency of praise appear to be as important as the particular techniques used (for example, written memos, comments to others, public address announcements, pats on the back). It is important to stress that teachers in our study often spoke of praise *not as an influence strategy used by a principal, but as a part of the principal's character*. Praise was sincere, genuine, and even natural for these principals.

Blumberg and Greenfield (1986) argued that the effective principals they studied had high personal needs to express warmth and affection. Consistent with these findings, our teachers found praise to be a pervasive aspect in the schools of effective principals. Clearly, our results indicate that praise is a very effective strategy for bringing out the best in teachers and their work.

Tips from Teachers

Our data indicated that in spite of the "endemic uncertainties" and structural isolation of teaching, effective principals find many opportunities to commend teachers and that, to be effective, praise need not be formal or lengthy. The particular behaviors for which the teachers in our study were praised also are revealing. In every case reported, teachers indicated that the praise that influenced them most was evoked by their work. Thus on the basis of our teachers' reports, we offer the following suggestions for you to consider in the context of your own school setting.

1. Praise sincerely.

Teachers view praise from effective principals as genuine. Rather than perceiving it only as an influence strategy, teachers see its expression as comfortable and natural for their principals. Praise does not appear contrived or awkward; it is congruent with other behaviors and personal characteristics of principals.

2. Maximize the use of nonverbal communication.

Effective principals use nonverbal gestures such as smiles, nods, and touches to communicate approval. Although not used as an exclusive form of praise, this technique is commonly employed during classroom observations to avoid the disruption of verbal praise.

3. Schedule time for teacher recognition.

Many teachers reported that their principals praise them on a regular basis. Some principals choose the beginning or the end of faculty meetings. Recognition of faculty at student assemblies also is common. Others choose to announce faculty accomplishments over the public address system at the end of each week. Many principals routinely praise teachers during their tours of schools. It is clear that open and effective principals build time for praise into their busy schedules. Although the use of praise seems "natural" to them, the neophyte might become more adept at the use of this strategy by consciously *scheduling* opportunities for recognition. As the practice becomes automatic and comfortable, additional forums for praise might be added.

4. Write brief personal notes to compliment individuals.

To praise individual teachers, effective principals often rely on written messages. These brief notes are always handwritten and *personalized*. The teachers in our study did not report being influenced by written acknowledgment of *group* efforts.

5. Show pride in teachers by boasting!

Teachers often learn of their principals' judgments of their work from others. Principals express pride in their teachers to parents, colleagues, and others in the community.

6. Praise briefly.

To be effective, praise need not be formal or lengthy. Teachers appreciate many forms of recognition that last only seconds. Thus short accolades delivered in a variety of forums using both verbal and nonverbal techniques can be effective without placing excessive demands on the principal's time.

7. Target praise to teachers' work

Because of the isolation and uncertainty characteristic of the profession, teachers are most responsive to praise bestowed for school-related success. Whenever possible, principals should commend specific professional accomplishments of individual teachers. Group praise can be used to increase the opportunities for recognition, but it too should be tied to specific achievements.

References

Blumberg, A., & Greenfield, W. (1986). Toward a theory of leading a school. In *The effective principal: Perspectives on school leadership* (2nd ed., pp. 229–249). Boston: Allyn & Bacon.

Deal, T. (1987). Effective school principals: Counselors, engineers, pawn brokers, poets . . . or instructional leaders? In W. Greenfield (Ed.), *Instructional leadership: Concepts, issues, and controversies* (pp. 230–245). Boston: Allyn & Bacon.

Greenfield, W. (1987). Moral imagination and interpersonal competence: Antecedents to instructional leadership. In W. Greenfield (Ed.), *Instructional leadership: Concepts, issues, and controversies* (pp. 56–73). Boston: Allyn & Bacon.

Lortie, D.C. (1975). *Schoolteacher: A sociological study*. Chicago: University of Chicago Press.

Chapter 9.* Mirrors to the Possible

> Our principal is supportive and personally concerned with his teachers' professional careers and outside interests. He is involved with students' extracurricular activities such as Special Olympics. He takes an interest in classroom activities and takes time to visit classrooms informally. He brags to visitors about his teachers and their programs. He has a positive attitude about his job which encourages a good attitude [among others]. He is very concerned with keeping an upbeat attitude in a school situation that tends to be depressing and discouraging. It works. Teachers in the school are as concerned and involved with the principal as he is with us.
>
> —An elementary school teacher

To this point we have discussed strategies of effective school principals that teachers in our study recognize as particularly powerful in influencing their behavior. But the teachers also commented extensively on the *personality* of leaders. They identified certain aspects of their principals' personality and demeanor that contributed to principals' effectiveness as leaders. In particular, the teachers found that effective principals are highly visible and model attitudes and behaviors consistent with personal values and with the expectations they hold for teachers. Teachers see these principals as expressing changes in schooling that are both desirable and possible.

Personality has long been recognized as an important dimension of leader effectiveness. Some people are more inspiring, more likable, more appealing than others. These persons frequently emerge as leaders. *Referent power* is often the term used to refer to one's ability to influence based on personality. In the extreme form, it is called *charisma*.

Weber borrowed the concept of charisma from theology, where it was considered to be a gift bestowed by God. For Weber, charisma was a mystical, magnetic attraction that some individuals acquired in times of crisis. Others followed the charismatic, believing that they too would be connected to transcendent powers by virtue of association with the charismatic (Bass, 1988).

The definition of charisma has evolved since Weber's conceptualization. Many theorists no longer believe that charismatic leadership only emerges in situations of crisis, for example. But the exact qualifications of the charismatic are no less clear today than they were when charisma was believed to be a gift from God. According to Bass (1988), two essential elements of the charismatic relationship are a strong desire by followers to identify with the leader, and the leader's possession of certain abilities, traits, and interests. Among the latter, he included emotional expressiveness or dramatic flair, self-confidence, conviction in one's beliefs, eloquence, insight, and high levels of energy.

Are the effective principals described in our study charismatic? According to teachers, aspects of principals'

personality that were most influential were their *honesty, optimism,* and *consideration*. Further, they were able to (and did) *model* the behavior they expected from teachers, and they were highly *visible* in their schools. Although the principals described to us were certainly liked and respected by their teachers, they were not simply depicted as dramatic, highly inspirational, and magnetic; that is, few were described in terms typically associated with charisma.

Lawler (1984) argued that more educated followers were less influenced by charisma than were the less educated. Thus, in organizations of workers with higher levels of skill and training, dramatic appeal is a less powerful form of persuasion than are expertise and consideration. Furthermore, there may be less magic and more logic to the personality of leaders than formerly acknowledged. Kouzes and Posner (1990) studied the personal traits and characteristics most admired in leaders. In study after study, they found that the overwhelming choice of managers and executives—the most essential test of one's ability to influence—was honesty. Inspiration ranked fourth, after honesty, competence, and being forward-looking.

The responses of teachers in our study are consistent with Kouzes and Posner's findings. Effective principals were repeatedly described as honest. They demonstrated their competence by modeling the skills and behaviors they expected from teachers, and they maintained very positive attitudes and sincere beliefs that they would improve education for students. Teachers also added consideration as an important personal attribute.

Leadership based on the values of honesty, optimism, and consideration differs in fundamental ways from leadership based on charisma. Most notable among the differences is that the former is grounded in morality whereas the latter is grounded in personality. Moral leaders incorporate an ethic of caring into a vision of what is best and possible for all students. In achieving their vision, they ask no more of others than they expect from themselves. Their actions and words are consistent, and they are genuine in their interactions with others.

William Foster (1991, p. 20) criticized the field of educational administration for its "bureaucratic concern with efficiency" and banning of values from discourse. In the scientific-positivist tradition that has dominated educational administration, he argued, decisions are evaluated on the basis of rules and procedures, rather than on the basis of what is moral or right. Education, however, can no more be amoral than can it be apolitical. Foster argued that administrators could help transform schooling through open critique, caring, and inclusion. Administrators who are able to make things happen in schools do so "not because of their scientific training and their judicious use of principles of management, but because of their personal and moral presence, their sense of 'what's right,' and their attention to people's needs" (p. 7).

It appears, then, that principals in our study may have been effective largely because they were viewed as *moral* leaders by teachers. The first standard in the American Association of School Administrators' (1976) code of ethics

---

* Editor's note: Chapter notation refers to this excerpt.

states, "A school administrator makes the well-being of students the fundamental value of all decision making and actions." A key theme in the data generated by our study is that goals associated with principals' influence strategies truly focus on "what's best for children." It may be that whatever the strategies used, principals' behaviors are ultimately judged against teachers' own moral codes.

The Personality of Leaders

Effective school leaders were frequently described as optimistic, honest, and considerate. Behaviors such as modeling and visibility conveyed these values.

Optimism

The positive attitude of principals was noted by several teachers in our study. These principals were perceived as enjoying their jobs and believing in the abilities of their staffs. They also were described as problem solvers who had particularly good relationships with their faculties and students. Teachers reported increases in self-esteem, security, and motivation resulting from principals' optimism. Some indicated that their attitudes also became more positive:

> She has a very positive feeling about our school. She enjoys her job and it is reflected to the rest of the teachers. . . . She faces every day as a new day with new challenges. I try to do the same. I don't mind coming to school this year. When the alarm goes off, I'm "up and at them" this year.

Extra effort was reported by other teachers: "The strategy makes me give 100 percent effort to the school and my class." Another summarized the benefits of a positive approach: "I makes me feel good about what I do."

Martin Seligman (1991), a noted psychologist, recently published a compelling book on the power of optimism. In *Learned Optimism*, Seligman is careful to define optimism as the power of nonnegative thinking, not as unjustifiable positivity (p. 221). The optimist avoids catastrophizing; in times of adversity, consequences are not distorted and seen as insurmountable. Thus the school principal who sees education as being in a state of crisis is neither positive nor negative. The optimist will explain the causes of the crisis in terms that are external, specific, and temporary. The pessimist will explain the crisis as internal ("I should have done more"), pervasive (for example, "teachers are less competent than they used to be"), and permanent. By monitoring our explanations of the events in our lives, Seligman claims, we can learn to be more optimistic.

Seligman presents forceful research evidence to suggest that optimists are happier and healthier and live longer than pessimists. More relevant to the present discussion, optimists tend to be liked more and are more successful in their work. Through analysis of campaign speeches, for example, Seligman and his colleagues found that successful U.S. presidential candidates tended to be more optimistic than their opponents. Our findings confirm that optimism may indeed be a significant factor in leader effectiveness.

Honesty

As used by teachers in our study, *honesty* referred to the principal's truthfulness, as well as openness and consistency between words and actions. One teacher explained: "There is no phony baloney. . . . She [the principal] will not tell you one thing and do another." Honesty was noted in principals' ability to communicate straightforwardly both positive and negative feedback to teachers. Honest principals confront teachers' weaknesses and acknowledge their strengths:

> Our principal is totally honest in his dealings with the faculty. He is direct with what he feels are our strengths and weaknesses and is always willing to help solve any problem that might arise. . . . [This] keeps me open-minded in my dealings with my students . . . and others on the faculty.

Also, nonmanipulation of teachers is viewed as a dimension of honesty that fosters collaboration: "I feel that the principal is working with me and I with him, not for him." Teacher satisfaction and effort also are associated with honesty: "You enjoy working for people of this nature, thus you want to improve."

Consideration

Consideration has been recognized as a major dimension of leader behavior in most theories of organizational effectiveness. Alternately termed "people orientation" or "concern for people," consideration was reported to be related to employee satisfaction by most major leadership theorists (see, for example, Bass [1985], Blake and Mouton [1964], Fiedler [1967], Hersey and Blanchard [1977], and Stogdill [1963]). It is not surprising, then, that consideration emerged as an important aspect of leadership in our study of effective principals.

Our teachers defined consideration as exhibiting a sincere interest in "teachers as human beings." A considerate principal was described as one who "shows a genuine concern for how I am doing . . . [one who] makes a point to say hello." Considerate principals were viewed as nondiscriminating; they show concern for all teachers. They express interest in their teachers' lives during both happy and sad events. One high school teacher gives an example:

> My principal was very understanding and flexible the times that I had to be absent due to hospitalization of family members. His cooperation and attempts to make my return to school smoother were above and beyond the call of duty. I feel that I've been treated with kindness and respect. I, in turn, tend to have a more compassionate attitude toward my students and their individual situations.

Effects associated with consideration include enhanced self-esteem ("If he believes in me, then I can believe in myself") and improved performance ("I come early and stay late and do maximum work because I know my work is appreciated"). Considerate principals serve as models for teachers. Several teachers reported becoming more considerate and empathic in their dealings with children and fellow teachers. Thus principals serve as mirrors of appropriate human interaction:

◆ "Teachers act more as friends, helpers, and resource persons. Students know we care about them and provide encouragement for them to meet their daily challenges."

◆ "[The principal's consideration] helps to promote warmth in our faculty. We cooperate with each other and express concern for each other."

◆ "Because our principal shows caring and concern, I feel the need to reciprocate; I want to give him back what he gives us."

Personality Manifested: Mirroring the Possible

The optimism, honesty, and consideration of effective principals are revealed in their daily interactions with students and teachers. These traits reflect the principals' values. As such, effective teachers also are expected to be optimistic, honest, and considerate. The principals described in our study offered countless opportunities for teachers to acquire similar values by revealing themselves as *mirrors to the possible*. Effective principals were highly visible and served as models of appropriate attitudes and behaviors.

Modeling

In earlier chapters, we discussed how effective principals encourage participation by participating as equal members in groups of teachers. As promoters of teacher development, they themselves are avid readers of professional literature, seeking new means of improvement. Expecting teachers to use positive disciplinary approaches with students, they provide examples of such techniques. At times, they also demonstrate teaching techniques. Thus *modeling* is used quite effectively to reinforce other strategies of influence.

Modeling as a general influence strategy was recognized by several teachers in the study. Principals enacted their expectations for teacher performance through their own behavior. As one teacher explained, "My principal seems to administer by behavior [rather than by] policy. For example, he asks that we dress professionally, monitor the halls between classes, attend extracurricular activities, and contribute to the United Way. He does all of these." Another explained:

[My principal] is a very positive person. She conveys her feelings about school and the kids to us without being overbearing or obnoxious. She does not ask us to do anything she has not already done herself or would not do. She does not complain about things that she cannot change. She makes

the best of all situations. She is a good role model. When I get angry about something, I think about how she would handle the situation.

Expected behaviors modeled by the principals included appropriate dress, punctuality, effective teaching, positive discipline, praise for students, and extra effort. Without exception, teachers reported that modeling influences them to behave in ways consistent with the principal's implicit expectations. With regard to extra effort, for example, a teacher commented that "many of [the principal's] requests might be viewed as beyond the call of duty, but, because of the principal's modeling, they seem to be part of the job." Another remarked that she tried approaches to student behavior in the hallways that she had seen her principal use effectively. Overall, teachers reported that modeling is a highly effective strategy of influence that leaves them feeling "comfortable," "proud," "aware" (of alternative techniques), and "positive."

Visibility

As a principal's visibility increases, so too do his or her opportunities to model effective behavior. According to our teachers, some principals clearly are more comfortable in hallways and classrooms than in their offices. Several researchers have identified visibility as a key component of instructional leadership. Reitzug (1989) compared leadership in two elementary schools, one instructionally effective and the other "ordinary." He found that there were substantially more interactions between the principal and teachers in the effective school. As Reitzug concluded, opportunities for influencing/improving performance may increase as the number of interactions between principals and teachers increases.

Andrews and Soder (1987) related gains in mathematics and reading scores of low-achieving students to four instructional leadership roles: instructional resource, resource provider, communicator, and visible presence. In later work, visibility was found to be particularly influential when new programs or techniques are being implemented (Bamburg & Andrews, 1989). As Kouzes and Posner (1990) observed, "[leaders] demonstrate what is important by how they spend their time, by the priorities on their agenda, by the questions they ask, by the people they see, the places they go, and the behaviors and results that they recognize and reward" (p. 200).

Teachers reported that effective principals are *visible*, both in the hallways and in classrooms. Different goals were attributed to visibility in each setting. Visibility in the hallways was deemed to be an effective manner of communicating support to both teachers and students. Implicit in the principal's presence was an expectation for appropriate student behavior between classes and an offer of assistance to teachers in matters of discipline should they so desire. Visibility in the classroom was associated more typically with expectations for instruction. Expectations for the use of allocated instructional time were implied by the principal's presence, as were expectations regarding implementation of specific instructional strategies. One elementary teacher described her principal's influence through visibility:

> The principal is extremely involved with all grades and their curricula. She visits the classrooms regularly (two times per week) to make sure that all teachers are on task. She walks around to see if the children are involved and participating in that particular subject. If not, she would place her hands on their shoulders to get their attention and make sure that they are then attentive. This type of discipline is very effective for all children.

The teachers experienced visibility as positive and nonthreatening. They indicated that visibility in the hallways helps to preempt some discipline problems: "It helps him to see problems before they snowball into serious ones." The principal's presence also afforded the opportunity to model optimism: "My principal frequently roams the halls during breaks between classes. He is very friendly and supportive. His positive attitude overflows both to students and to faculty."

Classroom visibility was sporadic for some of the principals and routine for others; some informed teachers of classroom visits, whereas others dropped in unannounced. The length of classroom visits also varied widely, as reported in our study, from a few minutes to a whole class period. Some principals walked around the class to "see what the student are busy doing." Others became more fully involved with the class activity: "She visits my class while we are doing laboratory activities . . . participates with the students . . . ask them questions . . . asks me questions. She demonstrates to the students that learning is a lifelong activity."

Teachers indicated that principals usually provide some form of feedback to teachers after visiting their classrooms. Consistent with the strategy of *suggestion* discussed in Chapter 7, feedback is presented as advisory. The teachers viewed visibility as an effective and acceptable strategy because it was accompanied by genuine interest and support. It was not viewed as obtrusive or punitive. Instead, the teachers associated visibility with opportunities for improvement ("You can correct weak points with her help") and increased accountability ("Even though I am a conscientious teacher, I need monitors. Unscheduled pop-in visits are motivational").

The motivational effect of principals' visibility in the classroom is quite powerful. Numerous examples suggest that although anxiety levels are heightened somewhat by the principal's visit, teachers work harder, are more innovative, and feel better about their own performance as a result:

◆ "As much as [visits] scare me, I like them because they bring me back to task."
◆ "Not knowing when I might be visited, I stay on task more often than I might if these visits didn't occur."

◆ "I try things I previously frowned on—outside labs, field trips."
◆ "[The principal's visits] caused me to think more about my class and my role as a teacher. I am aware that I am accountable for performance."

Mirrors Seldom Lie

We have presented three personality traits—honesty, consideration, and optimism—that appear to be common to effective and open principals. These traits are evident in principals' frequent interactions with their staffs (that is, in their visibility) and in the consistency between their expectations and their own actions (that is, modeling). If modeling and visibility are particularly effective in producing desirable outcomes in teachers for honest, caring, and positive principals, the implications for schools led by manipulative, inconsiderate, and negative principals are terrifying. Principals in the middle—those whose values are less explicit, who are sometimes thoughtful and positive, sometimes distant and gloomy—also emit constant messages to teachers. Teachers learn to be guarded and protective, afraid to trust the unpredictable. The implications for principals are weighty indeed.

Leaders may serve as mirrors to what is possible and what is right for the individuals they serve. But mirrors also can reflect barriers to human potential—lack of trust, feeling, and hope. As all of us who have stopped counting birthdays will attest, mirrors seldom lie. What is reflected to the observer is what the observer has become. If principals are reliable mirrors of what schools will become, we must develop moral leaders. Our data suggest that moral leaders abide by these principles:

1. **Do not become so concerned with becoming effective as to ignore the affective.**
   Consideration of others—an ethic of caring—is fundamental to moral leadership. Although this aspect of leadership can be improved through careful attention to others, the implications for leader selection should be obvious. Attention to moral fortitude should precede all other qualifications, including demonstrated mastery of certain managerial and instructional skills, in the selection of school leaders.

2. **Practice being more optimistic.**
   According to Seligman (1991), a more positive attitude can be acquired by monitoring our explanations of life's successes and failures. Specifically, we must learn to recognize that adversity is usually temporary, specific, and externally created. Although learning to become more optimistic is a difficult task, its advantages are clearly documented.

3. **Be visible, but beware the power of the mirror.**
   Effective leaders know that their behavior is regarded as the standard of performance. They, therefore, avail themselves of all opportunities to model the behaviors they expect in others. To become mirrors to what is right and

possible, their behavior must be above reproach. They must be honest in their interactions with others; the values they convey must be consistent in words and actions as well as over time. As long as principals are in contact with teachers, they are transmitting their values and expectations. The burden of the mirror is that it never stops reflecting.

References

American Association of School Administrators. (1976). *AASA statement of ethics for school administrators and procedural guidelines*. Arlington, VA: Author.

Andrews, R. L., & Soder, R. (1987). Principal instructional leadership and school achievement. *Instructional Leadership, 44*, 9–11.

Bamburg, J. D., & Andrews, R. L (1989, March). *Putting effective schools research to work: The process of change and the role of the principal*. Paper presented at the annual meeting of the American Educational Research Association, San Francisco.

Bass, B. M. (1985). *Leadership and performance beyond expectations*. New York: Free Press.

Bass, B. M. (1988). Evolving perspectives on charismatic leadership. In J.A. Conger & R.N. Kanungo (Eds.), *Charismatic leadership: Behind the mystique of exceptional leadership* (pp. 40–77). San Francisco: Jossey-Bass.

Blake, R., & Mouton, J. (1964). *The managerial grid*. Houston, TX: Gulf.

Fiedler, F. (1967). *A theory of leadership effectiveness*. New York: McGraw-Hill.

Foster, W. (1991, April). *Moral theory, transformation, and leadership in school settings*. Paper presented at the annual meeting of the American Educational Research Association, Chicago.

Hersey, P., & Blanchard, K. (1977). *Management of organizational behavior: Utilizing human resources*. Englewood Cliffs, NJ: Prentice-Hall.

Kouzes, J.M., & Posner, B.Z. (1990). *The leadership challenge: How to get extraordinary things done in organizations*. San Francisco: Jossey-Bass.

Lawler, E. E., III (1984). Leadership in participative organizations. In J. G Hunt, D. Hosking, C. A. Schreisheim, & R. Stewart (Eds.), *Leaders and managers: International perspectives on managerial behavior and leadership*. Elmsford, NY: Pergamon.

Reitzug, U. C. (1989). Principal-teacher interactions in instructionally effective and ordinary elementary schools. *Urban Education, 24*(1), 38–58.

Seligman, M. E. P. (1991). *Learned optimism*. New York: Knopf.

Stogdill, R. (1963). *Manual for the LBDQ-Form 12: An experimental revision*. Columbus: Bureau of Business Research, The Ohio State University.

Involving Staff in the In-Service Process

Knipper, C., and D. Suddarth. 1991. In *Capital wisdom: Papers from the Principals Academy 1991*, 29–34. Washington, D.C.: National Catholic Educational Association.

Educational research has repeatedly demonstrated that introducing change in teaching is a process which requires training in both content and method of instruction. Teachers and administrators realize that learning is a life-long process, therefore schools provide the perfect environment for challenging educators to improve their teaching skills so as to meet societal demands and to provide the best possible and most relevant student instruction.

An effective in-service program is a means of organizing and involving staff members in this change process. This in-service program has several purposes:

◆ to gain new knowledge and understanding of the content and process of education

◆ to gain an understanding and appreciation of the growth and development of students

◆ to provide for evaluation of school programs, citing both strengths and weaknesses in a continuous effort of school improvement

◆ to provide an environment where administrators and staff can work together to acquire the skills and methods necessary for making improvements

◆ to bring cohesiveness to the school's instructional program

◆ to unify and involve the total staff in understanding the educational language, philosophy and program development unique to the school

◆ to enable teachers to study alternative approaches, and to select the information and methods that will enhance their capabilities as educators

◆ to strengthen the self-confidence of each teacher through mutual sharing

Many times in-service programs are planned as one-day or half-day presentations given by visiting experts, area educators or administrators. These are held on a local, regional or diocesan level, with little regard for implementation, assistance or follow-up assessment. Under these conditions, initial enthusiasm seldom leads to lasting or effective change.

Research has shown that relatively few teachers, presented with new approaches to teaching, will make the skill a part of their regular practice unless there is an opportunity to learn theory, practice the theory with feedback, and receive additional instructional input as needed.

Gene Hall, in his report to the American Educational Research Association in 1982, identified seven levels of use of new learning by teachers. They are: non-use, orientation, preparation, mechanical use, refinement, integration, and renewal. Many in-service programs address only the orientation or preparation levels. It is important that teachers and administrators work together to progress through the other levels with an effectively planned program.

Many sources of information are available for presentation at the orientation level. These include:

◆ NCEA
◆ Association for Supervision and Curriculum Development (ASCD)
◆ Master Teacher
◆ published materials
◆ public school districts
◆ diocesan or regional offices
◆ textbook consultants
◆ state department of education consultants
◆ colleges and universities
◆ health care agencies

All of these resources enable teachers and administrators to gain new information, which can be used most effectively when followed by an organized program of development, with the encouragement by the administrator, at the local level.

School Model

Let's visit St. Regina School to observe the in-service process as it can be used to enable the staff to work collaboratively toward growth.

Mr. Roberts, the new principal of St. Regina, arrives at the school and discovers that the diocesan office does not have an in-service program for use by new administrators. Furthermore, the school has not formulated goals for curriculum improvement.

Realizing the importance of teacher involvement in staff in-service planning, Mr. Roberts meets with the faculty prior to the opening of school for an all-day planning session. Although he could have arranged for another staff member or an outside person to serve as facilitator, Mr. Roberts decides to take that role. He leads the staff through a brainstorming activity during which they list the strengths of their educational program and areas for growth. The completed lists look like this:

Strengths	Areas for Growth
❖ enthusiastic staff	❖ meeting individual needs of students
❖ supportive parents	
❖ warm, orderly environment	❖ discipline
❖ concern for students	❖ motivation of students
❖ Christian values	❖ cooperative learning
❖ cooperative staff	❖ computer education

The staff members then examine the areas for growth and each determines the area that he or she finds of most interest or concern. Each staff member indicates his or her choice on the master list, thus determining the priority concern for the entire group. The new list appears as follows:

Areas for Growth

❖ meeting individual needs of students	|
❖ motivation of students	┼┼┼
❖ cooperative learning	|||
❖ computer education	||

The staff determines that student motivation is a priority interest. It will be a topic for in-service planning. Mr. Roberts invites three staff members to form an in-service committee to assist him in determining directives for staff consideration in regard to student motivation.

Mr. Roberts meets with the in-service committee for a discussion of several alternatives. The committee decides to provide articles for the staff regarding current research and methods of increasing student motivation. This is the first step in increasing staff awareness.

The committee also invites a faculty member, recognized for successful work in student motivation, from the education department of a local university to meet with them. A full-day workshop is scheduled for late October.

Following the full-day workshop, teachers are encouraged to integrate the motivational techniques and theory presented into their own teaching. They are likewise encouraged to note which techniques and activities are of greatest benefit to increasing student motivation.

In early February, all staff members meet again to discuss problems and successes regarding student motivation, and to critique the effectiveness of the information gained during the October in-service. Teachers ask questions and list areas where clarification or additional information would be helpful. All teachers have an opportunity for sharing what they have learned and introduced in their classrooms.

The in-service committee decides to meet again to discuss the questions and concerns generated by the staff members, and to determine if additional support is needed in regard to student motivation. Committee members invite the instructor from the university to return in early April for an additional half-day session to address existing questions and concerns. The committee also suggests that some teachers may find it helpful to schedule visits with teachers in other schools to observe motivational techniques.

The staff members meet again in early May to evaluate the effects of the in-service programs. Because of the amount of input they have generated from the planning stage through the implementation stage, staff members are supportive of the program.

This process is enhanced by consideration of the following areas:

◆ the school benefits from administrator and staff participation
◆ the school budget allocates financial resources
◆ an ongoing staff development committee is established

Resources for Staff Development

Educational Leadership
    Association for Supervision and
      Curriculum Development
    225 North Washington Street
    Alexandria, VA 22314

Elementary School Journal
    University of Chicago Press
    Journals Division
    P.O. Box 37005
    Chicago, IL 60637

Journal of Staff Development
    National Staff Development Council
    5198 Westgate Drive
    Oxford, OH 45056

American Association of School Administrators
    1801 North Moore Street
    Arlington, VA 22209

Exemplary Center for Reading Instruction (ECRI)
    3310 South 2700 East
    Salt Lake City, UT 84109

Institute for Development of Educational Activities (I/D/E/A)
    259 Regency Ridge
    Dayton, OH 45459

National Catholic Educational Association
    1077 30th Street, NW, Suite 100
    Washington, DC 20007-3852

National Council of States on Inservice Education
    Syracuse University, School of Education
    364 Huntington Hall
    150 Marshall Street
    Syracuse, NY 13210

National Diffusion Network
    Division of Educational Replication
    U.S. Office of Education, Room 3616
    Seventh and D Sts., SW
    Washington, DC 20201

New England School Development Council
    85 Speen Street
    Framingham, MA 01701

Research and Development Center for Teacher Education
    Education Annex 3203
    The University of Texas at Austin
    Austin, TX 78712

Science and Mathematics Education Center
    B 302 Ellsworth
    Western Michigan University
    Kalamazoo, MI 49008

The Network, Inc.
    290 South Main Street
    Andover, MA 01810

The Role of the Principal in the Ongoing Education of Teachers

Ristau, K. 1989. In *Reflections on the role of the Catholic school principal*, ed. R. Kealey, 60–62.
Washington, D.C.: National Catholic Educational Association.

Principles of Adult Learning

Leaders have available to them a wealth of information concerning growth and development of the human person. Russell (1985) has presented helpful ideas for understanding the adult learner and planning the learning process for teachers. Principals need to use these generally accepted precepts about adult learning in planning for good staff development.

Ego-Involvement. The first point to consider in adult learning is ego-involvement. Learning a new skill, technique, or concept may promote a positive or negative view of self. There is always fear of external judgment that we as adults are less than adequate. Adults will resist learning situations they believe are an attack on their competence or are viewed as an insult to what they are presently doing. Many attempts at inservice or staff development fail because planners do not pay attention to this point.

Self-Planning. Adults want to be the originators of their own learning; that is involved in the selection of objectives, content, activities, and assessment of those activities. Faculty development prescribed by others and spoon-fed to passive adults rarely has any lasting effects and is more likely to be met with resistance. Therefore, it stands to reason, teachers themselves must be included in the planning and design of any staff development. The principal's role in the planning process is one of empowering the teachers to take charge of their own development.

The recent literature on businesses that succeed (Kantor, 1983 and Peters, 1982) describes employees working with leaders who allow people to have their own power instead of with leaders who control and tell others what to do. Bennis (1985) talks about a style of leadership that pulls rather than pushes, attracts and energizes people to an exciting vision of the future. The principal is the person who can articulate and embody the ideal toward which the school is striving.

Prior Learning. Adults come to any learning experience with a wide range of previous experiences, knowledge, skills, self-direction, interests, and competence. The design of education for adults needs to be very respectful of the attributes the person brings to the learning situation. Educators of children and young adults spend a good deal of time planning for teaching, including in each lesson discussion, reading activities, media experiences, and concluding work. New knowledge not only builds upon what is already known but fits the developmental level of the students.

Learning Styles. Effective teachers plan for the learning style of the student and include activities matched to the needs of the learner. However, when it comes to education for teachers we seem to throw good teaching/learning principles out. Teachers are asked to sit and absorb a forty-five minute lecture on a topic not of their own choosing at a time when most of them are weary from the work of the day. The activities, the reading, the critical thinking, the opportunity to practice the skills are missing.

Teachers would never present to children or young adults a topic totally disconnected from what went on before or what will come tomorrow. No high school class assembles for a period to consider linear regression statistics when the course addresses English literature for a semester. Yet, we offer to teachers scattered topics and then, perhaps only once. It is no wonder a peek into an inservice or staff development session often reveals a teacher checking papers, another grading student work, and usually someone knitting. It is a vision of passive learners. Adult learning is enhanced by behaviors that demonstrate respect, trust, and concern for the learner. Well-planned sessions that consider who the learners are and the gifts and background the learners bring with them display a respectfulness to the person of the teacher.

Relevance to Personal Needs. Several other points about adult learners that principals should keep in mind include the realization adults will commit to learning something when the goals and objectives of the learning are considered realistic and important to the learner. In other words, adults will learn, retain, and use what they perceive is relevant to their personal and professional needs. Another vote should be cast here for involvement of the teachers in the selection of the staff development activities.

Adult Interaction. Adults also prefer to learn in informal situations where social interaction can take place among the learners. This would speak again to the avoidance of the lecture-only approach.

Motivation. The most difficult aspect of adult learning for principals to wrestle with is motivation. Adult motivation for learning and doing one's job has two levels. One is to participate and do an adequate job. This first level comes as the result of good salary, benefits, and fair treatment. But the second and more important is to become deeply involved, going beyond the minimum or norm. The second builds on the first, but comes from recognition, achievement, and increased responsibility—the result of behavior, the leader's behavior, and not more dollars. While the need to supply recognition and share responsibility must be designed by the principal, it is comforting to realize that true motivation is produced by the learner. The principal can encourage and create conditions which nurture what already exists in the adult.

References

Bennis, Warren & Burt Nannis. *Leaders: The Strategies for Taking Charge.* New York: Harper and Row, 1985.

Kanter, Rosabeth Moss. *The Change Masters.* New York: Simon and Schuster, 1983.

Peters, Thomas. *Thriving on Chaos.* New York: A. Knopf, 1982.

Robinson, Russell D. *An Introduction to Helping Adults Learn and Change.* Milwaukee: Omnibook, 1983.

Moral Leadership:
Getting to the Heart of School Improvement

Sergiovanni, T. J. 1992. 59–65. San Francisco: Jossey-Bass.

What Is Rewarding Gets Done

The importance of the work itself as a motivator has only a recent history in psychology. Frederick Herzberg's famous motivation hygiene theory (Herzberg, Mausner, and Snyderman, 1959) was a pioneering effort. In one of the most replicated studies in the history of management, Herzberg and his colleagues were able to identify two fairly independent sets of job factors that seemed to be important to workers.

One set of factors affects whether people are dissatisfied with their jobs. These, the so-called hygiene factors, seem related to poor performance. Research has suggested that if administrators take care of these factors, so that they are no longer sources of dissatisfaction, workers' performance will improve to the level of "a fair day's work for a fair day's pay"; rarely, however, will workers be motivated to go beyond this minimum contract. For this reason, Herzberg coined the term hygiene factors to describe this set, suggesting that they can cause trouble if neglected but are not sources of motivation. They are concerned with the conditions of work, not with the work itself. Conditions of work are the source of extrinsic rewards. Herzberg, Mausner, and Snyderman (1959) concluded that extrinsic rewards are not potent enough to motivate people—at least not for very long, and not without a great deal of effort from administrators.

The second set of factors, called *motivators*, seem not to cause dissatisfaction or poor performance if neglected or even absent. As long as the hygiene factors are in place, people seem to do their jobs in a satisfactory way. The motivators, however, seem to motivate people to go beyond the "fair day's work for a fair day's pay" minimum contract. Motivators are concerned with the work itself, rather than with the conditions of work. The work itself is the source of intrinsic motivation (Herzberg, Mausner, and Snyderman, 1959).

When the motivation-hygiene theory has been tested in school settings (Sergiovanni, 1967), what have tended to emerge as the motivators are a sense of achievement, recognition for good work, challenging and interesting work, and a sense of responsibility for one's work. By contrast, pleasant interpersonal relationships on the job, nonstressful and fair supervision, reasonable policies, and an administrative climate that does not hinder are what have tended to emerge as the hygiene factors. This research has led to the idea that if one can arrange jobs so as to accent opportunities for the motivation factors to be experienced, people will become self-motivated.

The motivation-hygiene theory is not without controversy. Many of its critics feel that the specific findings may well have been artifacts of the methods used by the researchers, portraying an oversimplified version of reality. Nevertheless, few dispute the overall conclusion derived from this research tradition: that, for most people, the work itself counts as an important motivator of work commitment, persistence, and performance.

Carrying this theme further, researchers on job enrichment have identified ways in which jobs can be restructured to allow for workers to experience greater intrinsic satisfaction. Perhaps the best-known study is Hackman and Oldham's (1976). These researchers and their colleagues have identified three psychological states believed to be critical in determining whether a person will be motivated at work:

> *Experienced meaningfulness*: "The extent to which a person perceives work as being worthwhile or important, given her or his system of values."
>
> *Experienced responsibility*: "The extent to which a person believes that she or he is personally responsible or accountable for the outcomes of efforts."
> *Knowledge of results*: "The extent to which a person is able to determine on a regular basis whether or not the outcomes of her or his efforts are satisfactory" (Hackman, Oldham, Johnson, and Purdy, 1975, p. 57).

When the three psychological states are present, people are likely to feel good, perform well, and continue to perform well, in the effort to experience more of these feelings in the future. When these feelings are experienced, people do not have to depend on someone else to motivate or lead them.

How can school leaders restructure jobs so that the likelihood of experiencing meaningfulness, responsibility, and knowledge of results will be increased? The answer, provided by Hackman and Oldham (1976), is to build in opportunities for teachers to do the following:

◆ Use more of their talents and skills (skill variety).

◆ Engage in activities that allow them to see the whole and understand how their contributions fit into the overall purpose or mission (task identity).

◆ View their work as having a substantial and significant impact on the lives or work of other people (task significance).

◆ Experience discretion and independence in scheduling work and in deciding classroom arrangements and instructional procedures (autonomy).

◆ Get firsthand, and from other sources, clear information about the effects of their performance (feedback).

Experiencing Flow at Work

Carrying this work even further, Mihalyi Csikszentmihalyi's research (1990) has led him to conclude that the key to intrinsic motivation is a optimal experience that he calls *flow*, "the state in which people are so involved in an activity that nothing else seems to matter; the experience itself is so enjoyable that nothing else seems to matter; the experience itself is so enjoyable that people will do it even at great cost, for the sheer sake of doing it" (p. 4).

Searching our own experience, to identify occasions when we have experienced flow, can help us understand the concept. Recall, for example, instances when you were intensely involved in something. Perhaps it was hobby work; hunting or fishing; researching and writing a proposal to change some important aspect of your school; solving a complex problem; giving a talk to the faculty on a topic dear to your heart; teaching a class—an occasion when you were so absorbed in your work and so committed to its outcome that you completely lost track of time. As you worked, you were in total command of your thoughts and actions. It seemed as if you could even anticipate future moves with ease. You knew instinctively how parts fit together and where to get the information you needed. Your concentration was so intense, and everything seemed to be in such harmony, that at the end of this experience your feelings of competence and well-being were enhanced.

Csikszentmihalyi and others who are studying flow believe that it is commonly experienced by people engaged in a wide range of activities, including rock climbing, hunting, surgery, sports playing, rug weaving, long-distance swimming, writing, playing music, and gardening. All that is needed is for the activity to result in a high level of personal enjoyment and satisfaction, on the one hand, and the enhancement of one's feelings of competence and efficacy, on the other. Csikszentmihalyi (1990) believes that there are eight elements that contribute to these feelings:

> First, the experience usually occurs when we confront tasks we have a chance of completing. Second, we must be able to concentrate on what we are doing. Third and fourth, the concentration is usually because the task undertaken has clear goals and provides immediate feedback. Fifth, one acts with a deep but effortless involvement that removes from awareness the worries and frustrations of everyday life. Sixth, enjoyable experiences allow people to exercise a sense of control over their actions. Seventh, concern for the self disappears, yet paradoxically the sense of self emerges stronger after the flow experience is over. Finally, the sense of the duration of time is altered;

hours pass by in minutes, and minutes can stretch out to seem like hours. The combination of all these elements causes a sense of deep enjoyment that is so rewarding people feel that expending a great deal of energy is worthwhile simply to be able to feel it [p. 49].

To experience flow, one must be convinced that one's skills and insights are strong enough to cope with the challenges at hand. The matching of skills to challenges is critical, for this is a condition of growth. Csikszentmihalyi (1990, p. 74) explains, "In our studies, we found that every flow activity, whether it involved competition, chance, or other dimensions of experience, had this in common: It provided a sense of discovery, a creative feeling of transporting the person into a new reality. It pushed the person to higher levels of performance, and led to previously undreamed-of states of consciousness. In short, it transformed the self by making it more complex. In this growth of the self lies the key to flow activities."

The balance is delicate. Too much challenge in one's job, without the skills necessary for success, can lead to anxiety. Unless skills improve enough to match the challenge, one is likely to withdraw in search of less challenging alternatives. If levels of anxiety are only moderate, one way out is to seek ways in which one's skills can be enhanced. Long-term anxiety, however, can lead to psychological withdrawal from work and to personality disorders.

By the same token, not experiencing enough challenge at work, given one's skills, is likely to lead to boredom. Teachers, for example, can become "deskilled" by having to work narrowly or repetitiously or by using a restricted range of their talents. This condition ultimately takes its toll in loss of commitment and poor performance. When challenge and skills are high enough to matter and are properly balanced, flow can be experienced. Low challenge and skills may lead to a kind of low-level contentment, which can hardly be considered flow, or at least not for long.

The issue of control is also important. Experiencing flow requires one to be in charge of one's own work. But the amount of control wanted is an individual matter, and so a fixed amount of control for everyone can have differential effects. Relationships between challenge and skill seem also to hold for the amount of control wanted, as compared with the amount of control received. Receiving more control than one wants, like having more challenge than skills, results in anxiety, with the same consequences; wanting more control than one receives results in frustration and long-run boredom, with the same consequences.

A match between low levels of control wanted and low levels of control received may lead to a kind of short-term contentment but not to flow; the match between moderate to high levels of control wanted and control received are the conditions needed for flow to occur.

Flow can be a powerful substitute for leadership. Sometimes flow just happens as teachers close the classroom door and, on their own, get into the rhythm of their work. But the obstacles are too great for this to happen often enough. In many schools, for example, teaching is heavily scripted by a bureaucratic system that programs what teachers do, when they do it, how they do it, and even why. Few teachers following a script are challenged to work anywhere near their abilities. By the same token, we often give some teachers, particularly new ones, responsibilities for which they are not ready. Teaching jobs are often fragmented and compartmentalized. This makes it difficult for teachers to sense the wholeness of what they are doing. Schedules are beyond their reach. Curricula are mandated from afar. Materials and books are selected by someone else. Teaching is routinized to the point where it becomes habit. And to make it all work, "what gets rewarded gets done" is a rule that is firmly entrenched as the only motivational strategy.

If we want to harness the power of the work itself as a substitute for leadership, then teaching jobs will have to be redesigned, and systems of support will have to be developed in a way that helps teachers work in conditions of job enrichment. Motivation-hygiene theory, job-enrichment theory, and flow theory can help in this effort.

Intrinsically satisfying work makes sense because it leads to higher levels of commitment and performance. That is the effectiveness side of the equation. Intrinsically satisfying work also makes sense because it is right and good for teachers and others to find their jobs satisfying and meaningful. That is the moral side of the equation.

References

Csikszentmihalyi, M. *Flow: The Psychology of Optimal Experience*. New York: HarperCollins, 1990.

Hackman, J. R., and Oldham, G. "Motivation Through the Design of Work: A Test of a Theory." *Organizational Behavior and Human Performance*, 1976, *16* (2), 250–279.

Hackman, J. R., Oldham, G., Johnson, R., and Purdy, K. "A New Strategy for Job Enrichment." *California Management Review*, 1975, *17* (4), 57–71.

Herzberg, F., Mausner, B., and Snyderman, B. *The Motivation to Work*. New York: Wiley, 1959.

Sergiovanni, T. J. "Factors Which Affect Satisfaction and Dissatisfaction of Teachers." *Journal of Educational Administration*, 1967, *5* (1), 66–87.

Improving Schools from Within

Barth, R. S. 1991. 133–46. San Francisco: Jossey-Bass.

The Principal and a Community of Leaders

Principals, by virtue of the authority of their position, are seen as school leaders. Many principals attempt to exercise an authoritarian, hierarchical kind of leadership: They arrange schedules that mandate who is supposed to be where and doing what; they maintain tight control over money supplies and behavior; they dictate curriculum, goals, and means. An inevitable consequence of this patriarchal model of leadership—aside from a certain amount of order and productivity—is the creation of a dependent relationship between principal and teacher. Furthermore, many tasks in schools, such as helping disturbed children, coordinating curriculum, and evaluating pupils, are too complex and frightening for any one person to deal with. Consequently, the model of the principal who unilaterally "runs" a school no longer works very well.

Successful principals, like successful college presidents these days, are successful less as charismatic authority figures than as coalition builders. The increasing specialization of teachers, for instance, signals that the principal can no longer be the master teacher well versed in instructing handicapped children, students who are gifted and talented, beginning reading, and advanced math. Hence, it has become increasingly important to share leadership and to no longer even aspire to fully understand and control every aspect of the school.

Recently I participated in a lengthy conversation about shared leadership with an elementary school principal and a junior high school teacher. We agreed on several assumptions about teachers as leaders: All teachers have leadership tendencies; schools badly need teachers' leadership; teachers badly need to exercise that leadership; teachers' leadership has not been forthcoming; the principal has been at the center of both successes and failures of teachers' leadership; and principals who are most successful as leaders themselves are somehow able to enlist teachers in providing leadership for the entire school.

What, then, can principals do to develop a community of leaders within a school? What do principals do that thwarts the development of teacher leadership? What do principals do that makes the emergence of school leadership from teachers more likely?

Articulating the Goal. In order to move a school from where it is to where one's vision would have it be, it is necessary to convey what the vision is. As we will see in the following chapter, this is risky. Many principals may not be sure of what their vision is. They may not want to face the faculty and parental dissonance that might surface if they shared their vision. They may not want to expose their thinking to the central office, which may not see the connection between, say, "a community of leaders" and minimum competence in three-place multiplication. Consequently, few administrators telegraph their vision to the school community, preferring to believe that "they'll figure it out." A community of leaders and the involvement of teachers, students, and parents in school leadership is more likely to occur when the principal openly articulates this goal in meetings, conversations, newsletters, faculty memos, and community meetings. In this way shared leadership becomes part of the school culture.

Relinquishing Authority to Teachers. As we have seen, there are short lists and long lists of behaviors of "effective principals." They include continuous monitoring of performance, exercising strong leadership, and involving parents. I have never seen the "ability to relinquish" on such a list. Many principals feel they have too little authority over a tottering building. To convey any authority to others is illogical. It is against human nature for us to relinquish power when we will probably be held accountable for what others do with it. One should accumulate and consolidate, not relinquish. This leads to the common belief that "I cannot leave my building." A most important item in any list of characteristics of effective principals is the capacity to relinquish, because only then can the latent, creative powers of teachers be released.

It is important for a principal to relinquish decision-making authority to teachers. But teachers will not become leaders in the school community if, when the going gets tough and the angry phone calls come from the central office, the principal violates the trust and reasserts authority over the issues. It takes only one or two incidents where the rug is pulled from beneath teachers' leadership before teachers secede from the community of leaders. The principal must bet on a horse and have the courage and trust to stick with it and help it finish. To change the bet in the middle of the race is to create conditions under which everyone loses.

Involving Teachers Before Decisions Are Made. It is common in the world of teachers and principals for a problem, like inadequate fire safety, to emerge, and for the principal to quickly reach a solution (bringing in the fire chief to lecture students and teachers) and then invite a teacher to "handle" the situation. This is an opportunity for maintenance, not leadership, which few teachers will embrace. The energy, the fun, the commitment around leadership comes from brainstorming one's *own* solutions and then trying to implement them. For a community of leaders to develop, tough important problems need to be conveyed to teachers before, not after, the principal has played them out.

Which Responsibility Goes to Whom? Wanting desperately to resolve a problem, the principal often selects a responsible, trusted teacher who has successfully handled similar challenges. But, by relying on the tried and proven teacher, the principal rewards competence with additional hard work. The tried teacher is a tired teacher. It will be only a matter of time before the overburdened teacher burns out and leaves teaching or leaves the school, concluding that if one is going to *act* like an assistant principal, one might as well be *paid* like an assistant principal. Other often-chosen teachers will one day declare, "I'm drowning and I must return my attentions to the classroom. I'm sorry, but I can't do it."

The better match, as in Sparky's case, may be between an important school issue and a teacher who feels passionately about that issue. For one teacher, it is fire safety; for another, the supply closet; while another would favor reforming the science curriculum, finding both fire safety and the supply closet menial tasks, not leadership opportunities. Teacher leadership is less a question of according trusted teachers responsibility for important issues than of ensuring that all teachers are given ownership for a responsibility about which they care deeply. One person's junk is another person's treasure.

Reliance on a few proven teachers for schoolwide leadership also excludes the majority of untried teachers from the community of leaders, contributing to divisiveness and developing little of a community. For Sparky, the opportunity to have the "key" had far more meaning than for other teachers who had been offered and accepted many keys. His inclusion expanded the community by one.

Too often the criterion for bestowal of the "key" of leadership is evidence that a person knows how to do it. Yet the innovative solutions come more often from teachers who do not know how to do it but want to learn how. This is where leadership and staff development intersect. The moment of greatest learning for any of us is when we find ourselves responsible for a problem that we care desperately to resolve. Then we need and seek out assistance. We are ready to learn. At this moment, the principal (and faculty) have a responsibility and an opportunity to assist the teacher in developing leadership skills and finding success with responsibility. Mere delegation or "being kept informed" is not sufficient involvement on the principal's part for the development of a community of leaders. Unsuccessful leaders do not make a community of leaders. Most teachers, like most principals, need assistance in becoming successful school leaders. The principal who supports and teaches the "beginning school leader" assumes a burden of considerable risk, time, and patience. "It would be safer, easier, and quicker to handle it myself." Yet this is what is really meant by shared leadership. It is interactive, interdependent. Communities of leaders beget communities of learners.

By turning for leadership to untried and perhaps untrusted teachers who express a passionate interest in an issue, as Sparky did, everyone can win. The overburdened teacher receives no further burden; the teacher who displays excitement or anger about an issue is enlisted in the growing community of leaders. The teacher comes alive as an adult learner as well as a leader. And I think the principal wins. If the principal can help anoint and support the initial efforts of teacher-leaders this year, those efforts will be rewarded next year by a level of independence when much less will be needed from the principal.

Shared Responsibility for Failure. If the principal conveys responsibility to a teacher for an important schoolwide issue and the teacher stumbles, the principal has several options. Blame the teacher. "I entrusted leadership and authority for fire safety to Sparky and he blew it. Now I'll find someone more trustworthy who can do it better or I'll do it myself." This may protect the principal in the short run, but in the long run neither Sparky nor other teachers will choose to play again. Without the provision of a safety net by the principal, few teachers will aspire to walk the high wire—no community of leaders. Or the principal can become the lone lightning rod. "I am captain of the ship; it has gone aground. I assume responsibility." A needlessly lonely and self-punitive position.

If the principal bets on this horse and it runs poorly, "we" are responsible, for together we have given our best efforts. Both have wrestled with something of importance to them and to the school that bonds them. Responsibility for failure is shared. Usually the world of schools deals more kindly with mistakes made by a coalition of teacher and administrator than when either errs alone. The important question to ask is not "Whose fault is it?" but "What happened, what can we learn from it, and how might we do it better next time?" The principal and teacher who share leadership have hope for developing collegiality, staff development, and morale. There is much to be gained, then, by both teacher and principal from failing together.

Teachers Take Credit for Success. Whereas it is important to the development of a community of leaders that failures be shared by teacher and principal, I think it equally important that success reflect on the teacher, not the principal. The principal has many visible occasions during the school day and year to be the "hero": running the assembly, coming in over the loudspeaker, sending the notice to parents, meeting with the press about the National Merit Finalists. For the teacher, there are precious few opportunities to experience and enjoy recognition from the school community. For the principal to hog or share the limelight is to reduce the meaning and the recognition for the teacher and make less likely continuation of membership in the community of leaders.

Visible, schoolwide success replenishes the teacher personally and professionally. I have seen classroom performance, morale, commitment to teaching, and relationships with colleagues all benefit from public recognition. Additionally, teachers should enjoy the success because they have done most of the work. My part in the fire safety plan occupied a fraction of the time Sparky put in. Mine were prime minutes, perhaps, but there were few of them.

Principals, of course, have their own needs for success and recognition that often impede the development of a community of leaders. But, in the long run, teacher success begets further teacher leadership and success. The school improves. And the principal comes in for ample credit as "the one who pulled it off." Everyone wins.

All Teachers Can Lead. Just as high expectations that "all children can learn" have been associated with unexpected learning on the part of children whose background might not predict such achievement, high expectations on the part of principals and others that all teachers can be responsible, committed school leaders make more likely the emergence of leadership tendencies that all teachers possess.

How might principals' expectations for teachers as leaders be raised and conveyed? Principals can articulate a community of leaders as a goal, ask teachers to think about a piece of the school for which each would like responsibility, and then look for and celebrate examples of teacher leadership when they emerge.

"I Don't Know How." The foregoing discussion about principals helping induct teachers as citizens of a community of leaders implies that the principal knows how to do something, but, for a variety of reasons, would prefer that the teacher do it. I probably could have handled the problem of fire safety, although not as well as Sparky. Yet principals who always know how to do something perpetuate that "burden of presumed competence." A principal is hired from among 100 candidates because the selection committee supposes he or she knows how to do it. Therefore, for principals to admit that they do not know how is a sign of weakness, at best, and incompetence at worst. As we have seen, many principals succumb to the burden of presumed competence by pretending, and sometimes even *convincing* themselves, that they know how. This can kill the development of a community of leaders. The invitation for a teacher to take on fire safety may often be framed, then, as a veiled challenge to see if the teacher can do it as well as the principal. Competition on the part of the teacher to exceed the principal's knowledge and skills in turn may engender a wish on the part of the principal that the teacher fail. In such a case, school leadership becomes an occasion to renew adversarial relationships all too latent among teachers and principals.

Teachers know that principals do not know how to do it all. Surprising results are achieved when a principal initiates conversations with a teacher by announcing honestly, "I've never set up a fire safety system before. I've got some ideas, but I don't know how." *I don't know how.* This declaration by the principal becomes a powerful invitation to teachers. It suggests that the principal and school need help, and that the teacher can provide the help. And it gives the teacher room to risk not knowing how either and perhaps to fail. More likely, the teacher can emerge a genuinely helpful leader of the school and friend and colleague of the principal. *I don't know how* is an attractive,

disarming, and realistic invitation likely to be accepted and handled with responsibility—and with collegiality.

Personal Security. These suggestions for teacher and principal to move a school toward a community of leaders imply a level of personal security on the part of principal as well as teacher. To publicly articulate a personal vision, relinquish control, empower and entrust teachers, involve teachers early, accord responsibility to untried teacher-leaders, share responsibility for teacher failure, accord responsibility to teachers for success, and have confidence that all teachers can lead, principals have to be psychologically secure individuals who are willing to take risks. The principal's personal security is a precondition on which development of communities of leaders rests. With some measure of security on the part of principals these ideas have plausibility; without security they have little. Yet, as I have suggested earlier, there are many forces at work that give principals good reason to feel insecure. Who will supply *their* safety net?

The security of principals might be strengthened in several ways. During the preservice preparation of aspiring principals, including certification requirements, university course work, and peer interaction, the concept of shared leadership can be introduced and legitimized, so that candidates might become familiar and comfortable with the idea of teachers as colleagues in leadership.

During the process to select a new principal, criteria are put forth and decisions made on the basis of a host of factors usually determined within the school district. Seldom is "personal security" among them. Yet interview techniques and other oral and written instruments exist that might help identify this important quality.

A third promising point of possible influence on principals' security occurs at the *inservice* level. Principals have as a context the school over which they preside, a sense of the faculty's and of the student body's differences and strengths, and teachers and fellow principals with whom to explore the unfamiliar, perhaps threatening idea of shared leadership.

But, as we have seen, schools are organizations that suffer from scarce resources and recognition. Teachers compete with teachers; principals compete with principals; and teachers compete with principals for these precious commodities. For principals to feel sufficiently secure and in control in order to share authority with others, their own needs for recognition, success, and safety must be acknowledged and addressed.

The Program Advisory Board at the Principals' Center at Harvard recently selected shared leadership as a focus for one semester in the belief that "shared leadership expands the possibilities for school improvement, increases commitment, complicates decision-making, and makes for more effective education for children" (Graduate School of Education, Harvard University, 1987). Two-hour workshops with titles such as "Building School Coalitions"; "A Nation Prepared: Teachers for the 21st Century"; "The Principal and the Conditions of Teaching"; "A Case for Shared Leadership"; "The Revolution That Is Overdue"; "Who Owns the Curriculum?"; "School Improvement Councils"; and "Working Together for Quality Education" occupied the attention of many principals as well as teachers. These discussions may not have transformed the insecure into the secure, but they have made the concept of school as a community of leaders more compelling and less risky.

Communities of Leaders. The vision of a school as a community of leaders is not a fantasy. When the National Education Association (NEA) was founded in 1870, its membership included not only teachers but many teacher-educators, principals, and superintendents, all banded together in the cause of good schools.

A century later, the NEA—now a teachers' organization—has joined with the National Association of Secondary School Principals to create *Ventures in Good Schooling* (1986), a project that seeks collaborative schools in which the professional autonomy of teachers and managerial authority of principals are harnessed. Among the recommendations of this effort are that principals involve faculty members in decision-making; that teachers participate in the school budgeting process and in evaluating principals' performance; that principals seek teachers' advice on staffing needs and decisions; and that principals and teachers jointly devise a schoolwide plan for instructional improvement and for recognizing student achievement. This is but one promising step toward a community of leaders.

Several secondary schools, including the Cambridge School of Weston and Brookline and Andover High Schools in Massachusetts and Hanover High School in New Hampshire, have been working to create what they call "democratic schools." A town meeting form of school government provides teachers and students a structure for participating in the major decisions confronting these schools. Teachers and students join with administrators in determining policies about such matters as smoking, pupil evaluation, and use of space, as long as decisions are not illegal or in violation of school board policy. The principal has one vote in the assembly, but may veto its actions, subject to an override by a two-thirds vote of the whole. These assemblies, modeled after state and federal governments, with an executive, a legislative, and a judicial branch, are demonstrating that schools can not only teach about democracy, they can *be* democracies. In fact, these schools raise the question of whether it is possible for a school to teach democracy through nondemocratic means.

Alaskan small schools are places to watch, too. Their isolation makes them promising laboratories, uncontaminated by the rest of the world, for growing all sorts of unusual cultures. For instance, in Alaska, where one might routinely find a K–12 school staffed by three or four adults, no one knows that teachers are not supposed to be leaders. In many schools, all teachers, whether called *teacher*, *teaching-principal*, or *principal*, enjoy schoolwide leadership over issues from leaky roofs to parent involvement.

And many parochial schools thrive under what is often referred to as *servant leadership* on the part of the principal or headmaster. Principals, like parish priests, lead adults by serving adults. This invariably means involving teachers in important decisions of the schools. It is impossible to serve teachers by excluding them.

Quaker schools, too, have traditionally worked with great success by creating for students and adults a culture of participatory leadership, similar to the leadership of Quaker meetings. They assume that everyone has an "inner light," something to offer the group, if given the opportunity. And every member has something to learn from others. Members work together as equals, sharing ideas, planning, giving feedback, and supporting each other in new efforts. Leaders emerge in various ways at various times and then give way to other leaders. The work and the leadership of the group are responsibilities and an opportunities for all, as one observer at a faculty meeting in a Massachusetts Friends school discovered:

> One teacher sat down in the large circle of staff with a box of tangled yarn which had been donated for art projects. The teacher quietly took a mass of the yarn and began winding it into a ball, while listening to and discussing staff issues. Soon the person on her left reached into the box and began unraveling and winding another ball of yarn. The person to her right did the same, and soon the yarn had spread around the circle with *everyone* winding while participating in the meeting. No one had ever said a word about the yarn.

These examples suggest that it is possible for adults and students in schools to work and lead together, to everyone's benefit. A community of leaders—neither a new nor an imaginary concept—seems foreign only to the majority of public schools in this country.

Conclusion

> . . . I found out that those geese can fly from way up north to way down south, and back again. But they cannot do it alone, you see. It's something they must do in *community*. Oh, I know, it's a popular notion, and people swell with pride and emotion to think of themselves on the eagle side—strong, self-confident, solitary. Not bad traits. But we are what we are—that's something we can't choose. And though many of us would like to be seen as the eagle, I think God made us more like The Goose [Stomberg, 1982, p. 1].

The relationship between teacher and principal is currently under sharp scrutiny. The top-down model is too unwieldy, is subject to too much distortion, and is too unprofessional. Problems are frequently too big and too numerous for any one person to address alone. Schools need to recognize and develop many different kinds of leadership among many different kinds of people to replace the venerable, patriarchal model.

School leadership can come from principals who transform adversaries into colleagues; from teachers who individually or collectively take responsibility for the well-being of the school; from parents who translate a basic concern for their children into constructive actions; and from students who guide tours or in other ways offer community service. School leadership, then, can realistically be considered not only in terms of roles but also in terms of functions. School people with different titles frequently share similar goals and tasks and need the same skills in enlisting disparate individuals and groups in a search for good schools.

Each school faces the task of constructing an effective educational and intellectual community around a unique set of issues and individuals. What is needed is leadership from within, from parents, teachers, principals, and students. Coalition building and the replacement of competitive relationships with collegial ones does not occur easily, let alone naturally. Schoolpeople need skills, insight, and vision that will equip them to assume responsibility for their schools. Such tools are seldom won through experience as classroom teachers or principals, or in courses at schools of education. Yet they are skills and values that educators committed to the importance—and inevitability—of many forms of leadership at the school level can develop.

Leaders need to be able to set general directions and create environments and structures that enable everyone in the school community to discover their own skills and talents and thereby be free to help students discover theirs. For students' needs will not be fully addressed until teachers and administrators together have worked out their own. This role must be one of enabling rather than controlling. Shared school leadership is a timely, volatile, and I think very promising issue for the improvement of schools from within, because public schools are strapped for adequate personal resources at the same time that extraordinary personal resources lie unacknowledged, untapped, unrewarded, and undeveloped within each schoolhouse.

I have suggested a reconfiguration of the relationships among student, teacher, and principal. A community of leaders offers independence, interdependence, resourcefulness, and collegiality. While much of the current literature suggests that effective principals are the heroes of the organization, I suspect that more often effective principals enable others to provide strong leadership. The best principals are not heroes; they are hero makers.

Few of the tea leaves before us suggest that public schools are heading toward communities of leaders. But the important question is not what our schools will become, but what they might be. There is a critical difference. The question of what will be implies the exercise of purely rational faculties, calling for trend analyses, projections, extrapolations, and probability curves. A view of what could be is not confined to these means. It embraces intuition, creativity, morality, reason, and above all, vision. It extends inquiry from the realm of the probable to the realm of the possible. Clear vision offers inventive, promising, and powerful ideas for improving schools from within.

References

Principals' Center Spring Calendar. Cambridge, Mass.: Graduate School of Education, Harvard University, January 1987.

Stomberg, R. D. "The Goose." Unpublished poem, 1982.

Ventures in Good Schooling. Washington, D.C.: National Education Association and National Association of Secondary School Principals, 1986.

The Challenge:
To Provide Leadership within Catholic Schools

Ristau, K. 1991. In *Leadership of and on behalf of Catholic schools*, eds. K. Ristau and J. Rogus, 12–17.
Washington, D.C.: National Catholic Educational Association.

Reconceptualizing the Definition of Leadership

In suggesting what might be done about leadership and the deliberate development of leaders, Catholic educators should understand what leadership means. Ideas about a great leader, one in a position at the "top," who has all the answers and who can make anything happen are out of date. The former concept of the "hero" and the "charismatic" personality do not work today. In fact, there may be good people at the "top," who are doing the wrong things well. There is a need for a new kind of leadership.

What people currently understand leadership to be is not wrong. It simply is not adequate to the challenge of a new age. Like an umbrella in a hurricane, the current concept is of some use, but does not provide enough coverage. A sturdier structure is needed (Nanus, 1989).

The Catholic school today is affected by emerging pluralism, a desire for full participation and a higher valuation of human independence and capability as much as are all other national institutions. There is a demand for recognition, involvement and sense of worth by both individuals and organizations. People ask for dignity, meaning and commitment. The issue is not control, but a dedication to developing people and maximum delegation. The management books that taught leaders to be aloof, to keep workers off balance to increase motivation have become irrelevant. John Naisbitt and Patricia Aburdene (*Reinventing the Corporation*, 1986) describe today's workplace as "an environment for nurturing personal growth . . . a place in which topdown authoritarianism is yielding to a networking style and where everyone is a resource for everyone else." The new age of leadership should see the leader standing at the center of a dynamic system. The new system is circular. Leaders should see themselves not at the top, but in the center connected to those around them; not reaching down, but reaching out. The image of a web, of an interrelated structure built around a central point fits well. Nanus (1989) speaks about the need for leaders to be both the head and the heart. Helgesen (1990) speaks about the need for attention to both the efficient and the humane.

This model of leadership is aligned with the powerful message of Robert Greenleaf in *Servant Leadership* (1977) that the leader is seen as servant first. But, it is not the servant who is neutral, dull or immobile. It is the person Greenleaf describes as fully human. Servants, by definition, are fully human.

> Servant-leaders are functionally superior because they are closer to the ground—they hear things, see things, know things and their intuitive insight is exceptional. Because of this they are dependable and trusted...and they have the willingness to undertake the hard and high risk tasks of building better institutions in an imperfect world, who see the problem as residing in here and not out there (pp. 42, 45).

Developing leaders who understand and deal with new situations will build a stronger infrastructure than relying on traditional hierarchies and bureaucracies—but, this will have to be an effort of balance beam and tightrope walking to lead far in a church that is decidedly hierarchical.

Educating for Leadership

There always has been intense discussion around education for leadership. Can it be done? Can people learn how to be leaders? Who would be arrogant enough to understand such an all-encompassing subject well enough to teach it? People who still believe that leaders are born and not made would find teaching leadership skills unnecessary. Others would argue that leadership is elitist and no special training should be given to a select few. Since much about leadership is elusive and unscientific, what body of knowledge should be presented? All of these arguments are valid to a point, but they simply forestall the agenda. It is more than likely true that people cannot be taught to be leaders. But much can be and should be done. Cronin, in an article entitled, "Thinking and Learning about Leadership," offers an extensive list to consider.

◆ Anyone can be exposed to leadership, discussion of skills and styles, strategies and theories.
◆ People can learn about the paradoxes and contradictions and ironies of leadership.
◆ Students can appreciate the diversity and dilemmas of problem solving and organizational behavior. They can also learn countless problem solving strategies and theories and participate in role playing to sharpen their own skills.
◆ People can understand the linkage of ends and means; recognizing bad as well as good leadership. Students can learn from reading biographies about both the best and worst leaders.

◆ Learning opportunities exist to sharpen skills as a speaker, debater, negotiator, problem clarifier and planner.
◆ Much can be learned from mentors and intern participation.
◆ Would-be leaders need to get away from their own culture and examine how leaders in other circumstances go about the task.
◆ And most importantly students of leadership can make an appointment with themselves and begin to appreciate their own strengths and deficiencies. Personal mastery is important. So too the ability to use one's intuition, and to enrich one's creative impulses. . . . [T]hey learn to cast aside dull routines and habits that enslave most of us. Would-be leaders learn how to be truly sharing and caring people—in their families, their professions and in their communities (p. 34).

It is possible to prepare people for leadership. It is impossible, however, to teach people how to act in every contingency. Therefore, well-educated people are needed —people who are well grounded in the liberal arts, who can think and make decisions, people who have vision and can align others and motivate them to action.

Immediate Needs—School Leaders

In simpler times, Catholic education may have needed only a few hundred people to fill all the major leadership positions. Now not just hundreds are required, but perhaps thousands are needed to steer the system through endless squalls, scann the horizon for new opportunities and threats, interpret accelerating change, global complexity and ambiguity. Catholic education needs—now, and in the immediate future—leaders who

1. know education and work in the service of education
2. know the "church"
3. understand the connection
4. have new ideas, and
5. know what it means to lead.

To ensure the future of Catholic education, programs for leadership, scholarships and support for leaders are needed. Traditionally, the Catholic school system has not promoted the breadth and depth of education necessary for leadership. Education for leadership is not cherished. Seminars and workshops often have been deemed sufficient. They are not. Catholic educators should not be willing to settle for anything less than the best for themselves and for others. There are now degree programs (but probably not enough), which offer the occasion for leaders to study and reflect, not as a luxury, but as a commitment to life-long learning.

Even at some of the colleges and universities where these programs exist, support is shaky at best. Not only is there insufficient funding for students in terms of scholarships or tuition reduction, but also there often is little backing for the program from the institution of higher education itself. Without support and scholarships, the programs are too expensive for many; some too distant; others impossible for people with families to attend. People in higher education should continue to find ways to bring solid, thoughtful degree work to Catholic school leaders. Off-campus degree work, extension programs, the use of such technologies as interactive television should all be considered.

Dioceses and parishes should support mentor and internship programs for people with leadership potential, along with academic preparation. Too many Catholic school principals are placed in a very demanding position without any on-the-job training. Almost all public school principals are required in licensure programs to complete an internship, at least one semester to learn the work of administration alongside a practicing principal. Catholic school principals, who in most cases are expected to do all of the tasks of the ordinary public school superintendent with none of the accompanying staff, rarely get this experience. Learning from a role model and observing how others handle important challenges is far better than learning by trial and error. For the cost of one average teacher salary, a promising individual could begin some successful leadership experiences, and an effective principal could impart a way of thinking, acting and reflecting on educational leadership, while renewing himself or herself.

The church always has been good at building buildings. It is time to invest in people. Far too many people are solidly entrenched in a belief that this is a time of scarce resources. It simply does not have to be true. In parishes where there is life and hope and dreams, resources are always found. The history of the Catholic Church in America, particularly the history of Catholic education, proves this repeatedly. The past should reassure Catholics of ample resources for the future.

Future Preparation—Within Schools and Family

Educators bear a large responsibility for the development of leadership. Leadership can be promoted within and outside the regular classroom, if leadership is prized. Unfortunately, most students learn more from movies and television than they do in classrooms. Without much extra work, but with decided emphasis, students can learn leadership skills. Both in classrooms and in outside activities, students can learn a philosophy of leadership, interpersonal skills and strategies for problem solving. Too much schooling teaches children to be passive and dependent on adults. Dependence on fellow students is not allowed in many cases. Students are required to work by themselves most of the time. Classwork designed around cooperation and teamwork can enhance leadership skills and increase student confidence. Team captains and class officers are not enough. Students should be required to take turns leading or directing others. All students should have at least one or two leadership experiences during their school years.

Families have a responsibility as well. It may be up to the educators to help parents understand how to provide an environment which encourages leadership. Children should be urged to seek challenges and to understand that they have it in their ability to make the world a better place. Cynicism at home restricts children's thinking, as well as their ability to act. Parents also are the best people to demand that media act more responsibly in presenting leadership as valued and appreciated.

Community Attitudes

Christians are called to care about the health of public life as well as the health of our own institutions. To withdraw from this responsibility is not the message of Jesus. Christians are called to live fully amid the tension of our time. That means to develop the possibility of leadership in public organizations, in church and in education. There is the opportunity for growth and service for all. Leadership is not an elitist activity. Yet, many who could lead do not do so because of lack of community support. The final requirement for developing the leadership needed in the future is that society not make the task an impossible one. Institutions should not be allowed to become so complex that they are unmanageable, nor should those who are willing to lead be allowed to do so without support and encouragement. Perhaps in all this serious business, people would be better off to remember that leadership is about vision and meaning, about new ideas and going to new places. Educators might do well to heed the advice of Ray Bradbury (1984):

> If your meeting room, your board room or your office (take your pick) isn't a nursery for ideas, a rumpus room where seals frolic, forget it. Burn the table, lock the room, fire the clerks. You will rarely come up with any ideas worth entertaining. The dull room with the heavy people trudging in with long faces to solve problems by beating them to death is very death itself. Serious confrontations rarely arrive at serious ends. Unless the people you meet with are fun loving kids out for a romp, tossing ideas like confetti, and letting the bits fall where they may, no spirit will ever rouse, no notion will ever birth, no love will be mentioned, no climax reached. You must swim at your meetings, you must jump for baskets, you must take hefty swings for great or missed drives, you must run and dive, you must fall and roll, and when the fun stops, get out.

Conclusion

The challenge to provide leadership for Catholic education appears to be formidable. It will not be easy or instant. If the axiom, "grace builds on nature," once taught and well learned still holds true, then nothing can be left to chance. Particular effort should be given to the education and development of leaders for schools. That education should help leaders acquire a thoughtful view of the broader context in which Catholic education happens, provide an understanding of what educational leadership means in contrast to management, and supply the experiences to develop necessary skills. Retelling the stories of the heroic school founders can demonstrate to a new generation the value of taking a risk and trying new things, as well as encourage a renewed spirit for present leaders. In the hope of enhancing the quality of leadership, Catholic organizations can do a lot. A community, not a hierarchical structure, clear in its vision, in meaning, and purpose, offers rich opportunity for growth. Encouragement, modeling and especially, commitment to one another, will ensure the development of leadership.

References

Bradbury, R. "Management from Within." *New Management*. (1984), pp. 1, 4, 15.

Cronin, T. "Thinking and Learning about Leadership." *Presidential Studies Quarterly*. 14 (1984), pp. 22–34.

Greenleaf, R. *Servant Leadership*. New York: Paulist Press, 1977.

Helgesen, Sally. *The Female Advantage*. New York: Currency Books, 1990.

Naisbitt, J., and Aburdene, P. *Reinventing the Corporation*. New York: Warner Books, 1986.

Nanus, B. *The Leader's Edge*. Chicago: Contemporary Books, 1989.

Moral Leadership:
Getting to the Heart of School Improvement

Sergiovanni, T. J. 1992. 67–72. San Francisco: Jossey-Bass.

Chapter 6*
Followership First, Then Leadership

Professionalism and leadership enjoy high standing in the lexicon of education. Both are frequently prescribed as cures for our school problems. But in many ways the two concepts are antithetical. Beyond a certain point, the more professionalism is emphasized, the less leadership is needed; the more leadership is emphasized, the less likely professionalism is to develop. The point is not to get rid of leadership. Leadership can add a measure of quality to the most professional of school settings. But leadership becomes less urgent and less intensive once the wheels of professionalism begin to turn by themselves. When this happens, superintendents and principals can spend less time trying to figure out how to push and pull teachers toward goals and more time dealing with the broad issues of teaching and learning, on the one hand, and ensuring financial, moral, political, and managerial support for the school, on the other.

When conditions are right, professionalism has a way of encouraging teachers and principals to be self-managers. By the same token, providing too much leadership discourages professionalism. For example, the principal who insists on being a strong instructional leader, even though teachers are perfectly capable of providing all the necessary leadership, forces teachers into dependent roles and removes opportunities and incentives for them to be self-managers. Self-management and professionalism, by contrast, are complementary concepts. One can be self-managed without being a professional, but one cannot be a professional without being self-managed.

In Chapter Four, it was suggested that professionalism could be understood as competence plus virtue. *Virtue* was defined as commitment to the professional ideal of exemplary practice in the service of valued social ends and as concern for the practice of teaching itself. The professional ideal, and the norms and values that define the school as a

learning community, comprise two powerful substitutes for leadership. When the substitutes are present, teachers and administrators need less leading from the outside; instead, they are moved to action by inner forces—the motivational power of emotion and social bonds.

The relationship between professionalism and self-management can be understood by considering still another dimension of professionalism. The term *professionalism* was derived from the religious setting, where it pertained to the public statement of what one believed and was committed to (Camenisch, 1988). Commitment goes beyond the commitment of those who have made no such "profession"; carried into the modern professions, the concept of professing something, of believing in something, and of bringing an unusual commitment to this idea remains strong and forms the basis of self-management.

One could argue convincingly that while the establishment of the professional ideal in teaching may be a worthy goal, school must still be run somehow until professionalism is fully established. It follows that teachers, principals, parents, and students will still have to be "motivated" and "led" if the work of the school is to be done and done well. But what about the possibility that self-management could be encouraged by school leaders even if the professional ideal were not fully established? I believe that is possible. Professionalism helps, but so does the power of community norms. Schools as learning communities also publicly proclaim what they believe, and this center of shared values can also become the basis of self-management. Moving in this direction, however, means changing our understanding of leadership.

The Old Leadership Recipe

If self-management is our goal, then leadership will have to be reinvented in a fashion that places *followership* first. At the operational level, leadership is about two things: trying to figure out what needs to be done to make the school work and work well, and trying to figure out

---

* Editor's note: Chapter notation refers to this excerpt.

how to get people to do these things. For most of the last forty years, we were successful in accomplishing these goals, relying on a very simple management recipe:

◆ State your objectives.
◆ Decide what needs to be done to achieve these objectives.
◆ Translate these work requirements into role expectations.
◆ Communicate these expectations.
◆ Provide the necessary training.
◆ Put people to work.
◆ Monitor the work.
◆ Make corrections when needed.
◆ Throughout, practice human relations leadership, to keep morale up.

In a nutshell, the heart of the recipe was the simple management rule "expect and inspect." Anyone who did not comply with the system was punished in a variety of ways.

But things are different today. The standard recipe does not quite work as well as it used to. The times are different, the situations we face are different, and the people are different. The standard management recipe was based on two kinds of authority (see Chapter Three): bureaucratic (the authority of hierarchy, rules and regulations, job specifications, and assignments) and psychological (the authority of rewards that comes from practicing human relations leadership and fulfilling human needs). There is a place for both, but there are also problems with their use, particularly when bureaucratic and psychological authority comprise the overall strategy for how school administrators manage and lead. One problem is that teachers tend to respond to this kind of authority by becoming subordinates.

From Subordinate to Follower

A major theme of *Value-Added Leadership* (Sergiovanni, 1990) is the importance of building followership in the school, as an alternative to subordination. The argument presented in that work is summarized here.

Subordinates do what they are supposed to do, but little else, and what they do is often perfunctory. Subordinates want "marching orders." They want to know exactly what is expected of them and often gladly do it. For subordinates, life can be uncomplicated and even easy. After all, it does not take much talent or effort to be a good subordinate. If you want to be sure that subordinates are doing what they are supposed to do, in the right way, you have to monitor them and watch over them—either directly, through systems of supervision and evaluation, or indirectly, by monitoring lesson plans, collecting growth plans, analyzing test scores, and using other means.

Relying on psychological authority as the major basis of leadership practice breeds a different kind of subordination, one in which commitment to work depends on the satisfactory exchange of work for rewards: when the right rewards are provided, you get committed work in exchange. But the absence of rewards will mean no committed work, as will the wrong rewards. When rewards get used up—that is, when people are bored with them or no longer interested in them—people are no longer willing to give committed work.

It would be unfair to denigrate the importance of subordination. After all, everyone must adhere to certain minimal responsibilities and minimum standards. Moreover, there are always times when schools would be better if we could only get people to be good subordinates. But can bureaucratic and psychologically based leadership inspire and enhance extraordinary commitment and performance? Can they get people to go beyond—to strive for excellence? Can they build from within the kind of self-management that enables people to function fully, in the absence of rewards and without monitoring? I believe that, in the overwhelming majority of cases, the answer is no. If we want sustained and committed performance from teachers, then we must think about a leadership practice that helps teachers transcend subordination—one that cultivates followership.

What characteristics distinguish followers from subordinates? The ability to be self-managed is primary, of course. Robert E. Kelly (1988) says that followers work well without close supervision, assessing what needs to be done when and how, and making necessary decisions on their own. Followers are people committed to purposes, a cause, a vision of what the school is and can become, beliefs about teaching and learning, values and standards to which they adhere, and convictions. Whatever they are committed to, it is some kind of idea system to which they are connected. In other words, followership requires an emotional commitment to a set of ideas. Once in place, an idea structure constitutes the basis of a leadership practice based on professional and moral authority.

Normally, we think of followers as following charismatic people, or people who have persuasive interpersonal skills. This form of leadership is in the tradition of the managerial mystique, wherein leaders' styles and personalities take precedence over what they believe, intend, and say (see Chapter One). The mystique is an important contributor to the failure of leadership. In the extreme, emphasizing personality over ideas leads to the "messiah syndrome," in which emotional attachment to a leader is so blind and so strong that reason falters.

Neither the managerial mystique nor the messiah syndrome can form the basis of the kind of followership needed in schools. Followership emerges when leadership practice is based on compelling ideas. The concept of followership poses a number of paradoxes. It turns out that effective following is really the same as leadership (Kelly, 1988). Leaders and followers alike are attracted to and compelled by ideas, values, and commitments.

When followership and leadership are joined, the traditional hierarchy of the school is upset. It changes from a fixed form, with superintendents and principals at the top and teachers and students at the bottom, to one that is in flux. The only constant is that neither superintendents and principals nor teachers and students are at the apex; that position is reserved for the ideas, values, and commitments at the heart of followership. Further, a transformation takes place, and emphasis shifts from bureaucratic, psychological, and technical-rational authority to professional and moral authority. As a result, hierarchical position and personality are not enough to earn one the mantle of leader. Instead, it comes through one's demonstrated devotion and success as a follower. The true leader is the one who follows first.

References

Camenisch, P. F. "On Being a Professional, Morally Speaking." In A. Flores (ed.), *Professional Ideals*. Belmont, Calif.: Wadsworth, 1988.

Kelly, R. E. "In Praise of Followers." *Harvard Business Review*, 1988, 88 (6), 142–148.

Sergiovanni, T. J. *Value-Added Leadership: How to Get Extraordinary Performance in Schools*. Orlando, Fla.: Harcourt Brace Jovanovich, 1990.

Catholic Schools Make a Difference:
Twenty-Five Years of Research

Convey, J. J. 1992. 6–8, 33–34, 59, 62. Washington, D.C.: National Catholic Educational Association.

Self-Selection and Selectivity Bias

Any study of school effects must contend with the problem of self-selection. Self-selection occurs because students are not randomly assigned to schools nor do they choose schools randomly. Researchers know that self-selection, which may lead to selectivity bias, is a threat to the internal validity of a study; that is, the ability of the researcher to conclude that the effects noted are due to the differences in the treatments applied.

Self-selection prevents a conclusive answer to whether or not Catholic schools are more effective than public schools. Studies that compare Catholic schools with public schools can never eliminate the possibility that some unmeasured or otherwise uncontrolled attribute of students that is associated with self-selection is responsible for a significant amount of the differences between Catholic schools and public schools.

Researchers use either experimental or statistical means to control for the selectivity bias that can be associated with self-selection. Random assignment, which is the most adequate control for selectivity bias, is not possible in studies that compare different types of schools. Most studies, therefore, apply some statistical controls for selectivity bias. Many studies that compare Catholic schools with public schools use multiple regression analysis to control for the problems associated with self-selection. The ability of these models to control for self-selection depends upon whether they contain all of the important variables that are related to the differences in the characteristics of students in Catholic and public schools and that contribute to the differences in outcomes between the schools.

Moreover, it is not possible to know how well even the most sophisticated statistical models achieve the degree of control necessary to eliminate or substantially minimize the effects of selectivity. Therefore, the possibility that the observed differences between Catholic schools and public schools are more a function of the type of students who enroll in each, rather than anything that the schools do, can never be completely eliminated.

Identifying the Effects: Mode Specification

Closely related to the problems of self-selection and selectivity bias is the proper specification of statistical models. Improper model specification can occur in three ways, which vary significantly in the seriousness of their effects. The most serious error associated with improper model specification is the omission of relevant variables that would have a significant effect on the variables that are in the model. Properly-specified models must include all variables that have important relationships with those variables that are in the model. Failure to include important variables may result in spurious relationships among the variables in the model, which in turn, could lead to erroneous conclusions concerning the effectiveness of the schools or the identification of important predictors of school effectiveness.

The second type of model misspecification, inclusion in the model of irrelevant variables, may lead to an erroneous interpretation if not corrected. This problem, however, is correctable at the analysis stage. In a regression analysis, for example, irrelevant variables usually will be discovered because they often receive small and non-significant weights. However, if the same analysis also fails to include one or more important variables, an irrelevant variable may elude detection if it receives a large weight due to an inflated relationship that it may enjoy with another variable.

The third type of model misspecification is incorrectly stating the nature of the mathematical relationships among the variables in the model. This misspecification occurs when the model fails to include significant interactions between predictors (the model postulated is additive rather than non-additive) or other nonlinear terms (e.g., squared terms). This problem also is correctable at the analysis stage by examining a series of alternative models. Often, the theoretical framework that guides the analysis will assist the researcher in identifying variables that may interact with each other and those that may have nonlinear relationships in the model. A model that fails to specify the correct mathematical relationships among the variables will underestimate the prediction of the outcome variable.

Proper model specification always is an issue in the study of school effects. Two things should be noted. First, the results of such studies are only as good as the models on which they are based. Theory is the best safeguard against specification error. Second, the charge of model misspecification, which can never adequately be refuted, is a common attack used by critics of studies that show the superiority of Catholic schools over public schools.

Cross-Sectional Versus Longitudinal Data

Studies that use longitudinal data to determine school effects generally are methodologically superior to those that use cross-sectional data. Cross-sectional data are obtained from students in different grades at the same time, whereas longitudinal data are obtained from the same students at two different grade levels. The use of longitudinal data permits the direct examination of school effects since each student acts as his or her own control. Longitudinal data facilitate the proper interpretation of change in performance between grades. The analysis of cross-sectional data must presume that the older group of students would be comparable to the younger group on all measures if the older group had been measured at the age of the younger group. As a result, the studies that use the longitudinal data from *High School and Beyond* generally are in a better position to deal adequately with questions concerning school effects than are the studies that use only the base-year data.

Researchers usually use statistical significance as one criterion in judging the importance of research findings. Statistical significance means that the likelihood of the result of a particular statistical test is less than some pre-specified probability value, usually .05. In other words, if a result is likely to occur by chance about five or fewer times in every 100 tests, the researcher is willing to conclude that it represents a true difference in whatever is being compared.

In comparing schools, the statistical significance of the difference in performance between students from two or more schools or types of schools depends upon three things: (1) the number of students in each school; (2) the size of the effects; and (3) the level of significance chosen. For a given level of significance, the number of students and the size of the effects are inversely related; that is, the larger the number of students, the smaller the effect size that is necessary for statistical significance.

In some studies, the number of students is so large that very small effects are significant. In these situations, a legitimate question is: What is the practical significance of the effects? To answer this question, the researcher must decide upon the minimum effect size which he or she considers important. Some critics of the research on Catholic schools have argued that, while the differences between Catholic schools and public schools are often statistically significant, these differences are too small to have any practical significance.

The Tyranny of the Average

The research reviewed in this book reveals a Catholic school advantage over public schools on most student outcomes and school organizational measures. As is indicated above, the nonexperimental nature of these studies prevents the complete separation of school effects from student effects. Furthermore, the findings of better outcomes from Catholic schools, compared with public schools, which usually are based on a comparison of the average (mean) scores of Catholic and public schools on achievement tests and other outcome measures, cannot be applied universally to all Catholic and public schools.

What the data from the studies do support is that, on average, students from Catholic schools score higher on virtually all outcome measures than do students from public schools, even when relevant demographic characteristics of the students are controlled. However, this finding alone does not imply that: (1) every Catholic school is an effective school; (2) every Catholic school is more effective than every public school or even those public schools with similar characteristics; or (3) more Catholic schools than public schools are effective schools. Neither does this finding alone provide evidence that Catholic schools are more effective than public schools. The effectiveness of a particular school must be individually ascertained. Individual Catholic schools, as well as individual public schools, vary in their degree of effectiveness. Each school must be judged on its own merits.

Summary

1. The major studies on Catholic schools between 1965 and 1990 focused on a variety of religious, academic, social, and personal outcomes of Catholic schools. The early studies, those prior to 1978, concentrated mostly on the religious outcomes of Catholic schools. *Catholic Schools in Action* helped Catholic educators to understand more about students' religious understanding, attitudes, and opinions. The studies by Greeley and his colleagues produced convincing evidence concerning the beneficial effects of Catholic schools on the religious attitudes and practices of their graduates.

2. The studies after 1978 concerned the academic, social, and personal outcomes of Catholic schools, as well as their organizational effectiveness, more so than their religious outcomes. The few studies that did examine values and religious outcomes, particularly *The Heart of the Matter*, continued to find that Catholic students in Catholic schools fared better than did Catholic students who attended other schools. The Catholic-school effects appeared to be not totally due to selection factors or out-of-school experiences.

3. The most convincing results of these later studies concerned academic outcomes and organizational effectiveness. The studies by Coleman and his colleagues, as well as those of other researchers who used the data from *High School and Beyond*, showed that Catholic schools had better academic outcomes, more effective discipline, a more structured curriculum, a greater sense of collegiality among faculty, and a higher sense of community than did public schools. Moreover, Catholic schools were particularly effective for students from disadvantaged backgrounds.

4. Several studies documented the contribution of Catholic schools to the students of the inner city, particularly minority students. Offsetting the data concerning the special problems of inner-city schools, such as declining enrollments, difficulties experienced by parishes in financially supporting the schools, and older facilities were many positive findings, including the egalitarian nature of the schools, their strong communities, their

high expectations, and their ability to produce higher quality results than the public schools in their areas. These studies also showed the children in inner-city Catholic schools typically had responsive parents who sought sound educational placements for their children and the reinforcement of the values they stressed at home.

5. NCEA studies described the condition of Catholic high schools, the beliefs and values of Catholic high school teachers, and the support of Catholic schools by bishops and priests. *The Catholic High School: A National Portrait* and the study on low-income-serving Catholic high schools established a comprehensive database for Catholic high schools. Catholic schools attracted lay teachers because of the schools' religious mission and the teachers' commitment to Catholic education. Many teachers considered teaching as ministry and desired to participate in the spiritual development of their students. Finally, priests and bishops strongly affirmed the value of Catholic schools and rated their quality as high. The support of priests for Catholic schools varied according to the location of the parish, the number of years they were ordained, and whether they themselves had attended a Catholic school.

Outcomes

In most studies of school effectiveness, researchers concentrate on outcomes of an academic nature when examining the effects of schools on students. Typically, the outcomes involve indicators of the students' academic success: performance on standardized tests, perseverance in school, and success in postsecondary endeavors. Catholic schools are academic institutions, so these academic outcomes are important to consider when examining the effectiveness of Catholic schools.

Catholic schools, however, do more than simply teach academic subjects. Catholic schools are faith communities that strive to develop in their students an understanding of the Catholic faith, a commitment to the practice of their religion, and a set of values that will influence the students' present and future lives. Thus, the examination of the effectiveness of Catholic schools must go beyond the traditional academic outcomes and include the effects of Catholic schools on the religious education and value development of their students.

Achievement in Catholic High Schools

The superior performance of students in Catholic schools on achievement tests continues to occur in high school. As in the case of elementary schools, some studies showed that Catholic high school students attained average scores that were higher than the average scores of students in the national norm group. For example, the average scores of high school seniors in *Catholic Schools in Action* ranged from the 55th to the 79th percentile on the subtests of the

Metropolitan High School Battery (Neuwien, 1966), and those of Catholic high school sophomores in Boston were about one standard deviation unit above the mean of the national norm group on subtests of the *Differential Aptitude Test* (Walsh et al., 1969). Other studies showed that Catholic high school students scored higher on achievement tests than did students from public high schools. In NAEP [National Assessment of Educational Process], for example, Catholic high school juniors scored significantly higher than their public school counterparts in the reading, mathematics, writing, and science tests (Lee, 1985, 1987; Lee & Stewart, 1989; Marks & Lee, 1989). These studies, however, were descriptive, lacked longitudinal data, and applied no controls for important student background variables. As a result, none was able to verify whether the apparent Catholic school advantages were a result of what the schools themselves did or due to other factors, such as the presence of a selective student body.

The strongest evidence of a significant advantage for Catholic high schools over public high schools in academic performance came from the studies based on *High School and Beyond*, particularly those that utilized its longitudinal data. In analyzing the base-year data from *High School and Beyond*, Coleman, Hoffer, and Kilgore (1982) found that the test performance of both the sophomores and seniors in Catholic schools was higher than that of students in public schools.[7] On the sophomore tests, the average scores for Catholic school students were 10 percent higher in science and 12 percent higher in civics, and from 17 percent to 21 percent higher in mathematics, writing, reading, and vocabulary than were the average scores of students from public high schools. Compared with public school seniors, the averages of Catholic school seniors were from 10 percent to 17 percent higher in reading, mathematics, and vocabulary, and from 3 percent lower to 7 percent higher on three tests that measured ability more than achievement: mosaic, picture number, and visual.[8] Even after controlling for differences in family background, the Catholic school advantage remained, although it was reduced by about 50 percent.

Notes

7. The test performance of students from Catholic schools was about the same as that of students from other private high schools and lower than that of students from high-performing public and private high schools. The high-performing high schools were identified according to the percentage of students in them who scored high on these tests. Coleman and his associates did not analyze the test performance of high-performing Catholic high schools.

8. The tests for sophomores and seniors were different; however, the mathematics, reading, and vocabulary tests had some items in common. The senior tests were the same as those given in the *National Longitudinal Study of 1972*. The sophomore tests were given in 1980 were repeated in 1982 in the longitudinal follow-up. The percentages reported were calculated from the data provided in Tables 6-1 and 6-2 of Coleman, Hoffer, and Kilgore (1982, p. 125).

References

Coleman, J. S., Hoffer, T., & Kilgore, S. (1982). *High school achievement: Public, Catholic, & private schools compared*. New York: Basic Books.

Guerra, M. J., Donahue, M. J., & Benson, P. (1990). *The heart of the matter: Effects of Catholic High Schools on student values, beliefs and behaviors*. Washington, DC: National Catholic Educational Association.

Lee, V. E. (1985). *1983–84 National Assessment of Educational Progress reading proficiency: Catholic school results and national averages*. Washington, DC: National Catholic Educational Association.

Lee, V. E. (1987). *1983–84 National Assessment of Educational Progress writing proficiency: Catholic school results and national averages*. Washington, DC: National Catholic Educational Association.

Lee, V. E., & Stewart, C. (1989). *National Assessment of Educational Progress proficiency in mathematics and science 1985–86: Catholic and public schools compared*. Washington, DC: National Catholic Educational Association.

Marks, H. M., & Lee, V. E. (1989). *National Assessment of Educational Progress proficiency in reading 1985–86: Catholic and public schools compared*. Washington, DC: National Catholic Educational Association.

Neuwien, R. (Ed.) (1966). *Catholic schools in action*. Notre Dame: The University of Notre Dame Press.

Walsh, J. J., Airasian, P. W., Cahill, R. J., Jenson, J. A., & Rakow, E. A. (1969). *Archdiocese of Boston education study: Assessment of academic and religious outcomes*. Chestnut Hill, MA: New England Catholic Education Center.

Sharing the Light of Faith:
National Catechetical Directory for Catholics of the United States

National Conference of Catholic Bishops. 1979. No. 223. Washington, D.C.: United States Catholic Conference.

Chapter X.*
Organization for Catechesis

Part A. General Organizational Guidelines

223. Research

Rapid developments in the Church, society, and education underline the great need for research related to catechesis. Wherever possible, dioceses and parishes ought to examine themselves in order to ascertain their requirements and make plans for meeting them.

Diocesan, regional, and national groups are responsible for developing research instruments and projecting and testing models for local use. It is the responsibility of the religious education representative of the USCC Department of Education to coordinate efforts on the various levels and disseminate the results of research to diocesan offices and other interested parties. The other offices of the Department of Education, the departments of the United States Catholic Conference, and the agencies of the National Conference of Catholic Bishops provide the same services to their constituents, with regard to the catechetical components of their ministries.

The Office of Research, Policy and Program Development of the USCC Department of Education has the following functions: to maintain a listing of current and completed research in Catholic education, including catechetics; to help identify present and future research needs; to make a continuing study of trends in Catholic education, including projections for the immediate and distant futures. The staff works closely with Catholic colleges, universities, learned societies, and research groups in performing these functions.

Associated with the Office of Research, Policy and Program Development is the United States Center for the Catholic Biblical Apostolate. In relation to catechesis its pastoral purpose is to ascertain the needs of the dioceses with respect to Bible study programs, especially in adult education, and to promote popular biblical publications as well as wide distribution of the scriptures.[2]

It is highly desirable that catechists at all levels know and use the results of research. Useful research at any level should be shared as widely as possible with the rest of the Church.

Note

2.   Cf. Revelation, 22.

---

* Editor's note: Chapter notation refers to this excerpt.

What Works: Research about Teaching and Learning

United States Department of Education. 1986.
19, 21–23, 25, 27, 29, 31–39, 41–43, 45–47, 49–53, 55, 57, 59–62.
Washington, D.C.: Office of Educational Research and Improvement.

Getting Parents Involved

Research Finding: **Parental involvement helps children learn more effectively. Teachers who are successful at involving parents in their children's school-work are successful because they work at it.**

Comment: Most parents want to be involved with their children's schoolwork but are unsure of what to do or how to do it. Many say they would welcome more guidance and ideas from teachers. But it takes more than occasional parent-teacher conferences and school open houses to involve parents. Teachers who are successful at promoting parent participation in the early grades use strategies like these:

★ Some teachers ask parents to read aloud to the child, to listen to the child read, and to sign homework papers.

★ Others encourage parents to drill students on math and spelling and to help with homework lessons.

★ Teachers also encourage parents to discuss school activities with their children and suggest ways parents can help teach their children at home. For example, a simple home activity might be alphabetizing books; a more complex one would be using kitchen supplies in an elementary science experiment.

★ Teachers also send home suggestions for games or group activities related to the child's school-work that parent and child can play together.

Teachers meet parents' wishes for face-to-face contact by inviting them to the classroom to see how their children are being taught. This first-hand observation shows parents how the teacher teaches and gives parents ideas on what they can do at home.

References

Becker, H.J., and Epstein, J. (November 1982). "Parent Involvement: A Survey of Teacher Practices." *The Elementary School Journal*, Vol. 83, No. 2, pp. 85–102.

Cattermole, J., and Robinson, N. (September 1985). "Effective Home/School/Communications—From the Parents' Perspective." *Phi Delta Kappan*, Vol. 67, No. 1, pp. 48–50.

Rich, D.K. (1985). *The Forgotten Factor in School Success—the Family*. Washington, DC: Home and School Institute.

Walberg, H.J. (February 1984). "Families as Partners in Educational Productivity." *Phi Delta Kappan*, Vol. 65, No. 16, pp. 397–400.

Phonics

Research Finding: **Children get a better start in reading if they are taught phonics. Learning phonics helps them to understand the relationship between letters and sounds and to "break the code" that links the words they hear with the words they see in print.**

Comment: Until the 1930s and 1940s, most American children learned to read by the phonics method, which stresses the relationships between spoken sounds and printed letters. Children learned the letters of the alphabet and the sounds those letters represent. For several decades thereafter, however, the "look-say" approach to reading was dominant: children were taught to identify whole words in the belief that they would make more rapid progress if they identified whole words at a glance, as adults seem to. Recent research indicates that, on the average, children who are taught phonics get off to a better start in learning to read than children who are not taught phonics.

Identifying words quickly and accurately is one of the cornerstones of skilled reading. Phonics improves the ability of children both to identify words and to sound out new ones. Sounding out the letters in a word is like the first tentative steps of a toddler: it helps children gain a secure verbal footing and expand their vocabularies beyond the limits of basic readers.

Because phonics is a reading tool, it is best taught in the context of reading instruction, not as a separate subject to be mastered. Good phonics strategies include teaching children the sounds of letters in isolation and in words (s/i/t), and how to blend the sounds together (s-s-i-i-t).

Phonics should be taught early but not over-used. If phonics instruction extends for too many years, it can defeat the spirit and excitement of learning to read. Phonics helps children pronounce words approximately, a skill they can learn by the end of second grade. In the meantime, children can learn to put their new phonics skills to work by reading good stories and poems.

References

Anderson, R.C., et al. (1985). *Becoming a Nation of Readers: The Report of the Commission on Reading*. Urbana, IL: University of Illinois, Center for the Study of Reading.

Becker, W.C., and Gersten, R. (1982). "A Follow-up of Follow-Through: The Later Effects of the Direct Instruction Model on Children in Fifth and Sixth Grades." *American Educational*

Research Journal, Vol. 19, No. 1, pp. 75–92.

Chall, J.S. (1983). *Learning to Read: The Great Debate* (2nd ed.). New York: McGraw-Hill.

Perfetti, C.A., and Lesgold, A.M. (1979). "Coding and Comprehension in Skilled Reading and Implications for Reading Instruction." In L.B. Resnick and P.A. Weaver (Eds.), *Theory and Practice of Early Reading*, Vol. 1, pp. 57–84. Hillsdale, NJ: Erlbaum Associates.

Smith, N.B. (1965). *American Reading Instruction: Its Development and Its Significance in Gaining a Perspective on Current Practices in Reading*. Newark, DE: International Reading Association.

Reading Comprehension

Research Finding: **Children get more out of a reading assignment when the teacher precedes the lesson with background information and follows it with discussion.**

Comment: Young readers, and poor readers of every age, do not consistently see connections between what they read and what they already know. When they are given background information about the principal ideas or characters in a story before they read it, they are less apt to become sidetracked or confused and are more likely to understand the story fully. Afterwards, a question-and-answer discussion session clarifies, reinforces, and extends their understanding.

Good teachers begin the day's reading lesson by preparing children for the story to be read—introducing the new words and concepts they will encounter. Many teachers develop their own introductions or adapt those offered in teachers' manuals.

Such preparation is like a road map: children need it because they may meet new ideas in the story and because they need to be alerted to look for certain special details. Children who are well prepared remember a story's ideas better than those who are not.

In the discussion after the reading lesson, good teachers ask questions that probe the major elements of the story's plot, characters, theme, or moral. ("Why did Pinocchio's nose grow? Why did he lie? What did his father think about his lying? Did their feelings for each other change?") Such questions achieve two purposes: they check students' understanding of what they have just read, and they highlight the kind of meanings and ideas students should look for in future reading selections. These questions also lay the groundwork for later appreciation of the elements of literature such as theme and style. When children take part in a thought-provoking discussion of a story, they understand more clearly that the purpose of reading is to get information and insight, not just to decode the words on a page.

References

Beck, I.L., McCaslin, E.S., and McKeown, M.G. (1981). "Basal Readers' Purpose for Story Reading: Smoothly Paving the Road or Setting Up a Detour?" *The Elementary School Journal*, Vol. 81, No. 3, pp. 156–161.

Durkin, D. (1983). *Is There a Match Between What Elementary Teachers Do and What Basal Reader Manuals Recommend?* Urbana, IL: University of Illinois, Center for the Study of Reading, Reading E. Rep. No. 44. ERIC Document No. ED 235470.

Hansen, J. (1981). "The Effects of Inference Training and Practice on Young Children's Reading Comprehension." *Reading Research Quarterly*, Vol. 16, No. 3, pp. 391–417.

Mason, J. (1983). "An Examination of Reading Instruction in Third and Fourth Grades." *The Reading Teacher*, Vol. 36, No. 9, pp. 906–913.

Mason, J. and Osborn, J. (1983). *When Do Children Begin "Reading to Learn?": A Survey of Classroom Reading Instruction Practices in Grades Two Through Five*. Urbana, IL: University of Illinois, Center for the Study of Reading. Tech. Rep. No. 261. ERIC Document No. ED 220805.

Science Experiments

Research Finding: **Children learn science better when they are able to do experiments, so they can witness "science in action."**

Comment: Reading about scientific principles or having a teacher explain them is frequently not enough. Cause and effect are not always obvious, and it may take an experiment to make that clear. Experiments help children actually see how the natural world works.

Scientific explanations sometimes conflict with the way students may suppose that things happen or work. For example, most students would probably think that a basketball will fall faster than a ping-pong ball because the basketball is larger and heavier. Unless a teacher corrects this intuitive assumption by having the students perform an experiment and see the results, the students will continue to trust their intuition, even though the textbook or the teacher tells them the effect of gravity on both objects is exactly the same and that both will reach the floor at the same instant.

Many students have misconceptions even after taking a science course because they have not had opportunities to test and witness the evidence that would change their minds. To clear up misconceptions, students need to be given the chance to predict the results they anticipate in an experiment. For example, the mistaken idea that the basketball will fall faster than the ping-pong ball can be tested experimentally. The teacher can then explain why the original hypothesis was faulty. In this way experiments help students use the scientific method to distinguish facts from opinions and misconceptions.

References

Champagne, A., and Klopfer, L. (1984). "Research in Science Education: The Cognitive Psychology Perspective." In D. Holdzkom and P. Lutz (Eds.) *Research Within Reach: Science Education*. Charleston, WV: Appalachia Educational Laboratory, Research and Development Interpretation Service. ERIC Document No. ED 247148.

Gentner, D. and Stevens, A.L. (Eds.). (1983). *Mental Models*. Hillsdale, NJ: Erlbaum Associates.

Gunstone, R. and White, R. (1981). "Understanding of Gravity." *Science Education*, Vol. 65, pp. 291–299.

McCloskey, M. Caramazza, A., and Green, B. (1980). "Curvilinear Motion in the Absence of External Forces: Naive Beliefs about the Motion of Objects." *Science*, Vol. 210, pp. 1139–1141.

Storytelling

Research Finding: **Telling young children stories can motivate them to read. Storytelling also introduces them to cultural values and literary traditions before they can read, write, and talk about stories by themselves.**

Comment: Elementary school teachers can introduce young students to the study of literature by telling them fairy tales such as the *Three Billy Goats Gruff* or *Beauty and the Beast* and myths such as *The Iliad*. Even students with low motivation and weak academic skills are more likely to listen, read, write, and work hard in the context of storytelling.

Stories from the oral tradition celebrate heroes who struggle to overcome great obstacles that threaten to defeat them. Children are neither bored nor alienated by learning literature through storytelling; they enjoy, understand, and sympathize naturally with the goats on the bridge, Beauty in a lonely castle, and Hector and Achilles outside the walls of Troy. With the help of skillful questioning, they can also learn to reflect on the deeper meanings of these stories.

Children also benefit from reading stories aloud and from acting out dramatic narrations, whether at home or at school. Parents can begin reading to their children as infants and continue for years to come.

Storytelling can ignite the imaginations of children, giving them a taste of where books can take them. The excitement of storytelling can make reading and learning fun and can instill in children a sense of wonder about life and learning.

References

Applebee, A. N. (1978). *The Child's Concept of Story: Ages Two to Seventeen*. Chicago: University of Chicago Press.

Baker, A., and Greene, E. (1977). *Storytelling: Art and Technique*. New York: R.R. Bowker Co.

Bettelheim, B. (1975). *The Uses of Enchantment: The Meaning and Importance of Fairy Tales*. New York: Alfred A. Knopf.

Cook, E. (1969). *The Ordinary and the Fabulous: An Introduction to Myths, Legends and Fairy Tales for Teachers and Storytellers*. Cambridge and New York: Cambridge University Press.

Sawyer, R. (1962, Revised Edition). *The Way of the Storyteller*. New York: The Viking Press.

Thach, E. (June 1980). "Storytelling: Classics of the Oral Tradition." Report to the National Endowment for the Humanities, Washington, D.C.

Teaching Writing

Research Finding: **The most effective way to teach writing is to teach it as a process of brainstorming, composing, revising, and editing.**

Comment: Students learn to write well through frequent practice. A well-structured assignment has a meaningful topic, a clear sense of purpose, and a real audience. Good writing assignments are often an extension of class reading, discussion, and activities; not isolated exercises.

An effective writing lesson contains these elements:

★ *Brainstorming*: Students think and talk about their topics. They collect information and ideas, frequently much more than they will finally use. They sort through their ideas to organize and clarify what they want to say.

★ *Composing*: Students compose a first draft. This part is typically time consuming and hard, even for very good writers.

★ *Revising*: Students re-read what they have written, sometimes collecting responses from teachers, classmates, parents, and others. The most useful teacher response to an early draft focuses on what students are trying to say, not the mechanics of writing. Teachers can help most by asking for clarification, commenting on vivid expressions or fresh ideas, and suggesting ways to support the main thrust of the writing. Students can then consider the feedback and decide how to use it to improve the next draft.

★ *Editing*: Students then need to check their final version for spelling, grammar, punctuation, other writing mechanics, and legibility.

Prompt feedback from teachers on written assignments is important. Students are most likely to write competently when schools routinely require writing in all subject areas, not just in English class.

References

Elbow, P. (1981). *Writing With Power: Techniques for Mastering the Writing Process*. New York: Oxford University Press.

Emig, J. (1971). *The Composing Processes of Twelfth Graders*. Urbana, IL: National Council of Teachers of English. NCTE Research Rep. No. 13. ERIC Document No. ED 058205.

Graves, D.H. (1978). *Balance the Basics: Let Them Write*. New York: The Ford Foundation. ERIC Document No. ED 192364.

Graves, D.H. (1983). *Writing: Teachers and Children at Work*. Exeter, NH: Heinemann.

Hillcocks, G., Jr. (November 1984). "What Works in Teaching Composition: A Meta-Analysis of Experimental Treatment Studies." *American Journal of Education*, Vol. 93, No. 1, pp. 133–170.

Humes, A. (1981). *The Composing Process: A Summary of the Research*. Austin, TX: Southwest Regional Laboratory. ERIC Document No. ED 222925.

Learning Mathematics

Research Finding: **Children in early grades learn mathematics more effectively when they use physical objects in their lessons.**

Comment: Numerous studies of mathematics achievement at different grade and ability levels show that children benefit when real objects are used as aids in learning mathematics. Teachers call these objects "manipulatives."

Objects that students can look at and hold are particularly important in the early stages of learning a math concept because they help the student understand by visualizing. Students can tie later work to these concrete activities.

The type or design of the objects used is not particularly important; they can be blocks, marbles, poker chips, cardboard cutouts—almost anything. Students do as well with inexpensive or homemade materials as with costly, commercial versions.

The cognitive development of children and their ability to understand ordinarily move from the concrete to the abstract. Learning from real objects takes advantage of this fact and provides a firm foundation for the later development of skills and concepts.

References

Carmody, L. (1970). "A Theoretical and Experimental Investigation into the Role of Concrete and Semi-Concrete Materials in the Teaching of Elementary School Mathematics." Ph.D. Dissertation, Ohio State University, Columbus.

Fennema, E. (1972). "The Relative Effectiveness of a Symbolic and a Concrete Model in Learning a Selected Mathematical Principle." *Journal for Research in Mathematics Education*, Vol. 3, No. 4, pp. 233–238.

Jamison, D., Suppes, P., and Wells, S. (1974). "The Effectiveness of Alternative Instructional Media: A Survey." *Review of Educational Research*, Vol. 44, No. 1, pp. 1–67.

Piaget, J. (1952). *The Child's Conception of Numbers*. London: Routledge and Kegan Paul.

Suydam, M., and Higgins, J. (1977). "Activity-based Learning in Elementary School Mathematics: Recommendations from Research." Columbus, OH: ERIC Clearinghouse on Science, Mathematics and Environmental Education. ERIC Document No. ED 144840.

Estimating

Research Finding: **Although students need to learn how to find exact answers to arithmetic problems, good math students also learn the helpful skill of estimating answers. This skill can be taught.**

Comment: Many people can tell almost immediately when a total seems right or wrong. They may not realize it, but they are using a math skill called estimating.

Estimating can also be valuable to children learning math.

When students can make good estimates of the answer to an arithmetic problem, it shows they understand the problem. This skill leads them to reject unreasonable answers and to know whether they are "in the ballpark."

Research has identified three key steps used by good estimators; these can be taught to all students:

★ Good estimators begin by altering numbers to more manageable forms—by rounding, for example.

★ They change parts of a problem into forms they can handle more easily. In a problem with several steps, they may rearrange the steps to make estimation easier.

★ They also adjust two numbers at a time when making their estimates. Rounding one number higher and one number lower is an example of this technique.

Before students can become good at estimating, they need to have quick, accurate recall of basic facts. They also need a good grasp of the place value system (ones, tens, hundreds, etc.).

Estimating is a practical skill; for example, it comes in very handy when shopping. It can also help students in many areas of mathematics and science that they will study in the future.

References

Bestgen, B., et al. (1980). "Effectiveness of Systematic Instruction on Attitudes and Computational Estimation Skills of Preservice Teachers." *Journal for Research in Mathematics Education*, Vol. 11, pp. 124–136.

Reed, S.K. (1984). "Estimating Answers to Algebra Word Problems." *Journal of Experimental Psychology: Learning, Memory and Cognition*, Vol. 10, pp. 778–790.

Reys, R., et al. (1982). "Processes Used by Good Computational Estimators." *Journal for Research in Mathematics Education*, Vol. 12, pp. 165–178.

Schoen, H.L., et al. (1981). "Instruction in Estimating Solutions of Whole Number Computation." In *Developing Computational Skills, 1978 Yearbook*, Reston, VA: National Council of Teachers of Mathematics.

Trafton, P.R. (1978). "Estimation and Mental Arithmetic: Important Components of Computation." In *Developing Computational Skills, 1978 Yearbook*. Reston, VA: National Council of Teachers of Mathematics.

Teacher Expectations

Research Finding: **Teachers who set and communicate high expectations to all their students obtain greater academic performance from those students than teachers who set low expectations.**

Comment: The expectations teachers have about what students can and cannot learn may become self-fulfilling prophecies. Students tend to learn as little—or as much—as their teachers expect.

Students from whom teachers expect less are treated differently. Such students typically:

★ are seated farther away from the teacher,
★ receive less direct instruction,
★ have fewer opportunities to learn new material, and
★ are asked to do less work.

Teachers also call on these students less often and the questions they ask are more likely to be simple and basic than thought-provoking. Typically, such students are given less time to respond and less help when their answers are wrong. But when teachers give these same students the chance to answer more challenging questions, the students contribute more ideas and opinions to class discussions.

References

Brothy, J.E. (1981). "Teacher Praise: A Functional Analysis." *Review of Education Research*, Vol. 51, pp. 5–32.

Good, T.L. (December 1982). "How Teachers' Expectations Affect Results." *American Education*, Vol. 18, No. 10, pp. 25–32.

Good, T.L., and Brothy, J.E. (1984). *Looking In Classrooms* (3rd edition). New York: Harper and Row.

Marine-Dershimer, G. (Winter 1983). "Instructional Strategy and the Creation of Classroom Status." *American Educational Research Journal*, Vol. 20, No. 4, pp. 645–661.

Purkey, S., and Smith, M. (March 1983). "Effective Schools: A Review." *The Elementary School Journal*, Vol. 83, No. 4, pp. 427–452.

Student Ability and Effort

Research Finding: **Children's understanding of the relationship between being smart and hard work changes as they grow.**

Comment: When children start school, they think that ability and effort are the same thing; in other words, they believe that if they work hard they will become smart. Thus, younger children who fail believe this is because they didn't try hard enough, not because they have less ability.

Because teachers tend to reward effort in earlier grades, children frequently concentrate on working hard rather than on the quality of their work. As a result, they may not learn how to judge how well they are performing.

In later elementary grades, students slowly learn that ability and effort are not the same. They come to believe that lower ability requires harder work to keep up and that students with higher ability need not work so hard. At this stage, speed at completing tasks replaces effort as the sign of ability; high levels of effort may even carry the stigma of low ability.

Consequently, many secondary school students, despite their ability, will not expend the effort needed to achieve their potential. Underachievement can become a way of life.

Once students begin believing they have failed because they lack ability, they tend to lose hope for future success. They develop a pattern of academic hopelessness and stop trying. They see academic obstacles as insurmountable and devote less effort to learning.

Teachers who are alert to these beliefs in youngsters will keep their students motivated and on task. They will also slowly nudge their students toward the realism of judging themselves by performance. For example, teachers will set high expectations and insist that students put forth the effort required to meet the school's academic standards. They will make sure slower learners are rewarded for their progress and abler students are challenged according to their abilities.

References

Doyle, W. (1983). "Academic Work." *Review of Educational Research*, Vol. 53, No. 2, pp. 159–199.

Harari, O., and Covington, M.V. (1981). "Reactions to Achievement Behavior From a Teacher and Student Perspective: A Developmental Analysis." *American Educational Research Journal*, Vol. 18, No. 1, pp. 15–28.

Stipek, D. (1981). "Children's Perceptions of Their Own and Their Classmates' Ability." *Journal of Educational Psychology*, Vol. 73, No. 3, pp. 404–410.

Weiner, B. (1979). "A Theory of Motivation for Some Classroom Experiences." *Journal of Educational Psychology*, Vol. 71, pp. 3–25.

Weinstein, R., et al. (1982). "Student Perceptions of Differential Teacher Treatment in Open and Traditional Classrooms." *Journal of Educational Psychology*, Vol. 74, pp. 678–692.

Managing Classroom Time

Research Finding: **How much time students are actively engaged in learning contributes strongly to their achievement. The amount of time available for learning is determined by the instructional and management skills of the teacher and the priorities set by the school administration.**

Comment: Teachers must not only know the subjects they teach, they must also be effective classroom managers. Studies of elementary school teachers have found that the amount of time the teachers actually used for instruction varied between 50 and 90 percent of the total school time available to them.

Effective time managers in the classroom do not waste valuable minutes on unimportant activities; they keep their students continuously and actively engaged. Good managers perform the following time-conserving functions:

★ *Planning Class Work*: choosing the content to be studied, scheduling time for presentation and study, and choosing those instructional activities (such as grouping, seatwork, or recitation) best suited to learning the material at hand;

★ *Communicating Goals*: setting and conveying expectations so students know what they are to do, what it will take to get a passing grade, and what the consequences of failure will be;

★ *Regulating Learning Activities*: sequencing course content so knowledge builds on itself, pacing instruction so students are prepared for the next step, monitoring success rates so all students stay productively engaged regardless of how quickly they learn, and running an orderly, academically focused classroom that keeps wasted time and misbehavior to a minimum.

When teachers carry out these functions successfully and supplement them with a well-designed and well-managed program of homework, they can achieve three important goals:

★ They capture students' attention.

★ They make the best use of available learning time.

★ They encourage academic achievement.

References

Berliner, D. (September 1983). "The Executive Functions of Teaching." *The Instructor*, Vol. 93, No. 2, pp. 28–40.

Brothy, J. (1979) "Teacher Behavior and Its Effects." *Journal of Educational Psychology*, Vol. 71, No. 6, pp. 733–750.

Hawley, W., and Rosenholtz, S. with Goodstein, H. and Hasselbring, T. (Summer 1984). "Good Schools: What Research Says About Improving Student Achievement." *Peabody Journal of Education*, Vol. 61, No. 4.

Stallings, J. (1980). "Allocated Academic Learning Time Revisited, or Beyond Time on Task." *Educational Researcher*, Vol. 9, No. 11, pp. 11–16.

Wallberg, H.J. (1984). "What Makes Schooling Effective? A Synthesis and a Critique of Three National Studies." *Contemporary Education: A Journal of Reviews*, Vol. 1, No. 1, pp. 22–34.

Direct Instruction

Research Finding: **When teachers explain exactly what students are expected to learn, and demonstrate the steps needed to accomplish a particular academic task, students learn more.**

Comment: The procedure stated above is called "direct instruction." It is based on the assumption that knowing how to learn may not come naturally to all students, especially to beginning and low-ability learners. Direct instruction takes children through learning steps systematically, helping them see both the purpose and the result of each step. In this way, children learn not only a lesson's content but also a method for learning that content.

The basic components of direct instruction are

★ setting clear goals for students and making sure they understand those goals,

★ presenting a sequence of well-organized assignments,

★ giving students clear, concise explanations and illustrations of the subject matter,

★ asking frequent questions to see if children understand the work, and

★ giving students frequent opportunities to practice what they have learned.

Direct instruction does not mean repetition. It does mean leading students through a process and teaching them to use that process as a skill to master other academic tasks. Direct instruction has been particularly effective in teaching basic skills to young and disadvantaged children, as well as in helping older and higher ability students to master more complex materials and to develop independent study skills.

References

Berliner, D., and Rosenshine, B. (1976). *The Acquisition of Knowledge in the Classroom*. San Francisco: Far West Laboratory for Educational Research and Development.

Doyle, W. (1985). "Effective Secondary Classroom Practices." In R.M.J. Kyle (Ed.), *Reaching for Excellence: An Effective Schools Sourcebook*, Washington, D.C.: U.S. Government Printing Office.

Good, T., and Grouws, D. (1981). *Experimental Research in Secondary Mathematics Classrooms: Working with Teachers*. Columbia, MO: University of Missouri.

Hansen, J. (1981). "The Effects of Inference Training and Practice on Young Children's Reading Comprehension." *Reading Research Quarterly*, Vol. 16, No. 3, pp. 391–417.

Rosenshine, B. (1983). "Teaching Functions in Instructional Programs." *Elementary School Journal*, Vol. 83, No. 4, pp. 335–351.

Tutoring

Research Finding: **Students tutoring other students can lead to improved academic achievement for both student and tutor, and to positive attitudes toward coursework.**

Comment: Tutoring programs consistently raise the achievement of both the students receiving instruction and those providing it. Peer tutoring, when used as a supplement to regular classroom teaching, helps slow and underachieving students master their lessons and succeed in school. Preparing and giving the lessons also benefits the tutors themselves because they learn more about the material they are teaching.

Of the tutoring programs that have been studied, the most effective include the following elements:

★ highly structured and well-planned curricula and instructional methods,

★ instruction in basic content and skills (grades 1–3), especially in arithmetic, and

★ a relatively short duration of instruction (a few weeks or months).

When these features were combined in the same program, the students being tutored not only learned more than they did without tutoring, they also developed a more positive attitude about what they were studying. Their tutors also learned more than students who did not tutor.

References

Cohen, P.A., Kulick, J.A., and Kulick, C-L. C. (Summer 1982). "Educational Outcomes of Tutoring: A Meta-Analysis of Findings." *American Educational Research Journal*, Vol. 19, No. 2, pp. 237–248.

Devin-Sheehan, L., Feldman, R.S., and Allen, V.L. (1976) "Research on Children Tutoring Children: A Critical Review." *Review of Educational Research*, Vol. 46, No. 3, pp. 355–385.

Mohan, M. (1972). *Peer Tutoring as a Technique for Teaching the Unmotivated.* Fredonia, NY: State University of New York Teacher Education Research Center. ERIC Document No. ED 061154.

Rosenshine, B. and Furst, N. (1969). *The Effects of Tutoring Upon Pupil Achievement: A Research Review.* Washington, D.C.: U.S. Department of Education. ERIC Document No. ED 064462.

Memorization

Research Finding: **Memorizing can help students absorb and retain the factual information on which understanding and critical thought are based.**

Comment: Most children at some time memorize multiplication tables, the correct spelling of words, historical dates, and passages of literature such as the poetry of Robert Frost or the sonnets of Shakespeare. Memorizing simplifies the process of recalling information and allows its use to become automatic. Understanding and critical thought can then build on this base of knowledge and fact. Indeed, the more sophisticated mental operations of analysis, synthesis, and evaluation are impossible without rapid and accurate recall of bodies of specific knowledge.

Teachers can encourage students to develop memory skills by teaching highly structured and carefully sequenced lessons, with frequent reinforcement for correct answers. Young students, slow students, and students who lack background knowledge can benefit from such instruction.

In addition, teachers can teach "mnemonics," that is, devices and techniques for improving memory. For example, the mnemonic "Every Good Boy Does Fine" has reminded generations of music students that E, G, B, D, and F are the notes to which the lines on a treble staff correspond. Mnemonics helps students remember more information faster and retain it longer. Comprehension and retention are even greater when teachers and students connect the new information being memorized with previous knowledge.

References

Anderson, L., Evertson, C.M., and Brothy, J.E. (1979). "An Experimental Study of Effective Teaching in First-grade Reading Groups." *The Elementary School Journal*, Vol. 79, No. 4, pp. 193–223.

Bellezza, F. (1981). "Mnemonic Devices: Classification, Characteristics, and Criteria." *Review of Educational Research.* Vol. 51, No. 2, pp. 247–275.

Carlson, R.F., et al. (January 1976). "Spontaneous Use of Mnemonics and Grade Point Average." *The Journal of Psychology*, Vol. 92, first half, pp. 117–122.

Gregg, L. (Ed.). (1972). *Cognition in Learning and Memory.* New York: John Wiley and Sons.

Rosenshine, B.V. (1983). "Teaching Functions in Instructional Programs." *The Elementary School Journal*, Vol. 83, No. 4, pp. 335–351.

Questioning

Research Finding: **Student achievement rises when teachers ask questions that require students to apply, analyze, synthesize, and evaluate information in addition to simply recalling facts.**

Comment: Even before Socrates, questioning was one of teaching's most common and most effective techniques. Some teachers ask hundreds of questions, especially when teaching science, geography, history, or literature.

But questions take different forms and place different demands on students. Some questions require only factual recall and do not provoke analysis. For example, of more than 61,000 questions found in the teacher guides, student workbooks, and tests for 9 history textbooks, more than 95 percent were devoted to factual recall. This is not to say that questions meant to elicit facts are unimportant. Students need basic information to engage in higher level thinking processes and discussions. Such questions also promote class participation and provide a high success rate in answering questions correctly.

The difference between factual and thought-provoking questions is the difference between asking: "When did Lincoln deliver the Gettysburg Address?" and asking: "Why was Lincoln's Gettysburg Address an important speech?" Each kind of question has its place, but the second one intends that the student analyze the speech in terms of the issues of the Civil War.

Although both kinds of questions are important, students achieve more when teachers ask thought-provoking questions and insist on thoughtful answers. Students' answers may also improve if teachers wait longer for a response, giving students more time to think.

References

Berliner, D.C. (1984). "The Half-Full Glass: A Review of Research on Teaching." In P.L. Hosford (Ed.), *Using What We Know About Teaching.* Alexandria, VA: Association for Supervision and Curriculum Development.

Brothy, J., and Evertson, C.M. (1976). *Learning from Teaching: A Developmental Perspective.* Boston, MA: Allyn and Bacon.

Redfield, D.L., and Rousseau, E.W. (1981). "A Meta-Analysis of Experimental Research on Teacher Questioning Behavior." *Review of Educational Research*, Vol. 51, No. 2, pp. 237–245.

Rowe, M.B. (1974). "Wait-Time and Rewards as Instructional Variables: Their Influence on Language, Logic, and Fate Control: Part One—Wait-Time." *Journal of Research in Science Teaching*, Vol. 11, No. 2, pp. 81–94.

Trachtenberg, D. (1974). "Student Tasks in Text Material: What Cognitive Skills Do They Tap?" *Peabody Journal of Education*, Vol. 52, No. 1, pp. 54–57.

Study Skills

Research Finding: **The ways in which children study influence strongly how much they learn. Teachers can often help children develop better study skills.**

Comment: Research has identified several study skills used by good students that can be taught to other students. Average students can learn how to use these skills. Low-ability students may need to be taught when, as well as how, to use them.

Here are some examples of sound study practices:

★ Good students adjust the way they study according to several factors:
  ☆ the demand of the material,
  ☆ the time available for studying,
  ☆ what they already know about the topic,
  ☆ the purpose and importance of the assignment, and
  ☆ the standards they must meet.

★ Good students space learning sessions on a topic over time and do not cram or study the same topic continuously.

★ Good students identify the main idea in new information, connect new material to what they already know, and draw inferences about its significance.

★ Good students make sure their study methods are working properly by frequently appraising their own progress.

When low-ability and inexperienced students use these skills, they can learn more information and study more efficiently.

References

Bransford, J.D. (1979). *Human Cognition: Learning, Understanding and Remembering*. Belmont, CA: Wadsworth.

Brown, A.L., and Smiley, S.S. (1978). "The Development of Strategies for Studying Texts." *Child Development*, Vol. 49, pp. 1076–1088.

Craik, F.I.M., and Watkins, M.J. (1973). "The Role of Rehearsal in Short-Term Memory." *Journal of Verbal Learning and Verbal Behavior*, Vol. 12, pp. 599–607.

Hayes-Roth, B., and Goldin, S.E. (1980) *Individual Differences in Planning Processes*. Santa Monica, CA: The Rand Corporation.

Segal, J., Chipman, S., and Glaser, R. (1985). *Thinking and Learning Skills, Vol. 1: Relating Instruction to Research*. Hillsdale, NJ: Erlbaum Associates.

Homework: Quantity

Research Finding: **Student achievement rises significantly when teachers regularly assign homework and students conscientiously do it.**

Comment: Extra studying helps children at all levels of ability. One research study reveals that when low-ability students do just 1 to 3 hours of homework a week, their grades are usually as high as those of average-ability students who do not do homework. Similarly, when average-ability students do 3 to 5 hours of homework a week, their grades usually equal those of high-ability students who do no homework.

Homework boosts achievement because the total time spent studying influences how much is learned. Low-achieving high school students study less than high achievers and do less homework. Time is not the only ingredient of learning, but without it little can be achieved.

Teachers, parents, and students determine how much, how useful, and how good the homework is. On average, American teachers say they assign about 10 hours of homework each week—about 2 hours per school day. But high school seniors report they spend only 4 to 5 hours a week doing homework, and 10 percent say they do none at all or have none assigned. In contrast, students in Japan spend about twice as much time studying outside school as American students.

References

Coleman, J.S., Hoffer, T. and Kilgore, S. (1982). *High School Achievement: Public, Catholic and Private Schools Compared*. New York: Basic Books.

Keith, T.Z. (April 1982). "Time Spent on Homework and High School Grades: A Large-Sample Path Analysis." *Journal of Educational Psychology*, Vol. 74, No. 2, pp. 248–253.

National Center for Education Statistics. (April 1983). *School District Survey of Academic Requirements and Achievement*. Washington, D.C.: U.S. Department of Education, Fast Response Survey Systems. ERIC Document No. ED 238097.

Rohlen, T.P. (1983). *Japan's High Schools*. Berkeley, CA: University of California Press.

Walberg, H.J. (1984). "Improving the Productivity of America's Schools." *Educational Leadership*, Vol. 41, No. 8, pp. 19–36.

Homework: Quality

Research Finding: **Well-designed homework assignments relate directly to classwork and extend students' learning beyond the classroom. Homework is most useful when teachers carefully prepare the assignment, thoroughly explain it, and give prompt comments and criticism when the work is completed.**

Comment: To make the most of what students learn from doing homework, teachers need to give the same care to preparing homework assignments as they give to classroom instruction. When teachers prepare written instructions and discuss homework assignments with students, they find their students take the homework more seriously than if the assignments are simply announced. Students are more willing to do homework when they believe it is useful, when teachers treat it as an integral part of instruction, when it is evaluated by the teacher, and when it counts as a part of the grade.

Assignments that require students to think, and are therefore more interesting, foster their desire to learn both in and out of school. Such activities include explaining what is seen or read in class; comparing, relating, and experimenting with ideas; and analyzing principles.

Effective homework assignments do not just supplement the classroom lesson; they also teach students to be independent learners. Homework gives students experience in following directions, making judgments and comparisons, raising additional questions for study, and developing responsibility and self-discipline.

References

Austin, J. (1976). "Do Comments on Mathematics Homework Affect Student Achievement?" *School Science and Mathematics*, Vol. 76, No. 2, pp. 159–164.

Coulter, F. (1980). "Secondary School Homework: Cooperative Research Study Report No. 7." ERIC Document No. ED 209200.

Dick, D. (1980). "An Experimental Study of the Effects of Required Homework Review Versus Review on Request Upon Achievement." ERIC Document No. ED 194320.

Featherstone, H. (February 1985). "Homework." *The Harvard Education Letter*.

Walberg, H.J. (April 1985). "Homework's Powerful Effects on Learning." *Educational Leadership*, Vol. 42, No. 7, pp. 76–79.

Assessment

Research Finding: **Frequent and systematic monitoring of students' progress helps students, parents, teachers, administrators, and policymakers identify strengths and weaknesses in learning and instruction.**

Comment: Teachers find out what students already know and what they still need to learn by assessing student work. They use various means, including essays, quizzes and tests, homework, classroom questions, standardized tests, and parents' comments. Teachers can use student errors on tests and in class as early warning signals to point out and correct learning problems before they worsen. Student motivation and achievement improve when teachers provide prompt feedback on assignments.

Students generally take two kinds of tests: classroom tests and standardized tests. Classroom tests help teachers find out if what they are teaching is being learned; thus, these tests serve to evaluate both student and teacher. Standardized tests apply similar gauges to everyone in a specific grade level. By giving standardized tests, school districts can see how achievement progresses over time. Such tests also help schools find out how much of the curriculum is actually being learned. Standardized tests can also reveal problems in the curriculum itself. For example, a recent international mathematics test showed that U.S. students had encountered only 70 percent of what the test covered.

References

Freeman, D.J., et al. (1983). "Do Textbooks and Tests Define a National Curriculum in Elementary School Mathematics?" *The Elementary School Journal*, Vol. 83, No. 5, pp. 501–513.

Good, T.L., and Grouws, D.A. (1979). "The Missouri Mathematics Effectiveness Project: An Experimental Study in Fourth Grade Classrooms." *Journal of Educational Psychology*. Vol. 71, No. 3, pp. 355–362.

Rosenshine, B. (1983). "Teaching Functions in Instructional Programs." *The Elementary School Journal*, Vol. 83, No. 4, pp. 335–351.

Rutter, M. (1983). "School Effects on Pupil Progress: Research Findings and Policy Implications." In L.S. Shulman and G. Sykes (Eds.). *Handbook of Teaching and Policy* (pp. 3–41). New York: Longman.

Stallings, J.A., and Kaskowitz, D. (1974). *Follow Through Classroom Observation Evaluation*, 1972–73. Menlo Park, CA: Stanford Research Institute. ERIC Document No. ED 104969.

Effective Schools

Research Finding: **The most important characteristics of effective schools are strong instructional leadership, a safe and orderly climate, school-wide emphasis on basic skills, high teacher expectations for student achievement, and continuous assessment of pupil progress.**

Comment: One of the most important achievements of education research in the last 20 years has been identifying the factors that characterize effective schools, in particular the schools that have been especially successful in teaching basic skills to children from low-income families. Analysts first uncovered these characteristics when comparing the achievement levels of students from different urban schools. They labeled the schools with the highest achievement as "effective schools."

Schools with high student achievement and morale show certain characteristics:

★ vigorous instructional leadership,

★ a principal who makes clear, consistent, and fair decisions,

★ an emphasis on discipline and a safe and orderly environment,

★ instructional practices that focus on basic skills and academic achievement,

★ collegiality among teachers in support of student achievement,

★ teachers with high expectations that all their students can and will learn, and

★ frequent review of student progress.

Effective schools are places where principals, teachers, students, and parents agree on the goals, methods, and content of schooling. They are united in recognizing the importance of a coherent curriculum, public recognition for students who succeed, promoting a sense of school pride, and protecting school time for learning.

References

Bossert, S. (May 1985). "Effective Elementary Schools." In R. Kyle (Ed.), *Reaching for Excellence: An Effective Schools Sourcebook*, (pp. 39–53). Washington, D.C.: U.S. Government Printing Office.

Corcoran, T. (May 1985). "Effective Secondary Schools." In R. Kyle (Ed.), *Reaching for Excellence: An Effective Schools Sourcebook*, (pp. 71–97). Washington, D.C.: U.S. Government Printing Office.

Doyle, W. (May 1985). "Effective Secondary School Practices." In R. Kyle (Ed.), *Reaching for Excellence: An Effective Schools Sourcebook* (pp. 55–70). Washington, D.C.: U.S. Government Printing Office.

Finn, C.E., Jr. (April 1984). "Toward Strategic Independence: Nine Commandments for Enhancing School Effectiveness." *Phi Delta Kappan*, Vol. 65, No. 8, pp. 513–524.

Purkey, S.C., and Smith, M.S. (March 1983). "Effective Schools: A Review." *The Elementary School Journal*, Vol. 83, No. 4, pp. 427–452.

School Climate

Research Finding: **Schools that encourage academic achievement focus on the importance of scholastic success and on maintaining order and discipline.**

Comment: Good schools focus sharply on learning. In effective schools, the school climate—some call it the "learning environment"—puts academics first. Principals and teachers believe they can make a difference in what students learn. Teachers and students believe each student is capable of making significant academic progress. Students understand and agree that their first priority is to learn.

School activities reinforce these attitudes. Routines discourage disorder and disruptions. Teachers and principals protect the classroom from interruptions. Academic success is expected and rewarded. Public ceremonies honor student achievement.

Incoming students know the school's reputation and experienced students affirm the value placed on learning. Teacher morale is high and turnover is low. When there are openings, principals recruit and select teachers who share the school's goals and standards.

Principals work with teachers, students, parents, and community members to develop the school's learning environment. Once established, that learning environment becomes a durable part of the school's tradition.

References

Basualdo, S.M., and Basualdo, E.A. (1980). "Models to Prevent and Deal with Disruptive Behavior(s) in the Classroom: A Review of the Literature." ERIC Document No. ED 202812.

Brookover, W.B., et al. (1979). *School Systems and Student Achievement: Schools Make a Difference*. New York: Praeger.

Coleman, J.S., Hoffer, T., and Kilgore, S. (1982). *High School Achievement: Public, Catholic and Private Schools Compared*. New York: Basic Books.

Grant, G. (Summer 1981). "The Character of Education and the Education of Character." *Daedalus*, Vol. 110, No. 3, pp. 135–149.

Grant, G. (1985). "Schools That Make an Imprint: Creating a Strong Positive Ethos." In J.H. Bunzel (Ed.), *Challenge to American Schools: The Case for Standards and Values*, (pp. 127–143). New York: Oxford University Press.

Rutter, M., et al. (1979). *Fifteen Thousand Hours: Secondary Schools and Their Effects on Children*. Cambridge: Harvard University Press.

Discipline

Research Finding: **Schools contribute to their students' academic achievement by establishing, communicating, and enforcing fair and consistent discipline policies.**

Comment: For 16 of the last 17 years, the public has identified discipline as the most serious problem facing its schools. Effective discipline policies contribute to the academic atmosphere by emphasizing the importance of regular attendance, promptness, respect for teachers and academic work, and good conduct.

Behavior and academic success go together. In one recent survey, for example, high school sophomores who got "mostly A's" had one-third as many absences or incidents of tardiness per semester as those who got "mostly D's." The same students were 25 times more likely to have their homework done and 7 times less likely to have been in trouble with the law. Good behavior as a sophomore led to better grades and higher achievement as a senior.

The discipline policies of most successful schools share these traits:

★ Discipline policies are aimed at actual problems, not rumors.

★ All members of the school community are involved in creating a policy that reflects community values and is adapted to the needs of the school.

★ Misbehavior is defined. Because not everyone agrees on what behavior is undesirable, defining problems is the first step in solving them. Students must know what kinds of behavior are acceptable and what kinds are not.

★ Discipline policies are consistently enforced. Students must know the consequences of misbehavior, and they must believe they will be treated fairly.

★ A readable and well-designed handbook is often used to inform parents and students about the school's discipline policy.

References

Brodinsky, B. (1980). "Student Discipline: Problems and Solutions." AASA Critical Issues Report. Arlington, VA: American Association of School Administrators. ERIC Document No. ED 198206.

DiPrete, T.A. (1981). *Discipline, Order, and Student Behavior in American High Schools*. Chicago: National Opinion Research Center. ERIC Document No. ED 224137.

Duke, D. L., and Jones, V.F. (1983). "Assessing Recent Efforts to Reduce Student Behavior Problems." Paper presented at

Annual Meeting of the American Educational Research Association, Montreal, Canada. ERIC Document No. ED 233440.

Goldsmith, A.H. (February 14, 1982). "Codes of Discipline: Developments, Dimensions, Directions. *Education and Urban Society* (pp. 185–195). ERIC Document No. ED 260932.

Myers, D., et al. (1985). "Student Discipline and High School Performance." Paper presented at the Annual Meeting of the American Education Research Association, Chicago.

Unexcused Absences

Research Finding: **Unexcused absences decrease when parents are promptly informed that their children are not attending school.**

Comment: Absences are a major problem at all levels of school. Students who miss a lesson lose an opportunity to learn. Too many missed opportunities can result in failure, dropping out of school, or both. Research indicates parents want to hear promptly if their children have poor grades, are creating discipline problems, or have unexcused absences.

Schools have different ways of letting parents know when their children aren't in school. Some use staff members to check attendance records and phone the parents of absent students. Others have begun using automatic calling devices that leave a recorded message with parents. The usual message is a request to contact the school about the absence. These devices can be programmed to call back if no answer is received. Schools using such devices report substantial increases in attendance.

Good attendance in school is another example of the connection of time and learning. Just as homework amplifies learning, regular attendance exposes students to a greater amount of academic content and instruction. Students, of course, must concentrate on their lessons in order to benefit from attendance.

References

Brodinsky, B. (1980). "Student Discipline: Problems and Solutions." AASA Critical Issues Report. Arlington, VA: American Association of School Administrators. ERIC Document No. ED 198206.

Collins, C.H., Moses, O. and Cross, M. (1982). *The Home-School Connection: Selected Partnership Programs in Large Cities.* Boston: Institute for Responsive Education.

deJung, J., and Duckworth, K. (Spring 1985). "Study Looks at Student Absences in High Schools." *Outlook.* Eugene, OR: College of Education, Division of Educational Policy and Management, University of Oregon.

Gotts, E.E. (No Date). "Ways That Effective Home-School Communications Change Across Grade Levels." Charleston, WV: Appalachia Educational Laboratory (mimeographed).

Effective Principals

Research Finding: **Successful principals establish policies that create an orderly environment and support effective instruction.**

Comment: Effective principals have a vision of what a good school is and systematically strive to bring that vision to life in their schools. School improvement is their constant theme. They scrutinize existing practices to assure that all activities and procedures contribute to the quality of the time available for learning. They make sure teachers participate actively in this process. Effective principals, for example, make opportunities available for faculty to improve their own teaching and classroom management skills.

Good school leaders protect the school day for teaching and learning. They do this by keeping teachers' administrative chores and classroom interruptions to a minimum.

Effective principals visibly and actively support learning. Their practices create an orderly environment. Good principals make sure teachers have the necessary materials and the kind of assistance they need to teach well.

Effective principals also build morale in their teachers. They help teachers create a climate of achievement by encouraging new ideas; they also encourage teachers to help formulate school teaching policies and select textbooks. They try to develop community support for the school, its faculty, and its goals.

In summary, effective principals are experts at making sure time is available to learn, and at ensuring that teachers and students make the best use of that time.

References

Bird, T., and Little, J.W. (1985). *Instructional Leadership in Eight Secondary Schools.* Final Report to the U.S. Department of Education, National Institute of Education, Boulder, CO: Center for Action Research. (Available from ERIC).

Bossert, S. (May 1985). "Effective Elementary Schools." In R. Kyle (Ed.), *Reaching for Excellence: An Effective Schools Sourcebook* (pp. 45–49). Washington, D.C.: U.S. Government Printing Office.

Carnine, D.R., Gersten, R., and Green, S. (December 1982). "The Principal as Instructional Leader: A Second Look." *Educational Leadership,* Vol. 40, No. 3, pp. 47–50.

Corcoran, T. (May 1985). "Effective Elementary Schools." In R. Kyle (Ed.), *Reaching for Excellence: An Effective Schools Sourcebook* (pp. 82–85). Washington, D.C.: U.S. Government Printing Office.

Educational Leadership. (February 1984). Entire Issue.

Morris, V.C., et al. (1984). *Principals in Action: The Reality of Managing Schools.* Columbus, OH: Charles E. Merrill Publishing Co.

Collegiality

Research Findings: **Students benefit academically when their teachers share ideas, cooperate in activities, and assist one another's intellectual growth.**

Comment: Although high student achievement is most likely in a school with high faculty morale and a sense of shared responsibility, most teachers are independent and believe that the responsibility of running their classrooms is theirs alone. In some studies, as many as 45 percent of the teachers report no contact with each other during the workday; another 32 percent say they have infrequent contact.

As a result, these teachers fail to share experience and ideas or to get support from their colleagues. Isolation may undermine effective instruction.

Good instruction flourishes when teachers collaborate in developing goals that emphasize student achievement. Effective schools have a climate of staff collegiality and use mutual support as a means of improving pupil achievement. School leaders in such schools set aside time for faculty interaction and provide specific opportunities for teachers and administrators to work together on such tasks as setting school policies, improving instructional practice, selecting textbooks, and strengthening discipline.

References

Glidewell, J., et al. (1983). "Professional Support Systems: The Teaching Profession." In A. Nadler, J. Fisher, and B. DePaulo, (Eds.), *Applied Research in Help-Seeking And Reactions to Aid.* New York: Academic Press.

Little, J.W. (1982). "Norms of Collegiality and Experimentation: Workplace Conditions of School Success." *American Educational Research Journal*, Vol. 19, No. 3, pp. 325–340.

Lortie, D. (1975). *Schoolteacher: A Sociological Study.* Chicago: University of Chicago Press.

Phi Delta Kappa. (1980). *Why Do Some Urban Schools Succeed? The Phi Delta Kappa Study of Exceptional Urban Elementary Schools.* Bloomington, IN: Phi Delta Kappa.

Tye, K.A., and Tye, B.B. (1984). "Teacher Isolation and School Reform." *Phi Delta Kappan*, Vol. 65, No. 5, pp. 319–322.

Teacher Supervision

Research Finding: **Teachers welcome professional suggestions about improving their work, but they rarely receive them.**

Comment: When supervisors comment constructively on teachers' specific skills, they help teachers become more effective and improve teachers' morale. Yet, typically, a supervisor visits a teacher's classroom only once a year and makes only general comments about the teacher's performance. This relative lack of specific supervision contributes to low morale, teacher absenteeism, and high faculty turnover.

Supervision that strengthens instruction and improves teachers' morale has these elements:

★ agreement between supervisor and teacher on the specific skills and practices that characterize effective teaching,

★ frequent observation by the supervisor to see if the teacher is using these skills and practices,

★ a meeting between supervisor and teacher to discuss the supervisor's impressions,

★ agreement by the supervisor and teacher on areas for improvement, and

★ a specific plan for improvement, jointly constructed by teacher and supervisor.

Principals who are good supervisors make themselves available to help teachers. They make teachers feel they can come for help without being branded failures.

References

Bird, T. and Little, J.W. *1985). "Instructional Leadership in Eight Secondary Schools." Final Report to the National Institute of Education. Boulder, CO: Center for Action Research.

Fielding, G.D., and Schalock, H.D. (1985). *Promoting the Professional Development of Teachers and Administrators.* Eugene, OR: ERIC Clearinghouse on Educational Management.

Natriello, G. (1984). "Teachers' Perceptions of the Frequency of Evaluation and Assessments of Their Effort and Effectiveness." *American Educational Research Journal*, Vol. 21, No. 3, pp. 579–595.

Natriello, G., and Dornbusch, S.M. (1981). "Pitfalls in the Evaluation of Teachers by Principals." *Administrator's Notebook*, Vol. 29, No. 6, pp. 1–4.

Wise, A.E., et al. (1984). *Teacher Evaluation: A Study of Effective Practices.* Santa Monica, CA: Rand Corporation. ERIC Document No. ED 246559.

Cultural Literacy

Research Findings: **Students read more fluently and with greater understanding if they have background knowledge of the past and present. Such knowledge and understanding is called cultural literacy.**

Comment: Students' background knowledge determines how well they grasp the meaning of what they read. For example, students read passages more deftly when the passages describe events, people, and places of which the students have some prior knowledge. The more culturally literate students are, the better prepared they will be to read and understand serious books, magazines, and other challenging material.

Most school teachers, college professors, journalists, and social commentators agree that the general background knowledge of American students is too low and getting lower. Surveys document great gaps in students' basic knowledge of geography, history, literature, politics, and democratic principles. Teaching is hindered if teachers cannot count on their students sharing a body of knowledge, references, and symbols.

Every society maintains formal and informal mechanisms to transmit understanding of its history, literature, and political institutions from one generation to the next. A shared knowledge of these elements of our past helps foster social cohesion and a sense of national community and pride.

In the United States, the national community comprises diverse groups and traditions; together they have created a rich cultural heritage. Cultural literacy not only enables students to read better and gain new knowledge; it enables them to understand the shared heritage, institutions, and values that draw Americans together.

References

Anderson, R.C., Soiro, R.J., and Montague, W. (1977). *Schooling and the Acquisition of Knowledge*. Hillsdale, NJ: Erlbaum Associates.

Finn, C.E., Jr., Ravitch, D., and Roberts, P. (Eds.) (1985). *Challenges to the Humanities*. New York: Holmes and Meier.

Hirsch, E.D., Jr. (Spring 1983). "Cultural Literacy." *The American Scholar*, Vol. 52, pp. 159–169.

Hirsch, E.D., Jr. (Summer 1985). "Cultural Literacy and the Schools." *American Educator*, Vol. 9, pp. 8–15.

Levine, A. (1980). *When Dreams and Heroes Died: A Portrait of Today's College Student*. San Francisco: Jossey-Bass, Inc.

Resnick, D.B., and Resnick, L.B. (August 1977). "The Nature of Literacy: An Historical Exploration." *Harvard Educational Review*, Vol. 47, No. 5, pp. 370–385.

History

Research Finding: **Skimpy requirements and declining enrollments in history classes are contributing to a decline in students' knowledge of the past.**

Comment: Earlier generations of American students commonly learned the history of American institutions, politics, and systems of government, as well as some of the history of Greece, Rome, Europe, and the rest of the world. Today, most States require the study of only American history and other course work in social studies. Indications are that students now know and understand less about history.

In most State requirements for high school graduation, a choice is offered between history on the one hand and courses in social science and contemporary social issues on the other. Most high school students, even those in the academic track, take only one history course. Students enroll in honors courses in history at less than half the rate they enroll for honors courses in English and science. Typically, requirements have also declined for writing essays, producing research-based papers, and reading original sources. Similar declines are reported in the requirements for such reasoning skills as evaluating sources of information, drawing conclusions, and constructing logical arguments.

As a result, students know too little about the past. The National Assessment of Education Progress has pilot-tested the knowledge of 17-year-olds about American history. The preliminary results

of this study, due for release in 1987, indicate that two-thirds of the students tested could not place the Civil War within the period 1850-1900; half could not identify Winston Churchill or Stalin.

The decline in the study of history may hinder students from gaining an historical perspective on contemporary life.

References

Fitzgerald, F. (1979). *America Revised: History School Books in the Twentieth Century*. Boston: Atlantic Little-Brown.

Owings, J.A. (1985). "History Credits Earned by 1980 High School Sophomores Who Graduated in 1982." *High School and Beyond Tabulation*. Washington, D.C.: National Center for Education Statistics.

Ravitch, D. (November 17, 1985). "Decline and Fall of Teaching History." *New York Times Magazine*, pp. 50–52; 101; 117.

Ravitch, D. (1985). "From History to Social Studies." In *The Schools We Deserve: Reflections on the Educational Crisis of Our Times* (pp. 112–132). New York: Basic Books.

Shaver, J.P., Davis, O.L., Jr., and Helburn, S.W. (February 1979). "The Status of Social Studies Education: Impressions from Three NSF Studies." *Social Education*, Vol. 43, No. 2, pp. 150–153.

Thernstrom, S. (1985). "The Humanities and Our Cultural Challenge." In C.E. Finn, D. Ravitch, and P. Roberts (Eds.), *Challenges to the Humanities*: New York: Holmes and Meier.

Foreign Language

Research Finding: **The best way to learn a foreign language in school is to start early and to study it intensively over many years.**

Comment: The percentage of high school students studying foreign language declined from 73 percent in 1915 to 15 percent in 1979. Some States and schools are beginning to emphasize foreign language study. However, even with this new emphasis, most students who take a foreign language study it for 2 years or less in high school and do not learn to communicate with it effectively.

Students are most likely to become fluent in a foreign language if they begin studying it in elementary school and continue studying it for 6 to 8 years. Although older students may learn foreign languages faster than younger ones, students who start early are likely to become more proficient and to speak with a near-native accent.

"Total immersion" language study programs in the United States and Canada that begin instruction in the early grades and teach all subjects in the foreign language have been highly successful in teaching all students both the language and regular academic subjects.

If new foreign language requirements are really to improve students' language competence, experience has shown that schools will need to:

★ find qualified teachers,

★ set consistent goals,

★ select appropriate materials, and

★ continue a coherent program of instruction from elementary to junior to senior high school.

References

Eddy, P.A. (1981). "The Effect of Foreign Language Study in High School on Verbal Ability as Measured by the Scholastic Aptitude Test-Verbal." Washington, D.C.: Final Report of the Center for Applied Linguistics. ERIC Document No. ED 196312.

Grittner, F.M. (1981). "Teaching Issues in Foreign Language Education: Current Status and Future Directions for Research." Madison, WI: Department of Public Instruction. ERIC Document No. ED 203711.

Hortas, C.R. (1984). "Foreign Languages and Humane Learning." In C.E. Finn, D. Ravitch, and R.T. Fancher (Eds.), *Against Mediocrity: The Humanities in America's High Schools*. New York: Holmes and Meier.

Krashen, S.D., Long, M.A., and Scarella, R.C. (December 1979). "Age, Rate, and Eventual Attainment in Second Language Acquisition." *TESOL Quarterly*, Vol. 13, No. 4, pp. 573–582.

Stern, H.H., and Cummins, J. (1981), "Language/Teaching/Learning Research: A Canadian Perspective on Status and Directions." In J.K. Phillips (Ed.), *Action for the '80's: A Political, Professional, and Public Program for Foreign Language Education*. Skokie, IL: National Textbook Co.

Vigorous Courses

Research Finding: **The stronger the emphasis on academic courses, the more advanced the subject matter, and the more rigorous the textbooks, the more high school students learn. Subjects that are learned mainly in school rather than at home, such as science and math, are most influenced by the number and kind of courses taken.**

Comment: Students often handicap their intellectual growth by avoiding difficult courses. In order to help young people make wise course choices, schools are increasingly requiring students to take courses that match their grade level and abilities; schools are also seeing to it that the materials used in those courses are intellectually challenging.

The more rigorous the course of study, the more a student achieves, within the limits of his capacity. Student achievement also depends on how much the school emphasizes a subject and the amount of time spent on it: the more time expended, the higher the achievement. Successful teachers encourage their students' best efforts.

References

Chall, J., Conard, S., and Harris, S. (1977). *An Analysis of Textbooks in Relation to Declining SAT Scores*. New York: College Entrance Examination Board.

Ginsburg, A., Baker, K., and Sweet, D. (1981). "Summer Learning and the Effects of Schooling: A Replication of Heyns." Paper presented at the Annual Meeting of the American Educational Research Association, Los Angeles, CA. ERIC Document No. ED 204367.

Holsinger, D. (1981). "Time, Content and Expectations as Predictors of School Achievement in the USA and Other Developed Countries: A Review of IEA Evidence." Paper presented to the National Commission on Excellence in Education, New York, ERIC Document No. ED 227077.

Pallas, A.M., and Alexander, K.L. (Summer 1983). "Sex Differences in Quantitative SAT Performance: New Evidence on the Differential Coursework Hypothesis." *American Educational Research Journal*, Vol. 20, No. 2, pp. 165–182.

Walberg, H.J., and Shanahan, T. (1983). "High School Effects on Individual Students." *Educational Researcher*, Vol. 12, No. 7, pp. 4–9.

Acceleration

Research Finding: **Advancing gifted students at a faster pace results in their achieving more than similarly gifted students who are taught at a normal rate.**

Comment: Advocates of accelerating the education of gifted and talented students believe that this practice furnishes the extra challenge these students need to realize their full potential. Critics believe acceleration may result in emotional and social stress if a child is unable to get along with older students. Some, concerned about those who remain behind, characterize acceleration as unfair or undemocratic.

Research evidence generally supports acceleration. When abler students are moved ahead in school, they typically learn more in less time than students of the same age and ability who are taught at the conventional rate. Accelerated students score a full grade level or more higher on achievement tests than their conventionally placed schoolmates. Some may score several years ahead of their schoolmates.

Acceleration does not damage students' attitudes about school subjects. Nor do accelerated students necessarily become drudges or bookworms; they ordinarily continue to participate in extracurricular activities. Such students often become more sure about their occupational goals.

Accelerated students perform as well as talented but older students in the same grade. Despite being younger, accelerated students are able to capitalize on their abilities and achieve beyond the level available to them had they remained in the lower grade.

References

Cohn, S.J., George, W.C., and Stanley, J.C. (Eds.) (1979). "Educational Acceleration of Intellectually Talented Youths: Prolonged Discussion by a Varied Group of Professionals." In W.C. George, S.J. Cohn, and J.E. Stanley (Eds.), *Educating the Gifted: Acceleration and Enrichment*, (pp. 183–238). Baltimore: Johns Hopkins University Press.

Getzels, J.W., and Dillon, J.T. (1973). "The Nature of Giftedness and the Education of the Gifted." In R.M.W. Travers (Ed.), *Second Handbook of Research on Teaching*, (pp. 689–731). Chicago: Rand McNally.

Goldberg, M. (1958). "Recent Research on the Talented." *Teachers' College Record*, Vol. 60, No. 3, pp. 150–163.

Gowan, J., and Demos, G.D. (1964). *The Education and Guidance of the Ablest*. Springfield, IL: Charles C. Thomas.

Kulik, J.A., and Kulik, C.C. (1984). "Synthesis of Research on Effects of Accelerated Instruction." *Educational Leadership*, Vol. 42, No. 2, pp. 84–89.

Extracurricular Activities

Research Finding: **High school students who complement their academic studies with extracurricular activities gain experience that contributes to their success in college.**

Comment: High school class rank and test scores are the best predictors of academic success in college, but involvement sustained over time in one or two extracurricular activities contributes to overall achievement in college. On the other hand, when these activities become ends in themselves, academic performance may suffer.

Students who participate in extracurricular activities gain some significant advantages. Among them are

★ opportunities for recognition, personal success, and broader experience to complement their academic achievement,

★ the chance to develop intellectual, social, cultural, and physical talents to round out their academic education, and

★ the opportunity to extend the boundaries of the classroom by acquiring direct experience with the content and worth of a subject; for example, when drama club members study and present the plays of Shakespeare, or when debaters gain practice in applied logic, research, and public presentations.

Although such activities as athletics are less clearly related to academic goals, they do provide opportunities for physical growth and self-discipline. Indeed, all these activities can extend the range of experience that schools can offer.

But when extracurricular activities get out of balance, problems can arise, as when high school athletes treat sports as an alternative to learning rather than an addition to it. Distracted by the prestige they earn in sports, student athletes may fail to prepare adequately for the academic requirements of college or the workplace. This situation has worsened in recent years, and many abuses have come to light, such as lowering (or winking at) the academic requirements for sports eligibility. There have been recent attempts to rectify this situation by reinstating academic criteria as a condition for participation in all extracurricular activities.

References

Braddock, J.H., II. (1981). "Race, Athletics, and Educational Attainment." *Youth and Society*, Vol. 12, No. 3, pp. 335–350.

Purdy, D., Eitzen, D.S., and Hufnagel, R. (1982). "Are Athletes Students? The Educational Attainment of College Athletes." *Social Problems*, Vol. 79, No. 4, pp. 439–448.

Spady, W. (1970). "Lament for the Letterman: Effects of Peer Status and Extracurricular Activities on Goals and Achievement." *American Journal of Sociology*, Vol. 75, No. 4, pp. 680–702.

Spady, W. (1971). "Status, Achievement, and Motivation in the American High School." *School Review*, Vol. 79, No. 3, pp. 379–403.

Willingham, W.W. (1985). *Success in College: The Role of Personal Qualities and Academic Ability*. New York: College Board Publications.

Preparation for Work

Research Finding: **Business leaders report that students with solid basic skills and positive work attitudes are more likely to find and keep jobs than students with vocational skills alone.**

Comment: As new technologies make old job skills obsolete, the best vocational education will be solid preparation in reading, writing, mathematics, and reasoning. In the future, American workers will acquire many of their job skills in the workplace, not in school. They will need to be able to master new technologies and upgrade their skills to meet specialized job demands. Men and women who have weak basic skills, or who cannot readily master new skills to keep pace with change, may be only marginally employed over their lifetimes.

Business leaders recommend that schools raise academic standards. They point to the need for remedial programs to help low-achieving students and to reduce dropping out.

Business leaders stress that the school curriculum should emphasize literacy, mathematics, and problem-solving skills. They believe schools should emphasize such personal qualities as self-discipline, reliability, perseverance, teamwork, accepting responsibility, and respect for the rights of others. These characteristics will serve all secondary students well, whether they go on to college or directly into the world of work.

References

Center for Public Resources. (1982). *Basic Skills in the U.S. Work Force: The Contrasting Perceptions of Business, Labor, and Public Education*. New York.

Committee for Economic Development. (1985). *Investing in Our Children: Businesses and the Public Schools: A Statement*. New York and Washington, D.C.

National Academy of Science, National Academy of Engineering, Institute of Medicine, and Committee on Science, Engineering and Public Policy. (1984). *High Schools and the Changing Workplace: The Employer's View*. Washington, D.C.: National Academy Press.

National Advisory Council on Vocational Education. (1984). *Conference Summary: Vocational Education and Training Policy for Today and Tomorrow*. Washington, D.C.

Zemsky, R., and Meyerson, M. (1986). *The Training Impulse*. New York: McGraw Hill.

What Influences Learning?
A Content Analysis of Review Literature

Wang, M. C., G. D. Haertel, and H. J. Walberg. 1990. *Journal of Educational Research* 84(1):30–43.

Abstract

This paper reported a comprehensive "meta-review" and synthesis of research on variables related to learning, including both cognitive and affective schooling outcomes.[1] A conceptual framework was developed encompassing 228 items related to school learning, organized a priori into 30 scales within six categories. Search and selection procedures yielded 179 selected handbook and annual review chapters, commissioned papers, and other authoritative reviews. Content analysis yielded over 3,700 ratings of the strength of influence of the variables on learning. The variables confirmed the primacy of student, classroom, home, and community influences on learning relative to more distal policy variables such as state and district characteristics. Additionally, the variables also highlighted the importance of metacognition, classroom management, quantity of instruction, classroom interactions and climate, and the peer group.

Educational research has identified a large number of variables related to school learning. Because such a multiplicity of distinct influences on achievement have been found, educators may be perplexed as to which items are most important. Educational researchers, policy makers, and practitioners all require clearer guidance concerning the relative importance of different learning influences and the particular variables most likely to maximize school learning. To address this need, we did a comprehensive review and synthesis of handbooks, review annuals, and other highly synthetic prior reviews. We characterized the most authoritative scholarly opinion about ways to optimize educational conditions and settings. This research synthesis is distinguished by its comprehensiveness, its orientation toward practical school improvement strategies, and its focus on comparing the relative contributions of different items to learning. To organize the synthesis, we developed a conceptual framework that draws heavily on major theoretical models of school learning. Before turning to this framework, we briefly describe the evolution of these earlier theoretical models.

Evolution of Models of School Learning

J. B. Carroll (1963) introduced educational researchers to models of school learning in his aptly entitled article, "A Model of School Learning" in the *Teachers College Record*. In his model, he developed six constructs: aptitude, ability to comprehend instruction, perseverance, clarity of instruction, matching the task to student characteristics, and opportunity to learn. These constructs, which succinctly capture the psychological influences on school learning, became a point of departure for other models to follow. The

1960s and 1970s were marked by the introduction of several additional important models of learning, including those of Bruner (1966), Bloom (1976), Harnischfeger and Wiley (1976), Glaser (1976), and Bennett (1978).

All of those models recognized the primary importance of student ability, and included constructs such as aptitude, prior knowledge, verbal IQ, and pupil background. Most of the models also addressed the importance of motivation, by employing such constructs as perseverance, self-concept of the learner, and attitude toward school subject matter. This acknowledgment of individual difference variables among learners contrasted with the more narrowly psychological studies of influences on learning, which generally treated individual differences as a source of error, and focused instead on instructional-treatment variables (Hilgard, 1964).

In addition to student variables, each of the models of school learning noted above also gave salience to constructs developed from studies of classroom instruction. These constructs varied in generality, some being as broad as "instructional events" or "clarity of instruction" and others as narrow as "use of cues" or "feedback and correctives."

Although later models brought some refinement in the ways in which individual difference variables and instructional variables were defined and the ways in which they were related to one another, the primary contributions of more recent models have been in extending the range of influences considered. Haertel, Walberg, and Weinstein (1983), for example, identified nine theoretical constructs that exhibit consistent causal influences on academic learning: student age or developmental level, ability (including prior achievement), motivation, amount or quantity of instruction, quality of instruction, psychological environment of the classroom, influence of the home, influence of the peer group outside of school, and exposure to mass media. The researchers showed that previous models of school learning neglected extramural and social-psychological influences.

The evolution of models of school learning was further advanced with the introduction of models of adaptive instruction (Wang & Lindvall, 1984; Wang & Walberg, 1985). School-based implementation of models of adaptive instruction are designed to help schools create learning environments that maximize each student's opportunities for success in school. The models focused on new variables associated with instructional delivery systems, program design, and implementation. Also, the models emphasized those features that Glaser (1982) referred to as the "large practical variables" and included efficient allocation and use of teacher and student time, a practical classroom management system, systematic teacher feedback and reinforcement of student learning behavior and progress, instructional interactions based on the diagnosed learning needs of individual students, and flexible administrative and organizational patterns responsive to program implementation and staffing needs.

Another contribution to models of school learning came from sociologists concerned with the identification of effective schools. Edmonds (1979) is most strongly associated with this identification of variables associated with exceptionally effective schools, especially for the urban poor. Significant contributions to effective school models also were made by Brookover (1979), Brookover and Lezotte (1979), and Rutter, Maughan, Mortimore, Ouston, and Smith (1979). Illustrations of the types of variables characterizing effective schools included degree of curriculum articulation and organization, schoolwide staff development, parental involvement and support, schoolwide recognition of academic success, maximized learning time, district support, clear goals and high expectations, orderly and disciplined school environment, and leadership of principal characterized by attention to quality of instruction (Purkey & Smith, 1983).

Those various models of school learning all contributed a variety of items, or variables, that may be useful to educational practitioners. Individual researchers may focus their work on particular variables or constructs, but the purpose of this synthesis was to try to provide a synoptic view of the entire panoply of variables.

Methods and Procedures

The first step in developing the meta-review described in this paper was to delineate a comprehensive set of variables organized into an inclusive conceptual framework. Next, we identified a corpus of over 150 books, book chapters, reports, and other sources. The 228 items in the conceptual framework were listed on a detailed, 15-page coding form, and each of the sources was then coded using that form. In all, over 2,500 pages of coding forms were completed. Each citation or discussion of an item influencing learning outcomes was coded by page number, together with a notation of the reported strength of its influence on learning. Those detailed text citations by page number were placed in an archive.[2]

The detailed ratings were then recoded onto a set of summary forms, one for each chapter or other source, which gave overall ratings of strength of influence for each of the items discussed in that source. Those summary ratings were entered into machine-readable files and analyzed to determine the emergent consensus on which items exert the most powerful influence on learning outcomes. The initial coding tabulated well over 10,000 separate statements in the research literature concerning the strength of association between 1 of the 228 items and learning outcomes. Those statements were reduced to over 3,700 summary ratings, which were then keyed and analyzed.[3]

The development of the conceptual framework, selection of the corpus of studies, and coding procedures are described briefly below.

Conceptual framework for items related to learning. The identification of a comprehensive set of items began with a close examination of the models of school learning described above, as well as selected sources, including Brophy (1986), Keogh, Major-Kingsley, Omori-Gordon, and Reid (1982), Wang and Walberg (1985), and Wittrock (1986). Potential variables were written on separate index cards, then consolidated and organized into a preliminary version of the final coding scheme. This draft coding scheme was sent to members of the Scientific Advisory Panel of the Center for Research in Human Development and Education at Temple University.[4] Based on detailed commentaries received from the panel members, the framework was revised to include four additional items and to improve its organization.

The final framework organized the 228 items related to learning into 30 a priori scales within six broad categories. The six categories were ordered roughly from more distal to more proximal factors. Brief descriptions of the categories are presented in Figure 1, together with illustrative items from each scale.

Selection of a corpus of studies. A vast research literature addresses one or more of the potential learning influences represented by the conceptual framework, and one could not possibly examine all of the thousands of original studies relevant to a synthesis of this scope. Even the literature of *review* articles is massive. For this reason, we focused on authoritative reviews and handbook chapters, especially those sponsored by the American Educational Research Association and other organizations, and we selected additional syntheses in government documents and other sources. A preliminary list of sources was reviewed by the Scientific Advisory Panel and revised following their recommendations. Following this review, the sources chosen included chapters from the past decade or more of the *Review of Research in Education*, the *Annual Review of Psychology*, and the *Annual Review of Sociology*, as well as the *Handbook of Research on Teaching* (Wittrock, 1986), *Designs for Compensatory Education* (Williams, Richmond, & Mason, 1986), more specialized handbooks, and a small number of journal articles chosen to ensure coverage of all of the areas addressed in the comprehensive framework. Initially, over 200 articles, chapters, and other sources were identified. All of those sources were read, but some were excluded from the final corpus because they failed to address kindergarten through grade 12 instruction in regular school settings, because they addressed exceptionally narrow and atypical learning outcomes, or because they were relevant only to rare or special learner populations.

A total of 179 sources were included in the final corpus of studies (see Appendix at the end of this article for a complete bibliography). All of those sources were relevant to a range of cognitive and affective learning outcomes for kindergarten through grade 12 learners in formal educational settings. Table 1 presents a summary by type of the source documents included in the final synthesis.

Coding procedures. Each source document was coded initially onto a detailed rating form, which allowed the recording of multiple references in a single document to the same item. In addition to coding references to the 228

Figure 1. Conceptual Framework with Illustrative Examples

Category/Subcategory[a] **Illustrative Variable**

Category 1. State and District Variables: These variables are associated with state- and district-level school governance and administration. They include state curriculum and textbook policies, testing and graduation requirements, and teacher licensure, as well as specific provisions in teacher contracts, and some district-level administrative and fiscal variables.

District-Level Demographics and Marker	School district size
State-Level Policy	Teacher licensure requirements

Category 2. Out-of-School Contextual Variables: These variables are associated with the home and community contexts within which schools function. They include community demographics, peer culture, parental support and involvement, and amount of time students spend out of school on such activities as television viewing, leisure reading, and homework.

Community	Socioeconomic level of community
Peer-Group	Level of peers' academic aspirations
Home Environment and Parental Support	Parental involvement in assuring completion of homework
Student Use of Out-of-School Time	Student participation in clubs and extracurricular school activities

Category 3. School-Level Variables: These variables are associated with school-level demographics, culture, climate, policies, and practices. They include demographics of the student body, whether the school is public or private, and levels of funding for specific categorical programs; school-level decision-making variables, and specific school-level policies and practices, including policies on parental involvement in the school.

Demographic and Marker	Size of school
Teacher/Administrator Decision-Making	Principal actively concerned with instructional program
School Culture (Ethos conducive to teaching and learning)	School-wide emphasis on and recognition of academic achievement
School-Wide Policy and Organization	Explicit school-wide discipline policy
Accessibility	Accessibility of educational program (overcoming architectural, communication, and environmental barriers)
Parental Involvement Policy	Parental involvement in improvement and operation of instructional program

Category 4. Student Variables: These variables are associated with individual students, including demographics, academic history, and a variety of social, behavioral, motivational, cognitive, and affective characteristics.

Demographic and Marker	Gender
History of Educational Placement	Prior grade retentions
Social and Behavioral	Positive, nondisruptive behavior
Motivational and Affective	Attitude toward subject matter instructed
Cognitive	Level of specific academic knowledge in subject area instructed
Metacognitive	Comprehension monitoring (planning: monitoring effectiveness of attempted actions, monitoring outcomes of actions; testing, revising, and evaluating learning strategies)
Psychomotor	Psychomotor skills specific to area instructed

Category 5. Program Design Variables: These variables are associated with instruction as designed and with the physical arrangements for its delivery. They include the instructional strategies specified by the curriculum and characteristics of instructional materials.

Demographic and Marker	Size of instructional group (whole class, small group, one-on-one instruction)
Curriculum and Instructional	Alignment among goals, contents, instruction, assignments, and evaluation
Curriculum Design	Materials employ advance organizers

Category 6. Implementation, Classroom Instruction, and Climate Variables: These variables are associated with the implementation of the curriculum and the instructional program. They include classroom routines and practices, characteristics of instruction as delivered, classroom management, monitoring of student progress, and quality and quantity of instruction provided, as well as student-teacher interactions and classroom climate.

Classroom Implementation Support	Establishing efficient classroom routines and communicating rules and procedures
Classroom Instructional	Use of clear and organized direct instruction
Quantity of Instruction	Time on task (amount of time students are actively engaged in learning)
Classroom Assessment	Use of assessment as a frequent, integral component of instruction
Classroom Management	Group alerting (teacher uses questioning/recitation strategies that maintain active participation by all students)
Student and Teacher Interactions: Social	Student responds positively to questions from other students and from teacher
Student and Teacher Interactions: Academic	Frequent calls for extended, substantive oral and written response (not one-word answers)
Classroom Climate	Cohesiveness (members of class are friends sharing common interests and values and emphasizing cooperative goals)

[a]Subcategories are listed below the description of each broad category and are each illustrated with representative variables. For example, the first broad category includes two subcategories, "District-Level Demographics and Marker Variables" and "State-Level Policy Variables."

prespecified items, space was provided for the coding of any additional items related to learning outcomes, referred to on the form as supplementary items. Brief notes also were recorded for most sources, including page references, comments on the source's overall relevance, and any limitations on the learner populations or varieties of learning outcomes addressed. This archived documentation has been retained by the first author.

Each reference to an item's relation to learning outcomes was coded on a 3-point scale, with 1 representing a weak, uncertain, or inconsistent relation to learning, 2 representing a moderate relation, and 3 representing a strong relation. Where "vote counts" or proportions of confining studies were reported, a 3 indicated that more than 80% of the studies discussed had found a statistically significant association of an item to achievement, a 2 indicated that between 40% and 80% of the studies found support for the relationship, and a 1 indicated less than 40% in support. Where results were summarized in terms of effect sizes, we assigned a code of 3 to effect sizes greater than .33, 2 to effect sizes of .10 to .33, and 1 for smaller effect sizes. Where correlations were reported, we used 3 for correlations greater than .40, 2 for correlations of .15 to .40, and 1 otherwise.

In many cases, the source documents did not present quantitative indices like effect sizes or correlations, so we had to judge the strength of the evidence presented from prose descriptions of the conclusions from bodies of research. In those cases, the strength of the evidence presented was judged weak, moderate, or strong, and coded accordingly. Even though all of the 228 items were defined in such a way that they were expected to relate positively to learning, in rare instances the literature reported negative conclusions.[5]

Following the coding of all specific references by page number, we transcribed ratings onto a second summary form for each source, prior to keying for data analysis. At this stage, a single summary code—the average of all the ratings for each source document—was recorded indicating the strength of association for each item discussed in the source, according to the preponderance of the specific references noted.[6]

Data Analysis

After inspecting univariate frequency distributions for each of the 228 separate items to ensure that no values were out of range, we aggregated the separate items to the level of the 30 scales described in Figure 1. We accomplished this procedure by taking the average of all nonmissing values in a scale, for each source. In cases where a source document did not discuss any of the separate items in a scale, we entered a missing data code. In those rare cases where negative findings were coded, we retained their negative signs when averages were taken.

In a second stage of data reduction, six additional variables were created corresponding to the categories described in Figure 1. The values of those variables for each source were weighted averages of all nonmissing scale

Table 1. Number and Percentage of Source Documents by Type

Type of source[a]	N	%	Total pages
Chapters for annual review series	86	48	3,179
Handbook chapters	44	25	1,089
Government documents and commissioned reports	20	11	772
Book chapters	18	10	563
Review articles in journals	11	6	152
Total	179	100	5,755

values comprising that category.[7] Means, standard deviations, and alpha reliabilities for the six categories and 30 scales are presented in Table 2. The reliabilities for documents (not raters) ranged from .71 to .99; all but four were greater than .80 and most exceeded .90.[8]

Table 2 also reports the number of sources that discussed items in each scale. Surprisingly, the frequency with which different scale items are discussed in the literature was not a reliable guide to their importance for learning outcomes. The Spearman rank correlation between frequencies and means across the 30 scales was only .10.

Summary of Results

Table 2 presents the importance of many distinct influences on school learning outcomes. Over all 30 scales, the mean rating was roughly 1.8, a little below the level designated "moderate relation to learning." More important, however, the synthesis shows which categories, scales, and specific items are most strongly associated with learning outcomes. In discussing results by category and by scale, we presented relevant findings concerning specific items to clarify or elaborate the category- and scale-level findings reported in Table 2.

At the highest level of generality, this synthesis confirmed the importance of the quality of schooling for learning outcomes. Of the six categories, the highest ratings overall were assigned to Program Design Variables, followed by Out-of-School Contextual Variables. The category reflecting the quality of instruction as delivered, Classroom Instruction and Climate Variables, ranked third in importance, closely followed by Student Variables. The last two categories, School-Level Variables and State and District Variables, received markedly lower ratings overall. This overall ranking of sources of influence contrasted sharply with the "conventional wisdom" because the Equality of Educational Opportunity (EEO) Survey (Coleman et al., 1966) stated that quality of schooling has relatively little impact on schooling outcomes relative to out-of-school socioeconomic variables.

The importance of proximal psychological variables may be seen in the scales that obtained the highest ratings.[9]

Table 2. Reliabilities, Means, Standard Deviations, and Frequencies for Source Ratings

Category/subcategory	Reliability[a]	M	SD	Frequency
State and district variables	.90	1.22	.81	27
District demographics and marker	.95	1.46	.50	14
State-level policy	N.C.	1.24	1.00	19
Out-of-school contextual variables	.99	1.87	.39	59
Community	N.C.	1.80	.41	15
Peer-group	.98	2.00	.34	18
Home environment and parental support	.95	1.90	.40	47
Student use of out-of-school time	N.C.	1.94	.46	17
School-level variables	.95	1.54	.96	102
Demographics and marker	.91	1.74	.56	25
Teacher/administrator decision making	.87	1.65	.95	21
School culture	.87	1.84	.43	49
School-wide policies and organization	.76	1.40	1.14	74
Accessibility	N.C.	2.00	.00	2
Parental involvement policy	N.C.	1.67	.56	23
Student variables	.92	1.83	.57	155
Demographics and marker	.71	1.70	.77	90
History of educational placements	N.C.	.16	1.80	19
Social and behavioral	.80	1.98	.34	35
Motivational and affective	.91	1.93	.42	81
Cognitive	.88	1.98	.33	101
Metacognitive	.91	2.08	.36	76
Psychomotor	N.C.	2.33	.52	6
Program design variables	.90	1.90	.38	142
Demographic and marker	N.C.	1.97	.54	23
Curriculum and instruction	.90	1.92	.46	108
Curriculum design	.89	1.88	.34	97
Classroom instruction and climate variables	.97	1.84	.66	165
Classroom implementation support	.85	1.84	.38	66
Classroom instructional	.89	1.85	.74	156
Quantity of instruction	.94	2.02	.64	69
Classroom assessment	N.C.	1.89	.30	61
Classroom management	.98	2.07	.23	42
Student/teacher interactions: social	.73	2.02	.41	44
Student/teacher interactions: academic	.77	1.89	.44	29
Classroom climate	.99	2.01	.38	75

[a]Coefficient alpha reliabilities were estimated for each scale from average variances and inter-item covariances. Due to missing data, ratings for some cases are based on fewer items. Thus, obtained reliabilities are somewhat lower than the figures reported in this table. N.C. indicates values that were not calculable, either because scales consisted of only a single item or because of patterns of missing data.

Those scales with mean ratings of 2.00 or greater (beginning with the highest) were:

Metacognition	$X = 2.08$
Classroom management	$X = 2.07$
Quantity of instruction	$X = 2.02$
Student/teacher interactions: Social	$X = 2.02$
Classroom climate	$X = 2.01$
Peer group influences	$X = 2.00$

In the remainder of this section, the categories and scales are discussed in turn, and those scales and items that received exceptionally high ratings are highlighted. The categories representing instruction as designed and instruction as delivered are discussed first. Those categories are followed by out-of-school context and student characteristics. Finally, the more distal variable categories of school-level variables and state and district variables are addressed.

Program Design Variables

This category includes instruction as designed, and the physical arrangements for its delivery, organized into three scales, as shown in Figure 1 and Table 2. The scale Demographic and Marker Variables was rated highest of the three, and, within this scale, the most highly rated items are size of instructional group (whole class, small group, or one-on-one instruction), number of classroom aides, and resources needed. (Ratings for those items ranged from 1.95 to 2.00). Thus, the most important aspect of program design appeared to be the intensity of educational services provided to each learner. More aides, smaller groups, or increased material resources were associated with significantly higher learning outcomes.

Curriculum and Instructional Variables includes items with average ratings above 2.0 (moderate relation to learning). The highest rated of those suggest that the key to effective instructional design is the flexible and appropriate use of a variety of instructional strategies, while maintaining an orderly classroom environment. The highest overall rating in this scale was for use of . . . techniques to control classroom disruptiveness. This item was followed by use of prescriptive instruction combined with aspects of informal or open education and presence of information in the curriculum on individual differences and commonalities, both of which explicitly relate to student diversity and individualization. Other highly rated items referred to specific instructional strategies, including use of mastery learning techniques, . . . instructional cues, engagement, and corrective feedback . . . use of cooperative learning strategies, and use of diagnostic-prescriptive methods.

Curriculum Design also includes several items with average ratings near 2.0, although none exceeds the moderate level. High ratings were given to, materials employ alternative modes of representation and degree of structure in curriculum accommodates needs of different learners, both of which reinforce the importance of offering a variety of instructional materials and approaches to accommodate individual differences. The importance of the organization of curriculum content is revealed by two highest rated items in this scale, materials employ learning hierarchies and material is presented in a cognitively efficient manner.

Implementation, Classroom Instruction, and Climate Variables

This category includes support of the curriculum and the instructional program, classroom routines, specific instructional, assessment, and classroom management practices; quantity of instruction, academic and nonacademic student-teacher interaction, and classroom climate. By far the largest of the six categories, this group constitutes 79 of the 228 items and 8 of the 30 scales. Half of those scales had mean ratings above 2.00, placing them overall among the most influential scales.

High ratings in the areas of implementation, classroom instruction, and climate again highlight the importance of maintaining an orderly classroom environment and providing clear, well-organized instruction appropriate

to the needs of individual learners. In the overall ranking of all 30 scales, Classroom Management ranked second, and its most critical items were group alerting (teacher uses questioning/recitation strategies that maintain active participation by all students) and learner accountability (teacher maintains student awareness of learning goals and expectations). Smooth transitions from one instructional activity to another, minimal disruptions, and teacher awareness of classroom activity at all times also received mean ratings above 2.00.

Quantity of Instruction was ranked third overall, following Classroom Management. This included scale time spent in direct instruction, especially direct instruction on basic skills, time spent on homework, and length of the school day and year. The importance accorded quantity of instruction is not surprising. This construct has appeared in many of the most widely cited models of school learning (Haertel, Walberg, & Weinstein, 1983).

Student/teacher interactions. Social ranked fourth overall, and Classroom Climate was ranked fifth. The high ranking for social interactions was almost entirely caused by two items with mean ratings of 2.00 or greater: teacher reacts appropriately to correct and incorrect answers and student responds positively to questions from other students and from teacher.[10] Classroom climate included 15 items with ratings of 2.00 or greater. Together, the highly rated items in those two scales characterize a classroom in which teacher and students interact considerably and cooperatively, where students work with several classmates, share common interests and values, and pursue cooperative goals. In that type of classroom, students are actively engaged in learning and are involved in making some types of classroom decisions. Concurrently, the class is well organized and well planned, with a clear academic focus. Objectives of learning activities are specific and explicit, and students feel continually and appropriately challenged, with the pacing of instruction appropriate for the majority.

The remaining scales under Implementation, Classroom Instruction, and Climate Variables had much lower overall ratings, but they included more than 20 specific items with means of 2.00 or greater. The majority of those items referred to instructional organization and to mechanisms for assuring that students understand that organization and the goals of instruction. For example, high ratings were given to the use of advance organizers and directing students' attention to the content to be learned, as well as to clear and organized direct instruction, systematic sequencing of lesson events, and clear lesson transitions. Other highly rated items included corrective feedback in case of student error, frequent academic questions, and accurate measurement of skills. Finally, the literature strongly supported the teaching of skills in the context of meaningful applications, use of good examples and analogies, and teaching for meaningful understanding, together with explicit promotion of student self-monitoring of comprehension and gradual transfer of responsibility for learning from the teacher to the student.

Extramural Variables

This category included items associated with the home and community contexts within which schools function. As presented above, Peer-Group Variables was ranked sixth among all scales. This ranking was primarily caused by the emphasis placed on peers' educational and occupational aspirations, both of which had mean ratings of 2.00 or higher.

Additional highly rated items in this category reflected parental interest and involvement in students' schoolwork. For example, parental involvement in assuring completion of homework, parental participation in school conferences and related activities, and parental interest in students' schoolwork all received high ratings. The educational environment of the home (e.g., number of books and magazines) also was cited in numerous sources and received consistently high ratings. Student participation in clubs and extracurricular school activities and time spent on leisure reading also were moderately related to learning outcomes.

Student Variables

Student Variables items were associated with individual students themselves, including demographics, academic history, and various social, cognitive, and affective characteristics. Among those items, psychomotor skills specific to area instructed had the highest rating, which was 2.33. This item was the only one included in the Psychomotor Variables scale. However, as explained above, this mean was based on only six sources. This mean was best regarded as a statistical artifact and will not be further discussed.

Metacognitive Variables received the highest mean ratings of any of the remaining scales in the entire framework. Highly rated metacognitive items included comprehension monitoring (planning; monitoring effectiveness of attempted actions; testing, revising, and evaluating learning strategies), self-regulatory, self-control strategies (e.g., control of attention), and positive strategies to facilitate generalization of concepts.

Several specific items in the remaining Student Variables scales also had high ratings, including positive behavior and ability to make friends with peers, motivation for continual learning, and perseverance on learning tasks. Highly rated items from the Cognitive scale included several representing general mental abilities, levels of basic skills sufficient to profit from instruction, and prior knowledge in the subject area instructed.

School-Level and State and District Variables

Educational policy items at the school, district, and state levels appeared from this research synthesis to have relatively little association with learning outcomes, as shown by low mean ratings for categories and scales. A few items in this area received mean ratings of 2.00 or higher, but nearly all of those were based on fewer than 10 sources. Nonetheless, several school-level educational practices emerged as important. Those practices included the presence of an effective schools program, explicit school grading, academic progress, and attendance policies, and a safe and orderly school climate. Peer and cross-age tutoring, which were classified as school-level variables when their implementation required coordination among self-contained classrooms, also received moderate or higher ratings based on discussions in more than 10 sources.

Discussion

This research synthesis confirms that distal policy variables are less important to schooling outcomes than quantity and quality of instruction, home environment, or student characteristics. Of the six categories in the conceptual framework (see Figure 1 and Table 2), State and District Variables and School-Level Variables, both comprising mainly policy variables, had markedly lower mean ratings than the remaining four categories. The items most important to learning outcomes were those that were directly tied to students' engagement with the material to be learned.

In contrast to the earlier view that quality of schooling is of little importance relative to out-of-school factors (Coleman et al., 1966), our synthesis also suggests that from kindergarten through Grade 12, across a range of content areas and educational contexts, quality and quantity of instruction are roughly equal in importance to student characteristics and out-of-school contextual items.

Furthermore, the present synthesis of educational research is considerably more comprehensive than *What Works: Research About Teaching and Learning*, the widely distributed pamphlet of the U.S. Department of Education (1986), and it contains both highly effective and relatively less-effective practices. The present synthesis, moreover, draws on a larger body of literature and contains a more explicit methodology that can be replicated by other investigators. This research contains some 228 practices in comparison with 41 in the original *What Works* (and 62 in the second edition), and it gives a numerical rating to each one as well as composites. Yet none of the findings of *What Works* and the present work are discordant. *What Works* contains specific findings and elaborates on and illustrates various techniques. Such techniques are described specifically enough to be understood by parents and teachers; perhaps they might even be put into practice without assistance.

Regarding the 30 scales, those identified as most important to good learning outcomes are student metacognition, effective classroom management, quantity of instruction, positive and productive student/teacher interactions, a classroom climate conducive to learning, and a peer culture supportive of academic achievement. Those broad conclusions are supported by more specific findings from the research synthesis. Those selected findings are highlighted below.

Student characteristics. Individual differences among students have long been recognized as critical determinants of learning outcomes, but we were surprised and encouraged that in this synthesis the metacognitive items emerged as most important, including comprehension monitoring, use of self-regulatory, self-control strategies, and use of strategies to facilitate generalization of concepts. Metacognitive variables are heavily cited in the current literature, in contrast to an earlier focus on relatively stable general mental abilities. A better understanding of those alterable variables may ultimately help the great majority of students to reach higher achievement levels through appropriate training in metacognition. Two additional student items accorded importance in the research literature are perseverance on learning tasks and motivation for continual learning. Both of those factors reinforce the conclusion that consistent engagement with the subject matter to be learned is critical to school success.

Quality and quantity of instruction. Classroom management and climate and student-teacher interactions represent an important constellation of variables related to effective instruction. Detailed examination of the highly rated items in those areas reveals a portrait of cooperative, cohesive, goal-directed classrooms, in which a variety of educational approaches and activities are employed. Items heavily cited in the research literature include sound organization and systematic sequencing of instruction and effective use of direct, teacher-centered instruction. Among other instructional approaches frequently linked to positive learning outcomes are peer and cross-age tutoring and cooperative group-learning strategies.

Several items associated with quantity of instruction also emerged as important, including student time on task, length of school day and year, amount of time allocated to direct instruction in basic skills, and time spent out of school on homework and on leisure reading. Of these variables, the most frequently cited one is time on task. These time-related variables have clearly become well established and widely accepted as determinants of learning outcomes, in spite of criticisms cited by Shulman (1986) of time as an "empty vessel."

Out of school context. Researchers are giving increasing attention in the research literature to the role of parental involvement and support variables in promoting student learning. The synthesis affirms the importance of those items, as well as peer-group influences. Those findings are reflected in ratings for parental involvement in school activities, interest in schoolwork, and monitoring of school attendance and homework completion. Parental support might also be mediated through influence on students' selection of friends. Peer group variables, especially academic and occupational aspirations, are strongly related to school success.

Strength of influences on school learning. Physical processes can often be explained as functions of a small number of variables interacting in simple ways. In contrast, schooling processes respond to a multitude of influences interacting in kaleidoscopic patterns. This research synthesis has confirmed

that a large number of variables are moderately related to learning outcomes, but few, if any, single variables are strongly related to learning. Authors of original research studies and of reviews and syntheses are appropriately cautious in stating the importance of particular items, and their caution is reflected in the relatively narrow range of mean ratings presented in Table 2. Nonetheless, taken together, the items examined in this synthesis are powerful determinants of school effects.

Notes

1. This research was supported in part by the Temple University Center for Research in Human Development and Education and in part by a grant from the U.S. Department of Education's Office of Special Education and Rehabilitative Services. The opinions expressed herein are solely those of the authors, and no official endorsement should be inferred.

2. Copies of the detailed coding form and complete bibliographic citations for the 179 sources, as well as copies of the data archive, are available from Margaret C. Wang, Center for Research in Human Development and Education, Ritter Hall Annex, 9th Floor, Temple University, Philadelphia, PA 19122.

3. In addition to the coding and analysis of the 179 source documents, a survey also was conducted of the authors of all major source documents examined. The summary coding form described below was distributed to authors, with a request to provide overall ratings of the importance of the 228 items to learning outcomes. A total of 78 forms were returned. Those expert ratings were analyzed separately from the source document ratings, following identical procedures. Results were highly similar, with the exception that the experts generally tended to give somewhat higher numerical ratings.

4. This panel included 12 prominent experts in areas of research on teaching, education, educational psychology, and special education.

5. Most of those occurred for items in the scale History of Educational Placements, which accounts for the low mean of this variable in Table 2.

6. If any supplementary items had been coded, those were reexamined as the forms were transcribed and, whenever possible, were included under one of the prespecified items. This procedure was generally possible because most supplementary items documented authors' more detailed or specific empirical conclusions, for example, specific types of motivation related to learning or particular variants of instructional practices. Such detailed findings were incorporated into the broader variable prespecified on the form. The other supplementary items were those documenting two-way or occasionally higher order interactions. Because interactions represent more subtle findings and frequently fail to replicate, they were not transferred from the detailed form to the summary form. The summary forms were keyed and verified, and files were prepared for data analysis using standard statistical software packages.

7. The weights used were equal to the numbers of original items included in the respective scales. Note that if there were no missing data, this procedure would result in giving all of the original items in a broad category equal weight. Where some items in a scale are missing, this procedure in effect assigns the mean of the nonmissing scale items to those missing observations. For any given scale, about 15% of the values of items on average were missing.

8. As noted in the footnote to the table, those reported reliabilities are for means of all the items in a given category or scale. Due to missing data, values for some sources were based on means of fewer items.

9. The highest ratings overall were assigned to Psychomotor Variables and a moderately high rating also was assigned to the scale Accessibility Variables. However, only one item was included in each of those scales, and those items were referred to in 6 or fewer of the 179 sources analyzed. Thus, Psychomotor Variables and Accessibility Variables were set aside. The list of scales with the highest ratings include the 28 scales with more items and ratings.

10. A third item in this scale, teacher provides explicit coaching to reduce aggression, also received a mean rating above 2.00 but was mentioned in only 4 of the 179 sources. That item is of limited relevance in most regular educational settings.

APPENDIX

Bibliographic References for the 179 Sources Synthesized in This Article

Adams, M. J. (1986). Teaching thinking to Chapter 1 students. In B. I. Williams, P. A. Richmond, & B. J. Mason (Eds.), *Designs for compensatory education: Conference proceedings and papers* (pp. IV–85 to IV–119). Washington, DC: Research and Evaluation Associates.

Algozzine, R., & Mercer, C. D. (1980). Labels and expectancies for handicapped children and youth. In L. Mann & D. A. Sabatino (Eds.), *Fourth review of special education* (pp. 287–313). New York: Grune & Stratton.

Allington, R. L., & Johnston, P. (1986). The coordination among regular classroom reading programs and targeted support programs. In B. I. Williams, P. A. Richmond, & B. J. Mason (Eds.), *Designs for compensatory education: Conference proceedings and papers* (pp. VI–3 to VI–40). Washington, DC: Research and Evaluation Associates.

Alter, M., & Gottlieb, J. (1987). Educating for social skills. In J. Gottlieb & B. W. Gottlieb (Eds.), *Advances in special education* (Vol. 6, pp. 1–61). Greenwich, CT: JAI Press.

Ambramson, M. (1980). Implications of mainstreaming: A challenge for special education. In L. Mann & D. A. Sabatino (Eds.), *Fourth review of special education* (pp. 315–340). New York: Grune & Stratton.

Anderson, L. (1985). A retrospective and prospective view of Bloom's "Learning for Mastery." In M. C. Wang & H. J. Walberg (Eds.), *Adapting instruction to individual differences* (pp. 254–268). Berkeley, CA: McCutchan.

Archambault, F. X., Jr. (1986). Instructional setting: Key issue and bogus concern. In B. I. Williams, P. A. Richmond, & B. J. Mason (Eds.), *Designs for compensatory education: Conference proceedings and papers* (pp. 111–59 to 111–93). Washington, DC: Research and Evaluation Associates.

Armento, B. J. (1986). Research on teaching social studies. In M. C. Wittrock (Ed.), *Handbook of research on teaching* (3rd ed., pp. 942–951). New York: Macmillan.

Baldwin, A. L. (1973). Social learning. In F. N. Kerlinger (Ed.), *Review of research in education* (Vol. 1, pp. 34–57). Itasca, IL: Peacock.

Barr, R., & Dreeban, R. (1977). Instruction in classrooms. In L. S. Shulman (Ed.), *Review of research in education* (Vol. 5. pp. 89–162). Itasca, IL: Peacock.

Bennett, W. J. (1986). *First lessons. A report on elementary education in America.* Washington, DC: U.S. Department of Education.

Bereiter, C., & Scardamalia, M. (1986). Levels of inquiry into the nature of expertise in writing. In E. Z. Rothkopf (Ed.), *Review of research in education* (Vol. 13, pp. 259–282). Washington, DC: American Educational Research Association.

Berliner, D. C., & Cahen, L. S. (1973). Trait-treatment interaction and learning. In F. N. Kerlinger (Ed.), *Review of research in education* (Vol. 1, pp. 58–94). Itasca, IL: Peacock.

Biddle, B., & Anderson, D. S. (1986). Theory, methods, knowledge, and research on teaching. In M. C. Wittrock (Ed.), *Handbook of research on teaching* (3rd ed., pp. 230–252). New York: Macmillan.

Blackhurst, A. E., Bott, D. A., & Cross, D. P. (1987). Noncategorical special education personnel preparation. In M. C. Wang, M. C. Reynolds, & H. J. Walberg (Eds.), *Handbook of special education: Research and practice. Volume 1: Learner characteristics and adaptive education* (pp. 313–329). Oxford: Pergamon.

Blanton, L. P., Sitko, M. C., & Gillespie, P. H. (1976). Reading and the mildly retarded: Review of research and implications. In L. Mann & D. A. Sabatino (Eds.), *Third review of special education* (pp. 143–162). New York: Grune & Stratton.

Block, J. H., & Burns, R. B. (1975). Mastery learning. In L. S. Shulman (Ed.), *Review of research in education* (Vol. 4, pp. 3–49). Itasca, IL: Peacock.

Brainin, S. S. (1985). Mediating learning: Pedagogic issues in the improvement of cognitive functioning. In E. W. Gordon (Ed.), *Review of research in education* (Vol. 12, 121–155). Washington, DC: American Educational Research Association.

Brantlingr, E. A., & Guskin, S. L. (1987). Ethnocultural and social-psychological effects on learning characteristics of handicapped children. In M. C. Wang, M. C. Reynolds, & H. J. Walberg (Eds.), *Handbook of special education: Research and practice. Volume 1: Learner characteristics and adaptive education* (pp. 7–34). Oxford: Pergamon.

Brophy, J. E. (1986). Research linking teacher behavior to student achievement: Potential implications for instruction of Chapter I students. In B. I. Williams, P. A. Richmond, & B. J. Mason (Eds.), *Designs for compensatory education: Conference proceedings and papers* (pp. IV–121 to IV–179). Washington, DC: Research and Evaluation Associates.

Brophy, J. E., & Good, T. L. (1986). Teacher behavior and student achievement. In M. C. Wittrock (Ed.), *Handbook of research on teaching* (3rd ed., pp. 328–375). New York: Macmillan.

Brown, B. W., & Saks, K. H. (1981). The microeconomics of schooling. In D. C. Berliner (Ed.), *Review of research in education* (Vol. 9, pp. 217–254). Washington, DC: American Educational Research Association.

Bryan, T. H., & Bryan, J. H. (1981). Some personal and social experiences of learning disabled children. In B. K. Keogh (Ed.), *Advances in special education. Volume 3: Socialization influences on exceptionality* (pp. 147–186). Greenwich, CT: JAI Press.

Calfee, R. (1981). Cognitive psychology and educational practice. In D. C. Berliner (Ed.), *Review of research in education* (Vol. 9, pp. 3–73). Washington, DC: American Educational Research Association.

Calfee, R. (1986). Curriculum and instruction: Reading. In B. I. Williams, P. A. Richmond, & B. J. Mason (Eds.), *Designs for compensatory education: Conference proceedings and papers* (pp. IV–29 to IV–83). Washington DC: Research and Evaluation Associates.

Calfee, R., & Drum, P. (1986). Research on teaching reading. In M. C. Wittrock (Ed.), *Handbook of research on teaching* (23rd ed., pp. 804–849). New York: Macmillan.

Carpenter, R. L., & Apter, S. J. (1988). Research integration of cognitive interventions for behaviorally disordered children and youth. In M. C. Wang, M. C. Reynolds, & H. J. Walberg (Eds.), *Handbook of special education. Volume 2: Mildly handicapped conditions* (pp. 155–159). Oxford: Pergamon.

Carroll, J. B., & Maxwell, S. E. (1979). Individual differences in cognitive abilities. *Annual Review of Psychology, 30,* 603–640.

Cazden, C. B. (1986). Classroom discourse. In M. C. Wittrock (Ed.), *Handbook of research on teaching* (3rd ed., pp. 432–463). New York: Macmillan.

Clark, R., & Salomon, G. (1986). Media in teaching. In M. C. Wittrock (Ed.), *Handbook of research on teaching* (3rd ed., pp. 464–478). New York: Macmillan.

Colarusso, R. P. (1987). Diagnostic-prescriptive teaching. In M. C. Wang, M. C. Reynolds, & H. J. Walberg (Eds.), *Handbook of special education: Research and practice. Volume 1: Learner characteristics and adaptive education* (pp. 155–166). Oxford: Pergamon.

Cook, S. B., Scruggs, T. E., Mastropieri, M. A., & Glendon, C. C. (1985–86). Handicapped students as tutors. *Journal of Special Education, 19,* 483–492.

Cooper, H. M. (1986). Chapter 1 programs reduce student-to-instructor ratios but do reduced ratios affect achievement? In B. I. Williams, P. A. Richmond, & B. J. Mason (Eds.), *Designs for compensatory education: Conference proceedings and papers* (pp. 111–35 to 111–57). Washington, DC: Research and Evaluation Associates.

Corno, L., & Snow, R. E. (1986). Adapting teaching to individual differences among learners. In M. C. Wittrock (Ed.), *Handbook of research on teaching* (3rd ed., pp. 605–29). New York: Macmillan.

Cosden, M., Pear, R., Bryan, T. H. (1985). The effects of cooperative and individual goal structures on learning disabled and non-disabled students. *Exceptional Children, 52,* 103–114.

Craik, F. (1979). Human memory. *Annual Review of Psychology, 30,* 63–102.

Crittenden, K. S. (1983). Sociological aspects of attribution. *Annual Review of Sociology, 9,* 425–446.

Curtis, M. E., & Glaser, R. (1981). Changing conceptions of intelligence. In D. C. Berliner (Ed.), *Review of research in education* (Vol. 9, pp. 111–148). Washington, DC: American Educational Research Association.

DeCharms, R., & Muir, M. S. (1978). Motivation: Social approaches. *Annual Review of Psychology, 29,* 91–114.

de Kanter, A., Ginsburg, A. L., & Milne, Am. M. (1986). Parent involvement strategies: A new emphasis on traditional parent roles. In B. I. Williams, P. A. Richmond, & B. J. Mason (Eds.), *Designs for compensatory education: Conference proceedings and papers* (pp. V3–V26). Washington, DC: Research and Evaluation Associates.

Diaz, R. (1983). Thought and two languages: The impact of bilingualism. In E. W. Gordon (Ed.), *Review of research in education* (Vol. 10, pp. 23–54). Washington, DC: American Educational Research Association.

Divesta, F., & Palermo, D. S. (1974). Language development. In F. N. Kerlinger & J. B. Carroll (Eds.), *Review of research in education* (Vol. 2, pp. 55–107). Itasca, IL: Peacock.

Doyle, W. (1977). Paradigms for research on teacher effectiveness. In L. S. Shulman (Ed.), *Review of research in education* (Vol. 5., pp. 163–198). Itasca, IL: Peacock.

Doyle, W. (1986a). Classroom organization and management. In M. C. Wittrock (Ed.), *Handbook of research on teaching* (3rd ed., pp. 392–431). New York: Macmillan.

Doyle, W. (1986b). Vision and reality: A reaction to issues in curriculum and instruction for compensatory education. In B. I. Williams, P. A. Richmond, & B. J. Mason (Eds.), *Designs for compensatory education: Conference proceedings and papers* (pp. IV–259 to IV–271). Washington, DC: Research and Evaluation Associates.

Epps, S., & Tindel, G. (1987). The effectiveness of differential programming in serving students with mild handicaps: Placement options and instructional programming. In M. C. Wang, M. C. Reynolds, & H. J. Walberg (Eds.), *Handbook of special education: Research and practice. Volume 1: Learner characteristics and adaptive education* (pp. 213–247). Oxford: Pergamon.

Epstein, M. H., Cullinan, D., & Rose, T. L. (1980). Applied behavior analysis and behaviorally disordered pupils: Selected issues. In L. Mann & D. A. Sabatino (Eds.), *Fourth review of special education* (pp. 61–107). New York: Grune & Stratton.

Erickson, J. R., & Jones, M. R. (1978). Thinking. *Annual Review of Psychology, 29,* 61–90.

Farr, M. (1986). Language culture and writing: Sociolinguistic foundations of research on writing. In E. Z. Rothkopf (Ed.), *Review of research in education* (Vol. 13, pp. 195–224). Washington, DC: American Educational Research Association.

Faust, M. S., & Faust, W. L. (1980). Cognitive constructing: Levels of processing and developmental change. In B. K. Keogh (Ed.), *Advances in special education. Volume 1: Basic constructs and theoretical orientations* (pp. 1–54). Greenwich, CT: JAI Press.

Fillmore, L., & Valdez, C. (1986). Teaching bilingual learners. In M. C. Wittrock (Ed.), *Handbook of research on teaching* (3rd ed., pp. 648–658). New York: Macmillan.

Ford, B. G., & Jenkins, R. C. (1980). Changing perspectives in the education of the gifted. In L. Mann & D. A. Sabatino (Eds.), *Fourth review of special education* (pp. 151–174). New York: Grune & Stratton.

Frase, L. (1975). Advances in research and theory in instructional technology. In F. N. Kerlinger (Ed.), *Review of research in education* (Vol. 3, pp. 43–74). Itasca, IL: Peacock.

Gardner, M. (1985). Cognitive psychological approaches to instructional task analysis. In E. W. Gordon (Ed.), *Review of research in education* (Vol. 12, pp. 157–196). Washington, DC: American Educational Research Association.

Gayne, R. (1973). In F. N. Kerlinger (Ed.), *Review of research in education* (Vol. 1, pp. 3–33). Itasca, IL: Peacock.

Gayne, R. M., & Dick, W. (1983). Instructional psychology. *Annual Review of Psychology, 34,* 261–296.

Gecas, V. (1982). The self-concept. *Annual Review of Sociology, 8,* 1–33.

Gerber, M. M. (1987). Application of cognitive-behaviorist training methods to teaching basic skills to mildly handicapped elementary school students. In M. C. Wang, M. C. Reynolds, & H. J. Walberg (Eds.), *Handbook of special education: Research and practice. Volume 1: Learner characteristics and adaptive education* (pp. 167–186). Oxford: Pergamon.

Good, T., & Brophy, J. (1986). School effects. In M. C. Wittrock (Ed.), *Handbook of research on teaching* (3rd ed., pp. 570–604). New York: Macmillan.

Gordon, E. W., DeStefano, L. M., & Shipman, S. (1985). Characteristics of learning persons and the adaptation of learning environments. In M. C. Wang & H. J. Walberg (Eds.), *Adapting instruction to individual differences* (pp. 44–65). Berkeley, CA: McCutchan.

Gottlieb, B. W. (1987). Social facilitation effects in mainstream classes. In J. Gottlieb & B. W. Gottlieb (Eds.), *Advances in special education* (Vol. 6, pp. 75–85). Greenwich, CT: JAI Press.

Graves, M. F. (1986). Vocabulary learning and instruction. In E. Z. Rothkopf (Ed.), *Review of research in education* (Vol. 13, pp. 49–90). Washington, DC: American Educational Research Association.

Greenspan, S. (1981a). Defining childhood social competence. In B. K. Keogh (Ed.), *Advances in special education. Volume 3: Socialization influences on exceptionality* (pp. 1–39). Greenwich, CT: JAI Press.

Greenspan, S. (1981b). Social competence and handicapped individuals: Practical implications of a proposed model. In B. K. Keogh (Ed.), *Advances in special education. Volume 3: Socialization influences on exceptionality* (pp. 41–82). Greenwich, CT: JAI Press.

Gresham, F. M. (1988). Social competence and motivational characteristics of learning disabled children. In M.. C. Wang, M. C. Reynolds, & H. J. Walberg (Eds.), *Handbook of special education. Volume 2: Mildly handicapped conditions* (pp. 283–302). Oxford: Pergamon.

Griffin, G. (1986). Chapter 1 and the regular school: Staff development. In B. I. Williams, P. A. Richmond, & B. J. Mason (Eds.), *Designs for compensatory education: Conference proceedings and papers* (pp. VI–41 to VI–58). Washington, DC: Research and Evaluation Associates.

Griswold, P. A., Colton, K., & Hansen, J. B. (1985). *Effective compensatory education sourcebook. Volume 1-A review of effective educational practices.* Washington, DC: U.S. Government Printing Office.

Gump, P. V. (1980). The school as a social situation. *Annual Review of Psychology, 31,* 553–582.

Hall, R. J. (1981). An information-processing approach to the study of exceptional children. In B. K. Keogh (Ed.), *Advances in special education. Volume 2: Perspectives and applications* (pp. 79–110). Greenwich, CT: JAI Press.

Hallahan, D. P., & Reeve, R. E. (1980). Selective attention and distractibility. In B. K. Keogh (Ed.), *Advances in special education. Volume 1: Basic constructs and theoretical orientations* (pp. 141–181). Greenwich, CT: JAI Press.

Hallinan, M. T. (1986). Chapter 1 and student achievement: A conceptual model. In B. I. Williams, P. A. Richmond, & B. J. Mason (Eds.), *Designs for compensatory education: Conference proceedings and papers* (pp. VI–59 to VI–78). Washington, DC: Research and Evaluation Associates.

Hamilton, S. F. (1984). The secondary school in the ecology of adolescent development. In E. W. Gordon (Ed.), *Review of research in education* (Vol. 11, pp. 227–258). Washington, DC: American Educational Research Association.

Hodges, W. L., & Buzzeli, C. A. (1984). School change and evaluation: Follow Through revisited. In B. K. Keogh (Ed.), *Advances in special education. Volume 4: Documenting program impact* (pp. 163–192). Greenwich, CT: JAI Press.

Irvin, L. K., Close, D. W., & Wells, R. L. (1987). Programming independent living skills for handicapped learners. In M. C. Wang, M. C. Reynolds, & H. J. Walberg (Eds.), *Handbook of special education: Research and practice. Volume 1: Learner characteristics and adaptive education* (pp. 187–212). Oxford: Pergamon.

Jackson, P. W. (1985). Private lessons in public schools: Remarks on the limits of adaptive instruction. In M. C. Wang & H. J. Walberg (Eds.), *Adapting instruction to individual differences* (pp. 66–81). Berkeley, CA: McCutchan.

Johnson, D. W., & Johnson, R. T. (1985). Cooperative learning and adaptive education. In M. C. Wang & H. J. Walberg (Eds.), *Adapting instruction to individual differences* (pp. 105–134). Berkeley, CA: McCutchan.

Johnson, W. A., & Dark, V. J. (1986). Selective attention. *Annual Review of Psychology, 37,* 43–75.

Karweit, N. (1985). Time spent, time needed, and adaptive instruction. In M. C. Wang & H. J. Walberg (Eds.), *Adapting instruction to individual differences* (pp. 281–297). Berkeley, CA: McCutchan.

Kaufman, M., Agard, J. A., & Semmel, M. I. (1985). Learner competence in school. In M. Kaufman, J. A. Agard, & M. I. Semmel, *Mainstreaming: Learners and their environment* (pp. 99–150). Cambridge, MA: Brookline Books.

Kaufman, M., Agard, J. A., & Semmel, M. I. (1985). Teacher and peer characteristics. In M. Kaufman, J. A. Agard, and M. I. Semmel, *Mainstreaming: Learners and their environment* (pp. 153–191). Cambridge, MA: Brookline Books.

Kaufman, M., Agard, J. A., & Semmel, M. I. (1985). The socioemotional climate. In M. Kaufman, J. A. Agard, and M. I. Semmel, *Mainstreaming: Learners and their environment* (pp. 193–221). Cambridge, MA: Brookline Books.

Kaufman, M., Agard, J. A., & Semmel, M. I. (1985). The instructional conditions. In M. Kaufman, J. A. Agard, and M. I. Semmel, *Mainstreaming: Learners and their environment* (pp. 223–295). Cambridge, MA: Brookline Books.

Kaufman, M., Agard, J. A., & Semmel, M. I. (1985). Academic competence. In M. Kaufman, J. A. Agard, and M. I. Semmel, *Mainstreaming: Learners and their environment* (pp. 307–364). Cambridge, MA: Brookline Books.

Kaufman, M., Agard, J. A., & Semmel, M. I. (1985). Social competence. In M. Kaufman, J. A. Agard, and M. I. Semmel, *Mainstreaming: Learners and their environment* (pp. 365–400). Cambridge, MA: Brookline Books.

Kavale, K. A. (1988). The long-term consequences of learning disabilities. In M. C. Wang, M. C. Reynolds, & H. J. Walberg (Eds.), *Handbook of special education. Volume 2: Mildly handicapped conditions* (pp. 303–344). Oxford: Pergamon.

Kavale, K. A., & Glass, G. V. (1984). Meta-analysis and policy decisions in special education. In B. K. Keogh (Ed.), *Advances in special education. Volume 4: Documenting program impact* (pp. 195–247). Greenwich, CT: JAI Press.

Kavale, K. A., & Nye, C. (1985–86). Parameters of learning disabilities in achievement, linguistic, neuropsychological, and social/behavioral domains. *Journal of Special Education, 19*(4), 443–458.

Kelley, H. H., & Michela, J. L. (1980). Attribution theory and research. *Annual Review of Psychology, 31,* 457–502.

Kennedy, M. M., Jung, R. K., & Orland, M. E. (1986). Poverty, achievement and the distribution of compensatory education services. In B. I. Williams, P. A. Richmond, & B. J. Mason (Eds.), *Designs for compensatory education: Conference proceedings and papers* (pp. 11–3 to 11–8). Washington, DC: Research and Evaluation Associates.

Keogh, B. K. (1988). Learning disability: Diversity in search of order. In M. C. Wang, M. C. Reynolds, & H. J. Walberg (Eds.), *Handbook of special education: Research and practice. Volume 2: Mildly handicapped conditions* (pp. 225–251). Oxford: Pergamon.

Keogh, B. K., & Pullis, M. E. (1980). Temperament influences on the development of exceptional children. In B. K. Keogh (Ed.), *Advances in special education. Volume 1: Basic constructs and theoretical orientations* (pp. 239–276). Greenwich, CT: JAI Press.

Klausmeier, H. J. (1985). A design for improving secondary education. In M. C. Wang & H. J. Walberg (Eds.), *Adapting instruction to individual differences* (pp. 160–190). Berkeley, CA: McCutchan.

Klausmeier, H. J., & Hooper, F. (1974). Conceptual development and instruction. In F. N. Kerlinger & J. B. Carroll (Eds.), *Review of research in education* (Vol. 2, pp. 3–54). Itasca, IL: Peacock.

Kluwin, T. N., & Moores, D. F. (1985). The effects of integration on the mathematics achievement of hearing-impaired adolescents. *Exceptional Children, 52,* 153–160.

Kramer, J. J., Piersel, W. C., & Glover, J. A. (1988). Cognitive and social development of mildly retarded children. In M. C. Wang, M. C. Reynolds, & H. J. Walberg (Eds.), *Handbook of special education. Research and practice. Volume 2: Mildly handicapped conditions* (pp. 43–58). Oxford: Pergamon.

Krupski, A. (1980). Attention processes: Research, theory and implications for special education. In B. K. Keogh (Ed.), *Advances in special education. Volume 1: Basic constructs and theoretical orientations* (pp. 101–140). Greenwich, CT: JAI Press.

Langer, J. A., & Applebee, A. N. (1986,). Reading and writing instruction: Toward a theory of teaching and learning. In E. Z. Rothkopf (Ed.), *Review of research in education* (Vol. 13, pp. 171–194). Washington, DC: American Educational Research Association.

Leyser, V., & Cole, K. B. (1987). The reconceptualization and delivery of quality inservice education under Public Law 94-142. In J. Gottlieb & B. W. Gottlieb (Eds.), *Advances in special education* (Vol. 6, pp. 87–117). Greenwich, CT: JAI Press.

Liebert, R. M., & Schwartzberg, N. S. (1977). Effects of mass media. *Annual Review of Psychology, 28,* 141–174.

Lloyd, J. W. (1988). Direct academic interventions in learning disabilities. In M. C. Wang, M. C. Reynolds, & H. J. Walberg (Eds.), *Handbook of special education. Volume 2: Mildly handicapped conditions* (pp. 345–366). Oxford: Pergamon.

Lloyd, J. W., Hallahan, D. P., & Kaufman, J. M. (1980). Learning disabilities: A review of selected topics. In L. Mann & D. A. Sabatino (Eds.), *Fourth review of special education* (pp. 35–60). New York: Grune & Stratton.

Macdonald-Ross, M. (1978). Language in texts: The design of curricular materials. In L. S. Shulman (Ed.), *Review of research in education* (Vol. 6, pp. 229–275). Itasca, IL: Peacock.

MacMillan, D. L., Keogh, B. K., & Jones, R. L. (1986). In M. C. Wittrock (Ed.), *Handbook of research on teaching* (3rd ed., pp. 686–724). New York: Macmillan.

MacMillan, D. L., & Meyers, C. E. (1979). Educational labeling of handicapped learners. In D. C. Berliner (Ed.), *Review of research in education* (Vol. 7, pp. 151–194). Washington, DC: American Educational Research Association.

Mahoney, G., Crawley, S., & Pullis, M. (1980). Language intervention: Models and issues. In B. K. Keogh (Ed.), *Advances in special education. Volume 2: Perspectives and applications* (pp. 135–164). Greenwich, CT: JAI Press.

Mason, J. M., Liz Allen, J. (1986). A review of emergent literacy with implications for research and practice in reading. In E. Z. Rothkopf (Ed.), *Review of research in education* (Vol. 13, pp. 3–47). Washington, DC: American Educational Research Association.

McConkie, G. W. (1977). Learning from test. In L. S. Shulman (Ed.), *Review of research in education* (Vol. 5. pp. 3–48). Itasca, IL: Peacock.

McLaughlin, M. W., & Shields, P. M. (1986). Involving parents in the school: Lessons for policy. In B. I. Williams, P. A. Richmond, & B. J. Mason (Eds.), *Designs for compensatory education: Conference proceedings and papers* (pp. V–27 to V–46). Washington, DC: Research and Evaluation Associates.

Meisgeier, C. (1976). A review of critical issues underlying mainstreaming. In L. Mann & D. A. Sabatino (Eds.), *Third review of special education* (pp. 245–269). New York: Grune & Stratton.

Merrill, M. D., & Boutwell, R. C. (1973). Instructional development: Methodology and research. In F. N. Kerlinger (Ed.), *Review of research in education* (Vol. 1, pp. 95–131). Itasca, IL: Peacock.

Morrison, G. M. (1987). Relationship among academic, social, and career education in programming for handicapped students. In M. C. Wang, M. C. Reynolds, & H. J. Walberg (Eds.), *Handbook of special education: Research and practice. Volume 1: Learner characteristics and adaptive education* (pp. 133–154). Oxford: Pergamon.

Morsink, C. V., Thomas, C. C., & Smith-David, J. (1987). Noncategorical special education programs: Process and outcomes. In M. C. Wang, M. C. Reynolds, & H. J. Walberg (Eds.), *Handbook of special education: Research and practice. Volume 1: Learner characteristics and adaptive education* (pp. 287–311). Oxford: Pergamon.

Nelson, C. M., & Rutherford, R. B. (1988). Behavioral interventions with behaviorally disordered students. In M. C. Wang, M. C. Reynolds, & H. J. Walberg (Eds.), *Handbook of special education: Research and practice. Volume 2: Mildly handicapped conditions* (pp. 125–153). Oxford: Pergamon.

Nelson-LeGall, S. (1985). Help-seeking behavior in learning. In E. W. Gordon (Ed.), *Review of research in education* (Vol. 12, pp. 55–90). Washington, DC: American Educational Research Association.

Nevin, A., & Thousand, J. (1987). Avoiding or limiting special education referrals: Changes and challenges. In M. C. Wang, M. C. Reynolds, & H. J. Walberg (Eds.), *Handbook of special education: Research and practice. Volume 1: Learner characteristics and adaptive education* (pp. 273–286). Oxford: Pergamon.

Niemiec, R., & Walberg, H. J. (1987). Comparative effects of computer-assisted instruction: A synthesis of reviews. *Journal of Educational Computing Research, 3,* 19–37.

Olsen, K. R. (1986). *Effectiveness indicators for special education.* Hampton, NH: Center for Resource Management. (Developed by the National RRC Panel on Indicators of Effectiveness in Special Education, K. R. Olsen, chair.)

Palincsar, A. S., & Brown, A. (1987). Advances in improving the cognitive performance of handicapped students. In M. C. Wang, M. C. Reynolds, & H. J. Walberg (Eds.), *Handbook of special education: Research and practice. Volume 1: Learner characteristics and adaptive education* (pp. 93–112). Oxford: Pergamon.

Paris, S. G., Wixson, K. K., & Palincsar, A. S. (1986). Instructional approaches to reading comprehension. In E. Z. Rothkopf (Ed.), *Review of research in education* (Vol. 13, pp. 91–128). Washington, DC: American Educational Research Association.

Passow, A. H. (1974). Compensatory instructional intervention. In F. N. Kerlinger and J. B. Carroll (Eds.), *Review of research in education* (Vol. 2, pp. 145—175). Itasca, IL: Peacock.

Pea, R. D., & Kurland, D. M. (1987). Cognitive technologies for writing. In E. Z. Rothkopf (Ed.), *Review of research in education* (Vol. 14, pp. 277–326). Washington, DC: American Educational Research Association.

Peterson, P. L. (1986). Selecting students and services for compensatory education: Lessons from aptitude-treatment interaction research. In B. I. Williams, P. A. Richmond, & B. J. Mason (Eds.), *Designs for compensatory education: Conference proceedings and papers* (pp. 11–15 to 11–62). Washington, DC: Research and Evaluation Associates.

Pintrich, P. R., Cross, D. R., Kozma, R. B., & McKeachie, W. J. (1986). Instructional psychology. *Annual Review of Psychology, 37,* 611–651.

Polirstok, S. R. (1987). A specialized peer tutoring program for academically and behaviorally handicapped adolescents. In J. Gottlieb & B. W. Gottlieb (Eds.), *Advances in special education* (Vol. 6, pp. 63–74). Greenwich CT: JAI Press.

Polloway, E. A., & Smith, J. D. (1988). Current status of the mild mental retardation construct: Identification, placement, and programs. In M. C. Wang, M. C. Reynolds, & H. J. Walberg (Eds.), *Handbook of special education: Research and practice. Volume 2: Mildly handicapped conditions* (pp. 7–22). Oxford: Pergamon.

Price-Williams, D., & Gallimore, R. (1980). The cultural perspective. In B. K. Keogh (Ed.), *Advances in special education. Volume 2: Perspectives and applications* (pp. 165–192). Greenwich, CT: JAI Press.

Ramey, C. T., Yeates, K. O., & MacPhee, D. (1984). Risk for retarded development among disadvantaged families: A systems theory approach to preventive intervention. In B. K. Keogh (Ed.), *Advances in special education. Volume 4: Documenting program impact* (pp. 249–272). Greenwich, CT: JAI Press.

Reschly, D. J. (1987). Learning characteristics of mildly handicapped students: Implications for classification, placement and programming. In M. C. Wang, M. C. Reynolds, & H. J. Walberg (Eds.), *Handbook of special education: Research and practice. Volume 1: Learner characteristics and adaptive education* (pp. 35–58). Oxford: Pergamon.

Resnick, L. B. (1981). Instructional psychology. *Annual Review of Psychology, 32,* 659–704.

Reynolds, M. C. (1984). Classification of students with handicaps. In E. W. Gordon (Ed.), *Review of research in education* (Vol. 11, pp. 63–92). Washington, DC: American Educational Research Association.

Reynolds, M. C., & Lakin, K. C. (1987). Noncategorical special education: Models for research and practice. In M. C. Wang, M. C. Reynolds, & H. J. Walberg (Eds.), *Handbook of special education: Research and practice. Volume 1: Learner characteristics and adaptive education* (pp. 313–329). Oxford: Pergamon.

Rich, D. (1986). The parent gap in compensatory education and how to bridge it. In B. J. Williams, P. A. Richmond, & B. J. Mason (Eds.), *Designs for compensatory education: Conference proceedings and papers* (pp. V–47 to V–62). Washington, DC: Research Evaluation Associates.

Romberg, T. (1986). Mathematics for compensatory school programs. In B. I. Williams, P. A. Richmond, & B. J. Mason (Eds.). *Designs for compensatory education: Conference proceedings and papers* (pp. IV–3 to IV–28). Washington, DC: Research and Evaluation Associates.

Romberg, T. A., & Carpenter, T. P. (1986). Research on teaching and learning mathematics. Two disciplines of scientific inquiry. In M. C. Wittrock (Ed.), *Handbook of research on teaching* (3rd ed., pp. 850–873). New York: Macmillan.

Rosenshine, B., & Stevens, R. Teaching functions. (1986). In M. C. Wittrock (Ed.), *Handbook of research on teaching* (3rd ed., pp. 376–391). New York: Macmillan.

Ruble, D. N., & Boggiano, A. K. (1980). Optimizing motivation in an achievement context. In B. K. Keogh (Ed.), *Advances in special education. Volume 2: Perspectives and applications* (pp. 183–238). Greenwich, CT: JAI Press.

Sarason, S. B., & Klaber, M. (1985). The school as a social situation. *Annual Review of Psychology, 36,* 115–140.

Scardamalia, M., & Bereita, C. (1986). Research on written composition. In M. C. Wittrock (Ed.), *Handbook of research on teaching* (3rd ed., pp. 778–803). New York: Macmillan.

Schmidt, M., Weinstein, T., Niemiec, R., & Walberg, H. J. (1985–86). Computer-assisted instruction with exceptional children. *Journal of Special Education, 19*(4), 493–501.

Scott-Jones D. (1974). Family influences on cognitive development and school achievement. In E. W. Gordon (Ed.), *Review of research in education* (Vol. 11, pp. 259–304). Washington, DC: American Educational Research Association.

Semmel, M. I., & Frick, T. (1985). Learner background characteristics. In M. Kaufman, J. A. Agard, & M. I. Semmel, *Mainstreaming: Learners and their environment* (pp. 75–98). Cambridge, MA: Brookline Books.

Semmel, M. I., Gottlieb, J., & Robinson, N. M. (1979). Mainstreaming: Perspectives on educating handicapped children in the public school. In D. C. Berliner (Ed.), *Review of research in education* (Vol. 7, pp. 223–279). Washington, DC: American Educational Research Association.

Shipman, S., & Shipman, V. C. (1985). Cognitive styles: Some conceptual, methodological, and applied issues. In E. W. Gordon (Ed.), *Review of research in education* (Vol. 12, pp. 229–291). Washington, DC: American Educational Research Association.

Shores, R. E., Burney, J. D., & Wiegerink, R. (1976). Teacher training in special education: A review of research. In L. Mann & D. A. Sabatino (Eds.), *Third review of special education* (pp. 199–216). New York: Grune & Stratton.

Skiba, R. J., Casey, A., & Center, B. A. (1985–86). Nonaversive procedures in the treatment of classroom behavior problems. *Journal of Special Education, 19*(4), 459–481.

Slavin, R. E. (1985). Team-assisted individualization: A cooperative learning solution for adaptive instruction in mathematics. In M. C. Wang & H. J. Walberg (Eds.), *Adapting instruction to individual differences* (pp. 236-253). Berkeley, CA: McCutchan.

Smith, C. R., Wood, F. H., & Grimes, J. (1988). Issues in the identification and placement of behaviorally disordered students. In M. C. Wang, M. C. Reynolds, & H. J. Walberg (Eds.), *Handbook of special education: Research and practice. Volume 2: Mildly handicapped conditions* (pp. 95-123). Oxford: Pergamon.

Snow, R. E. (1976). Learning and individual differences. In L. S. Shulman (Ed.), *Review of research in education* (Vol. 4, pp. 50–105). Itasca, IL: Peacock.

Spady, W. G. (1973). The impact of school resources on students. In F. N. Kerlinger (Ed.), *Review of research in education* (Vol. 1, pp. 135–177). Itasca, IL: Peacock.

Stainback, W., Stainback, S., Courtnage, L., & Jaben, T. (1985). Facilitating mainstreaming by modifying the mainstream. *Exceptional Children, 52,* 144–152.

Stein, N. L. (1986). Knowledge and process in the acquisition of writing skills. In E. Z. Rothkopf (Ed.), *Review of research in education* (Vol. 13, pp. 225–258). Washington, DC: American Educational Research Association.

Taylor, R. L. (1988). Psychological intervention with mildly retarded children: Prevention and redemption of cognitive deficits. In M. C. Wang, M. C. Reynolds, & H. J. Walberg (Eds.), *Handbook of special education: Research and practice. Volume 2: Mildly handicapped conditions* (pp. 59–75). Oxford: Pergamon.

Tobias, S. (1985). Computer-assisted instruction. In M. C. Wang & H. J. Walberg (Eds.), *Adapting instruction to individual differences* (pp. 135–159). Berkeley, CA: McCutchan.

Torgesen, J., & Kail, R. V. (1980). Memory processes in exceptional children. In B. K. Keogh (Ed.), *Advances in special education. Volume 1: Basic constructs and theoretical orientations* (pp. 55–99). Greenwich, CT: JAI Press.

Torrance, P. (1986). Teaching creative and gifted learners. In M. C. Wittrock (Ed.), *Handbook of research on teaching* (3rd ed., pp. 630–647). New York: Macmillan.

Tyler, W. B. (1985). The organizational structure of the school. *Annual Review of Sociology, 11,* 49-74.

U.S. Department of Education. (1986). *What works.* Washington, DC: U.S. Government Printing Office.

Wachs, H., & Furth, H. (1980). Piaget's theory and special education. In B. K. Keogh (Ed.), *Advances in special education. Volume 2: Perspectives and applications* (pp. 51–78). Greenwich, CT: JAI Press.

Walberg, H. J. (1976). Psychology of learning environments: Behavioral, structural or perceptual? In L. S. Shulman (Ed.), *Review of research in education* (Vol. 4, pp. 142–178). Itasca, IL: Peacock.

Walberg, H. J. (1984). Improving the productivity of America's schools. *Educational Leadership, 41*(8), 19-27.

Walberg, H. J. (1985). Instructional theories and research evidence. In M. C. Wang & H. J. Walberg (Eds.), *Adapting instruction to individual differences* (pp. 3–23). Berkeley, CA: McCutchan.

Walberg, H. J. (1986). Syntheses of research on teaching. In M. C. Wittrock (Ed.), *Handbook of research on teaching* (3rd ed., pp. 214–229). New York: Macmillan.

Walberg, H. J., & Wang, M. C. (1987). Effective educational practices and provisions for individual differences. In M. C. Wang, M. C. Reynolds, & H. J. Walberg (Eds.), *Handbook of special education: Research and practice. Volume 1: Learner characteristics and adaptive education* (pp. 113–128). Oxford: Pergamon.

Wallace, R. C., Jr. (1985). Adaptive education: Policy and administrative perspectives. In M. C. Wang & H. J. Walberg (Eds.),

Adapting instruction to individual differences (pp. 269–280). Berkeley, CA: McCutchan.

Wang, M. C., & Baker, E. T. (1985–86). Mainstreaming programs: Design features and effects. *Journal of Special Education, 19,* 503–521.

Wang, M. C., Gennari, P., & Waxman, H. C. (1985). The adaptive learning environments model: Design, implementation, and effects. In M. C. Wang & H. J. Walberg (Eds.), *Adapting instruction to individual differences* (pp. 191–235). Berkeley, CA: McCutchan.

Wang, M. C., & Lindvall, C. M. (1984). Individual differences and school learning environments. In E. W. Gordon (Ed.), *Review of research in education* (Vol. 11, pp. 161–225). Washington, DC: American Educational Research Association.

Wang, M. C., & Peverly, S. T. (1987). The role of the learner: An individual difference variable in school learning and functioning. In M. C. Wang, M. C. Reynolds, & H. J. Walberg (Eds.), *Handbook of special education: Research and practice. Volume 1: Learner characteristics and adaptive education* (pp. 59–92). Oxford: Pergamon.

Wang, M. C., Peverly, S. T., & Catalano, R. (1987). Integrating special needs students in regular classes: Programming, implementation, and policy. In J. Gottlieb & B. W. Gottlieb (Eds.), *Advances in special education* (Vol. 6, pp. 119–149). Greenwich, CT: JAI Press.

Waxman, H. C., & Walberg, H. J. (1982). The relation of teaching and learning: A review of reviews of process-product research. *Contemporary Education Review, 1,* 103–120.

Weiner, B. (1976). An attributional approach to education psychology. In L. S. Shulman (Ed.), *Review of research in education* (Vol. 4, pp. 179–209). Itasca, IL: Peacock.

Weinstein, C. F., & Mayer, R. F. (1986). The teaching of learning strategies. In M. C. Wittrock (Ed.), *Handbook of research on teaching* (3rd ed., pp. 315–327). New York: Macmillan.

White, R. T., & Tisher, R. P. (1986). Research on natural sciences. In C. Wittrock (Ed.), *Handbook of research on teaching* (3rd ed., pp. 874–905). New York: Macmillan.

Wickelgren, W. A. (1981). Human learning and memory. *Annual Review of Psychology, 32,* 21–52.

Wilkinson, L. C. (1986). Grouping low achieving students for instruction. In B. I. Williams, P. A. Richmond, & B. J. Mason (Eds.), *Designs for compensatory education: Conference proceedings and papers* (pp. IV–181 to IV–206). Washington, DC: Research and Evaluation Associates.

Wittrock, M. C. (1986). Student thought processes. In M. C. Wittrock (Ed.), *Handbook of research on teaching* (3rd ed., pp. 297–314). New York: Macmillan.

Wittrock, M. C., & Lumsdaine, A. A. (1977). Instructional psychology. *Annual Review of Psychology, 24,* 417–460.

Zabel, R. H. (1988). Preparation of teachers for behaviorally distorted students: A review of the literature. In M. C. Wang, M. C. Reynolds, & H. J. Walberg (Eds.), *Handbook of special education: Research and practice. Volume 2: Mildly handicapped conditions* (pp. 171–193). Oxford: Pergamon.

Zigmond, N., & Sainatom, D. (1981). Socialization influences on educationally handicapped adolescents. In B. K. Keogh (Ed.), *Advances in special education. Volume 3: Socialization influences on exceptionality* (pp. 187–207). Greenwich, CT: JAI Press.

References

Bennett, S. N. (1978). Recent research on teaching: A dream, a belief and a model. British *Journal of Educational Psychology, 48,* 127–147.

Bloom, B. S. (1976). *Human Characteristics and School Learning.* New York: McGraw-Hill.

Brookover, W. B., Beady, C., Hood, P., Schweitzer, J., & Wisenboker, J. (1979). *School social systems and student achievement: Schools can make a difference.* New York: Praeger.

Brookover, W. B., & Lezotte, L. W. (1979). Changes in school characteristics coincident with changes in student achievement. East Lansing, MI: Michigan State University, Institute for Research on Teaching. (ERIC Document Reproduction Service No. ED 181 005)

Brophy, J. (1986). Research linking teacher behavior to student achievement: Potential implications for instruction of Chapter I students. In B. I. Williams, P. A. Richmond, & B. J. Mason (Eds.), *Designs for compensatory education: Conference proceedings and papers.* Washington, DC: Research and Evaluation Associates, Inc.

Bruner, J. S. (1966). *Toward a theory of instruction.* New York: W. W. Norton.

Carroll, J. B. (1963). A model of school learning. *Teachers College Record, 67,* 723–733.

Cowman, J. S. et al. (1966). *Equality of educational opportunity.* Washington, DC: U.S. Department of Health, Education, and Welfare, Office of Education.

Edmond, R. (1979). Effective schools for the urban poor. *Educational Leadership, 37*(1), 15–27.

Obey, R. (1976). Components of a psychological theory of instruction: Toward a science of design. *Review of Educational Research, 46,* 1–24.

Glaser, R. (1982). Instructional psychology: Past, present, and future. *American Psychologist, 37,* 292–305.

Haertel, G. D., Walberg, H. J., & Weinstein, T. (1983). Psychological models of educational performance: A theoretical synthesis of constructs. *Review of Educational Research, 53,* 75–92.

Harnischfeger, A., & Wiley, D. E. (1976). The teaching-learning process in elementary schools: A synoptic view. *Curriculum Inquiry, 6,* 5–43.

Hilgard, E. R. (1964). A perspective of the relationship between learning theory and educational practices. In E. R. Hilgard (Ed.), *Theories of learning and instruction* (Sixty-third yearbook of the National Society for the Study of Education, pp. 402–415). Chicago: University of Chicago Press.

Keogh, B. K., Major-Kingsley, S., Omori-Gordon, H., & Reid, H. P. (1982). *A system of marker variables for the field of learning disabilities.* Syracuse, NY: Syracuse University Press.

Purkey, S. C., & Smith, M. S. (1983). Effective schools: A review. *Elementary School Journal, 83,* 427–452.

Rutter, M., Maugham, B., Mortimore, P., Ouston, J., & Smith, A. (1979). *Fifteen thousand hours: Secondary schools and their effects on children.* Cambridge, MA: Harvard University Press.

Shulman, L. S. (1986). Paradigms and research programs in the study of teaching. In M. C. Wittrock (Ed.), *Handbook of research on teaching* (3rd ed., pp. 3–36). New York: Macmillan.

U.S. Department of Education. (1986). *What works: Research about teaching and learning.* Washington, DC: Author.

Wang, M. C., & Lindvall, C. M. (1984). Individual differences and school learning environment. In E. W. Gordon (Ed.), *Review of Research in Education* (pp. 161–225). Washington, DC: American Educational Research Association.

Wang, M. C., & Walberg, H. J. (1985). *Adapting instruction to individual differences.* Berkeley, CA: McCutchan.

Williams, B. I., Richmond, P. A., & Mason, B. J. (Eds.). (1986). *Designs for compensatory education: Conference proceedings and papers.* Washington, DC: Research and Evaluation Associates, Inc.

Wittrock, M. C. (Ed.). (1986). *Handbook of research on teaching* (3rd ed.). A project of the American Educational Research Association. New York: Macmillan.

Supervision as a Proactive Process

Daresh, J. C. 1991. 129–30, 137–40. Prospect Heights, Ill.: Waveland.

Chapter 9.* Change Processes

As the late James Lipham (1965) pointed out in what has become a classic statement about leadership, the fundamental essence of leadership must always be conceived of as the process of bringing about needed change. Implicit within any leadership role, whether director of a private corporation or educational supervisor, is a responsibility to foster the type of change that will stimulate continuous growth and development in an organization. Administration or management, on the other hand, deals with maintaining the status quo in an organization. This distinction confronts us directly with a classic continually perplexing problem that school supervisors must face. As we noted in Chapter 3, supervisors who wish to be effective in that role must generally engage in administrative duties and behaviors on occasion. As a result, the supervisor who is charged with the responsibility of providing leadership or organizational change, in Lipham's terms, must also take care to guard the status quo when that is the most appropriate route for a school to follow. Is effective educational supervision an impossibility, then? Or at best a case of trying to walk an exceedingly narrow line between the competing demands of "changing" and "maintaining"? *No change* can mean organizational stagnation; *change for the sake of change* can result in organizational dysfunction. Being effective in this paradox of leadership and administration is like Goldilocks trying to find the perfect bowl of porridge: We need to be careful not to select something either "too hot" or "too cold"; it must be "just right." The supervisor has to know just the right times to push for change, and also when to hold the line.

In this chapter we explore organizational change processes as they relate to the practice of proactive educational supervision. We will review a number of conceptualizations of change that have appeared frequently in the literature and then some of the most typical and consistent barriers to promoting needed change in organizations. While change is a necessary condition for the improvement of organizations, it is in no way an easy condition either to promote or sustain. As a result, this chapter concludes with a consideration of some of the strategies that may be followed to reduce the typical constraints that inhibit needed organizational change.

Barriers to Organizational Change

One overriding concern about change must be addressed by the practitioner of supervision as a proactive process. Because of a number of existing barriers, change is difficult to initiate, implement, and maintain in an organization such as a school.

John Lovell and Kimball Wiles (1983) recognized the importance of the educational supervisor's role in stimulating change and identified the following typical barriers to organizational change in schools. For each barrier, we have suggested a way in which this issue is often played out in schools.

1. *Lack of commitment to system goals:* If the teachers or other staff members of a school do not either understand or accept the school's goals, they will not endorse a change to ensure that those goals are being met. This often occurs in settings where the administrative team assumes total control over the establishment of goals. Teachers typically will do little to support an agenda mandated by others, particularly if substantive change is required.

2. *Inadequate feedback:* Teachers frequently lack concrete information and evaluative feedback concerning their performance. We will consider this problem in greater depth in Chapter 14, but it has implications for change processes as well. Teachers' feelings of being left to drift lead to tension, anxiety, and the type of low morale that causes people to withdraw into their roles and avoid any risks required for change.

3. *Inadequate knowledge about the conditions of teaching and learning:* Change implies that some ideal way of behaving is fixed in people's minds as a goal. A high percentage of classroom teachers and others in schools, while serving quite successfully, are nevertheless lacking in the kind of knowledge base that would suggest desirable goals for improved performance and change.

4. *Attitudes toward or values about the proposed change:* If people start out with negative views about an innovation, that attitude will be hard to change. When the concept of team teaching was introduced as an innovation to teachers a number of years ago, it did not take root in many settings because teachers started with negative assumptions even before the practice was formally introduced.

5. *Satisfaction with status quo:* Teachers demonstrate the same reluctance to change their behaviors that others do. The old saying "if it ain't broke, don't fix it" applies equally to educators, who are not always convinced of the need to change the way they have done

---

* Editor's note: Chapter notation refers to this excerpt.

things in the past. This phenomenon is likely to be strongest in schools where there is a highly stable and mature teaching staff.

6. *Inadequate skill development:* If people lack the skills needed to carry out a new program, they will resist change. A teacher who has little ability to work with groups of gifted students, for example, will resist being required to do just that as part of a new thinking-skills program.

7. *Strong vested interests in the status quo:* People may believe that they will lose something for which they have worked if changes are made in the system around them. Consider, for example, a case where a teacher foresees losing leadership status as chair of a subject department in a junior high school under a new organizational pattern for a middle school that proposes to dissolve departments.

8. *Lack of organizational support:* People will resist supporting a change if they believe that the larger system will not reward or endorse the change. Teachers often express resentment toward engaging in practices that they believe the central office will not wholeheartedly endorse.

9. *Closedness rather than openness in the system:* Teachers who work in schools in what Halpin calls an "open" organizational climate will be more likely to accept change. "Closed"-climate schools offer fewer opportunities for social interaction that might, in turn, spark greater interest in and support for change.

10. *Lack of compatibility between the change proposal and other dimensions of the organization:* When a change is introduced to one grade level team of teachers, for example, other teams may be affected by the change. If the reports from the first team are not positive, resistance will follow. On the other hand, when a small group gets "turned on" by an idea, others may follow readily.

11. *Threat to individuals:* The issue here is simple yet powerful: People fear new situations. Even a seemingly minor innovation introduced into school practices represents a new situation, and some resistance can be anticipated on that basis alone.

12. *Inadequate knowledge about restraints and possibilities in a situation:* People sometimes avoid participating in a change process because they assume that some unknown conditions will necessarily prohibit the change from being successfully implemented.

13. *Static organizational role structure:* Organizations do not always enjoy the kind of leadership that supports needed change. The majority of a teaching staff may push for some type of curricular or program change, but the principal may prohibit the change from taking place.

14. *Inadequate expertise for solving problems:* Change often brings with it certain problems related to transition. For the most part, people lack expertise in working with ambiguity and other problems that often accompany organizational change. In schools, teachers are generally well-prepared to serve in their assigned instructional roles, but they have had little or no preparation in handling the acceptance of innovation.

15. *Threat to officials in the organization:* The implementation of change in an organization implies significant modifications in existing power structures. Traditional leadership roles and the agendas held by those who inhabit these roles may need complete revision. Such modification, or even the possibility of such change, often carries with it great threats to those who have been "in charge" in the past. This potential "changing of the guard" causes the old guard to dig in its heels and resist. In schools, we often see resistance when principals or other administrators who have held their leadership positions for a long time are suddenly confronted with a change that they believe will erode their control of the schools. Teacher union activities in recent years have caused a considerable amount of negative reaction among some administrators, who believed that teachers wanted to change things "too fast and too much." Recent suggestions by educational reformers that the role of the principal as now defined is obsolete are, of course, not winning many administrative supporters.

16. *Inadequate rewards for change efforts:* People are often aware of the need for some type of organizational change and have the competence to bring the change about, but they do nothing simply because they decide that the rewards of the change effort will not be sufficient. Teachers might be asked to adopt a new language arts curriculum, for example, but decide that the costs for doing so, in terms of extra meetings, lack of additional pay, and so forth, far outweigh possible rewards.

These identified barriers to organizational change are useful to us in more accurately understanding the nature of organizational behavior. Simply stated, people generally have a tendency to remain constant in their behaviors. Change requires effort; it is easier not to move. Fortunately, people sometimes do engage in innovative practices. To encourage them in that process, proactive supervisors may find recent research on the phases of change useful.

References

Lipham, James M. (1965). Leadership and administration. In Daniel Griffiths (Ed.), *Behavioral science and educational administration*. Chicago: National Society for the Study of Education.

Lovell, John T., & Wiles, Kimball. (1983). *Supervision for better schools* (5th Ed.). Englewood Cliffs, NJ: Prentice-Hall.

Getting Reform Right: What Works and What Doesn't

Fullan, Michael G., and Matthew B. Miles. 1992. *Phi Delta Kappan* 73(10):745–52.

There are as many myths as there are truths associated with change, Messrs. Fullan and Miles assert, and educators need to deepen the way they think about change. To that end, the authors analyze seven reasons change fails and offer seven "propositions" for successful change.

After years of failed education reform, educators are more and more in the habit of saying that "knowledge of the change process" is crucial. But few people really know what that means. The phrase is used superficially, glibly, as if saying it over and over will lead to understanding and appropriate action.

We do believe that knowing about the change process is crucial. But there are as many myths as there are truths associated with change, and it is time to deepen the way we think about change. We need to assess our knowledge more critically and describe what we know. One needs a good deal of sophistication to grasp the fundamentals of the change process and to use that knowledge wisely.

We also believe that serious education reform will never be achieved until there is a significant increase in the number of people—leaders and other participants alike—who have come to internalize and habitually act on basic knowledge of how successful change takes place. Reformers talk of the need for deeper, second-order changes in the structures and cultures or schools, rather than superficial first-order changes.[1] But no change would be more fundamental than a dramatic expansion of the capacity of individuals and organizations to understand and deal with change. This generic capacity is worth more than a hundred individual success stories of implementing specific innovations. As we shall see, even individual success stories don't last long without an appreciation of how to keep changes alive.

Rather than develop a new strategy for each new wave of reform, we must use basic knowledge about the do's and don'ts of bringing about *continuous improvement*. In this article we present this knowledge in the form of seven basic reasons why reform fails—and seven propositions that could lead to success.

Why Reform Fails

Schools and districts are overloaded with problems —and, ironically, with solutions that don't work. Thus things get worse instead of better. Even our rare success stories appear as isolated pockets of excellence and are as likely to atrophy as to prosper over time. We get glimpses of the power of change, but we have little confidence that we know how to harness forces for continuous improvement. The problem is not really lack of innovation, but the enormous overload of fragmented, uncoordinated, and ephemeral attempts at change.

We begin with reasons why typical approaches do not work. In our view there are seven basic reasons why reforms fail. Though each one has its own form, these seven should be understood in combination, as a set.

1. Faulty maps of change.

It's hard to get to a destination when your map doesn't accurately represent the territory you're to traverse. Everyone involved in school reform—teachers, administrators, parents, students, district staff members, consultants, board members, state department officials, legislators, materials developers, publishers, test-makers, teacher educators, researchers—has a personal map of how change proceeds. These constructs are often expressed in the form of a proposition or statement.

1. Resistance is inevitable, because people resist change.
2. Every school is unique.
3. *Plus ça change, plus c'est la même chose.*
4. Schools are essentially conservative institutions, harder to change than other organizations.
5. You just have to live reform one day at a time.
6. You need a mission, objectives, and a series of tasks laid out well in advance.
7. You can never please everyone, so just push ahead with reforms.
8. Full participation of everyone involved in a change is essential.
9. Keep it simple, stupid: go for small, easy changes rather than big, demanding ones.
10. Mandate change, because people won't do it otherwise.

People act on their maps. But maps such as these don't provide reliable or valid guidance. Some, like number 1, are simply self-sealing and tautological. Others, like number 2, are true in the abstract but totally unhelpful in providing guidance. Imagine if a Michelin guide book were to tell you that "each restaurant is unique," refuse to make ratings, and tell you that you're on your own.

Some, like number 3, have the seductive appearance of truth, though they are mostly false. It stretches the bounds of credulity to say that the schools we see today are no different from those of yesteryear or that all change efforts are self-defeating. Such maps are self-defeating. At their worst, they tell us that nothing really changes—and that nothing will work. On such self-exculpatory propositions as number 4, there's simply very little evidence, and what there is leads to the verdict of "not proven."[2]

Sometimes our maps are in conflict with themselves or with the maps of colleagues. For example, number 5 advocates the virtues of improvisation, while number 6 lauds rational planning. In fact, the literature on organizational change and a recent study of major change in urban high schools show that *neither* statement is valid as a guide to successful school reform.[3] The same appears to be true for propositions 7 and 8.

Still other mapping statements are directly contradicted by empirical evidence. For example, though number 9 looks obvious, studies of change have repeatedly found that substantial change efforts that address multiple problems are more likely to succeed and survive than small-scale, easily trivialized innovations.[4]

And number 10, as attractive as it may be politically, simply doesn't work. Indeed, it often makes matters worse. You can't mandate important changes, because they require skill, motivation, commitment, and discretionary judgment on the part of those who must change.[5]

Our aim here is not to debunk all our maps. Maps are crucial. But unless a map is a valid representation of the territory, we won't get where we want to go. Later in this article, we will outline a map that, we believe, corresponds well with the real territory of change.

2. Complex problems.

Another major reason for the failure of reform is that the solutions are not easy—or even known in many cases. A number of years ago Arthur Wise labeled this problem the "hyperrationalization" of reform:

> To create goals for education is to will that something occur. But goals, in the absence of a theory of how to achieve them, are mere wishful thinking. If there is no reason to believe a goal is attainable—perhaps evidenced by the fact that it has never been attained—then a rational planning model may not result in goal attainment.[6]

The reform agenda has broadened in fundamental ways in the last five years. One need only mention the comprehensive reform legislation adopted in virtually every state and the scores of restructuring efforts in order to realize that current change efforts are enormously complex —both in the substance of their goals and in the capacity of individuals and institutions to carry out and coordinate reforms.

Education is a complex system, and its reform is even more complex. Even if one considers only seemingly simple, first-order changes, the number of components and their interrelationships are staggering: curriculum and instruction, school organization, student services, community involvement, teacher inservice training, assessment, reporting, and evaluation. Deeper, second-order changes in school cultures, teacher/student relationships, and values and expectations of the system are all the more daunting.

Furthermore, higher-order educational goals for all students require knowledge and abilities that we have never demonstrated. In many cases, we simply don't know how to proceed; solutions have yet to be developed. This is no reason to stop trying, but we must remember that it is folly to act as if we know how to solve complex problems in short order. We must have an approach to reform that acknowledges that we don't necessarily know all the answers, that is conducive to developing solutions as we go along, and that sustains our commitment and persistence to stay with the problem until we get somewhere. In other words, we need a different map for solving complex rather than simple problems.

3. Symbols over substance.

In the RAND-sponsored study of federal programs supporting educational change, Paul Berman and Milbrey McLaughlin found that some school districts adopted external innovations for opportunistic reasons rather than to solve a particular problem. These apparent reforms brought extra resources (which were not necessarily used for the intended purpose), symbolized that action was being taken (whether or not follow-up occurred), and furthered the careers of the innovators (whether or not the innovation succeeded). Thus the mere appearance of innovation is sometimes sufficient for achieving political success.

Education reform is as much a political as an educational process, and it has both negative and positive aspects. One need not question the motives of political decision makers to appreciate the negative. Political time lines are at variance with the time lines for education reform. This difference often results in vague goals, unrealistic schedules, a preoccupation with symbols of reform (new legislation, task forces, commissions, and the like), and shifting priorities as political pressures ebb and flow.

We acknowledge that symbols are essential for success. They serve to crystalize images and to attract and generate political power and financial resources. Symbols can also provide personal and collective meaning and give people faith and confidence when they are dealing with unclear goals and complex situations.[7] They are essential for galvanizing visions, acquiring resources, and carrying out concerted action. When symbols and substance are congruent, they form a powerful combination.

Nonetheless, reform often fails because politics favors symbols over substance. Substantial change in practice requires a lot of hard and clever work "on the ground," which is not the strong point of political players. After several experiences with the dominance of symbolic change over substantive change, people become cynical and take the next change that comes along much less seriously.

Symbolic change does not have to be without substance, however. Indeed, the best examples of effective symbols are grounded in rituals, ceremonies, and other events in the daily life of an organization. While we cannot have effective reform without symbols, we can easily have symbols without effective reform—the predominant experience of most educators and one that predisposes them to be skeptical about *all* reforms.

4. Impatient and superficial solutions.

Reforms also fail because our attempts to solve problems are frequently superficial. Superficial solutions, introduced quickly in an atmosphere of crisis, normally make matters worse.[8] This problem is all the more serious now that we are tackling large-scale reforms, for the consequences of failure are much more serious.

Reforms in structure are especially susceptible to superficiality and unrealistic time lines, because they can be launched through political or administrative mandates. Two examples at opposite ends of the political spectrum provide cases in point. A recent study of the impact of statewide testing in two states found that, while new testing mandates caused action at the local level, they also narrowed the curriculum and created adverse conditions for reform:

> [C]oping with the pressure to attain satisfactory results in high-stakes tests caused educators to develop almost a "crisis mentality" in their approach, in that they jumped quickly into "solutions" to address a specific issue. They narrowed the range of instructional strategies from which they selected means to instruct their students; they narrowed the content of the material they chose to present to students; and they narrowed the range of course offerings available to students.[9]

Site-based management—opposite in many ways to the strategy of centralized testing—also shows problems associated with structural reforms. Daniel Levine and Eugene Eubanks, among others, have indicated how school-based models often result in changes in formal decision-making structures but rarely result in a focus on developing instructional skills or on changing the culture of schools.[10] There are numerous other examples of new legislation and policies—career ladders, mentoring and induction policies, testing and competency requirements, and so on—being rushed into place with little forethought about possible negative consequences and side effects.

A related bane of reform is faddism. Schools, districts, and states are under tremendous pressure to reform. Innovation and reform are big business, politically and economically. The temptation is great to latch on to the quick fix, to go along with the trend, to react uncritically to endorsed innovations as they come and go. Local educators experience most school reforms as fads.

There are two underlying problems. One is that mistaken or superficial solutions are introduced; the other is that, even when the solution is on the right track, hasty implementation leads to failure. Structural solutions are relatively easy to initiate under the right political conditions, but they are no substitute for the hard work, skill, and commitment needed to blend different structural changes into a successful reform effort. In other words, changes in structure must go hand in hand with changes in culture and in the individual and collective capacity to work through new structures. Because education reform is so complex, we cannot know in advance exactly which new structures and behavioral patterns should go together or how they should mesh. But we do know that neglecting one or the other is a surefire recipe for failure.

5. Misunderstanding resistance.

Things hardly ever go easily during change efforts. Since change necessarily involves people, and people can commit willed actions, it seems natural to attribute progress that is slower than we might wish to their "resistance." Before a recent workshop, one of us asked a group of principals to list the problems they faced in a specific change project. More than half said resistance—variously known as intransigence, entrenchment, fearfulness, reluctance to buy in, complacency, unwillingness to alter behaviors, and failure to recognize the need for change. These traits were attributed to teachers and other staff members, though not to the principals themselves.

But it is usually unproductive to label an attitude or action "resistance." It diverts attention from real problems of implementation, such as diffuse objectives, lack of technical skill, or insufficient resources for change. In effect, the label also individualizes issues of change and converts everything into a matter of "attitude." Because such labeling places the blame (and the responsibility for the solution) on others, it immobilizes people and leads to "if only" thinking.

Change does involve individual attitudes and behaviors, but they need to be framed as natural responses to transition, not misunderstood as resistance. During transitions from a familiar to a new state of affairs, individuals must normally confront the loss of the old and commit themselves to the new, unlearn old beliefs and behaviors and learn new ones, and move from anxiousness and uncertainty to stabilization and coherence. Any significant change involves a period of intense personal and organizational learning and problem solving. People need supports for such work, not displays of impatience.

Blaming resistance for the slow pace of reform also keeps us from understanding that individuals and groups faced with something new need to assess the change for its genuine possibilities and for how it bears on their self-interest. From computers across the curriculum, to mainstreaming, to portfolio assessments, to a radical change in the time schedule, significant changes normally require extra effort during the transitional stage. Moreover, there's little certainty about the kinds of outcomes that may ensue for students and teachers (and less assurance that they will be any better than the status quo). These are legitimate issues that deserve careful attention.

Many reform initiatives are ill-conceived, and many others are fads. The most authentic response to such efforts is resistance. Nevertheless, when resistance is misunderstood, we are immediately set on a self-defeating path. Reframing the legitimate basis of most forms of resistance will allow us to get a more productive start and to isolate the real problems of improvement.

6. Attrition of pockets of success.

There are many examples of successful reforms in individual schools—cases in which the strong efforts of teachers, principals, and district administrators have brought about significant changes in classroom and school practice.[11] We do not have much evidence about the durability of such successes, but we have reason to believe that they may not survive if the conditions under which they developed are changed.

Successful reforms have typically required enormous effort on the part of one or more individuals—effort that may not be sustainable over time. For example, staff collaboration takes much energy and time to develop, yet it can disappear overnight when a few key people leave. What happens outside the school—such as changes in district policies on the selection and transfer of teachers and principals—can easily undo gains that have been made.

Local innovators, even when they are successful in the short run, may burn themselves out or unwittingly seal themselves off from the surrounding environment. Thus schools can become hotbeds of innovation and reform in the absence of external support, but they cannot *stay* innovative without the continuing support of the district and other agencies. Innovative schools may enjoy external support from a critically important sponsor (e.g., the district superintendent) or from a given agency only to see that support disappear when the sponsor moves on or the agency changes policies. Of course, the failure to institutionalize an innovation and build it into the normal structures and practices of the organization underlies the disappearance of many reforms.[12]

We suspect that few things are more discouraging than working hard against long odds over a period of time to achieve a modicum of success—only to see it evaporate in short order as unrelated events take their toll. It is not enough to achieve isolated pockets of success. Reform fails unless we can demonstrate that pockets of success add up to new structures, procedures, and school cultures that press for continuous improvement. So far there is little such evidence.

7. Misuse of knowledge about the change process.

The final problem is related to a particular version of faulty maps: "knowledge" of the change process is often cited as the authority for taking certain actions. Statements such as "Ownership is the key to reform," "Lots of inservice training is required," "The school is the unit of change," "Vision and leadership are critical," and so on are all half-truths. Taken literally, they can be misused.

Reform is systemic, and actions based on knowledge of the change process must be systemic, too. To succeed we need to link a number of key aspects of knowledge and maintain the connections before and during the process of change. In the following section we offer seven such themes, which we believe warrant being called propositions for success.

Propositions for Success

The seven basic themes or lessons derived from current knowledge of successful change form a set and must be contemplated in relation to one another. When it comes to reform, partial theories are not very useful. We can say flatly that reform will not be achieved until these seven orientations have been incorporated into the thinking and reflected in the actions of those involved in change efforts.

1. Change is learning—loaded with uncertainty.

Change is a process of coming to grips with new personal meaning, and so it is a learning process. Peter Marris states the problem this way:

> When those who have the power to manipulate changes act as if they have only to explain, and when their explanations are not at once accepted, shrug off opposition as ignorance or prejudice, they express a profound contempt for the meaning of lives other than their own. For the reformers have already assimilated these changes to their purposes, and worked out a reformulation which makes sense to them, perhaps through months or years of analysis and debate. If they deny others the chance to do the same, they treat them as puppets dangling by the threads of their own conceptions.[13]

Even well-developed innovations represent new meaning and new learning for those who encounter them initially and require time to assimilate them. So many studies have documented this early period of difficulty that we have given it a label—"the implementation dip."[14] Even in cases where reform eventually succeeds, things will often go wrong before they go right. Michael Huberman and Matthew Miles found that the absence of early difficulty in a reform effort was usually a sign that not much was being attempted; superficial or trivial change was being substituted for substantial change.[15]

More complex reforms, such as restructuring, represent even greater uncertainty: first, because more is being attempted; second, because the solution is not known in advance. In short, anxiety, difficulties, and uncertainty are *intrinsic to all successful change*.

One can see why a climate that encourages risk-taking is so critical. People will not venture into uncertainty unless there is an appreciation that difficulties encountered are a natural part of the process. And if people do not venture into uncertainty, no significant change will occur.

Understanding successful change as learning also puts ownership in perspective. In our view, ownership of a reform cannot be achieved *in advance* of learning something new. A deep sense of ownership comes only through learning. In this sense, ownership is stronger in the middle of a successful change process than at the beginning and stronger still at the end. Ownership is both a process and a state.

The first proposition for success, then, is to understand that all change involves learning and that all learning involves coming to understand and to be good at something new. Thus conditions that support learning must be part and parcel of any change effort. Such conditions are also necessary for the valid rejection of particular changes, because many people reject complex innovations prematurely, that is, before they are in a sound position to make such a judgment.

2. Change is a journey, not a blueprint.

If change involved implementing single, well-developed, proven innovations one at a time, perhaps we could make blueprints for change. But school districts and schools are in the business of implementing a bewildering array of innovations and policies simultaneously. Moreover, reforms that aim at restructuring are so multifaceted and complex that solutions for any particular setting cannot be known in advance. If one tries to account for the complexity of the situation with an equally complex implementation plan, the process will become unwieldy, cumbersome, and usually unsuccessful.

There can be no blueprints for change, because rational planning models for complex social change (such as education reform) do not work. Rather, what is needed is a guided journey. Karen Seashore Louis and Matthew Miles provide a clear analysis of this evolutionary planning process in their study of urban high schools involved in major change efforts:

> The evolutionary perspective rests on the assumption that the environment both inside and outside organizations is often chaotic. No specific plan can last for very long, because it will either become outmoded due to changing external pressures, or because disagreement over priorities arises within the organization. Yet there is no reason to assume that the best response is to plan passively, relying on incremental decisions. Instead, the organization can cycle back and forth between efforts to gain normative consensus about what it may become, to plan strategies for getting there, and to carry out decentralized incremental experimentation that harnesses the creativity of all members to the change effort.... Strategy is viewed as a flexible tool, rather than a semi-permanent expansion of the mission.[16]

The message is not the traditional "Plan, then do," but "Do, then plan . . . and do and plan some more." Even the development of a shared vision that is central to reform is better thought of as a journey in which people's sense of purpose is identified, considered, and continuously shaped and reshaped.

3. Problems are our friends.

School improvement is a problem-rich process. Change threatens existing interests and routines, heightens uncertainty, and increases complexity. The typical principal in the study of urban schools conducted by Louis and Miles mentioned three or four major problems (and several minor ones) with reform efforts. They ranged from poor coordination to staff polarization and from lack of needed skills to heart attacks suffered by key figures. Problems arise naturally from the demands of the change process itself, from the people involved, and from the structure and procedures of schools and districts. Some are easily solved; others are almost intractable.

It seems perverse to say that problems are our friends, but we cannot develop effective responses to complex situations unless we actively seek and confront real problems that are difficult to solve. Problems are our friends because only through immersing ourselves in problems can we come up with creative solutions. Problems are the route to deeper change and deeper satisfaction. In this sense, effective organizations "embrace problems" rather than avoid them.

Too often, change-related problems are ignored, denied, or treated as an occasion for blame and defense. Success in school reform efforts is much more likely when problems are treated as natural, expected phenomena. Only by tracking problems can we understand what we need to do next to get what we want. Problems must be taken seriously, not attributed to resistance or to the ignorance and wrongheadedness of others.

What to do about problems? In their study of urban schools, Louis and Miles classified coping styles, ranging from relatively shallow ones (doing nothing at all, procrastinating, "doing it the usual way," easing off, or increasing pressure) to deeper ones (building personal capacity through training, enhancing system capacity, comprehensive restaffing, or system restructuring/redesign). They found that schools that were least successful at change *always* used shallow coping styles. Schools that were successful in changing could and did make structural changes in an effort to solve difficult problems. However, they were also willing to use Band-Aid solutions when a problem was judged to be minor. It's important to note that successful schools did *not* have fewer problems than other schools— they just coped with them better.

The enemies of good coping are passivity, denial, avoidance, conventionality, and fear of being "too radical." Good coping is active, assertive, inventive. It goes to the root of the problem when that is needed.

We cannot cope better through being exhorted to do so. "Deep coping"—the key to solving difficult problems of reform—appears to be more likely when schools are working on a clear, shared vision of where they are heading and when they create an active coping structure (e.g., a coordinating committee or a steering group) that steadily and actively tracks problems and monitors the results of coping efforts. Such a structure benefits from empowerment, brings more resources to bear on problems, and keeps the energy for change focused. In short, the assertive pursuit of problems in the service of continuous improvement is the kind of accountability that can make a difference.

4. Change is resource-hungry.

Even a moderate-sized school may spend a million dollars a year on salaries, maintenance, and materials. And that's just for keeping schools as they are, not for changing them. Change demands additional resources for training, for substitutes, for new materials, for new space, and, above all, for time. Change is "resource-hungry" because of what

---

it represents—developing solutions to complex problems, learning new skills, arriving at new insights, all carried out in a social setting already overloaded with demands. Such serious personal and collective development necessarily demands resources.

Every analysis of the problems of change efforts that we have seen in the last decade of research and practice has concluded that time is the salient issue. Most recently, the survey of urban high schools by Louis and Miles found that the average principal with a schoolwide reform project spent 70 days a year on change management. That's 32% of an administrator's year. The teachers most closely engaged with the change effort spent some 23 days a year, or 13% of their time on reform. Since we have to keep school while we change school, such overloads are to be expected.

But time is energy. And success is likely only when the extra energy requirements of change are met through the provision of released time or through a redesigned schedule that includes space for the extra work of change.

Time is also money. And Louis and Miles discovered that serious change in big-city high schools requires an annual investment of between $50,000 and $100,000. They also found some schools spending five times that much with little to show for it. The key seemed to be whether the money simply went for new jobs and expensive equipment or was spent for local capacity-building (acquiring external assistance, training trainers, leveraging other add-on funds, and so on). Nevertheless, some minimum level of funding is always needed.

Assistance itself can be a major resource for change. It may include training, consulting, coaching, coordination, and capacity-building. Many studies have suggested that good assistance to schools is strong, sustained over years, closely responsive to local needs, and focused on building local capacity. Louis and Miles found that at least 30 days a year of *external* assistance—with more than that provided internally—was essential for success.

We can also think of educational "content resources" —such big ideas as effective schools, teaching for understanding, empowerment, and school-based management —that guide and energize the work of change. In addition, there are psychosocial resources, such as support, commitment, influence, and power. They're supposedly intangible, but they are critical for success.

The work of change requires attention not just to resources, but to "resourcing." The actions required are those of scanning the school and its environment for resources and matching them to existing needs; acquiring resources (buying, negotiating, or just plain grabbing); reworking them for a better fit to the situation; creating time through schedule changes and other arrangements; and building local capacity through the development of such structures as steering groups, coordinating committees, and cadres of local trainers.

Good resourcing requires facing up to the need for funds and abjuring any false pride about self-sufficiency. Above all, it takes willingness to invent, to go outside the frame in garnering and reworking resources. (We are reminded of the principal who used money for the heating system to pay for desperately needed repainting and renovation, saying, "I knew that, if the boiler broke, they'd have to fix it anyway.") The stance is one of steady and tenacious searching for and judicious use of the extra resources that any change requires. Asking for assistance and seeking other resources are signs of strength, not weakness.

5. Change requires the power to manage it.

Change initiatives do not run themselves. They require that substantial effort be devoted to such tasks as monitoring implementation, keeping everyone informed of what's happening, linking multiple change projects (typical in most schools), locating unsolved problems, and taking clear coping action. In Louis and Miles' study, such efforts occurred literally 10 times more frequently in successfully changing schools than in unchanging ones.

There appear to be several essential ingredients in the successful management of change. First, the management of change goes best when it is carried out by a *cross-role group* (say, teachers, department heads, administrators, and often—students and parents). In such a group different worlds collide, more learning occurs, and change is realistically managed. There is much evidence that steering a change effort in this way results in substantially increased teacher commitment.

Second, such a cross-role group needs legitimacy—i.e., a clear license to steer. It needs an explicit contract, widely understood in the school, as to what kinds of decisions it can make and what money it can spend. Such legitimacy is partly conferred at the front end and partly earned through the hard work of decision making and action. Most such groups do encounter staff polarization; they may be seen by others as an unfairly privileged elite; or they may be opposed on ideological grounds. Such polarization —often a sign that empowerment of a steering group is working—can be dealt with through open access to meetings, rotation of membership, and scrupulous reporting.

Third, even empowerment has its problems, and cooperation is required to solve them. Everyone has to learn to take the initiative instead of complaining, to trust colleagues, to live with ambiguity, to face the fact that shared decisions mean conflict. Principals have to rise above the fear of losing control, and they have to hone new skills: initiating actions firmly without being seen as "controlling," supporting others without taking over for them. All these stances and skills are learnable, but they take time. Kenneth Benne remarked 40 years ago that the skills of cooperative work should be "part of the general education of our people."[17] They haven't been, so far. But the technology for teaching these skills exists. It is up to steering groups to learn to work well together, using whatever assistance is required.

Fourth, the power to manage change does not stop at the schoolhouse door. Successful change efforts are most likely when the local district office is closely engaged with the changing school in a collaborative, supportive way and places few bureaucratic restrictions in the path of reform.

The bottom line is that the development of second-order changes in the culture of schools and in the capacity of teachers, principals, and communities to make a difference *requires* the power to manage the change at the local school level. We do not advocate handing over all decisions to the school. Schools and their environments must have an interactive and negotiated relationship. But complex problems cannot be solved from a distance; the steady growth of the power to manage change must be part of the solution.

6. Change is systemic.

Political pressures combine with the segmented, uncoordinated nature of educational organizations to produce a "project mentality."[18] A steady stream of episodic innovations—cooperative learning, effective schools research, classroom management, assessment schemes, career ladders, peer coaching, etc., etc.—come and go. Not only do they fail to leave much of a trace, but they also leave teachers and the public with a growing cynicism that innovation is marginal and politically motivated.

What does it mean to work systemically? There are two aspects: 1) reform must focus on the development and interrelationships of all the main *components* of the system simultaneously—curriculum, teaching and teacher development, community, student support systems, and so on; and 2) reform must focus not just on structure, policy, and regulations but on deeper issues of the *culture* of the system. Fulfilling both requirements is a tall order. But it is possible.

This duality of reform (the need to deal with system components and system culture) must be attended to at both the state and district/school levels. It involves both restructuring and "reculturing."[19] Marshall Smith and Jennifer O'Day have mapped out a comprehensive plan for systemic reform at the state level that illustrates the kind of thinking and strategies involved.[20] At the school/district level, we see in the Toronto region's Learning Consortium a rather clear example of systemic reform in action.[21] Schools, supported by their districts, avoid ad hoc innovations and focus on a variety of coordinated short-term and mid- to long-term strategies. The short-term activities include inservice professional development on selected and interrelated themes; mid- to long-term strategies include vision building, initial teacher preparation, selection and induction, promotion procedures and criteria, school-based planning in a system context, curriculum reorganization, and the development of assessments. There is an explicit emphasis on new cultural norms for collaborative work and on the pursuit of continuous improvement.

Systemic reform is complex. Practically speaking, traditional approaches to innovation and reform in education have not been successful in bringing about lasting improvement. Systemic reform looks to be both more efficient and more effective, even though this proposition is less proven empirically than our other six. However, both conceptually and practically, it does seem to be on the right track.[22]

7. All large-scale change is implemented locally.

Change cannot be accomplished from afar. This cardinal rule crystallizes the previous six propositions. The ideas that change is learning, change is a journey, problems are our friends, change is resource-hungry, change requires the power to manage, and change is systemic all embody the fact that *local* implementation by everyday teachers, principals, parents, and students is the only way that change happens.

This observation has both an obvious and a less obvious meaning. The former reminds us all that any interest in systemwide reform must be accompanied by a preoccupation with how it plays itself out locally. The less obvious implication can be stated as a caution: we should not assume that only the local level counts and hand everything over to the individual school. A careful reading of the seven propositions together shows that extra-local agencies have critical—though decidedly not traditional—roles to play. Most fundamentally, their role is to help bring the seven propositions to life at the local level.

Modern societies are facing terrible problems, and education reform is seen as a major source of hope for solving them. But wishful thinking and legislation have deservedly poor track records as tools for social betterment. As educators increasingly acknowledge that the "change process is crucial," they ought to know what that means at the level at which change actually takes place. Whether we are on the receiving or initiating end of change (as all of us are at one time or another), we need to understand why education reform frequently fails, and we need to internalize and live out valid propositions for its success. Living out the seven propositions for successful change means not only making the change process more explicit within our own minds and actions, but also contributing to the knowledge of change on the part of those with whom we interact. Being knowledgeable about the change process may be both the best defense and the best offense we have in achieving substantial education reform.

About the Authors

Michael G. Fullan is dean of the Faculty of Education at the University of Toronto. Matthew B. Miles is a senior research associate with the Center for Policy Research, New York, N.Y.

Notes

1. Larry Cuban, "Reforming, Again, Again, and Again," *Educational Researcher*, April 1990, pp. 3–13; Richard F. Elmore, ed., *Restructuring Schools* (San Francisco: Jossey-Bass, 1990); and Michael Fullan, with Suzanne Steigelbauer, *The New Meaning of Educational Change* (New York: Teachers College Press, 1991).
2. Matthew H. Miles, "Mapping the Common Properties of Schools," in Rolf Lehming and Michael Kane, eds., *Improving Schools: Using What We Know* (Santa Monica, Calif.: Sage, 1981), pp. 42–114; and Matthew B. Miles and Karen Seashore Louis, "Research on Institutionalization: A Reflective Review," in Matthew B. Miles, Mats Ekholm, and Rolf Vandenberghe, eds., *Lasting School Improvement: Exploring the Process of Institutionalization* (Leuven, Belgium: Acco, 1987), pp. 24–44.

3. Karen Seashore Louis and Matthew B. Miles, *Improving the Urban High School: What Works and Why* (New York: Teachers College Press, 1990).

4. Paul Berman and Milbrey W. McLaughlin, *Federal Programs Supporting Educational Change, Vol VIII: Implementing and Sustaining Innovations* (Santa Monica. Calif.: RAND Corporation, 1977); and Michael Huberman and Matthew B. Miles, *Innovation Up Close: How School Improvement Works* (New York: Plenum, 1984).

5. Milbrey W. McLaughlin, "The Rand Change Agent Study Revisited: Macro Perspectives and Micro Realities," *Educational Researcher*, December 1990, pp. 11–16.

6. Arthur Wise, "Why Educational Policies Often Fail: The Hyperrationalization Hypothesis," *Curriculum Studies*, vol. 1, 1977, p. 48.

7. Lee Bolman and Terrence Del, *Reframing Organizations* (San Francisco: Jossey-Bass, 1990).

8. Samuel D. Sieber, *Fatal Solutions* (Norwood, N.J.: Ablex, 1982).

9. H. Dickson Corbett and Bruce Wilson, *Testing, Reform, and Rebellion* (Norwood, N.J.: Ablex, 1990), p. 207.

10. Daniel U. Levine and Eugene E. Eubanks, "Site-Based Management: Engine for Reform or Pipedream? Pitfalls and Prerequisites for Success in Site-Based Management," unpublished manuscript, University of Missouri, Kansas City.

11. Bruce Joyce et al., "School Renewal as Cultural Change," *Educational Leadership*, November 1989, pp. 70–77; Louis and Miles, op. cit.; and Richard Wallace, Paul LeMahieu, and William Bickel, "The Pittsburgh Experience: Achieving Commitment to Comprehensive Staff Development," in Bruce Joyce, ed., *Changing School Culture Through Staff Development* (Alexandria, Va.: Association for Supervision and Curriculum Development, 1990), pp. 185–202.

12. Miles and Louis, op. cit.: and Matthew B. Miles and Mats Ekholm, "Will New Structures *Stay* Restructured?", paper presented at the annual meeting of the American Educational Research Association, Chicago, 1991.

13. Peter Marris, *Loss and Change* (New York: Doubleday, 1975), p. 166.

14. Fullan, with Steigelbauer, op. cit.

15. Huberman and Miles, op. cit.

16. Louis and Miles, p. 193.

17. Kenneth D. Benne. "Theory of Cooperative Planning," *Teachers College Record*, vol. 53, 1952, pp. 429–35.

18. Marshall Smith and Jennifer O'Day, "Systemic School Reform," in Susan Fuhrman and Bruce Malen, eds., *The Politics of Curriculum and Testing* (Philadelphia: Falmer Press, 1990), pp. 233–67.

19. "Systemic reform" is both a more accurate and a more powerful label than "restructuring" because it explicitly encompasses both structure and culture. See Andy Hargreaves, "Restructuring Restructuring: Postmodernity and the Prospects for Educational Change," paper presented at the annual meeting of the American Educational Research Association, Chicago, 1991.

20. Smith and O'Day, op. cit.

21. Nancy Watson and Michael Fullan, "Beyond School District-University Partnerships," in Michael Fullan and Andy Hargreaves, eds., *Teacher Development and Change* (Toronto: Falmer Press, 1992), pp. 213–42.

22. See Peter Senge, *The Fifth Discipline* (New York: Doubleday, 1990); and Michael G. Fullan, *Productive Educational Change: Going Deeper* (London: Falmer Press).

Introducing Change with Success

Luby, M. A., M. S. Moser, and L. Posey. 1991. In *Capital wisdom: Papers from the Principals Academy 1991*, 48–54. Washington, D.C.: National Catholic Educational Association

As competitors in the developing free-enterprise educational system of the 21st century, Catholic school leaders are building our tomorrows. The ability to effect quality change is critical. The following provides a model for administrators who wish to facilitate this quality change.

As administrators study the model (charted on page 108), we ask them to recall the story of the tortoise and the hare, and to identify with the tortoise. Success in implementing quality change will not be determined by how quickly administrators "run the race" or by how superbly administrators razzle dazzle others with their swiftness. We contend that change will be the result of comprehensive, thoughtful planning which entails "running the race" slowly but surely.

Many agents of change enter our lives. Administrators attend a meeting or conference and are intrigued with a new idea. A teacher sits at the lunch table and poses a problem or question to his/her peers. A student remarks in all sincerity, "I'm bored." A parent responds to an annual school evaluation survey. Each of these is a possible agent of change that provides an administrator with the opportunity to begin a slow but sure journey into the future.

The challenge has been made; let the race begin.

Agents of change

Agents of change include a variety of concepts, people and events. Conceptual agents of change include: diocesan, local and course mission statements; state department of education directives; and central office directives. In reviewing mission statements, directives and philosophies, administrators become aware of the need to change and/or introduce change in order to be who we say we are or to meet requirements. Annual reviews and recommitments to our philosophy should include time to be open to change and a willingness to dream.

People who initiate change include administrators, teachers, parents, students and community members. In the past year, a parent response on an annual survey and a teacher request initiated a consideration of expanding the kindergarten program 15 minutes each day. A class remark that "Mondays are boring" initiated a study of weekly mini-classes (on Mondays) for the next year.

Events can also initiate change. Through attendance at conferences and meetings, coursework and professional journals, administrators receive many ideas and inspirations.

When we encounter an agent of change, we can act and facilitate or we can react and do nothing. Thus, as administrators, the first questions we need to ask are: Will I listen with an open mind to this agent of change? Will I ignore or dismiss this agent of change?

Listen and respond

If an administrator chooses to respond openly to an agent of change, we suggest that he/she complete two initial steps. First, he/she will need to conduct preliminary research on the possible change. This research can be very informal: obtaining information from other administrators; verbal surveys of teachers, parents and/or students; brainstorming sessions with faculty; and reviewing written information about the suggested change. Formal research could include written surveys of teachers, parents and/or students; attendance at informational sessions; and/or a study of available materials.

Second, the administrator must evaluate the suggested change in light of the school mission statement and philosophy. The change needs to be compatible with, supportive of, and enhancing to the mission statement and philosophy. Ultimately change is initiated in order to enable our schools to live their philosophy more fully and faithfully. Therefore, this step is crucial to the success of any change.

Questions at this stage are

◆ What are the characteristics of the suggested change?
◆ What are the positive aspects?
◆ What are the negative aspects?
◆ Is this change something our school would like to pursue?
◆ Will this change enable us to meet the needs of our students? staff?
◆ Will this change enable us to live our philosophy more fully?
◆ Is this change consistent with our values and vision?
◆ Is this a change that merits further investigation or can the administrator handle it managerially?

At this stage, the administrator has three choices. The first choice is to declare the idea invalid and drop it. The second choice is to declare the idea valid and handle it managerially at the administrative level. The third choice is to declare the idea valid and continue the change process through a staff committee. Examples of options two and three are indicated below.

Managerial	Committee
Extending kindergarten hours	Mini classes
Field trip opportunity	Dress code
Student council clash day	Study skills program
Advent prayer service	Soccer program

Remember: A turtle only makes progress by sticking out its neck.

Form committee for possible change

It is time to involve others more fully in the process. The administrator's enthusiasm and knowledge of the proposed change will enable him/her to generate interest and help in taking the next steps. The involvement of others will require a committee, keeping these steps in mind.

Define membership. To clearly define the membership of the committee, consider why you are choosing the members. Select members who will look at all facets involved and who have a clear understanding of the school philosophy and mission. Membership in the committee may include principal, pastor, teachers, parents, students and community members.

Define responsibilities. The members must understand their specific committee responsibilities as well as their overall responsibility to the school and its future. Specific responsibilities will be defined by the nature of the proposed change. Subcommittees may be necessary. Committee members do need to know who will make the final decision.

Conduct investigation. The investigation will include in-depth research, observations of existing programs, and attendance at workshops and in-services. Part of the investigation should include a cost analysis.

Evaluate in relation to mission statement. When the proposed change is understood more fully, the committee will evaluate it in light of the school philosophy and mission. If compatibility, support and enhancement exist, the proposed change continues to be viable.

Submit recommendation. The final recommendation of the committee should be submitted in writing. Three recommendation options are

◆ Drop: Include reasons for a recommendation not to consider the change.
◆ Hold: If a proposed change is not financially feasible, it can be placed on hold until funding is secured.
◆ Continue: If the committee concludes that the program is viable and recommends continuance toward an action plan, the recommendation should include the rationale for continuance.

Prepare action plan

The action plan will include the why, what, who, when and how of implementing the proposed change.

◆ Why: Include the rationale submitted with the recommendation to continue.
◆ What: Name the tasks to be accomplished.
◆ Who: Individuals responsible for tasks should be identified.
◆ When: A timeline for preparation, implementation and evaluation should be determined.
◆ How: Prepare the budget; include resources and training.

In preparing the action plan, the administrator and committee need to consider two key components. First, a

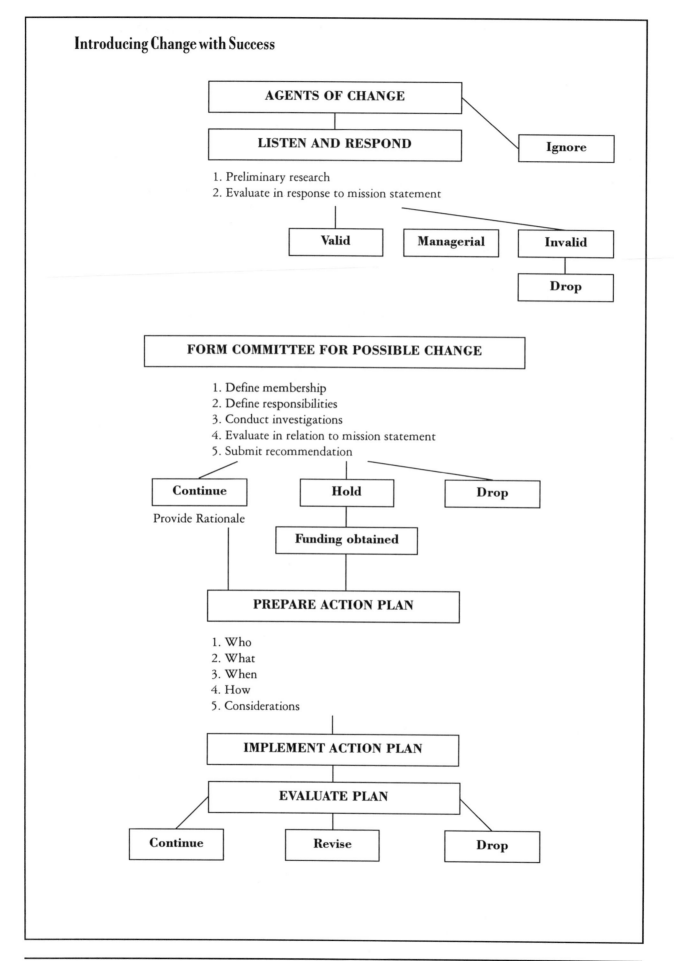

AGENTS OF CHANGE

LISTEN AND RESPOND   **Ignore**

1. Preliminary research
2. Evaluate in response to mission statement

Valid   **Managerial**   **Invalid**

Drop

FORM COMMITTEE FOR POSSIBLE CHANGE

1. Define membership
2. Define responsibilities
3. Conduct investigations
4. Evaluate in relation to mission statement
5. Submit recommendation

Continue   **Hold**   **Drop**

Provide Rationale

Funding obtained

PREPARE ACTION PLAN

1. Who
2. What
3. When
4. How
5. Considerations

IMPLEMENT ACTION PLAN

EVALUATE PLAN

Continue   **Revise**   **Drop**

unified approach to a completed action plan is essential. Including and informing faculty, staff, parents, students and community during the process will go a long way. Look for opportunities to plant seeds and reap benefits later. Saphier advises administrators to "involve all parties whose working conditions will be affected by the decision."[1]

Second, comprehensive planning is necessary and will take time. Sizer notes that "planning requires a major investment of time; the time needed to think through . . . matters carefully must not be underestimated."[2]

Implement action plan

Now that the finish line is in sight, keep the momentum going. It is important to communicate the action plan clearly and fully to all those affected. Ask for and consider the feedback of all parties involved. People feel a decision to implement is fair when administrators involve them in the change process and invite them to take ownership of the change.

Comprehensive support and appropriate training to accomplish the action plan are vital to successful, quality change.

Evaluate plan

Monitoring and evaluating the implementation of the change is essential. Include an evaluation process and timeline in the action plan. The evaluation process should include a component to ensure that the change is supportive of the school's vision and values. At the end of evaluation, options are: to continue the change, to continue with a revised version of the change, or to drop the change.

Our tomorrows will be changing continually. Just as the tortoise kept the finish line in sight, administrators for tomorrow need to keep the constancy of quality change before them in order to educate children for the 21st century.

Notes

1. Jon Saphier, *How to Make Decisions That Stay Made*, Alexandria, VA, Association for Supervision and Curriculum Development, 1989.
2. Ron Brandt, "On Changing Secondary Schools: A Conversation with Ted Sizer," *Leadership*, vol. 45, no. 5, pp. 30–36.

About the Authors

Mary Ann Luby
    Sacred Heart School
    Emporia, Kansas
Mary Sue Moser
    Blessed Sacrament School
    Omaha, Nebraska
Lyne Posey
    Mary Immaculate Star of the Sea School
    Key West, Florida

Improving Schools from Within

Barth, R. S. 1991. 68–78. San Francisco: Jossey-Bass.

The Principal as Learner

As learners, principals have a bad reputation. Many in my own school community wondered whether, as principal, I was educable. Parents, teachers, students, central office personnel, and even other principals sometimes had their doubts. Sometimes, so did I. Let me share some very good reasons why it is so difficult for school principals to become learners as well as leaders.

One, of course, is lack of time. "If I participate in that teachers' math workshop, the schedules for next semester and the phone messages from parents will go unattended." Yet we all find time for what is important and comfortable to us. Protesting a lack of time is another way of saying that other things are more important and perhaps more comfortable. Pushed harder, many principals reveal that "the consequences of my *not* engaging in my own learning appear to be far less severe than the consequences of my not answering the phone messages or attending to the kids in need of discipline at my door." When one's own learning is neglected there appears to be no "downside."

A second impediment comes from principals' prior experiences as learners. Most come to new opportunities for learning with old baggage. District inservice training and university course work have often left principals unsatisfied and turned off. Few retain much confidence that staff development will be engaging, let alone helpful, to them in running their schools. Skepticism, if not cynicism, abounds. Principals build up antibodies against attempts by others to remediate them. Many become gifted and talented at resisting fiercely, if covertly, a deficiency model of staff development that says, "Here's what I expect of you," and asks, "How well are you doing it?" Many attend, few succumb, fewer learn. And even if principals have been successfully trained by means of these staff development activities, without feedback and skillful, ongoing coaching little comes of it. Principals find that the linkages between their behavior in a workshop setting and their behavior in a school are convoluted and tenuous indeed.

Third, many principals consider it unethical, if not sinful, to use public funds and "company time" for their own learning. Like teachers, they see themselves and are seen as public servants whose place is to serve, not to be served. The purpose of schools is to promote student learning. Taking money from the school budget to engage in professional growth opportunities is tantamount to snatching bread from the mouths of babes. Think of what the school could purchase with that money—teacher aides, books, magic markers. And think of what you could accomplish at your school during that two-hour workshop! A strong measure of Calvinism remains deeply embedded in the school culture.

Another obstacle to principals becoming learners is that by publicly engaging in learning they reveal themselves as flawed. To be a learner in many school settings is an admission of imperfection, a scarlet letter. One principal told me that, when he left his district to come to the Harvard Summer Institute, another said to him, only half in jest, "I'm glad the superintendent chose the one who needed it the most." Few principals enjoy the respect and authority they desire and need. They can ill afford to render themselves more vulnerable by telegraphing their inadequacies to the school community. Consequently, principals find themselves forbidden not to know. To become a learner is to admit that the screening committee and superintendent made a mistake; it is somehow to suggest that the principal is not one to whom parents can entrust their children. "Principals," as one put it, "suffer under the burden of presumed competence. Everyone supposes we know how to do it. We get trapped into pretending we know how to do it."

Many principals also consider it inappropriate to be a learner. Just as teachers want children to learn but see their own learning as less necessary, principals want teachers to learn but do not feel that a math workshop is appropriate for them. Reform always begins one rung on the ladder below the reformer. The moral order of the school universe places the principal in authority as knower. The principal as learner is out of place. The principal running faculty meetings or answering phone messages is in place.

Finally, if principals do engage in a learning experience and learn something—a new way of thinking about curriculum, a new interpersonal skill, a new idea about improving school climate—they are then faced with having to *do* something with it. They are rewarded for their efforts at learning by additional work. A most curious reinforcement! Small wonder that many principals, contemplating their own professional development, hesitate because they fear such experiences will further deplete time and energy, already in too short supply.

Any one of these impediments to the principal becoming a serious learner is a force to be reckoned with. Together, they suggest why so few school leaders are learners. These road blocks to principals' learning help to explain why, after much fanfare announcing the birth of the Principals' Center at Harvard and a mailing of 1,500 invitations to administrators in the Boston area, only five persons showed up for the first event. And two of us were the staff of the Center!

Given this massive inertia working against the principal as learner, why bother What does it matter? Why can't learning for the leader be dismissed as another "it would be nice but"? There are, I believe, compelling reasons that make addressing these impediments not only important, but essential to the health of any school, especially to one that would become a community of learners.

Many of the skills recognized as important for an effective principal are *learned* skills. Take, for instance, the effective schools literature. A principal can *learn* how to continuously monitor the performance of pupils; can *learn* how to convey high expectations to teachers and pupils alike; and can *learn* how to orchestrate a safe, orderly environment. In designing the Principals' Center at Harvard, we enlisted twenty-eight outstanding principals in the Boston area to help us. We found that all of them were vitally interested in the professional development of principals—in their own development and that of others. This offered a bit of early evidence that the quality of the school and the learning of the principal are highly correlated.

Learning is replenishing. We deplore teachers who mindlessly repeat every move this year that they made last year. Yet after several years, principals face equally severe tendencies to switch on to "automatic pilot." One of the reasons I left the principalship was a growing feeling that I was becoming a tape recorder, replaying the same tape for the same events each year. I had a tape for parent orientation night, for new teachers, for the parent concerned about Johnny's reading score—for, it seemed, every occasion. It dawned on me that parents and teachers and students deserved more than a tape—and I deserved to be more than a tape recorder, a sure sign of clinical death. The school suffers. Parents suffer. Students suffer. And the principal suffers. Learning is the best antidote to the deadening routinization so endemic to schools.

Perhaps the most powerful reason for principals to be learners as well as leaders, to overcome the many impediments to their learning, is the extraordinary influence of modeling behavior. Do as I do, as well as I say, is a winning formula. If principals want students and teachers to take learning seriously, if they are interested in building a community of learners, they must not only be head teachers, headmasters, or instructional leaders. They must, above all, be *head learners*. I believe it was Ralph Waldo Emerson who once said that what you *do* speaks so loudly that no one can hear what you *say*.

And, finally, the impediments to the leader becoming the head learner are worth confronting and addressing because principals are people. The most noble and distinguishing characteristic of human life is the capacity to learn. Learning is a sign of life. A school can become a community of learners. And principals are as entitled as others to engage in its central activity, whether or not students' achievement scores improve accordingly. Learning is in and of itself a precious value of which too many principals have been deprived or have deprived themselves. Learning is the lifelong expression of our sense of wonder and of worth.

Fostering Professional Growth

Like most who work in schools these days, principals walk a narrow edge between being able and not being able to fulfill their complex job. Exhaustion and discouragement are high; discretionary energy and time are low. In such a climate, opportunities to participate in a new activity, even one addressed to the principal's own renewal, entail risks and demand that the principal give up something to make room for the new activity or else risk becoming further overextended and depleted. A major paradox confronting any who would assist principals as well as teachers in becoming learners in their schools, then, is that professional development is energy and time depleting as well as energy and time replenishing.

Now that links between principal performance and pupil performance are beginning to be forged in the research community and the importance of continued professional education for principals more widely recognized, there is a clear need for more inventive models and formats for promoting their professional growth. Sustaining the development of school leaders is crucial to the quality of life and to the best interests of all who inhabit the schoolhouse—and to their development as a community of learners. Principals, no less than teachers, need replenishment and invigoration and an expanded repertoire of ideas and practices with which to respond to staggering demands. And even more, principals need a clear vision and a sense of their own professionalism. It is to the development of these qualities that I now turn.

Learning to Lead

In order not only to survive but to flourish, principals need to be able to discuss promising school practices without fear of violating a taboo; they need to learn to share problems without worrying about appearing inadequate. They need to recognize that adult learning is not only legitimate but essential. They need help clarifying and becoming confident about their goals, ideas, and practices so they can act thoughtfully.

This constellation of crucial and largely unmet needs led in 1981 to the creation of the Principals' Center at Harvard. Over 100 other centers have been established in the United States and abroad. A National Network of Principals' Centers—with its headquarters at the Harvard Graduate School of Education—now supports emerging and existing centers through newsletters, conferences, an annual journal, and year-long informal interactions.

What Is a Principals' Center?

While there is no orthodox model of a "principals' center," while diversity among centers is part of the energy that propels the Network, the Principals' Center at Harvard shares with others many common purposes:

◆ To provide helpful assistance to principals and other school leaders that will enable them to become more successful in fulfilling their goals and providing leadership to their school

- ◆ To help principals cope with the changing realities of school administration, including increased time demands, collective bargaining, declining resources, and new state and federal guidelines
- ◆ To bring together principals from across districts to share experiences, ideas, concerns, and successes
- ◆ To identify promising school practices and arrange for principals who wish to engage in similar practices to visit one another's schools
- ◆ To encourage the formation of networks among principals, school districts, state departments, private foundations, professional associations, and universities
- ◆ To provide a mechanism for practitioners to take responsibility for promoting their own professional growth
- ◆ To provide assistance to principals in sharing leadership with teachers, parents, and students within their schools
- ◆ To provide a national forum for discussion of school leadership and professional training
- ◆ To bring attention to the relationship of principals' professional development to good schools
- ◆ To explore new conceptions of school leadership

Teacher centers in the 1960s and 1970s demonstrated that practitioners can take an active role in determining their professional training needs and provide a significant portion of that training. Although principals' centers frequently draw on the resources of universities, central offices, and state departments of education, they too are places where school practitioners play the major role in their own professional development. In short, a principals' center is *principal-centered*. Its activities emanate from the concerns and aspirations of the principals themselves, and its vitality relies heavily on the resources principals have to offer one another.

Like teachers, principals have a great capacity to stimulate professional growth and improved practice in their colleagues because they occupy the same rung on the bureaucratic ladder. They neither evaluate nor are evaluated by one another. In short, principals constitute a potential cohort—a potential "group 3," in the terminology of Chapter Five. However, because the culture of schools neither rewards nor encourages the sharing of ideas and resources among principals any more than among teachers, there is a pronounced need for a mediator leading toward their professional interdependence.

Principals are capable of interdependence and learning if the conditions are right. Considering the importance of the principalship, of the professional development of principals, the lack of success with principals' staff development, and the host of impediments that prevent leaders from becoming learners, what have we learned at the Principals' Center at Harvard during the past decade about the conditions necessary for principals' learning? A major proposition underlies our efforts: *Principals will be seriously involved in designing and conducting their professional development*. It is our belief that the critical element in principals' learning—indeed in anyone's learning—is ownership. Learning must be something principals do, not something others do to or for them. The questions asked at the Principals' Center at Harvard, then, are the following: Under what conditions will principals become committed, lifelong learners in their important work? Under what conditions will principals assume major responsibility for their learning? And, What conditions can principals devise to encourage and support their own learning?

As I have mentioned, our conviction that a principals' center must be principal-centered led to enlisting twenty-eight Boston-area principals as designers of the Center. After six months of deliberations, this group came up with several building blocks for the Center, each of which, ten years later, surprisingly is still in place, attached to the cornerstone of principals' involvement and ownership. Let me share what these principals put in place.

There are no more important decisions affecting principals' staff development than those determining the content and format of activities. An advisory board, chaired by a principal and joined by eighteen other Boston-area principals and four Harvard faculty members, was established to ensure that the major voice about the program was the principals'. Discussions at board meetings follow a common pattern: brainstorming about issues about which principals want to learn more (for example, new technologies, dealing with diversity); sharpening questions related to each theme (for instance, How can a new Apple II be used both as a management tool and an instructional tool?, or How can the principal come to use differences of age, gender, race, and ability within a school as opportunities for school improvement?). The board then identifies consultants, university professors, and principals as possible resources. Then members develop an idea, select resource persons, and devise formats. Finally, a staff member of the center, often a doctoral student interested in the principalship, takes the plan and invites speakers, secures a room, advertises the seminar, and evaluates the session.

Many observers initially questioned the wisdom of turning responsibility for programs over to principals, fearing that their decisions, like those made by some high schoolers in an "open campus," might be frivolous. Many feared that the Principals' Center would offer what principals "want" rather than what they "need." Conversely, principals were suspicious that the Center would be a disguised attempt by Harvard to "inservice" them. Over time, suspicions abated as principals demonstrated enthusiasm and inventiveness in planning programs for their colleagues. A list of some of the themes addressed at the Center would probably pass muster in most quarters:

- ◆ Curriculum improvement
- ◆ Shared leadership
- ◆ Using and not being used by the national reports
- ◆ New conceptions of school leadership
- ◆ Adult development

- Staff development within the school
- Special needs students and mainstreaming
- Gifted and talented students
- Dealing with minimum competency requirements
- The impact of standardized testing
- Issues facing a woman principal
- Instructional skills
- Proposal writing for grants
- Pupil and teacher evaluation
- Supervision of teachers
- Involving parents productively in a school
- Constructing a budget
- Decision making
- Priority setting
- Time management
- Dealing with stress
- Assertiveness training
- Self-understanding
- Racial and cultural awareness
- Vision

We are finding that principals, like teachers, carry with them extraordinary insights about their work that are seldom explicit for them, let alone accessible to others. The work of the Center is to reveal this abundance of thinking and practice so it may be more widely available to improve schools. We have engaged in a long and difficult struggle against the belief held by many practitioners that one's success in schools is a private matter, best kept from potential competitors or critics. Equally difficult to overcome is the belief harbored by some principals that the knowledge base for improving schools lies more in universities than within themselves. Many worried, for instance, that when principals talked they would reveal, not craft knowledge, but war stories. But more and more principals are acknowledging the importance of what they know and finding ways of making it available and valuable to others.

Soar with Your Strengths

Clifton, D. O., and P. Nelson. 1992. 111–22. New York: Delacorte Press.

Mission and the Bottom Line

Though mission seems like a spiritual pursuit, it can have an impact on worldly matters.

Even in our studies of insurance sales agents, we found that some of the top performers felt guided by a sense of mission. They would see an insured family where the father had died and feel satisfaction because they contributed to the family's ability to stay together and educate the children.

Some great insurance agents are so driven by mission that they were moved to tears during interviews because they were so concerned for someone they could not help.

When Mission Grows Thin, Organizations Deteriorate

Peter Drucker has said that foremost in the minds of executives must be the reality that their organization exists because it serves people outside of their organization.

When companies think only of how many units they can produce or sell, something happens to the spirit of the organization, and sales decrease rather than increase.

When the Detroit automakers focused only on how many cars they could move rather than how well they could serve the American people with quality transportation (their mission), they lost 30 percent of the market share.

When hospitals think only of how to fill their beds rather than how to be a quality place for people to claim their health, they have financial problems.

This phenomenon has been so clear in our study of companies that we voice strong concern whenever an organization, whether business, church, or school, emphasizes selling units over providing quality service to customers.

In business, when a manager communicates a genuine sense of mission to co-workers, profits and productivity usually follow. The more frequently a salesperson speaks of his or her mission, the higher his or her sales will be. Mission and profits are interdependent.

Mission as Motivator

Selling can be a selfish experience, serving the seller more than the customer. Mission is the antidote to selfishness.

When strengths are driven by mission, a circle is created. Strengths feed mission. For example, a salesperson's desire to contribute to the world by selling medical supplies is a mission. But it is put into practice by his or her sales strengths. The successful use of these strengths creates a pleasant feeling of satisfaction in the salesperson, which reinforces the sense of mission. And so we emphasize that "strengths function best in the framework of mission."

Goals Die; Mission Lives On

Mission is at the heart of why you do what you do. Goals, on the other hand, are often the steps to its achievement. Mission is altruistic. A goal does not necessarily have to better the world. Mission has an eternal quality—the benefits often extend far beyond a lifetime. Goals are timebound. They die because they are achieved, to be replaced by others. Memorable political leaders often had a mission. Getting elected was only one goal in the achievement of it.

Roark Stratton told us recently of a conversation he had with an SRI client who explained that his mission was "to be number one." That's not a corporate mission statement; that's a corporate goal. A true mission statement expresses the company's *raison d'etre*, the purpose for its existence, and often becomes the invisible life force that drives and unifies.

The mission statement at Federal Express is brief, elegant, and obviously effective: "Help the world through better and faster communications." At the Menninger Foundation in Topeka, Kansas, the mission statement is elaborate and eloquent:

Improving the quality of life . . .
By developing, utilizing and disseminating
psychiatric knowledge.
To help people who are ill
as well as those who are not ill
find greater personal fulfillment and satisfaction
through personal autonomy and enhanced
capacity to cope with the stress of life.

The Ringling Bros.' Mission of Amusement, first penned in 1899, is heartfelt and long lasting:

To be good, mankind must be happy. To wreathe the face of humanity in smiles for a time, to loosen the chains that hold man captive to his duties and return him to them better fitted for his obligations, is the mission of amusement and the one great desire of moralists is, and ought to be, that it be pure and wholesome.

Amusement unfetters the mind from its environs and changes the dreary monotony of the factory's spindles to the joyous song of the meadowlark. It gives light to the caged soul to treat in airy places. It softens the wrinkles of sorrow, makes smiles of frowns.

This is the mission of amusement—and the circus, with its innocent sights of joy for the children and its power to make all men and women children again for at least one day, comes the nearest of any form of amusement to fulfilling this mission.

A Mission, Not a Goal:
Designing Your Own Mission Statement

As we begin this exercise, which may involve a few minutes or many months, let us state clearly the purpose: to write a personal or corporate mission statement that will help you to focus your strengths.

We would like to ask you to set aside some time (not necessarily now) to answer the following question in writing: *What is it that you believe you do that makes a difference to other people and to mankind? or, in other words, Why do you do what you do?*

Write fast—don't worry about spelling, logic, or grammar. The objective is to let your thoughts flow. Remember, we are not talking about goals here, we are talking about mission. Your quest is to define your life purpose.

When you have finished, go back and look over your words. You can then begin to edit them.

Let's clarify some immediate questions that nearly always arise:

1. How long should a mission statement be?

A mission statement should be simple enough to be remembered and frequently reflected upon. The length of the mission statement can be anywhere from one paragraph to several pages—provided you can summarize its essence. One restaurateur, in referring to his mission statement, simply said, "To delight our customers."

2. Should your mission statement show how the mission is to be accomplished?

No. A mission statement does not show actual plans. It is designed to direct and express your values and beliefs. It provides guides, not goals.

3. Should everyone (in a company) have a mission statement?

Ideally, yes, though naturally the statements will not all be the same, but there should be commonality.

4. Does everyone have to believe or agree with your mission?

No. The goal is not to proselytize or convert, but to express your true desires without regard to what others will think. Often others with a mission will be supportive of yours since they understand the value of having one. People without a mission may also be supportive if yours fits with their beliefs. (Hence the power of a leader with a popular mission!) People want to follow a person who knows where he or she is going.

However, there will always be detractors. Some people may not understand the importance of mission and how it relates to success. Those lacking purpose in their own lives may feel compelled to dismiss your purpose or even feel negative about it.

5. Do mission statements change over the years?

Ideally, yes. If you begin your life or career with an awareness of mission, you can assume that it will grow as you grow. You may even find you take on several missions that relate to different areas of your life.

6. Do one's mission and work have to coincide?

If our work gives us purpose, then we have an advantage. But many people have a mission separate from their work, and their job is the means to support it. Here are some examples:

- Kent Pelz, a banker in Los Angeles, devotes twenty hours a week to world peace.
- Ann Blank, a single mother in Chicago, works as an executive secretary to fund her mission—the education of her children.
- Jane Fonda uses her earnings from acting to fund humanitarian and political campaigns.
- Paul Newman launched Newman's Own food products line to generate profits for his favorite causes.

Here are some typical mission statements:

- Life Insurance Agent: To provide financial security to families.
- Clothing Salesperson: To help people look their best.
- Farmer: To provide food for people of the world.
- Manager: To help people develop their capabilities.
- Law Enforcement Officer: To help people understand lawfulness and live together lawfully, and to give them security in their neighborhood communities.

Living a Mission Statement

Claim Your Mission

As we said earlier, personal mission is rare. To live a mission requires that you realize you can make a difference in this world. It also requires that you practice the strengths to fulfill your mission. Writing and developing your mission statement is neither instant nor easy. It's not like choosing a style of bank checks for your new account. Discovering that inner drive and matching it with real-world activities requires time and the commitment to your drives and needs. Mission statements can grow out of a strong sense of responsibility or a strong sense of rage. Leaders of the women's movement are clearly driven by mission, motivated by legal and financial inequities. Environmentalists are motivated by a sense of responsibility to future inhabitants of the earth. Some corporate leaders, on the other hand, have a mission about literacy motivated by their belief that a competitive workforce is a literate one.

Talk Your Mission Whenever You Get a Chance

"I just sold that lady her first Cadillac, and I know she's going to be happy."

"It was really exciting to see the looks on their faces when they understood that success and failure, strengths and weaknesses, were not opposites."

These statements are examples of talking mission. The Cadillac salesman has a mission to help people have safe, reliable transportation. To him the discussion of a Cadillac sale is talking his mission statement.

Enjoy Your Mission

Mission, like exercise, is most effective when experienced as often as possible. A person exercising his or her strengths on a daily basis is both developing strengths and fulfilling a sense of purpose. It becomes a win/win situation. Mission statements that live only on paper are a win/lose proposition. Having a mission statement and not living it is perhaps worse than having no mission at all. The only result would be guilt.

Mission: The Ultimate Empowerer

You are talking with your seatmate on a cross-country flight. During the conversation it becomes clear that your seatmate is very successful. In the course of your mile-high chat, you learn about his lifestyle, including not-so-passing references to his house, car, swimming pool, private schools, and all the requisite perks of success. But as the conversation progresses the tone switches from one of apparent satisfaction to one of emptiness, conjuring up the haunting message of the old Peggy Lee song, "Is That All There Is?" Your seatmate is the victim of a common syndrome: the search for purpose. Life goals have been reached, the brass ring has been won, and suddenly the question is "Now what?"

As the great leaders know, mission is the resolution to this malaise.

Mission gives purpose to life. It adds meaning to what one does. In its purest form, it is so deeply felt that it explains why one does what one does. One's mission will touch the heart versus the head. A mission must benefit the world.

Mission is a quality made most vivid by the great leaders of the world, from Jesus Christ to contemporary leaders. Consider President John F. Kennedy's famous statement, "Ask not what your country can do for you, ask what you can do for your country."

Dr. Martin Luther King, Jr., spoke from a sense of mission with his refrain "I have a dream, I have a dream."

President Bush conveyed it in his inaugural address when he made reference to his famous "thousand points of light."

Each of these statements captured the imagination and hearts of millions and is appropriately etched in the pages of history. The power of mission is well known to leaders who realize that humankind has a longing for it. Lacking a mission, people are likely to have only materialistic goals. But mission is not the exclusive territory of great leaders. It is the right of every person interested in developing his or her strengths, and it's one of the essential ingredients of excellence.

Ministry: A Theological, Pastoral Handbook

McBrien, R. P. 1987. 77–81. New York: Harper Collins.

What Is Ministerial Spirituality?

It is never enough simply to be a competent, efficient minister. The minister must embody and live by the spiritual values that she or he represents, proclaims, and tries to persuade others to embrace.

In keeping with the principle of sacramentality the minister is not only an instrument of God's grace; the minister is also a *sign* of God's grace. The invisible reality of grace must be made visible in the sign. And the sign in turn must truly embody the invisible reality it signifies. The sign signifies what it bears within itself.

To be in touch with the sign, therefore, is to be in touch with the reality it signifies. Otherwise it is a false sign, disconnected from the reality of grace it is supposed to signify. For this reason this century's greatest Catholic theologian, Father Karl Rahner, S.J., insisted that "it is not a matter of indifference to the meaning and nature of ministry in the Church whether it is exercised and administered with holiness or not" *(The Church and the Sacraments* [New York: Herder, 1963] p. 98). In fact, there would be no holy Church if all of its members, ministers and non-ministers alike, were sinners. Why? Because the Church is people, the People of God. The "holiness of the Church is only present and existent in the holiness of individuals, the multitude in fact who actually form the Church which is holy" *(The Church and the Sacraments*, p. 105). Moreover, there would be no sacraments and no ministerial life at all if the Church's ministers were "unbelieving and void of divine love." For it is "believing love" that "induces even the faithless and the loveless in the Church to deeds which essentially really spring from faith and love" *(The Church and the Sacraments*, p. 102).

Every ministry calls for a response of faith and love. But faith and love can only be called forth by "believing love" and loving faith. The minister, therefore, does more than provide a "service." The minister *witnesses* to the reality he or she communicates. In Rahner's view, "it is only really possible to bear witness to the faith by being a Christian oneself, that is, by one's own 'holiness'" *(The Church and the Sacraments*, p. 105).

This final chapter is concerned with the unity of sign and spiritual reality in those who minister in and for the Church. It is concerned, that is, with integrity, wholeness, and holiness.

Spirituality

"For those who live according to the flesh are concerned with the things of the flesh, but those who live according to the spirit with the things of the spirit" (Rom. 8:5). To be spiritual means to know and to live according to the knowledge that there is more to life than meets the eye. To be spiritual means, beyond that, to know and to live according to the knowledge that God is present to us in grace as the principle of personal, interpersonal, social, and even cosmic transformation. To be open to the Spirit is to accept explicitly who we are and who we are called always to become and to direct our lives accordingly.

The term *spirituality*, therefore, embraces everything that we are, think, and do in relation to the triune God who is present in and yet transcends all that is. Spirituality might be defined as *a style of life that flows from the presence of the Spirit within us and within the Church, the Temple of the Holy Spirit*.

The Second Vatican Council laid to rest, once and for all, the assumption that spirituality is for priests and nuns alone. The fifth chapter of its keynote Dogmatic Constitution on the Church is entitled, "The Call of the Whole Church to Holiness." The Lord himself was addressing *all* his disciples, regardless of their status or situation, when he said, "So be perfect, just as your heavenly Father is perfect" (Matt. 5:48).

We are, of course, already holy by reason of the Spirit's indwelling within us, and that indwelling is in turn rooted in the creative act of the Father and the redemptive work of the Son. Christian spirituality is a matter of living in accordance with who we have become in the Spirit, of manifesting the fruits of the Spirit's presence: mercy, kindness, humility, meekness, patience, and the like (Col. 3:12; Gal. 5:22; Rom. 6:22).

"Thus it is evident to everyone," the council declared, "that all the faithful of Christ of whatever rank or status are called to the fullness of the Christian life and to the perfection of charity." Significantly the council amplified on this declaration: "By this holiness a more human way of life is promoted even in this earthly society" (Dogmatic Constitution on the Church, n. 40). Holiness, therefore, is not only for everyone. It also comprehends much more than the soul's personal relationship with God. It has a social, even a political, dimension.

Furthermore there is no single mode or style of spirituality for Christians. Each of us must adapt the call to perfection to his or her own identity and situation. What will always be common to each is love of God and love of neighbor. "For charity, as the bond of perfection and the fulfillment of the law (cf. Col. 3:14; Rom. 13:10), rules over all the means of attaining holiness, gives life to them, and makes them work. Hence it is the love of God and of neighbor which points out the true disciple of Christ" (Dogmatic Constitution on the Church, n. 42).

Elsewhere the council reaffirms or elaborates upon these basic principles of Christian spirituality. The call to holiness is a call issued to laity as well as to clergy and religious. According to the Decree on the Apostolate of the Laity, their spiritual life will be rooted in the mysteries of creation and redemption, in the presence of the Holy Spirit, and in the mission of Christ and the Church (n. 29).

The Christian enters upon the spiritual life in response to the Word of God (Dogmatic Constitution on Divine Revelation, n. 21), and this in turn is proclaimed and celebrated in the liturgy of the Church, which is the "summit" and the "fountain" of the whole Christian life: "From the liturgy, therefore, and especially from the Eucharist, as from a fountain, grace is channeled into us; and our sanctification in Christ and the glorification of God, to which all other activities of the Church are directed as toward their goal, are most powerfully achieved" (Constitution on the Sacred Liturgy, n. 10).

And what the council taught about Catholic spirituality applies to the whole Body of Christ: "Let all Christ's faithful remember that the more purely they strive to live according to the gospel, the more they are fostering and even practicing Christian unity" (Decree on Ecumenism, n. 7). The more all Christians "enjoy profound communion with the Father, the Word, and the Spirit," the more surely will they "achieve depth and ease in strengthening mutual brotherhood [and sisterhood]." The council insisted that this is, in fact, "the soul of the whole ecumenical movement, and can rightly be called 'spiritual ecumenism.'" Indeed "there can be no ecumenism worthy of the name without a change of heart," that is, without *conversion* (Decree on Ecumenism, n. 7).

Adjustment and Growth: The Challenges of Life

Rathus, Spencer A., and Jeffrey S. Nevid. 1986. 273–79. New York: Holt, Rinehart, and Winston.

Controlling Irrational and Catastrophizing Thoughts

Have you had any of these experiences?

1. You have difficulty with the first item on a test and become absolutely convinced that you will flunk?
2. You want to express your genuine feelings but think that you might make another person angry or upset?
3. You haven't been able to get to sleep for 15 minutes and assume that you will lie awake the whole night and feel "wrecked" in the morning?
4. You're not sure what decision to make, so you try to put your conflicts out of your mind by going out, playing cards, or watching TV?
5. You decide not to play tennis or go jogging because your form isn't perfect and you're in less than perfect condition?

If you have had these or similar experiences, it may be because you harbor a number of the irrational beliefs. . . . These beliefs may make you overly concerned about the approval of others (experience 2, above) or perfectionistic (experience 5). They may lead you to think that you can best relieve yourself of certain dilemmas by pretending that they do not exist (experience 4), or that a minor setback will invariably lead to greater problems (experiences 1 and 3).

How, then, do we change irrational or catastrophizing thoughts? The answer is theoretically simple: We change these thoughts by changing them. However, it may take some work, and before we can change them we must often first become more aware of them.

Cognitive psychologist Donald Meichenbaum (1976) suggests a three-step procedure for controlling the irrational and catastrophizing thoughts that often accompany feelings of pain, anxiety, frustration, conflict, or tension:

1. Develop awareness of these thoughts through careful self-examination. Study the examples at the beginning of this section or in Table 10.3 to see if these experiences and thought patterns characterize you. . . . When you encounter anxiety or frustration, pay careful attention to your thoughts. Are they helping to point toward a solution, or are they compounding your problems?

2. Prepare thoughts that are incompatible with the irrational and catastrophizing thoughts, and practice saying them firmly to yourself. (If nobody is nearby, why not say them firmly aloud?)

3. Reward yourself with a mental pat on the back for effective changes in beliefs and thought patterns.

Controlling catastrophizing thoughts along with lowering the arousal of your alarm reaction—which we shall discuss next—serves to significantly reduce the impact of the stressor, whether it is pain, anxiety, or feelings of frustration. It gives you the chance to develop a plan for effective action. When effective action is not possible, controlling our thoughts and our levels of arousal dramatically increases our capacity to tolerate discomfort.

Lowering Arousal

One reason that a squash does not become as aroused as a person when it is assaulted is that it does not catastrophize. Another reason is that it does not have an autonomic nervous system. Thus it has no alarm reaction.

Once you are aware that a stressor is acting upon you, and have developed a plan to cope with it, it is no longer helpful to have blood pounding so fiercely through your arteries. Psychologists and other scientists have developed many methods for teaching people to lower excessive bodily arousal. They include meditation, biofeedback, and progressive relaxation.

Meditation

In meditation, one lowers one's level of arousal by focusing on relaxing, repetitive stimuli, and thereby narrowing consciousness. There are many ways to meditate. One is simply counting your breaths. The Yogi stares intently at a pattern on a vase or mandala. Thousands of Americans regularly practice *Transcendental Meditation* (TM) by repeating *mantras*—relaxing words or sounds such as *ieng* and *om*.

TM produces a *relaxation response* in many people that is characterized by a lower rate of metabolism, as measured by oxygen consumption (Benson, 1975). This lowered rate of metabolism, or *hypometabolism*, differs from sleep in that the drop-off rate is steeper and the decrease greater. The blood pressure of people with hypertension decreases; people who meditate twice daily tend to show normalized blood pressure throughout the day (Benson et al., 1973). Meditators also produce more frequent and intense alpha waves, which are associated with relaxation but infrequent during sleep.

Other researchers agree that meditation lowers a person's level of arousal, but argue that the same effects can be achieved by simply resting quietly for the same amount of time (Holmes et al., 1983; Holmes, 1984). The Holmes group found no differences between experienced Transcendental Meditators and novice "resters" in heart rate, respiration rate, blood pressure, and sweat in the palms of the hands (that is, galvanic skin response, or GSR). Critics of meditation do not argue that meditation is useless, but rather that "meditation" may have no special effects as

compared with simply taking a restful break from an anxiety-inducing routine.

If you want to try out meditation for yourself, note that what you *don't* do is more important than what you do. Limit your awareness to a constant or repetitive stimulus—a word or phrase (Benson 1975 suggests "one"), your breathing, a pleasant sight or odor. Adopt a passive, "what happens, happens" attitude. Create a quiet, nondisruptive environment. Don't directly face a light. You may seat yourself before a calming object like a plant or burning incense. Do not eat for an hour beforehand; avoid caffeine for at least two. Assume a comfortable position. Change it as needed. It's okay to scratch or yawn. Begin by meditating once or twice daily for 10 to 20 minutes.

Meditation appears to facilitate adjustment to stress without decreasing awareness. In this way it does not reduce perception of potential threats. In one experiment, Orne-Johnson (1973) exposed meditators and nonmeditators to unpredictable loud noises. Meditators stopped showing a stress reaction—as measured by GSR—earlier than nonmeditators. In another experiment, Goleman and Schwartz (1976) used heart rate and GSR to measure stress reactions to a film that explicitly portrayed accidents and death. Meditators showed a greater alarm reaction than nonmeditators when the contents of the film were announced, but recovered normal levels of arousal more rapidly during the showings. Meditators in this study thus

TABLE 10.3	**Irrational Catastrophizing Thoughts**	**Incompatible (Coping) Thoughts**
Controlling Irrational, Catastrophizing Beliefs and Thoughts	"Oh my God, I'm going to lose all control!"	"This is painful and upsetting, but I don't have to go to pieces."
	"This will never end."	"This will come to an end, even if it's hard to see right now."
	"It'll be awful if Mom gives me that look."	"It's more pleasant when Mom's happy with me, but I can live with it if she isn't."
	"How can I get out there? I'll look like a fool."	"So you're not perfect; it doesn't mean you'll look stupid. And if someone thinks you look stupid, you can live with that too. Just stop worrying and have fun."
	"My heart's going to leap out of my chest! How much can I stand?"	"Easy—hearts don't leap out of chests. Stop and think! Distract yourself. Breathe slowly, in and out."
	"What can I do? There's nothing I can do!"	"Easy—stop and think. Just because you can't think of a solution right now doesn't mean there's nothing you can do. Take it a minute at a time. Breathe easy."
	Do irrational beliefs and catastrophizing thoughts compound the stress you experience? Cognitive psychologists suggest that we can cope with stress by becoming aware of self-defeating beliefs and thoughts and replacing them with rational, calming beliefs and thoughts.	

The Principal as Educational Leader

QUESTIONNAIRE: Locus of Control Scale

Do you believe that you are in charge of your own life? That you can exert an influence on other people and the environment to reach your goal? Or do you believe that your fate is in the "stars"? That you are ruled by luck, chance, and other people?

People who believe that they are in control of their lives are said to have an internal locus of control, or to be "internals." People who view their fates as being out of their hands are said to be "externals." Are you more of an "internal" or more of an "external"? To learn more about your perception of your locus of control, respond to the following questionnaire developed by Nowicki and Strickland (1973). These are the directions used by the authors of the Questionnaire:

We are trying to find out what men and women think about certain things. We want you to answer the following questions the way you feel. There are no right or wrong answers. Don't take too much time answering any one question, but do try to answer them all.

One of your concerns during the test may be: "What should I do if I can answer both yes and no to a question?" It's not unusual for that to happen. If it does, think about whether your answer is just a little more one way or the other. For example, if you'd assign a weighting of 51 percent to "yes" and assign 49 percent to "no," mark the answer "yes." Try to pick one or the other response for all questions and not leave any blank.

Mark your responses to the questions on the answer sheet in the next column. When you are finished, turn to the end of the chapter to score your test.

1. Do you believe that most problems will solve themselves if you just don't fool with them?
2. Do you believe that you can stop yourself from catching a cold?
3. Are some people just born lucky?
4. Most of the time do you feel that getting good grades means a great deal to you?
5. Are you often blamed for things that just aren't your fault?
6. Do you believe that if somebody studies hard enough he or she can pass any subject?
7. Do you feel that most of the time it doesn't pay to try hard because things never turn out right anyway?
8. Do you feel that if things start out well in the morning it's going to be a good day no matter what you do?
9. Do you feel that most of the time parents listen to what their children have to say?
10. Do you believe that wishing can make good things happen?
11. When you get punished does it usually seem it's for no good reason at all?
12. Most of the time do you find it hard to change a friend's opinion?
13. Do you think that cheering more than luck helps a team to win?
14. Did you feel that it was nearly impossible to change your parents' minds about anything?
15. Do you believe that parents should allow children to make most of their own decisions?
16. Do you feel that when you do something wrong there's very little you can do to make it right?
17. Do you believe that most people are just born good at sports?
18. Are most of the other people your age stronger than you are?
19. Do you feel that one of the best ways to handle most problems is just not to think about them?
20. Do you feel that you have a lot of choice in deciding who your friends are?
21. If you find a four-leaf clover, do you believe that it might bring you good luck?
22. Did you often feel that whether or not you did your homework had much to do with what kinds of grades you got?
23. Do you feel that when a person your age is angry with you there's little you can do to stop him or her?
24. Have you ever had a good-luck charm?
25. Do you believe that whether or not people like you depends on how you act?
26. Did your parents usually help you if you asked them to?
27. Have you felt that when people were angry with you it was usually for no reason at all?
29. Do you believe that when bad things are going to happen they are just going to happen no matter what you try to do to stop them?
30. Do you think that people can get their own way if they just keep trying?
31. Most of the time do you find it useless to try to get your own way at home?
32. Do you feel that when good things happen they happen because of hard work?
33. Do you feel that when somebody your age wants to be your enemy there's little you can do to change matters?
34. Do you feel that it's easy to get friends to do what you want them to do?
35. Do you usually feel that you have little to say about what you get to eat at home?
36. Do you feel that when someone doesn't like you there's little you can do about it?
37. Did you usually feel that it was almost useless to try in school because most other children were just plain smarter than you were?
38. Are you the kind of person who believes that planning ahead makes things turn out better?
39. Most of the time do you feel that you have little to say about what your family decides to do?
40. Do you think it's better to be smart than to be lucky?

showed greater alertness to potential threat—a factor that could allow them to develop a plan for dealing with a stressor more rapidly—but also more ability to control arousal.

Biofeedback: Getting in Touch with the Untouchable

Through biofeedback training (BFT), people (and lower animals) have learned to voluntarily regulate many functions, like heart rate and blood pressure, that were previously thought to be beyond conscious control. BFT can also make us more aware of bodily responses we can normally influence, such as our level of muscle tension.

In the 1960s it was first reported that laboratory rats had been trained by biofeedback to raise or lower their heart rates. Neal E. Miller (1969) connected electrodes to the "pleasure centers" in the rodents' brains. Some rats were rewarded with a small burst of electric current whenever they raised their heart rates, which first occurred at random. Others were rewarded when their heart rates were lowered. After a single 90-minute training session, Miller's rats altered their heart rates by as much as 20 percent in the rewarded direction.

Since then people, too, have learned to gain control of their heart rates and other bodily functions through BFT—not for a "reward" of electric shock, but simply for a "bleep" or other electronic signal that indicated a change in the desired direction. Some people have gained control over their blood pressure; others over the temperature in a finger (useful in decreasing migraine), the sweat in the palm, or the emission of alpha waves. The electroencephalograph (EEG) is used in BFT for emission of certain brain waves, and the electromyograph (EMG), which monitors muscle tension, is used in BFT for control of muscle tension in the forehead and the rest of the body.

In research on BFT and stress, Sirota and his colleagues (1976) trained college women to slow their heart rates voluntarily, after which they reported a painful electric shock to be less stressful. College students at another campus reduced speech anxiety through BFT, which taught them to control their heart rates (Gatchel & Proctor, 1976).

Progressive Relaxation

Edmund Jacobson (1938) noted that people tense their muscles when they are under stress, compounding their discomfort, but they are often unaware of these contractions. Jacobson reasoned that if they could learn to relax these contractions they could directly lower the tension they experienced. But when he asked clients to focus on relaxing muscles, they often had no idea what to do.

Jacobson developed the method of progressive relaxation to teach people how to relax these tensions. In this method, people purposefully tense a muscle group before relaxing it. This sequence allows them to (1) develop awareness of their muscle tensions; and (2) differentiate between feelings of tension and relaxation. The method is "progressive" because people progress from one muscle group to another. Since its beginnings in the 1930s, progressive relaxation has undergone development by several behavior therapists such as Joseph Wolpe and Arnold Lazarus (1966).

Progressive relaxation decreases the sympathetic arousal of the alarm reaction and has been found useful with "diseases of adaptation" ranging from headaches (Tasto & Hinkle, 1973) to hypertension (Agras et al., 1983; Taylor et al., 1977).

Diaphragmatic Breathing

Diaphragmatic breathing tends to lower arousal by slowing breathing and, perhaps, by stimulating parts of the nervous system that counteract feelings of anxiety and tension (Harvey, 1978). Thus, it may also develop feelings of relaxation.

To use diaphragmatic breathing, lie on your back. Place your hands lightly on your stomach. Breathe so that you can feel your stomach rise as you inhale and lower with every outbreath. You are now breathing "through" the diaphragm. The following methods help maintain slow, regular breathing:

1. Breathe through the nose only.
2. Take the same amount of time to inhale and exhale.
3. Make inhaling and exhaling continuous and leisurely. You may count 1,001; 1,002; 1,003; etc.) as you breathe in and out.
4. To breathe diaphragmatically while sitting in a chair, keep one hand on your chest to see that it remains still. Keep the other on your stomach to see that it rises and falls.

References

Benson, H. (1975). *The relaxation response*. New York: Morrow.

Benson, H., Manzetta, B.R., & Rosner, B. (1973). Decreased systolic blood pressure in hypertensive subjects who practiced meditation. *Journal of Clinical Investigation, 52,* 8.

Gatchel, R.J., & Proctor, J.D. (1976). Effectiveness of voluntary heart rate control in reducing speech anxiety. *Journal of Consulting and Clinical Psychology, 44,* 381–389.

Goleman, D.J., & Schwartz, G.E. (1976). Meditation as an intervention in stress reactivity. *Journal of Consulting and Clinical Psychology, 44,* 456–466.

Harvey, J.R. (1978). Diaphragmatic breathing: A practical technique for breath control. *The Behavior Therapist, 1*(2), 13–14.

Holmes, D.S. (1984). Meditation and somatic arousal reduction: A review of the experimental evidence. *American Psychologist, 39,* 1–10.

Holmes, D.S., Soloman, S., Cappo, B.M., & Greenburg, J.L. (1983). Effects of transcendental meditation versus resting on physiological and subjective arousal. *Journal of Personality and Social Psychology, 44,* 1244–1252.

Jacobson, E. (1938). *Progressive relaxation*. Chicago: University of Chicago Press.

Meichenbaum, D. (1976). Toward a cognitive theory of self-control. In G. Schwartz & D. Shapiro (Eds.), *Consciousness and self-regulation: Advances in research*. New York: Plenum Press.

Miller, N.E. (1969). Learning of visceral and glandular responses. *Science, 163,* 434–445.

Orne-Johnson, D. (1973). Autonomic stability and transcendental meditation. *Psychosomatic Medicine, 35,* 341–349.

Sirota, A.D., Schwartz, G.E., & Shaprio, D. (1976). Voluntary control of human heart rate: Effect on reaction to aversive stimulation. *Journal of Abnormal Psychology, 85,* 473–477.

Tasto, D.L., & Hinkle, J.E. (1973). Muscle relaxation treatment for tension headaches. *Behavior Research and Therapy, 11,* 347–350.

Taylor, C.B., Farquhar, J.W., Nelson, E., & Agras, D. (1977). Relaxation therapy and high blood pressure. *Archives of General Psychiatry, 34,* 339–343.

Wolpe, J., & Lazarus, A.A. (1966). *Behavior therapy techniques*. New York: Pergamon.

Curriculum and Instruction

Curriculum Components for Catholic Education

Sr. Donna Innes, CSA, Ph.D.

The National Conference of Catholic Bishops of the United States explicitly states that "the educational efforts of the" Church must encompass the twin purposes of personal sanctification and social reform in light of Christian values (*To Teach as Jesus Did* 1972, p. 3). Thus, the Catholic school has a clear mandate from its institution, the Catholic Church, to instill values into the curriculum of the school and to work with parents to create a community that fosters the acquisition of values within the child. Imparting values, while allowing for the free will and the development of the student's conscience, is central to the mission of the Catholic school. The curriculum is the major vehicle by which this mission is achieved.

The curriculum of the Catholic school takes on unique characteristics because religious values are integrated with human values. As the curriculum addresses the spiritual, moral, physical, intellectual, emotional, social, and aesthetic development of the students, it enfleshes the school philosophy. The curriculum reflects Catholic beliefs, develops the student's responsibility to self, home, community, and the world, and includes a sensitivity to social justice and global peace concerns, while always being mindful that "the ultimate goal of all Catholic education is salvation in Jesus Christ" (*The Catholic School of the '80s* 1987, no. 8).

In light of the distinctive mission of Catholic schools, the following ten areas require careful deliberation when developing a comprehensive curriculum:

- philosophy;
- family, church, state/nation (background influences);
- global vision/world view;
- policies, guidelines, goals, and objectives;
- instructional strategies that apply appropriate

learning theory;
- staff development;
- content (scope and sequence);
- instructional materials;
- systematic and periodic assessment/evaluation;
- an ongoing curriculum assessment cycle.

Philosophy

Through the clear articulation of its philosophy and by meeting definite curriculum standards, Catholic schools manifest "a clear sense of their identity and the courage to follow all the consequences of their uniqueness." (*The Catholic School* 1977, no. 66). The Catholic theology and philosophy of education that permeates the Catholic school forms the basis on which each of the other nine elements of the curriculum model are based.

A Catholic school curriculum model must recognize the individual as empowered by God, an individual with freedom and dignity. It must address beliefs and values to be inculcated through the *Message* element of the curriculum, augmented through *Worship* occasions, supported through the *Community*, and manifested in *Service* opportunities (*Sharing the Light of Faith* 1979). Values to be imparted in the Catholic school include

> affection, respect, obedience, gratitude, gentleness, goodness, helpfulness, service and good example [as well as] a love for all that excludes no one because of religion, nationality or race; prayer for all, so that all may know God; laboring together in apostolic works and in efforts to relieve human suffering; a preferential option for the less fortunate, the sick, the poor, the handicapped, the lonely (*The Religious Dimension of Education in a Catholic School* 1988, no. 87).

Family, church, state/nation

Each individual lives within the context of the social forces of society. These social forces include the family, the Church and the local parish, the local community, and the community-at-large in the state and nation. The curriculum of a Catholic school needs to assist each individual in identifying how the social forces of society can be balanced with gospel beliefs and values.

The intrinsic right of parents to educate their children is clearly acknowledged by the Catholic Church (*Declaration on Christian Education* 1966, no. 6, *The Religious Dimension of Education in a Catholic School,* no. 43). When the Catholic school integrates the fullness of Christ's message into the total curriculum and includes parents in the design, implementation, and evaluation of the curriculum, it supports parents in their responsibilities toward their children.

All members of the Catholic school community are called upon to develop an environment in which the curriculum and instruction appropriate for a Catholic school can challenge students and impart gospel values. A sense of community is created within the school as parents, students, administrators, teachers, staff, clergy, and parishioners witness to the Gospel in their lives and support each other. In such an environment students are influenced and come to understand "the meaning of [their] faith experiences and their truths" (*The Catholic School* no. 27). Thus in a successful Catholic school the people involved with the school and the sharing of values through the curriculum merge to create a meaningful school climate.

Global vision/worldview

The need to assist students in developing a global vision and world view is based on the two preceding areas: the philosophical core and the relationship of the individual to the family and to society. This phase of a good curriculum model focuses on the Gospel message and considers the cultural conditions of the times (*The Catholic School* no. 9).

Creating a global vision is a difficult task. However, this task is made easier in Catholic education because of the belief in the dignity of each person which is integral to the Gospel message of Jesus.

When this basic integrity is applied to each human being in all of creation, multicultural understanding and a sense of oneness or universality becomes an essential part of the curriculum.

A global vision/world view can only be a true part of the curriculum when it is possessed by teachers, administrators, and parents and when it is consciously incorporated into all aspects of the curriculum.

Policies, guidelines, goals, and objectives

In the process of curriculum development, the procedures for assessing needs and for setting goals and objectives are tools used to facilitate the ongoing development of the curriculum. Here the curriculum process moves from its philosophical base to its implementation, i.e., from theory to practice.

Curriculum implementation occurs best when policies are established and clearly recognized by the school community.

The policies and guidelines for the curriculum need to be the connection links from the philosophical base of the curriculum to the applied theory of contact areas.

The goals and objectives of the curriculum should reflect the philosophy and policies of the school and be in harmony with gospel values. The total curriculum, composed of each of the content areas, should recognize the needs of each student and interact appropriately with the content of the total curriculum.

Instructional strategies/learning theory

The faculty of the school makes learning theory a reality as they apply it in the curriculum. Through staff development, teachers can consistently be updated in current learning theories. As teachers become knowledgeable about learning styles and apply teaching strategies appropriate to the individual student, they bridge the education gap from theory to practice.

Staff development

The importance of teachers in transmitting the Christian message, not only through the curriculum but also by their whole being, is reiterated in each of the church documents on Catholic education. *Lay*

Catholics in Schools: Witnesses to Faith (1982) states unequivocally that in the future it will be lay teachers who will substantially determine whether or not the school realizes its aims and accomplishes its objectives. Teachers are challenged to live and reflect the Christian message of Christ; to integrate religious truth, values, culture, and faith in their own lives; and to understand the mission and uniqueness of the Catholic school (*The Catholic School* nos. 43, 66; *To Teach as Jesus Did* no. 104). Teachers' attitudes about life influence the decisions they make. Therefore, the identity of the teacher has a great influence upon the school, curriculum, and students. The Catholic school teacher must not only be an educator, but also a model of the values promoted by the school.

Content (scope and sequence)

The scope and sequence of learning objectives should provide the student with necessary and appropriate information and skills and must integrate gospel values and the teachings of the Catholic Church into the content areas. When such integration occurs, the Catholic school is successful.

The scope and sequence, as one area of curriculum development, not only concentrate on theory and skills for specific subject areas such as religion, language arts (reading, writing, and speaking), mathematics, science, social studies, music, art, physical education, health, foreign languages, and especially religion, but they also must recognize and impart gospel (religious) values relevant to the content area (*The Catholic School of the '80s* no. 7).

Students need processes and procedures that will enable them to think, to plan, to cooperate, and to act by their own decisions. Learning how to learn, understanding one's own world view, knowing how to plan, being able to create one's own environment, knowing oneself and one's own values, as well as understanding how to interact with others—all are curriculum goals for today's world (Hanlon 1973).

Instructional materials

The quality and type of instructional materials used in the Catholic school should reflect the teaching of the Catholic Church and the philosophy of the school. They should meet the needs of the students and enable them to learn properly the content and skills of the curriculum. These materials include not only textbooks but also manipulative materials, maps, globes, charts, science equipment, games, audiovisual equipment, calculators, library books, computers, and computer software. The instructional materials augment the scope and sequence and the learning objectives of the curriculum.

Periodic assessment/evaluation

Evaluation needs to occur at every level of the curriculum. Ongoing evaluation is called formative evaluation. At the completion of a course, project, or activity, it is important to have a structured summative evaluation.

An achievement-testing program is one source of summative evaluation. However, standardized testing programs have several limitations; therefore, other types of student assessment are needed to evaluate the spiritual, cognitive, affective, and psycho-motor growth of the students.

Ongoing curriculum assessment

Curriculum planning needs to be systematic. Curriculum development is an ongoing process and having a long-range curriculum plan allows the school a consistency in curriculum planning. The curriculum of any Catholic school needs to be centered on the message of Christ as reflected in Scripture and through the teaching of the Church. A cyclical plan for curriculum development includes the review and assessment of philosophy, policies, guidelines, goals and objectives, scope and sequence of subject areas, instructional strategies, staff development, instructional materials, testing program, quality of parent involvement, and the impact of current social forces.

A Catholic school is successful when students possess the knowledge, skills, and values necessary to live out a life in which their faith life is integrated into their actions as they live out Christian values.

Reflection Questions

The following questions are posed to provide a framework for summarizing the ten components integral to a comprehensive Catholic school curriculum:

1. How does the school's philosophy reflect the Catholic nature of the school and influence the curriculum? Which gospel values are identified in the philosophy?

2. How do the curriculum decisions and activities include parents and project a positive image of the Catholic school to the public?

3. Are students assisted in gaining a balanced world view and an understanding of global interdependence? Are peace and justice concepts integrated into the curriculum and actually taught to students?

4. Is there an established procedure (perhaps recommended by the [arch]diocese) for developing curriculum policies and guidelines? Is it used by the board, principal, and faculty? What curriculum policies and/or guidelines currently exist? How are they evaluated?

5. Do the instructional strategies used in the school reflect learning theories that are in harmony with the Catholic philosophy of the school?

6. How are teachers and the school staff assisted in understanding their role in imparting gospel values in a Catholic school? Are faculty and staff involved in planning and assessing the curriculum and instructional strategies?

7. How does the content of the curriculum consider the needs and expectations of the learner, society, and the Church? How does the scope and sequence reflect gospel values?

8. Do the instructional materials reflect the school's philosophy, gospel values, and individual student's learning style?

9. Is there an organized plan for assessing curriculum? Is this cycle in harmony with curriculum planning in the (arch)diocese?

10. How is the curriculum assessed in light of the mission of the school? Does the assessment include a review of the philosophy, the scope and sequences for each content area, the instructional strategies, parent involvement in curriculum planning, the instructional materials and, how the curriculum is evaluated?

Resources

Abbott, W. M., ed. 1966. *Declaration on Christian education (Gravissimum educationis)*. In *The documents of Vatican II*, trans. Joseph Gallagher, 637–51. New York: Guild Press.

Congregation for Catholic Education. 1977. *The Catholic school*. Washington, D.C.: United States Catholic Conference.

————. 1982. *Lay Catholics in schools: Witnesses to faith*. Boston: Daughters of Saint Paul.

————. 1988. *The religious dimension of education in a Catholic school: Guidelines for reflection and renewal*. Washington, D.C.: United States Catholic Conference.

Hanlon, J. M. 1973. *Theory, practice and education*. Fond du Lac, Wis.: Marian College Press.

John Paul II. 1987. The Catholic school of the '80s. *Origins* 17(17).

National Conference of Catholic Bishops. 1972. *To teach as Jesus did: A pastoral message on Catholic education*. Washington, D.C.: United States Catholic Conference.

————. 1979. *Sharing the light of faith: National catechetical directory for Catholics of the United States*. Washington, D.C.: United States Catholic Conference.

Pius XI. 1929. *On the Christian education of youth*. Boston: Daughters of St. Paul.

Area of Responsibility: Curriculum and Instruction

Bernadine Robinson, OP; Donna Innes, CSA, Ph.D.; Jean Barton, Ph.D.;
Maria Ciriello, OP, Ph.D.

Glatthorn (1987) defines *curriculum* in terms of the plans made for guiding learning. The plans are usually presented in the form of documents or charts. Curriculum and instruction, he maintains, are two entities that are almost inseparable. *Instruction* is the curriculum as it is taught. One of the tasks of curriculum leadership is to use the right methods to bring the written and the taught curriculum into closer alignment.

The principal, in providing leadership in curriculum and instruction, is required to have a broadly developed set of understandings and skills. Heft (1991) notes that if one is a leader of a Catholic school, he or she is expected to support a vision of achieving excellence in academics within the context of a community of faith. The Congregation for Catholic Education (1988) emphasizes the necessity of infusing Gospel values, explicitly mentioning these values.

The principal as educational leader in a Catholic school is called to the following expectations:

C1. To demonstrate that he or she has a knowledge of the content and the methods of *religious education*

C2. To be knowledgeable of the *developmental stages of children and youth*

C3. To recognize and provide for *cultural and religious differences*

C4. To provide leadership in *curriculum development,* especially for the integration of Christian values

C5. To give evidence of an understanding of a variety of *educational and pedagogical skills*

C6. To recognize and *accommodate the special learning needs* of children within the mainstreamed classroom

C7. To effectively *supervise instruction*

C8. To demonstrate an understanding of effective procedures for *evaluating the learning* of students

C9. To demonstrate the ability to *evaluate* the general effectiveness of the *learning program* of the school

The following pages address each curriculum and instruction expectation separately. In an introduction a rationale is presented to clarify the importance of the expectation as a basic competency for the Catholic school administrator. Learning activities, including readings and interactions with experienced professionals, are prescribed. To foster optimum growth and insight, the learner is encouraged to seek a mentor and to make every effort to interact with personnel actively involved in the day-to-day functioning of Catholic educational institutions. A written journal record of all related readings and activities is integrated to enhance personal development and to provide a systematic chronicle of professional experiences. Finally, outcome activities are listed to provide the learner opportunities to demonstrate mastery of the specific competency.

Role: Principal as Educational Leader

Area: Curriculum and Instruction

Competency: C1
Religious Education

The United States Catholic Conference, in its directory, *Sharing the Light of Faith* (1979), states that Catholic schools are to be communities of faith in which the Christian message, the experience of community, worship, and social concerns are integrated with the total experience of students, their parents, and members of the faculty.

Administrators and teachers of religion enjoy great opportunities for their own faith development with the wide assortment of workshops and professional publications being offered. Excellent teaching resources are also available for developing good programs for the teaching of religion.

Gilbert (1983) reviews some of the religious education trends: the use of videotapes and other media, the art of story telling, parent participation in the sacramental programs, as well as a variety of ways to celebrate faith with children in liturgies and para-liturgies.

Attention given by the principal to integrating religious instruction, value formation, and faith development into the academic education of students is attending to the very reason for the existence of the Catholic school.

To support and give evidence of professional growth in demonstrating a knowledge of the content and the methods of religious education, the learner will engage in the listed activities under the direction of the diocese (Model I) or through a self-directed program and/or with the guidance of a mentor (Model II).

The primary means of keeping a consistent record of activities is to keep an ongoing JOURNAL which would contain:

1) a *Dated Log* section recording when activities were undertaken and completed,

2) a *Reading/Response* section in which notes from suggested readings and the response reactions are systematically organized, and

3) an *Experience (Activity)/Reflection* section in which one records ideas and insights gained through interacting with people or seeking out additional information in the course of completing the activities.

Learning Activities: C1
Religious Education

1. Read the following and respond with reactions in a journal.* Ideally, you should discuss these readings and your reactions with a mentor. These integral readings are reprinted for your convenience on pages 169–86.

Di Giacomo, J. 1989. *Teaching religion in a Catholic secondary school*. Washington, D.C.: National Catholic Educational Association, 64–66.

Groome, T. H. 1992. Catechesis and religious education: "Let's stay together". *The Living Light* 29(1):40–46.

Kelly, F. D. 1989. Catechesis for the Third Millennium. *Momentum* 20(4):6–10.

O'Malley, W. J. 1992. Catechesis for conversion. *The Living Light* 29(2):55–63.

United States Catholic Conference. 1990. *Guidelines for doctrinally sound catechetical materials*. Washington, D.C.: 11–25.

Also, read the following sections from the *Catechism*.

Libreria Editrice Vaticana. 1994. *Catechism of the Catholic Church*. Washington, D.C.: United States Catholic Conference.

Nos. 1–10: The call to know, love, and serve God is specified and the challenge to proclaim the gospel through catechesis is explored.

No. 25: Charity as an end is the concern of all doctrine and teaching.

Nos. 426–29: Christ is the heart of catechesis. The transmission of the Christian faith consists primarily in proclaiming Christ to bring others to Him.

Nos. 1074–75: Liturgy is the privileged place for catechizing.

Nos. 1674–76: Pious devotions and activities extend the liturgical life but should not replace it.

Nos. 1697–98: Characteristics of catechesis which lead to Christ are specified.

No. 2688: Catechesis aims at teaching people to meditate on the word of God in personal prayer and practice it in liturgical prayer. Memorization of basic prayers has value but it is important that learners come to savor their meaning.

---

* In your journal, note insights gained concerning a) the teaching of religion in a meaningful way, b) how to choose materials and resources, and c) your understanding of the term *catechesis*.

2. Tour a diocesan religious education office for the purpose of seeing the variety of resources available for the teaching of religion. Review two videos (or other like media) recommended for use with students. How would you suggest these materials be used with children?

3. Attend a parent meeting for sacrament preparation. Who led or presided at the meeting? Did the meeting appear organized and purposeful? What messages did the format convey to the participants? What type of dynamic took place? Take note of the expectations placed on parents. Were any provisions made to address any unique or special needs of the parents?

4. Investigate methods used by parishes to involve young people in the parish community. If possible, visit more than one parish and compare the approaches in the programs. What age levels are addressed? What is the personnel investment made? Are the persons paid or volunteers? What time commitments are expected? How will this information be helpful to you as a principal?

5. Attend a liturgy designated for children. What, if any, adaptations were made? How were the children involved? To what age level did the liturgy seem to be directed? Was that appropriate for those who attended? Try to talk to the person involved in the planning to discuss the process used to involve children. What other liturgical/spiritual opportunities are provided for the children and youth? What application will these have in the school you lead?

As a result of study, reflection, and interaction with knowledgeable individuals, the learner will be able to complete the following activities. The quality of response to these activities should give some indication of the level of expertise the learner is able to bring to the situation.

Outcome Activities: C1
Religious Education

1. Develop a long-range curriculum outline for some aspect of religious education (liturgy, sacramental preparation, etc.) within a school. Explain how the elements integral to a good religious education program will be present, why they are needed, and how they will be implemented.

2. Acquire at least two different textbooks, if possible, from different series. (Check your parish or diocesan office for resources or contact a publisher for examination copies.) Assess the content of texts in terms of appropriateness for the age and development of the child. What features are appealing and conducive to learning? Are any aspects lacking? If you were using the text in your instruction of students, how would you compensate for its deficiencies or complement its presentation? Search for a series which seems to follow the goals you envision for a religious education program and give reasons for your choice.

3. Compare and contrast the appropriate methods to be used in teaching religion on an elementary level and on a high school level. Support your assertion by making references to authorities in the field.

Role: Principal as Educational Leader

Area: Curriculum and Instruction

Intrinsic to the philosophy of a Catholic school is respect for and the valuing of each student. A vital aspect, therefore, of a successful school program is a sensitivity to the different intellectual, emotional, social, physical, and spiritual growth patterns of students. The theories of Piaget, Gesell, Kohlberg, Erikson, and Bandura each offer insights into behavior and needs and the subsequent implications for education (Crain 1992).

Hawker (1985) summarizes characteristics of students at various grade levels. The primary-level child learns through the senses and needs security and structure. The intermediate-level child is developing the power to think abstractly, is cultivating a sense of responsibility, has an acute sense of justice, and is legalistic. The junior high youth is able to think abstractly, is searching for a positive self-image, is being influenced by peer relationships, and is formulating personal values. The high school youth tends to test and question, is confused and insecure, needs significant adults, and asks religious questions.

Understanding growth patterns will influence curricular and instructional decisions on the part of the principal concerning class size, selection of materials, criteria for entrance into school, disciplinary policies, evaluation procedures, school activities, types of prayer experiences, sacramental programs, and teaching strategies.

In giving attention to the developmental stages of children and youth, the school demonstrates its valuing of its students by responding to their needs.

To support and give evidence of professional growth in demonstrating a knowledge of the developmental stages of children and youth, the learner will engage in the listed activities under the direction of the diocese (Model I) or through a self-directed program and/or with the guidance of a mentor (Model II).

The primary means of keeping a consistent record of activities is to keep an ongoing JOURNAL which would contain:

1) a *Dated Log* section recording when activities were undertaken and completed,

2) a *Reading/Response* section in which notes from suggested readings and the response reactions are systematically organized, and

3) an *Experience (Activity)/Reflection* section in which one records ideas and insights gained through interacting with people or seeking out additional information in the course of completing the activities.

Learning Activities: C2
Developmental Stages of Children and Youth

1. Read the following and respond with reactions in a journal.* Ideally, you should discuss these readings and your reactions with a mentor. These integral readings are reprinted for your convenience on pages 187–202.

   Crain, W. 1992. *Theories of development: Concepts and applications.* Englewood Cliffs, N.J.: Prentice Hall. (Note: Gesell's Maturation Theory, 17–18; Piaget's Cognitive-Developmental Theory, 102–03, 124; Kohlberg's Stages of Moral Development, 136–41; Bandura's Social Learning Theory, 188–90; and Erikson's Eight Stages of Life, 262–68.)

   Haney, R. 1991. Seize the day! *Momentum* 22(2): 6–8.

   Hawker, J. 1985. *Catechetics in the Catholic school.* Washington, D.C.: National Catholic Educational Association, 10–13.

   National Conference of Catholic Bishops. 1979. *Sharing the light of faith: National catechetical directory for Catholics of the United States.* Washington, D.C.: United States Catholic Conference, nos. 173–75, 177–80.

   * In your journal, list the major tenets of each of the theories about child development as well as the implications these various theories would have for education.

2. Visit at least one but preferably two classrooms on preschool, primary, middle, and high school

---

levels. Focus your attention on the students. Take note of levels of concentration and behavior exhibited by students. Were there differences between classes at the same level? What might account for them? What were the differences among levels? Was the behavior you saw typical or atypical of the textbook descriptions for that level? Give specific examples in your reflection.

3. While visiting the above classroom(s), focus on the teacher: Record actions of the teacher which demonstrate or do not demonstrate a knowledge of the stages of development in several aspects of the growth of student(s). Relate the behaviors you specify to particular theories. If you observe practices that seem to be at odds with the level of the students, what suggestions would you make to the teacher and how would you support your "better" ideas? What ideas do you want to remember in your interpersonal relations with teachers on matters that might be sensitive?

As a result of study, reflection, and interaction with knowledgeable individuals, the learner will be able to complete the following activities. The quality of response to these activities should give some indication of the level of expertise the learner is able to bring to the situation.

Outcome Activities: C2
Developmental Stages of Children and Youth

1. Develop ways to show how a curriculum program of a school meets the needs of students—evidencing knowledge of intellectual, emotional, social, physical, and spiritual growth patterns. These could be submitted as photographs of activities with written descriptions or videos with commentaries.

2. Identify specifically five instances (scenarios) in the daily life of the school (discipline or control issues, curriculum aspects, delegating responsibility, etc.). Discuss how and why a principal would deal differently in each instance with second graders versus eighth graders, or with sixth versus twelfth graders.

Role: Principal as Educational Leader

Area: Curriculum and Instruction

Competency: C3
Cultural and Religious Differences

Banks (1989) defines *culture* as shared beliefs, symbols, and interpretations within a human group. Grant and Sleeter (1989) classify *multicultural* education as a term used by educators for a certain approach, namely, that of changing the curriculum and instructional program to produce an awareness, acceptance, and affirmation of cultural diversity.

The educational leader, in providing for multicultural education, faces the challenge of assisting students from diverse groups to mediate between their home and community cultures and the school culture (Grant and Sleeter 1989).

Another challenge facing the principal is that of helping all students develop more positive attitudes toward different cultural, racial, ethnic, and religious groups. The goal is not simply one of tolerance, but rather appreciation of variety and diversity. Banks (1989) asserts that when students are able to view the world from the perspectives of different groups, their views of reality are broadened and they gain important insights into their own behavior.

Uphoff (1989) reminds educators they must be aware that religion is an important element in the lives of many people, a source of strength in times of trouble. Recognition and provision for cultural differences is linked with a respect for religious differences.

Attention given by the Catholic school principal to the value of every person through recognizing and providing for cultural and religious differences is to reflect Gospel values and to ensure that all students have an equal chance to achieve.

To support and give evidence of professional growth in demonstrating a knowledge of the skills of recognizing and providing for cultural and religious differences, the learner will engage in the listed activities under the direction of the diocese (Model I) or through a self-directed program and/or with the guidance of a mentor (Model II).

The primary means of keeping a consistent record of activities is to keep an ongoing JOURNAL which would contain:

1) a *Dated Log* section recording when activities were undertaken and completed,

2) a *Reading/Response* section in which notes from suggested readings and the response reactions are systematically organized, and

3) an *Experience (Activity)/Reflection* section in which one records ideas and insights gained through interacting with people or seeking out additional information in the course of completing the activities.

Learning Activities: C3
Cultural and Religious Differences

1. Read the following and respond with reactions in a journal.* Ideally, you should discuss these readings and your reactions with a mentor. These integral readings are reprinted for your convenience on pages 203–15.

Banks, J. A. 1989. Multicultural education: Characteristics and goals. In *Multicultural education: Issues and perspectives*, eds. J. A. Banks and C. M. Banks, 2–3, 19–23. Boston: Allyn and Bacon.

Hall, S., ed. 1992. *The people: Reflections of native peoples on the Catholic experience in North America.* Washington, D.C.: National Catholic Educational Association, 73–78.

Hall, S., R. Doyle, and P. Tran, eds. 1990. *A Catholic response to the Asian presence.* Washington, D.C.: National Catholic Educational Association, 85–91.

Hall, S., and C. Reck, eds. 1987. *Integral education: A response to the Hispanic presence.* Washington, D.C.: National Catholic Educational Association, 48–51.

Jones, N. 1987. An Afro-American perspective. In *Faith and culture*, 77–80. Washington, D.C.: United States Catholic Conference.

Also, read the following sections from the *Catechism*.
Libreria Editrice Vaticana. 1994. *Catechism of the Catholic Church.* Washington, D.C.: United States Catholic Conference.

Nos. 1204–06: Liturgical celebration should celebrate the genius and culture of diverse peoples with a purpose of expressing fidelity to a common faith. Cultural adaptation requires conversion of heart.

* In your journal, note insights gained concerning ways of developing a better understanding of and appreciation for various cultural groups and ways to help students from diverse groups to function in the school and parish community. Also reflect and take notes about the approach that could be employed to address multicultural education in a school where there is little or no diversity in the enrollment of the school or in the local community.

2. Interview two or three teachers who teach ethnic or immigrant students. Discuss the types of problems the students experience and how the school or the classroom is addressing them. If it is permitted, try to engage the students in a discussion to determine the students' ideas and feelings about how they are getting along in school. Compare the views of the teachers and the students. Where were the consistencies? Were there any discrepancies? What factors in the school or local community might contribute to the perceptions of both the teachers and the students?

3. To develop a better understanding of various cultural groups and how people worship differently even within the Catholic faith, attend a Hispanic, an African American Catholic, and an Eastern rite liturgy. What difference did you note between this liturgy and the one you usually attend? What particular accommodations were made for the group attending? Do you think the spiritual needs of the people attending were being met? Why or why not?

4. If you were hired to be a principal in a school that attracted students from diverse backgrounds, what accommodations would you make? Frame your answer by considering the students, faculty, curriculum, and parish as a context. What if the school employing you has no ethnic diversity? Then what obligation, if any, do you have to the teachers, students, parents, and larger community?

5. Catholic schools, particularly near large centers of population, are attracting larger numbers of non-Catholic (and, perhaps, non-Christian) students to their student bodies. Check with your diocese to determine if any policies exist pertaining to this situation. In the absence of a policy, how would you proceed in developing a community within the school while taking pains to preserve the Catholic identity of the school and taking into account the needs of the students and faculty?

As a result of study, reflection, and interaction with knowledgeable individuals, the learner will be able to complete the following activities. The quality of response to these activities should give some indication of the level of expertise the learner is able to bring to the situation.

Outcome Activities: C3
Cultural and Religious Differences

1. Develop a plan that a principal could use for one or two faculty meetings that would lead the faculty in a reflection on ways they are recognizing (or could recognize) the uniqueness of each student and the variety of cultures present in their school/classrooms. (Include time line, resources, objectives, possible themes for prayer services.)

2. Obtain samples of textbooks in different subject areas from at least three publishers. Analyze the samples to determine how cultural and religious differences are (or are not) recognized and addressed.

Role: Principal as Educational Leader

Area: Curriculum and Instruction

Because the Catholic school program, or its curriculum, flows from a Christian philosophy, an educational program can be developed to help students grow in all areas of learning, integrating Catholic teaching and values and allowing for the inclusion of topics that relate to the social forces of our times (e.g., an AIDS curriculum designed by the National Catholic Educational Association).

Kealey (1985) affirms that although every Catholic school follows a philosophy of education that transcends a particular school population, the goals, learning objectives, and instructional activities address a particular group of students. So, "with the cooperation of the faculty, the principal, in continuous fashion, reflects on the curriculum" (Gilbert 1983).

Glatthorn (1987) outlines the basic steps in improving curriculum in a field of study such as mathematics or science in *Curriculum Renewal*. He emphasizes the necessity of engaging teachers in new ideas and programs.

Lunenburg and Ornstein (1991) state that if the new program is a major change, the principal may want to use such communication vehicles as workshops, role playing, and demonstrations. Basic to any curriculum change is the creating of an environment which encourages openness and trust and gives feedback.

Attention given by the Catholic school principal to providing leadership in the development of curriculum ensures the systematic charting of a course for each curricular area so that the school continues to grow as a place of education.

To support and give evidence of professional growth in demonstrating a knowledge of skills in providing leadership in curriculum development, the learner will engage in the listed activities under the direction of the diocese (Model I) or through a self-directed program and/or the guidance of a mentor (Model II).

The primary means of keeping a consistent record of activities is to keep an ongoing JOURNAL which would contain:

1) a *Dated Log* section recording when activities were undertaken and completed,

2) a *Reading/Response* section in which notes from suggested readings and the response reactions are systematically organized, and

3) an *Experience (Activity)/Reflection* section in which one records ideas and insights gained through interacting with people or seeking out additional information in the course of completing the activities.

Learning Activities: C4
Curriculum Development

1. Read the following and respond with reactions in a journal.* Ideally, you should discuss these readings and your reactions with a mentor. These integral readings are reprinted for your convenience on pages 216–33.

   Brophy, J. 1992. Probing the subtleties of subject-matter teaching. *Educational Leadership* 49(7): 4–8.

   Glatthorn, A. A. 1987. *Curriculum renewal: A rationale for a consensus curriculum*. Alexandria, Va.: Association for Supervision and Curriculum Development, 20–27.

   Kealey, R. 1985. *Curriculum in the Catholic school*. Washington, D.C.: National Catholic Educational Association, 11–42.

   * In your journal, list recommended steps for implementing curriculum change. Note any differences you perceive in a comparison between public and Catholic schools in the designing and implementing of a new program in the curriculum. Identify ways that you as a principal could influence the infusion of Gospel values into the school curriculum.

2. Visit a Catholic school in the inner city. (If there is no "inner city" in your area, visit an educational setting that works with children who come from either very limited socio-economic or very privileged circumstances.) How does

the school meet the philosophy of the diocese (or its own philosophy) and the particular needs of its students in its curriculum? If the community is very homogeneous, what provisions are being made for increasing students' awareness of other cultures? If no such provisions are being made, what do you suggest? What criteria would you use in planning a program or activities?

3. One of the services offered by most dioceses is that of investigating new educational approaches and materials. Visit the curriculum department of your diocese to see what opportunities are available. How would you assess the resources? If asked, what suggestions or comments would you make?

4. Interview a group of teachers who are involved in interdisciplinary efforts (e.g., teachers of literature, history, physics, and math, who are coordinating instruction using an integrative theme), or—if you are not aware of teachers involved in interdisciplinary instruction—seek out several teachers (at least four) who work with children of various ages and/or in various disciplines). Inquire whether these teachers use strategies to integrate interdisciplinary content and/or how they encourage their students to make such connections (e.g., Does the physical education instructor ever use music or math? How are reading skills deliberately fostered in math instruction or math skills incorporated in history?). How is the curriculum designed?

How is it implemented? What are the benefits and the difficulties of using an interdisciplinary approach in curriculum design? What possibilities exist for synthesizing educational experiences for students when teachers engage in some interdisciplinary teaching?

As a result of study, reflection, and interacting with knowledgeable individuals, the learner will be able to complete the following activities. The quality of response to these activities should give some indication of the level of expertise the learner is able to bring to the situation.

Outcome Activities: C4
Curriculum Development

1. The statement of philosophy expresses ideals and beliefs. Goals are more precise delineations. Objectives are statements of learner outcomes. Write an illustration of a curriculum goal and two objectives derived from the goal.

2. Develop a plan indicating the specific steps you would take if you felt that there was a need for initiating a course in human sexuality in the school curriculum.

3. As new curriculum programs or new curriculum materials are adopted, identify problems that teachers and principals might have with some parents. What are some methods of handling a controversy?

Role: Principal as Educational Leader

Area: Curriculum and Instruction

> ### Competency: C5
> ### *Educational and Pedagogical Skills*

As an educational leader, the principal is expected to know educational theory and promote teaching techniques that benefit and challenge students.

Currently, the educational field is rich with advanced knowledge about the teaching/learning process. Dunn (1990) insists that attention to learning styles is becoming crucial because of the challenge to educate all children at high levels of performance. Marzano (1992) highlights an emphasis on teaching strategies that call for the learning of particular content with meaningful understandings as student outcomes. There are in place new content reforms suggested for the teaching of math, science, language arts, geography, and history (O'Neil 1990). Caine (1992) encourages educators to capitalize on what the learner already knows and values and how information and experiences connect.

The Catholic school principal is faced with a large repertoire of educational theories and methodologies. In order to meet expectations of knowing and promoting the best procedures for broadening professional skills and offering new instructional strategies, Perri (1989) suggests that a principal collaborate with a companion principal. As a pair, they might share readings, learning, problems, and experiences.

Attention given to understanding a variety of educational and pedagogical skills will enable the principal actually to see what is happening in the teaching/learning situations in classrooms and creatively to introduce the necessary changes to ensure learning experiences that are challenging, appropriate, diverse, and meaningful.

To support and give evidence of professional growth in demonstrating a knowledge of a variety of educational and pedagogical skills, the learner will engage in the listed activities under the direction of the diocese (Model I) or through a self-directed program and/or with the guidance of a mentor (Model II).

The primary means of keeping a consistent record of activities is to keep an ongoing JOURNAL which would contain:

1) a *Dated Log* section recording when activities were undertaken and completed,

2) a *Reading/Response* section in which notes from suggested readings and the response reactions are systematically organized, and

3) an *Experience (Activity)/Reflection* section in which one records ideas and insights gained through interacting with people or seeking out additional information in the course of completing the activities.

Learning Activities: C5
Educational and Pedagogical Skills

1. Read the following and respond with reactions in a journal.* Ideally, you should discuss these readings and your reactions with a mentor. These integral readings are reprinted for your convenience on pages 234–54.

Caine, R. N., and G. Caine. 1991. *Making connections: Teaching and the human brain*. Alexandria, Va.: Association for Supervision and Curriculum Development, 48–50, 59–61, 80–87, 102–05, 112–13.

Dunn, R. 1990. Rita Dunn answers questions on learning styles. *Educational Leadership* 48(2): 15–19.

Marzano, R. J. 1992. *A different kind of classroom*. Alexandria, Va.: Association Supervision and Curriculum Development, 25–27, 124–26, 135–39.

National Conference of Catholic Bishops. 1979. *Sharing the light of faith: National catechetical directory for Catholics of the United States*. Washington, D.C.: United States Catholic Conference, nos. 176, 185.

Reck, C. 1988. *The small Catholic elementary school*. Washington, D.C.: National Catholic Educational Association, 64–70.

* In your journal, note specific teaching approaches or practices that seem usable and that engage and empower students. Generally, what learning tasks are more meaningful to students and offer long-term benefits?

2. Visit one or two schools and observe lessons of two teachers recommended by the principal(s). In light of what you have read, how did each of the teachers create good learning situations? If the lessons seemed lacking, what improvements would you suggest?

3. Watch a videotape or film which deals with meaningful learning for children. (Suggestions: Fadiman, D. *Why Do These Children Love School?* Menlo Park, Calif: Concentric Media, or the movie *Little Man Tate,* available on video.) The purpose of this activity is to help you understand the importance of meaningful learning. What assumptions are made about the child, the teacher, and the learning? What was meaningful, or not so meaningful, about the learning that took place? Do you think the child and the teacher or significant adults in these films were communicating effectively? What lessons, either supporting or not supporting learning, were conveyed to the child and from the child to the teacher?

4. Teach a lesson to a class of at least fifteen students. (This might be in a regular classroom, at a CCD session, with a scout troop, or in some other information situation.) Have it videotaped. Later review the lesson (with a mentor, if possible). Concentrate not only on your teaching, but watch for students' reactions and involvement. In a journal, write reflections on:
   a. why you designed the lesson as you did,
   b. how successful the lesson seemed (from your perspective and the students' perspective) before and after the review of the tape, and
   c. any suggestions for what might have worked better if you were to do it again.
(If this activity is not possible, describe your style of teaching. Be specific about various techniques you use.)

As a result of study, reflection, and interaction with knowledgeable individuals, the learner will be able to complete the following activities. The quality of response to these activities should give some indication of the level of expertise the learner is able to bring to the situation.

Outcome Activities: C5
Educational and Pedagogical Skills

1. Select a student population and subject you know best. Based on your readings, design a ten-point program that would characterize excellence in the teaching of that subject to that particular group of students.

2. Select two content areas that may require contrasting pedagogical approaches and describe at least three ways the teaching skills would be similar or different (e.g., physical education and mathematics, science and literature, language arts and art, etc.). How could these two areas be integrated? What measures would need to be taken to be sure the integration was a meaningful application rather than cosmetic? What would justify integrating or keeping lessons/content areas separate?

Role: Principal as Educational Leader

Area: Curriculum and Instruction

Competency: C6
Accommodate Students' Special Needs[1]

Catholic Educators are charged with the mission to "teach as Jesus taught." To fulfill this mission, the principal as educational leader needs to reflect upon what this really means. Teaching in the Catholic school must be more than just training, instructing, or helping students to acquire facts and skills. To "teach as Jesus taught" seems closer to the Latin derivative of educating, *educare*, to lead out —to bring out all the potential in each student. This means that teachers need to see their role to be one of guiding each pupil in the process of becoming all that he or she can be in a climate that recognizes the worth of each individual and appreciates all gifts as equally valuable, albeit different. Such an attitude is reflective of St. Paul's concept of "many gifts but one spirit." This means, too, that the focus is on the aptitude development of the student, not solely on the delivery of content or covering a text. To be effective, instruction must be delivered in a flexible enough way that all students are helped to see themselves as lovable and capable, in the words of John Paul II, "unique and unrepeatable gifts of God." To achieve this goal, the principal must not only foster a climate where each student develops a healthy sense of self but the principal also must understand how to lead teachers in adapting instruction and classroom practices to match students' learning differences. Only then can all students learn to capitalize on their strengths while compensating for differences that might limit achievement.

In almost any mainstream Catholic school classroom, there are three types of learners who have unrecognized and unaddressed special needs that impede achievement and school performance. These students may have learning disabilities or attention deficit disorder or are gifted but unchallenged. If the manifestations of the problems are left unattended, they have the potential to lead to eroding self-esteem, feelings of inadequacy, declining motivation, and ultimately under-achievement despite considerable ability.

Unrecognized learning disabilities (LDs) can mask a student's ability for conceptualization and reasoning because they also impede the acquisition and application of basic skills such as reading, writing, spelling, and the algorithmic aspects of mathematics. A language-based LD, in particular, often makes a student appear less "able" because so much of the instruction and assessment in the classroom is language based.

Similarly, students with unrecognized Attention Deficit (Hyperactivity) Disorder (ADHD) will often appear immature and irresponsible or have motivation and/or behavior problems in the classroom. ADHD students often have increasing difficulty with peer relationships, organization, independence, and rule-following as they progress through school. Such behavior often results in lack of production and underachievement. Moreover, these students often frustrate both parents and teachers in attempts to "socialize" the ADHD child to the demands of the school routine. As a result, intense parent-school conflicts, parent-child conflicts, and school-student conflicts ensue.

Although often less overtly troublesome in the classroom, many gifted and talented (GT) students can also underachieve. If left underchallenged, they coast on a "conservation of energy policy." They develop many maladaptive habits and beliefs about the nature of intelligence and the role of effort in achievement. Such misconceptions may impede their ability later in their academic careers to respond appropriately to challenges for which they are cognitively quite capable. If they finish work quickly, get few answers wrong, and exert little effort for "easy grades," they can come to believe that a hallmark of "smart" people is minimal effort for maximal results. Nothing is further from reality for creative, productive, gifted contributors in any domain in society. If gifted children come to believe

---

1 Editor's note: The competency—to recognize and accommodate the special learning needs of children within the mainstream classroom—is not in the original list developed by the NCEA/USCC/NCGELP committee. It is included because the students coming to our schools have increasingly complex learning needs. Teachers are often stymied and need special guidance in this area from the principals. I am indebted to Dr. Jean Barton for sharing her special expertise by writing this section.

that all learning should be effortless for them, they often feel inadequate when they do encounter challenging problem-solving tasks that require considerable effort and perseverance and/or involve frustration and trial and error resolution. Often they begin avoiding the very kind of courses and activities that will develop their intelligence, choosing instead easy courses that guarantee high grades for little effort. They have learned to underachieve.

In the vast majority of cases, once these special needs are identified, a Catholic school can adapt instruction with minimal investment of resources. The result is a classroom climate in which these children can not only succeed, but also thrive. The Catholic school that makes provisions for a wider spectrum of student needs with an effective classroom learning environment is truly working as a partner with those parents who want to provide their children the benefits of a Catholic education.

To support and give evidence of professional growth in understanding the unique educational needs of ADHD, learning-disabled, and gifted students and how to adapt instruction to meet them, the learner will engage in the listed activities under the direction of the diocese (Model I) or through a self-directed program and/or with the guidance of a mentor (Model II).

The primary means of keeping a consistent record of activities is to keep an ongoing JOURNAL which would contain:

1) a *Dated Log* section recording when activities were undertaken and completed,

2) a *Reading/Response* section in which notes from suggested readings and the response reactions are systematically organized, and

3) an *Experience (Activity)/Reflection* section in which one records ideas and insights gained through interacting with people or seeking out additional information in the course of completing the activities.

Learning Activities: C6
Accommodate Students' Special Needs

1. Read the following and respond with reactions in a journal.* Ideally, you should discuss these readings and your reactions with a mentor. These integral readings are reprinted for your convenience on pages 255–396.

Barkley, Russell A. 1990. Primary symptoms and conceptualization. In *Attention deficit hyperactivity disorder: A handbook for diagnosis and treatment*, ed. R. A. Barkley, 39–73. New York: The Guilford Press.

Bos, C., and S. Vaughn. 1991. *Strategies for teaching students with learning and behavior problems*. Boston: Allyn and Bacon. (Note: Approaches to learning and teaching 24–57.)

Durbin, Karen. 1993. Attention deficit hyperactivity disorder. *Streamlined Seminar* 11(4). Alexandria, Va.: National Association of Elementary School Principals.

Mann, Virginia. 1991. Language problems: A key to early reading problems. In *Learning about learning disabilities*, ed. B. Y. L. Wong, 129–62. San Diego: Academic Press, Inc.

National Conference of Catholic Bishops. 1979. *Sharing the light of faith: National catechetical directory for Catholics of the United States*. Washington, D.C.: United States Catholic Conference, nos. 192–96.

Parke, B. 1989. *Gifted students in regular classrooms*. Boston: Allyn and Bacon. (Note: Gifted students: Who they are and what they need 3–16, Planning the programs 42–63, Designing the curriculum 127–42.)

Pfiffner, Linda J., and Barkley, Russell A. Educational placement and classroom management. In *Attention deficit hyperactivity disorder: A handbook for diagnosis and treatment*, ed. R. A. Barkley, 498–539. New York: The Guilford Press.

Swanson, H. Lee, and John B. Cooney. 1991. Learning disabilities and memory. In *Learning about learning disabilities*, ed. B. Y. L. Wong, 103–22. San Diego: Academic Press, Inc.

Willows, Dale M. Visual processes in learning disabilities. In *Learning about learning disabilities*, ed. B. Y. L. Wong, 163–93. San Diego: Academic Press, Inc.

Wong, Bernice Y. L. 1991. The relevance of metacognition to learning disabilities. In *Learning about learning disabilities*, ed. B. Y. L. Wong, 231–57. San Diego: Academic Press, Inc.

* In your journal, make a list of the identifying characteristics of each of the three special needs groups. Note your insights into how specific characteristics of each of these groups can lead to underachievement and/or behavior problems in the classroom when they are unaddressed. Reflect and comment upon how the suggestions made in the reading could be implemented in your school. What kind of teacher

in-service program would be needed? Are there students with these needs in your school? How are they perceived by their peers and teachers? What interventions does your school use now with these students? How well are the specific needs understood and addressed by the teachers, staff, and parents of these children? Are they achieving at their potential?

2. Interview a sample of your teachers across primary, intermediate, and upper grades. (If you are in a secondary school, interview across grade levels and departments.) Informally ask them about their knowledge and experience in identifying and working with LD, ADHD, and GT students. Discuss with each of them the students in their classes whose behavior and/or achievement are troubling to the teacher. Do these students exhibit any of the characteristics described in the readings? Make a list of the student and teacher comments/concerns. Observe some of these students during the times when they are engaged in the problematic activities described by the teachers. With your list of identifying characteristics from your journal before you, take notes on the behaviors observed: What happened before the troublesome incident; what was the antecedent? What were the consequences of the behavior for the student, the class, and the teacher? Are there patterns? Do they relate to the primary identifiers from the reading?

3. Make arrangements for yourself and, if possible, one or two teachers to visit at least one, but preferably two or three, other classrooms at different grade levels in a school where these populations are labeled and strategies are developed for them. Explain to the principal of the visited school that the purpose of your visit is to gain a greater understanding of the unique characteristics of these children as well as the techniques used to address their needs. Observe and identify behaviors, antecedents, and consequences, but also focus on the teacher's response and the proactive techniques used to provide for the student's needs. Note the effectiveness of the interventions and compare with the suggestions made in your readings. If possible,

interview the teacher and/or the principal. Have prepared in advance a list of your specific questions about identifying characteristics and procedures, teacher training, staff development, parent-school collaboration, programming techniques, etc. Be sure to ask about the local support groups for parents such as ACLD (Association for Children with Learning Disabilities) and CHADD (Children with ADD) or gifted summer/enrichment programs. After your visit, review your notes and reflect in your journal on the comparison of what you observed and what you read. If you had the opportunity to observe across grade levels, note the trends you saw regarding motivation, self-esteem, and production. Did you observe use of technology in meeting the needs of the children? To summarize each observation/interview in your journal, prepare a "PMI" chart with three columns: Plus-Minus-Interesting. In the "P" column list good/effective ideas. In the "M" column list bothersome incidents or problems you saw or can foresee. In the "I" column list things you want to think about more later. Discuss the visit with the teachers; if possible, compare notes and problem-solve how to incorporate the effective strategies into your school.

4. Contact two or three principals in other Catholic schools. Survey what provisions they make for the targeted students. As with the teachers, informally survey their knowledge and experience with these populations. Invite them to form an informal study group with you to investigate how better to serve these children within the Catholic schools. Meet on a regular basis to discuss readings and activities and to share ideas about interventions planned or implemented. Collaboratively problem-solve how to support one another in helping teachers to gain an understanding of these students' needs and to gain skill in coping constructively with them in the classroom. Perhaps you could pool resources for joint in-service activities and joint acquisition of materials, and even special personnel to supplement the efforts of the teachers. Consider linking with college or university resources to develop a pilot program or writing a grant proposal to generate funds for your projects.

As a result of study, reflection, and interaction with knowledgeable individuals, the learner will be able to complete the following activities. The quality of response to these activities should give some indication of the level of expertise the learner is able to bring to the situation.

Outcome Activities: C6
Accommodate Students' Special Needs

1. Develop a five-year plan that a principal could use to implement a process that provides for the special needs of LD, GT, and ADHD children within the mainstream classroom. Consider issues such as identification of children, staff development, collaborating with parents, and devising support systems.

2. Outline a plan of teacher in-service training to prepare teachers in the identification of students, planning of appropriate strategies, proper assessment and evaluation techniques, and working with parents of the targeted children.

3. Using your PMI list, decide which items in the "P" column could or should be adapted to your local circumstance. How might the items in the "M" column be remedied and perhaps adapted to your situation? Concerning the "I" column: What aspect of a comprehensive program is addressed? In which areas do you need more information or experience? Why do these ideas intrigue you?

4. Devise a three-year proposal/plan to be submitted to the diocese that would specify the services/resources and information/education needed by the diocesan principals and teachers to learn about and to develop viable programs for each school to address the needs of these special populations.

Do not forget about the needs of parents and the school-community relations aspect in developing the project.

Role: Principal as Educational Leader

Area: Curriculum and Instruction

**Competency: C7
Supervise Instruction**

One of the major responsibilities of the Catholic school principal is to assure that quality education is provided through the supervision of instruction. Darish (1989) defines *supervision* as the process of overseeing the ability of people to meet the goals of the organization in which they work.

There are a variety of approaches for supervising instruction recommended to administrators. Glickman (1990) proposes that the first order of business is to build the staff into a team. They must share a common purpose for their instruction with confidence that their collective action will make a difference in their students' lives. Ristau (1989) and Glatthorn and Shields (1983) portray the existing caring community in the Catholic school as a distinct advantage.

Personal assumptions, beliefs, and values influence a principal when working with teachers. Darish (1991) sees this as a useful tool for sharing important values and a help to developing a supervisory style.

Effective supervision requires knowledge, interpersonal skills, and technical skills. Ristau (1989) sees the process as one where teacher and principal focus together on deepening wisdom, improving skills, and enriching teaching techniques.

Attention given by the Catholic school principal to the effective supervision of instruction increases the probability that each teacher in the school is a successful and artistic instructor and that quality education is being provided.

To support and give evidence of professional growth in demonstrating a knowledge of effective supervision of instruction skills, the learner will engage in the listed activities under the direction of the diocese (Model I) or through a self-directed program and/or with the guidance of a mentor (Model II).

The primary means of keeping a consistent record of activities is to keep an ongoing JOURNAL which would contain:

1) a *Dated Log* section recording when activities were undertaken and completed,

2) a *Reading/Response* section in which notes from suggested readings and the response reactions are systematically organized, and

3) an *Experience(Activity)/Reflection* section in which one records ideas and insights gained through interacting with people or seeking out additional information in the course of completing the activities.

Learning Activities: C7
Supervise Instruction

1. Read the following and respond with reactions in a journal.* Ideally, you should discuss these readings and your reactions with a mentor. These integral readings are reprinted for your convenience on pages 396–411.

Daresh, J. C. 1991. *Supervision as a proactive process.* Prospect Heights, Ill.: Waveland, 29–36.

Glatthorn, A. A., and C. R. Shields. 1983. *Differentiated supervision for Catholic schools.* Washington, D.C.: National Catholic Educational Association, 15–27.

Glickman, C. D. 1990. *Supervision of instruction: A developmental approach.* Boston: Allyn and Bacon, 189–91.

Nolan, J., and P. Francis. 1992. Changing perspectives in curriculum and supervision. In *Supervision in transition, 1992 yearbook,* 52–60. Alexandria, Va.: Association for Supervision and Curriculum Development.

Ristau, K. 1989. The role of the principal in the ongoing education of teachers. In *Reflections on the role of the Catholic school principal,* ed. R. Kealey, 57–60. Washington, D.C.: National Catholic Educational Association.

* In your journal, keep a record of knowledge, skills, and procedures that can be used by you as you supervise instruction. This will help you to begin to formulate your own style of supervision.

2. View *Another Set of Eyes* (1987)—videotapes available from Alexandria, Va.: Association for Supervision and Curriculum Development. (The first tape [one hour] describes selected classroom observation techniques. The second

tape [30 minutes] enables viewers to practice the techniques.) What observation skills and procedures are necessary on the part of the principal to balance tasks and human needs?

3. Observe or talk with an administrator about his or her philosophy of supervision. How much time does the administrator engage in supervisory activities? Is the administrator satisfied that the time devoted is adequate to the task? What methods are used to supervise? What perspective does he or she take regarding supervision versus evaluation of staff? (Does this administrator differentiate between the two?)

As a result of study, reflection, and interaction with knowledgeable individuals, the learner will be able to complete the following activities. The quality of response to these activities should give some indication of the level of expertise the learner is able to bring to the situation.

Outcome Activities: C7
Supervise Instruction

1. A primary teacher, who has taught for five years, has a good grasp of the skills for teaching beginning reading, but with her habitual lack of enthusiasm, the children are bored and disinterested. Identify two factors that could be causing the low level of motivation. Then choose one of the factors and explain in detail the steps you would take to help the teacher and improve instruction.

2. Describe the model of supervision you would use with a beginning teacher who plans well and is creative but is having discipline problems with some of her fifth grade students.

3. Develop a plan that involves time management for the school week to allow for supervision of instruction.

4. Based on your readings, develop your personal professional profile. Such a profile should include your assumptions or beliefs about the way children grow, the purposes of schooling, the nature of learning, your style of teaching and administration, and the kind of school programs and environment that are best for teaching and learning. As a future administrator, include as part of this profile your philosophy of supervision.

Role: Principal as Educational Leader

Area: Curriculum and Instruction

Instructional leaders need to be aware of the variety of ways in which student progress can and should be assessed and to know the strengths and limitations of each method (Krug 1992).

Caine (1991) finds it acceptable to use formal tests and standardized tests in an assessment program but urges educators to extend the evaluation to a range of performance activities for the purpose of genuinely appreciating what the learners know. Some types of activities encourage active processing and provide invaluable feedback.

Saphier (1987) states that since true evaluation is tied to objectives, it is important in every assessment to look for a direct way of asking if objectives have been met. Maehr (1992) emphasizes how important it is for administrators to influence classroom level practices in this regard by recommending appropriate evaluation practices as well as effective methods for giving students clear and honest feedback.

In accordance with the philosophy of the Catholic school, evaluation occurs in a climate of respect and acceptance, looking to the development of the individual to his or her full potential.

Attention given to an understanding of effective procedures for evaluating the learning of students is an important investment for the Catholic school principal because it forces one to be clear about (1) what is to be accomplished and (2) what is evidence of mastery.

To support and give evidence of professional growth in understanding effective procedures for evaluating the learning of students, the learner will engage in the listed activities under the direction of the diocese (Model I) or through a self-directed program and/or with the guidance of a mentor (Model II).

The primary means of keeping a consistent record of activities is to keep an ongoing JOURNAL which would contain:

1) a *Dated Log* section recording when activities were undertaken and completed,

2) a *Reading/Response* section in which notes from suggested readings and the response reactions are systematically organized, and

3) an *Experience (Activity)/Reflection* section in which one records ideas and insights gained through interacting with people or seeking out additional information in the course of completing the activities.

Learning Activities: C8
Evaluate the Learning

1. Read the following and respond with reactions in a journal.* Ideally, you should discuss these readings and your reactions with a mentor. These integral readings are reprinted for your convenience on pages 412–30.

Caine, R. N., and G. Caine. 1991. *Making connections: Teaching and the human brain.* Alexandria, Va.: Association for Supervision and Curriculum Development, 105–06, 154–58.

Maehr, M. L., C. Midgley, and T. Urdan. 1992. School leader as motivator. *Educational Administration Quarterly* 28(3):410–29.

Maeroff, G. I. 1991. Assessing alternative assessment. *Phi Delta Kappan* 73(4):272–81.

* In your journal, note insights concerning various approaches to the measurement of learning. What are the assets and limitations to standardized testing, to alternative performance or authentic assessments? What are some ways of giving feedback to students that will give them a chance to improve performance?

2. Collect two or three different types of report cards (perhaps from different school systems or on different grade levels). From the general appearance and format of the card, what can you deduce about the philosophy of the school concerning evaluation of learning and reporting to parents? What kinds of information are listed on the card? Is the information listed on the card and the system used to report progress sensitive to the age level and development of

the student? Does the information listed on the card allow for and report individual differences? Evaluate the usefulness of the format in helping the student and/or parent to understand the student's progress. What suggestions would you make to improve the reporting instrument?

3. Interview principals, counselors, and, if possible, a kindergarten teacher to ascertain the skills being required for entry into the first grade. How are the skills evaluated? What is your assessment of the methods used?

4. Discuss with a school principal or a school or diocesan test coordinator the criteria used in choosing the formal and informal methods of evaluating students. If a standardized testing program is in place, what type is used? What purposes do the specific tests serve for the student, the parent, the teacher, the school, and the system? How is record keeping accomplished? How are parents educated and informed about their children's results? In lieu of the test results: (1) What types of interventions for students are planned and (2) what, if any, specific support measures are provided for teachers to implement the interventions?

As a result of study, reflection, and interaction with knowledgeable individuals, the learner will be able to complete the following activities. The quality of response to these activities should give some indication of the level of expertise the learner is able to bring to the situation.

Outcome Activities: C8
Evaluate the Learning

1. General guidelines, developed in a democratic framework, are essential for schoolwide directives to evaluate the learning of students. Outline some probable school guidelines on testing, grading, and reporting for a faculty presentation to teachers new to a school.

2. Explain the procedure you would use to manage the problem of the student and the teacher in this situation: A teacher tells you (as principal) that one of her eighth grade students is getting a quarterly grade of "F" for failing to hand in many written assignments. The teacher feels justified in giving the failing grade since the importance of the written assignments was emphasized from the very beginning of the course. You have worked with this student in the past and know she has a problem with organization. You are aware of her giftedness and more than adequate knowledge of the subject matter.

Role: Principal as Educational Leader

Area: Curriculum and Instruction

Ideally, every Catholic school under the leadership of the principal continuously clarifies its vision and evaluates the extent to which its program is balanced, goal-oriented, and integrated.

Oliva (1989) names several areas to examine in an evaluation of the effectiveness of the school program, namely: curriculum and instructional goals and objectives, parents' and other persons' reactions to the curriculum, quality of materials, organization of curriculum, specific programs (in formative stage and at the end of a trial period), projections for the future, and the evaluation program itself.

Convey (1992) states that since commitment to the religious formation of its students and the building of community are so essential to the nature of the Catholic school, monitoring effectiveness in these areas should receive high priority.

Reck (1988) points out that when the process of evaluation is well utilized and input on important issues is asked of all segments of the school community, regular evaluations can effectively build a unified community. Just by taking steps to do a self-study, the school shows its interest in improvement and accountability.

Attention given by the Catholic school principal to the continuous evaluation of the effectiveness of the learning program of the school enables the school to clarify its direction, to build shared beliefs, and to identify aspects of its program that require improvement.

To support and give evidence of professional growth in demonstrating a knowledge of the procedures for evaluating the general effectiveness of the learning program of the school, the learner will engage in the listed activities under the direction of the diocese (Model I) or through a self-directed program and/or with the guidance of a mentor (Model II).

The primary means of keeping a consistent record of activities is to keep an ongoing JOURNAL which would contain:

1) a *Dated Log* section recording when activities were undertaken and completed,

2) a *Reading/Response* section in which notes from suggested readings and the response reactions are systematically organized, and

3) an *Experience(Activity)/Reflection* section in which one records ideas and insights gained through interacting with people or seeking out additional information in the course of completing the activities.

Learning Activities: C9
Evaluate the Learning Program

1. Read the following and respond with reactions in a journal.* Ideally, you should discuss these readings and your reactions with a mentor. These integral readings are reprinted for your convenience on pages 431–49.

Convey, J. J. 1992. *Catholic schools make a difference: Twenty-five years of research*. Washington, D.C.: National Catholic Educational Association, 177–90.

Doyle, R., N. Kinate, A. Langan, and M. Swanson. 1991. Evaluation of the school's Catholicity. In *Capital wisdom: Papers from the Principals Academy 1991*, 1–6. Washington, D.C.: National Catholic Educational Association.

Reck, C., and J. Coreil. 1983. *School evaluation for the Catholic elementary school: An overview*. Washington, D.C.: National Catholic Educational Association, 3–20.

Savary, L. M. 1992. *Creating quality schools*. Arlington, Va.: American Association of School Administrators, 27–32.

*In your journal, list any recommended steps for evaluating school programs, particularly those of Catholic schools. How is the philosophy of the school important to guiding the evaluation? What further questions do you have?

2. Obtain one or two published instruments for school evaluation. (These have been produced

by some state, local, and diocesan education departments. *Verifying the Vision* [1984] is a self-evaluation tool which can be purchased from the National Catholic Educational Association in Washington, D.C. Also, most principals have at least one copy of a self-study instrument which was used or is being used.) Examine the sections that seem to be directly related to the evaluation of curriculum or instructional programs. Which criteria used for judging effectiveness would you consider adopting for future use? Record in your journal any usable information concerning the research design. What problems or reservations (if any) do you have with the questions being asked or the process for gathering, reporting, and reviewing of the information by outside parties?

3. Interview three or four principals or teachers for information involving research and/or evaluation of pilot programs or new textbook adoptions to improve the effectiveness of their school programs. How would you assess the processes used?

As a result of study, reflection, and interaction with knowledgeable individuals, the learner will be able to complete the following activities. The quality of response to these activities should give some indication of the level of expertise the learner is able to bring to the situation.

Outcome Activities: C9
Evaluate the Learning Program

1. A neighboring school has asked you to visit and make recommendations for their evaluation of their K–3 math program. Develop a written plan giving them suggestions for evaluating their math program. Base your plan and the resources you suggest on your own research.

2. Choose a curriculum guide in any subject and critique it according to a criterion supported by your readings and your related activities. If necessary, present a plan or revision of a section of the guide that is not consistent with what you have learned.

Curriculum and Instruction Bibliography

Role: Principal as Educational Leader

Area of Responsibility:
Curriculum and Instruction

Introduction

Congregation for Catholic Education. 1988. *The religious dimension of education in a Catholic school: Guidelines for reflection and renewal.* Washington, D.C.: United States Catholic Conference.

Glatthorn, A. A. 1987. *Curriculum renewal: A rationale for a consensus curriculum.* Alexandria, Va.: Association for Supervision and Curriculum Development, 20–27.

C1. To demonstrate that he/she has a knowledge of the content and the methods of religious education

Bohr, D. 1986. Imagination: The motivating force in catechesis. *Momentum* 17(3):10–12.

Di Giacomo, J. 1989. *Teaching religion in a Catholic secondary school.* Washington, D.C.: National Catholic Educational Association, 64–66.

Gilbert, J. R. 1983. *Pastor as shepherd of the school community.* Washington, D.C.: National Catholic Educational Association, 42–43.

Groome, T. H. 1992. Catechesis and religious education: "Let's stay together". *The Living Light* 29(1):40–46.

Kelly, F. D. 1989. Catechesis for the Third Millennium. *Momentum* 20(4):6–10.

Libreria Editrice Vaticana. 1994. *Catechism of the Catholic Church.* Washington, D.C.: United States Catholic Conference, nos. 1–10, 25, 426–29, 1074–75, 1674–76, 1697–98, 2688.

O'Malley, W. J. 1992. Catechesis for conversion. *The Living Light* 29(2):55–63.

United States Catholic Conference. 1990. *Guidelines for doctrinally sound catechetical materials.* Washington, D.C., 11–25.

C2. To be knowledgeable of the developmental stages of children and youth

Crain, W. 1992. *Theories of development: Concepts and applications.* Englewood Cliffs, N.J.: Prentice Hall, 17–18, 102–03, 124, 129, 136–41, 188–90, 262–68.

Haney, R. 1991. Seize the day! *Momentum* 22(2):6–8.

Hawker, J. 1985. *Catechetics in the Catholic school.* Washington, D.C.: National Catholic Educational Association, 10–13.

National Conference of Catholic Bishops. 1979. *Sharing the light of faith: National catechetical directory for Catholics of the United States.* Washington, D.C.: United States Catholic Conference, nos. 173–75, 177–80.

C3. To recognize and provide for cultural and religious differences

Banks, J. A. 1989. Multicultural education: Characteristics and goals. In *Multicultural education: Issues and perspectives*, eds. J. A. Banks and C. M. Banks, 2–3, 19–23. Boston: Allyn and Bacon.

Grant, C. A., and C. E. Sleeter. 1988. *Making choices for multicultural education.* Columbus: Merrill, 2–3.

Hall, S., ed. 1992. *The people: Reflections of native peoples on the Catholic experience in North America.* Washington, D.C.: National Catholic Educational Association, 73–78.

Hall, S., R. Doyle, and P. Tran, eds. 1990. *A Catholic response to the Asian presence.* Washngton, D.C.: National Catholic Educational Association, 85–91.

Hall, S., and C. Reck, eds. 1987. *Integral education: A response to the Hispanic presence.* Washington, D.C.: National Catholic Educational Association, 48–51.

Jones, N. 1987. An Afro-American perspective. In *Faith and culture*, 77–80. Washington, D.C.: United States Catholic Conference.

Kennedy, M. M., ed. 1991. *Teaching academic subjects to diverse learners.* New York: Columbia University, 239, 267.

Libreria Editrice Vaticana. 1994. *Catechism of the Catholic Church.* Washington, D.C.: United States Catholic Conference, nos. 1204–06.

United States Catholic Conference. 1990. *Guidelines for doctrinally sound catechetical materials.* Washington, D.C., 23–25.

Uphoff, J. K. 1989. Religious diversity and education. In *Multicultural education: Issues and perspectives*, eds J. A. Banks and C. M. Banks, 89–90. Boston: Allyn and Bacon.

C4. To provide leadership in curriculum development, especially for the integration of Christian values

Brophy, J. 1992. Probing the subtleties of subject-matter teaching. *Educational Leadership* 49(7):4–8.

Dede, C. 1986. The implications of emerging technologies for the value-oriented curriculum. *Momentum* 17(3): 42–44.

English, F., and J. C. Hill. 1990. *Restructuring: The principal and curriculum change.* Reston, Va.: National Association of Secondary School Principals, 4–5, 10–12.

Gilbert, J. 1983. *Pastor as shepherd of the school community.* Washington, D.C.: National Catholic Educational Association, 10–11.

Glatthorn, A. A. 1987. *Curriculum renewal: A rational for a consensus curriculum.* Alexandria, Va.: Association for Supervision and Curriculum Development, 20–27.

Kealey, R. 1985. *Curriculum in the Catholic school.* Washington, D.C.: National Catholic Educational Association, 11–42.

Lunenburg, F. C., and A. C. Ornstein. 1991. *Educational administration: Concepts and practices.* Belmont, Calif.: Wadsworth, 401–08.

Welch, M. L. 1990. *A beginning: Resource book for incorporating values and Church teachings in the Catholic school curriculum.* Washington, D.C.: National Catholic Educational Association, 17–124.

C5. To give evidence of an understanding of a variety of educational and pedagogical skills

Barton, J. 1990. The teacher as critical thinker. *Momentum* 21(4):20–22.

Caine, R. N., and G. Caine. 1991. *Making connections: Teaching and the human brain.* Alexandria, Va.: Association for Supervision and Curiculum Development, 48–50, 59–61, 80–87, 102–05, 112–13.

Dunn, R. 1990. Rita Dunn answers questions on learning styles. *Educational Leadership* 48(2):15–19.

Kealey, R., ed. 1989. *Reflections on the role of the Catholic school principal.* Washington, D.C.: National Catholic Educational Association, 70–73.

Marzano, R. J. 1992. *A different kind of classroom.* Alexandria, Va.: Association for Supervision and Curriculum Development, 25–27, 124–26, 135–39.

National Conference of Catholic Bishops. 1979. *Sharing the light of faith: National catechetical directory for Catholics of the United States.* Washington, D.C.: United States Catholic Conference, nos. 176, 185.

O'Neil, J. 1990. New curriculum agenda emerges for the '90s. *Curriculum Update* 32(6):2–7.

Reck, C. 1988. *The small Catholic elementary school.* Washington, D.C.: National Catholic Educational Association, 64–70.

Slavin, R. E. 1991. Synthesis of research on cooperative learning. *Educational Leadership* 48(5):71–82.

Zukowski, A. A. 1992. Re-thinking Catholic education: A dialogue. *Momentum* 23(1):24–27.

C6. To recognize and accommodate the special learning needs of children within the mainstreamed classroom.

Alley, G., and D. Deshler. 1979. *Teaching the learning disabled adolescent: Strategies and methods.* Denver: Love Publishing Company.

Ames, C., and C. Ames. 1984. *Research on motivation in education.* San Diego: Academic Press.

Armstrong, T. 1987. *In their own way.* Los Angeles: Jeremy Tarcher, Inc.

Barkley, R. 1990. *Attention deficit hyperactivity disorder: A handbook for diagnosis and treatment.* New York: The Guilford Press.

Bos, C., and S. Vaughn. 1991. *Strategies for teaching students with learning and behavior problems.* Boston: Allyn and Bacon.

Clarke, B. 1988. *Growing up gifted.* Columbus, Ohio: Merrill.

Clarke, J. 1990. *Patterns of thinking.* Boston: Allyn and Bacon.

Collins, C., and J. Mangieri. 1992. *Teaching thinking.* Hillsdale, N.J.: Erlbaum.

Davis, G., and S. Rimm. 1989. *Education of the gifted and talented.* Englewood Cliffs, N.J.: Prentice-Hall.

DeBono, E. 1985. *Thinking six hats.* Boston: Little Brown.

Durbin, K. 1993. Attention deficit hyperactivity. *Streamlined Seminar* 11(4). Alexandria, Va., National Association of Elementary School Principals.

Farmham-Diggory, S. 1992. *The learning disabled child.* Cambridge, Mass.: Harvard University Press.

Fox, L., L. Brody, and D. Tobin. 1983. *Learning disabled/ gifted children.* Baltimore: University Park Press.

Gallagher, J. 1985. *Teaching the gifted child.* Boston: Allyn and Bacon.

Gardner, H. 1985. *Frames of mind: The theory of multiple intelligences.* New York: Basic Books.

———. 1991. *The unschooled mind: How children think and how schools should teach.* New York: Basic Books.

Hyde, A., and M. Bizar. 1989. *Thinking in context.* White Plains, N.Y.: Longman.

Jones, B., and A. Palinscar. 1987. *Strategic teaching and learning.* Alexandria, Va.: Association for Supervision and Curriculum Development.

Karnes, M. 1986. *The underserved: Our young gifted children.* Reston, Va.: Council for Exceptional Children.

Marzano, R. 1992. *A different kind of classroom: Teaching with dimensions of learning.* Alexandria, Va.: Association for Supervision and Curriculum Development.

Mercer, C. 1987. *Student with learning disabilities.* 4th ed. New York: Macmillan Publishing Company.

National Conference of Catholic Bishops. 1979. *Sharing the light of faith: National catechetical directory for Catholics of the United States.* Washington, D.C.: United States Catholic Conference, nos. 192–96.

Novak, J., and D. Gowin. 1986. *Learning how to learn.* New York: Cambridge University Press.

Parke, B. 1989. *Gifted students in regular classrooms.* Boston: Allyn and Bacon.

Paul, R. 1990. *Critical thinking.* Rohnert Park, Calif.: Center for Critical Thinking.

Pehrsson, R., and H. Robinson. 1985. *The semantic organizer approach to writing and reading instruction.* Rockville, Md.: Aspen.

———. 1989. *Semantic organizers: A study strategy for special needs learners.* Rockville, Md.: Aspen.

Perkins, D. 1986. *Knowledge as design.* Hillsdale, N.J.: Erlbaum.

Smith, S. 1991. *Succeeding against the odds.* Los Angeles: Jeremy Tarcher, Inc.

Resnick, L., and L. Klopfer. 1989. *Towards the thinking curriculum.* Alexandria, Va.: Association for Supervision and Curriculum Development.

Sternberg, R. 1983. *How can we teach intelligence?* Philadelphia, Pa.: Research for Better Schools.

Whitmore, J., and J. Maker. 1985. *Intellectual giftedness in disabled persons.* Rockville, Md.: Aspen.

Wlodowski, R., and J. Jaynes. 1990. *Eager to learn.* San Francisco: Jossey-Bass Publishers.

Wong, B. Y. L. 1991. *Learning about learning disabilities.* San Diego: Academic Press, Inc.

C7. To effectively supervise instruction

Conley, D.T., and K. Dixon. 1990. The evaluation report: A tool for teacher growth. *NASSP Bulletin* 74(527): 10–14.

Daresh, J. D. 1991. *Supervision as a proactive process.* Prospect Heights, Ill.: Waveland, 29–36.

Glatthorn, A. A., and C. R. Shields. 1983. *Differentiated supervision for Catholic schools.* Washington, D.C.: National Catholic Educational Association, 15–27.

Glickman, C. D. 1981. *Developmental supervision.* Alexandria, Va.: Association for Supervision and Curriculum Development, 17–36.

———. 1990. *Supervision of instruction: A developmental approach.* Boston: Allyn and Bacon, 189–91.

Nolan, J., and P. Francis. 1992. Changing perspectives in curriculum and instruction. In *Supervision in transition, 1992 yearbook,* 52–60. Alexandria, Va: Association for Supervision and Curriculum Development.

Pope, C. A. 1990. Indirect teaching and assessment: Are they mutually exclusive? *NASSP Bulletin* 74(527):1–5.

Ristau, K. 1989. The role of the principal in the ongoing education of teachers. In *The role of the Catholic school principal,* ed. R. Kealey, 57–60. Washington, D.C.: National Catholic Educational Association.

Root, D., and D. Overly. 1990. Successful teacher evaluation: Key elements for success. *NASSP Bulletin* 74(527):34–38.

Sergiovanni, T. J., and R. J. Starratt. 1988. *Supervision: Human perspectives.* New York: McGraw-Hill, 226–38.

Smith, W., and R. L. Andrews. 1989. *Instructional leadership.* Alexandria, Va.: Association for Supervision and Curriculum Development, 36–38, 42–45.

C8. To demonstrate an understanding of effective procedures for evaluating the learning of students

Caine, R. N., and G. Caine. 1991. *Making connections: Teaching and the human brain.* Alexandria, Va.: Association for Supervision and Curriculum Development, 105–06, 154–58.

Krug, S. E. 1992. Instructional leadership. *Educational Administration Quarterly* 28(3):430.

Maehr, M. L., C. Midgly. and T. Urdan. 1992. School leader as motivator. *Educational Administration Quarterly* 28(3): 410–29.

Maeroff, G. I. 1991. Assessing alternative assessment. *Phi Delta Kappan* 73(4):272–81.

Marzano, R. J. 1992. *A different kind of classroom.* Alexandria, Va.: Association for Supervision and Curriculum Development, 171–75.

Saphier, J., and R. Gower. 1987. *The skillful teacher.* Carlisle, Mass.: Research for Better Teaching, 377–85.

C9. To demonstrate the ability to evaluate the general effectiveness of the learning program of the school

Convey, J. J. 1992. *Catholic schools make a difference: Twenty-five years of research.* Washington, D.C.: National Catholic Educational Association, 177–90.

Doyle, R., N. Kinate, A. Langan, and M. Swanson. 1991. Evaluation of the school's Catholicity. In *Capital wisdom: Papers from the Principals Academy 1991,* 1–6. Washington, D.C.: National Catholic Educational Association.

Guskey, T. R., and D. Sparks. 1991. What to consider when evaluating staff development. *Educational Leadership* 49(3):73–75.

Oliva, P. 1989. *Supervision for today's schools.* White Plains, N.Y.: Longman, 302–06.

Reck, C., and J. Coreil. 1983. *School evaluation for the Catholic elementary school: An overview.* Washington, D.C.: National Catholic Educational Association, 3–20.

Savary, L. M. 1992. *Creating quality schools.* Arlington, Va.: American Association of School Administrators, 27–32.

Integral Readings for Curriculum and Instruction

C1 RELIGIOUS EDUCATION

Teaching Religion in a Catholic Secondary School

Di Giacomo, J. 1989. 64–66. Washington, D.C.: National Catholic Educational Association.

Developmental Perspective

Let's take one more look at the young people we try to teach in religion class. We have already said a great deal about them—their world, their values, their hopes and fears. Is there a way of looking at them and relating to them that could bring some kind of unity to our many impressions and help us to focus our efforts and concerns?

Developmental theory, which looks at persons not as static beings, but as engaged in a process of growth, offers helpful insights into the hearts and minds of the adolescents teachers deal with every school day. It asks: How do people grow and learn? What are the changes taking place in our students which affect their hearing of what we say? Are there any predictable passages, any universal experiences through which each unique person must pass? Are there attitudes toward religious faith and moral concerns that are peculiar to the adolescent? And if so, are there any strategies of response that would have universal validity?

There are many developmentalists with many different approaches to human growth. The popularity of their theories waxes and wanes from time to time. Nevertheless, when used with discretion, they can be of genuine assistance.

> The behavioral sciences . . . help us understand how people grow in their capacity for responding in faith to God's grace. They can therefore make a significant contribution to catechesis. At the same time catechists should not be uncritical in their approach to these sciences . . . (and) should not imagine that any one school or theory has all the answers. Finally, behavioral sciences do not supply the doctrinal and moral content of catechetical programs. Their discoveries and developments must be constantly and carefully evaluated by competent persons before being integrated into catechetics.[13]

With these precautions in mind, some observations that are general enough to earn consensus but practical enough to be of value can be made. The evolution of cognitive and affective capacities in the child and the young person are determining facts in what they can absorb on the intellectual and emotional levels. We have always known this, but it is only in recent decades that observation has been refined and strategies elaborated to capitalize on what we know. Thus, we have always tailored language to the age of children, reserving abstract and universal ideas for later, and in motivating them we have recognized that young children can hardly respond to appeals to altruism. The impact of cognitive and affective development on the quality of faith and on the capacity for moral judgment and decision-making is a matter of great importance to the religious educator. Our task is not to become amateur psychologists, but to be more sophisticated in assessing student capabilities and behavior and in choosing teaching materials an strategies.

Earlier we briefly discussed the ways in which adolescents tend to make judgments of right and wrong, and we suggested strategies for encouraging movement to more mature levels of moral analysis.[14] Ninth and tenth graders should be emerging from a kind of pre-moral phase in which right and wrong are calculated purely in terms of reward and punishment. During the high school years most of them can move through what some developmentalists call the "good boy/good girl" stage in which morality and immorality are synonymous with the approval or disapproval of significant others, toward a stage at which the norm is the needs or expectations of the wider community (conventional morality). Many middle and older adolescents can also begin to appreciate and admire, if not totally understand, models of moral behavior based on universal principles.

On the cognitive level these passages depend on the growing capacity for abstract thinking which usually increases significantly in the teen years. As we have pointed out, structuring discussions in the Socratic mode to create cognitive dissonance can help promote movement to more mature levels of judgment. A few qualifications are in order here. First, according to developmental theory, people can usually understand moral reasoning at a level somewhat higher than that at which they operate. Thus, most teenagers can grasp the viewpoint of conventional morality even while they habitually operate from the more narrow foci of self-interest and peer group concerns. Second, movement to more mature levels of judgment cannot be rushed; youngsters need time and experience at different levels before they are ready to move on. Finally, as Craig Dykstra reminds us, the moral agent is more than just a thinking person.[15] The classroom is a good vehicle for addressing the cognitive aspects of moral development but the growth of the whole person, especially the crucial affective dimension, takes place elsewhere. Religion teachers can make a significant but limited contribution.

Not only in moral matters but in those that touch on faith we must also attend to developmental concerns, for young people face tasks of growth not only in the way they make judgments of right and wrong but also in the stance they take toward religious faith. Our eventual goal should be a mature adult who takes responsibility for his or her religious identity. One of the most impressive examples of such autonomy was the late Frank Sheed, an engaging and persuasive Catholic apologist. Once, after a talk to a gathering of physicians, a doctor observed that while the talk was interesting, Sheed's beliefs could be accounted for by the fact that he had been brought up to think as a Catholic while he, the doctor, had been raised as an agnostic. Sheed responded with a little personal history: his father was an atheist and his mother was a Protestant! So much for brainwashing. Many of our students think that they and their peers are all programmed to be what they are. We cannot expect them to exhibit a great deal of independence at this age, but we can provide experiences which will promote such outcomes later on. The suggestions we made earlier for stimulating the asking of religious questions and for dealing with questions of religious authority and conscience can help toward this end.

We should not, however, be so intent on these processes that we fail to give proper consideration to content. Youngsters need a more than rudimentary knowledge of what this faith is about, or their critical thinking will take place in a vacuum of ignorance. Autonomy without religious literacy leads to the kind of religious subjectivism that we are trying to avoid. This point about content shows the limitations of the developmental perspective; i.e., it is not the only important consideration. There should be a kind of rhythm in high school religion classes, moving from content to process and back again, as students absorb information even while learning to process it in more and more sophisticated ways. The teacher's function is to orchestrate this rhythm, never settling for the mere uncritical accumulation of information, but also making sure that critical thinking is exercised by students who know what they are talking about.

Notes

13. *Sharing the Light of Faith*, op. cit., pp. 100–101.
14. Ibid., chapter 3.
15. Craig Dykstra, *Vision and Character* (New York: Paulist Press, 1981), pp. 7–29.

Catechesis and Religious Education: "Let's Stay Together"[1]

Groome, Thomas H. 1992. *The Living Light* 29(1):40–46.

Groome revisits an ongoing debate and argues that true knowing always involves a transformation of personal identity and agency.

The title of this essay may sound like the rehashing of a tired old topic. Yet, some recent bickering between these pugnacious partners advises us to return again to their relationship. Clearly they can be distinguished by emphasis, but serious and reputable voices from the perspective of both catechesis and religious education are now advising their separation.

For example, religious educator Graham Rossiter calls for "a creative divorce between catechesis and religious education."[2] He assigns the former, and more "personal," to the parish and the latter, and more "intellectual," to the school. From a catechetical perspective, Robert Duggan and Maureen Kelly claim that children's catechesis should be based on an RCIA model that shifts "from education to initiation." With a strong polemic against religious education, they recommend a catechesis centered on the liturgy and that "there . . . be no religious education program for youngsters prior to junior high other than the regular gathering for children's liturgy of the word on every Sunday and holy day."[3] The former proposes that religious education abandon concern for catechesis, while the latter proposes that catechesis abandon religious education. This essay challenges such sentiments as unwise and misguided, at least in the social context of American Catholicism.

The "What Will We Call It Debate": Not Again!

For more than twenty years, theorists have made valiant efforts to establish linguistic clarity and precision regarding the "terms" we use to name whatever it is that we do (and I've joined in that fray myself). Yet we have reached little theoretical consensus. And, much as some might regret, my impression is that most people in U.S. Catholic parishes and schools use the terms "religious education" and "catechesis" as if they are synonymous. I suspect that this is encouraged by curriculum materials that cannot be easily differentiated in orientation between catechesis or religious education; while their pedagogy is designed to personally engage participants in a community of dialogue and nurture, they also prompt critical reflection and informed appropriation of the tradition, and they encourage both clarity and conversion in faith that is owned and lived. Perhaps there may be some wisdom in this pastoral practice of using the terms interchangeably; at least this emphasizes that religious education and catechesis are essential partners. Even if the two can be distinguished conceptually around their emphasis, in our parishes and schools they should not be divided or separated.

My intent here is not to re-engage the "what to call it debate," although clearly that debate is important. My sense is that people have become bored with it or that they are more concerned about the naming that goes on *within* "whatever we call it" (e.g., of ourselves and the dangers of exclusive language, or of God and the need for expansive language), and that we should wait before taking up the debate again. And yet we need some sense of how the two terms are typically used, at least in the theoretical literature, in order to proceed.

The dominant trend I notice is to use "catechesis" for what John Westerhoff calls a "faith enculturation" paradigm, and to understand it as the process of socializing people into Christian identity through the formative power of a Christian community.[4] Then, it seems that "religious education" refers to the more academic and school-located study of religious tradition(s), either to learn about it or from it, but typically not teaching in a confessional manner or with the intent to form people in a particular way of being religious. Rossiter, for example, calls religious education "an intellectual study" that leads to "knowledge and understanding of religion."[5]

Clearly these distinctions have validity, both conceptually and existentially. Participating in and reflecting on a parish liturgy is not the same experience as a classroom conversation; parishes are more likely to be effective at catechesis, and likewise schools at religious education. I'm convinced, however, that in the context of American Catholicism (i.e., given our history, culture, and social/political structures), religious education and catechesis should be complementary activities; to separate them will work to the detriment of both. (I nuance my claim because in other cultures or political contexts, a division between the two might seem advisable. For example, religious education is a required discipline in the British school system, but the law mandates that this be an academic study of religion that avoids attempting to shape people's religious identity. Or, a more extreme case, the Catholic schools in Pakistan are strictly forbidden to catechize their Muslim students, often 99 percent of the student body.)

"Divorcing" them can be tempting and seems to make for a neat "division of labor." I'm convinced, however, that they do far better together than apart, albeit without honeymoon bliss. I fear for the catechesis that is not also good religious education, and for the religious education that deliberately avoids shaping people's identity and agency in faith. The first has a very limited understanding of both faith and reason, while the latter has an impoverished sense of "education." In the American Catholic community, school-based religious education programs should be good education that helps to nurture people in Christian faith. (Why else did parochial schools originate and continue without public funding?) Likewise, the socializing power of a parish community to form people in Christian identity needs moments and programs of intentional catechesis, available to all age groups, that assemble people into communities of dialogue and reflection on their lives in faith, that enable them to study rigorously and appropriate critically their Scriptures *and* traditions, and that teach people how to live as disciples—personally and communally—in this time and place.

To appreciate and maintain the partnership of religious education and catechesis calls for transcending two modern sets of dichotomies and returning instead to two ancient unities, namely, the solidarity of "knowing" and "being," and the alliance of reason and faith.

Knowing and Being: A Solidarity

The separation of religious education from catechesis reflects the false dichotomy that grew up in Western philosophy between "knowing" and "being," or, more technically, between epistemology and ontology. This is a long and complex story than cannot be fully traced here.[6] In gist, reflecting their ancient unity, early Greek philosophy agreed that knowledge pertained to one's very "being," that what we know is to shape who we are and how we live, and that who we are and how we live shapes what we know. Both Plato and Aristotle were convinced of this solidarity of life and knowledge and held that true happiness is found only when our knowing forms us as people of virtue. Likewise in the Hebrew and Christian traditions, "to know" means something far beyond having information; it refers to a wisdom of life that brings one's very "being" into "right relationship" with God, self, others, and creation. Rather than something only "applied" to life, knowing both arises from and returns to life; in fact, it is through living as disciples that we come to "know the truth"—the truth that sets us free (see Jn 8:31–32). Ultimately, in the biblical perspective, to know is to love—"the one without love knows nothing of God" (1 Jn 4:8). But Western philosophy and theology did not maintain this ancient unity of "knowing" and "being."

At the beginning of the modern era, Rene Descartes limited knowing to rational thinking and severed the mind from life in the world ("I think, therefore I am"). Immanuel Kant, at the pinnacle of the Enlightenment era, tried to reestablish the importance of "practical reasoning" that Descartes had so disparaged, but Kant left it severed from "pure reason" and thus encouraged a theoretical knowing that has no ethic of life or influence on people's identity and values. With the advent of industrialization and then of modern technology, "knowing" came to emphasize "know how" and productivity. This "technical rationality" further diminished the humanizing, ethical, and aesthetic potential of "knowing" and thus of education of any kind.

This division of knowing from being and, some would say, the triumph of "technical rationality" also came to hold sway in theological and religious studies. In the first centuries of Christian scholarship, theology and spirituality were as one, and the purpose of all efforts to bring faith to understanding was holiness of life. But since theology left the monasteries and went to school with the Scholastics (circa 1200), it has been severed from spirituality. And it would seem that the "sacred disciplines" frequently fall prey to a "technical rationality" that treats the text or symbol for study as a kind of "object" over against the learner, as a thing to be "mastered" through reasoned and "objective" analysis, while avoiding all personal engagement with it.

Religious education needs to abandon this impoverished sense of "knowing" that dominates Western education of all kinds, and return to the ancient philosophical tradition of knowledge arising from life and shaping identity, and to the old biblical tradition of wisdom that refers to both intellect and character, mind and heart. Beyond "knowledge about" or "understanding of" religious tradition(s), the intent of religious education should be to enable people personally to appropriate religious wisdom in a way likely to shape their identity and agency in the world. Likewise, catechesis must recognize that the "being" and "becoming" of people in faith is shaped and deepened by their "knowing," that enabling people to "put on the mind of Christ" (Phil 2:5) is enhanced by engaging their own minds. This brings into focus the second dichotomy that must be transcended for the partnership between catechesis and religious education to flourish.

Faith and Reason: An Old Alliance

From its beginning, Christianity has recognized that faith is deepened by understanding, that revelation is enhanced by reason. Undoubtedly, there were skeptics like Tertullian who insisted that "Jerusalem has no need of Athens," but wiser voices prevailed. At Alexandria (circa end of 2nd c.), Clement and then Origen began to forge a "Christian paideia," a system of thought that would wed Christian revelation and Greek philosophy. Augustine (354–430), advancing this work, insisted on the priority of faith and repeated often that we must "believe in order to understand," but he recognized too that faith should move beyond blind assent; it needs to be made intelligible and complete by reason. Aquinas (1225–1274) saw faith as a gift of God's grace that is personally appropriated and enhanced by human reason; he wrote: "Faith is a habit of the mind whereby eternal life is begun in us. . . ."[7] In understandable reaction to the impoverished rationalism of the later Scholastics, the Reformers made a strong commitment to *sola scriptura*, but Trent reiterated the partnership of reason and revelation. Later, in its Constitution on Faith *(Dei Filius)*, Vatican I (1869–70) declared:

> Faith and reason can never disagree; but more than that, they are even mutually advantageous.
> For right reason demonstrates the foundations of

faith and, enlightened by the light of faith, it pursues the science of divine things; faith, on the other hand, sets reason free and guards it from errors and furnishes it with extensive knowledge.[8]

What a bold statement of this ancient alliance, with no talk of "divorce" at all.

Defenders of the Bond: Newman and Lonergan

In light of this long tradition, it is little wonder that two of the great Catholic thinkers of modern times, John Henry Newman and Bernard Lonergan, offer antidotes to the separation of catechesis from religious education. These two complex thinkers are beyond brief analysis, but we can draw a point from each that is relevant to our topic. *To catechists*, Newman advises that *forming* people as Christians is aided by *informing*, them well, and by thorough study in their "notions" of faith in order to prompt the "real" apprehension and assent that encourages faithful commitment. *To religious educators*, Lonergan cautions that on epistemological grounds alone they cannot settle for bringing people to know the "data" of a tradition, nor even to understand it. For authentic knowing, the kind that promotes humanization of the knower, every pedagogy should also invite participants to judgment and decision about how to live what they understand.

In the *Grammar of Assent*, Newman describes "apprehension" as a kind of coming to see for oneself and "assent" as a moment beyond apprehension when we take a personal position on what we have apprehended. Within each, Newman distinguishes what is "notional" from what is "real." These are interrelated activities, but the "notional" is more conceptual, whereas "real" apprehension and assent wed mind and heart, theory and practice, knowledge and life.[9] Apprehension and assent to a faith into which we have been socialized is often no more than "notional," whereas "real" apprehension and assent requires that we question, test, understand, and know the tradition for ourselves. The kind of "knowing" more likely to nurture identity and agency in faith advises personal coming to see and assent for oneself; this requires critical thinking, communal testing, and personal appropriation beyond what is prompted by socialization alone. In other words, catechesis without religious education is less likely to promote owned and lived Christian faith.

Lonergan transcends Kant's dangerous separation of theoretical from practical reasoning; he insists that authentic cognition should always eventuate into responsible decision making and action. Further, Lonergan detects in the operations of human consciousness a pattern of dynamic and cumulative activities that all people perform in the act of true cognition, namely, attending, understanding, judging, and deciding. Cognition begins by intentionally attending to data of experience or tradition. From attending, one moves by intelligent inquiry to understanding. In our existential lives, however, to truly "know" we must push on to judgment regarding the truth or falsehood of what we understand, and then, beyond that, to decide responsibly according to what we perceive as true and good. These four activities give rise to what Lonergan calls four transcendental imperatives that we must fulfill if we are to truly know and to know truly, namely, "be attentive, be intelligent, be reasonable, be responsible."[10]

The point I draw from Lonergan is that "religious knowledge," if reached by authentic cognition, will shape people's very "being." No religious educator, not even in the most academic of contexts and least of all, it would seem, in Catholic schools, can ever claim to be concerned solely with information sharing and understanding. Epistemology, not to speak of the commitment of faith, advises religious educators to employ a pedagogy that not only promotes understanding but also nurtures the very "being" of their students in personal judgment and responsible living.

I find encouragement in these insights from Newman and Lonergan for my own position that catechesis and religious education are essential partners; one without the other is impoverished. Catechesis forever needs a component of good religious education, education of the participative, critically reflective, dialogical kind that promotes what Freire calls "critical consciousness," or what Newman calls "real" apprehension and assent. Such catechesis is essential to promote the ongoing conversion of the person and the constant reformation of the community. And Catholic religious education, both within its very pedagogy and through the whole ethos of the schooling context, parish or parochial, should educate people in the Christian tradition in a way that not only *informs* their minds but also *forms* their values and *transforms* their lives—educates their very "being"—in the meaning and ethics of Christian faith.

I contend further that we have a number of approaches to both religious education and catechesis that are likely to maintain their partnership. I have made my own proposal of a "shared praxis" approach in some detail elsewhere.[11] Such an approach can be used in both religious education and catechesis, albeit with different emphases and with adaptation for age, theme, context, etc. In brief, "shared praxis" advises that religious education and intentional catechesis (1) engage students personally as active participants in a dynamic marked by dialogue and conversation; (2) bring them to look at, to express, and to reflect critically on the "data" of their own lives; (3) be informed by the best of scholarship to study the story and encounter the vision of Christian faith; (4) encourage people to personally and critically appropriate the faith tradition to their own lives and situations; (5) invite decision making out of the dialogue between peoples own lives and Christian story/vision. I also submit that posing catechesis and religious education as partners is a very "Catholic" perspective; the tradition advises their close working relationship. As we muddle along without consensus on exactly what to call what we do,[12] let us at least be convinced that for our Catholic community the activities named as religious education and catechesis are complementary; they need each other, something like the wings of a bird. And a bird never flew . . .

About the Author

Thomas H. Groome Is professor of theology and religious education at Boston College. He is the principal author of Sadlier's *God With Us* (1984) and *Coming to Faith* (1990) curricula; his most recent book is *Sharing Faith: A Comprehensive Approach to Religious Education and Pastoral Ministry* (Harper, San Francisco, 1990).

Notes

1. A version of this essay was published in *Living the Vision: 20th Anniversary*, East Coast Conference for Religious Education, edited by James A. Corr, Janaan Manternach, and Carl Pfeifer (Morristown, NJ.: Silver Burdett and Ginn, 1992).

2. Graham Rossiter, "The Need for a 'Creative Divorce' Between Catechesis and Religious Education in Catholic Schools," *Religious Education* 77:1 (January/February 1982).

3. Robert Duggan and Maureen Kelly, *The Christian Initiation of Children: Hope for the Future* (New York: Paulist Press, 1991), p. 72. In my opinion, far too much RCIA literature has had a polemic against anything like "education," and to the great loss of the movement.

4. See John Westerhoff, *Will Our Children Have Faith* (New York: Seabury Press, 1976).

5. Graham Rossiter, "Perspectives on Change in Catholic Religious Education since the Second Vatican Council." *Religious Education* 83:2 (Spring, 1988), pp. 268–9.

6. See Thomas H. Groome, *Sharing Faith* (San Francisco: Harper Collins, 1992), esp. chap. 2, for a review of this severing of knowing from people's "being" in the world.

7. Thomas Aquinas, *Summa Theologica*, II–II, 4, I; in Christian Classics edition, vol. 3, p. 1184.

8. *The Church Teaches: Documents of the Church in English Translation*, translated and compiled by John F. Clarkson, et al. (Rockford, Ill.: Tan Books, 1973), p. 34.

9. See John Henry Newman, *An Essay in Aid of a Grammar of Assent* (Oxford: Clarendon Press, 1985), esp. pt. I. Ian Kerr explains: "the famous notional/real distinction, which is at the heart of Newman's phenomenology, stems from a philosophy of mind which takes into account not only of the logical or ratiocinative intellect but also of the imagination." *The Achievement of John Henry Newman* (Notre Dame: Univ. of Notre Dame Press, 1990), p. 69. And again, "The whole theory of real assent demands that there should be notional concepts so vividly realized as to become facts in the imagination, that is, in Newman's terminology, images." (ibid, p. 60).

10. See Bernard Lonergan, *Method in Theology* (New York: Seabury Press, 1972), esp. pt. I.

11. See *Sharing Faith: A Comprehensive Approach to Religious Education and Pastoral Ministry*, (San Francisco: Harper San Francisco, 1991), esp. pt. II.

12. Personally, I still find that "Christian Religious Education," while a cumbersome title, is the most adequate way to name what I do and what I perceive a great host of others are doing by way of education in Christian faith in the North American context. I find it appropriate and adequate because: 1) "education" affirms the educational aspect of the enterprise; 2) as "religious" it is located within and thus in partnership and dialogue with the universal human effort to live in "right relationship" as an expression of what is perceived as ultimate in life; 3) "Christian" signifies its particularity within the religious universal, and that it is to inform, form, and transform people in Christian identity and discipleship.

Catechesis for the Third Millennium

Kelly, Rev. Francis D. 1989. *Momentum* 20(4):6–10.

Father Kelly is executive director of NCEA's religious education department and a member of the International Commission on Catechesis of the Holy See.

Introduction

Religious education is a multi-faceted ministry in the modern church. Its essential task is to share the light of Christian faith with persons of all ages and backgrounds.

This task takes place in a wide variety of settings and contexts, and employs many methodologies. Not only the perennial task but also the rich possibilities for carrying it out into the third millennium are explored in this special issue of *Momentum*.

Several articles examine the broader questions of catechetical principles and philosophy from the perspectives of a bishop, a national director, university professors of catechesis, and school and parish practitioners.

Also included are articles about religious education for the growing Hispanic population and the special challenges of adolescent catechesis in our culture. The use of modern telecommunications and art for the deepening of the faith are highlighted. A number of significant recent books on religious education are reviewed.

We cannot pretend to have covered all aspects of catechesis in this issue, but we believe we have brought together a collection of articles that will be both intellectually enriching and practically useful.

The "traditio"—renewal and vision

The church is a community of faith, a covenant fellowship forged by a shared meaning system and the shared values flowing from that meaning. Religious education or catechesis is the structured way through which the church passes on Christian meaning and values.

This ministry, then, is at the heart of the church's mission and life. An indispensable and constitutive element of the church's existence, it must be at the service of all the members of the community—adults and young people.

There is a central, timeless element to the catechetical task. It is the "traditio," the communication of the revealed truth about God and his saving plan for the human family, reaching its fulfillment in Jesus Christ. The importance of this traditio has been recovered in the revised Rite for the Christian Initiation of Adults (RCIA), in which the Creed is solemnly given and accepted by the candidate for church membership.

The timeless traditio is echoed in the words of the New Testament. We hear Paul saying: "I handed on to you what I myself received." (1 Cor. 15:3) The church's steadfast insistence on the importance of dogma and doctrine and its vigilance for the purity of faith are significant reminders that the faith contains the revealed, objective and eternally valid truth about God, the world, history and the dignity and destiny of each human person. Surely this is what is being conveyed in the words of the Letter to the Hebrews: "Jesus Christ is the same yesterday, today and forever." (13:8)

While catechesis has this essential and timeless quality, it also has a contingent and historical dimension. Its methodologies are legitimately influenced by the development of other human enterprises such as psychology, education, communications, technology.

Moreover, just as the content of the four Gospels reflect the pastoral needs of the communities to which they were addressed, so the content of catechesis over the centuries must address the specific concerns and needs of the communities in which it takes place.

It may be helpful to be reminded of the phases of catechetical renewal through which we have passed and which have so influenced the way the faith is taught today in the Catholic Church in the United States. We can then look to the future and to the challenges it holds for the catechetical ministry.

Phases of catechetical renewal

Evangelization, community and doctrine. The focus of catechesis in the early centuries of Christianity was clearly on forming vibrant, adult, faith communities. In those times of frequent and brutal persecution, the commitment required to embrace and practice the faith often bordered on the heroic. The level of commitment is reflected in the centuries of conflict about how to deal with the "lapsi," those who, in face of persecution, either denied or feigned a denial of the faith. Furthermore, entrance into the early faith community was not casual; it involved a lengthy and demanding catechumenate.

Columban monks from Ireland undertook the evangelization of Northern Europe during the various waves of barbarian invasion. The faith witness of the monks and the establishment of their monastic centers incorporated these new peoples into the community of faith.

Benedictine monks built upon their historic ministry by helping the nomadic peoples to adopt a settled farming economy and to acquire the rudiments of education, which also deepened their faith understanding and commitment.

Medieval Christians enjoyed a visual catechesis in cathedral environments. A series of festivals, folk celebrations, mystery and morality plays also vividly involved them in the celebration of the mysteries of Christ and a call to faith commitment.

Counter Reformation Catholics responded to the Protestant challenge by developing a strong doctrinal catechesis. It used a set question-and-answer method whose clarity and precision was an effective response for the times.

The Jesuits augmented this academic exercise with catechetical dramas based on the gospel stories. Philip Neri invited the musicians of Rome—especially Palestrina—to put the gospel dialogues to music. These works were performed in his Oratory, giving rise to the oratorio artform so effectively developed by Bach and Handel.

The catechism of the Council of Trent established a classic pattern of Creed, Code and Cult for transmitting the content of the faith. Soon to be recaptured in the universal catechism of Vatican II, now being developed, this approach is harmonious with that of the ancient catechumenate.

Many adaptations of the Trent catechism were developed in different countries. The Baltimore Catechism appeared in the United States in 1885 and, in various versions, was widely used until the post-World War II period.

Methods and content. At the turn of the 20th century, efforts to find a more effective catechetical method than the traditional question-answer approach began with the so-called Munich Method. This included presentation, explanation and application of the catechetical content.

This approach, it was felt, corresponded to the steps in the learning process: perception, understanding and practice. It would engage all the faculties of the student—not just the intellect. An application of this method was popularized in the United States by Msgr. Rudolph Bandas of St. Paul Seminary in Minnesota.

The second major development of the modern catechetical renewal involved the actual content. It was sparked by the Austrian Jesuit, Joseph Jungmann, and the publication in 1937 of his landmark book *The Good News: Yesterday and Today*.[1]

Jungmann called on the church to recapture the dynamism of its primitive, Christocentric kerygma as the focus of catechetical content, rather than the scholastic, abstract language that characterized the existing catechism. He also reintroduced the concept of "salvation history" as expressing the great sweep of God's redeeming plan, unfolding over the 4000 years of God's self-revelation, beginning with Abraham and looking forward to culmination in the Parousia.

The content of catechesis was also affected by a renewed focus on evangelization as Europe saw its Catholic character eroding. The writings of persons such as Emmanuel Suhard and Canon Cardijn were reinforced by the reflections of those catechizing in missionary lands. These trends culminated in the *Apostolic Exhortation on Evangelization*[2] of Pope Paul VI, and found structural embodiment in the promulgation of the revised RCIA.

Developmental psychology. The third major development of the modern catechetical renewal was the influence of modern developmental psychology. The research and insights of psychologists such as Piaget, Kohlberg and Fowler were accepted, sometimes uncritically, by religious educators and publishers.

On balance, this has been a positive development, endorsed in the *National Catechetical Directory* by an entire chapter titled "Catechesis Toward Maturity in Faith."[3] Pope John Paul II in *Catechesi Tradendae* has utilized this principle with exquisite pastoral sensitivity in his suggestions regarding content appropriate for various stages of human growth.[4]

This development is one factor that has helped to refocus attention and energy on the catechesis of adults. It points to the norm of the mature, adult believer as the goal of youth catechesis, and identifies the stages of adult change cycles with their special religious needs and possibilities.

Furthermore, developmental psychology has rescued catechesis from being too "other worldly" and has encouraged catechesis to use inductive and life-issue oriented approaches to bridge the gap between faith and life. Occasionally, however, this development led to an anthropocentric focus in which catechesis was reduced to a species of "pop psychology."

Prophecy and social consciousness. A fourth major phase of the modern catechetical renewal, one still in progress, might be called its prophetic phase. The content now includes the implications of the Gospel for societal renewal, for justice, charity and peace among groups and nations. The consciousness-raising educational methodology of pioneers such as Paolo Freire has been applied to religious education by writers such as Thomas Groome in his *Christian Religious Education*,[5] and is greatly influencing catechesis, especially in Latin America.

Signs of the times

It is easier to rehearse the past than to predict the future. Yet, as the *Pastoral Constitution on the Church in the Modern World (Gaudium et Spes)* affirms: "The Church always has the duty of scrutinizing the signs of the times in the light of the Gospel."[6]

Perhaps, after 25 years of the "post-conciliar period," it would be helpful to think ahead, as John Paul II urged in his first encyclical *Redemptor Hominis*, to the new millennium as a time for reawakening an awareness of the power of the coming of Christ.

The content of the Vatican II documents still give us an agenda for authentic renewal. But as we approach the third millennium of Christianity, should we not attempt to truly recapture enthusiasm about the church's external mission and its humanizing message for a rapidly changing world?

Catechists and religious educators need to read "the signs of the times" in the light of their responsibilities to adults and young people. The world in which the faith must be witnessed needs confident and courageous religious educators.

Our message is revealed and transcendent in a culture that, as Robert Bellah and his colleagues noted, is self-absorbed and individualistic.[7] We proclaim absolute truth and call for the "obedience of faith" (Rom. 1:5) in a culture where every assertion is taken as relative and subjective. Our morality calls for "denial of self" in a culture that reflects the primacy of personal pleasure and the avoidance of responsibility.

On the world scene, a dramatic symbol of political and social change occurred this past spring. The "Iron Curtain" —the barbed wire fence between Hungary and Austria— was cut down and carted away. While we must not be naive about the great ideological differences between East and West, many are now focusing on the chasm between the affluent, consumer-driven Northern Hemisphere and the exploited, poverty-ridden Southern Hemisphere as an equally significant world view.

Pope John Paul II, in his encyclical *Solicitudo Rei Socialis*, encouraged the church to take a prophetic view of this polarity.[8] He has also affirmed the call of many for the church to represent "a preferential option for the poor."

In the face of these and other striking realities, the religious educator who looks ahead realizes the challenge involved in forming joyful, confident Christian witnesses for the 21st century. Such Christians will be a "sign of contradiction" in many prophetic ways.

On a more pragmatic level, the transformation of large, anonymous parishes into smaller communities of faith seems imperative. The adult catechesis represented by such efforts as Renew and Cursillo must be vigorously promoted and expanded. At the same time, we must be sure that such groups are not merely "lifestyle enclaves" narcissistically reinforcing a comfortable suburban lifestyle with a patina of Christianity.

Each parish must reflect the richness, diversity and problems of all its members. More outward looking, it must seek ways to be a light and a leader to the local community and a participant in the church's worldwide evangelizing and liberating ministry.

Only in the environment of truly renewed, adult faith communities will catechesis for children and young people flourish and be effective.

New models and structures for child catechesis and youth ministry must be responsibly explored, with sensitivity to changing family patterns and lifestyles, e.g., working parents, one-parent families, domestic and economic pressures. Alternative models might include the largely untapped preschool stage, when faith is first evoked and expressed, and summer periods when more intensive instructional activities can be scheduled for older children.

Religious literacy will be more important than ever in the 21st century as social pressures for religious belonging continue to evaporate. Deep, personal understanding and conviction about the truths of faith will be needed to motivate religious practice and witness. A solid grasp of the meaning of revelation, of the Scriptures, of church doctrine and history will be indispensable.

It will be necessary to challenge directly the subjectivism and relativism that dominate our culture. People today speak of "my truth" or "your truth" as if all assertions are of equal validity. The prevailing maxim is "be true to yourself." This approach runs counter to the Gospel, which proclaims an objective truth that transcends personal opinions: "You shall know the truth and the truth shall set you free" (Jn. 8:32).

In the area of conscience formation, our purpose must be to help young people to think for themselves in accordance with solid Christian principles, not peer pressure or media hype. Young people will need to make sound judgments and to defend these judgments with skill and conviction. This is going to require a moral catechesis far more serious than that currently in vogue.

Clearly, more rather than less will be required. Parish directors of religious education will need to be true professionals, recognized and treated as such. While the recent burgeoning of parish ministries has many positive elements, the progress made by the presence of a full-time, competent, professional religious educator could be quickly eroded by a diffusion of energy and attention from catechesis to other, less defined "pastoral activities."

Quality religious education in a largely volunteer setting requires sustained and focused direction and leadership. At the same time, the now largely lay administrators and teachers of our Catholic schools will need a serious program of doctrinal and catechetical training and inservice.

As we look ahead, no better encouragement could be given than the words of Pope John Paul II in *Catechesi Tradenae*:

> The more the Church, whether on the local or the universal level, gives catechesis priority over other works and undertakings the results of which would be more spectacular, the more she finds in catechesis a strengthening of her internal life as a community of believers and of her external activity as a missionary Church. As the twentieth century draws to a close, the Church is bidden by God and by events—each of them a call from him—to renew her trust in catechetical activity as a prime aspect of her mission. She is bidden to offer catechesis her best resources in people and energy, without sparing effort, toil or material means, in order to organize it better and to train qualified personnel. This is no mere human calculation; it is an attitude of faith.[9]

Notes

1. *Joseph Jungmann, The Good News: Yesterday and Today.* New York, Sadlier Publishing Co., 1962.

2. Pope Paul VI, *Apostolic Exhortation on Evangelization*, Washington, DC, United States Catholic Conference, 1975.

3. *Sharing the Light of Faith*, Washington, DC, United States Catholic Conference, 1979.

4. Pope John Paul II, *Catechesi Tradendae*, Washington, DC, United States Catholic Conference, 1979, Nos. 35–44.

5. Thomas Groome, *Christian Religious Education*, San Francisco, Harper and Row, 1980.

6. Vatican Council II, *Pastoral Constitution on the Church in the Modern World*, Washington, DC: United States Catholic Conference, 1965, No. 4.

7. Robert Bellah et al., *Habits of the Heart*, Los Angeles, University of California Press, 1985.

8. Pope John Paul II, *Solicitudo Rei Socialis*, Washington, DC, United States Catholic Conference, 1988.

9. *Catechesi Tradenae*, op. cit., No. 15.

Catechesis for Conversion

O'Malley, William J. 1992. *The Living Light* 29(2):55–63.

O'Malley offers a thorough lesson plan that brings the Gospel to the lives of high school students.

A single soul outweighs all summae. Yet all catechetical directories belie that fact. Completeness contravenes personal acceptance: conversion. Let this foray offer an alternative, a rough medieval chart more expert seafarers might improve.

Ten Commandments for Catechists

I. *Know Where They Are:* Unconverted, with solid resistance to authority, trust, commitment, limitation of freedom, or challenges to materialism; self-absorbed—thus insinuations against self-image (whether ads or morality) are both repellent and intriguing. "Maybe I'm not OK?" Use reaction papers: How does all this honestly affect you personally? Family, peers, parish? Comment on every page. They honestly want attention.

II. *Do Not Be Thoroughgoing:* Don't begin with the Trinity, and don't even mention Chalcedon. Pare to the nonnegotiables and *focus* on them. You can drive a car without knowing all the mysteries of the internal combustion engine.

III. *Do Not Overwhelm:* Fundamentalists succeed because they strip down to sinfulness and surrender to the Lord Jesus. But we do the opposite: smother with details and distinctions. When you study prophets, for instance, no need to cover all of them. Take only one who speaks of topics of interest to this audience.

IV. *Blindside:* Always begin at an unthreatening distance from the core of each lesson, especially if it will call in question some certitude they believe to be unquestionable, e.g., the moral indifference of rock lyrics. Always start with a story or a riddle. That is what Jesus did. Jesus knew his audience.

V. *Avoid Authority:* Kids are at the most *anti*authoritarian stage of their lives. Use reason alone, and show that acting human and Christian is in their own self-interest; for instance, being honest when caught earns credibility later when they are innocent but look guilty. Very few can even comprehend altruism.

VI. *Remember the Authorities They Do Trust:* TV, music, science. Have more than a passing knowledge of the mindless media that make terminal adolescents like "Cheers'" Sam Malone role models. Find support from psychology for your doctrinal claims.

VII. *Imitate Salespeople:* They know, if communication fails, it's the *sender's* fault. They haven't found a way—yet—to make this information desirable to this audience. Rework the pitch.

VIII. *"Rejoice When They Hate You!":* It's working! You're threatening false certitudes. If they just sit smiling, you're either training sheep or they're thinking quite unChristian thoughts behind those vacuous faces. We did, didn't we?

IX. *Remember Love Is Not a Feeling:* Love is an act of the will; it takes over when the beloved is no longer even likable. It is an act of love to say, "I have not killed Ingeborg yet."

X. *Remember the First Christian School:* They secondguessed Jesus at every turn, ran when they were first needed, and didn't do a bloody thing until two months after they'd graduated.

Ninth Grade

Big-shot eighth graders just became minnows in a shark tank. Ordinarily, schools have an orientation, but those activities end too quickly. If they continued through the year, there is a better chance the school might eventually become a community. Also, for most, puberty has begun. Not only does it trigger mystifying urges, but it also turns a child with no concern for looks into a mirror addict. Even the best are not interested in wrestling with big questions like "The Meaning of Life." They are more puzzled by reactions of others and relationships: family, friend-to-friend, boy-to-girl. If that's where they are, begin there.

Relationships (Faith and Morality). Start with a film that centers on friendships, such as *Stand by Me.* Show that each of us sits at the focus of a series of broadening concentric circles: family, best friends, pals, "friends," acquaintances, out into the formless mass of anonymous faces. At one time, your best friend was a stranger. How did he or she penetrate the doors in those circles into your inmost heart? The very first step? Being *noticed,* fixated out of the crowd. If you wear blinders, you'll have few friends. The person becomes an acquaintance, as most people you "know" remain. Only with time and talk do they become "friends," people you habitually sit with at lunch. But pals have sacrificed with one another: the team, the yearbook, the show. To become best friends, you have to open yourself up all the way down, let the friend see all the knots and tangles, and if he or she comes out and says, "So what, we're still friends," you have something more precious than gold.

Each doorway in those circles has only one handle, and it's on the inside. Every time you let someone in further, it's a risk, an act of faith. Nine times out of ten, both of you are enriched. One out of ten times you'll be burned, so many give up nine friends to avoid one hurt. Sad. Faith usually pays off.

In studying the obligations living together places on us (morality), keep it small. Focus on relationships with family, friends, steadies, studies. If your parents subsidize you, learning is your job. Do you give an honest day's work for an honest day's pay? What do stealing, lying, cheating do to the web of our small society here in school? Who are the ones left out among us; what obligation does their need place on you?

The circles of our relationships also extend beyond the human family into the life of God. You can make a pretty good logical case for the highly probable existence of a Mind Behind It All. But all the logic in the world isn't the way we "prove" persons. As with all others, we have to notice God, spend time and talk with God, sacrifice with God, even forgive God.

With the Earth Science teachers (this is a Catholic school), take them on nature trips—not only to admire flora and fauna but to puzzle out the personality of the One who created such alive, diverse, fascinating things. It is easier to teach centering prayer to ninth graders than to twelfth graders; a park is a fine place to introduce it. We also have a relationship with nature, which places objective obligation on us to protect the environment and not to destroy it. Show the connection between some profiting by "enlightened self-interest" and all of us footing the bill.

Service should begin in first year, and the first step is insistently breaking down ego defenses. Extracurriculars are fine, but only the already skilled risk tryouts. At least once a week there ought to be an "ice-breaker"; make them switch lunch tables. By the end of freshman year, let there be no "nobodies."

Also, what is their relationship with their parishes? Do they really belong, or just "go"? Are there kids in the grade school who do not play basketball as well as you can? Old people who'd enjoy your reading to them or shopping for them?

Stories Tell Truth. A major barrier to the credibility of Scripture is that it's "just made up." Youngsters believe that nonfiction, like newscasts, tells the truth, but fiction is merely to pass the time. It takes work to show (not just tell) them that fiction most often can say *more* than a scholarly treatise can. Start from a distance with *Star Wars.* Ask what the film is trying to "say," through Luke and Leia, about growing up.

Then Aesop, who serves up exactly what he was trying to say at the end. Arthurian legends, folktales (See Bettelheim, *The Uses of Enchantment*), *The Gospel According to Peanuts.* Then the Hebrew patriarchs, a "retelling" to avoid the exaggerations of the scriptures. If they're not psychologically and literately ready for *Hamlet* or Adam Smith, why Moses' rules for priests? But they *are* ready for more than "The Ten Commandments."

Finally, look at gospel stories that focus on a single idea, say, Jesus' treatment of sinners: the Samaritan woman, the Prodigal Father, the adulterous woman. Ask (don't tell) what each story is trying to "say." What do all of them together tell us about how we must treat those who "trespass against us"? (Amazing what they learn if the teacher just learns to shut up.)

The Old Testament. Leave all talk of authorship, inspiration, revelation, canonicity, or inerrancy for graduate school. Stress that, like the Arthurian legends, the initial event was most likely historically rooted, but the tales have been reworked and reworked for generations to bring out a new theological insight into a long-past event. They aren't history, but history-as-lessons for "today's" problems—just as we now read Scripture.

Start with the liberating Exodus rather than the Fall. It changes the whole focus. Begin with the film *The Color Purple.* (Why?) Again, at this stage, "retelling" is less confusing than the actual scriptures. Stick to the core of the story and what its authors tried to reveal about human beings and God. In the historical books, when the people stray, Yahweh punishes. The point is not that God smashes our lives when we are bad, but that when we violate the natures God programmed into things, they blow up in our faces. And people keep making the *same* mistakes, even when they're as powerful as David and as wise as Solomon.

Dealing with the prophets, start with *Silkwood.* Who have been the whistle blowers over the past fifty years? The two tasks of a prophet are to see the situation with open eyes and to have courage to stand up and shout, however unwillingly. Read only the call of Isaiah (6:1–8), the lament of Jeremiah over Yahweh's shoddy treatment (15:10–21), and the book of Jonah, rather than a whole prophetic book; they tend to be long-winded, repetitious, and fulminant. Nearly all the heroes God picked were very reluctant—and, almost without exception, unexceptional: stammering Moses, spindly David, cowardly Gideon. If God asked you to convert—not Nineveh or L.A.—but this school . . . ? Don't say, "Oh, I'm just a kid!" God is on the prowl for you nobodies. (And that question and denial is as true for the religion teacher. That is our job.)

For a taste of Wisdom literature, make a selection from Proverbs and Wisdom that applies to *them*, e.g., Prv 1:7–15, the father's instructions to his son. Take a selection of psalms *as* poetry first, analyzing them just as they would in English class, but on the final day of the unit meet in a darkened room with candles and have the best actors in class read them.

By the end, ninth graders should be able to tackle one of the thorniest questions in the Old Testament: the opening of Genesis—but team-taught with the Earth Science teachers.

Tenth Grade

Sophomore year is the endless tunnel. Still getting used to the fit of their new limbs, far more interested in the opposite sex, more restless, and generally reverting to the Neanderthal.

Heroes (Jesus). Begin with stories or films about Terry Anderson, Mother Hale, Oscar Romero. What makes a hero? What kind of "heroes" did God pick in the Old Testament? (You *do* remember!)

Big paper: Choose a living or only recently deceased person who made a difference. Research all you can find about that person; send letters to people who know/knew him or her well, until you have at least five replies. Write a biography. You've just done precisely what Mark did: write a biography of someone he'd never met, using the best sources available.

Don't go right to Jesus' doctrine; focus first on Jesus' personality and, more important students' *image* of Jesus. Their image comes from bad biblical movies; in even the best, Jesus has blue eyes, very uncarpenter fingers, and a spacey look. For people so overly image-conscious, a real obstacle. Few would like to spend much time listening to him. Paper your class with *National Geographic* pictures of Israeli males. Jesus' message was "feminine": forgive, have compassion, but his method was "masculine": "Go!" Even girls aren't attracted to a "domesticated" male.

Before analyzing Jesus' message (remember: it's not their first time!), ask what Christianity means. Most say "being moral, keeping your slate clean"—which would make any ethical atheist Christian. In thirty years, I have never had anyone— young or adult—mention Jesus being the embodiment of God, liberation from the fear of death, adoption into the Trinity Family.

Concentrate on only nine gospel passages: Jesus' inaugural, the Sermon on the Mount, the Prodigal Father, the disciples at the arrest and at Pentecost, the Sanhedrin, the crucifixion, the resurrection, and Matthew 25.

In Jesus' inaugural (Lk 4:18–19), he laid out his whole platform: I have come to proclaim the amnesty of God. Sum up the whole gospel: "forgiveness" and "stand up and shout forgiveness." The only ones Jesus couldn't forgive were those who felt they had no need (pharisees) or who couldn't merit forgiveness (Judas). What was the one thing Jesus did his entire public life? Healing.

"Repent" does not mean to be sorry for a few sins but a total turnabout, conversion from self-absorbed narcissism. The Sermon on the Mount is in grinding conflict with everything we hear in the media. The Prodigal Father says that God—and we—have no choice when a sinner returns but to greet him or her with open arms: no groveling, no scrutiny, no need for restitution to a fiscal God. To see what conversion means, study the disciples in the garden and then on Pentecost and throughout the events described in Acts.

No one can legitimately call Jesus "one more moral teacher." He didn't leave that option open. On Palm Sunday, they cheered him through the streets; the next Friday the same crowd screamed, "Crucify him!" What happened between? The high priest asked, "Are you the Son of the Blessed?" And Jesus answered, "I AM." No question why Jesus was executed. Either he was a con artist, or mad, or what he claimed. Which do you think? Why?

But why was the crucifixion so cruel? Surely not to placate some Moloch slavering for revenge over one piece of fruit. Avoid all talk of "the Paschal Lamb." It turns the Father into Quetzalcoatl. Jesus died that way to show us how it's done. Suffering is a given. How do you face it with dignity and turn it into a resurrection? Suffering is—or can be—the great conversion.

As Paul wrote, all Christianity hinges on the resurrection. No one saw it. Judging from other writings of the time, they could have made a real Spielberg scene out of it.

They didn't. Why? Yet think of the disciples' conversion, from arrant cowards to martyrs. What could have occasioned that? They claimed it was because they'd seen Jesus alive again. What reason would they have had to deceive? They surely didn't profit from it.

Matthew 25, the Last Judgment, sums up our purpose: "I was outcast. What did you do about that?" With whom did Jesus deal? Who are the outcasts today? Not just homeless, addicts, homosexuals, prisoners. Right at your elbows. If you don't help them, there is little likelihood your life will make much difference. You can't heal them all. Neither could Jesus. He healed the ones he had. Now, sum it up again: What does being Christian mean?

Relationships (Morality). What comments do you think Jesus might have on our politics, schools, sex, rock lyrics, advertising, soap operas, sports? (Cf. Christopher Lasch, *The Culture of Narcissism*.) Let us explore each of them, one at a time. In forming your conscience—your guide to making choices—what has had *the* greatest influence: parents, school, church, or media? Is it in fact *your* conscience at all, or a confused rag bag? What then?

Scripture. Teach them how to read scripture for themselves, but begin with baby steps. Don't presume they learned how figurative language works in English class; they didn't. If you're not an English teacher, team teach with one. Spend at least a month on nonscriptural figures of speech and symbols in ordinary speech and life, in poems and prose, before getting to the gospels.

For most, a metaphor is merely a comparison without "like" or "as." Useless. Why metaphor at all? Why not just say things flat out? First of all, flat out is boring; read them the documentation for a computer program! Metaphors explain what you don't know in terms of what you do know; they make you figure things out for yourself. Start with their own speech: "My chick's got a brick for a heart." Literally, ludicrous, but we automatically "translate." You have got to do the same with the Scriptures. "If you want the first place, take the last place." Is that possible, unless you're alone in the race? "If your eye scandalizes you, pluck it out." If Jesus really meant that, why're there not more blind Christians? When asked who was the first in the Kingdom, Jesus just picked up a child. What was he saying through the child? *The* symbol that distills Christianity is a crucifix: a corpse on a cross. What does this symbol "say"?

Sacraments. Each of the sacraments is an act that symbolizes—physicalizes—an empowerment. Before focusing on each, explore (with the fine arts teacher) the symbolism of water, eating and drinking together, light and fire, oil (heating, healing, lubricating, binding the elements of bread). Actions "talk": clenched fist, hugging, head down on the desk, a pat on the shoulder—without a word. Only then move on to Baptism and Eucharist, with as little mention of sin as possible in either case. Try to get the whole class to the same parish on a day a baptism is actually done, and have a Mass in the classroom that segues into a meal.

Eleventh Grade

At the outset of junior year, kids are "former sophomores," but it is marvelous to see them begin to grow as learners. By second semester, many are becoming genuinely critical, trying to poke holes in Scripture and the Church—often because those are the only two obstacles they see to having all the immoral fun nonbelievers enjoy. Most have begun to date seriously and, if statistics hold, 50 percent of girls and 60 percent of boys have had sex. By second semester, most are ready to encounter logical complexity in math, but still do not know how to reason verbally or outline their thoughts in a sequential development of an idea.

Scripture. Back to the biography you wrote last year. Research everything written about that person since you handed it in last. Write letters to different people who knew the person until you get five replies; then rewrite the original paper. You'll have done just what Luke and Matthew did with Mark's earlier edition.

Read the synoptic passions, starting with the arrest, in parallel. (See Throckmorton, *Gospel Parallels*). When Mark wrote the first, he could call on Peter's memories, since he was very likely Peter's interpreter. But he had other sources: an account of the passion already written as well as stories he gleaned from others who had known Jesus. Notice his breathy style, "And then . . . and then . . ." almost as if he was dictating on the run. See how Luke "cleans up" Mark's style. Why? At the arrest, why does Matthew insert the little speech about useless violence; why is Luke the only one who doesn't show Judas actually kissing Jesus but who does show Jesus healing the soldier's ear? If Matthew and Luke had copies of Mark as they wrote, why did they omit the young man who ran off naked, *after* "they *all* deserted him"?

This approach is completely new, not something "we heard before." It fascinates most because it is detective work, and as they progress, not only do the different perspectives of the three synoptics begin to emerge, but students move painstakingly through the gospels, and assertions that "It's all exaggeration" fade into perspective. Conclude with a paper in which they take one pericope and exegete it, using at least three commentaries.

Church History. Stick to Acts and one or two epistles. Leave the rest to the history department, trusting they too are committed Christians who will wisely stick to the essentials and not burden the young with the niceties of Nicea. Focus on the community as an apostolic union, who haggled and made up, a pope who changed his mind about what he once had thought essential, a brave and prophetic group who stood up to be counted.

World Religions. All philosophers from Buddha to Karl Marx began with suffering: what caused it, what would fulfill human beings despite suffering. Studying how other religions view God and human fulfillment, we can check them out by comparing them with our own, finding insights the same as those of Jesus, or insights about women, for instance, which show that Christianity is really not as "bad" as many students had thought. (See C.S. Lewis, *The Abolition of Man*, "Illustrations of the Tao.")

Epistemology. By second semester junior year, most should be ready to discover what validates opinions—about religion or anything else: *objective evidence*, not "everybody says," not opinion polls, but data that originates "out there." It's painful trying to show the radical difference between objective evidence and subjective opinion, because if they ever admitted the difference, they would have to change their attitudes and behavior.

The tree comes to me; it tells me what it is and how I can legitimately use it. The objective fact that human beings have conscience (or the capacity for it) and animals don't tells me that I cannot use a human being like an ox. The fact that a cat has feelings tells *me* I cannot legitimately throw a live cat into boiling water as if it were as unfeeling as a cabbage. The fact that food can feed hungry people shows I cannot lob it around the cafeteria as if it had no more inherent value than snowballs.

Natural Law—out there—God-programmed into the natures of things and people, long before God found need to write commandments for people too busy to discover that law for themselves.

Relationships (Morality). Having established that, now we're ready to start talking about the objective nature of a fetus, the objective nature of human (vs. animal) sexuality, the objective right of all humans to life, liberty, and the pursuit of happiness, to private property, to honest answers to legitimate questions. And it all comes from "out there," not from "all those Catholic rules" or "the Bible says." The things and people themselves "tell" me how they can be legitimately used. Think for yourself, or someone will do it for you.

At this point, most students should be ready to read, with the guidance of the economics teacher, *one* of the social encyclicals that critiques the excesses both of communism and *laissez-faire* capitalism.

If one must be moral merely to be a good human being, no matter what one's religious beliefs, what's the difference between being moral and being Christian? What does being Christian add? Hints: Reread the parable of the Prodigal Father, the Samaritan woman, the adulterous woman; look at a crucifix.

Sacraments. Having studied morality based on reason alone, it might be fitting, in conjunction with the service program, to study the sacraments of healing: Reconciliation and the Sacrament of the Sick. The point to stress is that neither is miraculous: the penitent is sure to sin again; the patient may even die. Sacraments heal the soul, not the body, relieve fear, anguish, guilt and, like the passion of Jesus, open us to renewal of life.

Twelfth Grade

Hot-shots, self-delusively worldlywise, beer-drinking, convinced that acting adult is the same as being adult. Some fall into "senioritis" before the end of the first week, convinced they can cruise through with the minimum input. Tragically, they can and will. And they will get into *some* college. The crime is that they impoverish not only their present but their future. It is our task to offer them the enjoyment of the consequences of their choices: Flunk 'em. If we don't, we're the enemy.

The God Questions. Begin with a review of the epistemology study at the end of junior year. *Repetitio est mater studiorum.* It's the core of everything education is about: gather data from "out there," sift it to find what's important, put the data into some kind of logical sequence to draw a conclusion and ask someone wiser to critique it. If you don't know how to see or how to outline, you don't know how to think.

What does faith mean? Most say a blind leap in the dark, which is ludicrous. Eating strange berries is a blind leap, and lunacy. Nor is submission to prescriptive authority an act of faith in *God*, in the *objective evidence*. An act of faith is a *reasoned* risk. Remind them of the analogy in ninth grade between the faith in a growing friendship and faith in God.

What do atheists honestly believe and why? What effect on the value of your own life if they are right? What happens to you at death—all your triumphs and tragedies? Wiped out like a computer failure. We're all on the *Titanic*, and Mother Teresa and Adolf Hitler get the same "reward." Have them read or see *Waiting for Godot*, the distillation of atheism.

Again with the help of the science teachers, study the objective facts of human intelligence, the organized universe, the development of evolution. How could such design emerge without a Designer? By mere chance? How do you get order out of a series of blind accidents? How do you get laws out of luck?

Finally in this unit, a retreat is essential, preferably with faculty other than the teacher—or even religion teachers. All the head-trip proofs will not let God "prove" himself. Thus, make this not just a lower-the-barriers-between-classmates experience, but a genuine attempt to be alone with God and meet God.

Relationships (Morality). What is conscience? Surely not something inborn, or we would never have had Hitler. Evolving a conscience—personally validated moral guidelines—is not a requirement but an invitation. But if you don't evolve your own, someone will be happy to impose one.

Freud wrote that each of us is born a healthy little animal (Id), but in the course of growing when the child starts "getting into things," the parents have to impose rules the child has no way of critiquing (Superego), a survival manual the child can follow till he or she can form a personal one (Ego). Adolescence is the time to do that. Unfortunately, most find it too much effort. Thus, around forty, they often desert their families to "find themselves," a process most psychologists think should have been at least tentatively concluded at the end of adolescence.

Just as we are in a web of physical relationships with the biological ecology, so we are in a web of moral relationships with the human ecology (society). If we want the benefits of not being completely on our own, we have to make certain commitments or the whole ecology collapses —and each of us along with it. Beyond the self, we must make commitments regarding spouses, children, extended families, communities, careers, nations, and the whole human family. You may not like the impositions these commitments cause, but this is an objective fact, and if you want to live here, you've got to pitch in. The Golden Rule is not a Christian monopoly; it is a matter of human survival.

Sacraments. Graduation is a kind of sacrament for seniors, a physicalization of empowerment. Deal, then, with sacraments that involve adult life change: confirmation, marriage, orders, but with a direct analogy to the very real change they *feel* in graduating: moving into the scarcely known. What girds your courage along the way? Why is one never free until one gives up freedom in order to commit oneself? Is it better to be alone? Study at length the difficulties all three sacraments involve.

By no means a perfect syllabus. But different from what they are used to, written not by a theologian but by a teacher. Which might be an advantage. They rarely have been met there before, where they are. Where Jesus met people.

About the Author

William J. O'Malley, SJ, teaches theology and English at Fordham Preparatory School, Bronx, N.Y. Tabor Publishing Co. has published his collection of essays under this title.

Guidelines for Doctrinally Sound Catechetical Materials

United States Catholic Conference. 1990. 11–25. Washington, D.C.

Abbreviations Used

CL   *Christifideles Laici* ("The Vocation and the Mission of the Lay Faithful in the Church and in the World"). Post-Synodal Apostolic Exhortation of Pope John Paul II (Rome, December 30, 1988).

CT   *Catechesi Tradendae* ("On Catechesis in Our Time"). Apostolic Exhortation of Pope John Paul II (Rome, 1979).

EFJA   *Economic Justice for All: Pastoral Letter on Catholic Social Teaching and the U.S. Economy*. National Conference of Catholic Bishops (Washington, D.C., 1986).

FC   *Familiaris Consortio* ("On the Family"). Apostolic Exhortation of John Paul II (Rome, 1981).

GCD   *General Catechetical Directory*. Congregation for the Clergy (Rome, 1971).

LG   *Lumen Gentium* ("Dogmatic Constitution on the Church"). Second Vatican Council (Rome, October 28, 1965.)

JJPC   *Notes on the Correct Way to Present the Jews and Judaism in Preaching and Catechesis of the Roman Catholic Church*. Commission for Religious Relations with the Jews (Rome, 1985).

NA   *Nostra Aetate* ("Decree on the Relationship of the Church to Non-Christian Religious"). Second Vatican Council (Rome, October 28, 1965).

NCD   *Sharing the Light of Faith: National Catechetical Directory for Catholics of the United States*. Department of Education, United States Catholic Conference (Washington, D.C., 1979).

SC   *Sacrosanctum Concilium* ("Constitution on the Sacred Liturgy"). Second Vatican Council (Rome, December 4, 1963). This document is frequently referred to as simply *Constituion on the Liturgy*.

UR   *Unitatis Redintegratio* ("Decree on Ecumenism"). Second Vatican Council (Rome, November 21, 1964).

I. Guidelines for Doctrinally Sound Catechetical Materials

The following guidelines are based on major catechetical documents of the Church; the constitutions, decrees, and declarations of Vatican II; recent papal encyclicals and apostolic exhortations; and the pastoral letters of the U.S. bishops. The guidelines, even taken as a whole, are not a synthesis of the gospel message nor an exhaustive list of Catholic beliefs. They are not intended to supplant—and in fact should be studied in conjunction with—the outline of the "Principal Elements of the Christian Message for Catechesis" (NCD, ch. V) and any exposition of doctrine found in a future *Catechism for the Universal Church*.

The guidelines differ from the *National Catechetical Directory* and our earlier document *Basic Teachings for Catholic Religious Education* in two ways: First, they incorporate teachings and principles stated in recent papal encyclicals and in pastoral letters issued by the National Conference of Catholic Bishops; second, they single out certain doctrines that seem to need particular emphasis in the life and culture of the United States at this time. The guidelines take into account a hierarchy of truths of faith insofar as they give priority to the foundational mysteries in the Creed, but they do not prescribe a particular order in which the truths are to be presented (cf. GCD, 46). The guidelines are intended to present church teachings in a positive and meaningful way so that authors, editors, and publishers of catechetical materials can better assist the faithful to integrate the truth of Catholic doctrine and moral teachings into their lives.

General Doctrinal Content

Doctrinally sound catechetical materials . . .

[1] help the baptized, as members of the Church founded by Christ, appreciate Catholic tradition, grounded in the Scriptures and celebrated in the Divine Liturgy, in such a personal way that it becomes part of their very identity.

[2] present the teaching of the Church in a full and balanced way that includes everything necessary for an accurate understanding of a particular doctrine and express it in a manner appropriate to the audience and purpose of a given catechetical text.

[3] situate the teachings of the Church in the context of God's saving plan and relate them to one another so that they can be seen as parts of an organic whole and not simply as isolated and fragmented truths (see GCD, 39).

[4] describe the many ways that God has spoken and continues to speak in the lives of human beings and how the fullness of revelation is made known to Christ (see Heb 1:1–2; CT 20, 52).

[5] explain the inspired Scriptures according to the mind of the Church, while not neglecting the contributions of modern biblical scholarship in the use of various methods

of interpreation, including historical-critical and literary methods (see *1964 Instruction* Pontifical Biblical Commission).

[6] are sensitve to distinctions between faith and theology, church doctrine and theological opinion, acknowledging that the same revealed truth can be explained in different ways. However, every explanation must be compatible with Catholic tradition (see NCD, 16).

[7] reflect the wisdom and continuing relevance of the church Fathers and incorporate a sense of history that recognizes doctrinal development and provides background for understanding change in church policy and practice.

[8] explain the documents of the Second Vatican Council as an authoritative and valid expression of the deposit of faith as contained in Holy Scripture and the living tradition of the Church (see 1985 Extraordinary Synod of Bishops, *The Final Report*, n. 2).

[9] present the uniqueness and preeminence of the Christian message without rejecting anything that is true and holy in non-Christian religions, show a high regard for all religions that witness to the mystery of divine presence, the dignity of human beings, and high moral standards (see NA, 2).

Father, Son, and Holy Spirit

Doctrinally sound catechetical materials . . .

[10] are trinitarian and christocentric in scope and spirit, clearly presenting the mystery of creation, redemption, and sanctification in God's plan of salvation (see NCD, 47).

[11] help Christians contemplate with eyes of faith the communal life of the Holy Trinity and know that, through grace, we share in God's divine nature (see GCD, 47).

[12] arouse a sense of wonder and praise for God's world and providence by presenting creation, not as an abstract principle or as an event standing by itself, but as the origin of all things and the beginning of the mystery of salvation in Jesus Christ (see GCD, 51; NCD, 85).

[13] focus on the heart of the Christian message: salvation from sin and death through the person and work of Jesus, with special emphasis on the paschal mystery—his passion, death, and resurrection.

[14] emphasize the work and person of Jesus Christ as the key and chief point of Christian reference in reading the Scriptures (see JJPC, II:5,6).

[15] present Jesus as true God, who came into the world for us and for our salvation, and as true man who thinks with a human mind, acts with a human will, loves with a human heart (see NCD, 89), highlighting the uniqueness of his divine mission so that he appears as more than a great prophet and moral teacher.

[16] describe how the Holy Spirit continues Christ's work in the world, in the Church, and in the lives of believers (see NCD, 92).

[17] maintain the traditional language, grounded in the Scriptures, that speaks of the Holy Trinity as Father, Son, and Spirit and apply, where appropriate, the principles of inclusive language approved by the NCCB (see, *Criteria for the Evaluation of Inclusive Language Translations of Scriptural Texts Proposed for Liturgical Use*, [Washington, D.C.: United States Catholic Conference, 1990]).

Church

Doctrinally sound catechetical materials . . .

[18] recognize that the Church, a community of believers, is a mystery, a sign of the kingdom, a community of divine origin, that cannot be totally understood or fully defined in human terms (see NCD, 63).

[19] teach that the Church's unique relationship with Christ makes it both sign and instrument of God's union with humanity, the means for the forgiveness of sin as well as a means of unity for human beings among themselves (see NCD, 63).

[20] emphasize the missionary nature of the Church and the call of individual Christians to proclaim the Gospel wherever there are people to be evangelized, at home and abroad (see NCD, 71; 74e).

[21] nourish and teach the faith and, because there is often a need for initial evangelization, aim at opening the heart and arousing the beginning of faith so that individuals will respond to the Word of God and Jesus' call to discipleship (see CT, 19).

[22] emphasize that Jesus Christ gave the apostles a special mission to teach and that today this teaching authority is exercised by the pope and bishops, who are successors of St. Peter and the apostles.

[23] highlight the history and distinctive tradition of the Church of Rome and the special charism of the pope as successor of St. Peter in guiding and teaching the universal Church and assuring the authentic teaching of the Gospel.

[24] explain what it means when the Church professes to be "one, holy, catholic and apostolic" (see NCD, 72, 74i, ii).

[25] show how the Church of Christ is manifest at the local level in the diocesan church and the parish, gathered in the Holy Spirit through the Gospel and the eucharist (see CD, 11; LG, 26).

[26] present the Church as a community with a legitimate diversity in expressing its shared faith according to different ages, cultures, gifts, and abilities.

[27] foster understanding and unity by accurately presenting the traditions and practices of the Catholic Churches of the East (see NCD, 73, 74g).

[28] are sensitive in dealing with other Christian Churches and ecclesial communities, taking into account how they differ from the Catholic tradition while at the same time showing how much is held in common (see NCD, 76).

[29] foster ecumenism as a means toward unity and communion among all Christians and recognize that division in the Church and among Christians is contrary to the will of Christ (see UR, 1).

[30] integrate the history of the Jews in the work of salvation so that, on the one hand, Judaism does not appear marginal and unimportant and, on the other hand, the Church and Judaism do not appear as parallel ways of salvation (see JJPC, 1:7).

[31] explain the pastoral role and authority of the magisterium—the bishops united with the pope—in defining and teaching religious truth.

[32] emphasize that individuals reach their full potential and work out their salvation only in community—the human community and the community that is the Church (see EJFA, 63, 65, and passim).

[33] support the family as the basic unit of society and underline its role as "domestic church" in living the Gospel (see FC, 12).

Mary and the Saints

Doctrinally sound catechetical materials . . .

[34] explain the sacramental meaning of "communion of saints," linking it to the eucharist which, bringing the faithful together to share the "holy gifts," is the primary source and sign of church unity.

[35] explain the biblical basis for the liturgical cult of Mary as Mother of God and disciple *par excellence* and describe her singular role in the life of Christ and the story of salvation (see LG, 66, 67).

[36] foster Marian devotions and explain the Church's particular beliefs about Mary (e.g., the Immaculate Conception, Virgin Birth, and Assumption) (see GCD, 68; NCD, 106).

[37] explain the Church's teaching on angels and its veneration of saints, who intercede for us and are role models in following Christ (see GCD, 68).

Liturgy and Sacraments

Doctrinally sound catechetical materials . . .

[38] present the sacraments as constitutive of Christian life and worship, as unique ways of meeting Christ, and not simply as channels of grace.

[39] emphasize God's saving and transforming presence in the sacraments. In the eucharist, Christ is present not only in the person of the priest but in the assembly and in the

Word and, uniquely, in the eucharistic species of bread and wine that become the Body and Blood of Christ (see SC, 7).

[40] link the eucharist to Christ's sacrifice on the cross, explaining it as a sacrament of his presence in the Church and as a meal of communal solidarity that is a sign of the heavenly banquet to which the faithful are called (see SC, 7, 47; GS, 38).

[41] call attention to the special significance of Sunday as the day of the Lord's resurrection, emphasizing active participation in Sunday Mass as an expression of community prayer and spiritual renewal.

[42] explain the liturgical year, with special attention to the seasons of Advent-Christmas, Lent-Easter (see NCD, 144c).

[43] promote active participation in the liturgy of the Church not only by explaining the rites and symbols but also by fostering a spirit of praise, thanksgiving, and repentance, and by nurturing a sense of community and reverence (see NCD, 36).

[44] explain the Catholic heritage of popular devotions and sacramentals so that they serve as a means "to help people advance towards knowledge of the mystery of Christ and his message . . ." (CT, 54).

[45] embody the norms and guidelines for liturgy and sacramental practice found in the *praenotanda* of the revised rites, with special attention to those that preface the sacraments of initiation.

[46] assist pastors, parents, and catechists to inaugurate children into the sacraments of penance and eucharist by providing for their proper initial preparation according to Catholic pastoral practice as presented by the magisterium.

[47] promote lifelong conversion and an understanding of the need for reconciliation that leads to a renewed appreciation of the sacrament of penance.

[48] establish the foundations for vocational choices—to the married life, the single life, the priesthood, the diaconate, and to the vowed life of poverty, chastity, and obedience —in the framework of one's baptismal commitment and the call to serve.

[49] respect the essential difference between the ministerial priesthood and the common priesthood, between the ministries conferred by the sacrament of orders and the call to service derived from the sacraments of baptism and confirmation (see CL, 22, 23).

[50] foster vocations to the priesthood and religious life in appropriate ways at every age level.

Life of Grace and Moral Issues

Doctrinally sound catechetical materials . . .

[51] teach that from the beginning, God called human beings to holiness, but from the very dawn of history, humans abused their freedom and set themselves against

God so that "sin entered the world" (Rom 5:12), and that this "original sin" is transmitted to every human being (see GS, 13).

[52] introduce prayer as a way of deepening one's relationship with God and explain the ends of prayer so that a spirit of adoration, thanksgiving, petition, and contrition permeates the daily lives of Christians (see NCD, 140).

[53] promote the continual formation of right Catholic conscience based on Christ's role in one's life; his ideals, precepts, and examples found in Scripture; and the magisterial teaching of the Church (see NCD, 190).

[54] cultivate the moral life of Christians by inculcating virtue and nurture a sense of responsibility that goes beyond external observance of laws and precepts.

[55] discuss the reality and effects of personal sins, whereby an individual, acting knowingly and deliberately, violates the moral law, harms one's self, one's neighbor, and offends God (see GCD, 62).

[56] make it clear that the dignity of the human person and sanctity of life are grounded in one's relation to the Triune God, and that individuals are valued not because of their status in society, their productivity, or as consumers but in themselves as beings made in God's image (see EJFA, 28, 78).

[57] go beyond economic and political concerns in describing ecological and environmental issues and define human accountability for the created universe in moral and spiritual terms (see SRS, 38).

[58] present a consistent ethic of life that, fostering respect for individual dignity and personal rights, highlights the rights of the unborn, the aged, and those with disabilities and explains the evils of abortion and euthanasia.

[59] explain the specifics of Christian morality, as taught by the magisterium of the Church, in the framework of the universal call to holiness and discipleship; the Ten Commandments; the Sermon on the Mount, especially the Beatitudes; and in Christ's discourse at the Last Supper (see NCD, 105).

[60] include the responsibilities of Catholic living, traditionally expressed in the precepts of the Church.

[61] present Catholic teaching on justice, peace, mercy, and social issues as integral to the gospel message and the Church's prophetic mission (see NCD, 170).

[62] explain that the Church's teaching on the "option for the poor" means that while Christians are called to respond to the needs of everyone, they must give their greatest attention to individuals and communities with greatest needs (see EJFA, 86–87).

[63] state the Church's position on moral and social issues of urgent concern in contemporary society, for example, the developing role of women in the Church and in society, racism and other forms of discrimination.

[64] present human sexuality in positive terms of life, love, and self-discipline, explain the responsibilities of a chaste Christian life, and teach that love between husband and wife must be exclusive and open to new life (see FC, 29).

[65] link personal morality to social issues and professional ethics and challenge the faithful to make responsible moral decisions guided by the Church's teaching (see NCD 38, 170).

[66] teach that all legitimate authority comes from God and that governments exist to serve the people, to protect human rights and secure basic justice for all members of society (see EJFA, 122).

[67] teach that though sin abounds in the world, grace is even more abundant because of the salvific work of Christ (see NCD, 98).

Death, Judgment, and Eternity

Doctrinally sound catechetical materials . . .

[68] explain the coming of Christ "in glory" in the context of the Church's overall teaching on eschatology and final judgment (see NCD, 110).

[69] teach, on the subject of the last things, that everyone has an awesome responsibility for his or her eternal destiny and present, in the light of Christian hope, death, judgment, purgatory, heaven, or hell (see NCD, 109; GCD, 69).

II. Guidelines for Presenting Sound Doctrine

A second set of guidelines—no less important than the first if catechesis is to be effective—are based on pastoral principles and practical concerns. They are reminders that catechetical materials must take into account the community for whom they are intended, the conditions in which they live, and the ways in which they learn (cf. GCD, Foreword). Publishers are encouraged to provide catechetical materials that take into consideration the needs of the Hispanic community and other ethnic and culturally diverse groups that comprise the Church in the United States. No single text or program can address the many cultures and social groups that make up society in the United States, but all catechetical materials must take this diversity into account. Effective catechesis, as we have noted above, requires that the Church's teaching be presented correctly and in its entirety, and it is equally important to present it in ways that are attractive, appealing, and understandable by the individuals and communities to whom it is directed.

To present sound doctrine effectively, catechetical materials . . .

[70] take into account the experience and background of those being catechized and suggest ways that the Christian message illumines their life (see NCD, 176e).

[71] must be based on accepted learning theory, established pedagogical principles, and practical learning strategies (see NCD, 175).

---

[72] use language and images appropriate to the age level and developmental stages and special needs of those being catechized (see NCD, 177–188).

[73] integrate biblical themes and scriptural references in the presentation of doctrine and moral teaching and encourage a hands-on familiarity with the Bible (see NCD, 60a).

[74] challenge Catholics to critique and transform contemporary values and behaviors in light of the Gospel and the Church's teaching.

[75] maintain a judicious balance between personal expression and memorization, emphasizing that it is important both for the community and themselves that individuals commit to memory selected biblical passages, essential prayers, liturgical responses, key doctrinal ideas, and lists of moral responsibilities (see CT, 55; NCD, 176e).

[76] provide for a variety of shared prayer forms and experiences that lead to an active participation in the liturgical life of the Church and private prayer (see NCD, 145, 264).

[77] continually hold before their intended audience the ideal of living a life based on the teachings of the Gospel.

[78] include suggestions for service to the community that is appropriate to the age and abilities of the persons who are being catechized.

[79] stress the importance of the local church community for Christian living, so that every Catholic contributes to building up the spirit of the parish family and sees its ministries as part of the Church's universal mission.

[80] are sensitive to the appropriate use of inclusive language in the text and avoid racial, ethnic, and gender stereotypes in pictures (see NCD, 264).

[81] reflect the catholicity of the Church in art and graphics by presenting the diverse customs and religious practices of racial, ethnic, cultural, and family groups (see NCD, 194, 264).

[82] assist catechists by including easy-to-understand instructions regarding scope, sequence, and use of texts.

[83] suggest a variety of strategies, activities, and auxiliary resources that can enrich instruction, deepen understanding, and facilitate the integration of doctrine and life.

[84] include material that can be used in the home to aid parents in communicating church teaching and nurturing the faith life of the family.

[85] instruct teachers and catechists on how to respond to the needs of persons with disabilities and individuals with special needs (see NCD, 195, 196, 264).

[86] help teachers and catechists distinguish between church doctrine and the opinions and interpretations of theologians (see NCD, 264).

[87] help develop the catechists' own faith life, experience of prayer, and mature commitment to the Church and motivate them toward ongoing enrichment.

Theories of Development: Concepts and Applications

Crain, W. 1992. 17–18, 102–03, 124, 136–41, 188–90, 262–68. Englewood Cliffs, N.J.: Prentice Hall.

Principles of Development

The Concept of Maturation

The child's growth or development, Gesell said, is influenced by two major factors. First, the child is a product of his or her environment. But more fundamentally, Gesell believed, the child's development is directed from within, by the action of the genes. Gesell called this process *maturation* (Gesell and Ilg, 1943, p. 41).

An outstanding feature of maturational development is that it always unfolds in fixed sequences. This can first be seen in the developing embryo, where, for example, the heart is always the first organ to develop and function. Soon afterward, the rapidly differentiating cells begin to form the central nervous system—the brain and the spinal cord. The development of the brain and the head, in turn, begins before the other parts, such as the arms and the legs. This order, which is directed by the genetic blueprint, is never violated.

Similarly, sequential development continues after birth. For example, just as the head develops early in the embryo, it also takes the lead in early postnatal development. Babies first have control over their lips and tongues, then gain control over their eye movements, followed by control over the neck, shoulders, arms, hands, fingers, trunk, legs, and feet. In both prenatal and postnatal development there is a head-to-foot (cephalocaudal) trend (Gesell, 1946, p. 339).

As babies grow, they learn to sit up, to stand, to walk, and to run, and these capacities, too, develop in a specific order. They emerge with the growth of the nervous system, which itself is mediated by the genes.

Children, of course, vary in their rates of development. They do not all stand up and walk at the same age. Nevertheless, they all proceed through the same sequences. Moreover, individual differences in growth rates, in Gesell's view, are largely controlled by the internal genetic mechanism. (Gesell, 1945, p. 161).

As indicated, the effects of maturation are contrasted with those of the environment. In prenatal development, this means that maturation is distinguished from aspects of the internal environment, such as the embryo's temperature and the oxygen it receives from its mother. These environmental factors are certainly vital—they support proper growth—but they play no direct role in the sequential unfolding of structures and action patterns. This is the work of the maturational mechanism.

Once the baby is born, it enters a different kind of environment. It is not only an environment that meets its physical needs, but a social and cultural environment which tries to induce it to behave in the proper ways. Gesell said that the child clearly needs the social environment to realize his or her potentials, but he also argued that socializing forces work best where they are in tune with inner maturational principles (Gesell and Ilg, 1943, p. 41).

Gesell was particularly opposed to efforts to teach children things ahead of schedule. Children will sit up, walk, and talk when they are ready, when their nervous systems have sufficiently matured. At the right moment, they will simply begin to master a task, from their own inner urges. Until then, teaching will be of little value, and may create tensions between caretakers and children.

Some evidence for the maturational position on teaching has come from studies with identical twins. For example, Gesell and Thompson (1929) gave one twin practice at such activities as stair-climbing and the grasping and manipulation of cubes. This twin did show some skill superior to that of the other, but the untrained twin soon caught up, with much less practice. And he did so at about the age at which we would expect him to perform the various tasks. Apparently, then, there is an inner timetable that determines the readiness to do things, and the benefits of early training are relatively temporary. The question of early stimulation is controversial, but it does seem that our efforts to speed up early motor development produce only small effects (Sroufe and Cooper, 1988, pp. 162–68; Cole and Cole, 1989, pp. 186–88).

Maturation, then, refers to the process by which development is governed by intrinsic factors—principally the genes, which are chemical substances contained within the nucleus of each cell. The genes determine the sequence, timing, and form of emerging action-patterns.

However, the precise mechanism by which the genes work, in Gesell's day as today, is still mysterious. We know that the genes do not work in isolation from one another, and they appear to receive some cues from the cytoplasm, the cellular substance outside the nucleus (Gesell, 1945, p. 99; Gilbert, 1988, pp. 10, 442). Since the cytoplasm is, in effect, the environment of the genes, we see how difficult it becomes to draw sharp distinctions between internal and environmental factors. Nevertheless, we can still think of maturation as the process by which the genes direct development, albeit in conjunction with other factors.

So far, I have primarily been illustrating maturational growth with early motor behavior, which was Gesell's main scientific focus. However, Gesell believed that maturation governs the growth of the entire personality. He said, for example,

[The child's] nervous system matures by stages and natural sequences. He sits before he stands; he babbles before he talks; he fabricates before he tells the truth; he draws a circle before he draws a square; he is selfish before he is altruistic; he is dependent on others before he achieves dependence on self. All his capacities, including his morals, are subject to the laws of growth.

(Gesell and Ilg, 1943, p. 11)

Overview of the Theory

Although Piaget's research changed over the years, each part of it contributes to a single, integrated stage theory. The most general stages, or periods, are listed in Table 6.1.

Before we examine these stages in detail, it is important to note two theoretical points. First, Piaget recognized that children pass through his stages at different rates, and he therefore attached little importance to the ages associated with them. He did maintain, however, that children move through the stages in an *invariant sequence*—in the same order.

Second, as we discuss the stages, it is important to bear in mind Piaget's general view of the nature of *developmental change*. Because he proposed an invariant stage sequence, some scholars (e.g., Bandura and McDonald, 1963) have assumed that he was a maturationist. He was not. Maturationists believe that stage sequences are wired into the genes and that stages unfold according to an inner timetable. Piaget, however, did not think that his stages are genetically determined. They simply represent increasingly comprehensive ways of thinking. Children are constantly exploring, manipulating, and trying to make sense out of the environment, and in this process they actively construct new and more elaborate structures for dealing with it (Kohlberg, 1968).

Piaget did make use of biological concepts, but only in a limited way. He observed that infants inherit reflexes, such as the sucking reflex. Reflexes are important in the first month of life but have much less bearing on development after this.

In addition, Piaget sometimes characterized children's activities in terms of biological tendencies that are found in all organisms. These tendencies are assimilation, accommodation, and organization. *Assimilation* means taking in, as in eating or digestion. In the intellectual sphere, we have a need to assimilate objects or information into our cognitive structures. For example, adults assimilate information by reading books. Much earlier, a baby might try to assimilate an object by grasping it, trying to take it into his or her grasping scheme.

Some objects do not quite fit into existing structures, so we must make *accommodations*, or changes in our structures. For example, a baby girl might find that she can grasp a block only by first removing an obstacle. Through such accommodations, infants begin constructing increasingly efficient and elaborate means for dealing with the world.

Table 6.1 The General Periods of Development

Period I. Sensori-Motor Intelligence (birth to two years). Babies organize their physical action schemes, such as sucking, grasping, and hitting, for dealing with the immediate world.

Period II. Preoperational Thought (two to seven years). Children learn to think—to use symbols and internal images—but their thinking is unsystematic and illogical. It is very different from that of adults.

Period III. Concrete Operations (seven to 11 years). Children develop the capacity to think systematically, but only when they can refer to concrete objects and activities.

Period IV. Formal Operations (11 to adulthood). Young people develop the capacity to think systematically on a purely abstract and hypothetical plane.

The third tendency is *organization*. For example, a four-month-old boy might have the capacity to look at objects and to grasp them. Soon he will try to combine these two actions by grasping the same objects he looks at. On a more mental plane, we build theories. We seem to be constantly trying to organize our ideas into coherent systems.

Thus, even though Piaget did not believe that stages are wired into the genetic code, but constructed by children themselves, he did discuss the construction process in terms of biological tendencies (Ginsburg and Opper, 1988, pp. 16–19).

If Piaget was not a maturationist, he was even less a learning theorist. He did not believe that children's thinking is shaped by adult teachings or other environmental influences. Children must interact with the environment to develop. but it is they, not the external environment, who build new cognitive structures.

Development, then, is not governed by internal maturation or external teachings. It is an *active construction process*, in which children, through their own activities, build increasingly differentiated and comprehensive cognitive structures.

Implications for Education

Piaget did not write extensively on education, but he did have some recommendations. Essentially, his overall educational philosophy is similar to that of Rousseau and Montessori. For Piaget, too, true learning is not something handed down by the teacher, but something that comes from the child. It is a process of spontaneous invention and discovery. This is clearly true of infants, who make incredible intellectual progress simply by exploring and manipulating the environment on their own, and it can be true of older children as well. Accordingly, the teacher should not try to impose knowledge on the child, but he or she should find materials that will interest and challenge the child and then permit the child to solve problems on his or her own (Piaget 1969, pp. 151–53, 160).

Like Rousseau and Montessori, Piaget also stressed the importance of gearing instruction to the child's particular level. He did not agree with Montessori's maturational view of stages, but the general principle still holds: The educator must appreciate the extent to which children's interests and modes of learning are different at different times.

Say, for example, a boy is just entering the stage of concrete operations. He is beginning to think logically, but his thinking is still partly tied to concrete objects and activities. Accordingly, lessons should give him opportunities to deal actively with real things. If, for example, we wish to teach him about fractions, we should not draw diagrams, give him lectures, or engage him in verbal discussions. We should allow him to divide concrete objects into parts (Flavell, 1963, p. 368). When we assume that he will learn on a verbal plane, we are being egocentric; we are assuming that he learns just as we do. The result will be a lesson that sails over his head and seems unnatural to him.

Kohlberg's Six Stages
Level I. Preconventional Morality

Stage 1. Obedience and Punishment Orientation. Kohlberg's stage 1 is similar to Piaget's first stage of moral thought. The child assumes that powerful authorities hand down a fixed set of rules which he or she must unquestioningly obey. To the Heinz dilemma [Heinz must decide whether he should steal a drug to save his dying wife.], the child typically says that Heinz was wrong to steal the drug because "It's against the law," or "It's bad to steal," as if this were all there were to it. When asked to elaborate, the child usually responds in terms of the consequences involved, explaining that stealing is bad "because you'll get punished" (Kohlberg, 1958b).

Although the vast majority of children at stage 1 oppose Heinz's theft, it is still possible for a child to support the action and still employ stage 1 reasoning. A child might say, "Heinz can steal it because he asked first and it's not like he stole something big; he won't get punished" (see Rest, 1973). Even though the child agrees with Heinz's action, the reasoning is still stage 1; the concern is with what authorities permit and punish.

Kohlberg calls stage 1 thinking *preconventional* because children do not yet speak as members of society. Instead, they see morality as something external to themselves—something the big people say they must do (Colby et al., 1987a, p. 16).

Stage 2. Individualism and Exchange. At this stage children recognize that there is not just one right view that is handed down by the authorities. Different individuals have different viewpoints. "Heinz," they might point out, "might think it's right to take the drug, the druggist would

not." Since everything is *relative*, each person is free to pursue his or her *individual* interests. One boy said that Heinz might steal the drug if he wanted his wife to live, but that he doesn't have to if he wants to marry someone younger and better-looking (Kohlberg, 1963, p. 2). Another boy said Heinz might steal it because

> maybe they had children and he might need someone at home to look after them. But maybe he shouldn't steal it because they might put him in prison for more years than he could stand. (Colby et al.; 1987b, p. 208)

What is right for Heinz, then, is what meets his own self-interests.

You might have noticed that children at both stages 1 and 2 talk about punishment. However, they perceive it differently. At stage 1 punishment is tied up in the child's mind with wrongness; punishment "proves" that disobedience is wrong. At stage 2, in contrast, punishment is simply a risk that one naturally wants to avoid.

Although stage 2 respondents sometimes sound amoral, they do have some sense of right action. There is a notion of fair exchange or fair deals. The philosophy is one of returning favors— "If you scratch my back, I'll scratch yours." To the Heinz story, subjects often say that Heinz was right to steal the drug because the druggist was unwilling to make a fair deal; he was "trying to rip Heinz off." Or they might say that he should steal for his wife "because she might return the favor some day" (Colby et al., 1987c, pp. 16–17).

Respondents at stage 2 are still said to reason at the preconventional level because they speak as isolated individuals rather than as members of society. They see individuals exchanging favors, but there is still no identification with the values of the family or community.

Level II. Conventional Morality

Stage 3. Good Interpersonal Relationships. At this stage children—who are by now usually entering their teens—see morality as more than simple deals. They believe that people should live up to the expectations of the family and community and behave in "good" ways. Good behavior means having good motives and interpersonal feelings such as love, empathy, trust, and concern for others. Heinz, they typically argue, was right to steal the drug because "He was a good man for wanting to save her," and "His intentions were good, that of saving the life of someone he loves." Even if Heinz doesn't love his wife, these subjects often say, he should steal the drug because "I don't think any husband should sit back and watch his wife die" (Kohlberg, 1958b; Colby et al., 1987c. pp. 27–29).

If Heinz's motives were good, the druggist's were bad. The druggist, stage 3 subjects emphasize, was "selfish," "greedy," and "only interested in himself, not another life." Sometimes the respondents become so angry with the druggist that they say that he ought to be put in jail (Colby et al., 1987c, pp. 20–33). A typical stage 3 response is that of Don, age 13:

> It was really the druggist's fault, he was unfair, trying to overcharge and letting someone die. Heinz loved his wife and wanted to save her. I think anyone would. I don't think they would put him in jail. The judge would look at all sides, and see that the druggist was charging too much. (Kohlberg, 1963, p. 25)

We see that Don defines the issue in terms of the actors' character traits and motives. He talks about the loving husband, the unfair druggist, and the understanding judge. His answer deserves the label "conventional morality" because it assumes that the attitude expressed would be shared by the entire community—"anyone" would be right to do what Heinz did (Kohlberg, 1963, p. 25).

As mentioned earlier, there are similarities between Kohlberg's first three stages and Piaget's two stages. In both sequences there is a shift from unquestioning obedience to a relativistic outlook and to a concern for good motives. For Kohlberg, however, these shifts occur in three stages rather than two.

Stage 4. Maintaining the Social Order. Stage 3 reasoning works best in two-person relationships with family members or close friends, where one can make a real effort to get to know the other's feelings and needs and try to help. At stage 4, in contrast, the respondent becomes more broadly concerned with *society as a whole.* Now the emphasis is on obeying laws, respecting authority, and performing one's duties so that the social order is maintained. In response to the Heinz story, many subjects say they understand that Heinz's motives were good, but they cannot condone the theft. What would happen if we all started breaking the laws whenever we felt we had a good reason. The result would be chaos; society couldn't function. As one subject explained,

> I don't want to sound like Spiro Agnew, law and order and wave the flag, but if everybody did as he wanted to do, set up his own beliefs as to right and wrong, then I think you would have chaos. The only thing I think we have in civilization nowadays is some sort of legal structure which people are sort of bound to follow. [Society needs] a centralizing framework. (Colby et al., 1987c, p. 89)

Because stage 4 subjects make moral decisions from the perspective of society as a whole, they think from a full-fledged member-of-society perspective (Colby et al., 1987a, p. 17).

You will recall that stage 1 children also generally oppose stealing because it breaks the law. Superficially, stage 1 and stage 4 subjects are giving the same response, so we see here why Kohlberg insisted that we must probe into the reasoning behind the overt response. Stage 1

children say, "It's wrong to steal" and "It's against the law," but they cannot elaborate any further, except to say that stealing can get a person jailed. Stage 4 respondents, in contrast, have a conception of the function of laws for society as a whole—a conception that far exceeds the grasp of the younger child.

Level III. Postconventional Morality

Stage 5. Social Contract and Individual Rights. At stage 4, people want to keep society functioning. However, a smoothly functioning society is not necessarily a good one. A totalitarian society might be well organized, but it is hardly the moral ideal. At stage 5, people begin to ask, What makes for a good society? They begin to think about society in a very theoretical way, stepping back from their own society and considering the rights and values that a society ought to uphold. They then evaluate existing societies in terms of these prior considerations. They are said to take a "prior-to-society," perspective (Colby et al., 1987a, p.20).

Stage 5 respondents basically believe that a good society is best conceived as a social contract into which people freely enter to work toward the benefit of all. They recognize that different social groups within a society will have different values, but they believe that all rational people would agree on two points. First, they would all want certain basic *rights,* such as liberty and life, to be protected. Second, they would want some *democratic* procedures for changing unfair laws and for improving society.

In response to the Heinz dilemma, stage 5 respondents make it clear that they do not generally favor breaking laws; laws are social contracts that we agree to uphold until we can change them by democratic means. Nevertheless, the wife's right to live is a moral right that must be protected. Thus, stage 5 respondents sometimes defend Heinz's theft in strong language:

> It is the husband's duty to save his wife. The fact that her life is in danger transcends every other standard you might use to judge his action. Life is more important than property.

This young man went on to say that "from a moral standpoint," Heinz should save the life of even a stranger, since to be consistent, the value of a life means any life. When asked if the judge should punish Heinz, he replied:

> Usually the moral and legal standpoints coincide. Here they conflict. The judge should weight the moral standpoint more heavily but preserve the legal law in punishing Heinz lightly. (Kohlberg, 1976, p. 38)

Stage 5 subjects, then, talk about "morality" and "rights" that take some priority over particular laws. Kohlberg insisted, however, that we do not judge people to be at stage 5 merely from their verbal labels. We need to look at their social perspective and mode of reasoning. At stage 4, too, subjects frequently talk about the "right to life," but for them this right is legitimized by the authority of their social or religious group (e.g., by the Bible). Presumably, if their group valued property over life, they would too. At stage 5, in contrast, people are making more of an independent effort to think out what any society ought to value. They often reason, for example, that property has little meaning without life. They are trying to determine logically what a society ought to be like (Kohlberg, 1981, pp. 21–22: Colby et al., 1987c, pp. 53–55).

Stage 6. Universal Principles. Stage 5 respondents are working toward a conception of the good society. They suggest that we need to (a) protect certain individual rights and (b) settle disputes through democratic processes. However, democratic processes alone do not always result in outcomes that we intuitively sense are just. A majority, for example, may vote for a law that hinders a minority. Thus, Kohlberg believed that there must be a higher stage—stage 6—which defines the principles by which we achieve justice.

Kohlberg's conception of justice followed that of the philosophers Kant and Rawls, as well as great moral leaders such as Gandhi and Martin Luther King. According to these people, the principles of justice require us to treat the claims of all parties in an impartial manner, respecting the basic dignity of all people as individuals. The principles of justice are therefore universal; they apply to all. Thus, we would not vote for a law that aids some people but hurts others. The principles of justice guide us toward decisions based on an equal respect for all.

In actual practice, Kohlberg said, we can reach just decisions by looking at a situation through one another's eyes. In the Heinz dilemma, this would mean that all parties—the druggist, Heinz, and his wife—take the roles of the others. To do this in an impartial manner, people can assume a "veil of ignorance" (Rawls, 1971), acting as if they do not know which role they would eventually occupy. If the druggist did this, even he would recognize that life must take priority over property; for he wouldn't want to risk finding himself in the wife's shoes with property valued over life. Thus, they would all agree that the wife must be saved—this would be the fair solution. Such a solution, we must note, requires not only impartiality, but the principle that everyone is given full and equal respect. If the wife were considered of less value than the others, a just solution could not be reached.

Until 1975 Kohlberg had been scoring some of his subjects at stage 6, but he then stopped doing so. One reason was that he and other researchers had found very few subjects who consistently reasoned at this stage. Also, Kohlberg concluded that his interview dilemmas did not draw out differences between stage 5 and stage 6 thinking. Theoretically, stage 6 has a clearer and broader conception of universal principles (including justice as well as individual rights), but the interview did not draw out this broader understanding. So he dropped stage 6 from his manual, calling it a "theoretical stage" and scoring all postconventional responses at stage 5 (Colby et al., 1987a, pp. 35–40).

One issue that would distinguish stage 5 from stage 6 is civil disobedience. Stage 5 would be more hesitant to endorse civil disobedience because of its commitment to the social contract and to changing laws through democratic agreements. Only when an individual right is clearly at stake does violating the law seem justified. At stage 6, in contrast, a commitment to justice makes the rationale for civil disobedience stronger and broader. Martin Luther King argued that laws are only valid insofar as they are grounded in justice, and that a commitment to justice carries with it an obligation to disobey unjust laws. King also recognized, of course, the general need for laws and democratic processes (stages 4 and 5), and he was therefore willing to accept the penalties for his actions. Nevertheless, he believed that the higher principal of justice required civil disobedience (Kohlberg, 1981, p. 43).

Summary

At stage 1 children think of what is right as what authority says is right. Doing the right thing is obeying authority and avoiding punishment. At stage 2 children are no longer so impressed by any single authority: they see that there are different sides to any issue. Since everything is relative, one is free to pursue one's own interests, although it is often useful to make deals and exchange favors with others.

At stages 3 and 4 young people think as members of the conventional society, with its values, norms, and expectations. At stage 3 they emphasize being a good person, which basically means having helpful motives toward people close to one. At stage 4 the concern shifts toward obeying laws to maintain society as a whole.

At stages 5 and 6 people are less concerned with maintaining society for its own sake, and more concerned with the principles and values that make for a good society. At stage 5 they emphasize basic rights and the democratic processes that give everyone a say, and at stage 6 they define the principles by which agreements will be most just.

Practical Implications

Bandura's work should do a good deal to increase our awareness of the importance of models in child-rearing and education. Although most parents and teachers are already somewhat aware of the fact that they teach by example, they probably have also overlooked just how influential modeling can be. A case in point is physical punishment. Many parents try to prevent their children from fighting by spanking them when they fight—only to find, it seems, that their children fight all the more (Bandura and Walters, 1963, p. 129). The likely explanation is that the parents, by spanking, are inadvertently providing a good demonstration of how to hurt others (Bandura, 1967). Similarly, whenever we find that we are unable to rid a child of some distressing bit of behavior, we might ask whether we have been inadvertently modeling the behavior ourselves.

Modeling, according to Bandura, takes many forms. The familiar kind is behavioral modeling; we exemplify an activity by performing it. Modeling may also be done verbally, as when we give instructions or issue commands. Social learning researchers have evaluated the effectiveness of the various kinds of modeling, and their findings should be of importance to parents and educators. Of particular interest are studies such as G. M. White's (1972), which examined the effects of commanding children to share. At first, the commands seemed to work, but their impact diminished over time, and the commands also produced resentment and rebelliousness. In the long run, we may do better simply to model generosity and helpfulness through our own behavior. Then children can follow our example without feeling forced to do so.

Social learning theorists have also shown that behavior is influenced not only by personal or live models, but also by those presented in the mass media. Filmed models, in particular, seem to exert a powerful impact, and one major implication is that television, which many children watch for hours on end, is shaping young lives. Social learning theorists have been especially concerned with the effects of televised violence on children and have found that, in fact, it can increase children's aggressiveness in their daily lives. The findings are complex—the effects seem strongest, for example, on young children—but the findings are substantial enough to warrant our concern (Gardner, 1982, pp. 334–36; Huston et al., 1989).

The kinds of models presented in the mass media have been of concern to those seeking social change, such as African-Americans and women's groups. These activists have pointed out that films, books, and magazines have typically depicted women and people of color in stereotyped roles and, by doing so, have restricted people's sense of what they might become in life. Accordingly, these groups have tried to get the media to present new kinds of models, such as women and African-Americans as doctors and scientists, rather than housewives and delinquents. The social learning research suggests that the activists have, in this case, adopted a good strategy for social change.

Because modeling can have a strong impact on behavior, it has significant promise as a therapeutic device. You might recall that in Mary Cover Jones's (1924) famous experiment, modeling was part of the method used to eliminate Peter's fear of furry objects. Bandura and others have conducted a number of studies that have more systematically shown how modeling can help reduce fears. In one experiment (Bandura et al., 1967), for example, four-year-olds who were afraid of dogs observed a child calmly play with one, and then the children themselves became less fearful. Modeling can also help in other ways, such as making overly submissive clients more assertive (Rosenthal, 1976).

Bandura (1986) has begun to urge therapists to pay special attention to self-efficacy appraisals when they diagnose and treat their clients. For example, Bandura believes that whatever technique a therapist uses to treat a phobia —whether it is modeling or some other technique—the treatment will work best if it gives the client the sense that he or she can now exert some control over the feared stimulus. Similarly, techniques for dealing with pain, such as relaxation or guided imagery, work best when they give clients the feeling that they can now exert some influence on the amount of pain they feel (1986, pp. 425–445).

Theoretical Issues
Why Erikson's Theory Is a Stage Theory

In Chapters 6 and 7 we saw that Piaget and Kohlberg believed that cognitive stages should meet several criteria. Erikson's stages deal more with emotional development, but they basically meet the same criteria. That is, the stages (1) describe qualitatively different behaviors, (2) refer to general issues, (3) unfold in an invariant, sequence, and (4) are culturally universal. Let us examine these points in turn.

1. The stages refer to qualitatively different behavior patterns. If development were just a matter of gradual quantitative change, any division into stages would be arbitrary. Erikson's stages, however, give us a good sense of how behavior is qualitatively different at different points. Children at the autonomy stage sound very different from those at the trust stage; they are much more independent. Children at the initiative stage are different again. Whereas children who are establishing a sense of autonomy defy authority and keep others out, children with a sense of initiative are more daring and imaginative, running vigorously about, making big plans, and initiating new activities. Behavior has a distinctive flavor at each stage.

2. The stages describe general issues. As we have emphasized, stage refers to general characteristics or issues. Erikson has gone beyond Freud's relatively specific focus on body zones and has attempted to delineate the general issues at each period. At the oral stage, for example, he shows that it is not just the stimulation of this zone that is important but the general mode of taking in and, more generally still, the development of sense of trust in one's providers. Similarly, at each stage Erikson tries to isolate the most general issue faced by the individual in the social world.

3. The stages unfold in an invariant sequence. All stage theories imply an invariant sequence, and Erikson's is no exception. He says that each stage is present in some form throughout life, but each reaches its crisis at a specific time and in a specific order.

Erikson's claim is based on the assumption that his sequence is partly the product of *biological maturation*. As he puts it, the child obeys "inner laws of development, namely those laws which in his prenatal period had formed one organ after another and which now create a succession of potentialities for significant interaction with those around him" (1963, p. 6). At the second stage, for example, biological maturation ushers in a sense of autonomy. Because of maturation, children can stand on their own two feet, control their sphincter muscles, walk, use words such as "me," "mine," and "no," and so on. At the third stage, maturation prompts a new sexual interest, along with capacities for imaginative play, curiosity, and vigorous locomotion.

At the same time, *societies* have evolved such that they invite and meet this inner, maturational succession of potentialities. When, for example, the child at the autonomy stage demonstrates a new degree of self-control, socializing agents consider the child ready for training. For example, they begin toilet-training. The result is the battle of wills, between child and society, which creates the crisis of this period. Similarly, when children become recklessly ambitious with respect to sexual matters, societies decide it is now time to introduce their particular sexual prohibitions, creating the core conflict at the third stage. Thus, the succession of crises is produced by inner maturation on the one hand and social forces on the other.

4. The stages are cultural universals. Erikson believes that his stages can be applied to all cultures. Readers might see how the stages would be universal to the extent that they are maturationally governed, but they may still be skeptical, for they know how widely cultures differ.

Erikson, too, is aware of the vast differences among cultures. In fact, one of his goals is to show how cultures handle the stages differently according to their different value systems. For example, the Sioux provide their children with a long and indulgent period of nursing; one of their goals is to get children to trust others and to become generous themselves (1963, pp. 134–40). Our society, in contrast, discourages dependency. Compared to other cultures, we wean our infants very early. We do not seem to want our children to learn to depend on or trust others too much, but to become independent. Independence and free mobility seem part of our cultural ethos, from the pioneer days to the present time (1963, Ch. 8.).

What Erikson does claim is that all cultures address themselves to the same issues. All cultures try to provide their children with consistent care, regulate their extreme wish to do everything their own way, and instill incest taboos. And, as children grow, all cultures ask them to learn the tools and skills of their technology, to find a workable adult identity, to establish bonds of intimacy, to care for the next generation, and to face death with integrity. All cultures attempt to achieve these tasks because culture itself is a part of the evolutionary process; in the course of evolution, those groups that failed in these tasks had less chance of surviving. Unless cultures could get their members to sacrifice some of their independence or the needs of others (at the autonomy stage), to begin to learn the skills and tools of the society (at the industry stage), and to care for the next generation (at the generativity stage), they probably did not endure.

The question of hierarchic integration. Piagetians, you may recall, define their stages in terms of a fifth point; they view them as hierarch integrations. This concept has been used somewhat differently by different writers, but in a stage theory it basically means that earlier structures are reintegrated into new, dominant structures. In Erikson's theory, such a process does occur at certain stages, such as

adolescence. As people achieve a new sense of identity, they reorganize a good deal of their personality in the pursuit of dominant goals or life-plans. However, the concept of hierarchic integration does not apply to all the stages. For example, the issues at the stage of autonomy vs. shame and doubt are not reorganized or reintegrated into the next stage, initiative vs. guilt. The new stage simply raises new concerns, leaving the earlier stage in the background, in much the same form as before. Thus the concept of hierarchic integration does not seem to characterize development at all of Erikson's stages (see Kohlberg, 1969a, p. 353).

Must One Go through All the Stages?

We sometimes hear that if one doesn't achieve a good measure of success at one of Erikson's stages, one may be unable to go on to the next stage. This is wrong. In Erikson's theory, one must, if one lives long enough, go through all the stages. The reason has to do with the forces that move one from stage to stage: biological maturation and social expectations. These forces push one along according to a certain timetable, whether one has been successful at earlier stages or not. Consider, for example, a boy who has been unable to attain much of a sense of industry. When he reaches puberty, he must grapple with the issues of identity even though he is not really ready to do so. Because of biological changes, he finds himself troubled by an upsurge of sexual feelings and by a rapidly changing body. At the same time, social pressures force him to cope with problems of dating and to start thinking about his future occupation. It matters little to the larger society that he is still unsure about his own skills. His society has its own timetable, and by the time he is 20 years or so, he will feel pressure to decide on a career. In the same way, he will find himself confronting each new stage in the sequence.

Each person, then, must go through all the stages, whether he or she has traversed the earlier stages well or not. What is true is that success at earlier stages affects the chances of success at later ones. Children who developed a firm sense of trust in their caretakers can afford to leave them and independently explore the environment. In contrast, children who lack trust—who are afraid to let caretakers out of sight—are less able to develop a sense of autonomy. (Conceptualized slightly differently, it is the child who has developed a favorable balance of trust over mistrust who ventures into the world full of hope and anticipation, energetically testing new powers of independent action.) In a similar way, a favorable outcome at each stage affects the chances of a positive outcome at the subsequent stage. But whatever the outcomes, maturational and social forces require the child to face the issues at each new stage.

Comparison with Piaget

We have now reviewed the two most influential stage theories in the developmental literature: Piaget's cognitive-developmental theory and Erikson's psychoanalytic theory. In many respects, the theories are different, as briefly noted before. Broadly speaking, the most basic differences are these: Erikson describes a variety of feelings we bring to tasks; Piaget focuses on intellectual development. This development, for Piaget, is not motivated by biological maturation and social forces, but by the child's efforts to solve cognitive problems. As children encounter problems they cannot handle with their existing cognitive structures, they become challenged and curious and construct more elaborate structures. Since the driving force is the child's curiosity, there is no reason why the child must go through all the stages; if a child is not curious about an area (e.g., mathematics), he or she may never reach the highest stages in that area. Thus, where maturation and social pressures drive us though all of Erikson's stages, ready or not, we only go through Piaget's stages to the extent we are intellectually motivated to build new structures.

Such differences seem large. Nevertheless, both Erikson and Piaget are presenting stage theories, attempting to describe the most general qualitative shifts in behavior. Moreover, they often seem to be presenting different perspectives on the same basic developments. Let us look at how this is so.

1. Trust. As Erikson (16L. pp 116–117) observes, both Piaget and he are concerned with the infant's development of a secure image of external objects. Erikson points to the child's growing reliance on the predictability and dependability of people, whereas Piaget documents the developing sense of permanent things. Thus, both are concerned with the child's growing faith in the stability of the world.

2. Autonomy. As children develop a sense of trust in their caretakers, they become increasingly independent. Secure in their knowledge that others will be there when needed, they are free to explore the world on their own.

Piaget points to a similar process. As children gain the conviction that objects are permanent, they can act increasingly independently of them. For example, when his daughter Jacqueline's ball rolled under the sofa, she was no longer bound to the spot where she last saw it. She now knew that the object was permanent, even if hidden, and could therefore try out alternative routes for finding it. (For further thoughts on the parallels at this stage, see Kohlberg and Gilligan, 1971, p. 1076.) [For research exploring these parallels, see Gouin-Décarie, 1965; Bell, 1970; and Flavell, 1977, p. 54.]

3. Initiative. At this stage, between about three and six years, Erikson and the Freudians emphasize the child's consuming curiosity, wealth of fantasy, and daring imagination. As Erikson says, "Both language and locomotion permit him to expand his imagination over so many things that he cannot avoid frightening himself with what he has dreamed and thought up" (1959, p. 75).

Piaget's view of the thinking at this period is remarkably similar. As Flavell says:

The preoperational child is the child of wonder; his cognition appears to us naive, impression-bound, and poorly organized. There is an essential lawlessness about his world without, of course,

this fact in any way entering his awareness to inhibit the zest and flights of fancy with which he approaches new situations. Anything is possible because nothing is subject to lawful constraints. (1963, p. 211)

For Piaget, then, the fantasy and imagination of the phallic-age child owes much to the fact that the child is in the preoperational period—a time in which thoughts run free because they are not yet tied to the systematic logic that the child will develop at the next stage.

4. Industry. For Erikson and the Freudians, the fantasies and fears of the oedipal child are temporarily buried during the latency stage, which lasts from about six to 11 years. Frightening wishes and fantasies are repressed, and the child's interests expand outward: the child intently tries to master the realistic skills and tools of the culture. In general, this is a relatively calm period: children seem more self-composed.

Piaget, too, would lead us to believe that the six- to 11-year-old is more stable, realistic, and organized than the younger child. For Piaget, this change is not the result of the repression of emotions and dangerous wishes; rather, it comes about because, intellectually, the child has entered the stage of concrete operations. The child can now separate fact from fancy, can see different perspectives on a problem, and can work logically and systematically on concrete tasks. Intellectually, then, the child is in a stage of equilibrium with the world, and this contributes to his or her overall stability and composure. Erikson himself seems to have concrete operations in mind when he describes this period: He says that at this time the child's "exuberant imagination is tamed and harnessed by the laws of impersonal things . . ." (1963, p. 258).

5. Identity. In Erikson's view, the calm of the preceding period gives way to the turbulence and uncertainty of adolescence. Adolescents are confused by physical changes and pressures to make social commitments. They wonder who they are and what their place in society will be.

Piaget has little to say about physical changes in adolescence, but his insights into cognitive development help us understand why this can be an identity-searching time. During the stage of concrete operations, the child's thought was pretty much tied to the here-and-now. But with the growth of formal operations, the adolescent's thought soars into the distant future and into the realm of the purely hypothetical. Consequently, adolescents can now entertain limitless possibilities about who they are and what they will become. Formal operational capacities, then, may contribute to the self-questioning of this period (see Inhelder and Piaget, 1955, Ch. 18).

Practical Implications

Clinical Work: A Case Illustration

Clinical psychologists and other mental health workers have found Erikson's concepts very useful. We can get a sense of this from Erikson's own work with one of his cases, a four-year-old boy he calls Peter.

Peter suffered from a psychogenic megacolon, an enlarged colon that resulted from Peter's emotionally based habit of retaining his fecal matter for up to a week at a time. Through conversations with Peter and his family, Erikson learned that Peter developed this symptom shortly after his nurse, an Asian girl, had been dismissed. Peter, it seems, had begun "attacking the nurse in a rough-housing way, and the girl had seemed to accept and quietly enjoy his decidedly 'male' approach" (Erikson, 1963, p. 56). In her culture, such behavior was considered normal. However, Peter's mother, living in our culture, felt there was something wrong about Peter's sudden maleness and the way the nurse indulged it. So she got rid of the nurse. By way of explanation, the nurse told Peter that she was going to have a baby of her own, and that she preferred to care for babies, not big boys like Peter. Soon afterward, Peter developed the megacolon.

Erikson learned that Peter imagined that he himself was pregnant, a fantasy through which he tried to keep the nurse by identifying with her. But, more generally, we can see how Peter's behavior regressed in terms of stages. Initially, he had begun displaying the attacking, sexual behavior of the initiative stage, but he found that it led to a tragic loss. So he regressed to an anal mode. He was expressing, through his body, his central need: *to hold on*. When Erikson found the right moment, he interpreted Peter's wishes to him, and Peter's symptom was greatly alleviated.

Sometimes students, upon hearing of Peter's behavior, suggest that his symptom was a means of "getting attention." This interpretation is used frequently by the behaviorists. We note, however, that Erikson's approach was different. He was concerned with the meaning of the symptom for Peter, with what Peter was trying to express through it. Through his body, Peter was unconsciously trying to say, "I need to hold on to what I've lost." Erikson and other psychoanalysts believe that instead of changing a child's behavior through external reinforcements such as attention, it is best to speak to the child's fears and to what the child may be unconsciously trying to say.

Thoughts on Child-Rearing

Over the years, Erikson has applied clinical insights to many problems including those in education, ethics, and politics. He has also had a special interest in child-rearing.

As we briefly mentioned in our discussion of trust, Erikson is concerned with the problem facing parents in our changing society. American parents are often unable or unwilling simply to follow traditional child-rearing precepts; they would like to bring up their children in more personal, tolerant ways, based on new information and education (Erikson, 1959, p. 99). Unfortunately, modern child-rearing advice is often contradictory and frightens the new parent with its accounts of how things can go wrong. Consequently, the new parent is anxious and uncertain.

This is a serious problem, Erikson thinks, for, as we have seen, it is important that the parent convey to the child a basic security, a feeling that the world is a calm and secure place.

Erikson suggests that parents can derive some inner security from religious faith. Beyond this, he suggests that parents heed their fundamental "belief in the species" (1963, p. 267). By this, Erikson means something similar to Gesell. Parents should recognize that it is not all up to them to form the child: children largely grow according to an inner, maturational timetable. As Erikson says, "It is important to realize that . . . the healthy child, if halfway properly guided, merely obeys and on the whole can be trusted to obey inner laws of development . . ." (1963, p. 67). Thus, it is all right for parents to follow their inclination to smile when their baby smiles, make room for their child to walk when he or she tries to, and so on. They can feel secure that it is all right to follow the baby's own biological ground plan.

Erikson also hopes that parents can recognize the basic inequality between child and adult. The human child, in contrast to the young of other species, undergoes a much longer period of dependency and helplessness. Parents, therefore, must be careful to resist the temptation to take out their own frustrations on the weaker child. They must resist, for example, the impulse to dominate the child because they themselves feel helpless with others. Parents should also be careful to avoid trying to shape the child into the person they wanted to become, thereby ignoring the child's own capacities and inclinations. Erikson says, in conclusion, "If we will only learn to let live, the plan for growth is all there" (1959, p. 100).

References

Bandura, A. (1967). The role of modeling processes in personality development. In W. W. Hartup and W. L. Smothergill (Eds.), *The Young Child: Reviews of Research*. Washington, DC: National Association for the Education of Young Children.

———. (1986). *Social Foundations of Thought and Action: A Social Cognitive Theory*. Englewood Cliffs, NJ: Prentice Hall.

———, Grusec, J. E., and Menlove, F. L. (1967). Vicarious extinction of avoidance behavior. *Journal of Personality and Social Psychology, 5*, 16–23.

———, and McDonald, F. J. (1963). Influence of social reinforcement and the behavior of models in shaping children's moral judgments. *Journal of Abnormal and Social Psychology, 67*, 274–81.

———, and Walters, R. H. (1963). *Social Learning and Personality Development*. New York: Holt, Rinehart & Winston.

Bell, S. M. (1970). The development of the concept of object as related to infant-mother attachment. *Child Development, 41*, 291–311.

Colby, A., Kohlberg, L., and Kauffman, K. (1987a). Theoretical introduction to the measurement of moral judgment. In A. Colby and L. Kohlberg, *The Measurement of Moral Judgment* (Vol. I). Cambridge, England: Cambridge University Press.

———, Kohlberg, L. and Kauffman, K. (1987b). Instructions for moral judgment interviewing. In A. Colby and L. Kohlberg, *The Measurement of Moral Judgment* (Vol. I). Cambridge, England: Cambridge University Press.

———, Kohlberg, L., Speicher, B., Hewer, A., Candee, D., Gibbs, J., and Power, C. (1987c). *The Measurement of Moral Judgment* (Vol. II). Cambridge, England: Cambridge University Press.

Cole, M., and Cole, S. R. (1989). *The Development of Children*. New York: Scientific.

Erikson, E. H. (1959). Identity and the life cycle. *Psychological Issues, 1:* 1. New York: International Universities Press.

———. (1963). *Childhood and Society* (2nd ed.). New York: W. W. Norton & Co.

Flavell, J. H. (1963). *The Developmental Psychology of Jean Piaget*. New York: Van Nostrand Reinhold.

———. (1977). *Cognitive Development*. Englewood Cliffs, NJ: Prentice Hall.

Gardner, H. (1982). *Developmental Psychology: An Introduction* (2nd ed.). Boston: Little, Brown.

Gesell, A. (1945). *The Embryology of Behavior*. New York: Harper & Row, Pub.

———. (1946). The ontogenesis of infant behavior. In L. Carmichael (Ed.), *Manual of Child Psychology* (2nd ed.). New York: John Wiley, 1954.

———, and Ilg, F. L. (1943). *Infant and Child in the Culture of Today*. In A. Gesell, and F. L. Ilg, *Child Development*. New York: Harper & Row , Pub., 1949.

———, and Thompson, H. (1929). Learning and growth in identical infant twins: An experimental study by the method of co-twin control. *Genetic Psychology Monographs, 6,* 1–124.

Gilbert, S. F. (1988). *Developmental Biology* (2nd ed.). Sunderland, MA: Sinauer.

Ginsburg, H., and Opper, S. (1988). *Piaget's Theory of Intellectual Development* (3rd ed.). Englewood Cliffs, NJ: Prentice Hall.

Gouin-Décarie, T. (1965). *Intelligence and Affectivity in Early Childhood*. New York: International Universities Press.

Huston, A. C., Watkins, B. A., and Kunkel, D. (1989). Public policy and children's television. *American Psychologist, 44,* 424–33.

Inhelder, B., and Piaget, J. (1955). *The Growth of Logical Thinking from Childhood to Adolescence*. (A. Parsons and S. Milgram, trans.). New York: Basic Books, 1958.

Jones, M. C. (1924). A laboratory study of fear: The case of Peter. *Pedagogical Seminary, 31,* 308–15.

Kohlberg, L. (1958b). *Global Rating Guide with New Materials*. School of Education, Harvard University.

——— (1963). The development of children's orientations toward a moral order: I. Sequence in the development of moral thought. *Human Development, 6,* 11–33.

——— (1968). Early education: A cognitive-developmental approach. *Child Development, 39,* 1013-62.

——— (1969a). Stage and sequence: A cognitive-developmental approach to socialization. In D. A. Goslin (Ed.). *Handbook of Socialization Theory and Research*. Chicago: Rand McNally.

——— (1976). Moral stages and moralization: The cognitive-developmental approach. In T. Lickona (Ed.), *Moral Development and Behavior: Theory, Research, and Social Issues*. New York: Holt, Rinehart & Winston.

——— (1981). *Essays on Moral Development* (Vol. I). New York: Harper & Row.

———, and Gilligan, C. (1971). The adolescent as philosopher. *Daedalus, 100,* 1051–86.

Piaget, J. (1969). *Science of Education and the Psychology of the Child* (D. Coltman, trans.). New York: Viking, 1970.

Rawls, J. (1971). *A Theory of Justice*. Cambridge, MA: Harvard University Press.

Rest, J. (1973). The hierarchical nature of moral judgment: The study of patterns of preference and comprehension of moral judgments made by others. *Journal of Personality, 41,* 86–109.

Rosenthal, T. L. (1976). Modeling therapies. In M. Herson, R. M. Eisler, and P. M. Miller (Eds.), *Progress in Behavior Modification* (Vol. II). New York: Academic Press.

White, G. M. (1972). Immediate and deferred effects of model observation and guided and unguided rehearsal on donating and stealing. *Journal of Personality and Social Psychology, 21,* 139–48.

Seize the Day!

Haney, Sr. Regina, OSF. 1991. *Momentum* 22(2):6–8.

If the abundant energy of our young adolescents is to be positively directed, Catholic schools must invest in middle level programs.

The story takes place in the 1950s in a regimented boarding school in New England. A new faculty member enthusiastically challenges his senior high school English class to approach life from a new perspective. At first, he dramatizes this challenge by having each student stand on his desk to report what he sees from that point. Over time, the teacher leads the adolescents to the threshold of their own knowledge as they take his advice to "seize the day."

Anyone who has seen the movie *Dead Poets Society* will recognize this scenario.

This movie, along with the 1989 report of the Carnegie Council on Adolescent Development, *Turning Points*,[1] raised two crucial questions for me: What can I do to ensure that schools lead adolescents, particularly young adolescents, to the threshold of their own knowledge? How do I convince people that money invested in programs for these young persons is an investment for the future of church and society?

The Carnegie report reminds parents, the primary educators, and all teachers that they must be knowledgeable about the developmental stages of the young adolescent in order to effectively meet the needs of this age group. What are their needs?

Diversity.

All adolescents are not the same. Therefore, different adolescents need varied relationships with people, options for learning, and ample opportunities for personal reflection and self-exploration.

This diversity enables them to have a new sense of identity, a realistic matching of interests and opportunities to develop abilities for a future career, and a knowledge of appropriate sexual and social behavior.

Self-exploration and self-definition.

Young adolescents need to establish a sense of who they are and what they can do, incorporating not only their physical development and social status, but also their past, present and future.

They need time alone to cope with changes. At the same time, association with peers and adults is essential in order to test and talk about their personal concerns and ideas.

Meaningful participation.

As this age group becomes more independent and begins to think about other people and social problems, the individual wants to assume new responsibilities in school and in the community.

Positive social interaction.

Adolescents look to peers for companionship and criticism regarding new social roles. They need the sense of being liked which comes from positive social interaction. They also are observing adults whom they admire for examples of appropriate social and sexual behavior.

Physical activity.

Adolescents have a high level of energy which must be expended. This may be followed by a period of laziness. The energy relates to rapid physical growth, while fatigue may be the result of a preoccupation with emotional issues.

Competency and achievement.

Success is imperative for the young adolescent's sense of self-worth. An important part of establishing a sense of identity is finding out what one does well.

Structure and clear limits.

Adolescents are feeling their way. They need to know what is expected of them. They need the security provided by clear limits.

Appropriate curricula.

Older kids in the "same old setting" need to have a new school experience when they reach the middle grades. Therefore, educators must strive to provide curricula that recognize the middle level student's unique position in our K–eight Catholic schools.

By incorporating a course of study and teaching techniques that keep interest level high, classwork challenging and enthusiasm unlimited, the needs of young adolescents can be met in traditional Catholic school settings.

Knowledgeable and understanding educators.

One of the most vital aspects of a successful middle school program is a staff committed to effectively teaching the young adolescent. Educators must have open minds and a willingness to try innovative methods and different teaching styles. A great deal of planning and discussion among and between school personnel is required to develop and implement the necessary changes.

Integrated learning.

Young adolescents require teachers who are aware of their total needs rather than teachers skilled in specific content areas. This calls for team teaching. Team teachers need to meet at least weekly to support and motivate one another and to share ideas. The team sets yearly and short-term goals. At regularly scheduled meetings, all team members participate in discussions and in decision making.

In *Dead Poets Society*, the students were for the most part deprived of the opportunities for diversity, for self-exploration and self-definition, for meaningful participation in school and community, and for positive social interaction with adults.

Only one teacher knew and understood the developmental needs of the students. How moving it was to see students respond to that educator. It renewed my commitment to be such an educator, one who makes a significant difference in the lives of students.

The Carnegie report also revitalized my endeavors to continue to work with middle level students within Catholic education. *Turning Points: Preparing American Youth for the 21st Century* presents several recommendations for transforming these schools, among them:

◆   to create small communities for learning
◆   to emphasize critical thinking and community service
◆   to promote opportunities for cooperative learning and flexible instruction time
◆   to provide teacher in-service for understanding and working effectively with this age group[2]

During my tenure as the superintendent of schools for the Diocese of Raleigh, North Carolina, these recommendations were incorporated into the Catholic school system. I am certain that we wisely invested our dollars in a middle level program that has the potential to shape the future of our society. That diocesan investment contrasts powerfully with the state dollars spent in North Carolina in 1989 as the result of 18,478 offenses committed by juveniles (18% were violent crimes),[3] or to decrease the state's 6.6% dropout rate,[4] or in response to teen pregnancies, 16% of all births in the state.[5] The resources and energy we invest in young adolescents not only enable them to "seize the day," but also to confidently seek meaning within themselves and throughout our diverse society.

About the Author

Sister Regina, OSF, former superintendent of schools for the Diocese of Raleigh, North Carolina, is the executive director of the National Association of Boards of Education at NCEA. This article was written in cooperation with Sarah Almon, Carol Connelly, Mary Hogan and Judy Soyars, teachers in the Diocese of Raleigh.

Notes

1. Task Force on Education of Young Adolescents, *Turning Points: Preparing American Youth for the 21st Century*, Washington, DC, Carnegie Council on Adolescent Development, Carnegie Corporation of New York, June 1989.
2. Ibid.
3. *Annual Report of the Administration Office of the Courts*, North Carolina, 1989.
4. *Dropout Prevention Program: Students At Risk*, Division of Student Services, North Carolina Department of Public Instruction.
5. *North Carolina Reported Pregnancies*, 1989, Division of Statistics and Information Services, North Carolina Department of Environment, Health and Natural Resources.

Catechetics in the Catholic School

Hawker, J. 1985. 10–13. Washington, D.C.: National Catholic Educational Association.

The Stages of the Human Development of Children and Youth

A description of the characteristics of the child and young person may be structured in relation to the following levels: Primary (grades 1–3); Intermediate (grades 4–6); Junior High (grades 7–8); High School (grades 9–12).

The descriptions for each level are divided into four categories: intellectual, emotional, social, and moral. These descriptions are stereotypical, and may not apply to all students in all circumstances.

1. Primary Level

a. Intellectual

The child likes to be involved, active and doing. Curiosity is strong and imagination is lively. Unable to conceptualize, the child learns through the senses—needs to feel, touch, see, explore, manipulate—and is primarily interested in the world of the concrete. The child is able to repeat words, but doesn't always know their meaning. Although growing in the ability to distinguish between reality and fantasy, the child is interested in the magical and has a relatively short attention span. The gradual dawning of reason leads the child to question whether things are really true. The child slowly develops the faculty for reaching conclusions from observation and separate facts.

b. Emotional

The child is egocentric and self-centered and needs love, acceptance, security, and a sense of belonging. The child is emotionally responsive.

c. Social

The child is dependent upon the family and other adults. Parental guidance and support are essential. The child manifests a need to receive attention and gradually moves away from total dependence.

d. Moral/Faith

The child likes and needs structure and guidelines and matures in moral awareness and responsibility. Possessing the ability to marvel, the child has a sense of wonder.

2. Intermediate Level

a. Intellectual

While developing the power to think abstractly, the child is interested in the concrete and the real. Attention span is increasing, and interests are broadening. The child manifests intense curiosity and thirst for knowledge. The child likes to collect and clarify information, is better oriented to grasp a sense of history, questions and is willing to experiment.

b. Emotional

The child is entering a period of transition, begins to discard childish patterns and is growing in control and cultivating a sense of responsibility. Toward the end of this period, the child tends to be restless, sensitive, moody and begins to become conscious of sexual development and curious about the opposite sex.

c. Social

The child is increasingly independent of adults and more dependent on peers; friendships are important and the child needs opportunities for group sharing and cooperation. Dependable and loyal, the child has an acute sense of justice and fairness. Hero worship is common.

d. Moral/Faith

Conscience is developing and the child begins to appreciate the importance of intention in relation to actions. The child is legalistic; rules and regulations are important. The child has a greater sensitivity to others, a growing sense of responsibility and seeks to develop personal attitudes and values.

3. Junior High Level

a. Intellectual

The child manifests an increasing ability to think and reason. The child reaches for knowledge, generalizes, forms insights, appreciates symbols and the mind begins to probe and ponder. The child begins to develop a critical spirit. The power of making synthesis grows. Because of the ability to analyze, interpret and think in abstract terms, the child is interested in problems and discussions.

b. Emotional

The child is searching for a self-image during this period of confusion and change. Extremely concerned with self, the child tends to be insecure and insensitive.

c. Social

While the child desires the respect and understanding of adults, social involvement with the peer group is predominant and the standards of peers tend to be more important than those of the adult world. The child enters into close friendships with those of the same sex.

d. Moral/Faith

The child is interested in evaluating and integrating a new set of values and is growing in moral accountability. The child rejects childhood notions of God. A strong sense of social values is being cultivated.

4. High School Level

a. Intellectual

The young person is capable of deeper reasoning and understanding, can evaluate and analyze logically and needs to test, criticize and question. The ability to concentrate is growing in intensity and duration. The adolescent tends to vacillate between idealism and cynicism, and may make snap judgments.

b. Emotional

The young person is concerned with cultivating and expressing his or her self-image. The adolescent craves affection, acceptance, understanding, guidance, and needs to be secure, to belong, to be recognized, to achieve. The young person tends to be confused and insecure.

c. Social

The young person tends to be insecure about position in the peer group. The adolescent is more interested in the opposite sex, and is capable of sustaining interpersonal relationships. The young person needs significant adults.

d. Moral/Faith

The young person asks authentically religious questions and may experience a crisis of faith. The adolescent cultivates personal ideals and values, and may reject church laws and rules, viewed as impinging on freedom. The young person is concerned with social issues. Prayer tends to become more personal.

Sharing the Light of Faith:
National Catechetical Directory for Catholics of the United States

National Conference of Catholic Bishops. 1979. Nos. 173–75, 177–80.
Washington, D.C.: United States Catholic Conference.

Chapter VIII.[*]
Catechesis Toward Maturity in Faith

Part A. Faith and Human Development

173. The development character of the life of faith

Jesus's words, "You are my friends if you do what I command you" (Jn 15,14), point to the fact that the life of faith involves a relationship, a friendship, between persons. As the quality of a friendship between human beings is affected by such things as their maturity and freedom, their knowledge of each other, and the manner and frequency of their communication, so the quality of a friendship with God is affected by the characteristics of the human party. Because people are capable of continual development, so are their relationships with God. Essentially, development in faith is the process by which one's relationship with the Father becomes more like Jesus' (cf. Jn 14,6f): it means becoming more Christlike. This is not just a matter of subjective, psychological change, but involves establishing and nurturing a real relationship to Jesus and the Father in

the Holy Spirit, through a vigorous sacramental life, prayer, study, and serving others.

174. The relationship of growth in faith to human development

Because the life of faith is related to human development, it passes through stages or levels; furthermore, different people possess aspects of faith to different degrees. This is true, for example, of the comprehensiveness and intensity with which they accept God's word, of their ability to explain it, and of their ability to apply it to life.[1] Catechesis is meant to help at each stage of human development and lead ultimately to full identification with Jesus.

175. The role of the behavioral sciences

The Church encourages the use of biological, social, and psychological sciences in pastoral care.[2] "The catechetical movement will in no way be able to advance without scientific study."[3] Manuals for catechesis should take into account psychological and pedagogical insights, as well as suggestions about methods.[4]

The behavioral sciences cause neither faith nor growth in faith; but for that matter, neither does the catechist.

---

* Editor's note: Chapter notation refers to this excerpt.

The behavioral sciences cause neither faith nor growth in faith; but for that matter, neither does the catechist. Faith is from God: "This is not your own doing, it is God's gift." (Eph 2,8)

These sciences do, however, help us understand how people grow in their capacity for responding in faith to God's grace. They can, therefore, make a significant contribution to catechesis. At the same time, catechists should not be uncritical in their approach to these sciences, in which new discoveries are constantly being made while old theories are frequently modified or even discarded. There are different schools of psychology and sociology which do not agree in all respects; nor are all developments of equal merit. Catechists should not imagine that any one school or theory has all the answers. Finally, behavioral sciences do not supply the doctrinal and moral content of catechetical programs. Their discoveries and developments must be constantly and carefully evaluated by competent persons before being integrated into catechetics.

The framework used here to describe the stages of human development is one of a number that could be used. Other models offer valuable insights. One's understanding of catechesis should not be linked exclusively to a single explanation of the stages of human development and its implications for growth in faith.

Part B. Catechesis and Human Development

Section I: The Stages of Human Development

177. Infancy and early childhood (birth to age 5)[8]

Life's beginning stages are of critical importance to individual growth and development. Here foundations are laid which influence the ability to accept self, relate to others, and respond effectively to the environment. Upon these foundations rests the formation of the basic human and Christian personality—and so also one's human capacity for relating to God.

Healthy growth is most likely in a positive, nurturing environment—normally, the immediate family. Family relationships and interaction provide young children with their most powerful models for developing attitudes, values, and ways of responding to external influences which foster or hinder Christian and human growth.

God's love is communicated to infants and young children primarily through parents. Their faith, their confidence in human potential, and their loving and trusting attitude toward God and human beings strongly influence the child's faith. Parents are best prepared for this role by prior education for parenthood and by prenatal and prebaptismal catechesis concerning the religious upbringing of children. During this stage in the lives of children, catechesis is directed primarily to their parents, to help them in their task. This also contributes to strengthening the conjugal bond and deepening their Christian commitment.

Parents and others in intimate contact with infants and small children should speak naturally and simply about God and their faith, as they do about other matters they want the children to understand and appreciate. Catechesis for prayer, accommodated to age and understanding, is part of this religious formation; it encourages the child to call upon God who loves and protects us, upon Jesus, God's Son and our brother, who leads us to the Father, and upon the Holy Spirit who dwells in our hearts. The child is also encouraged to pray to Mary, Jesus' mother and ours, and to the saints.[9] Parental example, including the practice of prayer, is particularly important.

Catechetical programs for preschool children seek to foster their growth in a wider faith community. While they should build upon and reinforce everything positive in the family and home environment, they can also be of particular importance for children who lack certain opportunities at home, children in one-parent families, and those whose parents do not spend much time with them, either because they both work outside the home or for some other reason.

Early childhood catechetical programs allow 3- to 5-year-olds to develop at their own pace, in ways suited to their age, circumstances, and learning abilities. They encourage appropriate attitudes toward worship and provide occasions of natural celebration with other children and adults, including religious and clergy. They seek, by deepening the child's sense of wonder and awe, to develop the capacity for spontaneous prayer and prayerful silence.

In formal catechetical programs for young children, groups should be small and at least one adult should work with the children of each level. The staff should be composed of parents and other adults, and should include persons with training in such areas as theology, scripture, early childhood growth and development, and methodology.

The learning of young children can also be fostered through coordinated courses for the entire family, which help parents become active, confident, and competent in encouraging their children's emerging faith.

178. Childhood (ages 6–10)

Emotional development at this age is mainly a matter of growing in the capacity for satisfactory relationships with a wider circle of children and adults. Self-acceptance, trust, and personal freedom undergo significant changes, with acceptance of self coming to involve an awareness of specific talents (or their absence), unqualified trust of others giving way to a qualified trust which excludes some people and situations, and the expression of personal freedom being modified by recognition that other people, too, have rights and freedom.

Intellectual capacity gradually expands. Before, the world was viewed in very concrete terms drawn from direct personal experiences; now, the ability to form abstract ideas or concepts based on experience increases.

Catechesis calls attention to God's self-revelation and His invitation to us to be His children and friends; it points out that the revelation, the invitation, and the capacity to respond are all supernatural gifts. How children understand these realities still depends largely on analogous experiences in their relationships with other people. But "other people" now include a community much larger than the immediate family, notably the community to which children are exposed through media, particularly television which occupies so much of most children's time. TV should be evaluated in relation not only to the behavior it may encourage but that which it prevents—for instance, conversations, games, family festivities, and other activities which foster learning and character development.

The immediate environment, normally the home, remains the principal setting in which children experience a relationship with God. But now the support of the larger community becomes highly important to education in the faith, and its absence a more serious matter. Children accustomed to seeing others give witness to their faith are more likely to be ready for a fuller, more systematic presentation of concepts, forms of liturgical expression, and religious practices.

The child's first serious experience of work, usually in school, is relevant to catechesis. It serves as an introduction to values important in both the secular and religious spheres of life: the joy of doing things well, cooperation with others, and discipline experienced as something understandable and reasonable.[10]

Catechesis seeks to help children make an increasingly personal response to God's word and gifts. This response is not just a matter of external expressions, however useful they may be, but is truly heartfelt and prayerful. Catechesis approaches young persons with reverence and aids them in discovering and developing their unique, God-given gifts with the help of the gospel.

In presenting the values and teachings of Jesus, catechesis takes note of children's experience and encourages them to apply the same teachings and values to their lives.

At this stage significant changes occur in the ability to learn and understand. Certain prayer formulas become more intelligible. Stories like the parables take on deeper meaning. Practices like sharing and helping others make a great deal more sense. Memorization can be used very effectively, provided the child has a clear understanding of what is memorized and it is expressed in familiar language.

In the Western Church and in most Eastern Churches in the United States, catechesis is ordinarily provided at this stage for the sacraments of Reconciliation and Eucharist. Preparation for the reception of these sacraments is discussed in articles 122 and 126.

179. Pre-adolescence and puberty (ages 10–13)

Important physical changes have a direct bearing on how pre-adolescents perceive other people and relate to them. Young people at this stage face the task of coming to terms with themselves and others as sexual beings. While the foundations for doing so are laid in infancy, the effort now becomes conscious. They need to accept themselves precisely as male or female and to acquire a whole new way of relating to others. Usually, too, this involves some confusion, uncertainty, curiosity, awkwardness, and experimentation, as young people "try on" different patterns of behavior while searching for their unique identity. Puberty also adds a new dimension to the practice of personal freedom: increased responsibility for directing one's actions, together with increased readiness to accept their consequences.

Now more than ever interests extend beyond the home to the peer group, which exercises an increasing influence on attitudes, values, and behavior. Sensitivity toward others is growing, and efforts to develop a sense of community and of membership in the Church should continue.

While each child develops at his or her own rate, girls are generally more advanced than boys of the same age. The characteristics typical of this stage will be more or less intense according to an individual's physical and emotional attributes, home influences, previous experiences, and cultural background.

Catechesis should make use of all aspects of the pre-adolescent's experience, including the needs generated by rapid, radical change. The example of living faith given by others—at home and in the larger community—remains highly important and catechetically effective.

Topics like the nature of scripture, the Church, the sacraments, and the reasons which underlie moral norms can be discussed in greater depth than before. Reading and lectures can be used more effectively. But the life of faith is still best presented through concrete experiences which afford the pre-adolescent opportunities to incorporate Christian values into his or her life. These experiences are a point of departure for presenting the deeper aspects of the faith and its mysteries. Audio-visuals, projects, and field trips can be effective catechetical tools for this purpose. This is the age of hero worship, and it is helpful to present—in a manner which appeals to contemporary youth—the lives and deeds of the saints and other outstanding persons,[11] and especially the words and example of Jesus.

Growing more aware of themselves as individuals, pre-adolescents become better able to experience faith as a personal relationship with God. Prayer and service to others can become more meaningful. However, while it is possible for pre-adolescents, with the help of grace, to commit themselves to God, their faith is not that of fully mature persons.

Participation in the Mass, sacraments, and other rituals of the adult community can also become more meaningful. Young people can take a greater part in planning, preparing, and celebrating the liturgy.

As the sense of personal responsibility for behavior comes into sharper focus, specific Christian principles of conduct become more important, and the Sacrament of Reconciliation takes on deeper meaning.

Crises of faith, particularly relating to identification with the Church, occur among some pre-adolescents today. It is therefore extremely important that catechists with appropriate theoretical and practical expertise design catechetical programs which anticipate and ease such crises.

180. Adolescence

a) No specific age bracket

There are generally accepted age brackets for earlier stages, but not for adolescence. Different cultural, racial, and ethnic groups have their own standards for determining the length of time between puberty and adulthood.

b) Development of conscious spiritual life

The transition from childhood can be marked by an experience of emptiness. The self-awareness, relationship with others, sense of personal freedom, and intellectual understanding of reality achieved in childhood no longer suffice, but there is often nothing at hand to take their place. Now—and later, too—many have profound lack of self-confidence, magnified by life's complexity and ambiguity. The Church's ministry of service and healing richly equips it to respond to their need for interior reconciliation.

Interior turmoil and self-doubt are often expressed in external symptoms popularly associated with adolescence: boredom, frustration, sharp changes in mood, withdrawal, rebelliousness, apathy toward religion. Adolescents should be encouraged to understand that these symptoms are typical of many maturing persons and to be patient with themselves even while seeking to acquire the skills which will enable them to deal with their problems. Unfortunately, at precisely this time many experience difficulty in articulating their feelings, particularly to their parents.

Yet adolescents also commonly manifest increasing spiritual insight into themselves, other people, and life in general. A growing self-awareness and self-acceptance and a resultant greater capacity for authentic love of others begin to emerge, as well as increasing ability to respond with a mature faith.

A new sense of responsibility matching their expanded capacity for independent action often leads adolescents to reject, or seem to reject, laws and rules which they regard as arbitrary, external restrictions on their personal freedom. Many substitute a kind of inner law or norm of behavior based on personal ideals.

As idealism grows, so does the desire for continuous growth, even perfection, in the life of faith—or at least the ability to appreciate its value. Adolescents are increasingly critical of real or imagined imperfections in the Church and the adult faith community. The example of the adult community is extremely important at this time, although the direct influence of family and parents generally declines. For good or evil, peers exert the strongest influence of all; thus the need for developing strong youth ministry programs. School and media, especially television, also exert strong influences.

As they become more intellectually competent, adolescents need more intellectual stimulation and growth. At this time catechesis seeks to make clear the inner coherence of the truths of faith, their relation to one another and to humanity's final end. Careful attention must be given to the rational bases for faith; the intellectual investigation and articulation of religious belief are not "merely a kind of addition," but should be "counted as an essential need for the life of faith."[12] Appropriate experiences, involving participation by adolescents, provide a context in which doctrine can be systematically presented and reflected upon most effectively.

While the foundations of vocations—to marriage, the single life, priesthood and religious life, etc.—are laid and nurtured from early childhood on, vocational choices are imminent in adolescence. Now is the time to address the question directly and study the possibilities open to individuals, taking into account such things as youthful idealism, God's call, and the grace of the Holy Spirit. Catechists should be aware, however, that more and more young people are today delaying vocational and career choices until later in life.

Private prayer tends to become more personal and reflective now, while ritualized prayer often loses its attraction. Young people who see no point to prayer and meditation should be introduced—or reintroduced—to the idea that it is personal communication with Jesus and, through and in Him, with the Father. This can help make prayer an attractive reality in their lives. Prayer in all forms should be an integral and appealing part of catechesis for this age group.

Most people pass through adolescence during their teens, but in some cases the transition is delayed. The awakening of a conscious spiritual life is normally an impetus to move to the next stage of development, adulthood.

Notes

1. Cf. *General Catechetical Directory*, 30, 38.
2. For the use of the social and psychological sciences in pastoral care, cf. Modern World, 52, 62.
3. GCD, 131; cf. Christian Education, 1.
4. Cf. GCD, 121.
8. Cf. *Ibid.*, 78.
9. Cf. *Ibid.*
10. Cf. *Ibid.*, 79.
11. Cf. *Ibid.*, 83.
12. *Ibid.*, 88.

Multicultural Education: Characteristics and Goals

Banks, James A. 1989. In *Multicultural education: Issues and perspectives*,
eds. J. A. Banks and C. M. Banks, 2–3, 19–23. Boston: Allyn and Bacon.

The Nature of Multicultural Education

Multicultural education is at least three things: an idea or concept, an educational reform movement, and a process. Multicultural education incorporates the idea that all students—regardless of their gender and social class, and their ethnic, racial, or cultural characteristics—should have an equal opportunity to learn in school. Another important idea in multicultural education is that some students, because of these characteristics, have a better chance to learn in schools as they are currently structured than do students who belong to other groups or have different cultural characteristics.

Some institutional characteristics of schools systematically deny some groups of students equal educational opportunities. For example, in the early grades, girls and boys achieve equally in mathematics and science. However, the achievement test scores of girls fall considerably behind those of boys as children progress through the grades.[1] Girls are less likely than boys to participate in class discussions and to be encouraged by teachers to participate. Girls are more likely than boys to be silent in the classroom. However, not all school practices favor males. As Sadker, Sadker, and Long point out in Chapter 6, boys are more likely to be disciplined than are girls, even when their behavior does not differ from the girls'. They are also more likely than girls to be classified as learning disabled. Ethnic minority males, especially Afro-American males, experience a highly disproportionate rate of disciplinary actions and suspensions in school. Some writers have described the situation of black males as a "crisis" and have called them "endangered" in U.S. society.[2]

In the early grades, the academic achievement of such ethnic minorities as Afro-Americans, Hispanics, and American Indians is close to parity with the achievement of White mainstream students. However, the longer these ethnic minority students remain in school, the more their achievement lags behind that of White mainstream students. Social-class status is also strongly related to academic achievement. Persell, in Chapter 4, describes how students from the middle and upper classes are treated more positively in schools than are lower-class students and are given a better chance to learn. Exceptional students, whether they are physically or mentally disabled or gifted and talented, often find that they do not experience equal educational opportunities in the schools. The chapters in Part V of this book describe the problems that such exceptional students experience in schools and suggest ways that

teachers and other educators can increase their chances for educational success.

Multicultural education is also a reform movement that is trying to change the schools and other educational institutions so that students from all social-class, gender, racial, and cultural groups will have an equal opportunity to learn. Multicultural education involves changes in the total school or educational environment: it is not limited to curricular changes. The variables in the school environment that multicultural education tries to transform are identified and discussed later in this chapter (see Figure 1.4).

Multicultural education is also a process whose goals will never be fully realized. Educational equality, like liberty and justice, are ideals toward which human beings work but never fully attain. Racism, sexism, and handicapism will exist to some extent no matter how hard we work to eliminate these problems. When prejudice and discrimination are reduced toward one group, they are usually directed toward another group or they take new forms. Because the goals of multicultural education can never be fully attained, we should work continually to increase educational equality for all students.

Multicultural education must be viewed as an ongoing process, and not as something that we "do" and thereby solve the problems that are the targets of multicultural educational reform. When I asked one school administrator what efforts were being taken to implement multicultural education in his school district he told me that the district had "done" multicultural education last year and that it was now initiating other reforms, such as improving the students' reading scores. This administrator not only misunderstood the nature and scope of multicultural education, but he also did not understand that it could help raise the students' reading scores. A major goal of multicultural education is to improve academic achievement.

The Goals of Multicultural Education

I have discussed the goals of multicultural education throughout this chapter, *the major goal being to transform the school so that male and female students, exceptional students, as well as students from diverse cultural, social-class, racial, and ethnic groups will experience an equal opportunity to learn in school.* Thus, an important goal of multicultural education is to increase the academic achievement of all students. A major assumption of multicultural education is that educators can increase the academic achievement of students from diverse groups if they transform the total school environment and make it more consistent with their cultures, behaviors, and learning styles.

Another major goal of multicultural education is to help all students develop more positive attitudes toward different cultural, racial, ethnic, and religious groups.[46] Researchers have documented the negative attitudes, beliefs, and stereotypes that students have about various groups. Students acquire their attitudes about various groups from people among whom they are socialized and from the mass media. Cortés calls these institutions the "societal curriculum."[47] Children enter kindergarten with many misconceptions, negative beliefs, and stereotypes about people. If the school does not help students develop more positive attitudes about various groups, they will become even more negative as they grow older. Consequently, the school should take steps to help students develop more democratic cultural, ethnic, and racial attitudes, beginning in the earliest grades. Such prejudice-reduction strategies should be consistent, ongoing and an integral part of the school curriculum.[48] They should not be one-shot interventions that are reserved for special days or for celebrations such as Women's History Week or Black History Month.

Negative misconceptions about groups harm both members of those groups and people outside them. Many women, ethnic minorities, and disabled persons have internalized the negative stereotypes of themselves perpetuated by the larger society. Consequently, they often develop a low self-concept and other characteristics that prevent them from realizing their potentials. Researchers have described how fear of success in women students often prevents them from experiencing high levels of academic success, particularly in such areas as science and mathematics,[49] in which many women tend to have less confidence. Teachers often reinforce this attitude by giving boys more positive feedback in these courses than they give girls. Negative views of groups also harm individuals outside the groups because they develop a false and misleading sense of superiority.

Multicultural education should help empower students from victimized groups and help them develop confidence in their ability to succeed academically and to influence social, political, and economic institutions. Women, ethnic minorities, and people from other victimized groups often lack a sense of control over their environments, are external in orientation, and lack a sense of political and social efficacy. In his massive study in 1966, Coleman found that a sense of control over one's environment is one of the most important correlates of academic success.[50] Schools can help members of marginalized groups become empowered by providing them with opportunities to experience success, by recognizing and giving visibility to their cultures throughout the school, and by teaching them decision-making and social action skills. I describe these skills and ways to teach them in Chapter 10.

Multicultural education should help students to develop perspective-taking skills and to consider the perspectives of different groups. Most of the concepts, events, and issues taught in the school are from the perspective of mainstream middle- and upper-class White males. Students are rarely given the opportunity to view them from the perspectives of women, disabled persons, lower class people, and ethnic minority groups. Consequently, students gain only a limited conception of the development of the nation and the world. When students are able to view the world from the perspectives of different groups, their views of reality are broadened and they gain important insights into their own behavior. We gain a better view of ourselves when we look at ourselves from the perspectives of other cultures. Students can view a concept such as institutionalized discrimination from the perspectives of several groups and examine how it is manifested in various ways as sexism, racism, and handicapism.

The School as a Social System

To implement multicultural education successfully, we must think of the school as a social system in which all of its major variables are closely interrelated. Thinking of the school as a social system suggests that we must formulate and initiate a change strategy that reforms the total school environment to implement multicultural education. The major school variables that must be reformed are presented in Figure 1.4.

Reforming any one of the variables in Figure 1.4, such as the formalized curriculum or curricular materials, is necessary but not sufficient. Multicultural and sensitive teaching materials are ineffective in the hands of teachers who have negative attitudes toward different cultural groups. Such teachers are rarely likely to use multicultural materials or to use them detrimentally. Thus, helping teachers and other members of the school staff gain knowledge about cultural groups and democratic attitudes and values is essential when implementing multicultural programs.

To implement multicultural education in a school, we must reform its power relationships, the verbal interaction between teachers and students, the culture of the school, the curriculum, extracurricular activities, attitudes toward minority languages, the testing program, and grouping practices. The institutional norms, social structures, cause-belief statements, values, and goals of the school must be transformed and reconstructed.

Major attention should be focused on the school's hidden curriculum and its implicit norms and values. A school has both a manifest and a hidden curriculum. The manifest curriculum consists of such factors as guides, textbooks, bulletin boards, and lesson plans. These aspects of the school environment are important and must be reformed to create a school culture that promotes positive attitudes toward diverse cultural groups and helps students from these groups experience academic success. However, the school's hidden or latent curriculum is often more cogent than its manifest or overt curriculum. The latent curriculum has been defined as the one that no teacher explicitly teaches but that all students learn. It is that powerful part of the school culture that communicates to students the school's attitudes toward a range of issues and problems including how the school views them as human

Figure 1.4 The School as a Social System.

The total school environment is a system consisting of a number of major identifiable variables and factors, such as a school culture, school policy and politics, and the formalized curriculum and course of study. Any of these factors may be the focus of initial school reform, but changes must take place in each of them to create and sustain an effective multicultural school environment.

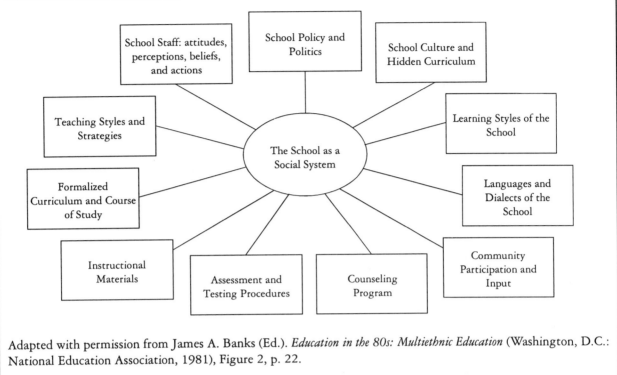

Adapted with permission from James A. Banks (Ed.). *Education in the 80s: Multiethnic Education* (Washington, D.C.: National Education Association, 1981), Figure 2, p. 22.

beings and its attitudes toward males, females, exceptional students, and students from various religious cultural, racial, and ethnic groups.

When formulating plans for multicultural education, educators should conceptualize the school as a microculture that has norms, values, statuses, and goals like other social systems. The school has a dominant culture and a variety of microcultures. Almost all classrooms in the United States are multicultural because White students, as well as Black and Brown students, are socialized within diverse cultures. Teachers also come from many different groups. Many teachers were socialized in cultures other than the Anglo mainstream, although these may be forgotten and repressed. Teachers can get in touch with their own cultures and use the perspectives and insights they acquired as vehicles for helping them relate to and understand the cultures of their students.

The school should be a cultural environment in which acculturation takes place: teachers and students should assimilate some of the views, perspectives, and ethos of each other as they interact. Teachers and students will be enriched by this process, and the academic achievement of students from diverse groups will be enhanced because their perspectives will be legitimized in the school. Both teachers and students will be enriched by this process of cultural sharing and interaction.

Summary

Multicultural education is an idea stating that all students, regardless of the groups to which they belong, such as those related to gender, ethnicity, race, culture, social class, religion, or exceptionality, should experience educational equality in the schools. Some students, because of their particular characteristics, have a better chance to succeed in school as it is currently structured than have students from other groups. Multicultural education is also a reform movement designed to bring about a transformation of the school so that students from both genders and from diverse cultural and ethnic groups will have an equal chance to experience school success. Multicultural education views the school as a social system that consists of highly interrelated parts and variables. Therefore, to transform the school to bring about educational equality, all the major components of the school must be substantially changed. A focus on any one variable in the school, such as the formalized curriculum, will not implement multicultural education.

Multicultural education is a continuing process because the idealized goals it tries to actualize—such as educational equality and the eradication of all forms of discrimination—can never be fully achieved in a human society. Multicultural education, which was born during the social protest of the 1960s and 1970s, is an international movement that exists in various nations on the European continent and in Australia, the United Kingdom, and Canada. A major goal of multicultural education is to help students to develop the knowledge, attitudes, and skills needed to function within their own microcultures, the U.S. macroculture, other microcultures, and within the global community.

Notes

1. Myra P. Sadker and David M. Sadker, *Sex Equity Handbook for Schools* (New York: Longman, 1982).
2. Jewelle Taylor Gibbs, ed., *Young, Black, and Male in America: An Endangered Species* (Dover, Mass.: Auburn House Publishing, 1988).
46. Stephen J. Gould, *The Mismeasurement of Man* (New York: Norton, 1981).
47. Neil Davidson, ed., *Cooperative Learning in Mathematics: A Handbook for Teachers* (Menlo Park, Calif.: Addison-Wesley, 1990).

The People: Reflections of Native Peoples on the Catholic Experience in North America

Hall, S., ed. 1992. 73–78. Washington, D.C.: National Catholic Educational Association.

Practical Helps for Teachers

Our first task in approaching another people, another culture, another religion, is to take off our shoes, for the place we are approaching is holy. Else we may find ourselves treading on another's dream. More serious still, we may forget . . . that God was there before our arrival.

Guidelines for Cultural Sensitivity with Native Americans

North American society provides a multicultural context for the experience of the Roman Catholic Church.

◆ Assimilation is no longer the guiding principle among the various racial, ethnic and national groups in our society.

◆ The preservation and practice of one's own culture, traditions and languages are of primary value.

◆ North American society is a blend of various groups: each maintaining its own identity while producing a North American tapestry.

◆ Native Americans hold a unique place in this tapestry as the original inhabitants of this land.

◆ While Native Americans are a minority, their cultures, languages and traditions have equal value with other racial/ethnic groups in a multicultural society.

The value and integrity of all racial, ethnic and cultural groups must be respected. North American society is not the assimilation of all groups into one, but the experience of a community of communities.

Native Americans are diverse in their own cultures and traditions.

◆ The primary identification of Native Americans is with their village, tribe or nation.

◆ North of the Rio Grande, there are over 300 extant Native languages and cultures.

◆ The cultural differences among Native Americans are as diverse as among other cultural groups, such as Asians and Europeans.

Native peoples must be viewed through their own cultural tapestry. Programs must avoid an attempt to present a monocultural understanding of Native Americans.

Native Americans have had a variety of experiences of European contact.

◆ Some Native Americans had their initial European contact almost 500 years ago. Others have had substantial contact only in the last 150 years.

◆ The experience of European contact varied, partially because of the different European groups (English, French, Spanish, Russian) and their different approaches to colonization.

◆ A number of Native American peoples had their primary European contacts with Americans of European descent who no longer considered themselves to be immigrants.

◆ The experience of initial conversion to Catholic Christianity ranges from over 400 years to less than 100 years.

The variety of Native American histories with Europeans needs to be taken into account in programs and policies.

Native Americans have a diversity of experiences of living in a multicultural society.

◆ Some Native Americans live among their own people on their own land (reservations).

◆ Some Native Americans have grown up on their reservations and have migrated to an urban setting. For most, this is a real and dramatic experience of immigration.

◆ Many urban Native Americans (who constitute at least half of the Native population) maintain some contact with their cultures through Native centers and/or visits to their reservations.

◆ In urban areas, there will be Native Americans who are native to the area and others who have migrated there from other parts of North America.

◆ Not all Native Americans have reservations. Some urban Natives belong to landless tribes. Their primary community is the multicultural urban experience of North American society.

The variety of reasons why Native Americans live where they do in our society needs to be understood and appreciated. Programs need to reflect their pluralistic experience.

Native Americans have a variety of experiences in regard to their own culture and to the dominant North American culture.

◆ After European contact, a number of Native American tribes lost their cultures and languages through the destruction of their villages. Some tribes disappeared while others continued with a few survivors.

◆ Through the experience of Christian missionization, some Native Americans lost their own culture and language and adopted European ones.

◆ Some Native Americans maintained two strictly divided cultural lives: one for the village or reservation and the other for the larger society and often for the church.

◆ Some Native Americans lost their culture and language because of the governmental assimilation efforts of previous years.

◆ Presently, a revival of Native cultures, traditions and languages is occurring. Many are regaining their culture.

The many diverse ways in which Native Americans relate to their own societies and to North American society must be appreciated in any program.

Native Americans continue to experience racial stereotyping and racism.

◆ Through centuries of contact, certain stereotypes have developed around Native Americans. The media has played a significant role in dispersing and supporting these stereotypes.

◆ Native Americans experience among themselves various forms of racism through tribal prejudices.

◆ Due to the experience of reservations, Native peoples have known the experience of forced segregation. The reservation system developed as a consequence of the Native people being a conquered people.

◆ Some Native Americans mistrust the institutions of the dominant culture, e.g., governmental agencies, church.

The reality of centuries of prejudice, racial stereotypes and racism needs to be acknowledged. Programs need to

develop and support trusting relationships between Native Americans and the larger North American society.

Among Native Americans, the understanding of relationships provides some shared elements, as well as a means to embrace them in a pluralistic society.

◆ Native Americans arrive at their self-identity through the various relationships in which they share.

◆ How Native Americans experience these primary relationships will help in understanding a particular group. These relationships are with word, time, land and all creatures.

◆ Native Americans view themselves as living through these relationships in a sacred and spiritual world.

Programs need to appreciate the deeply spiritual world of Native Americans. An understanding of Native peoples' primary relationship will be of help in this area.

Native Americans experience relationships through words.

◆ The spoken word has a higher value than the written word. The use of story has primary importance; through the telling of one's tribe's stories, the people are given and sustained in life.

◆ The speaker's personal integrity gives credence and value to the words he or she speaks.

◆ The value of words lessens with their quantity. Some Native Americans may appear reticent when, in fact, they are respecting the value of the conversation.

◆ Silence has an intrinsic value. It is important to spend time in silence with people.

Any program must appreciate the Native relationship with word and must rely more on the spoken word than on the written word.

Native Americans experience relationships with time.

◆ The primary understanding of time is how it relates to the days, months, seasons of the world. Time is the expression of one's unity and harmony with the world.

◆ While the understanding of time by hours and minutes used in the dominant society has importance, it is secondary to the Native understanding of time.

◆ Through the use of ritual, one can place oneself in greater harmony with the rhythm of the world. History is not seen as linear but rather as cyclical; it reflects the movement of the world, of the seasons.

◆ Through respect for one's elders, this appreciation of one's history is reflected. The elders carry in their bodies the traditions and values of the people.

The Native understanding of time needs to be appreciated to avoid confusion. History is not viewed as a chronicle of past events but rather a reflection of living with the universe.

Native Americans experience relationships with the land.

◆ Native Americans view the world on which we live as mother earth, the giver and sustainer of our life.

◆ The land has a unique relationship with Native peoples. The sense of ownership differs. Native people do not "own" the land, but they and the land belong to one another.

◆ Native Americans view their relationship with the land as characterized by care, for our mother earth makes us who we are.

The unique Native relationship with the land needs to be reflected in any program. This relationship is characterized by mutual love and respect.

Native Americans experience relationships with all living creatures.

◆ All life is sacred and shared by all living creatures.

◆ No one form of life has a greater intrinsic value than another since all creatures form one family and share one common life.

◆ By living in harmony with all creatures, humans can live the life for which the Creator made them.

The Native understanding of life needs to be reflected in programs. The Creator's creatures share a common life.

Native Americans have a diverse cultural experience which is deeply spiritual.

◆ Native American culture is a spiritual one.

◆ In the faith expression of Native Americans, Catholic Christianity needs to be enculturated in the Native traditions and cultures. Otherwise, the adoption of Catholic Christianity would mean the loss of one's culture.

◆ Native spirituality and Catholic Christianity are compatible with one another.

Catholic Christianity needs to be enculturated in the various Native traditions and cultures, which are deeply spiritual. Such an approach reflects the acceptance of the pluralistic world in which we live.

Pedagogical Way of Entering Into and Sharing Native American Cultures

Use oral tradition, primarily storytelling, as the vehicle of instruction. This is a natural, exciting and memorable way.

Experience realities through personal presence in the family, tribe and sacred ceremonies as the ordinary manner of learning. This is the best way to come to know the people and to form friendships.

Understand that traditional ways require leaders to give instructions. These leaders will let one know what and when to do things.

Respect older people teaching younger people. This is countercultural but needs to be maintained and restored.

Know that every culture has its etiquette in communication. It is necessary to know and respect the differences.

Take advantage of clear pictorial expressions which communicate best.

Abstractions and theory may cloud the teachings.

Remember Native peoples live in a close relationship with the Creator. A religion of words alone is foreign to the people.

Catechize in such a way as to reflect the values, traditions and customs of the tribes. This comes easily out of gospel values.

Take time to listen to the elders (men and women) of the tribes to relearn, rediscover, reinforce their values. These are strengths which will be handed down to the next generation.

Seek out the tribes' storytellers and learn their history, traditions and customs. This is a source of pride for the people.

Study and pray the Scriptures. This deepens the faith experience in relation to tribal history.

Explore spiritual insights God has given to the tribes. Ask what Christian teachings can be added or developed.

Integrate cultural values into religious education programs. This catechesis offers new experiences for the tribes as well as for the missionaries.

Turn to the gifts of creation as easy meditation for tribal people. Use them as tools for family gatherings.

Stress and affirm the following Native traditions. Awake to creation, reverence, respect, generosity. Challenge what seems to deny the best in them: harshness toward and neglect of children, choosing the way of noise and speed, and not passing on the most sacred values. This affirmation has helped others to be sensitive and to listen, no matter what the environment. This will make it possible for catechesis to happen.

Suggestions for a Native American Liturgy

◆ Conduct in the language and culture of the people.
◆ Base on the seasons and events important to the life of the people.

- ◆ Incorporate Native American symbolism, art and music in a meaningful way.
- ◆ Freely express their own faith in God.
- ◆ Celebrate the community's love for the Creator.
- ◆ Involve diverse forms for differing occasions.
- ◆ Include an intertribal sharing or liturgical experiences and experiments.
- ◆ Promote total Native American participation in preparation and planning of liturgies.
- ◆ Incorporate Native American prayer forms and customs approved by the people.
- ◆ Come from a catechized people (elders, etc.).
- ◆ Call for additional ministerial roles and affirm the gifts of the people.

- ◆ Express the identity of the people in Christ.
- ◆ Stress preaching (homilies) that forms the people in the Word of God.
- ◆ Clearly identify with Catholic worship.
- ◆ Allow for spontaneity.

Helps with Symbols and Sacred Ceremonies

The Native American world is one of meaningful symbols which help to encounter God, Creator, Great Spirit. Symbols and ceremonies express and present meaning which helps to provide purpose and understanding in the lives of human beings.

A Catholic Response to the Asian Presence

Hall, S., R. Doyle, and P. Tran, eds. 1990. 85–91. Washington, D.C.: National Catholic Educational Association.

Educational Considerations

A fundamental goal of Catholic educational institutions is to provide quality education and equality of opportunity. In spite of this altruistic purpose, however, many ethnic groups have suffered as a result of the assimilationist philosophy which equates equality with a systematic absorption into the dominant culture.

Assimilationist education often encourages one pattern of behavior commonly accepted by the majority and one distinct language and style pertinent to that particular culture. The goal of assimilationist education is to provide a mechanism for socializing immigrants and lower class students. Its symbol is the "melting pot" which suggests a single, all-embracing culture.

Schools with a multi-ethnic population and an assimilationist philosophy tend to have lower levels of educational achievement due to some students' poor self-esteem and others' negative attitudes toward their own cultural group. In such schools teachers are more inclined to blame the students for their failure. Furthermore, ethnic gangs, negative stereotyping, school evasion, vandalism and antisocial behavior easily develop.

In recent years we have been witnessing an increasing concern for the implementation of a different approach to education, that of cultural pluralism. This stresses the integration of cultural values and customs not only in the school's stated goals and objectives, but also in all aspects of school life.

Multicultural education, as opposed to assimilationist education, is a process whereby cultural behavior and cultural differences are regarded as teaching and learning tools, used to create a fair system that may ensure all students an equal chance to acquire social, academic, and spiritual skills. It is not limited to the study of ethnicity and it is not viewed only as a concern for minorities.[1]

A multicultural approach to teaching periodically searches and researches values, customs, cultural norms and gifts of its students in order to properly and effectively incorporate them into the school's formal and informal curriculum. Empathy, cultural awareness and willingness to alter and modify are basic principles of multiculturalism. Its symbol is the "mixed salad or fruit bowl" or the "mosaic picture."

Schools with a multicultural population and a multicultural approach to education often demonstrate higher levels of cooperation, integration and educational achievement. They generate a sense of belonging, equal status among students and freedom to pursue opportunities.

"Multicultural education recognizes cultural diversity as a fact of life in American society, and it affirms that this cultural diversity is a valuable resource that should be preserved and extended. It affirms that major educational institutions should strive to preserve and enhance cultural pluralism."[2]

This multicultural approach, although conceptually understood and accepted by many, has yet to gain significant status in the restructuring of present educational practices. All educators should be aware of the negative principles of the assimilationist philosophy so that they may apply the multicultural one. In the meeting of many cultures, all groups can find identity and enrichment.

The Process of Inculturation

The people being educated in Catholic schools and in all parish programs should feel "at home" with what they learn, with the matter in which they are being taught, and with the way they are being encouraged to express and live their faith. This will happen only if the religious education they are receiving is integrated with the "familiar"—with their own culture.

Since the 1977 Synod of Bishops on Catechesis, the dimension of *inculturation* has become a focal point in religious education, alerting educators to the importance of culture in the development and education of the total person.

Inculturation enables the Church to speak *with* and not only to the people of today, in a language that expresses, through signs and symbols, their genuine problems and needs. Obviously, these needs are to be considered in their totality: physical, intellectual, spiritual, material, personal, and communal.

Inculturation takes into account all these human aspects and must not be limited to the cognitive dimension. The evaluation of whether or not a program of religious education has been planned and carried out with inculturation in mind, should be extended to the affective and behavioral dimensions.

Rather than a method or approach, inculturation is an attitude of respect for and faith in God and each individual person, whoever he or she might be.

Respect comes from the awareness that the cultural roots of every individual are integral to his or her personality. Respect for these roots implies that they are not simply taken for granted, but that they are recognized as a particular aspect of the gift of life given by God to the person. To get to know and teach anyone in an integral way, it is imperative that his or her cultural roots be taken into consideration.

Faith asserts that everything that is good and true has its source in God; and it is a fact that, no matter how "primitive" and "under-developed" a culture might seem in the eyes of "modern" society, it has elements of goodness and truth. These elements are, therefore, signs of God's salvific presence. Faith gives the Christian educator the awareness that God, Creator and Father of all, is actively engaged in every aspect of the human development of each individual person.

Inculturation is, in fact, the discovery of Gospel values already contained in and lived in any given culture, whether or not the people themselves are aware of the Christian dimension in their lives. It is the role of the religious educator to point these values out, affirm them and explicitly associate them with Christ.

Religious education and catechetical programs have to meet the challenge of an existential reality; there is no one culture which, to the exclusion of others, is capable of fully understanding and assimilating the meaning of God's revelation, and adequately expressing the human response to God's invitation to every human being, "to be saved and come to the knowledge of truth" (Timothy 2:4). Therefore, aware of the enrichment every culture can bring a deeper Christian faith and a more Catholic formation, catechesis now stresses more and more the important role of inculturation.

On the other hand, the cultural root paradigm which molds and dictates the attitudes, customs, actions and reactions of individuals in a particular society, may not always reflect Christian values. All cultures, therefore, must be "tested," so that only those aspects must be purified. Thus, genuine inculturation calls for a double discernment:

◆ to discover the goodness already inherent in a given cultural characteristic or custom, in order to affirm it;

◆ to detect whatever is evil or destructive, in order to help eradicate it.

Enculturation and Acculturation

The Catholic educator, sensitive to the value of inculturation must be involved in facilitating both the enculturation and acculturation of Asians and other ethnic groups.

Enculturation is the process by which every individual from the time of conception is molded by the culture of his or her people. Even though culture is integral to the mentality and value system of generations, and its root paradigm goes deeper than a few generations of people, it is usually the extended family that provides the environment where the child absorbs and learns the language, customs, rituals, and beliefs peculiar to its culture.

Tragically, when families migrate and are uprooted from their native country, they can no longer provide for their growing children the same environment where cultural values can be experienced and appreciated. This is especially so when immigrants are made to feel "inferior" and unwanted. They become "ashamed" of their ethnicity, language, customs and religiosity and in many ways try to hide it. Religious educators should be ready to help immigrants recall, understand and explain to their children the values of their customs and especially the religious symbols underlying what they do.

Acculturation is the sociological tendency to accommodate to a new culture. As immigrants are confronted with a multiplicity of demands and pressure to survive, they gradually tend to adopt the life style of American society. This tendency has a two-fold danger: that of stifling their cultural values and characteristics (so that they are not passed on to their children), and that of imitating some of the evil aspects of a materialistic society. This is a danger that affects everyone in the Church.

The Catholic educator responds to these two realities by encouraging and facilitating the on-going transmission of culture *enculturation*, and by helping Asians to learn from and adopt the values of the "new" American culture in which they now live, while recognizing and rejecting its evil aspects—*acculturation*.

This requires knowledge and appreciation of both the cultural values of the particular ethnic groups and the demands of the multicultural society where they have to live and work. It requires also some degree of compromise.

For instance, Asians have a strong sense of family. In order to help young Asians experience these values (enculturation), school and parish programs should provide opportunities for Asian families to come together to celebrate their special feast days, inviting all members of the extended families to participate. Everyone is encouraged to prepare and bring their own special food and play their typical music. This responds to a genuine need in their culture.

Thus, enculturation and *acculturation* are not contradictory but complementary to *inculturation*, and of real value to Catholic education in a multicultural society.

The Principal as Educational Leader

Because church educators and ministers recognize the Asian presence as valuable and desirable, the following recommendations are given in order to foster a more Christian integration.

Catholic Centers for Enculturation and Acculturation

Church/Parish

1) Asians should not perceive the church as an "Americanizing agency," but as the sign and instrument of intimate union with God and with all people regardless of their ethnic, cultural and economic condition.

2) Ways must be found to encourage Asians to share their
   ❖ family values,
   ❖ religious traditions, especially their devotion to the Blessed Mother,
   ❖ sense of celebration.

3) In the church it is incongruous to speak of evangelization and education and, at the same time, to remain ignorant of the people being evangelized and educated. Before ministering to specific Asians, the church should first conduct an in-depth study of their cultures to avoid the repeated mistake of blending and homogenizing the various Asian groups.

4) Asians must be called forth to minister from leadership positions and should be adequately prepared to serve others, mainly from their own people.

5) Many Asians are not accustomed to parish boundaries and consequently seldom formally register within a parish. Therefore, there is a need to directly approach Asians within the home to evangelize. This should be the function of trained lay ministers, preferably Asians themselves.

Diocesan Education Office

1) The Education Office is more effective when it is representative of the people in the diocese. Therefore, if a significant number of Asian students are enrolled in the Catholic schools, the office should have at least one Asian staff member.

2) The office should publish information regarding the different Asian cultures present in the diocese: percentages, history, demographic characteristics, values, religious devotions, customs, art, music, festivities, family structures, and basic governing principles.

3) The office should engage in regular collaboration and cooperation with local colleges and universities to provide scholarships and low cost programs for the poor.

4) The office should investigate and pursue public and private subsidies to reduce school tuition, thereby increasing educational opportunities.

Catholic Schools

1) Catholic educators are to be prophetic promoters of the mission of Christ by teaching students, from every educational discipline, to interpret the signs of the time in the light of the Gospel and commit their given aptitudes and qualities "to enlarge the human family" (*Populorum Progressio*, No. 17).

2) An important responsibility of Catholic educators, by virtue of their Christian identity, is to free their students from any oppressing conditions such as inequality of opportunities and discrimination of any kind.

3) Language plays a powerful role in creating emotional responses. The significance given to words in the early stages of learning prepares children for understanding or for prejudice. Educators should make every effort to learn Asian phrases and expressions that may serve to build bridges. They should also allow natural communication in the native language during informal activities.

4) High schools which have a number of Asian students should set up "outreach" programs that may allow the students to work with their less privileged brothers and sisters. These programs are geared to develop in the students some social awareness which later may have significant bearing on their ministerial and political options.

5) Cultural celebrations which include the folklore and significant national and religious feast days need to be integrated within the school's special events.

6) Asian cultures need to be studied from an interdisciplinary perspective:
   ❖ Cultural values ought to be examined and discussed from different angles during Religion, Social Studies and Literature courses;
   ❖ Music, Art, Drama and Physical education may concentrate on the symbolic expression of these values;
   ❖ Different food values, clothing and family structures should be compared and analyzed during Home Economics;
   ❖ Physical characteristics and their influence on cultural relationships are important topics in Science;
   ❖ Mathematics expands the understanding of peoples by the way numbers have been grouped and systematized.

7) The hidden curriculum, which may reflect the norms and values characteristic of Anglo-Saxon culture, must give due consideration to the ethnic groups who may not accept them or value them equally.

8) Teachers need to be educated in countering classroom discrimination by methods such as:
   ❖ examining their own attitudes, biases, and stereotypes and trying to identify their origin;
   ❖ examining the biases and stereotypes present among the students;
   ❖ recognizing biases and stereotyping within textbooks and learning how to deal with them;

❖ learning to build interdependence among students in order to encourage positive association.

9) If the number of Asian students exceeds 40%, an Asian administrator should be hired to facilitate teacher/student and parent/teacher communication.

Conclusion

It is important for Catholic educators to understand the history, culture and language abilities of their Asian students before planning the curriculum for them. The best approach will be the one that effectively meets the needs of the specific group of Asian students, yet responds to the reality of available resources of personnel and finances.

During the Asian hearings, parents strongly indicated that they wanted their children to learn English in school; however, they were quick to add that they desired their children to learn and use their native language at home. This continued openness to the native language at home can be encouraged by teachers who take time to learn at least a few phrases of the student's language and use it with the child. This acceptance of the native language by the teacher will give a positive message to the child regarding his or her native culture and language.

It is interesting to note that children all over the world learn an additional language in elementary school and begin studying a third language around middle school years. This is not true in the United States.

Kjolseth (1983) states that the United States has spent millions of dollars of public funds teaching foreign languages to English monolinguals while at the same time engaging in systematic efforts to ignore and actively discourage the use and maintenance of these same languages by native speakers.

Kjolseth continues, saying that:

There is much at stake at home and abroad. . . . Internationally, our ability to deal effectively with other nations on diplomatic, political, economic, scientific, and social levels is affected by our attitudes towards other languages and by the availability of appropriately trained persons with bilingual skills.[3]

"This world is multilingual and it is unwise for us to remain on its fringes," Kjolseth cautions.[4]

The Catholic schools of the United States enjoy a reputation of providing quality education. They are now in a position to expand programs that show special sensitivity to the language and cultural backgrounds of Asian students. These programs would respond to students needs in terms of personal and cultural support and language assistance as needed.

Notes

1. Jack Kehoe, "Enhancing the Multicultural Climate of the School," *History and Social Science Teacher*, vol. 19, no. 2, December, 1983, p. 65.
2. Theresa McCormick, "Multiculturalism: Some Principles and Issues," *Theory Into Practice*, vol. 23, no. 2, Spring, 1984, p. 94.
3. Rolf Kjolseth, "Cultural Politics of Bilingualism," *Socio-linguistics Today*, May/June, 1983, p. 40.
4. *Ibid.*, p. 48.

Integral Education: A Response to the Hispanic Presence

Hall, S., and C. Reck, eds. 1987. 48–51. Washington, D.C.: National Catholic Educational Association.

Factors Related to Effective Teaching

The reasons for the Catholic school success with the Hispanic student are not totally clear. The Greeley analysis of the Coleman report suggests that the community setting of the Catholic school contributes to the success of the Hispanic as well as the black student. The National Assessment of Educational Process (NAEP) report correlated Catholic students' reading superiority with factors such as more substantial course content and additional homework.

During the NCEA Hispanic hearings, participants reported other factors that contribute to the success of the Catholic educational setting:

◆ evidence of personal caring;
◆ sensitivity to different cultures;
◆ respect for the student as an individual person;
◆ deliberate building of a youngster's self-esteem;
◆ special dimension of the religious community setting;

◆ ability to integrate religious values within the curriculum.

These human factors are an essential part of the philosophy and reality of the Catholic educational setting.

The research by Dr. J. U. Ogbu (1978) reinforces the special need to build the self-esteem of the Hispanic student. He explains that Hispanics in the United States are perceived by the Anglos as a lower class of immigrants than others, such as the Asians. He further explains that many Hispanics have accepted that perception and therefore achieved at lower levels. Only with educators who make intentional decisions to build self-esteem through respect of culture and language will these students begin to actualize their real potential. One can assume from studies by Dr. Ogbu and others that the learning environment is as important as the course of studies for the Hispanic student.

This importance of the learning environment is again affirmed by Ramirez and Casteneda (1974) in their recently developed cognitive theory which posits that there are two kinds of learners:

◆ field independent learners (mostly Anglos) and
◆ field dependent learners.

The *field independent* learner
1) can work well alone;
2) perceives the specific, then the totality;
3) is motivated by individual competition and achievement;
4) is usually more task oriented and is not affected as much by outside stimuli such as the instructor or the environment;
5) has well developed analytical abilities.

The *field dependent* or field sensitive learner
1) works well in groups;
2) perceives the totality, then the specific;
3) is motivated by group competition and achievement;
4) is more affected by outside stimuli such as the instructor or the environment when solving a problem or performing a task;
5) is influenced more by affective variables in learning.

Ramirez and Casteneda conclude that Hispanics are field *dependent* learners; thus the environment is crucially important to their learning processes.

Equally important is the respect for culture and language that is so closely associated with respect for the individual student. The educator who rejects a student's mother language rejects that student's culture and personhood—with devastating effects on his or her student's self-esteem.

The learning process, to be effective with Hispanic students, must include deliberate strengthening of self-esteem and building a positive community learning environment. Other considerations are teaching methodologies and language programs that are particularly suited to the Hispanic student.

Teaching Methodologies

The fact that most Hispanics are field dependent or field sensitive learners should determine the teaching methods to be used extensively in classrooms with Hispanic children. Although field dependent approaches represent good pedagogy and, therefore, will prove effective with most students, they are especially needed by the Hispanic student.

Based on the qualities of the *field dependent* learner, the following methods are recommended. First they are presented in basic outline form, then discussed in terms of general considerations (*see chart*).

General Considerations

The consistent emphasis on "caring" and "sensitivity" during the NCEA hearings underlines the need for personal rapport. Until Hispanics know that the teacher cares about them and their progress, learning will probably not occur.

Field Dependent Qualities	Recommended Methodology
1. values affective dimension	personal rapport in teaching and discipline
2. works well in groups	group discussion and activities
3. values group achievement	group goals
4. grasps totality, then specifics	overall picture or goal first
5. responds to outside stimuli	experiential learning

At times, these youngsters will need to experience a series of small incremental successes before having the self-confidence to assume and complete larger tasks.

The fact that Hispanics work well in groups indicates that *dialogue and group activities* should play an important role in the teaching/learning process—in short, a focus on "talk and do." Each individual needs to be involved. The placement of desks or chairs in the classroom should facilitate this group interaction. Because the family is so central to the life of the Hispanic youngster, family dialogue and activities related to the lesson should be encouraged.

Motivation for this group will not be engendered by rules or assignments as such. Neither will the opportunity for personal competition or achievement produce results. On the other hand, a call to group cooperation will motivate the Hispanic child to accountability. Individual tasks, which are required for a small group to complete a common project, will more likely be done than isolated individual assignments.

The inclination to grasp the totality first, then to move to specifics suggests that lessons should lead students to "figure it out." Many of the approaches currently designed for the "right-brain, intuitive learner" prove successful with the Hispanic youngster.

In a math class, for example, the teacher might show various newspaper advertisements offering "1/4 off," "1/3 off," etc. and promise the students they will soon be able to figure which are the best buys. Then only would the class proceed to the specifics involved in studying fractions. The importance of outside stimuli will suggest, for example, that teaching should involve the *experiential, tactile*, and *kinesthetic*. In other words, the learning experience should be "hands on," involving the total person. Some tips for working with non-English-speaking or limited-English-speaking students are the following:

◆ encourage students to teach words from their language to teachers and friends;
◆ don't discourage students from speaking their language with their friends—they need this release because they can't express their deep feelings in English yet;

- don't try to teach them to read words if they don't already use those words in speaking;
- don't teach them to sound out words they don't know;
- don't believe that, because they can't respond, they don't understand—there are two different tasks: listening comes first, speaking follows.

In addition, it is important to keep in mind that good teachers speak clearly and distinctly, avoiding syntactic complexities and sophisticated words. Most importantly, good teachers match what they say with concrete, visual referents so that students hear their new language within the context of clearly defined classroom experiences. When the kindergarten teacher says, "Take your blue crayon and draw a big circle on your paper" while demonstrating simultaneously, her students are receiving comprehensible input. When the science teacher conducts a classroom experiment with magnets while carefully identifying the materials used and describing the process, her students are acquiring simultaneously both new concepts and the language to discuss them.

References

Ogbu, J. U. *Minority Education and Caste*, Academic Press, New York, 1978.

Ramirez, Manuel, and A. Casteneda. *Cultural Democracy, Bicognitive Development and Education*, Academic Press, New York, 1974.

An Afro-American Perspective

Jones, Nathan. 1987. In *Faith and culture*, 77–80. Washington, D.C.: United States Catholic Conference.

When planning catechetical programs for Afro-American adults, youths, and children, we must necessarily build upon the inherent strengths of the people. Blacks, because of our history, have come to expect certain things from our religion that other persons may not.

Catholic educators generally fail to unravel the marvels of black cultural styles and behaviors. We prefer to insist on rigid conformity to white monocultural teaching/learning styles and act as if blacks were simply "black-skinned whites."

Our starting point in program development will be to acknowledge Afro-Americans as richly endowed. The untrained eye tends to overlook these qualities, underrate their significance, and insist on standard, white middle-class norms. Given the national tendency to view cultural differences as suggestive of inferiority, pastoral leaders are frustrated continuously by low attendance, passivity, and a general lack of interest in parish religious education programs.

This has been said before. We must ask ourselves the following critical questions: What is God asking of us now and in the future? What educational program, then, is required? What are the principal stumbling blocks to effective implementation of culturally appropriate catechetical designs?

Building upon Black Cultural Strengths

Learning takes place in a wide arena in black communities: family, relations, streets, institutions, media, music, and so forth. A broad spectrum of agencies shape the lives and values and determine the behavior and commitment of people. Normally, religious educators neglect to take these learning environments seriously. We fail to acknowledge what the community already provides by way of value formation, rituals, and optimal mental and spiritual health.

Program development begins by examining the distinctive ways black people display the courage to be themselves, to display their own style and unique characteristics.

In short, catechists must rigorously study culture, black expressive styles, and behaviors if we are to ever reverse the pattern of sterile, repetitive, and maladaptive religious education modalities that simply don't work.

The study of culture is not a single act, but a process. Films, study texts, guest speakers, field trips, and listening are a means to the end. Here are some questions to guide your inquiry: (1) What are the espoused goals, values, and norms of your local community? (2) What are the practiced realities, values, and norms of this community? (3) What are the personal and community behaviors that support the community goals? (4) What are the behaviors that deviate from these goals? (5) How might these behaviors be brought into line with community goals? (6) Who are the key players and carriers of the culture? (7) How are the community's values and norms related to transcendent and Christian values?

Frequently, our ways of ministering are at odds with black styles. Uninitiated educators normally view black culturally specific styles and behaviors with a great deal of suspicion and misunderstanding such as the open expression of feelings; self-glorification; braggadocio in words and body language; coined interjections; loud colors; the use of profanity; and the deliberate violations of structured English syntax.

Educators, guided by the American ethos, prefer to emphasize the rationalistic, repress sexuality, and deny suffering. Conversely, black styles are marked by considerable feeling and movement: a refusal to deodorize life; a resistance to formality and sameness; a comfort with the body, its shape, drives, and scars.

Either style can be, at times, dysfunctional. Therefore, catechists must make an objective appraisal of cultural styles based on the people's needs and community goals. One of the aims of catechesis is to bring the community to an awareness of its own God-given strengths, to reverse negative programming, and to draw religion out of the people rather than pump religion into them.

Pastoral and educational leaders cannot afford to be information-poor. We need to be aware of the context of our learners' lives, use it appropriately, and reflect on it deliberately. Jesus taught in the context of people's lives. He pointed them back to their own experience: farming, relationships, banquets. He invited them to grow and change in the context of their own lives.

Program Imperatives

The following elements are regarded widely as foundational for religious education in black communities: a sense of self, a sense of history, a sense of community, a sense of disciplined growth, and a sense of the sacred. These elements designate key assumptions that programs typically enflesh. An evaluation of your existing program—its philosophy and approaches—is a starter. The aim is not only to order new teaching aids but to understand the need for systemic change in our whole catechetical concept and its interrelated parts. By paying close attention to these imperatives, you can design effective programs, curricula, and select appropriate resources.

1. A Sense of Self

The development of a healthy identity is endemic to catechesis. It involves freeing people from forces (inner/outer) that prevent them from moving toward their full potential.

◆ Does the program foster self-esteem?
◆ How does the program aid the search for cultural identity?
◆ How does the program confront the learner with what it means to be a black Catholic-Christian in America?

2. A Sense of History

We are never isolated from our past or future, although some Christians find it easier to ignore their history than to examine it. History invites us to dream not only of what has been but what has *not yet* been. Now that we are driving the bus, where is the bus going?

◆ Does the program foster an appreciation of Africa as motherland? Afro-American heritage?
◆ Are students urged to search history to discover ways of making their own personal contribution?
◆ Does the program include truthful and relevant black content (saints, freedom fighters, liberation movements, arts)?

3. A Sense of Community

The black community is comprised of a repository of natural talent. Look for positive role models among the successful business persons, parents, law enforcement officers, reformed offenders, artists, and activists.

◆ Does the program recognize and engage the talent of the larger community?

4. A Sense of Disciplined Growth

Allowing blacks to think of themselves only as "victims" stigmatizes and further impedes the quest for affirmation and liberation. Challenge prevailing practices such as crime, recreational sex, eating disorders, severe dependency on artificial stimuli, the dissolution of the family, and so forth. Stress *development* rather than simply *survival* mentalities.

◆ Does the program motivate learners to examine their attitudes and behavior while comprehending their responsibilities?

5. A Sense of the Sacred

Build upon the ability of many blacks to feel deeply and express their feelings without reserve, to relax and enjoy everything they do. Educators who insist on formality and control can suppress affectivity and psychomotor expressions. Boredom is a direct response to the excessively low activity level of many classrooms. Handclaps, yells of approval, pantomime, hugs, linked arms, nonverbal cues, hot colors, movement, and rhythms are cultural avenues to the Divine. The absence of words in much of black communication signifies a very healthy readiness for the sacramental—expressing outwardly what we feel inside. Feeling and faith belong together.

◆ Does the program draw upon the spiritual insights of the people (stories, folk wisdom, songs)?
◆ Does the program seek to enable blacks to be at home with Catholic tradition and bring to the tradition black gifts and insights?

Conclusion

Answers to these questions for multicultural catechesis are not easy and are never fully satisfied by simple solutions —a gospel choir, a red/black/green altar covering. Maturity mobilizes us to generate a plan for local black church development, that is, total pastoral renewal. Looking backwards, we affirm that past practices and programs were helpful but also limiting. Today, we must move beyond routine and yesterday's agenda. The bishops of the Church have given us the "Go!" signal. It's all up to us!

Probing the Subtleties of Subject-Matter Teaching

Brophy, Jere. 1992. *Educational Leadership* 49(7):4–8.

Building on the effective schools research of the 1970s, studies today focus on teaching for understanding and use of knowledge.

Research on teaching, if interpreted appropriately, is a significant resource to teachers: it both validates good practice and suggests directions for improvement. All too often, however, reviews of the research assume an "out with the old, in with the new" stance, which fosters swings between extremes. Practitioners are left confused and prone to believe that research is not helpful. This summary of the research conducted during the last 25 years attempts not only to highlight the changing implications of research but also to emphasize how the research has built on what was learned before.

Process-Outcome Research

Especially relevant findings come from studies designed to identify relationships between classroom processes (what the teacher and students do in the classroom) and student outcomes (changes in students' knowledge, skills, values, or dispositions that represent progress toward instructional goals). Two forms of process-outcome research that became prominent in the 1970s were school effects research and teacher effects research.

School effects research (reviewed in Good and Brophy 1986) identified characteristics in schools that elicit good achievement gains from their students: (1) strong academic leadership that produces consensus on goal priorities and commitment to instructional excellence; (2) a safe, orderly school climate; (3) positive teacher attitudes toward students and expectations regarding their abilities to master the curriculum; (4) an emphasis on instruction in the curriculum (not just on filling time or on nonacademic activities); (5) careful monitoring of progress toward goals through student testing and staff evaluation programs; (6) strong parent involvement programs; and (7) consistent emphasis on the importance of academic achievement, including praise and public recognition for students' accomplishments.

Teacher effects research (reviewed in Brophy and Good 1986) identified teacher behaviors and patterns of teacher-student interaction associated with student achievement gains. This research firmly established three major conclusions:

1. *Teachers make a difference.* Some teachers reliably elicit greater gains than others, because of differences in how they teach.

2. *Differences in achievement gains occur in part because of differences in exposure to academic content and opportunity to learn.* Teachers who elicit greater gains: (a) place more emphasis on developing mastery of the curriculum, in establishing expectations for students, and defining their own roles; (b) allocate most of the available time for activities designed to foster such mastery; and (c) are effective organizers and managers who make their classrooms efficient learning environments, minimize the time spent getting organized or making transitions, and maximize student engagement in ongoing academic activities.

3. *Teachers who elicit greater achievement gains do not merely maximize "time on task"; in addition, they spend a great deal of time actively instructing their students.* Their classrooms feature more time spent in interactive lessons, featuring much teacher-student discourse and less time spent in independent seatwork. Rather than depend solely on curriculum materials as content sources, these teachers interpret and elaborate the content for students, stimulate them to react to it through questions, and circulate during seatwork times to monitor progress and provide assistance. They are active instructors, not just materials managers and evaluators, although most of their instruction occurs during interactive discourse with students rather than during extended lecture presentations.

The process-outcome research of the 1970s was important not only for contributing the findings summarized above but also for providing education with a knowledge base capable of moving the field beyond testimonials and unsupported claims toward scientific statements based on credible data. However, this research was limited in several respects. First, it focused on important but very basic aspects of teaching. These aspects differentiate the least effective teachers from other teachers, but they do not include the more subtle points that distinguish the most outstanding teachers.

Second, most of this research relied on standardized tests as the outcome measure, which meant that it focused on mastery of relatively isolated knowledge items and skill components without assessing the degree to which students had developed understanding of networks of subject-matter content or the ability to use this information in authentic application situations.

Research on Teaching for Understanding and Use of Knowledge

During the 1980s, research emerged that emphasized teaching subject matter for understanding and use of knowledge. This research focuses on particular curriculum units or even individual lessons, taking into account the teacher's instructional goals and assessing student learning accordingly. The researchers find out what the teacher is trying to accomplish, record detailed information about classroom processes as they unfold, and then assess learning using measures keyed to the instructional goals. Often these include detailed interviews or portfolio assessments, not just conventional short-answer tests.

Current research focuses on attempts to teach both the individual elements in a network of related content and the connections among them, to the point that students can explain the information in their own words and can use it appropriately in and out of school. Teachers accomplish this by explaining concepts and principles with clarity and precision and by modeling the strategic application of skills via "think aloud" demonstrations. These demonstrations make overt for students the usually covert strategic thinking that guides the use of the skills for problem solving.

Construction of Meaning

Current research, while building on findings indicating the vital role teachers play in stimulating student learning, also focuses on the role of the student. It recognizes that students do not merely passively receive or copy input from teachers, but instead actively mediate it by trying to make sense of it and to relate it to what they already know (or think they know) about the topic. Thus, students develop new knowledge through a process of *active construction*. In order to get beyond rote memorization to achieve true understanding, they need to develop and integrate a network of associations linking new input to preexisting knowledge and beliefs anchored in concrete experience. Thus, teaching involves inducing conceptual change in students, not infusing knowledge into a vacuum. Students' preexisting beliefs about a topic, when accurate, facilitate learning and provide a natural starting place for teaching. Students' misconceptions, however, must be corrected so that they do not distort the new learning.

To the extent that new learning is complex, the construction of meaning required to develop clear understanding of it will take time and will be facilitated by the interactive *discourse* that occurs during lessons and activities. Clear explanations and modeling from the teacher are important, but so are opportunities to answer questions about the content, discuss or debate its meanings and implications, or apply it in authentic problem-solving or decision-making contexts. These activities allow students to process the content actively and "make it their own" by paraphrasing it into their own words, exploring its relationships to other knowledge and to past experience, appreciating the insights it provides, or identifying its implications for personal decision making or action. Increasingly,

research is pointing to thoughtful discussion, and not just teacher lecturing or student recitation, as characteristic of the discourse involved in teaching for understanding.

Researchers have also begun to stress the complementary changes in teacher and student roles that should occur as learning progresses. Early in the process, the teacher assumes most of the responsibility for structuring and managing learning activities and provides students with a great deal of information, explanation, modeling and cueing. As students develop expertise, however, they can begin regulating their own learning by asking questions and by working on increasingly complex applications with increasing degrees of autonomy. The teacher still provides task simplification, coaching, and other "scaffolding" needed to assist students with challenges that they are not yet ready to handle on their own. Gradually, this assistance is reduced in response to gradual increases in student readiness to engage in self-regulated learning.

Principles of Good Subject-Matter Teaching

Although research on teaching school subjects for understanding and higher-order applications is still in its infancy, it already has produced successful experimental programs in most subjects. Even more encouraging, analyses of these programs have identified principles and practices that are common to most if not all of them (Anderson 1989, Brophy 1989, Prawat 1989). These common elements are

1. The curriculum is designed to equip students with knowledge, skills, values, and dispositions useful both inside and outside of school.
2. Instructional goals underscore developing student expertise within an application context and with emphasis on conceptual understanding and self-regulated use of skills.
3. The curriculum balances breadth with depth by addressing limited content but developing this content sufficiently to foster understanding.
4. The content is organized around a limited set of powerful ideas (key understandings and principles).
5. The teacher's role is not just to present information but also to scaffold and respond to students' learning.
6. The students' role is not just to absorb or copy but to actively make sense and construct meaning.
7. Activities and assignments feature authentic tasks that call for problem solving or critical thinking, not just memory or reproduction.
8. Higher-order thinking skills are not taught as a separate skills curriculum. Instead, they are developed in the process of teaching subject-matter knowledge within application contexts that call for students to relate what they are learning to their lives outside of school by thinking critically or creatively about it or by using it to solve problems or make decisions.
9. The teacher creates a social environment in the classroom that could be described as a learning community where dialogue promotes understanding.

In-Depth Study of Fewer Topics

Embedded in this approach to teaching is the notion of "complete" lessons carried through to include higher-order applications of content. The breadth of content addressed, thus, is limited to allow for more in-depth teaching of the content. Unfortunately, typical state and district curriculum guidelines feature long lists of items and subskills to be "covered," and typical curriculum packages supplied by educational publishers respond to these guidelines by emphasizing breadth over depth of coverage. Teachers who want to teach for understanding and higher-order applications of subject-matter will have to both: (1) limit what they teach by focusing on the most important content and omitting or skimming over the rest, and (2) structure what they do teach around important ideas, elaborating it considerably beyond what is in the text.

Besides presenting information and modeling skill applications, such teachers will need to structure a great deal of thoughtful discourse by using questions to stimulate students to process and reflect on the content, recognize relationships among and implications of its key ideas, think critically about it, and use it in problem-solving or decision-making applications. Such discourse downplays rapid-fire questioning and short answers and instead features sustained examination of a small number of related topics. Students are invited to develop explanations, make predictions, debate alternative approaches to problems, or otherwise consider the content's implications or applications. Some of the questions admit to a range of possible correct answers, and some invite discussion or debate (for example, concerning the relative merits of alternative suggestions for solving problems). In addition to asking questions and providing feedback, the teacher encourages students to explain or elaborate on their answers or to comment on classmates' answers. The teacher also capitalizes on "teachable moments" offered by students' comments or questions (by elaborating on the original instruction, correcting misconceptions, or calling attention to implications that have not been appreciated yet).

Holistic Skills Instruction

Teaching for understanding and use of knowledge also involves holistic skills instruction, not the practice of skills in isolation. For example, most practice of writing skills is embedded within activities calling for authentic writing. Also, skills are taught as strategies adapted to particular purposes and situations, with emphasis on modeling the cognitive and metacognitive components involved and explaining the necessary conditional knowledge (of when and why the skills would be used). Thus, students receive instruction in when and how to apply skills, not just opportunities to use them.

Activities, assignments, and evaluation methods incorporate a much greater range of tasks than the familiar workbooks and curriculum-embedded tests that focus on recognition and recall of facts, definitions, and fragmented skills. Curriculum strands or units are planned to accomplish

gradual transfer of responsibility for managing learning activities from the teacher to the students, in response to their growing expertise on the topic. Plans for lessons and activities are guided by overall curriculum goals (phrased in terms of student capabilities to be developed), and evaluation efforts concentrate on assessing the progress made.

Reading. Reading is taught as a sense-making process of extracting meaning from texts that are read for information or enjoyment, not just for practice. Important skills such as decoding, blending, and noting main ideas are taught and practiced, but primarily within the context of reading for meaning. Activities and assignments feature more reading of extended texts and less time spent with skills worksheets. Students often work cooperatively in pairs or small groups, reading to one another or discussing their answers to questions about the implications of the text. Rather than being restricted to the artificial stories written for basal readers, students often read literature written to provide information or pleasure (Anderson et al. 1985, Dole et al. 1991).

Writing. Writing is taught as a way for students to organize and communicate their thinking to particular audiences for particular purposes, using skills taught as strategies for accomplishing these goals. Most skills practice is embedded within writing activities that call for composition and communication of meaningful content. Composition activities emphasize authentic writing intended to be read for meaning and response. Thus, composition becomes an exercise in communication and personal craftsmanship. Students develop and revise outlines, develop successive drafts for meaning, and then polish their writing. The emphasis is on the cognitive and metacognitive aspects of composing, not just on mechanics and editing (Englert and Raphael 1989, Rosaen 1990, Scardamalia and Bereiter 1986).

Mathematics. Mathematics instruction focuses on developing students' abilities to explore, conjecture, reason logically, and use a variety of mathematical models to solve nonroutine problems. Instead of working through a postulated linear hierarchy from isolated and low-level skills to integrated and higher-level skills, and only then attempting application, students are taught within an application context right from the beginning through an emphasis on authentic problem solving. They spend less time working individually on computation skills sheets and more time participating in teacher-led discourse concerning the meanings of the mathematical concepts and operations under study (Carpenter et al. 1989; National Council of Teachers of Mathematics 1989, 1991; Steffe and Wood 1990).

Science. In science, students learn to understand, appreciate, and apply connected sets of powerful ideas that they can use to describe, explain, make predictions about, or gain control over real-world systems or events. Instruction connects with students' experience-based knowledge and beliefs, building on accurate current knowledge but also producing conceptual change by confronting and correcting misconceptions. The teacher models and coaches the students' scientific reasoning through scaffolded tasks and dialogues that engage them in thinking about scientific issues. The students are encouraged to make predictions or develop explanations, then subject them to empirical tests or argue the merits of proposed alternatives (Anderson and Roth 1989, Neale et al. 1990).

Social studies. In social studies, students are challenged to engage in higher-order thinking by interpreting, analyzing, or manipulating information in response to questions or problems that cannot be resolved through routine application of previously learned knowledge. Students focus on networks of connected content structured around powerful ideas rather than on long lists of disconnected facts and they consider the implications of what they are learning for social and civic decision making. The teacher encourages students to formulate and communicate ideas about the topic, but also presses them to clarify or justify their assertions rather than merely accepting and reinforcing them indiscriminately (Brophy 1990, Newmann 1990).

Greater Efforts, Greater Rewards

The type of teaching described here is not yet typical of what happens in most schools. For it to become more common several things must occur. First, researchers need to articulate these principles more clearly. Second, states and districts must adjust their curriculum guidelines, and publishers must modify their textbooks and teachers' manuals. Finally, professional organizations of teachers and teacher educators must build on the beginnings that they have made in endorsing the goals of teaching subjects for understanding, appreciation and life application by creating and disseminating position statements, instructional guidelines, videotaped examples, and other resources for preservice and inservice teachers. Clearly, the kind of instruction described here demands more from both teachers and students than traditional reading-recitation-seatwork teaching does. However, it also rewards their efforts with more satisfying and authentic accomplishments.

Author's note: This work is sponsored in part by the Center for the Learning and Teaching of Elementary Subjects, Institute for Research on Teaching, Michigan State University. The Center for Learning and Teaching of Elementary Subjects is funded primarily by the Office of Educational Research and Improvement, U.S. Department of Education. The opinions expressed here do not necessarily reflect the position, policy, or endorsement of the Office or Department (Cooperative Agreement No. G0087C0226).

References

Anderson, L. (1989) "Implementing Instructional Programs to Promote Meaningful, Self-Regulated Learning." In *Advances in Research on Teaching*, Vol. 1, edited by J. Brophy, pp. 311–343. Greenwich. Conn.: JAI.

Anderson, C. and K. Roth. (1989). "Teaching for Meaningful and Self-Regulated Learning of Science." In *Advances in Research on Teaching*, Vol. 1, edited by J. Brophy, pp. 265–309. Greenwich. Conn.: JAI.

Anderson, R., E. Hieben, J. Scott, and I. Wilkinson. (1985). *Becoming a Nation of Readers: A Report of the Commission on Reading*. Washington. D.C.: National Institute of Education.

Brophy, J., ed. (1989). *Advances in Research on Teaching*, Vol. 1. Greenwich, Conn.: JAI.

Brophy, J. (1990). "Teaching Social Studies for Understanding and Higher-Order Applications." *Elementary School Journal* 90: 351–417.

Brophy, J., and T. Good. (1986). "Teacher Behavior and Student Achievement." In *Handbook of Research on Teaching*, 3rd. ed., edited by M. Wittrock, pp. 328–375. New York: Macmillan.

Carpenter, T., E. Fennema, P. Peterson, C. Chiang, and M. Loef. (1989). "Using Knowledge of Children's Mathematics Thinking in Classroom Teaching: An Experimental Study." *American Educational Research Journal* 26: 499–532.

Dole, J., G. Duffy, L. Roehler, and P. D. Pearson. (1991). "Moving From the Old to the New: Research on Reading Comprehension Instruction." *Review of Educational Research* 61: 239–264.

Englert, C., and T. Raphael. (1989). "Developing Successful Writers Through Cognitive Strategy Instruction." In *Advances in Research on Teaching*, Vol. 1, edited by J. Brophy, pp. 105–151. Greenwich. Conn.: JAI.

Good, T., and J. Brophy. (1986). "School Effects." In *Handbook of Research on Teaching*, 3rd ed., edited by M. Wittrock, pp. 570–602. New York: Macmillan.

National Council of Teachers of Mathematics. (1984). *Curriculum and Evaluation Standards for School Mathematics*. Reston, Va.: NCTM.

National Council of Teachers of Mathematics. (1991) *Professional Standards for Teaching Mathematics*. Reston, Va.: NCTM.

Neale, D., D. Smith, and V. Johnson (1990). "Implementing Conceptual Change Teaching in Primary Science." *Elementary School Journal* 91: 109–131.

Newman, F. (1990). "Qualities of Thoughtful Social Studies Classes: An Empirical Profile." *Journal of Curriculum Studies* 22: 253–275.

Prawat, R. (1989). "Promoting Access to Knowledge, Strategy, and Disposition in Students: A Research Synthesis." *Review of Educational Research* 59: 1–41.

Rosaen, C. (1990). "Improving Writing Opportunities in Elementary Classrooms." *Elementary School Journal* 90: 419–434.

Scardamalia, M., and C. Bereiter. (1986). "Written Composition." In *Handbook of Research on Teaching*, 3rd ed., edited by M. Wittrock, pp. 778–803. New York: Macmillan.

Steffe, L., and T. Wood, eds. (1990). *Transforming Children's Mathematics Education: International Perspectives*. Hillsdale, N.J.: Erlbaum.

About the Author

Jere Brophy is University Distinguished Professor of Teacher Education and Co-director, Institute for Research on Teaching. He can be contacted at Michigan State University, Center for the Learning and Teaching of Elementary Subjects, College of Education, Erickson Hall, East Lansing, MI 48824-1034.

Curriculum Renewal: A Rationale for a Consensus Curriculum

Glatthorn, Allan A. 1987. 20–27. Alexandria, Va.: Association for Supervision and Curriculum Development.

Before explaining the recommended process, it might be useful to offer some general guidelines about what such a process should look like. Doing so may help you think through your own modifications of the process recommended here.

1. Use a process that brings the recommended, the written, and the taught curriculum into closer congruence. Remember in Chapter One you learned about these three types of curriculum: the recommended curriculum, the curriculum that professional organizations and experts recommend; the written curriculum, the curriculum embodied in the district documents (scope-and-sequence charts and curriculum guides); and the taught curriculum, the curriculum actually being taught in your classrooms.

In too many schools, these three curriculums are often quite discrepant. The recommended curriculum seems not to have influenced the written curriculum or the taught curriculum; and the written curriculum is not fully reflected in what teachers teach. So you want a process that will bring the three into closer congruence—but you do not want a complete overlap. You want a written curriculum that reflects the best—but not all—of the recommended curriculum, because the experts don't have all the answers. And you want teachers to be giving primary attention to that written curriculum, while still having some autonomy.

2. Use a process that will result in a teacher-supported curriculum. The goal is to develop a consensus curriculum that teachers will want to implement because they have had a large measure of input in developing it and because they believe in its professional quality. This guideline is important because of what has been learned about the teacher as a curriculum maker. In general, the research yields the following composite picture. (The picture is drawn from several sources, chiefly Connelly and Ben-Peretz 1980; MacDonald and Leithwood 1982; Doyle 1986; Floden and others 1980; and Cusick 1983.)

> The teacher is an active curriculum maker who, day by day, makes important decisions about what is taught and how it will be taught; in making those decisions the teacher responds to numerous pressures and influences. The written curriculum plays a varying role in influencing teacher decision making—but at best, it is only one of several factors that the teacher considers.

Some have responded to this situation by attempting to develop stronger and more stringent controls over teachers to limit their influence on the curriculum. They hope in this fashion to mandate teacher compliance with the written curriculum. Such attempts seem doomed to failure: When teachers close the doors, they become the curriculum, regardless of all your efforts to make them behave differently. On the other hand, some have responded to the situation by simply tolerating it, either because they have an unrealistic view of the teacher's ability as a curriculum decision maker or because they value curricular diversity. Total diversity leads to anarchy—and tolerance of curricular anarchy does not seem to be a wise policy for the organization.

It seems more reasonable to use a curriculum-improvement process that will elicit active teacher support of a consensus curriculum—one that reflects their best judgment about what should be taught. Notice the emphasis on *should be*. You want teacher input, not about what they actually are teaching but about what they believe should be taught. The reason for the emphasis on the ideal rather than the real is that teachers know better than they teach. Their decisions about the curriculum typically reflect compromises they have made. They would like to emphasize other skills and concepts but, rightly or wrongly, believe that they are prevented from doing so—by administrators, by tests, by texts, or by subtle community pressures. So you want to use a process that will capture their best thinking about curriculum.

3. Use a process that will focus district efforts on the mastery curriculum. Remember that the mastery curriculum includes only objectives that are essential for all students and that require careful structuring. There are two main advantages for such a focus. First, it results in a kind of curricular parsimony—an uncluttered district curriculum that omits everything except structured essential content. Second, it explicitly provides for teacher autonomy in the organic, the team-planned, and the student-determined components.

The process explained below follows these guidelines. Feel free to modify it as you see fit.

The Basic Process Explained

1. Determine where you will begin and develop broad-based support for the project.

The first step is to decide where you will start with field improvement and to develop broad-based support for the project. Some districts develop a five-year schedule that ensures that, once every five years, each of the major fields and one of the so-called "minor" fields is reviewed. Others rely on a more formal needs-assessment process that uses a comprehensive assessment of district strengths and deficiencies. (For a useful survey of needs-assessment approaches, see Kaufman 1983.) Some simply monitor achievement-test scores to detect signs of trouble. Still others make intuitive judgments based on their knowledge of current developments in education and their informal assessments of curricular quality. Regardless of how you decide where to begin, it is important, as noted above, to build broad-based support for the project. The teachers should be involved in whatever needs assessment or evaluations are conducted. If no formal process is used, then inservice time should be used to sensitize teachers to the importance of curriculum review and to solicit their support for and input into the process.

2. Establish project parameters.

The next step is to decide how comprehensive and ambitious your curriculum project will be. To do so, consider these questions.

1. How much time and money do we have? Limited time and money will make it necessary to take some shortcuts. The whole process can be simplified and accelerated. In my work with some districts with limited time and funds, we have been able to accomplish the entire project in as little as six months.

2. What grades will the project include? Usually it makes sense to develop the curriculum for all grade levels in which that subject is required. For example, if your district requires the study of art between kindergarten and grade eight, then the project should include K–8. You can handle the high school elective art courses separately, rather than including them in the comprehensive revision. However, you do not have to include all of the required levels in one project. In some districts where I have worked, we have begun with the high school curriculum and then worked on the middle school curriculum, since the elementary curriculum seemed to be in good shape.

3. How will the project provide for different ability levels? You have several choices here. One choice is to develop a separate curriculum for each ability level. A second choice is to develop a common curriculum for all students and train teachers in responding to individual differences. A third choice is a compromise between these two positions—develop a common curriculum for the general population and then develop supplements for the less able and the gifted. (Chapter Seven explains some additional ways in which the mastery curriculum can be adapted so that it is more responsive to individual differences.)

4. What materials will be produced? Based on your assessment of the resources available and teacher needs, make a tentative decision about the kinds of materials you will produce. You may change your mind once you are into the project, but you should start with some tentative ideas. Here are the options:

◆ *A scope-and-sequence chart.* This is a basic document that will display in chart form what is emphasized from grade to grade. Although some districts manage without such charts, they are very useful in checking on

articulation of content between levels and development of skills from grade to grade.

◆ *Curriculum guides or other materials for teachers*, to guide them in their own planning. These tend to be rather general documents organized by grade level.

◆ *Detailed units of study.* Detailed units of study including specific plans for instruction are sometimes needed, especially by inexperienced teachers. They are also useful when the curriculum is attempting to integrate content from more than one field of study or more than one area within a field (such as integrating speaking, listening, reading, and writing in language arts).

◆ *Teacher-written learning materials for student use.* Some districts find it useful to develop model student-learning materials that teachers can then use in fashioning their own.

◆ *Curriculum-referenced tests.* Increasingly districts see the need for valid and reliable curriculum-referenced tests, to assist in aligning the curriculum and in assessing student achievement.

The process described below focuses on what seem to be the essential elements: the scope-and-sequence chart and the curriculum guides for teacher use.

3. Become acquainted with available materials in the field.

The next step is to collect and review the best available resources in the field. In doing this you are both developing your own knowledge base and accumulating resources for future use. Here are some of the materials you should gather.

◆ *State guidelines, requirements, and curriculum guides.* Analyze them closely to see how prescriptive they are and what help they can give you.

◆ *Exemplary curriculum guides from other school districts.* Most professional associations, including ASCD (Association for Supervision and Curriculum Development), provide for displays of such guides at their annual conferences. Such guides can give you some direction and some specific ideas for your own project. However, avoid outright plagiarizing. You want your guide to reflect your district's special needs and resources. If you do adapt any materials from other guides, be sure to ask permission and acknowledge the source in your publications.

◆ *Curriculum projects developed by nationally recognized professional groups.* Even though the days of buying and implementing "teacher proof" curricula are fortunately over, it still makes sense to examine the products of recent curriculum projects. If you find one that looks especially good, it might make sense to use it as the basis of your own work, involving your teachers in modifying it and adapting it for local use. In science and mathematics especially, where there seems to be a strong consensus among the profession about what should be taught, such adaptation might be a useful strategy.

◆ *Materials from appropriate professional associations.* Almost every professional association has produced curriculum guidelines for its field. As noted below, such materials can be very useful in the staff-development aspect of the project.

◆ *Textbooks and other instructional materials.* We all agree that the text should not determine the curriculum—but it does make sense to learn what the most recent texts are emphasizing. There is a caution, here, however. Remember that most texts are developed to sell in a national market. As a consequence, they make compromises. They leave out any potentially controversial content. And they repeat much content from grade to grade.

In the Appendix are some useful resources for both informing yourself and training your teachers. I have tried to include only materials that seem professionally reliable and are easy to use.

4. Orient and train the staff.

The next task is to conduct staff development to accomplish two goals: orient the staff about the nature and emphasis of the project and inform the staff about the best current thinking about that curriculum.

To accomplish the first is relatively simple. I have usually found that one carefully worded memo (something like the one shown in Figure 3.1) and one faculty meeting are sufficient. The ideas make so much sense to teachers that they ordinarily have no difficulty in accepting them.

The second task will require more time and effort. The intent here is to inform the teachers about current developments in that field, to give them an opportunity to discuss the recommendations of experts, and to help them reconceptualize the way they think about that subject. This last objective is important. There is a growing body of evidence that the way teachers think about a particular subject profoundly influences how they teach it. (See, for example, Gudmundadattir, Carey, and Wilson 1985.)

How do you accomplish this second task? First, review all the materials you have previously gathered and select those that seem to be most useful. Then disseminate those materials as background reading for what I call "staff development dialogs." (My thinking about these dialogs has been much influenced by Margaret Buchman's writings; see, for example, her 1985 article.) The intent of these dialogs is not to coach the teachers in acquiring a set of instructional skills; instead it is to help them think about the subject they teach—and to think about it in a reflective and inquiring manner. Here is the general tenor you wish to establish in these dialogs (and what you might say in a preliminary announcement and invitation):

> We are coming together to think about social studies and its place in our curriculum. We will be reading some brief reports summarizing the recommendations of experts in the field. The hope is that we will listen to those recommendations with an open mind. However, we will attempt to reflect about our own experiences as educational professionals—about what we have learned by teaching our students, in our classrooms. In the process we hope we can achieve a synthesis of the best of expert knowledge and our own lived experience.

In conducting these dialogs, you or a committee of teachers should read through the materials and identify four or five key issues in that field—the ones you consider most important from the standpoint of your faculty and your schools. Then take each of these key issues and proceed as follows.

1. Summarize the views of the experts about that issue.
2. Let teachers ask questions only to get greater clarity about what the experts recommend.
3. Ask each teacher to write a brief statement summarizing what he or she believes about that issue, based on the teacher's professional experience. These statements should be written prior to any discussion.
4. Have the teachers then meet in groups of five or six. Each teacher has a chance to read and explain his or her own statement. The rest of the group listen, ask questions, and respond briefly.

5. Each group makes a one-minute report to the large group. You listen closely to each report, limit each to one minute, and identify the extent of agreement and the source of disagreements.

6. Involve the entire group in thinking together about the major areas of disagreement. Don't push the group to premature and superficial agreement. If major differences exist, let them continue to be matters for further reflection and investigation.

7. Summarize the discussion.

The intent of these dialogic sessions is to create an atmosphere of open inquiry, not heated debate. The teachers first listen to the experts and are sure they understand before they differ. Then they work individually, so that each has an opportunity to discern and express a position, rather than having a few powerful members monopolize the discussion. Then they meet in small groups to listen to each other. Finally, after that reflection, expression, and sharing, they come together to explore remaining differences.

Through this process they all will know what the experts recommend. They all will know what their colleagues believe about key issues. And many will have begun the challenging process of rethinking their subject matter.

5. Survey the teachers.

Now you prepare to "map the ideal," to learn from the teachers what they believe should be taught for mastery at their grade level. The first important task in accomplishing this goal is to prepare the form for the mapping step. The structure and quality of the form will very much influence the nature and quality of the results.

To begin the preparation of the forms, first develop a goal statement for that field of study. Remember that the goals are the very general long-term outcomes to be attained after several years of study, like "communicate effectively," "acquire the skills and knowledge for good citizenship," and so on. The goal statement lists two kinds of mastery goals: those that the field will be primarily responsible for and those that the field will contribute to. If you have used the process explained in Chapter Two, you can use the final chart you have produced as a basis for the goal statement. If you have not used that process, then you and a group of teachers, administrators, and supervisors should produce a statement that includes both types of goals.

The next step is to determine what strands you will use in mapping that field of study. The term strands is used here in the following sense: divisions of a field of study that are used in planning for learning over a multiyear period. The strands are the horizontal elements on a scope-and-sequence chart; taken together, they determine the scope of that field of study. Thus, I have identified these strands for English-language arts: critical reading and literature, speaking and listening, written composition, critical and creative thinking, study and information processing skills, and grammar and language study. (I usually recommend that beginning reading, spelling, and handwriting be handled separately.) Obviously, others would conceptualize English-language arts differently; however, those strands seem to have worked well in projects where I served as a consultant. It is apparent from this example that the way the strands are conceptualized will influence the kinds of data you get.

Curriculum in the Catholic School

Kealey, R. 1985. 11–42. Washington, D.C.: National Catholic Educational Association.

3. What Is Special about Curriculum Development for a Catholic School?

Having examined how students learn and what is included in any school's curriculum, what are the implications for Catholic educators? Another way of phrasing this question is: What is special about the Catholic school program? Seven characteristics set the Catholic school apart from other schools.

1. Sponsorship

The local faith community sponsors the school.

The local Catholic school represent a concrete expression of the faith and hope of the community. The community believes that passing on the Catholic faith and tradition in a complete and systematic manner is an essential part of its heritage. The community also expresses the hope that future generations of graduates of the school will continue to be the Christian leaven in American society. While the local community of faith founds and sustains the school, it is linked to the local church and the world church through its association with the arch/diocese and/or religious community, and its adherence to Catholic church teachings. Essentially, the Catholic school is a visible sign of the church and the teaching mission of the church in the community, even in communities that are substantially non-Catholic.

Sponsorship implies two aspects. Sponsors provide direction for a school. Thus the parishioners, graduates, parents, students, clergy, administrators, faculty, staff and any others who make up the school community, provide some input into the program of the school. Under the leadership of the pastor and principal, this information is molded into a coherent program which is both educationally and theologically sound. The development of the school's program is a living expression of the community of faith that exists among the sponsors.

Sponsorship also implies support. The entire faith community has the responsibility of maintaining the school, which includes both personal efforts and financial support. If the school is only supported by the parents of its current students, it is then not an expression of the faith of the community. If people claim not to support the school because they do not send their children to it, they express a lack of understanding of the theology of the community of faith. The school faculty has a major responsibility to correct both of these situations.

2. Philosophy of Education

A philosophy of education expresses the shared beliefs of the school community. For a Catholic school, the good news of the gospels forms the foundation for these beliefs. The written philosophy elucidates these gospel values. Parents seeking to register their children in the school immediately learn the nature of the school from a reading of its philosophy.

One section of the philosophy speaks about the nature of the learner. A Catholic school philosophy does this in most positive and hopeful terms.

3. Goals

The goals state the end results of the school's program. These results refer to how the students will be different at the end of their fourth, eighth or twelfth year experience in a Catholic school. The goals are phrased in such a way that they can be easily evaluated.

In 1972, the American bishops stated the goals of Catholic education in their pastoral *To Teach as Jesus Did*. The purposes of Catholic education are to communicate the message of the gospel, to develop a faith community, to motivate the students to serve others, and to provide worshipping activities that reflect the faith of the community. Therefore, the local school community, in developing its goals, specifically addresses these four areas. What is the message? How do students grow in their sense of a faith community? What service activities do the students provide? How do they express their faith through worship?

The bishops did not intend to limit the goals of Catholic schools to the above four. Thus, the school will have specific academic goals according to the age of the students, social and affective goals reflecting the maturity of the students, physical and health goals, addressing the developmental level of the students.

4. Total Educational Program

Because the Catholic school program flows from a Christian philosophy, an educational program can be developed to help the students grow in all areas of learning, i.e., academic, affective, social, and physical. The Catholic school gives high priority to the religious development of students. This comprises three areas. First, the students learn the academic content of the Catholic religion. Certain facts, definitions, people, dates, rules, and readings exist that an intelligent Catholic should know. The religious studies courses provide this information. A second area of learning is growth in the faith. The whole atmosphere of the school is designed in such a way as to model and encourage the students to internalize the academic content of their religion and to act in a way reflecting the principles of their faith. The religious formation of the students is not limited to any one teacher or class, rather this is a prime responsibility of the entire faith community of the school. Finally, the students grow in the expression of their faith through worship. Students experience a variety of prayer form, different paraliturgical services, and eucharists, which reflect the mood and theme of the celebration.

The Catholic school recognizes that students have feelings and emotions. The program helps students learn about their feelings and appreciate these reactions, as well as how to deal with their feelings in a rational manner.

The Catholic school program also is a total program because of the intimate involvement of the parents in the education of their children. Parents provide the primary education to their children. It is primary in the sense that children learn first from their parents. It is primary in the sense that children learn at the deepest level of their being from their parents. It is primary in the sense that home learning is the most lasting. When parents elect to send their children to a Catholic school, they make a conscious choice about the type of education that they desire for their children. Parents' financial support of the Catholic school represents a monthly commitment to the ideals of that school. Catholic educators involve parents in their children's education. This is seen not only in the academic program but also in the programs related to the reception of the sacraments.

5. Academic Quality

While the Catholic school has a unique religious purpose and dimension to it, it also functions in a civil society and thus must prepare students for this work world. Over the last 20 years, Catholic school parents from different geographic areas, from multiple socioeconomic levels, from diverse national and ethnic backgrounds have been surveyed regarding their reasons for sending their children to Catholic schools. The answer that has appeared again and again in these research studies is their perception of the high quality of the educational program of the Catholic school. One of the highest expressions of Christianity is to teach others, to instruct the ignorant. Thus, a Catholic school cannot exist unless it is a good school.

The Catholic school faculty cannot be content merely with providing the fundamentals of learning, it also must train the higher thinking powers of the students. The Catholic school graduate is able to critically evaluate, to pass reasoned judgments on current events, to understand the wonders of science, to appreciate the arts.

Finally, the academic quality of the Catholic school is ensured by a regular evaluation of its program.

6. Values Development

A Catholic school is different from all other types of schools because it seeks to inculcate its students with Christian values. Other schools may be concerned with civic values, or with teaching students how to form values. The Catholic school has at the heart of the curriculum, the values contained in the gospels. These values are identified and activities are developed to help students internalize them.

This values development takes place in all classes. Therefore, students see the application of the value of justice in social studies, science, health, literature and mathematics. All classes provide students with the opportunity to examine the value and to reflect on its meaning in their daily lives. As the teacher teaches a skill to help students learn the content, so the content is designed to move students to act in a particular way. The teacher also provides opportunities for students to act in ways consistent with their values.

7. Teaching Ministers

The final distinguishing characteristic of the Catholic school is the teacher. The teacher is not merely a teacher, but is a minister performing a sacred ministry in the church. St. Paul has discussed the variety of ministries in the church. Teaching is one of them. This understanding that the teacher is a minister is crucial for the success of the school's program. Because teachers are conscious of their ministry, they actively become involved in all of the above areas of service. These are not regarded as extras; rather they are regarded as an exercise of their ministry.

Summary

1. The Catholic school is sponsored and supported by the faith community.
2. The Catholic school's philosophy reflects the gospel values.
3. The goals of the Catholic school indicate the breadth of its program.
4. The Catholic school's curriculum assists students to grow in all areas of life.
5. A Catholic school provides an excellent academic education.
6. The training of students in values and how to form values is central to the curriculum of a Catholic school.
7. Teachers view themselves as teaching ministers of the Catholic church.

Readings

Declaration on Christian Education. In Abbot, Walter (Ed.), *Documents of Vatican II*. New York: American Press, 1966. This statement for Vatican II sets the tone for the present understanding of Catholic education.

Gilbert, John, *Pastor as Shepherd of the School Community*. Washington, D.C.: National Catholic Educational Association, 1983.

Father Gilbert presents a model of a team ministry in managing the Catholic school.

National Conference of Catholic Bishops. *Sharing the Light of Faith*. Washington, D.C.: United States Catholic Conference, 1979. This is a presentation of the reforms of Vatican II for the American Catholic church.

National Conference of Catholic Bishops. *Teach Them*. Washington, D.C.: United States Catholic Conference, 1976. This represents the thinking of the American bishops on the Catholic school.

National Conference of Catholic Bishops. *To Teach as Jesus Did*. Washington, D.C.: United States Catholic Conference, 1972. This represents the thinking of the American bishops on all phases of Catholic education.

4. How Is the Catholic School Curriculum Developed?

This chapter attempts to make practical what has been stated in previous chapters. In order to do this, a seven-step process will be explained in detail.

Step 1. Formation of School Community Curriculum Committee

The leadership in this entire process resides in the school principal. This leadership directs, organizes and facilitates the work of the committee. This leadership does not imply developing and advocating certain positions. The school administrator provides the leadership which enables the group to move efficiently through its charge. The principal provides leadership in schools that currently exist and wish to reexamine their curricula and in schools that are only in the process of being formed. The principal stimulates ideas, leads the group to consider these ideas, moves the group to arrive at a consensus, records the decisions made, suggests further action for the committee, and implements the program.

The chief administrators of the parish and the school appoint the committee. A limited number of people form the committee, about 10 to 15 members. Limiting the number provides an opportunity for all to actively participate. At the same time, the committee includes all groups in the school community: school and parish administration (schools that are not parish schools may wish to include clergy from some of the parishes from which the school draws its population); diocesan school office; teachers (religious and/or lay), students (this is especially important for junior and senior high schools); parents of students currently in the school and parents of graduates; parishioners; non-parish community members; graduates; and any other significant groups in the community. The committee members demonstrate knowledge of education, commitment to Catholic education, facility in expressing ideas, willingness to work, adherence to principles, and ability to compromise. The formulators of the committee give it a clear purpose and a timeline in which to complete its work. The school community curriculum committee is best described as an ad hoc committee. Its chief purpose is to develop the school philosophy and goals, and to ensure that the school program adheres to them.

Step 2. Development of School Philosophy

The committee first examines what their beliefs about education include. These beliefs revolve around several key areas: the nature of the learner; how a person learns; the purposes of education (schooling); the function of the teacher; the responsibility of the school for ensuring learning; the interrelationship between home and school.

The Catholic school curriculum committee should reflect on several documents before arriving at answers to these questions: the gospels; *Declaration on Christian Education; To Teach as Jesus Did; Teach Them; Sharing the Light of Faith; Lay Catholics*. These will introduce the committee to the most recent thinking on Catholic education.

The philosophy is a written document to enable all people to more closely examine it and understand it. This philosophy need not be long and wordy. It avoids using slogans and stereotypical language. The more specific the committee makes the statement of the philosophy, the greater the likelihood that it will be implemented in the school's program. The more specific the committee makes the statement of the philosophy, the easier it will be to evaluate the school program. The more specific the committee makes the philosophy, the more understandable it will be to parents seeking to place their children in the school.

A school philosophy sets the tone for the school. Everything flows from this clear statement. All the parts of the school program are in harmony with this statement. Everyone involved in the school accepts the school philosophy. A teacher who does not accept the philosophy or has some difficulty with it does not belong on the school staff.

Chief responsibilities of the principal include regularly reminding the faculty of the philosophy, and inaugurating new programs only in light of the current school philosophy.

Step 3. Determination of Student Characteristics

In this step, the committee examines carefully the student population. The committee considers the learning potential, learning rate, special learning needs, and future educational opportunities of the students. Before proceeding in the development of the school's program, the committee paints a very clear picture of the students who will attend the school. The emerging documents in this curriculum process evolve in light of the particular student population. While a philosophy of education transcends a particular school population, the goals, learning objectives, and instructional activities address a particular group of students.

In examining the student population, the committee determines the percentage of students who function on level, two years above level, or two years below level; are expected to continue their education; are non-Catholics; speak a language other than English; have different handicapping conditions; are from a particular national or ethnic group; come from a single parent home; have had some previous formal educational experiences; come from different economic levels.

Answers to all of these questions will affect the school's program. If many students academically function substantially below level, they require a remedial program. If many students come from a particular national background, they deserve some attention given to their national origins. If many students are from a low socioeconomic level, they can only afford a certain level of tuition.

Step 4. Development of School Goals

The school goals picture the students at the end of their school experience. They state what the students will be able to do as a result of having attended the school for a period of years. The school's goals refer to the students. They do not talk about teaching or instruction. Rather, they state what the learning will be, i.e., how will the students demonstrate by their behavior that they have learned what the school sought to teach them. The school exists for the benefit of the students. Therefore, concentration is given to the development of the students.

A school goal exists for each area in which the school community believes that the school has some responsibility in helping students grow. This responsibility may belong solely to the school, e.g., learning higher level mathematical operations. It may be shared by the school and home, e.g., understanding human sexuality. Or, it may be shared by the school, home and larger community, e.g., developing civic responsibility. Through dialogue, the school community curriculum committee formulates the outcomes that it expects the graduates to achieve. The goals address: areas related to academic learning; areas related to religious development; areas related to socialization; areas related to physical development; and areas related to affective development. Formulation of too many goals tends to make them trivial and prevents a person from discovering the major thrust of the school.

The school goals, written in behavioral form, identify the learners, state the behavior the learners will perform, indicate the exact nature of the learning, and fix the degree to which the learners will have achieved this learning. This type of formulation permits the faculty to measure the progress of the students as they progress toward acquiring the goals. Students merit graduation because they have achieved the goals.

School goals indicate what the vast majority of students will be able to achieve. School goals do not express an ideal; they express the hoped-for reality for the students. If goals state unattainable ideals, students may be discouraged and faculty may begin to set their own goals, which may be unrealistic in their simplicity. The school's handbook for parents lists these goals and clearly indicates that students are required to achieve them. The teacher regularly reminds the students of these goals and their progress toward achieving them.

Writing and publishing the school's goals complete the major responsibility of the school community curriculum committee. The school faculty addresses the remaining three steps. These professionals have the expertise to implement the instructional program within the guidelines established by the school community curriculum committee. The committee has set the policy and now the details are developed by those who have the necessary knowledge and experience. The school community curriculum committee may review the work of the faculty to ensure that it does implement a program to lead students to acquire the goals within the framework of the school's philosophy. This committee also may set a timeline for the completion of the remaining three steps. However, the school community curriculum committee should not become involved in matters that require technical knowledge, which they do not possess. The faculty trusts that the school community curriculum committee has developed a sound philosophy and an attainable set of goals. The school community curriculum committee respects the professional competence of the faculty to create a specific program which will implement their desired ideals.

Step 5. Writing Specific Learning Objectives

The faculty now sets down in print the specific steps that lead students to the attainment of the goals. These specific steps outline the learnings that move students from neophytes to scholars. Learning objectives are established for each of the subject areas that are part of the school's course of study. Learning objectives address each of these subjects in the three areas of learning, i.e., psychomotor, cognitive, and affective.

This writing process consists of five steps:

a. Adaptation

This step may sound like a monumental task for the faculty. However, there is no need to re-invent the wheel. Scope and sequence charts exist for each of the major subject areas. State education departments, professional associations, or textbook writers have created these, and they represent the best current educational thinking. A faculty would be foolhardy to ignore them. The faculty's task involves taking one of these existing scopes and sequences and adapting it to the unique school population in light of the school's philosophy in order to enable the students to arrive at the set goals.

The word adapt means "to make apt." Probably no currently existing scope and sequence developed by the three groups mentioned above suits a particular school 100 percent. State education departments and arch/diocesan school offices attempt to provide a program that all schools in the state can follow to some degree. In every state, vast distinctions exist between urban schools and rural schools. Professional associations tend to concentrate on their own subject areas. Many of their guidelines miss the opportunity to integrate instruction across the subject areas. Textbook publishers wish to sell their books in the 50 states. They, therefore, list what is common to most of the states.

Therefore, many items in textbooks will not be appropriate to a particular community and the textbook may neglect to mention items that are most important to that community.

The faculty uses one of these listings of instructional objectives. Each objective is examined in light of the student characteristics discovered in Step 3. Faculty members ask themselves, "Is this objective appropriate and necessary for our students?" They also ask themselves, "Is this objective too easy or too difficult for our students?" Depending upon the answers, the faculty may decide to include the objective in its scope and sequence, to omit the objective, or to place it at a different grade level. The faculty also may decide that some learning objectives should be added. These may relate to specific requirements of the state, local government or arch/diocesan school office, to needs of a particular ethnic or national group, or to the learning style of students. The faculty begins this adaptation procedure at its lowest grade and follows the procedures through all grade levels. The faculty reminds itself that the learning objectives for all the grades must enable the students to acquire the goals of the school. Thus, the adaptation process moves from one grade to the next and develops a sequential learning plan.

In this adaptation process, the faculty lists for each subject by each grade level, the essential learnings the students need to acquire. These essential learnings include specific knowledges, e.g., the steps taken for a bill to become a law, definition of a noun, characteristics of specific elements. These essential learnings also include specific skills, e.g., determining a conclusion from a set of facts, reducing a run-on sentence, safety procedures followed in a chemistry laboratory. Students are held accountable for this list of essential learnings. The mastery of these learnings determines if a student will be moved to a higher grade.

b. Values

A further aspect of adaptation exists for Catholic schools. This involves taking these listings of knowledges and skills and integrating into them the Christian values that the students are to acquire. This integration of Christian values into every curriculum area distinguishes the Catholic school from other schools. As the scope and sequence for each subject area clearly indicates the skills to be learned, and the knowledges to be memorized, so this scope and sequence must list the gospel values to be acquired from the particular content.

What are these gospel values? The National Catholic Educational Association's program of *Vision and Values* has identified eight values: faith; hope; courage; reconciliation; community; service; justice; and love. A careful reading of the beatitudes will enable the reader to match these eight values to the eight beatitudes. A school may seek to take the Ten Commandments and turn each of these into a value. Another school may develop its own set of values based upon the teaching of Christ in the New Testament. These lists of values probably will not differ greatly from one another, because certain aspects of Christ's teaching are so clear. The essential element is that each faculty member knows the specific values that the students are to acquire. These are no longer hidden behind abstract terms such as "gospel values," "Christian values," or Catholic principles. The identification of particular values enables the teacher to structure the learning environment to ensure that the students will acquire the values. The identification of the particular values enables the teacher to measure the growth of the students in the acquisition of values. The identification of the particular values enables the entire school community to see exactly what it is seeking to accomplish.

Therefore, the Catholic school's list of learning objectives includes not only the knowledges and skills to be learned, but it also includes (1) a clear statement of the values to be internalized by the students; (2) the content that will be used to present these values to the students; (3) a variety of activities that the students will do in order to give them practice in acting in a way, reflecting the particular value; and (4) behaviors that the students will display, which show that they have internalized the values.

Since a basic tenet of Catholic education is that values are infused into all subject areas, this listing is done by grade for each subject. This enables each teacher to foster particular values that are pertinent to the content and in a way that respects the developmental stage of the students. It also enables each teacher to regularly measure the growth of the students as they internalize these values.

c. Sequential

This listing of knowledges, skills and values follows a sequential presentation. This means that the students learn the easier material first, then move to more difficult concepts, and finally end with the most demanding ideas. The school's listing of the scope and sequence of learnings resembles a staircase. A gradual and even progression takes place from one level to the next. Each step is dependent on the previous step and prepares the way for the next step. A teacher looks at what is to be taught this year in light of what the students learned last year and will be expected to learn the following year.

This sequential progression takes place in small steps. Success forms the foundation of internal motivation. Small steps ensure the likelihood of students achieving success. Small steps demonstrate to the students that they have learned something. Small steps make the work of the teacher easier since the teacher can develop an entire lesson around one particular learning. Small steps enable the teacher to more clearly evaluate the students' progress and then go back and reteach what has not been learned.

By the time students leave elementary school or secondary school, they do not need to have learned everything in the world. Students have their whole lives to learn. The school's task is to teach key concepts and to teach them well. Therefore, students leave the school having a basic fund of information, knowing how to learn, and most importantly, having a desire to continue to learn.

d. Behavioral Objectives

The learnings are written in the form of behavioral objectives in order to clearly emphasize the behavior that the students will exhibit, which indicates to the teacher that the students have learned the material. As the faculty write these objectives, they constantly ask one another to examine the objectives to discover if each states what is intended, and if all members of the faculty understand the objective in the same way.

The objectives, as they are written in the school's scope and sequence, include five aspects:

---

1. Learners

Who are the students who will demonstrate this activity? These are the learners. The learners may include the entire class, the average students in the class, the slower students, the faster learners, or an individual student. A teacher using the scope and sequence needs to know who is expected to learn this material.

When it writes its scope and sequence of learnings, the school focuses on a vast majority of students on a particular grade level. The stated learnings address this vast group of students. Some of the students will learn the material after only a very brief exposure to it, others will need more time. Nevertheless, all the students will be able to learn the material. An adaptation of the school's curriculum is made for students who will have problems learning the stated material.

Obviously, each learning objective need not repeat the definition of the learner. However, since the teacher needs to know who are the intended learners, that information should appear somewhere in the document.

---

2. Action

The objective identifies the specific action that the students will exhibit. A difference in learning exists between defining, identifying, evaluating, and creating. At one grade level, students may be asked to define a noun. At another grade level, they may be required to identify a noun in a given sentence. At another grade level, they may be expected to evaluate the use of a noun as opposed to the use of a pronoun in a particular sentence. Finally, they may be expected to create sentences with different types of nouns in them. These four acts require the students to display different levels of mastery. Therefore, the faculty very carefully selects the most fitting verb to identify the degree of learning.

Since the students display an action (writing, outlining, matching, constructing a timeline, drawing a picture or diagram, pronouncing, etc.), the teacher can very easily determine if the students have learned the concept.

---

3. Learning

Now the faculty states the particular learning, e.g., multiplication of a three-digit number by a two-digit number, causes of the Revolutionary War, stages in the development of a frog, mysteries of the rosary, a pattern II sentence, a main idea and details, actions that display a sense of justice, or behaviors that indicate a commitment to the community. These learnings come from one of the three sources mentioned above. The faculty limits the learnings to those skills, concepts, values that are essential for students at this stage of their development.

4. Limitations

The objective may include some limitation on the part of the learners as they demonstrate their learnings. At one stage, the students may be required to place words in alphabetic order using the alphabet chart. At another stage, the students may be required to place the words in alphabetic order using only their memory. At one level, students may create a timeline of events leading to the outbreak of the Civil War, using the information in the textbook, while later they may be required to evaluate the causes of the Civil War as presented by two authors. These are examples of limitations.

Language arts, social studies, religious studies, and science are examples of a spiral curriculum. This means that certain key ideas are presented each year, but each year the learning is deeper and broader. Thus, students in the first grade will write very simple sentences. As they move up the grades, students are taught to create more complex, colorful, and precise sentences. The limitations distinguish the learning at one stage from the learning at another stage.

5. Degree of Mastery

Finally, the objective states what degree of mastery is expected of the students. Must the learners demonstrate 100 percent mastery or is 80 percent mastery sufficient to indicate learning has taken place? Spelling requires 100 percent mastery for each word. Social studies may require only 80 percent mastery of specific content. Even within a subject like social studies, the faculty may signify 1 percent of mastery for some content and a different percent of mastery for other content. The degree of mastery also can be used to separate the level of learning at one grade level from that at another grade level.

By stating the degree of mastery, every teacher and all the students know exactly what is expected. The teacher knows when to move on to new material, because the students have mastered the present material. The students know what they must do in order to achieve a certain grade on an examination.

e. Accountability

Many educational writers have criticized the use of behavioral objectives. While some of this criticism is valid, other statements hold little validity. Each faculty member decides the format for its scope and sequence. The format is consistent from one grade to the next. Faculty members know that their work lasts long after they leave the school. In today's mobile society, some teachers only spend a few years on a particular faculty and then move to another school or to other employment. The school's program remains and provides an unbroken guide for the education of the students. As new teachers join the faculty, the scope and sequence, written in the form of behavioral objectives, helps to ensure the continuity of the program because each instructional objective is phrased so precisely.

A clearly-stated listing of learnings enables the students, teacher, administrator, and parent to demand accountability. The students know what it is they should learn each year. The teacher has a list of the knowledges, skills, and values to be mastered by the students on this grade level. The administrator knows which teacher is responsible for the students learning this specific content. The parent can judge if the students have acquired the goals of the school, since the achievement of the learning objectives results in the acquisition of the goals.

Such accountability does not lead to divisiveness. Rather, it builds community. All members of the school community realize that they play a decisive role in the school's educational mission. All members of the school community work together to achieve the goals. All members of the school community support and help one another to master the learning objectives. Such a school community has achieved a high degree of a faith community.

Step 6. Determination of Specific Learning Activities

Having set down what is to be learned, the faculty now sets down how it is to be taught. This includes the four areas of materials, learning activities, teaching/learning styles, and correlation across the subject areas.

a. Materials

Some educational writers have indicated that the textbook is used in over 90 percent of American classrooms and they go on to say that the textbook then becomes the scope and sequence for 90 percent of these classrooms. This manual has tried to make the point that each school has its own scope and sequence that is independent of the textbook. This scope and sequence serves as a road map through the textbook. The scope and sequence indicates parts of the textbook that will be emphasized, and parts that will be ignored.

An important step in the curriculum process is the selection of textbooks and other educational materials. These are all selected in light of the school's scope and sequence. The textbook is chosen after the school has developed its own scope and sequence. The faculty seeks a textbook that most closely addresses the instructional objectives and reflects the philosophy of the school. Catholic educators have the responsibility of selecting instructional materials that reflect Christian values or are, at least, not antagonistic to them. Since Catholic school editions of textbooks no longer exist, the importance of the school's scope and sequence listing the Christian values associated with the content can be seen.

Other learning materials include audio visual aids, supplementary textbooks, TV programs, computer programs, and field trips.

The school considers its present materials and associates them with particular learning objectives. Through this process, the teacher sees the skills to be acquired, the content to be memorized, the values to be internalized, and the materials that will help the students do these things. It also tells the teacher that such material is available and tells other teachers that they should not use this material because it is intended for a specific lesson.

Requests for additional materials by teachers indicate how these new materials relate to the school's instructional program.

b. Learning Activities

A visitor to many kindergarten classes in the early spring will notice small jars on the windowsill with bean plants growing out of them. The first grade often has the same activity. The visitor may notice the same project in all the classrooms of a given elementary school. While this is a fine learning activity, it probably does not deserve repetition eight years in a row. Such a school probably has not designated certain learning activities for particular learnings and for specific grades.

Learning activities include: term papers; library projects; field trips; community service; community involvement; reading lists; guest speakers; demonstrations; creation of dioramas, collages, or posters; and debates. The faculty takes these special projects and associates them with specific learnings. A learning activity is not repeated on another grade level unless there is some unique aspect to it, which requires a different degree of learning or slightly changes the learning activity.

c. Learning/Teaching Styles

Much has recently been written about the differences in learning styles. Again some of this research is quite controversial. However, students do learn in different ways. This simply means that when a person is trying to learn some information, a preference is made in the way it will be learned. One student will learn by listening, another by reading, and a third by viewing a film. Each teacher also teaches in a different way. The teacher also tends to emphasize one of the above modalities in presenting information. The ideal is to match the learning style of the student with the teaching style of the teacher. While this is most difficult in a classroom of 30 students and one teacher, the teacher needs to be flexible in using different presentation styles for different students.

The teacher, therefore, builds into the lesson a variety of activities and approaches in order to provide some options for students because they learn through different channels. In giving a book report, students can draw pictures, record a commercial for the book, read an exciting section to the class, write a summary, or discuss it with another student. In teaching new vocabulary words, the teacher may use a phonetic approach (auditory), use the word several times in blackboard activities (visual), and have the students write the word and its meaning (kinesthetic).

While these different approaches need not be listed in the school's written scope and sequence, each teacher needs to be aware of the need for variety in the instruction. The faculty may choose to include a short selection on this need for variety as part of the introduction to the school's scope and sequence.

d. Correlation Across the Subject Areas

In a self-contained classroom, the teacher knows the expected learnings of the students in all the subject areas. In a departmental system, the teacher concentrates on one area and may not be aware of the expected learnings of the students outside that area. This should not happen. The teacher should have a general idea of the students' programs in all subject areas. At least two reasons require this across-the-board knowledge of learnings.

In school, each teacher works with students and each one of these students is a holistic being. This means that what a student experiences affects the entire personhood of that student. Each experience changes the student and makes the student more receptive or less receptive for the next learning. In order to teach students, each teacher presents specific content. Subject areas are broken down into subdivisions and subdivisions are broken down into gradations of instructional objectives. The way schools operate, in a certain sense, violates the way students learn. This division between holistic learning and specific instructional objectives is necessary for a school to function. The way to correct the situation is for the teacher to provide for transfer of learning from one class to another. For example, the literature teacher may remind the students of their knowledge of a specific historical period, or the science teacher may recall to the minds of the students some basic principles of mathematics, or the foreign language teacher may refer to a particular English grammatical construction. Such activities help students to discover the interrelationships that exist in the intellectual world.

The teacher needs to be aware of the students' expected learning in all subjects, especially when assignments are presented. The English teacher may require the students to write essays of only two short paragraphs, while the social studies teacher may ask the students to write a term paper. The science teacher may require the students to work out some scientific formulas while the students have not yet learned the mathematical principles involved. Such situations can easily be avoided by the teacher knowing the expected learnings of the students in all areas.

Learning is much deeper when the students can hook their new learning on to information they already possess. The more "hooks," the deeper the learning. Transfer of learning occurs when the new situation closely mirrors the original situation. Efforts that the faculty make to correlate the learning objective from one subject to another in the development of the school's scope and sequence will both deepen the degree of learning and provide for easy transfer to new situations.

Step 7. The Evaluation of the School Curriculum

The most fundamental question that the faculty asks itself or that an outside evaluation team asks the school is, "Are the students learning?" A school exists to achieve this objective. The curriculum, the school program, outlines what the students learn and how they are to learn it.

A number of different levels exist on which a school can be evaluated. The question, "What is the purpose of the school?" will lead to an examination of the school's philosophy and its goals. A faculty may call in an "expert" to investigate the sequencing of learning objectives in a particular subject area. A principal may visit all classes in a particular discipline to determine if the teaching staff is implementing the written scope and sequence. An outside team may visit classrooms to determine if the instructional activities and materials are truly effective. The success of the graduates may provide some information on whether the school is achieving its goals. The students may be given a school test or a standardized test. All of these procedures will help to evaluate parts of the curriculum. Since all of these have been discussed extensively in other publications, only two things will be said about the evaluation process.

First, evaluation is an integral part of the curriculum development process. Evaluation is an integral part of the school's program. Evaluation should be carried out on a regular basis. In developing the school's curriculum, or program, the school community curriculum committee and the faculty have built into the program procedures for periodic evaluation. This evaluation process is quite specific and includes timetables for evaluation and reporting results of the evaluation.

The second point regarding the evaluation concerns who does the evaluation. Growth comes from within both a person and an institution. Therefore, the prime characteristic of any school evaluation is that it is self-evaluation. The school community curriculum committee and the faculty carry out the major portion of the evaluation. This concerns both the evaluation itself and the program to correct the discovered weaknesses. Change takes place when the people most affected are intimately part of the change process.

Summary

1. The school leadership establishes a school community curriculum committee.
2. The school community curriculum committee formulates the school philosophy, identifies the unique characteristics of the students, and develops the school goals.
3. The faculty writes the specific learning objectives and determines the learning activities.
4. The school community curriculum committee and the school faculty develop and implement an evaluation plan.

Readings

Kibler, Robert, et al. *Objectives for Instruction*. Boston: Allyn and Bacon, Inc., 1975. This is a clear and concise explanation of educational objectives.

Reck, Carleen and Coreil, Judith. *School Evaluation of the Catholic Elementary School: An Overview*. Washington, D.C.: National Catholic Educational Association, 1983. This explains the process of evaluation, lists 109 criteria for Catholic schools, and lists possible evaluation procedures.

Reck, Carleen and Coreil, Judith. *Verifying the Vision—A Self-Evaluation Instrument for the Catholic Elementary School*. Washington, D.C.: National Catholic Educational Association, 1984. This instrument provides a comprehensive plan for the evaluation of an elementary school.

Reck, Carleen (Ed.). *Vision and Values*. Washington, D.C.: National Catholic Educational Association, 1980. This is a step-by-step program for helping a school develop its philosophy and infusing values into all curriculum areas.

Secondary School Department. *Self-Study Guide for Catholic High Schools*. Washington, D.C.: National Catholic Educational Association, 1981. This is one format for a comprehensive evaluation of a school.

5. How Is the Curriculum Implemented in the Classroom?

No matter how well the school community works together to develop the school curriculum, no matter how clear is the written listing of learning objectives, no matter how interrelated are the learning objectives, the materials, and the activities, the success of the school's program depends on the individual teacher in each classroom. Unless the teacher internalizes the school's philosophy, the program is a shell without substance. Unless the teacher actively implements the school's learning objectives, the goals of the school are not achieved. Unless the teacher fosters the implementation of the program, the learnings are diverse and uncoordinated. The classroom teaching minister remains the most essential element in the curriculum development process. What are the responsibilities of the classroom teacher in regard to the implementation of the program?

This brief manual does not afford an opportunity to examine in detail many specific responsibilities of the classroom teacher. Such responsibilities include school organization, grouping procedures, management techniques, testing and grading procedures and homework assignments. Nor does this brief manual afford an opportunity to explore the relationships among the members of the school community. Because these are not considered here, an inference should not be drawn that these are unimportant. However, when examining the procedures, one should examine them in light of the school's philosophy and goals. The procedures represent the implementation of the program and, therefore, they reflect and embody the principles contained in the philosophy and goals. The procedures and relationships model and exemplify the philosophy and goals. If the procedures don't embody the philosophy and the goals, then new procedures and relationships need to be created. Three aspects of the many-faceted role of the teacher are presented here.

Adherence to the Program

The success or failure of a program can only be determined if the program is implemented. Therefore, the classroom teacher needs to adhere very closely to the written curriculum of the school. This involves three aspects of the school's program.

First, the teacher accepts the philosophy of the school as written by the school community curriculum committee. This philosophy details the beliefs of the community regarding the purposes of education and how children learn. This philosophy sets the tone for the entire school program. When a teacher accepts the philosophy, the teacher allows it to influence his/her actions and the teacher becomes a living model of the philosophy. If a teacher cannot accept the philosophy, the teacher should neither be hired nor accept a position on the faculty. To do so would be dishonest to the school's philosophy and to oneself.

Second, the teacher believes that the students can achieve the goals set by the school community. The vast majority of the students can attain the goals. The teacher cannot say that certain students will never be able to achieve the goals, because these goals reflect the realistic examination and expectations of the school community.

Finally, the teacher develops daily lesson plans which move students toward the attainment of the school goals. These lesson plans spring from the specific listing of knowledges, skills, and values. The school's scope and sequence of learning objectives serves as a constant guide for classroom instruction. Instruction from the beginning of the school year to the end of the school year mirrors these learning objectives. Deviation from these central learnings should only happen when this departure enhances or enriches the stated learning objectives.

Fosters the Development of Values

The Catholic school teacher considers the development of values in the students an essential part of the role of the teaching minister. This personal consideration leads the teacher to create programs in the classroom which deepen in the students the Christian values listed in the school's scope and sequence of learning objectives. The teaching minister also embodies the values contained in the school's scope and sequence.

Today, more than at any other time in the history of Catholic education, the American Catholic church calls on the teaching minister to announce the good news of the gospel as it applies to modern society. At times, the teaching minister will need to announce and vigorously support unpopular positions, e.g., the right to life of all people whether they be the unborn, the elderly, or the prisoner; the halt of nuclear armament, the distribution of economic resources for the good of all. A Catholic school teacher who does not actively foster the development of values in students does not deserve the title of minister.

A Concern for all Students

Students come in many varieties: fast learners and slow learners; visual learners and auditory learners; active learners and passive learners; intuitive learners and incremental learners; emotionally-charged learners and emotionally-neutral learners. They all reflect the uniqueness of God. The teaching minister seeks to meet the unique characteristics of all these learners. This challenge the teacher cannot disregard.

By structuring the classroom lessons and using a variety of approaches, the teacher attempts to meet these needs. While the teacher may not be successful every time, the teacher must never stop trying to assist each individual student.

Summary

1. The teaching minister adheres to the school's written curriculum.
2. The teaching minister fosters values among students.
3. The teaching minister shows a deep concern for all students.

Readings

Code of Ethics for the Catholic School Teacher. Washington, D.C.: National Catholic Educational Association, 1982. This lists the attitudes and practices required of Catholic school teachers as they relate to students, parents and the community.

Teacher as Minister Weekly Plan Book. Washington, D.C.: National Catholic Educational Association, 1985. This practical teaching aid includes many statements on the ministry role of the teacher.

6. Who Are the Personnel Needed to Implement the Catholic School Curriculum?

The chief need of the American Catholic school is for teachers and administrators to reflect the above desired reality. The American Catholic school will survive only if its staff truly internalizes the meaning of the term, "teaching minister."

Role of Principal

The principal plays the pivotal role in this call to ministry. Educational research has repeatedly shown that the local building principal has the greatest effect on a school's program. A new principal can completely change the entire school program. The principal's class is the faculty of the school. The principal accepts as a primary responsibility the development of professional and competent teachers, who regard their teaching ministry as a gift from Christ, to be used to lead students to the knowledge of the truths of the gospels.

The principal can deepen in teachers their sense of ministry by:

◆ Hiring only teachers who are willing to grow in their commitment to the teaching ministry in a Catholic school;

- Providing cognitive information to the teacher about the teaching ministry;
- Initiating occasions for the faculty to pray and worship together;
- Challenging the teaching minister to truly live a life reflecting gospel values;
- Discussing with the teachers the meaning of faith in their lives as adult Catholics;
- Assisting the minister to become an effective and competent teacher;
- Reducing as much as possible the amount of unnecessary work for the teacher; and
- Supporting the teacher in times of trials.

Needs of the Teaching Minister

While the teacher has many responsibilities, the teacher also has many needs. The school administrator, the pastor and local clergy, the local school community, the diocesan school office, and the American church come to the aid of the teaching minister. The teacher lives a lonely life. The teacher spends the day in the privacy of the classroom. No other adult observes what happens. No one praises the teacher for a fine lesson or suggests ways to improve a weak lesson. The teacher leaves school at three o'clock, attends to family responsibilities, and finally prepares lessons. No opportunity may present itself to discuss what happened in the classroom that day. Quickly another day begins. What can the school community do to assist the teacher and what can the teacher do to become a more effective minister?

First, the teacher needs feedback about the work done in the classroom. While the principal may provide some of this feedback at the time of a formal class evaluation, this is not enough. The principal shows an interest in what happens in the classroom by being available to talk to the teacher, by asking the teacher about the day, by frequently visiting the classroom, and by regularly praising the teacher. The teacher seeks help from the administrator and from other teachers. The teacher asks how a particular lesson is taught, how classroom routines are managed, how records are maintained. The talk of teachers in school is not about the weather or last night's TV show. Discussions center on the task of the teacher, helping children learn. Faculty meetings do not deal with routine matters, but provide a forum to discuss teaching/learning problems.

Second, every teacher needs inservice. Only one teacher is the master teacher. Every other teacher tries to imitate his/her example. The teacher seeks staff development programs, actively participates, and implements the ideas in the classroom. This inservice includes practical approaches to classroom instruction in the various subject areas. It also includes techniques for integrating activities and programs which help students acquire values and how these values are manifested in the students' daily lives.

Finally, today's teacher needs help in growing in a deeper understanding and commitment to the gospel message. While the typical teacher is a product of at least 12 years of Catholic education, the teacher had only two to four courses in religious studies in college. Catholicism is an adult religion. The knowledge gained in elementary and secondary school about one's religion is not enough to foster continued growth as an adult. Through the teaching of the pope, the local hierarchy, theologians, and spiritual writers, new insights are provided into the mysteries of God. The principal takes the lead in helping the teacher learn about these developments. The teacher anxiously seeks to obtain a fuller understanding of these matters. Discussion with other adults leads to clarity of one's own ideas and the ideas of others. These discussion sessions may naturally lead to the group sharing prayer or worshipping together to express their faith.

Needs of the Principal

While the principal has great and many responsibilities, the principal also has needs. When the classroom teacher is lonely, frequently the principal is lonelier. When the classroom teacher needs praise, the principal needs more recognition. When the classroom teacher spends hours preparing lessons for students, the principal spends days writing reports for agencies.

What are some things a principal can do to help satisfy these needs?

1. Regularly spend some time in reflective prayer to recall the purpose of administrative ministry.
2. Regularly spend some time with other administrators to creatively discuss common problems.
3. Actively seek to improve one's administrative skills by attendance at programs or reading in the field.
4. Flexibly follow a realistic and well thought out schedule, making modifications only when necessary.
5. Frequently visit classes merely to observe the joy in students' faces as they learn something.

Summary

1. The principal plays the decisive role in staff development at the local level.
2. Teaching ministers have needs that the entire school community helps to satisfy.
3. The principal has needs which can be satisfied.

Readings

Glatthorn, Allan and Shields, Sister Carmel R. *Differentiated Supervision for Catholic Schools*. Washington, D.C.: National Catholic Educational Association, 1983. The authors present a variety of approaches to help teachers become more effective educators.

Hennessy, Sister Rosemarie. *The Principal as Prophet*. Washington, D.C.: National Catholic Educational Association, 1981. This is a series of reflection comparing the principal to an Old Testament prophet.

McBride, Alfred. *The Christian Formation of Teachers*. Washington, D.C.: National Catholic Educational Association, 1981. A presentation on the role of the teacher and model inservice programs.

Making Connections: Teaching and the Human Brain

Caine, R. N., and G. Caine. 1991. 48–50, 59–61, 80–87, 102–05, 112–13.
Alexandria, Va.: Association for Supervision and Curriculum Development.

Comparison of Route and Map Approaches to a Lesson

Let us look at two ways of conducting a lesson built around the lowly potato. It may be that some specific information is to be learned. A science student, for instance, might need to know that there are more than 1,000 varieties of potato and be familiar with the position of the potato in the vegetable kingdom. Another issue might be the chemical composition of the potato, including starch, protein, minerals, and water.

Route Learning, Emphasizing Taxon Systems

The Lesson Plan. We would have a predetermined lesson plan complete with specified outcomes all relating to the potato. Relevant facts about the potato would be identified through lecture and textbook information. The teacher acts as the primary authority, judging right and wrong responses. By and large, information from other subject areas would be considered irrelevant. A variety of memory strategies might be employed that focus on practice and rehearsal, but the object would remain memorization of facts. Testing would likely be in a formal, standardized mode.

Motivation. Motivation would be primarily extrinsic for all students who do not have some interest in or internal purpose or reason for knowing about potatoes. In general, desire for a high grade or fear of getting a low grade are the primary motivators.

Brain Activation. Activation of the brain would be fairly specific. What we mean by this is that, in addition to its normal global operation, for the purposes of memorization a relatively small number of neurons is firing repeatedly. Such specific effort results in rapid and substantial fatigue. Hence regular rest breaks must be taken between trials, and the process is unlikely to be enjoyable or stimulating unless part of a larger pattern invoking intrinsic motivation.

Results. Many students will remember some information in the short term, but forget it soon after the test. A few will remember a significant amount for longer periods. Testing for specific memories will be easy and relatively simple minded. However, the tests will reveal very little about what else students learned. And, in fact, the students will learn very little that they could apply in a broader or practical context or in a creative way.

Map Learning, Based on the Locale System

The Lesson Plan. Some of the facts to be learned would still be specified, but the lesson plan would be different because the objective would be to use the information to build maps. That can only be possible if there are additional objectives being met, basically aimed at helping a student build internal relationships. Thus subject boundaries would be crossed and the potato could be used for explorations in history, geography, science, literature, music, sociology, art, and so on. But this is not just a memorization strategy. One purpose would be to actually use the potato to help students understand the other areas.

For example, the teacher might begin by bringing to class a rather interesting looking and generously sprouting potato, accompanied by a story from history about a war or incident of extreme prejudice that involved the potato. It could become apparent that the history of the potato really is fascinating. Did students know it was the vegetable of the poor until a famine hit England and the wealthy were forced to eat it? The class could study the famine and the historical and social implications, including the relevance of prejudice and social class distinctions. Relationships would be drawn between the past, our own society, and actual student experiences. This could lead to a study of the effect of economic realities on societies both past and present. Even the laws of supply and demand could be better understood. Geographic features of different countries could be tied to a scientific exploration of soil needs and the consequential effect on nutrition. Ecology issues can be introduced. All of this will be enriched by the use of art, music, literature, field trips, visits from those actively working in relevant areas in the community, and creative projects that directly relate content to life. Thus many subjects could be integrated around the potato—and in a way that would allow the brain to tie the facts together.

Motivation. The student's personal curiosity is invoked. This is not always easy to do, but it is at the heart of locale learning. The teacher has a much better chance to engage the student because personal interests can be incorporated through the provision of choices and personal experience can be invoked. In many respects, this motivation is similar to the curiosity associated with mastering a hobby and the complexity of the experiences that relate to the hobby.

Brain Activation. The global operations of the brain are more directly engaged in learning because many areas of learning, including the senses and emotions, are brought into play. This type of learning disperses learning throughout the brain, and there is much less stress on specific brain cells. Hence students can participate in this type of learning for much longer periods of time. They will be more deeply involved and more excited.

Results. Most students will remember some information in the short term. Many more will recall a significant amount of information in the long term and will also be able to invoke it in different contexts and for different purposes. They will also have developed some understanding of many other issues than those of the original subject. Thus mapping also means that the subject itself can subsequently be used by the student automatically in the development of further maps. There will be a small amount of formal and standardized testing, but most evaluation will be complex and will be integrated into the instructional process in a challenging but nonthreatening way.

We have used the potato as one example, but thematic teaching of this kind can be done around any object, appropriate picture, or metaphor.

Acknowledging the Triune Brain in Teaching

Ritualistic Behaviors Need to Be "Played Out" in Positive Ways.

Sports and physical games fulfill basic instinctual drive. They are also the natural vehicles to begin more sophisticated learning. All types of games are natural to children and adults. Exploring language, formulas, and new information through games can bind one of our basic R-complex needs to learning.

Social Interactions and Emotional Well-Being Are Critical to Our Survival, Play a Crucial Role in Understanding, and Are Deeply Motivating.

Cooperative learning, communication skills, and learning how to live in a complex society with people of similar and conflicting needs and emotions should receive as much attention as "cognitive development." Our deep need for interconnectedness with others, which is often played out negatively in the form of gangs or exclusive groups, can also be a vehicle for expanding knowledge. Participating in debates, telling stories, role-playing historical figures, reenacting historical events, and generating "expert panel" solutions to social and medical or other scientific problems are only a few of the intellectually challenging behaviors that involve our need for social belonging and interaction. Such methods can also address the need to "stand out" (preening) and develop our own talents or expertise.

Schools Need to Redirect R-complex Preferences.

Much of the energy of the secondary school day is currently devoted to social activities—deciding how to dress, what shampoo to use, and where and how to engage in preening or mating rituals. It is extremely important that students do not come away with the belief that social rituals and emotional highs devoid of intellectual challenge are the limits of the joy and fulfillment that they can experience.

The alternative is to help students experience the genuine excitement inherent in any subject through, say,

research in science or the expression of their creative abilities. It is also a matter of helping students reflect on their own ritualistic behaviors and search for more sophisticated and challenging ways of living and learning. One issue, of course, is whether this redirection is possible.

Hope for the Future—Our Prefrontal Cortex

Though compassion and concern for others long preceded the 20th century, they are extremely important. Teaching becomes critical because it can help students appreciate complex issues in order to make better choices. But so far we know of no test for compassion, empathy, and other related qualities that is given with the same enthusiasm as IQ tests are. Why are we so enamored of cognitive and mechanistic notions of learning and artificial intelligence while our higher human functions remain uninvestigated? In our society, we do not yet appear to value accomplishments that can be attributed to the intelligence of our motives and values.

Acknowledging emotional factors and the power of ritualistic, reptilian behaviors may not, by itself, lead to the enhancement of education because the "locus of control" may still be in the more primitive parts of the brain. Our ability to sense beauty, experience compassion, and gain appreciation for life also needs to be enhanced in the classroom. To that end, MacLean, among others, sees the prefrontal cortex as one part of the brain that provides hope for our survival as a species.

The prefrontal cortex is that region of the neocortex inside our foreheads. Even though the removal of the prefrontal cortex results in no apparent change in IQ as we now measure it, it appears to be largely responsible for a wide range of abilities that neuropsychologists call "adaptive behaviors." These include planning, analysis, sequencing, and learning from errors, as well as the inhibition of inappropriate responses and the capacity for abstraction. Thus increased compassion and empathy become possible because we can acquire the cognitive capacity to "put ourselves in another's shoes."

Until recently, survival has meant physical victory against "the enemy" and such obvious foes as disease, hunger, and natural disasters. There are new threats that are much more subtle and less well understood. They involve our understanding of ecological issues that tie our existence to the survival of the rain forests and to the capacity to see common interests and overlapping concerns. They require an appreciation of the problems for all of us posed by such facts as that the United States alone, with 4 percent of the world's population, uses 60 percent of the world's resources; that 1,000 children are born each day to drug-dependent mothers; and that 27 percent of Native American children are born with fetal alcohol syndrome.

Interrelational thinking and action require, among other things, the ability to delay gratification and to act on the basis of complex understanding and with compassion and empathy, for all of which the prefrontal cortex is necessary. MacLean believes that these qualities may well be critical new survival features. He states

Have you seen the fish squirm and wiggle in the heron's crop as it is swept along to be slowly peeled away by burning juices? Have you heard birds cough themselves to death from air-sacculitis? Have you risen in the night to give them cough syrup? Have you seen the cat play with a mouse? Have you seen cancer slowly eat away or strangle another human being? The misery piles up like stellar gases tortured by a burning sun. Then why, slowly, progressively, did nature add something to the neocortex that for the first time brings a heart and a sense of compassion into the world? Altruism, empathy—these are almost new words. Altruism—"to the other." Empathy —"compassionate identification with another individual. . . ." In designing for the first time a creature that shows a concern for suffering of other living things, nature seems to have attempted a 180 degree turnabout from what had been a reptile-eat-reptile and dog-eat-dog world (pp. 340–449).

1. The Brain Is a Parallel Processor.

The human brain is always doing many things at one time (Ornstein and Sobel 1987). Thoughts, emotions, imagination, and predispositions operate simultaneously and interact with other modes of information processing and with the expansion of general social and cultural knowledge.

Implications for Education. Good teaching so "orchestrates" the learner's experience that all these aspects of brain operation are addressed. Teaching must, therefore, be based on theories and methodologies that guide the teacher to make orchestration possible. No one method or technique can adequately encompass the variations of the human brain. However, teachers need a frame of reference that enables them to select from the vast repertoire of methods and approaches that are available.

2. Learning Engages the Entire Physiology.

The interaction of the different parts of the triune brain attest, for instance, to the importance of a person's entire physiology. The brain is a physiological organ functioning according to physiological rules. Learning is as natural as breathing, but it can be either inhibited or facilitated. Neuron growth, nourishment, and interactions are integrally related to the perception and interpretation of experiences (Diamond 1985). Stress and threat affect the brain differently from peace, challenge, boredom, happiness, and contentment (see Ornstein and Sobel 1987). In fact, some aspects of the actual "wiring" of the brain are affected by school and life experiences.

Implications for Education. Everything that affects our physiological functioning affects our capacity to learn. Stress management, nutrition, exercise, and relaxation, as well as other facets of health management, must be fully incorporated into the learning process. Because many drugs, both prescribed and "recreational," inhibit learning,

their use should also be curtailed and their effects understood. Habits and beliefs are also physiologically entrenched and therefore resistant or slow to change once they become a part of the personality.

In addition, the timing of learning is influenced by the natural development of both body and brain, as well as by individual and natural rhythms and cycles. There can be a five-year difference in maturation between any two children of the same age. Expecting equal achievement on the basis of chronological age is therefore inappropriate.

3. The Search for Meaning Is Innate.

The search for meaning (making sense of our experiences) and the consequential need to act on our environment are automatic. The search for meaning is survival oriented and basic to the human brain. The brain needs and automatically registers the familiar while simultaneously searching for and responding to novel stimuli (O'Keefe and Nadel 1978). This dual process is taking place every waking moment (and, some contend, while sleeping). Other research confirms the notion that people are meaning makers. The search for meaning cannot be stopped, only channelled and focused.

Implications for Education. The learning environment needs to provide stability and familiarity; this is part of the function of routine classroom behaviors and procedures. At the same time, provision must be made to satisfy our curiosity and hunger for novelty, discovery, and challenge. Lessons need to be generally exciting and meaningful and offer students an abundance of choices. The more positively lifelike such learning, the better. Many programs for gifted children take these implications for granted by combining a rich environment with complex and meaningful challenges. In our view, most of the creative methods used for teaching gifted students should be applied to all students.

4. The Search for Meaning Occurs through "Patterning."

Patterning (Nummela and Rosengren 1986) refers to the meaningful organization and categorization of information. In a way the brain is both artist and scientist, attempting to discern and understand patterns as they occur and giving expression to unique and creative patterns of its own (Hart 1983, Lakoff 1987, Nummela and Rosengren 1986, Rosenfield 1988). The brain is designed to perceive and generate patterns, and it resists having meaningless patterns imposed on it. "Meaningless" patterns are isolated pieces of information unrelated to what makes sense to a student. When the brain's natural capacity to integrate information is acknowledged and invoked in teaching, then vast amounts of initially unrelated or seemingly random information and activities can be presented and assimilated.

Implications for Education. Learners are patterning, or perceiving and creating meanings, all the time in one way or another. We cannot stop them, but can influence the direction. Daydreaming is a way of patterning, as are problem solving and critical thinking. Although we choose much of what students are to learn, the ideal process is to present the information in a way that allows brains to extract patterns, rather than attempt to impose them. "Time on task" does not ensure appropriate patterning because the student may actually be engaged in "busy work" while the mind is somewhere else. For teaching to be really effective, a learner must be able to create meaningful and personally relevant patterns. This type of teaching is most clearly recognized by those advocating a whole-language approach to reading (Altweger, Edelsky, and Flores 1987; Goodman 1986), thematic teaching (Kovalik 1986), integration of the curriculum (Shalley 1987), and life-relevant approaches to learning.

5. Emotions Are Critical to Patterning.

We do not simply learn things. What we learn is influenced and organized by emotions and mind sets based on expectancy, personal biases and prejudices, degree of self-esteem, and the need for social interaction. Emotions and cognition cannot be separated (Halgren, Wilson, Squires, Engel, Walter, and Crandall 1983; Ornstein and Sobel 1987; Lakoff 1987; McGuinness and Pribram 1980). Emotions are also crucial to memory because they facilitate the storage and recall of information (Rosenfield 1988). Moreover, many emotions cannot be simply switched on and off. They operate on many levels, somewhat like the weather. They are ongoing, and the emotional impact of any lesson or life experience may continue to reverberate long after the specific event.

Implications for Education. Teachers need to understand that students' feelings and attitudes will be involved and will determine future learning. Because it is impossible to isolate the cognitive from the affective domain, the emotional climate in the school and classroom must be monitored on a consistent basis, using effective communication strategies and allowing for student and teacher reflection and metacognitive processes. In general, the entire environment needs to be supportive and marked by mutual respect and acceptance both within and beyond the classroom. Some of the most significant experiences in a student's life are fleeting "moments of truth," such as a chance encounter in a corridor with a relatively unknown teacher or, possibly, a "distant" administrator. These brief communications are often instinctive. Their emotional color depends on how "real" and profound the support of teachers, administrators, and students is for one another.

6. The Brain Processes Parts and Wholes Simultaneously.

There is evidence of brain laterality, meaning that there are significant differences between left and right hemispheres of the brain (Springer and Deutsch 1985). In a healthy person, however, the two hemispheres are inextricably interactive, whether a person is dealing with words, mathematics, music, or art (Hand 1984; Hart 1975; Levy, J. 1985). The "two brain" doctrine is most valuable as a metaphor that helps educators acknowledge two separate but simultaneous tendencies in the brain for organizing information. One is to reduce information into parts; the other is to perceive and work with it as a whole or series of wholes.

Implications for Education. People have enormous difficulty in learning when either parts or wholes are overlooked. Good teaching necessarily builds understanding and skills over time because learning is cumulative and developmental. However, parts and wholes are conceptually interactive. They derive meaning from and give it to each other. Thus vocabulary and grammar are best understood and mastered when incorporated in genuine, whole-language experiences. Similarly, equations and scientific principles should be dealt with in the context of living science.

7. Learning Involves Both Focused Attention and Peripheral Perception.

The brain absorbs information of which it is directly aware and to which it is paying attention. It also directly absorbs information and signals that lie beyond the field of attention. These may be stimuli that one perceives "out of the side of the eyes," such as grey and unattractive walls in a classroom. Peripheral stimuli also include the "light" or subtle signals that are within the field of attention but are still not consciously noticed (such as a hint of a smile or slight change in body posture). This means that the brain responds to the entire sensory context in which teaching or communication occurs (O'Keefe and Nadel 1978).

One of Lozanov's fundamental principles is that every stimulus is coded, associated, and symbolized (Lozanov 1978a, b). Thus every sound, from a word to a siren, and every visual signal, from a blank screen to a raised finger, is packed full of complex meanings. For example, a simple knock on the door engages attention and is processed for possible meaning by reference both to much of a learner's prior knowledge and experience and to whatever is happening at the moment. Peripheral information can therefore be purposely "organized" to facilitate learning.

Implications for Education. The teacher can and should organize materials that will be outside the focus of the learner's attention. In addition to traditional concerns with noise, temperature, and so on, peripherals include visuals such as charts, illustrations, set designs, and art, including great works of art. Barzakov (1988) recommends that art exhibits be changed frequently to reflect changes in learning focus. The use of music has also become important as a way to enhance and influence more natural acquisition of information. And the subtle signals that emanate from a teacher have a significant impact. Our inner state shows in skin color, muscular tension and posture, rate of breathing, and eye movements. Teachers need to engage the interests and enthusiasm of students through their own enthusiasm, coaching, and modeling, so that the unconscious signals appropriately relate to the importance and value of what is being learned. One reason that it is important to practice what we preach and, for example, to be genuinely compassionate rather than to fake compassion, is that our actual inner state is always signaled and discerned at some level by learners. Lozanov (1978b) coined the term "double planeness" to describe this internal and external congruence in a person. In the same way, the design and administration of a school send messages to students that shape what is learned. In effect, every aspect of a student's life, including community, family, and technology, affects student learning.

8. Learning Always Involves Conscious and Unconscious Process.

We learn much more than we ever consciously understand. "What we are discovering . . . is that beneath the surface of awareness, an enormous amount of unconscious processing is going on" (Campbell 1989, p. 203). Most signals that are peripherally perceived enter the brain without the learner's awareness and interact at unconscious levels. "Having reached the brain, this information emerges in the consciousness with some delay, or it influences the motives and decisions" (Lozanov 1978b, p. 18). Thus we become our experiences and remember what we experience, not just what we are told. For example, a student can learn to sing on key and learn to hate singing at the same time. Teaching therefore needs to be designed in such a way as to help students benefit maximally from unconscious processing. In part, this is done by addressing the peripheral context (as described previously). In part, it is done through instruction.

Implications for Education. Much of the effort put into teaching and studying is wasted because students do not adequately process their experiences. What we call "active processing" allows students to review how and what they learned so that they begin to take charge of learning and the development of personal meanings. In part, active processing refers to reflection and metacognitive activities. One example might be students' becoming aware of their preferred learning style. Another might be the creative elaboration of procedures and theories by exploring metaphors and analogies to help in the reorganization of material in a way that makes it personally meaningful and valuable.

9. We Have at Least Two Different Types of Memory: A Spatial Memory System and a Set of Systems for Rote Learning.

We have a natural, spatial memory system that does not need rehearsal and allows for "instant" memory of experiences (Bransford and Johnson 1972; Nadel and Wilmer 1980; Nadel, Wilmer, and Kurz 1984). Remembering where and what we had for dinner last night does not require the use of memorization techniques. We have at least one memory system actually designed for registering our experiences in ordinary three-dimensional space (O'Keefe and Nadel 1978). The system is always engaged and is inexhaustible. It is possessed by people of both sexes and all nationalities and ethnic backgrounds. It is enriched over time as we increase the items, categories, and procedures that we take for granted. Thus there was a time when we did not know what a tree or a television was. The system is motivated by novelty. In fact, this is one of the systems that drives the search for meaning mentioned previously.

Facts and skills that are dealt with in isolation are organized differently by the brain and need much more practice and rehearsal. The counterpart of the spatial memory system is a set of systems specifically designed for storing relatively unrelated information. Nonsense syllables are an extreme case. The more separated information and skills are from prior knowledge and actual experience, the more dependence there needs to be on rote memory and repetition. We can compare this memory system to the inventory of an automobile shop. The more items are available, the more the shop can repair, build, and even design cars. It can also do so with greater ease and speed and less stress. At the same time, if management becomes too enamored of the stocking of inventory, and mechanics and designers fail to see how to use the materials available, then an imbalance has been created. In the same way, emphasizing the storage and recall of unconnected facts is an inefficient use of the brain.

Implications for Education. Educators are adept at the type of teaching that focuses on memorization. Common examples include multiplication tables, spelling words, and unfamiliar vocabulary at the lower levels, and abstract concepts and sets of principles in different subjects for older students and adults. Sometimes memorization is important and useful. In general, however, teaching devoted to memorization does not facilitate the transfer of learning and probably interferes with the subsequent development of understanding. By ignoring the personal world of the learner, educators actually inhibit the effective functioning of the brain.

10. We Understand and Remember Best When Facts and Skills Are Embedded in Natural, Spatial Memory.

Our native language is learned through multiple interactive experiences involving vocabulary and grammar. It is shaped both by internal processes and by social interaction (Vygotsky 1978). That is an example of how specific "items" are given meaning when embedded in ordinary experiences. All education can be enhanced when this type of embedding is adopted. That is the single most important element that the new brain-based theories of learning have in common.

Implications for Education. The embedding process is complex because it depends on all the other principles discussed here. Spatial memory is generally best invoked through experiential learning, an approach that is valued more highly in some cultures than in others. Teachers need to use a great deal of real-life activity, including classroom demonstrations, projects, field trips, visual imagery of certain experiences and best performances, stories, metaphor, drama, and interaction of different subjects. Vocabulary can be experienced through skits. Grammar can be learned in process, through stories or writing. Mathematics, science, and history can be integrated so that much more information is understood and absorbed than is currently the norm. Success depends on using all of the senses and immersing the learner in a multitude of complex and interactive experiences. Lectures and analysis are not excluded, but they should be part of a larger experience.

11. Learning Is Enhanced by Challenge and Inhibited by Threat.

The brain downshifts under perceived threat and learns optimally when appropriately challenged. The brain will downshift under threat (Hart 1983). The central feature of downshifting is a sense of helplessness. [I]t is accompanied by a narrowing of the perceptual field (Combs and Snygg 1949). The learner becomes less flexible and reverts to automatic and often more primitive routine behaviors. Downshifting is roughly like a camera lens that has a reduced focus. The hippocampus, a part of the limbic system, which appears to function partially as a relay center to the rest of the brain, is the region of the brain most sensitive to stress (Jacobs and Nadel 1985). Under perceived threat, portions of our brain function suboptimally.

Implications for Education. Teachers and administrators need to create a state of relaxed alertness in students. This combines general relaxation with an atmosphere that is low in threat and high challenge. This state must continuously pervade the lesson, and must be present in the teacher. All the methodologies that are used to orchestrate the learning context influence the state of relaxed alertness.

12. Each Brain Is Unique.

Although we all have the same set of systems, including senses and basic emotions, they are integrated differently in every brain. In addition, because learning actually changes the structure of the brain, the more we learn, the more unique we become.

Implications for Education. Teaching should be multifaceted to allow all students to express visual, tactile, emotional, and auditory preferences. There are other individual differences that also need to considered. Providing choices that are variable enough to attract individual interests may require the reshaping of schools so that they exhibit the complexity found in life. In sum, education needs to facilitate optimal brain functioning.

The Objective of Education Is the Expansion of Natural Knowledge

A major source of confusion in educational debates has concerned learning outcomes. It seems to us that almost all learning objectives are, in fact, specified in terms of memorization or the acquisition of surface knowledge. If people are to be genuinely competent in their fields in complex and unpredictable situations, then what they need is an expansion of natural knowledge. We must teach as though teaching for genuine expertise. This is not the same as mastery. Mastery usually refers to memorization of a skill to the point of automaticity, but not to the point of complex understanding. A person may "master" some math equations but still be totally unable to apply them in a real-life problem. One of our goals must be to have students who can carry out procedures on demand and who understand what they are doing.

Of course, there can be levels of natural knowledge in any field. A person may be at home with some types of computer software and be a novice with others. We may

all be good communicators in some respects and yet have a great deal to learn about communication. The same notion applies to any subject or skill. Thus a student may be able to read simple stories very well but have a great deal of difficulty with more complex material. But a student is often like an expert at some level, even though still a novice by reference to other criteria. Educators must grasp the notion of degrees of expertise and teach for them. Moreover, because natural knowledge is not intrinsically limited, educators must refrain from interrupting its acquisition simply because their own expectations have or have not been met.

Natural knowledge is not the equivalent of absolute truth. People may organize their perceptions in bigoted, prejudiced, and limited ways and can have very different conceptual systems. Hence it is important for educators to continually push for an expansion of students' frames of reference. We may wish them to become competent in fields ranging from economics and history to art and science so that they can interpret events in many different ways. Moreover, we need to take advantage of cultural diversity. This, indeed, is also what business is beginning to seek. In addition, people may become competent in a domain at a basic level. It is extremely important that students be capable of thinking in more demanding ways, both conceptually and contextually. On the one hand, students need to grasp formal operations, without which some types of abstract thought are impossible. On the other, they need to become sensitive to the human and ecological issues inherent in any issue because there is always more involved than meets the eye. Put more simply, students need to be able to think and to care.

Finally, we need to foster in students a predisposition toward expansion. The more they are internally motivated to explore, the easier it is to teach for the generation of natural knowledge. We have shown that the desire to understand is inherent in the human brain. Perhaps the most devastating consequence of disregarding meaningfulness is the ensuing demotivation of students. Our task, then, is to capitalize on and encourage their innate need to know.

How Do We Teach for the Expansion of Natural Knowledge?

> You are never given a wish without also being given the power to make it true. You may have to work for it, however (Bach 1977, p. 92).

> All I ever needed to know about how to live and what to do and how to be I learned in Kindergarten (Fulghum 1988, p. 4).

Teaching for memory is fundamentally different from teaching for the expansion of natural knowledge. The former tends to be like laying bricks, in the hope that in due course those bricks will turn into a wall or a building. The latter begins with the notion of a building. The former is an accumulation of parts. The latter is an expansion and refinement of wholeness and interconnectedness. As we mentioned in the preceding section, this is the difference between a novice and an expert. The question, then, is *how to teach for expertise from the very beginning, when a person is still a novice.*

Prietula and Simon pointed out

> Expertise . . . involves much more than knowing a myriad of facts. Expertise is based on a deep knowledge of the problems that continually arise on a particular job. It is accumulated over years of experience tackling these problems and is organized in the expert's mind in ways that allow him or her to overcome the limits of reasoning (1989, p. 120).

What has been very little understood is that we are teaching all learners for expertise. The general answer to our question, therefore, is that we need to provide all students with *a sufficient accumulation of appropriate experiences.*

The notion that much of what we learn is gathered from experience is not new. It is part of what links many prominent writers and educators, such as John Dewey (1962, 1965, 1966), Alfred North-Whitehead (1979), and Maria Montessori (1965). Unfortunately, their message and the phrase "learn from experience" have a great deal of hidden depth that is almost invariably ignored. In particular, many educators subscribe to the notion that learning from experience is only one type of learning. This is illustrated by those who differentiate between lectures and experiential learning, and who equate experience with some sort of participative activity closely linked to vocational training. As is perhaps abundantly clear at this point, our definition of *experience* far surpasses such a narrow conceptualization.

We have established that we are all immersed in complex, global experiences every moment of our lives, much as a fish is surrounded by water. The locale system constantly monitors our movement in space; our sensory and motor systems are engaged in every life activity; we explore every event for meaning in a way that involves our emotions and thoughts and visceral body. One of the most important lessons to derive from the brain research is that, in a very important sense, *all* learning is experiential. What we learn depends on the global experience, not just on the manner of presentation. Dewey fully realized this. He wrote

> We never educate directly, but indirectly by means of the environment. Whether we permit chance environments to do the work, or whether we design environments for the purpose makes a great deal of difference. And any environment is a chance environment so far as its educative influence is concerned unless it has been deliberately regulated with reference to its educative effect (Dewey 1966, p. 19).

We do not, however, automatically learn enough from our experience. What matters is how experience is used. Our conclusion is that in deliberately teaching for the expansion of natural knowledge, we need both to help students have appropriate experiences and to help them capitalize on the experiences. Three interactive elements are essential to this process, and all three are implicit in the previous quote by Prietula and Simon (1989).

1. Teachers need to *orchestrate the immersion of the learner in complex, interactive experiences* that are both rich and real. A good example is the use of immersion in the teaching of a second language (Dolson 1984).
2. There must be a personally meaningful challenge. This is the intrinsic motivation that is part of the state of mind that we identify as *relaxed alertness.*
3. There must be intensive analysis so that the learner gains insight about the problem, about the ways in which it could be approached and about learning generally. We call this the *active processing of experience.*

Encouraging Complex, Real Projects of Personal Interest to Students

Students must be exposed to subject matter in many different ways, a great number of which must be complex, real projects. These projects should be developmental in nature and link work over time. They should assist in connecting content to the world in which the student actually lives. They can generate the sort of communication and group interaction upon which many people thrive. And they can be vehicles for teaching much more than the specific content of any one course.

Teachers often seem to fear that the use of real-life activities and large-scale projects will interfere with the coverage of the prescribed materials. In effect, they often feel that invoking locale memory will jeopardize the treatment of taxon information. Our experience is directly to the contrary. The proper use of complex activities makes it possible to deal with substantially more material than would otherwise be the case. The teacher or students may model or demonstrate the subject, bring in experts, engage in genuine problem solving, interview authorities, and create learning games.

If the topic to be studied is the eagle, for example, students deal with it in many different ways. They may explore nesting, feeding, and reproductive patterns and the eagle's ecological requirements, together with relevant information spanning several subject areas. They listen to recordings of the live eagle as it moves through the air, and they read literature featuring eagles. They study the eagle as a political symbol and its role in the arts. Students develop areas of expertise or experts are brought to class or are recorded or videotaped. Computer simulations and tracking programs are made available to students to help them identify where eagles are located and whether they are thriving. The mood that should prevail is that of a team of researchers or explorers engaged in a meaningful, exciting adventure.

References

Altweger, B., C. Edelsky, and B. Flores. (1987). "Whole Language: What's New?" *The Reading Teacher* 41, 2: 144–154.

Bach, R. (1977). *Illusions*. London: Heinemann.

Barzakov, I. (July 14, 1988). Unpublished workshop notes. *Optimalearning™ Workshop*.

Bransford, D., and M. Johnson. (1972). "Contextual Prerequisites for Understanding: Some Investigations of Comprehensive Recall." *Journal of Verbal Learning and Verbal Behavior* 11: 717–721.

Campbell, J. (1989). *The Improbable Machine*. New York: Simon and Schuster.

Combs, A. W., and D. Snygg. (1949). *Individual Behavior: A Perceptual Approach to Behavior*. New York: Harper and Row.

Dewey, J. (1962). *Reconstruction in Philosophy*. New York: The Beacon Press.

Dewey, J. (1965). *Experience and Education*. New York: Collier.

Dewey, J. (1966). *Democracy and Education: An Introduction to the Philosophy of Education*. New York: The Free Press.

Diamond, M. (March 23, 1985). *Brain Growth in Response to Experience*. Seminar, University of California, Riverside.

Dolson, D. P., project leader. (1984). *Studies on Immersion Education: A Collection for United States Educators*. A report prepared under the direction of the Office of Bilingual and Bicultural Education. Sacramento, Calif.: California State Department of Education.

Fulghum, R. (1988). *All I Really Need to Know I Learned in Kindergarten*. New York: Ivy Books.

Goodman, K. (1986). *What's Whole in Whole Language?* Portsmouth, N.H.: Heinemann.

Halgren, E., C. L. Wilson, N. K. Squires, J. Engel, R. D. Walter, and P. H. Crandall. (1983). "Dynamics of the Hippocampal Contribution to Memory: Stimulation and Recording Studies in Humans." In *Molecular, Cellular and Behavioral Neurobiology of the Hippocampus*, edited by W. Seifert. New York: Academic Press.

Hand, J. D. (1984). "Split Brain Theory and Recent Results in Brain Research: Implications for the Design of Instruction." In *Instructional Development: The State of the Art, Vol. 2*, edited by R. K. Bass and C. R. Dills. Dubuque, Iowa: Kendall/Hunt.

Hart, L. (1975). *How the Brain Works: A New Understanding of Human Learning, Emotion, and Thinking*. New York: Basic Books.

Hart, L. (1983). *Human Brain, Human Learning*. New York: Longman.

Jacobs, W. J., and L. Nadel. (1985). "Stress-Induced Recovery of Fears and Phobias." *Psychological Review* 92, 4: 512–531.

Kovalik, S. (1986). *Teachers Make the Difference—With Integrated Thematic Instruction*. Oak Creek, Ariz.: Susan Kovalik and Associates.

Lakoff, G. (1987). *Women, Fire, and Dangerous Things*. Chicago: University of Chicago Press.

Levy, J. (May 1985). "Right Brain, Left Brain: Fact and Fiction." *Psychology Today* 19: 38.

Lozanov, G. (1978a). *Suggestology and Outlines of Suggestopedy*. New York: Gordon and Breach.

Lozanov, G. (1978b). *Suggestology and Suggestopedia—Theory and Practice*. Working document for the Expert Working Group, United Nations Educational, Scientific and Cultural Organization (UNESCO). (ED–78/WS/119).

MacLean, P. D. (1969). "New Trends in Man's Evolution." In *A Triune Concept of the Brain and Behavior*. Papers presented at Queen's University, Ontario, 1969. Ann Arbor, Mich. Books on Demand, University Microfilms International.

McGuinness, D., and K. Pribram. (1980). "The Neuropsychology of Attention: Emotional and Motivational Controls." In *The Brain and Psychology*, edited by M. D. Wittrock. New York: Academic Press.

Montessori, M. (1965). *The Montessori Method*. Cambridge, Mass.: Robert Bentley.

Nadel, L., and J. Wilmer. (1980). "Context and Conditioning: A Place for Space." *Physiological Psychology* 8: 218–228.

Nadel, L., J. Wilmer, and E. M. Kurz. (1984). "Cognitive Maps and Environmental Context." In *Context and Learning*, edited by P. Balsam and A. Tomi. Hillsdale, N.J.: Lawrence Erlbaum.

Nummela, R., and T. Rosengren. (1986). "What's Happening in Students' Brains May Redefine Teaching." *Educational Leadership* 43, 8: 49–53.

O'Keefe, J., and L. Nadel. (1978). *The Hippocampus as a Cognitive Map*. Oxford: Clarendon Press.

Ornstein, R., and D. Sobel. (1987). *The Healing Brain: Breakthrough Discoveries about How the Brain Keeps Us Healthy*. New York: Simon and Schuster.

Prietula, M. J., and H. A. Simon. (January-February 1989). "The Experts in Your Midst." *Harvard Business Review* 1: 120.

Rosenfield, I. (1988). *The Invention of Memory*. New York: Basic Books.

Shalley, C. (1987). "Humanities Program: Hightstown High School. Curriculum for the Integrated Humanities Program at Hightstown High School, Hightstown, N.J." Unpublished manuscript.

Springer, S., and G. Deutsch. (1985). *Left Brain, Right Brain*. 2nd ed. New York: W. H. Freeman.

Vygotsky, L. S. (1978). *Mind in Society*. Cambridge: Harvard University Press.

Whitehead, A. N. (1979). *Process and Reality*. New York: The Free Press.

Rita Dunn Answers Questions on Learning Styles

Dunn, R. 1990. *Educational Leadership* 48(2):15–19.

How valid is the research on learning styles? Is it really necessary for teachers to diagnose styles and match instruction to individual differences? *Educational Leadership* asked Rita Dunn, consultant and author on learning styles, for her answers to these and other questions.

Q: Why are there so many learning styles models?

A: Different pioneers recognized individual differences based on their particular experiences, named the characteristics they observed, and described them in nomenclature that made sense to them.

Q: In what ways are the models similar to and/or different from each other?

A: ❖ Each of the models advocates acknowledging and honoring the diversity among individuals.

❖ Most models urge that teachers adapt instruction to the ways in which *individuals*, rather than *groups* learn. Some believe in "matching" to learning style characteristics all the time; others believe in matching some of the time. Still others believe in changing the child's characteristics.

❖ Most models are designed around one or two characteristics on a bipolar continuum, suggesting that people are either one way or another. Three "comprehensive" models include many characteristics and describe which trait is important to whom and the extent to which individuals can flex.

❖ One or two models have a great deal of both history and research behind them; most are based on limited research. And the quality of the research concerning each model varies widely.

❖ Many models are relatively new and cannot be observed in a variety of geographically, socioeconomically, and ethnically different schools or districts; others are well established and can be observed in diverse programs.

Q: Aren't we labeling children when we say they have one style or another?

A: No more than categorizing them as "students" or as "humans." *Everybody* has a learning style, and everybody has learning style strengths. Different people just have different strengths.

Q: Why do you call students' preferences their "strengths"?

A: Because many researchers have repeatedly documented that, when students are taught with approaches that match their preferences as identified by the *Learning Style Inventory* (LSI) (Dunn, Dunn, and Price 1975, 1979, 1981, 1985, 1989), they demonstrate statistically higher achievement and attitude test scores— even on standardized tests—than when they are taught with approaches that mismatch their preferences. If learning through your preference consistently produces significantly better test scores and grades, then your preference is your strength.

Q: Why should students be "matched" with complementary resources? Shouldn't they learn to flex?

A: It is important to note that three-fifths of learning style is biologically imposed (Restak 1979, Thies 1979). Thus, those students with strong preferences for specific learning style conditions/environments/approaches cannot flex; if they could, the would not be failing. Only those for whom a specific characteristic is relatively unimportant have the luxury of flexing.

Q: Why do learning styles have to be identified with an instrument?

A: Teachers cannot correctly identify all the characteristics of learning style (Dunn et al. 1989). Some aspects of style are not observable, even to an experienced educator. In addition, teachers often misinterpret behaviors or misunderstand symptoms.

Q: How strong is the instrumentation to identify individual styles?

A: Two separate reports agree on the reliability and validity of various instruments (Curry 1987, DeBello 1990). These help educators decide which should— and should not—be used with K–12 students. Because it is crucial to use a reliable and valid diagnostic assessment, people should become familiar with those studies.

Another alternative is to request the research manual of any instrument you are considering. Read its reliability and validity data carefully and be certain that the instrument has been widely used with the age group you are planning to test.

Q: How good is the Dunn, Dunn, and Price *Learning Style Inventory*?

A: It is the most reliable, most valid, and most widely used learning style diagnostic instrument for school-aged children in the United States. It assesses multiple characteristics that have been shown to significantly affect individual students' achievement, has been tested at every grade level (14), has been incorporated into research at more than 60 institutions of higher education, is easy to administer and score, and is inexpensive. Further, students *understand* it and rarely feel threatened by its questions. In addition, it has had the advantage of being developed, scrutinized, field-tested, redesigned, and consistently improved by university researchers for more than 22 years. Few instruments have had that kind of research and development.

Q: Has the research on the LSI been conducted only at St. John's University?

A: The research on the LSI has been conducted at more than 60 institutions of higher education in the United States and abroad (Annotated Bibliography, 1990).

Q: But aren't those all doctoral dissertations?

A: Many are; many are not. But if they *were* all doctoral dissertations, would that be a negative?

Q: Are doctoral dissertations considered good research?

A: St. John's University's doctoral dissertations have received 1 regional, 12 national, and 2 international awards/citations for the quality of their research between 1980 and 1989. In addition, I have read many outstanding and superior dissertations from other universities. In well-designed and conducted doctoral dissertations, a team of people examine each facet of the investigation. Errors are far less likely to occur under those circumstances than when individuals or pairs of authors undertake research without thorough understanding of the field or knowledge of multiple research strategies. However, if some universities do occasionally produce poor dissertations, it is the responsibility of the faculty at those institutions.

Q: Do you use an experimental/control design?

A: With few exceptions, learning styles research at St. John's University has been experimental research. Some of our experimental studies involved two or more equivalent groups of subjects differentially treated; in others, one group of subjects received multiple treatments. In all of our experimental investigations, however, we strive to control for potentially confounding factors through either random assignment of students to treatments and/or through the use of pretesting and the use of appropriate statistical analyses, including ANCOVA and repeated measures ANOVA.

Q: How well does learning styles-based instruction really work in the schools?

A: After having been shown how to study and do homework through their learning style strengths, students at many institutions and at varying academic levels have demonstrated statistically significant increases in academic achievement and improved attitudes toward school, less tension in classes, and significantly increased school retention (Dunn et al. 1990a). And that progress continues over years. Here are a few examples.

❖ The Center for Educating Students with Handicaps in Regular Education Settings (CESHRES) in North Carolina, established under contract to the U.S. Department of Education, was seeking to identify educational movements in the United States that had seriously affected student achievement. *Our* model of learning style was one of a limited number of movements designated as having positively affected special education students, and that determination was made only after visiting sites, examining test data, and reading a great deal of research.

❖ The mean language arts scores of the *Iowa Test of Educational Achievement* for middle school students at Sacred Heart Seminary in Hempstead, New York, changed from 8.5 in 1985–86 to 10.5 in 1986–87, when Principal Mary Giannitti began testing the students at the times of day that best matched their time-of-day preferences. The youngsters attending the school are bussed in from 34 separate districts; many are the offspring of military personnel and transient professionals. Many students had failed in their former schools; often both of their parents work; and many share a single parent environment barely above the national poverty level. But, if you visited Sacred Heart, you would believe that every student in attendance was an angel—brilliant, charming, beautifully bred, and independent. Results like these happen within three weeks of students' participation in that school's learning style program.

❖ Carole Marshall of the Center for Slower Learners, Richardson, Texas, reported the most success when using learning styles-based instruction with poor achievers.

❖ The Frontier and Hamburg School Districts working with the International Learning Styles Center, ERIE Board of Cooperative Educational Services, Depew, New York, reported the best gains they ever had with both special education and underachieving populations when working with a combination of learning styles and Mastery Learning.

❖ The Brightwood Elementary School in Greensboro, North Carolina had reading and mathematics scores in the 30th percentile in 1986 when its principal, Roland Andrews, came to New York to study with us for one week. Next year (1987), his school's scores on the *California Achievement Test* (CAT) rose to the 40th percentile. So impressed were the parents in that low socioeconomic area with their children's achievement gains that they paid for sending five Brightwood teachers to New York for one week of training during the summer of 1987. Brightwood's children then scored at about the 75th percentile in reading and math in 1987—and its African American children achieved 21 percent above the system's and the state's average. They also scored as well as the Caucasian youngsters. By 1989, Brightwood's CAT scores reached the 83rd percentile. During the past three years, those children have consistently shown between 15–21 percent improved achievement above their own previous test scores, and the *only* thing that teachers did differently between 1986 and 1989 was to introduce our model of learning styles.

❖ After placing its dropout population in a learning styles alternative program, Amityville High School in New York has witnessed dramatic effects on these students' academic achievement, retention, and behavior. And those youngsters are poor and minority, who experience traumatic family upheavals and neighborhoods overrun by drugs and local gangs.

❖ When (then) Principal Jeff Jacobson initiated a learning styles-based program at his high school in Midwest, Wyoming, the average number of absences per year decreased, and overall achievement gains reflected that 73 percent of the students moved onto grade level or higher as measured by the Stanford Achievement Test. Later, when he became Superintendent in Douglas, Wyoming, Jacobson was telephoned by the U.S. Department of Agriculture and asked why the district's special education students had achieved so much better than they had previously. When he explained that his teachers were teaching to the students' learning style, he was flown to Washington, D.C., to describe how to accommodate individual students' styles in the Department's newly conceived "agriculture-in-the classroom" international curriculum. Subsequently, a prototype elementary curriculum based on learning style was developed by Jacobson and his colleagues and is being evaluated for production.

❖ At Corsicana High School, in Texas, former Math Department Chairperson Sherrye Dotson attested to the fact that students who had never or barely passed math in the first three years of high school had, through their learning style strengths, learned all they needed during their senior year to pass the statewide TEAMS tests!

❖ Principal Jacqueline Simmons of Robeson High School in South Chicago enthusiastically describes how her seasoned faculty "took to" learning styles-based instruction, taught the students how to use their strengths, and reported better behavior, attitudes, and achievement for each grade.

❖ Principal Patricia Sue Lemmon of the Hutchinson Elementary School, Hutchinson, Kansas, reported statistically higher reading and math scores on the *Iowa Basic Skills Tests* when she responded to her

students' preferences for time-of-day and seating design during test administration. Her school has maintained consistently high scores for the past seven or eight years while it has provided learning styles-based instruction.

❖ Principal Mary A. Lafey of Oakland Junior High School, Columbia, Missouri, reported that her 8th and 9th grade reading teacher converted her classroom into a learning style pilot project to see if reading achievement could be increased at a greater rate. Whereas only 12 percent of the students during 1988–89 had reached nine months or more of growth, 64 percent of the students in the learning styles program reached four months or more of growth in only a *four-month* period.

Q: Wouldn't it be just as effective to change the curriculum?

A: Students are not failing because of the curriculum. Students can learn almost any subject matter when they are taught with methods and approaches responsive to their learning style strengths; those same students fail when they are taught in an instructional style dissonant with their strengths.

For example, global students achieved statistically higher test scores when the curriculum was translated into a global instructional approach. Those same students achieved statistically less well with analytic material (Dunn et al. 1990b). That also was true in high school mathematics (Brennan 1984), science (Douglas 1979), social studies (Trautman 1979), and nutrition (Tanenbaum 1981). The curriculum did not have to be changed; it merely had to be taught correctly to those students.

Similarly, students have to be taught in sociological patterns in which they feel comfortable. For example, prescribing cooperative learning for everyone is to fail to consider individuals' distinct differences. In every class, a percentage of youngsters can learn more rapidly and effectively by themselves than they can either in whole or small-group instruction. Many children learn competitively and enjoy it; others prefer competing against their own growth. Some children can learn in a pair—with one classmate—but place them into a group, and they destroy the group. Some need to be in direct contact with the teacher; they need adult closeness and supervision. Children with strong preferences for learning alone, in a pair, in a small group, or with the teacher achieve statistically higher test scores in matched, rather than in mismatched, instructional patterns (Dunn et al. 1989).

These statements apply equally to other learning style characteristics. Students learn more effectively and retain what they learn longer when taught through

The Principal as Educational Leader

their perceptual strengths and in instructional environments responsive to *how* they learn (Dunn et al. 1989).

Q: Then why isn't everyone teaching to students' learning styles?

A: For a number of reasons. First, many educators neither read nor understand research. Second, some teachers do not really care; for them, teaching is just a job. Further, certain people need to be doing what is "in"; they often adopt popular strategies without examining whether they have a strong research base or not.

In addition, because there are many competing learning styles models, people often do not know which is appropriate for their school or grade level. And although many are experimenting with various methods, practitioners rarely publish their results; thus, it takes a long time for the outcomes to reach widespread audiences. For whatever reason, there are still people who don't know about the concept, and they certainly do not know about the impact it has had on children's achievement and attitudes toward school.

Still another explanation is that certain administrators provide a one-day "motivating" introduction to a concept and say that their teachers are "doing it." Because what is being implemented under those circumstances is superficial, they never realize the benefits that might accrue.

Q: Isn't learning styles instruction a lot of work for teachers?

A: Perhaps initially, because it is different from what they have been trained to do. But relatively early in our program—after the first few months—teachers begin to teach students how to teach themselves. Once that is undertaken, teaching becomes enjoyable and easy for both students and their teachers. Besides, when students cannot learn the way we teach them, we must teach them the way they learn.

Q: With 30 students in a class, isn't it impossible for teachers to respond to students' multiple learning styles?

A: By just redesigning a classroom to respond to individual learning style differences, teachers can immediately address 12 elements—and that takes one hour once a semester for each class. Teaching both globally and analytically—and every class has both types of processors—eradicates another major problem. By learning how to lecture and simultaneously respond to each student's perceptual strengths, teachers eliminate a third problem. By teaching students to study and do their homework at their best times of day and by scheduling students for their most difficult or most important core subject at their best times of day, teachers can manage that component. A few simple strategies respond to students who are nonconforming and who are not persistent, and structure merely needs to be acknowledged and provided for those who need more or less. No, it is neither "impossible" nor difficult to respond to individuals' strengths; one merely needs to learn how.

References

Annotated Bibliography. (1990). Jamaica, N.Y. Center for the Study of Learning and Teaching Styles, St. Johns University.

Brennan, P. (1984). "An Analysis of the Relationships Among Hemispheric Preference and Analytic/Global Cognitive Style, Two Elements of Learning Style, Method of Instruction, Gender, and Mathematics Achievement of Tenth-Grade Geometry Students." Doctoral diss., St. Johns University, Jamaica, N.Y.

Curry, L. (1987). *Integrating Concepts of Cognitive Learning Style: A Review with Attention to Psychometric Standards*. Ontario: Canadian College of Health Science Executives.

DeBello, T. (1990). "Comparison of Eleven Major Learning Styles Models: Variables, Appropriate Populations, Validity of Instrumentation, and the Research Behind Them." *Journal of Reading Writing, and Learning Disabilities International* 6, 3: 203–222.

Douglas, C. (1979). "Making Biology Easier to Understand." *American Biology Teacher* 41. 5: 277–299.

Dunn, R., J. Beaudry, and A. Klavas. (1989). "Survey of Research on Learning Styles." *Educational Leadership* 46, 6: 50–58.

Dunn, R., J. Bruno, R.I. Sklar, R. Zenhausern, and J. Beaudry (May/June 1990b). "Effects of Matching and Mismatching Minority Developmental College Students' Hemispheric Preferences on Mathematics Scores." *Journal of Educational Research* 83, 5: 283–288.

Dunn, R., L. Deckinger, P. Withers, and H. Katzenstein. (1990a). "Should College Students Be Taught How to Do Their Homework? The Effects of Studying Marketing Through Individual Perceptual Strengths." *Illinois School Research and Development Journal* 26, 2: 96–113.

Dunn, R, K. Dunn, and G.E. Price. (1975, 1979, 1981, 1985, 1989). *Learning Style Inventory*. Lawrence, Kans.: Price Systems.

Restak, R. (1979) *The Brain: The Last Frontier*. New York: Doubleday.

Tanenbaum, R. (1981). *An Investigation of the Relationships Between Selected Instructional Techniques and Identified Field Dependent and Field Independent Cognitive Styles as Evidenced Among High School Students Enrolled in Studies of Nutrition*. Doctoral diss., St. John's University (*Dissertation Abstracts International* 43, 68A).

Theis, A. P. (1979). "A Brain-Behavior Analysis of Learning Style." In *Student Learning Styles: Diagnosing and Prescribing Programs*. Reston, Va.: National Association of Secondary School Principals, pp 55–61.

Trautman, P. (1979). "An Investigation of the Relationship Between Selected Instructional Techniques and Identified Cognitive Style." Doctoral diss., St. John's University, Jamaica, N.Y. (*Dissertation Abstracts International* 40, 1428A).

About the Author

Rita Dunn is Director of St. John's University's Center for the Study of Learning and Teaching Styles, Grand Central and Utopia Parkways, Jamaica, NY 11439.

A Different Kind of Classroom

Marzano, R. J. 1992. 25–27, 124–26, 135–39.
Alexandria, Va.: Association for Supervision and Curriculum Development.

Fostering Positive Attitudes and Perceptions About Classroom Tasks

Proficient learners believe that the tasks they are asked to perform have value, that they have a fairly clear understanding of what the tasks require, and that they have the resources necessary to complete the tasks. Teachers can use specific classroom techniques to bolster these beliefs.

Task Value

Of the beliefs listed above, the perceived value of tasks is probably the most important to the learner's success. Current research and theory on motivation (McCombs 1984, 1987; Schunk 1990) indicate that learners are most motivated when they believe the tasks they're involved in are relevant to their personal goals. Glasser (1981) and Powers (1973) hypothesize that human beings operate from a hierarchical structure of needs and goals: they must satisfy basic physical needs (e.g., food, shelter) and psychological needs (e.g., acceptance, safety) before being able to form goals—to decide what they are "consciously trying to accomplish" (Schunk 1990). From this perspective, working to develop a positive mental climate, discussed in the previous section, focuses on meeting students' psychological needs. A growing body of research indicates that when students are working on goals they themselves have set, they are more motivated and efficient, and they achieve more than they do when working to meet goals set by the teacher (Hom and Murphy 1985, Schunk 1985). This research strongly implies that if educators expect students to be motivated to succeed at classroom tasks, they must somehow link those tasks to student goals. Some powerful ways of doing this include allowing students to structure tasks around their interests, allowing students to control specific aspects of tasks, and tapping students' natural curiosity.

Overtly gearing tasks to student interests is a simple matter of knowing what students are interested in and then linking tasks to their interests. For example, knowing that many students in her class are fans of professional basketball, a mathematics teacher might use the box scores from the newspaper to illustrate the concept of the "average." Oddly enough, there is little research evidence indicating that teachers are using student interests, except in the area of reading instruction. Morrow (1991) notes that within that body of research, the trend is toward identifying and capitalizing on student interests, especially within literature-based instructional approaches.

Allowing students to specify how tasks will be completed means that assigned tasks are relatively open-ended. For example, an English teacher might review the rules for using commas and then, as a practice activity, ask students to find examples of each rule in whatever kind of material they want to read. A student interested in baseball might use the sports page. A student interested in music might use the written lyrics to popular songs, and so on.

Capitalizing on the natural curiosity of students is another way of making tasks relevant. Human beings are naturally curious. In effect, we are "hard-wired" to want to know why things happen, how they work, what the parts are, what will happen if . . ., and so on (Lindsay and Norman 1977). Teachers can tap this natural curiosity by offering interesting "tidbits" along with content. For example, I once observed a teacher present students with some of the details of Hemingway's life before she asked them to read one of his short stories. Specifically, she described how Hemingway had established a counterintelligence organization called the Crook Factory to deal with the influx of German spies in Cuba and the presence of submarines off its coast during World War II. Students were fascinated by the account and their enthusiasm carried over into their reading of the story.

Task Clarity

Fundamentally, if learners do not have a clear model of how a task will look when it is completed, their efforts to complete the task will often be ineffective. Educators like Hunter (1982) have provided teachers with strong guidelines about how to make tasks and expectations about tasks clear for students. In general, the guidelines suggest that teachers provide models of completed tasks. For example, following the Hunter guidelines, a language arts teacher who has asked students to write an essay might give students an example of a completed essay that illustrates all of the assigned criteria.

Resources

Obviously, students must perceive that they have the necessary materials, time, equipment, and so on, to complete a task. These are external resources. Not so obviously, students must also perceive that they have the necessary internal resources—the "right stuff." Contrary to popular belief, the "right stuff" is not necessarily ability. In fact, current research and theory in psychology indicate that learners commonly attribute success to any one of four causes (Schunk 1990; Weiner 1972, 1983): ability, effort, task difficulty, or luck.

The first two of these, ability and effort, are key elements of motivation. Learners who believe they have the inner resources to successfully complete a task attribute their success to effort; there is no task they consider absolutely beyond their reach. Learners who believe they are good at some things but not so good at others attribute their success to ability; they perceive themselves as incapable of success at some tasks. In the classroom, teachers should continually reinforce the importance of effort and boost students' sense of their ability. Teachers might give powerful examples of how effort paid off in their own lives or in others'. Covington (1983, 1985) suggests that students should occasionally receive rewards (such as grades) based on their efforts rather than on their successful completion of tasks.

Teachers can improve learning by planning ways to improve students' attitudes and perceptions about the classroom climate and about assigned tasks.

What Makes These Tasks Meaningful?

In this chapter I have asserted that decision making, investigation, experimental inquiry, problem solving, and invention are types of tasks that involve students in the meaningful use of knowledge. But what makes these tasks meaningful? In general, meaningful classroom tasks fall into three categories: application-oriented tasks, long-term tasks, and student-directed tasks.

Application-Oriented Tasks

All the tasks described in this chapter focus on the application of knowledge. Each can be conceptualized as answering specific types of questions. For example, decision making answers the question "What is the best?" Definitional investigation answers questions like "What are the defining characteristics?" These tasks require students to use their knowledge to accomplish specific goals or to apply their knowledge when answering specific questions. Their emphasis is not learning for learning's sake, but learning as a by-product of trying to accomplish something, of trying to answer questions that are common human concerns. This is always the most powerful kind of learning.

Long-Term Tasks

The length of the class period and the length of the course determine the lower and upper limits of long-term tasks in the classroom. In the traditional fifty-minute class period, a long-term task should last at least three classes. It could, however, last as long as the course itself: a quarter, a semester or a year, depending on the classroom setting. In most classrooms, though, the most practical way to use long-term projects is to tie them to units of instruction. Many teachers break instruction into theme units that last from one to six weeks. Within a unit of instruction, then, a task could last up to six weeks.

Unfortunately, the principle that classroom tasks should be long-term flies in the face of current practice. These learning tasks rarely take even one or two periods to finish; besides that, they are usually directed by the teacher and require little higher-order thinking (Doyle 1983, Fisher and Hiebert 1988). The most common task is probably reading a selection from a textbook and then answering questions at the end of the selection or completing a textbook exercise.

Student-Directed Tasks

The characteristic that is most important if a task is to be called meaningful is the extent to which it is student directed. This means two things: (1) students have control over the construction of the tasks, and (2) students have control over the products generated from the task.

At the very least, students should have control over the construction of tasks: they should identify the questions they would like to answer about the topic they are studying. The teacher and students might first discuss issues that have come up in the unit, but students should then be able to identify questions relating to these issues and construct appropriate tasks. Of course, when an issue of particular importance surfaces, the teacher may still devise tasks for students. And when students are first introduced to the five types of tasks described in this chapter, they will no doubt need a great deal of guidance from the teacher. In general, though, students should have the freedom to create their own tasks and be encouraged to do so.

Students should also have some control over the products generated from the tasks. Generally, outcomes and products in school are limited to written and oral reports (Durst and Newell 1989). That is, students are commonly required to write an essay or make an oral report describing what they have learned. As useful as these methods of presentation are, they exclude other methods of presenting information.

Video- or audiotaped reports, newscasts, graphic organizers accompanied by explanations, slide shows, dramatic presentations, demonstrations, debates, and panel discussions are all valid ways of reporting the results of the tasks described in this chapter.

For instance, the students in Ms. Haas' class might have presented the results of their investigation of the most important person of the 1960s in a video or in a debate. And the students in Mr. Kendall's class might have presented the results of their investigation of the greenhouse effect in a newscast or dramatic presentation.

The products of meaningful-use tasks can be expanded even beyond the list presented above if students are allowed and encouraged to develop artifacts along with their tasks. Artifacts are artistic or symbolic representations of affective experiences associated with a task. For example, in a decision-making task about which action would have been best for the United States to take in the conflict between Iraq and Kuwait, a student might develop a sketch to supplement her written report. The written report would be used to communicate the process used in the decision-making task and the conclusions drawn from it, while the artifact (the sketch) would be used to communicate a specific feeling associated with the learner's conclusions. In short, the learner would use the sketch to represent the emotion she had experienced while gathering information for the decision-making task.

Introducing Meaningful-Use Tasks

Because of the complexity of the meaningful-use tasks described in this chapter, students generally need to be taught the critical aspects of the processes underlying the tasks. It is in introducing the meaningful-use tasks that Beyer's (1988) five-step process for teaching a complex process makes sense:

1. The teacher introduces the process by describing and demonstrating the steps of the process, explaining when the process should be used, and naming the process.
2. Students experiment with the strategy using "neutral" content; that is, the teacher provides students with familiar and interesting content, allowing them to focus on the process without the interference of struggling with new or uninteresting content.
3. Students think about what goes on in their minds as they use the process. This may be done in cooperative groups.
4. As a result of their reflection or group discussion, students may make changes in the strategy.
5. Finally, students try out the modified process and again reflect on its use.

If the processes underlying the meaningful-use tasks are not taught in this manner, then teachers should be prepared to guide students through the tasks or to provide them with highly structured tasks. Over time, then, tasks can shift to a more student-structured format.

Helping Students Develop and Maintain Effective Habits of Mind

The process of helping students develop effective habits of mind is qualitatively different from the processes of

---

Figure 6.2: Students' Suggestions of Situations When the Habits of Mind Might Be Useful

Self-Regulation
- Being aware of your own thinking:
  - When you're not doing well on a task, being aware of your own thinking can help you figure out what you're doing wrong.
- Planning:
  - Any time you have to do something that takes a long time and is fairly complex—like completing assignments that take two weeks or even a semester.
- Being aware of necessary resources:
  - Any time you want to make or do something that requires resources. Not having the resources might put limits on what you can do.
- Being sensitive to feedback:
  - When you are doing something that is repetitious (e.g., doing a very long arithmetic problem), being sensitive to feedback helps prevent careless mistakes.
- Evaluating the effectiveness of your actions:
  - When you are doing something new or something you are not very good at, evaluating your actions helps you learn from your mistakes.

Critical Thinking
- Being accurate and seeking accuracy:
  - Whenever you are doing mathematical calculations.
  - Whenever you are doing anything that requires precision.
- Being clear and seeking clarity:
  - Whenever someone is trying to persuade you of something.

- Whenever you are trying to explain something to someone.
  - Whenever you are not sure of what you are saying or writing.
- Being open-minded:
  - Whenever you find yourself immediately rejecting an idea.
- Resisting impulsivity:
  - Whenever you find yourself responding to a question immediately without much thinking prior to your response.
- Taking and defending a position:
  - Whenever you are fairly confident about a specific position and it has not been expressed by someone else.
- Being sensitive to others:
  - Whenever you are dealing with a "touchy" topic that others might feel strongly about.

Creative Thinking
- Engaging intensely in tasks even when answers or solutions are not immediately apparent:
  - Whenever you continue to fail at something that's important to you.
- Pushing the limits of your knowledge and ability.
  - Whenever you find yourself falling into a routine way of doing things.
- Generating, trusting, and maintaining your own standards of evaluation:
  - Whenever you are doing something primarily to please yourself.
- Generating new ways of viewing situations outside the boundaries of standard convention:
  - Whenever you are stuck on a particularly difficult problem.
  - Whenever it is important to consider a variety of options.

---

helping students develop any of the other dimensions of learning. Unlike positive attitudes and perceptions (Dimension 1), which can be reinforced in a fairly unobtrusive manner by the teacher, the habits of mind must be overtly taught and reinforced. But they do not lend themselves to instruction in explicit strategies as do Dimensions 2, 3, and 4. Rather, the habits of mind must be introduced and then reinforced as they are exhibited.

The habits of mind must be introduced to students because students rarely see these habits of mind being used in the world around them. Few people plan and manage resources well. Few people seek clarity or accuracy. Few people work at the edge, rather than the center, of their competence. In fact, it is rather remarkable how infrequently human beings use these mental habits. After describing some of the dire consequences of ignoring these mental habits, Gilovich (1991) says, "As individuals and as a society, we should be less accepting of superstition and sloppy thinking and should strive to develop those 'habits of mind' that promote a more accurate view of the world" (p. 6).

There are, however, some striking examples of the use of these mental habits that teachers can employ in the classroom. I have seen teachers use specific events from the lives of Gandhi, Abraham Lincoln, George Bush, and others to illustrate one or more of the mental habits. This is what Mr. Nachtigal was doing by relating the story of Dan King: providing students with a real-life example of some of the mental habits. In fact, using stories and literature is probably one of the most popular ways of demonstrating the habits of mind. As Bloome (1991) explains, literature and stories are a society's way of passing on the important values of a culture.

I once observed a very powerful demonstration of how literature can be used to introduce some of the mental habits. The teacher was reading *The Island of the Blue Dolphins* by Scott O'Dell to her 4th grade students. The book is about a young Indian girl named Karana who with her little brother is left on an island off the coast of California when the tribe leaves to avoid a hostile rival tribe. Soon her brother is killed by a pack of wild dogs and Karana must fend for herself for many years. While waiting to be rescued, she builds a house, makes weapons and utensils,

finds and preserves food, and eventually adopts the leader of the dog pack, who protects her in a variety of situations. As the teacher read the story, she would periodically stop and ask students to identify the things they admired about Karana and the things that made her successful.

By the time the teacher had finished the book, students had generated a list of nearly thirty characteristics. As I recall, virtually all of the habits of mind described in this chapter, or variations of them, had been identified: Karana had made plans, she had been aware of resources, she had set her own standards, and so on. The teacher then highlighted the habits of mind that were to be the focus for the year. Although this lesson had taken some time and energy, it was a very powerful way of introducing specific habits of mind.

Once students have a basic awareness of the mental habits, the teacher can ask them to find examples among people they know. For example, in a 7th grade classroom in which the teacher had asked students to find examples of people using the mental habit of "hanging in there when answers and solutions aren't apparent," one student returned the next day with a story about how her brother had used that mental habit while trying to make the football team. Another girl told about how her father tried for more than two years to invent a new type of battery, persevering until he finally succeeded.

Another important aspect of introducing students to the habits of mind is asking them to identify specific situations in which each might be useful. Students from a variety of grade levels generated the list of situations in Figure 6.2.

Reinforcement is important too. Teachers should reinforce positive instances of the mental habits. For example, a teacher might notice that a student has paid particular attention to the resources necessary to complete a task, and say to her, "Amina, you're doing a great job of collecting all the material you need before you begin working," thus reinforcing the self-regulatory habit of managing resources. Or a teacher might notice and acknowledge that a student was trying to be particularly accurate: "Bill, I noticed that you looked up the facts in the encyclopedia. Good. That's a great way of making sure you're accurate," reinforcing the critical-thinking habit of seeking accuracy.

Sharing the Light of Faith:
National Catechetical Directory for Catholics of the United States

National Conference of Catholic Bishops. 1979. Nos. 176, 185.
Washington, D.C.: United States Catholic Conference.

Chapter VIII.*
Catechesis Toward Maturity in Faith

Part A. Faith and Human Development

176. Elements of methodology

a) A new methodology

In the covenant of the Old Testament, God announced His plan of salvation prophetically and by means of types. He revealed the truth about Himself gradually over centuries.

Now, in the fullness of time when revelation has been consummated in Christ, the Church uses a pedagogy adapted to the final age of salvation history, one in which the message is presented in its entirety while also being expressed according to the circumstances and ability of those being catechized. The principal elements of the Christian message (cf. Chapter V) must be central in all Catholic catechesis; they must never be overlooked or minimized, and must receive adequate and frequent emphasis.

b) No single methodology

Catechesis is not limited to one methodology. Although certain norms or criteria apply to all catechesis, they do not determine a fixed methodology, nor even an order for presenting the truths of faith. For instance, catechesis can begin with God and proceed to Christ, or do the reverse; it can proceed from God to humanity, or from humanity to God; and so on.

Whatever the method, catechists are responsible for choosing and creating conditions which will encourage people to seek and accept the Christian message and integrate it more fully in their living out of the faith.

c) Induction and deduction

All methods used in catechesis employ both induction and deduction, each with a different emphasis. The inductive approach proceeds from the sensible, visible, tangible experiences of the person, and leads, with the help of the Holy Spirit, to more general conclusions and principles. The deductive approach proceeds in the opposite manner, beginning with general principles, such as a commandment, whether from the decalogue or the Sermon on the Mount, and applying it to the real world of the person being catechized. The deductive approach produces its fullest impact when preceded by the inductive.[5]

d) Experience

Experience is of great importance in catechesis. Experiential learning, which can be considered a form of inductive methodology, gives rise to concerns and questions, hopes and anxieties, reflections and judgments, which increase one's desire to penetrate more deeply into life's meaning. Experience can also increase the intelligibility of the Christian message, by providing illustrations and examples which shed light on the truths of revelation. At the same time, experience itself should be interpreted in the light of revelation.

The experiential approach is not easy, but it can be of considerable value to catechesis.[6] Catechists should encourage people to reflect on their significant experiences and respond to God's presence there. Sometimes they will provide appropriate experiences. They should seek to reach the whole person, using both cognitive (intellectual) and affective (emotional) techniques.

e) Formulations[7]

In every age and culture Christianity has commended certain prayers, formulas, and practices to all members of the faith community, even the youngest. While catechesis cannot be limited to the repetition of formulas and it is essential that formulas and facts pertaining to faith be understood, memorization has nevertheless had a special place in the handing-on of the faith throughout the ages and should continue to have such a place today, especially in catechetical programs for the young. It should be adapted to the level and ability of the child and introduced in a gradual manner, through a process which, begun early, continues gradually, flexibly, and never slavishly. In this way certain elements of Catholic faith, tradition, and practice are learned for a lifetime and can contribute to the individual's continued growth in understanding and living the faith.

Among these are the following:

1. Prayers such as the Sign of the Cross; Lord's Prayer; Hail Mary; Apostles' Creed; Acts of Faith, Hope and Charity; Act of Contrition.

2. Factual information contributing to an appreciation of the place of the word of God in the Church and the life of the Christian through an awareness and understanding of: the key themes of the history of salvation; the major personalities of the Old and New Testaments; and certain biblical texts expressive of God's love and care.

3. Formulas providing factual information regarding worship, the Church Year, and major practices in the

---

* Editor's note: Chapter notation refers to this excerpt.

devotional life of Christians including the parts of the Mass, the list of the sacraments, the liturgical seasons, the holy days of obligation, the major feasts of our Lord and our Lady, the various eucharistic devotions, the mysteries of the rosary of the Blessed Virgin Mary, and the Stations of the Cross.

4. Formulas and practices dealing with the moral life of Christians including the commandments, the beatitudes, the gifts of the Holy Spirit, the theological and moral virtues, the precepts of the Church, and the examination of conscience.

Part B. Catechesis and Human Development

Section I: The Stages of Human Development

185. Some guidelines for the catechesis of adults

A number of catechetical norms and guidelines for adult catechesis have already been mentioned in this chapter. Others are noted elsewhere. What follows is intended to offer further assistance with regard to the Christian message as it pertains to adults, as well as to methodology.

a) The Christian message

The content of adult catechesis is as comprehensive and diverse as the Church's mission. It should include those universally relevant elements which are basic to the formation of an intelligent and active Catholic Christian and also catechesis pertaining to the particular needs which adults identify themselves as having.

The following description of content is not exhaustive.[17] Its elements have been selected either because of their relationship to the fundamental objectives of catechesis or their relevance to the present social scene in the United States.

Adult catechesis includes the study of scripture, tradition, liturgy, theology, morality, and the Church's teaching authority and life.[18] Church history is important for placing events in proper perspective.

Adult catechesis seeks to present the Church in all its dimensions, including its missionary nature, its role as sign or sacrament of Christ's presence in the world, its ecumenical commitment, and its mandate to communicate the whole truth of Christ to all persons in all times. (Cf. Mt 28,20)

Because Christ commissioned the apostles to teach people to observe everything He had commanded (cf. Mt 28,20), catechesis includes "not only those things which are to be believed, but also those things which are to be done."[19] Adult catechesis seeks to make adults keenly aware that an authentically Christian moral life is one guided and informed by the grace and gifts of the Holy Spirit, and that

decisions of conscience should be based on study, consultation, prayer, and understanding of the Church's teaching.

Adult catechesis gives parents and guardians additional instruction to help them in carrying out their particular responsibilities. It also provides similar instruction, at least of a general kind, to all adults, since the entire community has obligations toward the young.

It addresses the Church's mission to promote justice, mercy, and peace, including the vindication of religious, human, and civil rights which are violated.

Adult catechesis offers education for change, including the skills essential for dealing with the rapid changes typical of life today.

Adult catechesis gives special attention to spiritual life and prayer.

b) The methods

Adults should play a central role in their own education. They should identify their needs, plan ways to meet them, and take part in the evaluation of programs and activities.

Catechesis for adults respects and makes use of their experiences; their cultural, racial, and ethnic heritages; their personal skills; and the other resources they bring to catechetical programs. Whenever possible, adults should teach and learn from one another.

Much effective learning comes from reflecting upon one's experiences in the light of faith. Adults must be helped to translate such reflection into practical steps to meet their responsibilities in a Christian manner. Where appropriate experiences have not been part of a person's life, the catechetical process attempts to provide them, to the extent possible. This suggests the use of discussion techniques, especially in small groups, and the cultivation of communication skills.

Other methods of adult catechesis include reading, lectures, workshops, seminars, the use of the media, the Catholic press and other publications, and audio-visuals: in fact, all methods available to sound secular education. Specifically religious experiences—retreats, prayer meetings, and the like—provide extremely valuable opportunities for people to pause and reflect on their lives.

All catechetical programs, including those for adults, should be evaluated periodically.

Notes
5. Cf. *General Catechetical Directory*, 72.
6. Cf. *Ibid.*, 74.
7. Cf. *Ibid.*, 73.
17. Cf. *Ibid.*, 97, for a treatment of the special functions of catechesis for adults.
18. Cf. Church, 14.
19. GCD, 63.

The Small Catholic Elementary School

Reck, C. 1988. 64–70. Washington, D.C.: National Catholic Educational Association.

IV. Teaching Effectively

B. Assessing Needs of Old and New Students

1. Old students

As in any school, the teacher can acquire information for decisions about grouping and individualizing by studying standardized test results—both the class averages and the extremes of student achievement. Because a small number of students are involved, this study can suggest major adjustments in the curriculum such as the omission of certain skill areas, thus saving hours spent preparing to teach the standard curriculum.

2. New students

Students from other schools often experience difficulty when transferring into the small school; the Small Schools Study participants agreed that most students transferring from single-grade classrooms do not know how to proceed without extensive teacher assistance and supervision.

When new students enter the school, the teacher can assess the need for special steps such as the following:

a. To help kindergarten students and first graders feel welcome, a late-summer home visit may be a good introduction.

b. The teacher or principal, after studying the new student's testing record, arranges additional testing as needed to assure accurate placement.

c. Immediately after registration, the teacher appoints a student "buddy" to help the new student feel at home and develop the needed skills.

d. The teacher or "buddy" makes certain that the new student is introduced to the students and the total staff.

e. The teacher and "buddy" emphasize the importance of and teach practical steps toward effective study habits and self-discipline.

C. Outlining the Year's Curriculum

1. In Religion

The teacher, after learning the school plan, determines the following:

a. the key knowledge, attitudes, values, and experience for the assigned students;

b. the peripheral areas that may be used individually for enrichment or may be omitted;

c. the best way to combine basic areas to allow cross-graded classes to the extent desirable;

d. how to emphasize sacramental preparation with one grade only, e.g., while the other grade has a unit in

reading Bible stories or works on a special theme project;

e. any other responsibilities, e.g., liturgy planning.

2. In skill areas

Based on any schoolwide plans for skills areas (math, reading, phonics, language arts, spelling), the teacher determines the following for the levels within his/her responsibility:

a. the key concepts and skills to be mastered in each area;

b. any areas that can be taught to combined grades, e.g., in mathematics—statistics, division, problem solving—with differentiation in the level of problems;

c. an approximate assignment of the areas to be taught to the time available, dividing the required material first by semester, then by quarter, next by month, finally by week; when possible, trying to plan natural conclusions at the end of grading periods;

d. concepts and skills that can be omitted (because of alternation of textbooks, duplication within teaching materials, or total class mastery);

e. concepts and skills that can be used as enrichment (because of their non-essential nature);

f. any areas which are unfamiliar to the teacher; the teacher may benefit from reviewing related material in the preceding student text;

g. any feasible year-long options to regular teacher presentation, e.g., all spelling words introduced on and practiced with audiotape or with a student "practice partner"; all spelling tests by parent volunteer at school or by parent at home;

h. location or preparation of self-checking materials (print, audio, computer) for individual or small group practice exercises as well as unit self-tests.

3. In science and social studies

Within the school plan, the teacher identifies classroom curricular responsibilities and determines the following:

a. the key concepts and skills to be learned by all students within the classroom;

b. the best way to structure the following:

1) the teaching of those concepts and skills—as classroom, grades, groups, or individuals; (Groups and individualization will be considered below in Section D, "Planning Groups and Individualization.")

2) the allocation of available time to those concepts and skills;

3) the best use of available materials. This could mean, for example, that the teacher decides to use the materials assigned by the school plan in one of the following ways:

a) to alternate the two assigned texts, using, for example, World Geography one year and American History the next;

b) to use only the higher text;

c) to alternate state and federal Constitutions when both are required;

d) to use sections from both available texts each year;

e) to focus on science in one semester and social studies in the other;

f) to use general ungraded material when possible to lessen the focus on the graded text-book (from the State Conservation Department, the American Dairy Council, American Cancer Society, etc.);

g) to build a science program on low-cost experiments with supplementary study from textbooks and other resources.

4. In music, art, physical education

Using the schoolwide plan or another basic guide, the teacher identifies the following:

a. the knowledge and skills appropriate to the assigned levels;

b. possible interdisciplinary approaches to lessons and student activities involving these areas;

c. the best timing for each area, especially when a gym is not available, e.g., whether to allot more time for physical education in the fall and spring with more time for fine arts in the winter;

d. whether to use any of the fitness plans available from various agencies and companies;

5. In general

After reviewing all areas of required learning, the teacher may wish to schedule simultaneously any studies that could be treated in an interdisciplinary manner:

a. combining two subjects when related, e.g., science and math for probability or graphing; Religion and social studies to link the geography of the Holy Land with Scripture; social studies and literature for a unit on black history, women's studies, an historical era, or a regional study;

b. using a common vehicle to teach all subjects for one week, e.g., the newspaper, reference books;

c. planning an interdisciplinary field trip, e.g., one trip during which the students can study varied trees, see the effects of a lake on its environment, use scale measures to show the relative distances between cities, draw landscape scenes, compare the rhythmic sounds of nature to music, etc.

D. Planning Groups and Individualization

After studying available records—standardized tests, any other diagnostic or readiness measures, annotated records about last year's groupings—and talking with veteran educators at the school, the teacher's tasks are these:

◆ to group the students who have similar skills and needs;

◆ to identify students who have unique needs—
  ❖ those with learning difficulties,
  ❖ those with above-average achievement,

◆ to design a plan to track each student's mastery.

1. In religion

Although religion ordinarily is taught to total classes of students, the teacher can be alert for any students who seem to lack background, understanding, or a positive attitude regarding the faith or its expressions. Such areas may be strengthened by arranging special reading, audio-visual programs, or brief conferences.

2. In skill subjects

In skill subjects—reading, mathematics, phonics, language arts, and spelling—a checklist of skills can serve as a basis for grouping as well as for record keeping. Such lists of skills are provided in standardized testing manuals, textbook manuals, and in specialized professional books.

Generally, the younger the student, the more care will be needed to assure a firm foundation in skill development. With that foundation, students can handle more self-instruction, with most youngsters becoming very independent. The teacher can then spend more time with those who need and want more assistance.

3. In science and social studies

With science and social studies, many children can discuss the same topics and issues, but then they need varied ways to learn about those areas—with different levels of expected learning outcomes. Especially when combining the younger students in Grades 3 and 4, modifications in expectations will be needed.

The publication, *Challenging Gifted Students in the Catholic School*, (Hall, 1985) suggests practical ways to vary assignments to meet differing needs within the same classroom by modifying the content, process, product, or learning environment. Two examples from the publication follow:

◆ Content Modification—Degree of abstractness
The regular activity studies types of dinosaurs. Some students can also study the relationship between dinosaurs and their environment with possible reasons for their extinction.

◆ Process Modification—Questioning strategies
The regular curriculum asks two questions, What are the parts of an insect? and What are some types of insects? Some students can also address other questions: How are the parts of an insect similar to the parts of other animals? to people? How are they different from other animals? from people? How does the environment influence the development of any species of animal?

4. In music, art, and physical education

Because music, art, and physical education are participatory classes, children's skills must be considered when planning the class. This is especially important when a two- or three-year age range is involved.

In music, some students may be "allowed" to play the xylophone, finger cymbals, or recorders for a while until they are able to match the tones vocally. With art, all students could use the same media (e.g., poster paint)—with different degrees of design detail (e.g., a basic seascape or a boat or a fisherman) suggested according to experience and ability; or all could work on the same designs (e.g., still life)—with different media (e.g., crayon or charcoal or water color) according to experience and coordination.

In physical education, for example, before playing basketball, it is essential to begin with small groups working on specific needed skills, e.g., passing, dribbling, shooting. These skill groups could be led by student leaders.

5. Variety

A Grade 5–6 classroom could have the following groupings:

three reading groups,

two math groups,

total classroom sessions for religion, science, social studies,

classes combined with Grades 7–8 for music, art, and physical education.

In this classroom, a Grade 5 student could be working with a variety of youngsters:

Grade 6 students for reading,

a group composed predominantly of Grade 5 students for math,

Grades 5 and 6 for religion, science, and social studies,

Grades 5–8 for music, art, and physical education.

6. Flexibility

Occasionally a time could be allowed for "catchup" or for any work "contracted" between student and teacher. Sometimes students who have completed their work may be allowed to audit an upper class.

After work required of groups or individuals is completed, enrichment materials which match the students' interests and abilities should be available. These need not be paper-and-pencil exercises, but may include reusable puzzles, special books, computer programs, audio- or video-cassettes. Every student should have a fair chance to enjoy occasional enrichment activities.

Reference

Hall, Suzanne E. (Ed.). (1985). *Challenging gifted students in the Catholic school*. Washington, DC: National Catholic Educational Association.

Primary Symptoms and Conceptualization

Barkley, R. 1990. In *Attention deficit hyperactivity disorder: A handbook for diagnosis and treatment*, ed. R. Barkley, 39–73. New York: The Guilford Press.

Chapter 2[*]

The value of a principle is the number of things it will explain; and there is no good theory of a disease which does not at once suggest a cure.

—Ralph Waldo Emerson (1803–82)

A tremendous amount of research has been published on children with Attention-deficit Hyperactivity Disorder (ADHD)—their primary characteristics and related problems, the situational variability of these problems, their prevalence, and their etiologies. It was estimated by 1979 that over 2,000 studies existed on this disorder (Weiss & Hechtman, 1979), and this figure has surely doubled in the past 10 years. I have attempted to cull from this substantial fund of research the information that I believe is most useful for clinical work with these children; this information is described in this chapter. It is surely not the intent of the chapter, or of this book, to provide a critical review of the scientific literature—only to glean from it that which has a direct bearing on the clinical assessment and management of this condition. The clinically useful findings on the primary symptoms of ADHD are reviewed here, along with those pertaining to situational variability and prevalence. A modern reconceptualization of ADHD is also discussed. The associated features and comorbid disorders often seen with ADHD, and the etiologies proposed for the disorder, are reviewed in Chapter 3. The developmental course and outcome of ADHD children are described in Chapter 4. Those findings pertaining to the family interactions of these children and characteristics of their parents are discussed in Chapter 5.

Throughout this chapter and the remainder of this book, the term ADHD is used, although the research on which this discussion is based may have employed the related diagnoses of "hyperactivity," "hyperactive child syndrome," or "Attention Deficit Disorder with Hyperactivity" (ADD/+H). I realize that these terms and the diagnostic criteria used for them in this research are not completely identical. However, I believe that the clinical description of the children studied and the criteria used to select them for study are of sufficient similarity to permit one to argue that they pertain to quite similar groups of children. For gaining a general impression of the disorder and for the clinical purposes of this text, the minor differences that may exist among these groups because of these somewhat different terms and selection criteria do not

seem, at least to me, of sufficient import to justify qualifying each finding to be discussed by the manner in which the particular subjects were selected and diagnosed. But in so doing, I fully appreciate that for research purposes such differences among sample selection criteria are quite significant for both qualifying and interpreting one's findings.

Primary Symptoms

ADHD children are commonly described as having chronic difficulties in the areas of inattention, impulsivity, and overactivity—what one might call the "holy trinity" of ADHD. They are believed to display these characteristics early; to a degree that is inappropriate for their age or developmental level; and across a variety of situations that tax their capacity to pay attention, inhibit their impulses, and restrain their movement. As noted in Chapter 1, definitions have varied considerably throughout the history of this disorder, as have the recommended criteria for obtaining a diagnosis. The currently recommended criteria are set forth in Chapter 6, along with guidelines for distinguishing this disorder from other conditions that may be comorbid with it or that present with superficially similar features to it.

Inattention

By definition, children having ADHD display marked inattention, relative to normal children of the same age and sex. However, "inattention" is a multidimensional construct that can refer to problems with alertness, arousal, selectivity, sustained attention, distractibility, or span of apprehension, among others (Hale & Lewis, 1979). Research to date suggests that ADHD children have their greatest difficulties with sustaining attention to tasks or vigilance (Douglas, 1983). These difficulties are sometimes apparent in free-play settings, as evidenced by shorter durations of play with each toy and frequent shifts in play across various toys (Barkley & Ullman, 1975; Routh & Schroeder, 1976; Zentall, 1985). However, they are most dramatically seen in situations requiring the child to sustain attention to dull, boring, repetitive tasks (Luk, 1985; Milich, Loney, & Landau, 1982; Ullman, Barkley, & Brown, 1978; Zentall, 1985) such as independent schoolwork, homework, or chore performance.

The problem is not so much one of heightened distractibility, or the ease with which children are drawn off task by extraneous stimulation, although many parents and teachers will describe these children in such terms. Research

---

[*] Editor's note: Chapter notation refers to this excerpt.

on the distractibility of ADHD children has been somewhat contradictory on this issue, but in general finds these children to be no more distractible than normal children by extratask stimulation (Campbell, Douglas, & Morgenstern, 1971; Cohen, Weiss, & Minde, 1972; Rosenthal & Allen, 1980; Steinkamp, 1980). The findings for irrelevant stimulation provided within the task are more conflicting, however: Some studies find that such stimulation worsens the performance of ADHD children (Rosenthal & Allen, 1980), while others find no effect (Fischer, Barkley, Edelbrock, & Smallish, in press) or even an enhancing effect on attention (Zentall, Falkenberg, & Smith, 1985). Instead, the problem appears consistently to be one of diminished persistence or effort in responding to tasks that have little intrinsic appeal or minimal immediate consequences for completion (Barkley, 1990). The clinical picture may be different, however, in those situations where alternate, competing activities are available that promise immediate reinforcement or gratification, in contrast to the weaker reinforcement or consequences associated with the assigned task. In such cases, the ADHD child may appear distracted and in fact is likely to shift "off task" in order to engage the highly rewarding competing activity. It is not clear whether this represents true distraction as described above (i.e., the child orients to extraneous stimuli) or behavioral disinhibition (i.e., the child fails to follow rules or instructions when provided with competing, highly rewarding activities). It is my view that the latter is more likely to account for these attentional shifts than is a generalized problem with orienting to extraneous stimuli.

Parents and teachers will often describe these attentional problems in terms such as "Doesn't seem to listen," "Fails to finish assigned tasks," "Daydreams," "Often loses things," "Can't concentrate," "Easily distracted," "Can't work independently of supervision," "Requires more redirection," "Shifts from one uncompleted activity to another," and "Confused or seems to be in a fog" (Barkley, DuPaul, & McMurray, 1993; Stewart, Pitts, Craig, & Dieruf, 1966). Many of these terms are the most frequently endorsed items from rating scales completed by these caregivers (see Chapter 9). Studies using direct observations of child behavior find that "off-task" behavior or not paying attention to work is recorded substantially more often for ADHD children and adolescents than learning-disabled or normal children (Abikoff, Gittelman-Klein, & Klein, 1977; Barkley, DuPaul, & McMurray, 1993; Luk, 1985; Fischer et al., in press; Ullman et al., 1978). What is not so clear in these studies is whether this deficit in paying attention reflects a primary deficit in sustained attention or is secondary to the problem of behavioral disinhibition described below.

Behavioral Disinhibition

Intertwined with the difficulty in sustained attention is a deficiency in inhibiting behavior in response to situational demands, or impulsivity—again, relative to children of the same mental age and sex. Like "inattention," "impulsivity" is multidimensional in nature (Milich & Kramer, 1985), and it remains unclear which aspects of impulsivity are problematic for ADHD children. Clinically, these children are often noted to respond quickly to situations without waiting for instructions to be completed or adequately appreciating what is required in the setting. Heedless or careless errors are often the result. They may also fail to consider potentially negative, destructive, or even dangerous consequences that may be associated with particular situations or behaviors and so seem to engage in frequent, unnecessary risk taking. Taking chances on a dare or whim, especially from a peer, may occur more often than is normal. Consequently, accidental poisonings and injuries are not uncommon, and ADHD children may carelessly damage or destroy others' property considerably more frequently than normal children. Waiting their turn in a game or in a group lineup before going to an activity is often problematic for them. When faced with tasks or situations in which they are encouraged to delay seeking gratification and work toward a longer-term goal and larger reward, they often opt for the immediate, smaller reward that requires less work to achieve. They are notorious for taking "short cuts" in their work performance, applying the least amount of effort and taking the least amount of time in performing tasks they find boring or aversive.

When the children desire something to which others control access and they must wait a while to obtain it, as in a parent's promise to eventually take them shopping or to a movie, they may badger the parent excessively during the waiting interval, appearing to others as incessantly demanding and self-centered. Situations or games that involve sharing, cooperation, and restraint with peers are particularly problematic for these impulsive children. They often say things indiscreetly without regard for the feelings of others or the social consequences to themselves. Blurting out answers to questions prematurely, and interrupting the conversations of others, are commonplace. The layperson's impression of them, therefore, is often one of irresponsibility, immaturity or childishness, laziness, and outright rudeness. Little wonder that they experience more punishment, criticism, censure, and ostracism by adults and their peers than do normal children.

The problem of impulsivity is often scientifically defined as a pattern of rapid, inaccurate responding to tasks (Brown & Quay, 1977) such as Kagan's Matching Familiar Figures Test (MFFT; Kagan, 1966). In this task, a child is shown a picture below which are six very similar pictures. The child is to select from among the six that which is identical to the sample. ADHD children are noted to respond more quickly than others on the MFFT and to make more mistakes. Most often, it is their number of errors rather than their rapidity of responding that sets them apart from normal children (Brown & Quay, 1977), but even here recent findings have been conflicting (Fischer et al., in press; Barkley, DuPaul, & McMurray, 1993b; Milich & Kramer, 1985). Impulsivity may also refer to poor sustained inhibition of responding (Gordon, 1979), poor delay of gratification (Rapport, Tucker, DuPaul, Merlo, & Stoner, 1986), or impaired adherence to commands to regulate or inhibit behavior in social contexts (Kendall & Wilcox, 1979). Furthermore, studies that have factor-analyzed ratings of impulsive behavior mixed in with ratings or objective laboratory measures of inattention, overactivity, and oppositional behavior (Achenbach & Edelbrock, 1983; Milich & Kramer, 1985) have failed to differentiate an Impulsivity dimension from that measuring Hyperactivity—that is, overactive children are also impulsive children, and vice versa. This calls into serious question the existence of impulsivity as a separate dimension of behavioral impairment apart from hyperactivity in these children. It also strongly implies that the more global problem of behavioral disinhibition is what unites these two symptoms.

Evidence that behavioral disinhibition, or poor regulation and inhibition of behavior, is in fact the hallmark of this disorder has been accumulating recently from several sources. First, as noted at several points in this chapter, studies have typically shown that it is not inattention that distinguishes ADHD children from children with other clinical disorders or from normal children as much as it is their hyperactive, impulsive, and disinhibited behavior. Second, when objective measures of the three symptoms of ADHD are subjected to a discriminant-function analysis (a statistical method of examining the variables that contribute most to group discrimination), the symptoms of impulsive errors (typically on vigilance tasks) and excessive activity level are typically what best discriminate ADHD children from non-ADHD children (Barkley, DuPaul, & McMurray, 1993; Grodzinsky, 1990). A third source of evidence was derived from the field trial (Spitzer, Davies, & Barkley, in press) that tested the sensitivity and specificity of the 14 descriptors now comprising the diagnostic criteria for ADHD in the *Diagnostic and Statistical Manual of Mental Disorders*, third edition, revised (DSM-III-R; see below). These descriptors were rank-ordered by their discriminating power and are presented in the DSM-III-R in descending order. Careful inspection of this rank ordering reveals that again symptoms characteristic of disinhibition, such as poorly regulated activity and impulsivity, are more likely to discriminate children with ADHD from children with psychiatric disorders and normal children. For these reasons, I believe that the evidence available is sufficient to allow us to conclude that behavioral disinhibition rather than inattention is the hallmark of ADHD. In fact, this disinhibition or poor inhibitory regulation of behavior may result in the attention problems often noted in these children. That is, the attention problems may be secondary to a disorder of behavioral regulation and inhibition, rather than being a primary and distinct deficit apart from such disinhibition. This idea is developed further in the concluding section of this chapter.

Hyperactivity

The third primary characteristic of ADHD children is their excessive or developmentally inappropriate levels of activity, be it motor or vocal. Restlessness, fidgeting, and generally unnecessary gross bodily movements are commonplace (Stewart et al., 1966; Still, 1902). These movements are often irrelevant to the task or situation and at times seem purposeless. Parents often describe the problem in such terms as "Always up and on the go," "Acts as if driven by a motor," "Climbs excessively," "Can't sit still," "Talks excessively," "Often hums or makes odd noises," and "Squirmy." Observations of the children at school or while working on independent tasks find that they are out of their seats, moving about the class without permission, restlessly moving their arms and legs while working, playing with objects not related to the task, talking out of turn to others, and making unusual vocal noises (Abikoff et al., 1977; Barkley, DuPaul, & McMurray, 1993; Cammann & Miehlke, 1989; Fischer et al., in press; Luk, 1985). Making running commentaries on the activities around them or about others' behavior is not unusual. Direct observations of their social interactions with others also indicate generally excessive speech and commentary (Barkley, Cunningham, & Karlsson, 1983; Zentall, 1985).

Numerous scientific studies attest to these complaints that ADHD children are more active, restless, and fidgety than normal children throughout the day and even during sleep (Barkley & Cunningham, 1979b; Porrino, Rapoport, Behar, Sceery, Ismond, & Bunney, 1983). Again, however, there are many different types of "overactivity" (Barkley & Ullman, 1975; Cromwell, Baumeister, & Hawkins, 1963), and it is not always clear exactly which types are the most deviant for ADHD children. Measures of ankle movement and locomotion seem to differentiate them most reliably from normal children (Barkley & Cunningham, 1979b), but even some studies of wrist activity and total body motion have found them to be different as well (Barkley & Ullman, 1975; Porrino et al., 1983). There are also significant situational fluctuations in this symptom (Jacob, O'Leary, & Rosenblad, 1978; Luk, 1985; Porrino et al., 1983), implying that it may be the failure to regulate activity level to setting or task demands that is so socially problematic in ADHD (Routh, 1978), rather than just a greater-than-normal absolute level of movement. However, it has not been convincingly shown that excessive activity level distinguishes ADHD from other clinic-referred groups of children (Firestone & Martin, 1979; Sandberg, Rutter, & Taylor, 1978; Shaffer, McNamara, & Pincus, 1974). Recent studies suggest that it may be the pervasiveness of the hyperactivity across settings (home and school) that separates ADHD from these other diagnostic categories (Taylor, 1986b). As discussed below, this distinction may have more to do with our sources of information (parents vs. teachers) than with real differences in situational versus pervasive ADHD (Rapoport, Donnelly, Zametkin, & Carrougher, 1986).

As noted above for impulsivity, studies of objective measures or behavior ratings of hyperactivity have usually not found that it forms a separate factor or dimension apart from impulsivity. Typically, studies that factor-analyze behavioral ratings often find that items of restlessness may load on a factor comprising primarily poor attention and organization, while other types of overactivity load on a factor constituting impulsive or disinhibited behavior. This factor, not that of inattention, is what best distinguishes ADHD from other clinical conditions and from the normal state, as noted above. Hence, in our ranking of the importance of these primary symptoms, greater weight should be given to the behavioral class of impulsive and hyperactive characteristics than to inattention in conceptualizing this disorder and its clinical presentation. Again, the poor regulation and inhibition of behavior are the distinctive features of this disorder.

Deficient Rule-Governed Behavior

Although the idea is not yet widely accepted, many have stated that difficulties with adherence to rules and instructions may also be a primary deficit of ADHD children (American Psychiatric Association, 1987; Barkley, 1981, 1982, 1990; Kendall & Braswell, 1984). Care is taken here to exclude poor rule-governed behavior that may stem from sensory handicaps (e.g., deafness), impaired language development, or defiance or oppositional behavior. ADHD children have demonstrated significant problems with compliance to parental and teacher commands (Barkley, 1985a; Whalen, Henker, & Dotemoto, 1980), to experimental instructions in the absence of the experimenter (Draeger, Prior, & Sanson, 1986), and to prohibitions to defer gratification (Rapport, Tucker, et al., 1986). In fact, I have previously argued that most prior research demonstrating impaired attention and impulse control in ADHD children actually demonstrated poor rule-governed behavior, in that all of these studies involved experimenter instructions to subjects (Barkley, 1984, 1990). What the studies actually showed was that ADHD children have problems sustaining responding to experimenter rules and instructions, particularly when the instructions are not repeated or when the experimenter leaves the setting (Douglas, 1983; Draeger et al., 1986). Once again, "rule-governed behavior" is a multidimensional construct having various components, such as "pliance" (compliance to an immediately preceding stated rule) and "tracking" (correspondence over time between a previously stated rule and an individual's behavior), to name a few (Zettle & Hayes, 1983). It remains to be shown which of these are specifically impaired in ADHD children. However, there is little doubt in my mind that poor rule-governed behavior is closely associated with the behavioral disinhibition that is the distinctive feature of ADHD.

Zentall (1985), after reviewing the literature concerning the relationship of setting factors to the expression of ADHD symptoms, has concluded that noncompliance is not the primary difficulty of these children. This line of reasoning is based on the fact that the presence of an adult with them does not always lead to noncompliance, and may even improve their task performance. It is also based on observations that ADHD children may be inattentive and overactive in isolated or free-play settings even where no adults are present. But Zentall apparently has confused the notion of noncompliance or defiance with that of problems with rule-governed behavior, described above. "Defiance" is an active refusal to obey, through verbal or physical resistance or both. As I discuss below, over 60 percent of clinic-referred ADHD children will eventually develop a significant degree of this type of oppositional behavior. In contrast, "rule-governed behavior" refers to the extent to which behavior is under the stimulus control of preceding verbal stimuli that specify contingencies (if-then relations between behavior and consequences). The crux of this construct is whether correspondence exists between a child's behavior and previously stated rules. These rules may have been provided immediately prior to the performance of the desired behavior or may have been previously stated to the child earlier in time. ADHD children may display significant problems with initiating or sustaining responses to commands and rules, either immediately (pliance) or over time (tracking or sustained correspondence), without necessarily verbally refusing to obey or physically resisting the guidance of adults. Moreover, children are expected to adhere to previously stated rules of conduct, whether adults are present or not and whether the situation is free-play or task-oriented. This conceptualization of ADHD is further developed later in this chapter. Suffice it to say here that the fact that ADHD children are more active and inattentive in free-play settings or in the absence of adults does not eliminate the probability that they manifest impairments in rule following in these situations.

In any case, it is quite common clinically to hear these children described as not listening, failing to initiate compliance to instructions, unable to maintain compliance to an instruction over time, and poor at adhering to directions associated with a task. All of these descriptors are problems in the regulation and inhibition of behavior, especially by rules; their failure to develop adequately in ADHD children suggests serious problems with behavioral disinhibition in this disorder.

Greater Variability of Task Performance

Another characteristic that some believe to be a primary deficit in ADHD children is their excessive variability of task or work performance over time. Douglas (1972) noted this problem in observations of ADHD children performing reaction time tasks or serial problem solving, and many others have reported it since. It is a finding repeatedly noted on other tasks as well. One often finds that their standard deviation of performance on multitrial tasks is considerably larger than that seen in normal children. Both the number of problems or items completed and their accuracy of performance change substantially from moment to moment, trial to trial, or day to day in the same setting. Teachers often report much greater variability in homework and test grades, as well as in-class performance, than is seen in normal children. An inspection of the teacher's grade book for an ADHD child is often revealing of this pattern of performance. Similarly, parents may find that their children perform certain chores swiftly and accurately on some occasions, but sloppily if at all on other days.

As some have noted (Kupperman, 1988), the fact that these children have done their work well on a few occasions will be held against them for the rest of their academic careers. They are seen as capable but merely lazy. Yet this excessive variability may in fact be a hallmark of this disorder relative to other behavioral disorders, and that it may even be diagnostic of it. Rather than using such observations to rule out a potentially disabling condition in the children, clinicians may find that this variability in task performance is actually useful for ruling it in.

A Consensus Definition of ADHD

The foregoing discussion suggests that a consensus definition of ADHD might be phrased as follows:

Attention-deficit Hyperactivity Disorder is a developmental disorder characterized by developmentally inappropriate degrees of inattention, overactivity, and impulsivity. These often arise in early childhood; are relatively chronic in nature; and are not readily accounted for on the basis of gross neurological, sensory, language, or motor impairment, mental retardation, or severe emotional disturbance. These difficulties are typically associated with deficits in rule-governed behavior and in maintaining a consistent pattern of work performance over time.

Despite this apparent consensus view of ADHD, evidence is increasingly suggesting that it is the behavioral class of impulsivity and hyperactivity, or poor response regulation and inhibition, that underlies this disorder. A definition based on this view is presented later, in the section of this chapter dealing with a reconceptualization of ADHD.

Consensus Diagnostic Criteria for ADHD

At present, the primary characteristics of ADHD and the diagnostic criteria officially developed for clinical use are set forth in the DSM-III-R (American Psychiatric Association, 1987), used primarily in the United States, and the *International Classification of Diseases*, 10th edition (ICD-10; World Health Organization 1990), used mainly in Europe. The DSM-III-R criteria are presented in Table 2.1, and the ICD-10 criteria are shown in Table 2.2.

The DSM-III-R criteria for ADHD constitute a considerable improvement over those provided in the earlier versions of the DSM (American Psychiatric Association, 1968, 1980) and in the ICD-10 in many respects:

1. The items used to make the diagnosis were selected primarily from factor analyses of items from parent and teacher rating scales; thus, the items had already shown high intercorrelation with each other and validity in distinguishing ADHD from other groups of children (Barkley, Spitzer, & Costello, 1990). This is not the case for ICD-10.

2. In contrast to the DSM-III, the items in the DSM-III-R are no longer clustered within the separate categories or constructs of Inattention, Impulsivity, and Hyperactivity, with each having a separate cutoff score for determining its diagnostic significance. This polythetic approach to the symptoms of ADHD is more consistent with the dimensional view taken of other psychiatric disorders in the DSM-III-R, and with a similar view taken in more empirical approaches to a taxonomy of childhood disorders (Achenbach & Edelbrock, 1983).

3. The DSM-III-R avoids clustering particular items underneath a given construct (e.g., Inattention, Hyperactivity, etc.) purely on the basis of committee consensus, as was done in the DSM-III and has been done in the ICD-10. Attempts at factor-analyzing the older DSM-III items have shown that they do not cluster into three dimensions the way they are listed in the formal criteria, but in fact form two dimensions: Inattention-Restlessness and Impulsivity-Hyperactivity. The ICD-10 criteria, however, remain clustered under two dimensions, these being Attention Problems and Activity Problems. It is not at all clear whether these items would empirically cluster in this fashion.

4. As was not the case for either DSM-III or ICD-10, the cutoff point in the DSM-III-R was determined in a field trial (Spitzer et al., in press), and so had some empirical basis for its selection.

5. The specification of guidelines in DSM-III-R for establishing the severity of the disorder is important and reflects the research finding that the disorder has a significant range of expression and situational variation in its symptoms (see above). The degree of pervasiveness of the symptoms may be a particularly important indicator of the severity of the disorder, and both DSM-III-R and ICD-10 acknowledge this importance. However, they differ in that ICD-10 requires pervasiveness across situations for the diagnosis to be made, whereas DSM-III-R uses it simply to rate the severity of the disorder. Research shows that this insistence on agreement across home, school, and clinic in ICD-10, would severely restrict the diagnosis to approximately 1 percent or less of the childhood population (Lambert, Sandoval, & Sassone, 1978; Szatmari, Offord, & Boyle, 1989a).

6. Removing the requirement that the presence of affective disorders exclude the diagnosis of ADHD is a significant improvement of the DSM-III-R. Follow-up research clearly shows that ADHD children are not more likely to develop a major affective disorder; thus, when such a disorder is present it should not rule out ADHD, nor should ADHD rule out diagnosing an affective disorder when it is present. ICD-10 continues to labor under the outdated impression that a depressive or anxiety disorder should pre-empt the diagnosis of Hyperkinetic Disorder.

7. The DSM-III-R removed the subtyping of Attention Deficit Disorder with and without Hyperactivity (ADD/

Table 2.1. Diagnostic Criteria for Attention-Deficit Hyperactivity Disorder

A. A disturbance of at least six months during which at least eight of the following are present:
  (1) often fidgets with hands or feet or squirms in seat (in adolescents, may be limited to subjective feelings of restlessness)
  (2) has difficulty remaining seated when required to do so
  (3) is easily distracted by extraneous stimuli
  (4) has difficulty awaiting turn in games or group situations
  (5) often blurts out answers to questions before they have been completed
  (6) has difficulty following through on instructions from others (not due to oppositional behavior or failure of comprehension), e.g., fails to finish chores
  (7) has difficulty sustaining attention in tasks or play activities
  (8) often shifts from one uncompleted activity to another
  (9) has difficulty playing quietly
  (10) often talks excessively
  (11) often interrupts or intrudes on others, e.g., butts into other children's games
  (12) often does not seem to listen to what is being said to him or her
  (13) often loses things necessary for tasks or activities at school or at home (e.g., toys, pencils, books, assignments)
  (14) often engages in physically dangerous activities without considering possible consequences (not for the purpose of thrill-seeking), e.g., runs into street without looking
  Note: The above items are listed in descending order of discriminating power based on the data from a national field trial of the DSM-III-R criteria for Disruptive Behavior Disorders.
B. Onset before the age of seven.
C. Does not meet the criteria for a Pervasive Developmental Disorder.

Criteria for Severity of Attention-deficit Hyperactivity Disorder:
Mild: Few, if any, symptoms in excess of those required to make the diagnosis *and* only minimal or no impairment in school and social functioning.
Moderate: Symptoms or functional impairment intermediate between "mild" and "severe."
Severe: Many symptoms in excess of those required to make the diagnosis *and* pervasive impairment in functioning at home and school and with peers.

Note. From the *Diagnostic and Statistical Manual of Mental Disorders* (3rd ed., rev., pp. 52–53) by the American Psychiatric Association, 1987, Washington, DC: Author. Copyright 1987 by the American Psychiatric Association. Reprinted by permission.

+H and ADD/–H). Instead, ADD/+H is now ADHD, while ADD/–H is relegated to a relatively undefined disorder called Undifferentiated ADD. This was said to be necessary because little research was available at the time the DSM-III-R was drafted to indicate whether ADD/–H was a true subtype of ADHD, having the same attention disturbance, or whether it was an entirely separate and distinct disorder. This appears to have been a prudent gesture: Subsequent research, reviewed in Chapter 3, has pointed to ADD/–H as having a different attention disturbance from that in ADHD. ICD-10, by contrast, provides no mention of the existence of this subtype.

However, this review is not intended to suggest that the DSM-III-R criteria cannot be improved. Continuing research on the disorder and its characteristics suggests that the following would further improve the rigor of these criteria in distinguishing children with ADHD from children having other clinical disorders. One problem is that the placement of items into a single list or dimension in DSM-III-R is not as consistent with research findings as it

could be. Factor analyses of the 14 items suggest that they form two relatively separate behavioral dimensions, these being Inattention-Restlessness and Impulsivity-Hyperactivity (DuPaul, 1990a). It would therefore seem wise to present these symptoms in two separate lists, each having a separate cutoff score empirically determined in a field trial. Fortunately, this is now underway as part of a field trial test of possible DSM-IV criteria for this disorder. The ICD-11 would do well to follow suit and cluster its items on the basis of research on their interrelations rather than committee consensus.

Another difficulty in both approaches rests in the use of a fixed cutoff score across such a wide age range, from children through adolescents and even adults. It is well recognized that the symptoms of ADHD are present to a considerably greater degree in all preschool children and decline significantly over development into young adulthood. If the goal of a cutoff score is to restrict the diagnosis to a standard level of prevalence—say, the 97th percentile—then a single cutoff score simply will not achieve this aim across development. It will prove overly inclusive at

Table 2.2. ICD-10 Diagnostic Criteria for Hyperkinetic Disorders

A. Demonstrable abnormality of attention and activity at HOME, for the age and developmental level of the child, as evidenced by at least three of the following attention problems:
  (1) short duration of spontaneous activities;
  (2) often leaving play activities unfinished;
  (3) over-frequent changes between activities;
  (4) undue lack of persistence at tasks set by adults;
  (5) unduly high distractibility during study, e.g., homework or reading assignment;
  and by at least two of the following activity problems:
  (6) continuous motor restlessness (running, jumping, etc.);
  (7) markedly excessive fidgeting and wriggling during spontaneous activities;
  (8) markedly excessive activity in situations expecting relative stillness (e.g., mealtimes, travel, visiting, church);
  (9) difficulty in remaining seated when required.

B. Demonstrable abnormality of attention and activity at SCHOOL or NURSERY (if applicable), for the age and developmental level of the child, as evidenced by at least two of the following attention problems:
  (1) undue lack of persistence at tasks;
  (2) unduly high distractibility, i.e., often orienting towards extrinsic stimuli;
  (3) over-frequent changes between activities when choice is allowed;
  (4) excessively short duration of play activities;
  and by at least two of the following activity problems:
  (5) continuous and excessive motor restlessness (running, jumping, etc.) in situations allowing free activity;
  (6) markedly excessive fidgeting and wriggling in structured situations;
  (7) excessive levels of off-task activity during tasks;
  (8) unduly often out of seat when required to be sitting.

C. Directly observed abnormality of attention or activity. This must be excessive for the child's age and developmental level. The evidence may be any of the following:
  (1) direct observation of the criteria in A or B above, i.e., not solely the report of parent and/or teacher;
  (2) observation of abnormal levels of motor activity, or off-task behavior, or lack of persistence in activities, in a setting outside home or school (e.g., clinic or laboratory);
  (3) significant impairment of performance on psychometric tests of attention.

D. Does not meet criteria for pervasive developmental disorder (F84), mania (F30), depressive (F32) or anxiety disorder (F41).

E. Onset before the AGE OF SIX YEARS.

F. Duration of AT LEAST SIX MONTHS.

G. IQ above 50.

NOTE: The research diagnosis of Hyperkinetic Disorder requires the definite presence of abnormal levels of inattention and restlessness that are pervasive across situations and persistent over time, that can be demonstrated by direct observation, and that are not caused by other disorders such as autism or affective disorders.

Eventually, assessment instruments should develop to the point where it is possible to take a quantitative cut-off score on reliable, valid, and standardized measures of hyperactive behavior in the home and classroom, corresponding to the 95th percentile on both measures. Such criteria would then replace A and B above.

Note. From the *International Classification of Diseases* (10th ed.) by the World Health Organization, 1990, Geneva: Author. Copyright 1990 by the World Health Organization. Reprinted by permission.

young ages and overly restrictive or exclusive at adolescence and adulthood. The DSM-III-R field trial data in fact show such a problem with the cutoff score of 8 of 14 symptoms, in that the sensitivity and specificity of this cutoff score declined significantly with age (Spitzer et al., in press). More recent studies suggest that a score of 10 of 14 would be more appropriate for preschool-age children (those aged 5 or below), while 8 of 14 remains satisfactory with 6- to 11-year olds (DuPaul, 1990a). For adolescents, 6 of 14 would be more appropriate, respecting the decline in the prevalence of the ADHD symptoms in the normal population at this age (Barkley, Fischer, Edelbrock, & Smallish, 1993a). Although the ICD-10, acknowledges that eventually some objective measure of hyperactive behaviors should be used with a cutoff score of the 95th percentile, it does not yet apply this cutoff score to its own item listing, nor does it recommend using well-standardized behavior rating scales to assist in this task. Both the DSM and ICD criteria should begin to acknowledge the usefulness of rating scales in the diagnosis of this disorder.

A related problem with the DSM and ICD criteria is their failure to distinguish different cutoff scores for girls and boys. Research on rating scales and in developmental psychopathology has repeatedly shown that the prevalence of these symptoms is strongly related to gender, with girls showing considerably less of these characteristics than boys within community samples. Again, applying a fixed cutoff score will overidentify ADHD in boys and underidentify it in girls. The DSM-IV and ICD-11 should address this oversight by providing separate cutoff scores for boys and girls.

The requirement that the symptoms have lasted at least 6 months in both the DSM-III-R and ICD-10 requires some refinement, especially for use with preschool children. Ample evidence is now available that 3-year-olds with significant symptoms of inattention and hyperactivity have a high likelihood of remission of these concerns within 12 months (Campbell, 1987; see also Chapter 4). However, those whose problems last at least 12 months, or beyond 4 years of age, appear to have a very stable set of behavioral features that is predictive of ongoing ADHD in the later school years. Consequently, the duration of symptoms should be extended to 12 months.

The findings discussed thus far in this chapter indicate that behavioral disinhibition is the hallmark of ADHD, and so clinicians should place greater emphasis on the Impulsivity-Hyperactivity than on the Inattention symptoms in describing the disorder. Because behavioral disinhibition is what discriminates ADHD most clearly from other disorders, meeting a cutoff score for these items

should be a first requirement in the diagnostic criteria. Also, the Inattention items are as likely to be diagnosed in children with ADD/–H, who do not have this problem of behavioral disinhibition.

Finally, as discussed in Chapter 3, Undifferentiated ADD or ADD/-H should be provided with its own distinct label and diagnostic criteria apart from ADHD (or Hyperkinetic Disorder in ICD-10), as evidence points to its being a distinct childhood disorder and not a subtype of ADHD.

Is ADHD a Clinical Syndrome?

A troublesome issue for attempts to define ADHD as a disorder or syndrome has been the frequent finding that objective measures of these behaviors do not correlate well with each other (Barkley, 1993; Barkley & Ullman, 1975; Routh & Roberts, 1972; Ullman et al., 1978). Typically, for a disorder to be viewed as a syndrome, its major features should be related: The more deviant an individual is on one symptom, the more deviant he or she should be on the other major symptoms. The relatively weak or insignificant correlations among laboratory measures of hyperactivity, inattention, and impulsivity have often been used as evidence against the existence of ADHD as a disorder or syndrome by both scientists (Shaffer & Greenhill, 1979) and social critics (Kohn, 1989; Schrag & Divoky, 1975).

However, these weak relationships may have more to do with the manner in which we define the attention deficit or overactivity problems in ADHD children (Rutter,

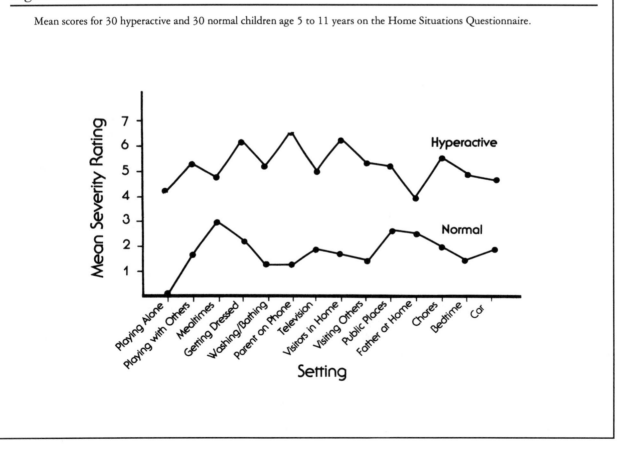

Figure 2.1.

Mean scores for 30 hyperactive and 30 normal children age 5 to 11 years on the Home Situations Questionnaire.

Figure 2.2.

Mean hourly activity scores and *SEMs* over period of 4 days for 12 hyperactives (open bars) and 12 controls (solid bars) during school hours (baseline week). Asterisks indicate significant differences on two-tailed *t* tests: triple asterisk, $p < .001$; double asterisk, $p < .01$. From "A Naturalistic Assessment of the Motor Activity of Hyperactive Boys" by L. J. Porrino, J. L. Rapoport, D. Behar, W. Sceery, D. R. Ismond, & W. E. Bunney, Jr., 1983, *Archives of General Psychiatry, 40,* 681–687. Copyright 1983 by the American Medical Association. Reprinted by permission of the authors and publisher.

Figure 2.3.

Mean hourly activity scores and *SEMs* over period of 4 days for 12 hyperactives (open bars) and 12 controls (solid bars), calculated for specific situations during after-school hours (baseline week). Asterisk indicates significant difference ($p < .05$) on two-tailed *t* tests. From "A Naturalistic Assessment of the Motor Activity of Hyperactive Boys" by L. J. Porrino, J. L. Rapoport, D. Behar, W. Sceery, D. R. Ismond, & W. E. Bunney, Jr., 1983, *Archives of General Psychiatry, 40,* 681–687 Copyright 1983 by the American Medical Association. Reprinted by permission of the authors and publishers.

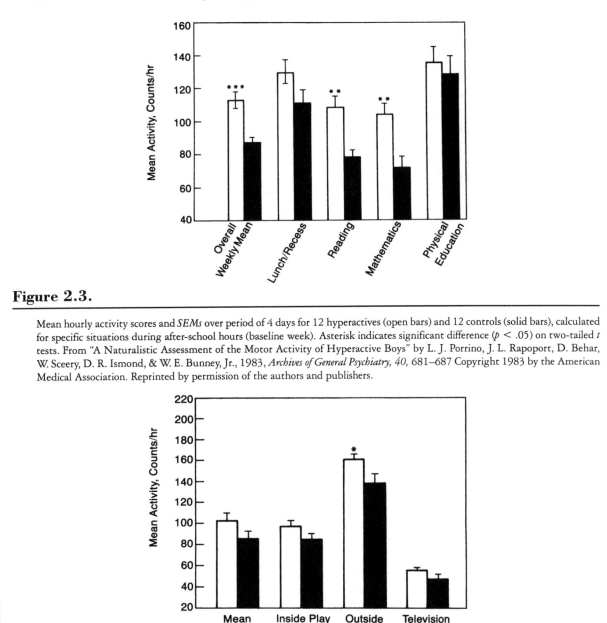

1989), and, more likely, with the measures we choose to assess these behaviors. How long a child attends to a classroom lecture may be a very different type of attentional process from that required to perform a vigilance test or that required to search out important from unimportant features in a picture (Barkley, 1988d; Ullman et al., 1978). Similarly, taking adequate time to examine a picture before choosing one identical to it from a number of similar pictures (as in Kagan's MFFT; see above) may be a different type of impulsivity from that seen when children are asked to draw a line slowly, or when they are asked whether they wish to work a little for a small reward now or do more work for a large reward later (Milich & Kramer, 1985; Rapport, Tucker, et al., 1986). It may be a source of wonder, then, that these types of measures correlate at all with each other.

In contrast, studies that factor-analyze parent or teacher ratings of ADHD symptoms often find that they are highly interrelated (Achenbach & Edelbrock, 1981; Barkley, 1988c, 1993; DuPaul, 1990a; Hinshaw, 1987), such that they can be combined into a single dimension

(Hyperactivity) or at most two dimensions (Inattention-Restlessness and Impulsivity-Hyperactivity). Similarly, when measures of attention and impulsivity are taken within the same task, as in scores for omission and commission errors on a continuous-performance test, they are highly related to each other (Barkley, 1990; Gordon, 1983). This suggests that the frequent failure to find relationships among various lab measures of ADHD symptoms has more to do with the source or types of measures chosen; their highly limited sampling of behavior (typically 20 minutes or less per task); and their sampling of quite diverse aspects of inattention, impulsivity, or hyperactivity than to a lack of relationships among the natural behaviors of these children.

Furthermore, the fact that such symptoms may not occur to a uniform degree in the same children does not rule out the value of considering ADHD as a syndrome. As Rutter (1977, 1989) has noted, a disorder may not show uniform variation but may still be clinically useful as a syndrome. If such children show a relatively similar course and outcome, their symptoms predict differential responses to certain treatments relative to other disorders, or they tend to share a common etiology or set of etiologies, then it may still be valuable to consider children with such characteristics as having a syndrome of ADHD. I and others (Douglas, 1983; Rutter, 1989; Taylor, 1986b) believe that the evidence supports such an interpretation of ADHD.

More problematic for the concept of a syndrome, however, is whether the defining features of ADHD can discriminate ADHD from other types of psychiatric disturbance in children. The evidence here is certainly conflicting and less compelling (Reeves, Werry, Elkind, & Zametkin, 1987; Werry, Reeves, & Elkind, 1987). Mentally retarded, autistic, psychotic, depressed, conduct-disordered, anxious, and learning-disabled children may show deficits in attention or be overactive. When studies compare such groups, they often find few differences among them on measures of ADHD characteristics (see Werry, 1988, for a review). However, such studies must first take into account the comorbidity of many of these disorders with each other. "Comorbidity" means that children with one disorder have a high likelihood of having a second. Some children may have only one of the disorders, some the other, and many have both. This is often noted with ADHD, Oppositional Defiant Disorder, Conduct Disorder, and learning disabilities. Many studies of this issue have not taken care to choose subjects who have only one of these disorders to compare against those who have "pure" cases of the other disorders. As a result, they compare mixed cases of ADHD with mixed cases of other disorders; this greatly weakens the likelihood that differences among the groups will emerge. When subjects have been more carefully selected, differences between pure ADHD and other disorders have been more significant and numerous (August & Stewart, 1982; Barkley, DuPaul, & McMurray, 1993; Barkley, Fischer, Edelbrock, & Smallish 1993a; McGee, Williams, & Silva, 1984a, 1984b).

Differences in approaches to defining ADHD can also contribute to the difficulties in evaluating ADHD as a distinct clinical syndrome. Research in the 1960s and 1970s was characterized by poorly specified and often subjective criteria for deciding on which subjects would be called hyperactive, or ADHD, with tremendous discrepancies across studies in these selection criteria (Barkley, 1982). Such criteria guaranteed not only that the studies would differ greatly in their findings, but also that many would employ subjects of mixed comorbidity, assuring a very conflicting pattern of results across the literature. With the development of consensus criteria for clinical diagnosis (as in the DSM-III and the more recent DSM-III-R) or for research (Barkley, 1982; Sergeant, 1988), and with greater attention to the study of pure cases of the disorder, better and more critical tests of the notion of ADHD as a distinct disorder can now be undertaken.

Situational and Temporal Variation

As already noted, all of the primary symptoms of ADHD show significant fluctuations across various settings and caregivers (Barkley, 1981; Zentall, 1984). This can be seen in Figure 2.1, which shows the severity of behavior problems across a variety of home and public situations as reported by parents of ADHD children. Play alone, washing and bathing, and when fathers are at home are a few of the situations that are less troublesome for ADHD children, whereas instances where children are asked to do chores, when parents are on the telephone, when visitors are in the home, or when children are in public places may be times of peak severity of their disorder.

Figures 2.2 and 2.3 show the mean activity level for 12 hyperactive and 12 normal children monitored during school hours and after school activities on school days, respectively (Porrino et al., 1983). Again, significant fluctuations in activity are evident across these different contexts for both ADHD and normal children, with the differences between them becoming most evident during school classes in reading and math. Despite these situational fluctuations, ADHD children appear to be more deviant in their primary symptoms than normal children in most settings; yet these differences can be exaggerated greatly as a function of several factors related to the settings and to the tasks children are required to perform in them (Zentall, 1985).

Degree of Environmental Demands for Inhibition

Some of the variables determining this variation have been delineated. One of these—the degree of "structure," or more specifically the extent to which caregivers make demands on ADHD children to restrict behavior—appears to affect the degree of deviance of these children's behavior from that of normal children. In free-play or low-demand settings, ADHD children are less distinguishable from normal children than in highly restrictive settings (Barkley,

The Principal as Educational Leader

1985a; Jacob et al., 1978; Luk, 1985; Routh & Schroeder, 1976).

Related to this issue of setting demands is the effect of task complexity on ADHD children. The more complicated the task, and hence the greater its demand for planning, organization, and executive regulation of behavior, the greater the likelihood that ADHD children will perform more poorly on the task than normal children (Douglas, 1983; Luk, 1985). Obviously, the symptoms of ADHD are only handicapping when the demands of the environment or task exceed a child's capacity to sustain attention, regulate activity, and restrain impulses. In environments that place few or no demands on these behavioral faculties, ADHD children will appear less deviant and will certainly be viewed by others as less troublesome than in settings or tasks that place high demands on these abilities. As Zentall (1985) has rightly noted in her comprehensive review of setting factors in the expression of ADHD symptoms, we must look closely at the discriminative stimuli in the task and setting to which the children are being required to respond, to gain a better understanding of why these children have so much trouble in some settings and with some tasks than others.

Behavior Toward Fathers Compared to Mothers

ADHD children appear to be more compliant and less disruptive with their fathers than with their mothers (Tallmadge & Barkley, 1983; Tarver-Behring, Barkley, & Karlsson, 1985). There are several possible reasons for this. For one, mothers are still the primary custodians of children within the family, even if they are employed outside the home; they may therefore be the ones who are more likely to tax or exceed the children's limitations in the areas of persistence of attention, activity regulation, impulse control, and rule-governed behavior. Getting children to do chores and schoolwork, to perform self-care routines, and to control their behavior in public remains predominantly a maternal responsibility and so mothers may be more likely to witness ADHD symptoms than fathers. It would be interesting to examine families of ADHD children in which these roles are reversed, to see whether fathers become the ones reporting more deviance of the children's behavior.

Another reason may be that mothers and fathers tend to respond to inappropriate child behavior somewhat differently. Mothers may be more likely to reason with children, to repeat their instructions, and to use affection as a means of governing child compliance. Fathers seem to repeat their commands less, to reason less, and to be quicker to discipline children for misconduct or noncompliance. The larger size of fathers and their consequently greater strength (among other characteristics) may also be perceived as more threatening by children, and hence may be more likely to elicit compliance to commands. For whatever reason, the greater obedience of ADHD children to their fathers than to their mothers is now well established. It should not be construed as either a sign that a child does not actually have ADHD or that the child's problems are entirely the result of maternal mismanagement.

Repetition of Instructions

On tasks where instructions are repeated frequently to the ADHD child, problems with sustained responding are lessened (Douglas, 1980a, 1980b, 1983). Research has shown that when directions for a laboratory task or psychological test are repeated by the examiner, better performance is derived from ADHD children. However, it is not clear

Figure 2.4.

Mean hourly activity scores and *SEMs* over period of 3–5 days for hyperactives and controls, calculated for typical weekday. Small squares indicate hours during which hyperactives were significantly more active than controls ($p < .05$, by Sheffe procedure after analysis of variance). From "A Naturalistic Assessment of the Motor Activity of Hyperactive Boys" by L. J. Porrino, J. L. Rapoport, D. Behar, W. Sceery, D. R. Ismond, & W. E. Bunney, Jr., 1983, *Archives of General Psychiatry, 40*, 681–687. Copyright 1983 by The American Medical Association. Reprinted by permission of the authors and publisher.

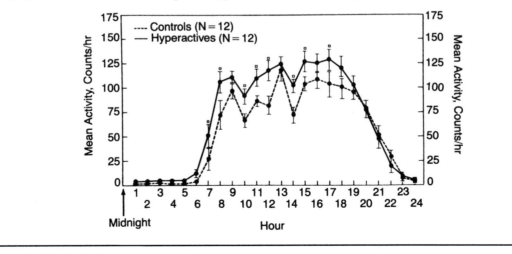

whether this is specific to these laboratory tasks and the novel examiner, or can be generalized to activities with routine caregivers. I raise this doubt because, as noted above, it is not uncommon for parents and teachers frequently to complain that repeating their commands and instructions to ADHD children produces little change in compliance.

Novelty and Task Stimulation

ADHD children display fewer behavioral problems in novel or unfamiliar surroundings, or when tasks are unusually novel, but increase their level of deviant behavior as familiarity with the setting increases (Barkley, 1977a; Zentall, 1985). It is not uncommon to find that ADHD children are rated as far better in their behavior at the beginning of the academic year, when they are presented with new teachers, classmates, classrooms, and even school facilities. Their behavioral control, however, usually deteriorates over the initial weeks of school. Similarly, when ADHD children visit with grandparents whom they have not seen frequently, who are likely to provide them with considerable one-to-one attention, and who are unlikely to make numerous demands of their self-control, it seems likely that the children will be at their best levels of behavioral control.

Task stimulation also seems to be a factor in the performance of ADHD children. Research suggests that these children are likely to pay much more attention to colorful or highly stimulating educational materials than to relatively less stimulating or uncolored materials (Zentall, 1985). Interestingly, such highly stimulating materials may not affect the attention of normal children as much or may even worsen it.

Magnitude of Consequences

Settings or tasks that involve a high rate of immediate reinforcement or punishment for compliance to instructions result in significant reductions in, or in some cases amelioration of, attentional deficits (Barkley, 1990; Barkley, Copeland, & Sivage, 1980; Douglas, 1983; Douglas & Parry, 1983). Few ADHD children seem to demonstrate attention deficits when they play popular video games, such as Nintendo, or when large amounts of money or salient rewards are promised them immediately upon completion of a task. Certainly, differences in activity level between hyperactives and normals while watching television may be minimal or nonsignificant, yet such differences are substantially evident during reading and math classes at school (Porrino et al., 1983). In these instances where ADHD children are engaged in highly reinforcing activities, they may even perform at normal or near-normal levels. However, when the schedule and magnitude of reinforcement are decreased, the behavior of ADHD children may become readily distinguishable from that of normals (Barkley et al., 1980). Such dramatic changes in the degree of deviance of behavior as a function

of motivational parameters in the setting has led several scientists to question the notion that ADHD is actually a deficit in attention at all. Instead, they suggest that it may be more of a problem in the manner in which behavior is regulated by its effects or consequences (Barkley, 1990; Draeger et al., 1986; Haenlein & Caul, 1987; Prior, Wallace, & Milton, 1984)—in essence, that ADHD is a motivational deficit rather than an attentional one. This issue is discussed further below in conceptualizing this disorder.

A situational factor related to motivation appears to be the degree of individualized attention being provided to the ADHD child. In one-to-one situations, ADHD children may appear less active, inattentive, and impulsive; in group situations, where there is little such attention, ADHD children may appear at their worst. Some studies, for instance, have found that whether the experimenter sits in the room with a child or not greatly determines whether differences between ADHD and normal children on visual or auditory attention tasks or on attention to arithmetic work will be found (Draeger et al., 1986; Steinkamp, 1980).

Fatigue

Fatigue or time of day (or both) may affect the degree to which ADHD symptoms are exhibited. Zagar and Bowers (1983) observed the behavior of ADHD children in their classrooms and during various problem-solving tasks, and found that they performed significantly better on these tasks when given in the mornings, whereas their classroom behavior was significantly worse in the afternoons. These changes in behavior with time of day did not appear to be a function of boredom or fatigue with the task, as efforts were made to counterbalance the order of administration of the tests across mornings and afternoons. Performance in the afternoon was routinely worse, whether it was the first or second administration of the task. However, there is the possibility that general fatigue, defined simply as time since the last resting or sleeping period, may still explain these results. Similar effects of time of day were noted in the study by Porrino et al. (1983), which monitored 24-hour activity levels across school days and weekends separately. These findings are shown in Figure 2.4 for school days and indicate the hours of 1 p.m. to 5 p.m. to be the peak times of activity for ADHD children.

This is not to say that differences between hyperactive and normal children do not exist in early mornings but emerge only as time of day advances, for this is not the case (Porrino et al., 1983). Normal children show similar effects of time of day upon their behavior, and so hyperactive children appear to be more active and inattentive than normal children, regardless of time of day. It remains true, however, that relatively better performances on tasks and in classrooms by ADHD children may be obtained at some times of the day rather than others. The findings so far suggest that educators would do well to schedule overlearned, repetitive, or difficult tasks that require the greatest powers of attention and behavioral restraint for morning periods, while placing recreational, entertaining, or physical activities in the afternoons (Zagar & Bowers, 1983). Such findings certainly raise serious doubts about the adequacy of the practice of scheduling homework periods for ADHD children in late afternoons or early evenings.

Implications for Diagnosis and Management

These situational fluctuations in symptom levels have significant implications for clinical diagnosis of ADHD. It is clear that the disorder is not completely pervasive across all settings. As a result, the previous and common clinical practice of establishing places where the ADHD child can behave "normally" and then ruling out the diagnosis is no longer tenable. Many clinicians have interrogated parents as to how their ADHD children behave while watching television, playing video games, or spending time with their fathers, grandparents, or babysitters. Having learned that the children are much better behaved or "normal" in these settings, the clinicians have proceeded to conclude that such children can not have ADHD because the symptoms are neither persistent nor pervasive. Some have even gone so far as to state that because the children behave better for their fathers (and often better during the office exam with the clinician!), the problem must rest with the mothers' inept management of their children. Such a prejudice against mothers, in fact, is still rather pervasive among laypersons and even some professionals. It is now quite clear that ADHD children show a tremendous variability in their symptom severity across settings, tasks, and time. And, although they are typically more deviant than normal children in their levels of activity and inattention in most settings, the factors within the setting and especially in the demands of the task are highly related to the level of deviance noted (Zentall, 1985). It therefore seems best, in searching for information to assist with the diagnosis, to focus clinical attention more on the ability of ADHD children to sustain attention, regulate activity, control impulses, and follow rules under conditions of tedium (especially boring, repetitive, or protracted work assignments) or under social conditions demanding restraint.

As already noted, these situational changes in behavior and performance can also have some impact on the management of ADHD children. An awareness of the situational or task factors that can enhance performance may greatly empower a parent or teacher to devise methods or schedules of work that best fit with the ADHD child's limited capacities for sustaining attention and regulating activity level. Difficult, complex, or tedious work can be organized into smaller units, provided with greater clarity, assisted by having the child think aloud and talk himself or herself through the task, and enhanced by providing more immediate and salient reinforcers for task completion. Scheduling such activities during morning hours, as suggested earlier, may further enhance task performance. Permitting some motion and talking during task completion, and interspersing periods of restraint with periods of exercise or movement, may also help. These and other suggestions are reviewed in the chapters on parent training and classroom management of this text, but clearly stem from a knowledge of these important situational and task parameters.

Prevalence and Sex Ratio

Because ADHD cannot be strictly defined and precisely measured, its true incidence cannot be accurately determined. Some social critics have used this point to challenge whether a disorder of ADHD exists at all (Kohn, 1989; Schrag & Divoky, 1975). This same problem, however, plagues all psychiatric disorders and even many medical conditions (e.g., Alzheimer's disease, Reye's syndrome, etc.), and yet this hardly makes them clinically useless or fictitious disorders. The consensus of opinion seems to be that approximately 3 to 5% of the childhood population has ADHD (American Psychiatric Association, 1987), but this greatly hinges on how one chooses to define ADHD, the population studied, the geographic locale of the survey, and even the degree of agreement required among parents, teachers, and professionals (Lambert et al., 1978). Estimates vary between 1 and 20% (DuPaul, 1990a; Ross & Ross, 1982; Szatmari et al., 1989a).

Certainly, behaviors similar to the symptoms of ADHD can be found in a large percentage of normal children. In 1958, Rema Lapouse and Mary Monk had teachers evaluate a large sample of school-age children as to the presence of various behavior problems. Their findings revealed that 57% of the boys and 42% of the girls were rated as overactive. Similarly, John Werry and Herbert Quay (1971) also surveyed a large population of school children and found that teachers rated 30% of the boys and 12% of the girls as overactive, 49% of the boys and 27% of the girls as restless, and 43% of the boys and 25% of the girls as having short attention spans.

Critics of the concept of ADHD as a disorder have used such figures to argue that if so many normal children have these features, how can one choose to label some of them as having a clinical or psychiatric disorder (Kohn, 1989; Schrag & Divoky, 1975)? These critics ignore the requirement that the degree of these behavioral characteristics must be developmentally inappropriate for the children's age and sex before it can be considered as clinically deviant or meaningful (American Psychiatric Association, 1987; Barkley, 1981, 1982). In other words, a statistical criterion is applied in which the referred children are compared to their peers in their level of these problematic behaviors, to determine how deviant they are from same-age, same-sex children. The further the children are from their peers in these behaviors, the greater the odds that they will be impaired in their educational and social adjustment and will eventually be diagnosed as having ADHD.

Defining Deviance

A problem here, admittedly, is deciding what cutoff point is needed to determine that children are "developmentally inappropriate" in their behavior. Some have used

Figure 2.5.

Prevalence of "hyperactivity" in metropolitan area of Ottawa, Ontario, and Hull, Quebec, Canada, 1977; southeast view. From *Hyperactivity in Children: Etiology, Measurement, and Treatment Implications*, by R. L. Trites, 1979, Baltimore: University Park Press. Copyright 1979 by University Park Press. Reprinted by permission of the publisher.

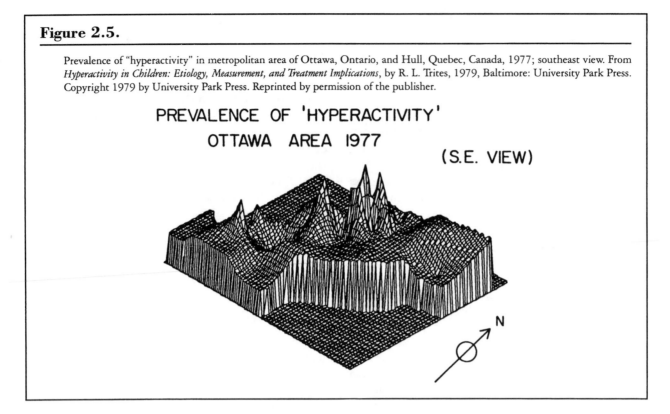

PREVALENCE OF 'HYPERACTIVITY'
OTTAWA AREA 1977
(S.E. VIEW)

the criterion of 1.5 standard deviations above the normal mean on parent or teacher rating scales of these ADHD symptoms. However, surveys of large samples of children, such as that done by Ronald Trites and colleagues (Trites, Dugas, Lynch, & Ferguson, (1979) using 14,083 school children, find that this cutoff score can identify an average of 14% of the population as hyperactive. In other studies (see Szatmari et al., 1989a; Taylor, 1986b), estimates can range from less than 1% to over 22% when cutoff scores ranging from 1 to 2 standard deviations above the mean on structured psychiatric diagnostic interviews are used. However, when others have applied the cutoff of two standard deviations above the mean using DSM-III-R symptoms, a more acceptable range of 2 to 9% has been labeled as hyperactive or ADHD (DuPaul, 1990a). Applying a more stringent statistical criterion, such as two standard deviations from the mean, is obviously somewhat arbitrary, but it is in keeping with tradition in defining other conditions (such as learning disabilities and mental retardation) as deviant. It also ensures that an excessive number of children are not being given a psychiatric diagnosis and reserves the diagnosis for the most severely afflicted. When such a stringent criterion as the 97th percentile is applied (two standard deviations above the mean), it does appear to identify a group of children whose ADHD symptoms are not only seriously deviant, but are also stable over as long a time as 8 to 10 years and highly predictive of later maladjustment, particularly in academic adjustment and attainment (Barkley, Fischer, et al., 1993a).

More recently, Szatmari et al. (1989a) have reported the results of a survey of the entire province of Ontario, Canada, in which they found the prevalence of ADHD to be 9% in boys and 3.3% in girls. These rates varied somewhat by age for boys: There was a prevalence of slightly more than 10% in the 4-to-11 age group, dropping to 7.3% in the 12-to-16 age group. The prevalence for girls, however, did not vary significantly across these age groupings (3.3 vs. 3.4%, respectively). The findings are quite similar to those of the much smaller community survey conducted by DuPaul (1990a), using DSM-III-R symptoms. Overall, then a prevalence of approximately 5 to 6% of children between 4 and 16 years of age are likely to be diagnosed as ADHD.

The Problem of Agreement Among Caregivers

Much is often made by social critics of the fact that the prevalence of ADHD appears to differ significantly as a function of how many people must agree on the diagnosis (Kohn, 1989). The study by Lambert et al. (1978) on this issue is the one most often cited. In this study, parents, teachers, and physicians of 5,000 elementary school children were asked to identify children they considered to be hyperactive. Approximately 5% of these children were defined as hyperactive when the opinion of only one of these caregivers (parent, teacher, physician) was required—a prevalence figure very close to that found both by Szatmari et al. (1989a) in their Canadian survey and by DuPaul (1990a) in the United States. However, this prevalence figure dropped to about 1% when agreement among all three was required. This should hardly be surprising, considering that no effort was made to provide these "social definers" with any criteria for making their judgments or any training in the actual symptoms believed to constitute this disorder. Research routinely finds agreements among people to be low to modest when judging the behavior of another, unless more specific and operational definitions of the behavior being judged and training in the application of the definitions are provided.

It is well established, for instance, that parent and teacher ratings of many different types of child behavior problems are likely to have interrater agreement coefficients of less than .50 (Achenbach, McConaughy, & Howell, 1987). Even fathers and mothers may have agreements of little more than .60 to .70. Certainly, the fact that children behave differently in different situations and with different adults can be a major factor contributing to this lack of agreement. The often subjective judgments required in determining whether a child's behavior occurs "often" or is "deviant" can be another. Undoubtedly, the fleeting or ephemeral nature of behavior and the constant stream of new behaviors or actions of children can create further confusion as to which of these actions should be considered in the judgment. Finally, the use of adult opinions to determine the diagnosis of hyperactivity will always be somewhat confounded by the characteristics and mental status of the adult informant, in addition to the child's actual behavior. As discussed in more detail in Chapter 9 on behavior rating scales, psychological distress, depression, family discord, and social biases can affect the judgments adults make about children, and can therefore add to the lack of agreement among adults about the presence and degree of a child's ADHD. Hence the lack of agreement across caregivers and the variations in the prevalence of ADHD that may arise as a result of it are hardly indictments of the concept of ADHD as a disorder, but apply to many other types of human behavior and virtually all mental disorders.

Culture and Socioeconomic Status

Rates of occurrence of ADHD also fluctuate to a small degree across cultures (O'Leary, Vivian, & Nisi, 1985; Ross & Ross, 1982) and socioeconomic status (SES; Taylor, 1986b; Trites, 1979). This variation in prevalence as a function of SES or geographic area was nicely illustrated in the survey by Trites and colleagues (see Trites, 1979), which is graphically depicted in Figure 2.5. Rates of hyperactivity, defined using the Conners rating scales, varied considerably across the metropolitan area of Ottawa and Hull, Canada, with apparently poorer regions showing higher rates of the disorder. Szatmari et al. (1989a) also found prevalence rates to vary between urban (7.0%) and small urban or rural areas (4.6%).

One reason for such fluctuations may be that women in lower-SES groups are likely to have poorer care and nutrition during their pregnancies and a higher incidence of pregnancy and birth complications. These may affect their children's developing brains and thus predispose the children to a greater risk for ADHD. Second, lower-SES groups are known to have higher rates of family instability, divorce, and parental psychiatric difficulties; these may exacerbate the characteristics of a child with marginal

ADHD, so that his or her symptoms are much more prominent. A third explanation may be that a phenomenon known as "social drift" may occur. Children with ADHD may inherit this condition and grow up to have less education than their peers, regardless of their SES level of origin. Upon reaching adulthood, they then drift into a level of employment, and hence a particular SES level, commensurate with their lower educational experience. Given that their condition is hereditary, they are likely to have children with similar problems, thereby inflating the incidence of ADHD within that SES level to which ADHD adults are likely to drift. It is not clear which if any of these explanations accounts for these differences in prevalence across geographic and SES levels. Nevertheless, these differences are relatively minor, and one is likely to find ADHD children coming from virtually all walks of life.

Sex Differences in Prevalence

The prevalence of ADHD is also known to vary significantly as a function of sex of the children being studied. The proportion of males versus females manifesting the disorder varies considerably across studies, from 2:1 to 10:1 (American Psychiatric Association, 1980; Ross & Ross, 1982), with an average of 6:1 most often cited for clinic-referred samples of children. However, epidemiological studies find the proportion to be approximately 3:1 among nonreferred children displaying these symptoms (Szatmari et al., 1989a; Trites et al., 1979).

The considerably higher rate of males among clinic samples of children compared to community surveys seems to be due to referral bias, in that males are more likely than females to be aggressive and antisocial, and such behavior is more likely to get a child referred to a psychiatric center. Hence, more males than females with ADHD will get referred to such centers. In support of this explanation are the following findings: Aggression occurs far more frequently in clinic-referred ADHD children than in those identified through epidemiological sampling (community surveys); hyperactive girls identified in community surveys are often less aggressive than hyperactive boys (see "Sex Differences in the Nature of ADHD," below), but girls who are seen in psychiatric clinics are likely to be as aggressive as boys with ADHD (Befera & Barkley, 1985; Breen & Barkley, 1988). Even so, males remain more likely to manifest ADHD than girls even in community-based samples, indicating that there is a sex-linked mechanism in the expression of the disorder.

Has ADHD Increased in Incidence?

A related issue is the question of whether the incidence of ADHD has increased within the past few decades. The question is difficult to address, as no community surveys of ADHD have been repeated in the same populations or geographic areas over sufficiently long time periods to permit such trends to be evaluated. Some writers (Block, 1977; Ross & Ross, 1982) believe that it may be increasing as a result of increasing cultural tempo or the rate of stimulation and change in a culture. Such speculations based on "tempo," however, are quite difficult to prove scientifically. Others intimate that the more sophisticated and successful life-saving efforts of the medical profession, as seen in neonatal intensive care units, may be increasing the incidence of ADHD by saving babies who would otherwise have died or have been more severely developmentally handicapped. Such logic would suggest that a higher-than-normal incidence of ADHD should be seen in long-term survivors of such intensive care units, and this does appear to be the case. However, this research can be faulted for failing to account for the higher-than-normal association of low SES with babies in these medical units; in other words, it may be the variable of lower SES and not the presence of perinatal complications that accounts for the higher incidence of ADHD. Finally, the actual occurrence of ADHD may not be increasing, while its detection may well be. This may partly stem from a greater awareness on the part of the public about the nature of the disorder, leading to more identification of such children. It could also be due to the trend toward earlier enrollment in preschool for many children, such that their difficulties of inattention, overactivity, and impulsivity will be noticed earlier as well.

Sex Differences in the Nature of ADHD

As noted above, boys are three times more likely to have ADHD than girls, and six to nine times more likely than girls to be seen with ADHD among clinic-referred children. Given these differences in prevalence, one might wonder whether there are differences in the expression of the disorder or its related features between boys and girls. A recent study conducted at Emory University in Atlanta (Brown, Abramowitz, Madan-Swain, Eckstrand, & Dulcan, 1989) evaluated a sample of clinic-referred children diagnosed as having ADHD. They found that girls ($n = 18$) were more socially withdrawn and had more internalizing symptoms (anxiety, depression) than boys ($n = 38$). Other studies based on school-identified hyperactive children have tended to find that hyperactive girls are rated as having fewer behavioral and conduct problems (such as aggressiveness) than hyperactive boys, but usually are not different on any laboratory measures of their symptoms (deHaas, 1986; deHaas & Young, 1984; Pascaulvaca, Wolf, Healey, Tweedy, & Halperin, 1988).

In contrast, two early studies using children referred to pediatric learning and developmental disability clinics suggested that hyperactive girls had lower verbal IQ scores, were more likely to have language disabilities, had a greater prevalence of problems with mood and enuresis, and had a lower prevalence of conduct problems (Berry, Shaywitz, & Shaywitz, 1985; Kashani, Chapel, Ellis, & Shekim, 1979). These studies may have been biased toward finding greater cognitive and developmental problems in their samples because of the source of referrals (learning disorder clinics). Subsequent studies that have used referrals to psychology or psychiatry clinics have found virtually no differences between ADHD boys and girls on measures of intelligence, academic achievement, peer relations, emotional problems, or behavioral disorders (Breen, 1989; Horn, Wagner, & Ialongo, 1989; McGee, Williams, & Silva, 1987). The exception to this was the finding reported by Taylor (1986a, pp. 141–143) that girls referred to a child psychiatry service at Maudsley Hospital in London had a greater degree of intellectual deficits than boys, but were otherwise equivalent in the onset and severity of their hyperactive symptoms. Slight differences have been found in mothers' treatment of their ADHD boys compared to mothers of ADHD girls: Boys received greater praise and direction from their mothers, but boys were less compliant than girls with their mothers' commands (Barkley, 1989b; Befera & Barkley, 1985). No sex differences were noted in the effects of stimulant medication on these interactions (Barkley, 1989b).

In general, ADHD girls within community samples may have fewer conduct problems than boys, but otherwise appear little different from them in their pattern of ADHD symptoms on objective tests. In clinic samples, few sex differences are noted, suggesting that girls who get referred to psychiatric clinics may be as aggressive or conduct-disordered as boys. Sex differences in cognitive performance are not routinely found, and, where they have been, are probably an artifact of the types of clinics from which the children were recruited.

Current Conceptualization of the Disorder

Although numerous studies have consistently demonstrated that ADHD children have deficits in impulse control, attention to tasks, and the regulation of their activity levels, recent reviews question whether these are the fundamental behavioral disturbances in ADHD. The global and multidimensional nature of such constructs as "inattention," "impulsivity," and "overactivity"; the well-demonstrated situational variation in ADHD symptoms; and the lack of testability of many of the theories of ADHD predicted on these constructs have led recent researchers to posit more specific behavioral impairments that may better account for the results of research in this area.

In the first edition of this text (Barkley, 1981) and in a more recent paper (Barkley, 1990), I raised the notion that a behavioral or functional analysis of the primary characteristics of ADHD could prove quite heuristic. Skinner (1953) has presented an analysis of the constructs of attention, impulsiveness, and self-control from this perspective that seems quite useful in understanding what the actual underlying behavioral deficit of ADHD children might be. Skinner proposes that attention itself is not a behavior or response of the individual. Instead, it is a term we use to represent a *relationship* between something in the environment (a discriminative stimulus) and the behavior of the individual. When children look at, orient to, move toward, or manipulate a stimulus in the environment, they are said to be attending to the event or object. Attention, then, is actually a form of stimulus control—a functional relationship between a stimulus or event and a child's response to it. When the relationship between an environmental stimulus and children's behavior is weak, we say that the children are inattentive to that stimulus. When children do not maintain their behavior toward an environmental event for as long as other children do, we say that they have poor sustained attention or poor attention span. When they respond too quickly but incorrectly to the presentation of a stimulus, we say that they are impulsive. And when children show problems with waiting for an event or consequence to occur, we say again that they are impulsive or, more specifically, cannot delay gratification.

Hence, poor attention and impulsivity are not actually behaviors or cognitive faculties of the children, but represent *relationships* between environmental events and child behavior. In particular, they represent temporal relationships among these events. We can therefore no more blame the weakness of these relationships as the problem in ADHD children than we can blame a low correlation coefficient for the failure of two events to covary. Perhaps if we referred to ADHD as "Correlation Deficit Disorder," it would help to illustrate this point and reveal the fallacy of present models of ADHD based on cognitive constructs of attention or impulse control. Blaming a relationship is not helpful in understanding the problem, misses the more crucial aspects of the problem of ADHD, and stifles further analysis by appearing to provide an adequate explanation of the problem. Instead, we should explore these temporal relationships between stimuli and behavior more thoroughly, and in particular should evaluate what other factors are important in conditioning and maintaining these relationships in children.

The Problem of Stimulus Control

From this perspective, the problem of ADHD children is a problem of control of behavior by socially important stimuli. If we are to better understand the nature of ADHD, we must ask why these important stimuli fail to control behavior adequately. Whether stimulus control develops in children is a function of not only the kinds of stimuli we present to them, but primarily the types of consequences we use in training them and the scheduling or arrangement of these consequences. A functional analysis of ADHD symptoms directs our investigation to the kinds of tasks or stimuli to which ADHD children have so much trouble responding, and the types of consequences and their schedules of occurrence under which they cannot maintain persistent responding or effort to these tasks. These are likely to tell us why ADHD children show so much difficulty with these functional relationships between certain stimuli and the socially desired responses to them.

As I have elsewhere indicated (Barkley, 1990), there are many reasons why certain stimuli deemed important by society, such as certain rules, tasks, or events, may fail to adequately control, or set the occasion for, the occurrence of the socially desired responses to these stimuli in ADHD children. These can be summarized as follows: (1)

inadequate detection of the stimulus, task, or event by the children (a sensory detection problem); (2) an inability of the children to perform the desired response (as in a physical or motor disability); (3) an inadequate conditioning history (the children have not been properly trained by their caregivers, leading to a lack of skills or knowledge of how to behave); (4) a deficit in the effects of consequences on the children's behavior (those consequences normally used to condition or train normal children are weaker in controlling the behavior of ADHD children); (5) unusually rapid satiation or habituation of the children to these consequences, such that consequences lose their value more quickly in ADHD children (rapid boredom); or (6) a deficiency in the manner in which the schedules of consequences maintain behavior over time (a diminished effectiveness of partial reinforcement schedules to maintain the behavior of ADHD children over time—i.e., persistence of effort toward a task). Unfortunately, these task or setting parameters have not been studied very methodically or rigorously in ADHD children. However, from the information reviewed earlier, we can rule out sensory deficits, physical or motor handicaps, and poor child-rearing skills of parents and teachers as likely sources of this inadequate stimulus control in ADHD children.

Deficient Regulation of Behavior by Rules and Consequences

Different laboratories are beginning to converge on the notion that the manner in which behavior is regulated by its consequences may be the fundamental problem in ADHD. Some hypothesize that ADHD children have higher-than-normal thresholds for arousal by stimulation; as environmental stimulation decreases, hyperactivity and inattention increase as means of compensating for this reduction, so as to maintain an optimal level of central nervous system arousal (Zental, 1985). Others have proposed that thresholds for reinforcement within the brain may be set too high (Haenlein & Caul, 1987). Reinforcers or consequences are therefore less reinforcing or weaker to ADHD children, leading to decreased persistence of responding to tasks.

Compelling but indirect evidence for this view comes from the research on the effects of stimulant drugs on brain reward centers. Such medications appear to lower the threshold for reinforcement, making the individual more sensitive to available reinforcers in the environment; that is, existing reinforcers become more reinforcing and therefore maintain behavior to tasks or stimuli longer than in unmedicated states (see the review by Haenlein & Caul, 1987). Quay (1988) has argued that ADHD may be due to decreased activity in the brain's behavioral inhibition system, such that punishment or its threat fails to inhibit and regulate behavior as well as in normal children. This may explain the symptoms of impulsivity and behavioral disinhibition in ADHD where punishment is used to inhibit or maintain responding. I (Barkley, 1984, 1990) have previously indicated that the problem may rest in several deficits: (1) decreased control by partial schedules of behavioral consequences; (2) rapid habituation or satiation to behavioral consequences, leading to rapid extinction of responding; and (3) diminished regulation of behavior by rules.

Both the first and second of these deficits are similar to the hypotheses of diminished sensitivity to magnitude of consequences by Haenlein and Caul (1987) and diminished inhibition of behavior by threat of punishment by Quay (1988). However, the third deficit requires elaboration here, as it is neither an obvious nor a commonly used construct in the field of child psychopathology. In rule-governed behavior, children's behavior occurs in response to immediately preceding linguistic stimuli and corresponds to that behavior stated in the rule (Skinner, 1953; Zettle & Hayes, 1983). A rule is a contingency-specifying stimulus—a linguistic cue that a particular behavior, if performed, is likely to be followed by a particular consequence. "If you do your homework, you can play with the Nintendo video game for a while" is such a rule. There are different components to rule-governed behavior. "Pliance" refers to behavior that occurs immediately following the presentation of the rule, while "tracking" refers to continued correspondence between behavior and the rule for much longer periods of time after the rule has been presented. Children may recall and subvocally repeat previously presented rules when in future situations in which the original rule giver is absent. We often think of this as a form of self-control. They can also be trained to generate their own rules through the commonly taught steps of problem solving (i.e., "State the problem, generate a list of possible solutions or rules, consider the outcomes for each, select and apply the solution, evaluate its success," etc.), or what Skinner has called "second-order" rules.

It virtually goes without saying that ADHD children have problems with self-control and problem solving, but problems with the other components, especially tracking, seem to be just as troublesome. It is also notable that rule-governed behavior seems important in training children to control impulsive responses and delay gratification. One function of a rule, in fact, is to state the contingency between present behavior and consequences relatively distant in the future. By training children to use rules to control behavior, we free them up from control by the immediate and occasionally spurious consequences associated with impulsive behavior, and bring them under the control of the longer-term consequences of their actions. This is achieved by using socially arranged and often artificial rewards for obeying rules. For these reasons, I have hypothesized that ADHD children have a deficiency in rule-governed behavior relative to their developmental level, along with these other deficits in sensitivity to consequences.

All of these deficits with responding to consequences and rule-governed behavior are believed by their proponents to be neurologically based deficits in ADHD children and are not due to purely environmental or social causes. This is not to say that environmental conditions may not exacerbate (or improve!) the symptoms of ADHD children, but that their problems do not originate in some defect in the environment.

Summary of the Conceptualization

It appears that the primary symptoms of ADHD described earlier can be more heuristically conceptualized as deficits in the functional relationships between child behavior and environmental events than as cognitive constructs or capacities. ADHD is therefore a problem with the stimulus control or regulation of behavioral responses, particularly in the area of behavioral inhibition. Evidence suggests that this deficit in behavioral regulation may stem from one or more of the following impairments: (1) diminished sensitivity to behavioral consequences, (2) diminished control of behavior by partial schedules of consequences, and (3) poor rule-governed behavior. Which of these may prove to be primarily involved in ADHD is not yet clear. However, there is little doubt that present cognitive conceptualizations of ADHD as a problem in attention or impulsivity are losing their explanatory and prescriptive value, and are likely to be replaced by theories founded on motivational deficits rather than on attentional ones.

ADHD Redefined

I have come to view ADHD as follows:

ADHD consists of developmental deficiencies in the regulation and maintenance of behavior by rules and consequences. These deficiencies give rise to problems with inhibiting, initiating, or sustaining responses to tasks or stimuli, and adhering to rules or instructions, particularly in situations where consequences for such behavior are delayed, weak, or nonexistent. The deficiencies are evident in early childhood and are probably chronic in nature. Although they may improve with neurological maturation, the deficits persist in comparison to same-age normal children, whose performance in these areas also improves with development.

These apparently biological deficiencies in the regulation and maintenance of behavior emanate into the social ecology of the child's social interactions in the family, school, and community, resulting in increased controlling responses by caregivers and peers in return. Over time, as these controlling responses meet with little success in managing the ADHD child's behavioral problems, family members, peers, and classmates may come to reject the child, avoiding unnecessary interactions as a means of limiting conflict. In families where other factors (such as parental psychopathology, marital discord, or family hardships) result in inconsistent, unpredictable, coercive, or simply diminished efforts at child management, defiant, oppositional, and aggressive behaviors may increase in the ADHD child. Left untreated, the development of these early antisocial behaviors appears to increase the risk of early and recurrent patterns of delinquent and antisocial conduct in the community that may be maintained into young adulthood (Patterson, 1982; Farrington, Loeber, & van Kammen, 1987). Managed properly, these social interaction conflicts of ADHD children may be maintained at relatively low levels, such that difficulties with school performance may be the primary area of difficulty for ADHD children during adolescence (Paternite & Loney, 1980).

Clinical Implications

The clinical implications of this reconceptualization of ADHD as a motivational disorder are enormous. Only a few of the more significant ones are mentioned here. First, the notion that these are biologically based handicaps in the response of ADHD children to environmental contingencies and consequences should at once direct society to desist from blaming these children for not behaving normally. They are not intentionally lazy, naughty, or simply unwilling to conform. Second, it should also relieve parents and teachers of believing that they are guilty of mismanaging these children. Yet it simultaneously burdens them with the notion that the disorder is relatively permanent and presently incurable.

Third, this view directly specifies the types of environments and tasks in which ADHD children will perform well or even normally (clear, external rules with immediate, salient, and frequent reinforcement) and where they will be most handicapped by their deficits (numerous implicit rules with low reinforcement). The design of prosthetic educational settings and the modification of child management skills and family functioning are seen as straightforward recommendations from this approach. Consequently, this view is highly heuristic and clinically prescriptive in planning interventions for ADHD. Fourth, the relative permanence of the condition argues for much longer interventions and periodic reintervention if treatment gains are to be maintained over time. A corollary of this is that short-term interventions that are withdrawn are likely to result in a rapid return to baseline or pretreatment levels of symptoms. And fifth, assessment procedures must take into account the tremendous variations across settings and caregivers and over time that result from such deficits. Suffice it to say here that these and other implications of this view are woven throughout the chapters on assessment and treatment that follow.

In any case, future conceptualizations of the disorder are likely to rely more heavily on motivational deficiencies with a physiological basis than on attentional deficits in accounting for the behavioral symptoms of ADHD children. These theories provide for more testable hypotheses, coincide better with known neurophysiological effects of drugs used to treat the disorder, offer better explanatory value for the tremendous situational fluctuations seen in ADHD symptoms, and are much more prescriptive of necessary treatments than has been the case for cognitive models of attention deficits in ADHD.

Summary

This chapter has described in detail the primary symptoms of ADHD and concluded that behavioral disinhibition, or the inability to adequately regulate behavior by rules and consequences, is the sine qua non of this disorder. Such disinhibition creates difficulties with maintaining attention to tasks, especially in settings where other activities offer competing immediate consequences of a higher magnitude than those inherent in the task assigned to the children. The manner in which the ADHD symptoms may be affected by situational variation, and possible contributors to this variation, have been discussed.

A review of epidemiological studies suggests that the prevalence of the disorder is approximately 3 to 5 percent, and that it occurs in boys almost three times as often as in girls. Despite this sex difference in prevalence, clinical studies suggest that girls and boys referred to clinics are quite similar in their presenting symptoms. However, epidemiological studies imply that in community samples, girls are considerably less likely to manifest aggressive behavior or conduct problems. Evidence for a syndrome of ADHD has been briefly reviewed; the conclusion is that although such evidence is not always consistent, it is sufficiently compelling and clinically useful to permit us to view the disorder as a syndrome. Finally, a reconceptualization of ADHD has been presented that emphasizes biologically based deficiencies in the regulation of behavior by rules and consequences, rather than an attentional deficit, as being the core problems in ADHD.

References

Abikoff, H., Gittelman-Klein, R., & Klein D. (1977). Validation of a classroom observation code for hyperactive children. *Journal of Consulting and Clinical Psychology, 45,* 772–783.

Achenbach, T. M., & Edelbrock C. S. (1981). Behavioral problems and competencies reported by parents of normal and disturbed children aged four through sixteen. *Monographs of the Society for Research in Child Development, 46*(1), 1–82.

Achenbach, T. M., & Edelbrock C. S. (1983). *Manual for the Child Behavior Checklist and Revised Child Behavior Profile.* Burlington: University of Vermont, Department of Psychiatry.

Achenbach, T. M., McConaughy, S. H., & Howell, C. T. (1987). Child/adolescent behavioral and emotional problems: Implications of cross-informant correlations for situational specificity. *Psychological Bulletin, 101,* 213–232.

American Psychological Association. (1968). *Diagnostic and statistical manual of mental disorders* (2nd ed.). Washington, DC: Author.

American Psychiatric Association. (1980). *Diagnostic and statistical manual of mental disorders* (3rd ed.). Washington, DC: Author.

American Psychiatric Association. (1987). *Diagnostic and statistical manual of mental disorders* (3rd ed., rev.). Washington, DC: Author.

August, G. J., & Stewart, M. A. (1982). Is there a syndrome of pure hyperactivity? *British Journal of Psychiatry 140,* 305–311.

Barkley, R. A. (1977a). The effects of methylphenidate on various measures of activity level and attention in hyperkinetic children. *Journal of Abnormal Child Psychology, 5,* 351–369.

Barkley, R. A. (1981). *Hyperactive children: A handbook for diagnosis and treatment.* New York: Guilford Press.

Barkley, R. A. (1982). Specific guidelines for defining hyperactivity in children (Attention Deficit Disorder with Hyperactivity).

In B. Lahey & A. Kazdin (Eds.), *Advances in clinical child psychology* (Vol. 5, 137–180). New York: Plenum.

Barkley, R. A. (1984). *Do as we say, not as we do: The problem of stimulus control and rule-governed behavior in children with Attention Deficit Disorder with Hyperactivity*. Paper presented at the Highpoint Conference, Toronto.

Barkley, R. A. (1985a). The social interactions of hyperactive children: Developmental changes, drug effects, and situational variation. In R. McMahon & R. Peters (Eds.), *Childhood disorders: Behavioral-developmental approaches* (pp. 218–243). New York: Brunner/Mazel.

Barkley, R. A. (1988c). Child behavior rating scales and checklists. In M. Rutter, A. H. Tuma, & I. Lann (Eds.), *Assessment and diagnosis in child psychopathology* (pp. 113–155). New York: Guilford Press.

Barkley, R. A. (1988d.) Attention. In M. Tramontana & S. Hooper (Eds.), *Issues in child clinical neuropsychology*. New York: Plenum.

Barkley, R. A. (1989b). Hyperactive girls and boys: Stimulant drug effects on mother-child interactions. *Journal of Child Psychology and Psychiatry, 30*, 379–390.

Barkley, R. A. (1990). *ADHD adolescents: Family conflicts and their treatment*. Grant from National Institute of Mental Health, MH41583.

Barkley, R. A. (1993). The problem of stimulus control and rule-governed behavior in children with Attention Deficit Disorder with Hyperactivity. In J. Swanson & L. Bloomingdale (Eds.), *Attentional deficit disorders* (Vol. 4). New York: Pergamon Press.

Barkley, R. A., Copeland, A. P., & Sivage, C. (1980). A self-control classroom for hyperactive children. *Journal of Autism and Developmental Disorders, 10*, 75–89.

Barkley, R. A., & Cunningham, C. E. (1979b). Stimulant drugs and activity level in hyperactive children. *American Journal of Orthopsychiatry, 49*, 491–499.

Barkley, R. A., Cunningham, C. E., & Karlsson, J. (1983). The speech of hyperactive children and their mothers: Comparisons with normal children and stimulant drug effects. *Journal of Learning Disabilities, 16*, 105–110.

Barkley, R. A., DuPaul, G. J., & McMurray, M. B. (1993a). A comprehension evaluation of Attention Deficit Disorder with and without Hyperactivity defined by research criteria. *Journal of Consulting and Clinical Psychology*.

Barkley, R. A., DuPaul, G. J., & McMurray, M. B. (1993b). Attention Deficit Disorder with and without Hyperactivity: Clinical response to three dose levels of methylphenidate. *Pediatrics*.

Barkley, R. A., Fischer, M., Edelbrock, C. S., & Smallish, L. (1993a). The adolescent outcome of hyperactive children diagnosed by research criteria: I. An 8 year prospective follow-up study. *Journal of the American Academy of Child and Adolescent Psychiatry*.

Barkley, R. A., Spitzer, R., & Costello, A. (1990). *Development of the DSM-111-R criteria for the Disruptive Behavior Disorders*. Unpublished manuscript, University of Massachusetts Medical Center, Worcester.

Barkley, R. A., & Ullman, D. G. (1975). A comparison of objective measures of activity and distractibility in hyperactive and nonhyperactive children. *Journal of Abnormal Child Psychology, 3*, 213–244.

Befera, M., & Barkley, R. (1985). Hyperactive and normal boys and girls: Mother-child interaction, parent psychiatric status, and child psychopathology. *Journal of Child Psychology and Psychiatry, 26*, 439–452.

Berry, C. A., Shaywitz, S. E., & Shaywitz, B. A. (1985). Girls with Attention Deficit Disorder: A silent minority? A report on behavioral and cognitive characteristics. *Pediatrics, 76*, 801–809.

Block, G. H. (1977) Hyperactivity: A cultural perspective. *Journal of Learning Disabilities, 110*, 236–240.

Breen, M. J. (1989). ADHD girls and boys: An analysis of attentional, emotional, cognitive, and family variables. *Journal of Child Psychology and Psychiatry, 30*, 711–716.

Breen, M. J., & Barkley, R. A. (1988). Child psychopathology and parenting stress in girls and boys having attention deficit disorder with hyperactivity. *Journal of Pediatric Psychology, 13*, 265–280.

Brown, R. T., Abramowitz, A. J., Madan-Swain, A., Eckstrand, D., & Dulcan, M. (1989, October). *ADHD gender differences in a clinic referred sample*. Paper presented at the annual meeting of the American Academy of Child and Adolescent Psychiatry, New York.

Brown, R. T., & Quay, L. C. (1977). Reflection-impulsivity of normal and behavior-disordered children. *Journal of Abnormal Child Psychology, 5*, 457–462.

Cammann R., & Miehlke, A. (1989). Differentiation of motor activity of normally active and hyperactive boys in schools: Some preliminary results. *Journal of Child Psychology and Psychiatry, 30*, 899–906.

Campbell, S. B. (1987). Parent-referred problem three-year-olds: Developmental changes in symptoms. *Journal of Child Psychology and Psychiatry, 28*, 835–846.

Campbell, S. B., Douglas, V. I., & Morganstern, G. (1971). Cognitive styles in hyperactive children and the effect of methylphenidate. *Journal of Child Psychology and Psychiatry, 12*, 55–67.

Cohen, N. J., Weiss, G., and Minde, K. (1972). Cognitive styles in adolescents previously diagnosed as hyperactive. *Journal of Child Psychology and Psychiatry, 13*, 203–209.

Cromwell, R. L., Baumeister, A., & Hawkins, W. F. (1963). Research in activity level. In N. R. Ellis (Ed.), *Handbook of mental deficiency*. New York: McGraw-Hill.

deHaas, P. A. (1986). Attention styles and peer relationships of hyperactive and normal boys and girls. *Journal of Abnormal Child Psychology, 14*, 457–467.

deHaas, P. A., & Young, R. D. (1984). Attention styles of hyperactive and normal girls. *Journal of Abnormal Child Psychology, 12*, 531–546.

Douglas, V. I. (1972). Stop, look, and listen: The problem of sustained attention and impulse control in hyperactive and normal children. *Canadian Journal of Behavioral Science, 4*, 259–282.

Douglas, V. I. (1980a). Higher mental processes in hyperactive children: Implications for training. In R. Knights & D. Bakker (Eds.), *Treatment of hyperactive and learning disordered children* (pp. 65–92). Baltimore: University Park Press.

Douglas, V. I. (1980b). Treatment and training approaches to hyperactivity: Establishing internal or external control. In C. Whalen & B. Henker (Eds.), *Hyperactive children: The social ecology of identification and treatment* (pp. 283–318). New York: Academic Press.

Douglas, V. I. (1983). Attention and cognitive problems. In M. Rutter (Ed.), *Developmental neuropsychiatry* (pp. 280–329). New York: Guilford Press.

Douglas, V. I., & Parry, P. A. (1983). Effects of reward on delayed reaction time task performance of hyperactive children. *Journal of Abnormal Child Psychology, 11*, 313–326.

Draeger, S., Prior, M., & Sanson, A. (1986). Visual and auditory attention performance in hyperactive children: Competence or compliance. *Journal of Abnormal Child Psychology, 14*, 411–424.

DuPaul, G. J. (1990a). *The ADHD Rating Scale: Normative data, reliability, and validity*. Unpublished manuscript, University of Massachusetts Medical Center, Worcester.

Farrington, D. P., Loeber, R., & van Kammen, W. B. (1987, October). *Long-term criminal outcomes of hyperactivity–impulsivity–attention deficit and conduct problems in childhood*. Paper presented at the meeting of the Society for Life History Research, St. Louis.

Firestone, P., & Martin, J. E. (1979). An analysis of the hyperactive syndrome: A comparison of hyperactive, behavior problem, asthmatic, and normal children. *Journal of Abnormal Child Psychology, 7*, 261–273.

Fischer, M., Barkley, R. A., Edelbrock, C. S., & Smallish, L. (in press). The adolescent outcome of hyperactive children diagnosed by research criteria: II. Academic, attentional, and neuropsychological status. *Journal of Consulting and Clinical Psychology*.

Gordon, M. (1979). The assessment of impulsivity and mediating behaviors in hyperactive and non-hyperactive children. *Journal of Abnormal Child Psychology, 7*, 317–326.

Gordon, M. (1983). *The Gordon Diagnostic System*. Boulder, CO: Clinical Diagnostic Systems.

Godzinsky, G. (1990). *Assessing frontal lobe functioning in 6 to 11 year old boys with attention deficit hyperactivity disorder*. Unpublished doctoral dissertation. Boston College.

Haenlein, M., & Caul, W. F. (1987). Attention deficit disorder with hyperactivity: Specific hypothesis of reward dysfunction. *Journal of the American Academy of Child and Adolescent Psychiatry, 26*, 356–362.

Hale, G. A., & Lewis, M. (1979). *Attention and cognitive development*. New York: Plenum.

Hinshaw, S. P. (1987). On the distinction between attentional deficits/hyperactivity and conduct problems/aggression in child psychopathology. *Psychological Bulletin, 101*, 443–463.

Horn, W. F., Wagner, A. E., & Ialongo, N. (1989). Sex differences in school-aged children with pervasive attention deficit hyperactivity disorder. *Journal of Abnormal Child Psychology, 17*, 109–125.

Jacob, R. G., O'Leary, K. D., & Rosenblad, C. (1978). Formal and informal classroom settings: Effects on hyperactivity. *Journal of Abnormal Child Psychology, 6*, 47–59.

Kagan, J. (1966). Reflection-impulsivity: The generality and dynamics of conceptual tempo. *Journal of Abnormal Psychology, 71*, 17–24.

Kashani, J., Chapel, J. L., Ellis, J., & Shekim, W. O. (1979). Hyperactive girls. *Journal of Operational Psychiatry, 10*, 145–148.

Kendall, P. C., & Braswell, L. (1984). *Cognitive-behavioral therapy for impulsive children*. New York: Guilford Press.

Kendall, P. C., & Wilcox, L. E. (1979). Self-control in children: Development of a rating scale. *Journal of Consulting and Clinical Psychology, 47*, 1020–1029.

Kohn, A. (1989, November). Suffer the restless children. *Atlantic Monthly*, pp. 90–100.

Lambert, N. M., Sandoval, J., & Sassone, D. (1978). Prevalence of hyperactivity in elementary school children as a function of social system definers. *American Journal of Orthopsychiatry, 48*, 446–463.

Lapouse, R., & Monk, M. (1958). An epidemiological study of behavior characteristics in children. *American Journal of Public Health, 48*, 1134–1144.

Luk, S. (1985). Direct observations studies of hyperactive behaviors. *Journal of the American Academy of Child Psychiatry, 24*, 338–344.

McGee, R., Williams, S., & Silva, P. A. (1984a). Behavioral and developmental characteristics of aggressive, hyperactive, and aggressive-hyperactive boys. *Journal of the American Academy of Child Psychiatry, 23*, 270–279.

McGee, R., Williams, S., & Silva, P. A. (1984b). Background characteristics of aggressive, hyperactive, and aggressive-hyperactive boys. *Journal of the American Academy of Child Psychiatry, 23*, 280–284.

McGee, R., Williams, S., & Silva, P. A. (1987). A comparison of girls and boys with teacher-identified problems of attention. *Journal of the American Academy of Child and Adolescent Psychiatry, 26*, 711–717.

Milich, R., & Kramer, J. (1985). Reflections on impulsivity: An empirical investigation of impulsivity as a construct. In K. D. Gadow & I. Bialer (Eds.), *Advances in learning and behavioral disabilities* (Vol. 3). Greenwich, CT: JAI Press.

Milich, R., Loney, J., & Landau, S. (1982). The independent dimensions of hyperactivity and aggression: A validation with play-room observation data. *Journal of Abnormal Psychology, 91*, 183–198.

O'Leary, K. D., Vivian, D., & Nisi, A. (1985). Hyperactivity in Italy. *Journal of Abnormal Child Psychology, 13*, 485–500.

Pascaulvaca, D. M., Wolf, L. E., Healey, J. M., Tweedy, J. R., & Halperin, J. M. (1988, January) *Sex differences in attention and behavior in school-aged children*. Paper presented at the 16th annual meeting of the International Neuropsychological Society, New Orleans.

Paternite, C., & Loney, J. (1980). Childhood hyperkinesis: Relationships between symptomatology and home environment. In C. K. Whalen & B. Henker (Eds.), *Hyperactive children: The social ecology of identification and treatment* (pp. 105–141). New York: Academic Press.

Patterson, G. R. (1982). *Coercive family process*. Eugene, OR: Castalia.

Porrino, L. J., Rapoport, J. L., Behar, D., Sceery, W., Ismond, D. R., & Bunney, W. E., Jr. (1983). A naturalistic assessment of the motor activity of hyperactive boys. *Archives of General Psychiatry, 40*, 681–687.

Prior, M., Wallace, M., & Milton, I. (1984). Schedule-induced behavior in hyperactive children. *Journal of Abnormal Child Psychology, 12*, 227–244.

Quay, H. C. (1988). Attention deficit disorder and the behavioral inhibition system: The relevance of the neuropsychological theory of Jeffrey A. Gray. In L. Bloomingdale & J. Sergeant (Eds.), *Attention deficit disorder: Criteria, cognition, and intervention* (pp. 117–126). New York: Pergamon Press.

Rapport, M. D., Tucker, S. B., DuPaul, G. J., Merlo, M., & Stoner, G. (1986). Hyperactivity and frustration: The influence of control over and size of rewards in delaying gratification. *Journal of Abnormal Child Psychology, 14*, 191–204.

Reeves, J. C., Werry, J., Elkind, G. S., & Zametkin, A. (1987). Attention deficit, conduct, oppositional, and anxiety disorders in children: II. Clinical characteristics. *Journal of the American Academy of Child Psychiatry, 26*, 133–143.

Rosenthal, R. H., & Allen, T. W. (1980). Intratask distractibility in hyperkinetic and nonhyperkinetic children. *Journal of Abnormal Child Psychology, 8*, 175–187.

Ross, D. M., & Ross, S. A. (1982). *Hyperactivity: Current issues, research, and theory* (2nd ed.). New York: Wiley.

Routh, D. K. (1978). Hyperactivity. In P. Magrab (Ed.), *Psychological management of pediatric problems* (pp. 3–48). Baltimore: University Park Press.

Routh, D. K., & Roberts, R. D. (1972). Minimal brain dysfunction in children: Failure to find evidence for a behavioral syndrome. *Psychological Reports, 31*, 307–314.

Routh, D. K., & Schroeder, C. S. (1976). Standardized playroom measures as indices of hyperactivity. *Journal of Abnormal Child Psychology, 4*, 199–207.

Rutter, M. (1977). Brain damage syndromes in childhood: Concepts and findings. *Journal of Child Psychology and Psychiatry, 18*, 1–21.

Rutter, M. (1989). Attention deficit disorder/hyperkinetic syndrome: Conceptual and research issues regarding diagnosis and classification. In T. Sagvolden & T. Archer (Eds.), *Attention deficit disorder: Clinical and basic research* (pp. 1–24). Hillsdale, NJ: Erlbaum.

Sandberg, S. T., Rutter, M., & Taylor, E. (1978). Hyperkinetic disorder in psychiatric clinic attenders. *Developmental Medicine and Child Neurology, 20,* 279–299.

Schrag, P., & Divoky, D. (1975). *The myth of the hyperactive child.* New York: Pantheon.

Sergeant, J. (1988). From DSM-III attentional deficit disorder to functional defects. In L. Bloomingdale & J. Sergeant (Eds.), *Attentional deficit disorder: Criteria, cognition, and intervention* (pp. 183–198). New York: Pergamon Press.

Shaffer, D., & Greenhill, L. (1979). A critical note on the predictive validity of "the hyperkinetic syndrome." *Journal of Child Psychology and Psychiatry, 20,* 61–72.

Shaffer, D., McNamara, N., & Pincus, J. H. (1974). Controlled observations on patterns of activity, attention, impulsivity in brain-damaged and psychiatrically disturbed boys. *Psychological Medicine, 4,* 4–18.

Skinner, B. F. (1953). *Science and human behavior.* New York: Macmillan.

Spitzer, R. L., Davies, M., & Barkley, R. A. (in press). The DSM-III-R field trial for the Disruptive Behavior Disorders. *Journal of the American Academy of Child and Adolescent Psychiatry.*

Steinkamp, M. W. (1980). Relationships between environmental distractions and task performance of hyperactive and normal children. *Journal of Learning Disabilities, 13,* 40–45.

Stewart, M. A., Pitts, F. N., Craig, A. G., & Dieruf, W. (1966). The hyperactive child syndrome. *American Journal of Orthopsychiatry, 36,* 861–867.

Still, G. F. (1902). Some abnormal psychical conditions in children. *Lancet, i,* 1008–1012, 1077–1082, 1163–1168.

Szatmari, P., Offord, D. R., & Boyle, M. H. (1989a). Ontario child health study: Prevalence of attention deficit disorder with hyperactivity. *Journal of Child Psychology and Psychiatry, 30,* 219–230.

Tallmadge, J., & Barkley R. A. (1983). The interactions of hyperactive and normal boys with their mothers and fathers. *Journal of Abnormal Child Psychology, 11,* 565–579.

Tarver-Behring, S., Barkley, R., & Karlsson, J. (1985). The mother-child interactions of hyperactive boys and their normal siblings. *American Journal of Orthopsychiatry, 55,* 202–209.

Taylor, E. A. (1986a). (Ed.) *The overactive child.* Philadelphia: J. P. Lippincott.

Taylor, E. A. (1986b). Childhood hyperactivity. *British Journal of Psychiatry, 149,* 562–573.

Trites, R. L. (1979). *Hyperactivity in children: Etiology, measurement, and treatment implications.* Baltimore: University Park Press.

Trites, R. L., Dugas, F., Lynch, G., & Ferguson, B. (1979). Incidence of hyperactivity. *Journal of Pediatric Psychology, 4,* 179–188.

Ullman, D. G., Barkley, R. A., & Brown, H. W. (1978). The behavioral symptoms of hyperkinetic children who successfully responded to stimulant drug treatment. *American Journal of Orthopsychiatry, 48,* 425–437.

Weiss, G., & Hechtman, L. (1979). The hyperactive child syndrome. *Science, 205,* 1348–1354.

Werry, J. S. (1988). Differential diagnosis of attention deficits and conduct disorders. In L. Bloomingdale & J. Sergeant (Eds.), *Attention deficit disorder: Criteria, cognition, and intervention* (pp. 83–96). New York: Pergamon Press.

Werry, J. S., Elkind, G. S., & Reeves, J. C. (1987). Attention deficit, conduct, oppositional, and anxiety disorders in children: III. Laboratory differences. *Journal of Abnormal Psychology, 15,* 409–428.

Werry, J. S., & Quay, H. C. (1971). The prevalence of behavior symptoms in younger elementary school children. *American Journal of Orthopsychiatry, 41,* 136–143.

Whalen, C. K., Henker, B., & Dotemoto, S. (1980). Methylphenidate and hyperactivity: Effects on teacher behaviors. *Science, 208,* 1280–1282.

World Health Organization. (1990). *International classification of diseases* (10th ed.) Geneva: Author.

Zagar, R., & Bowers, N. D. (1983). The effect of time of day on problem-solving and classroom behavior. *Psychology in the Schools, 20,* 337–345.

Zentall, S. S. (1984). Context effects in the behavioral ratings of hyperactivity. *Journal of Abnormal Child Psychology, 12,* 345–352.

Zentall, S. S. (1985). A context for hyperactivity. In K. D. Gadow & I. Bialer (Eds.), *Advances in learning and behavioral disabilities* (Vol. 4, pp. 273–343). Greenwich, CT: JAI Press.

Zentall, S. S., Falkenberg, S. D., & Smith, L. B. (1985). Effects of color stimulation and information on the copying performance of attention-problem adolescents. *Journal of Abnormal Child Psychology, 13,* 501–511.

Zettle, R. D., & Hayes, S. C. (1983). Rule-governed behavior: A potential theoretical framework for cognitive-behavioral therapy. In P. C. Kendall (Ed.), *Advances in cognitive-behavioral research* (Vol. 1, pp. 73–118). New York: Academic Press.

Strategies for Teaching Students with Learning and Behavior Problems

Bos, C., and S. Vaughn. 1991. 24–57. Boston: Allyn and Bacon.

Chapter Two:[*]
Approaches to Learning and Teaching

Chapter Questions

◆ Within the operant learning model, what procedures can be used to increase desirable behavior? Decrease undesirable behavior?

◆ What are the stages of learning and how can they be applied using the operant learning model?

◆ What are the common characteristics of most cognitive behavior modification interventions?

◆ Using principles associated with cognitive behavior modification, design a strategy that one could use to solve subtraction problems with regrouping.

◆ What implications does a sociocultural perspective have on teaching and learning?

◆ How does long-term memory relate to working memory and perception?

◆ Using implications from information processing and schema theories, what could you do to assist a student who is having difficulties remembering the information needed to pass an objective social studies test?

Models and theories for learning can assist us in understanding and explaining how students learn. They also guide us in modifying our teaching and the learning context to promote effective and efficient learning. This chapter overviews four theories or approaches to learning and teaching: operant learning, cognitive behavior modification, a sociocultural theory of learning, and information processing and schema theory. The models are sequenced in the chapter from less cognitively oriented, operant learning, to more cognitively oriented, information processing and schema theory. Many of the general principles presented in this chapter will be applied to specific content areas in the subsequent chapters. As you read this chapter, we encourage you to think about students who you know are not succeeding in school and who have learning and behavior problems. How are their learning patterns and habits explained by the various approaches to learning described in this chapter? What general teaching principles do the different approaches suggest to help such students? We will begin by looking at operant learning, a theory that has provided educators with a variety of techniques for improving student behavior and learning.

Operant Learning

Operant learning theorists believe that behavior is learned and, for this reason, it can be unlearned or the student can be taught new behaviors. Operant learning focuses on identifying observable behaviors and manipulating the antecedents and consequences of these behaviors to change behavior. Operant learning theory is not concerned with what you think or tell yourself during the learning process.

In this section on operant learning we will discuss how to increase behaviors we want to see continued and how to eliminate undesirable behaviors through extinction, reinforcing incompatible behaviors, punishment, and time-out, and how to teach to different levels of learning.

Increasing Desirable Behaviors

During the past few weeks, Ms. Glenn has focused on teaching Marjorie, Sheila, and Jose subtraction with regrouping. During this time she demonstrated many of the principles by using "ten packs" of sticks. The students recently practiced applying the principles on the chalkboard. Ms. Glenn then asked the students to practice the skills independently by completing a math paper with twelve subtraction-with-regrouping problems. She watched them complete the first problem correctly. She then needed to teach another group, yet she wanted to be sure that these three students would continue the desirable behavior of working on their math while she was working with her other group.

According to operant learning, behavior is controlled by the consequences that follow it. Ms. Glenn needed to decide what consequences would follow "math performing behavior" in order to maintain or increase its occurrence. She told Marjorie, Sheila, and Jose, "If you complete this math sheet with 80 percent or better accuracy, I will let you have five minutes of free time in the Fun Corner." Free time in the Fun Corner was very reinforcing to all three students, and they accurately completed the math sheet while she worked with other students.

There are several principles to apply when attempting to maintain or increase behavior:

1. The behavior must already be in the student's repertoire. In the preceding example, Ms. Glenn's students knew how to perform the math task. Reinforcing them with free time in the Fun Corner would have been an ineffective consequence if they did not know how to perform the assigned task. If you want to maintain or increase social or academic behaviors, you must first be sure the student knows how to perform the target behaviors.

2. A consequence must follow the precise behavior you want to change or be linked to it through language. For example, "Because you completed all of your math

* Editor's note: Chapter notation refers to this excerpt.

assignments this week, I'll let you select a movie to watch on the VCR."

3. A reinforcer is whatever follows a behavior and maintains or increases the rate of the behavior.
4. To be most powerful, reinforcement should occur immediately following the behavior.

Thus, to control behavior all we need to learn is to control the consequence that follows the behavior. Consequences that increase behavior, such as reinforcement and the Premack Principle, will be discussed next.

Reinforcement

Reinforcement is the most significant means of increasing desirable behavior. There are two types of reinforcement, positive and negative; both increase responding. How do they differ? The major difference between positive and negative reinforcement is that *positive reinforcement* is the presentation of a stimulus to increase responding, whereas *negative reinforcement* is the removal of a stimulus to increase responding.

Positive reinforcement increases responding by following the target behavior with activities, objects, food, and social rewards, which include such things as ice cream, toys, clothes, and privileges such as helping the teacher or having an extra recess.

When using reinforcers it is important to start with more *intrinsic reinforcers* such as using activities that are reinforcing to the student (e.g., listening to records, coloring) and move to more *tangible reinforcers* such as tokens and food only as necessary. For example, Christian (1983) suggests a seven-level hierarchy of reinforcers, ranging from food and hugs to internal self-reinforcement ("I did a good job").

The practice of negative reinforcement is often misused because the term *negative* is misinterpreted to mean harmful or bad and, therefore, the implication is that positive reinforcement is good and negative reinforcement is bad. Negative reinforcement means taking away something unpleasant or punishing contingent on the performance of a specific behavior. If a teacher scowls at a student until the student works, removing the scowl is negative reinforcement. The learning that takes place through negative reinforcement is avoidance learning. A common use in schools is the completion of work assignments to avoid staying after school. The completion of work assignments is reinforced by the removal of the unpleasant task of staying after school. Children often use negative reinforcement with adults. An example is a child who throws a temper tantrum until he or she gets what he or she wants.

Secondary Reinforcer

A *secondary reinforcer* is a previously neutral behavior that is paired with a reinforcer and therefore takes on reinforcing properties of its own. Thus if the teacher always calls a student up to the teacher's desk prior to rewarding him or her, then being called to the teacher's desk becomes reinforcing—a secondary reinforcer.

Sincere praise and attention are the most frequently used secondary reinforcers. Teachers are often quite skillful at using such subtle but effective secondary reinforcers as a hand on the shoulder, a pat on the head, a smile, or a wink. Many teachers position themselves carefully in the room to be near students whose behavior they want to reinforce with their attention.

Token reinforcement systems are frequently used by special education teachers. Briefly, a *token system* is an economy in which a symbol (e.g., points, chips, or stars) is given contingent on designated behaviors. Tokens are symbols in that they usually have little inherent value themselves but can be exchanged for valuable things or privileges. Token systems can be very simple (e.g., receiving stars for completing writing assignments, with each star worth three minutes of extra recess); they can also be very complicated and may even involve a level system with rewards and privileges varying according to the level the student is on. Students are assigned to levels contingent upon their behavior. Being raised or lowered to a different level occurs as points are accumulated. Points are awarded and deducted for a full range of behaviors. More complicated token systems are typically used to manage aggressive behaviors displayed by severely disturbed students.

Shaping

If reinforcement maintains or increases the rate of behavior already occurring, what does the teacher do if the behavior is occurring at a very low rate or not at all?

For example, Mr. Kladder's goal is to shape Rhonda's behavior so that she is performing multiplication facts quickly and automatically. During the initial teaching phase Mr. Kladder rewards her for computing 3 × 5 by adding five threes. After Rhonda demonstrates she can perform this behavior with high accuracy, Mr. Kladder no longer reinforces her for adding the numbers but only for skip counting 5, 10, 15, and then writing the answer. After Rhonda is successfully able to skip count she is reinforced for computing the answer in her head and writing it down. Now Mr. Kladder begins to give Rhonda timed tests in which she is reinforced only for beating her best time. Like most good teachers, Mr. Kladder is *shaping* his student's behavior by reinforcing responses that more and more closely approximate the target response.

Premack Principle

If one activity occurs more frequently than another, the more frequently occurring activity can be used as a reinforcer to increase the rate of the less frequently occurring activity (Premack 1959). For example, Adam more frequently participates in outdoor play than in writing stories. His teacher can make outdoor play contingent on completing the writing assignment. The advantage of the Premack Principle is that a teacher can use events that are already occurring in the classroom. One possibility is to inventory the student and rank behaviors from most liked to least liked, for example, (1) reading, (2) math (3) spelling. Thus reading could be contingent on completing spelling. A more appropriate list for most students with learning and behavior problems might include five minutes of free time contingent on completing spelling. Reinforcing activities such as talking quietly with friends or listening to music can be used to increase the rate of less desirable activities such as completing a book report. Students who prefer activities that involve movement can be informed that they can engage in these behaviors contingent on their performance in less desirable activities such as sitting still and listening to the teacher.

Group Contingencies

Group contingencies can be used to increase desirable behavior or decrease undesirable behavior. When using *group contingencies*, a group of students, or an individual student, is either reinforced or loses reinforcement, contingent on the behavior of the entire group or a target student in the group. For example, the teacher could establish a twenty-minute block of free time at the end of the school day. Every time the noise level of the classroom exceeds the teacher's limits she subtracts one minute from the allocated free time. In addition to changing group behavior, group contingencies can be used to change the behavior of one student in the class. For instance, Carla is a twelve-year-old child who has been mainstreamed into a regular sixth-grade class. During Carla's first couple of weeks in the class she continually got into fights with her classmates during recess. The teacher told the class that she would extend their recess by ten minutes if Carla did not get into any fights during recess. The class included Carla in their group play and fighting was eliminated. However there are dangers in group contingencies being dependent on the behavior of an individual. It is possible the individual will use his or her situation to manipulate the behavior of others in the class. For example, Carla could say to the other students in the class, "You better let me be captain of the team. Otherwise I'll get into a fight and you won't get extra recess." It is also possible that the individual will view himself or herself negatively because of this position.

Contingency Contracting

Contingency contracting is an agreement between two or more persons that specifies their behaviors and consequences. A common example of a contingency contract is the agreement between parent and child regarding an allowance. The child agrees to perform certain behaviors in return for a specified amount of money each week. The objective of a contingency contract is to delineate the exchange of reinforcers between two or more persons (Hall, 1975).

The contingency contract should specify who is doing what, when, under what conditions, and for what consequences.

Decreasing Undesirable Behaviors

Unfortunately, students manifest behaviors that interfere with their learning or the learning of others. Techniques for decreasing these undesirable behaviors include: extinction, reinforcing incompatible behaviors, punishment, and time-out.

Extinction

Extinction is the removal of reinforcement following the behavior. For example, a teacher wants to extinguish a student's behavior of shouting out and determines that telling the student to raise his hand is reinforcing the shouting out. To extinguish shouting out, the teacher removes the reinforcer ("Raise your hand") and ignores the student's shouting out.

Extinction can be an effective means of decreasing undesirable behaviors, but it is often slow and can be impractical for many behaviors that occur within the classroom because the reinforcers for the undesirable behavior are often difficult for the teacher to control. For example, let's return to the student who continually shouted out in class. In this situation the student was being reinforced not only by the classroom teacher's attention ("Raise your hand") but also by other students who looked and attended to him when he shouted out. A teacher attempting to reduce this behavior through extinction would have to eliminate both the teacher's reinforcement and the reinforcement of others in the class. To compound the difficulty, slip-ups by the teacher or students would intermittently reinforce the behavior and maintain it for a long time. As we discussed in the section on reinforcement schedules, intermittent reinforcement is a powerful way to maintain behavior and it is difficult to extinguish behaviors maintained on an intermittent schedule.

Another characteristic of extinction is its effect on the rate the target behavior continues to occur. During extinction the target behavior will increase in rate or intensity before decreasing. Thus a teacher attempting to eliminate tantrums through extinction will observe the tantrums occurring more frequently, lasting longer, and perhaps even being louder and more intense than before extinction. As long as the teacher continues to withhold reinforcement, usually attention, the rate and intensity will decrease and tantrums can be eliminated. For this reason it is extremely important to chart behavior when using extinction. Taking *baseline*, a record of the frequency and/or duration of the behavior before implementing the intervention, and continuing to take data after intervention is implemented, will document behavior change.

Although extinction can be an effective means of decreasing undesirable behaviors, it requires patience and the ability to control all of the reinforcers. Ignoring, the most frequently applied form of extinction in the classroom, is an important skill for teachers to learn. A summary of points to remember about using ignoring as a means of decreasing undesirable behavior follows:

1. Ignoring can be effective when the behavior is being reinforced by the teacher's attention.
2. If the teacher attempts to eliminate a behavior through ignoring, the behavior must be ignored every time it occurs.
3. Ignoring will not be effective if the behavior is being maintained by other reinforcers, such as the attention of classmates.

Reinforcing Incompatible Behavior

Ignoring can be most effective when it is paired with reinforcing an incompatible behavior. *Reinforcing an incompatible behavior* requires the teacher to target the undesirable activity. For example, while ignoring the out-of-seat behavior of a student, the teacher targets and reinforces the desirable behavior that is incompatible, in this case, in-seat behavior. Therefore, when Scott is sitting in his seat the teacher is quick to catch his appropriate behavior and reinforce. In addition, the teacher would intermittently reinforce Scott for being in his seat. Reinforcing incompatible behavior requires you, the teacher, to do four things:

1. Identify the behavior you want to change (interfering behavior).
2. Identify the incompatible behavior.
3. Discontinue reinforcing the interfering behavior.
4. Reinforce the desirable behavior in the target child or others who are displaying it.

Punishment

Punishment, the opposite of reinforcement, is following a behavior with a consequence that decreases the strength of the behavior or reduces the likelihood the behavior will continue to occur. Unfortunately, punishment does not assure the desired behavior will occur. For example, a student who is punished for talking in class may stop talking, but may not attend to his or her studies for the remainder of the day.

There are many significant arguments against the use of punishment:

1. Punishment is ineffective in the long run.
2. Punishment often causes undesirable emotional side effects such as fear, aggression, and resentment.
3. Punishment provides little information to the person as to what to do, teaching the individual only what not to do.
4. The person who administers the punishment is often associated with it and also becomes aversive.
5. Punishment frequently does not generalize across settings, thus it needs to be readministered.
6. Fear of punishment often leads to escape behavior.

If there are so many arguments for not using punishment, why is it so frequently used as a means for changing behavior? There are many explanations, including lack of familiarity with the consequences of punishment and the inability to effectively use a more positive approach. Also, punishment is often reinforcing to the punisher, reducing the occurrence of the undesirable behavior, therefore reinforcing its use.

Punishment should be used only when behaviors are harmful to the child or others. In this case, the student should be told ahead of time what the consequence (punishment) for exhibiting the behavior will be. When the undesirable behavior occurs, the punishment should be delivered quickly and as soon as the inappropriate behavior is initiated. Punishment should be applied consistently every time the designated behavior occurs. If you choose to use punishment you should identify several other behaviors you would like to see maintained and give extensive reinforcement for their occurrence.

Time-Out

Time-out occurs when the student is removed from the opportunity to receive any reinforcement. Time-out occurs when the teacher asks a student to sit in the hall during the remainder of a lesson, when a young child is asked to leave the group, or when a student is asked to sit in a quiet chair until he or she is ready to join the group.

Unfortunately, time-out is frequently used inappropriately. The underlying principle behind the successful use of time-out is that the environment the student is leaving must be reinforcing and the time-out environment must be without reinforcement. This may not be as easy to achieve as you might think. For example, when Elizabeth was talking and interfering with others during the science lesson, her teacher thought she would "decrease" Elizabeth's behavior by sending her to time-out, which was a chair in the back of the room away from the group. The teacher became discouraged when Elizabeth's inappropriate behavior during science class increased in subsequent lessons rather than decreased. A likely explanation for the ineffectiveness of time-out in this situation is that Elizabeth did not enjoy science class and she found sitting in a chair in the back of the room looking at books and toys reinforcing. The efficacy of time-out is strongly influenced by environmental factors. If the environment the student is leaving is unrewarding, then time-out is not an effective means of changing the student's behavior.

Teachers who use secluded time-out areas or contingent restraint (holding the student down plus withdrawal, exclusion, and seclusion) should be aware of the legal implications of such intervention, and should obtain the necessary authorization from within the school setting and from parents or guardians. Recommended procedures for successfully implementing time-out are listed in Apply the Concept 2.1.

Levels of Learning
One way the principles of operant learning can be applied is through stages of learning. The stages of learning are the levels a student may pass through in acquiring

Apply the Concept 2.1. Procedures for Implementing Time-Out

Time-out, like punishment, should be used as a last resort. Teachers should discuss this intervention with school administrators and parents before implementing it.

1. The student should be told in advance which behaviors will result in time-out.
2. The amount of time the student will be in time-out should be specified ahead of time.
3. The amount of time the student is in time-out should be brief (between one to five minutes).
4. The student should be told once to go to time-out. If the student does not comply, the teacher should unemotionally place the student in time-out.
5. Time-out must occur every time the undesirable behavior occurs.
6. Contingencies should be set in advance for the student who fails to comply with time-out rules.
7. Do not leave the time-out area unmonitored.
8. When time-out is over, the student should return to the group.
9. Reinforce positive behaviors that occur after time-out.

proficiency in learning. For example, the first stage of learning, entry, is the level of performance the student is presently performing. During the second stage, *acquisition*, the components of the target behavior are sequenced into teachable elements. Each teachable element is taught to mastery through a high rate of reinforcement, shaping, and consistent use of cues. After the behavior is occurring at a high level of accuracy, the focus of the learning is on *proficiency*. During this level the teacher's goal is to increase the student's accuracy and fluency in performing the behavior. At the next level, *maintenance*, the goal is for the behavior to be maintained at the target level of accuracy and proficiency with intermittent reinforcement and a reduction in teacher assistance and cues. With reduced reinforcement and assistance, many students with learning and behavior disorders have difficulty maintaining behaviors. The next stage is *generalization*, in which the target behavior transfers across settings, persons, and materials. Stokes and Baer (1977) suggest that generalization may be a separate skill that needs to be taught. At the final level, *application*, the learner is required to extend and utilize the materials in new situations. Application is a difficult skill for special learners, and the teacher's role may be to demonstrate and delineate a range of opportunities for applying the newly acquired skill.

In summary, the principles of operant learning are applicable within the classroom for both instructional and classroom management purposes. Teachers can use such principles as positive and negative reinforcement, token reinforcement, shaping, the Premack Principle, and group contingencies to increase desired behaviors. Teachers who want to decrease undesirable behaviors can apply such principles as extinction, reinforcing incompatible behaviors, punishment, and time-out.

Cognitive Behavior Modification

Cognitive behavior modification integrates notions from operant, social, and cognitive learning theories, and assumes that cognitive behavior (thinking processes), like observable behaviors, can be changed. This model of teaching and learning incorporates many of the principles of operant learning, but it adds some additional techniques that seem relevant when the goal of instruction is to change the way one thinks. Let's look at how Mrs. Neal uses cognitive behavior modification to help Marlow and his classmates better understand their science textbooks.

Marlow, a seventh grader in a class for emotionally handicapped students, and several of his classmates consistently have difficulty comprehending the important ideas from their textbooks, particularly in science. Even though they can identify most of the words in the text, they only remember a few details from what they read. Mrs. Neal wants to teach Marlow and his classmates how to understand and remember the major points. She decided that if she wants to teach the students this cognitive behavior, she will have to give them a consistent set of steps to use in completing the process, much in the same way we use a consistent set of steps to tie shoes. She also knows that for the students to learn what to do, they need to observe someone else. But how can she do this?

Mrs. Neal uses cognitive behavior modification. First, she selects the steps she wants to teach Marlow and the other students to use when they read their science text. Next, she and the students discuss the strategies the students currently use and their effectiveness. They also discuss the importance of improving this skill and the payoff for improvement. Mrs. Neal then tells the students about the steps she uses when she reads. To model these steps, she reads and explains what she is thinking. Then she gets the students to try the steps as she talks them through the steps. Finally, Mrs. Neal gives the students lots of opportunities to practice the steps when reading their textbooks, encouraging them at first to say the steps aloud as they work through them. She provides feedback on how they are doing and she also teaches them how to evaluate their own performance.

Using these systematic techniques, Mrs. Neal finds that in several weeks Marlow and his classmates are improving in their ability to remember the important information from their science text. In addition, they are beginning not to rely so much on the strategy she taught them. It is almost as if they are using it automatically, without having to consciously remember to use it. Mrs.

Neal feels that she has taught her students a good strategy for thinking about what they are reading and that she has changed their cognitive behavior (thinking processes).

Mrs. Neal used *cognitive behavior modification* (CBM). This approach includes an analysis of the task as well as an analysis of the thinking processes involved in performing the task. It also includes a training regimen that utilizes modeling, self-instructional techniques, and evaluation of performance (Meichenbaum, 1977, 1983).

Several key learning and teaching principles are associated with CBM. One principle of CBM is *cognitive modeling*. When Mrs. Neal explained what she was thinking as she read, she was using cognitive modeling. Another principle is *guided instruction*. Mrs. Neal used this principle when she guided the students through the reading task by telling them the steps in the process as they read. *Self-instruction* is another principle. When learners use language to guide their performance, they are using self-instruction. For instance, if you talk or think through the steps in solving a complex algebra problem while completing it, you are using self-instruction. If you talk aloud, it is called *overt self-instruction*; if you think to yourself, it is referred to as *covert self-instruction*.

Self-evaluation and self-regulation are two more principles of CBM. *Self-evaluation* refers to making judgments concerning the quality or quantity of performance. Mrs. Neal had Marlow and his classmates judge the quality of the performance by having them pause at the end of each section of the science text and comment on how they were doing. *Self-regulation* refers to the learner monitoring his or her own thinking strategies through language mediation. Self-regulation also occurs when the learner corrects or uses fix-up strategies when he or she detects a problem. For example, Mrs. Neal taught Marlow and his classmates to say to themselves what the main idea was when they finished reading each paragraph or section of the text. If the students could not give the main idea, then she demonstrated and encouraged them to use a fix-up strategy. In this case, she showed them how to go back and reread the first sentence in the paragraph to see if that helped them to remember the main idea. If this did not work, she demonstrated how to review the paragraph quickly.

Origins of Cognitive Behavior Modification

Cognitive behavior modification has origins from several theories in the psychology of learning (Harris, 1982, 1985). From operant learning come the principles of behavior modification. Behavior modification techniques such as task-analyzing the skill to be learned, providing cues to the learner, and using reinforcement and corrective feedback have been incorporated into many CBM training programs.

Social learning theory (Bandura, 1977) has also influenced CBM. A major assumption of social learning theory is the notion that affective, cognitive, and behavior variables interact in the learning process. For example, the extent to which Eva understands the cognitive concepts of place value will affect how well she performs the behavior

of computing three-digit subtraction problems with regrouping. Motivation and other affective variables also interact. Eva will probably perform the subtraction more accurately and carefully if she is determining whether there is enough money in her bank to buy a new record than if she is doing the twenty-fifth problem on a page of assigned subtraction problems.

The notion that we learn through watching others is another assumption that comes from social learning theory (Bandura, 1977). In social learning theory the importance of modeling is emphasized in relation to social behaviors (e.g., aggressive and cooperative behaviors). In CBM, modeling has been expanded to include cognitive modeling. When Mrs. Neal "talked aloud" what she was thinking as she read, she was using cognitive modeling.

Cognitive theory and cognitive training have also had a strong influence on CBM. Like cognitive training, CBM explicitly teaches problem solving and relies heavily on principles of self-regulation and self-evaluation.

Common Features of CBM Interventions

Cognitive behavior modification interventions or training regimens have been used to develop a range of academic and social skills. Lloyd (1980) identified five common features found in most CBM techniques: strategy steps, modeling, self-regulation, verbalization, and reflective thinking.

Strategy Steps

A series of steps is usually identified for the student to work through when solving a problem or completing a task. These steps are based on a task analysis of the cognitive and observable behaviors needed to complete the task. Before Mrs. Neal began teaching, she determined the steps in the reading strategy she wanted to teach Marlow and his classmates.

Graham and Harris and their colleagues have developed a series of writing strategies to assist students in writing stories and other pieces (e.g., Graham and Harris, 1989a, 1989b; Harris and Graham, 1985). Each strategy has steps that the students learn to assist them with specific aspects of writing. For example, to help students write a story Graham and Harris (1989a) used the following strategy steps:

1. Look at the picture (picture prompts were used).
2. Let your mind be free.
3. Write down the story part reminder (W-W-W; What = 2; How = 2). The questions for the story part reminder were:
   ❖ Who is the main character? Who else is in the story?
   ❖ When does the story take place?
   ❖ Where does the story take place?
   ❖ What does the main character want to do?
   ❖ What happens when he or she tries to do it?
   ❖ How does the story end? How does the main character feel?

4. Write down the story part ideas for each part.
5. Write your own story; use good parts and make sense.

Modeling

In CBM, modeling is used as a primary means of instruction. Research in social learning theory as well as in CBM supports the notion that modeling is a very effective teaching technique. With CBM, students are asked not only to watch observable behaviors as the instructor performs the task, but also to listen to the instructor's self-talk. In this way the instructor is modeling both observable behaviors and the unobservable thinking processes associated with those behaviors. Being able to model unobservable thinking processes is an important component for teaching such cognitive skills as verbal math problem solving, finding the main idea in a paragraph, editing written work, and solving social problems. In most instances the person modeling is the teacher or a peer, but video and puppets have also been used effectively for modeling. Vaughn, Ridley, and Bullock (1984) used puppets as models for teaching interpersonal social skills to young, aggressive children. The puppets were used to demonstrate appropriate social behaviors and strategies for solving interpersonal problems.

Self-Regulation

Self-regulation refers to the learner monitoring his or her thinking and actions through language mediation. When Meichenbaum (1977) developed his CBM training for improving the self-control of hyperactive children, he used Vygotsky's notions about how language affects socialization and learning processes. Luria (1961) and Vygotsky (1962) suggest that children become socialized using verbal self-regulation. Children first use language to mediate their actions by overtly engaging in self-instruction and self-monitoring. Later, this language mediation becomes covert.

Using self-regulation, students act as their own teachers. Students are expected to take active roles in the learning process and to be responsible for their own learning. Although they work under the guidance of a teacher, students are expected to monitor their learning, change or modify strategies when difficulties arise, evaluate their performance, and in some cases provide self-reinforcement. For example, Kosiewicz, Hallahan, Lloyd, and Graves (1982) used self-instruction in combination with self-correction to improve the handwriting legibility of a ten-year-old, learning-disabled boy. The self-instruction consisted of having the child do the following:

1. Say aloud the word to be written.
2. Say the first syllable.
3. Name each of the letters in the syllable three times.
4. Repeat each letter as it is written.
5. Repeat steps 2 through 4 for each syllable

For self-correction, the student was asked to judge each letter and circle the errors in a list or paragraph he had copied on the previous day. Both of these techniques reflect self-regulation that the student is performing the techniques independently and is responsible for his learning.

Verbalization

Verbalization is typically a component of self-instruction and self-monitoring with overt verbalization being faded to covert verbalization. Many CBM programs rely on a "talk aloud" or "think aloud" technique. After listening to the teacher think aloud as he or she performs the targeted processes and task, students are encouraged to talk aloud as they initially learn the strategy. For example, Ramon might say the following as he completes a two-digit subtraction problem without regrouping, "Start at the one's place and take the bottom number away from the top. Write the answer in the one's place. Now go to the ten's place. Do the same thing." Usually these overt verbalizations only occur during the initial stages of learning. As the strategy becomes more automatic, students are encouraged to "think to themselves" instead of "aloud."

In addition to verbalization concerning the learning processes, students are also encouraged to make self-statements about their performance. For example, "That part is done. Now go to the next part." or "I'm getting much faster at this." or "I need to think about all my choices before I decide."

Meichenbaum (1977) has suggested several ways to encourage students to use self-talk:

1. The teacher can model self-talk and self-statements as he or she performs the task.
2. The teacher can begin with tasks for which the students are already somewhat proficient. Later, as the students are comfortable with self-talk, the teacher can switch to the targeted tasks.
3. Students can develop and use cue cards to help them remember the steps they are to talk through.

Reflective Thinking

Reflective thinking requires students to take the time to think about what they are doing. Teaching students who have learning and behavior problems to "stop and think" is an important skill to include in instruction. Many of these students are impulsive in their actions, seeming to act without thinking (Blackman and Goldman, 1982; Kauffman, 1985; Keogh and Donlon, 1972). These students have limited and ineffective strategies for approaching academic tasks or social situations. They approach these tasks and situations in a disorganized, haphazard way, and often without thinking about the consequence of the actions (Torgesen, 1982; Torgesen and Licht, 1983; Wallace and Kauffman, 1986). In using CBM training programs, teachers assist students in using reflective thinking.

Let's look at how Wong, Wong, Perry, and Sawatsky (1986) encouraged reflective thinking when they taught seventh-grade students to use self-questioning when summarizing social studies texts. After teaching the students how to identify the main idea of paragraphs and how to summarize paragraphs, Wong and colleagues taught the students a summarization strategy. The summarization form and the steps in this strategy required the students to be reflective in their reading. The questions the students asked themselves were:

1. In this paragraph, is there anything I don't understand?
2. In this paragraph, what's the most important sentence (main-idea sentence)? Let me underline it.
3. Let me summarize the paragraph. To summarize, I rewrite the main-idea sentence, and add important details.
4. Now, does my summary statement link up with the subheading?
5. When I have written summary statements for a whole subsection:
   a. Let me review my summary statements for the whole subsection. (A subsection is one with several paragraphs under the same subheading.)
   b. Do my summary statements link up with one another?
6. At the end of an assigned reading section: Can I see all the themes here? If yes, let me predict the teacher's test question on this section. If no, let me go back to step 4 (Wong et al., 1986, pp. 25–26).

Teaching Implications of CBM

Cognitive behavior modification is designed to actively involve students in learning. Meichenbaum (1977, 1983) characterizes the student as a collaborator in learning. General guidelines to consider when using CBM include:

1. Analyze the target behavior carefully.
2. Determine if and what strategies the student is already using.
3. Select strategy steps that are as similar as possible to the strategy steps used by good problem solvers.
4. Work with the student in developing the strategy steps.
5. Train the prerequisite skills.
6. Train the strategy steps using modeling, self-instruction, and self-regulation
7. Give explicit feedback.
8. Teach strategy generalization.
9. Help the students maintain the strategy.

Guidelines for assessing the effects of training have also been suggested (Rooney and Hallahan, 1985).

A substantial and growing body of research supports the use of cognitive behavior modification for developing academic, cognitive, and social skills in students with learning and behavior problems (Deshler, Warner, Schumaker, and Alley, 1983; Graham and Harris, 1989a; Hallahan, Hall, Ianna, Kneedler, Lloyd, Loper, and Reeve, 1983; Montague and Bos, 1986b; Palincsar and Brown, 1987; Paris and Oka, 1986; Schumaker, Deshler, and Ellis,

1986; Vaughn, Ridley, and Bullock, 1984; Wong and Wilson, 1984). Researchers at the Kansas Institute for Research in Learning Disabilities have developed a teaching model as well as a number of task-specific strategies that employ the principles of CBM.

Sociocultural Theory of Cognitive Development

The sociocultural theory of cognitive development (Vygotsky, 1978) is similar to cognitive behavior modification in that it highlights the importance of modeling and the use of language to facilitate learning. However, the theory also assumes that learning is a social activity highly influenced by the resources that learners bring to the learning environment.

One concept associated with this theory is that the teacher needs to consider and utilize these resources (Diaz, Moll, and Mehan, 1986), which include such aspects as culture and language as well as background knowledge the learners can apply to the task being completed or the problem to be solved. For example, Moll (in press) in assisting Hispanic elementary students in developing literacy began by first exploring the "funds of knowledge" that could be gained from the community and the Hispanic and southwestern cultures. He also examined how literacy functioned as a part of community and home life. He brought this information into the schools and used it to build a literacy program. In this way, culturally diverse students were given the opportunity to use sources of knowledge that are not often highlighted in traditional school curriculums.

Another important theoretical concept is the premise that learning occurs during social interactions; that is, learning is a social event in which language plays an important role. Using this concept, teachers and students discuss what they are learning and how they are going about learning. Such interactive dialogue between teachers and learners provides language models and tools for guiding one's inner talk about learning (Moll and Diaz, 1987). Initially, a more expert person may model the self-talk and vocabulary related to the cognitive processes. However, this gives way to a collaborative or social dialogue in which the learner assumes increasing responsibility. This type of teaching allows for the instruction of cognitive and metacognitive strategies within purposeful, meaningful discussions and also provides a means for selecting, organizing, and relating the content matter being discussed. For example, in reciprocal teaching (Palincsar and Brown, 1984), a technique designed to foster comprehension and comprehension monitoring, the teacher and students take turns leading dialogues which focus on their knowledge of the information they are studying and on the processes they are using for understanding and for checking their understanding.

Another concept of the sociocultural theory of learning relates to the role of the teacher or the expert, who encourages learners by providing temporary and adjustable support as they develop new skills, strategies, and knowledge.

The instruction is referred to as *scaffolded instruction* (Tharp and Gallimore, 1988). The metaphor of a scaffold captures the idea of an adjustable and temporary support that can be removed when no longer necessary. Vygotsky (1978) describes learning as occurring in the "zone of proximal development" or "the distance between the actual developmental level as described by independent problem solving and the level of potential development as determined through problem solving under adult guidance or in collaboration with more capable peers" (p. 86).

Thus, the sociocultural theory of learning implies the following for instruction:

1. Instruction is designed to facilitate scaffolding and cooperative knowledge sharing among students and teachers within a context of mutual respect and critical acceptance of others' knowledge and experiences.
2. Learning and teaching should be a meaningful, socially embedded activity.
3. Instruction should provide opportunities for mediated learning with the teacher or expert guiding instruction within the students' zones of proximal development.

Information Processing and Schema Theories

Whereas operant learning focuses on observable behaviors and views learning as the establishing of functional relationships between a student behavior and the stimuli in the environment, cognitive learning theory focuses on what happens in the mind and views learning as changes in the learner's cognitive structure.

Information processing theory, one of several cognitive theories, attempts to describe how sensory input is perceived, transformed, reduced, elaborated, stored, retrieved, and used (Hunt, 1985; Neisser, 1976; Swanson, 1987). Psychologists and educators studying information processing attempt to understand how thinking processes operate to allow humans to complete such complex cognitive tasks as summarizing a chapter in a textbook, solving complex math problems, writing a mystery novel, and comparing and contrasting theories of learning.

A visual model depicting the sequence of stages in which information is processed or learned is presented in Figure 2.6. Although the figure implies that each activity is relatively separate, these processes are highly interactive. This processing system is controlled by *executive functioning* or *metacognition* which assists the learner in coordinating, monitoring, and determining which strategies the learner should employ for effective learning (Campione, Brown, and Ferrara, 1982; Swanson, 1987).

We can use this model to explain how Greg, a learning-disabled, high-school student, might acquire and remember some new information about "seizure" as it relates to the Fourth Amendment of the United States Constitution. Mr. Gomez is explaining the concepts of "search and seizure" to Greg and the rest of the students in government class. He writes the word *seizure* on the board and says,

"Seizure is when the police take your possessions away from you because those possessions are illegal. Sometimes the police need a search warrant to seize your possessions and sometimes they do not. As you read this chapter see if you can determine the rules for when the police need a search warrant."

According to the model presented in Figure 2.6, the first step in learning and remembering the information on the concept of "seizure" is to receive the information through the senses or sensory receptors. Mr. Gomez exposed Greg to both visual and auditory information by writing the word on the board and by talking about it.

Next, the information is transported to the sensory store. Here, both the visual representation of "seizure" and the auditory information are stored. At this point Greg has neither attended to the information nor connected meaning to it.

Now Greg can attend to the information, but he has only a limited capacity for attending and he can selectively attend to some sensory information and not to other information. If most of Greg's attention is allocated to thoughts about a Friday night date or a comic book he is reading, the information Mr. Gomez shared with Greg cannot be learned because Greg has not selectively attended to it. For our example, we will assume that Greg was attending to Mr. Gomez.

Next, Greg can recognize or perceive the information by detecting the salient features in the information and using the context and his prior knowledge to assist in perception. For example, Greg can use salient visual features in the word *seizure* his sight word recognition for the word (prior knowledge), and Mr. Gomez's discussion of seizure (context) to perceive the word written on the board as *seizure* rather than the word *leisure* or *search*.

Once the information is perceived it can be held for a short period of time in working or short-term memory. However, if Greg wants to learn the information, he can either transfer and store the information in long-term memory or utilize a strategy to keep the information active in short-term memory. Unless some effort is made to remember the information, it will fade in about fifteen seconds. We can use a variety of memory strategies to keep information active. We can rehearse it (repeat it aloud and to ourselves), chunk it (group it together to make fewer pieces of information to remember), elaborate on it (expand on it by using information we already know), and so on. Greg rehearses the word and its definition by saying it several times to himself.

Greg is aware that the information related to "seizure" needs to be remembered for a long time or at least until the test next week. Therefore, the information must be meaningfully stored in long-term memory to become part of his cognitive structure. This way, he should be able to retrieve the information next week for the test. One efficient means of storing new information is to relate the new information to old information. Greg retrieves from his memory a story about a senior who tried to raise marijuana in his backyard. The police found it, arrested him, and seized the marijuana.

Figure 2.6.

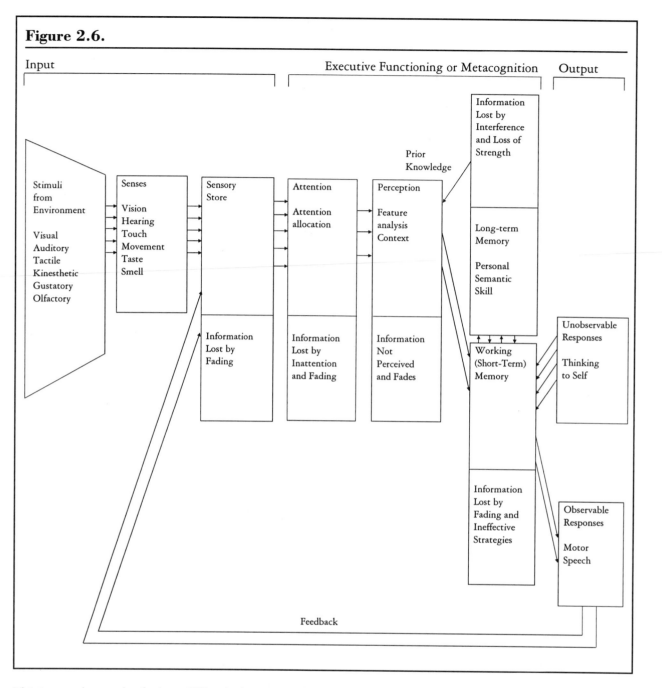

This is a good example of seizure. When he hears or reads the word *seizure*, he can think of the senior having the marijuana seized. Greg also retrieves from his memory that search and seizure are discussed in the Fourth Amendment. Greg can relate the new information to old information almost as if he were filing it away in an organized filing system. Greg can store the new information about seizure in the same file as the one containing the story about the marijuana and the information on the Fourth Amendment.

When the exam is given next week, and Mr. Gomez asks for the definition of seizure, Greg should be able to retrieve the information from long-term memory into working memory and then write the definition because he filed it in a meaningful way.

Throughout the process, learning is orchestrated by executive functioning or metacognition. For example,

when Greg decided to rehearse the word and its definition rather than write them down, he was using his executive functioning to coordinate the learning process.

Although we process information in a logical sequence (see Figure 2.6), we generally process information very quickly and don't think consciously about what we are doing. We do not necessarily say to ourselves, "Now I need to rehearse this so I won't forget it," or "I have to relate this information to what I already know so that I can remember it." Information processing is also very interactive. Feedback is possible both from observable responses we make and unobservable thinking responses. These interactions are depicted by the bi-directional arrows in Figure 2.6. Let's explore information processing further by looking at each component and at the overall coordinating processes of executive functioning and metacognition.

Sensing

Sensing involves the use of one or more of our senses to obtain information. It refers to our system's capacity to use the sensory processes to obtain information, not our system's ability to attend or discriminate. Stimuli from the environment are received through all our senses. However, much of the information we learn in school-related tasks is received through visual and auditory senses.

Sensory Store

The *sensory store* holds all incoming information for approximately a second, just long enough for us to attend and perceive it (Loftus and Loftus, 1976). Although we have the ability to retain large amounts of information in the sensory store, the information quickly fades unless we actively attend to and perceive it (Sperling, 1960).

Attention

Most of us use the term *attention* to refer to a wide range of behaviors. We speak of attending to details when we are concerned about the quality of a job, we ask people if they are attending to us when we want them to hear what we are about to say, and we measure students on the amount of time they attend to tasks. Attention is the capacity to focus awareness on selected incoming stimuli. At any one time a variety of information is being received by the senses and held in sensory store. However, as depicted in Figure 2.6, we attend only to some of the information, depending on the task demands. In other words, we selectively attend.

The importance of *selective attention* can be demonstrated in relation to the reading process. You have probably experienced reading a text by going through the mechanical motions (identifying the words) only to realize suddenly that you are not attending and cannot remember what you were reading. Instead, your mind has drifted to thoughts about a friend's problems, the music playing in the background, or how good the apple pie baking in the oven smells. All of these stimuli are being received by your senses and funneled into the sensory store. An effective learner must selectively attend to the relevant stimuli.

Attention can only be allocated to a few cognitive processes at a time. However. the more proficient you are at a process, the less attention it will require. Well-practiced processes require little attention and are said to be *automatic*, whereas processes requiring considerable attention have been referred to as *deliberate* (Anderson, 1980; Kolligian and Sternberg, 1987). LaBerge and Samuels (1974; Samuels, 1987) have applied these principles to the reading process. Poor readers, including many students with learning and behavior problems, must allocate so much of their attention to identifying the words in the text that little is left to allocate toward comprehension. Good readers, however, have word recognition at an "automatic" level, and therefore have more attentional capacity to allocate to understanding what they read.

Many students with learning and behavior disabilities have some sort of automation failure (e.g., Ackerman and Dykman, 1982; Samuels, 1987; Spear and Sternberg, 1986). As a result, the disabled students must allocate attention and exert effort to task and task components that nondisabled individuals have already mastered.

Not only do these students have to allocate more attention to some tasks than nondisabled students, they also have difficulty selectively attending to the relevant stimuli and attending for sustained periods of time (Anderson, Halcomb, and Doyle, 1973; Ross, 1976; Tarver, Hallahan, Cohen, and Kauffman, 1977).

Perception

Once we allocate our attention to incoming stimuli, the next step in processing is to recognize or perceive the information. *Perception* can be defined as "the process of 'recognizing' a raw, physical pattern in sensory store as representing something meaningful" (Loftus and Loftus, 1976, p. 23). *Perceptual learning* is the increased ability to gain new information from the environment (Gibson, 1969). Students who have perceptual disabilities usually have trouble interpreting and obtaining meaning from the stimuli in the environment (Schiff, 1980).

One explanation of how perception works entails the perceiver using feature analysis and the context in which the stimulus is presented to give the stimulus meaning. In *feature analysis*, the perceiver uses the critical features to recognize the stimuli. For example, the critical feature between *n* and *u* and *p* and *b* is orientation. We process more slowly and are prone to confuse letters that have minimal feature differences such as *C* and *G* or *b* and *d* (Kinney, Marsetta, and Showman, 1966). Similar findings have been shown with speech sounds (phonemes). Feature analysis is used across a variety of contexts. For instance, a listener might use the salient clue "Once upon a time" to recognize that she is listening to a story.

The perceiver also uses the *context* in which the stimulus is presented to assist in perception. Read the two words presented in Figure 2.7. Did you have any difficulty reading *THE CAT*? Now look closely at the *H* and the *A*. They are the exact same visual image. The context provided by the words facilitates the appropriate interpretation (Neisser, 1967). Context also plays an important role in perceiving auditory stimuli. Warren and Warren (1970) asked individuals to listen to sentences in which a nonspeech sound replaced a speech sound. The sentences were similar to the following:

It was found that the *eel was on the axle.
It was found that the *eel was on the shoe.
It was found that the *eel was on the orange.
It was found that the *eel was on the table.

In each case, the * represented a nonspeech sound. The individuals did not report hearing the nonspeech sound or the word *eel*, but they used the context to assist in perception and reported hearing the words *wheel, heel, peel*, and *meal*, respectively. Our store of background information, as represented in long-term memory (see Figure 2.6), interacts with the incoming stimuli to assist us in the perception process.

Figure 2.7. Effect of Context on Letter Recognition

THE CHT

Perception involves the simultaneous use of both feature analysis and use of context and prior knowledge. Feature analysis has been referred to as *bottom-up processing* "because information flows from little perceptual pieces (features), which serve as the foundation of perception, to larger units built from them (e.g., letters, words, pictures)" (Anderson, 1980, p. 43). If we processed every feature of every letter when reading a page, it is estimated that we would be making an average of 100 feature analyses per second. But because we can also use context and prior knowledge to assist in perception, we do not need to detect every feature, every letter, or even every word (Smith, 1978; Goodman, Smith, Meredith, and Goodman, 1987). When context or prior knowledge guide perception, we refer to the processing as *top-down processing*, since high-level general knowledge determines the interpretation of low-level perceptual units (Anderson, 1980). It is the interaction of bottom-up and top-down processing that makes for efficient perceptual processing (Anderson, 1977; Rumelhart, 1980).

Working Memory

Once information is perceived it can move into working or short-term memory. *Working memory* can be thought of as activated memory since it represents the information that is easily accessible. Working memory has a limited capacity in that we have the ability to store only a small amount of information in working memory at any one time (i.e., seven bits of information plus or minus two bits) (Miller, 1956). However, much of the information that enters through our senses is already lost (see Figure 2.6). We lose some information because we do not attend to it; we lose other information because we do not perceive it or because it will not fit into working memory.

Working memory can be contrasted with long-term memory. Long-term memory represents the information passively stored outside the attentional spotlight (Rumelhart, 1977). An example can clarify the difference between short term and long-term memory.

Study the following numbers so that you can remember them: 9-6-5-8-2-4-1-7. Now cover the numbers, wait for at least fifteen seconds, and then write them. After you attended and perceived the numbers, you probably studied them to keep them active in your working memory and then you wrote them. To keep the numbers active you may have rehearsed the numbers, closed your eyes and tried to visualize them, or used some other memory strategy.

Now write the phone numbers of your two best friends. This information is stored in long-term memory. You had to search your long-term memory for your two best friends. You probably used their names in searching, although you could have used their appearances or an idiosyncratic characteristic. Then you retrieved their phone numbers and transferred them to working memory. Once the information was in working memory you were ready to use the information, so you wrote their phone numbers.

Now, without looking back, write the numbers you were asked to remember earlier. You will probably have difficulty with this task. Since information fades from working memory if you do not work with it, and since you filled your working memory with the phone numbers of your two best friends, you probably cannot write the original numbers. If you had stored the original numbers in long-term memory, you might be able to retrieve them, but the task did not require you to do this. Consequently, they are lost forever.

Several concepts were demonstrated by this example:

1. Working or short-term memory is activated memory.
2. Working memory has a limited capacity. We can keep a limited amount of information in working memory (i.e., seven pieces of information plus or minus two pieces). These pieces can be of various size or comprehensiveness. For example, they may be seven single digits, seven phone numbers, seven sentences, or seven major concepts.
3. The more we cluster or group information into larger related concepts, the more information we can keep in working memory.
4. If we do not actively work with the information in working memory, it will fade rapidly (in about fifteen seconds).
5. We can use various strategies to keep information active in working memory. For example, we can rehearse the information, elaborate on it, create visual images of it, and so on.
6. Information in working memory is easily replaced by new incoming information (e.g., recalling your friends' phone numbers).
7. Information not stored in long-term memory cannot be retrieved.
8. Information that is stored in long-term memory is sometimes retrievable. How the information is organized in long-term memory affects how easily it can be retrieved.
9. Information from long-term memory is transferred to working memory. Then you can use that information (e.g., writing the phone numbers of your best friends).

Like attention and perception, some students with learning and behavior problems have difficulties with tasks requiring them to listen to or look at numbers, pictures, letters, words, or sentences, hold them in working memory, and then recall them (e.g., Howe, Brainerd, and Kingma, 1985; Swanson, 1985, 1987; Torgesen, Rashotte, Greenstein, Houck, and Portes, 1987).

Long-Term Memory and Schemas

We have already discussed the role that long-term memory plays in learning. Using Figure 2.6 as a reference, we see that *long-term memory* aids us in perceiving incoming stimuli. It provides the context that allows us to use top-down processing when perceiving information (e.g., to perceive the stimuli *THE CAT* even though visual images of the *H* and the *A* are the same). It helps us fill in the words or speech sounds of a conversation that we do not fully hear because we are at a noisy party. Long-term memory also interacts with working memory. Information is retrieved from long-term memory and transferred to working memory before it can be used to make responses. If long-term memory plays such an important part in the information processing system, how is it organized? If it has to hold all the information we know, including our store of knowledge about the world, procedural information on how to do numerous skills such as tie shoes and play basketball, and information about our goals and values, how does long-term memory keep all this information straight? Like the rest of the information processing system, cognitive psychologists do not know just how this vast array of information is organized, but they do have some logical hunches.

According to one theory, our knowledge is organized into schemas. *Schemas* can be defined as organized structures of stereotypic knowledge (Schank and Abelson, 1977). They are higher-order cognitive structures that assist in understanding and recalling events and information.

It is hypothesized that we have innumerable schemas for events and procedures and it is our schemas that allow us to make inferences about the events that happen around us (Rumelhart, 1980; Spiro, 1980). These schemas are organized in our cognitive structure in such a way that they can be retrieved and utilized in working memory to aid in understanding new events and ideas (Brewer and Nakamura, 1984).

Read the following short passage about an event John experienced.

John had been waiting all week for Friday evening. He skipped lunch just to get ready for the occasion. At 6:30 P.M. he got in his car and drove to the restaurant. He planned to meet several friends when he arrived. When he arrived, he got out of his car and waited outside for his friends.

At this point you are probably using a general schema for restaurants. You could answer such questions as "Is John going to eat dinner?" "Will John eat dinner with his

friends?" However, you have not been given enough information to utilize a more specific restaurant schema. Now read on to see how your schema is sharpened by the information given in the rest of the passage.

After a few minutes, John's friends arrived. They entered the restaurant and walked up to the counter. John placed his order first. After everyone ordered, they carried the trays of food to a booth.

How has your schema changed? You should be using a more specific schema for fast-food restaurants. Now you can probably answer more specific questions such as "What kind of food did John and his friends probably eat?" "Did John leave a tip?" Utilizing schemas (e.g., our prior knowledge about stereotypic events) allows us to make inferences, thereby filling in the gaps and giving meaning to incoming information. Schemas serve a crucial role in providing an account of how old or prior knowledge interacts with new or incoming information (Anderson, 1977; Rumelhart, 1980, 1985).

The early work in schema theory is usually credited to Bartlett (1932) who, in his book *Remembering* argued that memory is not simply recalling what one remembers almost in a template-like fashion, but it is reconstructive. In other words, in comprehending and recalling information, our prior knowledge interacts with incoming information, and to some extent it changes the information to fit with our prior knowledge. In this way we reconstruct the meaning in relation to our schemas. To verify his premise about schemas, Bartlett had English subjects read and then recall a folktale from another culture. He had the individuals recall the tale immediately after they read it and again at later times.

Bartlett's subjects showed clear distortions in their memory of the story. These inaccuracies appear to be systematic in that the individuals distorted the folktale to fit with their own cultural stereotypes. Many of the people omitted proper names, unfamiliar details, and hard-to-interpret aspects of the tale. They made the tale shorter, more coherent, and more consistent with their cultural expectations. In other words, understanding and memory do not simply reflect a rote process but a *reconstructive* process, resulting in the interaction of a person's schemas with the new infirmation.

Within and across schemas, concepts or ideas are organized so as to promote understanding and retrieval. Information can be stored in semantic networks composed of concepts and relationships between concepts (Kintsch, 1974; Rumelhart, 1980). The closer together the concepts are in the network, the better they serve as cues for each other's recall (Ratcliff and McKoon, 1978; Weisberg, 1969). For example, wings should serve as a better recall cue for *bird* than should *two*. Concepts do not exist in isolation in semantic memory but are related to other concepts at higher, lower, or the same levels. In the case of *birds*, it could be filed along with *reptiles* and *mammals*, under the superordinate concept of *animals*.

Schemas and semantic networks allow us to organize our knowledge in such a way that we can retrieve information and effectively add new information to long-term memory. They also assist us in determining the relationship among ideas.

Executive Functioning and Metacognition

The specific processes in the information processing system (i.e., attention, perception, working memory, and long-term memory) are controlled or coordinated by what has been referred to as *executive functioning* (see Figure 2.6). In the same way that a business executive has many departments that he or she has to coordinate, and many decisions that have to be made regarding how best to use those various departments, the learner has to coordinate his or her various learning processes and strategies and make decisions regarding learning. For example, as learners, we must decide (1) which stimuli to attend to (e.g., the book we are reading and/or the smell of the apple pie baking); (2) whether to rely more on feature analysis or context and prior knowledge when perceiving information; (3) what memory strategies are more effective for keeping the information active in working memory; and (4) what is an effective and efficient way to store the information so that we can retrieve it later. Making decisions allow us to control the learning process.

This executive functioning or control and coordination of our learning processes has also been referred to as metacognition (Brown, 1980; Flavell, 1976). *Metacognition* is generally considered to have two components (Brown, 1980):

1. An awareness of what skills, strategies, and resources are needed to perform a cognitive task
2. The ability to use self-regulatory strategies to monitor the thinking processes and to undertake fix-up strategies when processing is not going smoothly

In many ways, metacognition and executive functioning are similar to the concepts of self-evaluation and self-regulation presented in the section on cognitive behavior modification.

Flavell, one of the first cognitive psychologists to focus his research in the area of executive functioning, explains:

> For example, I am engaging in metacognition (metamemory, metalearning, metaattention, metalanguage, or whatever) if I notice that I'm having more trouble learning A than B; if it strikes me that I should double-check C before accepting it as a fact; if it occurs to me that I had better scrutinize each and every alternative in any multiple-choice type task situation before deciding which is the best one; if I sense that I had better make a note of D because I may forget . . . (1976, p. 232).

Metacognition and executive functioning require the learner to monitor the effectiveness of his or her learning and, based on feedback, regulate learning by activating task-appropriate strategies. Read the short essay in Apply the Concept 2.6 and see how you use your metacognition.

Students with learning and behavior problems certainly have potential for having difficulties with executive functioning or metacognition. For example, the essay you read in Apply the Concept 2.6 was also read by groups of learning-disabled and average-achieving seventh graders. They were asked to read the essay to see if it made sense. Although most of the average-achieving students recognized the inconsistency, most of the learning-disabled students reported that there was nothing wrong with the essay (Bos and Filip, 1984). Others have found similar metacognitive deficits for these students in reading, memory, and math tasks (Cherkes-Julkowski, 1985; Montague and Bos, 1986b; Torgesen, 1985; Torgesen and Houck, 1980; Wong, 1979, 1980).

Teaching Implications from Information Processing and Schema Theories

Information processing and schema theories have definite educational implications for students with learning and behavior problems. As you read the content chapters in this book, think about how information processing theory helped to shape the instructional techniques. When teaching, think about how you can modify your teaching and the learning environment to facilitate directing a student's attention to the relevant stimuli and his or her perception of the incoming information. What strategies can you teach students so that information can stay active in working memory, and how can you present information to facilitate its storage and organization of long-term memory? How can you teach students to use executive functioning to coordinate the various learning and memory strategies? Several general implications are:

1. *Provide cues to students so they might be guided to the relevant task(s) or salient features of the task.* For instance, when giving a lecture, provide cues to assist the students in attending to the key points by giving an overview of the lecture, writing important concepts on the board, providing the students with a written outline of the lecture, or teaching the students how to listen and look for behaviors that signal important information (e.g., raised voice, repetition).
2. *Have students study the critical feature differences between stimuli when trying to perceive differences.* For example, highlight the "stick" part of the letters *b* and *d*; provide instances and noninstances when discussing a concept.
3. *Have the students use the context to aid in perception.* Students are not likely to substitute *bog* for *dog* if they are reading a story or sentence about a dog.
4. *Facilitate the activation of schemas and provide labeled experiences.* In this way students can develop adequate schemas and modify their current schemas for better understanding of the concepts being presented in both skill and content area subjects.

Apply the Concept 2.6. Comprehension Monitoring

Read the following the short essay:

There are some things that almost all ants have in common. For example, they are all very strong and can carry objects many times their own weight. Sometimes they go very, very far from their nest to find food. They go so far away that they cannot remember how to go home. So, to help them find their way home, ants have a special way of leaving an invisible trail. Everywhere they go, they put out an invisible chemical from their bodies. This chemical has a special odor. Another thing about ants is they do not have noses to smell with. Ants never get lost (Bos and Filip, 1984, p. 20).

As you read the first part of the essay, you probably read along smoothly and quickly, comprehending the information and confirming that in fact what you are reading makes sense. However, when you read the last couple lines of the essay, you probably slowed your reading rate, possibly went back and reread, and/or stopping and thought about what you were reading. If these are the type of cognitive strategies in which you engaged, then you were using your executive functioning or metacognition to monitor your information processing system.

5. *Teach students to use memory strategies.*
6. *Use organization techniques to assist students in organizing their long-term memories.*
7. *Teach students to be flexible thinkers and how to solve problems, thereby encouraging them to use executive functioning.*

Much work is still to be completed before we fully understand how learners process information. Still, there is an accumulated body of research from which we, as educators, can draw implications for effective teaching and learning.

Summary

This chapter presents approaches to learning and teaching for guiding the teaching-learning process. The models provide principles that influence the way you, as a teacher, observe, record, interact, and evaluate the teaching-learning process with students.

The first model, operant learning theory, focuses on observed behavior and the antecedents and consequences that control the behavior. In this model the teacher is able to increase or maintain desirable behaviors through positive and negative reinforcement, secondary reinforcers, the Premack Principle, shaping, and group contingencies. Through operant learning the teacher is also able to decrease undesirable behaviors by using extinction, reinforcement of incompatible behavior, punishment, and time-out. Teachers can use the principles from operant learning to enhance students' progress through the stages of learning. These include entry, acquisition, proficiency, maintenance, generalization and application. The teaching-learning process in the operant learning model is highly teacher directed.

The second model, cognitive behavior modification, utilizes principles from both operant learning theories and cognitive-oriented theories. Key features of cognitive behavior modification interventions are that they include strategy steps, modeling, self-regulation, verbalization,

and reflective thinking. Through cognitive behavior modification the student and the teacher have a more interactive role in the teaching-learning process.

The third model, a sociocultural theory of learning, emphasizes the social nature of learning and encourages interactive discussions between students and teachers. In these discussions the teacher is encouraged to use the students' funds of knowledge and to provide the needed support for the student to acquire new strategies, skills, and knowledge.

The fourth model, information processing and schema theories, is a pair of cognitive theories that attempt to explain how information is received, transformed, retrieved, and expressed. Key features of information processing are sensing, sensory store, attention, perception, memory, executive functioning, and metacognition. The information processing model focuses on an interactive role between the teacher and the student, with the concentration on activating prior background knowledge in the student, relating new learning to information the learner already has learned, and maintaining the student as an active learner who thinks about how he or she thinks, studies, and learns.

Throughout the remaining chapters you will see many examples of the principles for teaching and learning that were presented in this chapter. These examples will assist you in understanding how the different approaches to learning and teaching can be applied when interacting with students. In a sense, this chapter provides the theoretical underpinnings for the strategies presented in the subsequent chapters. As you read the subsequent chapters, think about how theory guides the instructional practices and how it will guide your teaching as you work with students experiencing learning and behavior problems.

References

Ackerman, P. T., and Dykman, R. A. (1982). Automatic and effortful information-processing deficits in children with learning and attention disorders. *Topics in Learning and Learning Disabilities, 2,* 12–22.

Anderson, J. R. (1980). *Cognitive psychology and its implications*. San Francisco: W. H. Freeman.

Anderson, R. C. (1977). The notion of schemata and the educational enterprise. In R. C. Anderson, R. J. Spiro, and W. E. Montague (Eds.), *Schooling and the acquisition of knowledge*. Hillsdale, N.J.: Erlbaum, pp. 415–431.

Anderson, R. P., Halcomb, C. G., and Doyle, R. B. (1973). The measurement of attentional deficits. *Exceptional Children, 39,* 534–539.

Bandura, A. (1977). *Social learning theory*. Englewood Cliffs: N.J.: Prentice-Hall.

Bartlett, R. C. (1932). *Remembering*. Cambridge, Eng.: Cambridge University Press.

Blackman, S., and Goldman, K. M. (1982). Cognitive styles and learning disabilities. *Journal of Learning Disabilities, 15,* 106–115.

Bos, C. S., and Filip, D. (1984). Comprehension monitoring in learning disabled and average students. *Journal of Learning Disabilities, 17*(4), 229–233.

Brewer, W. R., and Nakamura, G. V. (1984). *The nature and functions of schemas* (Tech. Rep. 325). Champaign: University of Illinois, Center for the Study of Reading.

Brown, A. L. (1980). Metacognitive development and reading. In R. J. Spiro, B. C. Bruce, and W. F. Brewer (Eds.)., *Theoretical issues in reading comprehension*. Hillsdale, N.J.: Erlbaum, pp. 453–482.

Campione, J., Brown, A., and Ferrara, R. (1982). Mental retardation and intelligence. In R. J. Sternberg (Ed.), *Handbook of human intelligence*. New York: Cambridge University Press, pp. 392–473.

Cherkes-Julkowski, M. (1985). Metacognitive considerations in mathematics for the learning disabled. In J. Cawley (Ed.), *Cognitive strategies and mathematics for the learning disabled*. Rockville, Md.: Aspen.

Christian, B. T. (1983). A practice reinforcement hierarchy for classroom behavior modification. *Psychology in the Schools, 20,* 83–84.

Deshler, D. D., Warner, M. M., Schumaker, J. B., and Alley, G. R. (1983). Learning strategies intervention model: Key components and current status. In J. D. McKinney and L. Feagans (Eds.), *Current topics in learning disabilities* (Vol. 1). Norwood, N.J.: Ablex, pp. 245–283.

Diaz, S., Moll, L. C., and Mehan, H. (1986). Sociocultural resources in instruction: A content-specific approach. In *Beyond language: Social and cultural factors in schooling language minority students*. Sacramento, Calif.: Bilingual Education Office, California State Department of Education, pp. 187–229.

Flavell, J. H. (1976). Metacognitive aspects of problem solving. In L. B. Resnick (Ed.), *The nature of intelligence*. Hillsdale, N.J.: Erlbaum.

Gibson, E. J. (1969). *Principles of perceptual learning and development*. New York: Appleton-Century-Crofts.

Goodman, K. S., Smith, E. G., Meredith, R., and Goodman, Y. M. (1987). *Language and thinking in school: A whole-language curriculum* (3rd ed.). New York: Richard C. Owen.

Graham, S., and Harris, K. R. (1989a). Components analysis of cognitive strategy instruction: Effects on learning disabled students' compositions and self-efficacy. *Journal of Educational Psychology, 81,* 353–361.

Graham, S., and Harris, K. R. (1989b). Improving learning disabled students' skills at composing essays: Self-instructional strategy training. *Exceptional Children, 56,* 201–214.

Hall, R. V. (1975). *Behavior modification: Basic principles, managing behavior (Part 2)* (Rev. ed.). Lawrence, Kans.: H & H Enterprises.

Hallahan, D. P., Hall, R. J., Ianna, S. O., Kneedler, R. D., Lloyd, J. W., Loper, A. B., and Reeve, R. E. (1983). Summary of research findings at the University of Virginia Learning Disabilities Research Institute. *Exceptional Educational Quarterly, 4*(1), 95–114.

Howe, M. L., Brainerd, C. J., and Kingma, J. (1985). Storage-retrieval process of normal and learning disabled children: A stages-of-learning analysis of picture-word effects. *Child Development, 56,* 1120–1133.

Hunt, E. B. (1985). Verbal ability. In R. J. Sternberg (Ed.), *Human abilities: An information processing approach*. New York: Freeman, pp. 63–100.

Kauffman, J. M. (1985). *Characteristics of children's behavior disorders* (3rd ed.). Columbus, Ohio: Merrill.

Keogh, B. K., and Donlon, G. McG. (1972). Field dependence, implusivity, and learning disabilities. *Journal of Learning Disabilities, 5,* 331–336.

Kinney, G. C., Marsetta, M., and Showman, D. J. (1966). *Studies in display symbol legibility, Part XXI*. The legibility of alphanumeric symbols for digitized television (ESD-TR-66-117). Bedford, Mass.: Mitre Corporation.

Kintsch, W. (1974). *The representation of meaning in memory*. Hillsdale, N.J.: Erlbaum.

Kolligian, J., Jr., and Sternberg, R. J. (1987). Intelligence, information processing, and specific learning disabilities: A triarchic synthesis. *Journal of Learning Disabilities, 20*(1): 8–17.

Kosiewicz, M. M., Hallahan, D. P., Lloyd, J. W., and Graves, A. W. (1982). Effects of self-instructive and self-correction procedures on handwriting performance. *Learning Disabilities Quarterly, 5*(1), 71–78.

LaBerge, D., and Samuels, S. J. (1974). Toward a theory of automatic information processing in reading. *Cognitive Psychology, 6,* 293–323.

Lloyd, J. W. (1980). Academic instruction and cognitive behavior modification: The need for attack strategy training. *Exceptional Educational Quarterly, 1*(1) 53–64.

Loftus, G., and Loftus, E. R. (1976). *Human memory*. Hillsdale, N.J.: Erlbaum.

Luria, A. R. (1961). *The role of speech in the regulation of normal and abnormal behavior*. (J. Tizard, Trans.). New York: Liveright.

Meichenbaum, D. (1977). *Cognitive-behavior modification: An integrative approach*. New York: Plenum.

Meichenbaum, D. (1983). Teaching thinking: A cognitive-behavioral approach. In *Interdisciplinary voices in learning disabilities and remedial education*. Austin, Tex.: Pro-Ed.

Miller, G. A. (1956). The magical number seven, plus or minus two: Some limits on our capacity for processing information. *Psychological Review, 63,* 81–97.

Moll, L. C., and Diaz, S. (1987). Teaching writing as communication: The use of ethnographic findings in classroom practice. In D. Bloome (Ed.), *Literacy and schooling*. Norwood, N.J.: Ablex, pp. 193–221.

Montague, M., and Bos, C. S. (1986b). The effect of cognitive strategy training on verbal math problem solving performance of learning disabled adolescents. *Journal of Learning Disabilities, 19*(1), 26–33.

Neisser, U. (1967). *Cognitive psychology*. New York: Appleton.

Neisser, U. (1976). *Cognition and reality: Principles and implications of cognitive psychology*. San Francisco: Freeman.

Palincsar, A. S., and Brown, A. L. (1984). Reciprocal teaching of comprehension fostering and comprehension monitoring activities. *Cognition and Instruction, 1*(2), 117–175.

Palincsar, A. S., and Brown, D. A. (1987). Enhancing instructional time through attention to metacognition. *Journal of Learning Disabilities, 20*(2), 66–75.

Paris, S. G., and Oka, E. R. (1986). Instruction and cognitive development: Coordinating communication and cues. *Exceptional Children, 53*(2), 109–117.

Premack, D. (1959). Toward empirical behavior laws. *Psychological Review, 66*(4), 219–233.

Ratcliff, R., and McKoon, G. (1978). Priming in item recognition: Evidence for the propositional structure of sentences. *Journal of Verbal Learning and Verbal Behavior, 17,* 403–417.

Rooney, K. J., and Hallahan, D. P. (1985). Future directions for cognitive behavior modification research: The quest for cognitive change. *Remedial and Special Education, 6*(2), 46–51.

Ross, A. O. (1976). *Psychological aspects of learning disabilities and reading disorders.* New York: McGraw-Hill.

Rumelhart, D. E. (1977). *Introduction to human information processing.* New York: John Wiley.

Rumelhart, D. E. (1980). Schemata: The building blocks of cognition. In R. J. Spiro, B. C. Bruce, and W. F. Brewer (Eds.), *Theoretical issues in reading comprehension.* Hillsdale, N.J.: Erlbaum, pp. 33–58.

Rumelhart, D. E. (1985). Toward an interactive model of reading. In H. Singer and R. B. Ruddell (Eds.), *Theoretical models and processes of reading* (3rd ed.). Newark, Del.: International Reading Association.

Samuels, S. J. (1987). Information processing abilities and reading. *Journal of Learning Disabilities, 20*(1), 18–22.

Schank, R. C., and Abelson, R. (1977). *Scripts, plans, goals, and understanding.* Hillsdale, N.J.: Erlbaum.

Schiff, W. (1980). *Perception: An applied approach.* Boston: Houghton Mifflin.

Schumaker, J. B., Deshler, D. D., and Ellis, E. S. (1986). Intervention issues related to the education of LD adolescents. In J. K. Torgenson and B. Y. L. Wong (Eds.), *Psychological and educational perspectives on learning disabilities.* Orlando, Fla.: Academic Press, pp. 329–365.

Smith, F. (1978). *Understanding reading* (2nd ed.). New York: Holt, Rinehart and Winson.

Spear, L. D., and Sternberg, R. J. (1986). An information-processing framework for understanding learning disabilities. In S. Ceci (Ed.), *Handbook of cognitive, social, and neuropsychological aspects of learning disabilities.* (Vol. 2). Hillsdale, N.J.: Erlbaum, pp. 2–30.

Sperling, G. A. (1960). The information available in brief visual presentation. *Psychological Monographs, 74,* whole no. 498.

Spiro, R. J. (1980). Constructive processes in prose comprehension and recall. In R. J. Spiro, B. C. Bruce, and W. F. Brewer (Eds.), *Theoretical issues in reading comprehension.* Hillsdale, N.J.: Erlbaum, pp. 245–276.

Stokes, T. F., and Baer, D. M. (1977). An implicit technology of generalization. *Journal of Applied Behavior Analysis, 10,* 349–367.

Swanson, H. L. (1985). Verbal coding deficits in learning disabled readers. In S. J. Ceci (Ed.), *Handbook of cognitive, social and neuropsychological aspects of learning disabilities* (Vol. 1). Hillsdale, N.J.: Erlbaum, pp. 203–228.

Swanson, H. L. (1987). Information processing theory and learning disabilities: An overview. *Journal of Learning Disabilities, 20*(1), 3–7.

Swanson, H. L. (Ed.) (1987). *Advances in learning and behavioral disabilities* (Supplement 2). Greenwich, Conn.: JAI Press.

Tarver, S. G., Hallahan, D. P., Cohen, S. B., and Kauffman, J. M. (1977). The development of visual selective attention and verbal rehearsal in learning disabled boys. *Journal of Learning Disabilities, 10*(8), 491–500.

Tharp, R. G., and Gallimore, R. (1988). *Rousing minds to life: Teaching, learning, and schooling in social context.* New York: Cambridge University Press.

Torgesen, J. K. (1982). The learning disabled child as an inactive learner: Educational implications. *Topics in Learning and Learning Disabilities, 2*(1), 45–52.

Torgesen, J. K. (1985). Memory processes in reading disabled children. *Journal of Learning Disabilities, 18*(6), 350–357.

Torgesen, J. K. , and Houck, G. (1980). Processing deficiencies in learning disabled children who perform poorly on the digit span test. *Journal of Educational Psychology, 72,* 41–60.

Torgesen, J. K., and Licht, B. G. (1983). The learning disabled child as an inactive learner: Retrospect and prospects. In J. D. McKinney and L. Feagans (Eds.), *Current topics in learning disabilities.* Norwood, N.J.: Ablex.

Torgesen, J. K., Rashotte, C. A., Greenstein, J., Houck, G., and Portes, P. (1987). Academic difficulties of learning disabled children who perform poorly on memory span tasks. In H. L. Swanson (Ed.), *Advances in learning and behavioral disabilities* (Supplement 2). Greenwich, Conn.: JAI Press, pp. 305–333.

Vaughn, S. R., Ridley, C. A., and Bullock, D. D. (1984). Interpersonal problem solving skills training with aggressive young children. *Journal of Applied Developmental Psychology, 5,* 213–223.

Vygotsky, L. S. (1962). *Thought and language* (E. Hanfmann and G. Vakar, eds. and trans.). Cambridge, Mass.: MIT Press.

Vygotsky, L. S. (1978). *Mind in society: The development of higher psychological processes.* Cambridge, Mass.: Harvard University Press.

Wallace, G., and Kauffman, J. M. (1986). *Teaching students with learning and behavior problems* (3rd. ed.). Columbus, Ohio: Merrill.

Warren, R. M., and Warren, R. P. (1970). Auditory illusions and confusions. *Scientific American, 223,* 30–36.

Weisberg, R. W. (1969). Sentence processing assessed through inrasentence word associations. *Journal of Experimental Psychology, 82,* 332–338.

Wong, B. Y. L. (1979). Increasing retention of main ideas through questioning strategies. *Learning Disability Quarterly, 2*(2), 42–47.

Wong, B. Y. L. (1980). Activating the inactive learning: Use of questions/prompts to enhance comprehension and retention of implied information in learning disabled children. *Learning Disability Quarterly, 3,* 29–37.

Wong, B. Y. L., and Wilson, M. (1984). Investigating awareness of and teaching passage organization in learning disabled children. *Journal of Learning Disabilities, 17*(8), 447–482.

Wong, B. Y. L., Wong, R., Perry, N., and Sawatsky, D. (1986). The efficacy of a self-questioning summarization strategy for use by underachievers and learning disabled adolescents in social studies. *Learning Disabilities Focus, 2*(1), 20–35.

Attention Deficit Hyperactivity Disorder

Durbin, K. 1993. *Streamlined Seminar* 11(4).
Alexandria, Va.: National Association of Elementary School Principals.

Attention Deficit Hyperactivity Disorder (ADHD) has been defined as a collection of symptoms, all of which lead to disruptive behavior and are therefore expected to be seen in various combinations in most ADHD children.

The characteristic symptoms of ADHD are not abnormal in themselves. In fact, they are present in all children at one time or another, and only when excessive do they become disruptive behavioral problems. Three distinctions to keep in mind when examining the eight principal ADHD characteristics discussed here are their intensity, persistence, and patterning (Wender 1987). But also note that not all of these characteristics are present in every ADHD child.

1. Inattentiveness and Distractibility

ADHD children are nearly always easily distracted and have short attention spans. At home, these children don't listen to what their parents say to them; they don't mind; and they forget things. Their homework is never finished. When getting dressed, they may leave buttons unbuttoned and zippers unzipped, and even put shoes on the wrong feet. At school, their teachers notice that they have difficulty listening to and following directions, have trouble completing assignments, and often are off-task and out of their seats.

It is important to remember that inattentiveness and distractibility need not be present at all times. Many teachers report that these children do well when given one-to-one attention, and physicians and psychiatrists note good attention spans during brief office visits.

The paradox of ADHD children being attentive under specialized conditions, but unable to pay attention and complete tasks under normal conditions, is confusing to parents and teachers, especially when they see that these children are able to sit and watch television for long periods of time. But, as Pugliese (1992) has observed, television programming reinforces the way ADHD children think by switching rapidly from idea to idea and scene to scene, with numerous commercial interruptions. There is constant movement both on the screen and in the minds of the affected children.

2. Impulsiveness

ADHD children tend to speak and act first, and think later (Garber *et al.* 1990). They talk out in class and interrupt others. They rush across streets, oblivious to traffic, and have more than their share of accidents.

These children are often unable to tolerate delays, and become upset when people or things fail to respond as they wish. This may result in broken toys, as well as attacks on siblings and classmates (Wender 1987).

3. Hyperactivity

Hyperactivity, which involves such attributes as restlessness, excessive talking, difficulty awaiting turns in games, and shifting from one uncompleted activity to another (Garber *et al.* 1990), is not always exhibited by ADHD children. They may appear to be normally, or even less than normally, active until they have an important task to complete. It is then that these children, distracted by things that would barely be noticed by anyone else, display the classic symptoms of hyperactivity—constant motion, fidgeting, drumming fingers, and shuffling feet. In the classroom, hyperactive children talk constantly, jostle and annoy others, do a lot of clowning, and are generally disruptive.

4. Attention-Demanding Behavior

All children want and need adult attention, and ADHD children are no exception. The difference is in their insatiable desire for such attention. They have to have center stage, be the clown, monopolize the conversation, and show off. Wender (1987) explains the adult reaction to such behavior:

> The demand for attention can be distressing, confusing, and irritating to parents. Since the child demands so much, they feel they have not given him what he needs. Since they cannot understand how to satisfy him, they feel deficient. Finally, because the child may cling and poke simultaneously and endlessly, they feel angry.

5. Learning Difficulties

While ADHD is in no way related to mental retardation, some ADHD children do have similar problems. Their intellectual development may be uneven—advanced in some areas and behind in others. For example, a child may be able to do fifth-grade mathematics, but only second-grade reading.

Problems in perception are more difficult to define and are more complex than simple vision or hearing limitations. ADHD children may be unable to distinguish between similar sights or sounds, or to connect sensations in a meaningful way.

Such difficulties in children of normal intelligence are called specific developmental disorders (SDDs), a term that is replacing "learning disabilities." While the most common SDDs are in reading and arithmetic, not all ADHD children have these disorders. Nevertheless, because most ADHD children have learning difficulties, they are often viewed as underachievers.

6. Coordination Difficulties

About half of all ADHD children have problems with various types of coordination. For example, trouble with fine muscle control may result in difficulties in coloring, writing, tying shoelaces, and buttoning. For many of these children, handwriting is perceived as an awesome chore, and the results are often illegible. They may also have difficulty learning to ride a bike and throwing and catching a ball. Such difficulties are especially detrimental for boys because these abilities help win social acceptance, and their importance as building blocks for self-esteem should not be taken lightly.

7. Unacceptable Social Behavior

Probably the most disturbing feature of ADHD, and the one most likely to be the initial cause of referral, is the difficulty that ADHD children have in complying with adult requests and prohibitions. While some may appear to forget what they are told, others may obstinately refuse to comply. Parents often describe their ADHD children as obstinate, disobedient, stubborn, bossy, sassy, and uncaring (Wender 1987).

While these children are often very adept at making initial friendships, they are unable to maintain them because they have to be the leaders, the first ones in line, the ones that make the rules. Unable to see the connection between how they treat others and the way others respond to them, they wonder why they have no friends.

8. Immaturity

It is important to remember that while all of these characteristics can be seen in all children from time to time, in ADHD children they appear to reflect the behavior of children four or five years younger. It may be helpful to consider the actions of a ten-year-old ADHD child as being much like those of a normal five-year-old (Wender 1987).

Diagnosis and Implications

The first step parents should take for a child suspected of having ADHD is a medical examination to rule out physical problems that may show similar symptoms. The second step is for a qualified physician or psychologist to diagnose the child's condition, based in part on a parent questionnaire and teacher assessments.

What are the implications of an ADHD diagnosis on a child's relationships with family and peers? This is an important area, minimized in the past, that may continue to hinder the development of self-esteem even after most or all ADHD symptoms have disappeared.

Because managing these children requires such energy, parents are likely to give more direct orders, feel they need to supervise more, and not allow the kind of freedoms that other children of the same age would be able to handle. Parents may also demonstrate unresolved anger toward their ADHD children. If self-esteem is formed on the basis of how others respond to us, it is easy to see why ADHD children often form low opinions of themselves (Wender 1987).

Peer Relationships

This attack on self-esteem occurs not only within the family, but in the ADHD child's relationships with peers. Because these children lack social skills, they often find themselves without friends. They are not invited to parties; in choosing up sides for games, they are chosen last—or not at all; and they are often teased because they react highly to teasing (Wender 1987). The area of peer relationships is one that continues to be troubling for ADHD children even when most or all of their symptoms respond to treatment. While the attitudes and reactions of adults may improve, studies have shown that peers continued to reject ADHD children even after they had successfully learned social skills.

Treating ADHD: Medication

The most common treatment for ADHD children is stimulant medication, and the three most widely used stimulants are Dexedrine, Ritalin, and Cylert. All have been highly effective in improving attention span, impulse control, restlessness, and compliance with requests from parents and teachers (Anastopoulos and Barkley 1990). Also, by being less bossy, more obedient, and better students, these children are more readily accepted by the people around them at home and in school. They feel better about themselves and about their lives in general.

While treatment with stimulant medication alone makes ADHD children more manageable and attentive in the short term, it is not clear if it will have a long-term beneficial effect on learning. Studies have shown that this type of treatment is not always a panacea (Klein and Abikoff 1989).

Treating ADHD: Therapy

Other treatments that have shown some effectiveness in reducing ADHD symptoms are behavior therapy, cognitive therapy, and combinations of these, with and without medication.

At the Attention-Deficit Hyperactivity Disorder Clinic of the University of Massachusetts Medical Center, two of the most commonly recommended treatment services are parent training and parent counseling (Anastopoulos and Barkley 1990). Even when medication is used, parents must possess the knowledge and skills to manage their ADHD children on evenings and weekends, when medication is usually not taken, and medication-improved behavior may not be maintained.

Parents must also be aware that ADHD children often exhibit forms of psychosocial behavior that cannot be helped through medication, such as aggression, diminished self-esteem, depression, and lack of appropriate social skills (Anastopoulos and Barkley 1990).

Behavior Management

The use of behavior management principles is one way parents can minimize ADHD symptoms and establish positive new behaviors. Behavior therapy is based on the assumption that ADHD children need clear, consistent, and immediate consequences for their behavior (Gordon *et al.* 1991).

One approach for parents is the use of negative consequences. For example, simply ignoring an attention-seeking behavior is one effective way to eliminate it, particularly with younger children. There are a number of other effective behavior modification techniques, but of paramount importance is the coordination of such efforts between parents and educators.

How Educators Can Help

Because the problems of ADHD children spill over into school, effective classroom intervention is needed. Teachers should know and be able to use the same behavior modification principles used by parents. In addition, however, teachers can benefit from classroom management suggestions like these:

◆ Maintain a structured program for ADHD children.

◆ Have them practice positive behaviors repeatedly until they internalize them.

◆ Give them work paced to fit their capabilities.

◆ Keep a daily checklist to help them stay focused on their behavior (Pugliese 1992).

The success of school interventions is dependent not only on the range of cognitive strategies used, but on a high level of communication and cooperation between parents and educators. The main goal is to instill self-control and reflective problem-solving skills in ADHD children.

However, behavior and cognitive therapies also have some limitations. Research has found, for example, that treatment focused on one academic or social skill does not tend to transfer to another area. It appears that behavior therapy needs to be instituted in each specific setting, and that the success of cognitive therapy is highly dependent on the ability of an adult to provide the needed learning cues and encouragement.

Because successful treatment of ADHD by medication and/or therapy has thus far been elusive, we are left with the realization that affected children need individualized, broadly based, and long-term intervention, and that those who help these children must sustain a high level of optimism, enthusiasm, and energy throughout their involvement (Pfiffner and Barkley 1990).

Is ADHD Curable?

There is no one-shot cure for ADHD. One theory is that treatment intervention is required until the brain matures and is able to produce adequate amounts of required chemicals (Wender 1987). Another theory is that ADHD is a lifestyle rather than an acute disorder and therefore cannot be completely eliminated (Whalen and Henker 1991).

Even though symptoms may diminish or disappear in over half of all ADHD children as they move into adolescence and adulthood, many of them will continue to have symptoms well into their adult years. Psychiatrists recognize an adult form of ADHD as Attention Deficit Disorder, Residual Type (ADD/RT).

For the present, research indicates that ADHD children will derive the greatest benefit from multimodal treatment strategies that combine various therapeutic approaches. But such treatment requires a long-term, consistent effort by both parents and educators.

References

Anastopoulos, A.D.; and Barkley, R.A. "Counseling and Training Parents." In R.A. Barkley (ed.), *Attention-Deficit Hyperactivity Disorder: A Handbook for Diagnosis and Treatment*. New York: Guilford Press, 1990.

Garber, S.W.; Garber, M.D.; and Spizman, R.F. *If Your Child Is Hyperactive, Inattentive, Impulsive, Distractible: Helping the ADD (Attention Deficit Disorder)/Hyperactive Child*. New York: Villard Books, 1990.

Gordon, M.; Thomason, D.; Cooper, S.; and Ivers, C.L. "Nonmedical Treatment of ADHD/Hyperactivity: The Attention Training System." *Journal of School Psychology* 29 (Summer 1991): 151-152.

Klein, R.G.; and Abikoff, H. "The Role of Psychostimulants and Psychosocial Treatments in Hyperkinesis." In T. Sagvolden and T. Archer (eds.), *Attention Deficit Disorder: Clinical and Basic Research*. New York: Lawrence Erlbaum Associates, 1989.

Pfiffner, L.J.; and Barkley, R.A. "Educational Placement and Classroom Management." In R.A. Barkley (ed.), *Attention-Deficit Hyperactivity Disorder: A Handbook for Diagnosis and Treatment*. New York: Guilford Press, 1990.

Pugliese, Frank. Lecture notes by author, March 10, 1992.

Wender, P.H. The Hyperactive Child, Adolescent, and Adult: *Attention Deficit Disorder through the Lifespan*. New York: Oxford University Press, 1987.

Whalen, C.K.; and Henker, B. "Therapies for Hyperactive Children: Comparisons, Combinations, and Compromises." *Journal of Consulting and Clinical Psychology* 59: (February 1991): 126-135.

Whalen, C.K.; and Henker, B. "Social Impact of Stimulant Treatment for Hyperactive Children." *Journal of Learning Disabilities* 24:4 (April 1991): 231.

Language Problems: A Key to Early Reading Problems

Mann, V. 1991. In *Learning about learning disabilities*, ed. B. Y. L. Wong, 129–62. San Diego: Academic Press, Inc.

Editor's Notes[*]

You have read about memory-processing problems in children with learning disabilities in the previous chapter. You will discover that their phonetic short-term memory problems contribute to their difficulties in learning to read as you read the present chapter. Clearly, memory-processing problems are more than a characteristic of children with learning disabilities.

In this chapter, Mann's major theme concerns her exposition that extant research findings support a language-oriented view of reading disability. She approaches her task by first considering the question of what cognitive processes are involved in reading. This is an important question for a twofold reason: (1) it uncovers the commonalities between some of the processes in spoken and written language; and (2) the cognitive processes involved in reading differentiate importantly between good and poor readers.

Reading subsumes two component processes: language processing skills and phonemic awareness. Language-processing skills comprise speech perception, vocabulary skills as in naming, linguistic short-term memory, syntax, and semantics. Phoneme awareness is the sensitivity to the constituent phonemes in words. It is intricately associated with the English language system of alphabets. Mann examined the research in these two areas of component processes in reading. The research findings indicated poor readers were deficient in all aspects of language-processing skills, excepting syntax and semantics, and consistently pointed to the power of phonemic awareness in predicting future reading ability and achievements among beginning readers.

Although we subscribe to a language-oriented view of reading disability, we must not forget that for a minority of poor readers and students with learning disabilities visual factors apparently compound their reading difficulties. In the next chapter, Dale Willows examines the role of visual factors in reading disability.

I. Introduction: The Link between Reading Problems and Language Problems

What makes a poor reader a *poor reader*? Why do some children fail to learn to read in the very same classrooms where other children succeed and even excel? Although reading is a task that most children accomplish quite readily, it poses a specific difficulty for some 4–10% of children who may be labeled as dyslexic or reading-disabled. It is often noted that such children cannot be distinguished from their more successful peers by general intelligence, motivation, or prior classroom experience; in fact, this "unexpected" aspect of the problem is at the core of the definition of dyslexia. Are early reading problems really so

unexpected? Can we not identify some factor or factors that have limited certain children's success in learning to read? The objective of the following page is to introduce the very fruitful approach to the problem of early reading disability that is being guided by the assumption that reading is first, and foremost, a language skill. In Section II, we begin with the rationale behind this approach before turning to the many interesting results that it has produced. Psychologists, educators, and medical doctors have all, in one way or another, tried to identify the basis of early reading difficulty, and their efforts have always been guided by a rationale of some sort or another that reflects some basic assumptions as to what skilled reading is "all about." For this reason, a basic understanding of the assumptions behind the studies and experiments that seek to explain early reading problems is an obvious place to begin. To introduce these assumptions, Section II first describes how the English alphabet functions as "written language" by mapping onto the structure of spoken English. This theoretical point will then be complemented by a brief review of experimental evidence that shows that adult readers use certain spoken language skills to read well. Section III turns to the real substance of the chapter; it outlines two categories of spoken language skills—language processing and phoneme awareness—that are essential to beginning readers and then proceeds to a survey of research that links early reading difficulty to problems within each of these areas. This section also offers a few comments on some less successful accounts of early reading problems. Section IV presents some plausible explanations of the language deficiencies that have been found among poor beginning readers, considering constitutional factors and environmental factors in turn. Section V concludes the chapter with a brief summary and some concluding remarks about directions for future research and practical applications.

II. Why Spoken Language Is So Critical to Readers

A necessary first step toward understanding the role of language problems in poor reading is to understand something about how writing systems function as written language and the language skills that allow skilled readers to read. Those researchers who have approached the question "What makes a poor reader a *poor reader*?" by first identifying the skills that are involved in reading have made some of the greatest contributions to the field. The success of their approach will become obvious in Section III, when we turn to surveying the abilities and disabilities of poor readers.

What skills are involved in reading? Obviously, reading involves the processes of perceiving, recognizing, remembering, and interpreting the various letters and the words, sentences, etc. that they form. Certain aspects of

---

[*] Editor's note: These "Editor's Notes" are from this excerpt.

these processes are visual, but others are linguistic in that they use some of the spoken language skills that allow us to be speakers and hearers of our language. Two insights about the linguistic aspects of reading have been particularly helpful in pointing out potential causes of reading problems: (1) that writing systems are designed to make use of language skills as well as visual skills and (2) that skilled readers make active use of some of the same skills that allow them to be fluent speakers and hearers of their language. The following sections will review the basis for each of these two insights.

A. How Writing Systems Represent Language

Writing systems, or orthographies, are systems of symbols that represent, or transcribe, spoken language, which is to say that a writing system writes language. The focus of this section will be on how alphabets work, because most readers of this chapter will be interested in children who are having problems with the English alphabet. Like all writing systems, alphabets represent units of the spoken language. Various systems have come to exist because of the variety of different types of linguistic units that can be represented. Ideographies, like American Indian petroglyphs, represent language at the level of ideas: logographies, like the Chinese writing system (and Japanese Kanji), represent units called morphemes; syllabaries, like Hebrew and Japanese Kana, represent syllables; and alphabets, like those used for English, French, and most of the European languages, represent units called phonemes. Each of these systems makes slightly different demands on the beginning reader because each transcribes a different type of unit. Their history and diversity is quite fascinating to consider, and, for interesting discussions, the reader might want to read Hung and Tzeng (1981) and Watt (1989).

Because a writing system represents certain units of spoken language, the language user's realization that these units are a part of his or her speech will be an important key to understanding how written words relate to their spoken language counterparts (for a discussion, see Hung and Tzeng, 1981; Liberman et al., 1980a). Alphabets represent phonemes, so someone who wishes to learn how an alphabet functions should be sensitive to the fact that spoken language can be broken down into phonemes. As we shall see in Section III.D, much evidence indicates that this "sensitivity," which is referred to as phoneme awareness, is a problem for many young children and, in particular, for poor readers.

---

1. The English Alphabet:
A Morphophonological Transcription

Alphabets represent phonemes, the consonants and vowels of language. To be a bit more precise, the English alphabet does not provide the one-to-one mapping of letter to phonemes that one finds, for example, in Spanish. Rather, it provides a "deeper," more abstract level of representation, which has been referred to as a morphophonological

transcription (morphological and phonological transcription). Morphophonological transcription corresponds not so much to the consonants and vowels that speakers and hearers think they pronounce and perceive, as to the way theoretical linguists assume that words are abstractly represented in the ideal speaker/hearer's mental dictionary, or lexicon (Chomsky, 1964). According to these linguists, words are represented as sequences of systematic phonemes in such a way as to preserve (on the whole) the basic units of meaning that we refer to as morphemes. To convert the morphophonological representations of words in the lexicon to the less abstract, phonetic representations that are used in pronunciation and perception, language users are thought to employ ordered series of phonological rules that alter, insert, or delete segments.

As discussed in Liberman et al. (1980a), an example of the morphophonological nature of transcription by the English alphabet can be found by the way we use "ea" to transcribe the vowels in "heal" and "health," preserving their abstract morphological and phonological similarity, while blurring certain phonetic distinctions. Insofar as the letter sequences in "heal" and "health" stand for the morphophonological (morphological and phonological) representations of these words, they can provide a means of access to lexical information, including each word's meaning and grammatical properties. To pronounce a written word, the reader who has recovered the appropriate morphophonological representation need only apply the phonological rules of his language—the same rules that otherwise exist for the perception and pronunciation of "heal" and "health" in normal speech.

This account of the English orthography is, of course, somewhat idealized. Sometimes words are transcribed at a shallower, more phonetic level than the morphophonological ideal, hence the different spelling of the vowels in "well" and "wealth." Sometimes, too, the spelling of a word seems neither phonetically nor phonologically principled, as in the spelling of "sword." Some of these exceptions have the advantage of disambiguating homophones; others are historically based, but their existence does not seriously undermine Chomsky's claim about the basic operating principle of the English orthography (Liberman et al., 1980a).

---

2. Virtues of Alphabetic Systems

Why should English be transcribed with an alphabetic system? Are there any advantages to using an alphabetic orthography and to the English morphophonological system, in particular? One general benefit of alphabets stems from the fact that they transcribe phonemes as opposed to some other unit of language—syllables, for example, or words. This greatly reduces the number of characters that the would-be reader must learn to recognize and reproduce. There are only 26 letters in the English alphabet, whereas between 2,000 and 3,000 characters are needed to read a newspaper written in the Chinese logography.

A benefit of the English morphophonological system, in particular, stems from the fact that, by transcribing a deep, relatively abstract level of phonological structure, it preserves the relation between words such as "heal" and "health" and thereby can facilitate our appreciation of word meaning. The transcription of a morphophonological level of representation also avoids the need to create different spelling patterns for people who speak with different accents. Were English a more "shallow" alphabet, speakers from Boston would spell "cot" and "cart" the same way, and speakers from the South would spell "pen" and "pin" the same—imagine the inconveniences this could cause.

Another virtue to alphabets, aside from being economical, is that they are highly productive. In alphabets and morphophonological transcription, the relation between written words and spoken words is highly rule-governed. Knowledge of the rules that relate between written words and spoken words—the rules that relate letter sequences, morphophonological representations, and their pronunciation—allows the reader to read not only highly familiar words but also less familiar ones such as "skiff" and even nonsense words such as those that Dr. Seuss so cleverly employs. Consider that a skilled reader of the Chinese logography must have memorized thousands of distinct characters—and even then may encounter difficulty in reading a new word. In contrast skilled readers of English need to know only a limited set of phoneme-grapheme correspondences and the phonological rules of their spoken language to "decode" most words on the page (and any phonologically plausible nonword such as "bliggle").

This is not to imply that there is anything inherently undesirable about reading a syllabary or logography. Ultimately, the utility of a given orthography rests on the nature of the spoken language it transcribes. For example, a logography is appropriate for Chinese because it allows people to read the same text even though they cannot understand each other's speech. Likewise, for Japanese, the Kana syllabaries are quite well suited to the hundred or so syllables in the Japanese language. English, however, has less profound dialectical variation than Chinese, and English employs more than 1,000 syllables. Hence, an alphabet is appropriate, and it would be a disservice to present the English writing system otherwise. However, to present it in its true light requires that the would-be reader possess both language-processing skills and phonological sophistication.

---

3. Phoneme Awareness:
A Special Requirement of Alphabetic Systems

Alphabets may have clear advantages, but they nonetheless pose an obstacle for poor readers. There are a variety of reasons why children might become poor readers. They might have problems distinguishing between the various letter shapes. They might have problems with the linguistic units that the written words represent. But children must "know" these units when they "know" spoken English, so why isn't every child who speaks English able to become a successful beginning reader? The answer to this question is that "knowing" spoken English is not enough: Would-be readers must go one step further than merely being a

speaker/hearer of their language; they must be "aware" of certain aspects of their language and aware of phonemes in particular (Mattingly, 1972).

The awareness of phonemes is critical because alphabets work best for readers who are aware that letters represent phonemes; however, readers cannot be aware of this relationship unless they are aware of phonemes in the first place. Unless they are sensitive to the fact that words can be broken down into phonemes (i.e., units the size of consonants and vowels), the letter-phoneme correspondences will be useless. This sensitivity is not something that we use in the normal activities of speaking and hearing, although we use it in certain "secondary language activities" such as appreciating verse (i.e., alliteration), making jokes (i.e., Where do you leave your dog? In a barking lot.), and talking in secret languages (i.e., Pig Latin). We refer to this sensitivity as phoneme awareness.

One slight problem with the term phoneme awareness is that it is often used interchangeably with several other terms: phonological awareness, metalinguistic awareness, and linguistic awareness, to name a few. By using the term phoneme awareness, we confine the issue to sensitivity about phonemes. Phonological awareness would also include sensitivity to syllables, morphemes, and the phonological rules that operate upon them; linguistic awareness and metalinguistic awareness would further include sensitivity to syntax (i.e., grammar), semantics (i.e., meaning), and their rules. These broader levels of awareness are of interest in their own right and could be an interesting topic for research. To date, awareness of phonemes has been most often studied and appears to be directly related to the beginning reader's progress.

B. Language Skills that Skilled Readers Use

Considerations about the way in which the English alphabet transcribes language offer one form of evidence about the importance of spoken language skills to reading. A second source of evidence comes from studies of skilled readers. These show a clear involvement of certain spoken language skills in the skilled reading of words, sentences, and paragraphs. Such studies are important to consider, not only because they show that reading is really quite parasitic upon spoken language processes, but because they have inspired certain studies of the differences between good and poor beginning readers.

---

1. Language Skills and Word Recognition

The question of whether or not written words must be recoded into some type of "silent speech" has been a topic in much of the research on the psychology of skilled reading. It has especially preoccupied those who study the processes that make it possible to recognize the words of our vocabulary, a process often referred to as lexical access, or word perception (for recent reviews, see Crowder, 1982; Perfetti and McCutchen, 1982; Taylor and Taylor, 1983). Under some circumstances silent speech can appear unnecessary for word recognition: some words may be directly perceived as visual units, instead of decoded into a string of phonemes. But clear evidence also implicates at least some speech code involvement in word perception, making many psychologists favor a "dual access" or "parallel race-horse" model in which both phonetic and visual access occur in parallel. The speech code, or phonetic, route is most heavily used in the case of less frequent or unfamiliar words, the visual, or whole word, route is most important for very familiar words and words with irregular spelling patterns.

Regardless of how a word is recognized, it will be remembered from Section I that the mental lexicon of words contains the morphophonological representation of each word in the reader's vocabulary, and that representation is the key to realizing the word's semantic extensions (its meaning) and its syntactic properties (its part of speech: noun, action verb, etc.) as well as its pronunciation. Hence, it is appropriate that English transcribes spoken words in terms of their morphophonological representations. It may not be necessary to recode print into a speech code in the process of gaining access to this dictionary (referred to as the mental lexicon), and it may not even be feasible if we accept Chomsky's (1964) contention, but morphophonological recoding clearly must occur, or else the reading of phrases, sentences, etc. would not be possible.

---

2. Language Skills and the Reading
of Sentences and Paragraphs

From the point of word perception onward, the involvement of speech processes in reading is quite clear (Perfetti and McCutchen, 1982). First of all, considerable evidence indicates that temporary or short-term memory for written material involves recoding the material into some kind of silent speech, or phonetic representation. This type of representation is used whether the task requires temporary memory for isolated letters, printed nonsense syllables, or printed words. In all of these cases, both the nature of the errors that subjects make in recalling such material and the experimental manipulations that help or hurt their memory performance have shown us that a phonetic representation is being used; i.e., subjects are remembering the items in terms of the consonants and vowels that form the name of each item, rather than the visual shape of the letters, the shape of the words, etc. (cf., e.g., Baddeley, 1978; Conrad, 1964, 1972; Levy, 1977). Furthermore, subjects apparently rely on phonetic representation when they are required to comprehend sentences written in either alphabetic (Kleiman, 1975; Levy, 1977; Slowiaczek and Clifton, 1980) or logographic orthographies (Tzeng *et al.*, 1977). This is one reason why we may observe such significantly high correlations between reading and listening comprehension among a variety of languages and orthographies, including English (cf. Curtis, 1980; Daneman and Carpenter, 1980; Jackson and McClelland, 1979), Japanese, and Chinese (Stevenson *et al.*, 1982).

Thus, regardless of the way in which the reader recognizes each word, the processes involved in reading sentences

and paragraphs apparently place certain obvious demands on temporary memory, and temporary memory for language apparently makes use of phonetic representation in short-term memory. The fact that readers make active use of a phonetic representation is an important thing to keep in mind. In Section III.C, we will see that problems with phonetic representation are often found among poor beginning readers in the form of short-term memory problems.

III. Language Problems as Causes of Early Reading Problems

Without spoken English, there would be nothing for the English orthography to transcribe; the well-known difficulties of deaf readers attest to the importance of spoken language skills for successful reading. But deaf children are not the only ones for whom deficient language abilities are a cause of reading problems. As we will see, many hearing children who are poor readers also suffer from spoken language problems, and, although their problems are considerably more subtle than those of the deaf, they are no less critical. However, before discussing this fact, let us first summarize the language skills needed by beginning readers and then mention some of the previously held theories about the causes of reading problems and some of the general evidence that points to a link between reading and language problems. Then we may more appropriately turn to a more detailed survey of various forms of evidence about the types of language skills that are lacking in poor readers and are typical of kindergarten children who will become poor readers in the early elementary grades.

A. Two Types of Language Skills That Are Essential to Beginning Readers

What skills does a child need to learn to read well? Obviously, would-be readers need to possess the visual skills that allow them to differentiate and remember various letter shapes. They also need language-processing skills to perceive and recognize the teacher's words and to combine them into phrases, sentences, and paragraphs as well as to meet the requirements of skilled reading discussed in Section II.B. Finally, they will need to possess phoneme awareness if they are to make any real sense of the way in which the alphabet works.

---

1. Language-Processing Skills

Beginning readers should possess language-processing skills at four different levels. First, they need the speech perception skills that make it possible to distinguish the words of their vocabulary (e.g., the difference between "cat" and "hat"). They also need vocabulary skills, although they need not necessarily possess mature morphophonological representations in their lexicons, given some evidence that the experience of reading, in and of itself, serves to stimulate and further phonological development (Moskowitz, 1973;

Read, 1986). Beginning readers should also have an adequate linguistic short-term memory, because this is not only critical to skilled readers but also supports retention of sufficient words to understand sentences and paragraphs. Finally, they should further be able to recover the syntactic and semantic structure of phrases and sentences (although their mastery of these aspects of language, like their mastery of phonology, may be facilitated by the experience of reading [Goldman, 1976]).

---

2. Phoneme Awareness

Language-processing skills, however, are only one aspect of the language skills needed by would-be readers of English. As noted in Section II.A, the English orthography requires that successful readers not only be able to process spoken language but also be conscious of certain abstract units of that language—in particular, phonemes. Otherwise, the alphabet will make no sense as a transcription of spoken English. Whereas sophistication about words is sufficient for learning a logography, and sophistication about words and syllables is sufficient for syllabaries, children must know about these units and also about phonemes if the alphabet is to make sense and if they are to use it to its fullest advantage.

Section II.A hinted that phoneme awareness might pose a problem, but why should this be the case? One reason is that phonemes are quite abstract units of language, considerably more abstract than either words or syllables. We reflexively and unconsciously perceive them when we listen to the speech stream, because we have a neurophysiology uniquely and elegantly adapted to that purpose (cf. A. M. Liberman, 1982). However, phonemes cannot be mechanically isolated from each other nor produced in isolation (Liberman *et al.* 1967) as can syllables and words. There are some very interesting indications that infants may distinguish phonemes (for a recent review of the speech perception capabilities of infant listeners, see Miller and Elmas, 1983), and preschool-aged children most certainly employ phonetic representation when holding linguistic material in short-term memory (Alegria and Pignot, 1979; Elmas, 1975). Yet these are automatic, tacit aspects of language-processing ability, and the child who "knows" his or her language well enough to perceive and remember phonemes can still be blissfully unaware of the fact that these units exist—much the same way that you and I are blissfully unaware of the rods and cones that allow us to see.

The problems with using written language is that the tacit must also become explicit. Successful beginning readers must not only know the difference between words such as "cat" and "hat," and how to hold these words in memory. They must further possess the awareness of phonemes, which allows them to appreciate the fact that, among other things, "cat" and "hat" differ in one phoneme, namely the first, and share a final phoneme, which is the initial one in "top"; otherwise the alphabet will remain a mystery to them, and its virtues are unrealized.

B. The Problem of Specific Reading Difficulty

One way to discover the problems that limit success in learning to read is to examine the differences between children who become poor readers and those who become skilled readers. We have now developed some ideas about where to look for those differences, for it is clear that language-processing and phoneme awareness problems might lead to reading problems. But before we turn to a survey of research that concerns each of these two areas, a bit more background is in order. It is appropriate to consider some of the ways in which psychologists and educators have tried to explain reading disability in the past. We might also ask if there are any indications that a linguistic account of poor reading will be more successful than some of the previously popular theories have been.

---

1. Some Less Successful
Accounts of Poor Reading

As Rutter (1978) has noted, learning to read is a specific example of a complex learning task, which correlates about 0.6 with IQ. Yet a low IQ cannot be the sole basis of reading problems, because some children are backwards in reading ability but average in intelligence (Rutter and Yule, 1973). Children who possess a seemingly adequate IQ (typically 90 or higher) but nonetheless encounter reading problems are said to have a specific reading difficulty, as their actual reading ability lags between 1 and 2 yr behind that which is predicted on the basis of their age, IQ, and social standing. For these children, something other than general intelligence must be the primary cause of many instances of poor reading.

In attempting to discover the cause of early problems, many early theories were biased by an assumption that influenced psychologists and educators alike. That assumption stemmed from the view that reading is first and foremost a complex visual skill that demands differentiation and recognition of visual stimuli. Owing to it, models of skilled reading have often been biased toward clarification of how readers see and recognize the various letter and word shapes, and many studies of the cause of poor reading tried to blame early reading difficulty on some problem in the visual domain. Recently, however, visual theories of reading disability have become less and less popular, for it seems that, at best, only a few of the children who are poor readers actually suffer from perceptual malfunctions that somehow prevent recognition, differentiation, or memory of visual forms. In short, visual skills do not reliably distinguish among children who differ in reading ability (for recent reviews of these findings, see Rutter, 1978; Stanovich, 1982a; Vellutino, 1979), so visual problems would not seem to be the primary cause of many instances of reading problems.

Let me follow Mann and Brady (1988) in mentioning two pieces of supporting evidence that show just how unfair it is to blame the majority of early reading problems on visual problems. First, 5- to 6-yr-old children who were identified as having deficient visual perception and/or visuomotor coordinating skills show no more instances of reading difficulty at age 8–9 yr than do matched controls who possess no such deficits (Robinson and Schwartz, 1973). Second, while it is true that all young children tend to confuse spatially reversible letters such as "b" and "d" and "p" and "q" until they are 7 or 8 yr old (Gibson *et al.*, 1962), letter and sequence reversals actually account for only a small proportion of the reading errors that are made by children in this age range. Even children who have been formally diagnosed as dyslexic make relatively few letter and sequence reversal errors (Fisher *et al.*, 1977).

Theories that placed primary emphasis on cross-modal integration have also been popular at one time or another (Birch and Belmont, 1964; see reviews by Benton, 1975; Rutter and Yule, 1973). Their misconception was that reading involved translating visual information into auditory information and that this cross-modal match was the source of the problem. Such theories have met much of the same fate as theories that emphasized visual deficiencies as the cause of reading problems. When investigators carefully examined the behavior of skilled readers, they realized that the translation was not directly from visual to auditory information, visual information was first translated into an abstract linguistic code. When they considered children's ability to map between information presented to the visual and auditory modalities, they also began to realize that an abstract linguistic code was often the basis for the cross-modal integration. Finally, researchers began to realize that when visual-auditory integration problems were present, then so were auditory-auditory problems and even visual-visual ones. Thus, the poor reader's problems with visual-auditory integration have come to be viewed as one of the many consequences of a more general linguistic coding problem, which hurts integration within modalities as well as between them (for a review, see Vellutino, 1979).

Other theories have suffered from similar attempts to explain an observation about poor readers in terms that are somehow too general. For example, certain theories were preoccupied by the fact that reading involves remembering an ordered sequence of letters in a word and of words in a sentence, etc. Hence, it was suggested that poor sequential order memory (Corkin, 1974) or poor short-term memory (Morrison *et. al.*, 1977) might be a cause of poor reading. A focus on memory problems was not a bad direction for theories to take, but some other observations about the specific pattern of poor readers' disabilities and abilities indicate that some refinements are in order. Good and poor readers do not differ on all tasks that require temporary memory of items or their order. Good and poor beginning readers are equivalent, for example, in ability to remember faces (Liberman *et al.*, 1982) or visual stimuli that cannot readily be assigned verbal labels (Katz *et al.*, 1981; Liberman *et al.*, 1982; Swanson, 1978). Only when the to-be-remembered stimuli can be linguistically coded do children who are poor readers consistently fail to do as well as good readers (Liberman *et al.*, 1982; Katz *et al.*, 1981; Swanson, 1978).

Various other general or visual accounts of reading disability have been offered in the literature (for a review, see Carr 1981). These tend to be inadequate because they fail to explain why poor readers often do as well as good readers on nonlinguistic tasks, yet lag behind good readers in performance on many linguistic tasks (for recent reviews, see Mann and Brady, 1988; Stanovich, 1982a, b; Vellutino, 1979). For the sake of brevity, such general accounts will not be discussed here; instead, let us turn to the more positive task of reviewing that evidence which links language and reading problems.

---
2. A Language-Based Perspective May Offer a Better Account

The previous paragraphs mentioned several studies that demonstrate that good and poor readers are distinguished by their performance on certain linguistic tasks but not by their performance on comparably demanding nonlinguistic ones (e.g., as shown by Brady *et al.*, 1983; Katz *et al.*, 1981; Liberman *et al.*, 1982; Mann and Liberman, 1984; Swanson, 1978). That evidence receives further support from a consideration of the frequency of reading difficulties in children with various sorts of handicaps. As Rutter (1978) observes, whereas children deficient in visual-perceptual and/or visual-motor skills do not encounter reading difficulty any more frequently than matched controls (Money, 1973; Robinson and Schwartz, 1973), speech- and language-retarded children encounter reading problems at least six times often than controls do (Ingram *et al.*, 1970; Mason, 1976). But we can ask whether there is a more fine-grained analysis of the language problems found among poor readers. Are some areas of language skill more problematic than others? Considered broadly, the language disabilities that tend to be found among poor beginning readers fall within the two categories of language processing and phoneme awareness. Let us now proceed to examine the evidence within each area.

C. Language-Processing Problems Associated with Poor Reading

Since the mid-1970s, activity in the psychology of early reading problems has been considerable, and study after study has uncovered some link between difficulties in learning to read and difficulties with some aspect of spoken language processing. Such a link is clearly established beyond question, not only in English (for a review, cf. Mann, 1986) but in Swedish (Lundberg *et al.*, 1980), Japanese, and Chinese (Stevenson *et al.*, 1982) as well. In the case of English, there have also been considerable attempts to more precisely specify the nature of the language problems that typify poor beginning readers. These attempts can be organized in terms of the four levels of language processing that were identified in Section III.A.1 as being important to beginning reading: speech perception, vocabulary skills, linguistic short-term memory, and syntax and semantics.

---
1. Speech Perception

The possibility that some aspect of speech perception might be a special problem for poor readers receives support from a study by Brady *et al.* (1983). Their research considered a group of beginning readers who did not differ from each other in age, IQ, or audiometry scores but strongly differed in reading ability. The children were asked to identify spoken words or environmental sounds under a normal listening condition and under a noisy condition, and the performance of the good and poor readers was compared. The results indicated that the good and poor readers could equally identify the environmental sounds, whatever the listening condition. As long as the words were not masked by noise, the good and poor readers performed equivalently on these items as well, but the poor readers made almost 33% more errors than the good readers when they were asked to identify the spoken words in the noisy condition. This result implies, as other research has suggested (Goetzinger *et al.*, 1960), that poor readers have difficulties with speech perception when the listening conditions are less than optimal.

Another suggestion to this effect comes from studies that compare the categorical perception of synthetic speech stimuli by good and poor beginning readers. In such studies, categorical perception was evident in both groups of subjects; yet the poor readers differed from the good readers either in failing to meet the level of intercategory discrimination predicted on the basis of their identification responses (Brandt and Rosen, 1980) or in failing to give consistent identification responses (Godfrey *et al.*, 1981). These findings have been interpreted as the reflection of deficient speech perception processes on the part of poor readers (but they may also relate to a problem with remembering speech sounds, because memory plays an obvious role in discrimination tasks as well as in many identification tasks).

2. Vocabulary Skills

There are quite a few indications that reading ability is related to certain vocabulary skills, depending on how reading ability is measured and on what type of vocabulary skill is at issue. Reading ability can be measured in terms of the ability to read individual words (decoding) or to understand the meaning of sentences and paragraphs (comprehension). In the case of beginning readers, decoding and comprehension tests are correlated quite highly, implying that children who differ on one type of test will usually differ on the other as well. Still, in some cases the two types of tests identify different groups of good and poor readers that may lead researchers to different conclusions about the cause of poor reading (for a discussion, see Stanovich, 1988). Vocabulary skills are a case in point; future research may uncover other cases as well.

Vocabulary skills are also tested with two different types of test. One type is recognition vocabulary tests such as the Peabody Picture Vocabulary Test, which requires the child to point to a picture that illustrates a word. Recognition vocabulary has sometimes been related to early reading ability (see Stanovich *et al.*, 1984b), although it is not always a very significant predictor (see Wolf and Goodglass,

1986). The utility of this test may depend on how reading ability is measured, as the relationship seems stronger for tests of reading comprehension like the Reading Survey of the Metropolitan (see Stanovich *et al.*, 1988) than for tests of word recognition such as the Word Identification and Word Attack tests of the Woodcock (see Mann and Liberman, 1984).

The other type of vocabulary test is naming or productive vocabulary tests such as the Boston Naming Test, which requires the child to produce the word that a picture illustrates. Productive vocabulary gives clearer indications of a link between reading ability and vocabulary skill, and evidence indicates that this link exists whether reading skills are measured in terms of decoding or comprehension. Performance on the Boston Naming Test predicted both the word recognition and the reading comprehension ability of kindergarten children far more accurately than did performance on the Peabody Picture Vocabulary Test (Wolf, 1984; Wolf and Goodglass, 1986). Tests of continuous naming (sometimes called rapid automatized naming), which require children to name a series of repeating objects, letters, or colors, also show that children who are poor readers require more time to name the series than good readers do (see, e.g., Denckla and Rudel, 1976; Blachman, 1984; Wolf, 1984).

A causal link between naming problems and reading problems is indicated by the discovery that performance on naming tests can predict future reading ability. Wolf (1984) noted that, whereas continuous naming tests using objects and colors are predictive of early problems with word recognition, problems with rapid letter recognition and retrieval play a more prolonged role in the reading of severely impaired readers, even in reading comprehension. In the author's laboratory, students and the author have been using a test of letter-naming ability in longitudinal studies of kindergarten children (Mann, 1984; Mann and Ditunno, 1990) and have consistently found that kindergarteners who take more time to name a randomized array of the capital letters are significantly more likely to perform poorly on word decoding tests and comprehension tests that are administered in first grade. Furthermore, present letter naming apparently predicts future reading ability more consistently than present reading ability predicts future letter naming ability (for relevant evidence, see Mann and Ditunno, in press; also see Stanovich *et al.*, 1988). Thus, something other than a lack of educational experience probably is preventing these children from naming the letter names as fast as other children can, and that something could be a problem with productive vocabulary skills.

A final piece of evidence about the vocabulary problems of poor readers comes from a study by Katz (1986), who found that children who perform poorly on a decoding test are particularly prone to difficulties in producing low-frequency and polysyllabic names and suggested that, for such words, these children may possess less phonologically complete lexical representations than good readers do. On the basis of his research, he further suggests that, because poor readers often have access to aspects of the correct phonological representation of a word, even though they are unable to produce that word correctly, their problem may be attributable to phonological deficiencies in the structure of the lexicon rather than to the process of lexical access, per se.

3. Phonetic Short-Term Memory

The observation that poor readers perform less well than good readers on a variety of short-term memory tests has given rise to one of the more fruitful lines of research in the field (see Mann and Brady, 1988). It has often been noted that poor readers tend to perform less well on the digit span test and are deficient in the ability to recall strings of letters, nonsense syllables, or words in order, whether the stimuli are presented by ear or by eye. Poor readers even fail to recall the words of spoken sentences as accurately as good readers do (for references to these effects, see Jorm, 1979; Mann et al., 1980). Evidence that these differences are not merely consequences of differences in reading ability has come from a longitudinal study that showed that problems with recalling a sequence of words can precede the attainment of reading ability and may actually serve to presage future reading problems (Mann and Liberman, 1984).

In searching for an explanation of this pattern of results, researchers turned to the research that was discussed in Section II.B, namely that research that indicated that linguistic materials such as letters, words, etc. are held in short-term memory through use of phonetic representation. Liberman, Shankweiler, and their colleagues (Shankweiler et al., 1979) were the first to suggest that the linguistic short-term memory difficulties of poor readers might reflect a problem with using this type of representation. Several experiments have supported this hypothesis. These show that when recalling letter strings (Shankweiler et al., 1979), word strings (Mann et al., 1980; Mann and Liberman, 1984), and sentences (Mann et al., 1980) poor readers are much less sensitive than good readers to a manipulation of the phonetic structure of the materials (i.e., the density of words that rhyme). Indeed, good readers can be made to appear like poor readers when they are asked to recall a string of words in which all of the words rhyme (such as "bat," "cat," "rat," "hat," and "mat"), whereas poor readers perform at the same level whether the words rhyme or not. This observation had led to the postulation that poor readers—and children who are likely to become poor readers—are for some reason less able to use phonetic structure as a means of holding material in short-term memory (Mann et al., 1980; Mann and Liberman, 1984; Shankweiler et al., 1979).

One might ask, at this point, whether poor readers are avoiding phonetic representation altogether or merely using it less well. We have obtained little evidence that poor readers employ a visual form of memory instead of a phonetic one (Mann, 1984), although there have been indications that they may place greater reliance on word meaning (Byrne and Shea, 1979). Evidence that poor readers are attempting to use phonetic representation has been found in the types of errors that they make as they attempt to recall or recognize spoken words in a short-term memory task (Brady et al., 1983, 1989). These errors reveal that poor readers make use of many of the same features of phonetic structure as good readers do. They make the same sort of phonetically principled errors—they merely make more of them.

4. Syntax and Semantics

Do poor readers have a problem with the syntax (grammar) and the semantics (meaning) of language in addition to their problem with speech perception, vocabulary, and using phonetic structure in short-term memory? The observation that poor readers cannot repeat sentences as well as good readers has led to some obvious questions about these higher-level language skills and their involvement in reading problems.

Quite a few studies have examined the syntactic abilities of poor readers. An accumulating body of evidence indicates that poor readers do not comprehend sentences as well as good readers do (for a review, see Mann et al., 1989). It has been shown that good and poor readers differ in the ability both to repeat and to comprehend spoken sentences that contain relative clauses such as "the dog jumped over the cat that chased the monkey" (Mann et al., 1985). They also perform less well on instructions from the Token Test such as "touch the small red square and the large blue triangle" (Smith et al., 1987). They also are less able to distinguish the meaning of spoken sentences such as "he showed her bird the seed" from "he showed her the birdseed," which use the stress pattern of the sentence (its prosody) and the position of the article "the" to mark the boundary between the indirect object and the direct object.

To explain these and other sentence comprehension problems that have been observed among poor readers, the author and her colleagues have been struck by the fact that a short-term memory problem could lead to problems with comprehending sentences whose processing somehow stresses short-term memory. When they examined the results of the studies mentioned above, they found little evidence that the poor readers were having trouble with the grammatical structures being used in the sentences that caused them problems. In fact the structures were often ones that young children master within the first few years of life and ones that the poor readers could understand if the sentence was short enough (for a discussion, see Mann et al., 1989). Instead, they found much evidence that the comprehension problem was predominantly due to the memory problem discussed in the previous section. It seems as if poor readers are just as sensitive to syntactic structure as good readers; they fail to understand sentences because they cannot hold an adequate representation of the sentence in short-term memory (for a discussion, see Mann et al., 1985, 1989; Smith et al., in press).

At present, then, while it is clear that poor readers do have sentence comprehension problems, there is little reason to think that their difficulties reflect a problem with the syntax of the language. But the issue of whether or not poor readers are deficient in syntactic skills is far from resolved and will have to await further research. Goldman (1976) is correct in noting that such syntactic differences as have been reported among good and poor readers could be either the cause of reading difficulty or a consequence of different amounts of reading experience. It is also worth noting that such deficits as do exist are relatively subtle, with poor readers merely performing as somewhat younger children rather than as good readers.

As for the question of semantic impairments among poor readers, here, there is no reason to presume any real deviance exists. If anything, poor readers place greater reliance on semantic context and semantic representation than good readers do, perhaps in compensation for their other language difficulties (for a review, see Stanovitch, 1982b; also see Byrne and Shea, 1979; Simpson *et al.*, 1983).

D. Problems with Phoneme Awareness Associated with Poor Reading

Possessing adequate phonetic perception and short-term memory skills, an adequate mental lexicon, and the ability to recover the syntactic and semantic structure of utterances is only part of the requirement of reading success. As noted in Section II.B, successful readers of the alphabet must go beyond these tacit language-processing abilities to achieve an explicit awareness of phonemes. Let us now turn to studies concerned with the pertinence of phonological sophistication to success in learning to read an alphabetic orthography.

---

1. Evidence from the Analysis of Reading Errors

The errors that a person makes can be informative about the difficulties that produce those errors, and oral reading errors can offer an important source of evidence about the cause of reading problems. A consideration of these errors has shown that a lack of phoneme awareness is responsible for making beginning reading difficult for all young children (Shankweiler and Liberman, 1972), including dyslexic ones (Fisher *et al.*, 1977). As noted earlier, such errors do not tend to involve visual confusions or letter or sequence reversals to any appreciable degree. What they did apparently reflect is a problem with integrating the phonological information that letter sequences convey. Hence, children often tend to be correct as to the pronunciation of the first letter in a word but have more and more difficulty with subsequent letters, with a particular problem with vowels as opposed to consonants. For more detailed presentation of these findings and their implications, the reader is referred to papers by Shankweiler and Liberman (1972) and Fisher *et al.*, (1977) and also to a paper by Russell (1982), which suggests that deficient phoneme awareness may account for the reading difficulties of adult dyslexics.

---

2. Evidence from Tasks that Measure Awareness Directly

Most of the studies of phoneme awareness have concerned tasks that directly measure awareness. These tasks require children to play language "games" that manipulate the phonemes within a word in one way or another: counting them, deleting them, choosing words that contain the same phoneme, etc. The use of these tasks has revealed that phoneme awareness develops later than phonetic perception and the use of phonetic representation and remains a chronic problem for those individuals who are poor readers.

Research involving such tasks began with a study by Liberman and her colleagues who asked whether or not a sample of 4–6-yr-olds could learn to play syllable counting games and phoneme counting games in which the idea was to tap the number of syllables–phonemes in a spoken word (Liberman *et al.*, 1974). It was discovered that none of the nursery school children could tap the number of phonemes in a spoken word, while half of them managed to tap the number of syllables. Only 17% of the kindergarteners could tap phonemes, while again, about half of them could tap syllables. At 6 yr old, 90% of the children could tap syllables and 70% could tap phonemes. From such findings about children's sensitivity to the number of phonemes and syllables in spoken words, the awareness of phonemes and syllables clearly develops considerably between the ages of 4 and 6 yr. It is also clear that awareness of phonemes is slower to develop than awareness of syllables. Finally, both types of awareness markedly improve at just the age when children are learning to read (Liberman *et al.*, 1974).

Numerous experiments involving widely diverse subjects, school systems, and measurement devices have shown a strong positive correlation between a lack of awareness about phonemes and current problems in learning to read (see, e.g., Alegria *et al.*, 1982; Fox and Routh, 1976; Lundberg *et al.*, 1980; Liberman *et al.*, 1980b; Perfetti, 1985; Yopp, 1988). Also, evidence indicates that lack of awareness about syllables is associated with reading disability (Katz, 1986). Finally, studies of kindergarten children provide evidence that problems with phoneme segmentation (Blachman, 1984; Helfgott, 1976) and problems with syllable segmentation (Mann and Liberman, 1984; Wagner *et al.*, in press) can presage future reading difficulty. For example, we have found that 85% of a population of kindergarten children who went on to become good readers in the first grade correctly counted the number of syllables in spoken words, whereas only 17% of the future poor readers could do so (Mann and Liberman, 1984). In another study, a kindergarten battery of tests that assessed phoneme awareness accounted for 66% of the variance in children's first-grade reading ability (Stanovich *et al.*, 1984a).

IV. Some Plausible Origins of the Language Problems That Lead to Reading Problems

---

Having surveyed some, though certainly not all, of the many findings that link reading difficulty to problems with language skills, we can now appropriately consider a related line of research that concerns the causes of the language problems that lead to reading problems. Both theoretical and practical matters are at stake in such research, because if we knew why poor readers are lacking in certain language skills, then we might be able to develop more effective means of early diagnosis and more remedies for reading difficulty.

Much of the available literature on the causes of language-processing problems is centered on what will be referred to here to as constitutional causes. These involve those factors that are somehow intrinsic to the child, such as his or her brain structure, genetic makeup, and rate of physical development. Problems with phoneme awareness have also been explained in these terms, but it has been more common to attribute problems in this area to a lack of sufficient experience, such as insufficient exposure to instruction in the use of an alphabetic writing system. We shall consider constitutional explanations and experiential explanations in turn.

A. Constitutional Factors

As representative examples of theories that place the cause of a child's language problems within the child's constitution, genetic theories, neuropsychological theories, and the theories that postulate some type of developmental lag have been chosen. Each of the following sections contains a representative, but by no means exhaustive, summary of each type of account, and the different accounts should not be taken as mutually exclusive. For example, a genetic account might help a neuropsychological account to explain why the brains of poor readers are subtly different from those of good readers, and both of these accounts may help to explain why the language development of many poor readers seems delayed.

---
1. Genetic Theories

That reading problems and language problems do tend to run in certain families was first noted by Thomas (1905), and has received considerable attention in recent literature as well (see, e.g., Owen, 1978; Owen et al., 1971; Rutter, 1978). In fact, whether or not a child comes from a family that contains other dyslexic individuals is one of the most important factors to consider when attempting to predict that child's likelihood of becoming a poor reader (see Scarborough, 1988).

Further evidence about the genetic basis of dyslexia has become available through the use of more sophisticated forms of analysis. Ample evidence now indicates that the concordance rate of dyslexia in monozygotic (i.e., identical) twins is consistently higher than in dizygotic (fraternal) ones, and the Colorado Twin Study is addressing this point (see DeFries et al., 1987). There is also interesting information about the type of genetic transmission. Some instances of dyslexia have been linked to an aberration on chromosome 15 (Smith et al., 1983). There are also some indications of considerable genetic heterogeneity (Smith et al.,

1986). Research on the genetic basis of dyslexia will surely be an exciting area for years to come.

---
2. Neuropsychological Accounts

Neuropsychological accounts seek to place the cause of the language problem within the brain structure of the affected child. One of the first accounts of this sort was offered by Orton (1937) in his now famous theory of strephosymbolia. In that theory, mirror reversals (which Orton erroneously thought to be the predominant symptom of reading disability) were attributed to insufficiently developed cerebral dominance. This insufficiency further manifested itself, according to Orton, in such abnormalities of lateral preference as mixed dominance.

Orton's theory has given rise to considerable research. On the one hand, it has been falsified by findings that reading difficulty is not associated with any particular pattern of handedness, eyedness, or footedness (for a review, see Rutter, 1978). It has also motivated quite a number of studies of cerebral lateralization for language processing among good and poor readers, with mixed results. Some such studies have provided evidence that poor readers show a reversal of the normal anatomical asymmetries between the left and right hemispheres, in conjunction with a lower verbal IQ (Hier et al., 1978). Others have reported that poor readers may show a lack of cerebral dominance for language processing (see, e.g., Keefe and Swinney, 1979; Zurif and Carson, 1970). But, at best, only a weak association can exist between abnormal lateralization and poor reading, because not all of the individuals who display abnormal cerebral lateralization are poor readers (Hier et al., 1978). It must also be recognized that several other studies have failed to find that good and poor readers differ in the extent or direction of the lateralization for language processing (Fennell et al., 1983; McKeever and van Deventer, 1975).

Overall, the data are not particularly supportive of Orton's thesis about incomplete cerebral dominance as the explanation of reading difficulty; however, Orton may still have been correct in the spirit, if not the letter, of his explanation. If we accept the left hemisphere to be the mediator of language processing (in the majority of individuals), and if we accept that language processes are deficient among poor readers, then certainly we may suppose that some anatomical or neurochemical abnormality of the left hemisphere is involved in early reading difficulty. This is the position taken in a new neuropsychological theory by Geschwind and Galaburda (1987), which views developmental dyslexia as a consequence of slowed development of the left hemisphere. The slowed development is postulated to be a consequence of early exposure to the hormone testosterone, which explains the greater instance of reading problems among young boys. Thus far, the Geschwind and Galaburda theory is supported by autopsies of the brains of several adult dyslexics and by a certain profile of disabilities (language problems), abilities (spatial skills), and other traits (left handedness, allergies) that distinguish the population of dyslexics from the general population. Further tests of this theory are a topic for future research.

---

3. Maturational Lag Accounts

The third class of constitutional explanations seeks to explain poor readers' language difficulties as the consequence of a maturational lag in development (see, e.g., Fletcher *et al.*, 1981), which may be specific to language development (Mann and Liberman, 1984), especially in the case of dyslexic children (Stanovich, 1988). Maturational lag has been offered to explain the problems of young children who are poor readers, their word decoding problems (Stanovich, 1988), their speech perception difficulties (Brandt and Rosen, 1980), their problems with phonetic representation in temporary memory and their problems with phoneme awareness (Mann and Liberman, 1984; Watson and Engle, 1982), and their sentence comprehension problems (Mann *et al.*, 1989). Such theories also provide an interesting account of adolescent learning disability, (Wong *et al.*, 1989).

Maturational lag theories have the virtue of providing a ready explanation of one of the more common findings in the field, namely that the performance of poor readers never really deviates from that of good readers but, rather, merely involves more of the kinds of errors typical of slightly younger children (Mann *et al.*, 1989). They are also consistent with some other observations about the population of poor readers. First, there is the observation that boys encounter reading problems more often than girls (Mann and Liberman, 1980; Rutter and Yule, 1973). It is well known that boys mature less rapidly than girls do. It has also been shown that a slower rate of physical maturation tends to be associated with a pattern of mental abilities in which spatial processing skills are superior to language (Waber, 1977). Given these observations, one should expect to find disproportionately many boys with lesser language skills and, hence, disproportionately many boys who encounter reading difficulty among children at a given age. It is also the case that children with low birthweight are at risk for reading problems (Rutter and Yule, 1973). Low birthweight often reflects a premature birth, and prematurely born infants may reach the first milestones of language development relatively later in postgestational life than do those infants born at full term (Gleitman, 1981). Hence, they show a lag in language development and would be expected to encounter reading problems.

The primary difficulty with the concept of maturational lag is that it cannot, as yet, explain why only certain language difficulties tend to be found among poor readers. Perhaps we might want to conceive of a maturational lag that is confined to one area of language skill, given the findings summarized earlier. We will have more to say about the identity of this area in the final section of this chapter. Another problem with maturational lag theories is that the language-processing difficulties of poor readers can persist after early childhood to adolescence (McKeever and

van Deventer, 1975) and beyond (Scarborough, 1984; Jackson and McClelland, 1979); i.e., the language-processing skills of poor readers may never really catch up to those of good readers. Perhaps the concept of a lag in development will need to be refined to allow for the possibility that language development in poor readers is not only delayed but also reaches a premature plateau. In any event, such problems are not insurmountable, and the possibility that reading difficulty involves a specific maturational lag in the development of language-processing skills is a most intriguing one, which should spark considerable research in the years to come.

B. Experiential Factors

Rutter and Madge (1976) noted that poor reading and low verbal intelligence tend to associate with low socioeconomic status and large family size. In discussing their findings about "cycles of disadvantage," these investigators note that both genetic and environmental influences are to be held responsible. We have already discussed the possibility of a genetic basis for reading problems, so let us now turn to the evidence that the environment can play an important role in the language skills that are important to reading. Experience is no doubt important to the child's development of the language-processing skills involved in speech perception, vocabulary, etc.; however, the role of the environment in poor readers' problems in these areas has not been very well explored and remains a topic for future research. However, a wealth of evidence exists on the role of the environment—the educational environment—in the development of phoneme awareness.

In considering the role of the environment in the development of phoneme awareness, let us return to the spurt in phoneme awareness that occurs at the age of 6 yr (Liberman *et al.*, 1974). Why should such a spurt occur? Phoneme awareness is a cognitive skill of sorts, and, as such, must surely demand the attainment of a certain degree of intellectual maturity. Yet, 6 yr is the age at which most children in America begin to receive instruction in reading and writing, and there is reason to suspect that not only may phoneme awareness be important for the acquisition of reading, being taught to read may at the same time help to develop phoneme awareness (see, e.g., Alegria, *et al.*, 1982; Liberman *et al.*, 1980b; Morais, *et al.*, 1979).

It has been reported that illiterate adults are unable to manipulate the phonetic structure of spoken words (Morais *et al.*, 1979). Another study, conducted in Belgium, reveals that first graders taught largely by a phonics method did spectacularly better on a task requiring phoneme segmentation than did other children taught by a largely whole-word method (Alegria *et al.*, 1982). It would seem that awareness of phonemes is enhanced by methods of reading instruction that direct the child's attention to the phonetic structure of words, and it may even depend on such instruction.

However, experience alone cannot be the only factor behind some child failure to achieve phoneme awareness. This is aptly shown by a finding that among a group of

6-yr-old skilled readers and 10-yr-old disabled readers who were matched for reading ability, the disabled readers performed significantly worse on a phoneme awareness task, even though they would be expected to have had more reading instruction than the younger children (Bradley and Bryant, 1978). Here it could be argued that some constitutional factor limited the disabled readers' ability to profit from instruction and, thus, limited their attainment of phonological sophistication. Indeed, Pennington *et al.* (in press) have offered some new and interesting evidence that deficient phoneme awareness is the primary trait of individuals who are familiar dyslexics.

V. Summary and Concluding Remarks

This chapter has proceeded from a consideration of the importance of certain language skills to reading, to a survey of evidence that links problems with these language skills to early reading disability, to a consideration of some plausible origins of these problems. By way of a conclusion, a generalization about the type of language problems that cause reading problems and about how we might improve upon our characterization of the relation between reading and language problems is now offered. Also, a few words speculate about the prospects for future research in the prediction and prevention of reading problems.

A. The Phonological Core Deficit: A Language-Oriented Perspective on Reading Problems

The survey of the literature on the relation between language-processing skills and reading problems indicates that poor readers—and children who are likely to become poor readers—tend to have problems with phoneme awareness and also with three aspects of language-processing skill: (1) speech perception under difficult listening conditions; (2) vocabulary, especially when vocabulary is measured in terms of naming ability; and (3) using a phonetic representation in linguistic short-term memory. A logical interrelation exists among these difficulties, for they all involve phonological processes that concern the sound pattern of language. Hence, we may speculate that the cause of many instances of reading disability is some problem within the phonological system, something that could be referred to as a phonological deficit (see Mann, 1986; Stanovich, 1988).

In this chapter the emphasis has been on the language problems of reading-disabled children in general, and no attempt has been made to differentiate between dyslexic children and so-called "garden-variety" poor readers. From the perspective of present research, both groups of children seem to form a continuous distribution (see Stanovich, 1988). Both have problems with the phonological skills of primary interest in this paper, and t he phonological core deficit seems just as characteristic of dyslexic children as of garden-variety poor readers. To date, the only language measure that distinguishes the two groups of children is receptive vocabulary, which may account for the lack of consensus about the role of receptive vocabulary problems in reading, as discussed in Section III.C.2. All other differences among the groups seem to involve real word knowledge and strategic abilities: The dyslexic children possess superior skills in these nonlinguistic areas, hence the discrepancy between their IQ and their reading ability, whereas the garden-variety poor readers may show a developmental delay in these skills as well as in their phonological ones (for a discussion, see Stanovich, 1988).

Future research can help us approach a more accurate description of the phonological core deficit and its role in the reading problems of different groups of children. For example, it may also help us discern the extent of differences among children within each group, informing us as to whether there are different problems or different clusters of problems for different children. In this regard, it is interesting to note Pennington and his colleagues' observation that the language problems of adults from dyslexic families tend to be restricted to phoneme awareness, whereas those of individuals from nondyslexic families demonstrate problems with linguistic short-term memory as well as problems with phoneme awareness (Pennington *et al.*, in press). In the future, researchers will surely try to determine whether or not this distinction applies to the population of young children who have reading problems as well as it applies to that of adult disabled readers.

B. Practical Applications and Implications for Future Research

One of the practical benefits of the research described in this chapter is its potential for suggesting ways of predicting and remediating early reading difficulty. One obvious benefit concerns screening devices for identifying children at risk for early reading problems. Phonological processing skills such as the ability to rapidly access the names of objects and the ability to make effective use of phonetic representation in short-term memory have already been shown to be effective kindergarten predictors of first-grade reading success (see, e.g., Blachman, 1984; Mann and Liberman, 1984; Mann, 1984; Mann and Ditunno, 1990). It is a task for future research to consider other tests such as tests of speech perception and tests of the ability to comprehend sentences that place special demands on short-term memory. It will also be important for future studies to address the very practical matter of how to administer such tests to groups of children; thus far, the studies that have successfully predicted future reading problems have involved two or more sessions of individual testing and would not be practical for large-scale use in public school systems.

Some evidence indicates that tests of phoneme and syllable awareness may be even better predictors of reading ability than tests of language processing (Mann and Ditunno, 1990; Yopp, 1988). Thus, it is even more important that such tests be refined for practical administration to groups of children. In this regard, the author and her students have had some success in developing an "invented spelling test," in which preliterate children are asked to try to write some familiar words. Their responses are quite unconventional but show considerable creativity and considerable awareness of the fact that words can be broken down into smaller phonological units. When those responses are scored in terms of their ability to capture the sound of the word the child is trying to spell, we find this score to be a very successful kindergarten predictor of first-grade reading ability (for a discussion of the test, see Mann *et al.*, 1987; Mann and Ditunno, 1990).

The research surveyed by this chapter may also be of interest to those who are concerned with the remediation of reading problems. As we come closer to identifying the linguistic problems associated with specific reading difficulty —and their causes—we should also come closer to pointing the way toward more effective procedures for remediation of those problems. For example, if a maturational lag in language development is the cause of reading difficulty, then perhaps we should attempt to identify children at risk for such a lag and consider delaying beginning reading instruction until a point in time when those children have language skills that are more optimal. However, we would not want to delay all education—math, geography, etc.—for it is far from clear that poor readers, especially dyslexic ones, are lagging in those areas of development that support the ability to learn other types of curriculum (see Mann *et al.*, 1989; Stanovich, 1988). We might also want to continue researching the possibility that environmental enrichment can decrease the extent of these children's language-processing problems and pursue research to that effect.

Certainly the brightest prospects for remediation are offered by research that has shown that various types of training can facilitate phoneme awareness. Elsewhere, the author and her colleagues have suggested that the best favor we can do for all children is to promote their phoneme awareness so that we may let them in on the secrets of the alphabetic principle as early as possible (I.Y. Liberman, 1982; Liberman and Mann, 1980; Mann, 1986). Some very interesting and very practical advice on how to facilitate phoneme awareness is currently available from the work of such researchers as Liberman, Blachman, Bradley, and their colleagues (Blachman, 1984, 1989; Bradley and Bryant, 1985; I.Y. Liberman, 1982; Mann and Liberman, 1984; Liberman *et al.*, 1980b). They offer a variety of word games, nursery rhymes, and other prereading activities that will encourage the child's awareness of the way in which words break down into phonemes. Such activities will undoubtedly pave the way for phonics-oriented methods of instruction so obviously favored by current research (see Chall, 1979; Morais, in press) and so obviously in keeping with this chapter's focus on the importance of phoneme awareness in early reading.

Acknowledgments

Much of the research herein described was funded by NICHD Grant HD01994 and BRS Grant 05596 to Haskins Laboratories, Inc. Many of the same points were made in two other technical papers (Mann, 1986; Mann and Brady, 1988).

References

Alegria, J., and Pignot, E. (1979). Genetic aspects of verbal mediation in memory. *Ch. Dev.* 50, 235–238.

Alegria, J., Pignot, E., and Morais, J. (1982). Phonetic analysis of speech and memory codes in beginning readers. *Mem. Cognit.* 10, 451–456.

Baddeley, A. D. (1978). The trouble with levels: A reexamination of Craik and Lockhardt's framework for memory research. *Psycholog. Rev.* 85, 139–152.

Benton, A. (1975). Developmental dyslexia: Neurological aspects. *In* "Advances Neurology," Vol. 7 (W. J. Freelander, ed.). Raven Press, pp. 1–47. New York.

Birch, H. G., and Belmont, L. (1964). Auditory–visual integration in normal a retarded readers. *Am. J. Orthopsych.* 34, 852–861.

Blachman, B. (1984). Relationship of rapid naming and language analysis skills to kindergarten and first-grade reading achievement. *J. Educ. Psychol.* 76, 610–622.

Blachman, B. (1989). Phonological awareness and word recognition: Assessment intervention. *In* (A. G. Kamhi and H. W. Watts, eds.), "Reading Disabilities Developmental Language Perspective" pp. 133–158. College Hill, Boston.

Bradley, L., and Bryant, P. E. (1978). Difficulties in auditory organization as a possible cause of reading backwards. *Nature* 271, 746–747.

Bradley, L., and Bryant, P. (1985). "Rhyme and Reason in Reading and Spelling." University of Michigan Press, Ann Arbor.

Brady, S., Shankweiler, D., and Mann, V. (1983). Speech perception and memory coding in relation to reading ability. *J. Exp. Child Psychol.* 35, 345–367.

Brandt, J., and Rosen, J. J. (1980). Auditory phonemic perception in dyslexia: Categorical identification and discrimination of stop consonants. *Brain Lang.* 9, 324–337.

Bryden, M. P. (1972). Auditory-visual and sequential-spatial imaging in relation to reading ability. *Child Dev.* 43, 824–832.

Byrne, B., and Shea, P. (1979). Semantic and phonetic memory in beginning readers. *Mem. Cognit.* 7, 333–338.

Carr, T. H. (1981). Building theories of reading ability: On the relation between individual differences in cognitive skills and reading comprehension. *Cognition* 9, 73–114.

Chall, J. (1979). The great debate: Ten years later with a modest proposal for reading stages. *In* "Theory and Practice of Early Reading," Vol. I (L. Resnick and P. Weaver, eds.), pp. 29–55. Lawrence Erlbaum, Hillsdale, New Jersey.

Chomsky, N. (1964). Comments for project literacy meeting. Project Literacy Report No. 2, pp. 1–8. (M. Lester, ed.). "Reading in Applied Transformational Grammar" Reprinted *in* Holt Rinehart and Winston, New York.

Conrad. R. (1964). Acoustic confusions in immediate memory. *Br. J. Psychol.* 55, 75–84.

Conrad, R. (1972). Speech and reading. *In* "Language by Ear and by Eye: The Relationships between Speech and Reading" (J. F. Kavanaugh and I. G. Mattingly, eds.). pp. 205–240. MIT Press, Cambridge.

Corkin, S. (1974). Serial-order deficits in inferior readers. *Neuropsychologia* 12, 347–354.

Crowder, R. (1982). "The Psychology of Reading." Academic Press, New York.

Curtis, M. E. (1980). Development of components of reading skill. *J. Educ. Psychol.* 72, 656–669.

Daneman, M., and Carpenter, P. A. (1980). Individual differences in working memory and reading. *J. Verbal Learn. Verbal Behav.* 19, 450–466.

Daneman, M., and Case, R. (1981). Syntactic form, semantic complexity and shortterm memory: Influences on children's acquisition of new linguistic structures. *Dev. Psychol.* 17, 367–378.

DeFries, J. C., Fulker, D. W., and LaBuda, M. C. (1987). Evidence for genetic etiology in reading disability of twins. *Nature* 329, 537–539.

Denckla, M. B., and Rudel, R. G. (1976). Naming of object drawings by dyslexic and other learning-disabled children. *Brain Lang.* 3, 1–15.

Eimas, P. D. (1975). Distinctive feature codes in the short-term memory of children. *J. Exp. Child Psychol.* 19, 241–251.

Fennell, E. B., Satz, P., and Morris, R. (1983). The development of handedness and dichotic ear asymetries in relation to school achievement: A longitudinal study. *J. Exp. Child Psychol.* 35, 248–262.

Fisher, F. W., Liberman, I. Y., and Shankweiler, D. (1977). Reading reversals and developmental dyslexia: A further study. *Cortex* 14, 496–510.

Fletcher, J. M., Satz, P., and Scholes, R. (1981). Developmental changes in the linguistic performance correlates of reading achievements. *Brain Lang.* 13, 78–90.

Fox, B., and Routh, D. K. (1976). Phonemic analysis and synthesis as word-attack skills. *J. Educ. Psychol.* 69, 70–74.

Geschwind, N., and Galaburda, A. M. (1987). "Cerebral Lateralization." Bradford Books, Cambridge.

Gibson, E. J., Gibson, J. J., Pick, A. D., and Osser, R. (1962). A developmental study of the discrimination of letter-like forms. *J. Comp. Physiolog. Psychol.* 55, 897–906.

Gleitman, L. R. (1981). Maturational determinants of language growth. *Cognition* 10, 103–114.

Godfrey, J. L., Syrdal-Lasky, A. K., Millay, K. K., and Knox, C. M. (1981). Performance of dyslexic children on speech perception tasks. *J. Exp. Child Psychol.* 32, 401–424.

Goetzinger, C., Dirks, D., and Baer, C. J. (1960). Auditory discrimination and visual perception in good and poor readers. *Ann. Otol. Rhinol. Laryngol.* 69, 121–136.

Goldman, S. R. (1976). Reading skill and the minimum distance principle: A comparison of listening and reading comprehension. *J. Exp. Child Psychol.* 22, 123–142.

Hicks, C. (1980). The ITPA Visual Sequential Memory Test: An alternative interpretation of the implications for good and poor readers. *Br. J. Educ. Psychol.* 50, 16–25.

Hier, D., LeMay, M., Rosenberger, P., and Perlo, V. (1978). Developmental dyslexia. *Arch. Neurol.* 35, 90–92.

Hung, D. L., and Tzeng, O. J. L. (1981). Orthographic variations and visual information processing. *Psycholog.* 90, 377–414.

Ingram, T. T. S., Mason, A. W., and Blackburn, I. (1970). A retrospective study of 82 children with reading disability. *Dev. Med. Child Neurol.* 12, 271–281.

Jackson, M., and McClelland, J. L. (1979). Processing determinants of reading speed. *J. Exp. Psychol.: Gen.* 108, 151–181.

Jorm, A. F. (1979). The cognitive and neurological basis of developmental dyslexia: A theoretical framework and review. *Cognition* 7, 19–33.

Katz, R. B. (1986). Phonological deficiencies in children with reading disability: Evidence from an object naming task. *Cognition* 22, 225–257.

Katz, R. B., Shankweiler, D., and Liberman, I. Y. (1981). Memory for item order and phonetic recoding in the beginning reader. *J. Exp. Child Psychol.* 32, 474–484.

Keefe, B., and Swinney, D. (1979). On the role of hemispheric specialization in developmental dyslexia. *Cortex* 15, 471–481.

Kleiman, G. (1975). Speech recoding in reading. *J. Verbal Learn. Verbal Behav.* 14, 323–339.

Levy, B. A. (1977). Reading: Speech and meaning processes. *J. Verbal Learn. Verbal Behav.* 16, 623–638.

Liberman, A. M. (1982). On finding that speech is special. *Am. Psycholog.* 37, 148–167.

Liberman, A. M., Cooper, F. S., Shankweiler, D., and Studdert-Kennedy, M. (1967). Perception of the speech code. *Psycholog. Rev.* 74, 431–461.

Liberman, I. Y. (1982). A language-oriented view of reading and its disabilities *In* "Progress in Learning Disabilities," Vol. 5 (H. Mykelburst, ed.). pp. 81–101. Grune and Stratton, New York.

Liberman, I. Y., and Mann, V. A. (1980). Should reading remediation vary with the sex of the child? *In* "Sex Differences in Dyslexia" (A. Ansara, N. Geschwind, A. Galaburda, N. Albert, and N. Gartrell, eds.). pp. 151–168. The Orton Society, Towson, Maryland.

Liberman, I. Y., Shankweiler, D., Fisher, F. W., and Carter, B. (1974). Explicit syllable and phoneme segmentation in the young child. *J. Exp. Child Psychol.* 18, 201–212.

Libermann, I. Y., Shankweiler D., Liberman, A. M., Fowler, C., and Fisher, F. W. (1977). Phonetic segmentation and recoding in the beginning reader. *In* "Towards a Psychology of Reading: The Proceedings of the CUNY Conference" (A. S. Reber and D. Scarborough, eds.). Lawrence Earlbaum, Hillsdale, New Jersey.

Liberman, I. Y., Liberman, A. M., Mattingly, I. G., and Shankweiler, D. (1980a). Orthography and the beginning reader. *In* "Orthography, Reading and Dyslexia" (J. Kavanaugh and R. Venezky, eds.). University Park Press, Baltimore.

Liberman, I. Y., Shankweiler, D., Blachman, B., Camp, L., and Werfelman, M. (1980b). Steps towards literacy. Report prepared for Working Group on Learning Failure and Unused Learning Potential, President's Commission on Mental Health, November 1, 1977. *In* "Auditory Processing and Language: Clinical and Research Perspectives" (P. Levinson and C. H. Sloan, eds.). pp. 189–215. Grune & Stratton, New York.

Liberman, I. Y., Mann, V. A., Shankweiler, D., and Werfelman, M. (1982). Children's memory for recurring linguistic and non-linguistic material in relation to reading ability. *Cortex* 18, 367–375.

Lundberg, I., Olofsson, A., and Wall, S. (1980). Reading and spelling skills in the first school years predicated from phoneme awareness skills in kindergarten. *Scand. J. Pschol.* 21, 159–173.

Mann, V. A. (1984). Longitudinal prediction and prevention of early reading difficulty. *Ann. Dyslex* 34, 117–136.

Mann, V. A. (1986). Why some children encounter reading problems: The contribution of difficulties with language processing and linguistic sophistication to early reading disability. *In* "Psychological and Educational Perspectives on Learning Disabilities" (J. K. Torgesen and B. Y. Wong, eds.), pp. 133–159. Academic Press, New York.

Mann, V. A., and Brady, S. (1988). Reading disability: The role of language deficiencies. *J. Consult. Clin. Psychol.* 56, 811–816.

Mann, V. A., and Liberman, I. Y. (1984). Phonological awareness and verbal short-term memory: Can they presage early reading success? *J. Learn. Disabil.* 17, 592–598.

Mann, V. A., Liberman, I. Y., and Shankweiler, D. (1980). Children's memory for sentences and word strings in relation to reading ability. *Mem. Cognit.* 8, 329–335.

Mann, V. A., Shankweiler, D., and Smith, S. T. (1985). The association between comprehension of spoken sentences and early reading ability: The role of phonetic representation. *J. Child Lang.* 11, 627–643.

Mann, V. A., Cowin, E., and Schoenheimer, J. (1989). Phonological processing, language comprehension and reading ability. *J. Learn. Disabil.* 22, 76–89.

Mann, V. A., and Ditunno, P. (1990). Phonological deficiencies: Effective predictors of reading problems. *In* "Dyslexia: Neurophysiological and learning perspectives." (6, Pavlides, ed.) Wiley and Sons: New York.

Mann, V. A., Tobin. P., and Wilson R. (1987). Measuring phonological awareness through the invented spellings of kindergarten children. *Merill-Pelmer Quart.* **33**, 365–391.

Mason, W. (1976). Specific (developmental) dyslexia. *Dev. Med. Child Neurol.* **9**, 183–190.

Mattingly, I. G. (1972). Reading, the linguistic process, and linguistic awareness. *In* "Language by Ear and by Eye: The Relationship between Speech and Reading" pp. 133–148. MIT Press, Cambridge.

McKeever, W. F., and van Deventer, A. D. (1975). Dyslexic adolescents: Evidence of impaired visual and auditory language processing associated with normal lateralization and visual responsivity. *Cortex* **11**, 361–378.

Miller, J. L., and Eimas, P. D. (1983). Studies on the categorization of speech by infants. *Cognition* **13**, 135–166.

Money, J. (1973). Turner's syndrome and parietal lobe functions. *Cortex* **9**, 387–393.

Morais, J. (in press). Constraints on the development of phonological awareness. *In* "Phonological Processes in Literacy" (S. Brady and D. Shankweiler, eds.). Lawrence Erlbaum, Hillsdale, New Jersey.

Morais, J., Cary, L., Alegria. J., and Bertelson, P. (1979). Does awareness of speech as a sequence of phonemes arise spontaneously? *Cognition* **7**, 323–331.

Morrison, F. J., Giordani, B., and Nagy, J. (1977). Reading disability: An information processing analysis. *Science* **196**, 77–79.

Moskowitz, B. A. (1973). On the status of vowel shift in English. *In* "Cognitive Development and Acquisition of Language" (T. Moore, ed.), pp. 223–260, Academic Press, New York.

Orton, S. T. (1937). "Reading, Writing and Speech Problems in Children." Norton, New York.

Owen, F. W. (1978). Dyslexia—Genetic aspects. *In* "Dyslexia: An Appraisal of Current Knowledge" (A. L. Benton and D. Pearl, eds.), pp. 265–284. Oxford University Press, New York.

Owen, F. W., Adams, P. A., Forrest, T., Stolz, L. M., and Fischer, S. (1971). Learning disorders in children: Sibling studies. *In* "Monographs of the Society for Research in Child Development," **36**. University of Illinois Press, Chicago.

Pennington, B. F., Van Orden, G., Kirson, D., and Haith, M. (in press). Phonological processing skills in adult dyslexics. *In* "Phonological Processes in Literacy." Lawrence Erlbaum, Hillsdale, New Jersey.

Perfetti, C. A. (1985). "Reading Skill." Lawrence Erlbaum, Hillsdale, New Jersey.

Perfetti, C. A., and McCutchen, D. (1982). Speech processes in reading. *Speech Lang.: Adv. Basic Res. Practice* **7**, 237–269.

Read, C. (1986). "Children's Creative Spelling." Routledge & Kegan Paul, London.

Robinson, M. E., and Schwartz, L. B. (1973). Visuo-motor skills and reading ability: A longitudinal study. *Dev. Med. Child Neurol.* **15**, 280–286.

Russell. G. (1982). Impairment of phonetic reading in dyslexia and its persistence beyond childhood—Research note. *J. Child Psychol. Child Psych.* **23**, 459–475(b).

Rutter, N. (1978). Prevalence and types of dyslexia. *In* "Dyslexia: An Appraisal of Current Knowledge" (A. L. Benton and D. Pearl, eds.), pp. 3–28. Oxford Press, New York.

Rutter, M., and Madge, N. (1976). "Cycles of Disadvantage: A Review of Research." Heinemann Educational, London.

Rutter, M., and Yule, W. (1973). The concept of specific reading retardation. *J. Child Psych.* **16**, 181–198.

Scarborough, H. S. (1984). Continuity between childhood dyslexia and adult reading. *Br. J. Psychol.* **75**, 329–348.

Scarborough, H. S. (1988). Early language development of children who became dyslexic. Paper presented to the New York Child Language group.

Shankweiler, D., and Liberman, I. Y. (1972). Misreading: A search for the causes. *In* "Language by Ear and by Eye: The Relationships between Speech and Reading" (J. F. Kavanaugh and I. G. Mattingly, eds.), pp. 293–318. MIT Press, Cambridge.

Shankweiler, D., Liberman, I. Y., Mark, L. S., Fowler, C. A., and Fisher, F. W. (1979). The speech code and learning to read. *J. Exp. Psychol.: Hum. Percep. Perform.* **5**, 531–545.

Simpson, G. B., Lorsbach, T. C., and Whitehouse, D. (1983). Encoding and contextual components of word recognition in good and poor readers. *J. Exp. Child Psychol.* **35**, 161–171.

Slowiaczek, M. L., and Clifton, C. (1980). Subvocalization and reading for meaning. *J. Verbal Learn. Verbal Behav.* **19**, 573–582.

Smith, S. D., Kimberling, W. J., Pennington, B. F., and Lubs, H. A. (1983). Specific reading disability: Identification of an inherited form through linkage analysis. *Science* **219**, 1345–1347.

Smith, S. D., Pennington, B. F., Fain, P. E., Kimberling, W. J., and Lubs, H. A. (1986). Genetic heterogeneity in specific reading disability. *Am. J. Hum. Gen.* **39**, A169.

Smith, S. T., Macaruso, P., Shankweiler, D., and Crain, S. (in press). Syntactic comprehension in young poor readers. *Appl. Psycholing.*

Smith, S. T., Mann, V. A., and Shankweiler, D. C. (1986). Spoken sentence comprehension by good and poor readers: A Study with the Token Test. *Cortex* **22**, 627–632.

Spring, C. (1976). Encoding speech and memory span in dyslexia children. *J. Special Educ.* **10**, 35–40.

Stanovich, K. (1982a). Individual differences in the cognitive processes of reading: I. Word decoding. *J. Learn. Disabil.* **15**, 485–493.

Stanovich, K. (1982b). Individual differences in the cognitive processes of reading: II. Text-level processes. *J. Learn. Disabil.* **15**, 549–554.

Stanovich, K. (1988). Explaining the differences between the dyslexic and the garden variety poor reader: The phonological-core variable difference model. *J. Learn. Disabil.* **21**, 590–604.

Stanovich, K. E., Cunningham, A. E., and Cramer, B. B. (1984a). Assessing phonological awareness in kindergarten children: Issues of task comparability. *J. Exp. Child Psychol.* **38**, 175–190.

Stanovich, K. E., Cunningham, A. E., and Feeman, D. J. (1984b). Intelligence, cognitive skills and early reading progress. *Read. Res. Q.* **19**, 278–303.

Stanovich, K. E., Nathan, R. G., and Zolman, J. E. (1988). The developmental lag hypothesis in reading: Longitudinal and matched reading-level comparisons. *Child Dev.* **59**, 71–86.

Stevenson, H. W., Stiegler, J. W., Lucker, G. W., Hsu, C.-C., and Kitamura, S. (1982). Reading disabilities: The case of Chinese, Japanese and English. *Child Dev.* **53**, 1164–1181.

Swanson, L. (1978). Verbal encoding effects on the visual short-term memory of learning-disabled and normal children. *J. Educ. Psychol.* **70**, 539–544.

Taylor, I., and Taylor, M. M. (1983). "The Psychology of Reading." Academic Press, New York.

Thomas, C. C. (1905). Congenital 'word blindness' and its treatment. *Opthalmoscope* **3**, 380–385.

Torgesen, J. K. (1977). Memorization processes in reading-disabled children. *J. Educ. Psychol.* **69**, 551–578.

Torgesen, J. K., and Hoack, D. J. (1980). Processing deficiencies of learning-disabled children who perform poorly on the digit spaan test. *J. Educ. Psychol.* **72**, 141–160.

Tzeng, O. J. L., Hung, D. L., and Wang, W. S.-Y. (1977). Speech recoding in reading Chinese characters. *J. Exp. Psychol.: Hum. Learn. Mem.* **3**, 621–630.

Vellutino, F. R. (1979). "Dyslexia: Theory and Research." MIT Press, Cambridge.

Waber, D. P. (1977). Sex differences in mental abilities, hemispheric lateralization, and rate of physical growth at adolescence. *Dev. Psychol.* **13**, 29–38.

Wagner, R., Balthazor, M., Hurley, S., Morgan, S., Rashotte, C., Shaner, R., Simmons, K., and Stage, S. (1987). The nature of prereaders' phonological processing abilities. *Cog. Dev.* **2**, 355–373.

Watt, W. C. (1989). Getting writing right. *Semiotica* **75**, 279–315.

Wolf, M. (1984). Naming, reading and the dyslexias: A longitudinal overview. *Ann. Dyslexia* **34**, 87–115.

Wolf, M., and Goodglass, H. (1986). Dyslexia, dysnomia and lexical retrieval: A longitudinal investigation. *Brain Lang.* **28**, 159–168.

Wong, B. Y. L., Wong, R., and Blenkinsop, J. (1989). Cognitive and metacognitive aspects of learning-disabled adolescents' composing problems. *Learn. Disabil. Q.* **12**, 300–322.

Yopp, H. K. (1988). The validity and reliability of phonemic awareness tests. *Read. Res. Q.* **23**, 159–177.

Zurif, E. B., and Carson, G. (1970). Dyslexia in relation to cerebral: Dominance and temporal analysis. *Neuropsychologia* **8**, 351–361.

Sharing the Light of Faith:
National Catechetical Directory for Catholics of the United States

National Conference of Catholic Bishops. 1979. Nos. 192–96.
Washington, D.C.: United States Catholic Conference.

Chapter VIII.[*]
Catechesis Toward Maturity in Faith

Part C: Catechesis for Persons with Special Needs

192. Introduction

Articles 134–139 consider the liturgical needs of various special groups. Now we consider their catechetical needs.

193. Adapting catechesis to a pluralistic society

Catechesis is prepared to accommodate all social and cultural differences in harmony with the message of salvation. Within the fundamental unity of faith, the Church recognizes diversity, the essential equality of all, and the need for charity and mutual respect among all groups in a pluralistic Church and society.

Guidelines for catechesis by geographical area can easily be inferred from what follows concerning the catechesis of cultural, racial, and ethnic groups. Catechetical guidelines concerning the Catholic Church's relationship to other religious traditions are discussed in articles 75–79.

194. Catechesis of cultural, racial, and ethnic groups

At one time or another almost every cultural, racial, and ethnic group in the United States has held minority status in society and in the Church. Many still do. "Minority" can be understood either numerically or as referring to a group whose members are hindered in their efforts to obtain, keep, or exercise their rights.

In some cases, it is important that catechesis distinguish among subgroups within larger groups. For example, the Spanish-speaking, while sharing a common language, include Mexican-Americans, Puerto Ricans, Cubans, and others, each group with its distinct cultural characteristics,

customs, needs, and potential. The same is true of various tribes and nations of Native Americans, Afro-Americans, and others.

The preparation of catechists is of the greatest importance. Ideally, the catechist will be a member of the particular racial, cultural, or ethnic group. Those who are not should understand and empathize with the group, besides having adequate catechetical formation.

The language of the particular group should be used in the catechesis of its members: not just its vocabulary, but its thought patterns, cultural idioms, customs, and symbols. Catechetical materials should suit its characteristics and needs. Rather than simply translating or adapting materials prepared for others, it is generally necessary to develop new materials. To be appropriate, even adaptations must involve more than translations and picture changes. Catechetical materials should affirm the identity and dignity of the members of the particular group, using findings of the behavioral sciences for this purpose.

Catechesis takes into account the educational and economic circumstances of diverse groups, avoiding unrealistic demands on time, physical resources, and finances and making adjustments which correspond to the educational level of those being catechized.

Catechesis takes into account a group's special needs in relation to justice and peace, and prepares its members to assume their responsibility for achieving its just goals.

Even in culturally homogeneous areas and parishes catechesis should be multi-cultural, in the sense that all should be educated to know and respect other cultural, racial, and ethnic groups. Minority group members should be invited and encouraged to participate in religious and social functions.

The Church at all levels must make a special commitment to provide funds, research, materials, and personnel for catechesis directed to minority groups. Parishes in which there are no members of such groups have an obligation to

---

[*] Editor's note: Chapter notation refers to this excerpt.

help provide funds and personnel. Dioceses with many minority group members should be assisted by dioceses in which there are few or none. Parochial, regional, and national leadership and coordination are needed.

At the same time, the leaders of minority groups should support catechesis, especially by engaging in broad consultation to ascertain their people's catechetical needs. Community leaders can stimulate catechetical research, planning, and promotion, and participate in actual catechesis.

At all times catechesis must respect the personal dignity of minority group members, avoiding condescension and patronizing attitudes. The ultimate goal is that minority groups be able to provide for their own catechetical needs, while remaining closely united in faith and charity with the rest of the Church. This unity can be fostered in many ways, including the educational and informational efforts of mission agencies and missionaries.

195. Persons with handicapping conditions

Handicapped persons, approximately 12.5 percent of the total population of the United States, include the mentally retarded, those with learning disabilities, the emotionally disturbed, the physically handicapped, the hard of hearing, the deaf, the visually impaired, the blind, and others. Many handicapped persons are in isolating conditions which tend to cut them off from learning. Each handicapped person has special needs—including a need for catechesis—which must be recognized and met.

Catechetical programs should not segregate the handicapped from the rest of the community excessively or unnecessarily.

Catechesis for certain groups (e.g., the deaf, the blind, the mentally retarded) often requires specialized materials, training, and skills (such as the ability to sign). The entire Church has a responsibility for providing training and research; leadership preparation and funding are needed at the national, diocesan, and local levels. On the diocesan and parish levels, sharing of resources and personnel and collaboration in the preparation and sponsorship of programs are appropriate; the possibility of ecumenically sponsored and conducted programs should also be investigated.

It is particularly important for the families of the handicapped persons to be involved in their catechesis. Supportive participation by family members helps them better understand handicapped individuals.

The goal is to present Christ's love and teaching to each handicapped person in as full and rich a manner as he or she can assimilate.

196. Other persons with special needs

The list of groups with special needs is almost endless: the aged—often among the socially and economically disadvantaged; the illiterate and educationally deprived; young single people in college or vocational programs; young single workers; military personnel; unmarried people with children; young married couples with or without children; couples in mixed marriages; the divorced; the divorced and remarried; middle-aged singles; the widowed; the imprisoned; persons with a homosexual orientation; etc.

Catechesis is also needed by people in the "caring" professions—such as doctors, nurses, and social workers—who have their own special requirements along with many opportunities for witness and for catechizing in their dealings with the deprived, the sick, and the dying.

The Church is seriously obliged to provide catechesis suited to the special needs of these and other groups. Some were overlooked in the past, but in several cases these special needs are of relatively recent origin: for example, those of the aged, whose current difficulties are largely associated with increased longevity and the decline of the extended family; and those of young single people, whose needs are related to the recent emergence of new life styles.

Catechesis is part of a total pastoral ministry to people with special needs. It emphasizes aspects of the Church's teaching and practice which will help them make personal, faith-filled responses to their special circumstances. Sensitivity and careful planning are essential.

Catechetical programs should, whenever possible, be developed in consultation with representatives of those for whom they are intended. The aim should be to help them overcome the obstacles they face and achieve as much integration as they can into the larger community of faith.

Gifted Students in Regular Classrooms

Parke, B. 1989. 3–16, 42–63, 127–42. Boston: Allyn and Bacon.

Gifted Students: Who They Are and What They Need

It takes only a very few days in a classroom to become aware that there are a variety of abilities in the students we teach. Some learn very quickly with little effort, while others seem to struggle just to understand the basics. How can educators respond to the challenge that such ranges of ability present? How can they do the best possible job, making sure that all the students receive the types of instruction they need?

These are tough questions and ones that educators grapple with all their professional careers. The tasks can be made less difficult by learning more about how students differ and how to respond to their varying needs. Gifted and talented students require attention, for these students are not readily understood. "In all my years of teaching, I have never had a 'gifted' child in my class" and "It shows favoritism to put these students in 'special programs'" are among the comments often heard when discussing the plight of the gifted. However, neither is the case! There are gifted and talented students *throughout* our school systems who are in dire need of programs that are suited to their abilities. In order to deliver such programs and alter these misconceptions, it is first necessary to understand what is meant and not meant by the term *gifted*.

Who Are the Gifted? Dispelling the Myths

The misconceptions that have been held over the last century about the nature of giftedness have led to a mythology that surrounds persons of high ability. These myths can result in flawed educational decision making. One of the earliest myths was "genius is next to insanity." In other words, the smarter you are the more likely it is that you will also be a bit crazy. Following years of study (Terman, 1925), it has become very clear that this is not the case. The highly accomplished among us are not more likely to have psychological problems; in fact, they may have fewer. This is just one myth among many; let us now look at additional myths and actualities about the gifted and talented.

MYTH: Gifted students are a group of like individuals.
ACTUALITY: Gifted students vary greatly in their abilities, personalities, and interests.

There are no definitive lists of characteristics that indicate that people are gifted. Rather, the characteristics vary within the group as much as they do between the gifted and their age-peers. This is a very heterogeneous population. Not all gifted students are Einsteins, Mozarts, or Edisons, displaying eccentric or supernatural abilities. Most are students who have abilities that surpass those of other persons the same age and, therefore, are in need of educational programs other than or in addition to those typically offered at their grade levels. A fixed set of characteristics for the gifted and talented does not exist. Each student is an individual with his or her own strengths and weaknesses, likes and dislikes, quirks and flaws, and each should be judged on his or her own merits, accomplishments, and potential.

MYTH: Gifted children are "better."
ACTUALITY: All students in a classroom are of equal value.

All students in a classroom are of equal value. To believe that gifted children are "better" is to do a disservice to all the students in the class. It is not unusual to hear the objection to special programs for gifted and talented students based on the premise that taking the "good" students from the classroom will jeopardize the entire group. This sounds as if there are "good" and "bad" students in each class. The abilities of students do not make them better or worse as individuals; each child in a class is of equal value as a person. Each has the same right to be respected and to receive an appropriate educational experience. Gifted students are different, but their abilities do not make them inherently better individuals and they should not be treated as such as it makes other students question their own worth.

MYTH: Gifted students will make it on their own.
ACTUALITY: Gifted students need the guidance of teachers.

Many people believe that it is not necessary to focus on the education of gifted students because they will make it on their own, regardless of what schools do. Although they may appear to be achieving, it cannot be assumed that gifted students, when left to their own devices, will achieve at a level commensurate with their abilities. This fact has been a point of discussion for eighty years. Marland (1972) expressed this belief in his report to the Congress of the United States when he was the United States Commissioner of Education. His report states:

> Large scale studies indicate that gifted and talented children are, in fact, disadvantaged and handicapped in the usual school situation. Terman observed that the gifted are the most retarded group in the schools when mental age and chronological age are compared. Great discrepancies existed during his study (1904), and continue to persist today . . . (p. 26).

Since gifted students are usually able to display large amounts of information at any time, it is assumed that they possess the strategies necessary to be able to learn on their own. In fact, a gifted student may not know what a thesaurus is or how to locate information in the library, have difficulty deciding on a topic for an independent study, or be unable to reconstruct how he or she arrived at the correct answer to a complicated mathematics problem. Gifted students need to be given the opportunity to learn how to learn. Without such instruction, we cannot assume they will be able to use such skills when needed.

MYTH: **Gifted students are perfect.**
ACTUALITY: **Gifted students have strengths *and* weaknesses.**

Gifted students may be perfectionistic, but they are never perfect. Some frequent misconceptions about gifted students are that they do not make mistakes, always complete their work on time, never need remediation, and always have a positive attitude toward school. As with all children, the gifted vary in these behaviors. It is unrealistic to assume that they will constantly perform at their highest possible levels. Gifted students rarely have equal ability in all academic areas, they do not always behave as we may wish, and their attitudes toward school may range from enthusiastic to very negative. Gifted students do make mistakes; they may be behavior problems, underachieving, or handicapped in some manner. Just because these students are not perfect in all aspects of their lives does not mean that they are not gifted and/or talented, and they should not be disqualified, on that basis, from receiving programs commensurate with their abilities.

MYTH: **"Early ripe, early rot."**
ACTUALITY: **Gifted students' abilities do not "burn out."**

The belief that the performance levels of gifted students level off may be referred to as the "early ripe, early rot" theory of child development. This position holds that students who display precocity at a young age will eventually begin to lose their advantage, and their performance levels will more closely approximate that shown by their classmates. When gifted students are provided with appropriate programs that include challenging experiences and opportunities to learn new things, this phenomenon does not take place. However, when gifted students do not receive appropriate programs, there is evidence to suggest that they may lose much of the advantage that they have when they arrive at school (Ness and Latessa, 1979).

MYTH: **Gifted students like to be called gifted.**
ACTUALITY: **Gifted students feel they are basically like other students and have not been "given" anything.**

It will surprise many people to learn that gifted students do not like to be called *gifted*. They find the label to be a detriment both socially and emotionally. This is particularly the case when they reach the middle school or junior high school years and the peer group gains increasing importance. Gifted students report that they do not feel as though they have been "given" anything. Rather, they feel that they are regular people who happen to learn differently and sometimes enjoy different types of activities than their classmates. They do not like to be separated from their peers or made to be an example (positive or negative) for the rest of the class. By doing so, teachers position them for

peer sanctions, an event that can lead to the gifted students being less inclined to show their true abilities for fear of social ramifications.

These mythological beliefs have contributed to a condition in our schools and society in which gifted and talented students are often underserved. By understanding the actualities of giftedness we can see that this population, although unique in many ways, is in need of the same basic considerations we should afford all our students. Getting the facts straight about these students, then, becomes a necessity; the next step is to understand just what giftedness really is.

Definitions of Giftedness

Over the past century, the meaning of the term *gifted* has changed from single-dimensional (high IQ) definition (Terman, 1925) to one in which multiple abilities and intelligences are recognized (Guilford, 1956; Taylor; 1968; Sternberg, 1982; Gardner, 1983). This transition has opened the door to greater understanding of students and their needs in schools. It is clear that there are many students who, by virtue of their exceptional abilities, require programs that are beyond those typically offered to them. When such a case exists, the process of terming students *gifted and/or talented* can commence.

There are a number of definitions employed to describe people who are gifted and/or talented. These definitions usually recognize that giftedness is a multidimensional trait since there are *many* different areas in which students may have exceptional abilities. These capabilities are reflected in the definitions that are most commonly adopted for the operational and funding purposes of programs for the gifted and talented.

United State Department of Education definition. The most commonly used definition of *gifted and talented* is stated in the Educational Amendment of 1978 (P.L. 95-561, IX (A)). It is a multidimensional definition based on Marland's *Education of the gifted and talented, Volume 1. Report to the Congress of the United States by the U.S. Commissioner of Education* (Maryland, 1972). This definition, as revised, reads as follows:

> (The gifted and talented are) . . . children and, whenever applicable, youth who are identified at the preschool, elementary, or secondary level as possessing demonstrated or potential abilities that give evidence of high performance capability in areas such as intellectual, creative, specific academic or leadership ability or in the performing or visual arts, and who by reason thereof require services or activities not ordinarily provided by the school (U.S. Congress, Educational Amendment of 1978 [P.L. 95-561, IX (A)]).

There are a number of interesting facets to this definition. It notes that there are many areas in which a student may be gifted. Furthermore, it recognizes by its words, "demonstrated or potential abilities," that not all students display their abilities at all times, thereby allowing programs to be constructed for high potential/low or average performance students, such as gifted underachievers. Finally, it calls for specific programs to be instituted to meet the needs of these students by stating, " . . . and who by reason thereof require services and activities not ordinarily provided by the school."

All or part of this definition is used by over 94 percent of the states (Council of State Directors of Programs for the Gifted, 1986). In addition, many school districts use this definition for guiding their program development and establishing guidelines for program eligibility. However, critics point out shortcomings of this model. Renzulli, Reis, and Smith (1981) list three: failure to include nonintellective (motivational) factors; unparallel factors, with two relating to abilities and three to processes; and the misuse of the definition by persons who treat the categories as if they were mutually exclusive.

Renzulli's Three-Ring Conception of Giftedness. The Three-Ring Conception of Giftedness (Renzulli, 1978) is based on studies of creative and productive individuals. These data show three interlocking traits that are evident in this type of person: above average ability, creativity, and task commitment. When these abilities converge in one person, the result is an individual who is exceptional in performance and a significant contributor to society. It is Renzulli's belief that these are the factors that should be considered when determining which students are eligible for a program for the gifted. His definition of giftedness (Renzulli, 1978) is:

> giftedness consists of an interaction among three basic clusters of human traits—these clusters being above average general abilities, high levels of task commitment, and high levels of creativity. Gifted and talented children are those possessing or capable of developing this composite set of traits and applying them to any potentially valuable area of human performance. Children who manifest or are capable of developing an interaction among the three clusters require a wide variety of educational opportunities and services that are not ordinarily provided through regular instructional programs (p. 261).

This model is based on the premise that there are many ways in which the gifted and talented may demonstrate their abilities and that these demonstrations may come at different times and under varying circumstances. Thus, Renzulli calls for the identification processes to be ongoing and the programs to be multifaceted. The inclusion of the noncognitive factor of "task commitment" sets this definition apart from past definitions of gifted and talented students.

Gardner's Theory of Multiple Intelligences. Gardner (1983) posits that there are "intelligences" rather than a single intelligence. Seven distinct intelligences are described in this theory:

> . . . intelligence should be considered as a constellation of at least seven different competencies—linguistic, logical-mathematical, spatial, bodily-kinesthetic, musical, inter-personal and intra-personal (Hatch and Gardner, 1986, p. 148).

This theory, which results in profiles of ability, allows a person to be gifted in one area and average or below average in others. Although similar to the Department of Education's definition of giftedness, this is a *theory of intelligence*, with factors based in the author's research. However, it does provide a useful basis for discussing the nature and identification of giftedness.

Gagne's Differentiated Model of Giftedness and Talent. An attempt to integrate the above models has been made by Gagne (1985), author of the following definitions:

> *Giftedness* corresponds to competence which is distinctly above average in one or more domains of ability.

> *Talent* refers to performance which is distinctly above average in one or more fields of human intelligence (p. 108).

He elaborates:

> Talent, which is defined in the context of a large or narrow field of human activity, expresses itself through a set of behaviors linked to this field of activity. . . . Giftedness is somewhat different in that abilities are generally identified using more unidimensional and standardized measures so as to connect together in the purest form possible those individual characteristics which "explain" the observed performance (p. 108).

Gagne shows underlying abilities that, when coupled with the catalysts of environment, personality, and motivation, can result in the demonstration of high-level performance in talent areas. Thus, he combines the notions of multiple intelligences, personality factors, environment, and talents into one model of giftedness and talent.

Critical Points

You can now see that there is no agreement as to an absolute definition of giftedness and talent. Over the past thirty years, however, the notion of multiple abilities and multiple intelligences has gained wide acceptance. These are the critical points to remember when developing a definition of giftedness for program planning:

1. There are many intelligences.
2. Intelligences will vary in the extent to which they are developed and show strength.
3. Consideration of giftedness and talent should encompass multiple ability areas.

4. Developing, as well as developed, abilities should be considered.
5. High levels of ability may require programs beyond those typically provided in schools in order to nurture and develop students' abilities fully.
6. The definition that is adopted by a school district or for a particular program serves as the basis for the development of student selection and program design procedures.

Why Educators Should Be Concerned

Incidence

Gifted and talented students are everywhere—in every community and in every classroom. Keeping in mind the multiple ability notions of intelligence and the U.S. Department of Education's definition, which states that the gifted are those students who "(possess) demonstrated or potential abilities that give evidence of high performance capability . . . and who by reason thereof require services or activities not ordinarily provided by schools," it becomes apparent that there is a myriad of students who fall into these categories. Some set the number at 2 to 5 percent of the population (Council for Exceptional Children, 1978); others are more inclusive, identifying 16 to 20 percent of the school population as students who can potentially benefit from special programs (Renzulli, Reis, and Smith, 1981).

Regardless of the definition of giftedness to which one adheres and regardless of your specific teaching assignment, the fact is that every teacher probably has students in the classroom who could benefit from some type of differentiated programming because of the advanced abilities they possess. Whether or not they have been officially identified, or a designated program for the gifted and talented exists in your school, it is the responsibility of educational professionals to make sure that these students are receiving a proper education commensurate with their abilities.

This can be complicated and tricky to accomplish. One of the problems often encountered is a feeling by a faculty that there are *no* gifted and/or talented students in their school. They fail to realize that giftedness can be situationally specific and is relative to the environment. If a student displays abilities that transcend the other students in the class, that student may need some type of accommodation to have an appropriate education. The student does not have to score 95 to 99 percent on a standardized achievement test to merit such consideration. Rather, *the performance level of the student judged within the context of the environment should lead to the decision of whether or not alternative programming is needed.* Again, there is no absolute state of giftedness. There are gifted behaviors and situations in which students need differential treatment due to their advanced abilities, talents, and interests.

Current Programming Pattern

Another overwhelming reason why educators should be actively concerned about gifted and talented students is that the vast majority of such students are in regular classroom placements. This has historically been the case and continues to be the placement of choice in a preponderance of districts due to such factors as philosophical positions, convenience, and/or default. In the Council for Exceptional Children's 1977 *Survey of the States and Territories*, it was found that approximately 33 to 63 percent of the gifted students in the thirty-two states that had programs for the gifted at that time were receiving any type of special services. Although that number has increased over the last decade, the levels of service are still far below the incidence and need levels. Apparently, most gifted and talented students are in typical classroom placements.

Even when programs are instituted for the gifted and talented, the programs of choice tend to be those that center around the regular classroom. The Richardson Study Survey (Cox, Daniel, and Boston, 1985) reports that the five most frequently instituted programs for the gifted across the country were (1) part-time special classes, (2) enrichment, (3) independent study, (4) resource rooms, and (5) itinerant teachers. All five of these approaches center around the regular classroom. In each instance, students are in the regular class for all or part of the week—yet, their abilities are with them *all week long*. Part-time programs exist in abundance, but giftedness and talents are full-time capabilities. Therefore, provisions for these abilities must be thought of in the context of the entire school week, not just in the hour or two the students typically happen to be in a program for the gifted and talented.

Student Well-Being

The classroom teacher is one of the most influential persons in the students' school lives. Teachers hold a great deal of power within the classroom and have tremendous impact on the lives of their students. When eminent people are asked who influenced their lives the most, they usually respond that it was a teacher or a parent (Goertzel and Goertzel, 1962; Bloom, 1985). Thus, teachers play an integral role in the development of student abilities and talents.

These influences can be both positive and negative, however. Therefore, it becomes important for teachers to learn how to handle the wide range of abilities found in the average classroom in such a way that all students flourish. The gifted and talented students need guidance and direction as well as skill development. Independent studies and tutoring students of lesser ability will not sufficiently compensate for academic requirements that are below students' achievement levels. Teachers must develop the skills of managing the learning of children of all abilities if students are to survive school in a healthy manner.

Student well-being is based on teacher attitude as much as teacher skill. The gifted require teachers who value student abilities and encourage excellence and achievement. They need instructional leaders who will understand the costs as well as the benefits to being exceptional. Such compassion and understanding are vital to the gifted as they attempt to develop their abilities to the fullest extent.

Gifted students are not free of problems; they are children who face a different set of problems. The teacher is in a unique position to be of assistance as these students work through the difficult issues they face.

What Can Be Done?

What can educators do to make sure that their gifted and talented students receive appropriate educational experiences? The list is truly endless, but there are four guidelines that will serve you well in thinking about gifted students in regular classroom settings. They provide the philosophical underpinnings for this book.

1. *Accept all children as individuals with differing abilities.* We all know that there are many levels of student ability within a classroom. Recognizing this fact and designing instruction to respond to it are giant steps toward meeting the needs of gifted and talented students. Looking for the behaviors of students that may indicate exceptional ability is the beginning stage for providing appropriate programs for the gifted. But programs for these students *must* be considered within the context of appropriate programs for *all* students.

2. *Establish student-centered classrooms.* Classroom decisions should be based on the needs of the students. Allow students to become part of the team by enfranchising them with decision-making power. They are the ones who must ultimately be responsible for their own learning, so why not give them the power to do so? Running a student-centered classroom involves making students the center of the decision-making process. This seems only reasonable since schools exist so students can learn.

3. *Plan models of instruction that allow individual differences to be accommodated.* There are methods of instruction that will allow students to respond to instruction at their own levels of expertise. Such approaches to teaching are valuable because they accommodate the many ability levels within the classroom without designating who the slow and rapid learners are. Choosing the appropriate model for the given circumstances is the hallmark of an excellent teacher. Having many approaches available and using multiple methods to teach should result in students learning through their various learning styles and at their highest possible levels.

4. *Remember that gifted students are not "better"; they are just "different" in their abilities, needs, and interests.* Try to avoid placing a value judgment on the abilities of students. We do not do a favor for gifted children by placing them on a pedestal for other students to emulate. They are students with their own needs and problems who require the same compassion and care as the other students in the class. Their needs may be different, they are no less urgent than those of students with lesser ability.

Summary

Giftedness is a multidimensional trait seen through the behaviors of students who signal potential or actual performance levels that are at an exceptionally high level. Gifted and talented students are found throughout our schools and classrooms, as that is the placement of choice in most school districts. Therefore, it becomes the task of the regular classroom teacher to meet the needs of these students through whatever means necessary. Strategies do exist to accomplish this feat and will be discussed in later chapters. From the onset, however, it is important to keep in mind that there are many students in our classes with exceptional abilities who require differential programs for the full development of those abilities. It is the classroom teacher who is the vital link to assuring that such programs exist and flourish for the students who need them.

Action Steps

1. Choose or write a definition of giftedness and/or talent that fits your purposes and philosophical position. Keep this handy for future reference, as it will be the basis for assessment, program, and curricular planning. Remember to take multiple abilities into account and to provide for students who both display and have the potential to display levels of achievement that surpass their peers.

2. Inventory your own attitudes. Do you believe that any of the myths discussed in this chapter to be actualities? If so, try to go a step beyond recognizing these biases and begin to change your attitudes. This can be done through reading publications on the topic of gifted and talented students and by talking with experts, the students themselves, or their parents to find out exactly what it is like to be unusually adept.

3. Begin to evaluate the regular classroom settings. Are multiple ability levels being addressed within the instructional program? If so, in what ways can improvement be made? If not, what changes should be made? Begin to construct a written plan of action to bring an equal education to all your students. Write down your thoughts and put them in a folder along with the definition of giftedness that you wrote. You may want to refer to these later as you learn more about providing programs for the gifted and talented in the regular classroom.

References You Can Use

Bloom, B. (Ed.). (1985). *Developing talent in young people.* New York: Ballantine Books.

Clark, B. (1983). *Growing up gifted* (2nd ed.). Columbus, OH: Merrill Publishing Company.

Gallagher, J. (1985). *Teaching the gifted child* (3rd ed.). Boston: Allyn and Bacon.

Renzulli, J. (1978). What makes giftedness? Reexamining the Definition. *Phi Delta Kappan* 60(3), 180–184, 261.

Treffinger, D. (Ed.). (1982). *Gifted Child Quarterly* (Special issue on the myths in educating the gifted), 26(1).

3: Planning the Programs

Planning programs to accommodate gifted and talented students should commence under one circumstance only: If the needs of these students are not being met by an existing program, then an alternative program designed to address their needs should be instituted. Gifted students have unique abilities that may necessitate such a step, as it is the right of all students to have educational programs that will meet their learning needs.

Each child in the regular classroom has a unique learning schema, preferring to work alone or in small groups, to write a response to a question or answer orally, to take direction from the teacher or grapple with a problem alone. If you observe students as they work, you will find that they all have their own learning characteristics. These varying characteristics are what necessitate building programs with sufficient flexibility to accommodate multiple approaches to the learning process.

Learning Characteristics of Gifted Students

Many lists of characteristics exist that describe the population of gifted learners as a whole; one such list appears in Chapter 2. You may have observed many of these characteristics in the classroom. You may have noticed, in particular, that the learning characteristics of the gifted tend to differ from their chronological age-peers in three important ways (Maker, 1982).

First, gifted students tend to learn more quickly than other students. The *pace* of their learning is advanced. They can absorb information at a faster rate and process it efficiently. This is one reason that many gifted students seem to have minds like a sponge. They learn a great deal of information quickly and they rarely miss much. Second, gifted students are often able to comprehend information with greater *depth* than their classmates. They tend to ask the questions that show insight or understanding of more universal concepts. More than one teacher has been shocked at the understanding displayed by some six- and seven-year-olds about world conflict, death, or the monetary system. Finally, gifted students are often distinguished by *interests* that are different from others of the same age. Interests may be shown in areas more typical of older students or adults. A walk through a high school science fair will quickly demonstrate the wide variety of interests enjoyed by the student body.

These three primary characteristics are enhanced by others which complement them and add to the variance in the way these students learn. Dunn and Griggs (1985, p. 43) report that learning styles of gifted students, when considered as a group, can be characterized by the following descriptors; "(a) independence (self learners); (b) internal or external control; (c) persistence; (d) perceptual strengths; (e) nonconformity; (f) task commitment; and (g) high self motivation." They further comment that these categories of behaviors will vary with individual students and can only be used as indicators of group tendencies.

It quickly becomes obvious that gifted students come to their educational experiences with different credentials than most students, and they will likely require programs that allow them to work at their own pace, explore topics in greater depth, and pursue their own interests in addition to those topics covered by the conventional curriculum. The difficulty for the teacher comes in trying to establish programs that will be sufficiently flexible to meet the needs of all students in a classroom without segregating or isolating individuals and groups of students who are members of that class.

Differentiating the Educational Program

Differentiated educational programs are necessary for all students because each student has unique learning needs and styles. Any educational experience will not be equally beneficial for all students. In fact, it is not equal education to have all students receiving the same experiences. It is far more defensible to establish programs that have the flexibility to respond to various needs, interests, and learning styles of students. This *cannot* be accomplished if only a single program is in place. If all the students in the class are doing the same math problems or reading the same basal reader, it is most likely that the educational needs of some students are not being met—it may be the students of more advanced skill or those in need of remediation. Regardless, the needs, abilities, and interests of the students should determine their educational program.

It is essential for the educator to think in terms of a *multiple programming approach* in which options are available to the teacher and/or student to develop an individualized program based on the student's profile of abilities, achievements, needs, and interests. The programming options should include various ways to make a classroom program more flexible in the delivery of educational experiences to students. By so doing, all students, not just the gifted, will be better served with program that facilitate learning to a greater degree.

For the gifted student, then, the teacher will need to pay particular attention to those aspects of the program that influence the pace at which students learn, the depth that they are allowed to explore a topic, and the opportunity to pursue or incorporate their own interests into their studies. Questions similar to the following may arise: What options are available to a child who is reading at the second-grade level while enrolled in kindergarten? What options are available for a first-grade student who can multiply and divide accurately? What options are available for the sixth-grade math student who is able to begin the study of algebra? What can you do for the fifth-grade student who is involved in dissecting frogs at home and is aggressively studying anatomy on her own? If a teacher is not in the position to answer these questions with reasonable alternatives, then attention needs to be given to how the educational program can be differentiated to accommodate the individual learning profiles of students.

Differentiating programs for the gifted can begin by remembering the following guidelines for program planning:

1. The program should be characterized by its flexibility to respond to the individual needs of students.
2. Program options should be in place so that the varying skills, abilities, and interests of the students can be accommodated.
3. Patterns for grouping students should be based on the unique needs of the students and should allow students to progress at their own pace.
4. Decision making should be based on student needs. Individualized program planning should take place for all students.

Selecting Programming Options

Selecting programming options to institute in the classroom involves three steps. Each is essential to this decision-making process. The first step is to determine the academic, social, emotional, and physical needs of the students in the classroom. Among the questions to be investigated are: What is the range of ability the students display in reading? Are there students who have problems socializing with the other students? Do all the students complete their work at the same time, or are some students faster or slower than the norm? A look at the abilities and needs of the students will lead you to the next step in the process of selecting appropriate programming options. The next step is to establish learning objectives for all the students in the class. The objectives for gifted students may be similar to those for the rest of the class, but will differ in that the gifted students have unique requirements for appropriate programming. After you have investigated the needs of the students and have established objectives for their educational experiences, you can then begin the third step, selecting programming options that will address these needs and objectives in a comprehensive manner.

Step 1: Determining Student Needs

The needs of students can be determined through a number of methods. Some involve formal assessment procedures whereas others are very informal and subjective in nature. Regardless of the types of procedures cited, the purpose is still the same: Construct a profile of student abilities, achievements, needs, and interests from which program placement decisions can be made. It is critical that profiles be established for *all* students in the classroom. When the objectives are written and the program design is determined, they must reflect the needs of all students working in that environment, not just the gifted students. It is the intent of this program planning process to develop programming options that will facilitate the learning of all the students in the regular classroom, not just a few. Program designs must not discriminate among children unfairly or isolate certain students from the rest of the class, socially or physically. Establishing a sound program design

will assure that individual needs and differences are addressed and that learning is encouraged.

Various types of instruments can assess the needs and abilities of students. Tests of ability or achievement used in the assessment process for program placement can be reevaluated (see Chapter 2). Criterion-referenced tests, such as the placement tests provided by many textbook publishers, can provide a great deal of information regarding student level of achievement in subject areas. A look at the accumulative record file of a child may very well result in information that will prove useful in determining current levels of functioning and past activities. More informal methods, such as observations and interviews, can yield equally important information, particularly as you investigate the social and emotional developmental factors. Interest and learning style inventories can be useful tools for determining student needs and preferences. Parent questionnaires can produce clues to the abilities and interests of the students that may be exhibited outside of school. When these data are accumulated and profiles of individual students are completed, the information should be synthesized into a classroom profile to be used in determining the types of programs and curricular accommodations that are needed (see Figure 3-1).

Step 2: Establishing Student Objectives

Objectives for students are written so that the students and the teacher have a basis upon which to make decisions about the students' educational experiences. They are the guides to program planning and the foundation for curricular decision making. Some objectives will be the same for all the students in the class; others will vary depending on the profiles of the students. Objectives should reflect the unique composition of each student's profile, the total class profile, and the following six basic rights that should be afforded to all students.

◆ *All students have the right to learn at their own pace.* Those students who learn more quickly should be allowed to move through material at a faster pace. It is also the right of students who learn more slowly to progress at a rate that will allow them to learn with the greatest effectiveness.

◆ *All students have the right to receive instruction that is at their achievement levels.* Materials and methods of instruction should be determined by the abilities and achievements of the students, not the grade level to which they are assigned. A third grader capable of reading at a fifth-grade level should be receiving fifth-grade materials and reading experiences.

◆ *All students should be given the opportunity to develop independent thinking skills.* Students must be prepared to make decisions on their own. They cannot learn to think independently if they are not given the opportunity. Problem-solving techniques, inquiry, and higher level thinking skills are strategies that can benefit all children in a classroom. They should be

Figure 3-1 Student Profile Chart

Student Name: _____

Student Number: _____

Grade Level: _____

Teacher's name: _____

Date Profile Completed: _____

_____

               Grade Level Equivalency   Test

Curricular Area:

Reading
  (see attached skill chart) _____

Math
  (see attached skill chart) _____

Spelling
  Book level completed _____

_____

Writing Proficiency _____

Handwriting Proficiency _____

_____

Special Interests: _____

Special Talents: _____

Awards: _____

Projects: _____

Extracurricular Activities: _____

---

integrated into the classroom through the program design, curriculum, and interpersonal interactions.

◆ *All students should be prepared to be lifelong learners.* Objectives must be established in such a way as to give students the responsibility for learning and the tools to learn on their own. This will mean designing programs that allow students to make decisions and experience the consequences of their decisions. As well, this will necessitate that students become partners with teachers in the decision-making processes of the classroom. Their learning commenced before they began school and it will continue long after their formal schooling ends.

◆ *All students should be allowed multiple means of expressing what they know and how they feel.* Young children who have cognitive abilities that surpass their physical abilities must be given outlets to express their ideas that will not be hindered by an inability to write or speak. Children who can express themselves through artistic display should be given the opportunity to do so. By developing divergent modes of expression, children are better able to use all their abilities and develop new ones.

◆ *All students should be encouraged to develop a respect for themselves and others.* Schools can play an integral role in teaching children about themselves and those around them. By treating students with respect, we model appropriate behavior. By helping them gain insight into their behaviors and those of others, we assist them in understanding that all people are different and each deserves to be treated in a respectful manner.

Keeping these rights for all students in mind, individual and/or group objectives should be written to outline the types of learning experiences that are needed and the methods that will facilitate learning in the most effective and efficient manner. These objectives should address the academic, social, emotional, and physical needs of the students. Objectives typical for gifted students take into account their special need for accommodating the pace at which they learn, the depth at which they are capable of comprehending, and the unique interests they display (see Tables 3-1 and 3-2). Kaplan (1974) lists ten basic areas on which objectives can be built. They are:

◆ Awareness of environmental and academic learning opportunities;
◆ Leadership;
◆ Academic achievement;
◆ Interpersonal relationships;
◆ Self-awareness;
◆ Creativity;
◆ Research skills;
◆ Abstract thinking processes;
◆ Basic skill mastery; and
◆ Career and vocational opportunities (p. 39).

Actual objectives listed for any individual may include many but not necessarily all of these areas. Each area should be considered, however, in the process of generating the objectives. Objectives are central to the program planning process as they provide the focus for instruction. As the program develops and student abilities change, objectives must evolve also. They should be reviewed periodically and modified as necessary.

Step 3: Choosing Program Options

There are many administrative arrangements for delivering programs for gifted students. In choosing programming options to fit a particular set of circumstances, it is best to think in terms of combinations of programs rather than a single configuration. If you offer only one type of program, you can be assured that the needs of some of your students are not being met. It is far more valid to construct a mosaic of programming options from which to choose when making program placement decisions for students.

The range of programs recommended for gifted students is quite broad. The Pyramid Project (Cox, Daniel, and Boston, 1985) proposes program options that extend

---

from more typical programs to programs appropriate only for the highly gifted learner. As you climb the pyramid, the programs become more separated from the regular classroom and more segregated in their design. This is a reflection of the increasing difficulty teachers experience in trying to meet the needs of students in a regular classroom environment as abilities of gifted students become more and more advanced beyond those typically displayed by their classmates.

Program options can be combined or offered alone. For example, a school district may choose to have programming for gifted students strictly in a resource room arrangement with students coming to the program one-half day per week. Or the district may choose to employ a cluster grouping concept in addition to the resource room program, in which a group of gifted students are placed in a class, with provisions for a resource teacher to assist the regular classroom teacher in delivering their educational programs.

The types of program options used should be a reflection of the needs and abilities of the students, along with the objectives that were established from student profiles. The goal is to have all students in the classroom receiving appropriate programs that allow them to learn at their own pace, their own depth, and take into account their individual interests.

The Role of Creativity in Programs for the Gifted

Enhancing creativity is considered to be an integral component of many programs for gifted and talented students. When looking at the goals of programs or student objectives, creativity is usually mentioned as a priority. When thinking about student-centered programming within the regular classroom environment, it should also be seen as an important piece of the mosaic.

This does not mean, however, that creativity should be viewed as separate from the other subjects and processes we teach (Parke, 1985). Rather, creativity should permeate and enhance the classroom through such factors as accepting attitudes, open-ended questions, explorations, and choices. Thirty minutes of "creativity time" is not enough. Thoughtful attention should be given to how creativity relates to classroom activities at all times.

In Megatrends: *Ten New Directions Transforming Our Lives* (Naisbitt, 1982), our society is depicted as moving from one in which industrialization is paramount to one in which information processing is key and either/or decisions are becoming ones in which multiple options are sought. Preparing students for this type of future society has ramifications for school systems today. Our students need to learn how to use their resources to the fullest, work cooperatively, find innovative answers to questions, and not block their own creative abilities. Remaining cognizant of the role creativity can have in this pursuit and integrating creative expression and problem solving throughout the curriculum can help students be better prepared for the world in which they live.

Table 3-1 Typical Objectives for Gifted Students

The student will:

1. Develop different modes of expression.
2. Develop the ability to think critically.
3. Develop the ability to solve problems by using multiple resources.
4. Develop the ability to learn independently.
5. Master basic skills needed to study at advanced levels.
6. Develop curiosity and learn strategies to pursue questions and interests that arise.
7. Develop an awareness and acceptance of personal abilities.
8. Develop a love of learning for the intrinsic pleasure that it can bring.
9. Develop any special talents and skills to the highest level.

Table 3-2 Typical and Accelerated Learning Objectives in Length, Height, and Distance

Typical Objectives

The students will be able to:

1. Point to the longer/shorter-item.
2. Point to the longer/shorter-same length item.
3. Write line length to the nearest inch.

Accelerated Objectives

The student will be able to:

1. Write line length to nearest eighth inch.
2. Convert up to 10 feet to inches.
3. Write solutions to story problems.

Patterns for Grouping Gifted Students in the Regular Classroom

For philosophical or pragmatic reasons, many school districts choose to place gifted students within the regular classroom structure. Historically, this is where gifted students have received their educational programs. For some of these students this may not be an overwhelming handicap. However, to avoid underserving them, careful attention must be given to assuring that the programming in such an environment is done properly and that differentiated programming is occurring.

In order to meet these goals, attention must be given to the grouping patterns that will respond to the student and class profiles of ability. Six configurations are often found, singly or in combination, in classrooms with gifted students. These options are cluster groups, interest groups, skill groups, multiaged classes, grade skipping, and telescoping.

Cluster Groups

Cluster grouping is a procedure in which a group of high-ability students is placed together in a classroom. This type of grouping assumes that a teacher is more likely to build challenging programs if a number of students will benefit rather than just a few. A typical cluster may number as few as four students and as many as ten. Students within the cluster are an integrated part of the class, but may have some different learning opportunities and materials with which to work. Teachers have more latitude to adjust the pace and depth of learning when they are dealing with more than one student at a time. By grouping these students together, they also have the social/emotional advantage of being in contact with other students like themselves who have similar interests and abilities.

Cluster grouping differs from the typical grouping patterns in that all teachers may not have the same distribution of student ability levels in their classes. The traditional method of rank ordering students as to their achievement levels and then assigning them to classrooms so that all teachers have the same balance of abilities becomes obsolete (see Table 3-3). In its place, a grouping procedure emerges that has the top students in clusters (in one or more classes) and the other students evenly distributed, based on their ability (see Table 3-4).

As stated previously, the advantage to this type of system is two-fold. First, teachers have a defined group of students of similar ability for which to plan a program. Therefore, the students are more likely to receive accommodations that will meet their needs. Second, the students have others like them within the classroom. It is important for gifted students to have the opportunity to interact with their peers as it gives them a more accurate view of their own abilities and an assurance that there are other people like them in the world.

Interest Groups

Groups can also be established based on the interests of students. The purpose is to allow students who have similar interests to explore them together. For example, students who are interested in miming may work together on their art. Those who are interested in computers may meet to write programs. Students who are adept at writing and journalism may belong to a group that writes a classroom newspaper.

Interest groups are often used in conjunction with other types of groups, such as cluster groups and skill groups. They serve an important function in the regular classroom, providing a forum in which students group themselves according to interests rather than abilities. Students who are in the cluster groups may find that interest groups give them the opportunity to integrate themselves into the mainstream of the class, as all the students have a chance to work and meet together.

Skill Groups

Skill grouping can appear in concert with cluster and interest groups. They are established based on the academic needs of the students in the class. There is always a range of achievement levels in any classroom, whether it has the more typical mix of students or is a classroom solely for gifted students. It is not unusual to find gifted students with uneven skills and in need of remediation!

The teacher bases the skill groups on some type of assessment procedure, depending on the type of skill being addressed. For example, third-grade students may be tested on skills ranging from short vowel sounds and syllabication to character development and main idea. When an accurate assessment is made of the skills the students have and have not mastered, a class profile can be assembled from which the skill groups can be drawn (see Table 3-5). All students who have not mastered the short vowel sounds can work on that skill. Other students who know the short vowel sounds should not have to spend their time working on a skill they have already mastered. Rather, these students should be in other skill groups, studying topics they have not mastered, such as syllabification and contractions (see Table 3-6).

Table 3-3 Traditional Grouping Procedure Using Student Ranks

		Teacher		
A	B	C	D	E
1*	2	3	4	5
6	7	8	9	10
11	12	13	14	15
16	17	18	19	20
21	22	23	24	25

* Number 1 ranking student

Table 3-4 Cluster Grouping Procedure Using Student Ranks

		Teacher		
A	B	C	D	E
1*+	5	6	7	8
2+	10	11	12	13
3+	15	16	17	18
4+	20	21	22	23
9	25	26	27	28

* Number 1 ranking student
+ Cluster group member

As with interest groups, skill groups give the students opportunities to work together. Gifted students have varying skills and may need to be in a skill group studying at or below grade level. For instance, a child in a cluster group may not know his math facts and may compute problems by counting on his fingers. Since it is important that this child learn the facts and commit them to memory, an appropriate placement would be to assign this student to a group in which the students are memorizing their math facts.

Students do not remain in the same skill groups all year long. Rather, when a student has mastered skills to the teacher's and student's satisfaction, he or she is ready to move to another skill. Students may find that they are in more than one skill group at a time. Or they may be placed in the same skill group on more than one occasion if the teacher is rotating skill groups and finds that certain students either do not know the skill or have not retained the information from the last time the group was assembled.

Multiaged Classes

Multiaged classes can be of two types. The first type is assembled by having students from more than one grade assigned to one class. This may be a "split-grade" arrangement, in which a teacher has students from two contiguous grades in the same class, such as a second/third-grade combination. Or the class may be made up of students from a number of grades, such as a first/second/third-grade combination.

The second type of multiaged classroom arrangement is found when the typical class structures are in place and teachers have students in the class who are at the same grade level. In this design, when a student needs instruction at an advanced or lower level, that student travels to the appropriate grade classroom for instruction. A fourth-grade student may go to the sixth grade for reading, and a seventh grader may go to high school for an algebra class.

This type of grouping, again, allows students to receive instruction at the level that is appropriate for them. The disadvantage most frequently cited is that the scheduling of these arrangements is often difficult. The fourth-grade teacher may not have math at the same time or for the same amount of time as the sixth-grade teacher. The seventh grader may have to find her own transportation to and from the high school and may find that the algebra classes are conducted during her regular class's reading time. Cooperation among faculty members is necessary to employ this type of grouping efficiently.

Grade Skipping

Grade skipping is a way to group a child with students who more resemble the student's abilities than do the age-peers. This is accomplished by allowing the student to skip a particular grade and advance to the next. For example, a precocious first grader may be advanced to third grade; the second-grade year is omitted, allowing the child more educational experiences in keeping with his or her abilities.

Problems commonly associated with this technique can be minimized if certain guidelines are followed. First, if grade skipping is being seriously considered, it is important that the child be functioning at the 76 percent or above in the class *into which* the child is moving. Students who are used to performing at the top of the class should not be put in a situation where they will be average. This can be psychologically harmful to the student. In addition, social and emotional development should also be considered, along with the physical development of the child. This evaluation is best done by a psychologist who is familiar with high-ability children. Third, the time most conducive to skipping grades without trauma is when a natural break in the class patterns occurs. If a school district has a middle school that begins in fifth grade, then skipping a third grader to fifth might be a reasonable move. Since all the students are developing new peer groups, the child who has skipped a grade will seem less out of place. Another method to consider is early entrance, wherein a four-year-old begins kindergarten or a five-year-old goes directly to first grade.

Table 3-5 Class Profile of Reading Skills

Reading Skills	Bob	Jan	Sue	Jim	Ted	Ben
Recognizes and uses:						
1. Initial consonants	+	+	+	+	+	+
2. Final consonants	+	+	+	—	—	—
3. Blends	+	—	—	+	+	—
4. Long vowels	+	+	—	—	+	+
5. Short vowels	—	—	—	—	+	+
6. Double vowels	—	—	—	—	—	—
7. Silent consonants	+	+	+	—	—	—
8. Syllabication	—	—	—	—	—	—
9. Contractions	—	—	—	—	—	—

+ = Mastered skill
— = Instruction needed

Again, the peer group is established at the onset. Finally, if grade skipping is advised, it should be done on a trial basis. If the students are not flourishing in the new environment, they should be allowed to return to the class level originally skipped.

Telescoping

Many of the problems inherent in grade skipping are eased by telescoping, a procedure in which a student enters into a mixed grade situation with the understanding that two years of work will be completed in one (see Table 3-7). A student may be assigned to a fourth/fifth-grade split. The student comes into the class as a fourth grader and leaves at the end of one year with the fifth graders. This is possible because most students who are eligible for such consideration are already quite advanced for their age and probably already know most of what is being taught at their level. Care must be taken in this instance to assure that time is spent learning the fourth/fifth-grade skills that the student does not know so that no gaps appear in the student's skills.

One of the advantages most frequently mentioned regarding this approach is that the student maintains a peer group, as the students with whom the child is being advanced are already friends and classmates. The student is not arriving into an unknown world full of strangers who think she or he is an anomaly.

Grouping, then, is one way to begin thinking about ways to educate gifted children appropriately in the regular classroom. These six grouping techniques are administrative arrangements that can be employed to facilitate the learning of children and the teaching of the educators. When properly done, grouping can result in students receiving instruction at levels reflecting their abilities and in teachers organizing their classrooms to meet individual needs of students. It is this *student-centered* approach to teaching that allows students to engage in educational experiences in a way that will result in full and comprehensive programming.

Individualization as a Framework for Program Planning

With grouping as the base, individualizing is one of the primary frameworks upon which programs for gifted students in regular classrooms are built. In order to begin the process of educating students when a range of abilities exists, you must make a philosophical commitment to educating individual children with individual needs, rather than educating a mass of students termed, for example, "fifth graders."

Schools exist for the purpose of educating our youths. In order to be effective in this pursuit, we cannot forget the needs of the students we are instructing. Therefore, it becomes imperative that a student-centered approach to learning is adopted. This may sound self-evident, but the mechanics of delivering programs that are student-centered are difficult at best. Those people who are involved in the decision-making processes must be committed to this philosophy. Teachers must be trained to become managers of learning as well as oracles of knowledge. Schedules must be devised that allow flexible pacing for students. Materials need to be acquired that will allow students to pursue their broad interests at their own levels of ability. These conditions are not easily realized, but they are essential components to educating students in a student-centered environment.

Individualization Defined

The word *individualization* is often misused and misunderstood. Clark (1983) simply defines individualization as "a way of organizing learning experiences so that the rate, content, schedule, experiences, and depth of exploration available to all students stem from their assessed needs and interests" (p. 215). This does not suggest that each student must be doing something different than her or his classmates at all times. Rather, it outlines a process through which educational decisions are made—by assessment of individual needs and interests from which learning experiences are organized. These may appear in the form of large or small group instruction, if more than one student or the entire class is in need of the same experience. Or it may result in students working on their own for part of the day.

What Is Individualized?

Blackburn and Powell (1976) cite five facets of an educational program that can be individualized: (1) the rates at which students progress through their work, (2) the actual learning alternatives, (3) the schedule, (4) the

---

Table 3-6 Skill Groups Drawn from Class Profile

Final Consonants	Short Vowels	Blends
Jim	Bob	Jan
Ted	Jan	Sue
Ben	Sue	Ben
	Jim	

Table 3-7 Grade Skipping and Telescoping Compared

	Student Grade Progression						
Grade skipping	K	1	2	3	5	6	7
Telescoping	K	1	2	3/4	5	6	7

---

content of the instruction, and (5) the depth of exploration that is allowed. These areas correspond closely to the learning characteristics of gifted children that necessitate differentiating programs (see Table 3-8). This compatibility makes individualization of programs a highly defensible alternative for programming for these students.

Aspects of an Individualized Program

Dunn and Dunn (1975) have made great contributions to the practice of individualizing programs for students. They suggest that there are thirteen aspects of individualized programs. There are many such lists in the literature on this topic, but the Dunn and Dunn listing is one of the most inclusive. It mentions the following:

1. Diagnosis (teacher, student, cooperative, team);
2. Prescription (teacher, student, cooperative, team);
3. Publicly stated objectives (teacher, student, cooperatively or team prescribed);
4. Alternative resources through which to learn;
5. Alternative or optional activities;
6. Self-pacing;
7. Self-leveling;
8. Self-assessment and/or cooperative assessment, teacher and/or team assessment;
9. Self-selection of learning methods;
10. Objectives and prescriptions based on student abilities and interests;
11. Opportunities for student creativity incorporated into prescription;
12. Criterion-referenced evaluation; and
13. Performance-based evaluation (student demonstration of knowledge through means other than written tests) (p. 48).

Many of these aspects to individualized instruction appear in methods typically employed in the classroom, such as learning activity packages, contracts, programmed learning packages, computer-based tutorial programs, work-study experiences, mentorships, and commercially marketed instructional programs. Combining many approaches to individualization will most likely be necessary when building programs with multiple options. This variety serves only to strengthen a program, as it makes the program more flexible and responsive to student needs, abilities, and interests.

Advantage to Individualization

The greatest advantage to individualizing programs for students is that it allows them to receive instruction that is appropriate for their abilities in content and pace, achievement levels, and interests. In addition, individualizing programs for students allows the teacher more freedom to attend to the individual learning needs of the students. Dunn and Dunn (1975) list the following additional benefits accrued through individualizing educational programs:

1. Provides for student success rather than failure;
2. Builds self-image;
3. Permits peer interaction that causes retention;
4. Decreases student dependence on the teacher and initially transfers it to peers and eventually to self;
5. Provides for problem-solving experiences;
6. Develops internal motivation rather than peer competition; and
7. Develops critical analysis abilities (pp. 48–49).

The advantages to individualizing programming are many. It allows students an opportunity to take charge of their own learning and gain the tools to become life-long learners. The gifted students in the classroom must learn how to rely on themselves to gain information because much of their learning will be accomplished on their own. It is unrealistic to expect teachers to know everything the gifted students know or want to know. However, teachers can provide students with the tools to learn on their own. Certainly, allowing for individualization in the classroom is one way to begin this process.

Individualized Educational Plans (IEPs) for the Gifted

One strategy that has been proposed to plan and manage instruction for the gifted is the Individualized Educational Plan (IEP). It contains the following information about a student: student name, school, address, phone; current performance levels; annual goals for each area of special programming; short-term objectives for each goal;

Table 3-8 Correspondence Between Areas that Can Be Individualized and Learning Characteristics of Gifted Students

Area to Be Individualized	Gifted Students' Characteristics
1. Rate	Learns more quickly
2. Learning alternatives	Wide range of interests
3. Schedule	Learns more quickly
4. Content	Understands with greater depth
	Wide range of interests
5. Depth of exploration	Understands with greater depth

an evaluation plan for each goal; and date and signatures of all parties involved. Some IEPs also include information about support services and ancillary staff involvements. This document is usually brought to a meeting at which the teachers, administrator, psychologist, parents, and (sometimes) the child discuss the plan and approve its intent and contents.

IEPs have received mixed levels of acceptance among those people who work with gifted students. Many have found them to be a useful planning and management tool. In fact, in *The State of the State's Gifted and Talented Education* (Council of State Directors of Programs for the Gifted, 1986), it is reported that eleven states require IEPs for assessment and placement purposes. Although the use of this technique seems to be growing, there are still those people who believe that IEPs are too constricting for the gifted and that their use aligns gifted education too closely with special education.

Assembling the Mosaic

Devising a program schema for gifted and talented students is much like assembling a 2,000-piece jigsaw puzzle or an intricate stained glass window. Each piece is vital to the completed product; if pieces are missing, the entirety is marred. If visualized, the programming efforts for these students would look much like a mosaic. That is, they are composed of many parts of differing hues, intensity, and shapes, but when placed together a harmony emerges that is pleasing and tranquil to all who view it.

In order to construct a mosaic of program options that has these traits, balance must be attained between the key elements. First, the programs must be based in an environment that is conducive to learning and that respects the varying abilities of the students. This environment should include teachers who understand and have compassion for gifted students and who are willing to allow the students to enter into the process of decision making in a student-centered approach to living.

Second, a balance must be achieved between programs that will deal with the pace at which students learn (generally accelerated courses of study), the depth at which they learn (usually enrichment opportunities), and their unique interests. All are essential to the harmony of the mosaic for gifted and talented students. Too often, programs are heavily weighted in one direction. Either they deal only with acceleration or enrichment, or they are so intense in academic areas that they ignore the arts and extracurricular activities such as drama, gymnastics, and computer club. For the best results, many possible configurations for programming should be available, with the actual courses students take based on their own profiles of ability.

Finally, a balance must be struck between what a student can handle cognitively, emotionally, and physically. There are many instances in which a student has been pushed beyond the limit and has either failed, stopped participating, underachieved, or (in the extreme) become suicidal. Program mosaics must make room for students to work at comfortable (yet challenging) levels. For some students, highly rigorous, demanding, accelerative programs will be fine. However, for others, more conservative programs that include a smattering of accelerated options, along with enrichment opportunities, will suffice nicely. When dealing with young children, this balance is especially important. With these students, physical abilities often lag behind cognitive abilities, and being engaged in options that require them to write or draw beyond their abilities may lead to disaster. In one instance, a ten-year-old student was involved with radical acceleration and was taking his courses at the high school. He was able to comprehend the language and science courses fine, but he began to have headaches and was soon bedridden. The doctors determined that the child was physically exhausted by trying to keep up with the older students, carrying heavy textbooks and studying for prolonged hours. This is an obvious case of a student's program being out of balance. Programming options were being employed, but the results were not acceptable.

As you begin to think about programming for the gifted and talented students in regular classroom settings, remember that you should develop a mosaic of programming possibilities from which actual student programs can be matched to profiles of ability. Balance is essential to the success of the programs. What works for one student will not necessarily work for another. Having the capability to respond in many ways to the unique needs of students will allow you to provide educational experiences that will enhance the students' learning and your own satisfaction as an educator.

Summary

Planning programs for gifted students in regular classrooms requires many decisions to be made. These decisions are based on the needs, abilities, and interests of the students, as well as institutional requirements. However, it is critical that the needs of students take priority and that decisions are made based on what those needs are. This requires familiarity with the students involved and a commitment to their individual programming needs.

Profiles of student needs serve as the basis for program planning. These profiles should suggest multiple programming options, or programming mosaics, that will accommodate the pace and depth at which these students learn, as well as their interests. Grouping patterns and individualized program prescriptions that can best serve the students can then be outlined. Gifted students have unique learning needs that necessitate differentiated programming. These needs result in challenges for classroom teachers—to provide the types of programs needed for the students without making them feel different and without segregating them from the class in some way. When the gifted and talented are in the regular classroom, they need to feel a part of the class, not apart from the class; it is up to the classroom teacher to make sure this happens.

Action Steps

1. Review the programs that are currently available to students within and outside the regular classroom. Is there sufficient range to accommodate the educational needs of your students?
2. Make a list of these programs, adding a short description of each. Use this for reference in program planning when matching student profiles to programs.
3. Closely scrutinize the regular classroom offerings to determine the extent to which they allow individual student growth, flexible pacing, in-depth investigations, and interests to be pursued.
4. Spend some time thinking about the extent to which you feel prepared to open the regular classroom to student exploration and shared responsibility for learning.
5. Choose a group of three to five students and review their assessment data. Are their current programs sufficient? What is needed? Begin to plan comprehensive programs for them.
6. Expand the number of students receiving individualized programs as much as you are comfortably able.

References You Can Use

Cox, J., Daniel N., & Boston, B. (1985). *Educating able learners: Programs and promising practices*. Austin, TX: University of Texas Press.

Dunn, R., & Dunn, K. (1972). *Practical approaches to individualizing instruction. Contracts and other effective teaching strategies*. West Nyack, NY: Parker Publishing Company.

Juntune, J. (Ed.). (1986). *Successful programs for the gifted and talented* (2nd ed.). Circle Pines, MN: National Association for Gifted Children.

Kaplan, S. (1974). *Providing programs for the gifted and talented: A handbook*. Ventura, CA: Office of the Ventura County Superintendent of Schools.

Renzulli, J., & Reis, S. (1986). *The schoolwide enrichment model: A comprehensive plan for educational excellence*. Mansfield Center, CT: Creative Learning Press.

Renzulli, J., & Smith, L. (1979). *A guidebook for developing individualized educational programs for gifted and talented students*. Mansfield Center, CT: Creative Learning Press.

Part Three: Designing the Curriculum

Whereas programs are the administrative configurations in which students are placed, *curriculum* refers to the manner in which they are taught, the content that is presented, and the resources that are used. In programs for the gifted, differentiated curriculum must be instituted in order to give these students an equal opportunity to develop their abilities. Maker (1982) lists four ways in which curriculum for the gifted can be modified: the content, process, product, and environmental aspects of curriculum. Since environment has been covered in Part One, the other three areas will be discussed in the following chapters.

In Chapter 8, the issue of differentiation of curriculum is discussed along with the ways teachers can select the modifications that fit with their ways of teaching. To make this more clear, sample curricular plans for various subject areas are presented which can serve as models for future curriculum development.

The ten models most common to programs for the gifted are presented in Chapter 9. For each, the model is described, its relationship to the ways in which curriculum can be modified is explored, and the appropriate use of the model is explained. Although these models do not represent all those meaningful for the gifted, they do give a sampling of what is available and how models can be used.

The last chapter of this section is composed of a number of case studies that present problems inherent in providing programs for the gifted in the regular classroom. The nature of the problems are described along with alternative solutions and the strategies actually used. Each case study is followed by a sample of lessons that respond to the various learning levels of students in a regular classroom.

Adhering to any one model or approach to instruction will not meet the needs of the students in that class. Rather, accomplished teachers know when various methods will work and under what conditions they should use different approaches to the subject matter at hand. The challenge for the regular classroom teachers who are dealing with a wide range of abilities is to deliver instruction in a way to which students at all levels can relate. This is where the *art* of teaching comes about.

8: Prescribing the Appropriate Curriculum

The meaning of the word *curriculum* is not always fully understood. It refers to the content, manner of presentation, materials, and processes used to instruct students in the classroom. The most frequent misunderstanding is how the *curriculum* differs from the *program* that is being mounted. The program is the administrative structure employed, whereas the curriculum is that which is taught and the manner in which it is taught.

The curriculum, or course of study, may or may not be written down in such a way that it represents a formal plan. At times, scope and sequence charts are available or curriculum guides have been prepared. At other times, teachers are free to develop their own curricular plans. It is important that the curricular plan not be left to chance or haphazard preparation. It should be built on a philosophy of how children learn and contain a pattern for the presentation of skills so that there is a prepared progression in student learning. The plan should also contain suggested resources and ways to present the content. Individual teachers can then take the plan and modify it to meet their own teaching style and the differing needs of their students.

Differentiating Curriculum for the Gifted

Due to the unique needs and abilities of gifted and talented students, a separate consideration for these individuals is warranted when curriculum is being designed. Maker (1982) lists four areas in which the curriculum for the gifted may need modification from the norm: the content that is covered, the process or method of instruction, the products that are expected from the students, and the environment in which learning takes place. This chapter will look at the three areas that have not already been discussed (content, process/method, and product) in order to see how each applies in the case of gifted and talented students receiving appropriate curricular modifications in the regular classroom.

Modifying the Content of Curriculum

As we have seen, the gifted and talented students in a classroom may already have mastered the content of a particular unit or course of study before it is presented. Thus, they may be capable of going beyond the usual scope and sequence to more advanced skills and concepts. In order to facilitate student progress, curricular modifications must take place. This may mean making arrangements for more complex content, employing abstractions, arranging for more advanced materials, or finding alternative placements for the students so that they can take advantage of content modification through participation in a more advanced setting.

Programs such as fast-paced classes, cross-level grouping, independent studies, continuous progress curriculum, and curricular compacting can help make modifying curricular content more simple, but programmatic schema alone do not assure that appropriate curricular practice is taking place. You *must look beyond the program configuration to the instruction itself to determine if the students are involved in content that is appropriate to their abilities.*

A third-grade unit on the structure of the earth was modified by one teacher so that the content was differentiated for the students. The teacher was using such teaching techniques as whole group instruction, small group activities, an enrichment center on the unit, and demonstrations. It became obvious through the questions the students asked that some already knew the names of the layers in the earth and about the materials that composed those layers. Therefore, the teacher decided that some content modification was in order for those students, and created a small group for the study of earthquakes. This group met with the teacher while the other students were doing their small group activities. The earthquake group learned about why earthquakes occur and were assigned the task of finding out how the intensity of earthquakes is measured. Filmstrips, books, and charts were made available for their use in this project. After they found the answers to the questions, they were asked to design an activity to do with the rest of the class in order to instruct them in the information that they had learned. The outgrowth of this curricular modification was beyond the expected lecture and chart presentation. The students made a learning center for the class and arranged (with teacher assistance) for the students to visit the local university's seismology laboratory. In addition, two students pursued the idea further through an independent study on how scientists predict geological activity.

In another instance, a sixth-grade class was studying basic geometric shapes. As part of their study, students were to find shapes in the environment and make conjectures as to why particular shapes were used in those circumstances. They had little difficulty locating shapes, but justifying the use of the shapes was a far more difficult proposition. However, the investigation did lead three students to experiments using different shapes in design. After a number of toothpick and glue structures were made, the students were encouraged by the teacher to formalize their investigation by using the scientific method in their studies and recording their results in a journal format. Following their investigation, the results of their study were published in the school newspaper.

Both of these examples show how content modifications can be made. They can be as unobtrusive as asking questions that require students to think in abstract terms, or as obtrusive as setting up parallel lessons and conducting more than one course of study at the same time. Different circumstances call for different remedies. The key to successfully modifying the content of curriculum is to be flexible, on your guard to notice when it is needed, and equipped with access to a variety of resources for the students to use.

Modifying the Process/Method of Instruction

The process or method of presenting the content is the second way in which curricula can be differentiated for gifted and talented students Such students often display unbridled curiosities, desires to probe subjects in depth, preferences to study on their own, capacity for disciplined investigation, and a capacity to think in ways that may differ from the rest of the class. These and other abilities, when coupled with the goals of preparing students to be independent and lifelong learners, may require that the teacher modifies the way in which content is presented and the way students conduct themselves in the classroom.

Again, there are programs that will enhance the teacher's ability to make these modifications without a great deal of disruption to the rest of the class. Among these are programs using high-level questioning techniques, simulations, contracting, mentors, Future Problem Solving, and Junior Great Books. But, as with content modifications, program structure alone is not sufficient to insure that proper curriculum is occurring. Changes in the way in which material is presented and the very roles of the teacher and students may also need to be adjusted.

There are many modifications to process that a teacher can make in order to assure that the needs of all the students in the classroom are being met. Among those most necessary for the gifted and talented students are: good questioning techniques requiring the use of the upper levels of thought to answer; allowing students to become involved in their learning through choosing content, flexible pacing, self-monitoring progress, and selecting resources; using both convergent and divergent activities to enhance students' abilities to solve problems; and group process activities to help students learn to work together in a cooperative fashion.

Again, flexibility is a key ingredient to successfully modifying the processes and methods of instruction. Using any one delivery system for instruction is not appropriate, whether it is the lecture method or self-discovery method of learning. Master teachers know when a particular strategy will be most beneficial in helping the students to grasp the content being studied. They also are in tune with which methods of instruction are the most beneficial to each of their students, as learning styles will differ. Thus, many different methods may be used at one time.

In the instance where kindergarten students were engaged in a unit on transportation, the teacher tried to vary the methods of instruction in order to accommodate the different students' instructional needs and abilities. This was apparent in that students were given choices throughout the unit as to which of the activities they engaged in and the types of products they made. A whole-group brainstorming activity began the unit, with students listing as many types of transportation as they could think of. This was followed by separating students into interest groups which proceeded to investigate three common types of transportation in depth. One group studied cars and their impact on the way we live. The other two groups had the same focus with trains and airplanes. Creative dramatics, student story telling, block construction, and interviews of family members were used to assemble information and relate it to the students in the other groups. At the end of the unit, students were again given a choice as to how their products would be prepared. The teacher presented the options of story writing, picture drawing or construction, and dramatic presentation or demonstration. Students were also allowed to suggest ideas of their own which were approved or modified by the teacher.

In another circumstance, the teacher of a fifth-grade class presented a unit on theater, particularly plays. The main focus of the unit was to have students understand how plays are constructed. Following a whole-group presentation, a number of different methods were used to reinforce the information. The teacher had the students review four plays and make a list of how their structures were alike and how they differed; cut a five-scene play into pieces, with each scene being a piece, and had the students assemble the play in the order in which they thought it was written and create a rationale for that order; and had students present short plays in which certain components were missing (props, staging directions, dialog), asking other students to determine what the missing parts were. Then, as a culminating experience, students were allowed to choose the activity in which they would like to participate: play writing, play critique and written review, or analysis of the work of one playwright in a form of the student's choice.

Perhaps the most difficult aspect of modifying the process or method of instruction is that it may require teachers to relinquish some of the control they maintain over the curriculum and students' activities. But by doing so, they open the door to student involvement and student-centered environments, resulting in students who are more involved with taking responsibility for their own learning. This type of differentiation will also require teachers to be more agile in the skills they use to instruct and more diligent about the monitoring of individual student progress.

Modifying the Products of Learning

The products of student learning are another area that may be differentiated for the gifted and talented students in the class. These students can use their abilities to explore topics in depth and to show creativity and perseverance in designing divergent products uniquely representative of the learning they have experienced. Although learning to write reports is an important skill for all students, there are other ways to present information in a summative way. All students should be encouraged to explore many avenues to product development and be creative in the ways they present their work.

Obviously, the skills involved with presenting divergent products are ones that should be developed by as many students in the classroom as possible. You might find, however, that the gifted and talented students are more able to develop products that are on a larger scale, more complex, or most closely related to the products generated in real-life circumstances.

From the previous scenarios, you can see that the teachers gave students options for their products and the chance to design their own. This has been a successful strategy in classrooms of kindergarten through college-level students. The students in those examples did such things as demonstrations, journals, newspaper articles, dramatics, constructions, interviews, and critiques to synthesize and present the knowledge that they had gained over the course of study. But the list of possible products extends far beyond that. The possibilities are limited only by the students' imaginations, resources, time available—and the teacher's patience!

Surprisingly enough, students often have to be taught how to create divergent products. They are far more comfortable with continuing what is known (written reports and pictures) and often resist delving into the unknown of mobile construction or filmstrip producing. However, experience shows that when students are encouraged and given the material and psychological support necessary, they quickly find the new methods of presentation fun and a learning experience in and of themselves. Students have been known to be quite competitive in their product generation, which sometimes calls for tempering by the teacher. But on the whole, the excitement and products generated make the challenges for both the students and teacher well worth the effort.

Finding outlets for student products is one of the greatest challenges faced by the teacher. During the course of the year, students should have products that are judged in real-life circumstances with true-to-life results. Science fairs, young authors' conferences, recitals, and exhibitions are among the vehicles used extensively. Beyond those, student investigations and products often indicate an outlet that is appropriate. For example, if a student is delving into the problems associated with Dutch elm disease, she may wish to prepare a proposal for presentation to the town council or create a foundation for fund raising to save the trees through spraying. A student who is interested in writing may wish to send a poem or short story to a magazine that publishes student work or perhaps publish such a magazine on his own. In both instances there are real-life audiences, real-life requirements in preparing the product, and real-life evaluation of that product.

Choosing Modifications That Are Right for You

Installing modifications in content, process, and product in the classroom will require prior planning in order to be successful. It is the wise educator who begins on a conservative scale and escalates the changes as the students and the teacher become adept at the new procedures. As it is difficult for students to begin to make choices, to ask high-level questions, and to take responsibility for their learning at the onset, so it is difficult for teachers to relinquish total control over the classroom, to institute multiple programming options, and to make modifications to tried and true methods of instruction. The following guidelines should help make the transition easier.

1. Begin at a comfortable pace. Limit the scope by choosing one subject area or one group of students with which to begin. Gradually add more students and more subject areas to your programming mosaic as you feel comfortable. It would not be unusual for this process to take two to three school years to implement fully. So be patient and concentrate on the growth process. Do make a pact with yourself, however, to try at least one new approach per term. Designing a multiple-year plan will help you know in what direction you are going and help you keep track of the progress you have made (see Table 8-1).

2. Make a chart and list the programs you would like to institute and the curricular modifications that can be used with each one (see Table 8-2). Notice that most of the programs in the list can be modified in more than one way. For example, an independent study option will lend itself to curricular modifications in all three areas. Odyssey of the Mind is especially good for process and product modifications. This chart should help you coordinate your effort and demonstrate to you that it is not impossible to integrate programming options and curricular modifications.

3. Think about teaching style. How do teachers tend to interact with the students? What is the environment like in the classroom? What type of modifications are already being made for students of above average ability? Are there already modifications being made in content, process, and/or product? What do teachers do in their classroom of which they are most proud? What do the students seem to enjoy the most? Build the initial changes from the areas in

which you excel; make them even better. Begin with the area in which you feel most confidence and expand into other areas. If a teacher is a whiz in language arts and has a particularly good unit on Caldecott winning books, that may be the place to start. Think of how you can enhance the unit even more to accommodate the needs of all the students in the class. Perhaps you could invite an author to talk with the students or demonstrate illustrating to the class, include options for the final project, or arrange for a student-sponsored book fair with the profits going to a special charity project of the students. By building on successes, you are more likely to have even greater success. Do not be content to work only within your comfort zone, however. Be bold and expand your efforts to areas in which you are less comfortable and build them into areas in which you can be proud.

4. Consider the resources you have at your disposal. Think about the materials that are already in the classroom, those in the storeroom and the basement at home, people who are available to assist you both in the school and the community, the cultural institutions in your area, companies that have school programs and instructional materials available, audio-visual devices, and even old class notes from your university classes. When you first start, rely on what you have at hand. As you expand your options, expand your resources at the same time, and open the doors to learning even further. If you are interested in adding an art appreciation program to your programming mosaic and do not have a museum with an "Art Lady" program (volunteers who give art appreciation lectures in the classroom), you may be able to find a student or community person with an art history background who can do the job for you. Or, if you would like to investigate simulation gaming and have none available in your personal library, you may be able to order one through a computer software catalog, find one in the local library or media center, or make your own. Resource availability can make some techniques impossible to use, but there are plenty of others to take their place. Trusting your own ingenuity can often fill the gap that a lack of resources may make.

5. Give each option that you try an ample chance to develop. If you try one learning center and find that the students have trouble self-directing their activities, it can be tempting to give up on that option all together. However, as was stated earlier, students have to learn such skills as how to make choices, budget their time, work with other students, and read directions carefully. The gifted and talented are no exception. Teachers also have to be prepared to modify and experiment with their instructional techniques. This is not to say that everything you try will eventually work—only that sometimes it takes work to make things go the way we want them to.

6. Review your performance on a regular basis to see if you are moving in the right direction. Ask yourself these questions:

a. Are all students in this class working at levels commensurate with their abilities?

b. Do students have options from which they can choose some of their assignments?

c. Are the content, process, and products of instruction regularly being modified so that all students are involved in meaningful instruction?

d. Has a new strategy, program, or activity recently been tried with the students?

e. How well are the gifted and talented students integrated into the classroom activities? Have my attempts at providing appropriate instruction resulted in isolating them from the rest of the group?

f. Is the program more valid than it was prior to beginning the changes?

g. Am I happier? Are the students happier and more productive?

7. If you determine that a technique, program, or activity is not working out, try something else. Not all teachers will want to mount a guest lecture series. Remember: Your goal is to put together options in programming and curriculum that will form a balance for students in the areas of pacing, in-depth inquiry, content, methods of instruction, products, and student interests. An infinite number of configurations are possible.

8. Feel free to experiment. Educators are often afraid to try new things for fear that they will not work and they will look foolish. Discard those notions and have fun trying new techniques regardless of the anticipated outcome. How about staging a class debate, a make-your-own sundae production line, or a class meeting to discuss problems that arise? What is the worst thing that can happen? It might not work, but there is always tomorrow and lots of other new experiences to explore. Being willing to experiment can bring excitement to the classroom, new vigor to the teacher, and avid interests by the students about what is going to happen next. You may even want to set up half an hour a week as "Anything Goes Time," a time in which you try new ideas with the understanding of all involved that they are to give it a fair chance. You may end up enjoying it and it is good modeling for risk taking.

Table 8-1 Multiple-Year Plan for Curriculum Development and Modification

Year	Areas for Review
Year 1	1. Individualize the reading basal textbook.
	2. Make question cards for books in class library.
	3. Investigate Junior Great Books.
	4. Review each unit as presented for modifying content, process, and products.
	5. Review progress at end of year and develop detailed plan for Year 2.
Year 2	1. Individualize mathematics text.
	2. Alter units to reflect needed modifications.
	3. Continue work as needed in Language Arts.
	4. Review and plan for Year 3.
Year 3	1. Concentrate on the science curriculum, making it more participatory.

Table 8-2 Relationship between Programming Options and Curricular Modifications

Program Option	Curricular Modification		
	Content	Process	Product
Fast-Paced Classes	x	x	x
Self-Instruction	x	x	x
Early Admission	x		
Contracting	x	x	x
Correspondence Courses	x	x	
Independent Studies	x	x	x
Simulations	x	x	x
Mentorships	x	x	x
Guest Lectures	x		
Junior Great Books	x	x	
Odyssey of the Mind		x	x

x = Compatibility between program option and curricular modification

Sample Curricular Plans

There are many ways to begin the process of curricular planning to insure that all students in the classroom are engaged in instruction that is suited to their abilities and needs. Content can be accelerated, compacted, enriched, and extended; processes can be open-ended, discovery-based, teacher-centered, and student-centered; and products can be conventional, unconventional, true to real life, simple, or complex. The variations and additions to this list are endless, but the task is really quite simple. Three sample lesson plans appear below to show the manner in which curriculum can be differentiated for the gifted and talented in the regular classroom.

Discovering the Decimal System

One of the basic monetary units taught in elementary schools deals with the decimal system. Usually there are a number of students who know little about the system and several who already have it mastered. It then becomes the teacher's task to differentiate the curriculum so that all of these students have a meaningful instructional experience rather than allowing some of the students to be involved in lessons about which they already know the content. In this case, the teacher chose to modify the content that was being taught in order to enrich the students' understanding of the decimal systems. This was done in a rather simple manner by having all of the students engaged in basically the same activities but with different frames of reference. One group studied the U.S. monetary system while the other students were told to choose the system of another country, which also uses a decimal base, for investigation. The curricular plan (see Table 8-3) shows the objectives, activities, and resources that were used for one segment of the unit.

Creative Story Composing

Creative writing is one subject area in which differentiation seems to occur naturally. Students who are able writers show their talents in the products they create, at times appearing to be unaffected by the assignment that is given. This should not be interpreted to suggest that teachers do not have to plan modifications for the gifted and talented writers, for that is not the case! It is vital to their growth that they be given the opportunity to do so. This can be accomplished in a fairly unobtrusive way. The lesson plan shown (see Table 8-4) differentiates for the gifted and talented writing students through the open-ended process that is used. The primary resource used is the book, *The Silver Pony* by Lynd Ward (1973). This classic book tells the story of a little boy who lives on a farm and discovers a magical silver pony. When his father does not believe that the pony exists, the pony and the boy run away to have adventures throughout the world and return to the farm at the end of the story. What makes this book uniquely suited to the lesson is that there are no words in the story, only pictures, and the pictures are displayed on the right-hand pages only, leaving white space on the left-hand side for story composing (in the imagination or on the paper). Thus, the students can write the story at their own writing levels with as much dialog, embellishment, phraseology, and figurative language as they desire, using the pictures for inspiration. No special grouping, resources, or instructions are needed in order to give the students a chance to write at their individual levels.

Drawing a Still Life

Arranging instruction so that students can grow at their own rates in the arts is also an important matter to consider. This lesson (see Table 8-5) focuses on the discipline of drawing, with a still life as the subject. In this case, the

---

Table 8-3 Plan for Differentiated Lesson on Decimal System

TOPIC: The Decimal System

Objectives:
1. The students will be able to assign the monetary value to each coin presented.
2. The students will know that the decimal system is based on units of ten.

Activities:
1. Administer pretest and determine if any students already have mastery of concepts.
2. Students who do not will meet in group for instruction on the value of U.S. coins and the decimal equivalent of each.
3. Students who have mastered content will choose another country that has a decimal-based monetary system, study the value of each coin and its decimal equivalent, and report their results in a small group meeting with the teacher.
4. Students will show their knowledge through successfully using the monetary system (U.S. or foreign) in the class store.

Resources:
1. Mathematics textbooks and library books.
2. Filmstrip/Video on coins of the world.

---

teacher has designated the subject, the materials, and the products that are to be used. However, the lesson is differentiated for the more talented art students and has been done in an intriguing way. The challenge has been made greater for these students by *limiting* the materials that they can use. They sit in the same studio, draw the same still life under the same lighting, for the same amount of time, but they use only one color of crayon to do so. Requiring this limitation forces the students to seek alternative ways of showing gradations of color and shading in their composition. Therefore, they are working on techniques that are more advanced than those techniques being used by the other students, and are essentially receiving accelerated content in the same setting as the rest of the class. Again, this is an example of a lesson that has been differentiated for student abilities without special assignments, resources, or settings for some of the students. Although such alterations in the curriculum are sometimes needed in meeting the curricular needs of the gifted students in the regular classroom, this is not always the case and much can be done to provide suitable curriculum within that setting.

Student Outcomes from Appropriate Curriculum

Differentiating curriculum so that students receive meaningful instruction extends beyond presenting more and different information. The intellectual and emotional health of students is affected by the manner in which curriculum is implemented. Appropriate curriculum contributes to students' feelings of accomplishment, vitality, and growth, whereas inappropriate curriculum can lead to potential difficulties.

When students are involved in learning new skills and content rather than information they already know, they may be more active learners and less bored with their schooling. The challenge of learning new information and skills keeps the gifted and talented interested in school as they see its relevancy to their lives. It can also help deter

later problems such as underachievement and dropping out of school altogether.

Appropriate curricular experiences can also give students the tools to continue to learn on their own. By exposing the students to processes, information, and resources that are diverse and suited to their needs and interests, they may find doors opening for them in their own mind and lead to new areas of interest and exploration.

Summary

Because of the various abilities and needs of the students in a classroom, a single curricular plan may not be sufficient to instruct them appropriately. With the gifted and talented students, there are at least four factors (Maker, 1982) that may need to be modified in order to provide these students with instruction that is suited to them. These areas are the environment in which instruction takes place, the content of that instruction, the process or method of the instruction, and the products that are the results of the students' learning. By so doing, the students can continue as active learners in an environment that nurtures growth and development of new skills and abilities.

Action Steps

1. Consider how curriculum decisions are currently being made. Do you have a curriculum guide, teachers' manuals, or scope and sequence charts? If so, familiarize yourself with their content, if you have not already done so.
2. What curricular modifications are already being made in regular classrooms? Are these adequate for the needs of your students? If not, choose one modification to make tomorrow.
3. Design a plan for differentiated curriculum building for the next year. What areas are the strength of the curriculum? Begin here and then extend to areas that are less strong.

Table 8-4 Plan for Differentiated Lesson in Creative Writing

TOPIC: Story writing

Objective:
Students will write a story using dialog between at least two characters.

Activities:
1. The book *The Silver Pony* will be shown to the students.
2. Students will volunteer to tell the story for the first chapter, including dialog between the father and the boy.
3. The students will choose one chapter for which to write the story and include dialog between two characters. All chapters will have at least one writer so that the entire story will be told.
4. The composite story will be read and critiqued by the class.

Resource:
Lynd Ward, *The Silver Pony* (Boston: Houghton Mifflin Company, 1973).

Table 8-5 Plan for Differentiated Lesson in Drawing

TOPIC: Drawing a still life

Objective:
1. Students will draw a still life, including shadowing and gradations of color.

Activities:
1. The still life will be composed by two of the students from a variety of objects made available by the instructor.
2. The technique of shading will be reviewed.
3. Students will choose their own perspective for drawing and will then do so.
4. Advanced students will limit their color selection to one.
5. Drawings will be displayed and critiqued.

Resources:
1. Objects for the still life.
2. Books on still life.
3. Paper and crayons.

---

4. At the end of the first year, assess your progress and develop a multiple-year plan for programming and curricular development for dealing with multiple student abilities.
5. Meet with the school's curriculum committee and arrange for materials and inservice presentations to assist you and the staff in this activity.

References You Can Use

Gallagher, J. (1985). *Teaching the gifted child* (3rd. ed.). Boston: Allyn and Bacon.

Maker, J. (1982). *Curriculum development for the gifted.* Rockville, MD: Aspen Systems Corporation.

Ostrander, S., & Schroeder, L. (1979). *Superlearning.* New York: Dell Publishing Company.

Swassing, R. (Ed.). (1985). *Teaching gifted children and adolescents.* Columbus, OH: Merrill Publishing Company.

VanTassel-Baska, J. (1986). *Handbook on curriculum for the gifted.* Evanston, IL: Center for Talent Development.

Educational Placement and Classroom Management

Pfiffner, L. J., and R. A. Barkley. 1990. In *Attention deficit hyperactivity disorder: A handbook for diagnosis and treatment,* ed. R. A. Barkley, 498–539. New York: The Guilford Press.

Chapter 15[*]

Education does not mean teaching people to know what they do not know; it means teaching them to behave as they do not behave.

—John Ruskin (1819–1900)

Children with Attention-deficit Hyperactivity Disorder (ADHD) may exhibit a wider range of problems in the classroom than in any other setting. Inattention, impulsivity, and overactivity, the cardinal symptoms of ADHD, translate into a variety of classroom behavior problems including difficulty in staying seated, paying attention, working independently, and following directions and rules. ADHD children are also often disruptive and interrupt class lessons and quiet work periods. They also tend to be very disorganized and have great difficulty in keeping track of their academic materials (e.g., books, paper, pencils) and assignments.

In addition to problems stemming from the core symptoms, children with ADHD frequently exhibit a myriad of associated problems that may have an even more debilitating effect on school performance. Given their high rates of off-task and disruptive behavior, it is not surprising that ADHD children experience frequent academic problems ranging from failure to complete work and poor grades to significant underachievement, grade retentions, suspensions, and expulsions (see Chapters 3 and 4). In addition, these children exhibit a high incidence of specific learning disabilities (Cantwell & Satterfield, 1978; see Chapter 3).

More than half of all hyperactive children also have significant problems of an oppositional nature (Hinshaw, 1987). These problems run the gamut from defiance, tantrums, and refusal to follow class rules to more serious violations of social norms including stealing, fighting, lying, truancy, and destruction.

Seriously disturbed peer relations are also prominent among ADHD children. Despite their apparent interest in

---

* Editor's note: Chapter notation refers to this excerpt.

establishing interpersonal contacts, their attempts to interact with peers are typically high-rate, intrusive, and often negative. As a reflection of their lack of success in the social arena, these children are consistently rejected by their peers on sociometric indices (Milich & Landau, 1982).

Teachers frequently respond to the challenging problems exhibited by children with ADHD by becoming more interactive and commanding (e.g., Campbell, Endman, & Bernfield, 1977). Over time, teachers may become frustrated in working with these difficult children and become less positive and more negative in their interactions as well. Although the impact of these predominantly negative interactions on long-term functioning is not well understood, such interactions may further exacerbate poor academic and social achievement, reduce the children's motivation and self-esteem, and ultimately result in school failure. On the other hand, a positive teacher-student relationship may not only improve academic and social functioning in the short term, but may also increase the likelihood of long-term success. For instance, adults who had been hyperactive as children have reported that a teacher's caring attitude, extra attention, and guidance were "turning points" in helping them overcome their childhood problems (Weiss & Hechtman, 1986).

Given the range and significance of ADHD children's difficulties at school, a great need exists for effective school interventions. The purpose of this chapter is to review and describe the success of behavioral and cognitive-behavioral interventions in treating ADHD children in the classroom. It is important to point out that these interventions are intended to maximize children's likelihood for success, and are not intended to cure or normalize their problems. Although the interventions can have a powerful and positive impact, the refractory nature of ADHD symptomatology makes it likely that these children will continue to experience at least some difficulty in their academic and social endeavors.

Treatment Targets

Disruptive, off-task behaviors are probably the most salient problems exhibited by ADHD children in the classroom. As a result, it is not surprising that these problems have been the focus of numerous intervention studies. Off-task behaviors have been readily modified with a variety of behavioral techniques. However, improvement in classroom deportment is often not paralleled by improvement in academic functioning, suggesting that on-task behavior may be necessary but not sufficient for academic progress. As a result, many researchers have questioned the practice of limiting the focus of intervention to classroom behavior and have instead targeted academic measures. The results of these studies have demonstrated not only significant improvement in academic performance but also improvement in children's behavior, although the latter was not directly targeted for the intervention. Focusing solely on academic performance appears to be insufficient, however, since children's behavior does not always improve when academic performance is the target for intervention.

In addition, undesirable behavior is necessary to target directly when it occurs during nonacademic school periods (such as recess and lunch), and when it is of an especially severe nature (as in the case of aggression, stealing, or destruction).

More recently, the poor peer relations of ADHD children have been targeted for intervention. In these programs, contingencies have been placed on children's use of appropriate social skills such as sharing, cooperating, and initiating play with other children. Preliminary studies, finding improvement in these skills, point to the utility of directly targeting these problem areas (see Chapter 16).

In sum, effective management programs should directly target the areas in which change is desired (e.g., deportment, academic problems, social skills). The identification of target areas in individual cases will probably require a functional analysis. Such an analysis requires several steps. First, the behavior in question should be pinpointed and carefully defined so that the teacher is able to monitor the behavior reliably. Next, the antecedents and consequences to the behavior in the natural environment should be identified. Antecedents that set the occasion for problem behavior may include difficult or challenging work, a teacher direction or negative consequence, or disruption from another child.

These antecedent events need not immediately precede the problem behavior for to be important in this analysis. Distal events, or those occurring minutes to hours before the target behavior, may have some role to play in increasing the probability of disruptive behaviors. For instance, arguments or fights with other family members at home or with other children on the bus ride to school may alter certain affective states (e.g., anger, frustration), which may make the occurrence of aggressive or defiant behavior upon arrival at school more probable.

Consequences that follow and maintain problem behavior may include teacher or peer attention, or withdrawal of a task or teacher request. Identification of such antecedents and consequences should help isolate features in the classroom environment or teacher interactions requiring change. It is also important to identify appropriate classroom behaviors that can replace the problem behavior. For example, staying seated may be identified as an appropriate behavior to replace wandering around the class. If positive alternative behaviors are not taught and only problem behavior is targeted for intervention, children may simply replace one problem behavior with another.

Intervention Issues

Although the aforementioned discussion implies that the initial targets of intervention are the child's disruptive and poorly regulated behaviors, this is hardly the case. The actual initial target of intervention is the teacher's knowledge of and attitude toward the disorder of ADHD. For we have found that where teachers have a poor grasp of the nature, course, outcome, and causes of this disorder and misperceptions about appropriate therapies, attempting to establish behavior management programs within that classroom will have little impact. As with parent training, then, the initial step in classroom management is educating teachers about the disorder. This is done by providing brief reading materials similar to those mentioned in Chapters 12 and 13. We also have made a videotape that summarizes the disorder which many consumers have found to be more convenient to their busy schedules than reading the materials we provide. In either ease, some means of providing information to educators about ADHD is a critical first step.

A variety of behavioral interventions have been utilized to modify classroom behavior. The primary interventions include teacher- and peer-administered consequences, home-based consequences, cognitive-behavioral interventions, and modification of factors related to academic tasks and the classroom environment. Each of these strategies is described and evaluated below in terms of its usefulness with ADHD children.

The specific intervention selected is ideally based on a functional analysis of the problem behavior as described above. However, classroom resources and teacher characteristics often play important roles in the final selection of an intervention. To be successful, most teacher-based behavioral programs require accurate record keeping, close monitoring of the child, and administration of a range of rewards and/or negative consequences. Although teachers of small classes may have little difficulty in implementing such procedures, they can be quite time-consuming and impractical for a teacher of a class of up to 40 students to implement. Therefore, these programs may require simplification, as well as tailoring to the routine of individual classes, before they can be implemented successfully.

It is also important to note that teachers vary in their ability and motivation to implement behavioral programs according to their training, experience, and beliefs about the educational process. In some cases, intensive training in behavioral procedures may be required. Additional "booster" sessions following training may also be necessary in order to maintain a teacher's use of the procedures. Teachers who adhere to a nondirective approach to education are often averse to using behavioral approaches out of concern that these approaches are too mechanistic and fail to foster a child's natural development and motivation to learn. In some cases, these beliefs may be altered through the success of a behavioral program. In other cases, such beliefs may greatly impede the effective use of behavioral programs and a transfer to an alternative teacher with a behavioral orientation may prove to be beneficial. In such a case of poor teacher motivation, or a case where teacher philosophy greatly conflicts with the necessary interventions for an ADHD child, parents are encouraged to be assertive in pressing the school administrators for either greater teacher accountability or a transfer to another classroom or school rather than waste a year of an ADHD child's education.

The involvement of a consulting therapist is often useful in order to help plan the intervention and train the teacher and parents in its effective implementation. Weekly or biweekly meetings are typically scheduled among teacher, parent, and therapist in order for the therapist to provide instruction and coaching in behavioral management as well as continual monitoring and evaluation of the program. It is advisable that older children (e.g., ages 7 and older) be included during some of these meetings to help set goals and determine appropriate and valuable rewards. Involving the children in this way often enhances their motivation to participate and be successful in the program. During these meetings, behavioral contracts delineating the details of the programs are often written and signed by parent, teacher, and child. Contracts can help maintain the consistent use of the program over time; emphasize the different roles of teacher, parent, and child in the program (e.g., the teacher's role in monitoring child behavior, the parent's role in dispensing rewards, and the child's role in engaging in appropriate target behaviors); and also give the program a more formal appeal.

Overall, the importance of a close collaboration among members of the treatment team cannot be overemphasized. However, successful collaboration may be thwarted in several ways. Parents of ADHD children often have a long history of conflictual interactions with school personnel. In some cases, parents may feel that the school system is failing to address their children's needs. For instance, parents whose children are in mainstream classes may be frustrated when the children's teachers are unable to implement an intensive behavioral program. Some parents may also have unrealistic expectations that the school should cure their children's problems. In cases where parents are having few if any difficulties at home, they may believe that inadequate teaching or management are causing their children's difficulties at school.

On the other hand, teachers may believe that problems of ADHD are due to emotional problems stemming from conflictual family relationships or that medication is indicated because of the disorder's presumed biological origin. In either ease, some teachers may believe that changing their interactions will have little impact on the children. Other teachers may resent altering their teaching style if they believe this suggests that their own behavior is causing the children's problems. Because antagonism on a parent's or teacher's part will probably undermine any intervention, these problems need to be addressed. A consulting therapist may help mediate these problems by providing information regarding the nature of ADHD and its causes as well as information regarding the role of behavioral interventions (including both their strengths and limitations) in the treatment of ADHD. If need be, a change in classrooms can be requested when a teacher is reluctant to try any special management programs with an ADHD child.

As noted in Chapter 5 the psychological status of parents must be considered in evaluating the veracity and severity of parental reports about the disruptive behavior of ADHD children. It seems that a similar state of affairs exists in the evaluation of teacher complaints about ADHD children. There is little reason not to believe that affective status, degree of psychological distress, and extent of other stressors in the life of the teacher play some role in the teacher's level of tolerance for the ADHD child's behavior, the teacher's perceptions and reports of the child's degree of behavioral deviance to others, and the teacher's cooperation in behavioral intervention programs for the child. Although formal assessment of teachers' psychological integrity is not an acceptable aspect of the evaluation of ADHD children, clinicians and educators must be sensitive to the possible role these factors play in the degree of problems an ADHD child is having in a particular classroom and attempt to informally assess them as appropriate.

In many cases, behavioral interventions are used in conjunction with pharmacological approaches to treat ADHD children's school problems. Since recent research documents superior effects with combined as compared to single interventions for some children (Pelham & Murphy, 1986), it may be prudent to consider using medication to treat the school problems of some ADHD children (see Chapter 17).

Whether or not medication is used, a number of general principles apply to the classroom management of ADHD children. These stem from the model presented earlier (see Chapter 2) according to which ADHD is primarily an impairment in the regulation of behavior by its consequences and by rules. These principles apply as much to classroom management as they do to parent training in child management at home (see Chapters 12 and 13). This conceptualization of ADHD requires the following:

1.   Rules and instructions provided to ADHD children must be clear, brief, and often delivered through more visible and external modes of presentation than is required for the management of normal children. Stating directions clearly, having the children repeat them out loud, having the children utter them softly to themselves while following through on the instruction, and displaying sets of rules or rule prompts (e.g., stop signs, big eyes, big ears for "stop, look, and listen" reminders) prominently throughout the classroom are essential to proper management of ADHD children. Relying on the children's recollection of the rules as well as upon purely verbal reminders is often ineffective. Externally represented rules, therefore, are more influential at regulating behavior than are internally represented ones.

2.   Consequences used to manage the behavior of ADHD children must be delivered more swiftly and immediately than is needed for normal children. Delays in consequences greatly degrade their efficacy with ADHD children. As we note throughout this chapter, the timing and strategic application of consequences with ADHD children must be more systematic and are far more crucial to their management than with normal children.

3.   Consequences must be delivered more frequently, not just more immediately, to ADHD children in view of their motivational deficits. This means that feedback for ongoing task performance must be delivered more often if the children are to use such feedback to shape and regulate

behavior toward the task or instruction. Behavioral tracking, or ongoing adherence to rules after the rule has been stated and compliance initiated, appears to be problematic for ADHD children. Frequent feedback or consequences for rule adherence seem helpful in maintaining appropriate degrees of tracking to rules over time.

4.   The consequences used with ADHD children must often be of a higher her magnitude, or more powerful, than those needed to manage the behavior of normal children. The relative insensitivity of ADHD children to response consequences dictates that those chosen for inclusion in a behavior management program must have sufficient reinforcement value or magnitude to motivate these children to perform the desired behaviors. Suffice it to say, then, that mere occasional praise or reprimands are simply not enough to manage ADHD children effectively.

5.   Appropriate and often richer incentives or motivational parameters must be provided within a setting or task to reinforce appropriate behavior before punishment can be implemented. This means that punishment must remain within a relative balance with rewards or it is unlikely to succeed. It is therefore imperative that powerful reinforcement programs be established first and instituted over 1 to 2 weeks before implementing punishment in order for the punishment, sparingly used, to be maximally effective. Often ADHD children will not improve with the use of response cost or time-out if the availability of reinforcement is low in the classroom and hence removal from it is unlikely to be punitive. "Positives before negatives" is the order of the day with ADHD children. When punishment fails, this is the first area that clinicians, consultants, or educators should explore for problems before instituting higher magnitude or more frequent punishment programs.

6.   Those reinforcers or rewards that are employed must be changed or rotated more frequently with ADHD than with normal children, given the penchant of the former for more rapid habituation or satiation to response consequences, apparently rewards in particular. This means that even though a particular reinforcer seems to be effective for the moment in motivating an ADHD child's compliance, it is likely that it will lose its reinforcement value more rapidly than with a normal child over time. Reward menus in classes, such as those used to back up token systems, must therefore be changed periodically (say, every 2 to 3 weeks) to maintain the power or efficacy of the program in motivating appropriate child behavior. Failure to do so is likely to result in the loss of power of the reward program and the premature abandonment of token technologies based on the false assumption that they simply will not work any longer. Token systems can be maintained over an entire school year with minimal loss of power in the program provided that the reinforcers are changed frequently to accommodate to this problem of habituation. Such rewards can be returned later to the program once they have been set aside for a while, often with the result that

their reinforcement value appears to have been improved by their absence or unavailability.

7. Anticipation is the key with ADHD children. This means that teachers must be more mindful of planning ahead in managing ADHD children, particularly during phases of transition across activities or classes, to ensure that the children are cognizant of the shift in rules (and consequences) that is about to occur. It is useful for a teacher to take a moment to prompt a child to recall the rules of conduct in the upcoming situation, repeat them orally, and recall that the rewards and punishments will be in the impending situation *before* the child enters that activity or situation. "Think aloud, think ahead" is the important message to educators here. Following a three-step procedure similar to that used in parental management of ADHD children in public places (see Chapter 12) can be effective in reducing the likelihood of inappropriate behavior. As noted below, by themselves such cognitive self-instructions are unlikely to be of lasting benefit; however, when combined with contingency management procedures they can be of considerable aid to the classroom management of ADHD children.

With these seven principles in mind, the creative educator or consultant can readily devise an effective management program for the ADHD child in the classroom.

Teacher-Administered Intervention Strategies

Teacher-administered positive and negative consequences are the most commonly used behavioral interventions with ADHD children in the classroom. Positive consequences usually include positive teacher attention (e.g., praise), tokens, and tangible rewards. Commonly used negative consequences consist of ignoring, verbal reprimands, response cost, and time-out. Although these procedures are discussed separately, most classroom management programs involve a combination of these interventions. In fact, clinically significant improvement in classroom behavior and academic performance is likely to accrue only with a combination of different strategies.

Positive Consequences

Positive Teacher Attention

Praise and other forms of positive teacher attention, such as a smile, nod, or pat on the back, are some of the most basic management tools in a teacher's armamentarium. Positive attention is valued by most children, including hyperactive children, and numerous studies document positive effects of such attention on appropriate classroom conduct. Similarly, withdrawal of teacher attention contingent upon undesirable behavior (i.e., ignoring) tends to decrease that behavior, especially when it is maintained by teacher attention (e.g., calling out).

Although these procedures may seem unusually simplistic, the systematic and effective use of teacher attention in this manner requires great skill. In general, praise appears to be most effective when it specifies the appropriate behavior being reinforced and when it is delivered in a genuine fashion (see O'Leary & O'Leary, 1977). The latter may be facilitated by use of a warm tone of voice and varied content appropriate to the developmental level of the child. Praise is also more effective when it is delivered as soon as possible following the appropriate behavior. It is this *strategic* timing in the application of teacher attention contingent upon appropriate child conduct that is so crucial to its being effective as a behavior change agent.

Effective ignoring requires complete withdrawal of teacher attention. This procedure is most appropriate to use for nondisruptive minor motor and nonattending behaviors intended to gain teacher attention. Although ignoring can be very effective, the use of this procedure with annoying, somewhat disruptive behavior can be very difficult. Even an occasional verbal or nonverbal response (e.g., a glance) can maintain the behavior. In addition, when problem behavior is initially ignored, it often becomes worse before it improves since the child whose behavior is being ignored often attempts to gain the teacher's attention in any way he or she can. In these cases, it is important that ignoring be consistent in order to prevent the child from learning that an escalation of the problem behavior will eventually gain the teacher's attention. It should be noted, however, that ignoring is generally not effective in modifying problem behavior that is not maintained by teacher attention. Ignoring is also contraindicated in cases of aggression or destruction. It is our considered opinion that most child behavior problems of ADHD children are not purely bids for teacher attention and so this strategy alone is unlikely to result in dramatic changes in the behavior of these children.

The simultaneous use of praise and ignoring often increases the efficacy of both procedures. Thus, appropriate behavior (e.g., sitting in seat) that is incompatible with ignored behavior (e.g., wandering around the class) should be consistently praised. In addition, one of the most powerful uses of teacher attention for modifying problem behavior capitalizes on the positive spillover effects of positive attention. In this procedure, the teacher ignores the disruptive student and praises the student(s) who are working quietly. The behavior of the problem student often improves as a result, presumably due to the vicarious learning that has occurred through this modeling procedure and the child's desire for teacher attention.

Requiring teachers to increase their monitoring of ongoing child behavior and to readily consequate the occurrence of ongoing appropriate behavior may be easier said than done. The considerable demands on teacher time and attention in the average classroom often compete with the teacher's ability to monitor the activities of all children and intervene immediately. In particular, it may be difficult to watch for what seems like relatively modest appropriate behavior in ADHD children, especially when normal children perform such behaviors with minimal attention for doing so. To assist teachers with remembering to attend to and reinforce ongoing appropriate child conduct, several cue or prompt systems can be recommended. One such system involves placing large "smiley face" stickers around the classroom in places where the teacher may frequently glance, such as toward the clock on the wall. When these are then subsequently viewed, they serve to cue the teacher to remember to check out what the ADHD student is doing and to attend to it if it is at all positive.

A second system relies on tape-recorded cues. A soft tone can be taped onto a 90-minute or 120-minute cassette so that it occurs at random intervals. This tape is then played throughout the class time with the children. Whenever the tone is emitted, the teacher is to note briefly what the ADHD child is doing and provide a consequence to the child (praise, token, or response cost) for the behavior at that point in time. We recommend that the tape initially contain relatively frequent tone prompts for the first 1 to 2 weeks, which can then be faded to less frequent schedules of prompts over the next several weeks. We recommend that these be variable-interval prompts so that they occur relatively randomly on the tape. This tape can play openly to the class or can be used with a pocket-size tape player, such as a Sony Walkman, with an earpiece for private monitoring by the teacher.

Such a system can then be converted to a self-monitoring program for second-grade-level or older ADHD students by providing the children with small white file cards on their desks. Each card is divided down the middle to form two columns, with a plus sign (+) or smiley face over the top of the left column and a minus sign (−) or frowning face over the right column. The teacher then instructs the children that whenever they hear the tone, if they are doing as instructed for that activity, they can award themselves a hash mark in the plus column. If they were not obeying instructions or were off-task, they must place a hash mark in the minus column. The teacher's job at the sound of the tone is to rapidly scan the classroom and note the ADHD child's behavior, then note whether the child is delivering the appropriate consequence to himself or herself. Such scanning for honesty can be further aided by using two separate cards for pluses and minuses, with the plus card taped to the left corner of the child's desk and the minus card taped to the right corner. The program can also be made more effective by having an easel at the front of the classroom with a list of five or so rules that should be followed during that class period (i.e., the five rules for deskwork might be "Stay in seat, stay on-task, don't space out, don't bug others, do your work"). The teacher can then refer to the set of rules in force at that particular class period or activity when the activity begins and can flip to the appropriate chart at that time, calling the children's attention to these rules.

A third system for prompting strategic teacher attending and monitoring is to have the teacher place 10 or so Bingo chips in his or her left pocket that must be moved to the right pocket whenever positive attention has been given appropriately to the ADHD child. The goal is eventually to move all 10 chips to the right pocket by the end of that class period.

Overall, the systematic use of contingent praise and ignoring can be a powerful management tool and should be a mainstay in any classroom program. In addition, once the skills are learned, they generally do not require any more time or resources than procedures the teacher is currently using. Often, teachers of hyperactive children are spending a great deal of time attending to negative behavior. This procedure simply involves a teacher's altering his or her pattern of interaction from attending to negative to attending to positive behaviors. Again, it is the timing of the attention that is so important to its success in managing behavior.

Tangible Rewards and Token Programs

Despite the utility of praise and ignoring, these procedures, while necessary for success, are often not by themselves sufficient with ADHD children. Wender (1971) and others (see Chapter 2) have theorized that ADHD children evidence a diminished response to positive reinforcement or to consequences in general. Recent research supports this theory (e.g., Douglas, 1985) and suggests that ADHD children may have an elevated reward threshold, which reduces the magnitude of reward they experience (e.g., Haenlein & Caul, 1987). In addition, ADHD children have been shown to perform as well as non-ADHD children with continuous reinforcement, but perform significantly worse with a partial schedule of reinforcement (Douglas & Parry, 1983). Thus, as noted earlier, ADHD children seem to require more frequent and more powerful reinforcement. A variety of more powerful rewards, often in the form of special privileges, can be utilized to modify classroom performance. These activities may include helping the teacher, extra recess, special games, computer time, and art projects. Some tangible or backup rewards are distributed on a daily basis, while longer periods (e.g., weekly) of appropriate behavior or academic functioning may be required for more valuable rewards.

A study conducted by Pfiffner, Rosen, and O'Leary (1985) found that the contingent use of very frequent praise (e.g., six praise statements per child per hour) coupled with special activities and privileges (e.g., song-time, posting work on a "superstar" board, reading comic books, special recess activities, positive note home, stickers, running errands for the teacher) was much more effective than an approach consisting primarily of praise. In this study, the special activities and privileges were provided several times during the school day, contingent on academic and behavioral performance. The addition of an individualized reward program, wherein children selected their own rewards each day from a reward menu, proved to be particularly effective in maintaining high rates of on-task behavior and academic productivity. The individualized reward program also greatly reduced the need for negative consequences.

Token reinforcement systems have also been widely used with great success to modify behaviors of ADHD children (see Pfiffner & O'Leary, in press) These systems involve the distribution of tokens (e.g., poker chips, stars) or points contingent upon appropriate behavior. Children typically accumulate tokens or points throughout the day and later exchange their earnings for desired backup privileges, activities, or tangible objects (e.g., food, small toys). Backup rewards are typically assigned a purchase value so that rewards can be matched to the number of tokens or points earned. As we describe later, some programs also include a response cost component wherein children lose points for inappropriate behavior.

The identification of powerful backup consequences is critical for program success and may be achieved in a number of ways. For instance, teachers may interview children regarding the kinds of activities or other rewards they would like to earn. As indicated earlier, children's compliance with token programs may be greater when they have provided input regarding the rewards to be used. Potential reinforcers may also be identified through observation of the high-rate behaviors emitted by a child. For instance, Legos may be an effective reward for a child who spends much of his or her free time playing with Legos. That is, the child will probably improve his or her behavior if Lego play is made available only as a reward for appropriate behavior. In some cases, rewards available at school may not be sufficiently powerful to alter a child's behavior. Home-based reward programs, discussed in a subsequent section, may be considered in those cases. It is also possible to have parents provide a favored toy or piece of play equipment from home to the teacher for contingent use in the classroom as part of a classroom token or reward system. One very powerful reinforcer at this writing is access to video games, such as Nintendo. Having such a video game (either the larger systems or the newer hand-held models) can greatly enhance the power of a class reward program when children can earn time on the video game for accurate and timely completion of classwork and adherence to classroom rules of conduct. We have been successful in approaching local civic clubs (Rotary Club, Civitans, Lions Club, Knights of Columbus, etc.) to donate the equipment to a particular classroom or at least to partially offset its expense by providing presentations to them on the seriousness of classroom behavioral problems and the critical need for such reinforcers in the management of disruptive (and normal!) children. Otherwise, soliciting each parent of a child in that classroom to donate a mere $3.00 or so is often adequate to purchase these systems for reinforcement of child behavior.

When a teacher is in doubt as to what privileges to place on a token system menu for a particular child, it is often helpful to have the child construct the menu with the teacher's assistance. Where this is not helpful, then monitoring the manner in which the child spends free time activities over the next week may suggest what privileges or activities are especially rewarding to that particular child.

Token programs can be individual or group-based. In individual programs, children earn tokens and backup positive consequences contingent on their own behavior. In group programs, all class members earn rewards based on the behavior of one or more of their classmates. Individual and group programs appear to be equally effective, although they may be most useful in different situations. For instance, when only one child is evidencing a problem or the behavioral goals for several children are very dissimilar, individual contingency programs may be indicated. On the other hand, group programs may be particularly useful when peer contingencies are competing with teacher contingencies (e.g., when peers reinforce disruptive students by laughing or joining in on their off-task pursuits). In some group programs, the performance of an ADHD student serves as the criterion for distribution of rewards to the class. In other cases, tokens or points are dispensed to each child in the classroom, including the ADHD child, contingent upon the occurrence of the appropriate behavior of any student. A variation of this procedure involves the use of team contingencies. In these programs, children are divided into competing teams and earn or lose points for their respective team, depending on their behavior. The team with the greatest number of positive points or fewest negative points earns the group privileges.

Group programs targeting all students' behavior have the advantage of not singling out ADHD children. Given the concern that some teachers have about possible stigmatization or undue attention to problem children receiving treatment, this procedure may be preferable. This may also be the treatment of choice when there is concern that children not involved in treatment may increase their misbehavior in order to be a part of the program and receive reinforcement. It should be noted, however, that concerns of stigmatization and escalation of problem behavior have not been substantiated in research studies. When using group contingencies, however, teachers should take care to minimize possible peer pressure and subversion of the program by one or more children. Powerful reward-only programs may be effective in this regard

Token programs targeting academic functioning have proven successful in improving performance in both academic and behavioral domains. For example, in a widely cited study, Allyon, Layman, and Kandel (1975) investigated the effects of a token reinforcement system on three diagnosed hyperactive children after they had been withdrawn from medication. The token system involved the children's earning checks recorded on an index card for each correct academic response. The checks were exchanged for a large array of backup reinforcers (e.g., candy, free time, school supplies, picnics in the park) later in the day. The purchase price of backup reinforcers ranged from 1 to 75 checks. Discontinuation of medication resulted in a dramatic increase in inappropriate and disruptive behavior across all three children. Subsequent implementation of the token program sharply increased math and reading scores and reduced disruptive behavior to a level similar to that observed on medication.

Robinson, Newby, and Ganzell (1981) evaluated the effects of an innovative token reward system, targeting both academic performance and cooperative peer tutoring, on the academic performance of 18 disruptive hyperactive boys. Tokens were issued for successful completion of four tasks: two that involved learning to read and using new vocabulary words in sentences and two that involved teaching these tasks to another student. When tokens had been earned for completion of each of these four tasks, they were exchanged for 15 minutes of play on a pinball machine or electronic "pong" game, both of which were located in the classroom. Additional game time was earned whenever a child passed a unit skills test. This token intervention program dramatically increased task completion and performance on the school district's standardized weekly reading exams. Although no specific contingencies were established for nonacademic behavior, the contingencies for academic performance and peer tutoring resulted in a reduction in disruptive behavior. This study is particularly noteworthy for demonstrating that it is possible to design a powerful token program with a class of hyperactive boys that can be successfully administered by a single teacher.

The success of token programs in these and numerous other studies, and the utility of these programs with a wide range of problem behavior, have led to their widespread use in school settings. Tokens are portable so they can be administered in any situation and can usually be distributed immediately following desirable behavior. Token programs also tend to be very powerful because a wide range of backup rewards can be used to avoid satiation of any one reward. However, appropriate and realistic treatment goals are critical for the success of the program. In many typical classrooms, rewards are often reserved for exemplary performance. While this practice may be sufficient for some children, it is unlikely to improve the performance of children exhibiting severe attentional and behavioral problems. Regardless how motivated such a child may be initially, if the criterion for a reward is set too high, the child will rarely achieve the reward and will probably give up trying. To prevent this occurrence, rewards should initially be provided for approximations to the terminal response and should be set at a level that ensures the child's success. For instance, a child who has a long history of failing to complete work should be required to complete only a part, not all of his or her work, in order to earn a reward. Similarly, a child who is often disruptive throughout the day may initially earn a reward for exhibiting quiet, on-task behavior for only a small segment of the day. As performance improves, more appropriate behavior can be shaped by gradually increasing the behavioral criteria for rewards.

The nature in which token systems are constructed and implemented will certainly change as a function of the age of the ADHD children with whom they are to be used. We have found that tangible tokens, such as poker chips, are very important in managing young children (4- to 7-year-olds); points, numbers, or hash marks on a card can be used with older children (through high school). Also, with preschool- or kindergarten-age children, the plastic chips when awarded may actually serve as distracters and become objects of play or overly excite the children, if within their field of vision/reach. To counteract this, we have often used small fabric pockets that are pinned to the children's clothing on their backs. When tokens are dispensed, the teacher reaches to a child and slips the token in the child's "knapsack" along with a light affectionate squeeze to the shoulder. Several times each day, the pockets are removed and emptied and the children can exchange their tokens for various classroom privileges.

Negative Consequences

Ignoring

Ignoring, as discussed previously, is often used as one of the first interventions for mild misbehavior, especially in cases when children's misbehavior is maintained by teacher attention. Ignoring is not simply the failure to monitor child behavior but is the *contingent withdrawal* of teacher attention upon the occurrence of inappropriate child behavior. However, the use of ignoring alone or in conjunction with praise is often ineffective in shaping or maintaining high rates of on-task behavior and work productivity with ADHD children (Rosen, O'Leary, Joyce, Conway, & Pfiffner, 1984). Even in the context of a powerful reward program, ignoring may not be sufficient (e.g., Pfiffner & O'Leary, 1987). In these cases, additional negative consequences appear to be not only effective, but also necessary with ADHD children. In fact, negative consequences may be more important than praise for maintaining appropriate behavior (e.g., see Acker & O'Leary, 1987; Rosen et al., 1984).

Reprimands

The verbal reprimand is probably the most frequently used negative consequence in the classroom. However, the effectiveness of reprimands appears to vary, depending upon a number of parameters associated with the delivery style. A series of studies investigating these parameters were conducted by S. G. O'Leary and her colleagues at Point of Woods Laboratory School, a full-day educational program, with eight second- and third-grade children referred from regular classes because of inattention, overactivity, and conduct problems. In the first of these studies, Rosen et al. (1984) compared two multiple-component reprimands, one labeled "prudent" and the other labeled "imprudent." Prudent reprimands were immediate, unemotional, and brief, and were consistently backed up with time out or loss of a privilege for repeated noncompliance. Imprudent reprimands were delayed, long, and emotional, and concrete backup consequences were not utilized. The results strongly supported the superior effects of prudent reprimands.

Subsequent studies have examined the effects of a variety of individual parameters of negative consequences, including length, timing, consistency, and intensity (see Pfiffner & O'Leary, in press). Short reprimands appear to be more effective than long reprimands (e.g., a lecture), possibly because less attention is paid to children when a short reprimand is delivered. ADHD children also appear to respond more favorably to negative consequences delivered

The Principal as Educational Leader

early in the sequence of misbehavior. This appears to be particularly true in cases where peer attention is maintaining off-task behavior. With regard to consistency of feedback, mixing positive and negative feedback for inappropriate behavior appears to be particularly deleterious. For example, children who are sometimes reprimanded for calling out, but other times responded to as if they had raised their hands, are apt to continue if not to increase their calling out. Reprimands also appear to be more effective when delivered with eye contact and in close proximity to the child. In addition, children respond better to teachers who deliver consistently strong reprimands at the outset of the school year (immediate, brief, firm, and in close proximity to the child) than to teachers who gradually increase the severity of their discipline over time.

In sum, reprimands appear to be most effective when they are consistent, immediate, brief, delivered in close proximity to the child, and of sufficient intensity at the outset. These dimensions may be particularly critical with hyperactive children, who may be sensitive to these stylistic features. However, verbal reprimands are not always sufficient. More powerful backup consequences, including response cost and time out, may be necessary in these cases.

Response Cost

Response cost involves the loss of a reinforcer contingent upon inappropriate behavior. Lost reinforcers can include a wide range of privileges and activities. Response cost has often been used to manage the disruptive behavior of ADHD children in the context of a token program. This procedure involves the children's losing tokens for inappropriate behavior in addition to earning them for appropriate behavior. Similar to reward-only token programs discussed earlier, this procedure is convenient and readily adapted to a variety of target behaviors and situations. Furthermore, response cost has been shown to be more effective than reprimands with ADHD children and can also increase the effectiveness of reward programs.

Rapport, Murphy, and Bailey (1982) compared the effects of response cost with those of stimulant medication on the behavior and academic performance of two hyperactive children. In the response cost procedure, the teacher deducted 1 point every time she saw a child not working. Each point loss translated into a loss of 1 minute of free time. An apparatus was placed at each child's desk to keep track of point totals. One child's apparatus consisted of numbered cards that could be changed to a lesser value each time a point was lost. The teacher had an identical apparatus on her desk where she kept track of point losses. The child was instructed to match the number value on his apparatus with that of the teacher's on a continual basis. The second child had a battery-operated electronic "counter" with a number display. The teacher decreased point values on the display via a remote transmitter.

Both response cost procedures resulted in increases in both on-task and academic performance, which compared favorably with the effects of stimulant medication. The

immediacy with which consequences could be delivered in either procedure (the teacher was able to administer a consequence even when she was some distance away from the child) probably contributed to their efficacy. In addition, these procedures are particularly noteworthy for their practicality and ease of administration.

To aid in making the implementation of classroom token systems as convenient as possible, Michael Gordon has marketed the Attention Trainer® (available from Gordon Systems, DeWitt, N.Y.) This device was invented and field-tested in the aforementioned study by Rapport et al. (1982). A small plastic box containing a display counter on the face of the box and a red light on top is placed on the child's desk during individual work periods. The box is turned on and each minute a point is awarded to the child on the counter display. It is assumed that the child is on-task and following rules during this time. The teacher carries a small transmitter during this class time. If the child is observed to be off-task, not working, or disruptive, the teacher simply presses a button on the transmitter, and the red light is triggered on the child's box. A point is simultaneously deducted from the face of the counter. We have found this system to be highly useful for both children with Attention Deficit Disorder with hyperactivity (ADD/+H) and those without hyperactivity (ADD/−H; see Chapter 3). Although some teachers initially believe that such a device may result in negative social stigma or excessive peer attention, we have never found this to be the case. Encouraging the teachers to try the device for a few days is more than sufficient to convince them that this negative social reaction does not typically happen. Thereafter, they are often ardent supporters of using the device, frequently loaning it to other teachers who witness its use and effectiveness. The device can be faded out for use over 4 to 6 weeks and replaced by a less intensive class token system or self-monitoring program (such as the tone prompt system described above) or by a home-school report card (described below).

As with other punishment procedures, however, the use of response cost has met with concern regarding possible adverse effects including escalation of problem behavior, dislike of the teacher, or avoidance of school. However, several studies comparing response cost and reward procedures do not support such concerns. Response cost involving the contingent loss of tokens that had been distributed "for free" at the outset appears to be just as effective as reward procedures involving the receipt of tokens contingent on appropriate behavior (e.g., Sullivan & O'Leary, in press). In addition, teachers' and children's attitudes toward response cost programs appear to be as positive as those toward reward programs. It should be noted, however, that teachers may tend to be more positive with children when implementing a reward procedure. This may be due to the emphasis in these programs on tracking positive child behavior. Similarly, teachers implementing cost programs may be more critical, due to the emphasis in these programs on tracking negative child behavior. Therefore, a special effort should be made to continue monitoring and praising appropriate behavior when cost programs are in effect. It is also advisable that when rewards and response cost are used together, the opportunity to earn tokens should be greater than the possibility of losing them. The need for frequent costs will be greatly reduced by targeting appropriate behaviors judiciously (i.e., those that are incompatible with the inappropriate behaviors). As with any behavioral procedure, the effectiveness of such programs depends on the selection of appropriate behavioral goals that afford the child success. In all cost programs, care should be taken to avoid the use of unreasonably stringent standards that lead to excessive point or privilege losses.

Time-Out

Time out from positive reinforcement (i.e., "time-out") is frequently recommended for hyperactive children who are particularly aggressive or disruptive. This procedure involves the withdrawal of positive reinforcement contingent upon inappropriate behavior. Several variations of time-out are used in the classroom including removal of materials, removal of adult or peer attention, or removal of the student from the classroom situation. The last procedure, often referred to as "social isolation," usually involves placement in a small empty room (i.e., "time-out room") for short periods of time (e.g., 2 to 10 minutes).

Social isolation has been increasingly criticized over the years due to ethical concerns and difficulty with implementing the procedure correctly. Thus, less restrictive time-out procedures have been utilized. In these procedures, a child is not isolated or removed from the class but is removed from the area of reinforcement or the opportunity to earn reinforcement. This may involve having the child sit in a three-sided cubicle or sit facing a dull area (e.g., a blank wall) in the classroom. In other cases, children may be required to put their work away (which eliminates the opportunity to earn reinforcement for academic performance) and their heads down (which reduces the opportunity for reinforcing interaction with others) for brief periods of time. Another time-out procedure, implemented by Kubany, Weiss, and Sloggett (1971), involves use of a "good-behavior clock." In this procedure, rewards (e.g., penny trinkets, candy) are earned for both a target child and the class when the child has behaved appropriately for a specified period of time. A clock runs whenever the child is on-task and behaving appropriately, but is stopped for a short period of time when the child is disruptive or off-task. Kubany et al. (1971) found dramatic decreases in a hyperactive student's disruptive behavior for as a result of this procedure.

Most time-out programs set specific criteria that must be fulfilled prior to release from time-out. Typically, these criteria involve the child's being quiet and cooperative for a specified period during time-out. In some cases, extremely disruptive hyperactive children may fail to comply with the standard procedure, either by refusing to go to time-out or not remaining in the time-out area for the required duration. To reduce noncompliance in these cases, children may earn time-off for complying with the procedure (i.e., the length of original time-out is reduced). Alternatively, refusal to follow time-out rules may result in the length of the original time-out's being increased for each infraction, or the child may be removed from the class to serve the time-out elsewhere (e.g., in another class, or in the principal's office). Failure to comply with time-out may also be consequated with a cost procedure. For instance, activities, privileges, or tokens may be lost for uncooperative behavior in time-out. One strategy that may be particularly effective for reducing noncompliance to time-out involves children staying after school to serve their time-out when they are not cooperative in following time-out rules during school hours. The use of this procedure, however, depends on the availability of personnel to supervise the children after school.

Overall, time-out appears to be an effective procedure for reducing aggressive and disruptive actions in the classroom, especially when they are maintained by peer or teacher attention. Time-out may not be effective in cases where inappropriate behavior is due to a desire to avoid work or be alone, since in these cases time-out may actually be reinforcing. It is important that time-out be implemented with minimal attention from teacher and peers. In cases where a child's problem behavior consistently escalates during time-out and requires teacher intervention (e.g., restraint) to prevent harm to self, others, or property, alternative procedures to time-out may be indicated. Procedural safeguards and appropriate reviews are important to ensure that time-out is used in an ethical and legal way (see Gast & Nelson, 1977).

Suspension

Suspension from school (usually from 1 to 3 days) is sometimes used as punishment for severe problem behavior. However, it is recommended that this procedure be used with caution. Many children may find staying at home or going to day care more enjoyable than being in school, which can thereby undermine the effectiveness of the procedure. In addition, suspension is contraindicated in cases where parents do not have the appropriate management skills needed for enforcement or in cases where parents may be overly punitive or abusive.

Minimizing Adverse Side Effects

Despite the overall effectiveness of negative consequences, adverse side effects may occur it they are used improperly. O'Leary and O'Leary (1977) offer several guidelines to minimize possible adverse side effects. First, punishment should be used sparingly. Teachers who frequently use punishment to the exclusion of positive consequences may be less effective in managing children's behavior due to a loss in the teachers' reinforcing value and/or due to the children having satiated or adapted to the punishment. Excessive criticism or other forms of punishment may also cause the classroom situation to become aversive. As a result, a child may begin to avoid certain academic subjects by skipping classes, or to avoid school in general by becoming truant. Frequent harsh punishment may even accelerate a child's overt defiance, especially in cases where a teacher inadvertently serves as an aggressive model. When negative consequences are used, children should be taught and reinforced for alternative appropriate behaviors incompatible with inappropriate behaviors. This practice will aid in teaching appropriate skills as well as decrease the potential for the occurrence of other problem behaviors. In addition, punishment involving the removal of a positive reinforcer is usually preferable to punishment involving the presentation of an aversive stimulus. Use of the latter method, as exemplified by corporal punishment, is often limited for ethical and legal reasons.

Maintenance and Generalization

Despite the substantial success of teacher-administered behavioral interventions, little evidence exists that treatment gains persist once the programs are terminated. Furthermore, the improvements wrought by contingency management programs in one setting (e.g., reading class) often do not generalize to settings in which the programs are not in effect (e.g., math class, recess).

Technologies are currently being developed to improve the probability that treatment gains will transfer to other school settings as well as across academic years. One procedure involves implementing programs in all the settings in which behavioral change is desired. Maintenance of treatment gains may also be facilitated by withdrawing the classroom contingency program gradually. For example, a study conducted by Pfiffner and O'Leary (1987) found that the abrupt removal of negative consequences, even in the context of a powerful token program, led to dramatic deterioration in class behavior. However, when negative consequences were gradually removed, high on-task rates were maintained. Gradual withdrawal of contingency programs may be accomplished by reducing the frequency of feedback (e.g., fading from daily to weekly rewards) and by substituting natural reinforcers (e.g., praise, regular activities) for token rewards. One particularly effective procedure for fading management programs involves varying the range of conditions or situations in which contingencies are administered, in order to reduce the child's ability to discriminate when contingencies are in effect. The less the discriminability of the changes in contingencies when one is fading a program, the more successful fading appears to be.

Self-management skills such as self-monitoring and self-reinforcement (to be described in a subsequent section) have also been taught in order to improve maintenance of gains from behavioral programs and to help prompt appropriate behavior in nontreated settings. Although these procedures hare been found to improve maintenance following withdrawal of token programs, they are not effective in the absence of teacher supervision, and little evidence exists to suggest that they facilitate generalization across settings.

Continued development of programs to enhance maintenance and generalization of teacher-administered interventions appears to be critical for children's long-term success in school. Nevertheless, specially arranged interventions for ADHD children may be required across school settings and for extended periods of time over the course of their education, given the developmentally handicapping nature of their disorder.

Peer-Administered Contingencies

The disruptive and intrusive behavior of ADHD children often prompts their peers (both ADHD and non-ADHD) to respond in ways that promote and/or maintain the problem behavior. On the one hand, peers may reinforce a display of clowning behavior with smiles and giggles. On the other hand, peers may retaliate against provocative teasing or intrusiveness and thus further perpetuate the problem. As discussed previously, group contingencies are often effective in counteracting peer reinforcement of inappropriate behavior. However, studies show that peers can also intervene directly to produce desirable changes in their disruptive classmates.

One of the most powerful ways peers can intervene is by ignoring disruptive, inappropriate behavior. Peers can also increase their classmates' appropriate behavior through praise and positive attention. A common example of this effect occurs during sports events when team members cheer and congratulate one another for successful plays. However, peers can also be encouraged to praise one another for other accomplishments or appropriate behavior, such as being a good sport, getting a high grade on an exam (or accepting a low grade without a tantrum), contributing to a class discussion, or helping another student. Peer-monitored token programs in which peers monitor child behavior and distribute tokens to deserving students have also been successful when conducted under teachers' supervision.

In order to promote peers' use of reinforcement and ignoring, it is necessary that teachers reward their efforts. In some cases, praise is sufficient. However, with ADHD children, ignoring and positive attention will be reinforced more effectively with tangible rewards or with tokens in a token economy. Serving as a peer monitor or dispenser of reinforcers appears to be a particularly powerful reward and children will often purchase the privilege of distributing rewards with tokens they have earned.

The use of peers as "behavior modifiers" may be advantageous for several reasons. First, since teachers are unable to continually observe every student's behavior, peers may be better able to monitor their classmates' behavior and therefore better able to provide accurate, immediate, and consistent reinforcement. Second, training children to alter their interactions with peers not only improves peer behavior, but also directly improves the behavior of the children implementing the intervention. This would seem particularly beneficial for ADHD children who are at such a great risk for poor peer relations. Third, peer reinforcement systems may facilitate generalization, since peers may function as cues for appropriate behavior in multiple settings. Fourth, peer-mediated programs may be more practical and require less time than traditional teacher-mediated programs.

Despite these advantages, peer-mediated programs are successful only to the extent that peers have the ability and motivation to learn and accurately implement the program. Peers may be overly lenient and reward too liberally because of peer pressure, fear of peer rejection, or more lenient definitions of misbehavior. On the other hand, children may use the program in a coercive or punitive fashion. Due to these concerns, it is advisable that peers not be involved in implementing punishment programs such as response cost. In addition, when peers are utilized as change agents, they should be carefully trained and supervised and contingencies should be provided for accurate ratings.

Home-Based Contingencies

Home-based contingency programs have been effective in modifying a wide range of problems at school. Due to their high cost-effectiveness and involvement of both teacher and parents, they are often one of the first interventions used. In general, these programs involve the provision of contingencies in the home based on the teacher's report of the child's performance at school. Teacher reports usually consist of either a note or a more formal report card delineating the target behavior(s) and a rating for each behavior. Teacher reports are typically sent home on a daily basis. In some cases, notes are sent home only when a child has met the behavioral or academic goals for that day. In other cases, notes are sent home on both "good" and "bad" days. As children's behavior improves, the daily reports can readily be faded to twice weekly, biweekly, monthly, and finally to the reporting intervals typically used in the school. A variety of home-based programs may be developed and individualized for each child. Target behaviors may include both behavior and academic performance. Targeting inadequate academic performance may be especially effective since some home-based programs targeting only academic performance have resulted in improvements in both academic and social behaviors. Examples of target behaviors include completion of all (or a specified portion of) work, staying in assigned seat, following teacher directions, and playing cooperatively with others. Negative behaviors (e.g., aggression, destruction, calling out) may also be included as target behaviors to decrease. In addition to targeting in-class performance, homework-related activities may also be included. ADHD children often have difficulty in remembering to bring home assignments, completing the work, and then returning the completed work to school the next day. Each of these areas may be targeted in a note-home program.

The number of target behaviors may vary from as few as one to as many as seven or eight. Targeting very few behaviors may be indicated when a program is first being implemented (to maximize the child's likelihood of success), when few behaviors require modification, or in cases where teacher have difficulty monitoring many behaviors.

The daily ratings of each target behavior may be global and subjective (e.g., "poor," "fair," "good") or more specific and objective (e.g., frequency of each behavior or the number of points earned or lost for each behavior). We recommend including at least one or two positive behaviors that the child is currently reliably displaying, so that the child will be able to earn some points during the beginning of the program.

Typically, children are monitored throughout the school day. However, in order for some success to be achieved with particularly high-rate problem behaviors, children may initially be rated for only a portion of the day. As behavior improves, ratings may gradually include more periods/subjects until the children are being monitored throughout the day. In cases where children attend several different classes taught by different teachers, programs may involve some or all of the teachers depending upon the need for intervention in each of the classes. When more than one teacher is included in the program, a single report card may include space for all teachers to sign, or different report cards may be used for each class and organized in a notebook for a child to carry between classes.

The success of the program requires a clear, consistent system for translating teacher reports into consequences at home. Some programs involve rewards alone; others incorporate both positive and negative consequences. Some studies suggest that a combination of positive and negative consequences may be more effective than rewards alone. However, in cases where parents tend to be overly coercive or abusive, reward-only programs are preferable.

One advantage of home-based programs is that a wide variety of contingencies can be utilized. At a minimum, praise and positive attention should be provided whenever a child's goals are met. With ADHD children, however, tangible rewards or token programs are often necessary. For example, a positive note home may translate into TV time, a special snack, or a later bedtime A token economy or response cost program may also be utilized, in which a child earns points for positive behavior ratings and loses points for negative ratings. Both daily rewards (e.g., time with parent, special dessert, TV time) and weekly rewards (e.g., movie, dinner at a restaurant, special outing) may be utilized.

Overall, home-based reward programs can be as effective as (if not more effective than) classroom-based programs, but may be particularly effective when used in conjunction with classroom-based programs. Daily reports seem particularly well suited for ADHD children, since they often benefit from more frequent feedback than is usually provided at school. These programs also afford parents more frequent feedback regarding their child's performance than would normally be provided; this can prompt parents when to reinforce a child's behavior, as well as when behavior is becoming problematic and requires more intensive intervention. In addition, the type and quality of reinforcers available in the home are typically far more extensive than those available in the classroom—a factor that may be critical with hyperactive children, as reviewed earlier. Aside from these benefits, note-home programs generally require considerably less teacher time and effort than a classroom-based intervention. As a result, teachers who have been unable to implement a classroom management program may be far more likely to implement a note-home program.

Despite the impressive success of note-home programs, the effectiveness of such a system depends on accurate assessment of child behavior by the teacher as well as consistent and contingent consequences at home. In some cases, children may attempt to subvert the system by failing to bring home a report, forging a teacher signature, or failing to get certain teacher signatures. To discourage this practice, missing notes or signatures should be treated the same way as "bad" reports (e.g., a child fails to earn points, or privileges or points are revoked). In cases where parents may be overly punitive or lack skills to follow through with consequences, their implementation of appropriate consequences should be closely supervised (possibly by a therapist), or other adults (e.g., school counselors, principal) may implement the program.

We now describe several types of home-based reward programs that rely on daily school behavior ratings. One example is shown in Figure 15.1. This card lists four areas of potentially problematic behavior with ADHD children. Columns are provided for up to six different teachers to rate a child in these areas of behavior or for one teacher to rate the child multiple times across the school day. We have found that more frequent ratings are more effective forms of feedback to children and more informative to their parents. The teacher initials the bottom of the column after rating the child's performance during that class period to guard against forgery. Where getting the correct homework assignment home is a problem for some ADHD children, the teacher can require the child to copy the homework for that class period on the back of the card before completing the ratings for that period. In this way,

the teacher merely checks the back of the card for accuracy of copying the assignment and then completes the ratings on the front of the card. For particularly negative ratings, we also encourage teachers to provide a brief explanation to the parents of what resulted in that negative mark. The teachers rate the children using a 5-point system.

The child takes a new card to school each day, or these can be kept at school and a new card given out each morning, depending upon the parents' reliability in giving the card out each day. Upon returning home, a parent immediately inspects the card; discusses the positive ratings first with the child; and then proceeds to a neutral, business-like (not angry!) discussion with the child about any negative marks and the reason for them. The child is then asked to formulate a plan for how to avoid getting the negative mark tomorrow (parents are to remind the child of this plan the next morning before the child departs for school). The parent then awards the child points for each positive rating on the card and deducts points for each negative mark. For instance, a young elementary-age child may receive five chips for a 1, three for a 2, and one chip for a 3, while being fined three chips for a 4 and five chips for a 5 on the card. For an older child, the number of points assigned might be 25, 15, 5, -15, and -25, respectively, for these marks on the card. The chips or points are summed, the fines are subtracted, and the child may then spend chips on activities from a home reward menu.

A similar card system was devised for an aggressive ADHD child who was having problems with interactions with others during school recess periods each day. This card, shown in Figure 15.2, was to be completed by the recess monitor during each recess period, inspected by the teacher when the child returned to the classroom, and then sent home for use as described above in a home point system. The teacher was also instructed to use a "think aloud, think ahead" procedure with the child just prior to the child's exiting the class for recess. In this procedure, she reviewed

---

Figure 15.1. A daily school report card for controlling ADHD behavior at school, used with a home-based token reward system.

DAILY STUDENT RATING CARD

NAME_____   DATE_____

Please rate this child in each of the areas listed below as to how he performed in school today using ratings of 1 to 5. 1=excellent, 2 = good, 3 = fair, 4 = poor, 5 = terrible or did not work.

AREA	CLASS PERIODS / SUBJECTS 1	2	3	4	5	6
participation						
class work						
handed in homework						
interaction with other children						
teacher's initials						

Place comments on back if needed:

NAME_____ DATE_____

Please evaluate this child in the following areas of behavior during free or unstructured school time, especially during recess. Using a rating of 1 = excellent, 2 = good, 3 = fair, 4 = poor, please place a number beside each behavior listed below for each recess or free-time period this child is observed each day.

Free Time/Recess

	#1	#2	#3	#4
1. Keeps hands to self; does not push, shove, pinch, or touch others wrongly	—	—	—	—
2. Does not fight with other children (hitting, kicking, biting) or try to provoke them by tripping them, shoving them, or taking their things	—	—	—	—
3. Follows rules	—	—	—	—
4. Tries to get along well with other children	—	—	—	—

Other comments:

the rules for proper recess behavior with the child, noted their existence on the card, and directed the child to give the card immediately to the recess monitor. As these cards illustrate, virtually any child behavior can be targeted for intervention via these monitoring/rating systems.

Cognitive-Behavioral Interventions

Cognitive-behavioral interventions were originally developed in order to directly treat the impulsive, unorganized, and unreflective manner in which hyperactive children approach academic tasks and social interactions. With their emphasis on the development of self-control, it was thought that cognitive-behavioral therapies would result in better maintenance and generalization of behavioral improvement than that achieved with traditional behavioral interventions.

A variety of different classroom-based cognitive-behavioral strategies have been utilized with hyperactive children. These include behavioral self-control techniques such as self-monitoring and self-reinforcement as well as more comprehensive procedures. Behavioral self-control strategies focused on self-monitoring and self-reinforcement involve children's monitoring and evaluating their own academic and social behavior and rewarding themselves (often with tokens or points) on the basis of those evaluations. Training typically involves teaching children how to observe and record their own behavior and how to evaluate their behavior to determine whether they deserve a reward. Occurrences of appropriate as opposed to inappropriate behavior are usually monitored, and children often keep written records of their ratings. Accuracy of child ratings is usually assessed by comparing these ratings against the teacher's records.

Self-monitoring and self-reinforcement were first implemented in order to maintain gains in classroom behavior established through token reinforcement programs. For example, Turkewitz, O'Leary, and Ironsmith (1975) gradually transferred control of a token reinforcement program from the teacher to the children by teaching children to evaluate and reward their own behavior. Accuracy of children's self-evaluations was taught by rewarding children depending upon the extent to which their ratings matched the teacher's ratings. Results showed that children's appropriate classroom behavior was maintained as they assumed primary responsibility for evaluating and reinforcing their own behavior.

Hinshaw, Henker, and Whalen (1984b) extended the use of self-monitoring and self-reinforcement to children's peer interactions. They utilized a training program similar to Turkewitz et al.'s (1975) "Match Game" to teach children to self-evaluate and self-reward their cooperative interactions with peers. In this procedure, trainers first taught children behavioral criteria for a range of ratings by modeling various behaviors (e.g., paying attention, doing work, cooperative behavior) and rating the behaviors on a scale from 1 to 5 points (e.g., 1 = "pretty bad," 5 = "great!"). Thereafter, children participated in role plays followed by naturalistic playground games in which trainers rated each child's behavior on the 1-to-5 scale and instructed children to monitor and rate their own behavior using the same scale. Children were encouraged try to match the trainer's ratings. Initially, children were given extra points for accurate self-evaluations regardless of the actual point value of their behavior. However, once children learned the procedure, they were rewarded only when their behavior was desirable *and* matched the trainers' ratings. Results of this study revealed that reinforced self-evaluation was more effective than externally administered reinforcement in reducing negative and increasing cooperative peer contacts on the playground.

Many cognitive training programs involve teaching children self-instructional and problem-solving strategies in addition to self-monitoring and self-reinforcement. The self-instructional program introduced by Meichenbaum and Goodman (1971), or a variant of this program, is often utilized. This program involves teaching children a set of self-directed instructions to follow when performing a task. Self-instructions include defining and understanding the task or problem, planning a general strategy to approach the problem, focusing attention on the task, selecting an answer or solution, and evaluating performance. In the case of a successful performance, self-reinforcement (usually in the form of a positive self-statement, such as "I really did a good job") is provided. In the case of an unsuccessful performance, a coping statement is made (e.g., "Next time I'll do better if I slow down") and errors are corrected. At first, an adult trainer typically models the self-instructions while performing a task. The child then performs the same task while the trainer provides the self-instructions. Next, the child performs the task while self-instructing aloud. These overt verbalizations are then faded to covert self-instructions. Reinforcement (e.g., praise, tokens, toys) is typically provided to the child for following the procedure as well as selecting correct solutions.

A variety of training tasks have been utilized ranging from a host of psychoeducational tasks (e.g., reproducing designs, following sequential instructions, concept problems) to academic and/or social relationship tasks. Studies show that the use of training tasks similar to the area(s) in which improvement is desired is most successful. For instance, the use of academically related tasks seems to facilitate generalization from the training sessions to academic performance in the classroom more than does the use of psychological tasks, such as maze performance. Similarly, training regimens that focus primarily on cognitive problem solving with psychoeducational or academic tasks have failed to show the same degree of improvement in children's social behavior as that found when social interactions are the focus of the training. In addition, children's improvement in these comprehensive programs appears to occur most consistently when external or self-reinforcement is provided for accurate and positive self-evaluations in conjunction with self-instructional training. In fact, when programs are effective, it may be more a result of reinforcement than of self-instructions.

A multicomponent self-control training program, including both behavioral self-control and self-instructions, was examined in a study conducted by Barkley, Copeland, and Sivage (1980) with six 7- to 10-year-old hyperactive boys. The study was conducted in an experimental classroom, which children attended in the afternoon after attending their regular class in the morning. Self-instructional training was provided in small- and large-group activities, with training tasks including both academic and social problems. Tokens were distributed for accurate performance of the self-instruction procedure. During individual seatwork, children self-monitored and recorded their on-task behavior at intervals signaled by a prerecorded tone. Specifically, whenever children heard the tone, they evaluated their behavior with respect to the posted classroom rules (e.g., staying in seat, working quietly). If they had been following the rules, they recorded a check mark on an index card kept at their desk. Initially, the tone sounded on a variable 1-minute schedule, but was faded to a variable-interval 5-minute schedule. Accurate reports, defined as matching observers' reports, were rewarded with tokens that could be exchanged for privileges.

Results are shown in Figures 15.3 and 15.4. They revealed that on-task behavior improved during individual seatwork, pointing to the efficacy of the self-monitoring and reinforcement procedures. The frequent use of these procedures was most effective (i.e., 1-minute rating intervals) and older children profited more from the procedure than did younger children. In contrast, training in self-instruction did not reduce misbehavior during the group lessons. This finding was probably due to the lack of contingencies for appropriate behavior during this time. In addition, behavioral improvements made during individual seatwork did not generalize to the regular classroom. Thus, the effectiveness of self-monitoring and self-reinforcement seemed to be limited to the context in which they were taught and where contingencies were in effect for their use.

Social problem solving and stress inoculation, two additional cognitive-behavioral interventions, have been applied toward improving the peer interactions of ADHD children. For instance, Hinshaw, Henker, and Whalen (1984a) utilized these interventions to enhance ADHD children's ability to control their anger in response to peer provocation. The treatment began with instruction in problem-solving skills and self-instructional strategies applied to academic and fine motor tasks. Problem-solving skills were then extended to interpersonal conflict situations. This portion of training involved children's generating and evaluating solutions to vignettes of interpersonal problems. The children also practiced self-control skills during role plays of interpersonal problems (e.g., meeting a new boy, playing a competitive game). The final treatment procedure involved training in stress inoculation and social problem-solving skills to be used in coping with verbal taunting and provocation from peers during a brief group interaction. Stress inoculation procedures involved monitoring internal cues related to anger and aggression and developing and practicing selected self-control coping strategies under increasingly greater provocation from peers. Self-control strategies included such response as ignoring, initiating calm conversation with peers, looking out the window, counting to 10, or reading a book. This cognitive-behavioral treatment resulted in greater self-control and greater use of effective coping strategies than a control treatment focusing on social problem solving (without practice), perspective taking, and enhancement of empathy. However, it was not known whether the positive effects found during the staged situation would generalize to more naturalistic peer interactions.

Despite these promising results, many other studies fail to show positive effects of treatment (see Abikoff,

Figure 15.3.

The percentage of time on task (× 10) during individual work time for each of six hyperactive boys across baseline (A), treatment (B), and reversal (A) phases. The graphs are in order of highest to lowest mental age (MA) (upper left to lower right) for the boys: Brad (MA = 10 years, 2 months); Seth (MA = 10 years, 1 month); Karl (MA = 8 years, 6 months); Gene (MA = 8 years, 1 month); Jim (MA = 6 years, 9 months); and Tim (MA = 6 years, 6 months). From "A Self-Control Classroom for Hyperactive Children" by R. A. Barkley, A. Copeland, and C. Sivage, 1980, *Journal of Autism and Developmental Disorders, 10,* 75–89. Copyright 1980 by Plenum Publishing Corporation. Reprinted by permission.

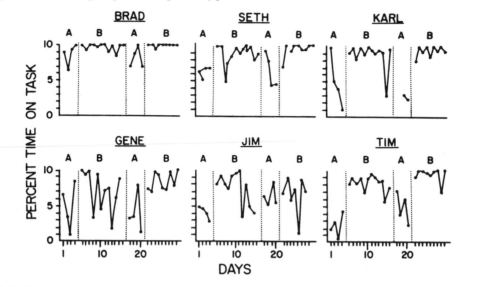

Figure 15.4.

Mean percentage of time spent on task by six hyperactive boys during all treatment conditions. From "A Self-Control Classroom for Hyperactive Children" by R. A. Barkley, A. Copeland, and C. Sivage, 1980, *Journal of Autism and Developmental Disorders, 10,* 75–89. Copyright 1980 by Plenum Publishing Corporation. Reprinted by permission.

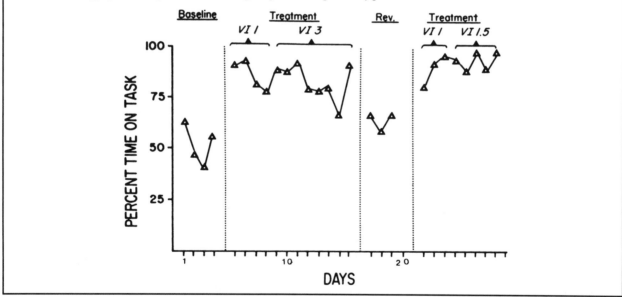

1985, for a review). Overall, the effects of cognitive-behavioral therapies are not as strong, as durable, or as generalizable as was once expected. Treatment gains usually are not maintained after the cognitive-behavioral procedures are withdrawn and rarely generalize to settings in which the procedures have not been implemented. Limited effects may be the result of failing to individualize treatment to the specific deficits of the child. The lack of generalization to academic and behavioral measures and to nontreated school settings found in many studies may be due to the brevity of the training (often only a few hours), and to little or no overlap between the skills taught during training and the requirements of the classroom or playground. Improved generalization may require training children in all settings in which self-control is desirable and training individuals in these settings (e.g., teachers, recess monitors) to encourage children's application of the skills.

Cognitive-behavioral treatments have also not been shown to be superior to traditional behavioral programs or to enhance the effects of behavioral programs on a consistent basis. In addition, cognitive-behavioral interventions frequently require an excessive amount of time and resources to implement properly. Trained experimenters or teachers are necessary to teach the children the procedures. Supervision of children's self-monitoring and evaluation is also required to ensure honest reports, since without supervision children become increasingly lenient in their self-evaluations and inappropriate behavior increases.

In light of these issues, the value of the widespread use of these procedures with ADHD children remains to be seen. It is our opinion that cognitive-behavioral techniques are most likely to be useful when they are taught directly to a child's caregivers (parents and teachers) for use within the myriad day-to-day interactions with that child, rather than having the child formally practice these skills in individual sessions in a clinic or outside of the classroom. A simple cognitive training strategy will therefore be necessary if it is to be conveniently implemented by the parents or teachers. One such approach is the "think aloud, think ahead" method mentioned above. Another is the "STAR" program where children learn to Stop, Think ahead about what they have been asked to do, Act or do the requested task while talking to themselves about the task, and Review their results. However, children must be adequately reinforced for displaying self-control skills in order to maintain this type of behavior—the training alone is insufficient.

Classroom Structure and Task Demands

A variety of factors related to the structure of the classroom environment, classroom rules, and the nature of task assignments have been recommended for modification in order to improve hyperactive children's school functioning. Early efforts focused on procedures to reduce stimulation in the classroom (i.e., minimal stimulation programs). These procedures were based on the premise that excessive distractibility was causing the problems of inattention exhibited by hyperactive children. Teachers were advised to remove as many visual distracters (e.g., colorful pictures and posters, brightly colored clothing and jewelry) and auditory distracters from the classroom as possible. In some cases, children were placed in desks facing a corner or wall; in other cases, three-sided cubicles were utilized to reduce exposure to distracting stimuli. Research evaluating these programs has generally not found that they lead to improvement in classroom behavior or academic performance of hyperactive children. Other investigators, proposing that traditional classrooms are too restrictive for hyperactive children, have advocated the use of classrooms that afford a greater degree of freedom and flexibility. However, this approach has also not been supported empirically.

Nevertheless, several specific features of the classroom environment may warrant modification when working with hyperactive children. Probably one of the most common classroom interventions involves moving the hyperactive child's desk away from other children to an area closer to the teacher. This procedure not only reduces the child's access to peer reinforcement of his or her disruptive behavior, but also allows the teacher to monitor the child's behavior better. As a result, the teacher can provide more frequent feedback which, as discussed earlier, is necessary with many ADHD children. It may also be beneficial for ADHD children to have individual and separated desks. When children sit very near one another, attention to task often decreases because of the disruptions that occur among children. Altering seating arrangements in this manner may sometimes be as effective as a reinforcement program in increasing appropriate classroom behavior.

Physically enclosed classrooms (with four walls and a door) are often recommended for hyperactive children over classrooms that do not have these physical barriers (i.e., "open" classrooms). An open classroom is usually noisier and contains more visual distractions since children can often see and hear the ongoing activities in nearby classes. In light of research showing that noisy environments are associated with less task attention and higher rates of negative verbalizations among hyperactive children (Whalen, Henker, Collins, Finck, & Dotemoto, 1979), open classrooms appear to be less appropriate for ADHD children.

It is also advisable that the classroom structure be well organized and predictable, with the posting of a daily schedule and classroom rules. Poster feedback charts regarding children's adherence to the classroom rules may also facilitate program success. In some cases, we have found the use of "nag tapes" to be particularly helpful in making rules more "externalized" and more effective in controlling child behavior. This involves tape-recording a set of reminders for the child ("Stay on task, don't space out, do your work, don't bug others," etc.) that are randomly interspersed on the audiotape. Obviously, they should be not so frequent as to disrupt the child's work. We often try to use the child's father as the voice on the tape, to capitalize on the somewhat greater compliance of ADHD children to their fathers than their mothers. When the child is about to do deskwork, he or she takes out a small portable tape recorder, plugs in an earpiece so the tape does not distract other students, and turns on the tape. The child then proceeds to do his or her work, while the tape is simultaneously providing reminders to remain on task. However, the efficacy of these types of procedures will depend greatly on their being combined with consistent methods of rule enforcement and the contingent use of rewards and punishments.

The following additional changes to classroom structure and curriculum are likely to prove beneficial to the management of ADHD children:

1. As with all children, academic tasks should be well matched to ADHD children's abilities. Increasing the novelty and interest level of the tasks through use of increased stimulation (e.g., color, shape, texture) seems to reduce activity level, enhance attention, and improve overall performance (Zentall, Falkenberg, & Smith, 1985).

2. Varying the presentation format and task materials (e.g., through use of different modalities) also seems to help maintain interest and motivation. When low-interest or passive tasks are assigned, they should be interspersed with high-interest or active tasks in order to optimize performance. Tasks requiring an active (e.g., motoric) as opposed to a passive response may also help hyperactive children to channel their disruptive behaviors into constructive responses (Zentall & Meyer, 1987).

3. Academic assignments should be brief (i.e., accommodated to the child's attention span) and feedback regarding accuracy of assignments should be immediate. Short time limits for task completion should also be specified and may be enforced with the use of external aids such as timers.

4. Children's attention during group lessons may be enhanced by delivering the lesson in an enthusiastic yet task-focused style, keeping it brief, and allowing frequent and active child participation.

5. Interspersing classroom lecture or academic periods with brief moments of physical exercise may also be helpful, so as to diminish the fatigue and monotony of extensive academic work periods (e.g., jumping jacks by the desk, a quick trip outside the classroom for a brisk 2-minute run or walk, forming a line and walking about the classroom in a "conga line" fashion, etc.).

6. Teachers should attempt to schedule as many academic subjects during morning hours as possible, leaving the more active, nonacademic subjects and lunch to the afternoon periods. This is suggested in view of the progressive worsening of ADHD children's activity levels and inattentiveness over the course of the day (see Chapter 2).

7. Whenever possible, classroom instructions should be supplemented with direct-instruction (e.g., DISTAR) drill of important academic skills, or, even better, with computer-assisted drill programs. ADHD children are considerably more attentive to these types of teaching methods than to mere lectures.

Managing Academic Programs with ADHD Adolescents

All of the recommendations above apply as much to adolescents with ADHD as to children. However, implementing these recommendations becomes considerably more difficult with adolescents because of the increased number of teachers involved in high school; the short duration of the class periods with each; the greater emphasis on individual self-control, organization, and responsibility for completing assignments; and the frequent changes that occur in class schedules across any given week. All of this is likely to result in a dramatic drop in educational performance in many ADHD children after they enter high school. There is little or no accountability of teachers or students at this level of education unless the students'

behavioral offenses become sufficiently heinous to attract attention or unless their academic deficiencies are grossly apparent. It is very easy for the average ADHD adolescent to "fall through the cracks" at this stage of education unless he or she has been involved with the special educational system before entering high school. Those who have will have been "flagged" as in need of continuing special attention. But most ADHD adolescents will not be in special education and so are likely to be viewed merely as lazy and irresponsible. It is at this age level that educational performance becomes the most common reason ADHD adolescents will be referred for clinical services (see Chapter 4).

Dealing with large educational institutions can be frustrating for parent, clinician, and ADHD teenager alike. Even the most interested teacher may have difficulties mustering sufficient motivation among his or her colleagues to help an ADHD adolescent in trouble at school. Below we have listed a number of steps that can be attempted to manage poor educational performance and behavioral adjustment problems in middle and high school. To the degree that other methods described above can also be implemented, so much the better.

1. A Public Law 94-142 evaluation of the adolescent should be immediately initiated, if one has not been done before or has not been done within the past 3 years (federal law requires a re-evaluation every 3 years a child is in special education). Special educational services will not be forthcoming until this evaluation is completed, and this can take up to 90 days or longer in some districts. The sooner it is initiated, the better.

2. ADHD adolescents invariably require counseling on the nature of their handicapping condition. Although many have certainly been previously told by parents and others that they are "hyperactive" or have ADHD, many of them still have not come to accept that they actually have a disability. In our opinion, this counseling is not intended to depress the individuals over what they cannot do, but to help them accept that they have certain limitations and to find ways to prevent their disability from creating significant problems for them. Such counseling is difficult, requiring a sensitivity to the adolescents' striving to be independent and to form their own opinions of themselves and their world. It often takes more than a single session to succeed in this endeavor but patience and persistence can pay off. Our approach is to stress the concept of individual differences: Everyone has a unique profile of both strengths and weaknesses in mental and physical abilities, and each of us must adjust to them. We often confide about our own liabilities and use humor to get the adolescent to see that they are not the only ones who have weaknesses. It is how we accept and cope with our weaknesses that determines how much they limit our successes in life. And yet we have personally sat at many school meetings where parents, teachers, school psychologists, and private tutors all had gathered to offer assistance

to ADHD teenagers, only to have the teens refuse the offers while promising that they could turn things around on their own. Until ADHD adolescents accept the nature of their disorder, they are unlikely to fully accept the help that may be offered them.

3. If ADHD adolescents have been on medication previously and responded successfully, they should be counseled on the advantages of returning to the medication as a means of both improving their school performance and obtaining those special privileges at home that may be granted as a result of such improved performance. (See Chapter 14 for an example of such counseling with a teenager about medication.) Many adolescents are concerned about others' learning that they are on medication. They can be reassured that only they, their parents, and the physician are aware of this and that no one at school need know unless the teenagers expose it. Therapists should be prepared in many cases, however, for ADHD adolescents to want to "go it alone" without the medication, believing that with extra applied effort they can correct the problem.

4. It is often essential that a team meeting be scheduled at the beginning of each academic year, and more often as needed, at an ADHD teen's school. The teachers, school psychologist, guidance counselor, principal, parents, *and the adolescent* are to be present. The therapist should take a handout describing ADHD to give to each participant (the chapter on ADHD by Barkley, 1989a, can be circulated as a condensed reading on the disorder and its treatments). The therapist should briefly review the nature of the adolescent's disorder and stress the need for close teamwork among the school, parents, and teen if the teen's academic performance is to be improved. The teachers should describe the current strengths and problems of the teen in their classes and make suggestions as to how they think they can help with the problem (e.g., being available after school a few days each week for extra assistance; reducing the length of written homework assignments; allowing the teen to provide oral means of demonstrating that knowledge has been acquired rather than relying on just written, time test grades; developing a subtle cueing system to alert the teen as to when he or she is not paying attention in class without drawing the whole class's attention to the fact; etc.). It is at this conference that the teen is asked to make a public commitment as to what he or she is going to strive to do to make school performance better. Once plans are made, the team should agree to meet again in 1 month to evaluate the success of their plans and troubleshoot any problem areas. Future meetings may need to be scheduled depending upon the success of the program to date. At the least, meetings twice a year are to be encouraged even for a successful program, so as to monitor progress and keep the school attentive to the needs of this teen. The adolescent always attends these meetings.

5. A daily home-school report card should be introduced as described above. These are often critical for teens more than any other age group; they give a teen and his or her parents daily feedback on how well the teen is performing in each class. Again, the back of the card can be used to record daily homework assignments, which are verified by each teacher before completing the rating on the card and initialing the front of the card. In conjunction with this, a home point system must be set up that includes a variety of desired privileges the teen can purchase with the points earned at school. Such things as telephone time, use of the family car, time out of the home with friends, extra money, clothes, musical tapes and compact discs, and special snacks kept in the house can be placed on the program. Points can also be set aside in a savings book to work toward longer-term rewards. It should be recalled, however, that the daily, short-term, immediately accessible privileges and not these longer-term rewards are what give the program its motivational power, and the reward menu should not contain too many long-term rewards. Once the adolescent is able to go for 3 weeks or so with no score of 4 or 5 (negative ratings) on the card, then the card is faded to a once- or twice-per-week schedule of completion. After a month of satisfactory ratings, the card can either be faded out or reduced to a monthly rating. The adolescent is then told that if word is received that grades are slipping, the card system will have to be reinstated.

6. The school should be encouraged to provide a second set of books to the family, even if a small deposit is required to do so, so that homework can still be accomplished even if a book required for homework is forgotten by the teen and left in his or her locker.

7. One of the teen's school teachers, the homeroom teacher, a guidance counselor, or even a learning disabilities teacher should be asked to serve as the "case manager." This person's role is to meet briefly with the teen three times a day for just a few minutes to help keep him or her organized. The teen can stop at this person's classroom or office at the start of school, at which time the manager checks to see that the teen has all the homework and books needed for the morning's classes. At lunch, the teen checks in again with this manager who sees that the teen has copied all necessary assignments from the morning classes, helps him or her select the books needed for the afternoon classes, and then sees that he or she has the assignments to be turned in that day for these afternoon classes. At the end of school, the teen checks in again with the manager to be sure that he or she has all assignments and books needed to go home for homework. Each visit takes no more than 3 to 5 minutes; however, interspersed as they are throughout the school day, these visits can be of great assistance in organizing the teen's schoolwork.

8. All parties should consider whether getting a private tutor for the teen may be beneficial. Many parents find it difficult to do homework with their teens or to tutor them in areas of academic weakness. The teens often resist these efforts as well, and the tension or arguments that can arise

may spill over into other areas of family functioning even after the homework period has passed. Where this is the case and a family can afford it, hiring a tutor to work with a teen even twice a week can be of considerable benefit to both improving the teen's academic weaknesses and "decompressing" the tension and hostility that arises around homework in the family.

9. The therapist should insist that the parents set up a special time each week to do something alone with this teen that is mutually pleasurable, so as to provide opportunities for parent-teen interactions that are not task-oriented, school-related, and fraught with the tensions that work-oriented activities can often bring with ADHD teens. This can often contribute to keeping parent-teen relations positive and counterbalance the conflicts that school performance demands frequently bring to such families.

Educational Placement

As reviewed earlier, a wide range of behavioral interventions have been shown to be effective in improving the classroom performance of hyperactive children. However, many of the programs described above are designed to be implemented by teachers of small classes who are well trained in behavioral procedures. In order to be implemented in mainstream classes, many of these programs may require the assistance of a classroom aide, or modification in terms of reduced time and resources (e.g., less frequent teacher monitoring and/or delivery of rewards). Teachers of mainstream classes may also require extensive training in behavior modification. Although intensive classroom programs are often not feasible in large classes, home-based programs are usually recommended, since they are often both practical and powerful.

In many cases, these procedures are sufficient, especially for children with mild to moderate ADHD symptoms or for children whose attentional and behavioral problems are controlled with pharmacological interventions. However, in other cases, especially when children have severe ADHD symptoms and accompanying problems of opposition, aggression, and/or learning disabilities, these simplified procedures are inadequate and alternative educational placements may be necessary (e.g., special education, private school). Ideally, these placements should include classes with a small student-teacher ratio that are taught by teachers with expertise in behavior modification. These factors will enable teachers to provide the intensive one-to-one instruction necessary, as well as the continuous monitoring, feedback, and use of intensive behavioral programs that appear necessary to maximize these children's success.

Special Educational Services

Obtaining special educational services that offer such classes for ADHD children is often a difficult process. Many ADHD children do not qualify for special educational services according to the guidelines specified in PL 94-142.

Clinicians need to keep in mind that diagnostic criteria for ADHD do not correspond in any direct way to eligibility criteria in federal and state laws governing placement within special educational programs. When ADHD children do qualify, they are often assigned to classes containing children with very different problems from their own (e.g., severe emotional disturbances or learning problems). Such placements often depend on the type of problem comorbid with the ADHD. For instance, ADHD children who are particularly aggressive and defiant are likely to be placed in programs for emotionally disturbed children, while those with coexisting learning disabilities but minimal aggression are likely to wind up in learning disability resource rooms. Certainly, ADHD children with significant speech and language or motor development problems are likely to receive language interventions, occupational and physical therapy, and adaptive physical education provided that these developmental problems are sufficient to interfere with academic performance. The ADHD child without these comorbid conditions is likely to be eligible for little special education in most states. Efforts are now underway by national parent support associations to force states and the federal government to reconsider the eligibility criteria for special services. Any change is likely to come after much debate and may be contingent upon the need to limit any cost that opening special education programs to another handicapped population would entail for school districts.

In the meantime, it is essential that clinicians be very familiar with the federal guidelines for special education, as well as with their own specific state guidelines and any particular local district guidelines. In addition, clinicians should become acquainted with the directors of special education within the school districts from which their clients most commonly come, so as to know their criteria for special education placement and be able to advocate knowledgeably for the children in their practice. The phrase "You are only as good as your Rolodex" is a truism in dealing with educational placements for ADHD children as well as locating resources within the private sector, such as private schools, formal and informal tutoring programs, and special summer camps for behavioral problem children. Sometimes the clinician will be contacted to give a "second opinion" on a case because of conflict between parents and school staff over the nature and extent of the child's problems and his or her eligibility for services. It is in such cases that clinicians must determine the precise nature of the school district's eligibility criteria and select assessment methods for addressing these criteria that are acceptable within school district policies.

It is also important that clinicians understand the principle of the "least restrictive environment" as it applies to decisions regarding special educational placement. PL 94-142 makes it clear that special services are to be provided in such a way that handicapped children may interact with nonhandicapped peers as much as possible. Hence, school districts are likely to err in the direction of placing ADHD children in the least restrictive environment necessary to manage the academic and behavioral problems—that is to say, in the program that provides the greatest contact with normal students. Some teachers are not always in agreement with this, preferring that even children with mild ADHD be removed to special educational settings, rather than having to adjust their own classroom curriculum and behavioral management style to accommodate the maintenance of these children in regular education. Parents may be equally biased toward special education believing that the smaller class sizes, better-trained teachers, and greater teacher attention are to be preferred over regular education. School districts are likely to resist these pressures so as not to violate the rights of the children to the least restrictive environment or risk legal action for doing so. Parents may find this frustrating, but must be helped to understand the philosophy behind this placement bias and its basis in law.

An Exemplary Program for ADHD Children

Only a few school-based treatment programs specifically serving ADHD children exist. One program, exemplary for specifically targeting the diverse needs of ADHD children, has been developed by James Swanson at the University of California–Irvine in collaboration with the Orange County Department of Education (UCI-OCDE). This program has been modeled after the summer programs developed by William Pelham at Washington State University, Florida State University, and the University of Pittsburgh, and by Barbara Henker, Stephen Hinshaw, and Carol Whalen at the University of California–Los Angeles.

The UCI-OCDE year-round program serves ADHD children in kindergarten through fifth grade. (For a full description, see Swanson et al., in press.) A full-day educational curriculum (approximately 12–15 children per class) and a comprehensive clinical program are provided to children over the course of approximately 1 year. The clinical component includes many of the techniques described above. First, an intensive behavior modification program based on a token economy is provided in the classroom. Children, working independently and in small groups, earn points every 30 minutes throughout the school day in the following areas: getting started, completing assignments, appropriate interaction with peers and adults, following instructions, and cleaning up. Points are tallied throughout the day and are exchanged for daily rewards (e.g., computer video games, Legos, games). Reward choices are dependent on the percentage of points earned (e.g., earning 90% of points results in choice of computer games, Legos, or any reward activity; earning 80% or better provides choice of a board game or art supplies; earning below 80% provides paper and pencil only). Weekly rewards (e.g., special outings, cooking, movies) are also earned, depending on the number of points accumulated over the course of the week. Teachers initially administer the point system. After demonstrating success with the system, children learn to self-monitor, self-evaluate, and self-reinforce their own performance. Once children

learn to evaluate their behavior accurately, teacher feedback is gradually reduced.

The second clinical component involves parent participation in a 6-week parent training class and weekly individual therapy sessions. This training focuses on the principles and techniques of behavior modification and includes development of an individual home program to address problems at home and to reinforce successful performance at school. Parent participation facilitates consistency across settings and promotes generalization of in-school gains to the home environment.

Social skills training is a third component and is delivered to the children in daily group sessions. This training focuses on teaching children the skills necessary to interact successfully with their peers and adults. Instruction, role plays, and *in vivo* practice during cooperative and competitive group games are used to teach a wide variety of social skills. Children's performance is monitored and reinforced by social skills counselors through the point system. Children are also taught to self-evaluate and reward their performance during social skills sessions. As their social behavior improves, the children are rewarded with increased privileges and counselor feedback is gradually reduced. Generalization of appropriate social skills to the playground and classroom is facilitated by involving the playground supervisors and classroom teachers in social skills training sessions, so that they reinforce children's use of these skills in each of these environments.

After meeting academic, behavioral, and social goals in the program, children are transferred back to their home schools. To facilitate a successful return to the home school, children may attend a transition school. At this school, advanced social skills groups are conducted, and classroom behavioral programs are established to facilitate transfer of learning. Individualized home-based reinforcement programs targeting school behaviors are typically implemented during the transition process.

The UCI-OCDE combined clinical and educational program appears to hold much promise in the treatment of ADHD children. Development and evaluation of this and other multifaceted school-based treatment programs may be important not only for serving these children, but also for preventing the development of more serious antisocial problems as the children enter adolescence and adulthood.

Summary

This chapter has reviewed a variety of behavior management methods that, when used in combination, can lead to substantial improvement in the classroom deportment, academic performance, and peer relations of ADHD children. Manipulation of teachers' attention (e.g., praising appropriate behavior and ignoring inappropriate behavior) is the basic ingredient in all interventions, but when used alone is usually not sufficient. ADHD children seem more responsive to frequent and powerful incentives such as tangible rewards or token economies. Prudent reprimands, backed up with a loss of privileges or time-out for severe behavior, are also necessary to reduce inappropriate disruptive behavior. Group contingencies and peer-administered consequences may be especially useful with ADHD children, since they may improve peer status in addition to behavioral and academic performance. Integrating schools and home contingencies is particularly useful to facilitate consistency and generalization across settings. Although recent studies show some success with cognitive-behavioral interventions, particularly in the area of social skills, the expectation that these interventions would result in greater maintenance and generalization than traditional approaches has not been realized. We therefore recommend that they be integrated with the teaching styles of the child's teacher for use in day-to-day exchanges, rather than taught in formal, one-to-one sessions outside of school.

The success of these procedures often depends on the ability of the teacher to monitor child behavior frequently, provide immediate feedback, and provide backup consequences (when needed) on a consistent basis. When these techniques are used in mainstream classes, practical issues often necessitate modifications and an emphasis on home-based contingencies. In cases requiring more intensive interventions, small classes with specialized programs designed to address the behavioral, academic, and social needs for ADHD children may be required.

The generalization and maintenance of treatment gains have thus far been elusive. Although the development of more sophisticated technologies may improve maintenance and generalization, the pervasive and durable problems exhibited by ADHD children seem to necessitate individualized, broadly based, long-term interventions. The effectiveness of these interventions requires not only a range of appropriate techniques, but also a high level of rapport and cooperation among those individuals working with the children, including school personnel, parents, and consultants. Moreover, the success of these interventions is undoubtedly a function of the ability of the treatment team to maintain a high level of optimism, enthusiasm, and energy throughout their work with these children.

Acknowledgment: Special thanks are extended to James Swanson and Cheryl Rosenau for their review of an earlier version of this chapter.

References

Abikoff, H. (1985). Efficacy of cognitive training intervention in hyperactive children: A critical review. *Clinical Psychology Review, 5,* 479–512.

Acker, M. M., & O'Leary, S. G. (1987). Effects of reprimands and praise on appropriate behavior in the classroom. *Journal of Abnormal Child Psychology, 15,* 549–557.

Allyon, T., Layman, D., & Kandel, H. (1975). A behavior-educational alternative to drug control of hyperactive children. *Journal of Applied Behavior Analysis, 8,* 137–146.

Barkley, R. A. (1989a). Attention Deficit Hyperactivity Disorder. In E. Mash & R. Barkley (Eds.), *Treatment of childhood disorders* (pp. 39–72). New York: Guilford Press.

Barkley, R. A., Copeland, A. P., & Sivage, C. (1980). A self-control classroom for hyperactive children. *Journal of Autism and Developmental Disorders, 10,* 75–89.

Campbell, S. B., Endman, M., & Bernfield, G. (1977). A three-year follow-up of hyperactive preschoolers into elementary school. *Journal of Child Psychology and Psychiatry, 18,* 239–249.

Cantwell, E., & Satterfield, J. H. (1978). The prevalence of academic underachievement in hyperactive children. *Journal of Pediatric Psychology, 3,* 168–171.

Douglas, V. I. (1985). The response of ADD children to reinforcement: Theoretical and clinical implications. In L. M. Bloomingdale (Ed.), *Attention deficit disorder: Identification, course, and treatment rationale* (pp. 49–66). New York: Spectrum.

Douglas, V. I., & Parry, P. A. (1983). Effects of reward on delayed reaction time task performance of hyperactive children. *Journal of Abnormal Child Psychology, 11,* 313–326.

Gast, D. C., & Nelson, C. M. (1977). Timeout in the classroom: Implications for special education. *Exceptional Children, 43,* 461–464.

Haenlein, M., & Caul, W. F. (1987). Attention deficit disorder with hyperactivity: Specific hypothesis of reward dysfunction. *Journal of the American Academy of Child and Adolescent Psychiatry, 26,* 356–362.

Hinshaw, S. P. (1987). On the distinction between attentional deficits/hyperactivity and conduct problems/aggression in child psychopathology. *Psychological Bulletin, 101,* 443–463.

Hinshaw, S. P., Henker, B., & Whalen, C. K. (1984a). Self-control in hyperactive boys in anger-inducing situations: Effects of cognitive-behavioral training and of methylphenidate. *Journal of Abnormal Child Psychology, 12,* 55–77.

Hinshaw, S. P., Henker, B., & Whalen, C. K. (1984b). Cognitive-behavioral and pharmacologic interventions for hyperactive boys: Comparative and combined effects. *Journal of Consulting and Clinical Psychology, 52,* 739–749.

Kubany, E. S., Weiss, L. E., & Sloggett, B. B. (1971). The good behavior clock: A reinforcement/time out procedure for reducing disruptive classroom behavior. *Journal of Behavior Therapy and Experimental Psychiatry, 2,* 173–179.

Meichenbaum, D., & Goodman, J. (1971). Training impulsive children to talk to themselves: A means of developing self-control. *Journal of Abnormal Psychology, 77,* 115–126.

Milich, R., & Landau, S. (1982). Socialization and peer relations in hyperactive children. In K. D. Gadow & I. Bialer (Eds.), *Advances in learning and behavioral disabilities* (Vol. 1, pp. 283–339). Greenwich, CT: JAI Press.

O'Leary, K. D., & O'Leary, S. G. (1977). *Classroom management: The successful use of behavior modification* (2nd ed.). New York: Pergamon Press.

Pelham, W. E., & Murphy, H. A. (1986). Attention deficit and conduct disorders. In M. Hersen (Ed.), *Pharmacological and behavioral treatments: An integrative approach* (pp. 108–148). New York: Wiley.

Pfiffner, L. J., & O'Leary, S. G. (1987). The efficacy of all-positive management as a function of the prior use of negative consequences. *Journal of Applied Behavior Analysis, 20,* 265–271.

Pfiffner, L. J., & O'Leary, S. G. (in press). Psychological treatments: School-based. In J. L. Matson (Ed.), *Hyperactivity in children: A handbook.* New York: Pergamon Press.

Pfiffner, L. J., Rosen, L. A., & O'Leary, S. G. (1985). The efficacy of an all-positive approach to classroom management. *Journal of Applied Behavior Analysis, 18,* 257–261.

Rapport, M. D., Murphy, H. A., & Bailey, J. S. (1982). Ritalin vs. response cost in the control of hyperactive children: A within-subject comparison. *Journal of Applied Behavior Analysis, 15,* 205–216.

Robinson, P. W., Newby, T. J., & Ganzell, S. L. (1981). A token system for a class of underachieving children. *Journal of Applied Behavior Analysis, 14,* 307–315.

Rosen, L. A., O'Leary, S. G., Joyce, S. A., Conway, G., & Pfiffner, L. J. (1984). The importance of prudent negative consequences for maintaining the appropriate behavior of hyperactive students. *Journal of Abnormal Child Psychology, 12,* 581–604.

Sullivan, M. A., & O'Leary, S. G. (in press). Differential maintenance following reward and cost token programs with children. *Behavior Therapy.*

Swanson, J., Simpson, S., Agler, D., Pfiffner, L., Bender, M., Kotkin, R., Rosenau, C., Mayfield, K., Ferrari, L., Lerner, M., Cantwell, D., & Youpa, D. (in press). *The UCI school-based treatment program for children with ADHD/ODD.* Excerpt. Medica International Congress Series.

Turkewitz, H., O'Leary, K. D., & Ironsmith, M. (1975). Generalization and maintenance of appropriate behavior through self-control. *Journal of Consulting and Clinical Psychology, 43,* 577–583.

Weiss, G., & Hechtman, L. (1986). *Hyperactive children grown up.* New York: Guilford Press.

Wender, P. H. (1971). *Minimal brain dysfunction in children.* New York: Wiley.

Whalen, C. K., Henker, B., Collins, B. E., Finck, D., & Dotemoto, S. (1979). A social ecology of hyperactive boys: Medication effects in systematically structured classroom environments. *Journal of Applied Behavior Analysis, 12,* 65–81.

Zentall, S. S., Falkenberg, S. D., & Smith, L. B. (1985). Effects of color stimulation and information on the copying performance of attention-problem adolescents. *Journal of Abnormal Child Psychology, 13,* 501–511.

Zentall, S. S., & Meyer, M. J. (1987). Self-regulation of stimulation for ADD-H children during reading and vigilance task performance. *Journal of Abnormal Child Psychology, 15,* 519–536.

Learning Disabilities and Memory

Swanson, H. L., and J. B. Cooney. 1991.
In *Learning about learning disabilities*, ed. B. Y. L. Wong, 103–22. San Diego: Academic Press, Inc.

Editor's Notes[*]

In the preceding chapter, you learned about attentional problems in children with learning disabilities. In the present chapter, you will learn about their memory skills and problems. Attentional and memory processes are closely related. Hence, from a teacher's point of view, to facilitate your learning, it makes good sense for us to proceed from addressing attentional problems to memory-processing problems in children with learning disabilities.

Here, Swanson and Cooney's chapter is organized around five themes. The first theme concerns the three types of memory research in learning disabilities: (1) descriptive, (2) instructional, and (3) theoretical. The second theme concerns how learning-disabled children's memory functions/skills resemble those in younger, normal-achieving children. They highlight these functional similarities in four specific areas: (1) the distinctions between automatic and effortful processing, (2) the use of cognitive strategies, (3) the development of a knowledge base, and (4) children's awareness of their own memory processes. The third lies in a model of memory and the outlining of processing stages in it. Swanson and Cooney use it to show where memory-processing problems of learning-disabled children occur. The fourth theme lies in a historical review of memory research in learning disabilities, which Swanson and Cooney have divided into early versus contemporary research. The last theme focuses on principles for memory strategy instruction.

I. Introduction

Simply defined, memory is the ability to encode, process, and retrieve information that one has been exposed to. As a skill, it is inseparable from intellectual functioning and learning. Individuals deficient in memory skills, such as the learning-disabled (LD), would be expected to have difficulty in a number of academic and cognitive domains (Stanovich, 1986; Torgesen *et al.*, 1988). Thus, helping students with learning disabilities (LDs) to better remember information is an important educational goal. The importance of this goal is also bolstered by studies suggesting that the memory skills used by students with LDs do not appear to exhaust, or even to tap, their ability (e.g., Barclay and Hagen, 1982; Brown and Palinscar, 1988; Kolligian and Sternberg, 1987; Scrugg and Mastropieri, 1989; Spear and Sternberg, 1987; Swanson, 1990; Wong, 1982). In the spirit of this broad educational goal, the objective of this chapter is to provide a foundation for our understanding of LD students' memory skills. The chapter attempts to characterize and selectively review current research on LD children's memory skills, describe the components and stages of processing that influence memory performance, and discuss the implication of memory research for the instruction of LD students.

II. Information Processing

Based mainly on the findings of descriptive and instructional studies, we may characterize LD students' memory skills as similar to those of younger children, particularly in the way they approach memory tasks. For a broader understanding of their immature memory functioning, however, it is necessary to provide a model of memory that outlines some important components that influence performance.

To date, the study of memory in LD students is conceptualized with an information-processing approach. Greatly simplified, the information processing approach is defined as the study of how input is transformed reduced, elaborated, stored, retrieved, and used (Newell, 1980). To understand how each of these processes plays a part in the flow of information, some general components must be identified. Three components that typically underlie information-processing models are (1) a constraint or structural

---

[*] Editor's note: These "Editor's Notes" are from this excerpt.

component, akin to the hardware of a computer, which defines the parameters within which information can be processed at a particular stage (e.g., sensory storage, short-term memory), working memory, long-term memory; (2) a control or strategy component, akin to the software of a computer which describes the operations of the various stages (to be described); and (3) an executive process, by which learners' activities (e.g., strategies) are overseen and monitored.

Briefly, the structural components are sensory, short-term, working, and long-term memory. Sensory memory refers to the initial representation of information that is available for processing for a maximum of 3–5 sec; short-term memory processes information between 3 and 7 sec and is primarily concerned with storage, via rehearsal processes. Working memory also focuses on the storage of information as well as the active interpretation of newly presented information, whereas long-term memory is a permanent storage with unlimited capacity. The executive component monitors and coordinates the functioning of the entire system. Some of this monitoring may be automatic, with little awareness on the individual's part, whereas other types of monitoring require effortful and conscious processing. These components will become clearer when we later discuss current research findings (for a review, also see Jorm, 1983).

Let us now consider research that identifies where in this memory model LD students' memory difficulties may lie. However, it is important to recognize that research findings on memory problems in LD children come primarily from contemporary research. Contemporary research focuses on control and, more recently, executive processes, whereas earlier research focused primarily on the hardware (structural) differences of LD children's memory difficulties.

A majority of the research published prior to 1976 was concerned with perceptual-motor behavior of brain-injured and/or reading-disabled children, and little experimental research dealt directly with memory difficulties (Hallahan and Cruickshank, 1973). Of the studies that were available prior to 1970, most stated merely that LD children perform poorly on certain tasks (e.g., digit span; for a recent review, see Mishra *et al.*, 1985), and the nature of their deficits were isolated to structural (hardware) problems. We now focus on more recent findings of LD children's memory processes/functions.

III. Contemporary Research

After 1975, the study of LD children's memory deficits dramatically increased. For example, a survey of LDs journals between 1976 and 1979 revealed that 18% of the reports were concerned with memory processes (Torgesen and Dice, 1980). Let us briefly review important research findings to date. This review is organized according to the basic components: sensory register, short-term memory, working memory, long-term memory, and executive function.

A. Sensory Register

Basic structural environmental information (e.g., visual, auditory) is assumed first to enter the appropriate sensory register. Information in this initial store is thought to be a relatively complete copy of the physical stimulus that is available for further processing for a maximum of 3–5 sec. An example of sensory registration for the visual modality is an image or icon. In a reading task, if an array of letters is presented tachistoscopically and the child is then asked to write out those letters after a 30-sec delay between instructions, the child can reproduce about six or seven letters. Incoming information from other modalities (auditory, kinesthetic) receives sensory registration, but less is known about their representation. For example, students who are presented a letter of the alphabet may produce a photographic trace that decays quickly, or they may physically scan the letter and transfer the information into an auditory (e.g., echo of sound)–visual–linguistic (meaning) representation. In other words, information presented visually may be recorded into other modalities (e.g., auditory). The transfer of visual image to the auditory–visual–linguistic store is made at the discretion of the person. In the reading process, each letter or word is scanned against information in long-term memory and the verbal name. Certainly this representation will facilitate transfer of information from the sensory register to a higher level of information processing.

In general, research on the sensory register of LD children suggests it is intact. For example, Elbert (1984) has provided evidence that LD and nonlearning-disabled (NLD) students are comparable at the encoding stage of word recognition, but that LD children require more time to conduct a memory search (also see Manis, 1985). Additional evidence that LD and NLD children are comparable at the encoding stage of information processing was provided by Lehman and Brady (1982). Using a release from the proactive inhibition procedure (see Dempster and Cooney, 1982), Lehman and Brady found that reading-disabled and normal readers were comparable in their ability to encode word information (e.g., indicating whether a word was heard or seen and information concerning a word's category). However, reading-disabled children relied on smaller subword components in the decoding process than did normal readers.

Many accounts of poor recognition of quickly presented information by LD students have been attributed to attention deficits—although this conclusion is in question. For example, using a psychological technique free of memory confounds, McIntyre *et al.* (1978) reported a lower-than-normal span of apprehension in children identified as LD. Subsequently, Mazer *et al.* (1983) attributed the lower span of apprehension to a slower rate of information pickup from the iconic sensory store. Despite the common assumption of differences between LD and NLD children in attentional to visual and auditory stimuli, Bauer (1977a) has argued that the attentional resources of the LD children are adequate for performance on a variety of memory tasks. In other words, the residual differences are not great enough to account for the differences in memory performance. For example, LD and NLD children are comparable in their ability to recall orally presented sets of three letters or three words within 4 sec after presentation (Bauer, 1979). Similarly, LD and NLD students are comparable in their ability to recognize letters and geometric shapes after a brief visual presentation when recognition is less than 300 msec after stimulus offset (Morrison *et al.*, 1977). In view of these findings, the retrieval of information from sensory storage apparently is an important, although not a major, factor in the memory deficits exhibited in LD children. Taken as a whole, research on attention suggests that the attentional resources of LD children are adequate for performance on most learning and memory tasks (also see Elison and Richman, 1988; Samuels, 1987a, b; Swanson, 1983a).

B. Short-Term Memory

From the sensory register, information is transferred into the limited-capacity short-term memory. Information lost in this memory is assumed to decay or disappear, but actual time of decay is longer than time available in the sensory register. Exact rate of decay of information cannot be estimated, because this component is greatly controlled by the subject. The short-term memory retains information in auditory-verbal-linguistic representations. Using the example of a child recalling letters, the child may subvocally rehearse a letter by voicing the letter as well as the place of articulation in the mouth.

Variation in short-term memory capacity of LD children has been attributed to control processes (such as rehearsal) and the meaningfulness of the material. The crucial factor in capacity is the person's ability to encode units or sequence the items so that they can be recoded into smaller units. Other factors that affect capacity include (1) information load, (2) similarity of items, (3) number of items processed during subsequent activities, and (4) passage of time. The exact nature of problems with the capacity of short-term memory is somewhat obscure in LD students (Cooney and Swanson, 1987). Research has been unclear as to whether the limitation is one of processing capacity, storage capacity, or some interaction between the two.

Control processes in short-term memory include a choice as to which information to scan and a choice of what and how to rehearse. Rehearsal refers to the conscious repetition of information, either subvocally or orally, to recall information at a later date. Learning a telephone number or street address illustrates the primary purpose of rehearsal. Additional control processes also involve organization (ordering, classifying, or tagging information to facilitate retrieval) and mediation (comparing new items with items already in memory). Various organization of strategies may include:

1. Chunking: Grouping items so that each one brings to mind a complete series of items (e.g., grouping words into a sentence).
2. Clustering: Organizing items in categories (e.g., animal, furniture).

3. Mnemonics: Idiosyncratic methods for organizing materials.
4. Coding: Varying the qualitative form of information (e.g., using images rather than verbal labels, substituting pictures for words).

Mediation may be facilitated by

1. Making use of preexisting associations, eliminating the necessity for new ones.
2. Utilizing instructions, either verbal or asking the child to imagine, to aid in retrieval and organization.
3. Cuing at recall by using verbal and imaginary information to facilitate mediation.

Concerning research on short-term memory control processes, Torgesen and Goldman (1977) studied lip movements of children during a memorization task. LD children were found to exhibit fewer lip movements than the NLD students. To the extent that these lip movements reflect the quantity of rehearsal, these data support a rehearsal-deficiency hypothesis. Haines and Torgesen (1979) and others (e.g., Dawson *et al.*, 1980; Koorland and Wolking, 1982) also reported that incentives could be used to increase the amount of rehearsal and, thus, recall by LD students. More recently, Bauer and Emhert (1984) have suggested that the difference between LD and NLD students is in the quality of the rehearsal rather than the quantity of rehearsal, per se.

Another major source of difficulty that LD children experience during their attempts to memorize material has been highlighted by Gelzheiser *et al.* (1983). These authors recorded a brief statement made by a LD student following an attempt to retain a passage containing four paragraphs about diamonds. The student reported that she could identify major themes of the story but could not categorize the various pieces of information under these major items. She was able to abstract the essence of the story but was unable to use this as a framework to organize the retention of the specific passage.

Swanson (1983c) found that LD children rarely reported the use of an organizational strategy when they were required to rehearse several items. He reasoned that, because these children were capable of rehearsal, the problem was not a deficiency in rehearsal but, instead, was a failure to perform elaborative processing of each word. Elaborative processing was defined as processing that goes beyond the initial level of analysis to include more sophisticated features of the words and ultimately the comparison of these features with others in the list.

Another major source of difficulty related to short-term memory processing has been related to LD children's lack or inefficient use of a phonological code (sound represented). Torgesen (1988) conducted studies on a small group of subjects who performed in the retarded range of verbatim recall on sequences of verbal information. His comprehensive analysis of LD students' performance deficits suggests that they are due to coding errors and represent the phonological features of language. He suggests that LD children's memory problems relate to the acquisition of fluent word identification and word analysis skills.

Additional support for the notion of phonological coding errors comes from studies suggesting that good and poor readers differ in the extent to which they recall similar- and dissimilar-sounding names. An interaction is usually found in which poor readers perform better on "rhyming-word and similar letter-sounding tasks" because they have poor access to a phonological code (e.g., Shankweiler et al., 1979; Siegel and Linder, 1984). That is, good readers recall more information for words or letters that have distinct sounds (e.g., mat vs. book, A vs. F) than words or letters that sound alike (mat vs. cat, b vs. d). In contrast, poor readers are more comparable in their recall of similar and dissimilar words or sounds than skilled readers. This finding suggests that good readers are disrupted when words or sounds are alike because they process information in terms of sound (phonological) units. In contrast, poor readers are not efficient in processing information into sound units (phonological codes) and, therefore, are not disrupted in performance if words or letters sound alike. In a recent study by Johnston et al. (1987), 8- and 11-yr-old good and poor readers of average and below-average intelligence were compared on their ability to recall strings of similar and dissimilar sounding letters. When a control was made of differences in memory span between ability groups, high- and low-IQ poor readers were comparable with their chronological age (CA) reading-level matched controls in similarity effects; i.e., the study did not directly support the contention that difficulties in immediate memory are primarily due to difficulty with phonological coding. Some other contrasting studies (e.g., Sipe and Engle, 1986) have suggested that poor readers may be adequate in phonological coding (echoic memory processes) but show a fast decline in their ability to recall as the retention interval (time between item presentation and recall) is increased.

In summary, LD children's poor short-term memory has been related to problems in rehearsal, organization, elaborative processing, and phonological coding; i.e., the previous studies suggest that LD children suffer short-term memory difficulties and these problems manifest themselves in terms of how information is strategically processed (e.g., rehearsal) and how information is mentally represented (e.g., phonological codes).

C. Long-Term Memory

The amount of information as well as the form of information transferred to long-term memory is primarily a function of control processes (e.g., rehearsal). Long-term memory is a permanent storage of information of unlimited capacity. How information is stored is determined by the uses of links, associations, and general organization plans. Information stored in long-term memory is primarily semantic. Forgetting occurs because of item decay (loss of information) or interference.

In comparison to the volume of research on short-term memory processes, research on LD children's long-term memory is meager; however, the available research provides considerable support for the assertion that storage and retrieval problems are primary sources of individual differences in long-term memory performance (e.g., Bjorklund, 1985; Ceci, 1986; Howe et al., 1985; Vellutino and Scanlon, 1987).

Numerous studies have also shown that LD children are less skilled than NLD peers in the use of rehearsal strategies used to store information in long-term memory (Bauer, 1977a,b, 1979; Tarver et al., 1976; Torgeson and Goldman, 1977). The main source of support for the assertion of rehearsal deficits in LD children is the diminished primary effect (i.e., better recall of items at the beginning of a list over the middle items of the list) of the serial position curve (Bauer, 1979). Primacy performance is a measure of the accessibility of items placed in long-term storage. Thus, the primacy effect is thought to reflect greater rehearsal of those items at the beginning of the list.

Concerning retrieving information from long-term memory, LD children can use organized strategies for selecting retrieval cues (Wong, 1982) and different word attributes (e.g., graphophonic, syntactic, semantic) to guide to retrieval (Blumenthal, 1980); however, they appear to select less efficient strategies, conduct a less exhaustive search for retrieval cues, and lack self-checking skills in the selection of retrieval cues (Wong, 1982). Swanson (1984b, 1987e) also provided evidence suggesting that long-term memory deficits may arise from failure to integrate visual and verbal memory traces of visually presented stimuli at the time of storage or retrieval. His findings suggested that semantic memory limitations underlie LD children's failure to integrate verbal and visual codes. In contrast, Ceci et al. (1980) presented data that suggested separate pathways for auditory and visual inputs to the semantic memory system and that LD children may have an impairment in one or both of these pathways. For children with visual and auditory impairments, the recall deficit arises in both storage and retrieval. When only one modality is impaired, the long-term memory deficit is hypothesized to arise at the time of storage. Furthermore, semantic orienting tasks were found to ameliorate the recall deficits of the children with single modality impairments but not those with impairments in both visual and verbal modalities (Ceci et al., 1980; experiment 2).

Some investigators (for a review, see Worden, 1986) have suggested that LD children's long-term memory is intact, but the strategies necessary to gain access to this information are impaired. This notion has been recently challenged (Baker et al., 1987), and evidence suggests that LD children's long-term memory for tasks that require semantic processing is clearly deficient when compared with that of NLD peers (Swanson, 1986a). Moreover, some experimental evidence suggests that LD children may have problems in the structural component of information processing (e.g., Baker et al., 1987; Cohen, 1981; Swanson, 1987c; Torgesen and Houck, 1980). Specifically, Torgesen and Houck (1980) completed a series of eight experiments in which subgroups of LD and NLD children were compared on a digit span task.

Treatment variations among the eight experimental conditions included manipulations of rehearsal, incentives, and related mnenomic activities. Not all LD subjects benefited from strategy intervention, suggesting that structural or capacity difficulties may exist in some children with LD (also see Swanson, 1986a, 1989).

Taken as a whole, the results reviewed here suggest that the processes involved in entering a memory trace into the long-term store are important sources of ability group differences in children's long-term recall. Additional research to discover methods for remediating these deficits is certainly warranted.

D. Working Memory

Working memory is viewed as a *dynamic* and active system because it simultaneously focuses on both processing and storage demands, whereas short-term memory primarily focuses on the storage of information and is considered a more passive system (Baddeley, 1981). Thus, short-term memory is partly understood as a component of a limited capacity system from accumulating and holding segments of information in order (e.g., speech or orthographic units) as they arrive during a listening or reading task. Material in short-term memory is retained if it is rehearsed. In contrast, working memory is concerned with the interpretation and integrating of information with previously stored information.

How does the formulation of working memory help us understand LD children's memory problems better than the concept of short-term store? First, it suggests that verbal rehearsal plays a smaller role in learning and memory (Baddeley, 1984) an important point because some studies do show that performance deficits of LD children are not related to rehearsal, per se (e.g., see Swanson, 1983b). For example, previous studies of LD children's short-term memory operations such as rehearsal (Bauer, 1979) have not explained how constraints in long-term memory contribute to academic performance; i.e., they have not shown how word knowledge, associations, and attentional capacity contribute to some of the problems we see occurring in short-term memory tasks. Furthermore, measures (e.g., digit span) commonly used in assessing differences between LD and NLD children's memory are weakly correlated with academic ability (Daneman and Carpenter, 1980, 1983), suggesting that such short-term tasks may not capture the essence of academic performance, namely the combination of processing and long-term memory storage functions. Second, the idea of a working memory system is useful because it is viewed as an active memory system directed by a central executive (to be discussed) and the resources stored in long-term memory.

A recent study (Swanson et al., 1989a) sought to determine the *extent* to which less skilled readers suffer from working memory deficiencies. A sentence span task (Daneman and Carpenter, 1980; also see Baddeley *et al.*, 1985) was used to measure the efficiency of storage and processing operations combined. The task requires recalling the last word of several sentences as well as answering a comprehension question about a sentence. Materials for the sentence span task were unrelated declarative sentences, 7–10 words in length. The sentences were randomly arranged into sets of two, three, four, or five. Examples of the sentences for recalling the last word in a series of three sentences for words are

1. We waited in line for a *ticket*.
2. Sally thinks we should give the bird *its food*.
3. My mother said she would write a *letter*.

To ensure that children comprehended the sentences (i.e., processed their meaning) and did not merely treat the task as one of short-term memory, they were required to answer a question after each group of sentences were presented. For the three-sentence set, for example, they were asked "Where did we wait?" The results of this study suggests that LD readers' working memory was inferior to NLD readers. Thus, studies that suggest LD children's memory deficiencies are localized to a short-term store system must be re-evaluated within the context of a model that incorporates the operations of working memory.

E. Executive Function

An executive function is a cognitive activity that determines the order in which processes will be performed (Neisser, 1967). In other words, it is the organization directive for various memory strategies. The executive function does not perform the searching task, or organize, and sort out material; instead, it directs the various mental activities to a goal. Computers have the executive built-in; humans can modify and develop overall routines for information retrieval.

Neisser sums up some important points related to executive processing:

1. Retrieval of information consists of many programmed searches simultaneously and independently (parallel search or multiple search).
2. Control of parallel and sequential processes is directed by the executive routine.
3. Executive function and search processes are learned and based on earlier processing, the implication being that:
   a. Individuals learn to organize and retrieve.
   b. There are individual styles of organization.
4. Failure to recall is failure to access, the implication being that there is a misguided search strategy.

Although executive functioning has been researched with respect to its importance and application to mentally retarded children's memory (Campione *et al.*, 1985), its application to LDs is just emerging (Brown and Palinscar, 1988; Pressley *et al.*, 1987b; Swanson, 1987a). A focus on executive processing is an important area of research because planning activities prior to solving a problem, monitoring behavior in action, reorganizing strategies, and evaluating the outcomes of any strategic action have characterized LD students' functioning in a number of academic domains (e.g., Palinscar and Brown, 1984). Strategy deficits in LD learners have been noted in terms of failing to monitor cognitive progress or to notice important task difference in learning tasks (for a review, Pressley *et al.*, 1989). Within this context, the important focus of memory research has been to determine whether or not LD students can review their own cognitive strategies, select and reject them appropriately, and persist in searching for the most suitable task strategies at various stages of performance (Palinscar and Brown, 1984; Pressley *et al.*, 1987). Support for possible problems in LD children's executive functioning can be found in studies where students with LDs have difficulty checking, planning, and monitoring control processes (Palinscar and Brown, 1984). This type of research focuses on how decisions or strategies are prioritized, the kinds of decisions LD children make at a specific point in implementing strategy, and how they make decisions related to an unresolved processing stage (e.g., cannot understand the gist of the passage). In summary, the focus of the executive function is to detail the LD students' coordination, direction, and organization of search strategies. The kinds of decisions that will be made and how decisions will be directed when a sequence of operations may provide unresolved steps is related to the child's metacognitive knowledge (see Chapter 8, later in this volume).

F. Summary

Overall, current research suggests that LD children experience problems with a number of information-processing components. Most of the research has focused on short-term memory, and problems in short-term memory may very likely influence processes related to working memory, long-term memory, and executive processes. As yet, research has not identified the independent effects and contributions of various memory components to LD students' overall memory functioning. Thus, it is best to view their memory difficulties as reflecting interactive problems between and among various memory-processing components.

IV. Implications from Contemporary Memory Research for Instruction

A number of memory researchers have converged on the notion that LD students' ability to access information remains inert, unless they are explicitly prompted to use certain cognitive strategies (e.g., for a review, see Swanson, 1989). For example, LD students may be taught to (1) organize lists of pictures and words in common categories, (2) rehearse the category names during learning, and (3) use the names and retrieval cues at the time of the test (e.g., for a review, see Cooney and Swanson, 1987; Swanson, 1987a). The data suggest that when LD children are explicitly encouraged to use such strategies on some tasks their performance improves and thus the discrepancy between their general intellectual ability and contextually related memory deficits is lessened.

Based on these findings, the LD learner has been viewed as having poor strategies for approaching the complex requirements of academic tasks and, thus, cannot meet his or her academic potential. Thus, he or she is described as an inefficient learner—one who either lacks certain strategies or chooses inappropriate strategies and/or generally fails to engage in self-monitoring behavior. Critical to the strategy-deficit model is the concept of access. Access refers to the notion that the information necessary for task performance resides within the child. Some children can flexibly access this information; i.e., a particular behavior is not delimited to a constrained set of circumstances (Campione *et al.*, 1985). In addition, some children are "aware" of these processes and can consciously describe and discuss their own cognitive activities that allow them to access information. Based on this extensive literature, some very practical concepts and principles from memory research can serve as guidelines for the instruction of LD students. We will briefly discuss eight in the following.

V. Principles of Strategy Instruction

A. Memory Strategies Serve Different Purposes

One analysis of the memory strategy research suggests there is no single best strategy for LD students within or among particular domains (for a review, see Cooney and Swanson, 1987). As can be seen from the studies reviewed in this chapter, research is in pursuit of the best strategy to teach LD students. Some of the memory strategies that have been used to enhance LD children's performance are shown in Table 4.1. A number of studies, for example, have looked at enhancing LD children's performance by using advanced organizers, skimming, asking, questioning, taking notes, summarizing, and so on. But apart from the fact that LD students have been exposed to various types of strategies, the question of which strategies are the most effective is not known. We know in some situations, such as remembering facts, the key word approach appears to be more effective than direct instruction models (Scruggs *et al.*, 1987), but, of course, the rank ordering of different strategies changes in reference to the different types of learning outcomes expected. For example, certain strategies are better suited to enhancing students' understanding of what they previously read, whereas other strategies are better suited to enhancing students' memory of words or facts. The point is that different strategies can effect different cognitive outcomes in a number of ways.

B. Good Memory Strategies for NLD Students Are Not Necessarily Good Strategies for LD Students and Vice Versa

Strategies that enhance access to information for NLD students will not, in some cases, be well suited for the LD child. For example, Wong and Jones (1982) trained LD and NLD adolescents in a self-questioning strategy to monitor reading comprehension. Results indicated that although the strategy training benefited the adolescents with LDs, it did not positively influence the performance of NLD adolescents.

To illustrate this point further, Swanson (1989) presented LD, mentally retarded, gifted, and average-achieving students a series of tasks that involved base and elaborative sentences. Their task was to recall words embedded in a sentence. The results of the first study suggested that LD children differ from the other group in their ability to benefit from elaboration. This finding was qualified in the next study (experiment 2) and suggested that the difficulty of the material must be taken into consideration when determining strategy effects, but the results suggest that LD children may require additional strategies to perform comparably to their cohorts. In another study (Swanson *et al.*, 1989b), LD college students were asked to recall words in a sentence under semantic and imagery instructional conditions. The results showed LD students were better able to remember words in a sentence during instructional conditions that induced semantic processing. In contrast, NLD readers favored imagery processing over semantic processing conditions. In summary, these results suggest that strategies that are effective for NLD students may, in some situations, be less effective for LD students.

C. Effective Memory Strategies Does Not Necessarily Eliminate Processing Differences

It is commonly assumed that if LD children are presented a strategy that enables efficient processing of information, then improvement in performance is due to the fact that the strategies are affecting the same processes as in NLD students (e.g., Torgesen *et al.*, 1979). This assumption has emanated primarily from studies that have imposed organization on seemingly unorganized material. For example, considerable evidence indicates that LD readers

---

Table 4.1. Classification of Memory Strategies

1. Rehearsal

Students are told to rehearse stimuli verbally or to write, look at, go over, study, or repeat the stimuli in some other way. The children may be instructed to rehearse items just once, a finite number of times, or an unlimited number of times.

2. Elaboration

Students are instructed to use elements of the stimulus material and assign meaning by, for instance, making up a phrase or sentence, making an analogy, or drawing a relationship based on specific characteristics found in the stimulus material.

3. Orienting (attention)

These strategies direct student's attention to a task. For example, teachers may instruct children to "follow along" or "listen carefully" during lessons.

4. Specific Attentional Aids

This strategy is similar to the attention strategy, but students are instructed to use objects, language, or a part of their body in a specific way to maintain orientation to a task.

5. Transformation

Transformation is a strategy suggested by teachers for converting unfamiliar or difficult problems into similar or simpler ones that can then be remembered more easily. Transformations are possible because of logical, rule-governed relationships between stimulus elements.

6. Categorical Information

Teachers might direct students to use taxonomic information (e.g., pictures accompanying a category) or to analyze the item into smaller units (e.g., looking for interitem associations).

7. Imagery

This strategy usually consists of nonspecific instructions to remember by taking a mental picture of something or to maintain or manipulate them in the mind.

8. Specific Aids for Problem-Solving and Memorizing

This strategy involves the use of specific aids in problem-solving or memorizing. For example, teachers may tell children to use blocks or other counters to represent addition or subtraction operations in a concrete way.

9. General Aids

In contrast to specific aids, teachers recommend the same general aid for a variety of different problems. These aids are designed and used to serve a general reference purpose. Examples include the use of dictionaries or other reference works.

10. Metamemory

Teachers instructing this strategy tell students that certain procedures will be more helpful for studying and remembering than others. The strategy frequently includes giving hints about the limits of memory, asking students about the task factors that will influence ease of remembering, or helping them understand the reasons for their own performance. Teachers can also tell students that they can devise procedures that will aid their memory or indicate the value of using a specific strategy.

[Adapted from Moely *et al.* (1986).]

---

do not initially take advantage of the organizational features of material (e.g., Dallego and Moely, 1980). When instructed to organize information into semantic or related categories (e.g., Torgesen et al., 1979), they improve considerably and perform comparably to NLD students. However, the notion that LD readers process the organizational features of information in the same fashion as NLD students is questionable. For example, Swanson and Rathgeber (1986) found in categorization tasks that LD readers can retrieve information without interrelating superordinate, subordinate, and coordinate classes of information as the NLD children do. Thus, LD children can learn to process information in an organizational sense without implicitly knowing the meaning of the material. Hence, just because LD children are sensitized to internal structure of material via some strategy (e.g., by cognitive strategies that require the sorting of material), it does not follow that they will make use of the organization qualities of the material in a manner consistent with what was intended from the instructional strategy.

D. Comparable Memory Performance Does Not Mean Comparable Strategies

Although the previous principle suggests that different processes may be activated during intervention that are not necessarily the intent of the instructional intervention, it is also likely that LD subjects use different strategies on tasks in which they seem to have little difficulty, and these tasks will probably be overlooked by the teacher for possible intervention. For example, it is commonly assumed that although LD children have isolated processing deficits and require general learning strategies to compensate for these processing deficits, they process information comparable with their normal counterparts on tasks in which they have little trouble. Yet several authors suggest that there are alternative ways for achieving successful performance (Newell, 1980), and some indirect evidence indicates that LD individuals may use qualitatively different mental operations (Shankweiler et al., 1979) and processing routes (e.g., Swanson, 1986a) when compared with their NLD counterparts. A recent study (Swanson, 1988) suggests that LD children use qualitatively different processes on tasks they have little difficulty with; i.e., their performance is comparable to NLD children, but they use different strategies to arrive at the same response as their NLD peers.

E. Memory Strategies in Relation to a Student's Knowledge Base and Capacity

Levin (1986) has suggested that a match must exist between strategy and learner characteristics. For example, Conca (1989), as well as others (Jenkins et al., 1986; Gelzheiser et al., 1987), suggests that LD children are not uniformly inactive strategy users but, rather, tend to be more proficient users when demands on verbal processing are not heavy.

One important variable that has been overlooked in the LD memory literature is the interaction between processing constraints (structures) and memory strategies. Most

LD strategy research, either implicitly or explicitly, has considered cognitive to be a confounding variable and has made very little attempt to measure its influence (Swanson, 1987c). Swanson (1984a) has recently conducted three experiments related to LD students' performance on a word-recall task and found that recall is related to cognitive effort (or the mental input) that a limited capacity system expends to produce a response. He found that LD readers were inferior in their recall of materials that made high-effort demands when compared with NLD readers. Furthermore, it was found that skilled readers accessed more usable information from semantic memory for enhancing recall than did LD readers. In a subsequent study, Swanson, (1986b) found that LD children were inferior in the quantity and internal coherence of information stored in semantic memory as well as in the means by which it is accessed.

F. Comparable Memory Strategy May Not Eliminate Performance Differences

It is commonly assumed that without instruction, LD students are less likely to produce strategies than their normal counterparts. However, several studies have indicated that residual differences remain between ability groups even when groups are instructed or prevented from strategy use (Gelzheiser, 1984; Swanson, 1983b, 1989; Wong et al., 1977). For example, in a study by Gelzheiser et al. (1987), LD and NLD children were compared on their ability to use organizational strategies. After relevant instruction, LD and NLD were compared on their ability to recall information on a post-test. The results indicated that LD children were comparable to NLD in strategy use but were deficient in overall performance. In another study, Swanson (1983c) found that the recall performance of the LD group did not improve from baseline level when trained with rehearsal strategies. They recalled less than normal-achieving peers, even though the groups were comparable in the various types of strategy use. The results support the notion that groups of children with different learning histories may continue to learn differently, even when the groups are equated in terms of strategy use.

G. Memory Strategies Taught Do Not Necessarily Become Transformed into Expert Strategies

One mechanism that promotes expert performance is related to strategy transformation (e.g., Chi et al., 1988). Children who become experts at certain tasks often have learned simple strategies and, through practice, discover ways to modify them into more efficient and powerful procedures. In particular, the proficient learner uses higher-order rules to eliminate unnecessary or redundant steps to hold increasing amounts of information. The LD child, in contrast, may learn most of the skills related to performing an academic task and perform appropriately on that task by carefully and systematically following prescribed rules or strategies. Although LD children can be taught strategies, recent evidence suggests that the difference between LD (experts in this case) and NLD children is that the latter have modified such strategies to become more efficient (Swanson and Cooney, 1985). It is plausible that the LD child remains a novice in learning new information because he or she fails to transform memory strategies into more efficient forms (see Swanson and Rhine, 1985).

H. Strategy Instruction Must Operate on the Law of Parsimony

A "number of multiple-component packages" of strategy instruction have been suggested for improving LD children's functioning. These components have usually encompassed some of the following: skimming, imagining, drawing, elaborating, paraphrasing, using mnemonics, accessing prior knowledge, reviewing, orienting to critical features, and so on. No doubt there are some positive aspects to these strategy packages in that:

1. These programs are an advance over some of the studies that are seen in the LDs literature as rather simple or "quick-fix" strategies (e.g., rehearsal or categorization to improve performances).
2. These programs promote a domain skill and have a certain metacognitive embellishment about them (see Chapter 8, later in this volume).
3. The best of these programs involve (a) teaching a few strategies well rather than superficially, (b) teaching students to monitor their performance, (c) teaching students when and where to use the strategy to enhance generalization, (d) teaching strategies as an integrated part of an existing curriculum, and (e) teaching that includes a great deal of supervised student practice and feedback.

The difficulty of such packages, however, at least in terms of theory, is that little is known about which components best predict student performance, nor do they readily permit one to determine why the strategy worked. The multiple-component approaches that are typically found in a number of LDs strategy intervention studies must be carefully contrasted with a component analysis approach that involves the systematic combination of instructional components known to have an additive effect on performance. As stated by Pressley (1986: 140), good strategies are "composed of the sufficient and necessary processes for accomplishing their intended goal, consuming as few intellectual processes as necessary to do so."

VI. Summary and Conclusion

In summary, we have briefly characterized research on memory and LDs. Our knowledge of LD individuals' memory somewhat parallels our knowledge about the differences between older and younger children's memory. The parallel relies in effortful processing, the focus on cognitive strategies, the development of a knowledge base, and the awareness of one's own memory processes. Memory research may be categorized into three types: (1) descriptive, (2) instructional, and (3) theoretical. Most memory research

emanates from an information-processing framework. Earlier research tends to emphasize the structural problems (hardware problems), i.e., brain deficits of memory, whereas more recent studies tend to focus on the representation, control, and executive process (e.g., strategies) of memory. Current research on memory is beginning to examine the interaction of structures and process on performance. A number of principles related to memory strategy instruction have emerged that have direct application to the instruction of children and adults with LDs. These principles are related to (1) the purposes of strategies, (2) parsimony with regard to the number of processes, (3) individual differences in strategy use and performance, (4) learner constraints, and (5) the transfer of strategies into more efficient processes.

References

Baddeley, A. D. (1981). The concept of working memory: A view of its current state and probable future development. *Cognition* 10, 17–23.

Baddeley, A. (1984). Reading and working memory. *Vis. Language* 18, 311–322.

Baddeley, A., Logie, R., Nimmo-Smith, T., and Brereton, N. (1985). Components of fluent reading. *J. Mem. Language* 24, 119–131.

Baker, J. G., Ceci, S. J., and Hermann, N. D. (1987). Semantic structure and processing: Implications for the learning disabled child. *In* "Memory and Learning Disabilities" (H. L. Swanson, ed.), pp. 83–110. JAI Press, Greenwich, Connecticut.

Barclay, C. R., and Hagen, J. W. (1982). The development of mediated behavior in children: An alternative view of learning disabilities. *In* "Theory and Research in Learning Disabilities" (J. P. Das, R. F. Mulcahy, and A. E. Wall, eds.), pp. 61–84. Plenum Press, New York.

Bauer, R. H. (1977a). Memory processes in children with learning disabilities: Evidence for deficient rehearsal. *J. Exp. Child Psychol.* 24, 415–430.

Bauer, R. H. (1977b). Short-term memory in learning disabled and nondisabled children. *Bull. Psychon. Soc.* 10, 128–130.

Bauer, R. H. (1979). Memory processes in children with learning disabilities: Evidence for deficient rehearsal. *J. Exp. Child Psychol.* 24, 415–430.

Bauer, R. H., and Emhert, J. (1984). Information processing in reading-disabled and nondisabled children. *J. Exp. Child Psychol.* 37, 271–281.

Blumenthal, S. H. (1980). A study of the relationship between speed of retrieval of verbal information and patterns of oral reading errors. *J. Learn. Disabil.* 3, 568–570.

Brown, A. L., and Palinscar, A. S. (1988). Reciprocal teaching of comprehension strategies: A natural history of one program for enhancing learning. *In* "Intelligence and Cognition in Special Children: Comparative Studies of Giftedness, Mental Retardation, and Learning Disabilities" (J. Borkowski and J. P. Das, eds.), Ablex, New York.

Campione, J. C., Brown, A. L., Ferrara, R. A., Jones, R. S., and Steinberg, E. (1985). Breakdown in flexible use of information: Intelligence related differences in transfer following equivalent learning performances. *Intelligence* 9, 297–315.

Ceci, S. J. (1986). Developmental study of learning disabilities and memory. *J. Exp. Child Psychol.* 38, 352–371.

Ceci, S. J., Ringstrom, M. D., and Lea, S. E. G. (1980). Coding characteristics of normal and learning-disabled 10 year olds:

Evidence for dual pathways to the cognitive system. *J. Exp. Psychol.: Hum. Learn. Mem.* **6,** 785–797.

Chi, M. T. H., Glaser, R., and Farr, M. (1988). "The Nature of Expertise." Lawrence Erlbaum, Hillsdale, New Jersey.

Cohen, R. L. (1981). Short-term memory deficits in reading disabled children, in the absence of opportunity for rehearsal strategies. *Intelligence* **5,** 69–76.

Conca, L. (1989). Strategy choice by LD children with good and poor naming ability in a naturalistic memory situation. *Learn. Disabil. Q.* **12,** 97–106.

Cooney, J. B., and Swanson, H. L. (1987). Overview of research on learning disabled children's memory development. *In* "Memory and Learning Disabilities" (H. L. Swanson, ed.), pp. 2–40. JAI Press, Greenwich, Connecticut.

Dallego, M. P., and Moely, B. E. (1980). Free recall in boys of normal and poor reading levels as a function of task manipulation. *J. Exp. Child Psychol.* **30,** 62–78.

Daneman, M., and Carpenter, P. A. (1980). Individual differences in working memory and reading. *J. Verbal Learn. Verbal Behav.* **19,** 450–466.

Daneman, M., and Carpenter, P. A. (1983). Individual differences in integrating information between and within sentences. *J. Exp. Psychol.: Learn. Mem. Cognit.* **9,** 561–584.

Dawson, M. H., Hallahan, D. P., Reeve, R. E., and Ball, D. W. (1980). The effect of reinforcement and verbal rehearsal on selective attention in learning-disabled children. *J. Abnorm. Child. Psychol.* **8,** 133–144.

Dempster, F. N., and Cooney, J. B. (1987). Individual differences in digit span, susceptibility to proactive interference, and aptitude/achievement test scores. *Intelligence* **6,** 399–416.

Elbert, J. C. (1984). Short-term memory encoding and memory search in the word recognition of learning-disabled children. *J. Learn. Disabil.* **17,** 342–345.

Forrest Pressley, D. D. L., and Gillies, L. A. (1983) Children's flexible use of strategies during reading. *In* "Cognitive Strategy Research: Educational Applications" (M. Pressley and J. R. Levin, eds.). Springer-Verlag, New York.

Gelzheiser, L. (1984). Generalization from categorical memory tasks to prose by learning disabled adolescents. *J. Educ. Psychol.* **76,** 1128–1138.

Gelzheiser, L. M., Solar, R. A., Shephard, M. J., and Wozniak, R. H. (1983). Teaching learning disabled children to memorize: Rationale for plans and practice. *J. Learn. Disabil.* **16,** 421–425.

Gelzheiser, L. M., Cort, R., and Shephard, M. J. (1987). Is minimal strategy instruction sufficient for learning disabled students. *Learn. Disabil. Q.* **10,** 267–275.

Haines, D., and Torgesen, J. K. (1979). The effects of incentives on short-term memory and rehearsal in reading disabled children. *Learn. Disabil. Res. Q.* **2,** 18–55.

Hallahan, D. P., and Cruickshank, W. M. (1973). Psychoeducational foundations of learning disabilities. Prentice-Hall, Englewood Cliffs, New Jersey.

Jenkins, J., Heliotis, J., Haynes, M., and Beck, K. (1986). Does passive learning account for disabled readers' comprehension deficits in ordinary reading situations? *Learn. Disabil. Q.* **9,** 69–76.

Johnson, R. S., Rugg, M., and Scott, T. (1987). Phonological similarity effects, memory span and developmental reading disorders. *Br. J. Psychol.* **78,** 205–211.

Jorm, A. F. (1983). Specific reading retardation and work memory: A review. *Br. J. Psychol.* **74,** 311–342.

Kolligian, J., and Sternberg, R. J. (1987). Intelligence, information processing, and specific learning disabilities: A triarchic synthesis. *J. Learn. Disabil.* **20,** 8–17.

Koorland, M. A., and Wolking, W. D. (1982). Effect of reinforcement on modality of stimulus control in learning. *Learn. Disabil. Q.* **5,** 264–273.

Koppitz, E. M. (1971). "Children with Learning Disabilities: A Five Year Follow-up Study." Grune & Stratton, Orlando, Florida.

Lehman, E. B., and Brady, K. M. (1982). Presentation modality and taxonomic category as encoding dimension from good and poor readers. *J. Learn. Disabil.* **15,** 103–105.

Levin, J. R. (1986). Four cognitive principles of learning strategy instruction. *Educ. Psycholog.* **21,** 3–17.

Manis, F. R. (1985). Acquisition of word identification skills in normal and disabled readers. *J. Educ. Psychol.* **27,** 28–90.

Mazer, S. R., McIntyre, C. W., Murray, M. E., Till, R. E., and Blackwell, S. L. (1983). Visual persistence and information pick-up in learning disabled children. *J. Learn. Disabil.* **16,** 221–225.

McIntyre, C. W., Murray, M. E., Coronin, C. M., and Blackwell, S. L. (1978). Span of apprehension in learning disabled boys. *J. Learn. Disabil.* **11,** 13–20.

Mishra, S. P., Shitala, P., Ferguson, B. A., and King, P. V. (1985). Research with the Wechsler digit span subtest: Implications for assessment. *School Psychol. Rev.* **14,** 37–47.

Moely, B. E., Hart, S. S., Santulli, K., Leal, L., Johnson, T., and Rao, N. (1986). How do teachers teach memory skills? *Educ. Psycholog.* **21,** 55–57.

Morrison, F. J., Giordani, B., and Nagy, J. (1977). Reading disability: An information processing analysis. *Science* **196,** 77–79.

Neisser, U. (1967). "Cognitive Psychology." Appleton-Century-Crofts, New York.

Newell, A. (1980). Reasoning, problem solving and decision processes: The problem space as a fundamental category. *In* "Attention and Performance VIII." (R. Nickerson, ed.). Lawrence Erlbaum, Hillsdale, New Jersey.

Palinscar, A. S., and Brown, A. L. (1984). Reciprocal teaching of comprehension-fostering and monitoring activities. *Cognit. Instruct.* **1,** 117–175.

Pressley, M. (1986). The relevance of the good strategy user model to the teaching of mathematics. *Educ. Psycholog.* **21,** 139–161.

Pressley, M., Borkowski, J. G., and O'Sullivan, J. T. (1984). Memory strategy instructions is made of this: Metamemory and durable strategy use. *Educ. Psycholog.* **10,** 94–107.

Pressley, M., Johnson, C. J., and Symons, S. (1987). Elaborating to learn and learning to elaborate. *J. Learn. Disabil.* **20,** 76–91.

Pressley, M., Symons, S., Snyder, B. L., and Cariglia-Bull, T. (1989). Strategy instruction research is coming of age. *Learn. Disabil. Q.*

Samuels, S. J. (1987a). Information processing and reading. *J. Learn. Disabil.* **20,** 18–22.

Samuels, S. J. (1987b). Why is it difficult to characterize the underlying cognitive deficits in special education populations. *Excep. Children* **54,** 60–62.

Schneider, W., and Pressley, M. (1989). "Memory Development between 2 and 20." Sringer-Verlag, New York.

Schneider, W., and Sodian, B. (1988). Metamemory–memory relationships in preschool children: Evidence from a memory-for-location task. *J. Exp. Child Psychol.* **45,** 209–233.

Scruggs, T. E., and Mastropieri, M. A. (1989). Mnemonic instruction of LD students: A field-based evaluation. *Learn. Disabil. Q.* **12,** 119–125.

Scruggs, T. E., Mastropieri, M. A., Levin, J. R., and Gaffney, J. S. (1987a). Facilitating the acquisition of science facts in learning disabled students. *Am. Educ. Res. J.* **22,** 575–586.

Scruggs, T. E., Mastropieri, M. A., and Levin, J. R. (1987b). Transformational mnemonic strategies for learning disabled students. *In* "Memory and Learning Disabilities" (H. L. Swanson, ed.), pp. 225–244. JAI Press, Greenwich, Connecticut.

Shankweiler, D., Liberman, I. Y., Mark, S. L., Fowler, L. A., and Fischer, F. W. (1979). The speech code and learning to read. *J. Exp. Psychol.: Hum. Learn. Mem.* **5**, 531–545.

Siegel, L., and Linder, B. A. (1984). Short-term memory processing in children with reading and arithmetic learning disabilities. *Dev. Psychol.* **20**, 200–207.

Sipe, S., and Engle, R. (1986). Echoic memory processes in good and poor readers. *J. Exp. Psychol.: Learn. Mem. Cognit.* **12**, 402–412.

Snow, J. H., Barnett, L., Cunningham, K., and Ernst, M. (1988). Cross-model development with normal and learning disabled children. *Int. J. Clin. Neuropsychol.* **10**, 74–80.

Spear, L. C., and Sternberg, R. J. (1987). An information-processing framework for understanding reading disability. *In* "Handbook of Cognitive, Social and Neuropsychological Aspects of Learning Disabilities (S. Ceci, ed.), pp. 3–32. Lawrence Erlbaum, Hillsdale, New Jersey.

Stanovich, K. (1986). Matthew effects in reading: Some consequences of individual differences in the acquisition of literacy. *Read. Res. Q.* **21**, 360–387.

Sternberg, R. J. (1987). A unified theory of intellectual exceptionality. *In* "Intelligence and Exceptionality: New Directions for Theory, Assessment, and Instructional Practices." (J. D. Day and J. G. Borkowski, eds.), pp. 135-172. Ablex, Norwood, New Jersey.

Swanson, H. L. (1983a). A developmental study of vigilance in learning disabled and non-disabled children. *J. Abnorm. Child Psychol.* **11**, 415–429.

Swanson, H. L. (1983b). A study of nonstrategic linguistic coding on visual recall of learning disabled and normal readers. *J. Learn. Disabil.* **16**, 209–216.

Swanson, H. L. (1983c). Relations among metamemory, rehearsal activity and word recall in learning disabled and nondisabled readers. *Br. J. Educ. Psychol.* **53**, 186–194.

Swanson, H. L. (1984a). Effects of cognitive effort and word distinctiveness on learning disabled and nondisabled readers' recall. *J. Educ. Psychol.* **76**, 894–908.

Swanson, H. L. (1984b.) Semantic and visual memory codes in learning disabled readers. *J. Exp. Child Psychol.* **37**, 124–140.

Swanson, H. L. (1986a). Do semantic memory deficiencies underlie disabled readers encoding processes? *J. Exp. Child Psychol.* **41**, 461–488.

Swanson, H. L. (1986b). Learning disabled readers' verbal coding difficulties: A problem of storage or retrieval? *Learn. Disabil. Res.* **1**, 73–82.

Swanson, H. L. (1987a). Information processing theory and learning disabilities: An overview. *J. Learn. Disabil.* **20**, 3–7.

Swanson, H. L. (1987b). The combining of multiple hemispheric resources in learning disabled and skilled readers' recall of words: A test of three information processing models. *Brain Cognit.* **6**, 41–54.

Swanson, H. L. (1987c). Verbal coding deficits in the recall of pictorial information in learning disabled readers: The influence of a lexical system. *Am. Educ. Res. J.* **24**, 143–170.

Swanson, H. L. (1988). Learning disabled children's problem solving: Identifying mental processes underlying intelligent performances. *Intelligence* **12**, 261–278.

Swanson, H. L. (1989). Central processing strategy differences in gifted, average, learning disabled and mentally retarded children. *J. Exp. Child Psychol.* **47**, 370–397.

Swanson, H. L. (1990). Intelligence and learning disabilities. *In* "Learning Disabilities and Research Issues" (H. L. Swanson and B. K. Keogh, eds.), pp. 97-113. Lawrence Erlbaum, Hillsdale, New Jersey.

Swanson, H. L., and Cooney, J. (1985). Strategy transformations in learning disabled children. *Learn. Disabil. Q.* **8**, 221–231.

Swanson, H. L., and Rathgeber, A. (1986). The effects of organizational dimensions on learning disabled readers' recall. *J. Educ. Res.* **79**, 155–162.

Swanson, H. L., and Rhine, B. (1985). Strategy transformation in learning disabled children's math performance: Clues to the development of expertise. *J. Learn. Disabil.* **18**, 596–603.

Swanson, H. L., Cochran, K., and Ewers, C. (1989a). Working memory and reading disabilities. *J. Abnorm. Child Psychol.* **17**, 745–756.

Swanson, H. L., Cooney, J. D., and Overholser, J. D. (1989b). The effects of self-generated visual mnemonics on adult learning disabled readers' word recall. *Learn. Disabil. Res.* **4**, 26–35.

Tarver, S. G., Hallahan, D. P., Kaufmann, J. M., and Ball, D. W. (1976). Verbal rehearsal and selective attention in children with learning disabilities: A developmental lag. *J. Exp. Child Psychol.* **22**, 375–385.

Torgesen, J. K. (1978). Memorization process in reading-disabled children. *J. Educ. Psychol.* **69**, 571–578.

Torgesen, J. K. (1988). Studies of children with learning disabilities who perform poorly on memory span tasks. *J. Learn. Disabil.* **21**, 605–612.

Torgesen, J. K., and Dice, C. (1980). Characteristics of research on learning disabilities. *J. Learn. Disabil.* **13**, 531–535.

Torgesen, J. K., and Goldman, T. (1977). Rehearsal and short-term memory in second grade reading disabled children. *Child Dev.* **48**, 56–61,

Torgesen, J. K., and Houck, D. G. (1980). Processing deficiencies of learning disabled children who perform poorly on the digit span task. *J. Educ. Psychol.* **72**, 141–160.

Torgesen, J. K., Bowen, C., and Ivey, C. (1978). Task structure vs. modality of the visual–oral digit span test. *J. Educ. Psychol.* **70**, 451-456.

Torgesen, J. K., Murphy, H. A., and Ivey, C. (1979). The effects of an orienting task on the memory performance of reading disabled children. *J. Learn. Disabil.* **12**, 396–402.

Torgesen, J. K., Rashotte, C. A., and Greenstein, J. (1988). Language comprehension in learning disabled children who perform poorly on memory span tests. *J. Educ. Psychol.* **80**, 480–487.

Vellutino, F. R., and Scanlon, D. M. (1987). Linguistic coding and reading ability. *In* "Advances in Applied Psycholinguistics," Vol. (S. Rosensberg, ed.), pp. 71–69. Cambridge University Press, New York.

Wong, B. Y. L. (1982). Strategic behaviors in selecting retrieval cues in gifted, normal achieving and learning disabled children. *J. Learn. Disabil.* **15**, 33–37.

Wong, B. Y. L., and Jones, W. (1982). Increasing metacomprehension in learning-disabled and normally-achieving students through self-questioning training. *Learn. Disabil. Q.* **5**, 228–240.

Wong, B. Y. L., Wong, R., and Foth, D. (1977). Recall and clustering of verbal materials among normal and poor readers. *Bull. Psychon. Soc.* **10**, 375–378.

Worden, P. E. (1986). Comprehension and memory for prose in the learning disabled. *In* "Handbook of Cognitive, Social and Neuropsychological Aspects of Learning Disabilities," Vol. 1. (S. J. Ceci, ed.), pp. 241–262. Lawrence Erlbaum, Hillsdale, New Jersey.

Worden, P. E., Malmgren, P., and Gabourie, P. (1982). Memory for stories in learning disabled adults. *J. Learn. Disabil.* **15**, 145–152.

Worden, P. E., and Nakamura, G. V. (1983). Story comprehension and recall in learning-disabled vs. normal college students. *J. Educ. Psychol.* **74**, 633–641.

Visual Processes in Learning Disabilities

Willows, D. M. 1991. In *Learning about learning disabilities*, ed. B. Y. L. Wong, 163–93.
San Diego: Academic Press, Inc.

Editor's Notes[*]

In this chapter, Willows' theme is that it is premature to dismiss the potential role of visual processing problems in reading disabilities. In support of her theme, she presents impressive data on early visual information processing where younger nondisabled and disabled readers clearly differ. Additionally, she examines data from visual memory research and concludes that the data suggest the possibility of a developmental lag in visual memory in younger disabled readers. She also points out the consistent discovery in subtype research studies in reading disabilities of a cluster of disabled readers sharing visual deficits.

However, it is pertinent to note that Willows does not dispute the research findings on the role of linguistic factors in reading disability, which are elucidated in Mann's previous chapter. Nor is she championing a visual deficits viewpoint about reading disabilities. In fact, she does not support research that attempts to link reading disabilities to one source of causal factors, be they linguistic or otherwise. Rather, she simply wants us to be researchers unfettered by self-imposed blinkers, to explore all possible factors or combinations of factors regarding the causes of reading disabilities.

I. Introduction

This chapter describes the visual perception and visual memory abilities of individuals who have difficulties in processing written language. A very high proportion of those designated as learning-disabled might more accurately be termed written-language-disabled, because their most salient difficulties are manifested in the areas of reading, spelling, handwriting, and written composition. Many learning-disabled individuals may also be language-disabled in a more general sense, showing problems in their receptive and expressive aural/oral language processes as well as in the written domain. Many others, however, seem to function very well in the aural/oral domain, but they have great difficulty when they have to deal with print. Despite the fact that spelling, handwriting, and written composition difficulties are almost invariably involved, the term reading-disabled is commonly used to refer to those individuals who have written-language disabilities. The many variants on this term include specific reading disability, developmental reading disability, congenital reading disability, dyslexia, specific dyslexia, developmental dyslexia, etc., but because there are no satisfactory distinctions in the definitions of these terms, the term reading disability will be used here to encompass them all.

Although listening, speaking, reading, and writing are all language processes, the latter two are distinct from the former by virtue of the fact that they involve a visual symbol system. For skilled readers/writers, the visual symbols in the writing system are so familiar that it is very difficult for them to recall a time when printed words were just meaningless marks on the page; however, for beginning readers/writers, young or old, this is exactly the case. The person who is just starting to learn to read and write must differentiate and remember the symbols in their writing system, be they alphabetic like the Arabic system, logographic like the Chinese, or syllabic like the Cree.

If people differ from each other in their abilities to perceive, discriminate, identify, and remember visual symbols (as they differ from each other in virtually every other area of cognitive–linguistic functioning), then it might be expected that those who have weaknesses in these visual abilities would have trouble learning the symbol system of their written language and, as a consequence, might become disabled in their learning to read and write. Despite this obvious possibility, the topic of visual processes in reading–writing disabilities is a very controversial one. This chapter is about why clinicians and educators have long considered visual processing deficits to be potential contributing factors in written-language disabilities, and about what current research tells us about the relation between visual processing deficits and reading disabilities. It is also about why some theorists and researchers dismiss the importance of visual factors in written-language disabilities, and why others believe that progress toward an understanding of reading disabilities is being hampered by a failure to consider the possibility of a contribution by visual processing factors.

The chapter begins by considering the visual demands of learning to read, write, and spell. It then goes on to present clinical case studies and correlational evidence that seem to support the long-standing belief that visual processing weaknesses play some role in written-language disabilities. The next section presents a review of the key basic research in the area, beginning with a discussion of a central point of controversy—whether reading disabilities are caused by one or more types of processing deficit. The research review covers a large number of studies that compare the visual processing abilities of disabled readers with those of normal readers. One major group of studies examines the initial stages of visual processing (visual perception), and another group of studies deals with later processing stages (visual memory). The chapter concludes with a discussion of the implications of the findings concerning visual processing deficits and reading disabilities for future research directions and practical applications.

II. Visual Components in Reading and Writing

Before considering potential areas of visual processing difficulty among the reading-disabled, the visual processing

---

[*] Editor's note: These "Editor's Notes" are from this excerpt.

demands of learning to read, spell, and write are examined. To understand what the child, or anyone just beginning to learn the written form of a language, is faced with, consider the messages printed in Figure 6.1. Unless you are familiar with the written languages of Chinese (1), Korean (2), Japanese (3), Hindi (4), Arabic (5), or Urdu (6), all of the characters and words in Figure 6.1 are just meaningless marks on the page. In fact, all six writing samples represent highly meaningful expressions—the first three languages all ask the question "How are you?" and the latter three ask the question "What is your name?" Despite the fact that the content of the messages is familiar, novice readers of the language (whether or not fluent in the oral language) must learn to pay close attention to the visual information on the page to extract the underlying meaning. For more experienced readers of these languages, the visual component is processed unconsciously and may seem to be of little or no importance. For the beginner, the visual task of dealing with written language involves several types of demands, including the following:

1. Accurate visual perception of letters and words

2. Visual analysis of letter forms and the extraction of invariant features (so that variations of handwriting and the type style will not interfere with reading)

3. Visual discrimination between similar forms in the writing system (in the English lowercase alphabet, letter-pairs such as "h" and "n," "f" and "t," "b" and "d," and "c" and "e" have a high degree of visual similarity)

4. Visual memory for the patterns of individual letters, of letter-strings (e.g., "ph," "ght," "oi," "th," "ing") that make up orthographic (i.e., spelling) patterns of the language, and of whole words—both to recognize them for reading and to recall or "revisualize" them for writing

5. Visual–spatial and scanning ability to track print from left to right and top to bottom on the page (or whatever direction is appropriate for the writing system involved)

6. Visual–motor ability to reproduce letters and words in writing

7. Visual–linguistic integration to associate letters and words with sounds and word meanings (Dunn-Rankin, 1978; Gibson and Levin, 1975; Rayner and Pollatsek, 1989; Vernon, 1971)

The above demands are present for all novice readers, but, over time, with maturation and reading experience, most individuals master them. The extent to which the visual demands of reading and writing serve as a barrier to progress may vary considerably from one individual to another.

III. Clinical Case Studies

A. Historical Perspectives

The earliest evidence suggesting that individual differences in visual processing abilities might be a basis for some reading disabilities comes from clinical reports before the turn of the century. In 1895, James Hinshelwood, a Scottish ophthalmologist with a special interest in neurology, began to present his observations of individuals who exhibited a mysterious phenomenon, the sudden loss of reading ability. This acquired word-blindness, as Hinshelwood described it, is a condition in which an individual with normal vision can no longer interpret written or printed language because of some brain injury. A series of fascinating clinical cases in which the ability to recognize faces and objects was retained but the ability to read words was lost led Hinshelwood to conclude that the "inability to read was . . . not due to any failure of visual power, but to a loss of the visual memory for words and letters" (Hinshelwood, 1917: 3).

On the basis of Hinshelwood's descriptions of acquired word-blindness, the medical community raised the possibility that there might be cases of congenital word-blindness in which an individual was impaired in her or his ability to process letters and words from birth. Pringle Morgan published a brief note in the *British Medical Journal* in 1896 describing a 14-yr-old boy who might represent such a case. Hinshelwood's book "Congenital Word-Blindness" (1917),

Figure 6.1. Samples of the written languages of Chinese (1), Korean (2), Japanese (3), Hindi (4), Arabic (5), and Urdu (6).

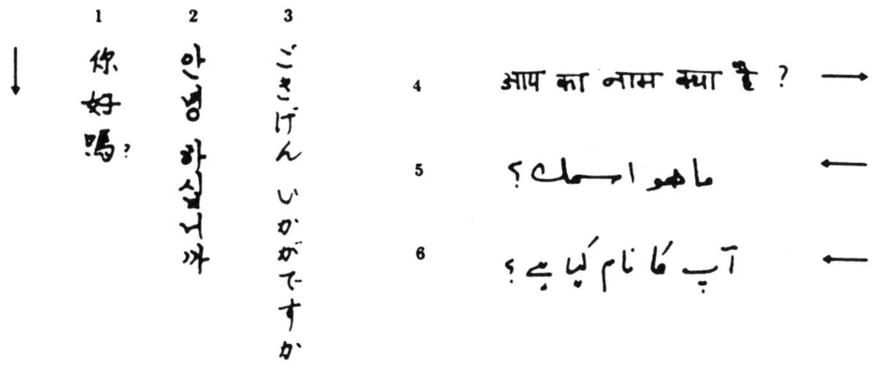

however, clearly described what seemed to be convincing evidence of congenital word-blindness. With its thorough and perceptive case histories it outlines what has now come to be known as "specific dyslexia," "specific reading disability," or, simply, "reading disability." The case descriptions in Hinshelwood's book match very well those currently reported by educators and clinicians.

A few years later, in 1925, Dr. Samuel Orton, a medical doctor with a special interest in neurology (who is now considered by many to be the father of the field of reading disabilities), published the article "Word-blindness in school children." In it he described a range of phenomena associated with congenital word-blindness with a particular emphasis on the confusions of letter and word orientation ("b" and "d," "was" and "saw"), the so-called reversal errors that clinicians often observe in the reading and writing of children with reading disabilities (e.g., see Fig. 6.2). Based on his observations of word-blindness, which he preferred to call strephosymbolia (twisted symbols), Orton developed a theory of reading disability that also focused on visual processes.

To understand why these early clinicians formulated visual processing interpretations of reading disabilities, it is instructive to read Hinshelwood's original descriptions of cases of congenital word-blindness. The discrepancy between the children's oral/aural language facility and their specific weaknesses in processing visual symbols is consistent with present-day observations. One such case is presented below.

Case 1. In March 1900 a boy, aged 11 years, was brought to me at the Glasgow Eye Infirmary by his father, who gave the following history: This boy had been at school for four and a half years, but was finally sent away, because he could not be taught to read. His father informed me that he was at school a considerable time before his defect was noticed, as he had such an excellent memory that he learned his lessons by heart; in fact, his first little reading book he knew so well that whenever it came to his turn he could from memory repeat his lesson, although he could not read the words. His father also informed me that in every respect, unless in inability to read, the boy seemed quite as intelligent as any of his brothers or sisters. His audio memory was excellent, and better than that of any of the other members of the family. When a passage was repeated to him aloud, he could commit it to memory very rapidly. When I first saw the boy and his father at the Eye Infirmary, I asked them to call at my house and I wrote down the address on an envelope. A few days thereafter the father could not find the envelope, but the boy at once told him my address correctly, having remembered it from hearing me state it once. When I examined the boy, he seemed a smart and intelligent lad for his years. He knew the alphabet by heart, repeating it rapidly and correctly. He could recognize by sight, however, only a very few letters, and these not with any degree of certainty, after being four and a half years at school. He could spell [aloud] correctly most simple words of one syllable, such as "cat," "dog," "man," "boy,"

Figure 6.2. Examples of the "reversal errors" that clinicians often observe in the writing of reading-disabled children.

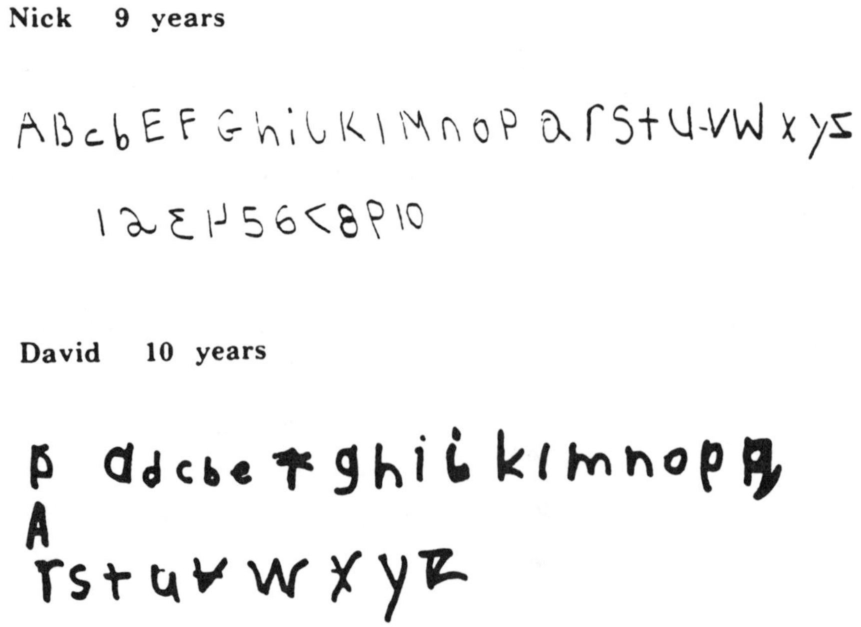

Nick   9 years

David   10 years

etc., but he could not recognize by sight even the simplest and commonest words such as "the," "of," "in," etc. He had no difficulty in recognizing all other visual objects such as faces, places and pictures. On each page of the little primer in which I tested him, there was a picture of some object, which was followed by some simple letterpress about it. He at once recognized and named the pictures, e.g., "a cat," "a dog." I would then ask him to spell [aloud] the word, which he nearly always did correctly. On asking him to pick out the word "cat" on the page, he was unable to do it. I repeated this experiment with the same result on page after page of the little primer. On testing him with figures [numbers] I found that he could repeat from memory fluently and correctly numbers up to a hundred. He could also perform mentally simple sums of addition. He could not, however, recognize all the figures by sight, but he knew them better than the letters, and recognized a greater number of them. (Hinshelwood, 1917: 45–46)

In the next section, a summary of common clinical characteristics of reading-disabled children based on more recent reports is presented. From a comparison of the case above with this more recent clinical profile, it should be evident that Hinshelwood's term congenital word-blindness was undoubtedly describing present-day specific dyslexia or reading disability.

B. Clinical Profile

Consistent with the thoughtful observations of Hinshelwood and Orton, the case reports of clinicians observing the patterns of difficulties in the reading, writing, and spelling of reading-disabled children have confirmed over the last 60–70 years that a substantial proportion of these individuals seem to have difficulties with the visual demands of the tasks. Although there are good reasons to exercise great caution in interpreting subjective clinical reports that have not been confirmed through properly controlled experimental testing (Nisbett and Ross, 1980), a type of information is available in clinical case studies that is extremely difficult to test directly with controlled research. Clinicians and educators who often work with the same individuals over weeks, months, and even years have an opportunity to observe patterns in the abilities and learning of reading-disabled individuals that short-term laboratory studies cannot assess. Only well-conceived longitudinal studies that follow the same children for an extended period can begin to capture the complex patterns of development over time. Few such studies exist.

A review of clinical reports suggests a common profile or pattern of difficulties in the reading and writing of many learning-disabled individuals over time, a pattern that seems to support the importance of some type of visual component processes. Students who experience great difficulty in their written-language acquisition, irrespective of whether or not they manifest any sign of processing difficulties in their aural/oral language (indeed, some may have superior oral-language abilities), often show the following characteristic set of problems as they are learning to read and write:

In reading:
- difficulty learning to recognize letters and numbers
- confusion between similar-looking letters and words
- great difficulty recognizing words "by sight"
- over-reliance on context for word recognition
- failure to analyze the internal structure of words
- low word-by-word reading

In writing:
- difficulty learning how to form letters
- confusion between similar-looking letters
- mirror-image printing of letters and numbers
- difficulty in remembering "how words look" to spell them
- phonetic spelling, based on the sounds in words

Aspects of this profile have been confirmed in a large number of clinical reports (e.g., Boder, 1973; Farnham-Diggory, 1978; Golick, 1978; Kaufman, 1980; Money, 1966; Rawson, 1982; Saunders, 1962; Simpson, 1979; Spache et al., 1981; Willows et al., 1986). A comparison of the above pattern of difficulties manifested by many disabled readers with the earlier section on the "visual demands" of learning to read suggests that overlap between the two lists is considerable; i.e., the difficulties of disabled readers seem to involve visual perception and visual memory of printed symbols. It's no wonder, then, that early workers in the field, such as Hinshelwood and Orton, focused on visual factors.

IV. Clinical and Neuropsychological Research

A. Standardized Psychometric Tests

During the 1960s, a considerable number of studies related children's development of visual–perceptual and visual–motor abilities to their development of reading skill. Much of this research relied on standardized paper-and-pencil psychometric measures such as the Bender Visual–Motor Gestalt Test, the Frostig Developmental Test of Visual Perception, and the Memory-for-Designs test. For example, several studies examined the relation between performance on the Bender Test and scores on tests of reading achievement. Based on such evidence, researchers reported a significant correlation between poor analysis of complex visual patterns and reading difficulties (e.g., Crosby, 1968; Lachmann, 1960). Moreover, two studies were predictive. The perceptual ability tests were administered before the children began learning to read, so inadequacy in reading could not have caused their poor visual analysis abilities (de Hirsch et al., 1966; Smith and Keogh, 1962).

This type of correlational evidence resulted in the development of visual discrimination exercises for the express purpose of improving reading skills (Frostig, 1968). Such training programs, often involving discriminating between geometric shapes, were notoriously unsuccessful because their effects were specific to the training stimuli and did not generalize to letters and words (Cohen, 1967; Rosen, 1966). One important conclusion that these training studies provide is that the type of training required to improve reading achievement is not a generic training of perceptual abilities but, rather, must be a more specific training of reading skills (e.g., letter and word recognition). An additional conclusion is that researchers must be careful in their interpretation of correlational findings. This caution is as important in the interpretation of present-day findings as it was 25–30 years ago. Evidence of a significant correlation between levels of performance on tests of perceptual skills, or any other type of processing, and reading achievement should not be assumed to reflect a causal link.

Performance on standardized psychometric tests is often open to a variety of interpretations because, although the test may be called a "visual" test and seem to assess some sort of visual ability, other types of factors such as verbal abilities and attentional processes may also be involved over and above what the test purports to measure. Although current research continues to employ standardized psychometric measures to examine the possible role of visual processes in reading disability, such tests are usually used in conjunction with more controlled experimental tasks designed to assess "purer" visual processes.

B. Visual Deficit Subtypes

More recently, some researchers, primarily clinicians and neuropsychologists, have investigated the possibility that groups of reading-disabled children might be subdividable into relatively homogeneous subgroups or subtypes; i.e., different types of processing deficits might play a role in the reading disabilities of different groups of reading-disabled individuals. Subtyping research usually involves administering a battery of tests (standardized and/or experimental) to groups of learning-disabled individuals. Based on a variety of methodological and statistical approaches, researchers have come up with two, three, or more classifications of reading disabilities, often including a visual deficit subtype, variously labeled visual dyslexic (Johnson and Myklebust, 1967), dyseidetic (Boder, 1973), visual–perceptual (Denkla, 1977; Lyon and Watson, 1981), visual–spatial (Bakker, 1979; DeFries and Decker, 1982; Petrauskas and Rourke, 1979; Pirozzolo, 1979), and visual perceptual–motor (Satz and Morris, 1981). Although the subtyping procedures vary widely from one study to another, the frequent finding of a subgroup of reading-disabled children who seem to have difficulties with visual aspects of reading and writing has convinced some that "resolution of problems regarding dyslexia in all likelihood depends on our identifying specific subgroups of dyslexia and treating them separately rather than continuing to view all dyslexia as a unitary syndrome" (Malatesha and Dougan, 1982: 89). This conclusion is not universally accepted, however. Other researchers strongly contend, on the basis of the type of basic research evidence discussed in the next section, that there is essentially only one type of reading disability. Vellutino, for example, has argued that "far from being a visual problem, dyslexia appears to be the consequence of limited facility in using language to code other types of information" (Vellutino, 1987: 34).

V. Basic Experimental Research

A. Unitary or Multiple Factors

A major source of contention among present-day theorists concerns the above issue of whether reading disabilities are the result of one or more than one type of processing problem. Theorists such as Vellutino argue that all reading disabilities are a result of subtle and not-so-subtle linguistic processing deficits (e.g., Mann, 1984; Swanson, 1984). Others, however, believe that a variety of factors may contribute to reading disabilities (e.g., Malatesha and Dougan, 1982; Rayner and Pollatsek, 1989), with different reading-disabled individuals being more or less affected by linguistic, visual, and other types of processing deficits.

Those who claim that the unitary cause of reading disabilities is some type of underlying linguistic deficit use as the basis for their argument (1) that an enormous amount of evidence relates language problems in phonology, syntax, and semantics to reading disabilities and (2) that a large body of evidence indicates that no visual processing differences exist between disabled and normal readers (Vellutino, 1979, 1987; Stanovich, 1982, 1985). Those who question the unitary causation position argue instead for a multiple causation position, suggesting either that there are different subtypes of reading disabilities or that two or more areas of processing weakness in combination may underlie reading disabilities. Those who hold a multiple-causation view agree with the unitary-causation theorists that research evidence suggests that linguistic processing factors are involved in some, if not all, cases of reading disabilities, but they question the validity of the second conclusion: that a large body of evidence indicates that no visual processing differences exist between disabled and normal readers (Di Lollo et al., 1983; Doehring, 1978; Fletcher and Satz, 1979a, b; Gross and Rothenberg, 1979; Lovegrove et al., 1986). Rather, on the basis of evidence demonstrating the existence of basic visual processing differences between disabled and normal readers, they argue that, in addition to linguistic factors, visual perceptual and/or visual memory factors may also be involved in causing reading disabilities.

The basic research reviewed in this section reflects directly on this main point of dispute between the unitary- and multiple-factor theorists. It deals with the question of whether or not disabled and normal readers demonstrate differences in their basic visual perceptual and visual memory processes.

B. Methodological Considerations

1. Operational Definitions

Throughout this section on basic research, the term reading disabilities will be defined by the conventional discrepancy definition that includes the following elements:

1. reading performance of 2 or more years below what is expected for an individual's age and general level of cognitive ability,[a]
2. evidence of at least normal cognitive ability as reflected by scores on standardized IQ tests and/or areas of school achievement that do not involve written language,
3. normal educational opportunity to learn to read,
4. no organic deficiencies of vision or hearing, and
5. no behavioral or emotional disorders.

Virtually all of the studies examining the role of visual processes in reading disabilities have compared the performance of a group of disabled readers with that of normal-achieving readers. Although most researchers have adopted an acceptable definition of reading disabilities, some have not. Because the operational definition of the groups of readers (i.e., how they are selected) is key to the interpretation of the data produced by research, this review focuses on studies that provide evidence of having met the conventional discrepancy definition for selecting the reading-disabled group and also of having employed an appropriate comparison group of nondisabled "normal" readers that differs from the disabled readers on measures of written language (e.g., reading, spelling) but that is similar to them on factors such as age and general cognitive ability.

2. Language–Labeling Confounds

Although intuitively the most direct way of assessing for visual processing differences between disabled and normal readers might be to test them with letters and words, this approach has serious problems. In view of the fact that linguistic processing deficits undoubtedly play a very significant role in reading disabilities (as Chapter 5 has clearly shown), an important factor to consider in defining experimental tasks thought to be assessing visual processes is whether or not performance on the task may involve the use of linguistic processes that are confounded with the visual processes of interest. Some studies attempting to assess visual processes in reading disabilities may inadvertently have been assessing verbal as well as visual factors. Most studies in which the goal has been to assess visual

factors free of linguistic–verbal confounds have avoided this pitfall by employing stimuli that are very difficult to label verbally, by using procedures in which performance could not be affected by verbal labeling, or by taking precautions of both types. This review reports only studies that have attempted to exclude the possibility that the "visual" task could have been performed by labeling the stimuli. Thus, studies that report the performance of subjects who apparently have visual processing strengths or weaknesses on a task but who, in fact, might have relied on linguistic–verbal rather than visual processes to complete it are not included in this review.

3. "Levels" of Visual Processing

Probably because of the longstanding views of clinicians and educators that reading disabilities have some underlying basis in visual processes, a great deal of basic research has attempted to examine the possibility that visual processing deficits play some role in reading disabilities. This research, which generally fits within an information-processing framework, has involved a wide range of methodologies. To understand the current status of our knowledge about visual processing, it is essential to review the research within the context of the types of methodologies involved.

The type of visual process investigated varies from one study to another. To understand the need to examine different aspects or levels of visual processing, it is helpful to consider that from the instant a visual stimulus reaches the eye, the visual information begins to undergo "processing," proceeding from the retina to the visual cortex, to various association areas of the brain. Deficits in any or all of the levels of visual processing might play some role in reading, spelling, and writing disabilities. Some researchers have focused their efforts on understanding the earlier levels of visual processing, immediately after the information has entered the visual system, whereas others have been more interested in later levels of processing in which higher cognitive processing may play a greater role. Some studies simply require that subjects indicate when they see a stimulus on a screen, whereas others may require that subjects correctly recognize what they saw at some later point or even that they be able to reproduce accurately what they saw. Because the interpretation of any particular study depends on the level of processing demanded in the experimental task, the studies reviewed in the following sections are roughly organized from earlier to later levels of visual processing.

C. Visual–Perceptual Processes

Clinical observations indicating that disabled readers seem to confuse similar-looking letters and words in their reading and writing suggest that, in comparison with normal readers, they may have some underlying difficulty in basic visual perception. A large number of studies have been undertaken to investigate this possibility. These studies have attempted to determine whether or not disabled

---

[a]   Note: For children who are below the age of 8 yr, and therefore cannot be more than 2 yr below grade level, it is commonly accepted in research to designate an individual who is at least 1 yr below age/grade at age 7 yr or at least 6 mo below age/grade expectation at age 6 yr as being reading-disabled.

and normal readers differ in their perception of visual stimuli in the early stages of processing before higher-level cognitive processes have had time to come into play.

Much of the research comparing the early stages of visual information processing of disabled and normal readers has involved two main techniques: temporal integration tasks and backward masking tasks. These tasks are used to determine whether or not disabled and normal readers differ in how quickly they can perceive and extract information from a visual stimulus. Because visual information processing occurs at very rapid rates, highly sophisticated procedures are required in this type of research. Tachistoscopes (or T-scopes), oscilloscopes, and computer presentation technologies are used to control the time intervals, which are measured in thousandths of a second (msec).

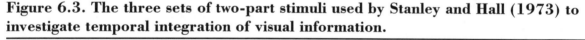

1. Temporal Integration

The visible trace of a stimulus persists for a fraction of a second after the stimulus has been removed from view. The duration of this visible persistence can be measured by presenting two stimuli in very close temporal sequence and assessing whether the stimuli have been perceived as two separate stimuli or as a single stimulus. Two main types of temporal integration task have been used to compare the initial stages of visual information processing in disabled and normal readers. One type involves the presentation of two different stimuli with a variable time interval, the interstimulus interval (ISI), between them. The minimum length of the ISI required for a person to perceive the two stimuli as separate is considered to reflect the duration of the visible persistence of the first stimulus. This is often referred to as the separation threshold. An example may

make this procedure clearer. In a well-known study by Stanley and Hall (1973), groups of disabled readers and normal readers were shown the pairs of stimuli in Figure 6.3. To begin with, each pair of stimuli was presented simultaneously so that they would be perceived as a single image. It can be seen from the examples in Figure 6.3 that if each pair of stimuli were displayed simultaneously in the same location they would combine to make the word NO, a cross, and a cross within a square, respectively. Next, the procedure involved increasing, by very small steps (20 msec), the time interval between each pair of stimuli until the child reported that he or she saw two shapes instead of one. The results of Stanley and Hall's research indicated that the disabled readers' separation threshold before they reported seeing two separate images was significantly longer than that of the normal readers. This pattern of results showing longer visual persistence among the reading-disabled has been found in other studies using similar procedures (Lovegrove and Brown, 1978; Stanley, 1975).

A second type of temporal integration task involves the presentation of two identical stimuli (such as two identical straight lines or sets of parallel lines called gratings) in close temporal sequence, also to assess the visible persistence of the first stimulus. The task begins by presenting the two stimuli simultaneously, and then the ISI is increased by very small steps until the subject reports that the stimulus is flashing rather than constant. Using this type of temporal integration task, researchers have amassed considerable evidence also indicating that disabled readers have longer visible persistence than normal readers (Di Lollo *et al.*, 1983; Lovegrove *et al.*, 1978; O'Neill and Stanley, 1976). The evidence suggests that the processing deficit is not at the level of the retina but occurs later in

Figure 6.3. The three sets of two-part stimuli used by Stanley and Hall (1973) to investigate temporal integration of visual information.

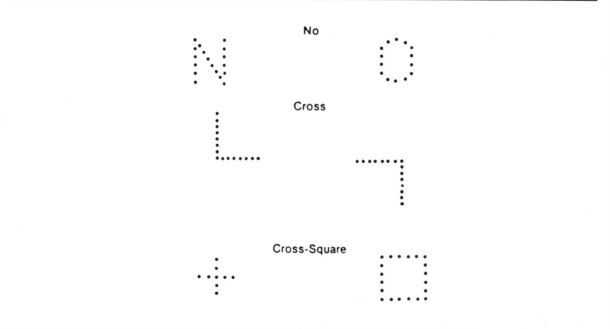

processing, at the level of the visual cortex (Slaghuis and Lovegrove, 1985, 1986). Moreover, 75% of disabled readers in a series of studies of early visual processing exhibited evidence of such deficits (Lovegrove *et al.*, 1986). An impressive program of research is still ongoing to clarify the nature of the processing mechanisms involved in these early visual processing deficits among disabled readers (Badcock and Lovegrove, 1981; Lovegrove, 1988; Lovegrove *et al.*, 1980a, b, 1982; Martin and Lovegrove, 1984).

2. Backward Masking

When the onset of one visual stimulus, called the target, is followed almost immediately by the onset of another visual stimulus (known as a masking stimulus or, simply, a mask), the second stimulus interferes with the processing of the first. This effect is known as backward masking. Whereas the temporal integration tasks described earlier are thought to provide an index of the visible persistence of a stimulus after its termination, backward masking tasks are thought to provide a measure of the rate of information pick up in the initial stages of visual information processing. In a typical backward masking experiment, a target stimulus (a figure or letter) is briefly presented, then a mask is presented and then a test stimulus is presented. The task involves a same–different paradigm (i.e., test format) such that one key is pressed to indicate that the test stimulus is the same as the target or another key is pressed to indicate that it is different. On every trial, there is a 50/50 chance of a "same" or "different" response being correct. The time interval between the target and the mask is varied until a performance level of 75% accuracy is achieved. The ISI at which a reader can perform at 75% accuracy is referred to as the critical ISI. The results of several experiments comparing performance on backward masking tasks have shown that disabled readers process visual information more slowly (their critical ISI is longer) than normal readers (Di Lollo *et al.*, 1983; Lovegrove and Brown, 1978; Mazer *et al.*, 1983; O'Neill and Stanley, 1976; Stanley and Hall, 1973).

Overall, then, the pattern of results from both types of temporal integration task and from studies involving backward masking indicates that disabled readers do not process visual information as quickly as normal readers of similar age and IQ. Some suggestive evidence also indicates that this visual processing deficit may diminish with increasing age (Badcock and Lovegrove, 1981; Di Lollo *et al.*, 1983; Lovegrove and Brown, 1978).

3. Consistency of Findings

Not all studies using temporal integration and backward masking tasks have produced the same patterns of early visual processing differences between disabled and normal readers reported here. A few studies have been repeatedly cited in the literature as sources of contrary evidence (e.g., Arnett and Di Lollo, 1979; Fisher and Frankfurter, 1977; Morrison *et al.*, 1977). Although the existence of studies reporting conflicting evidence suggests that caution is certainly warranted in drawing conclusions, the evidence in support of early visual processing differences between disabled and normal readers is almost overwhelming. Moreover, careful review of the research articles reporting conflicting findings has usually uncovered possible explanatory factors, often involving inadequacy of the operational definition of reading disabilities employed in the studies. For example, Di Lollo *et al.* (1983) point out that in the earlier study by Arnett and Di Lollo (1979), the fact that only a 1-yr discrepancy existed between the "disabled" and normal reader groups may account for the lack of significant difference between those two groups. Also the very unusual finding by Fisher and Frankfurter (1977) of a disabled reader superiority in early visual processes may be the result of these authors having failed to control for general cognitive ability of their disabled and normal groups. The disabled readers in their sample may, in fact, have been superior in IQ to the age- and reading-level-matched normal groups with which they were compared. Perhaps brighter children process visual information faster. Another often-cited source of contrary evidence is an article by Morrison *et al.* (1977) in which no early visual processing differences were found between disabled and normal readers. Like Fisher and Frankfurter (1977), however, these authors failed to match their disabled and normal groups on measures of general intelligence. In addition, the Morrison *et al.* (1977) study had a small sample size, with only nine disabled and nine normal readers. Their failure to find reading group differences in early visual processes may have resulted from their having tested too small a sample of children.

Virtually all of the studies cited here that have found early visual processing deficits among disabled readers have employed the conventional operational definition of reading disabilities and an age- and IQ-matched normal reader group. Also, the sample sizes in the studies reporting differences have been quite large, with most of the studies having a minimum of 15 subjects per reading-ability group, and many having sample sizes substantially greater. Thus, although this type of *post hoc* explanation of conflicting findings cannot be considered definitive, it does cast doubt on the reliability of the results of the studies. If the conflicting findings prove in the future to be replicable, then they should be considered more seriously. At this point, however, the evidence of early visual processing deficits among disabled readers is very persuasive.

4. Relation to Reading Processes

Some researchers argue that the types of methodologies used to assess early visual processing differences between disabled and normal readers "are remote from the perceptual conditions facing a child learning to read" (Hulme, 1988: 373), but others argue just as persuasively that the types of measures of visual perception described here are more sensitive and powerful approaches to comparing the visual–perceptual functioning of disabled and normal readers (Di Lollo *et al.*, 1983; Gross and Rothenberg, 1979; Lovegrove *et al.*, 1986). Other types of procedures may be confounded with higher cognitive processes (e.g., verbal labeling, rehearsal, cognitive strategies). Moreover, evidence from studies of letter, number, and word perception, stimuli that are more closely related to reading, seems to confirm that disabled readers require stimuli to be exposed for a longer duration than normal readers to produce a given level of correct response (e.g., Allegretti and Puglisi, 1986; Gross *et al.*, 1978; Stanley, 1976). These findings appear to confirm that when brief visual presentations are used to measure adequacy of visual–perceptual functioning disabled readers show deficits relative to normal readers.

5. Conclusions Concerning Early Visual Processes

Returning to the question of whether or not disabled readers differ from normal readers in their visual–perceptual processes, the answer seems to be in the affirmative. Many well-controlled studies have employed temporal integration and backward masking tasks to compare the early visual information processing abilities of disabled and normal readers, and most of them have resulted in similar patterns of results. In general, it seems quite clear that the early visual information processes of disabled readers are different from those of nondisabled normal readers (Di Lollo *et al.*, 1983; Hulme, 1988; Lovegrove *et al.*, 1986).

To answer the more fundamental question of whether or not perceptual deficits are among the causes of reading disabilities, more research is necessary. The role of these early visual processing differences in reading disabilities is not yet well understood. They may have some direct causal role in the perception, discrimination, and analysis of the visual features of letters and words. On the other hand, they may be reflecting some more basic underlying processing differences between disabled and normal readers, such as speed of information processing, which in turn may have some causal role in reading disabilities (Di Lollo *et al.*, 1983). It has even been suggested that disabled–normal reader differences could be a result of reading experience, although evidence argues against this interpretation (Di Lollo *et al.*, 1983; Lovegrove *et al.*, 1986). Whatever the case, the visual–perceptual differences between disabled and normal readers appear to be very real, and, whatever their explanation, theories and models of reading disabilities must take them into account.

D. Visual Memory Processes

To remember the letters and groups of letters that characterize the spelling patterns and words of the language —to recognize them for reading and to recall them for writing and spelling—an individual must retain a record of them in memory and have easy access to that stored information.

After visual information has passed from the very brief visual persistence level to a short-term memory storage level, the information must be processed further in long-term memory if it is to be retained for later recognition and recall (Craik and Lockhart, 1972; Rayner and Pollatsek, 1989). A variety of experimental procedures have been used to determine whether or not differences exist between disabled and normal readers at these later processing stages. Most of the studies designed to investigate visual memory differences between disabled and normal readers have employed one of four main types of task, involving visual recognition memory, reproduction from visual memory, visual–visual paired-associate learning, and serial learning of visual designs. All of these types of tasks are designed to investigate how well individuals remember visual information that they have perceived, to recognize or reproduce it from memory later.

1. Visual Recognition Memory

To recognize words with speed and accuracy, a reader must make use of information such as the overall shape of words. A series of investigations by Lyle and Goyen was designed to examine how accurately disabled readers and normal readers recognize unfamiliar visual stimuli that resemble "word contours" or "word shapes." Sample stimuli from their research are shown in Figure 6.4. In five experiments, Lyle and Goyen, using tachistoscopic procedures, presented a series of different word shapes to disabled and normal readers (Goyen and Lyle, 1971a, b, 1973; Lyle and Goyen, 1968, 1975). Shortly after the presentation of each word-shape target, one of two test formats was used. In one test situation, a set of several test word shapes was presented, and the child's task was to select the target stimulus she or he had just seen. In the other test format, involving a same-different paradigm, the child had to press one key to indicate that the test shape was the same as the target or another key if it was different. Lyle and Goyen were interested not only in determining whether or not disabled readers differed from normal readers in their visual recognition of the word shapes, but also whether or not younger children (age 6–8 yr) in the two reading groups differed from older children(age 8–10 yr). In addition, they wanted to know whether or not the exposure duration of a word shape (ranging from 0.10 to 5.0 sec) and the degree of similarity among the set of test alternatives affected accuracy of responding.

The results of Lyle and Goyen's research showed clearly that, at the younger age level, disabled readers were less accurate in recognizing word shapes than were normal readers. Such differences were not found at the older age level. These differences between disabled and normal readers were found at the shorter stimulus duration rates (0.10 and 1.0 sec) but not at longer ones (5.0 sec). Consistent with the findings of the studies described in the previous sections, Lyle and Goyen concluded from their research that "the perceptual deficit manifested by young [disabled] readers on tachistoscopic tasks involves the input or processing of visual information at rapid exposures. The relative deficit of young [disabled] readers appears to arise not through short-term memory deficits or difficulty in discriminating between alternatives on response cards but through incomplete analysis of the tachistoscopically presented stimulus, so that certain distinctive features or their interrelationships are not taken into account" (Lyle and Goyen, 1975: 675–676).

More recently, Willows *et al.* (1988) conducted a study of children's visual recognition memory for unfamiliar visual symbols (letters from the Hebrew alphabet) using a same–different paradigm in a "computer game" format. Disabled and normal readers at three age levels (6, 7, and 8 yr) were tested. On each trial in the computer game, the child was shown a target stimulus selected randomly from a pool of 18 Hebrew letters (shown in Fig. 6.5, in six sets of three). After a brief interval, they were shown the test stimulus, either the same letter again or a different, but similar-looking, letter from the same set. The child had to press one key to indicate that the test item was the same as the target and another if it was different. The delay between the target and test stimuli was varied to determine whether disabled readers' visual processing difficulty was at the level of initial input or it was a result of some memory difficulty. The results of this research were consistent with Lyle and Goyen's findings: Reading-disabled children were less accurate and slower in their visual recognition performance. Moreover, there was a developmental pattern (i.e., the effect was greater among younger than older disabled readers) and the deficit appeared to be at the level of initial visual perception rather than visual memory.

Taken together then, the pattern of results from studies of visual recognition that involve rapid stimulus presentation is clear and consistent. Younger disabled readers make more errors and are slower at responding than normal readers of similar age and IQ. The disabled readers' difficulty seems to occur at the initial input stage rather than at a later storage stage. In other words, the findings of these studies that assessed both early and later stages of processing add to the evidence of early visual information processing differences between disabled and normal readers.

2. Reproduction from Visual Memory

In learning to read and write, the child must attend to and remember the visual information in the symbols to recognize them for reading and reproduce them for writing. A widely cited series of studies was undertaken by Vellutino and his colleagues to investigate the possibility of visual memory differences between disabled and normal readers. These studies all involved having children view difficult-to-label visual shapes or strings of letters from the Hebrew alphabet and then, after the stimuli had been removed, "copy" them from memory. The performance of younger and older disabled and normal readers was compared. Based on the findings of the three key studies (Vellutino *et al.*, 1973a, 1975b,d) involving the ability to reproduce unfamiliar visual shapes from memory, Vellutino and his colleagues concluded that: "In all these investigations, poor readers performed as well as normals in short- and long-term memory of Hebrew letters and words—symbols unfamiliar to both groups." (Vellutino *et al.*, 1977: 57).

Other evidence, however, suggests that disabled and normal readers may differ in a draw-from-memory task (Lyle, 1968). In that research, Lyle compared the abilities of large samples of disabled and normal readers to draw unfamiliar visual patterns from memory using the Memory-for-Designs test. The results showed that the disabled were significantly inferior to the normal readers in their reproductions of the designs. Moreover, the previously mentioned findings by Willows *et al.* (1988), showing disabled–normal reader differences in visual recognition (a less demanding task than reproduction from visual memory) of Hebrew letters, the type of stimuli used in Vellutino and his colleagues' studies, suggest that caution is warranted in drawing definitive conclusions at this point.

The evidence reported by Vellutino and his colleagues on reproduction from visual memory does not contradict that from research on early stages of processing, because all of the studies by Vellutino and his colleagues involved

Figure 6.4. Samples of "word contours" used as stimuli in the research by Lyle and Goyen.

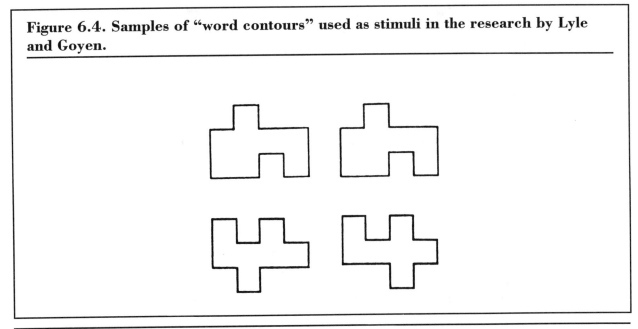

"long" stimulus exposures. In the studies using Hebrew letters as stimuli, for example, the children examined the string of letters for 3–5 sec. These are exposure durations that are longer than those at which the research on visual perception found disabled–normal reader differences in performance.

3. Visual–Visual Paired-Associate Learning

In the context of attempting to compare disabled and normal readers' abilities to associate unfamiliar visual shapes with sounds and words, as the child must do in learning to read, Vellutino and his colleagues undertook research in which they had disabled and normal readers learn to associate pairs of unfamiliar visual designs with each other. These studies also involved having the children associate visual designs with verbal responses, but this visual–verbal association aspect of the research is concerned with the children's ability to use verbal labels and is essentially irrelevant to questions about visual perception and memory processes. Thus, only the visual–visual paired-associate tasks are discussed here. In these tasks, the child was shown pairs of difficult-to-label shapes (such as those in Fig. 6.6) and told "to try to remember what two designs go together" (Vellutino et al., 1973b: 117). On test trials, the children were shown one of each stimulus pair and required to select its mate from a set of five choices. In both experiments, Vellutino and his colleagues found no differences between disabled and normal readers' abilities to associate visual designs with each other (Vellutino et al., 1973b, 1975a). These results have been interpreted as additional evidence that no visual processing differences exist between disabled and normal readers.

The consistency of these results, using a visual–visual paired-associate task, with the earlier findings, using a reproduction from visual memory task, appears to add weight to Vellutino et al.'s (1977) conclusion that no disabled–normal reader differences exist on tasks designed to measure visual memory; however, the results do not contradict the evidence on visual perception. The disabled and normal readers in these studies were in an older age range, between about 9.5 and 12.5 yr of age, and the stimulus presentation rates were relatively slow.

4. Serial Learning of Visual Designs

Based on the work of Vellutino and his colleagues, Swanson also undertook a series of studies designed to compare disabled and normal readers' abilities to remember difficult-to-label visual shapes under conditions in which verbal labels were either excluded or included. Swanson used a probe-type serial memory task in which he presented six nonsense shapes (such as those shown in Fig. 6.7). Again, the task involving the use of verbal labels, although interesting, is not relevant to the present discussion about visual memory processes. Only the unnamed condition is discussed here. In the unnamed condition, a set of six cards, each with a different shape printed on it,

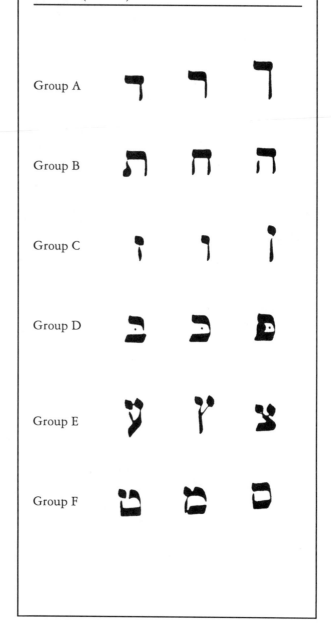

Figure 6.5. The stimulus pool of 18 Hebrew letters, grouped in six visually different sets of three visually similar items, used in the visual recognition studies by Willows et. al. (1988).

Group A

Group B

Group C

Group D

Group E

Group F

was placed face down in front of the child. From left to right, each of the cards was then turned up for a few seconds and then turned down again. A probe (one of the six shapes) was then shown, and the child had to point to the card in the row in front of her or him that matched the probe. Their task was essentially a visual–spatial task, because they were shown a probe and had to remember where they had seen it. In three experiments involving children from 7 to 12 yr of age, Swanson consistently found no differences between disabled and normal readers in serial memory for unnamed stimuli (Swanson, 1978, 1982, 1983).

Figure 6.6. Samples of the pairs of difficult-to-label shapes used in the visual–visual paired-associate learning research by Vellutino and his colleagues.

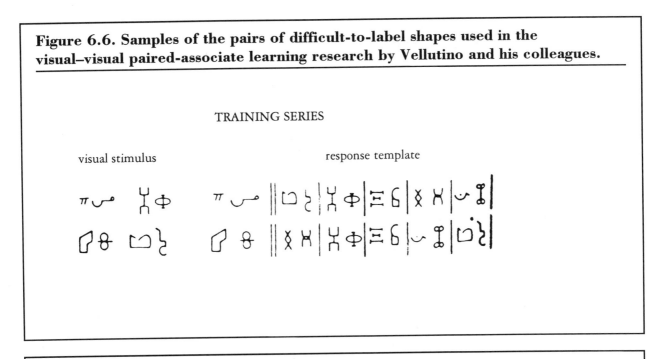

TRAINING SERIES

visual stimulus   response template

Figure 6.7. The six nonsense shapes (unnamed condition) used by Swanson in his studies involving a visual serial learning task.

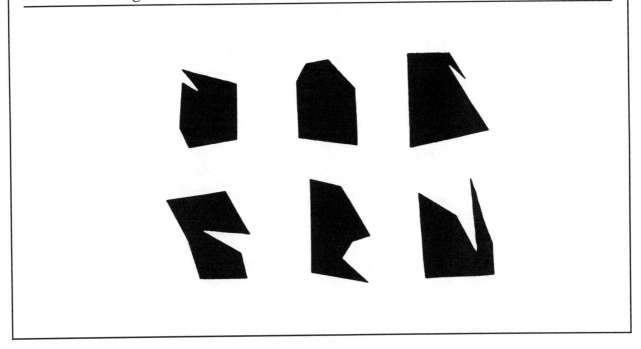

Other research examining visual–spatial memory has produced a different pattern of results, however. Willows *et al.* (1988) presented strings of Hebrew letters to 6–8-yr-old disabled and normal readers in a computer game. After each string of three visually distinct letters (each of the three was taken from a different set in Fig. 6.5), one of the same three letters was shown in one of the three spatial positions that the original string had occupied. The child's task was simply to press one of two keys to indicate whether the letter was in the same or a different position from the one she or he had just seen it in. The results on both accuracy and response speed measures indicated that disabled readers were less able than normal readers to remember visual–spatial information. The disabled–normal reader differences were greater at the younger age levels.

5. Statistical Limitations

Although the failure to find disabled–normal reader differences on tasks tapping visual memory is a consistent pattern in the studies by both Vellutino and Swanson, several other researchers have been critical of the "no-difference" conclusions from their findings. They argue that some of the studies have statistical ceilings and floors that prevent finding disabled–normal difference especially among the younger readers, even if such differences actually exist (Doehring, 1978; Fletcher and Satz, 1979a; Gross and Rothenberg, 1979; Satz and Fletcher, 1980; Singer, 1979; Willows *et al.* 1986). These statistical problems are very serious because they result in no-difference conclusions when real differences may exist. If, for example, 10-yr-old disabled and normal readers were compared on their ability to read first-grade-level words, all children might read the words almost perfectly; i.e., their performance might be at a statistical ceiling. Conversely, if 6-yr-old disabled and normal readers were compared on their ability to read fifth-grade-level words, all of the children might do very poorly, their performance being at the statistical floor. A failure to find disabled–normal reader differences with such tasks might simply indicate that the tasks were too easy (ceiling effect) or too difficult (floor effect) to detect differences.

---

6. Conclusions Concerning Later Visual Processes

The answer to the question of whether or not visual memory differences exist between disabled and normal readers is still uncertain. The evidence with respect to older children is fairly consistent. It seems quite unlikely that visual memory differences exist between older (over age 8 yr) disabled and normal readers on the types of tasks reviewed here. At the younger age level, however, the possibility of some sort of developmental lag in visual memory still exists. Evidence suggests that younger disabled readers have difficulty in remembering visual information in a variety of task types. These difficulties may be due to differences in early perceptual processes, because most of the studies that have found differences in visual memory tasks have involved brief stimulus presentation rates, whereas studies that have failed to find such differences have usually presented stimuli at slower rates. Further carefully done research is required to clarify the relation between "later" visual process and reading disabilities, particularly in the younger age range (up to age 8 yr).

VI. Conclusions and Future Direction

A. Research Directions

Combining the high degree of consistency of the early visual processing evidence with the inconclusiveness of the later visual processing evidence, it appears that visual–perceptual and visual memory deficits may be implicated in reading disabilities. The conclusion of the unitary–deficit theorists that disabled readers have no visual processing difficulties appears to have been premature. There may be more to reading disabilities than the verbal labeling and verbal memory problems that have been widely identified. It is incumbent on researchers to explore all factors that may contribute to reading disabilities and not to limit themselves to those that may seem to fit currently popular models.

Ultimately, the goal of research examining the visual processing of readers of different ability levels is to determine the role that visual processes play in learning to read

and in reading failure. However, establishing whether a weakness in any particular processing ability is causal in reading acquisition or reading failure is a difficult problem. Nearly all of the research examining the strengths and weaknesses of children who differ in reading abilities is correlational in nature. It can tell us which factors are related to levels of reading ability, but it cannot tell us why. Very little research on reading disabilities can validly be interpreted as demonstrating a causal link between a particular processing deficit and reading failure. Deficits in some well-documented correlates of reading ability, such as phonemic awareness, have been suggested as causes of reading disabilities, but even these have not passed crucial experimental tests (Hulme, 1987; Bryant and Goswami, 1987) demonstrating a causal link.

Future research examining the relation between visual processing deficits and reading disabilities should focus particular attention on the possibility of visual memory deficits among reading-disabled children in the age range from 6 to 8 yr. In addition, future research should attempt to explore the underlying causal factors that are responsible for the relation between visual deficits and reading disabilities. Perhaps, for example, both visual and linguistic deficits reflect a more basic weakness in the processing of the left hemisphere of the brain. The challenge for future researchers is not to demonstrate whether reading disabilities are related to visual, linguistic, or other types of processing factors but, rather, to explain how basic processing weaknesses of various types may be related to each other or may interact in causing reading disabilities.

B. Practical Implications

If some disabled readers have delays or deficits in their visual processing abilities, such weaknesses could be a factor in their apparent difficulties in differentiating between similar-looking letters and words, especially in analyzing and remembering the orthographic (i.e., spelling) patterns in words and in processing letters and words at rapid rates in text. Clinical observations and case reports, correlational evidence from studies using standardized psychometric instruments, and visual deficit subtypes from clinical and neuropsychological studies all point to some role of visual processing deficits in reading disabilities. Evidence from information-processing research involving basic visual perception and visual memory also suggests that some relation exists between visual processing deficits and reading disabilities. At this point, however, the potential role of visual processing weaknesses in written-language problems is not well enough understood to draw confident conclusions about practice.

Clinicians and educators in the field of learning disabilities should certainly keep an open mind about the possibility that visual processing deficits contribute in some way to reading disabilities. Prudence would dictate that both assessment approaches and teaching techniques should be devised on the assumption that the reading-disabled child may have some difficulty in coping with the visual demands of the task. The findings indicating that younger disabled readers (6–8 yr of age) may be more likely to have some sort of visual perceptual and/or visual memory deficits are worthy of special note. The visual demands of the beginning stages of reading acquisition are probably more significant than those at later stages of reading acquisition when linguistic processes may play a greater role (Chall, 1983; Vernon, 1977).

References

Allegretti, C. L., and Puglisi, J. T. (1986). Disabled vs nondisabled readers: Perceptual vs higher-order processing of one vs three letters. *Percep. Motor Skills* **63**, 463–469.

Arnett, J. L., and Di Lollo, V. (1979). Visual information processing in relation to age and to reading ability. *J. Exp. Child Psychol.* **27**, 143–152.

Badcock, D., and Lovegrove, W. (1981). The effects of contrast, stimulus duration, and spatial frequency on visible persistence in normal and specifically disabled readers. *J. Exp. Psychol.: Hum. Percep. Perform.* **7**, 495–505.

Bakker, D. J. (1979). Hemispheric differences and reading strategies: Two dyslexias? *Bull. Orton Soc.* **29**, 84–100.

Boder, E. (1973). Developmental dyslexia: A diagnostic approach based on three atypical reading–spelling patterns. *Dev. Med. Child Neurol.* **15**, 663–687.

Bryant, P. E., and Goswami, U. (1987). Development of phonemic awareness. *In* "Cognitive Approaches to Reading" (J. Beech and A. Colley, eds.), pp. 213–244. Wiley, Chichester, England.

Chall, J. S. (1983). "Stages of Reading Development." McGraw-Hill, New York.

Cohen, R. (1967). Remedial training of first grade children with visual perceptual retardation. *Read. Horizons* **45**, 60–63.

Craik, F. I. M., and Lockhart, R. S. (1972). Levels of processing: A framework for memory research. *J. Verbal Learn. Verbal Behav.* **11**, 671–684.

Crosby, R. M. N. (1968). "Reading and the Dyslexic Child." Souvenir Press, London.

de Hirsch, K., Jansky, J. J., and Langford, W. S. (1966). "Predicting Reading Failure." Harper & Row, New York.

DeFries, J. C., and Decker, S. N. (1982). Genetic aspects of reading disability: A family study. *In* "Reading Disorders: Varieties and Treatments" (R. N. Malatesha and P. G. Aaron, eds.), pp. 255–280. Academic Press, Toronto.

Denkla, M. B. (1977). Minimal brain dysfunction and dyslexia: Beyond diagnosis by exlusion. *In* "Topics in Child Neurology" (M. Blaw, I. Rapin, and M. Kinsbourne, eds.), pp. 223–268. Spectrum, New York.

Di Lollo, V., Hanson, D., and McIntyre, J. S. (1983). Initial stages of visual information processing in dyslexia. *J. Exp. Psychol.: Hum. Percep. Perform.* **9**, 923–935.

Doehring, D. G. (1978). The tangled web of behavioral research on development dyslexia. *In* "Dyslexia: An Appraisal of Current Knowledge" (A. L. Benton and D. Pearl, eds.). Oxford University Press, New York.

Dunn-Rankin, P. (1978). Visual characteristics of words. *Sci. Am.* **238**(1), 122–130.

Farnham-Diggory, S. (1978). "Learning Disabilities: A Psychological Perspective." Harvard University Press, Cambridge.

Fisher, D. F., and Frankfurter, A. (1977). Normal and disabled readers can locate and identify letters: Where's the perceptual deficit? *J. Read. Behav.* **9**, 31–43.

Fletcher, J. M., and Satz, P. (1979a). Unitary deficit hypotheses of reading disabilities: Has Vellutino led us astray? *J. Learn Disabil.* **12**(3), 155–159.

Fletcher, J. M., and Satz, P. (1979b). Has Vellutino led us astray? A rejoinder to a reply. *J. Learn. Disabil.* **12**(3), 168–171.

Frostig, M. (1968). Education of children with learning disabilities. *In* "Progress in Learning Disabilities" (H. R. Myklebust, ed.), pp. 234–266. Grune & Stratton, New York.

Gibson, E. J., and Levin, H. (1975). "The Psychology of Reading." MIT Press, Cambridge.

Golick, M. (1978). Learning disabilities and the school age child. *Learning Disabilities: Information Please*, 1–8.

Goyen, J. D., and Lyle, J. G. (1971a). Effect of incentives and age on the visual recognition of retarded readers. *J. Exp. Child Psychol.* **11**, 266–273.

Goyen, J. D., and Lyle, J. G. (1971b). Effect of incentives upon retarded and normal readers on a visual–associate learning task. *J. Exp. Child Psychol.* **11**, 274–280.

Goyen, J. D., and Lyle, J. G. (1973). Short-term memory and visual discrimination in retarded readers. *Percep. Motor Skills* **36**, 403–408.

Gross, K., and Rothenberg, S. (1979). An examination of methods used to test the visual perceptual deficit hypothesis of dyslexia. *J. Learn. Disabil.* **12**, 670–677.

Gross, K., Rothenberg, S., Schottenfeld, S., and Drake, C. (1978). Duration threshold for letter identification in left and right visual fields for normal and reading-disabled children. *Neuropsychologia* **16**, 709–715.

Hinshelwood, J. (1895). Word-blindness and visual memory. *Lancet* **2**, 1564–1570.

Hinshelwood, J. (1917). "Congenital Word-Blindness." H. K. Lewis & Co., London.

Hulme, C. (1987). Reading retardation. *In* "Cognitive Approaches to Reading" (J. Beech and A. Colley, eds.), pp. 245–270. Wiley, Chichester, England.

Hulme, C. (1988). The implausibility of low-level visual deficits as a cause of children's reading difficulties. *Cog. Neuropsychol.* **5**, 369–374.

Johnson, D. J., and Myklebust, H. R. (1967). "Learning Disabilities: Educational Principles and Practices." Grune & Stratton, New York.

Kaufman, N. L. (1980). Review of research on reversal errors. *Percep. Motor Skills* **51**, 55–79.

Lachmann, F. M. (1960). Perceptual-motor development in children retarded in reading ability. *J. Consult. Psychol.* **24**, 427–431.

Lovegrove, W. (1988). The relationship of visual deficits to short-term memory processes and phonological recoding in normal and specifically disabled readers. Paper presented in August 1988 as part of the symposium "Visual Factors in Learning Disabilities," at the XXIV International Congress of Psychology, Sydney, Australia.

Lovegrove, W., and Brown, C. (1978). Development of information processing in normal and disabled readers. *Percep. Motor Skills* **46**, 1047–1054.

Lovegrove, W., Billing, G., and Slaghuis, W. (1978). Processing of visual contour orientation information in normal and disabled reading children. *Cortex* **14**, 268–278.

Lovegrove, W., Bowling, A., Badcock, D., and Blackwood, M. (1980a). Specific reading disability: Differences in contrast sensitivity as a function of spatial frequency. *Science* **2102**, 439–440.

Lovegrove, W., Heddle, M., and Slaghuis, W. (1980b). Reading disability: Spatial frequency specific deficits in visual information store. *Neuropsychologia* **18**, 111–115.

Lovegrove, W., Martin, F., Bowling, A., Blackwood, M., Badcock, D., and Paxton, S. (1982). Contrast sensitivity functions and specific reading disability. *Neuropsychologia* **20**, 309–315.

Lovegrove, W., Martin, F., and Slaghuis, W. (1986). A theoretical and experimental case for a visual deficit in specific reading disability. *Cog. Neuropsychol.* **3**, 225–267.

Lyle, J. G. (1968). Performance of retarded readers on the Memory-for-Designs test. *Percep. Motor Skills* **26**, 851–854.

Lyle, J. G., and Goyen, J. D. (1968). Visual recognition, developmental lag, and strephosymbolia in reading retardation. *J. Abnorm. Psychol.* **73**, 25–29.

Lyle, J. G., and Goyen, J. D. (1975). Effect of speed of exposure and difficulty of discrimination on visual recognition of retarded readers. *J. Abnorm. Psychol.* **84**, 673–676.

Lyon, R., and Watson, B. (1981). Empirically derived subgroups of learning disabled readers: Diagnostic characteristics. *J. Learn. Disabil.* **14**, 256–261.

Malatesha, R. N., and Dougan, D. R. (1982). Clinical subtypes of developmental dyslexia: Resolution of an irresolute problem. *In* "Reading Disorders: Varieties and Treatments" (R. N. Malatesha and P. G. Aaron, eds.), pp. 69–92. Academic Press, Toronto.

Mann, V. (1984). Reading skill and language skill. *Dev. Rev.* **4**, 1–15.

Martin, F., and Lovegrove, W. (1984). The effects of field size and luminance on contrast sensitivity differences between specifically reading disabled and normal children. *Neuropsychologia* **22**, 73–77.

Mazer, S. R., McIntyre, C. W., Murray, M. E., Till, R. E., and Blackwell, S. L. (1983). Visual persistence and information pick up in learning disabled children. *J. Learn. Disabil.* **16**(4), 221–225.

Money, J. (1966). Case 1: Space-form deficit. *In* "The Disabled Reader: Education of the Dyslexic Child" (J. Money, ed.), pp. 263–276. Johns Hopkins Press, Baltimore.

Morgan, W. P. (1896). A case of congenital word-blindness. *Br. Med. J.* **2**, 1378.

Morrison, F. J., Giordani, B., and Nagy, J. (1977). Reading disability: An information-processing analysis. *Science* **19**, 77–79.

Nisbett, R., and Ross, L. (1980). "Human Inference: Strategies and Shortcomings of Social Judgement." Prentice-Hall, Englewood Cliffs, New Jersey.

O'Neill, G., and Stanley, G. (1976). Visual processing of straight lines in dyslexic and normal children. *Br. J. Educ. Psychol.* **46**, 323–327.

Orton, S. T. (1925). "Word-blindness" in school children. *Arch. Neurol. Psych.* **14**, 581–615.

Petrauskas, R. J., and Rourke, B. P. (1979). Identification of subtypes of retarded readers: A neuropsychological, multivariate approach. *J. Clin. Neuropsychol.* **1**, 17–37.

Pirozzolo, F. J. (1979). "The Neuropsychology of Developmental Reading Disorders." Praeger, New York.

Rawson, M. B. (1982). Louise Baker and the Leonardo syndrome. *Ann. Dyslexia* **32**, 289–304.

Rayner, K., and Pollatsek, A. (1989). "The Psychology of Reading." Prentice-Hall, Englewood Cliffs, New Jersey.

Rosen, C. (1966). An experimental study of visual perceptual training and reading achievement in first grade children. *Percep. Motor Skills* **22**, 979–986.

Satz, P., and Fletcher, J. M. (1980). Minimal brain dysfunctions: An appraisal of research concepts and methods. *In* "Handbook of Minimal Brain Dysfunctions: A Critical View" (H. E. Rie and E. D. Rie, eds.), pp. 669–715. Wiley, New York.

Satz, P., and Morris, R. (1981). Learning disability subtypes: A review. *In* "Neuropsychological and Cognitive Processes in Reading" (F. J. Pirozzolo and M. C. Wittrock, eds.), pp. 109–144. Academic Press, New York.

Saunders, R. E. (1962). Dyslexia: Its phenomenology. *In* "Reading Disability" (J. Money, ed.). Johns Hopkins Press, Baltimore.

Simpson, E. (1979). "Reversals: A Personal Account of Victory Over Dyslexia." Houghton Mifflin, Boston.

Singer, H. (1979). On reading, language and learning. *Han. Educ. Rev.* **49**, 125–128.

Slaghuis, W. L., and Lovegrove, W. J. (1985). Spatial-frequency-dependent persistence and specific reading disability. *Brain Cognit.* **4**, 219–240.

Slaghuis, W. L., and Lovegrove, W. J. (1986). The effect of physical flicker on visible persistence in normal and specifically disabled readers. *Aust. J. Psychol.* **38**, 1–11.

Smith, C. E., and Keogh, B. K. (1962). The group Bender-Gestalt as a reading readiness screening test. *Percep. Motor Skills* **15**, 639–645.

Spache, G. D., McIroy, K., and Berg, P. C. (1981). "Case Studies in Reading Disability." Allyn and Bacon, Inc., Boston.

Stanley, G. (1975). Two-part stimulus integration and specific reading disability. *Percep. Motor Skills* **41**, 873–874.

Stanley, G. (1976). The processing of digits by children with specific reading disability (dyslexia). *Br. J. Educ. Psychol.* **46**, 81–84.

Stanley, G., and Hall, R. (1973). Short-term visual information processing in dyslexics. *Child Dev.* **44**, 841–844.

Stanovich, K. E. (1982). Individual differences in the cognitive processes of reading: Word decoding. *J. Learn. Disabil.* **15**, 485–493.

Stanovich, K. E. (1985). Explaining the variance in terms of psychological processes: What have we learned? *Ann. Dyslexia* **35**, 67–96.

Swanson, L. (1978). Verbal encoding effects on the visual short-term memory of learning disabled and normal readers. *J. Educ. Psychol.* **70**(4), 539–544.

Swanson, L. (1982). Verbal short-term memory encoding of learning disabled, deaf, and normal children. *Learn. Disabil. Q.* **5**, 21–28.

Swanson, L. (1983). A study of nonstrategic linguistic coding on visual recall of learning disabled readers. *J. Learn. Disabil.* **16**(4), 209–216.

Swanson, L. (1984). Semantic and visual memory codes in learning disabled readers. *J. Exp. Child Psychol.* **37**, 124–140.

Vellutino, F. R. (1979). "Dyslexia: Theory and Research." MIT Press, Cambridge.

Vellutino, F. R. (1987). Dyslexia. *Sci. Am.* **256**(3), 34–41.

Vellutino, F. R., Steger, J. A., and Kandel, G. (1972). Reading disability: Investigation of the perceptual deficit hypothesis. *Cortex* **8**, 106–118.

Vellutino, F. R., Pruzek, R., Steger, J. A., and Meshoulam, U. (1973a). Immediate visual recall in poor and normal readers as a function of orthographic–linguistic familiarity. *Cortex* **9**, 368–384.

Vellutino, F. R., Steger, J. A., and Pruzek, R. (1973b). Inter-versus intra-sensory deficiency in paired-associate learning in poor and normal readers. *Can. J. Behav. Sci.* **5**, 111–123.

Vellutino, F. R., Harding, C. J., Phillips, F., and Steger, J. A. (1975a). Differential transfer in poor and normal readers. *J. Gen. Psychol.* **126**, 3–18.

Vellutino, F. R., Smith, H., Steger, J. A., and Kaman, M. (1975b). Reading disability: Age differences and the perceptual deficit hypothesis. *Child Dev.* **46**, 487–493.

Vellutino, F. R., Steger, J. A., DeSetto, L., and Phillips, F. (1975c). Immediate and delayed recognition of visual stimuli in poor and normal readers. *J. Exp. Child Psychol.* **19**, 223–232.

Vellutino, F. R., Steger, J. A., Kaman, M., and DeSetto, L. (1975d). Visual form perception in deficient and normal readers as function of age and orthographic linguistic familiarity. *Cortex* **11**, 22–30.

Vellutino, F. R., Steger, J. A., Moyer, B. M., Harding, S. C., and Niles, C. J. (1977). Has the perceptual deficit hypothesis led us astray? *J. Learn. Disabil.* **10**, 54–64.

Vernon, M. D. (1971). "Reading and Its Difficulties: A Psychological Study." The University Press, Cambridge, England.

Vernon, M. D. (1977). Varieties of deficiency in reading processes. *Harv. Educ. Rev.* 47, 396–410.

Willows, D. M., Kershner, J. R., and Corcos, E. (1986). Visual processing and visual memory in reading and writingdisabilities: A rationale for reopening a "closed case." Paper presented in April 1986 as part of the symposium "The Role of Visual Processing and Visual Memory in Reading and Writing," at

the Annual Meeting of the American Educational Research Association, San Francisco, California.

Willows, D. M., Corcos, E., and Kershner, J. R. (1988). Disabled and normal readers' visual processing and visual memory of item and spatial-order information in unfamiliar symbol strings. Paper presented in August 1988 as part of the symposium "Visual Factors in Learning Disabilities," at the XXIV International Congress of Psychology, Sydney, Australia.

The Relevance of Metacognition to Learning Disabilities

Wong, B. Y. L. 1991. In *Learning about learning disabilities*, ed. B. Y. L. Wong, 231–57.
San Diego: Academic Press, Inc.

Editor's Notes[*]

Metacognition is an important construct in reading research, and metacognitive strategies have been shown to differentiate between skilled and unskilled readers. More important, reading researchers have shown that teaching students metacognitive strategies in reading enhanced their reading comprehension.

What does all that have to do with us in learning disabilities? My chapter answers this question by explaining to you the relevance of metacognition to learning disabilities. This relevance concerns the invalidity in interpreting all learning and performance problems in individuals with learning disabilities as deep-seated cognitive deficiencies, as well as the necessity to include metacognitive strategies in reading and writing in instructional remediations of those individuals. The relevance of metacognition to learning disabilities is realized through an appreciation of A. L. Brown's conceptualization of the crucial role of metacognition in successful reading and learning and of the empirical research on metacognitive skills in reading that discriminated among younger, readers poor readers, and skilled readers.

I. Rationale

Every young science begins its development by adopting theories and experimental methods and approaches from other more established sciences. Psychology is a prime example. The psychologist Murray (1984) shows how the development of psychology as an experimental science has been shaped by various theories from other disciplines.

Learning disabilities (LDs) is a very young scientific discipline. Its development began in the late 1960s and is influenced by advances in the theories and research in related fields such as cognitive psychology, reading, and instructional psychology. In this chapter, we will see the influence of a theoretical construct from cognitive psychology, metacognition, and its research on the LDs field.

Metacognition is one of the important theoretical constructs in cognitive psychology. It was originated by Flavell (1976) and arose from the context of research in

memory processes. It has generated much theoretical and empirical interest. The construct was then applied to academic areas by A. L. Brown (1980), who conceptualized the important role of metacognition in effective learning and reading. Subsequently, research findings were obtained that clearly separated good and poor/learning-disabled (LD) readers in metacognitive skills in reading. Against the backdrop of Brown's conceptualizations and the metacognitive research findings differentiating between good and poor/LD readers, the question of the relevance of metacognition assumes research and practical significance for LD professionals.

II. Scope and Sequence

The topic of metacognition and LDs revolves around the relevance of this theoretical construct and its accompanying research to LDs. This chapter focuses on explicating that relevance. First, the theoretical construct of metacognition is defined. Then, its crucial role in effective learning and efficient reading is explained. A summary of research differentiating between the metacognitive skills of good and poor/LD readers follows. The preceding conceptual and empirical expositions provide the necessary framework for explaining the relevance of metacognition to LDs. Both the advantages and limitations of applying metacognition to LDs are then considered. The limitations appear to be redressed by the most recently developed model of, metacognition by Borkowski *et al.* (1989).

From this chapter, readers should understand the following:

1. why metacognition is crucial to effective learning and efficient reading,

2. why metacognition is relevant to LDs and the implications of this relevance for LDs professionals, and

3. the heuristic value of the model of metacognition developed by Borkowski *et al.* (1989) for instructional research with individuals with LDs.

Although both males and females have LDs and problems in metacognition, in the interest of clarity and a smoother flow of writing, reference will be made to the masculine gender throughout this chapter.

---

* Editor's note: These "Editor's Notes" are from this excerpt.

III. Metacognition: Definition, Aspects, and Characteristics

Flavell (1976: 232) stated that "metacognition refers to one's knowledge concerning one's own cognitive processes and products of anything related to them, e.g., the learning-relevant properties of information or data." Included in that statement are two kinds of activities: knowledge about cognition and regulation of cognition (Baker and Brown, 1984b).

Knowledge about cognition concerns an individual's knowledge about his own cognitive resources and the compatibility between himself as a learner and the learning situation. Specifically, Flavell (1987) proposes three categories of knowledge about cognition: person variables, task variables, and strategy variables. Person variables refer to an individual's knowledge and beliefs that he has learned through his experiences about human beings as cognitive organisms. Thus, an individual may believe that he is good at processing abstract, conceptual materials but poor at processing information about machines. He may consider himself to be more musically talented than his classmates but realizes that in other schools some peers surpass himself in musical talent. Then there is some universal or general knowledge that we gain in the course of growing up. For example, we all realize that we think and operate less efficiently when we are hungry or tired. The above examples correspond to the three subcategories of person variables proposed by Flavell (1987): intraindividual (within the individual, i.e., within oneself), interindividual (between individuals), and universal (applies to everyone).

Knowledge about task variables refers to the individual's learning from experience that different kinds of tasks exert different kinds of information-processing demands on him. For example, memorizing an entire poem word for word involves much more work (information processing) than remembering its theme. Realizing the need for different information processing for different tasks helps us plan appropriate allocation of our cognitive resources in completing them successfully.

Strategy variables refer to two kinds of strategies: cognitive and metacognitive. Cognitive strategy is a procedure that enables an individual to reach a goal. For example, one can learn a summarization strategy to record efficient notes from one's reading. A metacognitive strategy is a procedure that involves self-monitoring, self-testing, or self-evaluation. For example, one can learn a strategy that helps one to self-check whether or not one has properly carried out the summarization strategy. This self-monitoring strategy may consist of self-questions such as: "Have I included all the important points from this passage in my summary?" A self-evaluative strategy may have these self-questions: "How good is my summary? Is it sufficiently concise? Have I paraphrased all the important points?" Clearly both kinds of strategies, cognitive and metacognitive, are important in our successful learning and performance.

The studies of Flavell and Wellman (1977) and Flavell (1987) emphasize the interactions among person, task, and strategy variables. We develop intuitions about interactions among these variables. For example, we become aware of the superiority-inferiority of certain strategies, as we consider our own particular cognitive resources and the specific task (Flavell, 1987).

The regulation of cognition concerns the self-regulatory mechanisms used by an active learner during an ongoing attempt to solve problems (Brown, 1980; Baker and Brown, 1984a). The metacognitive activities here include planning, monitoring, testing, revising, and evaluating.

The two aspects of metacognition—knowledge about cognition and regulation of cognition—direct, guide, and govern successful learning, efficient reading, and effective studying (Brown, 1980; Baker and Brown, 1984a, b). Although they are very closely related, the two aspects of metacognition have different characteristics. Knowledge about cognition is "stable, statable but fallible, and late-developing"; i.e., we can verbalize our own awareness of our cognitive strengths and weaknesses. These cognitive strengths and weaknesses are, by and large, consistent. However, our knowledge about cognition is fallible in the sense that a child or an adult may "know" some facts about something (e.g., mathematics) that are untrue. Regulation of cognition, on the other hand, is "relatively unstable, rarely statable and relatively age independent" (Brown, 1987). The regulating activities as stated earlier (planning, monitoring, testing, revising, and evaluating) are unstable and age-independent in that their consistent use in individuals may not be assumed. For example, although older children and adults use self-regulating activities more often than younger children, they do *not* always use them. Even young children monitor their activities on a simplified task (Patterson *et al.*, 1980). Moreover, adults–fluent readers may only be aware of their regulating activities such as comprehension monitoring when they have a reading comprehension failure (Anderson, 1980). Thus, active comprehension monitoring is often an unconscious process and, therefore, an unstatable experience (Baker and Brown, 1984a,b).

IV. Origin of the Construct of Metacognition and Its Subsequent Application to Reading

The construct of metacognition originated in Flavell's research on young children's memory processes. He proposed this construct in an attempt to explain young children's failure to maintain and generalize learned mnemonic strategies. Metamemory, awareness of parameters that govern effective recall, was assumed to be deficient among young children, and this deficiency explained their problems in strategy maintenance and generalization (Flavell, 1976). Subsequently in a seminal paper, Ann Brown (1980) related the theoretical construct of metacognition to reading. Brown (1980: 456) stated: "Any description of effective reading includes active strategies of monitoring, checking and self-testing, whether the task under consideration is reading for remembering (studying) or reading for doing (following instructions)."

V. Metacognition and Effective Learning

Jenkins' (1979) model of memory outlines four basic sources of influence on a learner's remembering in a learning situation. These include characteristics of the learner, criterial task, nature of the materials to be learned, and learning activities engaged in by the learner. Jenkins' model was borrowed and modified for use by Bransford (1979). It was subsequently borrowed from Bransford by Brown (1982) to apply to the educational scene. Brown's (1980) model contained the same factors as Jenkins' original model.

The *characteristics of the learner* refer to the cognitive and strategic repertoires that the individual brings to the learning situation. Individual differences in knowledge and procedural repertoires affect how the individuals learn (Brown, 1982). For example, students with a psychology background would find it easier to understand the research summaries in this and other chapters of this book than someone without such a background. The *nature of the materials to be learned* refers to the organizational nature of the materials, materials that match the readers' prior knowledge, etc. The nature of the materials to be learned affects the individuals' learning outcome. For example, materials that match subjects' prior knowledge are more easily understood by subjects (Anderson, 1982; Brown, 1978). Organized lectures facilitate student understanding and notetaking. The *criterial task* is the end product in any learning. For example, the criterial task in this course in LDs comprises a midterm and a final examination. The efficient learner is aware of the criterial task and tailors his learning activities accordingly (Baker and Brown, 1984b). For example, knowing that the final examination in a course involves short essay questions would lead a student to rely less on memorization of materials. Instead, he would focus on understanding the course material and thinking hard about implications of what is read. Thus, the criterial task sets the learner's purpose in learning, as well as providing him with standards for evaluating his learning (Brown, 1980; Anderson, 1980). *Learning activities* refer to the activities the student engages in while learning. He could spontaneously deploy suitable learning activities or be taught to do so. As children grow older, they gradually learn a repertoire of learning activities. With extensive use, these learning activities-strategies become automatic and their deployment unconscious (Brown, 1982). Engaging in appropriate learning activities greatly influences students' learning outcome. For example, failure to categorize items into discrete categories such as food, clothing, furniture, or vehicles impairs recall in children with LDs. Unobtrusively prompting them to put related items into suitable categories remarkably improved their recall (Wong, 1978).

The literature in cognitive psychology and developmental psychology has shown us clearly how each of the above factors governs the likelihood of a student's successful learning. To demonstrate the point that these four factors and their interactions are important determinants of learning, two illustrative studies are described.

The influence of knowledge of criterial task on students' performances and perception of the ease/difficulty in task learning was shown by Wong *et al.* (1982). In two experiments involving normal-achieving and LD children, Wong *et al.* (1982) investigated the hypothesis that poor comprehension and recall in LD children might stem from a vague perception of criterion tasks (task demands) and\ that provision of clear knowledge of criterion tasks would enhance their performance. This performance enhancement comes about when students focus their study efforts on relevant parts of the exercise, in light of knowledge of criterion task.

In the comprehension task, children given knowledge of criterion task were explicitly told to attend to pre-paragraph questions in two expository passages, because they modeled test questions the children would receive later. In the recall task, the children in the treatment condition were told to study the two expository passages for subsequent recall.

The results in the comprehension task substantiated the hypothesis under investigation. Wong *et al.* (1982) found that both normal-achieving and LD children, given knowledge of criterion task, correctly answered more questions than their respective counterparts in the control condition. However, the results in the recall task did not indicate reliable differences between treatment and control groups. The investigators attributed this outcome to the imprecision in the instructions given to the treatment groups. It is recalled that these children were simply told to expect a recall test. Unlike the comprehension task, they were not guided on which parts of the text to focus on in studying.

In a follow-up experiment, Wong *et al.* (1982) improved the methodology in the recall task. They instructed the children in the treatment condition to study the passages for subsequent recall and to attend specifically to certain important parts of the passages in their study. The children in the control condition were simply told to study the passages for subsequent recall. The results clearly indicated that given explicit knowledge of criterion task, both normal-achieving and LD children recalled substantially more of the passages than their respective control groups. In summary, Wong *et al.* (1982) showed that explicit knowledge of criterion task induced appropriate studying activities in children. The children could focus their attention on relevant contents in the passages, because of knowledge of criterion task.

Equally important influences on a student's successful learning are exerted by the interactions between the four factors of characteristics of learner, nature of materials to be learned, criterial task, and learner activities. Miyake and Norman's (1979) study illustrates the interactive influences between the nature of the materials to be learned (in this case, conceptual difficulty) and learning activities employed by students. Miyake and Norman (1979) investigated the effects of prior knowledge on students' questioning behavior. They used two groups of college students. One group knew little about computers and text-editors. The other group was given sufficient training in the use of a text-editor. The criterion in training was the students' editing one text unaided. Subsequently, both groups were instructed to learn to operate a different text-editor by following either an easy nontechnical manual or a difficult technical manual. The students were further instructed to verbalize their thoughts and questions as they learned the new text-editor. Miyake and Norman (1979) found an interesting interaction in their study: Novice students in computer science asked more questions on the easy manual but very few on the hard manual. The reverse pattern of questioning was obtained for the trained students. Miyake and Norman interpreted the findings to suggest that to ask a question, you have to have an *optimal* amount of prior knowledge for the particular subject matter at hand. Because educators have long stressed the importance of cultivating questioning behaviors to facilitate learning in students, Miyake and Norman's findings imply that teachers should attend to students' existing prior knowledge as a concomitant condition in teaching students to generate questions. The preceding study of Miyake and Norman (1979) presents a mere glimpse into the web of interactions of various parameters underlying successful learning.

VI. Metacognition and Brown's Model

One impetus responsible for the development of metacognitive theory and research is that an individual's successful learning requires more than background knowledge or learning strategies. Equally, if not more important, the individual must be able to use his background and strategic knowledge effectively during learning (Brown, 1980). If an individual is unaware of his own repertoire of strategies, he would be unlikely to deploy suitable strategies flexibly and precisely in tune with task demands. Occasionally, children and adults fail to use appropriate strategies for learning despite having them in their repertoire of strategies (Brown, 1980). The term production deficiencies has been applied to these occasions by Flavell (1976) and called inert knowledge by Scardamalia and Bereiter (1987). For the learner to be able to use and control appropriately his background knowledge and knowledge of strategies, he needs to develop metacognitive skills (Brown, 1980; Baker and Brown, 1984b).

It is recalled that metacognition refers to the awareness of knowledge and control and regulation of that knowledge (Baker and Brown, 1984a,b). The distinction between cognition and metacognition is the "distinction between knowledge and the understanding of knowledge in terms of *awareness and appropriate use*" (Brown, 1980: 453, italics added). Metacognitive skills are those that have been attributed to the "executive" in numerous theories of human memory and artificial intelligence. They are the essential characteristics of efficient thinking in a broad range of learning situations, including efficient reading and effective studying (Anderson, 1980; Brown, 1980; Baker and Brown, 1984b). The following example gives some flavor of how good students deploy metacognitive strategies in their studying. After being informed that there will be a midterm examination involving short essay answers, the good students begin to plan their study schedule. With 3 weeks left before the midterm, they start reading their lecture notes and corresponding chapters from their textbooks. They underline important parts of the materials and denote parts that they understand well. In addition, they identify those sections not understood thoroughly. They seek out the teaching assistant and the professor for help over parts of their notes and texts on which they lack thorough understanding. Having received the necessary help, they concentrate their efforts at studying the important parts of their notes and texts. Remembering that short essay answers rather than multiple choice questions will be on the midterm, good students spend time thinking about what they are studying, in particular, the implications of what they have studied.

In the above example, the good students ascertain what they already know or understand and what they need to clarify in their lecture notes and texts (assessing own knowledge repertoire). Their awareness of the need to get clarification for certain parts of their notes and chapters leads them to seek help from the appropriate sources: the teaching assistant and the professor (awareness leads to proper action). Having clarified their notes and texts, they settle down to diligent studying (self-regulation). However, they are mindful of the criterial task (short essay answers in the midterm), which leads them to engage in appropriate studying behaviors (concentrating on thinking about rather than rote memorization of notes and text). Metacognition enables good students to coordinate their awareness of their state of knowledge with appropriate problem-solving behaviors and guides them to link up appropriate studying behaviors with the task demands of the midterm. Surely the consequence of such well-coordinated, planful, and intelligent studying behaviors is a first class performance on the midterm.

The above description indicates how good students consciously and deliberately coordinate their efforts in studying. The skills they have mobilized in coordinating and regulating their efforts in studying are metacognitive skills. What they have coordinated and regulated are their own knowledge, their notes and texts, their own learning activities, and the criterial task. These are factors depicted in Brown's model. Thus, it can be seen that metacognitive skills are essential in effective coordination of the four factors in that model, and this coordination greatly affects the student's success in learning. Put differently, executive processes are needed to direct, coordinate, and regulate the interactions among those four factors. It is effective coordination, or orchestration (to borrow the word from Brown, 1980), of these interactions that is responsible for the success of any learning outcome. These executive processes are the individual's metacognitive skills.

VII. Metacognitive Skills and Efficient Reading

Good readers who possess metacognitive skills in reading are aware of the purpose of reading and differentiate between task demands, for example, in reading a text for class assignment versus reading a magazine for pleasure. They actively seek to clarify the purposes or task demands through self-questioning prior to reading the given materials (Anderson, 1980). Their awareness of reading purpose leads to the use of suitable reading strategies. For example, a good reader varies his reading rate and concentration level as a function of materials being read—text or magazine. He reads his text slower and with more intense concentration than his magazine. The awareness of the purpose in reading also leads a good reader to monitor his state of reading comprehension. For example, when he encounters difficulty in comprehending material, he uses debugging problem-solving strategies. These problem-solving attempts indicate self-regulation (Anderson, 1980; Brown, 1980). Moreover, good readers evaluate their own comprehension of materials read. Evaluating one's own comprehension of given instructions or of materials read has important consequences (Markman, 1977, 1979). This last reading strategy involves a very basic form of self-awareness (Brown, 1980). If a reader does not realize that he has not understood a particular part of the given materials, he will not employ suitable "debugging devices" (problem-solving strategies) such as backtracking or scanning ahead for possible clues to shed light on the part that currently presents difficulties in comprehension (Anderson, 1980; Baker, 1979). In contrast, LD readers show little indication of such coordination between task demands and suitable reading strategies. They lack the requisite metacognitive skills in reading (Wong, 1985).

The fluent or mature reader is rarely conscious of his own comprehension monitoring. Only when a comprehension failure arises in reading does the fluent reader realize that comprehension monitoring has occurred (Anderson, 1980). The individual immediately slows down his rate of reading and either reviews the difficult section or reads on, seeking enlightenment in subsequent text.

It remains to be shown if younger or immature readers, poor readers, and children and adolescents with LDs have deficient metacognitive skills in the reading process. Two excellent summaries of metacognitive research in reading (Baker and Brown, 1984a,b) document deficiencies in metacognitive skills of reading in poor readers and young children. Readers should study those papers.

How does the importance of metacognitive skills in reading affect our understanding of reading problems in students with LDs? Put differently, what is the relevance of metacognitive skills in reading to LDs?

VIII. Metacognition and Learning Disabilities

Wong realized the relevance of the theoretical construct of metacognition and metacognitive research to special education, in particular, to the education of the LD. She sought to relate metacognition to LDs because basically she felt there has been an indiscriminate tendency among LDs professionals to interpret performance failures in children and adolescents with LDs as cognitive deficits. She felt there is a need to discern between performance failures that genuinely reflect more deep-seated processing problems versus problems that are of a strategic nature. Because metacognitive research unequivocally demonstrates that skilled reading involves decoding, reading comprehension, *and* metacognitive skills, Wong felt that LDs professionals need to look afresh at how they interpret reading problems manifested by LD students. Specifically, they would not be justified in indiscriminately inferring deep-seated processing deficits in any child or adolescent with LDs who has a reading disability. Likewise, they would not be justified in focusing exclusively on decoding and comprehension skills in remediating reading problems in students with LDs (Wong, 1985, 1986, 1987, 1990).

Essentially, metacognition is relevant to LDs because it broadens our perception and understanding of reading problems in LD students and highlights the need to teach them metacognitive skills in reading *in addition* to decoding and comprehension skills. However, we must not lose sight of the limitations of a metacognitive perspective in LDs (Wong, 1986). Specifically, we must not embrace a wholesale interpretation of academic failures in LD students in terms of strategic deficits because there will be occasions when failures are caused by insufficient knowledge and/or ability. Moreover, metacognition alone does not suffice in students' maintenance and generalization of what has been learned. Students' motivation is pivotal in such maintenance and generalization (Wong, 1986: 22–24).

Of more serious concern is Stanovich's point that linking metacognition to LDs may in fact attenuate the assumption of specificity, which underlies the concept of LDs (Stanovich, 1986a,b, 1988). The assumption of specificity holds that dyslexics have a severe disability in one particular cognitive domain, typically reading, but in other cognitive domains, they are relatively adequate. It is essential that the cognitive disability be restricted to one specific area, otherwise the individual would be labeled slow learner or mentally retarded. The latter type of learners characteristically have widespread cognitive deficits (Stanovich, 1986a).

Stanovich (1986a,b, 1988) pointed out that recent theoretical formulations in intelligence tend to include metacognition as an integral component, as shown, for example, in Sternberg's work. Thus, if metacognition is treated or seen as a characteristic of individuals with LD, it would logically lead to the conclusion or statement that they have lower intelligence. Clearly, this conclusion would undermine the discrepancy notion, and cause the disintegration of the assumption of specificity in LDs.

How can we resolve this problem? One way to resolve it is to invoke Stanovich's hypothesis of Matthews Effects (Stanovich, 1986b). In his phonological core-variable model (Stanovich, 1988), Stanovich posits that dyslexic children begin with a very specific, circumscribed cognitive problem in phonological processing. This phonological processing problem impedes the child's learning to read because he would experience enormous difficulties in learning letter-sound associations. Early and persistent failures to learn to read inevitably create motivational problems in the young child (Torgesen, 1977). The child becomes anxious with the reading task, comes to loathe reading, and develops problems with self-esteem.

These motivational problems eventually generalize to academic areas outside of reading (Butkowsky and Willows, 1980) and adversely affect the child's motivation to learn in school. Because the child cannot read and dislikes reading, because reading reminds him of his disability and presents continual frustrations, he ends up having substantially less reading experience outside of school. Similarly, in remedial reading sessions, the child typically receives phonics drills or drills in word recognition rather than passage reading; therefore, he is exposed to much less reading for meaning than his peers in school (Allington, 1980). These motivational and experiential deficiencies bode ill for the dyslexic child because many school subjects involve reading. Hence, the child's reading disability and the resultant motivational problems impede his learning of other academic subjects in school. Consequently, his academic problem is not confined to reading. In time, as he ages, the dyslexic child presents a picture of more generalized cognitive and cumulative deficits.

Stanovich uses the Biblical analogy of Matthews Effects to describe the generalized deficits that dyslexic individuals manifest. It's the case of the poor getting poorer as contrasted with the rich getting richer version of learning to read in the normal-achieving child. Normal-achieving children literally take off after mastering letter-sound associations or cracking the spelling to-sound code. They begin to read much more, enjoy reading more, and comprehend more. Independent reading for pleasure and in-class reading provide normal-achieving children with reading experiences that are essential for their growth in various kinds of knowledge: vocabulary, syntax, and, knowledge about the world and specific topics (e.g., dinosaurs). In turn, such growth in knowledge promotes knowledge acquisition in other related areas. Current schema theories and research in reading comprehension indicate the importance of prior knowledge in the acquisition of knowledge (Schallert, 1982). Thus, children who learned to read well can add much to this cognitive foundation. Cognitively speaking, they get richer and richer. The analogy is most apt *vis-à-vis* skilled readers.

The Matthews Effects hypothesis provides us with a potential solution for the problem of linking metacognition with LDs. We can treat metacognitive problems in the LD as a joint by-product of their lack of reading exposure or experience and motivational problems. Metacognition about reading develops in the context and experiences of reading. An individual cannot develop metacognition about reading in a vacuum. Similarly, the self-regulatory component of metacognition depends on motivation for its deployment. As children with LDs get poorer and poorer

in learning, they develop metacognitive problems, which are essentially a second-order problem. In the picture of more widespread and generalized cognitive problems, metacognitive deficiencies are also present.

It is important to remember that we can avoid the problem highlighted by Stanovich only by treating metacognitive problems as a second-order problem—a joint by-product of deficient reading experiences and motivation. It is not a first-order problem such as a phonological processing problem. Seen from the perspective of the negative effects of Matthews Effects, metacognitive deficits may be legitimately used to describe the LD.

Having addressed the issue of the relevance of metacognition to LDs and the caveats in embracing a metacognitive perspective, it is opportune to consider the question of metacognitive deficiencies in reading in students with learning disabilities.

IX. Metacognition in Students with Learning Disabilities

The assumption that LD students generally lack metacognitive skills in reading is invalid. Rather, they appear to have less sophisticated metacognitive skills than nonlearning-disabled peers in reading (Wong and Wong, 1986).

Wong and Wong (1986) investigated how metacognitive knowledge of vocabulary difficulty and passage organization of given passages affected study time of the same passages in above-average, average, and LD students from grades five through seven. The investigators first interviewed each subject individually on his knowledge/awareness of how easy/difficult vocabulary and the organized/disorganized nature of a passage affected the ease in studying a particular passage. Altogether, four passages were used. In two of these, level of vocabulary difficulty was manipulated. The "Oyster" passage contained difficult words such as "mollusks, plankton, immediate, environment, unexpectedly, especially, maturity." In comparison, the "Whooping Crane" passage contained relatively easy words. Passage organization was manipulated through two alternate versions of a passage either about a fox or polar bears. Each passage contained 12 short sentences, which clustered in fours around a specific subtopic about the respective animal: physical features, food, and habitat. One version of the "Fox" and the "Polar Bear" passages was organized so that the four sentences clustering each of the three subtopics were related to the particular subtopic and logically sequenced. In the disorganized version of the passages, thematic cohesion within each cluster of sentences was clearly lacking.

Each child was seen individually and, depending on order of passage presentation, was given either the organized/disorganized pair or the pair with hard/easy vocabulary first. With respect to the pair of passages with hard/easy vocabulary, the child was told that two students (A and B) studied the Oyster (hard vocabulary) and Whooping Crane (easy vocabulary) passages. Student A spent 15 min studying each passage. Student B spent 30 min on the Oyster passage and 15 min on the Whooping Crane passage. The child was asked which student would remember more of the passages, especially the Oyster passage, and why. To facilitate the child's responding, a schematic depiction of the hypothetical students' study behaviors and the Oyster and Whooping Crane passages were placed before the child. With respect to the organized/disorganized pair of passages, the child was told that again two students (C and D) studied them. Student C spent 15 min on the organized passage and 30 min on the disorganized passage. Student D, however, studied them for 15 min each. The child again was asked which student would remember more of the passages, especially the disorganized one, and why. Again, to facilitate the child's responding, a schematic depiction of the hypothetical students' study behaviors and the organized and disorganized passages were placed before the child.

About 3 weeks after the interview, the children were again seen individually. Half the children were randomly assigned to receive the passage-pair with hard/easy vocabulary first, followed by the organized/disorganized passage-pair. The remaining children had the passage-pairs in the reverse order. When given the previously seen organized/disorganized passage-pair, the child was told to study for subsequent recall of both passages. When given the passage-pair with hard/easy vocabulary, the child was told to study for a subsequent reading comprehension test on each passage. Within each pair of passages, the order of passage presentation was randomized. Moreover, there was a 3-min break between passages within a pair of passages and a 5-min break between the two sets of passages. The child was self-paced and given unlimited time to study the passages. Also, an aide pronounced and carefully explained the meanings of key vocabulary words in the Oyster and Whooping Crane passages. For the benefit of the LD readers, words that might pose decoding or vocabulary difficulties were pronounced clearly and explained thoroughly. Additionally, the child was encouraged to seek help with any other decoding or vocabulary difficulties. When ready for the recall or comprehension test, the child signaled to the experimenter. The child was told not to worry about spelling errors in written answers to the short comprehension questions. Study times in minutes and seconds were recorded with a stopwatch. The children's recall was tape-recorded and later transcribed.

The results indicated that above-average readers were substantially more aware that the level of vocabulary difficulty and passage organization affect the ease of studying a given passage. Examination of the children's individual protocols indicated that few fifth-grade children scored more than one point in the justification responses, which had a scoring range of 0–4. Those who obtained two points were above average. Among the sixth-grade children, above-average readers did very well because none had scores less than two points. Apart from one fifth-grade child, the average readers' performance was generally lackluster. Among LD readers, two seventh-grade subjects had

four points each in justifying why the hypothetical student studying the disorganized passage a longer time would do better. Their respective responses were "30 min for disorganized passage—disorganized passage would be harder to learn so would need more time," and "Studied longer on the disorganized passage . . . it's harder to remember . . . need to study longer." Thus, examination of individual protocols indicated that although above-average readers were substantially more advanced in metacognitive knowledge about vocabulary difficulty and passage organization, the same awareness appeared to be present in LD readers. Such awareness, however, appeared only in two out of four of the *oldest* (grade seven) readers.

More importantly, Wong and Wong (1986) found a significant interaction between reader and passage. This finding indicated that whereas LD readers were most sensitive to level of vocabulary difficulty in a passage, above-average readers were most sensitive to the organization of a passage. Within the pair of passages with easy and difficult vocabulary, only LD readers showed reliable differences in study times, studying significantly longer the passage with difficult vocabulary. Within the pair of passages with organized/disorganized sentences, only above-average readers showed reliable differences in study times, studying significantly longer the disorganized passage.

This pattern of differential study times among above-average readers and LD readers is important. The data for LD readers challenge the ubiquitous assumption of metacognitive deficiency in reading among LD readers. LD readers apparently do possess metacognitive knowledge about one particular aspect of reading investigated, namely level of vocabulary difficulty. Moreover, LD readers' sensitivity to differential vocabulary difficulty in the two passages led them to deploy suitable reading strategies. They studied the passage with difficult vocabulary much longer. One possible reason for LD readers' possession of such metacognitive awareness may be due to their decoding problems, from which ensues an acute awareness of vocabulary difficulty in the reading materials and the development of a strategy to overcome the problems, namely reading slowly.

X. Model of Metacognition

A very recently developed model of metacognition by Borkowski and his associates clearly establishes the relevance of metacognition to the instruction of individuals with LDs. The following is a condensed description of their model. However, before proceeding to that description, some explanatory notes are necessary. Specifically, the original term metamemory acquisition procedures (MAPs), used in Pressley *et al.* (1985), is equivalent to executive processes in later papers by Borkowski and his associates (see Borkowski *et al.*, 1989; Groteluschen *et al.*, 1990). Whereas Borkowski, Pressley, and their associates refer to a person's entire stock of knowledge of a particular strategy as specific strategy knowledge, others have used the term metamemorial knowledge. Lastly, in earlier versions of the models (e.g., Borkowski *et al.*, 1987), attributions were subsumed under General Strategy Knowledge. In the most recent paper, however, attributions are conceptualized as correlates of General Strategy Knowledge (Groteluschen *et al.*, 1990).

A. Model of Metacognition Developed by Borkowski *et al.* (1989)

1. Components of the Model

The components within this model of metacognition are specific strategy knowledge, relational strategy knowledge, general strategy knowledge, and MAPs.

Specific strategy knowledge refers to the individual's repertoire of cognitive-learning strategies, which enhance learning and performance, and his knowledge of their uses. For example, a child or an adolescent may know and use an elaboration strategy as an aid to learning French vocabulary. Children develop specific strategy knowledge slowly as they grow up. Such knowledge means they understand (1) what a particular strategy would achieve for them; (2) what tasks match its use in appropriateness; (3) the range of its usefulness, i.e., what tasks it should or should not be used for; (4) the benefits from regular use of the strategy; (5) how much effort is involved using the strategy; and (6) how enjoyable or laborious is the strategy used.

With specific strategy knowledge about various strategies and their uses, the child can make enlightened decisions about which to use to aid the learning of new tasks. Thus, specific strategy knowledge is requisite in intelligent deployment of strategies. Moreover, a reciprocal beneficial relationship exists between strategy use and specific strategy knowledge. While the individual's specific strategy knowledge guides his use of particular strategies, consistent use of them broadens and refines his specific strategy knowledge about those particular strategies. These elaborations and refinements result in detailed representations of them in specific strategy knowledge. In turn, the expanded and refined specific strategy knowledge improves future use of those strategies.

As specific strategy knowledge cumulates, two other components develop: relational strategy knowledge and general strategy knowledge. Relational strategy knowledge refers to the child's knowledge of the comparative characteristics of various strategies in his repertoire. This knowledge enables the child to choose the appropriate strategy to match task demands and to switch strategies when necessary.

General strategy knowledge refers to the child's awareness that strategy use involves effort expenditure, that a planned and strategic approach to learning is much more likely to result in successful learning. The conceptual uniqueness of general strategy knowledge is its motivational aspect. Borkowski and his associates highlight attributions as the motivational correlate of general strategy knowledge. Effort-related attributions enhance the individual's selfefficacy and self-esteem and induce him to value

strategy use in learning. The individual's enhanced self-efficacy motivates/energizes him to tackle difficult tasks and to maintain and generalize learned strategies.

2. MAPs

As conceptualized by Pressley *et al.* (1985), MAPs have a twofold function. First, these procedures refer to the child's problem-solving attempts to fill in gaps that occur in the teacher's incomplete instructions. Second, they refer to the child's self-regulation, i.e., his self-monitoring of proper use of strategy, the effects of it on his performance (evaluation of strategy use), and deciding on change or modification of strategy in use. MAPs are very important because they constitute the executive processes (self-control or self-regulation). Without knowledge of MAPs, the child would not be able to engage in self-monitoring or self-evaluation of strategy use. It is these executive processes that are energized by enhanced self-efficacy and self-esteem. Such enhanced self-efficacy and self-esteem are brought about by effort-related attributions and a new-found belief in the value of a strategy approach to learning. MAPs are manifested by the following behaviors: self-directed, self-initiated learning or behaviors, self-reliance (independence) in problem solving, and persistence at difficult tasks.

B. Relevance of the Model of Metacognition to LD

Although intervention research with LD students focuses on inculcation of cognitive strategies, it would be erroneous to assume that they have entirely no specific strategy knowledge; rather, it would be more valid to consider that these students possess faulty or ineffectual strategies. In support of this consideration, Garner (1981) found that poor readers read in a word-by-word fashion greatly straining short-term memory and that they showed "piece-meal processing" in that they did not integrate textual information across sentences, which may well impede inferential comprehension. Moreover, when LD students possess knowledge of appropriate strategies, their knowledge appears to be "inert" in that they do not spontaneously activate their use. External prompting for strategy mobilization is required (Wong, 1978; Torgesen, 1979; Torgesen and Goldman, 1977).

How do we explain such "inert" strategy knowledge in LD children and their failure to maintain and generalize learned strategies? One plausible answer to this question is their lack of executive control or self-regulation. Insufficient self-regulation in learning explains LD students' lack of initiation and selection of appropriate strategies, subsequent monitoring, evaluation, and modification of the strategy in use.

C. Empirical Support for the Suggestion That LD Students Lack Executive Control, or Self-Regulation

LD students lack executive control (self-regulation). Observations of deficient executive control in LD students span a number of areas. Specifically, LD students frequently need external prompting to mobilize strategy use (Wong, 1978). They tend not to spontaneously deploy strategies (Torgesen and Kail, 1980). They also have difficulty in choosing suitable problem-solving devices for tasks ranging from reading comprehension (Kavale, 1980), to analytical reasoning (Barton, 1988), to arithmetic problems (Fleischner and Garnett, 1987). Additionally, they show problems in comprehension monitoring, which is an important constituent of mature executive processing (Bos and Filip, 1982; Kotsonis and Patterson, 1980; Wong and Jones, 1982).

In turn, why do LD students show lack of executive control or self-regulation in learning? Put differently, why do LD students fail to develop self-regulation? How have they become passive learners?

The answer mainly resides in the self-systems in LD students. Self-system comprises self-efficacy, self-esteem, and attributions. LD students have a history of academic failure (Torgesen, 1977). Consistent academic failures have at least three negative consequences: (l) erode their motivation to learn, (2) result in nonbeliefs of the value of effortful strategic learning because applications of their own faulty strategies inevitably result in poor learning outcomes, and (3) produce low self-concept ("I am dumb"). At the same time, LD students develop maladaptive attributional patterns. They attribute success in learning to external factors such as luck or "teacher likes me," whereas they attribute failure to internal factors such as ability (Pearl et al., 1980, 1986; Pearl, 1982). These faulty attributions reinforce their incredulous attitudes toward expending effort at strategy-based learning as well as lower their self-esteem. Clearly, compared with normal-achieving students, the self-systems in LD students are warped in development.

The unwholesome self-systems of LD students lead them to avoid challenging tasks, to give up readily at difficult tasks after initial setbacks. Hence, they rob themselves of opportunities in generating problem-solving strategies and fail to apply and modify learned strategies flexibly to suit the task demands. The net result of such poorly developed self-systems is to restrict LD students' development in self-efficacy and self-regulation and make them into passive learners.

To turn LD students into active learners involves a direct assault on their maldeveloped self-systems. How can we achieve this turn-around in their self-systems? One feasible way has been suggested by Borkowski and his associates (Borkowski et al., 1988, 1989; Groteluschen et al., 1990). They advocate reattribution training. They reason that LD students have faulty attributions and need to learn to make effort-related attributions once they have mastered a cognitive strategy. When they succeed at the task, they should be shown clearly that their effortful use of an appropriate learning strategy is responsible for the positive learning outcome. When they fail, they should be taught to analyze the cause(s) of failure—is it due to insufficient effort or insufficient domain knowledge, or should the strategy be changed, etc.? Failure should be

depersonalized. It should in no way be taken to reflect low ability.

The goal of reattribution training is to change LD students into active learners by restoring responsibility of learning to them. They must be the agents of their own learning and learning outcomes. The end product of reattribution training is that LD students develop a sense of self-efficacy because, through such training, they come to realize that they are indeed in control of their own learning: They alone are responsible for their learning outcomes. This sense of self-efficacy (1) provides the confidence to select or activate the use of a learned strategy, (2) mobilizes self-regulation (executive control processes) to monitor and evaluate the impact of strategy use on learning and performance, and (3) motivates and energizes maintenance and generalization of strategy. Put differently, for the LD student, a sense of self-efficacy translates into self-statements such as "I can do it." It empowers LD students to select a task-appropriate strategy, take the responsibility of monitoring and evaluating it, and maintain and generalize its use. Concomitant to the development of self-efficacy, their self-esteem would soar as they experience increasing success in learning.

However, Borkowski and his associates are quick to point out the need to accompany reattribution training with training in executive processes or self-regulation procedures. LD students need to learn how to monitor and evaluate the impact or effect of strategy use on their learning and performance so that they can use and modify learned strategies adaptively. Earlier in this chapter, we summarized the research literature on their lack of self-regulation (executive control). Hence, we must not neglect to teach them requisite self-regulation procedures such as self-monitoring. In short, we need to teach them MAPs.

In light of the above account of how to turn LD students into active learners, we can see the relevance of the metacognition model put forth by Borkowski and his associates to LDs. Their model provides the most comprehensive framework in understanding the cognitive, metacognitive, and affective motivational needs of LD individuals. More importantly, it gives the most plausible conceptualization of their failure to maintain and transfer learned strategies. The model highlights the necessity of the interactive roles of specific strategy knowledge, executive processes (self-regulation), and general beliefs about self-efficacy (effort-related attributions) in inducing successful strategy maintenance and transfer in LD individuals. Borkowski and his associate's repeated emphasis on a twin foci in intervention research with the LD, i.e., an equal focus on executive process and reattribution training, is supported by Reid and Borkowski's (1987) study.

Reid and Borkowski (1987) investigated the effects of three instructional conditions on strategy maintenance and generalization in hyperactive children with LDs. Children in the control condition received specific strategy training, which involved learning the use of an interrogative associative strategy for a paired-associate task and a cluster-rehearsal strategy for a sort-recall readiness task. Children in the self-control (or executive process) condition learned the same strategies as those in the control condition. In addition, they learned self-regulatory procedures in the form of self-statements such as "look to see how the problem might be solved" and "stop and think before responding." These self-regulatory procedures were modeled for them by the instructor in the context of using those strategies. Children in the self-control plus attribution retraining group received specific strategies training and self-control (executive process) training as well as attribution retraining. Specifically, they received two forms of attribution retraining: (1) Antecedent attributional training involved a discussion between instructor and student on prevalent beliefs about the causes of success and failure; and (2) program-specific attributions comprised feedback from the instructor about the link between the child's strategic behavior or his lack of it and his performance during learning. The child was shown individual items in which right or wrong answers depended on whether or not he had used the learned strategy.

The results indicated substantially superior performance of those children in the self-control plus attribution retraining condition across a wide range of performance measures. Not only did they demonstrate better strategy maintenance and generalization, they also attained higher personal causality scores that endorsed effort. Moreover, these hyperactive children with LDs showed less impulsivity than the others in the remaining two conditions of self-control training and the control comparison condition.

Most significant was the finding that after 10 months, children in the combined self-control plus attribution retraining condition were found to use more strategies, maintained effort-related attributions, and showed more advanced metamemories. In short, the combined training appeared to have established some rather permanent improvements in the hyperactive children with LD.

The impressive results of Reid and Borkowski's (1987) intervention study speak to the importance of training both executive processes (self-control/self-regulation) and reattribution in children and adolescents with LDs. Training-specific strategies are clearly insufficient, as is training solely in executive processes (self-control).

XI. Research Issues

Concerning metacognition and LDs several areas appear to call for research. These are briefly discussed below.

A. Development of Metacognition
How normal-achieving children and children and adolescents with LDs develop the various kinds and levels (higher order versus lower order) of metacognitive skills in academic domains, such as reading and writing, remains an empirical question. At present, we only know that, compared with LD children, normal-achieving children possess more sophisticated metacognitive skills in reading (Wong and Wong, 1986). Understanding the developmental

processes here would greatly facilitate the design of instructions to inculcate metacognitive skills in reading.

B. Cumulative Strategy Instruction
The effects of long-term cumulative strategy instruction on normal-achieving children and LD children have not been researched. Conducting this kind of research appears to be very profitable because we would be informed about the nature of strategic learners that results from such training; how the learners modify the learned strategies for their own purposes: whether or not savings in learning occur across cumulative strategies inculcation; and how the learners transfer all the learned strategies.

C. Instructional Modes
Hitherto in research and in classroom practice, strategy instruction has been conducted by an adult. We have not researched the efficacy of peer instruction in strategy training. Having an older LD student teach a younger LD student a metacognitive strategy, such as comprehension monitoring ("Is there anything I don't understand in this story?") may be a worthwhile study. We would hypothesize that self-efficacy and self-esteem in the older LD student should increase as the younger one improves his reading comprehension by using comprehension monitoring in his reading.

D. Metacognitive Skills in Writing
Research in metacognitive skills in writing is nascent (Englert, 1990). We need to expand this area of research to better understand the role of metacognition in effective writing.

E. Metacognitive Model
The model of metacognition proposed by Borkowski and his colleagues invites research. It has much heuristic value for instructional research with LD individuals.

XII. Teaching Implications: Metacognitive Assessment and Curricula

To date, Scott Paris and his associates (Jacobs and Paris, 1987) have developed the only metacognitive strategies assessment device in reading. In the Index of Reading Awareness (IRA), Jacobs and Paris (1987) have produced a very useful questionnaire to measure students' strategies in reading. The questionnaire is divided into four sections: evaluation, planning, regulation, and conditional knowledge with five questions per section. It also contains multiple-choice answers. One example from each of the four sections is shown below:

Evaluation (Jacob and Paris, 1987; 269)

1. What is the hardest part about reading for you?
   a. Sounding out the hard words.
   b. When you don't understand the story.
   c. Nothing is hard about reading for you.

Planning (Jacob and Paris, 1987; 269)

4. Before you start to read, what kind of plans do you make to help you read better?
    a. You don't make any plans. You just start reading.
    b. You choose a comfortable place.
    c. You think about why you are reading.

Regulation (Jacob and Paris, 1987; 270)

2. Why do you go back to read things over again?
    a. Because it is good practice.
    b. Because you didn't understand it.
    c. Because you forgot some words.

Conditional Knowledge (Jacob and Paris, 1987; 270)

3. If you are reading for a test, which would help the most?
    a. Read the story as many times as possible.
    b. Talk about it with somebody to make sure you understand it.
    c. Say the sentences over and over.

Clearly, the IRA assessment is applicable to LD students. It can be used for both research and practical purposes. Currently, there is only information on its use in research. However, it can be profitably used by teachers of LD students as both a pretraining assessment and post-training measure.

Similarly, Paris has produced the only metacognitive curricula, the Reading and Thinking Strategies curricula. He has produced three sets/modules of reading and thinking strategies, one for each of the following grades: third-fourth, fifth-sixth, seventh, and eighth. There are clear merits to these metacognitive curricula, not the least of which is the theoretical framework and empirical base on which they were built.

The instructional principles underlying the Reading and Thinking Strategies curricula are direct explanation, metaphors for strategies, group dialogues, guided practice, and integration with content area reading (Paris *et al.*, 1986). Elsewhere I have detailed the uniqueness of Paris' Reading and Thinking Strategies curricula, its theoretical and empirical underpinnings (Wong, 1990).

XIII. Summary

As assessment of metacognitive practice in LDs suggests that practical applications may still only be at the stage of a promising start. This is due largely to the lack of development of metacognitive assessment tools and curricula. However, this state of affairs may not last. To date, Scott Paris and his associates have blazed the trail in developing a strategy assessment questionnaire that is immensely applicable in LDs research and practice. More importantly, he has developed a systematic set of metacognitive curricula for instructional purposes—the Reading and Thinking Strategies curricula. Close scrutiny of them suggests immediate possibilities for use with LD students in instructional research and actual remedial practices. Paris' strategy assessment device and curricula should serve as models for similar developments by LDs professionals in the future.

Acknowledgments

I greatly appreciate Jenny Alexander's helpful draft of this chapter. I thank Rod Wong for reading the final draft and Eileen Mallory for cheerfully word-processing the various drafts of this chapter.

References

Allington. R. L. (1980). Poor readers don't get to read much in reading groups. *Lang. Arts* 57, 872–876.

Anderson, R. C. (1982). Role of the reader's schema in comprehension, learning and memory. *In* "Learning to Read in American Schools: Basal Readers and Content Texts" (R. C. Anderson, J. Osborn, and R. J. Tierney, eds.), pp. 243–257. Lawrence Erlbaum, Hillsdale, New Jersey.

Anderson, T. H. (1980). Study strategies and adjunct aids. *In* "Theoretical Issues in Reading Comprehension," pp. 484–502. Lawrence Erlbaum, Hillsdale, New Jersey.

Baker, L. (1979). "Do I Understand or Do I Not Understand: That is the Question." Reading Education Report No. 10, July 1979. Center for the Study of Reading, University of Illinois, Urbana.

Baker, L., and Brown, A. L. (1984a). Cognitive monitoring in reading. *In* "Understanding Reading Comprehension" (J. Flood, ed.), pp. 21–44. International Reading Association, Newark, Delaware.

Baker, L., and Brown, A. L. (1984b). Metacognition skills of reading. *In* "Handbook on Research in Reading" (D. P. Pearson, ed.), pp. 353–394. Longman, New York.

Barton, J. A. (1988). Problem-solving strategies in learning disabled and normal boys: Developmental and instructional effects. *J. Educ. Psychol.* 80, 184–191.

Borkowskj, J. G., Johnston, M. B., and Reid, M. K. (1987). Metacognition, motivation and controlled performance. *In* "Handbook of Cognitive, Social and Neurological Aspects of Learning Disabilities," Vol. 2. (S. Ceci, ed.), pp. 147–174. Lawrence Erlbaum, Hillsdale, New Jersey.

Borkowski, J. G., Milstead, M., and Hale, C. (1988). Components of children's metamemory: Implications for strategy generalization. *In* "Memory Development: Universal Changes and Individual Differences" (F. E. Weinert and M. Perlmutter, eds.), pp. 73–100. Lawrence Erlbaum, Hillsdale, New Jersey.

Borkowski J. G., Estrada, M. T., Milstead, M., and Hale, C. A. (1989). General problem-solving skills: Relations between metacognition and strategic processing. *Learn. Disabil. Q.* 12(1), 57–70.

Bos, C., and Filip, D. (1982). Comprehension monitoring skills in learning disabled and average students. *Top. Learn. Learn. Disabil.* 2, 79–85.

Bransford, J. D. (1979). "Human Cognition: Learning, Understanding and Remembering." Wadsworth, Belmont, California.

Brown, A. L. (1978). Knowing when, where, and how to remember: A problem of metacognition. *In* "Advances in Instructional Psychology" (R. Glaser, ed.). Lawrence Erlbaum, Hillsdale, New Jersey.

Brown, A. L. (1980). Metacognitive development and reading. *In* "Theoretical Issues in Reading Comprehension" (R. J. Spiro,

B. B. Bruce, and W. F. Brewer, eds.), pp. 453–481, pp. 77–165. Lawrence Erlbaum, Hillsdale, New Jersey.

Brown, A. L. (1982). Learning and development: The problems of compatibility, access and induction. *Hum. Dev.* 25, 89–115.

Brown, A. L. (1987). Metacognition, executive control, self-regulation and other even more mysterious mechanisms. *In* "Metacognition, Motivation and Learning" (R. H. Kluwe and F. E. Weinert, eds.), pp. 65–116. Lawrence Erlbaum, Hillsdale New Jersey.

Brown, A. L., and Palincsar, A. S. (1982). Inducing strategic learning from texts by means of informed, self-control training. *Top. Learn. Learn. Disabil.* 2, 1–17.

Butkowsky, J. S., and Willows, D. M. (1980). Cognitive-motivational characteristics of children varying in reading ability: Evidence for learned helplessness in poor readers. *J. Educ. Psychol.* 72, 408–422.

Englert, C. S. (1990). Unravelling the mysteries of writing through strategy instruction. *In* "Intervention Research in Learning Disabilities" (T. E. Scruggs and B. Y. L. Wong, eds.), pp. 186–223. Springer-Verlag, New York.

Flavell, J. H. (1976). Metacognitive aspects of problem solving. *In* "The Nature of Intelligence" (L. B. Resnick, ed.), pp. 231–235. Lawrence Erlbaum, Hillsdale, New Jersey.

Flavell, J. H. (1987). Speculations about the nature and development of metacognition. *In* "Metacognition, Motivation and Learning" (R. H. Kluwe and F. E. Weinert, eds.), pp. 21–39. Lawrence Erlbaum, Hillsdale, New Jersey.

Flavell, J. H., and Wellman, H. M. (1977). Metamemory. *In* "Perspectives on the Development of Memory and Cognition" (R. V. Kail and J. W. Hagen, eds.), Lawrence Erlbaum, Hillsdale, New Jersey.

Fleischner, J. E., and Garnett, K. (1987). Arithmetic difficulties. *In* "Handbook of Learning Disabilities," Vol. 1, "Dimensions and Diagnosis" (K. Kavale, S. Forness, and M. Bender, eds.), pp. 189–209. Little, Brown & Co., Boston.

Garner, R. (1981). Monitoring of passage inconsistency among poor comprehenders: A preliminary test of the "Piecemeal Processing" explanation. *J. Educ. Res.* 74, 159–162.

Garner, R. (1987). "Metacognition and Reading Comprehension." Ablex, Norwood, New Jersey.

Groteluschen, A. K., Borkowski, J. G., and Hale, C. (1990). Strategy instruction is often insufficient: Addressing the interdependency of executive and attributional processes. *In* "Intervention Research in Learning Disabilities." (T. E. Scruggs and B. Y. L. Wong, eds.), pp. 81–102. Springer-Verlag, New York.

Hagen, J. W., and Barclay, C. R. (1981). The development of memory skills in children: Portraying learning disabilities in terms of strategy and knowledge deficiencies. *The Best of ACLD.*

Jacobs, J. E., and Paris, S. G. (1987). Children's metacognition about reading: Issues in definition, measurement and instruction. *Educ. Psycholog.* 22(3/4), 255–278.

Jenkins, J. J. (1979). Four points to remember: A tetrahedral model and memory experiments. *In* "Levels and Processing in Human Memory" (L. S. Cermak and F. I. M. Craik, eds.), pp. 429–446. Lawrence Erlbaum, Hillsdale, New Jersey.

Kavale, K. A. (1980). The reasoning abilities of normal and learning-disabled readers on measures of reading comprehension. *Learn. Disabil. Q.* 3, 34–45.

Kotsonis, M. E., and Patterson, C. J. (1980). Comprehension monitoring skills in learning disabled children. *Dev. Psychol.* 16, 541–542.

Markman, E. M. (1979). Realizing that you don't understand: Elementary school children's awareness of inconsistencies. *Child Development* 50, 643–655.

Markman, E. M. (1977). Realizing that you don't understand: A preliminary investigation. *Child Development* 43, 986–992.

Miyake, N., and Norman, D. A. (1979). To ask a question, one must know enough to know what is not known. *J. Verbal Learn. Verbal Behav.* 18, 357–864.

Murray, F. B. (1984). The application of theories of cognitive development. *In* "Applications of Cognitive-Developmental Theory" (B. Gholson and T. L. Rosenthal, eds.), pp. 3–18. Academic Press, New York.

Paris, S. G., Wixson, K. K., and Palincsar, A. S. (1986). Instructional approaches to reading comprehension. *In* (E. Z. Rothkopf, ed.), *Rev. Res. Educ.* 13, 91–128.

Patterson, C. J., Cosgrove, J. M., and O'Brien, R. G. (1980). Nonverbal indicants of comprehension and noncomprehension in children. *Dev. Psychol.* 16, 38–48.

Pearl, R. (1982). Learning-disabled children's attributions for success and failure: A replication with a labeled learning-disabled sample. *Learn. Disabil. Q.* 5, 183–186.

Pearl, R., Bryan, T. H., and Donahue, M. (1980). Learning-disabled children's attributions for success and failure. *Learn. Disabil. Q.* 3, 3–9.

Pearl, R., Donahue, M., and Bryan, T. (1986). Social relationships of learning-disabled children. *In* "Psychological and Educational Perspectives on Learning Disabilities" (J. K. Torgesen and B. Y. L. Wong, eds.), pp. 194–224. Academic Press, New York.

Pressley, M., Borkowski, J. G., and O'Sullivan, J. (1985). Children's metamemory and the teaching of memory strategies. *In* "Metacognition, Cognition and Human Performance" (D. L. Forrest-Pressley, D. MacKinnon, and T. G. Waller, eds.), pp 111–153. Academic Press, San Diego.

Reid, M. K., and Borkowski, J. G. (1987). Causal attributions of hyperactive children: Implications for training strategies and self-control. *J. Educ. Psychol.* 76, 225–235.

Scardamalia, M., and Bereiter, C. (1987). Knowledge telling and knowledge transforming in written composition. *In* "Advances in Applied Psycholinguistics," Vol. 2, "Reading, Writing and Language Learning" (S. Rosenberg, ed.), pp. 142–175. Cambridge University Press, Cambridge.

Schallert, D. L. (1982). The significance of knowledge: A synthesis of research related to schema theory. *In* "Reading Expository Material" (W. Otto and S. White, eds.), pp. 13–49. Academic Press, New York.

Stanovich, K. E. (1986a). Cognitive processes and the reading problems of learning-disabled children: Evaluating the assumption of specificity. *In* "Psychological and Educational Perspectives in Learning Disabilities" (J. K. Torgesen and B. Y. L. Wong, eds.), pp. 110–131. Academic Press, New York.

Stanovich, K. E. (1986b). Matthew effects in reading: Some consequences of individual differences in the acquisition of literacy. *Read. Res. Q.* XXI(4), 360–407.

Stanovich, K. E. (1988). Explaining the differences between the dyslexic and the garden-variety poor reader. The phonological-core variable-difference model. *J. Learn. Disabil.* 21(10), 590–612.

Torgesen, J. K. (1977). The role of nonspecific factors in the task performance of learning-disabled children: A theoretical assessment. *J. Learn. Disabil.* 10, 27–34.

Torgesen, J. K. (1979). Factors related to poor performance on rote memory tasks in reading-disabled children. *Learn. Disabil. Q.* 2, 17–23.

Torgesen, J. K., and Goldman, T. (1977). Rehearsal and short-term memory in reading disabled children. *Child Dev.* 48, 56–60.

Torgesen, J. K., and Kail, R. V. (1980). Memory processes in exceptional children. *Adv. Special Educ.* Vol 1., JAI.

Wong, B. Y. L. (1978). The effects of directive cues on the organization of memory and recall in good and poor readers. *J. Educ. Res.* **72**, 32–38.

Wong, B. Y. L. (1985). Metacognition and learning disabilities. *In* "Metacognition Cognition and Human Performance" (T. G. Waller, D. Forrest-Pressley and E. MacKinnnon, eds.), pp. 137–180. Academic Press, New York.

Wong, B. Y. L. (1986). Metacognition and special education: A review of a view. *J. Special Educ.* **20**(1), 9–29.

Wong, B. Y. L. (1987). Metacognition and learning disabilities. *Learn. Disabil. Q.* **10**(3), 189–195.

Wong, B. Y. L. (1991). Assessment of metacognitive research in learning disabilities: Theory, research and practice. *In* "Handbook on the Assessment of Learning Disabilities: Theory, Research and Practice" (L. Swanson and B. Keogh, ed.), pp. 265–283. College Hill Press.

Wong, B. Y. L., and Jones, W. (1982). Increasing metacomprehension in learning-disabled and normally-achieving students through self-questioning training. *Learn. Disabil. Q.* **5**, 228–240.

Wong, B. Y. L., and Wong, R. (1986). Study behavior as a function of metacognitive knowledge about critical task variables: An investigation of above average, average, and learning-disabled readers. *Learn. Disabil. Res.* **1**, 101–111.

Wong, B. Y. L., Wong, R., and LeMare, L. J. (1982). The effects of knowledge of criterion tasks on the comprehension and recall of normally-achieving and learning-disabled children. *J. Educ. Res.* **76**, 119–126.

Wong, B. Y. L., Wong, R., and Blenkisop, J. (1989). Cognitive and metacognitive aspects of composing problems in learning-disabled adolescents. *Learn. Disabil. Q.* **12**(4), 300–322.

Supervision as a Proactive Process

Daresh, J. C. 1991. 29–36. Prospect Heights, Ill.: Waveland.

Educational Platform Development

The supervisor's *educational platform*, developed by Thomas Sergiovanni and Robert Starratt (1988), is a model designed to help professional educators assess their views about a series of educational issues by stating their views in a straightforward manner, akin to the platform statements made by political candidates in an election campaign. The major difference between a politician's and an educator's platform is that the latter is structured to communicate the educator's deepest and truest attitudes, values, and beliefs, even if these are contrary to the sentiments of "the public." (An individual educational platform is very similar to a personal, informal theory, a concept explained in greater detail in Chapter 3.)

Sergiovanni and Starratt's model for formulating a supervisor's educational platform includes 12 major elements. Ten of these deal with general educational themes, and, as a result, they can serve as the basis for any professional educator's platform. The last two are linked specifically to the role of a supervisor.

1. The aims of education.
2. The major achievements of students this year.
3. The social significance of the student's learning.
4. The supervisor's image of the learner.
5. The value of the curriculum.
6. The supervisor's image of the teacher.
7. The preferred kind of pedagogy.
8. The primary language of discourse in learning situations.
9. The preferred kind of teacher-student relationship.
10. The preferred kind of school climate.
11. The purpose or goal of supervision.
12. The preferred process of supervision.

The following excerpts from one particularly well-developed statement prepared by a classroom teacher contemplating a change to a supervisory position in her school system illustrate how writing a platform helps define personal views.

Aims of Education

The aims of education are threefold. First, the schools must help each student to acquire a sense of self-fulfillment and self-worth in which all children can discover and realize their own unique talents, gifts, and abilities. . . . Secondly, the schools must help students create and maintain meaningful relationships with others. They must help students learn how to communicate . . . their needs, attitudes, concerns, and appreciations. . . . Finally, educators should enable students to become productive, responsible citizens in our society. Schools need to impart the basic knowledge, develop creative expression, and provide a variety of experiences that will enable each individual to assume a role within one's community, one's country, and one's world. . . .

Major Achievements of Students this Year

The major achievements I would hope to have my children display by the end of the year include both academic achievements and personal achievements. As a first-grade teacher, I hope that my children will acquire the basic skills, concepts, and information that they will need in order to continue in their educational pursuit. . . . Along with an ability to receive and absorb specific facts, concepts and skills, I hope that my children will achieve the necessary work habits that they will need in order to accomplish their present and future goals. . . . In order to meet the personal objectives that I deem important for my children I hope to create a safe and comfortable environment in which they can explore and discover themselves.

Social Significance of the Students' Learning

Our children are our future. Therefore, student learning profoundly affects us in that students' views of the world begin to take shape during the school years. Out of the student population will come the future leaders and decision makers of our country. Thus, the future quality of life in our society is directly related to the quality of education we provide for our students today.

The Image of the Learner

Children are unique. Therefore, their ability to acquire and retain new knowledge and skills is unique. One method of instruction, although it may be appropriate for a percentage of the children within a classroom, cannot adequately meet the individual needs and learning styles of the remainder of the children. Thus, in order to motivate children to greater degrees of personal success, it is necessary to provide a variety of learning strategies within a classroom. . . .

Value of the Curriculum

In essence, the curriculum is a composite of all experiences, planned and unplanned, that constitute the learning of the individual. These learnings occur both within and outside of the classroom. Those experiences which children encounter through the interaction with their families and peers, through the mass media such as television, radio, magazines, and newspapers, and through their social and religious organizations strongly impact the curriculum that is presented in the schools. Therefore, in designing and developing curricula for schools, this "hidden" curriculum needs to be recognized, acknowledged, and planned for specifically. In so doing, the teacher can be proactive rather than reactive in providing the optimal learning experiences for each child. . . .

The Image of the Teacher

A teacher is an individual with a specific purpose or mission. A teacher with a mission has a deep underlying belief that students can grow and attain self-actualization. Teachers believe that they have something of significance to contribute to other people, especially students, and believe with every fiber of their being that they can "make a difference." Teachers believe that children can learn and want to learn and are driven from within to find the technique or strategy that will assist that child to learn. . . . Teachers also receive high personal satisfaction and inner joy from the growth of their students. They seek out the resources necessary to stimulate and activate learning within the student and are excited when students think, respond, and learn. . . . A teacher is also a contributing member of the larger school setting and should value working closely with the principal and other staff personnel.

Preferred Kind of Pedagogy

As a first-grade teacher, I employ a multitude of ideas, materials, and experiences when helping my children to learn. Because of the age, experiences, and socialization of first-graders, at the beginning of the year I find it is necessary to assume a more directive role within my particular classroom. I feel that this is appropriate and necessary in order to help six- and seven-year-olds feel safe and secure in their new environment, and to help them make a transition from a more home-centered world into a more school-centered world. . . . As I work within my classrooms encouraging children to higher degrees of personal and academic achievement, I also utilize the larger resources of the school. These include students, the principal, the media specialist, the special area teachers . . . the guidance counselor, the psychologist, and our teacher aides. I believe that it takes many caring and concerned individuals to help a child learn and grow into a healthy, productive adult. . . .

Primary Language of Discourse in Learning Situations

Children learn best when they are involved and when the material presented is relevant to their interests and needs. Therefore, the language within the classroom should foster communication. This communication can take many forms: discussion, lecture, questions and answers, dialogue, and role-playing. But whatever form that it takes, it should have at its base the interests and needs of the child. . . .

Preferred Kind of Teacher-Student Relationship

The relationship established between the teacher and the student has a profound effect upon the child's ability to function and to learn to his or her optimal level. A teacher's priority is to foster a safe environment in which each child feels a sense of belonging, importance, and acceptance. If this is established, the child is able to channel his or her energy into positive learning rather than withdrawing from the learning situation in a negative way. . . . It is important for the teacher to understand that each child is unique and that a teacher's expectations for one student may not be the same expectations that one may have for another student. . . .

The Preferred Kind of School Climate

An atmosphere of trust and safety must be created within a classroom. Within this environment, each child's unique needs and interests can be met. Because all students are different, they have different requirements for openness and structure, for movement and control, for an opportunity to work in groups or the need to work alone. It is important to meet these differences and to help children create an awareness and understanding of the similarities and differences that they share. . . . A teacher needs to realize that no one best environment will meet the needs of every student. . . . A positive climate is essential throughout the total school building and should be realized districtwide. . . .

Allowing for and appreciating the special needs, interests, and styles of our colleagues—feeling valued and important as professionals and as people—ultimately transfers itself into an atmosphere that profoundly affects children and stimulates their capacity to learn.

Purpose of Supervision

The purpose of supervision is to maximize children's learning. This is accomplished by directly improving the quality of a teacher's instruction within the classroom. A supervisor, therefore, is an individual whose responsibility and desire is to help teachers recognize and capitalize on their strengths. A supervisor must also understand and assume responsibility for the goals and priorities of the organization as a whole. This requires that the supervisor must often bridge the gap between the interests and needs of the teachers and those of the administration. Thus, the supervisor's role is often one of effective communication and advocacy—advocacy of the teacher and advocacy of the administrator.

The supervisor must clearly visualize how each separate part of the organization fits together for the benefit of the whole and be able to take the steps necessary to accomplish this end. Thus, the supervisor must be genuinely concerned and comfortable with each group and be able to effectively merge their varied concerns and transcend the difficulties to a level of greater excellence for the total organization. In order to accomplish this, supervisors must clearly understand their personal platforms. This has the potential of creating a climate of trust and credibility between supervisors and all parties involved. When this is achieved, the needs of the child are enhanced, and that is our primary focus as educators.

Preferred Process of Supervision

As I grow in my understanding of supervision and the various modes of supervisory practice, I believe that there is no one best way to supervise. I realize that each situation is different and that each individual is unique. It is my responsibility as a supervisor to evaluate and to respond to each condition by gathering and accessing the data surrounding that particular situation.

I respond to the inherent worth and value of each individual, and this belief will be a strong guide within me as I interact with my colleagues. I believe that growth is attained most completely when the strengths of an individual are determined and those strengths are developed and encouraged. By identifying and developing strengths, I believe that the personal dignity of the individual is preserved and that this is the foundation upon which change and growth can occur. I feel that as I direct and encourage teachers to utilize their strengths to their greatest potential, they will, in turn, direct their abilities to more productive instruction of the children.

I realize that, at times, I will find it necessary to supervise a staff member who is minimally effective with children. I hope, by identifying that

person's strengths with him or her, that might increase the person's sense of self-worth and, possibly, minimize any confusion or anxiety that may be hindering the individual's effectiveness in the classroom. If it becomes apparent that this person's strengths could be utilized more appropriately in a different direction, working together with him or her to explore possible alternatives would be appropriate. I am aware that a high degree of trust needs to be established before this is even possible.

I see myself applying the human resources philosophy. When members of an organization understand the goals of that organization, and become the agents by which those goals are achieved, then growth within those members is attainable to a higher degree. Personal self-attainment is energizing, both to the individual and to the organization, and creates an atmosphere of good will, trust, and greater cooperation. This has a cyclic effect. Within the organization, participation should be encouraged at the level at which an individual is capable: understanding that each person has his or her own "timing" and will develop accordingly. It is necessary to stimulate learning for each staff member by offering many opportunities for personal and professional growth, such as inservices, workshops, conference attendance, and involvement in specific interest and support groups. Staff who had interest and skills in a particular area would be encouraged to share them, formally or informally, with their peers. In this fashion, a network of in-house expertise is developed for the recognition and the evolution of the presenter, the growth of the staff, and the benefit of the children. In this manner, supervisors can, by acknowledging the control of the growth of their teachers with their colleagues, internalize and expand the ownership of the goals of the district.

I have provided only excerpts for the first 10 issues, but the last two topics, "Purpose of Supervision" and "Preferred Process of Supervision," are quoted in their entirety. The "author" of this platform, like most readers of this text, is a classroom teacher who was thinking about pursuing professional career in a supervisory position. As a result, her statements in the last two sections are best understood as an attempt to find a personal vision of leadership or supervision.

Sergiovanni and Starratt's notion of the educational platform is useful for a number of reasons. First, writing a formal educational platform requires you to articulate many of the things that you may take for granted as you go about your business in a particular role. It is not unusual to hear highly experienced teachers praise the platform-writing process simply because it is a *disciplined* way to express sets of values, beliefs, and attitudes they may have forgotten over the years. Second, writing a platform results in a formal agenda that allows you to see and then confront ideas that are rarely stated.

A third benefit of preparing a platform is that it allows you to make your values more visible to others. Although we don't recommend circulating copies of a personal platform as a standard practice, a well-prepared platform can be a useful tool for sharing important personal feelings with others who need to know your beliefs. In sum, a formal statement can help you gain greater insights into your fundamental "nonnegotiable" or "sacred" values.

Everyone who works in any organization wonders from time to time whether or not to stay in a particular position. Sometimes an organization changes to the extent that it no longer seems to represent values that were once appealing. A formal platform statement is a visible and constant reminder of what an educator holds in greatest esteem. Its real value may be to help you answer the question, "What is *so important* to me that I would quit rather than compromise?"

Action Plan

Articulating an individual educational platform is an extremely powerful activity for reviewing professional and personal values, but it is little more than an exercise unless it is combined with an *action plan.* An action plan need not be a formal statement with a predetermined number of "elements" like the platform, but it should list actions that will allow you to put to use the platform's critical concepts. The action plan will enable you to look at your present role to determine how personal behavior actually matches both the platform and the characteristics of the job.

The elementary teacher quoted earlier moved from the initial platform statement to a statement of analysis, and finally to a personal action plan.

Platform Analysis

The writing of my platform has been a challenging and a valuable undertaking. I feel these beliefs and assumptions, but have never articulated them until now. This has been an affirming exercise, but, at the same time, I realize that I am also in process. I am not the same person today that I was yesterday. Nor will I be the same person tomorrow as I am today. . . . I know that should I ever step out of the process, I will stop growing as an individual and will lose any effectiveness that I might have as a teacher and a supervisor. . . . I found as I placed my thoughts on paper that

there was an element of interrelatedness among the different themes. In order to achieve one aspect of my platform, I needed to build upon the others. As a result, I sense a unified direction for myself. It is as though I have developed a focus, and that the confusion that accompanies indecision is removed. As a teacher, I know what I'm about and feel that what I do is valuable. Yet, as I began to express my thoughts concerning supervision, I found myself searching for clarity. My experience in personnel, in facilitating both student and adult groups . . . has given me a background of understanding. There are still gaps in this understanding. This is what is directing me to gain a better understanding of the field of supervision.

Personal Action Plan

I plan:

1. To exercise my belief that learning is a life-long adventure. This would include my present goals. . . .

2. To become a more effective classroom teacher, and to continually seek the resources that will permit children to reach their greatest potential.

3. To encourage and assist in the development of the staff within my particular school and within the district. To plan and implement with my principal a specific plan for staff support and supervision.

4. To plan and implement my field experience study. To evaluate my growth and needed areas of growth with my supervisors and the participants involved in my experience.

5. To continually clarify my educational platform by asking the question, "What is best for children?"

This teacher's action plan allows her to examine the major "nonnegotiable" issues described in her original platform statement and to select a series of important objectives. Action planning allows the teacher to come full cycle from original statement of philosophy to a statement of action.

Differentiated Supervision for Catholic Schools

Glatthorn, Allan A., and C. R. Shields. 1983. 15–27.
Washington, D.C.: National Catholic Educational Association.

Clinical Supervision

Clinical supervision, as explained in the previous chapter, is an intensive and systematic process of conferring, observing, analyzing, and de-briefing, a process designed to effect major improvements in teaching performance. In this chapter we would like to explain the basic process in some detail and then suggest a modification that could be used by very busy supervisors.

At the outset, however, it might be useful to discuss briefly the issue of which teachers can most profit from clinical supervision. Since it is an intensive form of supervision which focuses on the improvement of teaching skills, it can best be provided to beginning teachers and to experienced teachers who are encountering serious instructional problems. Even though beginning teachers might have had good clinical supervision during their student teaching, they still need the benefits of close observation and feedback while they are negotiating the transition to the real world of the classroom, where they are completely on their own. Experienced teachers who are having serious problems similarly need the help of a supervisor who knows how to observe a class, identify what is going wrong and help the teacher find ways to improve. Clinical supervision, of course, should also be provided to any experienced teacher new to the building—until the principal feels confident about the newcomer's teaching ability.

For these reasons we suggest that the supervisor should make it clear when the differentiated program begins that all beginning teachers will be required to have clinical supervision. The supervisor should also explain that he or she will be able to exercise a veto over the choices of experienced teachers. If an experienced teacher who is having problems asks for an option other than clinical, the supervisor should confer with the teacher and say, in effect, "I've had some concerns about your teaching. I think it would be better for both you and the school if you had the benefits of clinical supervision." Restricting clinical supervision to those who most need it will usually mean that the supervisor can focus his or her efforts on perhaps ten percent of the faculty, a manageable number even when the time-consuming clinical approach is used.

The Pre-Observation Conference

The cycle of clinical supervision begins with the pre-observation conference. This pre-observation conference is best seen as a dialogue between you and the teacher. The teacher informs you about the class and the teacher's tentative plans for that instructional period. You raise with the teacher your own questions about objectives and activities. While the pre-observation conference should be seen as a dialogue, you should also have in mind a clear agenda for the conference. Figure 4 shows one such agenda that we have found effective.

You begin by tying to get a sense of the class and individual students—their problems and their progress. You want to know the class as well as possible, so that you will understand well the context in which the lesson will be presented. You then move to a discussion of the four essential components of the lesson: objectives, activities, pacing and assessment. Then help the teacher think about alterative scenarios, in case things do not work out as planned. You close by exploring the teacher's special concerns about the lesson.

You need not, of course, follow this agenda like a script. If you know the pupils well, you can omit that part of the discussion. If you are working closely with the teacher, you probably have a general sense of class progress. In such cases you can move directly to a discussion of the four instructional issues—objectives, activities, pacing, and assessment.

Figure 4. Agenda for the Pre-Observation Conference

1. What are the general characteristics of this class? What should I know about them as a group?

2. Are there any individual students who are experiencing learning or behavior problems?

3. What general academic progress has the class made? Where is the class in relation to your goals for the year?

4. What are your specific objectives for the class session to be observed? Why have you chosen those objectives?

5. What teaching methods and learning activities do you plan to use to accomplish those objectives?

6. How do you plan to assess learning and give students feedback about progress?

7. What is your general pacing strategy? About how much time do you plan to devote to reach major objectives?

8. What alterative scenarios have you considered in case one of the planned activities does not work out?

9. Is there anything special you would like me to observe for?

While we have found that most teachers are very open to suggestions in the planning conference, we still believe it is unwise to be too directive at this time. If you tell the teacher what objectives to teach and what activities to use, then the teacher in essence takes your plan to that classroom. If the teacher returns to the de-briefing conference and says, "Your suggestion didn't work out too well," there isn't much you can say in response. Therefore, it makes better sense to help the teacher think through options and choices, but be sure that the teacher feels a sense of ownership about the plans for the class to be observed.

We should note here one of the clear limitations that results from holding such a conference: in effect all supervisory visits become announced. If you and the teacher wish to talk in detail about the class to be observed, then obviously the teacher must know when to expect your visit. There are some obvious drawbacks here. Knowing that a specific visit is planned will probably increase teacher anxiety. Most teachers will take special pains to prepare a good lesson, and some teachers will even coach the students about how to behave and respond during the observation. For these reasons we suggest later in the chapter a variation in the standard clinical model which omits the pre-observation conference and which enables you to make unannounced visits.

In general, however, the pre-observation conference has values that outweigh its potential drawbacks. It gives you a framework with which to view instruction. It gives you and the teacher an opportunity to talk about objectives and activities. And it enables you and the teacher to confer as professional peers, exchanging ideas about what is to happen—not judging what has already taken place.

The Observation

How do you observe a class for supervisory purposes? At the outset we would note that we speak of supervisory, not evaluative, purposes. If you are principal of a school, you are expected to evaluate teachers—to rate them "satisfactory" or "unsatisfactory." While that is a legitimate and important function of the principalship, we strongly believe that evaluation should be separated from supervision. If you evaluate, you observe to judge; if you supervise, you observe to help. So we will speak about the supervisory, not the evaluative, visit.

If at all possible, arrive at a natural break—when classes are passing or when the teacher in a self-contained classroom is shifting to a new activity or topic. Move as quickly as possible to a place in the room where you can observe. Find a spot where you will be relatively inconspicuous, where you can see students' faces, and where you can have a good view of the teacher. In a classroom arranged in a conventional fashion, a seat at the door-side of the room, about one-third the distance from the front of the classroom, will usually provide a good vantage point to observe both pupils and teacher.

Begin at once to take notes. You previously should have explained to the faculty how you would like to take

notes in a supervisory visit—and what use will be made of those notes. Some prefer an audio recorder. Others find a video tape recorder gives much fuller information, as long as someone is available to operate the equipment. If you use either an audio or video recorder, it is usually wise to secure the teacher's permission in advance.

Some prefer to take detailed notes of all the important transactions, simply noting in the margin the time. Such notes might look like those shown in Figure 5. Others prefer a somewhat more structured observation form, like the one shown in Figure 6. We have had a great deal of success in using the "Learning-Centered Observation Form" shown in Figure 7. The column headed "Stage" identifies the three basic stages of a learning episode: readiness, learning, closure. The desirable learning behaviors listed next to each stage have been derived from a review of learning theory and research. The theory and research on learning clearly suggest that those behaviors should be used if effective learning is to take place. The two wider columns provide space for the observer to note teacher behaviors that seem to be facilitating and those that seem to be impeding.

Regardless of the form you use, take pains to be sure that your notes are rather complete and focus on the important teaching and learning transactions: the teacher's objectives, the teacher's instructional behaviors, and the pupils' responses. Be concerned as well for those aspects of classroom climate involved in your own concept of the classroom as a "caring Christian community." Do not concern yourself with the following: teacher voice, teacher dress, teacher mannerisms, appearance of bulletin boards, position of shades, or other unimportant matters. Those trivial concerns, so often the focus of the observations of untrained administrators, draw your attention away from the more vital aspects of the complex teaching-learning transaction.

Occasionally we have worked with supervisors who told us, "We don't take any notes at all. We rely on our memories. Note-taking distracts the teacher." We don't believe that such a position is a wise one to take. Hundreds of transactions take place during a 5-minute period. Memories are fallible. Detailed notes help you analyze and understand what is going on. The distraction is minimized if you have previously assured the teacher that your notes are for supervisory purposes only—to help you remember and understand what took place.

At an appropriate break in the instructional session, you leave, as unobtrusively as you can. If possible, you should stay for at least thirty minutes, long enough to see how the teacher begins and ends a class or a learning episode. If the teacher stops you at the door and asks, "What did you think of the lesson?" the best response, we think is, "I learned a great deal from the observation. Why don't we try to find a time today or tomorrow when we can talk about it?" Such an answer enables you to avoid having to make snap judgments or off-the-cuff comments that might later complicate the de-briefing session.

Figure 5. Observational Notes

9:27   Jones explains concept of *simile:* "a simile is a comparison." Gives two examples: "red as a rose," "the bulls on Wall Street." Asks her pupils to give examples. One pupil raises hand; calls on her: "my dog is like a friendly terrier." Jones: "Good."

9:30   Jones explains concept of *metaphor:* "a metaphor is also a comparison. It doesn't use *like* or *as*." Six pupils in back of room seem inattentive; Jones does not seem to be aware of them.

Figure 6. Structured Observation Form

Teacher		Class	
Time	Teacher Objectives, Noted or Inferred	Teacher Actions	Student Responses

Analysis of Observation

You need some time for the analysis stage of the clinical cycle. You review your notes carefully, looking for patterns of recurring teacher and pupil behaviors. From all the data you have acquired, you are trying to identify the salient behaviors that were facilitating and impeding learning. It is probably most useful if you attempt to identify two or three recurring behaviors of each type. We believe, first of all, that a good supervisor always notes effective and facilitating behaviors, for teachers need to be aware of what they are doing well. The supervisory conference should not focus only on problems; instead, one of your objectives should be to build upon the strengths the teacher already has.

Note that we also suggest you identify a limited number of both strengths and weaknesses. Our experience suggests that the best growth comes about when teacher and supervisor work together on a relatively small number of critical skills. We have frequently observed supervisors overwhelming teachers with well-intentioned suggestions. The teacher leaves such a conference trying to remember ten or twelve suggestions, puzzled about which ones are most important, and anxious about trying to implement all of them.

In identifying the two or three areas where you wish to bring about some improvement, consider both the importance of that particular skill and the readiness of the teacher to acquire and use that skill effectively. Suppose, for example, you noted that in one class session the teacher seemed to be having some problems in these areas:

- keeping pupils on task
- explaining ideas clearly
- asking higher-level questions
- responding effectively to pupil answers
- using a variety of learning activities

You would probably decide to work initially on the ability to keep pupils on task. You know that such a skill is one of the most important, and you sense that the teacher can readily adopt some behaviors that will result in a higher proportion of on-task responses.

In preparing for the de-briefing conference, you might find it useful to crystallize your thinking by noting on an index card the important strengths and weaknesses—along with several specific examples. Figure 8 shows how such notes might look for a conference with the teacher who was explaining simile and *metaphor.*

This analysis phase of the cycle is obviously important. It gives you an opportunity to review the data, identify salient behaviors, and prepare for the de-briefing conference.

The De-Briefing Conference

Hold the de-briefing conference as soon after the observation as you can. The more immediate the feedback, the more useful it is. Be sure you have allowed yourself sufficient time: a half-hour seems to be the minimum

Figure 7. Learning-Centered Observation Form: Unfocused Observation

Teacher_____ Date_____ Period_____

Learning Episode: Time Begun_____ Time Completed_____ Central Objective _____

Stage	Desirable Learning Behaviors	Teacher Behaviors That Facilitated	Teacher Behaviors That Impeded
	THE LEARNER		
READINESS	1. Learns important skills, concepts at appropriate level of difficulty.		
	2. Believes in ability to learn, sets reasonably high standard.		
	3. Perceives learning as relevant.		
	4. Has prior skill, knowledge required.		
	5. Understands objectives.		
LEARNING	6. Has overview of learning.		
	7. Actively engages in task-related activities.		
	8. Uses appropriate materials.		
	9. Remains on task.		
	10. Paces learning appropriately.		
	11. Gets feedback about learning.		
	12. Practices, applies learning.		
	13. Experiences success with efforts.		
	14. Takes corrective measures when needed.		
CLOSURE	15. Reaches closure on task.		
	16. Anticipates next learning task.		

COMMENTS:

amount of time you will need. Arrange for the conference to be uninterrupted, except by emergencies. Ask your secretary to take all telephone calls and handle any unannounced visits. It is important that the teacher feels that this conference is your first priority.

The basic question you must resolve before embarking upon the conference itself is the general interactional style you think will be most effective. Here we would like you to consider three options: direct, indirect, and problem-solving. The direct style is one in which you tell, explain, advise. You want to control the agenda and to make your points clearly and directly. In the indirect style your objective is to listen and reflect. You want the supervisee to control the agenda, for your chief purpose is to be supportive as an empathetic listener.

The problem-solving style is more complex. It is neither direct nor indirect. Your purpose is to help the teacher solve important instructional problems. In a sense you serve as a "second mind" for the teacher, thinking along with the

teacher, offering data the teacher might have forgotten, helping the teacher move through the problem-solving sequence.

Here are examples of the three styles.

DIRECT

Teacher: I felt they weren't paying attention.

Principal: You're right. They weren't listening because you had been talking too much. They seemed bored. You ought to vary the activities you use.

INDIRECT

Teacher: I felt they weren't paying attention.

Principal: You must have felt some concern about that.

Teacher: Yes, I was worried about what you might be thinking.

Principal: You were afraid that I was making a negative judgment of your work?

Figure 8. Conference Notes

JONES

Explaining

Incomplete definition: s. is a comparison
examples confusing, misleading: bulls on WS
only two examples
did not check on pupils' prior knowledge
did not check on pupil understanding in
    explaining metaphor, also gave incomplete
    definition:
did not distinguish between literal and
    figurative comparisons.
Give 3 examples; these seemed more relevant to
    pupils' experience.

PROBLEM-SOLVING

Teacher: I felt they weren't paying attention.

Principal: I have some data that might help us look at that. Why don't we try to figure out what was going on. Almost all the students were attentive for the first ten minutes of class. Then the percentage who were on task dropped sharply. Can you guess what might have been happening?

Which of the styles is best? There is no research which is most effective in changing behavior, and the research on which one teachers prefer is somewhat ambiguous. (See, for example, Blumberg, 1974; and Zins, 1977.) Some teachers prefer a more direct style; some prefer the supportive indirect style; and still others seem to like a problem-solving orientation. While Glickman (1981) advocates matching style with teacher ability and commitment, we believe the question is more complex. These are the factors you must weigh as you think about the style you will use:

1.   Your own preferred way of interacting with people. Some supervisors are very effective with direct style and have so much difficulty being otherwise that they probably should go on using a direct approach.

2.   The teacher's general ability and maturity. Here, of course, we support Glickman's basic argument that less mature teachers probably prefer—initially at least—a style that is more direct.

3.   The developmental state of the supervisory relationship. We would argue from our experience that the style might change as the supervisory relationship develops. You might start with an indirect style, just to build a climate of acceptance and support. Then you might move to a somewhat more direct style until the supervisee seems to have developed some insight into the teaching-learning transaction. At that point you would move to the problem-solving

style, sensing that the teacher was ready for that more demanding interaction.

4.   The particular nature of the lesson observed and the teacher's reaction to it. If you have observed what you believe was a very poor lesson and you sense the teacher was unaware of the serious problems, you might choose a direct style. If the lesson had one or two serious problems but you perceived the teacher to be highly anxious and upset about it you might feel an indirect style more appropriate.

Our goal, then, is not to argue for a given style or to give you a simple formula for interacting with teachers. We want instead to help you become more reflective about the way you interact and more flexible in the approach you use. One way to become more reflective is to get a picture of how you interact now. Tape one of your supervisory conferences, with the permission of the teacher. Then play the tape back and analyze what you said. The form shown in Figure 9 is a relatively simple one that will enable you to compute the percentage of your comments that could be classified as direct, indirect or problem-solving.

How can you become more flexible? The answer is to make a conscious attempt to use the style you seem to be neglecting. Our experience suggests that most supervisors need help in making more use of the problem-solving style. They do a good job of telling and advising—and they know how to listen and be supportive when necessary, but they are uncertain about how to interact as a problem-solver. It, therefore, might be more useful to examine this style in some detail.

Think about it in two relationships: problem-solving for strength, problem-solving for weakness. In problem-solving for strength, you want to help the teacher identify and understand a facilitative behavior. Use a strategy something like this:

1.   Identify a part of the lesson that was successful:
"What part of the lesson do you feel was especially successful?"

2.   Provide objective data that will confirm the teacher's perception:
"You're right, according to my observations. They all seemed to be on task in their small groups."

3.   Help the teacher understand in detail what he or she was doing and why that behavior produced the desired results:
"Why do you think they wasted such little time in their small groups?"

4.   Help the teacher decide how to use that behavior again:
"Do you see any way you can structure their small group work when they're working on language arts?"

Figure 9. Analyzing Your Conference Style

INDIRECT RESPONDING		INSTRUCTIONAL SOLVING		DIRECT MANAGING		OTHER TALLY
Category	*Tally*	*Category*	*Tally*	*Category*	*Tally*	
Accepts feelings		Assists in recalling lesson		Evaluates behavior		
Reflects feelings		Offers observational data		Analyzes behavior		
Probes others' feelings		Asks for information about lesson		Analyzes questions		
Expresses feelings		Focuses on problem		Advises		
Re-directs		Probes for causes		Criticizes		
Accepts ideas		Asks for ideas		Evaluates others' ideas		
Agrees		Offers research data		Makes suggestions		
Praises		Poses alternatives		Gives directions		
Encourages		Probes consequences		Expresses personal opinion		
Converses		Assists in evaluating consequences		Recounts personal experience		
TOTAL		TOTAL		TOTAL		

Total Recorded Utterances:_____ % Indirect_____ % Problem Solving_____ % Direct_____

Notes:

When you problem solve for weakness, you use a somewhat different strategy that moves, however, through similar stages.

1. Help the teacher identify a part of the lesson when all were not learning:
   "What part of the lesson did not satisfy you?"

2. Provide objective data that will confirm the teacher's perception:
   "I also noted that several seemed unclear about the concept."

3. Help the teacher understand in detail what he or she was doing and why that behavior was impeding learning:
   "Why do you think they seemed uncertain about the meaning of osmosis?"

4. Help the teacher consider some alterative teaching strategies that might have been more effective:
   "What helps you understand a new concept or idea that seems very abstract to you?"

5. Help the teacher make specific plans to use the alternative behavior in the future:
   "Let's think about a concept you will be teaching tomorrow and see if we can find several examples of that concept that will relate to their experience."

In each case you are trying to help the teacher do some intellectual problem-solving. You are neither telling nor just listening; you are an active participant in the pedagogical dialogue.

Modifying the Clinical Model

As we noted above, the clinical model is usually effective —but it is very time-consuming. There is a way to simplify it, without losing all of its benefits.

Begin by omitting the planning conference. Instead of holding the planning conference, ask the teacher to give you a written sketch of his or her general plans for the week. You might say something like this to the teacher "I would like to come by for a supervisory visit some time next week. Could I take a look at your lesson plan book for next week, or could you outline for me what you think you might be doing?" Most of all, are you trying to develop a helping relationship that, as the Credo notes, is authentic and mutual?

By checking the teacher's plans and your own schedule, choose a day and time when you think you will be able to observe a class and also hold a de-briefing conference. For example, if the teacher has a preparation period during period three, you might decide to observe the first period, blocking out period two in your appointment book to allow yourself some time to analyze the data and prepare for the conference. If the teacher has no preparation period, you might decide to observe between 1:15 and 2:00 p.m., allowing yourself time to analyze before you hold an after-school de-briefing session.

You then make the observation as you have planned it, analyze the observational data, and hold the post-observational conference the same day. The whole cycle has now been condensed into a one-day process involving only an hour and a half of your time.

Supervision of Instruction: A Developmental Approach

Glickman, C. D. 1990. 189–91. Boston: Allyn and Bacon.

Teacher Problem Solving as Cueing Information for Deciding Supervisory Approach

Expertise refers to the body of knowledge, or know-how, an individual or a group possesses for improving instruction. *Competence* refers to the performance of an individual or group of teachers in achieving desired learning results with students. Therefore expertise is the knowledge (training and experience) that one brings to instructional problems; competence is one's on-the-feet performance with students. The process of problem solving is an integration of expertise and competence. One puts knowledge into action via decision making. This section will outline the rational decision-making method as providing cues to the supervisor in deciding which approach to use when working with a teacher. The rational decision-making method will be explained rather than a more intuitive method because teachers' rational decision making has been correlated with measures of teacher effectiveness (Clark and Joyce 1976; Hunt and Sullivan 1974; Porter and Brophy 1988; Riley 1980). Keep in mind that there are exceptions to the rules. Some teachers appear to be more intuitive and spontaneous, yet run exceptionally fine classrooms. Therefore, not all good rational planners are good teachers, nor are all poor rational planners poor teachers. More good teachers display rational problem-solving abilities than not, but the ultimate criterion must be whether teachers are achieving desired individual and collective goals of student learning.

Rational decision making can be viewed as an eight-step procedure with three major phases:

A. Goal identification phase
1. Awareness of situations to be improved
2. Identifying causes of situation
3. Identifying the goal

B. Planning phase
4. Generating alternative actions
5. Exploring consequences
6. Selecting actions to be taken

C. Implementation phase
7. Testing selected actions
8. Reviewing results

Steps 1, 2, and 3 identify the goal; steps 4, 5, and 6 plan the actions to reach the goal; and steps 7 and 8 monitor the actions to see if the goal is being achieved. Obviously, it is difficult to plan and achieve a goal that has not been identified correctly. One study has shown that when supervisors were given problem scenarios and asked to identify problems, over 80 percent of their responses were solutions (Clinton, Glickman, and Payne 1982). In other words, most supervisors tend to leap before they look. Rational decision-making skills are important for supervisors as well as for teachers. A supervisor might use the eight-step decision-making procedure when deciding which interpersonal approach is appropriate with which teachers. We first use our own expertise or knowledge about interpersonal skills and our own competence to perform the interpersonal skills. We then look at the teacher's decision-making abilities, gather information about teacher proficiency, generate alternative approaches toward working with the teacher, choose one, and try it out. Asking ourselves the following questions when assessing an individual teacher can help:

1. Is the teacher aware of improvements that can be made in the classroom? Can the teacher identify those needs?
2. Has the teacher considered possible causes of the instructional needs? Does the teacher gather information from multiple sources about the instructional needs?
3. Can the teacher generate several possible solutions? How carefully does the teacher weigh the merits of each solution? Does the teacher consider what he or she can do to reach the goal without looking unrealistically for outside help?
4. Can the teacher be decisive in choosing a course of action? Does the teacher commit himself or herself to an implementation procedure?
5. Does the teacher do what he or she says?

These are some questions to answer in determining the necessary degree of intervention with nondirective, collaborative, or directive approaches. A teacher who shows no inclination to improve and is considered less than competent by those with responsibilities for formal teacher evaluation is appropriately matched with a directive controlling approach. A teacher who desires to improve his or her performance but is at a loss for what to do is appropriately matched with a directive informational approach. A teacher who is aware, knowledgeable, and decisive about instructional improvement is appropriately matched with a nondirective approach. This application is obviously a bit simplistic, since each teacher will have variations of awareness, commitment, and thought depending on the particular topic or situation under consideration.

References

Clark, C.M., and Joyce, B.R. 1976. Teacher decision making and teacher effectiveness. Paper presented at the annual meeting of the American Educational Research Association, San Francisco.

Clinton, B.C., Glickman, C.D., and Payne, D.A. 1982. Identifying supervision problems: A guide to better solutions. *Illinois School Research and Development* 9(1).

Hunt, D.E., and Sullivan, E.V. 1974. *Between psychology and education*. Hinsdale, Ill.: Dryden Press.

Porter, A.C., and Brophy, J. 1988. Synthesis of research on good teaching? Insights from the work of the Institute for Research on Teaching. *Educational Leadership* 45(8):74–85.

Riley, J.F. 1980. Creative problem solving and cognitive monitoring as instructional variables for teaching training in classroom problem solving. Unpublished Ed.D. dissertation, University of Georgia.

Changing Perspectives in Curriculum and Supervision

Nolan, J., and P. Francis. 1992. In *Supervision in transition, 1992 yearbook*, 52–60. Alexandria, Va.: Association for Supervision and Curriculum Development.

Supervisors as Collaborators in Creating Knowledge

Just as the teacher's role will change when students are seen as active partners in constructing knowledge, so too the supervisor's role will change when teachers are viewed as constructors of their own knowledge about learning and teaching. From its traditional perspective, supervision is viewed as a process intended to help teachers improve instruction. The supervisor often, intentionally or unintentionally, takes on the role of critic whose task is to judge the degree of congruence between the teacher's classroom behavior and the model of teaching that the teacher is trying to implement or the generic research on teaching. When the supervisor is viewed as a critic who judges the teacher's performance, supervision tends to concentrate on surface-level issues because the supervisor is denied access by the teacher to the dilemmas, issues, and problems that every teacher experiences and struggles with on an ongoing basis (Blumberg and Jonas 1987). These dilemmas and problems reach to the very heart of the teaching enterprise and cannot be resolved by simply adding new models to our repertoires of teaching behaviors. They must be confronted head on and resolved through action and reflection in the classroom (Schon 1983). Supervision should play a central role in understanding and resolving complex, perennial problems such as:

◆ how to reconcile individual student needs and interests with group needs and interests;

◆ how to balance the need to preserve student self-esteem with the need to provide students with honest feedback on their performance;

◆ how to balance student motivation against the need to teach prescribed content that may not match students' current needs or interests; and

◆ how to maintain a reasonable amount of order while still allowing sufficient flexibility for the intellectual freedom needed to pursue complex topics and issues.

When the supervisor relinquishes the role of critic to assume the role of co-creator of knowledge about learning and teaching, the teacher is more willing to grant the supervisor access to these core issues and dilemmas of teaching because the teacher does not have to fear a critique from the supervisor. Relinquishing the role of critic also benefits the supervisor by removing the awesome burden of serving as judge, jury, and director of the supervisory process.

When supervision is viewed as a process for generating knowledge about learning and teaching, data collection is transformed from a mechanism for documenting behavior to a mechanism for collecting information. This information can be used to deepen both teacher's and supervisor's understanding of the consequences of resolving problems, dilemmas, and issues in alternative ways. Conferences are also transformed. In the traditional conference scenario, the supervisor provides a neat, well-documented list of praiseworthy behaviors, as well as some suggestion for future improvement. When the supervisor relinquishes the role of critic, conferences become collaborative work sessions in which both teacher and supervisor try to make sense of the almost always messy data that are gathered in the process of relating teacher action to its consequences for learners. Finally, the outcomes of conferences are transformed. In most current practice, both partners sign written narrative critiques, which are filed away to collect dust until next year's observation. When teacher and supervisor become co-creators of knowledge, they produce jointly developed, tentative understandings of the learning-teaching process. These insights can then be tested against the reality of the classroom in future cycles of supervision.

To engage effectively in inquiry-oriented supervision, supervisors need a different type of expertise. They will need a passion for inquiry; commitment to developing an understanding of the process of learning and teaching; respect for teachers as equal partners in the process of trying to understand learning and teaching in the context of the teacher's particular classroom setting; and recognition that both partners contribute essential expertise to the process. They will also need to feel comfortable with the ambiguity and vulnerability of not having prefabricated answers to the problems that are encountered in the process. Supervisors will need to trust themselves, the teacher, and the process enough to believe that they can find reasonable and workable answers to complex questions and problems.

Greater Variety in Data Collection

The emphasis in traditional conceptions of learning on observable behavior, coupled with the emphasis on the teacher as the central actor, has resulted in the use of paper-and-pencil observation instruments as the primary and often sole vehicle for data gathering in supervision. When the supervisor's task is viewed as capturing the observable behavior of one actor (the teacher), paper-and-pencil instruments seem to work reasonably well. However, when learning is viewed as an active process of knowledge construction by the learner, student cognition becomes the critical element in the learning process. Learning is then seen as a collaborative process between teacher and learner, and the task of gathering useful data changes dramatically. Now, the data-gathering task becomes one of simultaneously capturing information about multiple actors which can be used to make inferences about the thinking processes that are occurring in the minds of the actors. This type of data collection requires supplementing paper-and-pencil instruments with a wide range of data-gathering techniques including audiotapes, videotapes, student products (essays, projects, tests), student interviews, and written student feedback regarding classroom events.

The use of multiple sources of data will bring about another important change in the expertise required of those who function as supervisors. The supervisor will need to become an expert in helping the teacher match various types of data collection strategies to the questions that are being addressed in the supervisory process and in helping the teacher interpret and reflect on the data that have been gathered. This change in the focus of data collection techniques will parallel closely the changes that have taken place in educational research techniques over the past decade. Just as the paper-and-pencil instruments used in the process-product research on teaching have been augmented by qualitative data collection strategies, so too observation and data collection in supervision can be expanded to include many more data sources. Data alone, however, are never sufficient. They never tell the full story. Only human judgment, in this case the collaborative judgment of teacher and supervisor, can give meaning to the richness of the learning-teaching process. Human judgment functions much more effectively in capturing that richness when it is augmented by a wide variety of data sources.

Garman (1990) points out an additional factor that comes into play when we view the goal of data collection as capturing student and teacher thinking: the development of thinking over time. Data collection currently is almost always accomplished by the observation of a single period of instruction.

> [A] lesson generally means an episodic event taken out of context within a larger unit of study. It is time to consider the unfolding lesson as a major concept in clinical supervision. We must find ways to capture how a teacher unfolds the content of a particular unit of study and how students, over time, encounter the content (Garman 1990, p. 212).

By collecting data over longer periods of instruction, we would be likely to obtain a much more complete picture of both teacher and student thinking. We would also capture a much richer portrait of the teacher's view of how the discipline should be represented for students. Although it might at first seem that collecting data over several periods of instruction requires additional time for observation by the supervisor, this is not necessarily the case. When the teacher becomes a collaborator in the process, and multiple data collection techniques are used (e.g., videotapes, student homework, student tests), the supervisor need not be present for every period of instruction during which data are gathered. The teacher can take primary responsibility for much of the data collection and then meet with the supervisor to jointly interpret and discuss the meaning of the data.

Greater Balance Between General Concerns and Content-Specific Issues and Questions

Given the renewed emphasis and research on content-specific learning and teaching, the focus of supervision should shift from total emphasis on general concerns to the inclusion of content-specific issues and questions. This does not mean that we should exclude general behaviors. To do so would clearly be a mistake because process-product research has been successful in identifying some behaviors that seem to transfer across content (Gage and Needels 1989). However, as Shulman (1987) has pointed out, excluding content-specific strategies from the supervisory process has also been a mistake. We need to balance content-specific issues and general issues.

On the surface at least, this need to expand the focus of supervision poses a dilemma for many schools. Principals, who supervise teachers in many different content areas, carry out much of the supervision that takes place in schools. The question is whether a generalist can be an effective supervisor when the supervisory process focuses not only on general concerns but also on content-specific strategies and methods. Given the new supervisory mindscape, we believe it is possible.

If the supervisor is viewed as a collaborator whose primary task is to help teachers reflect on and learn about their own teaching practices through the collection and interpretation of multiple sources of data, and the teacher who has content expertise is allowed to direct the process, it seems reasonable to think that content-specific issues could be addressed through supervision. In addition, if supervision is viewed as a function—not merely a role—to which many people in a school can contribute (Alfonso and Goldsberry 1982), it would also be possible to use a process of group supervision, peer coaching, or colleague consultation to help address content-specific issues, provided the peers have the appropriate preparation and skills.

Whatever personnel are used to carry out the process, the scope of supervision needs to be expanded to include questions such as these: What content should be taught to this group of students? Are the content and the instructional approaches being used compatible? What beliefs about the content and its general nature are being conveyed to students by the teacher's long-term approach to the subject matter? Are students acquiring the thinking and learning strategies that are most important for long-term success in the discipline?

Emphasis on Group Supervision

Just as students seem to benefit when they are placed in groups to cooperate with each other in the learning process, teachers seem to benefit when they are allowed to work together in groups to help each other learn about and refine the process of teaching (Little 1982). Teachers learn by watching each other teach. In addition, the new roles they take on and the perspectives they gain promote higher levels of thinking and cognitive development (Sprinthall and Thies-Sprinthall 1983). This benefits students because teachers who have reached higher cognitive-developmental levels tend to be more flexible and better able to meet individual student needs (Hunt and Joyce 1967). Collaborative practices have been endorsed and employed in staff development circles for several years; however, supervisory practice, which also aims at professional development, typically continues to occur on a one-to-one basis between supervisor and teacher.

We concur with Fullan (1990), who pointed out the necessity of linking collaboration to norms of continuous improvement:

> There is nothing particularly virtuous about collaboration per se. It can serve to block change or put students down as well as to elevate learning. Thus, collegiality must be linked to norms of continuous improvement and experimentation in which teachers are constantly seeking and assessing potentially better practices inside and outside their own school (p. 15).

Similarly, group supervision must be viewed as an activity whose primary aim is learning about and improving teaching. Teachers are sometimes uncomfortable when they are asked to confront tough questions about their own teaching. Collaboration and mutual support from colleagues can be vehicles for enabling teachers to risk facing those tough questions. However, there is a danger that collaboration can be wrongly viewed as meaning to support one another without rocking the boat or causing any discomfort. When this happens, collaboration can degenerate into a mechanism for skirting tough questions through unwarranted assurances that things are just fine. To avoid this degeneration, all participants must understand that learning about the instructional process and improving student learning are the primary goals of group supervision. Collaboration is a means to an end, not an end in itself. It is a mechanism for providing support as teachers engage in the sometimes disquieting, uncomfortable process of learning.

Given the research on cooperative learning and teacher collegiality, we hypothesize that if supervision were carried out as a group process in which the supervisors and teachers were interdependent in achieving group and individual goals, the process of supervision would become more effective in helping teachers learn about and improve their teaching. In addition, enabling those teachers who may be less committed to growth to work together in groups with colleagues who are more committed to the process may be an effective strategy for creating shared norms that are supportive of the supervisory process. In discussing the concept of collaborative cultures, Hargreaves and Dawe (1989) eloquently describe what supervision might become when it is viewed as a cooperative group process. "It is a tool of teacher empowerment and professional enhancement, bringing colleagues and their expertise together to generate critical yet also practically-grounded reflection on what they do as a basis for more skilled action" (p. 7).

What we have labeled "the changing mindscape on learning and teaching" demands a new mindscape on supervision, a mindscape grounded in the following principles and beliefs:

◆ The primary purpose of supervision is to provide a mechanism for teachers and supervisors to increase their understanding of the learning-teaching process through collaborative inquiry with other professionals.

◆ Teachers should not be viewed only as consumers of research, but as generators of knowledge about learning and teaching.

◆ Supervisors must see themselves not as critics of teaching performance, but rather as collaborators with teachers in attempting to understand the problems, issues, and dilemmas that are inherent in the process of learning and teaching.

◆ Acquiring an understanding of the learning-teaching process demands the collection of many types of data, over extended periods of time.

◆ The focus for supervision needs to be expanded to include content-specific as well as general issues and questions.

◆ Supervision should focus not only on individual teachers but also on groups of teachers who are engaged in ongoing inquiry concerning common problems, issues, and questions.

These principles and beliefs are not completely new. They closely parallel the principles of clinical supervision as endorsed by Cogan (1973) and Goldhammer (1969). Unfortunately, these principles have not been widely adopted. We believe that the changing perspectives on learning and teaching provide a powerful impetus for putting these principles of supervision into practice. When these concepts begin to touch the mainstream of supervisory practice, supervision is much more likely to have a positive impact on teacher thinking, teacher behavior, and student learning.

References

Alfonso, R.J., and L. Goldsberry. (1982). "Colleagueship in Supervision." In *Supervision of Teaching*, edited by T.J. Sergiovanni. Alexandria, Va.: ASCD.

Anderson, L.M. (1989). "Classroom Instruction." In *Knowledge Base for the Beginning Teacher*, edited by M.C. Reynolds. New York:

Pergamon Press and the American Association of Colleges of Teacher Education.

Blumberg, A., and R.D. Jonas. (1987). "Permitting Access: The Teacher's Control Over Supervision." *Educational Leadership* 44, 8:12–16.

Brandt, R. (1988–89). "On Learning Research: A Conversation with Lauren Resnick." *Educational Leadership* 46, 4:12–16.

Brandt, R. (1989–90) "On Cooperative Learning: A Conversation with Spencer Kagan." *Educational Leadership* 47, 4:8–11.

Bransford J.D. and N.J. Vye. (l989). "A Perspective on Cognitive Research and Its Implications for Instruction." In *Toward the Thinking Curriculum: Current Cognitive Research*, edited by L.B. Resnick and L.E. Klopfer. Alexandria, Va.: ASCD.

Brooks, J.G. (1990). "Teachers and Students: Constructivists Forging New Connections." *Educational Leadership* 47, 5: 68–71.

Buchman, M. (1984). "The Priority of Knowledge and Understanding in Teaching." In *Advances in Teacher Education. Vol. 1*, edited by L.G. Katz and J.D. Raths Norwood, N.J.: Ablex.

Cochran-Smith, M., and S.L. Lytle. (1990). "Research on Teaching and Teacher Research: Issues That Divide." *Educational Researcher* 19, 2: 2–11.

Cogan, M. (1973). *Clinical Supervision*. Boston: Houghton-Mifflin.

Dewey, J. (1902). *The Child and the Curriculum*. Chicago: University of Chicago Press.

Fullan, M. (1990). "Staff Development, Innovation, and Institutional Development." In *Changing School Culture Through Staff Development. The 1990 ASCD Yearbook*, edited by B. Joyce. Alexandria, Va.: ASCD.

Gage, N.L., and M.C. Needels. (1989). "Process-Product Research on Teaching: A Review of Criticisms." *Elementary School Journal* 89, 3: 253–300.

Garman, N.B. (1986). "Reflection: The Heart of Clinical Supervision: A Modern Rationale for Professional Practice." *Journal of Curriculum and Supervision* 2,1: 1–24.

Garman, N.B. (1990). "Theories Embedded in the Events of Clinical Supervision: A Hermeneutic Approach." *Journal of Curriculum and Supervision* 5,3: 201–213.

Goldhammer, R. (1969). *Clinical Supervision: Special Methods for the Supervision of Teachers*. New York: Holt, Rinehart, and Winston.

Hargreaves, A., and R. Dawe. (1989). "Coaching as Unreflective Practice." Paper presented at the Annual Meeting of the American Educational Research Association, San Francisco.

Henry, G. (1986). "What Is the Nature of English Education?" *English Education* 18, 1: 4–41.

Hunt, D.E., and B.R. Joyce. (1967). "Teacher Trainee Personality and Initial Teaching Style." *American Educational Research Journal* 4: 253–59.

Joyce, B., and B. Showers. (1988). *Student Achievement Through Staff Development*. New York: Longman.

Lampert, M. (1990). "When the Problem is not the Question and the Solution is not the Answer: Mathematical Knowing and Teaching." *American Educational Research Journal* 27,1: 293.

Little, J. (1982). "Norms of Collegiality and Experimentation: Workplace Conditions of School Success." *American Educational Research Journal* 5, 19: 325–340.

Perkins, D.N., and G. Salomon. (1989). "Are Cognitive Skills Context-Bound?" *Educational Researcher* 8, 1: 16–25.

Putnam, R. (1990). "Recipes and Reflective Learning: 'What Would Prevent You from Saying It That Way?'" Paper presented at the Annual Meeting of the American Educational Research Association, Boston.

Resnick, L.B., and L.E. Klopfer. (1989). *Toward the Thinking Curriculum: Current Cognitive Research*. Alexandria, Va.: ASCD.

Schlechty, P.C. (1990). *Schools for the 21st Century*. San Francisco: Jossey-Bass.

Schon, D.A. (1983). *The Reflective Practitioner*. San Francisco: Jossey-Bass.

Schon, D.A. (1989). "Coaching Reflective Teaching." In *Reflection in Teacher Education*, edited by P.P. Grimmet and G.P. Erickson. New York: Teachers College Press.

Sergiovanni, T.J. (1985). "Landscapes, Mindscapes, and Reflective Practice in Supervision." *Journal of Curriculum and Supervision* 1, 1: 5–17.

Shulman, L.S. (1987). "Knowledge and Teaching: Foundations of the New Reform." *Harvard Educational Review* 57: 1–22.

Shulman, L.S. (1990). "Transformation of Content Knowledge." Paper presented at the Annual Meeting of the American Educational Research Association, Boston.

Slavin, R.E. (1989–90). "Research on Cooperative Learning: Consensus and Controversy. *Educational Leadership* 47, 4: 52–54.

Sprinthall, N.A., and L. Thies-Sprinthall. (1983). "The Teacher as Adult Learner: A Cognitive Developmental View." In *Staff Development. 82nd Yearbook of the National Society for the Study of Education*, edited by G.A. Griffin. Chicago: University of Chicago Press.

Wilson, S.M., L.S. Shulman, and A.E. Richert. (1987). "150 Different Ways of Knowing: Representations of Knowledge in Teaching." In *Exploring Teachers' Thinking*, edited by J. Calderhead. London: Cassel.

The Role of the Principal in the Ongoing Education of Teachers

Ristau, Karen. 1989. In *Reflections of the role of the Catholic school principal*, ed. R. Kealey, 57–60. Washington, D.C.: National Catholic Educational Association.

Reflection is a good thing. "Endless drama in a group clouds consciousness. Too much noise overwhelms the senses," says John Heidler in *The Tao of Leadership*. When we reflect, we can see more clearly what has happened and what is essential. In this brief reading, take time to step back and ponder the drama of adult development within the role of teacher and the responsibility of the leader in that process.

The Context

Teacher inservice has been around for a long time in the educational enterprise. In recent years, we use new vocabulary; we now talk about staff development. This newer term, staff development, has also become the current trend, the front page story. It is seen as a cure-all, an elixir for all the ills of schooling. Many educators are planning for, talking about, attending to, scheduling around, and even hiring special personnel to do staff development. I, on the other hand, am apprehensive about it! Education has had other antibiotics: accountability, tracking, effectiveness, individualization, and homogeneous grouping are some that come to mind. These terms are either a faint part of educational practice today, or have been shelved in the back of a medicine cabinet. My fear is the same thing will happen to staff development. It will go the way of other buzz words. Or worse still, it will be poorly done and Catholic school leaders will decide it either takes time which they do not have, or money and extra personnel of which they have even less.

Instead I would like to remind principals that staff development is an essential part of schools we do not dare let slip away. It is more important than some tasks we allow to fill our time, and it does not need great expenditures of money to do it well. Further, reflection upon the traditions and rituals of adult education in the church can offer educators a model for appropriate staff development.

The Need

Staff development, the on-going education of school personnel, has come into the limelight at this time for a variety of reasons. Perhaps it is because in some areas, schools are staffed by very young teachers, or in other areas, schools are filled with teachers whose length of service is between 15 and 25 years. New teachers need to refine skills once actually employed in school settings. Older and more stable faculties need to be excited about their work. Further, in recent years, the educational field has become rich with advanced knowledge about the teaching/learning process. This is information many need to acquire and utilize. Yet somehow staff development is necessary for reasons beyond these.

Staff development is about the real stuff of education. It is about new things. It is about deepening and broadening one's wisdom, improving one's skills, and increasing and enriching one's teaching techniques. It is life-long learning. It is paying attention to one's own scholarship. It focuses on all those things we say we believe as teachers. We must believe them for ourselves as well. Staff development is for teachers and also for principals. But it is the responsibility of the principal to see that staff development happens in the school.

Christian Context

The Catholic school is established in and draws strength from the life of the church community. It is that reality which brings us to share in the mystery of growth, liberation, and fulfillment. The theology of the Catholic church reflected in its sacramental life has never suggested we, as adults, are a finished product, that there is no more to know, no more to do. We are called to something ever new, to a level of relationship with God ever deeper. We can and do begin again. Our tradition is to look upon our lives as a journey, to envision ourselves a part of the pilgrim church. Our work is part of that journeying event.

The leaders and the teachers are often culled from unfamiliar surroundings, from a permanent oasis, to put forth to an unknown land. Children present a spectrum of joys, heart-rending problems, curiosities, difficulties, questions, talents and gifts which tug at the teacher's capabilities to fulfill students' needs. Parents present no less an array of comforts and challenges. Staff development assures, as the faculty strives to meet these demands, as they venture out seeking new ways, that journeyers do not become wanderers.

Process of Staff Development

Looking at staff development as a process rather than as a program would be more in keeping with this idea. "Program" presents images of set times, set topics, specific occasions, speakers, outside resources, something compartmentalized. Although some of these things will be included in staff development, it could be more helpful to consider the importance of "process," of journey, not "program."

Process brings to mind another set of images. It implies other activities, different ways of providing information and assistance, more conversations. There does not seem to be any compulsiveness or frenzy about the events. It suggests openness, changes at different times and occasions, a sense of rhythm that fits one's personal development, enough time to be respectful of persons, and to care for each teacher as a learner. The process of staff development pays attention to what is known about an adult learner.

Making Connections: Teaching and the Human Brain

Caine, R. N., and G. Caine. 1991. 105–06, 154–58.
Alexandria, Va.: Association for Supervision and Curriculum Development.

Indicators of Understanding: Evaluation

As educators, we have to be able to see that a learner understands. It is appropriate, of course, to use some formal tests and measures of performance in the assessment program. We suggest, however, that most formal testing simply measures limited aspects of the acquisition of surface knowledge. This is particularly true of multiple-choice questions. The use of such testing must be limited because it often forecloses on the options available to learners and changes the conditions of the performance. It has been said, for instance, that "behaviorally stated objectives reduce wasted time in temporary diversions, ephemeral entertainment, or other irrelevancies" (Popham 1968, quoted in Jenkins and Deno 1971). Our point is that those "irrelevancies" often include both the context and the creative insights that are indispensable for meaningful learning.

A solution that we find extremely practical is to evaluate our students by combining *measures of complex performance* with *indicators of understanding*. These emerge quite readily if we look at the acquisition of felt meaning and the development of natural knowledge in the workplace and elsewhere. We are asking exactly the same question when we seek to discover whether our child is learning to speak, whether a person has mastered a hobby, or whether someone really is an expert in a particular domain. What we use at work and at home are indicators of complex performance in real and often unplanned tasks. An expert, for example, is a person who can react appropriately in both predictable and unpredictable situations. A superb example is the capacity to engage in a conversation that unexpectedly calls one's knowledge into play. This happens all the time in the workplace and in social gatherings, whether we are talking about computers, change in Eastern Europe, art, or finance. We use similar indicators of unexpected competence to tell us that a child has genuinely begun to speak. At other times, a problem will be presented for which there is no known answer. The expert is the person who can be reliably called on to work on and solve the problem.

We can translate such evaluations into educational applications by developing complex contexts that call for competent performance and for both predictable and unpredictable, but appropriate, behaviors. Our task is to know when and how to look for evidence of understanding. It can be done. This contextual assessment is discussed further in Chapter 11.

Active Processing in Action

Here are some examples of the types of activities that can be used to encourage active processing.

Have students become resident experts in some field so that they are the ones who need to inform and assist other students. Their support may take the form of answering questions, helping to design projects, and providing advice. This takes advantage of peer teaching and provides invaluable feedback to teachers.

Simulate panels and discussion groups of various sorts, such as TV talk shows, presidential debates, United Nations forums, and congressional hearings. Simulate other real events. We know of a Spanish language class, for example, in which one half of the students act as the residents of a town, taking on the roles of shopkeepers and other inhabitants; and the rest of the class act as tourists.

Other classes engage in full congressional proceedings for the purpose of dealing with some social problem, such as pollution. One excellent example is the nationwide "law and community" project, in which students take the roles of advocates and jurors and argue socially relevant cases before panels of practicing lawyers and judges. At the college level, we have seen students develop sophisticated plans for community development: law students play a role in legal aid, engineering students participate in the development of solar power vehicles, and so on.

Elementary and secondary school students can also participate in community events, though in less sophisticated ways. In addition, students and teachers need to explore in more depth the power of the arts. For example, there are several outstanding programs in which students are given the opportunity to develop their singing, dancing, and other artistic talents and where their participation is directly linked to the content of their school curriculum in history or science.

There is a key to doing all this effectively. Some students may wish to develop professional expertise, whereas others may seek to win competitions. *It is extremely important, however, that many of the activities we discuss have no direct bearing on grades.* The students need to experience the joy of participating and to have the opportunity to be creative. They will receive more than enough feedback to give them a sense of what the community values. They must also have the freedom to experiment.

Testing and Evaluation

It should be apparent that much of what is done to aid processing is open-ended. Students are invited to explore

Figure 11.1 Checklist of Useful Questions

- ◆ Are students involved and challenged?
- ◆ Is there clear evidence of student creativity and enjoyment? Are students dealing appropriately with dissonance?
- ◆ Are students being exposed to content in many ways that link content to life?
- ◆ Are students' life themes and metaphors being engaged?
- ◆ Are there "hooks" that tie the content together in a big picture that itself can make sense to students?
- ◆ Is there some sort of continuity, such as through projects and ongoing stories, so that content is tied together and retains interest over time?
- ◆ Is there any sign of continuing motivation or student interest that expresses itself above and beyond the dictates of the class?
- ◆ Is the physical context being used optimally?
- ◆ What do the setting, decorations, architecture, layout, music, and other features of the context actually "say" to students?
- ◆ What sort of group atmosphere is emerging?
- ◆ Are there any signs of positive collaboration, and do they continue after the lesson and after school?
- ◆ Do students have opportunities to reorganize content in creative and personally relevant ways?
- ◆ Are there opportunities to reflect in an open-ended way on what does and does not make sense?
- ◆ Are students given the opportunity to apply the material in different contexts?
- ◆ Do students consciously and deliberately examine their performances in those different contexts and begin to appreciate their own strengths and weaknesses?

content in their own ways and express themselves uniquely. Yet it is also essential that students acquire socially prescribed information and skills. In practice neither is possible with a system of testing and evaluation that is mechanical, limited, and fixed. The reason is that our methods of evaluation govern the way we teach and the freedom to learn. The result is precisely what we have—a majority of teachers teaching to simplistic tests, teaching for memorization, and thereby limiting what else students can learn and the connections they can make.

Indicators of Performance and Understanding

As already stated, a solution that we find extremely practical is to evaluate our students by combining measures of complex performance with indicators of understanding. Teachers must dramatically extend the range of observations that they can make of students. Standardized tests are not excluded. They simply become a relatively small part of the global evaluation process. Immersion and active processing tend to come together here. We take advantage of the entire gamut of activities in which the students engage for the purpose of genuine grasping and coming to appreciate what they know.

This approach to evaluation can be systematized to some extent as follows, although this area is one educators urgently need to develop.

Performance in Multiple Contexts. Natural knowledge is knowledge that can be applied in real-world situations. Hence, we need to provide our students with realistic contexts within which to call on ideas and skills. Rather than ask questions about computers, for instance, we might ask them to build a database to record class attendance.

Their reading skill is shown in their ability to follow instructions that come with new equipment or in their ability to find information on current events as reported in the press. And dealing with numbers is involved in everything from weaving and art to managing the finances for a class outing or field trip.

Ability to Question. It is a maxim in many professions that a key to success is not knowing the answer but knowing how to find it. Similarly, a manager knows that new employees are beginning to have a sense of felt meaning for the job when they ask penetrating questions. We therefore suggest that the same ability be invoked by educators as an indicator that a student is acquiring felt meaning. Critical indicators of acquiring felt meaning for a new subject include (1) being able to ask the right questions, (2) knowing how to find the answers, and (3) knowing what to do with the answers.

Appropriate Performance in Unexpected Situations. Students need to be able to do more than perform in scheduled, planned situations. Such performance is indicative of competence, but not necessarily of understanding and natural knowledge. Students need to be able to respond appropriately to unanticipated events. An expert, for example, is a person who can react appropriately but often unpredictably in unanticipated situations. A superb example is the capacity to engage in a conversation that unexpectedly calls one's knowledge into play. This happens all the time in the workplace and in social gatherings, whether the conversation is about computers, changes in Eastern Europe, art, or finance. Similar indicators of competence in spontaneous or unexpected interactions can serve to tell us that a child has genuinely begun to synthesize what has been learned. This does not exclude times when a problem will be presented for which there is no known answer. The expert is the person who can be reliably called on to work on and solve the problem.

Evaluation Guidelines

We suggest that there are at least four relevant indicators that guide evaluation:

◆ The ability to use the language of the discipline or subject in complex situations and in social interaction.
◆ The ability to perform appropriately in unanticipated situations.
◆ The ability to solve real problems using the skills and concepts.
◆ The ability to show, explain, or teach the idea or skill to another person who has a real need to know.

The 15 questions in Figure 11.1 introduce general indicators of what should be taking place during brain-based learning. These questions underlie effective performance and the expansion of natural knowledge. They provide us with indicators concerning whether students are acquiring relaxed alertness, are being adequately immersed in orchestrated experience, and are being sufficiently active in processing their experience. Regardless of what particular educational model educators use, the key is the adequate engagement of the brain.

Cautions on Evaluations

Brain-based teaching demands a critical look at current methods of evaluation. First, it is impossible to communicate the scope and depth of a student's abilities by means of a letter or numerical grade. In business, an employee often has a performance appraisal. It includes assessments by nominated people, as well as observed performance on complex tasks. When done well, this is a complex, global and useful evaluation. This type of evaluation is also a helpful model for teaching.

Second, students' self-concept is also shaped by the type of feedback they get and the manner in which it is communicated. Whereas a student journal is an invaluable source of information regarding how a student really thinks, grading it or writing detached and insensitive comments can be quite destructive. All forms of assessment affect our feelings and perceived self. The more we risk personally, the more destructive simplistic evaluation will be.

Finally, there is a difference between looking for indicators and counting numbers of specific responses. One child may ask just one question and reveal profound understanding, whereas another may ask many questions and yet be relatively ignorant. There is a difference, therefore, between quality and quantity. That poses a challenge for teachers, because it is difficult to monitor what is happening in the classroom and also remember all the possible indicators and criteria. In our experience, the solution is for educators to acquire a grasp of these indicators as a part of their own natural knowledge. *Educators, in effect, must be experts at recognizing expertise in students.* This becomes easier when educators grasp the essence of levels of meaning and begin to identify real shifts in thinking.

Reference

Jenkins, J.R., and S.L. Deno. (1971). "Influence of Knowledge and Type of Objectives on Subject Matter Learning." *Journal of Educational Psychology* 62: 67–70.

School Leader as Motivator

Maehr, Martin L., Carol Midgley, and Timothy Urdan. 1992.
Educational Administration Quarterly 28(3):410–29.

Authors' Note: The authors are indebted to many colleagues, particularly Carole Ames.

These are turbulent times for schools. There are daily calls for reform, renewal, or restructuring (e.g., Cuban, 1990). There are regular reports on how the calls are being answered or ignored (e.g., Chira, 1991). There are fears that today's answers may be tomorrow's failures (Sarason, 1990). And as is so often true, there is a tendency to place these problems at the feet of the leaders with a succinct demand: DO SOMETHING!

But what can a leader do? Our answer is simple and direct: The leader can motivate. For a school to be effective, it must elicit the best efforts of all those concerned. The "bottom line" is the investment of children in learning. Of the multiple roles that school leaders play (see Sergiovanni, 1990), none is more critical than the one that is the subject of this article: school leader as motivator (see Gardner, 1990). As self-evidently important as the leadership-motivation connection may be, there has been surprisingly little systematic study of how leaders can elicit motivation. Generally, the literature reflects a greater interest in motives, beliefs, and personal predilections of leaders than on how leaders can enhance the motivation of followers (e.g., McClelland & Boyatzis, 1982). Indeed, it is interesting and curious that to this point, the literatures on motivation and leadership have, for all practical purposes, gone their own and separate ways. A notable exception is the work of Sergiovanni (1990), but he focused primarily on the motivation of school staff and only indirectly on how this translated into student motivation and learning.

We base this article on the assumption that leadership and motivation are more than incidentally related. Indeed, we argue that school leaders play an important role in determining the personal investment of students. More than argue, we will describe a program of research that demonstrates how they can play this role.

A Perspective on Leadership

Our research leads to the proposal that school leaders affect student motivation. They do so as they inaugurate, support, maintain, allow, or permit certain policies, practices, and procedures. Their action or inaction frames the learning environment of the school, that facet of the culture that is especially associated with the purposes of teaching and learning. As leadership and staff deal with fundamental questions of school management, they inevitably reflect a rationale for teaching and learning. They define the meaning of school for students and thereby affect the nature and quality of student investment.

Goals and Purposes

Recent research on motivation and school achievement has concentrated especially on the role of purposes and goals in determining the nature and degree of student investment in learning (Ames & Ames, 1989; Dweck, 1985; Maehr & Pintrich, 1991; Nicholls, 1992; Pervin, 1989). This work has generally revolved around two contrasting types of goals: "Task focused" and "ability focused." Given an ability focus, children will be concerned with being judged able (or avoiding being judged not able), with ability being evidenced by outperforming others or by achieving success even when the task is easy. In contrast, with a task focus, the goal of learning is to gain understanding, insight, or skill, to accomplish something that is challenging. Learning is the goal. The acquisition of knowledge and the attainment of mastery is seen as dependent on one's effort.

As children define the purpose of learning, there are profound motivational consequences. The goals they accept in performing a task are likely to affect their inclination to try hard, take on or avoid challenges, or persist or give up when faced with failure (Ames, 1984; Dweck & Leggett, 1988; Elliott & Dweck, 1988; Maehr, 1989; Nicholls, 1984). Different goals lead to broadly different approaches to learning and ultimately different learning outcomes. Children with a task orientation tend to use deep-processing strategies, including discriminating important from unimportant information, trying to figure out how new information fits with what one already knows, and monitoring comprehension. Children with an ability focus tend to use surface-level strategies, including rereading text, memorizing, and rehearsing (Golan & Graham, 1990; Meece, Blumenfeld, & Hoyle, 1988; Meece & Holt, 1990; Nolen, 1988; Powell, 1990). As such, goals are likely to affect understanding and retention (Anderson, 1980; Entwistle & Ramsden, 1983) as well as creativity (Archer, 1990). In brief, goal orientation has been shown to have a pervasive influence on the nature and quality of student motivation and learning.

Goals and the Learning Environment

That goals play such a role is noteworthy. Equally important is that the learning environment influences the goals that students adopt.

Implicit within any given learning environment is a differential stress on task and ability goals, a stress that affects how students approach learning. Thus recent research indicates that classrooms vary in how learning is defined and that these definitions affect the goals that students adopt, thereby influencing their motivation and learning (Ames & Archer, 1988; Meece et al., 1988; Nicholls Cobb, Wood, Yackel, & Patashnick, 1990; Nolen, 1988; Nolen & Haladyna, in press; Pintrich & DeGroot, 1990; Pintrich & Garcia, 1991; Powell, 1990).

Parallel to research at the classroom level, research indicates that *schools as a whole* reflect different goal stresses (Krug, 1989; Maehr, 1991; Maehr & Anderman, in press; Maehr & Buck, in press; Maehr & Fyans, 1989; Maehr & Midgley, 1991). Just as the smaller unit of the classroom has been found to define learning, it now appears that the larger unit of the school may likewise define learning and therewith have a pervasive influence on student motivation. Indeed, that goal stresses in the school as a whole may exist and have an influence on student investment in learning is a singularly important finding. Although students are exposed to different classrooms and a variety of curricular and cocurricular experiences, they are also exposed to pervasive schoolwide influences.

Changing the Definition of Learning and School

Armed with evidence that differential schoolwide stresses on task and ability goals are likely to affect the quality of student motivation and learning, a number of questions arise. What happens in a school context that results in a greater stress on task and a lesser stress on ability goals? Are these antecedent factors amenable to change? How do leaders effect such change? Answering these questions is a crucial next step in our program of research. That next step is under way. A progress report follows.

We initiated a program of intervention research in collaboration with a public school district situated in the greater metropolitan area of Detroit. The area embraced by the school district is a collection of housing areas interspersed by shopping centers, sprinkled with an assortment of small businesses and dominated by massive automobile manufacturing and assembly plants. The ill-defined urban sprawl is given some measure of cohesiveness and unity by the school district that now embraces it. The district serves a largely blue-collar population, with many of the parents in the district employed by the automotive industry and affected significantly by the economic fortunes of this industry. Currently, 16% of the students are African American, and 37% of the students qualify for the free or reduced-fee lunch program. As is true in many area communities, this district has had difficulty passing millage issues and has been engaged in serious and prolonged contract disputes. Individual teachers often exhibit creative approaches to instruction, but most would describe the curriculum, organization, and design of the schools in this district as "traditional."

We presented the project to the superintendent and director of instruction as well as to school leaders and staff as a collaborative effort. A school-university coalition would examine schoolwide policies, procedures, and practices and attempt to change those that militated against a focus on task goals. School staff, of course, were to play a major role in deciding what changes would be attempted and how such attempts would be managed. University staff primarily were to provide a framework for evaluating policy and practice options, interpreting them in terms of likely implications for student motivation and learning. A number of the schools expressed a willingness, in some cases a strong interest, in collaborating with us in this effort. After much deliberation, we selected one elementary school and one middle school to serve as "demonstration" schools and two schools in the same district to serve as "comparison" schools.

Additional features of our approach merit special comment (see Maehr & Midgley, 1991). We designed the intervention to engage the staff as a whole in the process. However, the focus of change was to be in the hands of a school leadership team. Thus the collaboration required the participation of not only the principal or an administrator but the teachers. For schoolwide changes to occur, both teachers and administrators must invest in the endeavor (see Rowan, Raudenbush, & Kang, 1991).

Operationally, the collaboration has proceeded as follows. Each week, a group from the university, consisting of two faculty members and six graduate students, meets for at least 1 hour with the leadership team of each school. At the elementary school, the leadership team initially consisted of the principal and members of a previously organized school improvement team. This team has now expanded to include approximately one third of the teachers in the school. The leadership team at the middle school consists of the assistant principal and a core group of five teachers, although we often have as many as 10 teachers at the meetings.

It is noteworthy that the school leadership teams have increasingly sought out their own ways to evaluate the current state of affairs and make plans for change. With information provided by the university group, leadership team members from both the elementary and middle schools visited other schools and programs. Both also invited outside experts on specific topics to present a case for one or another programmatic option. In all cases, these were staff members from other schools or school districts, and the focus was on the question of how one actually *does* something. The middle school staff held a special retreat on a selected Saturday, which they attended without reimbursement. The elementary school devoted several in-service days to options under discussion. In both the elementary and middle schools, certain staff members, including teachers who were not on the leadership team, began meeting on their own time to develop plans for specific programmatic action. In short, it is currently no longer a process in which

a school-university committee is doing the evaluating, the planning, and the acting. The school-university coalition has become the forum for coordinating what is happening —the hub around which the action revolves. But the action is clearly happening elsewhere: in various small groups and in late afternoon meetings in classrooms, over the phone, and over coffee on the weekend—as one would hope.

The focus of the effort from the research team's standpoint is understanding how change in school learning environments occurs. The primary goal of the school district and the participating schools is to effect change. We have agreed to operate within a theoretical framework that specifies the effects of goal stresses on motivation and learning. Together we are constructing knowledge about how schoolwide policy, practice, and procedures create these goal stresses.

Fortunately, there is a body of research that suggests possible guidelines for our efforts. Work broadly directed toward enhancing student motivation at the classroom level (e.g., Brophy, 1987; deCharms, 1976) was initially of considerable help. But the primary basis for action was a growing literature on how classroom practices increase students' perceptions of a task (or ability) focus and thereby affect their motivation and learning (see, e.g., Ames, 1990; MacIver, 1991; Meece, 1991; Nicholls et al., 1990). With some reason to believe that schoolwide practices might have analogous effects (see Baden & Maehr, 1986; Good & Weinstein, 1986; Maehr, 1991), we proceeded to hypothesize that one could increase the stress on task and decrease the stress on ability by (a) providing meaningful, challenging, contextualized tasks; (b) giving students an increased sense of control over their schooling through choice and decision-making opportunities; (c) recognizing students on the basis of their progress, effort, and improvement rather than on their performance compared to others; (d) grouping students heterogeneously and on the basis of interest rather than on the basis of relative ability; (e) using evaluation as a way to provide helpful feedback to students rather than to tell them how they compare to others; (f) allowing all students, regardless of their academic ability or attitudinal disposition, equal access to school resources, both tangible (e.g., computers, lab equipment) and intangible (e.g., participation in extracurricular activities); and (g) allowing some flexibility in how teachers and students use time during the school day to allow for innovative, interdisciplinary instruction and the pursuit of interests.

In summary, we identified seven areas that school leaders could examine in attempting to affect the learning environment of the school. In the following sections, we describe these areas of school activities in greater detail, illustrate their importance for student motivation, and suggest how leaders can promote a schoolwide task focus.

Antecedents of a Task-focused Learning Environment

Research by ourselves and others, discussions with the teachers and administrators at the two demonstration sites, and informal observations of the daily practices at these schools have given us insights into the dimensions of the school environment that influence the goal stresses in schools.

The Nature of Academic Tasks

The nature of the learning task is a first and critical feature of the school learning environment (Brophy & Alleman, 1991; Blumenfeld, Mergendoller, & Swarthout, 1987). Current reform efforts stress the need to move toward curricula that emphasize contextualized tasks and active learning rather than discrete facts and rote learning (Murphy & Beck, in press). The types of tasks that students undertake in the classroom can, in large part, determine the types of goals they will pursue and consequently their level of investment in school. For example, students can be given tasks that are relevant to their lives and require creative thinking and problem solving, or they can receive a daily dose of drill-and-practice dittos. In the former case, students are more likely to adopt task-focused goals and become personally invested; in the latter case, they are likely to adopt ability-focused goals, finding little intrinsic value in the activities involved. Indeed, given the inherent drudgery and boredom involved, teachers are likely to find themselves resorting to a variety of extrinsic incentives, ranging from tangible rewards to grades. They may even engender competition in the hope that this will make the task interesting. At some point, there will likely be a threat of punishment or failure. The nature of the tasks that children are required to do is often the first step in the process of determining whether they adopt a task-focused or an ability-focused goal orientation.

School leaders can and do play an important role in determining what children will be asked to do. Heck, Larsen, and Marcoulides (1990) found that one of the defining characteristics of effective principals is their direct involvement in decisions about curriculum and instructional strategies. Schoolwide resources and attention can be invested in activities that challenge students, stimulate the use of higher-order thinking skills, and engage their intrinsic interest. School policy—*and* school leaders—can stress adherence to textbooks or encourage teachers to think broadly and creatively about academic tasks, including interviewing knowledgeable persons, surveying constituencies, providing hands-on and project-oriented activities, allowing for independent study, facilitating field trips, and countless other possibilities. Teachers can be given (and expected to use) "teacher proof" materials, such as certain texts, worksheets, and preplanned exercises—or be given the freedom to design and use tasks that are action oriented, that flow from the interests of the students, and that are challenging and creative (see Meece, 1991). Indeed, as Hallinger, Bickman, and Davis (1990) suggested, it may be that one of the most powerful ways in which school leaders shape the environment of the school is by encouraging teachers to take risks and be creative in designing instructional tasks.

The point is that teachers alone do not decide what students do in the classroom. These decisions are also made in direct and subtle ways by school leaders when curricular issues are discussed and decided, teachers are recognized for their work, news reports are filed, textbooks are chosen, state mandates are interpreted, in-service training is planned, and resources are allocated. Everyday decisions by school leaders—their implicit and explicit gestures, their actions or inaction, the content of their communication to the central administration and to parents—influence the range of learning activities that will be made available to students. Thereby, they also define the operative meaning and purpose of learning for students.

Opportunities for Student Initiative and Responsibility

Schools vary considerably in the degree to which they grant opportunities for choice, initiative, and responsibility to students (Midgley & Feldlaufer, 1987). Motivation research indicates that this is likely to affect the goals and purposes that students adopt for their life in school (Ames, 1990; Deci, 1975; Deci & Ryan, 1985). As school leaders work toward enhancing the opportunities for student initiative and responsibility, they are likely to increase the task focus among students.

Long ago, John Dewey emphasized that the classroom can be an important precursor for participation in a democratic society. That is doubtless correct. To that we add: Participation in decision making by students leads to views of the nature of the school's mission, its relevance to their lives, and the intrinsic worth of learning (see Nicholls, 1989).

Recognition

Recognition consists of at least three parts. One part is *what* is recognized. Honor rolls that recognize students for getting higher grades than their classmates likely detract from a task goal focus. The goal becomes the demonstration of academic ability rather than learning per se. One encourages students to adopt task goals by paying attention to improvement and sustained effort and by recognizing the willingness to venture into a new area of study simply because it is intriguing. Another part, of course, is *who* is recognized. When one recognizes academic achievement in a socially competitive fashion, there are some who will seldom, if ever, be recognized. The likely result is their alienation from school. The third part is *how* students are recognized. One program that we have encountered rewards students for good conduct by letting them skip 15 minutes of their most dreaded class. That is hardly a positive statement about the nature and value of learning.

Research at the classroom level has repeatedly called attention to the problems created by such a unidimensional, indeed misplaced, attention to recognition and reward (e.g., Ames, 1990). But there is reason to believe that schools and school leaders have a major role to play in this regard as well. An example or two from our work might make the point. In working with teachers to encourage recognition on the basis of progress, improvement, and effort—and thereby foster a task focus in their classrooms—it was pointed out to us that our efforts were being undermined by a highly visible school practice. The school in question prominently displays an honor roll, recognizing students for high grades. Teachers are the first to admit that these grades are closely tied to the entering ability level of students. These students receive special attention (honor roll assemblies) and special privileges (raising and lowering the flag, acting as guides at school functions, and so on). Of course, it was virtually predetermined that some students would regularly appear on the honor roll; others would just as regularly never be so recognized, regardless of effort put forth. There was no "personal best" award as one commonly finds in the presumably competitive world of business. The honor roll was the overwhelming dominant instrument for recognizing students and for defining what the school was about. It was not a very effective instrument in defining the intrinsic worth of learning for all regardless of ability or place in society. Moreover, school leaders initiated it and promulgated it.

Some administrators have actively sought school-business partnerships that focus on student recognition, presumably for achievement. One of the more popular among these is a program sponsored by a pizza chain. This well-meaning effort rewards students—with pizza, no less—for the number of books they read. Students compete with each other, recognition is on the basis of relative ability, and the difficulty or challenge inherent in the task is ignored. Teachers tell us that some students do not even try, some cheat, and most read the easiest, shortest books they can find. As such, children participating in the program are unlikely to develop what we have termed a task goal orientation. Rather, as John Nicholls put it, we are most likely to end up with a lot of fat kids who hate reading.

Returning to the central point, it should be clear that administrators can and do affect how learning is perceived in the school through the recognition practices they promote or accede to. School leaders can undermine the efforts of individual teachers to promote a facilitative learning environment. It appears that they can do more than that. They can actually affect the overall learning environment of the school. By sponsoring programs or policies that publicly reward students for outperforming their peers, students and parents are put on notice that relative ability is more important than mastering the task.

Grouping

The practice of grouping students together homogeneously according to their ability level is widespread. Ability grouping within classrooms is common at the elementary level, while assigning students to classes on the basis of their ability is common in middle-level schools, particularly in mathematics. There is reason to believe that the resultant grouping sends powerful messages to everyone involved in the educational process, particularly students (Oakes, 1981). Students assigned to low-ability groups or classes are well aware that they are considered inferior to students in higher-ability groups. As one teacher we work with put it, "The kids in the 'Basic' classes (the low-ability track) know they are in the 'dummy' group." The practice of ability grouping enhances the perception that school is essentially a sorting mechanism, a place to define who is and who is not able. It encourages the emergence of a learning environment that stresses the demonstration of ability and minimizes the focus on learning.

Besides the message that homogeneous ability grouping sends to parents, teachers, and students, there are other very practical consequences that must be considered. We have often heard teachers speak of their dread of teaching low-ability classes. These feelings on the part of teachers reflect potentially harmful expectations that may inhibit effective teaching (Oakes, 1981). In addition to such negative feelings on the part of teachers, there is the fact that as students are grouped, different resources are assigned. Consider a specific example in this regard. We have often observed that computer usage is not broadly distributed across students. *Who* gets to use the computers and *for what* may effectively state what the school thinks about who can achieve and what that achievement is worth. Higher-level groups and classes may be encouraged to use the computer for desktop publishing, for simulations, for programming, and for complex problem solving. Students in lower-level groups typically use drill-and-practice software that gives them immediate feedback but fails either to motivate them or to develop higher-order thinking skills. Similarly, project-based science may be reserved for those in the advanced groups. All children can presumably profit from seeing the relevance of science and technology in their daily lives. Opportunities to use science while learning science should not be the province of an elite few—if learning, not just competitive performance, is the preeminent goal of the school. In short, school grouping policies and practices frame the purpose of teaching-learning.

The very pervasiveness and apparent influence of ability grouping practices make it evident that they should be attended to by those who are interested in school learning environments. Further, this appears to be an area in which school leaders can make a difference. With the many negative effects that ability grouping has for students, some have argued that school leaders have a responsibility to do away with the practice (Murphy & Beck, in press). Even though strong opinions in this regard are often held by teachers, school leaders typically can and do exert considerable influence over policies that encourage or discourage homogeneous grouping. In secondary schools, the leadership typically decides whether classes will be organized on the basis of ability. The schedule is then designed with this decision in mind. School leaders can encourage thoughtful discussion about the pros and cons of ability grouping by providing materials to teachers or through in-service training. At the very least, they can and should examine precisely how resources are assigned to different ability groups.

Evaluation Practices

A large body of literature is available on the effects of evaluation practices on student motivation and learning (Covington & Omelich, 1987a, 1987b; Hill, 1980; Hill & Wigfield, 1984; MacIver, 1991). Briefly summarized, the findings indicate that these practices are fraught with possibilities for encouraging students to approach academic tasks as competitive contests to see who is the smartest and the best. Focusing as they do on outcome and performance, regardless of the place at which the learner starts, many evaluation practices are likely to suggest that the purpose of learning is to define relative ability rather than to assess the individual's progress in mastering a particular skill or acquiring certain knowledge. Investing in the task for learning's sake, to understand, to gain new knowledge and skill is probably undermined by typical evaluation practices. Evaluation practices can and often do define the name of the game as one in which some win and others lose. Too often, they define some students as perpetual and inevitable losers.

Evaluation practices are critical factors in determining the learning environment of the school. Although evaluation is a part of schooling, it is practiced in different ways and given different emphases. By what we choose to evaluate, how we do it, and how we interpret what we do, we make important statements about the purpose of schooling. Some schools focus on effort put forth and on student progress. Some view evaluation as diagnosis leading to the development of goals and plans for improvement. Other schools are apparently quite proud of letter grades that sort out the able from the less able, perhaps as early as the primary grades.

No perfect system of evaluation has yet been devised. Clearly, however, schools can and do approach the issue quite differently. It is an area in which leaders can act to influence the learning environment. Decisions are made at the school level about reporting to parents. In addition, school leaders can influence classroom-level practices by advocating certain evaluation practices (e.g., weekly tests graded on a curve) and by providing resources (e.g., in-services) for teachers to learn about alternative forms of evaluation. But perhaps the role of a school leader relates especially to how evaluation is treated at the school level. Our own preliminary judgment is that a great deal of significant control does exist at the school level. Most of the interpretation of evaluative information (standardized tests, for example) occurs at the school level. Certainly, the recognition that is often associated with such evaluation is initiated at this level. Giving tests may not be a debatable issue. Assigning letter grades may also be a policy set in stone. Yet, at the very least, the school does provide an interpretative patina. It constructs meaning around these practices; it interprets what they mean for students and thus affects how students perceive learning and schooling and how they feel about themselves.

Resources

Budgets reflect goals; expenditures reflect values. What an organization believes and wants to do is reflected in the way it uses its resources. The more obvious use of resources involves what can be directly bought: computers, texts, science equipment, and library books. But in a more subtle and no less important way, it also includes intangibles such as in-service activities, retreats, camping experiences, extracurricular activities, school parties, and student government. A first point is that schools differ not only in total amount of resources but in the configuration of resources. Even within the bounds of extensive external regulation and policy definition, schools purchase different things in different amounts. They also distribute their resources in different ways. These points are obvious to any knowledgeable observer. What may be less obvious is that the array of resources purchased as well as the ways in which they are distributed affect the learning environment of the school. Our earlier example of the access to computers is relevant here, of course. But examples from a different realm may broaden the points at issue. Many schools have policies that prohibit some students (usually low-achieving students) from gaining access to school activities by establishing ability standards as admission criteria. Such policies create an environment that emphasizes that relative ability is the "coin of the realm." By making participation in some activity contingent on an ability standard, ability goals rather than task goals are stressed.

Those in leadership roles are called on to manage these resources. They do not have unlimited freedom in the resources they obtain and how they distribute them, but they do have choices. Heck et al. (1990) found that one hallmark of effective principals is that they allocate resources for in-services and instructional materials. We have seen administrators in relatively poor schools somehow manage to find a way to support a teacher who wants to try something new. In schools of similar circumstances, we have seen discretionary funds spent not on fostering instructional innovation but to support advanced placement classes, to send selected students to statewide competitions, and to buy equipment that will be used by a select population in the school. Teachers and students are sensitive to how resources are allocated, particularly because most schools operate on limited budgets, and in this way come to understand what is valued and not valued in the school.

Organization of the School Day

The scheduling of the school day and school activities is an important element in the determination of the learning environment of the school. All the previously discussed areas interlock and interact with each other, but this is most especially true in the case of scheduling. As noted earlier, scheduling influences how students are grouped. It relates to matters of student initiative and responsibility; students typically have no control over scheduling. Certain electives may be unavailable to students if the schedule is relatively inflexible. Scheduling dictates how time is to be used and how the curriculum is approached. Team teaching and interdisciplinary approaches to the curriculum are at the mercy of the schedule. Nowhere is this more evident than at the secondary school level, where the school day is typically divided into 45-minute periods in which different subjects are taught. With this type of schedule, teachers must design tasks that take no more than 40 minutes a day. Such time restrictions necessarily limit the types of tasks that students engage in, often resulting in more rote learning tasks and fewer interesting, hands-on types of activities that are more likely to motivate students. Science teachers who wish to engage students in challenging projects quickly learn that the 40- or 50-minute period may interrupt activities at the point of real insight. Much of the period may be spent first gathering together and then cleaning up materials. Perhaps a group of teachers would prefer to devote a whole day to math, or to integrate math and science instruction, or to capitalize on some current event or phenomenon that is in the news but is restricted by schoolwide mandates regarding the use of time. Any teacher wishing to move instruction beyond school walls to a museum or to a garden on the edge of the school grounds will be bound by scheduling policies to some significant degree. The 40–50-minute hour is well designed to conform to the teacher lecture and to preprogrammed group activities. It is not particularly well suited to a project approach to teaching. Indeed, it is likely to foster a didactic, teacher-oriented approach to instruction. Changing the organization of the school day will not alone produce a change in the learning environment, but a more flexible schedule does permit a broader range of freedom and self-determination for both teachers and students. That in itself is likely to have important effects. Furthermore, as flexible scheduling allows more engaging approaches to the curriculum, it should result in a greater stress on task goals and a reduced stress on ability goals. So often we hear teachers say, "The schedule won't allow that." The schedule should be the servant of instruction, not the boss. It is a significant purpose of leadership to make it that.

Observations on the Process of Change

In addition to identifying policies that school leaders might work to change, we have also learned something about the process of change.

The Empowerment of Teachers

Theoretically, there are at least two reasons for engaging teachers in the change process. The first is motivational. Stated simply, motivational theory suggests that people are likely to be more personally invested in their work within an organization when they have a voice in what happens to them and their work has meaning and significance in contributing to a higher purpose or goal (see Blase, 1990; Sergiovanni, 1990). Not only does such involvement and purpose affect the overall level, it affects the quality of

motivation. When teachers are treated in a way that allows them to develop a sense of self-determination and purpose, they, in turn, relate to students in a qualitatively different fashion (Ryan & Stiller, 1991). As one of the teachers working with us said, "If we are going to create a task-focused environment for students, we've got to work in one." By involving teachers in the change process and having teachers decide what policies and practices we will examine and change, both of these motivating conditions are satisfied.

The second reason for engaging teachers is a matter of harnessing their expertise and the knowledge of practice that they bring to the process. Teachers have a special awareness of the daily happenings in classrooms and schools that often surpasses that of principals—or outside "experts." Too often, interventions designed by researchers fail because they do not take account of the realities of school and classroom life.

Our work leads us to believe that teachers, given the opportunity, are eager to take an active role in deciding what happens in their school. We suggest, further, that empowering teachers not only enhances staff morale but is crucial to school change.

The Critical Role of the Principal

As important as teacher empowerment is, it should not detract from the importance of the role of the principal. A leadership team or the staff as a whole may decide to act, but it is typically a person in a formal leadership role who must defend the action.

We have observed how our collaborating administrators struggled with the proposals that their leadership teams put forward. We empathized as we sensed their (often unspoken) concerns about how to explain a new grouping policy to the Parent-Teacher Organization, an organization that might be expected to be pleased with ability grouping. We noted their initial resistance to discussing changes in assessment or evaluation because "central administration will never go along with that." With time, other teachers on the leadership teams began to challenge these assumptions rather than simply accept them—but they continued to believe that the principals had the final authority. Frequently, they would turn to the principal and say, "Can we really do this? Is this just pie-in-the-sky?"

But we also noted a change in the principals. Just as the teachers appeared to feel empowered by the process, the principals also began to believe that changes could be made and that parents and the superintendent's office could be convinced of their merit. They still reminded teachers of constraints such as scheduling, district policies, and budgetary limitations, but increasingly they became advocates for change. One of the principals began to say to less venturesome teachers, "Just try it. Give it a chance. Trust me."

Critical as the staff is in the change process, the role of the principal is not to be underrated. Like teachers, principals must not only be encouraged but empowered to make changes if changes are to occur.

The Need for Reflection

In a moment of frustration, one of our collaborators blurted out, "I'm simply too busy to think." To make effective, enduring changes, school staff need the time "to think." They need opportunities to review policies, procedures, and practices that are in place in their school and to consider their impact. The idea of the "reflective practitioner" (Schon, 1983) is one that is often voiced but probably seldom realized in the public schools. On more than one occasion, school staff expressed the view that the collaboration with a university group was of value primarily because it provided the occasion for such review and reflection. Yet there is no reason why schools themselves could not sustain dialogue on school improvement.

The Role of Models

The spirit of change is enhanced by the perception of possibilities. We found that school staff are encouraged to act in new ways as they observe concrete examples of programmatic options. Thus visits to "model" school sites and consultations with school staff who have initiated a given course of action are very useful. Early on, teachers in our middle school project appeared eager to move toward a "small house" concept. Yet they made little progress in their thinking until they observed the program in operation in another school. A principal resisted allowing a group of teachers to experiment with multiaged classrooms until she talked to fellow principals who were intrigued with the idea—and visited several schools to see how it was actually done. Taking school staff members to various demonstration schools and arranging for in-service programs provided comfort, encouragement, and inspiration. It also conveyed very practical information. In one form or another, we often hear "Sounds good, but what does that mean exactly? What do you do on a day-to-day basis?" These practical, procedural questions, if left unanswered, can threaten the change process before it gets beyond the talking stage. Examples of how other practitioners are doing things are invaluable and in many cases absolutely necessary.

The Importance of Theory

Perhaps in part because we are academics, we wonder about the role of an operating theoretical framework in fostering meaningful change. Certainly, something so important as school change ought to have a rationale and be guided by some coherent conceptual framework. The change process in which we are engaged is clearly theory driven. It is a framework that we found to be easily understood by, and largely compatible with, the biases and beliefs of teachers in our sample. Whether one accepts *this* framework, it seems appropriate to argue that school changes ought to be guided by and related to some system of purpose, mission, and goal. It ought to relate to a view about the nature of students and learning and the purpose of schools. In our case, goal theory serves as a guiding force in keeping the dialogue about change on a meaningful and coherent path. It provides language for staff to use in discussing change. It provides questions for examining practices. It helps in fending off the introduction of various "quick fixes." A teacher put it this way: "We need a framework to guide unified action."

Is an Outside Force Necessary to Effect Change?

The change that is occurring in the schools in which we are working is associated with an outside force: a university collaboration. Is an outside influence, such as our university research team, necessary to get schools to make qualitative changes in the goals they stress? We think not. The elements for change outlined here are not per se tied to some external force, university or otherwise. A variety of forces could serve equally well. In particular, the "right leader" might make the difference. This is a critical issue that must receive further attention.

Conclusion

Our story, of course, is a continuing one. What we have provided is a snapshot of what we see at the moment and a guess or two about what we might see at some future point. We trust that we have done more than urge school leaders to focus on student motivation and learning. We hope that we have presented a useful framework for considering how action can be taken. On that note, we pause. A conclusion is yet to be written.

References

Ames, C. (1984). Competitive, cooperative, and individualistic goal structures: A motivational analysis. In R. Ames & C. Ames (Eds.), *Research on motivation in education: Vol. 1.* New York: Academic Press.

Ames, C. (1990). Motivation: What teachers need to know. *Teachers College Record, 91,* 409–421.

Ames, C., & Ames, R. (Eds.). (1989). *Research on motivation in education: Vol. 3. Goals and cognitions.* New York: Academic Press.

Ames, C., & Archer, J. (1988). Achievement goals in the classroom: Students' learning strategies and motivation processes. *Journal of Educational Psychology, 80,* 260–270.

Anderson, J.R. (1980). *Cognitive psychology and its implications.* San Francisco: Freeman.

Archer, J. (1990). *Motivation and creativity: The relationship between achievement goals and creativity in writing short stories and poems.* Unpublished doctoral dissertation, University of Illinois, Urbana-Champaign.

Baden, B., & Maehr, M. L. (1986). Confronting culture with culture: A perspective for designing schools for children of diverse sociocultural backgrounds. In R. Feldman (Ed.), *Social psychology applied to education.* New York: Cambridge University Press.

Blase, J. J. (1990). Some negative effects of principal's control-oriented and protective political behavior. *American Educational Research Journal, 27,* 727–753.

Blumenfeld, P. C., Mergendoller, J., & Swarthout, D. (1987). Accomplishment as a heuristic for understanding student learning and motivation. *Journal of Curriculum Studies, 19,* 135–148.

Brophy, J. (1987). Socializing students' motivation to learning. In M. L. Maehr & D. A. Kleiber (Eds.), *Advances in motivation and achievement: Vol. 5. Enhancing motivation.* Greenwich, CT: JAI.

Brophy, J., & Alleman, J. (1991). Activities as instructional tools: A framework for analysis and evaluation. *Educational Researcher, 20,* 9–23.

Chira, S. (1991, May 15). Schools to help with life as well as learning. *New York Times,* pp. A1, B7.

Covington, M. V., & Omelich, C. L. (1987a). "I knew it cold before the exam": A test of the anxiety-blockage hypothesis. *Journal of Educational Psychology, 4,* 393–400.

Covington, M. V., & Omelich, C. L. (1987b). Item difficultly and test performance among high-anxious and low-anxious students. In R. Schwarzer, H. M. van der Ploeg, & C. D. Spielberger (Eds.), *Advances in test anxiety: Vol. 5.* Hillsdale, NJ: Lawrence Erlbaum.

Cuban, L. (1990). Reforming again, again, and again. *Educational Researcher, 19,* 3–13.

Deci, E. L. (1975). *Intrinsic motivation.* New York: Plenum.

Deci, E. L., & Ryan, R. M. (1985). *Intrinsic motivation and self-determination.* New York: Plenum.

deCharms, R. (1976). *Enhancing motivation.* New York: Irvington.

Dweck, C. S. (1985). Intrinsic motivation, perceived control, and self-evaluation maintenance: An achievement goal analysis. In C. Ames & R. Ames (Eds.), *Research on motivation in education: Vol. 2.* New York: Academic Press.

Dweck, C.S., & Leggett, E.L. (1988). A social-cognitive approach to motivation and personality. *Psychological Review, 35,* 256–273.

Elliott, E. S., & Dweck, C. S. (1988). Goals: An approach to motivation and achievement. *Journal of Personality and Social Psychology, 54,* 5–12.

Entwistle, N. J., & Ramsden, P. (1983). *Understanding student learning.* London: Croom Helm.

Gardner, J. W. (1990). *On leadership.* New York: Free Press.

Golan, S., & Graham, S. (1990, April). *Motivation and cognition: The impact of ego and task involvement on levels of processing.* Paper presented at the annual meeting of the American Educational Research Association, Boston.

Good, T. L., & Weinstein, R. S. (1986). Schools make a difference: Evidence, criticisms, and new directions. *American Psychologist, 41,* 1090–1097.

Hallinger, P., Bickman, L., & Davis, K. (1990). *What makes a difference? School context, principal leadership, and student achievement.* (Occasional Paper No. 3). Cambridge, MA: Center for Educational Leadership, Harvard Graduate School of Education.

Heck, R. H., Larsen, T. J., & Marcoulides, G. A. (1990). Instructional leadership and school achievement: Validation of a causal model. *Educational Administration Quarterly, 26,* 94–125.

Hill, K. T. (1980). Motivation, evaluation, and testing policy. In L.J. Fyans, Jr. (Ed.), *Achievement motivation: Recent trends in theory and research.* New York: Plenum.

Hill, K. T., & Wigfield, A. (1984). Test anxiety: A major educational problem and what can be done about it. *Elementary School Journal, 84,* 105–126.

Krug, S. (1989). Leadership and learning: A measurement-based approach for analyzing school effectiveness and developing effective leaders. In M. L. Maehr & C. Ames (Eds.) *Advances in motivation and achievement: Vol. 6. Motivation enhancing environments.* Greenwich, CT: JAI.

MacIver, D. (1991, April). *Enhancing students' motivation to learn by altering assessment reward and recognition structures: An evaluation of the incentives for improvement program.* Paper presented at the annual meeting of the American Educational Research Association, Chicago.

Maehr, M. L. (1989). Thoughts about motivation. In C. Ames & R. Ames (Eds.), *Research on motivation in education: Vol. 3. Enhancing motivation.* New York: Academic Press.

Maehr, M. L. (1991). The "psychological environment" of the school: A focus for school leadership. In P. Thurston & P. Zodhiates (Eds.), *Advances in educational administration.* Greenwich, CT: JAI.

Maehr, M. L., & Anderman, E. (in press). Reinventing schools for early adolescents. *Elementary School Journal.*

Maehr, M. L., & Buck, R. (in press). Transforming school culture. In H. Walberg & M. Sashkin (Eds.), *School leadership and culture: Current research and practice.* Chicago: National Society for the Study of Education.

Maehr, M. L., & Fyans, L. J., Jr. (1989). School culture, motivation and achievement. In M. L. Maehr & C. Ames (Eds.), *Advances in motivation and achievement: Vol. 6. Motivation enhancing environments.* Greenwich, CT: JAI.

Maehr, M. L., & Midgley, C. (1991). Enhancing student motivation: A school-wide approach. *Educational Psychologist, 25,* 333–427.

Maehr, M. L., & Pintrich, P. R. (Eds.). (1991) *Advances in achievement and motivation: Vol 7. Goals and self-regulatory processes.* Greenwich, CT: JAI.

McClelland, D. C., & Boyatzis, R. E. (1982). The leadership motive pattern and long term success in management. *Journal of Applied Psychology, 67,* 737–743.

Meece, J. L. (1991). The classroom context and students' motivational goals. In M. L. Maehr & P. R. Pintrich (Eds.), *Advances in motivation and achievement: Vol. 7. Goals and self-regulatory processes.* Greenwich, CT: JAI.

Meece, J. L., Blumenfeld, P. C., & Hoyle, R. H. (1988). Students' goal orientations and cognitive engagement in classroom activities. *Journal of Educational Psychology, 80,* 514–523.

Meece, J., & Holt, K. (1990, April). *Classification and validation of achievement goal patterns in elementary school children.* Paper presented at the annual meeting of the American Educational Research Association, Boston.

Midgley, C., & Feldlaufer, H. (1987). Students' and teachers' decision-making fit before and after the transition to junior high school. *Journal of Early Adolescence, 7,* 225–241.

Murphy, J., & Beck, L. (in press). *Understanding the principalship: A metaphorical analysis from 1920–1990.* New York: Teachers College Press.

Nicholls, J. G. (1984). Conceptions of ability and achievement motivation. In R. Ames & C. Ames (Eds.), *Research on motivation in education: Vol. 1. Student motivation.* New York: Academic Press.

Nicholls, J. G. (1989). *The competitive ethos and democratic education.* Cambridge, MA: Harvard University Press.

Nicholls, J. G. (1992). Students as educational theorists. In D. Schunk & J. Meece (Eds.), *Student perceptions in the classroom.* Hillsdale, NJ: Lawrence Erlbaum.

Nicholls, J. G., Cobb, P., Wood, T., Yackel, E., & Patashnick, M. (1990). Assessing students' theories of success in mathematics: Individual and classroom differences. *Journal for Research in Mathematics Education, 21,* 109–122.

Nolen, S. B. (1988). Reasons for studying: Motivational orientations and study strategies. *Cognition and Instruction, 5,* 269–287.

Nolen, S. B., & Haladyna, T. M. (in press). Personal and environmental influences on students' beliefs about effective study strategies. *Contemporary Educational Psychology.*

Oakes, J. (1981). Tracking policies and practices: School by school summaries (Study of Schooling Tech. Rep. No. 25). Los Angeles: University of California Graduate School of Education.

Pervin, L.A. (Ed.) (1989). *Goal concepts in personality and social psychology*. Hillsdale, NJ: Lawrence Erlbaum.

Pintrich, P. R., & DeGroot, E. (1990). Motivational and self-regulated learning components of classroom academic performance. *Journal of Educational Psychology, 82*, 33–40.

Pintrich, P. R., & Garcia, T. (1991). Student goal orientation and self-regulation in the college classroom. In M. L. Maehr & P. R. Pintrich (Eds.), *Advances in motivation: Vol. 7. Goals and self-regulatory processes*, Greenwich, CT: JAI.

Powell, B. (1990, April). *Children's perceptions of classroom goal orientation: Relationship to learning strategies and intrinsic motivation*. Paper presented at the annual meeting of the American Educational Research Association, Boston.

Rowan, B., Raudenbush, S.W., & Kang, S.J. (1991). Organizational design in high schools: A multilevel analysis. *American Journal of Education, 99*, 238–266.

Ryan, R., & Stiller, J. (1991) The social contexts of internalization: Parent and teacher influences on autonomy, motivation, and learning. In M. L Maehr & P. R. Pintrich (Eds.), *Advances in motivation and achievement: Vol. 7. Goals and self-regulatory processes*. Greenwich, CT: JAI .

Sarason, S. B. (1990). *The predictable failure of educational reform: Can we change course before it's too late?* San Francisco: Jossey-Bass.

Schon, D. (1983). *The reflective practitioner*. New York: Basic Books.

Sergiovanni, T.J. (1990). *Value-added leadership: How to get extraordinary performance in schools*. San Diego, CA: Harcourt Brace Jovanovich.

Assessing Alternative Assessment

Maeroff, Gene I. 1991. *Phi Delta Kappan* 73(4):272–81.

In looking closely at what is happening in Rhode Island, Mr. Maeroff notes, it is possible to get a preview of the satisfactions and frustrations that may spread as the movement toward large-scale alternative assessment mushrooms.

William, a tiny third-grader in a red sweatshirt, was sitting in an adult-sized chair, balancing on the edge of the seat as he listened intently to the woman across the table telling him that she was going to ask him about one of the several books that he had read recently. "If you know the questions I'm going to ask, it may help you decide which book you want to discuss," she said, going on to list the subjects of the questions. "I will want to know about the main part of the story, the main characters, the setting, the ending, and the major conflict or problem."

And so it was that William, aware in advance of what he would be asked, decided to answer questions about a biography of Marco Polo that he had read not long before. What ensued between child and adult resembled an informal conversation more than the assessment that it actually was. "They go quite a bit by camel through the desert," William said of the setting as he answered the questions, one by one. "He lived in Venice, and they were going to trade some things from Italy for some better things. A war broke out, and so they decided to go to China and stayed there."

"Does it end in China?" William was asked.

"No," he answered. "After 17 years he decided to go home and left on a fleet of Chinese junks. When Marco Polo got back to Italy, no one believed him, so they put him in prison. He wrote a book about it, and years later Christopher Columbus read it."

This encounter was an assessment of William's reading, and the only paper and pencil in evidence were in the hands of the adult who was questioning him and taking notes on his responses. None of the questions had multiple-choice or true-or-false answers, and nothing about this reading examination was norm-referenced or nationally standardized. It was an alternative assessment, which included the individual interview about the book on Marco Polo and a review of a portfolio containing samples of William's work. Later, with another assessor, William would be assessed on other tasks, participating in a small group in which he would be asked to read and discuss a different story and to write about it. Alternative assessments of this sort typify a movement that is capturing the imagination of educators across the country. Good teachers have historically used such methods to monitor the progress of their students, but now these approaches are being extended beyond individual classrooms to pose a challenge to traditional ways of mass testing. However, large-scale alternative assessment is still talked about more than it is used, and William's experience in his school in South Kingstown, Rhode Island, represents one of the early efforts by a state to develop a system of alternative assessments in its elementary schools.

Other states—notably California, Connecticut, Kentucky, and Vermont—as well as some school systems and individual schools are at various stages in this gentle upheaval that proponents hope will alter the way Americans think about evaluating schoolwork. Altogether, 40 states are planning some form of alternative assessment at the state level, with writing samples as the most common alternative.[1]

Rhode Island's pilot project, which began in 1989, is still inchoate as a small number of third-grade teachers in four school districts around the state collaborate with officials from the state education department and a researcher from the Educational Testing Service (ETS). Together they are struggling to devise methods of assessing students that can provide useful information while avoiding the shortcomings associated with norm-referenced tests. In looking closely at what is happening in Rhode Island, it is possible to get a preview of the satisfactions and frustrations that may spread as the movement mushrooms.

Those pursuing change in Rhode Island are continually administering and revising the pilot assessments, striving to create a framework for instruments that eventually might be used in schools throughout the state at various grade levels. They hope to forge a synergy of instruction and assessment in which each complements the other to raise learning to new levels. This approach allows a child to know in advance—as William did—what will be asked. The goal is not to spring surprises on students and catch them unawares; unlike the usual mode of testing, this is no "gotcha" game. The students, under the tutelage of their teachers, are trained to provide evidence of their own learning.

The original charge to the pilot group in Rhode Island was to try to determine how the state's "Outcomes for Third-Graders" might be measured through the use of portfolios. This goal, which fits comfortably within the nation's alternative assessment movement, has extended beyond portfolios to include other possibilities, such as performance tasks and group interviews, and it embraces outcomes in reading, writing, speaking, listening, and mathematics.

Schools presumably are doing their job if students learn something that is deemed worth knowing. This kind of assessment does not drive the curriculum; it grows out of the curriculum and is part and parcel of the curriculum. Such a philosophy is widely accepted at the elementary and secondary levels in the performing and studio arts, in athletics, and even in vocational education. But it is not readily accepted in formal academics. Think, for instance, how long it was before test-makers asked students to produce essays in order to demonstrate their writing skills instead of giving them tests with questions about writing.

A young pianist who is asked to master Beethoven's "Für Elise" becomes proficient by practicing the piece, knowing all the while that his examination will consist of playing it. A nonswimmer who is told that the measure of her ability to swim will be the completion of one lap of the pool endeavors to swim with full knowledge of the form the assessment will take. Being able to play Beethoven or to swim a lap of the pool is presumably indicative of the ability to play some other composition of equal difficulty or to swim a similar distance on another occasion.

Yet, for all its attractiveness, alternative assessment is fraught with complications and difficulties, not unlike having to endure life with a teenager as the price for the joys of parenthood. If they are to be used widely or even as supplements to nationally standardized, norm-referenced tests, these new assessments will have to be done more quickly, more efficiently, and less expensively than at first seems possible.

As experimenters in Rhode Island and elsewhere are discovering, the quest for alternative forms of mass testing could remain as elusive as Don Quixote's dream. The schools seem unable even to broker the logical marriage of alternative assessment and technology; they treat the two as if they dwelt on separate planets. For example, in elementary and secondary education, how often do we hear of alternative assessment that involves the manipulation of computer models or simulations?

Furthermore, there must be standardization of some sort, as Rhode Island hopes to achieve. Otherwise, there is no way to put the findings of an assessment in context. Even in Kentucky, which by 1995 is to have the first statewide assessment system that is completely based on performance, there is anguish over how to meet the state board's mandate that there be a way of comparing Kentucky students with those in other states.

Speed and low cost were the silver bullets that enabled the norm-referenced test—with its multiple-choice responses—to conquer the world of education and hold it in thrall. Meanwhile, alternative assessment, which is not so new an idea as some people think, tends to be a time-consuming, labor-intensive, imprecise exercise in which the expense mounts as nuances are weighed and scoring is done by humans, without even the benefit of grids that fit conveniently over answer sheets studded with blacked-in boxes.

On the other hand, there is the potential for teasing considerable consensus from an approach that seems at first to be hopelessly subjective. Consider the competition in such sports as diving and figure skating, in which experts have developed scoring criteria that are so extensively accepted around the world that judges find a remarkable level of concurrence. Some of the best work in assessing writing samples mirrors this sort of agreement on relevant criteria.

While it may be possible to be systematic about alternative assessment, there are ultimately no quick and easy ways to rate large numbers of performance-based tasks or portfolios or interviews or exhibits or even essays. American proponents of alternative assessment like to cite the example of England as a country that has used alternative assessments to the exclusion of norm-referenced and multiple-choice tests. That is generally true, but until recently it has mostly meant using essays for external assessment. Only lately has England made a large-scale attempt to develop for external assessment such nonwriting tasks as science experiments. Meanwhile, portfolios containing work done over time have been and will continue to be used in England for assessment within the classroom, though not for outside comparisons of students or for purposes of accountability.

Measurement experts from around the U.S. who gathered in California in March 1991 under the auspices of the federal government's Center for Research on Evaluation, Standards, and Student Testing commiserated over the difficulty of meeting the rapidly escalating demands of policy makers for alternative assessment tools. They noted the time that it will take to establish validity and reliability, the need to train teachers in alternative assessment procedures, and the amount of time needed to administer the examinations.[2]

Nonetheless, the pioneers in Rhode Island and other locales—like those who drove their Conestoga wagons into unfamiliar territory—steel themselves and press the journey forward, intent on building an assessment system that is embedded in instruction. They want an approach that attests to a student's progress over time, something that figuratively resembles a semester-length videotape rather than a Polaroid snapshot that, like a one-shot test, captures only a single moment of a child's learning.

The cynosure for each of five subject areas in Rhode Island is a set of literacy outcomes for third-graders. One aim is to assess outcomes in reading, writing, speaking, listening, and mathematics—both as individual subjects and in ways that integrate them. The intention is that teachers will then teach in this manner.

In this approach, assessment drives instruction, and instruction drives assessment, much the way the front and rear axles impel one another in a vehicle with four-wheel drive. In essence, the assessment task is part of the instruction. This notion may be revolutionary for elementary and secondary education, but in medical schools, where clinical education is often evaluated on the basis of performance tasks that may have an instructional component even during the examination, it is accepted practice.[3] When assessment is sheared off from instruction, as is customary in the commercially produced examinations given in the public schools, the findings may not tell a great deal about what students have learned from their classroom experience.

One must wonder, therefore, about the movement for a national examination system that is hurrying forward on several fronts. A great deal is heard about various plans to create tests that would be given to students at, say, fourth, eighth, and 12th grades. Yet these discussions are curiously reticent about the curriculum on which students are to be examined. Presumably, these tests will dictate the curriculum, a policy that is anathema to proponents of alternative assessment. The concern about widespread low achievement that is fueling the movement for a national test is understandable. But wouldn't it be more straightforward to decide what ought to be taught and to teach it, instead of first administering tests and hoping that they push the curriculum in the right direction?

Perhaps circuitous routes are chosen because the challenge of unifying teaching and assessment is so daunting. Assessment that is authentically embedded in instruction is not easy to fashion. This is no Operation Desert Storm. There are no smart bombs to wipe out specific problems, nor any flanking maneuvers to avoid the tedious process of repeatedly refining the assessment instruments. There is just the slow, mundane reconnoitering to find and frame the best ways of eliciting the most useful information. One can only hope that alternative assessment is not rushed onto the battlefield of testing so hastily as to produce in its unperfected form friendly fire that harms the very children who are supposed to be the beneficiaries.

And the work doesn't stop with declaring, for example, that students will submit portfolios. What should be in the portfolios? What should students be asked about the contents of their portfolios? How can some element of standardization be lent to the process so that one student's portfolio may be compared with another's? Putting less emphasis on comparisons is fine, but at some point a child and his parents have a right to know whether the child's progress is reasonable for his or her age and experience.

There is an inclination among proponents to regard alternative assessment as suitable for all purposes—diagnosis, selection, and accountability at all levels. It may be that an alternative assessment that is a marvelous indicator of an individual child's academic progress will prove fairly useless for other purposes. Americans may have to decide whether comparisons are what they seek in alternative assessment or whether they prefer to use the approach for other, more individualized purposes. Incidentally, the very idea of comparing the progress of young children is seldom embraced in Europe, where the practice is generally not to test students in the primary years. But America is different.

Thus, one crisp New England morning at South Road Elementary School, little William and some of his classmates played guinea pigs for the assessment developers, who had situated themselves at three separate sites in the school. It was part of a continuing process of refinement that has continued through this fall.

Grant Wiggins reminds us that the root of the word *assessment* means to "sit with" a learner and seek to be sure that a student's responses really mean what they seem to mean. He adds: "Does a correct answer mask thoughtless recall? Does a wrong answer obscure thoughtful understanding? We can know for sure by asking further questions, by seeking explanation or substantiation, by requesting a self-assessment, or by soliciting the student's response to the assessment."[4]

Next door to the conference room in which William met with his assessor, Mary Fowles of ETS, four other third-graders wearing name tags sat at a table with Susan Skawinski of the state department of education. She was also carrying out a pilot assessment, talking about a story that they had read and were going to write about. The idea at this point was not so much to assess the children's learning as to assess the assessment itself. Eventually, classroom teachers are to be the assessors of their own students. And when this happens, they will need a fully developed instrument.

This was a group interview in which Skawinski would assess each student's understanding of literature by having him or her discuss and write about what had been read. "I'm going to talk to you about something you've done, and I'm going to talk to you about reading," Skawinski said to the three girls and one boy who were gathered with her around the Formica-topped table.

"In this story we have some very important characters," she said, proceeding to list and discuss the characters in "The Rooster Who Understood Japanese," a tale about a Japanese-American family that owned a rooster whose crowing woke a neighbor each morning. Their home was on the outskirts of a city. Skawinski handed out copies of a "story map" to the youngsters and, following its scheme, mentioned the characters, the setting, the problem, the attempts to solve the problem—all of which had been briefly summarized on the story map. She took notes on a pad on her lap as the students—sometimes readily, sometimes reluctantly—entered the conversation.

The box labeled "solution" was blank on the story map, and the children were asked to write in the details of what had been done to deal with the crowing of the rooster, named Mr. Lincoln. The students were permitted to go back and look at the story if they wished. This, it turned out, was a warmup for the real task: the writing assessment. Skawinski asked the children to think about solutions in addition to the one offered by the author and prodded them to discuss their ideas with the group.

"Tie a rope around his beak," suggested Rebecca; causing Kevin, sitting next to her, to look crestfallen. He said that he had had the same idea.

"Send him to rooster obedience school," suggested Alicia.

And so it went as possible solutions to the conflict were proposed and discussed. "Pick a solution you think makes the most sense and write about it," Skawinski said. "It can be your own or someone else's that we talked about." In addition, the children were asked to address two other questions about the story. The following excerpts are part of what each third-grader wrote:

> "keep mr. licon in the dark because the moring he crows in but not at night."

> "I would put Mr. Lincoln in the dark so he would think it was still night and wouldn't crow."

> "talk to him in japaneas and then he will be quiete"

> "Put him in a room when it's dark to make him feel that it's still dark out side."

It took so long to complete the discussion and the writing that, as she collected their papers, Skawinski told the children that there would not be time for them to talk about their favorite books, which they had been asked to bring with them to the assessment. "It was a laboriously slow process," she said afterward. "I needed more time." Such complaints are frequent in the piloting of alternative assessments because a central problem is figuring out how to accomplish the assessment in a manageable time period.

Furthermore, in this case, the assessor would still have to devote time to sorting out the notes she took during the assessment. "You can't actually mark the sheets in front of the children," Skawinski remarked after the students had left.

She noted discreetly on the pad that had been perched on her lap throughout the interview the extent to which each child seemed to bring background knowledge to the story—ideas about living arrangements in a city, an awareness that roosters crow early in the morning, and so on. She noted their familiarity with a story map as a way of setting out the structure of the story. She also observed how long it took each child to read the story silently and what responses each one had to questions about the story—who had original ideas, who followed the ideas of others, how well individual students could go back and cite information from the story to justify what they were saying.

Mary Fowles of ETS expects that, as the assessment is improved, there will be less note-taking by the assessor. In the pilot assessments, attention has been paid to deciding what information is most important to gather about a student's reactions and what kinds of evaluation forms lend themselves to recording this information. Theoretically, it is possible for the evaluation form to be anything from a check-off list to a sheet on which detailed quotes from a discussion with a student are recorded.

Assessing a portfolio might seem to be a more straightforward job than assessing students' performance in a group interview, but the challenge is simply of a different sort. This was illustrated in the trial assessment of mathematics portfolios that Mary Ann Snider, a testing and evaluation specialist with the state education department in Rhode Island, was conducting with students at a desk in the corridor outside their classroom.

"Your teacher tells me you've been doing several things in math that you might want to share with me." Snider said to the first of the students, Nigel, as she began reviewing his math portfolio with him after a bit of casual chatter. Nigel was eager to talk and spoke enthusiastically about his work in conjunction with a medieval theme, used concurrently by many teachers in his school as a means of teaching various subjects in an interdisciplinary fashion. There had also been a schoolwide medieval festival for which the classes had gathered en masse.

Nigel showed Snider a pencil drawing he had made of intricately linked chain mail, and they discussed what he had learned about shapes by making the drawing. "What else did you do with math in the medieval project?" Snider eventually asked. The emphasis in this part of the assessment was on finding ways in which math had been integrated into other subjects, reflecting the goal of bringing about the interdisciplinary teaching that the assessment is intended to reinforce.

Nigel displayed a word puzzle that he had devised, using vocabulary words associated with the medieval period, and a separate math word problem that he had written on a medieval theme. But the math problem he had created was so convoluted that even he could not solve it. Then he showed some work that he had done on estimation. It called for counting the number of bricks in one portion of a castle wall and estimating the number in the entire wall. Snider initiated a discussion of how the drawing of the castle might be used to study shapes and asked Nigel to identity some of the shapes.

Moving beyond the contents of the portfolio and following a written script so that the assessment would be systematic, Snider posed a series of questions, some of which were more successful than others in eliciting responses that could help in assessing Nigel's understanding of math: "What has been your favorite thing to do in math this year?" "When you learn something new in math, when do you know that you understand it?" "Have any of the new things you've learned in math helped you outside of school?"

Finally, they reached the last part of the assessment, the task that Nigel would be asked to perform. A plastic bucket filled to the brim with small, square, colored tiles was put on the desk between them, and Snider held up a bag.

"I have something in this brown paper bag, and I have a riddle so you can figure out what is in it," she said. "I will give you some clues, and you can use these tiles to figure it out. Here's the first clue: there are fewer than 10 tiles in the bag. What does that mean?"

"Less than 10."

"Does that mean I could have 10 of them in the bag? Snider asked.

"Yes . . . ," Nigel answered hesitantly. Then, upon a moment's reflection, he changed his answer.

The goal was for Nigel to take from the bucket and put onto the desk tiles of the same number and color as the riddle indicated were in the bag. He took nine tiles of various colors from the bucket and spread them on the desk, now fairly certain that there could not be more than nine in the bag.

"Clue 2: there are two colors in the bag." And so it went, Nigel having to modify the number or color of the tiles in front of him in response to a series of clues. When he thought he had solved the problem, Snider gave him the bag so that he could take out the tiles and see if the number and color matched those he had assembled on the desk.

"Now," Snider said, "I'd like you to write a riddle for me using the tiles, and I will try to solve it."

This was not a wholly satisfactory assessment, according to Snider, who said afterward that she wished Nigel had accumulated more math work in his portfolio to reflect studies pursued more recently than the medieval project, completed some six weeks earlier. Furthermore, she worried that the warm-up period had not been adequate and that Nigel was not sufficiently at ease during the assessment. "I saw emerging evidence of understanding," she said. "He is logical but not confident. He doesn't have enough math vocabulary, and he has trouble talking about the work he did. He is not comfortable explaining. He remembered what estimation was, but he could not say enough about it to show that he understood it."

So it is that Snider and the others who are piloting Rhode Island's assessment are carrying out their work in selected schools in East Providence, Glocester, South Kingstown, and Newport. In each of the four participating districts, a lead teacher acts as a liaison between the project and other third-grade teachers in the district. One aim of the project is to develop a format for reporting indicators of a student's progress toward reaching the state's proposed literacy outcomes. Most experts believe that the reports should be more descriptive than just a row of numbers. But the reports will include numbers, and the experts are striving to determine what those numbers should represent.

This attempt to add meaning to the evaluative numbers can be appreciated by examining what happened in a place that preceded Rhode Island in the shift toward alternative assessment. When Mark Twain Elementary School in Littleton, Colorado, began moving into an assessment program that would be based on the actual performances

of students, a major part of the effort was devoted to developing criteria for scoring the performances. The criteria evolved through at least 10 stages, according to Monte Moses, the school's principal. "Every time we gave the assessment, we saw some student doing something we couldn't account for on the scoring rubric," Moses said.

One part of an assignment at Mark Twain, for example, calls for fifth-graders to submit a written research report. It is scored on a descending scale of 5 to 1. A report earns a 5 when it

clearly describes the question studied and provides strong reasons for its importance. Conclusions are clearly stated in a thoughtful manner. A variety of facts, details, and examples are given to answer the question and provide support for the answer. The writing is engaging, organized, fluid, and very readable. Sentence structure is varied, and grammar, mechanics, and spelling are consistently correct. Sources of information are noted and cited in an appropriate way.

By comparison, a 3 is awarded to a written report when the student

briefly describes the question and has written conclusions. An answer is stated with a small amount of supporting information. The writing has a basic organization although it is not always clear and is sometimes difficult to follow. Sentence structure and mechanics are generally correct with some weaknesses and errors. References are mentioned, but without adequate detail.[5]

The bottom line is that it is easier to propose outcomes than it is to set the criteria and establish the performance levels that are represented by various achievements. Moreover, if students themselves are to take responsibility for their own work, the criteria must be spelled out in ways that are understandable to children. Then the students can go about learning how to do what is expected of them. In general, it is desirable that a student spend time thinking about questions of the type that will be asked on the assessment; those questions should promote and direct the child's learning.

In Rhode Island, some individuals administering the pilot assessments wondered after one of the pilot sessions how useful it was, for instance, to ask a student, "When you learn something new in math, when do you know that you understand it?" or "What was the hardest thing about reading for you this year?" At each step of the Rhode Island project, the evaluation is being fine-tuned, as it was at Mark Twain. Questions are dropped, added, or modified.

The way that assessment can enhance the learning of students is illustrated in Rhode Island by the evaluation of speaking ability. An evaluation form serves the twin purposes of instruction and assessment. Proceeding on the assumption that the best way to get students to reach the expected outcomes is to familiarize them with the expectations, students see the criteria by which they will be rated.

In fact, the children are asked to apply these criteria to one another, using the same evaluation forms by which they will be rated. In most cases, the speech to be rated is an oral presentation of a book report. The student is supposed to be sufficiently conversant with the book to be able to deliver the report by referring to notes, not by reading a written text. One teacher found that students were somewhat reluctant to fill out the evaluation forms because they did not want to rate one another, especially if it meant saying something negative about a classmate. She encouraged them to think of the evaluation as "helping one another." The assessment consists of the following questions, each of which is answered by circling a yes or a no:

Did the student

◆ speak so that everyone could hear?
◆ finish sentences?
◆ seem comfortable in front of the group?
◆ give a good introduction?
◆ seem well-informed about the topic?
◆ explain ideas clearly?
◆ stay on the topic?
◆ give a good conclusion?
◆ use effective costumes, pictures, or other materials to make the presentation interesting?
◆ give good answers to questions from the audience?[6]

After giving a report, a student has only to sort through the evaluation sheets marked by classmates to discover what he or she must do to improve. The crucial point here is that the strands of instruction and assessment are so interwoven. The Rhode Islanders are trying to help create classroom assignments that both support the growth of students in the five specified literacy areas and prepare them for assessment, as the evaluation form in speaking does. The most promising practices will be documented so that they may be shared among the teachers.

The difficulty of banishing the glitches from alternative assessment may be sensed from a glimpse at England's attempt to develop sets of "standard assessment tasks" that are to be used nationally for the first time in conjunction with the new national curriculum. Despite England's considerable experience with alternative assessment, that nation's efforts have been marked by controversy. One teacher told of his frustration in carrying out the pilot assessment in science for 7-year-olds last spring. He said:

> Close observation of the pupils was necessary throughout. It was difficult deciding whether Dionne was counting with her fingers under the table or mentally sorting through the number bonds that she genuinely knew. During discussion about floating and sinking, it required considerable attention to assess the pupils against the 13 states of attainment.[7]

It took more than 35 minutes to test just four students on the scientific floating exercises alone, according to this teacher, and still the results were inconclusive. The proposed number of tasks to be performed in England's national assessment has been reduced by as much as two-thirds because the assessment, as originally conceived, demanded too much time. Students waiting to be assessed and those already assessed were supposed to work on their own while the teacher was off in a corner of the room assessing their classmates in small groups. But after students ended up being left unsupervised for long periods —and sometimes disrupting classmates who were being assessed—some schools sought to scrape up money to hire substitutes to oversee the classes while regular teachers were conducting assessments. There is even talk now in England of inserting some multiple-choice questions into the assessments to speed up the process.

The matter of time is also on the minds of those developing the alternatives in Rhode Island. One day, as they sat around evaluating yet another pilot assessment, the assessors wondered whether they should continue to review portfolios only in the presence of the students. "It might have been good to have had five or 10 minutes with the portfolios before the student walked into the room to discuss it," said one assessor, raising the prospect of adding even more time to a job that some believe lasts too long already.

Subsequently it was decided that each portfolio would be reviewed briefly before the student arrived. This step would not only increase the amount of time required for the assessment but would also mean that the portfolios would have to be more self-explanatory and more selectively assembled. In preparation for this change in policy, teachers were to reconsider the kinds of pieces that should go into the portfolio so as to reduce the amount of peripheral material. After all, a portfolio should not be like a kitchen gadget drawer, so chock-a-block with unrelated items that locating the corkscrew becomes a frustrating quest.

Among the sorts of writing to be weighed for inclusion in the portfolio were: 1) a favorite piece of writing of any genre, 2) a set of revisions showing the evolution of the writing process, 3) a creative and/or informative piece that responds to literature that the student has read, 4) a piece illustrating the student's understanding in a particular content area, and 5) a wild card that the student wants to include for whatever reason.

Since the content of the portfolio depends on what has been generated by assignments, the onus is on teachers to teach in ways that lead students to produce samples of appropriate work. At the same time, teachers must guide students in making proper selections from the various pieces they have written in each category, and they must prepare students to respond to an assessor in ways that will help him or her make a proper assessment. Ideally, the steps leading to an assessment and the assessment itself will be a learning experience for students.

This responsibility can be forbidding to a teacher unaccustomed to teaching in this manner. Judy Wood, a third-grade teacher in Rhode Island, who is in her 28th and probably final year of teaching, can now reflect on her participation in the development of the alternative assessment with a little less anxiety than she and her colleagues felt at the outset of the project. She said:

At first, when they were asked to get involved, the teachers thought they would be given something that had already been completed. They were uneasy when they realized that they were getting involved in something that was only in the development stage. After a while, they understood that there was not a finished product for them and that their input would count and that there was a big, messy ingredient—the papers that were needed from the children for the portfolios. Finally, this fall, we were organized enough to know what was needed and to help the teachers in the first week or two of school so that those who were interested in joining in could start getting the folders going.

The ways in which both learning and assessment might not be fully served were illustrated in one of the sessions in Rhode Island by a student who was asked to show her best work. (There has been some agonizing incidentally, over possible differences in responses when children are asked for their "best" work as opposed to their "favorite" work.) She kept displaying examples from the beginning of the school year, although as a third-grader her work had presumably improved during the term. Difficulties arose in assessing other students when their math portfolios contained only the final step in solving a problem and showed little evidence of how that point had been reached.

In yet another instance, the assessor's task was made more difficult by what was not contained in a student's math portfolio. "We wrote some word problems with circulars from Stop 'N' Shop," said the student, Stacy, reaching into a folder and pulling out a list of questions she had written using the grocery prices in an accompanying circular published by the store. One question asked, "If you had $8.99 and bought Head & Shoulders, how much would you have left?" The reader had to find the price listed for the product in the circular and then subtract it from the amount in Stacy's problem.

Stacy was asked why all her word problems involved only subtraction. She said that there were some that called for addition, but she hadn't been able to find them. When asked about her use of math in other subjects, Stacy pulled from her portfolio pages of graphs that she had drawn comparing temperatures on various dates in Rhode Island and Hawaii, apparently reflecting work in social studies. Stacy had nothing to show when she was asked about what she had learned of division and multiplication.

During their reviews of the pilot assessments, the assessors questioned whether even the settings might have affected the assessments, because some sessions were held in large rooms where other assessments were also taking place, while others were held in smaller rooms in which only one assessment at a time took place.

Such concerns have arisen elsewhere. Researchers at England's Bristol University who studied assessments of performance tasks conducted last spring in 57 of the county's primary schools wondered about the relationship of the settings to the comparability of outcomes. In some instances, students being assessed were regularly interrupted by comments directed at them by classmates working elsewhere in the room. At some other sites, the students being assessed were the only ones in the room and had the full attention of the assessor.[8]

Despite the existence of models on which to build, there is clearly much about alternative assessment that remains problematic. There are many hurdles that teachers must learn to leap before they assume responsibility for external assessment, as indeed they must if the activity is to be financially viable.

Nor can it be taken for granted that teachers will easily shift to alternative assessment. Many teachers do not fully understand the intricacies of the kinds of examinations with which they have been working until now. Most states require no training in assessment as a part of teacher certification—and, "even when assessment training is offered to teachers, it typically fails to provide the kinds of knowledge and skills needed to produce assessment literates."[9]

There is promise in what has been happening in such endeavors as Arts PROPEL in Pittsburgh, a program in which teachers of music, of the visual arts, and of writing have been altering their teaching to weave a blend of instruction and assessment that enables both students and teachers to be reflective throughout the process of creation. But money from the Rockefeller Foundation and expertise from Harvard University and from ETS have perhaps made this venture easier to carry out than it might be in schools without such financial and human resources on which to draw.

Another matter is seldom mentioned. Those who have cited the need for equity in their rush toward alternative assessment should recognize that students who score poorly on the much-maligned norm-referenced tests with their multiple-choice responses are not necessarily going to perform better on the alternatives. In fact, there is reason to suspect that the weakest students could look even worse—though they may avoid the embarrassment of being ranked and compared on a numerical scale.

In England in the late 1980s, when the assessments that make up the General Certificate of Secondary Education were changed to put more emphasis on performance tasks (which are assessed by classroom teachers) and less on written answers, the gaps between the average scores of various ethnic groups *increased* rather than narrowed.[10] While such findings should not dampen the ardor of those eager to court alternative assessment, the suitors must nonetheless be realistic and recognize that the bride has imperfections.

Then there are issues related to the significance of being able to perform a given task. As I pointed out above, it seems reasonable to let students know that they will be examined on their ability to play a certain composition or execute a specific athletic feat. But what about when it is less clear that the performance of the task is indicative of understanding that is transferable and not merely the result of memorization that barely outlasts the assessment?

For example, New York State has used the same tasks for three years to assess the manipulative skills of fourth-graders in science. Each year a new group of fourth-graders goes to the same five testing stations as did fourth-graders the year before, where their skills are assessed in: 1) recognizing the physical properties of an object, 2) predicting, 3) inferring, 4) creating a classification system, and 5) writing a generalization. The main reason why the tasks and the equipment have stayed the same for three years—changes are scheduled for 1992—is that making changes and training teachers to conduct new assessments are expensive.

Fourth-grade teachers throughout New York know which tasks are to be assessed, and there is nothing to prevent them from coaching their students for the performance that occurs each May. Douglas Reynolds, who oversees this science assessment for the state department of education, said that the tasks—such as knowing how and when to use a thermometer or a ruler or an equal-arm balance—are widely transferable, and, even if children practice them in advance, all they are doing is learning what they ought to know. He was quick to add, though, "If we weren't working on a shoestring and if I had an infinite pool of items and if I could go back and train people every year, then the tasks would not be the same each year."

Worries of this sort are not unique to science tests for fourth-graders. At medical schools using alternative assessments there has been concern about the impact of discussions between students who have taken the examinations and those who are waiting to do so. This worry arose in connection with a lengthy assessment that could accommodate only small numbers of students at a time, as they took turns diagnosing mock patients who simulated symptoms.[11]

Expense and time may turn out to be the brakes on the alternative assessment movement, both for the development of instruments and for their use. But thumbing through a portfolio with a student or watching a student perform a task—whatever the psychometric worth of such assessments—adds a degree of intimacy that can be refreshing in an age of depersonalized appraisal.

For instance, when the assessment in Rhode Island shifted from little William's reading to his writing, he was asked to show and discuss the story he considered his best. Asked what he found most troublesome about writing, William—the proud author of a story about a nobleman who has a feast for his friends—did not pause for a moment, issuing a response that is universal in its simplicity for authors of all ages: "The hardest part is covering the blank pages." And so it goes with alternative assessment.

About the Author

Gene I. Maeroff is a senior fellow at the Carnegie Foundation for the Advancement of Teaching, Princeton, N. J., and author of *The School-Smart Parent* (Henry Holt, 1990).

Notes

1. "Performance Assessments in the States," paper prepared by the Council of Chief State School Officers for presentation to the Secretary's Commission on Achieving Necessary Skills. January 1991.
2. Robert Rothman, "Supply of New Assessment Methods Said Trailing Behind Strong Demand," *Education Week*. 20 March 1991, p. 11.
3. Vicki Kowlowitz et al., "Implementing the Objective Structured Clinical Examination in a Traditional Medical School," *Academic Medicine*, June 1991, pp. 345–47.
4. Grant Wiggins. "A True Test: Toward More Authentic and Equitable Assessment," *Phi Delta Kappan*, May 1989, p. 708.
5. "Fifth-Grade Research Performance Assessment," Mark Twain Elementary School document.
6. Excerpted from assessment materials of the Rhode Island Literacy Portfolio Project, 1991.
7. Richard Stainton, "Sinking Rather Than Floating," *Times* (London) *Educational Supplement*, 1 March 1991, p. 15.
8. Diane Hofkins, "Testing Conditions Undermined SATs," *Times* (London) *Educational Supplement*, 9 August 1991, p. 9.
9. Richard J. Stiggins. "Assessment Literacy," *Phi Delta Kappan*, March 1991. p. 535.
10. Desmond L. Nuttall and Harvey Goldstein, "The 1988 Examination Results for ILEA," paper presented to the Inner London Educational Authority Committees, March 1990.
11. Jerry A. Colliver et al., "Test Security in Examinations That Use Standardized-Patient Cases at One Medical School," *Academic Medicine*, May 1991, pp. 279–82.

Catholic Schools Make a Difference: Twenty-five Years of Research

Convey, J. J. 1992. 177–90. Washington, D.C.: National Catholic Educational Association.

Chapter 9: *
Conclusions and Future Research

By design, Catholic schools are academic and faith communities that foster the academic, religious, and value development of their students. To achieve these ends, Catholic schools attempt to create an environment that is characterized by a strong sense of community, high academic standards, discipline and order, a highly committed and collegial faculty, and high levels of parental interest and participation. The evidence from the research suggests that Catholic schools generally are very successful in achieving these goals.

Are Catholic schools more effective than public schools in achieving their goals? This question is difficult to address and impossible to answer conclusively. Some of the observed differences in the outcomes of Catholic schools and public schools could be attributed to non-school factors, such as the type of students enrolled and high levels of parental involvement in their education. Recent studies, however, have produced better empirical evidence to support some measurable Catholic school effect. These same studies, however, also show that good public schools will produce similar effects. What evidence exists for a Catholic school effect?

The Relative Effectiveness of Catholic Schools

Academic Outcomes

The most convincing evidence for the effectiveness of Catholic schools comes from studies based on three national databases: the *National Assessment of Educational Progress*, the *National Education Longitudinal Study of 1988*, and, especially, *High School and Beyond*. Although no absolute criterion for what constitutes effectiveness is established, these and other studies demonstrate that Catholic elementary and secondary school students, on average, score better on tests of academic achievement than do public school students. The differences in the achievement between Catholic school and public school students increase with grade level, occur with cross-sectional and longitudinal data, and are reduced, but still significant, when analyses control for family background.

Catholic schools also send a higher percentage of their students to college than do public schools and are more successful in preventing dropouts than are public schools.

Moreover, for students who enter college, those from Catholic schools are more likely to complete college than are those from public schools.

Catholic schools seem to be particularly effective for disadvantaged students, especially minority students, but also for those from families with lower levels of parental education or family income.

Studies show that minority students in Catholic schools perform better on tests of academic achievement, have higher educational aspirations, and are less likely to drop out of school than are minority students in public schools. Further, the within-school achievement differences between minority students and other students are substantially less in Catholic schools than in public schools. Because of these findings, James Coleman and his associates portrayed Catholic schools as better examples than public schools of the "common school" ideal of American education.

On the other hand, some studies have found that no differences occur in the performance of students from higher social class Catholic and public high schools and, in some cases, students in public schools score slightly higher, but not significantly. Furthermore, early results from NELS:88 indicated that the achievement differences between elementary students from Catholic and public schools are smaller than differences observed for high school students. Moreover, some critics have argued that the Catholic school effects are really too small to have practical import or are based on tests that are too short to be of any significance.

Religious Outcomes and Values

Attending a Catholic school has a measurable effect on the behaviors and values of students, over and above the influence produced by the religiousness of their parents. Andrew Greeley and his associates conducted much of the research on the religious outcomes of Catholic schools in a series of studies, beginning in 1966 with *The Education of Catholic Americans*, and continuing into the 1980's. Greeley's work demonstrated that the relationship between attendance at a Catholic school and various measures of religious attitudes, knowledge and behaviors—church attendance, reception of the sacraments, prayer, attitude toward vocations, doctrinal beliefs, doctrinal orthodoxy, activity in parish organizations, and closeness to the church—increased from the 1960's to the 1980's. As a result, Greeley argued that Catholic schools are much more important in times of crises in the church than in times of stability.

* Editor's note: Chapter notation refers to this excerpt.

Other research indicates that Catholic students in Catholic high schools are more likely than Catholic students in public high schools to attend Mass regularly, view religion as more important in their lives, and have higher religious self-evaluations. In addition, Catholic school students generally place family values ahead of materialistic goals that equate success in life with having a good job and making a lot of money.

Alternative Explanations

Selection

As indicated earlier, the problem of separating student effects from school effects is a chronic one in school effectiveness research. Regardless of the methodology, the sophistication of the analysis, and the number and kinds of confounding variables included, the differences observed could be more a function of the students enrolled than of the school itself. Schools that enroll better students would be expected to have higher test scores, fewer dropouts, and higher educational aspirations than other schools.

Catholic schools do enroll students from a wide socioeconomic range and not all Catholic schools are highly selective. As the evidence presented in Chapter 3 indicates, families at the lowest and highest socioeconomic levels generally are somewhat underrepresented in Catholic schools.

However, studies also show that, on average, the socioeconomic status of students in Catholic schools, the educational level of their parents, and their family income are higher than those of students in public schools. Therefore, the possibility remains that the observed differences between Catholic schools and public schools are due mainly to differences in the ability, motivation, and family background of the students that each enroll.

Parents

Another possible non-school explanation for an apparent Catholic school advantage is the support provided in the home. Parents choose to send their children to Catholic schools for a variety of reasons, which include religious formation and value development. The research indicates that Catholics view the religious nature of Catholic schools as their most distinctive quality and their most important asset, and many parents send their children to Catholic schools primarily because of their religious nature. However, most studies confirm that the school's academic program is a necessary prerequisite for the majority of Catholic parents and a sufficient reason for some parents to enroll their children in a Catholic school. At the same time, most parents who select a Catholic school primarily for academic reasons also value the school's Catholic tradition, religious instruction, sense of community, and caring environment. Whatever reasons parents have for choosing Catholic schools, most parents seek the reinforcement of the values that they stress at home.

The high expectations that Catholic school parents have for their children, the extent to which they monitor their children's work, and their level of involvement in the school, each of which studies have shown is higher than that of the average public school parent, are important contributors to students' success. These factors and the quality and intensity of the interactions they produce are consistent with Coleman's hypothesis of social capital, to which he attributed a large degree of the Catholic school's success.

School Effects

While differences in student characteristics and family background, including parental involvement, remain as possible explanations of the differences between the performance of Catholic school and public school students, recent studies have produced empirical evidence that some school-related factors do in fact contribute to observed differences in student and teacher outcomes over and above the possible contributions of student background and family characteristics. The findings of Tony Bryk and Valerie Lee (Bryk & Raudenbush, 1989; Bryk & Thum, 1989; Lee & Bryk, 1988,1989; Lee, Dedrick, & Smith, 1991) regarding the contribution of school-related factors are particularly compelling. Moreover, Catholic schools tend to be higher on these school-related factors than do public schools. This evidence is important since it provides stronger empirical support for the possible effectiveness of Catholic schools that is separate from explanations that depend upon the type of students enrolled. What are these school-related factors and how do Catholic schools measure against them?

The school-related factors that research has identified as contributing to differences in student and teacher outcomes involve the organization of schools and their environments. Research shows that when these organizational and environmental factors are present in any school, public or Catholic, measurable differences in outcomes occur. For the most part, however, Catholic schools are more likely to evidence these school-related factors than are public schools. These factors are the school's academic and curricular policies and the school's characteristic culture, as indicated by its consensus on goals, its sense of community, its standard of order and discipline, and the collegiality, commitment, efficacy and satisfaction of its teachers.

Academic and Curricular Policies

Studies (Coleman & Hoffer, 1987; Lee & Bryk, 1988,1989) show that organizational differences among schools regarding academic and curricular policies substantially influence students' achievement. Furthermore, these organizational differences are under the control of individual schools, rather than a result of the types of students enrolled. Therefore, the presence of such policies provides evidence for a school effect.

Catholic schools have a focused curriculum, which includes a strong commitment to a core academic program for all students (Bryk et al., 1984). Lee and Bryk (1988) convincingly demonstrated that the course enrollment patterns of students in Catholic schools not only are a function of the type of students served, but also a reflection of a school philosophy that values academics. Instruction that is tailored to the needs of the students at different ability levels varies in pacing and intensity, but not content. Even the electives in Catholic schools ordinarily have an academic orientation (Bryk et al., 1984). Furthermore, school policies, rather than student choices, determine placements in different curricular tracks.

As a result of school policies, Catholic high school students, regardless of background, are more likely to be in an academic program than are public high school students (Coleman & Hoffer, 1987; Lee & Bryk, 1988). Catholic high school students also are more likely to take more and more rigorous academic courses than are public high school students (Bryk et al., 1984; Coleman et al., 1982; Rock et al., 1986). Moreover, the educational aspirations of Catholic school students correspond more closely to their academic placements than do those of public school students (Lee & Bryk, 1988). In Catholic schools, expectations are high for all students, regardless of background and ability.

The strong emphasis on academic work benefits all students, particularly disadvantaged students. As the research reviewed in this book indicates, the results of this commitment to academics are clearly evident in Catholic schools: homework is more likely assigned and more time is spent on it, attendance is better, dropouts are fewer, and interest and effort are higher.

Characteristic Culture

The culture or ethos of a school, the spirit that gives a school its distinctive character, has long been hypothesized as an important component of effective schools. Most studies provided either anecdotal or descriptive evidence that suggested the centrality of a school's culture to its success (Grant, 1988; Kleinfeld, 1979; Lesko, 1988; Lightfoot, 1983; Rutter et al., 1979). However, recent studies have produced stronger empirical evidence for the importance of the school's culture in affecting student and teacher outcomes (Bryk & Driscoll, 1988; Bryk & Thum, 1989; Lee et al., 1991; Newmann et al., 1989).

A school's culture develops intentionally from its goals and objectives, the vision and leadership of its administrators, the commitment and sense of purpose of its faculty, the shared values of the entire school community, including parents, and, in the case of a private school, the ideals of its founders. Students help fashion a school's culture; however, the adult members of the school community are its major architects. Thus, a school's culture is predominantly a school effect, rather than merely a function of the type of students enrolled.

Strong evidence exists that a sense of community dominates the culture of the typical Catholic school and plays a major role in the school's effectiveness. Called a "functional community" by Coleman, this faith community fosters an environment that supports the religious and academic norms of parents by establishing a strong academic curriculum, by exercising greater control within the school in order to place greater demands upon students, and by creating a communal atmosphere among faculty and students that is conducive to the social and spiritual development of students.

Research shows tènt of Catholic schools promotes student learning more than does the environment and climate of public schools. Catholic schools function more as communities than do public schools and have fewer disciplinary problems. Catholic schools generally place a stronger emphasis on academics and have more demanding academic requirements than do public schools. Catholic school teachers rate their students higher in cooperation, motivation, discipline, and school interest than public school teachers rate their students. In addition, compared with the typical public school student, the typical Catholic school student spends more time on homework, misses fewer days of school, and is less likely to cut class.

Teachers

Many teachers choose to work in Catholic schools because of their desire to minister to the faith community in the schools. At the same time, most teachers evidence a high commitment to students and to the professional aspects of teaching. Compared with public school teachers, Catholic school teachers generally enjoy higher levels of collegiality, are more committed, are happier with their relationships with their principals, and have higher job satisfaction and sense of efficacy. Catholic school teachers perceive that the goals of their schools are clearer, and they are more in agreement among themselves concerning the goals and policies of the schools than are public school teachers. Catholic school teachers feel they have more influence over matters of school policy and more control over instructional decisions than do public school teachers. In addition, students in Catholic schools rate the quality of their teachers and the instruction they receive higher than do students in public schools. Finally, students in Catholic schools, compared with students in public schools, report getting along better with their teachers and perceive the teachers to be more interested in them.

Conclusion

Empirical evidence is available that school effects clearly explain some of the differences in student outcomes that are not attributable to the types of students enrolled. These effects are found in schools with focused academic and curricular policies and with supportive cultures. Such school-related factors are likely to occur in all good schools; however, the average Catholic school is more likely than the average public school to possess them.

Although the research supports the higher average outcomes of Catholic schools and the greater likelihood of Catholic schools possessing effective school-related factors, not every Catholic school is necessarily an effective school. As indicated in Chapter 1, the effectiveness of a particular school must be separately ascertained. Schools vary in their degree of effectiveness and each school must be judged on its own merits. The research does suggest, however, that Catholic schools are more likely than public schools to possess those characteristics that research has associated with effective schools and that less variability occurs in the measures of effectiveness among Catholic schools than among public schools.

Future Priorities

Despite the dramatic increase in the number of studies dealing with Catholic schools during the past 25 years, the research agenda on Catholic schools is far from complete. A concerted research effort is needed that will enable researchers, policy makers, and consumers to understand Catholic schools better, monitor the quality of their products, and continue to identify those factors that contribute to the schools' effectiveness. This research effort requires three things: (1) the use of new methodologies, which will improve the quality of the studies on Catholic schools; (2) the establishment of national research priorities, which will require a coordinated, well-funded effort by Catholic educational leaders and researchers; and (3) the further examination, in greater depth, of the nature of Catholic schools and their effects, which individual researchers or graduate students, perhaps in doctoral dissertations or master's theses, could profitably explore.

Methodological Priorities

Three changes in the design of studies on Catholic schools would result in better information concerning the schools. The methodological priorities are: (1) an increase in studies using an ethnographic design, as opposed to a survey design; (2) the use of longitudinal, rather than cross-sectional, designs; and (3) the incorporation of more appropriate statistical models to analyze data.

Ethnographic Studies

The vast majority of major studies on Catholic schools are descriptive or comparative studies that employ a survey research methodology. Survey research typically uses questionnaires or interviews to determine opinions, attitudes, and perceptions. The advantage of survey research generally is that a considerable amount of data is obtained with a minimal investment of time and money. However, the quality of the data from survey research is limited by the quality of the questions asked and by both the knowledge of the person who responds to the information requested and his or her willingness to answer the questions accurately.

The research on Catholic schools would benefit from an increase in the use of an ethnographic methodology. Ethnographic research is a type of observational research in which the researcher performs an in-depth investigation of a situation, both as an observer and as a genuine participant. Ethnographic research usually occurs in a naturalistic setting; that is, the researcher records and studies behavior as it normally occurs. This type of research is labor-intensive because data are collected on many variables over an extended period of time. These data may come from interviews, field notes, diaries, chronologies, questionnaires, checklists, and audio or video recordings. The analysis of ethnographic data is largely qualitative and inductive, rather than statistical and deductive.

Since the late 1970's, educational researchers have recognized the value of ethnographic studies and, as a result, the frequency of these studies increased rapidly in the 1980's. A major reason educational researchers turned more to an ethnographic methodology, traditionally the principal methodology for many anthropologists and sociologists, was the ineffectiveness of survey research to provide for sufficient understanding of how schools work and how students learn.

With regard to research on Catholic schools, ethnographic studies would be particularly useful in examining how the transmission of values occurs in the school, to what extent values are integrated into the entire curriculum, how the faith community of the school is established and nurtured, and how the commitment of the teachers and the leadership of the principal affect the outcomes of Catholic schools. Two excellent examples of ethnographic studies involving Catholic schools are Lesko's (1988) study of the culture of a Catholic high school and Helm's (1990) study of the leadership of four elementary school principals.

Ethnographic research requires committed, well-trained, and disciplined researchers, who have the time and funding to devote to this intensive type of research. While ethnographic research demands substantial effort, the methodology has the potential to yield rich insights that may elude researchers who use a survey methodology.

Longitudinal Studies

Despite the increasing popularity and utility of ethnographic research, the majority of educational research, including studies on Catholic schools, will continue to collect data using tests, questionnaires, and surveys and will use quantitative, statistical methods to analyze these data. Thus, a second methodological priority involves an improvement in the design of quantitative studies about Catholic schools.

Longitudinal studies, which follow the same group of students over an extended period of time, would greatly assist Catholic educators in learning about the effects of Catholic schools. The major longitudinal studies involving Catholic schools are those associated with the federally-sponsored *National Longitudinal Study, High School and Beyond*, and *The National Education Longitudinal Study of 1988*. No important study of Catholic schools under Catholic auspices has used a longitudinal methodology. Some studies were retrospective examinations by adults on the effects of Catholic schools on their behavior. Other studies were cross-sectional, comparing two different groups of students at two grade levels with data collected at the same time. And some studies were snapshots of a group of students at a particular time.

A longitudinal study permits a microscopic view of development and growth. In such a study, the individual studied becomes his or her own control. Thus, a longitudinal study eliminates many of the limitations associated with retrospective, cross-sectional, and one-shot studies. A longitudinal study would assist in better understanding how Catholic schools promote the development of religious knowledge and values, and how successful the schools are in doing this, a topic of great importance to the American bishops, Catholic educational leaders, and consumers of Catholic education.

Longitudinal studies are very expensive; they require dedicated resources, careful management, and adequate funding. A nation-wide, longitudinal study of Catholic schools would require massive funding, especially if the data are collected over a period of years. However, longitudinal studies in local situations are feasible, particularly if the time between the data collections is somewhat short and the number of subjects is rather small.

Analytic Priorities

The use of modern advanced statistical methods for analyzing data, when their use is appropriate, would increase the potential of studies on Catholic schools to uncover the true relationship between the variables being studied and the credibility of the findings from these studies. Catholic school researchers have commonly used regression models and various multivariate methods to analyze data. However, other important statistical techniques, such as structural equations, path analysis, or LISREL models, have not been widely used by Catholic school researchers.

A promising recent analytic strategy for studying school effects is the hierarchical linear model (Raudenbush & Bryk, 1986). Educational researchers have long recognized the multilevel nature of the data used to study the effectiveness of schools. Some data are from individual students (student-level), while other data are from entire classrooms, schools, or districts (school-level). The use of different levels of data in regression models has always been unsatisfactory. A hierarchical linear model accommodates both student-level and school-level data, avoids problems associated with aggregation bias, and permits better estimates of the school effects. Anthony Bryk from the University of Chicago, one of the chief architects of this recent contribution to the statistical literature, and Valerie Lee from the University of Michigan already have applied the hierarchical linear model to data from Catholic schools (Bryk & Raudenbush, 1989; Bryk & Thum, 1989; Lee & Bryk, 1989; Lee, Dedrick, & Smith, 1991; Lee & Smith, 1990).

National Research Priorities

The two major initiatives proposed as national research priorities for Catholic education are: (1) a comprehensive

study of Catholic elementary schools, similar to the studies of Catholic secondary schools, such as *The Catholic High School: A National Portrait* and *Catholic High Schools: Their Impact on Low-Income Students*; and (2) a comprehensive study of the religious outcomes of Catholic schools.

Research on Catholic Elementary Schools

The national leaders of Catholic schools should give the highest priority to sponsoring a comprehensive, empirical study of Catholic elementary schools in the United States. Despite wide recognition that the elementary grades represent the most important formative years for the development of cognitive skills, values, and attitudes, no major study of Catholic elementary schools has occurred since *Catholic Schools in Action* in 1966.

Most of the research on Catholic schools has involved high schools. The research from *High School and Beyond*, portions of Greeley's research, and all of the major studies sponsored by NCEA during the 1980's collected data about high schools. Data concerning Catholic elementary schools were part of the recent preliminary studies from NELS:88 (Hafner et al. 1990; Rock & Pollack 1990) and the research on Catholic inner-city elementary schools, sponsored by the Catholic League for Civil Rights (Cibulka et al., 1982). However, these were not comprehensive studies of Catholic elementary education, and they included other types of schools, as well as Catholic schools.

A model for the study of Catholic elementary schools is the series of studies on Catholic high schools sponsored by NCEA and conducted by the Search Institute. *The Catholic High School: A National Portrait* (Yeager et al., 1985) provided an in-depth look at the modern Catholic high school. This study and its associated studies on low-income-serving Catholic high schools (Benson et al., 1986) and on the beliefs and values of high school teachers (Benson & Guerra, 1985) provided a rich database for researchers, policy makers, and practitioners. The Catholic educational community needs a similar database for Catholic elementary schools.

Religious Outcomes of Catholic Schools

A comprehensive study of the effects of Catholic schools on the religious knowledge, practice, and values of their graduates is a second research priority that the leaders of Catholic education should embrace.

Catholic schools do more than simply teach academic subjects. As faith communities with formal programs of religious instruction, Catholic schools strive to develop in their students a deeper understanding of the Catholic faith, a commitment to full participation in the life of the church, and a set of values which will influence students' lives. These are the reasons that the Catholic community will continue to support Catholic schools and parents will continue to make sacrifices to send their children to these schools.

Research (Convey, 1990; O'Brien, 1987) shows that most of the Catholic community and the vast majority of bishops and priests believe Catholic schools are more important today than they were in the past. Catholic schools receive this endorsement from most respondents because of the religious and spiritual dimensions of the schools, not the academic dimension. However, a few bishops and a significant number of priests around the country have expressed concern about the Catholic identity of the schools, and some feel that going to a Catholic school doesn't seem to make a difference in the religious practice of many graduates.

Because the commitment to the religious formation of students is so essential to the very nature of Catholic schools, monitoring the effectiveness of the schools in this regard should receive the highest priority. A few of the questions that a national study could address are: How effectively do Catholic schools teach religion? Why do some schools have effective religious education programs and others do not? Do Catholics who attend Catholic schools grow more in their understanding of Catholic doctrine than do Catholics who attend other schools? How do Catholic schools help to develop the commitment of their students toward full participation in the life of the church? Do Catholic school graduates differ from Catholics who are graduates of other schools in the active practice of their faith? How important is the cooperation between the school and the home regarding the religious education of children? What is the school's contribution to the religious development of its students, over and above the contribution of the home?

Other Research Priorities

The other areas of research to which Catholic educators and researchers should give priority are studies concerning: (1) the school as community, (2) leadership, (3) values, (4) parental choice, (5) teachers, and (6) single-sex and coed schools.

School as Community

A recurrent theme in the research on effective schools is that good schools have a sense of community, which has a positive effect on the quality of life for both teachers and students. The church asks that Catholic schools create and nurture a vibrant faith community. Research (Benson et al., 1986; Benson & Guerra, 1985; Yeager et al., 1985) indicates that Catholic schools attempt to build and sustain a successful faith community through: (1) the presence of specific community building structures; (2) a teaching staff whose members have a commitment to develop the faith community; and (3) the leadership of the principal in fostering the faith community of the school. However, more research is needed concerning what specific activities are effective in promoting the school as community, particularly as a faith community, and how this community contributes to the academic, religious, and social development of the students.

Coleman has hypothesized that part of the effectiveness of Catholic schools is explained by the functional community that resides in and surrounds the schools, and by the efficacious social capital produced by that community. Coleman's hypothesis concerning the importance of the functional community and social capital should be tested empirically. To what extent is a functional community present in a Catholic school, how extensive is that community within the school and outside the school, and how does the functional community influence the daily life of the school? In what ways does the functional community generate social capital and what are the effects of social capital on student outcomes? The study of these questions presents researchers with the challenging problems of developing both operational definitions of functional community and social capital, and appropriate scales to measure each construct.

Leadership

The research on effective schools emphasizes the importance of the principal as the instructional leader of the school (Purkey & Smith, 1985). Other research shows that the principal's leadership has a positive influence on teachers' sense of efficacy (Lee et al., 1991). Effective Catholic schools, however, must have principals who also exercise strong leadership in the creation of the faith community of the school.

Continuing research, analogous to Helm's (1990) study concerning the leadership role of Catholic school principals, is needed. The results of this research on leadership have practical implications for the hiring and training of Catholic school principals. Further, research on the leadership of the principal in a Catholic school will be increasingly more important in the 1990's as the schools strive to offer a quality academic and religious education in the face of increasing costs and a diminishing presence of administrators and faculty members from religious communities.

Some of the relevant research questions concerning the leadership of the principal are: How does the principal of a Catholic school facilitate the establishment and maintenance of the faith community of the school? How do effective principals deal with the faculty, students, and parents? What are the characteristics of principals who are recognized as effective leaders? Why are some principals effective leaders and others are not? How does the training of principals influence their style of leadership?

Another area of research on leadership concerns the development of student leaders. One goal of Catholic schools is to produce leaders for the church and for the community. What do Catholic schools do to nurture the leadership potential of their students, to encourage their involvement in their parishes and in their communities, and to foster vocations? Research (Convey, 1983) from *High School and Beyond* indicates that Catholic school students often place a higher value on community leadership as a life goal than do public school students; however, the research also shows that leadership generally receives a low priority from students. What do Catholic schools do to foster leadership in students while the students are still in school and to prepare them for future leadership roles? Are leadership skills and academic skills related? What are the qualities of a good student leader?

Values

Studies are needed concerning: (1) the relationship between Catholic schools and the home in the development of values; (2) the types of values Catholic schools are most successful in developing; and (3) how the development of values occurs in the schools.

The school's contribution to the development of a student's values, over and above the influence of the student's home, is still largely unresolved. Catholic schools generally complement the values that are promoted in the home. Students from homes with value systems that are congruent with the values of the schools are likely to benefit most from Catholic schools. However, Catholic schools seemingly are able to overcome and compensate for the disadvantaged backgrounds of some students who do not receive enough support in their homes. More research is needed on the relationship between the school and the home in the formation of values.

Are schools more successful in facilitating the development of one type of values over another? What is the relationship between social values, religious/moral values, family values, and academic values? Studies also are needed to explore why students do not give higher priority to certain issues involving social justice, such as working to correct social and economic inequalities (Convey, 1984; Guerra et al., 1990), despite Catholic schools placing a great deal of emphasis on social justice values (Yeager et al., 1985).

The role of the teacher in value development is widely recognized. Teachers are role models who, intentionally or not, communicate values. What are the mechanisms within the school community to assist in the development of student values and how effective are these mechanisms? What specific things do teachers do to help in the development of student values? How much emphasis does the school place on the teaching of values? Is more or less emphasis paid to values in high school than in elementary school? How are values integrated into the entire curriculum? Do some teachers "leave the teaching of values" to others? What is the relationship between the teachers' emphases on values and the strength of the functional community in Catholic schools?

Parental Choice

A considerable amount of research already exists concerning why parents choose Catholic schools. As noted earlier, the research suggests that parents send their children to Catholic schools for a variety of reasons, which include the school's academic program, Catholic tradition, religious education, emphasis on values, caring atmosphere, and discipline. For some parents, the perceived quality of the academic program of a particular Catholic school is sufficient reason to send their children to the school; however, most parents want more from the school than just a good academic program. On the other hand, very few parents will send their children to a school that they feel is not going to provide a good academic education.

Very little is known, however, as to how parents obtain and use information about a Catholic school to help them decide whether to enroll their children in that school. Some parents have firsthand information about the school from an older child already enrolled there, or they learn what they can about the school from a friend or neighbor or from personal visits. Other parents may act with incomplete information. A fascinating area of potential research, as yet completely untapped, is the extent to which parents use the representativeness and availability heuristics (Tversky & Kahneman, 1974) in making decisions about Catholic schools, what evidence the parents use in forming these heuristics, and whether parents attempt to verify any of this evidence. This area of research would have considerable consequences on how Catholic schools are marketed and portrayed to the public.

Yet another area of research concerns why Catholic parents who can afford to send their children to Catholic schools decide not to do so. To what extent is the lack of a conveniently-located Catholic school, the unavailability issue long championed by Greeley, a factor for many parents?

Do parents no longer value Catholic schools? If not, is it because parents have become increasingly secular and don't see the value of the religious aspect of Catholic schools? Or, do parents see a greater value in having their children attend public schools? Is it because parents lack courage or conviction, or are simply unwilling to change their financial priorities, despite having sufficient resources to afford Catholic schools? Again, the results of this research would be extremely helpful to those responsible for public relations and the marketing of Catholic schools.

Teachers

The presence of committed teachers in a school leads to a strong sense of community in the school. Research (Chubb & Moe, 1988; Salganik & Karweit, 1982) shows that teacher commitment is strongly related to value consensus and collegiality, each essential elements of community.

Catholic schools are fortunate to have many dedicated and committed teachers who work for far less compensation than they would receive if they taught in public schools. In addition to demonstrating commitment to students, teaching, and the school, Catholic school teachers often exhibit commitment to the mission of Catholic education. Research (Ciriello, 1988) shows the commitment to mission is precisely the major reason why many teachers choose to work in Catholic schools.

Additional studies are needed to understand more fully the commitment of Catholic school teachers and its relationship to their satisfaction, efficacy, and sense of ministry.

How does the commitment of lay teachers compare with the commitment of teachers from religious communities? Why do individuals decide to teach in Catholic schools, why do they remain teaching in these schools, and how satisfied are they? Clearly, the adult members of the community set the tone for the entire community. Do Catholic school teachers fully understand their role in developing the faith community of the school? Do the teachers perceive their teaching as ministry?

Single-Sex and Coed Schools

Research (Lee & Bryk, 1986; Lee & Marks, 1990; Riordan, 1990; Schneider & Coutts, 1982) shows that single-sex Catholic high schools seem to have specific advantages over coed Catholic high schools in the areas of academic achievement, educational aspirations, attitudes and behaviors related to academics, and stereotypes concerning sex roles. The advantages of single-sex schools are particularly notable for minority students, and overall for girls more than for boys.

While some studies have controlled for family and personal background variables, courses taken by students, and the social composition of the school, a number of issues are largely unresolved. Is the apparent effectiveness of single-sex schools due to the fact that they enroll students of one sex, or do other factors explain some of the differences between these schools and coed schools?

Why do females seem to benefit from single-sex education more than males do? Single-sex Catholic schools are more likely than coed Catholic schools to be highly academic and quite selective. Studies have found that boys' Catholic schools tend to have the highest average socioeconomic status, compared to other types of Catholic schools, raising the possibility that boys' schools are more selective than girls' schools. Have previous studies adequately controlled for the selectivity of single-sex schools? Is it possible that, in the case of boys' schools, the controls applied have resulted in an overadjustment, and hence an underestimate, of the outcome effects?

Studies are needed that compare the cultures of single-sex Catholic schools and coed Catholic schools. Do single-sex schools emphasize academics more than coed schools? Why does the separation of academic concerns from social concerns in single-sex schools seem to result in more favorable outcomes for girls than for boys? Why do single-sex schools seem to place a higher emphasis on discipline and order than do coed schools? Do girls in single-sex schools have better role models than do girls in coed schools? Research indicates that girls' schools seem to enjoy a higher sense of community than other types of schools. Is that because girls' schools tend to be smaller than other Catholic schools, or are there other factors at work here?

Finally, what is the influence of the sponsorship by a religious community on a single-sex school? In what ways do single-sex schools that are owned and operated by a religious community differ in their academic and spiritual cultures from parish or diocesan single-sex schools?

Planning for the Future of Catholic Schools

During the past 25 years, the research on Catholic schools has assisted the Catholic educational community to deepen its understanding about Catholic schools and their effects. This book has identified some of the major studies on Catholic schools and has presented some of their principal findings. While the number of studies on Catholic schools has increased dramatically in recent years, even more studies are needed to understand Catholic schools more fully and to keep abreast of changes.

This chapter identifies specific priorities for future research on Catholic schools. Three priorities concern changes in the methodology of studies; implementation of these changes would improve the quality of research on Catholic schools. Other priorities are for studies that focus on the uniqueness of Catholic schools and their effects. These studies will result in a better understanding of what makes Catholic schools different from other schools, why the schools deserve the support of the church and of parents, and what differences the schools make in the lives of their students and their roles as future Catholic leaders. Two of these studies are proposed as national research priorities: the comprehensive study of Catholic elementary schools and the study of the impact of Catholic schools on the religious knowledge, beliefs, practices, and attitudes of their students and their graduates.

At the same time, studies must continue to explore the academic effectiveness of Catholic schools. The results of these studies will permit Catholic educators to monitor the academic quality of the schools and to further their understanding of the factors that contribute to the excellence of the schools. In addition, the public dissemination of results of these studies will greatly assist the public relations and marketing efforts of individual schools.

One final word. The research discussed in this book provides evidence concerning the nature of Catholic schools and the effectiveness of their programs. However, two of the types of studies, each a type of institutional research, are needed to ensure the continued excellence of Catholic schools. The first is the monitoring of the entire school program by the school itself, through participation in diocesan and regional accreditation programs. The self-study activities that are part of most accreditation programs enable a school to identify aspects of its program that require improvement. The external review by a visiting team of educators, both immediately following the self study and periodically thereafter, and the accreditation decision provide motivation for the school to improve areas that are found deficient.

The second type of study is the long-range, strategic planning by a diocese of its Catholic schools. Diocesan strategic planning efforts should result in the development of policies concerning finances, governance, curriculum, marketing and public relations, and development programs for the schools, as well as a coordinated plan for the future placement of the schools in the diocese. By careful

The Principal as Educational Leader

planning, a diocese can help provide for the continuation of its Catholic schools and their future excellence.

References

Benson, P. L., & Guerra, M. J. (1985). *Sharing the faith: The beliefs and values of Catholic high school teachers*. Washington, DC: National Catholic Educational Association.

Benson, P. L., Yeager, R. J., Wood, P. K., Guerra, M. J., & Manno, B. V. (1986). *Catholic high schools: Their impact on low-income students*. Washington, DC: National Catholic Educational Association.

Bryk, A. S., & Driscoll, M. E. (1988). *The high school as community: Contextual influences, and consequences for students and teachers*. Madison, WI: Wisconsin Center for Education Research.

Bryk, A. S., Holland, P. B., Lee, V. E., & Carriedo, R. A. (1984). *Effective Catholic schools: An exploration*. Washington, DC: National Catholic Educational Association.

Bryk, A. S., & Raudenbush, S. W. (1989). Toward a more appropriate conceptualization of research on school effects: A three-level hierarchical model. In Bock, R. D. (Ed.) *Multilevel analysis of educational data*. New York: Academic Press.

Bryk, A. S., & Thum, Y. M. (1989). The effect of high school organization on dropping out: An exploratory investigation. *American Educational Research Journal, 26*, 353–383.

Chubb, J. E., & Moe, T. M. (1988). Politics, markets, and the organization of schools. *American Political Science Review, 82*, 1055–1087.

Cibulka, J. G., O'Brien, T. J., & Zewe, D. (1982). *Inner-city private elementary schools*. Milwaukee: Marquette University Press.

Ciriello, M. J. (1988). Teachers in Catholic schools: A study of commitment. (Doctoral dissertation, The Catholic University of America, 1987.) *Dissertation Abstracts International, 48*, 8514A.

Coleman, J. S., Hoffer, T., & Kilgore, S. (1982). *High school achievement: Public, Catholic, & private schools compared*. New York: Basic Books.

Coleman, J. S., & Hoffer, T. (1987). *Public and private high schools: The impact of communities*. New York: Basic Books.

Convey, J. J. (1983, April). *Religious practice and value orientation of Catholic adolescents*. Paper presented to the annual meeting of the National Catholic Educational Association, Washington.

Convey, J. J. (1984). Encouraging findings about students' religious values. *Momentum, 15(2)*, 47–49.

Convey, J. J. (1990). *Archdiocese of Boston planning study: Results of parent surveys*. Washington, DC: The Catholic University of America.

Grant, G. (1988). *The world we created at Hamilton High*. Cambridge, MA: Harvard University Press.

Greeley, A. M., & Rossi, P. B. (1966). *The education of Catholic Americans*. Chicago: Aldine Publishing Company.

Guerra, M. J., Donahue, M. J., & Benson, P. (1990). *The heart of the matter: Effects of Catholic High Schools on student values, beliefs, and behaviors*. Washington, DC: National Catholic Educational Association.

Hafner, A., Ingels, S., Schneider, B., & Stevenson, D. (1990). *A profile of the American eighth grader: NELS:88 students' descriptive summary*. Washington, DC: National Center for Education Statistics.

Helm, C. M. (1990). Cultural and symbolic leadership in Catholic elementary schools: An ethnographic study. (Doctoral dissertation, The Catholic University of America, 1989.) *Dissertation Abstracts International, 50*, 1156A.

Kleinfeld, J. S. (1979). *Eskimo school on the Andreafsky: A study of effective bicultural education*. New York: Praeger.

Lee, V. E., & Bryk, A. S. (1986). Effects of single-sex secondary schools on student achievement and attitudes. *Journal of Educational Psychology, 78*, 381–395.

Lee, V. E., & Bryk, A. S. (1988). Curriculum tracking as mediating the social distribution of high school achievement. *Sociology of Education, 61*, 78–94.

Lee, V. E., & Bryk, A. S. (1989). A multilevel model of the social distribution of high school achievement. *Sociology of Education, 62*, 172–192.

Lee, V. E., Dedrick, R. F., & Smith, J. B. (1991). The effect of the social organization of schools on teachers' efficacy and satisfaction. *Sociology of Education, 64*, 190–208.

Lee, V. E., & Marks, H. M. (1990). Sustained effects of the single-sex secondary school experience on attitudes, behaviors, and values in college. *Journal of Educational Psychology, 82*, 578–592.

Lee, V. E., & Smith, J. B. (1990). Gender equity in teachers' salaries: A multilevel approach. *Educational Evaluation and Policy Analysis, 12*, 57–81.

Lesko, N. L. (1988). *Symbolizing society*. Philadelphia: Falmer Press.

Lightfoot, S. L. (1983). *The good high school: Portraits of character and culture*. New York: Basic Books.

Newmann, F. M., Rutter, R. A., & Smith, M. S. (1989). Organizational factors that affect school sense of efficacy, community, and expectations. *Sociology of Education, 62*, 221–238.

O'Brien, J. S. (1987). *Mixed messages: What bishops and priests say about Catholic schools*. Washington, DC: National Catholic Educational Association.

Purkey, S. C., & Smith, M. A. (1985). Educational policy and school effectiveness. In Austin, G. R., & Garber, H. (Eds.) *Research on exemplary schools*. New York: Academic Press.

Raudenbush, S., & Bryk, A. S. (1986). A hierarchical model for studying school effects. *Sociology of Education, 59*, 1–17.

Riordan, C. (1990). *Girls and boys in school: Together or separate?* New York: Teachers College Press.

Rock, D. A., Ekstrom, R. B., Goertz, M. E., & Pollack, J. M. (1986). *Study of excellence in high school education: Longitudinal study, 1980–82 final report*. Washington, DC: U.S. Department of Education, Center for Education Statistics.

Rock, D. A., & Pollack, J. M. (1990, April). *Test achievement of NELS:88 eighth-grade students*. Paper presented to the annual meeting of the American Educational Research Association, Boston.

Rutter, M., Maughan, B., Mortimore, P., Ouston, J., & Smith, A. (1979). *Fifteen thousand hours: Secondary schools and their effects on children*. Cambridge, MA: Harvard University Press.

Salganik, L. H., & Karweit, N. (1982). Voluntarism and governance in education. *Sociology of Education, 55*, 152–161.

Schneider, F. W., & Coutts, L. M. (1982). The high school environment: A comparison of coeducational and single-sex schools. *Journal of Educational Psychology, 74*, 898–906.

Tversky, A., & Kahneman, D. (1974). Judgment under uncertainty: Heuristics and biases. *Science, 185*, 1124–1131.

Yeager, R. J., Benson, P. L., Guerra, M. J., & Manno, B. V. (1985). *The Catholic high school: A national portrait*. Washington, DC: National Catholic Educational Association.

Evaluation of the School's Catholicity

Doyle, R., N. Kinate, A. Langan, and M. Swanson. 1991. In *Capital wisdom: Papers from the Principals Academy 1991*, 1–6. Washington, D.C.: National Catholic Educational Association.

To Teach as Jesus Did, the American bishops' pastoral, is pivotal to any meaningful consideration of the catholicity of a Catholic school. What is unique and distinctive about a Catholic school can easily be blurred. For a Catholic school to be true to its mission as an agent of change in this world, its Catholic identity must be evident and operative.

At the heart of this Catholic identity is the love of God and others that motivates and permeates relationships and daily activities. Beyond this core reality, *To Teach as Jesus Did* and subsequent church documents describe characteristics that identify the four essential and interrelated concepts of message, worship, community and service.

These concepts form an evaluative instrument in enabling leadership to get a perspective on the catholicity of a school.

Objectives:

1. To assist local school leadership with a means of accountability for the catholicity of its school
2. To contribute to the continuance of Catholic schools, not only as communities of academic excellence but also as viable and credible communities of faith
3. To provide an instrument for evaluation, reflection and growth

Process:

Phase 1: Administrator evaluation
Phase 2: Review of results
Phase 3: Follow-up

Indicators of Catholic Identity

Principals, teachers, staff, students, parents and parishioners view each other as brothers and sisters in Christ.

The truths of the Gospel as proclaimed by the Catholic Church are taught with conviction.

Gospel values are incorporated into all aspects of school life.

A supportive environment enables the young to mature in the faith.

Students are challenged to live the gospel message.

An excellent and comprehensive program is provided by ministers of Catholic education.

Source: *The Religious Dimension of Education in a Catholic School*, Congregation for Catholic Education, Rome, 1988.

Phase 1: Administrator evaluation

Directions: Circle the response that best describes your school.

1. Consistently
2. Often
3. Sometimes
4. Seldom
5. Never

Message

There is evidence of systematic religious education.

   1   2   3   4   5

Updated theological and liturgical materials are used.

   1   2   3   4   5

Teachers are involved in ongoing religious formation and theological studies.

   1   2   3   4   5

The life and values of Jesus are consciously integrated into the curriculum.

   1   2   3   4   5

There is a definite effort between school and home to share faith activities.

   1   2   3   4   5

Visible signs and symbols of Catholic faith are displayed.

   1   2   3   4   5

The Bible is used as a primary source of religious education.

   1   2   3   4   5

Worship

Daily prayer experiences for children and staff are provided to nourish a personal relationship with Christ.

   1   2   3   4   5

Sacramental preparation and celebration hold high priority in the curriculum.

   1   2   3   4   5

Liturgical celebrations and the liturgical feasts are opportunities for integrating life and prayer on a regular basis.

   1   2   3   4   5

Faith stories and experiences are shared.

   1   2   3   4   5

Time is scheduled for retreats and/or days of reflection.

   1   2   3   4   5

Community

Specific means are provided for developing the Catholic lifestyle and spirituality of staff, students and parents.

   1   2   3   4   5

The atmosphere is Christian and caring.

   1   2   3   4   5

There is good morale.

   1   2   3   4   5

Parents are an integral part of this faith and learning community.

   1   2   3   4   5

Actions reflect what is stated in the school philosophy.

| 1 | 2 | 3 | 4 | 5 |

Students and their opinions are respected.

| 1 | 2 | 3 | 4 | 5 |

A cooperative relationship with the clergy is evident.

| 1 | 2 | 3 | 4 | 5 |

Service

Students are taught habits of heart and mind for service.

| 1 | 2 | 3 | 4 | 5 |

Students are involved in activities that reflect global awareness and environmental sensitivity.

| 1 | 2 | 3 | 4 | 5 |

Special consideration is given to those in need.

| 1 | 2 | 3 | 4 | 5 |

Specific outreach projects are done.

| 1 | 2 | 3 | 4 | 5 |

Phase II: Review of results

The entire staff reviews the results, identifies the weakest area and plans strategies.

Phase III: Follow-up

Worship	Strategy	Responsible Person	Timeline
Prayer	Whole school praying	Principal/ student	Weekly/ ongoing
	Home room prayer	Home room Teacher	Daily in classroom
	Faculty prayer	Principal	Every Friday before class
Sacraments			
Eucharist:	Teachers involve parents and children	Sacramental team	One meeting per month
Reconciliation:	Teachers involve parents and children	Sacramental team	One meeting per month
Confirmation: (if in 7th or 8th grades)	Teachers involve parents and children	Sacramental team	One meeting per month
Liturgy	Student involvement in preparation and participation	Principal/ teachers/music ministers/clergy	Once a month minimum
Faith Experiences	Two retreats outside school	Planning committee	Present to end of year
Theological Update	Each faculty member attends one program	Principal and faculty	Present to end of year

Resources

National Conference of Catholic Bishops, *To Teach as Jesus Did* Washington, DC, 1972.

The Catholic Identity of Catholic Schools, Washington, DC, National Catholic Educational Association (NCEA), 1991.

What Makes a School Catholic?, Washington, DC, National Catholic Educational Association (NCEA), 1991.

Congregation for Catholic Education, *The Religious Dimension of Education in a Catholic School*, Rome, 1988.

Congregation for Catholic Education, *The Catholic School*, Rome, 1977.

Congregation for Catholic Education, *Lay Catholics in Schools: Witnesses to Faith*, Rome, 1982.

National Conference of Catholic Bishops, *Sharing the Light of Faith* (National Catechetical Directory for Catholics of the United States), 1979.

About the Authors

Robert Doyle, St. Mary's School, Melrose, Minnesota

Nancy Kinate, OSF, St. Joseph School, Green Bay, Wisconsin

Aideen Langan, CP, Msgr. Matthew F. Clarke School, Wakefield, Rhode Island

Marcian Swanson, SSSF, St. Matthias School, Chicago, Illinois

School Evaluation for the Catholic Elementary School: An Overview

Reck, C., and J. Coreil. 1983. 3–20. Washington, D.C.: National Catholic Educational Association.

I. Why Regular School Evaluation

Some answers to this key question include: to facilitate improvement; to provide a means of accountability. In addition, many schools report accompanying advantages or byproducts: to foster community involvement; and to build public relations. The following section considers these four answers to "Why Evaluation?", beginning with the most important.

A. To Facilitate Improvement

Every school community—principal, faculty and staff, students, parents, board members, and clergy—is responsible to work constantly to maintain present quality and to improve each year. The question is not *if* the group wants a better school, but *how* they will assure a better one. Regular evaluation involving the total school staff offers one approach that has consistently proven effective to clarify the school's direction, to examine the total school, to study the school in a systematic way, to motivate growth, and to help plan future directions.

1. Evaluation clarifies the school's direction.

Just as "the unexamined life is not worth leading," the unexamined philosophy is not worth its space on the shelf. Time for reflection is essential—but is not likely to happen spontaneously. School evaluation, however, guarantees both a time and a process for all on the staff

◆ to ask why their Catholic school exists
◆ to share their individual visions of the school
◆ to shape a corporate vision for their school
◆ to determine specific objectives they should try to accomplish
◆ to discuss how they can fulfill the religious dimension of the school
◆ to determine academic excellence, and
◆ to assess the school's response to society and the mission of the Church.

Evaluation provides a process whereby a school can clarify its philosophy and goals—not as lifeless documents, but as ideals and visions of a living faith community.

2. Evaluation examines the total school.

In order to understand if the school program is achieving its goals, *all aspects* of the school must be examined, asking "Does our direction really affect our operation?" These aspects include: the philosophy and goals, the interpersonal relations among all the members of the school community, the academic program, the religious studies

and formation programs, the physical plant, and financial stability. The evaluation helps the school community to see how all these elements are integrated and are moving the school to live its philosophy and to achieve its goals.

3. Evaluation studies the school in a systematic way.

A school yearly sets goals in order to improve itself in one curricular area or in some other aspects. However, a school needs regularly to examine its total program in a systematic way. A systematic approach enables the school to determine if continuity exists among its many elements —philosophy, goals, program objectives, teaching/learning experiences, and manifested outcomes. The systematic approach assures that all aspects of all areas will be covered and that the interrelationships among the various areas will be examined. Actually, a school evaluation does not add any new areas of concern; it merely organizes and integrates the areas which demand attention separately.

4. Evaluation motivates growth.

A systematic study can and should be nonthreatening while raising staff awareness of challenges in both professional and religious areas. A greater awareness of the total picture, an expression of appreciation for consistent efforts, a sense of affirmation based on present achievements, and a spirit of shared responsibility for future improvement can bring a faculty together in a new way. The process can provide a genuine inservice growth experience for the staff. It not only motivates, but becomes a relevant and very thorough staff development program.

5. Evaluation helps to plan future directions.

The information surfaced by an evaluation serves as a sound basis for planning school improvement. With more surety, a school can maintain and improve its quality programs, can discard practices that are harmful or ineffective, can design a course of action for continual school improvement—all in keeping with its philosophy and goals. Some schools may stagnate, and some may use the "band-wagon" or faddish approach to change; other schools, however, choose regular evaluation and use a thorough needs assessment to help plan for future improvement.

B. To Provide a Means of Accountability

After a school community sets a clear direction, it seems reasonable to evaluate whether or not they have effectively followed that direction, to compare the view of outside evaluators with that of the school community, and ultimately to justify the faith and resources which others place in the school. To be more specific, evaluation provides a means of accountability by measuring the desired outcomes, verifying self-evaluation with external assessment and supporting confidence in the school.

1. Evaluation measures the desired outcomes.

Each Catholic school community must answer basic questions such as these:

Is it a Catholic school? How is it different?

Is its philosophy really "in effect"?

Is the school achieving its goals and objectives?

Do Gospel values really permeate the school community?

Is the staff effective? Are staff members fulfilling their call as Christian educators?

Is the faith community evident?

Does this school provide total Catholic education?

Does it provide a quality instructional program?

Are the needs of each student—the total student —being met?

Are parents appropriately involved?

Although many of these areas are difficult to measure, an honest evaluation can indicate a basic presence or absence of the desired outcomes.

2. Evaluation verifies self-evaluation with external assessment.

The school community necessarily brings an insider's view which—although essential—should be verified with a more objective view. A self-evaluation program—in conjunction with verification by qualified outside agents —provides conclusions that are objectively validated.

3. Evaluation supports confidence in the school.

Accountability is a good business practice; and although a school is not a "business" in the ordinary sense of the term, accountability is important to the publics who support an institution, especially to the students and to the parents who are the primary educators of their children. Evaluation is one way to assure those parents and other supporters that a particular school does indeed meet its desired goals and an appropriate set of criteria.

In the words of the Sacred Congregation for Catholic Education, "The Catholic school forms part of the saving mission of the Church, especially for education in the Faith." (*The Catholic School #9*) For that reason, Catholic schools—with all other forms of Catholic education—are accountable to the Church and its members. Moreover, Catholic schools ordinarily use resources provided by parents, parish, the broader school community, a religious community, or the diocese. The school should provide a clear picture of its effectiveness, thereby justifying the faith that has been placed in the institution. Many "talents" have been given and many should be included in the accounting.

Beyond the students, parents, parishioners, and Church members lies society at large. With or without accurate information, people will form an image of Catholic schools. The evaluation process provides better data which can, in turn, positively affect any public policy related to the schools.

C. To Foster Community Involvement

Ideally, a school evaluation does not remain the task of the staff and outside educators, but rather involves the broader school community. Several advantages flow from this extension: deeper community understanding of the school, a broader staff view of community expectations, and closer school/community collaboration.

1. Evaluation offers the community an opportunity to know and "own" the school.

Dinners, bazaars, sports events, meetings, and other activities which are designed for the broader community tend to present a peripheral view of the school. An evaluation, on the other hand, focuses on the present and future of the school itself. Through involvement in the evaluation process, a community gets to know the essential elements of the school, and the joint effort often increases a sense of ownership.

2. Evaluation gives the staff an opportunity to learn the expectations and perceptions of the community.

Although some individuals from the community initiate contact with the school, they may not represent the views of the typical members. A school evaluation process offers an excellent opportunity to discuss important issues with the local community.

This interchange can

◆ raise the staff's awareness of the professional expectations in the broader school community

◆ help to identify and understand the particular needs of the students and therefore more adequately provide service

◆ reflect the extent of parental support of the Catholic-Christian value system and other features of the school

◆ remind the staff that they are part of a picture larger than an isolated school, that they are part of the parish, the (arch)diocese, and the universal Church.

3. Evaluation facilitates a broad basis for the whole educational endeavor.

In addition to the above benefits that touch either the community members or the staff, an evaluation also brings representatives of both groups together. The process involves the larger community in school goal setting and assesses important issues with input from all segments of the school community. When the process is well utilized, regular evaluation can effectively build a unified community and prevent isolated education.

D. To Build Public Relations

The fact that a school takes a major step to facilitate improvement, to provide accountability, and to foster community involvement offers in itself a basis for excellent public relations. The potential of a school evaluation far exceeds the news value of school socials and other activities.

Well planned publicity about a school evaluation can spread not only the good news of Catholic education, but also the basic message of the faith. Some schools invite parents, parishioners, local superintendents, public school officials, civic leaders, and religious community representatives to the school's presentation of their philosophy and community reports; this presents an excellent opportunity for a good school to share its clear, positive self-image. After the evaluation, schools often share the many affirmations of outside evaluators with the entire community; they may also wish to state general recommendations for continued growth in the future. The process provides a newsworthy occasion to "tell" a school's story; as a P.R. tool, the evaluation often proves effective for recruiting, marketing and development as well as for general credibility.

Why regular evaluation? Basically to facilitate improvement, to provide a means of accountability, to foster community involvement, and to build public relations. Although presented in general terms, each school community can apply this section to its own situation—and perhaps even identify additional reasons for and advantages of regular evaluation for their own Catholic elementary school.

II. What Are the Basic Steps?

A. Basic Steps and Choices

1. Decide when to evaluate

2. Determine scope of evaluation

3. Review applicable criteria

4. Select an appropriate instrument

5. Identify persons to involve

6. Plan communication

7. Complete the self-study process

8. Verify the self-study report

9. Design and implement the improvement plan

10. Review progress

The basic steps and choices within a school evaluation process can be sub-divided in many ways; the above chart and the following explanation will treat the process in ten steps, including choices where appropriate.

1. Decide when to evaluate

After considering the reasons for a total school evaluation and weighing the readiness of the school staff, the principal and representatives of the school community with appropriate (arch)diocesan involvement should together decide on the time of the evaluation. Readiness considerations include the number of years since the last formal evaluation, (arch)diocesan policy, stability of present school leadership, the receptivity of the staff, availability of resources including opportunities for preservicing about school evaluation. Although its advantages are many, an evaluation will demand much time and attention; to begin without essential preparedness will be to no advantage.

If the representative group concludes "Not Ready!", the next step designs a plan to get ready; e.g., to develop an attitude of receptivity. If the decision is "Ready!", motivation and general preparation for the overall process will be in order.

2. Determine scope of evaluation

If the initial decision is positive, many automatically assume that the scope of the evaluation will be that of the total school, including all areas of philosophy, community, administration, faculty and staff, instruction, student services and facilities.

In some cases, however, a narrower scope may be preferred i.e., selecting only one or two components or programs of the school. Although the total study provides the advantage of a full perspective, there may be sufficient reason to consider a limited number of segments—especially if that approach allows a more thorough study. Determining the scope of the evaluation may not require much time, but it should be a conscious decision.

3. Review applicable criteria

Evaluation or judgment must be based upon some criteria. The criteria should be clarified and/or chosen deliberately. Certain criteria are universal for quality education and will be common to all good schools; others based on calls of the bishops to Catholic educators can be specified for Catholic schools. Section III of this handbook presents those criteria which NCEA considers essential for the quality school which calls itself Catholic.

Certain standards may also be established by a local authority. For that reason, a school should note criteria specified by the (arch)diocese as well as by local or state jurisdictions to the extent applicable.

Next, the school should review its own stated ideals and expectations. Although the evaluation process will provide time to reshape the school philosophy and goals, it will prove useful to have gathered any specific objectives previously stated by the school; e.g., the expected outcomes of its major programs.

Standards of an accrediting agency may also be reviewed, if applicable and desirable. An increasing number of regional accrediting associations are opening membership to elementary schools. While some schools find that such an agency fits their need for criteria and external verification, accrediting agencies do involve an on-going financial commitment and may hold some criteria that are not priorities for many Catholic elementary schools.

Although the task of clarifying criteria will demand time—especially if little attention has been given them in the past—the compilation of applicable criteria seems a worthwhile endeavor, whether or not an evaluation were to follow.

4. Select an appropriate instrument

Although experienced educators can adapt almost any instrument to suit their needs, an evaluation will stay on target more surely if the tool has a "good fit" with the appropriate criteria and the desired focus.

In practice, this means that a Catholic school will carefully assess available instruments, looking at points such as these:

◆ the religious orientation: an instrument that integrates the religious orientation throughout or a religion supplement with a secular tool

◆ the product/process balance: an instrument that concentrates on the right balance of outcomes (e.g., test scores) and inputs (e.g., school climate)

◆ the formative/summative emphasis: an instrument that provides for a statement of approval at the end of the process as well as a diagnostic approach for future improvements

◆ an objective/subjective format: the desired balance of objective data, checklists, rating scales, questionnaires, and open-ended items

◆ appropriateness for self-study/use by outside agents: adequate direction for self-study and, if applicable, sufficient information for outside agents. (All parties involved should use the same basic instrument.)

Although no two schools will have exactly the same desired focus, every school community should clarify its focus and try to identify an evaluation instrument that matches the focus well. No tool or process—of itself—is necessarily better than any other; one will, however, offer the "best fit" for the direction of a particular school.

5. Identify persons to be involved

a. School leadership team

Leadership in the evaluation process rests primarily with the school principal and faculty. A leadership team, composed wholly or mostly of administration and faculty members, should be involved in the instrument selection process and should become thoroughly familiar with the purpose and approach of the tool; for if leadership does not understand and is not committed, the tool is worthless.

b. Participants from total school community

Technically, a principal alone or a principal together with the staff can evaluate a school. In most situations, however, a *school* evaluation has come to mean a study involving in some way the *total school community*. Even though the instrument may include questionnaires for parents, students and clergy, some personal participation

of persons beyond the staff can build a sense of involvement and support.

For that reason, the evaluation leadership team should seek appropriate means whereby students, parents, board members, and other school personnel can participate in the self-study. They can, of course, provide auxiliary services during the evaluation; but they should also be considered seriously as contributors to the substance of the study. If the study is to be truly a *school* evaluation, these members of the school community can assist by sharing their ideals, observations, commendations as well as recommendations through some appropriate channel.

c. Visiting team for external verification

All of the reasons for regular school evaluation—to facilitate improvement, to provide accountability, to foster community involvement, to build public relations—underscore the value of including a visiting team in plans for any major evaluation. A visiting team can contribute much by offering their objective view of the school's progress along its chosen direction, based on the self-study. They can thereby add more credibility to the findings. Moreover, their recommendations can support a school's own statements of need; for example, those concerning budget or plant use. The very inclusion of participants beyond the school tends to build a sense of community involvement and opens many doors for building public relations.

Careful selection of the team members and chairperson is, of course, essential. Many groups can be surveyed for possible members:

◆ principals and teachers from other Catholic schools, preferably those who have already experienced an evaluation process

◆ local and neighboring (arch)diocesan education staff members

◆ educational personnel from local colleges/universities

◆ faculty of Catholic high schools, especially those who receive some of the school's graduates

◆ parents and/or members of the broader community

◆ local public and private school staff members

◆ religious community education personnel.

The team should be balanced as well as possible, with some diversity (e.g., age, education, experience, sex, race, present position). Although members will be selected from specific settings, they must be persons with broad views, willing and able to base their observations—not on their own educational views—but on the philosophy and goals stated by the school.

Many (arch)diocesan education offices not only encourage school evaluation, but facilitate the process in various degrees and ways. Some direct the process and help form visiting teams; a small number conduct evaluations personally—with or without actual membership on the visiting team; others merely observe the process or monitor the reports. The options are many and include evaluation in conjunction with local, state, or other agencies. Team membership ordinarily reflects all constituencies involved in such cooperative evaluations.

Other options for external validation could be a(n) (arch)diocesan board of education, a state Catholic conference, a regional or a national association of Catholic educators. Team membership would ordinarily include a member or designated representative of the group offering certification, accreditation, or other form of approval.

Decisions about involvement of the total school community and the selection of visiting team members will require much prayer, thought, dialogue, and planning.

6. Plan communication

The evaluation leadership team together with appropriate representatives form plans and share responsibility for keeping members of interested groups (e.g., home-school, board of education, parish council) informed about the evaluation. Other communication plans should include items for the parish bulletin as well as news releases for (arch)diocesan and appropriate local newspapers. The local school may wish to contact local and/or state education officials, diocesan offices, and religious community education personnel—in general, anyone who would be interested, but may not be involved. Every school should identify its own appropriate communication lines.

7. Complete the self-study process

Since the whole study must be done in the light of the desired thrust of the school, it is essential first to reassess, reshape, and then clarify the philosophy and goals until they are clearly understood by all involved. This foundation will be worth the time it demands if the process involves honest dialogue about values and directions which are basic to the school. The criteria which had been determined during the third step should raise for discussion some important but otherwise forgotten issues.

Every evaluation process and instrument proposes slight variations in the actual study. Most include subcommittees to assess and prepare draft reports regarding sections of the study, a total group response to preliminary findings, and a leadership team to coordinate the whole process.

The actual writing process—though time consuming—serves to organize and clarify important observations about the school. Although processes and tools vary, many schools spend almost a year in this self-study phase.

8. Verify the self-study report

Although a visiting team is the most common means of verification, other approaches can also be effective. The actual visit of an outside team—possibly one to three days—offers an extensive opportunity for multiple observers to examine, verify, and challenge the findings of the school community. On the other hand, even one objective visitor —especially an experienced, perceptive educator—can offer a limited assessment of the self-study.

9. Design and implement the improvement plan

A thoughtful, honest analysis of the self-study findings and of the visiting team report will direct a school toward specific areas for improvement. Any study not surfacing needed improvements would be quite unusual and probably defective.

Organized in some practical way, the school community weighs the validity of each recommendation, documenting reasons for considering any recommendation invalid and cautiously postponing any improvements that are judged to be impossible. Staff members determine priorities among the needed areas of improvement, set goals, then design a plan for action on a reasonable timeline. In general, vague plans remain plans; those with specifics are more likely to become reality. Although processes differ, most plans are charted over a course of several years.

The design as well as the implementation of the plan will rely heavily on the principal and other faculty leadership. To assure steady movement from plan to reality, some sort of coordinating team usually keeps the design for improvement before the staff, recalls checkpoints and deadlines, and helps with adjustments needed because of staff turnover or other changes.

10. Review progress

A little external pressure can sometimes stimulate more movement than internal deadlines. For that reason, some schools specify a time for an outside agent to review their progress. The visitor may or may not be a member of the former visiting team.

With or without external visitors, every school should systematically review its progress, comparing actual achievements with its own improvement plan.

B. Continuing Process

When a school has finally completed all ten steps, it is practically time to decide when the school will be ready to repeat the evaluation cycle. This handbook has referred to "regular" evaluation; only those who have experienced the total cycle and have begun again really understand the implications of that word "regular."

In general, the school staff which accepts its responsibility to improve each year regards a regular evaluation process—not as an extra task—but as a means for fulfilling the responsibility for improvement.

Creating Quality Schools

Savary, L. M. 1992. 27–32. Arlington, Va.: American Association of School Administrators.

Guidelines Some School Districts Have Found Helpful

Total quality management in education is still in its infancy. School leaders are learning from each other, service agencies, and the business community. In quality, there is no "cookbook" to follow. True to one of its key beliefs, total quality is a constantly evolving process.

The following guidelines are not intended to be a recipe or manual. Each school system must make its own journey to quality. However, the experiences of pioneer school districts provide some directions to follow when starting out.

1. Lay the groundwork for quality. Well-thought-out preparation offers the best hope for success. Build a quality system slowly; start by developing knowledge and interest in quality concepts and attitudes.

The cultural change required in a transformation to quality is the biggest hurdle and takes the longest time. "We have begun a two-year process of team building," explains David Fultz, superintendent of the Grand Blanc Community School District, Michigan. "Every employee receives team-building training. We are building quality principles in those who have to change their thinking the most. These are the ones who can make or break the transformation."

The conversion-to-quality process may take several years, as hundreds of employees, board members, and parents learn skills in team building, consensus building, decision making, empowerment, communication, problem solving, and data and information management.

Denny Dowd, a school administrator from Texas, has this advice for school districts starting total quality management:

> Plan out your strategy carefully. Realize you have to lay the groundwork for quality and give people a chance to grow into it. Have someone responsible keep up the momentum. Begin with a decision phase where a committee lays the foundations. This should be followed by a training phase, which is most critical. Provide a training curriculum for professional educators, nonprofessional employees, and parents, too.

Bill Borgers, superintendent of the Dickinson School District, Texas, adds, "Implementation of total quality management plans has been smooth since we began using consensus problem-solving techniques."

2. Provide everyone in the system with opportunities for learning about their processes and systems and how they work. For example, Borgers says, "All employees have completed a 30-hour course in total quality management." Myra De Byle, executive director for curriculum and instruction in the Duluth School District, Minnesota, discovers, "People need much more training before they go into quality management."

In some areas, people began studying the school system by making a flow chart of all its inputs, processes, and results. In studying a flow chart, school employees see how much they need each other in order for any of them to make a difference in the lives of children. "Each department of the Sacramento County Office of Education has identified its internal and external clients," explains David P. Meaney, superintendent, Sacramento County Schools, California. "Flow charts of each department's major processes and their relationship to internal and external clients have been completed."

3. Develop shared beliefs and understandings about children and schools. What is it that staff and the community really believe about humans and the learning process? Deming says, for example, "One is born with a natural inclination to learn and be innovative." Does everyone agree with that?

Everyone, from teachers to superintendents, should have some understanding of how and why children learn. The staff of Newman Smith High School in Carrollton, Texas, developed a set of shared beliefs about people and work. One example of these beliefs, says former Principal Charles Blanton, is the following:

> People work best when they are in, and feel part of, a team where they can be trusted and trust each other to do their jobs; share leadership and make decisions; are accepted and respected; resolve issues with sensitivity and understanding; have the opportunity to accomplish challenging goals; and contribute to continuing improvement.

4. Work with all stakeholders in the larger educational system to identify the shared aim for the school system. "Every school system must have a written statement of purpose," says quality consultant Ronald Moen. "This includes the mission, beliefs/values, and vision of how the system will be structured or will behave in the future to accomplish the mission. Administrators, teachers, support personnel, and board members must demonstrate constantly their commitment to this written statement."

In Arlington County, Texas, at the beginning of each school year during an opening convocation, the superintendent, Richard E. Berry, presents the school system's quality management vision statement to all employees, not just teachers.

5. Identify the key "customers" at all levels in the education system. List their requirements and design your system to meet and exceed their needs. In Sacramento, says Meaney, "Surveys assessing external client needs have been utilized. Client satisfaction surveys for external and internal clients have been and continue to be developed."

Focus on the external customers to identify purpose and general direction. "For us," explains Henry E. LaBranche, superintendent, Salem School District, New Hampshire, "students and parents are the direct customers of our school system, the rest of the community are indirect customers."

Although less than 20 percent of the American population have children in school, property values increase and people move into an area because of a good school system. As a consequence, the Salem School District has begun to restructure its learning system to provide learning for more than the traditional elementary and secondary school student. Says LaBranche:

> We sent out surveys to the community to find out how we could help the nontraditional learners, so we now offer eight-week courses and four-week courses for the underemployed, the unemployed, senior citizens, mothers for child care, etc. We are marketing ourselves as the educational service system of the community.

6. Consistently serving the school system's aim, identify key suppliers and help them learn how to help you exceed your requirements (as their customer). In Alaska's Mt. Edgecumbe High School, the students modified this principle into the following:

> Work with the educational institutions from which students come. Minimize total cost of education by improving the relationship with student sources and helping to improve the quality of students coming into your system. A single source of students coming into a system, such as junior high students moving into a high school, is an opportunity to build long-term relationships of loyalty and trust for the benefit of the students.

Families also are "suppliers" of students. Work with them so that the children they provide are able to meet the school system's requirements, such as being ready to learn, attentive in school, and well-disciplined.

7. Identify some indicators of a poor system. These counter-quality indicators send a signal that the system is not working as efficiently and effectively as it should. When a school district wants to begin managing for quality, improvement in the following areas will provide short-term results in the context of a long-term aim:

◆ Duplication of work (same data gathered two or three times, same material taught in more than one class).

"You never see the whole picture of the system as long as you keep focusing on individual people," explains David Gangel of Virginia. "Put more time into planning and less time into correcting errors.

In the Duluth School District, Myra De Byle says they are asking if teachers are wasting a lot of their time in noneducational tasks: "Must study hall supervisions be done by teachers? Must hall patrol be done by teachers? Does every teacher need to attend pep assemblies? How many evenings should teachers be required to invest at sports events or school social events?" Questions like these are being asked, and "the answers are not being taken for granted," comments De Byle.

◆ Relationships where fear is operating (lack of trust, not sharing information, covering up, providing false information). "Strive for an atmosphere conducive to risk-taking and experimentation without the fear of punishment for failure," says Charles A. Melvin, superintendent, School District of Beloit Turner, Wisconsin.

"We are also trying to break down barriers between district/school, union/district, and elementary/secondary," says Lee Jenkins, superintendent of the Enterprise School District, California. "We're driving out fear and creating more joy."

◆ Ineffective processes (bottlenecks, barriers, missing pieces, redundancies). Complicated procedures for registration, purchasing, or library use could be examples.

8. Start collecting and reviewing data that will provide knowledge for improving the school system and its variations. In the Crawford Central School District of northwestern Pennsylvania, data collection is being done by the administration, teachers, and students. As the superintendent, Robert Bender, explains: "Our focus is on improving the quality of the instructional process and those systems that support it."

One study measured the amount of time needed for psychological referrals, that is, from the date of the original referral for a gifted or special education child, to the date when the referral team made a decision. The studies used many standard statistical tools, such as control charts ("the workhorse of all tools," says Bender), cause and effect diagrams, and flow charts. Bender reports that four other studies have been designed for the coming school year.

9. Elicit suggestions for improvement from the people who are close to a process. For example, in classrooms, teachers are in the best position to identify and monitor the needs and progress of students. Teachers, therefore, "ought to have significant roles in the instructional planning and delivery. People don't feel as much responsibility for the outcome of something unless they have some degree of ownership," says Willis B. McLeod, superintendent, Petersburg Public Schools, Virginia. The suggestion technique works only if management has developed trust in the school atmosphere, which allows people to try out new ideas, make mistakes, and not fear punishment. "In Japan," explains Superintendent Meaney, "the average employee submits 32 suggestions for improvement annually. In the United States in companies that have employee suggestion systems, the average number of suggestions per employee is 0.12." Referring to his school district, Meaney adds, "In Sacramento, employees are guaranteed that their problem or suggestion will be addressed within 14 working days." More than 80 percent of these suggestions are implemented.

10. Talk with and learn from other people who are on the same quality management path as your school system. But do not blindly imitate them or use their procedures as a recipe for your system without first obtaining a thorough understanding of your own system and processes. For example, superintendents from three Wisconsin school districts began the process of restructuring their districts by applying Deming's beliefs on quality. All three had studied at the same school with the same professor and began the transformation in their districts at the same time as a consortium. "We soon learned that there was no specific Deming process to follow," explains Superintendent Charles Melvin of the School District of Beloit Turner. "Rather, Deming offers an alternative way of viewing an organization."

11. Get help from an outside consultant who knows quality management and understands how schools work as systems. Often people within a system cannot see how to transform it, since the prevailing management style is the only thing they know.

"The consortium," says Melvin, "used a different outside consultant for each of the strands [curriculum, governance, instruction, and decision-making evaluation]."

An outside expert can ask the questions that will give educators a new perspective and lead them carefully through this long and complex process. "One-shot workshops or inspirational speakers," cautions Melvin, "will not be sufficient to change instructional beliefs and methodologies. Boards of education and administrators need to become familiar with the change process and its application in schools."

12. Align the school district in partnership with a business corporation that has itself begun a quality transformation. "One thing is sure, as you begin to develop your quality program," says Houlihan, superintendent in Johnston County, North Carolina, "you will need outside experts who have demonstrated their knowledge/expertise. These persons must become partners with you on your road to total quality in schools."

A number of school districts have gone into quality partnerships with the Xerox Corporation. Other corporations that have "adopted" school districts include IBM,

---

Involving Students in the Quest for Quality

In Dickinson, Texas, the quality system is operational enough to involve students. Superintendent Bill Borgers says "students are starting to assess their own work for quality. They are allowed to improve their grades, and in some classes they are teaching each other the quality tools that were taught to the teachers."

Before involving students in quality assessment, Borgers explains, a district needs to lay the proper groundwork. In Dickinson, students follow a progression of quality exercises that ultimately leads to self-evaluation:

1. Students define quality by identifying a quality car, television program, or any object or person. The teacher encourages class discussion about what makes these things "quality."
2. Next, classes discuss quality in relation to schoolwork. A teacher can provide examples of different types of work and ask students to identify quality work and explain why.
3. Starting with one project or assignment, students are asked to put a "Q" on their work if they think it meets their agreed-on definition of quality.
4. In time, students are asked to grade their own assignments. The teacher also will grade them, and the two grades are averaged together.

Borgers says that initial reactions to this process have been "very enthusiastic. Kids are really buying into ownership of their work. They're setting high standards and being pretty tough on themselves."

General Motors, and Hewlett-Packard. Superintendent Borgers reports that a team approach to problem solving, a seven-step method taught to them by Monsanto and Sterling Chemicals, has been used to solve serious district problems. "The most success has come from using the model to solve our workers' compensation problems and gifted/talented identification problems."

When seeking a business partnership, look for local corporations committed to quality management as likely candidates for a long-term involvement with your school district. Superintendent David Fultz of Michigan, says, "We are in liaison with GM; we are following their model, and learning from their mistakes."

13. Involve the larger community in a school's quality enterprise. On quality steering committees, include not only teachers and principals, but parents, people from the community and its agencies, and employees from the central office.

Appendicies and Bibliography

General Bibliography

Abbott, W. M., ed. 1966. Declaration on Christian education *(Gravissimum educationis)*. In *The documents of Vatican II*, trans. Joseph Gallagher. New York: The Guild Press.

Alley, G., and D. Deshler. 1979. *Teaching the learning disabled adolescent: Strategies and methods*. Denver: Love Publishing Company.

Ames., C., and C. Ames. 1984. *Research on motivation in education*. San Diego: Academic Press.

Anderson, C. S. 1982. The search for school climate: A review of the research. *Review of Educational Research* 52(3):368–420.

Armstrong, T. 1987. *In their own way*. Los Angeles: Jeremy Tarcher, Inc.

Banks, J. A. 1989. Multicultural education: Characteristics and goals. In *Multicultural education: Issues and perspectives*, eds. J. A. Banks and C. M. Banks. Boston: Allyn and Bacon.

Barkley, R. 1990. *Attention deficit hyperactivity disorder: A handbook for diagnosis and treatment*. New York: The Guidford Press.

Barth, R. S. 1991. *Improving schools from within*. San Francisco: Jossey-Bass.

Barton, J. 1990. The teacher as critical thinker. *Momentum* 21(4):20–22.

Bass, B. M. 1985. *Leadership and performance beyond expectations*. New York: The Free Press.

Beaudoin, D. M. 1990. Diversity in spirituality in the Catholic elementary school. *Momentum* 21(2):34–36.

Bennis, W. 1984. Transformation power and leadership. In *Leadership and organizational culture*, eds. T. J. Sergiovanni and J. E. Corbally. Urbana-Champaign: University of Illinois Press.

Blase, J., and P. C. Kirby. 1992. *Bringing out the best in teachers*. Newbury Park, Calif.: Corwin Press.

Bohr, D. 1986. Imagination: The motivating force in catechesis. *Momentum* 17(3):10–12.

Bos, C., and S. Vaughn. 1991. *Strategies for teaching students with learning and behavior problems*. Boston: Allyn and Bacon.

Brophy, J. 1992. Probing the subtleties of subject-matter teaching. *Educational Leadership* 49(7):4–8.

Bryk, A. S., P. B. Holland, V. E. Lee, and R. Carriedo. 1984. *Effective Catholic schools: An exploration*. Washington, D.C.: National Catholic Educational Association.

Burns, J. M. 1978. *Leadership*. New York: Harper and Row.

Caine, R. N., and G. Caine. 1991. *Making connections: Teaching and the human brain*. Alexandria, Va.: Association for Supervision and Curiculum Development.

Clarke, B. 1988. *Growing up gifted*. Columbus, Ohio: Merrill.

Clarke, J. 1990. *Patterns of thinking*. Boston: Allyn and Bacon.

Clifton, D. O., and P. Nelson. 1992. *Soar with your strengths*. New York: Delacorte Press.

Collins, C., and J. Mangieri. 1992. *Teaching thinking*. Hillsdale, N.J.: Erlbaum.

Congregation for Catholic Education. 1982. *Lay Catholics in schools: Witnesses to faith*. Boston: Daughters of Saint Paul.

———. 1988. *The religious dimension of education in a Catholic school: Guidelines for reflection and renewal*. Washington, D.C.: United States Catholic Conference.

Conley, D. T., and K. Dixon. 1990. The evaluation report: A tool for teacher growth. *NASSP Bulletin* 74(527): 10–14.

Convey, J. J. 1992. *Catholic schools make a difference: Twenty-five years of research*. Washington, D.C.: National Catholic Educational Association.

Crain, W. 1992. *Theories of development: Concepts and applications*. Englewood Cliffs, N.J.: Prentice-Hall.

Csikszentmihalyi, M. 1990. *Flow: The psychology of optimal experience*. New York: Harper Collins.

Daresh, J. C. 1991. *Supervision as a proactive process*. Prospect Heights, Ill.: Waveland Press.

Davis, G., and S. Rimm. 1989. *Education of the gifted and talented*. Englewood Cliffs, N.J.: Prentice-Hall.

Deal, T. E. 1987. The culture of schools. In *Leadership: Examining the elusive, 1987 yearbook*. Alexandria, Va.: Association for Supervision and Curriculum Development.

Deal, T. E., and A. A. Kennedy. 1983. Culture and school performance. *Educational Leadership* 40(5):14–15.

Deal, T. E., and K. D. Peterson. 1990. *The principal's role in shaping school culture*. Washington, D.C.: United States Department of Education, Office of Educational Research and Improvement.

DeBono, E. 1985. *Thinking six hats*. Boston: Little Brown.

Dede, C. 1986. The implications of emerging technologies for the value-oriented curriculum. *Momentum* 17(3): 42–44.

Di Giacomo, J. 1989. *Teaching religion in a Catholic secondary school*. Washington, D.C.: National Catholic Educational Association.

Doyle, R., N. Kinate, A. Langan, and M. Swanson. 1991. Evaluation of the school's Catholicity. In *Capital wisdom: Papers from the Principals Academy 1991*. Washington, D.C.: National Catholic Educational Association.

Drahmann, T., and A. Stenger. 1989. *The Catholic school principal: An outline for action* (revised). Washington, D.C.: National Catholic Educational Association.

Dunn, R. 1990. Rita Dunn answers questions on learning styles. *Educational Leadership* 48 (2):15–19.

Durbin, K. 1993. Attention deficit hyperactivity. *Streamlined Seminar* 11(4). Alexandria, Va.: National Association of Elementary School Principals.

Edmonds, R. R. 1979. Effective schools for the urban poor. *Educational Leadership* 37(2):15–27.

English, F., and J. C. Hill. 1990. *Restructuring: The principal and curriculum change.* Reston, Va.: National Association of Secondary School Principals.

Farmham-Diggory, S. 1992. *The learning disabled child.* Cambridge, Mass.: Harvard University Press.

Fiedler, F. E. 1964. A contingency model of leadership effectiveness. In *Advances in experimental social psychology,* ed. L. Berkowitz. New York: Academic Press.

Fox, L., L. Brody, and D. Tobin. 1983. *Learning disabled/gifted children.* Baltimore: University Park Press.

French, J. R. P., and B. Raven. 1959. The bases of social power. In *Studies in social power,* ed. D. Cartwight. Ann Arbor, Mich.: Institute for Social Research.

Fullan, M. G. 1991. *The new meaning of educational change.* New York: Teachers College.

Fullan, M. G., and M. B. Miles. 1992. Getting reform right: What works and what doesn't. *Phi Delta Kappan* 73(10): 745–52.

Gallagher, J. 1985. *Teaching the gifted child.* Boston: Allyn and Bacon.

Galton, F. 1870. *Hereditary genius.* New York: Appleton.

Gardner, H. 1985. *Frames of mind: The theory of multiple intelligences.* New York: Basic Books.

———. 1991. *The unschooled mind: How children think and how schools should teach.* New York: Basic Books.

Gilbert, J. R. 1983. *Pastor as shepherd of the school community.* Washington, D.C.: National Catholic Educational Association.

Glatthorn, A. A. 1987. *Curriculum renewal: A rationale for a consensus curriculum.* Alexandria, Va.: Association for Supervision and Curriculum Development.

Glatthorn, A. A., and C. R. Shields. 1983. *Differentiated supervision for Catholic schools.* Washington, D.C.: National Catholic Educational Association.

Glickman, C. D. 1981. *Developmental supervision.* Alexandria, Va.: Association for Supervision and Curriculum Development.

———. 1990. *Supervision of instruction: A developmental approach.* Boston: Allyn and Bacon.

Grant, C. A., and C. E. Sleeter. 1988. *Making choices for multicultural education.* Columbus: Merrill.

Groome, T. H. 1992. Catechesis and religious education: "Let's stay together". *The Living Light* 29(1):40–46.

Guskey, T. R., and D. Sparks. 1991. What to consider when evaluating staff development. *Educational Leadership* 49(3):73–75.

Hall, S., ed. 1992. *The people: Reflections of native peoples on the Catholic experience in North America.* Washington, D.C.: National Catholic Educational Association.

Hall, S., R. Doyle, and P. Tran, eds. 1990. *A Catholic response to the Asian presence.* Washington, D.C.: National Catholic Educational Association.

Hall, S., and C. Reck, eds. 1987. *Integral education: A response to the Hispanic presence.* Washington, D.C.: National Catholic Educational Association.

Haney, R. 1991. Seize the day! *Momentum* 22(2):6–8.

Hanlon, J. M. 1973. *Theory, practice and education.* Fond du Lac, Wis.: Marian College Press.

Hawker, J. 1985. *Catechetics in the Catholic school.* Washington, D.C.: National Catholic Educational Association.

Heft, J. 1991. Catholic identity and the Church. In *What makes a school Catholic?,* ed. F. D. Kelly. Washington, D.C.: National Catholic Educational Association.

Helm, C. M. 1989. Cultural and symbolic leadership in Catholic elementary schools: An ethnographic study. Ph.D. diss., The Catholic University of America, Washington, D.C.

Hersey, P., and K. H. Blanchard. 1977. *Management of organizational behavior.* 3d ed. Englewood Cliffs, N.J.: Prentice-Hall.

Hollander, E. P. 1985. Leadership and power. In *Handbook of social psychology.* Vol. II. *Special fields and applications,* ed. E. Aronson, 3d ed. New York: Random House.

House, R. J. 1971. A path goal theory of leader effectiveness. *Administrative Science Quarterly* 16: 321–39.

———. 1977. A 1976 theory of charismatic leadership. In *Leadership: The cutting edge,* eds. J. G. Hunt and L. L. Larson. Carbondale: Southern Illinois University Press.

Hyde, A., and M. Bizar. 1989. *Thinking in context.* White Plains, N.Y.: Longman.

John Paul II. 1987. The Catholic school of the '80s. *Origins,* 17(17).

Jones, N. 1987. An Afro-American perspective. In *Faith and culture.* Washington, D.C.: United States Catholic Conference.

Jones, B., and A. Palinscar. 1987. *Strategic teaching and learning.* Alexandria, Va.: Association for Supervision and Curriculum Development.

Karnes, M. 1986. *The underserved: Our young gifted children.* Reston, Va.: Council for Exceptional Children.

Katz, R. L. 1955. Skills of an effective administrator. *Harvard Business Review* January-February:33–42.

Kealey, R. 1985. *Curriculum in the Catholic school.* Washington, D.C.: National Catholic Educational Association.

———, ed. 1989. *Reflections on the role of the Catholic school principal.* Washington, D.C.: National Catholic Educational Association.

Kellerman, B., ed. 1984. *Leadership: Multidisciplinary perspectives.* Englewood Cliffs, N.J.: Prentice-Hall.

Kelly, F. D. 1989. Catechesis for the Third Millennium. *Momentum* 20(4):6–10.

Kennedy, M. M., ed. 1991. *Teaching academic subjects to diverse learners.* New York: Columbia University.

Knipper, C., and D. Suddarth. 1991. Involving staff in the in-service process. In *Capital wisdom: Papers from the Principals Academy 1991.* Washington, D.C.: National Catholic Educational Association.

Krug, S. E. 1992. Instructional leadership. *Educational Administration Quarterly* 28(3):430.

Larranaga, R. 1990. *Calling it a day: Daily meditations for workaholics.* San Francisco: Harper and Row.

Levine, S. L. 1989. *Promoting adult growth in schools.* Boston: Allyn and Bacon.

Libreria Editrice Vaticana. 1994. *Catechism of the Catholic Church*. Washington, D.C.: United States Catholic Conference.

Lipham, J. M. 1981. *Effective principal, effective school*. Reston, Va.: National Association of Secondary School Principals.

Luby, M. A., M. S. Moser, and L. Posey. 1991. Introducing change with success. In *Capital wisdom: Papers from the Principals Academy 1991*. Washington, D.C.: National Catholic Educational Association.

Lunenburg, F. C., and A. C. Ornstein. 1991. *Educational administration: Concepts and practices*. Belmont, Calif.: Wadsworth.

Maehr, M. L., C. Midgly, and T. Urdan. 1992. School leader as motivator. *Educational Administration Quarterly* 28(3): 410–29.

Maeroff, G. I. 1991. Assessing alternative assessment. *Phi Delta Kappan* 73(4):272–81.

Mann, F. C. 1965. Toward an understanding of the leadership role in formal organization. In *Leadership and productivity*, eds. R. Dubin, G. C. Homans, F. C. Mann, and D. C. Miller. San Francisco: Chandler.

Marzano, R. J. 1992. *A different kind of classroom: Teaching with dimensions of learning*. Alexandria, Va.: Association for Supervision and Curriculum Development.

McBrien, R. P. 1987. *Ministry: A theological, pastoral handbook*. New York: Harper Collins.

McClery, L. E. 1992. The knowledge base for school leaders. In *School leadership: A blueprint for change*, ed. Thomson. Newbury Park, Calif.: The Corwin Press.

McClelland, D. 1970. The two faces of power. *Journal of International Affairs* 24(1):29–47.

———. 1975. *Power: The inner experience*. New York: Irvington.

McDermott, E. 1985. Distinctive qualities of the Catholic school. In *NCEA Keynote Series No. 1*. Washington, D.C.: National Catholic Educational Association.

Mercer, C. 1987. *Student with learning disabilities*. 4th ed. New York: Macmillan Publishing Company.

Miner, J. B. 1978. Twenty years of research on role motivation theory of managerial effectiveness. *Personnel Psychology* 31:739–60.

National Association of Secondary School Principals. 1990. Developing staff morale. *Practitioner* 16(4).

National Conference of Catholic Bishops. 1973. *To teach as Jesus did: A pastoral message on Catholic education*. Washington, D.C.: United States Catholic Conference.

———. 1977. *The Catholic school*. Washington, D.C.: United States Catholic Conference.

———. 1979. *Sharing the light of faith: National catechetical directory for Catholics of the United States*. Washington, D.C.: United States Catholic Conference.

———. 1990. *In support of Catholic elementary and secondary schools*. Washington, D.C.: United States Catholic Conference.

Nolan, J., and P. Francis. 1992. Changing perspectives in curriculum and instruction. In *Supervision in transition. 1992 yearbook*. Alexandria, Va.: Association for Supervision and Curriculum Development.

Nouwen, H. J. M. 1989. *In the name of Jesus: Reflections on Christian leadership*. New York: Crossroad.

Novak, J., and D. Gowin. 1986. *Learning how to learn*. New York: Cambridge University Press.

Oliva, P. 1989. *Supervision for today's schools*. White Plains, N.Y.: Longman.

O'Malley, W. J. 1991. Evangelizing the unconverted. In *What makes a school Catholic?*, ed. F. D. Kelly. Washington, D.C.: National Catholic Educational Association.

———. 1992. Catechesis for conversion. *The Living Light* 29(2):55–63.

O'Neil, J. 1990. New curriculum agenda emerges for the '90s. *Curriculum Update* 32(6): 2–7. Alexandria, Va.: Association for Supervision and Curriculum Development.

Owens, R. G. 1987. The leadership of educational clans. In *Leadership: Examining the elusive, 1987 yearbook*. Alexandria, Va.: Association for Supervision and Curriculum Development.

Parke, B. 1989. *Gifted students in regular classrooms*. Boston: Allyn and Bacon.

Parks, D., and W. Warner. 1992. Four essentials of leadership. *Streamlined Seminar* 10(3). Alexandria, Va.: National Association of Elementary School Principals.

Paul, R. 1990. *Critical thinking*. Rohnert Park, Calif.: Center for Critical Thinking.

Pehrsson, R., and H. Robinson. 1985. *Semantic organizers: Approach to writing and reading instruction*. Rockville, Md.: Aspen.

———. 1989. *The semantic organizer: A study strategy for special needs learners*. Rockville, Md.: Aspen.

Perkins, D. 1986. *Knowledge as design*. Hillsdale, N.J.: Erlbaum.

Perri, S. 1989. The principal as teacher of teachers. In *Reflections on the role of the Catholic school principal*, ed. R. Kealey. Washington, D.C.: National Catholic Educational Association.

Peters, T., and N. Austin. 1985. *A passion for excellence*. New York: Random House.

Pius XI. 1929. *On the Christian education of youth*. Boston: Daughters of St. Paul.

Pope, C. A. 1990. Indirect teaching and assessment: Are they mutually exclusive? *NASSP Bulletin* 4(527):1–5.

Purkey, S., and M. S. Smith. 1982. Synthesis of research on effective schools. *Educational Leadership* 40(3):64–69.

Rathus, S. A., and J. S. Nevid. 1986. *Adjustment and growth: The challenge of life*. New York: Holt, Rinehart, and Winston.

Reck, C. 1988. *The small Catholic elementary school*. Washington, D.C.: National Catholic Educational Association.

———. 1991. Catholic identity. In *The Catholic identity of catholic schools*, eds. J. Heft and C. Reck, 26–27. Washington, D.C.: National Catholic Educational Association.

Reck, C., and J. Coreil. 1983. *School evaluation for the Catholic elementary school: An overview.* Washington, D.C.: National Catholic Educational Association.

Resnick, L., and L. Klopfer. 1989. *Towards the thinking curriculum.* Alexandria, Va.: Association for Supervision and Curriculum Development.

Ristau, K. 1989a. In *Reflections on the role of the Catholic school principal*, ed. R. Kealey. Washington, D.C.: National Catholic Educational Association.

———. 1989b. The role of the principal in the ongoing education of teachers. In *Reflections on the role of the Catholic school principal*, ed. R. Kealey. Washington, D.C.: National Catholic Educational Association.

———. 1991. The challenge: To provide leadership within Catholic schools. In *Leadership of and on behalf of Catholic schools*, eds. K. Ristau and J. Rogus. Washington, D.C.: National Catholic Educational Association.

Roberts, W. 1985. *Leadership secrets of Attila the Hun.* New York: Warner Books.

Root, D., and D. Overly. 1990. Successful teacher evaluation: Key elements for success. *NASSP Bulletin* 74(527):34–38.

Saphier, J., and R. Gower. 1987. *The skillful teacher.* Carlisle, Mass.: Research for Better Teaching.

Savary, L. M. 1992. *Creating quality schools.* Arlington, Va.: American Association of School Administrators.

Sergiovanni, T. J. 1984. Leadership and excellence in schooling. *Educational Leadership* 41(5):4–13.

———. 1990. *Value-added leadership.* New York: Harcourt, Brace, Jovanovich.

———. 1992. *Moral leadership: Getting to the heart of school improvement.* San Francisco: Jossey-Bass.

Sergiovanni, T. J., and R. J. Starratt. 1988. *Supervision: Human perspectives.* New York: McGraw-Hill.

Sheive, L. T., and M. B. Schoenheit. 1987. Vision and the work of educational leaders. In *Leadership: Examining the elusive, 1987 yearbook.* Alexandria, Va.: Association for Supervision and Curriculum Development.

Slavin, R. E. 1991. Synthesis of research on cooperative learning. *Educational Leadership* 48(5):71–82.

Smith, S. 1991. *Succeeding against the odds.* Los Angeles: Jeremy Tarcher, Inc.

Smith, W. F., and R. L. Andrews. 1989. *Instructional leadership.* Alexandria, Va.: Association for Supervision and Curriculum Development.

Sternberg, R. 1983. *How can we teach intelligence?* Philadelphia, Pa.: Research for Better Schools.

Stogdill, R. M. 1974. *Handbook of leadership: A survey of theory and research.* New York: The Free Press.

Tagiuri, R. 1968. The concept of organizational climate. In *Organizational climate: Exploration of a concept*, eds. R. Tagiuri and G. H. Litwin. Boston: Harvard University, Division of Research, Graduate School of Business Administration.

United States Catholic Conference. 1990. *Guidelines for doctrinally sound catechetical materials.* Washington, D.C.

United States Department of Education. 1986. *What works: Research about teaching and learning.* Washington, D.C.: Office of Educational Research and Improvement.

Uphoff, J. K. 1989. Religious diversity and education. In *Multicultural education: Issues and perspectives*, eds. J. A. Banks and C. M. Banks. Boston: Allyn and Bacon.

Vaill, P. B. 1984. The purposing of high-performing systems. In *Leadership and organizational culture*, eds. T. J. Sergiovanni and J. E. Corbally. Urbana-Champaign: University of Illinois Press.

Vroom, V. H., and P. W. Yetton. 1973. *Leadership and decision-making.* Pittsburgh: University of Pittsburgh Press.

Wang, M. C., G. D. Haertel, and H. J. Walberg. 1990. What influences learning? A content analysis of review literature. *Journal of Educational Research* 84(1):30–43.

Weber, M. 1947. *The theory of social and economic organization.* New York: Oxford University Press.

Welch, M. L. 1990. *A beginning: Resource book for incorporating values and Church teachings in the Catholic school curriculum.* Washington, D.C.: National Catholic Educational Association.

Whitmore, J., and J. Maker. 1985. *Intellectual giftedness in disabled persons.* Rockville, Md.: Aspen.

Whyte, W. F. 1969. *Organizational behavior: Theory and applications.* Homewood, Ill.: Irwin.

Wlodowski, R., and J. Jaynes. 1990. *Eager to learn.* San Francisco: Jossey-Bass.

Wong, B. Y. L. 1991. *Learning about learning disabilities.* San Diego: Academic Press, Inc.

Yukl, G. A. 1981. *Leadership in organizations.* Englewood Cliffs, N.J.: Prentice-Hall, Inc.

Yukl, G. A., and W. Nemeroff. 1979. Identification and measurement of specific categories of leadership behavior: A progress report. In *Crosscurrents in leadership*, eds. J. G. Hunt and L. L. Larson. Carbondale: Southern Illinios University Press.

Zukowski, A. A. 1992. Re-thinking Catholic education: A dialogue. *Momentum* 23(1):24–27.

Appendix A.
Integral Readings

This appendix is a compilation of all integral readings cited.
They are listed by competency topic within each area of responsibility.

I. Leadership

L1. Symbolic and Cultural Leadership

Congregation for Catholic Education. 1988. *The religious dimension of education in a Catholic school: Guidelines for reflection and renewal*. Washington, D.C.: United States Catholic Conference, nos. 24–46.

Deal, T. E., and K. D. Peterson. 1990. *The principal's role in shaping school culture*. Washington, D.C.: United States Department of Education, Office of Educational Research and Improvement, 16–33.

Libreria Editrice Vaticana. 1994. *Catechism of the Catholic Church*. Washington, D.C.: United States Catholic Conference, nos. 1897–98, 1902–03.

National Conference of Catholic Bishops. 1979. *Sharing the light of faith: National catechetical directory for Catholics of the United States*. Washington, D.C.: United States Catholic Conference, nos. 206–11, 215.

Reck, C. 1991. Catholic identity. In *The Catholic identity of Catholic schools*, eds. J. Heft and C. Reck, 26–27. Washington, D.C.: National Catholic Educational Association.

Sergiovanni, T. J. 1990. *Value-added leadership*. New York: Harcourt, Brace, Jovanovich, 82–90, 151–52.

L2. Catholic Educational Vision

Libreria Editrice Vaticana. 1994. *Catechism of the Catholic Church*. Washington, D.C.: United States Catholic Conference, nos. 737–38.

National Conference of Catholic Bishops. 1973. *To teach as Jesus did: A pastoral message on Catholic education*. Washington, D.C.: United States Catholic Conference, no. 82.

————. 1979. *Sharing the light of faith: National catechetical directory for Catholics of the United States*. Washington, D.C.: United States Catholic Conference, nos. 30, 232.

————. 1990. *In support of Catholic elementary and secondary schools*. Washington, D.C.: United States Catholic Conference, p. 6.

Perri, S. 1989. Principal as teacher of teachers. In *Reflections on the role of the Catholic school principal*, ed. R. Kealey, 67–74. Washington, D.C.: National Catholic Educational Association.

Sergiovanni, T. J. 1990. *Value-added leadership*. New York: Harcourt, Brace, Jovanovich, 56–63.

Sheive, L. T., and M. B. Schoeneit. 1987. Vision and the work of educational leaders. In *Leadership: Examining the elusive, 1987 yearbook*, 94, 96–98. Alexandria, Va.: Association for Supervision and Curriculum Development.

L3. Staff Morale

Blase, J., and P. C. Kirby. 1992. *Bringing out the best in teachers*. Newbury Park, Calif.: Corwin Press, 10–21, 99–111.

Knipper, C., and D. Suddarth. 1991. Involving staff in the in-service process. In *Capital wisdom: Papers from the Principals Academy 1991*, 29–34. Washington, D.C.: National Catholic Educational Association.

Libreria Editrice Vaticana. 1994. *Catechism of the Catholic Church*. Washington, D.C.: United States Catholic Conference, nos. 1913–17, 1917.

Ristau, K. 1989. Role of the principal in the ongoing education of teachers. In *Reflections on the role of the Catholic school principal*, ed. R. Kealey, 60–62. Washington, D.C.: National Catholic Educational Association.

Sergiovanni, T. J. 1992. *Moral leadership: Getting to heart of school improvement*. San Francisco: Jossey-Bass, 59–65.

L4. Leadership Among Staff

Barth, R. S. 1991. *Improving schools from within*. San Francisco: Jossey-Bass, 133–46.

Libreria Editrice Vaticana. 1994. *Catechism of the Catholic Church*. Washington, D.C.: United States Catholic Conference, nos. 1878–80, 1882–85, 1889, 1905–12.

Ristau, K. 1991. The challenge: To provide leadership within Catholic schools. In *Leadership on behalf of Catholic schools*, eds. K Ristau and J. Rogus, 12–17. Washington, D.C.: National Catholic Educational Association.

Sergiovanni, T .J. 1992. *Moral leadership: Getting to the heart of school improvement*. San Francisco: Jossey-Bass, 67–72.

L5. Educational Research

Convey, J. J. 1992. *Catholic schools make a difference: Twenty-five years of research*. Washington, D.C.: National Catholic Educational Association, 6–8, 33–34, 59, 62.

National Conference of Catholic Bishops. 1979. *Sharing the light of faith: National catechetical directory for Catholics in the United States*. Washington, D.C.: United States Catholic Conference, no. 223.

United States Department of Education. 1986. *What works: Research about teaching and learning*. Washington, D.C.: Office of Educational Research and Improvement, 19, 21–23, 25, 27, 29, 31–39, 41–43, 45–47, 49–53, 55, 57, 59–62.

Wang, M. C., G. D. Haertel, and H. J. Walberg. 1990. What influences learning? A content analysis of review literature. *Journal of Educational Research* 84(1):30–43.

L6. Effecting Change

Daresh, J. C. 1991. *Supervision as a proactive process*. Prospect Heights, Ill.: Waveland, 129–30, 137–40.

Fullan, M. G., and M. B. Miles. 1992. Getting reform right: What works and what doesn't. *Phi Delta Kappan* 73(10): 745–52.

Luby, M. A., M. S. Moser, and L. Posey. 1991. Introducing change with success. In *Capital wisdom: Papers from the Principals Academy 1991*, 48–54. Washington, D.C.: National Catholic Education Association.

L7. Personal Growth and Development

Barth, R. S. 1991. *Improving schools from within*. San Francisco: Jossey-Bass, 68–78.

Clifton, D. O., and P. Nelson. 1992. *Soar with your strengths*. New York: Delacorte Press, 111–22.

McBrien, R. P. 1987. *Ministry: A theological, pastoral handbook*. New York: Harper Collins, 77–81.

Rathus, S. A., and J. S. Nevid. 1986. *Adjustment and growth: The challenges of life*. New York: Holt, Rinehart and Winston, 273–79.

❖ ❖ ❖ ❖ ❖ ❖ ❖ ❖ ❖ ❖ ❖ ❖ ❖ ❖

II. Curriculum

C1. Religious Education

Di Giacomo, J. 1989. *Teaching religion in a Catholic secondary school*. Washington, D.C.: National Catholic Education Association, 64–66.

Groome, T. H. 1992. Catechesis and religious education: "Let's stay together". *The Living Light* 29(1):40–46.

Kelly, F. D. 1989. Catechesis for the Third Millennium. *Momentum* 20(4):6–10.

Libreria Editrice Vaticana. 1994. *Catechism of the Catholic Church*. Washington, D.C.: United States Catholic Conference, nos. 1–10, 25, 426–29, 1074–75, 1674–76, 1697–98, 2688.

O'Malley, W. J. 1992. Catechesis for conversion. *The Living Light* 29(2):55–63.

United States Catholic Conference. 1990. *Guidelines for doctrinally sound catechetical materials*. Washington, D.C. 11–25.

C2. Developmental Stages

Crain, W. 1992. *Theories of development: Concepts and applications*. Englewood Cliffs, N.J.: Prentice Hall, 17–18, 102–103, 124, 136–41, 188–90, 262–68.

Haney, R. 1991. Seize the day! *Momentum* 22(2):6–8.

Hawker, J. 1985. *Catechetics in the Catholic school*. Washington, D.C.: National Catholic Educational Association, 10–13.

National Conference of Catholic Bishops. 1979. *Sharing the light of faith: National catechetical directory for Catholics of the United States*. Washington, D.C.: United States Catholic Conference, nos. 173–75, 177–80.

C3. Cultural and Religious Differences

Banks, J. A. 1989. Multicultural education: Characteristics and goals. In *Multicultural education: Issues and perspectives*, eds. J. A. Banks and C. M. Banks, 2–3, 19–23. Boston: Allyn and Bacon.

Hall, S., ed. 1992. *The people: Reflections of native peoples on the Catholic experience in North America*. Washington, D.C.: National Catholic Educational Association, 73–78.

Hall, S., R. Doyle, and P. Tran, eds. 1990. *A Catholic response to the Asian presence*. Washington, D.C.: National Catholic Education Association, 85–91.

Hall, S., and C. Reck, eds. 1987. *Integral education: A response to the Hispanic presence*. Washington, D.C.: National Catholic Educational Association, 48–51.

Jones, N. 1987. An Afro-American perspective. In *Faith and culture*, 77–80. Washington, D.C.: United States Catholic Conference.

Libreria Editrice Vaticana. 1994. *Catechism of the Catholic Church*. Washington, D.C.: United States Catholic Conference, nos. 1204–06.

C4. Curriculum Development

Brophy, J. 1992. Probing the subtleties of subject-matter teaching. *Educational Leadership* 49(7):4–8.

Glatthorn, A. A. 1987. *Curriculum renewal: A rational for a consensus curriculum*. Alexandria, Va.: Association for Supervision and Curriculum Development, 20–27.

Kealey, R. 1985. *Curriculum in the Catholic school*. Washington, D.C.: National Catholic Educational Association, 11–42.

C5. Educational and Pedagogical Skills

Caine, R. N., and G. Caine. 1991. *Making connections: Teaching and the human brain*. Alexandria, Va.: Association for Supervision and Curriculum Development, 48–50, 59–61, 80–87, 102–05, 112–13.

Dunn, R. 1990. Rita Dunn answers questions on learning styles. *Educational Leadership* 48(2):15–19.

Marzano, R. J. 1992. *A different kind of classroom*. Alexandria, Va.: Association for Supervision and Curriculum Development, 25–27, 124–26, 135–39.

National Conference of Catholic Bishops. 1979. *Sharing the light of faith: National catechetical directory for Catholics of the United States*. Washington, D.C.: United States Catholic Conference, nos. 176, 185.

Reck, C. 1988. *The small Catholic elementary school*. Washington, D.C.: National Catholic Educational Association, 64–70.

C6. Students' Special Needs

Barkley, R. A. 1990. Primary symptoms and conceptualization. In *Attention deficit hyperactivity disorder: A handbook for diagnosis and treatment*, ed. R. A. Barkley, 39–73. New York: The Guilford Press.

Bos, C., and S. Vaughn. 1991. *Strategies for teaching students with learning and behavior problems*. Boston: Allyn and Bacon, 24–57.

Durbin, K. 1993. Attention deficit hyperactivity disorder. *Streamlined Seminar* 11(4). Alexandria, Va.: National Association of Elementary School Principals.

Mann, V. 1991. Language problems: A key to early reading problems. In *Learning about learning disabilities*, ed. B. Y. L. Wong, 129–62. San Diego: Academic Press, Inc.

National Conference of Catholic Bishops. 1979. *Sharing the light of faith: National catechetical directory for Catholics of the United States*. Washington, D.C.: United States Catholic Conference, nos. 192–96.

Parke, B. 1989. *Gifted students in regular classrooms*. Boston: Allyn and Bacon, 3–16, 42–63, 127–42.

Pfiffner, L. J., and Barkley, R. A. Educational placement and classroom management. In *Attention deficit hyperactivity disorder: A handbook for diagnosis and treatment*, ed. R. A. Barkley, 498–539. New York: The Guilford Press.

Swanson, H. L., and J. B. Cooney. 1991. Learning disabilities and memory. In *Learning about learning disabilities*, ed. B. Y. L. Wong, 103–22. San Diego: Academic Press, Inc.

Willows, D. M. Visual processes in learning disabilities. In *Learning about learning disabilities*, ed. B. Y. L. Wong, 163–93. San Diego: Academic Press, Inc.

Wong, B. Y. L. 1991. The relevance of metacognition to learning disabilities. In *Learning about learning disabilities*, ed. B. Y. L. Wong, 231–57. San Diego: Academic Press, Inc.

C7. Supervision of Instruction

Daresh, J. C. 1991. *Supervision as a proactive process*. Prospect Heights, Ill.: Waveland, 29–36.

Glatthorn, A. A., and C. R. Shields. 1983. *Differentiated supervision for Catholic schools*. Washington, D.C.: National Catholic Education Association, 15–27.

Glickman, C. D. 1990. *Supervision of instruction: A developmental approach*. Boston: Allyn and Bacon, 189–91.

Nolan, J., and P. Francis. 1992. Changing perspectives in curriculum and supervision. In *Supervision in transition, 1992 yearbook*. Alexandria, Va.: Association for Supervision and Curriculum Development, 52–60.

Ristau, K. 1989. The role of the principal in the ongoing education of teachers. In *Reflections on the role of the Catholic school principal*, ed. R. Kealey. Washington, D.C.: National Catholic Educational Association, 57–60.

C8. Evaluating Learning

Caine, R. N., and G. Caine. 1991. *Making connections: Teaching and the human brain*. Alexandria, Va.: Association for Supervision and Curriculum Development, 105–06, 154–58.

Maehr, M. L., C. Midgley, and T. Urdan. 1992. School leader as motivator. *Educational Administration Quarterly* 28(3):410–29.

Maeroff, G. I. 1991. Assessing alternative assessment. *Phi Delta Kappan* 73(4):272–81.

C9. Evaluating School Program

Convey, J. J. 1992. *Catholic schools make a difference: Twenty-five years of research*. Washington, D.C.: National Catholic Educational Association, 177–90.

Doyle, R., N. Kinate, A. Langen, and M. Swanson. 1991. Evaluation of the school's Catholicity. In *Capital wisdom: Papers from the Principals Academy 1991*, 1–6. Washington, D.C.: National Catholic Educational Association.

Reck, C., and J. Coreil. 1983. *School evaluation for the Catholic elementary school: An overview*. Washington, D.C.: National Catholic Educational Association, 3–20.

Savary, L. M. 1992. *Creating quality schools*. Arlington, Va.: American Association of School Administrators, 27–32.

Appendix B.
Learning Activities

This appendix is a compilation of all learning activities listed.
They are listed by competency topic within each area of responsibility.

I. Leadership

L1. Symbolic and Cultural Leadership

1. Readings with log entries
2. School Visits: looking for signs and symbols indicating the culture of the school
3. Obtain printed material about the school: critique
4. Diocesan office contact: Principal's handbook, info on Educational philosophy of Diocese

L2. Catholic Educational Vision

1. Readings with log entries
2. Reflect on the impact of *To Teach as Jesus Did* today with implications for leadership
3. Interview persons associated with Church/school ministry about Message/Community/Service/Worship
4. Interview school principal: role of the parents in complementing the "vision"
5. Research resources and agencies that might support families in raising their children

L3. Staff Morale

1. Readings with log entries
2. School visits: presence of healthy staff morale
3. Interview teachers: about preferred qualities of leadership which enable personal growth

L4. Leadership Among Staff

1. Readings with log entries
2. Interview principal: qualities of ideal teachers
3. School visit to observe departmental/faculty meeting
4. Interview teachers: views of leadership/personal contribution to

L5. Educational Research

1. Readings with log entries
2. Compare practices from research with the lived experience
3. Interview principals: curriculum/policy issues

L6. Effecting Change

1. Readings with log entries
2. Interview principal about an agenda for change
3. Interview teachers: how have they been involved in change
4. Collect articles from newspaper and journals to begin a resource file, re: change efforts

L7. Personal Growth and Development

1. Readings with log entries
2. Investigate local opportunities for personal and professional learning
3. Interview Pastor/DRE about possible spiritual enrichment opportunities
4. Interview Principal: How does one maintain balance in life/time management

II. Curriculum

C1. Religious Education

1. Readings with log entries
2. Tour Diocesan Religious education office
3. Attend parent meeting on sacramental preparation
4. Investigate the ways various parishes involve young people in parish life
5. Attend a childrens' liturgy: reflect/critique

C2. Developmental Stages

1. Readings with log entries
2. Observe in classrooms focusing on students
3. During class observation focusing on teacher behavior demonstrating knowledge of child development

C3. Cultural and Religious Differences

1. Readings with log entries
2. Interview teachers of minority students
3. Attend liturgy/worship services of different ethnic groups
4. Reflection on meeting the challenge of ethnic diversity
5. Reflection on the issue of the non-Catholic in the school

C4. Curriculum Development

1. Readings with log entries
2. Visit an inner city school
3. Visit the Curriculum department of the Diocesan schools office
4. Interview teachers about interdisciplinary teaching efforts

C5. Educational and Pedagogical Skills

1. Readings with log entries
2. School visit with classroom observations: focus on learning situation
3. Watch videos of educational situations: analyze
4. Learner Videotapes a lesson taught by self

C6. Students' Special Needs

1. Readings with log entries
2. Interview teachers on prior knowledge regarding learning problems
3. Visit school with programs in place
4. Contact Catholic school principal to ascertain needs/develop support system

C7. Supervision of Instruction

1. Readings with log entries
2. View teaching videos: reflect and critique
3. Observe and Interview principal: supervision plan and strategies

C8. Evaluating Learning

1. Readings with log entries
2. Collect report card samples: critique
3. Interview principals, counselors, teachers: admission procedures into first year of schooling
4. Interview principals or Diocesan personnel: formal and informal methods of student evaluation

C9. Evaluating School Program

1. Readings with log entries
2. Obtain instruments used to evaluate schools: analyze
3. Interview principals, teachers: processes used to evaluate instructional materials/programs

Appendix C.
Outcome Activities

This appendix is a compilation of all outcome activities listed.
They are listed by competency topic within each area of responsibility.

I. Leadership

L1. Symbolic and Cultural Leadership

1. List values important for leaders to stress cultural and symbolic aspects
2. Designate occasions appropriate for celebration and present plans it
3. Reflection/critique of situation wherein cultural leadership was demonstrated
4. Design a brochure that exemplifies the spirit of the school

L2. Catholic Educational Vision

1. Develop a mission statement for a school that is sensitive to the needs of the families served. Propose a three year plan to implement the sentiments of the statement
2. Critique the value of a set of recommendations of a National Committee to improve education
3. Reflection on the "ideal" school

L3. Staff Morale

1. Generate list of strategies to create a positive learning/working environment
2. List factors that enrich the work environment and propose ways to implement or improve
3. Develop a process to include faculty input in developing staff development opportunities
4. Develop short and long term plans to improve and maintain faculty/staff morale

L4. Leadership Among Staff

1. Develop attitude survey for teachers to assess feelings about staff involvement and empowerment
2. Produce a plan that fosters the values of transformational leadership
3. Scenario addressing the "worthwhileness" of generating new ideas

L5. Educational Research

1. Critique article of a research journal
2. Analyze the implication of implementing an "innovation"
3. Scenario: Developing a policy about early age admission

L6. Effecting Change

1. Scenario: Athletes and academic excellence
2. Process to improve the climate for change in a school
3. Specify an area needing improvement and develop a plan to implement change
4. Collect articles from newspapers and journals to begin a resource file, re: change efforts

L7. Personal Growth and Development

1. Reflection: personal assessment of professional knowledge, skills, traits for leadership in Catholic school
2. Design a weekly time management program that integrates the various responsibilities of life
3. Reflection on personal and professional life goals

II. Curriculum

C1. Religious Education

1. Develop a long range curriculum outline for aspect of religious education
2. Assess the strengths and weakness of two different religious education texts

C2. Development Stages

1. Generate strategies/product to demonstrate ways the curriculum meets the needs of the students
2. Identify specific student problems/issues and specify age appropriate responses to them

C3. Cultural and Religious Differences

1. Generate staff development plan to address diversity issues
2. Critique various textbook on the handling of diversity issues

C4. Curriculum Development

1. Produce examples of curriculum goals and related objectives
2. Develop a plan for initiating a sexuality curriculum in a school
3. Generate problems/solutions likely to be generated by the introduction of new curricular programs/approaches

C5. Educational and Pedagogical Skills

1. Design a ten point excellence in teaching program for a selected population
2. Describe specific teaching strategies called for in contrasting academic areas

C6. Students' Special Needs

1. Develop a five year plan to address the issue
2. Outline a plan for teacher inservice on special needs of students
3. Use a PMI list to analyze issue
4. Develop a proposal to Diocese specifying the resources and services needed to cope with special problems in the classroom

C7. Supervision of Instruction

1. Scenario: teacher motivation
2. Describe model of supervision for specific teacher
3. Develop a time management plan
4. Develop a personal professional profile encompassing philosophy and beliefs

C8. Evaluating Learning

1. Outline school guidelines to evaluate student learning
2. Procedure to manage problem between teacher and student over an academic matter

C9. Evaluating School Program

1. Develop a plan to evaluate math curriculum
2. Critique a curriculum

About the Authors

Jean Barton, Ph.D., has over twenty-five years experience in the field of education, serving as a school psychologist, curriculum specialist, director of computer education, and teacher in both public and Catholic schools. She took her doctorate in cognitive psychology at The Catholic University of America where she specialized in learning, cognition, and instruction. She is presently the project coordinator of a United States Office of Education Jacob Javits Grant to the Maryland Montgomery County public schools. The aim of the project is to identify and nurture hidden giftedness in underserved populations, learning disabled, economically disadvantaged, and culturally-linguistically different children.

Sr. Maria Ciriello, OP, Ph.D., is presently the dean of the School of Education of the University of Portland in Oregon. Sister Maria spent eight years teaching and fourteen years in elementary and secondary school administration before pursuing her doctorate at The Catholic University of America. In 1987 she joined the faculty at Catholic University. As an associate professor, she taught in the areas of teacher education and education administration. She also collaborated nationally on strategic planning and evaluation studies of diocesan school systems. She earned her master's degree in education administration at the University of Dayton.

Claire Helm, Ph.D., is currently director of the Holy Child School in Jacksonville, Fla. She was previously the assistant superintendent for elementary schools in the Archdiocese of Washington, D.C., and prior to that was the archdiocesan director of personnel. Her area of particular interest is the identification and professional development of Catholic school administrators. As coordinator of professional services and director of professional development programs, she has developed a highly successful archdiocesan leadership institute for Catholic school principals. For the last twelve years she has also served as a consultant to Catholic dioceses in the areas of strategic planning, leadership training, and more recently, school advisory boards. She holds a master's degree in American history from the State University of New York at Albany and completed her doctoral degree in guidance and counseling at The Catholic University of America in 1989. Her dissertation was an ethnographic study of Catholic school leadership styles, particularly transformational leadership.

Sr. Donna Innes, CSA, Ph.D., is currently professor of graduate education at Marian College in Fond du Lac, Wisconsin. She holds a doctorate from The Catholic University of America. She has taught curriculum development to Catholic school administrators through the University of Saint Thomas in St. Paul, Minnesota. As curriculum coordinator for the Archdiocese of St. Paul and Minneapolis from 1980–88, she assisted 126 schools in designing, implementing, and evaluating curriculum. She was co-author of the "Media Mirror" program and has conducted research on imparting values in Catholic schools.

Sr. Rita K. O'Leary, IHM, is principal of Our Lady of Lourdes Regional High School in Shamokin, Pa. She holds a bachelor's of music degree from Immaculata College, a master's degree in music education from West Chester State University, and a master's degree in educational administration from The Catholic University of America. In the past twenty years she has taught or held school administration positions at the elementary, secondary, and college level.

Sr. Bernadine Robinson, OP, has been involved in Catholic education for 45 years. Twenty-six of those years were spent as principal at various schools in the Ohio dioceses of Cleveland and Toledo. She has served as a member of her Dominican community's Board of Education, and as regional representative to the Cleveland diocesan principal's association. She earned her master's degree in education, majoring in administration and supervision from Saint John College of Cleveland, Ohio.